THE EXPOSITOR'S
DICTIONARY OF TEXTS

THE EXPOSITOR'S
DICTIONARY OF TEXTS

CONTAINING OUTLINES, EXPOSITIONS, AND
ILLUSTRATIONS OF BIBLE TEXTS, WITH FULL
REFERENCES TO THE BEST HOMILETIC LITERATURE

EDITED BY THE REV.

SIR W. ROBERTSON NICOLL, M.A., LL.D.

AND

JANE T. STODDART

WITH THE CO-OPERATION OF THE REV.

JAMES MOFFATT, M.A., D.D.

Volume 2
Part 2
I Corinthians Through Revelation

BAKER BOOK HOUSE

Grand Rapids, Michigan

Reprinted 1978 by
Baker Book House Company
from the edition published in 1910
by George H. Doran Company

ISBN: 0-8010-6697-2

Printed in the United States of America

CONTENTS

THE FIRST EPISTLE TO THE CORIN-
THIANS 510

THE SECOND EPISTLE TO THE CORIN-
THIANS 593

THE EPISTLE TO THE GALATIANS . . 623

THE EPISTLE TO THE EPHESIANS . . 651

THE EPISTLE TO THE PHILIPPIANS . 702

THE EPISTLE TO THE COLOSSIANS . 738

THE FIRST EPISTLE TO THE THESSA-
LONIANS 761

THE SECOND EPISTLE TO THE THESSA-
LONIANS 771

THE FIRST EPISTLE TO TIMOTHY . 775

THE SECOND EPISTLE TO TIMOTHY . 790

THE EPISTLE TO TITUS 805

THE EPISTLE TO PHILEMON . . . 810

THE EPISTLE TO THE HEBREWS . . 813

THE EPISTLE OF JAMES 889

THE FIRST EPISTLE OF PETER . . . 920

THE SECOND EPISTLE OF PETER . . 935

THE FIRST EPISTLE OF JOHN . . . 944

THE SECOND EPISTLE OF JOHN . . 975

THE THIRD EPISTLE OF JOHN . . 977

THE EPISTLE OF JUDE 978

THE BOOK OF REVELATION . . . 981

OUTLINES FOR THE CHURCH YEAR . 1055

INDEX OF OUTLINES 1057

THE FIRST EPISTLE TO THE CORINTHIANS

1 CORINTHIANS

REFERENCES.—*Expositor* (4th Series), vol. ii. p. 69 ; *ibid.* **vol.** vii. p. 267. I. 1-9.—*Ibid.* (6th Series), vol. i. p. 25.

CALLED TO BE SAINTS
'Called to be saints.'—1 COR. i. 2.

MANY names are given to the followers of our Lord in the New Testament. But the name most frequently given is 'saint'. The word occurs sixty times in its pages, and it is plainly intended to describe the life which every Christian should earnestly seek after.

I. The idea of devotion—devoted to Christ ; that is the essence of the Christian life, that is the primary notion of sainthood. And really this is the basis of membership in the Church of Christ. This is the one thing to look for in every one who desires to join a Christian Church. The primary question to be asked is, What is Jesus Christ to you? Personal relation to Christ is the primary thing. I beg leave to say still further that this phrase, 'devoted to Christ,' expresses what every one of us professes who has been baptised. The pre-eminent idea in the ordinance is the absolute surrender of the life to Jesus Christ, that He may cleanse and use it. It is also the thing that we profess every time we come to the Lord's Table. We take again the vow of allegiance. This relation of devotion to Christ our Lord is the thing to watch and guard carefully and jealously.

II. And now comes the second idea clinging to the word saint, *viz.*, that of goodness as a result of our contact with Christ and His influence on our lives. One of the most serious questions in connection with organised Christianity at this moment—a question on which its future largely depends—is, are the people who profess the Christian faith by Church membership better people than others? You know, if you know anything, that the most eloquent evangelistic preaching in the world will be far less potent than character, and can never prevail against an unchristian spirit in a Church or in individuals connected with it. If we, bearing the name of Christ, have manifestly no joy in Him, there is no reality in our profession. Our business is to realise our calling. Our chief business is to be good, true, pure, loving, holy. The future of the Church depends on the character of its members. The way to goodness is devotion to Him.—CHARLES BROWN, *Christian World Pulpit*, vol. LXXIII. p. 280.

REFERENCES.—I. 2.—R. W. Dale, *Christian World Pulpit*, vol. xlviii. p. 264. R. J. Wardell, *Preacher's Magazine*, vol. xix. p 142. C. S. Horne, *Christian World Pulpit* vol. lii. p. 17. Spurgeon, *Sermons*, vol. viii. No. **434** F. W. Farrar, *Everyday Christian Life*, p 128. *Expositor* (4th Series), vol. x. p. 204 ; *ibid.* (5th Series), vol. x. p. 159. A. Maclaren, *Expositions of Holy Scripture—Corinthians*, p. 1. I. 3.—*Expositor*, vol. vii. p. 65. 1. 4-6. —*Ibid.* vol. ii. p. 103. I. 6.—Spurgeon, *Sermons*, vol. l No. 2875. *Expositor* (6th Series), vol. ix. p. 268. I. 7.— Bishop Creighton, *Christian World Pulpit*, vol. liv. p. 264. E. A. Askew, *The Service of Perfect Freedom*, p. 1. H. J. Wilmot-Buxton, *Sunday Sermonettes for a Year*, p. 193. W. H. Evans, *Short Sermons for the Seasons*, p. 1. *Expositor* (4th Series), vol. x. pp. 104, 440. I. 9.—Spurgeon, *Sermons*, vol. xi No. 616, and vol. xliv. No. 2580. R. W. Dale, *Fellowship with Christ*, p. 1. *Expositor* (4th Series), vol. iv. p. 426.

'I beseech you . . . that there be no divisions among you. For it hath been signified to me . . . that there are contentions among you.'—1 COR. i. 10, 11.

THE average man or woman is always at open discord with some one ; the great majority could not live without oft-recurrent squabble. . . . Verbal contention is, of course, commoner among the poor and vulgar than in the class of well-bred people living at their ease, but I doubt whether the lower ranks of society find personal association much more difficult than the refined minority above them. High cultivation may help to self-command, but it multiplies the chances of irritative contact. In mansion, as in hovel, the strain of life is perpetually felt—between the married, between parents and children, between relatives of every degree, between employers and employed. They debate, they dispute, they wrangle, they explode— their nerves are relieved, and they are ready to begin again.—GEORGE GISSING, *The Private Papers of Henry Ryecroft*, pp. 93, 94.

REFERENCE.—I. 10.—*Expositor* (5th Series), vol. v. p. 38.

'Each of you saith, I am of Paul ; and I of Apollos ; and I of Cephas ; and I of Christ.'—1 COR. i. 12.

IN a letter Vinet remarks, apropos of Thomas Erskine : 'If I did not abjure on principle such expressions as "I am of Apollos, and of Cephas," I should gladly allow myself to say "I am of Erskine". He does not wrap up the Gospel in shadows. He makes us feel that if the *how* of the mysteries of religion is inconceivable, the *why* is perfectly accessible to our reason.'

REFERENCES.—I. 12.—*Expositor* (6th Series), vol. viii. p. **73** ; *ibid.* (7th Series), vol. vi. p. 79. I. 13.—T. Arnold, *Sermons*, vol. iii. p. 186. H. Alford, *Sermons on Christian Doctrine*, p. 210. *Expositor* (6th Series), vol. v. p. 48. I. 14.—*Ibid.* (5th Series), vol. vi. p. 82.

'Not in wisdom of words, lest the cross of Christ should be made void.'—1 COR. I. 17.

'TAKE eloquence,' said Paul Verlaine once, 'and wring its neck.'

REFERENCES.—I. 17.—*Expositor* (4th Series), vol. vi. p. 367 ; *ibid.* (6th Series), vol. vi. pp. 212, 366. I. 17, 18.—*Ibid.* p. 29.

THE PREACHING OF THE CROSS

'The preaching of the cross.'—1 COR. I. 18.

CHRISTIANITY is the religion of redemption ; it is for that reason that the Apostle gives as the motto and the summary of the Gospel this little sentence in the text, 'The preaching of the cross'. For the cross is the symbol, as it once was the instrument, of our redemption. Whether it were to Galatia or to Corinth ; to rude and barbarous rustics in their impetuosity and changefulness ; or whether it were to the cultivated children of Greek wisdom, St. Paul had one message, and that message was, 'The preaching of the cross'. What did he mean?

I. Well, first of all, the Apostle announced an historical reality. The Apostle rejoiced in an historical redemption. Not in ideas, but in facts ; not in a code, but a Person ; not in impulses and sentiments, but in the flesh and blood reality of the dire struggle of our Lord with human guilt, wretchedness, and wrong. He rejoiced in an historical redemption when he preached the Gospel of the cross ; and if ever there was a doleful and desperate reality in this world, it was the cross of Jesus Christ. Paul spoke of this reality as a great thing effected here in this world, and on its dusty surface. He spoke upon events that transpired in a known place, under a known government, in known circumstances, on which eyes had been riveted, over which hearts had been broken. He spoke of Christ in Jerusalem nailed to the cross, placed in the tomb, and risen from the dead. Never forget that Christianity rests upon the great obdurate facts of human history.

II. Secondly, St. Paul, when he spoke of this preaching of the cross, meant an inward experience. He said, 'I am crucified with Christ'. 'The life I live in the flesh I live by faith of the Son of God, Who loved me and gave Himself for me.' 'God forbid that I should glory save in the cross of our Lord Jesus Christ.' Very personal, very inward, even mystical is the language, and it is the preaching of the cross that carries that message home into the living experiences of men and women.

III. Thirdly, the Apostle referred to 'the preaching of the cross' as a vivid and graphic description of Christ in His unseen power working among men. Do you recall those words from the letter to the Galatians? So powerful was the portraiture which Paul drew before the spiritual eyes of the Galatian hearers, that for a moment they seemed to have seen the extended arms, the bleeding brow, and pierced side of the crucified Jesus.

Now this, in brief, is what he meant by 'the preaching of the cross' ; he meant the historical redemption, he meant the inward experience, he meant the vivid portraiture and living presentation of an exalted but still potent Saviour, so as to reach the inward vision of the soul ; and such should be the preaching of the Gospel to-day.

REFERENCES.—I. 18.—Spurgeon, *Sermons*, vol. xxvii. No. 1611. T. D. Barlow, *Rays from the Sun of Righteousness*, p. 66. R. H. Conwell, *Baptist Times*, vol. liv. p. 396. A. Maclaren, *The Wearied Christ*, p. 296. H. P. Liddon, *Sermons on Some Words of St. Paul*, p. 17. W. M. Clow, *The Cross in Christian Experience*, p. 193. *Expositor* (4th Series), vol. i. p. 201 ; *ibid.* (6th Series), vol. x. p. 372. A. Maclaren, *Expositions of Holy Scripture—Corinthians*, p. 10. I. 18-24.—*Ibid.* (5th Series), vol. vii. p. 276.

'For it is written, I will destroy the wisdom of the wise, and the prudence of the prudent will I reject.'—1 COR. I. 19.

IT is for the punishment of our temeritie and instruction of our miserie and incapacitie, that God caused the trouble, downfall and confusion, of Babels Tower. What course soever man taketh of himself, it is God's permission that he ever commeth to that confusion whose image he so lively representeth unto us by the just punishment, wherewith he framed the presumptuous over-weening of Nembroth, and brought to nothing the frivolous enterprises of the building of his high-towering Pyramis or Heaven-menacing tower. 'I will destroy the wisdome of the wise, and refuse the praidence of them that are most prudent'. The diversitie of tongues and languages wherewith he disturbed that worke and overthrew that proudly-raised Pile ; what else is it but this infinit altercation and perpetual discord of opinions and reason which accompanieth and entangleth the frivolous frame of man's learning, or vaine building of human science?—MONTAIGNE, vol. II. p. 12.

REFERENCES.—I. 20.—*Expositor* (4th Series), vol. i. p. 31. I. 20, 21.—T. D. Bernard, *The Exclusion of Wisdom*, p. 1. I. 21.—H. P. Liddon, *Sermons on Some Words of St. Paul*, p. 37. *Expositor* (5th Series), vol. ix. p. 372.

CHRIST MEETS EVERY NEED

1 COR. I. 22, 23.

I. NOTE the testimony of heathenism to men's religious wants, or what men desire.

II. Note that Christianity seems to neglect and contradict many of men's ideas and wants. (1) We preach. Not *we do*—opposition to all requirements for signs, to all sacramentarianism and ritualistic notions. (2) We preach Christ. We deal with a Person. (3) We preach Christ crucified. The cross is the centre of His work.

III. Note that Christianity really meets and satisfies them all. (1) Christ crucified is Power. No other sign half as strong. (2) Christ crucified is Wisdom. Christ crucified meets the real wants of every age and of every man.—A. MACLAREN.

REFERENCE.—I. 22, 23.—*Expositor* (6th Series), vol. iv. p. 232.

THE POWER OF THE CROSS

For the Jews require a sign, and the Greeks seek after wisdom : but we preach Christ crucified, unto the Jews a stumbling-block, and unto the Greeks foolishness ; but unto them which are called, both Jews and Greeks, Christ the power of God, and the wisdom of God.'—1 Cor. I. 22-24.

'THE Jews ask for signs,' a request which is not necessarily indicative of a thirst. That is the bane and peril of all externalism. It may gratify a feverish curiosity without awakening the energies of a holy life.

'And the Greeks seek after wisdom.' They are the epicures in philosophies, the dainty tasters of intellectual subtilties. 'The Jews ask for signs,' and their religion degenerates into a despiritualised system of magic. 'The Greeks seek after wisdom,' and their religion becomes the domain of the disciplinist theorist, the heritage of a cultured and exclusive aristocracy.

'We preach Christ crucified,' says Paul, and we are not going to be diverted by the hunger for mere sensation ; 'we preach Christ crucified,' and we are not going to be disengaged from our high calling, and tempted to submit our Gospel as a piece of subtle and mincing controversy.

I. We preach Christ crucified, because it is the doctrine which incomparably preserves for us the sense of the holiness of God. The sense of the holiness of God is an element that is conspicuously lacking in our modern religious life. The idea of Fatherhood does not exclude or obscure the idea of holiness : it includes and intensifies it.

II. We preach Christ crucified, because it is the doctrine which incomparably creates and preserves the sense of the nature of sin. Any doctrine which unveils the holiness of God reveals also the horribleness of sin ; any doctrine which obscures God's holiness veneers man's sin. All true forgiveness throws a most lurid illumination on the sin that is forgiven. The cross is the place of great awakening for sinners.

III. We preach Christ crucified, because it is a doctrine in the experience of which we incomparably discern the realities of grace.

IV. We preach Christ crucified, because it is the doctrine in whose heart we find ample resources for the attainment of moral and spiritual health.

For ethical revivals we must first of all have evangelical revivals. We must first of all have the doctrine of the cross before we can hope for moral elevation.—J. H. JOWETT, *Apostolic Optimism*, p. 68.

CHRIST CRUCIFIED

For the Jews require a sign, and the Greeks seek after wisdom : but we preach Christ crucified, unto the Jews a stumbling-block, and unto the Greeks foolishness ; but unto them which are called, both Jews and Greeks, Christ the power of God, and the wisdom of God.'—1 Cor. I. 22-24.

I. LET us note the desire of Jew and Greek. 'The Jews require a sign and the Greeks seek after wisdom. A sign! Had not the Jew received signs sufficient ? He had seen the leper cleansed, he had seen the dead raised from their graves, and yet the Jews required a sign. This is quite explicable in consistency with the nature of men. If you look for external things you will never be satisfied with them. 'And the Greeks seek after wisdom.' There was nothing wrong in that. But the Corinthian Greek babbled of wisdom when he had nothing but the name left. And yet they were not willing to accept the message of eternal truth, because they preferred their own little puppets to the Gospel, just as a child prefers the little ragged doll it has made for itself to the best products of the market.

II. What does Paul do ? What is his message in the face of this ? Will he manufacture signs ? I believe Paul could have done so had he chosen. Did Paul dazzle the Greek by a display of wisdom ? No. 'We preach *Christ*.' And that is not all. 'We preach Christ *crucified*.' That is the gist of the matter ; that is where the difficulty comes in. The cross must be taken into account, and not only that, but the cross is the centre and secret of all Christian life and power. Of course, Paul does not mean that he remains constantly with the cross, that he has nothing further to say ; he does not mean that he never varies his discourse. What he means is, that all is built upon that, and though he may soar into the sunlight of the eternal glory, and tell men of all the vast expansion of God's purpose and kingdom in the future, he starts from the cross and comes back to it again.

III. Notice the various estimates here formed of this preaching. 'Unto the Jews a stumbling-block.' Shall we remove the cross that people may not stumble ? If you do you remove the world's redemption at the same time. 'Unto the Greeks foolishness.' Man redeemed by blood ! It is vulgar. So shouts the modern Greek in his polished frenzy. But the foolishness of God is wiser than men. The world *is* saved by blood. Those who know themselves and God, those who find themselves in Christ, understand the cross ; for its power has entered into their life. And because it is the power of God it is also the wisdom of God, for wisdom and power go together.—JOHN THOMAS, *Myrtle Street Pulpit*, vol. III. p. 99.

REFERENCES.—I. 22.—*Expositor* (5th Series), vol. ii. p. 265. I. 22-24.—Archbishop Magee, *The Gospel and the Age*, p. 3. E. M. Geldart, *Echoes of Truth*, p. 54.

THE WATERSHED

'We preach Christ crucified.'—1 Cor. I. 23.

WE preach Christ crucified. The phrase may be described as a watershed, and I will illustrate its different uses from a poem by Oliver Wendell Holmes :—

Behold the rocky wall
    That down its sloping sides
Pours the swift rain-drops, blending, as they fall
    In rushing river-tides !

Yon stream, whose sources run
    Turned by a pebble's edge,
Is Athabasca, rolling toward the sun
    Through the cleft mountain-ledge.

The slender rill had strayed,
But for the slanting stone
To evening's ocean, with the tangled braid
Of foam-flecked Oregon.

So from the heights of will
Life's parting stream descends,
And, as a moment turns its slender rill,
Each widening torrent bends,—

From the same cradle's side,
From the same mother's knee,—
One to long darkness and the frozen tide,
One to the Peaceful Sea !

Let me trace briefly the courses of the two streams. 'We preach Christ crucified' on one side, and on the other 'We, risen and crucified, preach Christ Divine, crucified, risen'.

I. It is the word Divine which turns the course. The essence of heresy is the assertion that Christ is a creature. No matter how loftily He may be conceived of, if His Deity is denied the end is the long darkness and the frozen tide.

(1) We begin with Arianism, which seems at first sight, to grant so much that it is barely distinguishable from Christianity. It affirms that Christ existed before He became Incarnate, that by Him God made the worlds, that He is, in a manner, to be worshipped, that He wrought miracles, and that He rose from the dead. But it affirms also that He had a beginning of existence, that He was created by God, that, being created by God, He could be annihilated by God. This conception of Christ was held at one time by many powerful intellects, and has at least one living representative who must be regarded with deep respect. Yet it is fair to say that it has practically no place in the actual world of thought.

(2) The stream descends, and we find it next as Socinianism, or, as it is now called, Unitarianism. Those who have read Socinus may be astonished to find how exalted is the place he accords to Christ. He differs from Arius in holding that Christ had no pre-existence, that His life began with His mortal birth. But he maintains that Christ was born of a virgin, that He was the Immaculate Son of God, that in a sense He is worthy of our homage, that He wrought miracles in the world, and visibly conquered death. Within living memory Unitarians made similar affirmations.

(3) But this, so far as I am aware, can no longer be said. The disciples of Socinus began to maintain that Christ would be more powerful if He were freed from the bandages of the supernatural. So gradually miracle was denied. The truth of the Resurrection was volatilised, or openly rejected. Christ, it was said, shared the lot of the departed, and left His body to become Syrian dust. Still, for a long time a strenuous effort was made to maintain His sinlessness. 'I know not,' said Channing, 'what can be added to the wonder, reverence, and love that belong to Jesus.' It was held that He towered over the rest of mankind in His moral and spiritual perfection, that He was the true Leader of faithful souls. I think it would be correct to say that this view is taken to-day by some representative Unitarians, including Stopford Brooke. But it has become clear to the majority that a sinless man is a miracle, and that if the order of the law is to remain inviolate, Christ must be, in another sense, numbered with the transgressors.

(4) So the stream still descends. When the miracles are denied, when the Resurrection becomes incredible, when the sinlessness is seen to be impossible, the question comes, How are we to estimate Christ's character? Francis Newman was tempted to call Him a conscious and wilful impostor. He could not recognise Him as really simple and straightforward, and put Fletcher of Madeley, Wesley's designated successor, far above Him in point of character. I confess that Renan's conclusion seems to me by far the most logical. His apologies for Christ are far more appalling than his accusation, but on his own premises he is compelled to recognise that Christ was a schemer as well as a dreamer. A certain shrinking holds most critics back, but it is significant enough that one declares that Jesus is no part of His own Gospel, while another finds the historical proof of His existence in what he evidently takes for tokens and acknowledgments of mortal frailty.

(5) Can the stream go lower? Yes. So desperate is the problem of the character of Christ as viewed by rationalistic criticism, that some have strenuously and ably argued that He has never existed at all. I cannot but think that this position will be much more widely adopted by the critics who deny the supernatural. Beside such a Christ as they conceive, the Christ of the Gospels is credible and simple.

One to long darkness and the frozen tide.

II. The other stream turns another way, and ends in another rest. We, risen and crucified, preach Christ Divine, crucified, and risen. The Divinity, or, rather, the Deity, is the dividing line. Christ was uncreated, not only the Son of God, but God the Son. He was perfectly and purely God, and as truly and really man. The Church lives only as she holds fast to this fact, and she knows it. No definitions or descriptions, theological or other, can do more than touch the fringe of His splendour. But, if we are to understand the preaching of Christ crucified, we must fill every word and every thought with the full meaning of Deity which belongs to the name of Christ. The more we do this, the more gloriously the river will expand and end. I can but touch on one or two points.

(1) It is the Deity of Christ which gives meaning to His atonement. We must not shrink from the strongest words that Scripture uses ; rather we must glory in them. The Church of God has been purchased by the blood of God. Whenever we preach Christ, whenever we sit at His Table, we show forth the Lord's death. It is the Deity of Christ that gave His death its significance in regard to sin.

(2) Nor is the Deity of Christ less important when we consider the relation of His death to human suffering. The sense of sin may be weak, but the sense of pain was never stronger than it is now. The springs

of sorrow are full to the very lips. Lightness of heart has gone out of us, and the monotone of sadness is to be heard in most of our noblest literature. We are already far past the optimism of even thirty years ago. If you tell a man that Christ was the chief of the noble army of martyrs, he will answer that you have merely increased his difficulty and despair. The line of martyrs has stretched so long and so far that men demand from us the news of the Suffering that hallows all sufferings, the sacrifice which consecrates all sacrifices. The optimism of Browning's—

> God's in His heaven,
> All's right with the world,

falls on deaf ears to-day. If God is merely in His heaven, all is wrong with the world. It is our business not to abandon but to expand the great truth that God in Christ suffered and died to take away our suffering and our death. The gospel to the generation of sufferers is that the sufferings of His people were the thorns in the crown which Christ wore as a fair mitre ; and that these sufferings ended when they clasped the Sacred Head.

(3) The Resurrection can only be understood as the Resurrection of the God-man. If Christ had been less than God, I could understand the force of many difficulties. If He was God, it was not possible that He should be holden of death. It was not possible that He should see corruption. He laid down His life of His own will, and of His own will He took His life again. Three days and three nights He was to lie in the grave, but for the elect's sake the days were shortened, and very early in the morning He burst the bonds of the tomb. Nor could the God-man rise for Himself alone—

> Among the sleeping dead alone He woke,
> And blessed with outstretched hands the host around.

Did He hear them say in their slumber, 'Think of me, I pray Thee, when it shall be well with Thee, and speak for me unto the King, that He may bring me out of this prison'. 'Draw me ; we will run after Thee.' He heard, understood, remembers, and at the voice of the Archangel these little hills in the churchyard will one day rejoice on every side. This is the end, then, of the stream—

> One to the Peaceful Sea.

III. But we must say a word on the preachers of this Gospel. We, risen and crucified, preach Christ Divine, crucified, risen. Note the order—risen and crucified. It is the order of St. Paul : 'That I may know Him, and the power of His Resurrection, and the fellowship of His sufferings'. Not the fellowship of His sufferings and the power of His Resurrection, but first the power and then the fellowship. When we believe in the risen Christ there flows into us the strength and joy of His Spirit, the power of His Resurrection.

Our own difficulties of faith we are to meet in the power of His Resurrection. Our own frequent failures and humiliations and trials in work we are to meet in the power of His Resurrection. Our own personal griefs of missing faces and loosened hands we must bear in the power of His Resurrection. The unbelieving world we must confront in the power of His Resurrection. Whatever there may be of indifference, of hostility, of persecution, we have to meet them all in the power of His Resurrection, and be made more than conquerors through Him that loved us.—W. Robertson Nicoll, *The Lamp of Sacrifice*, p. 76.

PREACHING CHRIST CRUCIFIED
1 Cor. i. 23.

Preaching is an agency, previously unknown, which Christianity has created to be its chosen mode of utterance. Jesus and His messengers are the only preachers. Notice :—

I. The great pulpit theme : 'Christ crucified'. This is the sum of our message, the central regulative idea in the Gospel of God. The Gospel offers itself to us as a plan of restoration, it proceeds upon the fact of a fall. A Gospel based on the Incarnation of God cannot but be the final end of all God's other doings on this earth. The Christian scheme of salvation through God incarnate is thus the world's centre of gravity, but its own centre of gravity is the cross : it is not ' Christ ' simply but ' Christ crucified ' whom we preach. Modern thought is strong, because it recognises the Incarnation, but it is weak because it fails to see the necessary issue of the Advent in the work of the cross. The fact that our Divine Helper came in human form showed that there was a man's work to be done before God's help could be extended, and for the doing of that Christ was born. Christ bore His cross before He was fastened to it. He was born that He might die. Thus we reach the heart of Christianity. Such is the twofold Gospel fact : Christ the Incarnate Son ; Christ crucified, our righteousness and ransom.

II. The utterance of the Divine message : 'We preach'. What is this peculiar instrument ? Preaching is the announcement of the Saviour, with the offer of His salvation, in its widest sense ; both being delivered as a message from God. So the Apostles preached ; so have all great and honoured preachers ; so must we. (1) As to *matter* ; everything should serve the preacher's main drift, and illustrate or commend his message. (2) As to the *form* of the message : it must be in the main declarative.

Preaching is at once historical and personal. (1) All that concerns the life of Christ, with its historical foreshadowings, its self-manifestation in word and miracle must be prominent in the pulpit. (2) The Jesus of biography is now the glorified Christ, a Person present, though absent, whose spiritual power we feel ; that ministry is best which leads straight to the living helping Saviour. Yet, even here, preaching will lose its savour unless it is sustained by a perpetual offer of the Saviour to men's hearts.—J. Oswald Dykes, *The Preacher's Magazine*, vol. xi. p. 229.

' We preach Christ crucified, unto the Jews a stumbling-block, and unto the Gentiles foolishness.'—1 Cor. i. 23.

Compare the curious use of this passage by Hazlitt in his *Winterslow* : 'It has always been with me a test of the sense and candour of any one belonging to the opposite party, whether he allowed Burke to be a great man. Of all the persons of this description that I have ever known, I never met with above one or two who would make this concession. . . . They did not know whom they had to contend with. The corner-stone, which the builders rejected, became the head-corner, though to the Jews a stumbling-block and to the Greeks foolishness; for, indeed, we cannot discover that he was much better understood by those of his own party, if we may judge from the little affinity there is between his mode of reasoning and theirs.'

REFERENCES.—I. 23.—*Sermons for the Church Year*, vol. ii. p. 119. H. S. Holland, *Vital Values*, p. 1. R. W. Church, *Village Sermons* (3rd Series), p. 101. *Expositor* (5th Series), vol. viii. p. 349; *ibid.* (6th Series), vol. vi. p. 471.

THE MESSAGE THAT CONVINCES

We preach Christ crucified, unto the Jews a stumbling-block, and unto the Greeks foolishness; but unto them that are called, both Jews and Greeks, Christ the power of God, and the wisdom of God.'—1 COR. I. 23, 24.

WE preach Christ crucified . . . the power of God, and the wisdom of God! The words ring out, not in protest or defence, but as the summons of a herald. It is the message of an ambassador from his Royal Master. For this to St. Paul was the essence of His Gospel, so vital, so essential, so comprehensive that, as he adds presently, he had deliberately resolved to exclude from his teaching whatever was not directly concerned with the person and the work of His Lord Jesus Christ, and Him crucified. The declaration, as you remember, is the climax of a natural argument. There had been divisions in the Corinthian Church, divisions that after their manner had grown to contentions. Incidents, perhaps trivial, had roused the party spirit. Sharply the Apostle calls the Christians back to first principles. What meant this ranging of themselves some under one name, some under another? Was Christ divided? Had Paul been crucified for them? Had they been baptised in his name? Nay, his only office had been the ministry of the good news, and to declare it with such definiteness and simplicity that its appeal to their consciences might come through no distorting medium, and that their faith should stand, not in the wisdom of men, but in the power of God.

I. This very plainness of speech, this absence of philosophy and rhetoric, were resented by a Church where the eloquent Apollos had just been labouring. Offence had been taken and on various grounds. The Apostle's preaching had come into conflict with the prejudices of one class of men, and not less with the postulates of another class. The pride of religion and the pride of reason both refused their assent. The man who sought for merit in some sterile series of acts, who based his hopes on national or ecclesiastical birthright, whose ethics were the practice of rules rather than the exercise of principles—such a man could have little sympathy with the message that offered life to the lost and grace to the guilty.

And to the other man, who had allowed reason to usurp the place of faith, whose range of research rose no higher than the plane of human thought, who measured the supernatural by the natural—to such a man the story of redemption would seem unreal and foolish. The cross, indeed, had its answer for each. It could tell them of forces far beyond their vision, of wisdom compared with which their own was as naked ignorance; for to those who will receive it in God's own way, it will reveal secrets for which ages have laboured in vain. So comes the fourfold experience which apart from Christ no human mind has ever conceived—'Christ Jesus, who of God is made unto us wisdom, and righteousness, and sanctification, and redemption'. World-wisdom, or, to borrow an alien but familiar word, *Zeitgeist*—the spirit of the times, knows not God, nor the things of God. It may talk about Him, and it may criticise them, but it knows not either. That knowledge, as the Apostle has reminded us, comes not by world-wisdom, but by the exercise of spiritual and God-given faculties.

II. The story of modern missions in this respect is the same as the story of the Apostolic day and the story of the living Church in every age. Conditions differ, of course, but the same causes are producing like results. The signs that follow the missionary to-day are just as much evidence of a Divine presence and of Divine forces at work with him as those seen by the early Church. When we hear, as, thank God, we so often hear, of some bitter Moslem turning to worship the Son of God, or some proud Brahmin counting all things lost for the excellency of the knowledge of Christ Jesus his Lord, or some poor pagan cleansed from loathsome vice and superstition, are we not face to face with facts which are just as truly 'signs and wonders' as those which were wrought in Apostolic times? And they can only be explained in the same way. They are also to be seen not only in separate instances but on a wider scale. The Cross draws men together still as it did then; it influences communities as well as individuals. In the ordered growth of Christian Churches, in the promotion of higher standards of social duty, in a new sense of brotherhood, in the elevation of home life, and not least in a wider outlook and in service for them that are without; in such facts as these, and many others of the same kind, must we not devoutly and gratefully recognise tokens of superhuman wisdom and supernatural power at work on the consciences and lives of men?

III. And we are still far from the end of the message. We have been thinking only of the manifestation of Christ with regard to ourselves—for us men and our salvation. We know, we think we know, what Christ did for us on the cross, and we speak of 'the innumerable benefits which by His precious blood-shedding He hath obtained for us': but there is another side on which I fancy few ponder. What is the Cross but Jesus Himself? Are the redemption and reconciliation of fallen man, marvellous, indeed, beyond all human thought, the final object of the Incarnation and the death and the Resurrection of the Lord? But may not reverent faith, led by the teaching of the Spirit, show us that an even greater purpose lies beyond? There is a profound saying of Jonathan Edwards, which runs thus: 'The emanation of His own infinite fulness was aimed at by God as the end of His creation'. How much more, then, of His creation restored in Christ? In one of those sublime glimpses of the other world which are given in the closing pages of the Bible, the occupants of the new heaven and the new earth are seen engaged in the highest acts of which created beings are capable; and there rises the united offering of angelic and human adoration before the throne of the eternal God, 'Blessing, and honour, and glory, and power be unto Him that sitteth upon the throne and unto the Lamb for ever and ever.— H. G. Fox, *Christian World Pulpit*, vol. LXXIX. p. 312.

REFERENCES.—I. 23-24.—Spurgeon, *Sermons*, vol. i. Nos. 7 and 8. H. Allen, *Penny Pulpit*, No. 1551, p. 41. J. C. M. Bellew, *Sermons*, vol. ii. p. 18. I. 24.—H. Bonar, *Short Sermons for Family Reading*, pp. 33 and 41. J. Oswald Dykes, *Christian World Pulpit*, vol. xlvi. p. 373. Spurgeon, *Sermons*, vol. iii. No. 132.

'The foolishness of God is wiser than men; and the weakness of God is stronger than men.'—I COR. I. 25.

THE philosopher aspires to explain away all mysteries, to dissolve them into light. It is mystery, on the other hand, which the religious instinct demands and pursues: it is mystery which constitutes the essence of worship, the power of proselytism. When the cross became the 'foolishness' of the cross, it took possession of the masses. And in our own day, those who wish to get rid of the supernatural, to enlighten religion, to economise faith, find themselves deserted, like poets who should declaim against poetry, or women who should decry love.—AMIEL's *Journal* (June, 1870).

REFERENCES.—I. 25.—J. B. Lightfoot, *Cambridge Sermons*, p. 265. *Expositor* (6th Series), vol. viii. p. 214.

'Not many wise after the flesh, not many mighty, not many noble, are called.'—I COR. I. 26.

'SATURDAY, 17th November (London).—I spent an hour,' writes Wesley in his *Journal* for 1759, 'agreeably and profitably with Lady G— H— and Sir C— H—. It is well a few of the rich and noble are called. O that God would increase their number! But I should rejoice (were it the will of God) if it were done by the ministry of others. If I might choose, I should still (as I have done hitherto), preach the Gospel to the poor.'

Nor many wise, rich, noble, or profound
In science, win one inch of heavenly ground.
And is it not a mortifying thought
The poor should gain it, and the rich should not?
No:—the voluptuaries, who ne'er forget
One pleasure lost, lose heaven without regret;

Regret would rouse them, and give birth to prayer,
Prayer would add faith, and faith would fix them there.
—COWPER, *Truth* (337 f.).

REFERENCES.—I. 26.—*Expositor* (5th Series), vol. ii. p. 275; *ibid.* (6th Series), vol. i. p. 98. I. 26, 27.—J. G. Greenhough, *The Cross in Modern Life*, p. 54. I. 26-28.—E. M. Geldart, *Faith and Freedom*, p. 15. Bishop Gore, *Christian World Pulpit*, vol. liv. p. 113. I. 26-29.—Spurgeon, *Sermons*, vol. x. No. 587.

'God chose the foolish things of the world that He might put to shame them that are wise; and God chose the weak things of the world, that He might put to shame the things that are strong.'—I COR. I. 27.

SIR JOHN HOOKER has pointed out a very remarkable illustration of this, in showing that . . . the English fly soon supersedes entirely the disgusting and enormous blue-bottle of New Zealand. The English rat drives out the Maori rat. The little clover competes successfully even with the *phormium tenax*, the sword-flax, 'a plant of the coarsest, hardest, and toughest description, that forms huge matted patches of woody rhizomes, which send up tufts of sword-like leaves six to ten feet high, and inconceivably strong in texture and fibre'. This is 'the weak things of the world confounding the mighty' over again, though in a purely physical sense.—R. H. HUTTON, *Theological Essays*, p. 53.

'And the base things of the world, and the things that are despised, did God choose, yea and the things that are nought.' I COR. I. 27, 28.

IN his essay on George Eliot's Life and Letters, Mr. R. H. Hutton declares 'that her ambition always took an intellectual form, that she despised the moral judgment of those who were not intellectual, and never shared a trace of sympathy with the Christian principle "embodied in the above verses". George Eliot had absolutely none of this feeling.'

IN modern Christendom it is not merely our theories of life but the facts of life that have changed. 'Weak things of the world and things that are despised hath God called.' With the recognition of rights in human beings as such, there comes a new realisation of human capacities, not only for the emancipated multitude, but for those whom Aristotle would have allowed to be previously sharers in the βίος πρακτικός. The problems of life become for them far more difficult indeed, but first on account of their greater range and complication, they become of such a kind as to elicit powers previously unused. — T. H. GREEN, *Prolegomena to Ethics* (III. 5).

REFERENCE.—I. 27.—J. B. Johnston, *Christian World Pulpit*, vol. lx. p. 252.

'But of him are ye in Christ Jesus, who was made unto us wisdom from God, and righteousness, and sanctification, and redemption.'—I COR. I. 30.

ALL early Christians taught in the same manner. They never cared to expound the nature of this or that virtue; for they knew that the believer who had Christ had all. Did he need fortitude? Christ was his rock: Equity? Christ was his righteousness: Holiness? Christ was his sanctification: Liberty?

Christ was his redemption : Temperance ? Christ was his ruler : Wisdom ? Christ was his light : Truthfulness ? Christ was the Truth : Charity ? Christ was love.—RUSKIN, *Stones of Venice*, vol. II. chap. VIII.

REFERENCES.—I. 30.—W. J. Knox-Little, *Christian World Pulpit*, vol. xlv. p. 211. R. Flint, *Sermons and Addresses*, pp. 213, 223, 234. J. Stalker, *Christian World Pulpit*, vol. lii. p. 282. W. B. Selbie, *The Servant of God*, p. 201. I. 30, 31.—Spurgeon, *Sermons*, vol. xvii. No. 991.

'He that glorieth, let him glory in the Lord.'—1 COR. I. 31.

'RELIGION,' says Butler in his thirteenth sermon, 'does not demand new affections, but only claims the direction of those you already have, those affections you daily feel. ... We only represent to you the higher, the adequate objects of those very faculties and affections. Let the man of ambition go on still to consider disgrace as the greatest evil ; honour, as his chief good. But disgrace, in whose estimation ? Honour, in whose judgment ? This is the only question.'

REFERENCE.—I. 31.—Spurgeon, *Sermons*, vol. xx. No. 1178.

'He that glorieth, let him glory in the Lord.'—1 COR. I. 31.

THE first text chosen by R. W. Dale as co-pastor at Carr's Lane Meeting, Birmingham.

REFERENCE.—II. 1, 2.—J. M. Neale, *Sermons Preached in Sackville College Chapel*, vol. ii. p. 187.

THE GREAT EXPIATION

'I determined not to know anything among you, save Jesus Christ, and Him crucified.'—1 COR. II. 2.

THE Corinth of St. Paul's day had inherited a revival of philosophy, and was a home of culture so much as to induce a rivalry with Athens herself. But it was not in an atmosphere of intellectual restlessness, in a society where energy was dissipated in an excessive love of dialectic, that the Apostle's ministry was carried on. It was a wisdom of the world, worldly ; brilliant yet pretentious, that led men no nearer to solving the deeper problems of life. When the gifted Alexandrian, Apollos, had appeared as a preacher of Christianity, a considerable section of the Church attached itself to him. The result of an adherence that ought to have been for good was a very grave misunderstanding—many of them were men in whom the old pagan temper was by no means exterminated, and they claimed the sanction of his name, as it would seem, for a great deal that he would have been the very first to disown. The issue was the beginning of a party spirit, which has been under the most widely diverse conditions the bane and hindrance of Christendom. That there ought to have been no such divisions because the methods of two men in the interpreting of their common belief were different goes without the saying. But so it was, and this was the distressful condition of affairs with which in his first extant letter to them the founder of the Corinthian Church had to deal.

I. Here at the outset we must be on our guard as to a possible misconception of St. Paul's determination. Let it be said at once (we shall find abundant reason to justify it later on) that there is no shadow of excuse in his words for a one-sided presentation of Christ's religion. Such partial treatment, to our great injury, is common enough, but it was not his way who had 'not shunned to declare the whole counsel of God'. In the conduct of our own life's occupation we all know that limitation of thought and labour for a while is an indispensable thing. It does not mean neglect of other responsibilities. Because the Bishop of Exeter found it requisite to concentrate two years' attention on the vast expansion of Plymouth, he did not overlook the claims of Devonshire at large. And St. Paul did not determine to know anything among the Corinthians 'save Jesus Christ, and Him crucified,' because he knew, not only, as few others, what human life really is, but he rightly judged that in the particular phase of it with which he had to deal a suffering Christ was the aspect under which he should preach His Lord.

II. The cross of Christ, the final act which crowned a life which was a sacrifice throughout, is the centre of the good tidings to all people. It discovered to us the inmost heart of mercy of our God. It was at once the measure of and the only remedy for sin. ' Can we make the sun go back in its course ? Can we recall the tide at its ebb ? No more can we do away with, and make as though it had never been done, one single sin that we have ever committed,' the condemning voice within, the plague of our own hearts, the unbearable burden of secret or open sin. This is it with which, in the end, each one of us must needs reckon, and the true meaning and value of the Sacrifice offered on Calvary is that it alone—

> Can give the guilty conscience peace,
> And wash away the stain.

Therefore he was more than willing to lay aside any ornament of speech and reputation for ability he might possess, so that he might recall them to the one essential point, that in the crucifixion ' God made Him to be sin for us Who knew no sin, that we might become the righteousness of God in Him '. The showy speculations of the schools might supply a passing interest ; they were absolutely worthless in view of the sorrows and degradation of humanity. ' Jesus Christ, and Him Crucified.' There is nothing else, we may be sure, to come between us and despair.

' Jesus Christ, and Him Crucified.' There is no power so attractive as that of the cross. And yet it is no wonder, for ' God commendeth His love toward us in that while we were yet sinners Christ died for us '. There is no other appeal like unto it. It calls out an instinctive homage which nothing else can. Two generations ago, during the terrible fire that broke out in York Minster, a line of soldiers was posted at the south-west side to keep back the multitude that thronged the streets. The flames spread toward the extreme point of the aisle, and suddenly from within lighted up the western window, revealing the figure of the crucified Christ. And the soldiers, moved by an overwhelming impulse, presented arms before the suffering King of kings.

A little child was present at that memorable scene who in after-life became a Canon of this Cathedral and is now the Bishop of an English See. Another incident thoroughly well attested, in a family that is still among us, will illustrate further what I say. A notorious libertine of bygone days was reading one evening, when he saw an unusual blaze of light fall on the page, and looking up he saw before him a representation of our Blessed Lord on the cross surrounded by a glory. At the same instant he heard a voice saying, 'O sinner, did I suffer this for thee, and are these thy returns?' The vision filled him with unutterable astonishment and agony of heart, and, pierced by a sense of his ingratitude to God, he from that moment forsook his evil life. Still, it is true that, as in Corinth of old, men will avoid the teaching and the application of the cross. They will go round it, so to speak, and admire the poetry of religion while they resent the self-surrender which the Passion of the Master must ever claim. There can be no place for half-measures with the appeal of the crucified Christ. It implies the crucifixion of self, the abolition of the whole body of sin, the consecration of the personality to work in some unequivocal way for God, and for our fellow-men. It must mean this, as it means 'so great salvation,' and therefore many to their peril falter and delay.—ARCHDEACON TETLEY, *The Guardian*, 26th August, 1910.

'I determined not to know anything among you, save Jesus Christ, and Him crucified.'—1 COR. II. 2.

'I AM determined,' said William Lloyd Garrison, the great abolitionist leader, 'to know nothing as a public man save Jesus Christ and Him crucified, and in this country I see Him crucified again in the person of the slave.'

REFERENCES.—II. 2.—R. J. Campbell, *Christian World Pulpit*, vol. lii. p. 264. Archbishop Benson, *Living Theology*, p. 191. A. L. N. *Christian World Pulpit*, vol. xlix. p. 350. W. C. Wheeler, *Sermons and Addresses*, p. 44. Joseph Parker, *Christian World Pulpit*, vol. liii. p. 67. Spurgeon, *Sermons*, vol. xxi. No. 1264, and vol. xlvi. No. 2673. J. G. Rogers, *Christian World Pulpit*, vol. lvii. p. 67. A. Barry, *The Doctrine of the Cross*, p. 5. A. Maclaren, *Expositions of Holy Scripture—Corinthians*, p. 19.

STRENGTH AND WEAKNESS

'And I was with you in weakness, and in fear, and in much trembling.'—1 COR. II. 3.

WHO is it that says so? Weakness and fear and much trembling! Surely he never did any great good. Surely, when he says, 'I was with you,' he might as well, or better, have stayed away altogether. Was it so? It is none other than the Apostle St. Paul, who was in so many dangers, who underwent so many labours.

What he felt none of us must be ashamed or discouraged if we feel also.

I. To feel our weakness—that is one great way to become strong. If we feel strong of ourselves, we are apt to look to ourselves, and to think that *we* can

manage very well, *we* can overcome our enemies, *we* can gain for ourselves a passage to the kingdom of heaven. But when we feel weak, then we are more disposed to go to Him who can give all strength, to Him who is all strength—our Lord Jesus Christ, as He said, 'The earth is weak and all the inhabitants of it; I bear up the pillars of it'.

II. 'I was with you in weakness and in fear.' There is enough to be afraid of in this world. But unfortunately we are all just like children, afraid of that which we ought not to be afraid of, and not the least afraid of what we ought to fear. A child will be afraid of a stuffed wild beast, and cry out in terror. The same child will play in a room where there is a most malignant fever, and have no sense of danger.

III. Every man is weak in that which is his besetting sin. Yet God would give us strength to overcome that completely if only we went to Him for it. 'The congregations of the ungodly have robbed me,' says David. So they have robbed us. The congregations of the ungodly are the devil and his wicked angels.

IV. 'I was with you in weakness, and in fear, and in much trembling.' See where all that ended. He went through fire and water, and he has long since been brought out into a wealthy place.—J. M. NEALE, *Sermons in Sackville College Chapel*, vol. II. p. 249.

'And my speech and my preaching were not in persuasive words of wisdom, but in demonstration of the Spirit and of power: that your faith should not stand in the wisdom of men, but in the power of God.'—1 COR. II. 4, 5.

'TREASURER WIGHTMAN, having glanced at the MS. on the *Fourfold State*,' says Thomas Boston in his memoirs for 1st January, 1719, 'wrote to me, that he found a vein of true Christianity in it, and therefore would contribute to the publication of it; and this requiring an answer, gave me an unlooked-for errand to the throne of grace at this time. He intimated withal, that the style would be nauseous to the polite world, and that no book had yet been written on the depraved state of man, with true spirit and elegancy of expression. This did not much move me; for I do not think that way of writing he is so fond of is the way the Lord has used much to countenance for the advancing of true Christianity.'

'I PREACH the Gospel not with the "enticing words of man's wisdom"'—this was the way of the Apostles' discoursing of things sacred,' says South. 'Nothing here of "the fringes of the north star"; nothing of "nature's becoming unnatural"; nothing of the "down of angels' wings"; or "the beautiful lock of cherubims": no starched similitudes introduced with a "Thus have I seen a cloud rolling in its airy mansion"; and the like. No, there were sublimities above the rise of the apostolic spirit. For the Apostles, poor mortals, were content to take lower steps. . . . It tickled not the ear, but sunk into the heart; and when men came from such sermons, they never commended the preacher for his taking voice or gesture; for the fineness of such a simile, or the quaintness of such a sentence ; but they spoke like men conquered with the overpowering force and evidence of the most concerning truths.'

WE ask questions perhaps about diction, elocution, rhetorical power ; but does the commander of a besieging force dream of holiday displays, reviews, mock engagements, feats of strength, or trials of skill, such as would be graceful and suitable on a parade ground when a foreigner of rank was to be received and *fêted ;* or does he aim at one and one thing only, *viz.,* to take the strong place ? Display dissipates the energy, which for the object in view needs to be concentrated and condensed. We have no reason to suppose that the Divine blessing follows the lead of human accomplishments. Indeed, St. Paul, writing to the Corinthians, who made much of such advantages of nature, contrasts the persuasive words of human wisdom ' with the showing of the Spirit,' and tells us that 'the kingdom of God is not in speech, but in power '.—NEWMAN, *The Idea of a University,* p. 407.

REFERENCES.—II. 4, 5.—T. Sadler, *Sunday Thoughts,* p. 177. J. H. Holford, *Memorial Sermons,* p. 24. II. 5.—C. Perren, *Revival Sermons in Outline,* p. 276. II. 6.—*Expositor* (5th Series), vol. v. p. 39. II. 6, 7.—J. Oswald Dykes, *Christian World Pulpit,* vol. xlvi. p. 373. II. 6-8.—*Expositor* (4th Series), vol. i. p. 31. II. 6-16.—*Ibid.* (5th Series), vol. ix. p. 353. II. 7.—H. Allen, *Penny Pulpit,* No. 1569, p. 185. J. Budgen, *Parochial Sermons,* vol. ii. p. 111. W. P. Du Bose, *The Gospel According to St. Paul,* p. 17. *Expositor* (4th Series), vol. i. p. 32. II. 8.—*Ibid.* (5th Series), vol. vi. p. 2 ; *ibid.* vol. ix. p. 93 ; *ibid.* (6th Series), vol. x. p. 180.

HEAVEN PREPARED FOR THOSE PREPARED FOR HEAVEN

' . . . things which God hath prepared for them that love Him.'—1 COR. II. 9.

To go to heaven when they die, to gaze upon the face of Jesus Christ and so to be blessed throughout all eternity, is the one great desire of all people, believers in the Christian religion, in their more serious moments of reflection—to go to heaven. But there is a question which confronts every one who has ever so desired, a question so extremely simple and natural that one wonders that a reply is not oftener made to it, *viz.,* What sort of place or state would one find heaven to be if he got there ? Granted that earth was done with, its toils and tears for ever over, and a free and full entrance ministered abundantly into that happy realm beyond time and the gloomy grave, what sort of experience would it afford, what sort of occupation would one have assigned him, what kind of society would he find himself mingling in ?

That heaven is a kingdom of unbounded delight, that Jesus is there, and that the ransomed and redeemed of the Lord are there, every one knows who has read even ten pages of the Bible in his lifetime. But this is not the question ; but would the newly arrived spirit find it a state of enjoyment if he entered it ? Granted that suddenly, as men on the

battle-field pass, a soul winged its way into the dread presence of God, and that in the twinkling of an eye the Spirit had sped. If the golden bowl were broken, and the silver cord loosed, and the pitcher broken at the fountain, as happens every hour somewhere in this world, suddenly, and the liberated soul appeared before his Maker, is it conceivable that merely because a man had died and the gates of heaven opened wide to welcome the newly arrived spirit that heaven would be found truly enjoyable irrespective of and wholly apart from the kind of life he had led and the tastes that deepened into habits during that life ?

I. Say that a man had led a tolerably forceful and busy life, and had by his personality forged out for himself a well-recognised place in the esteem of his friends and fellow-mortals, and that he was summoned suddenly, as people are constantly, and found himself among the celestial and blessed throng on high, and that gazing round his newly attained, newly entered on surroundings, he found that the company was too good for him, that the employment assigned him was certain to eventually prove uncongenial to him—that the presence of God and the holy Jesus and the blessed companionship of the pure angels and the ransomed and the redeemed liberated from earth's defilements and no longer trammelled by earth's limitations, all conduced to make up a state for him that he was convinced he could not possibly endure or ever be truly happy in ; but that, on the contrary, promised to make him miserable beyond the power of words to describe ; what would that heaven be ? What though its delights were pure and unbounded —its courts hallowed, its streets of gold, its citizens aglow with eagerness to serve the most High God, its infinite expanse pervaded to the remotest part by the consciousness in every heart but his own of the presence of an all-merciful, all-loving, everpresent God ! And all this to go on indefinitely perpetuated, with no break, no year of respite, and with no hope of ever terminating an engagement which opened with nothing more certain than the certainty that the experience so often sighed for on earth, and over the attainment of which countless religious services had been engaged in and perhaps occasionally a few insipid tears shed, would end in misery, and this called heaven—longed for, sung of, it may be even prayed for and now at last won ! Why, such a heaven would prove itself to one unprepared for it a veritable hell, the torture and horror of which would burn into a man's being like a bar of hot iron into his flesh.

II. Now in these circumstances what can be said in answer to this plain pointed question which every Bible reader finds himself face to face with, nay, which lies before every one who has even once sighed for the joy of heaven and longed to enter there. That question is, What sort of heaven am I prepared for entering here and now? To that plain and most serious question, can any reliable reply be given ? Or must we shut and hasp our Bibles and go our ways into the world again, sad at heart, because we are unable to answer the question, and must we live and die unable to say what sort of heaven we are best fitted for inhabiting? Nay! There is no need for this.

We have only to turn our searching scrutiny within—to gaze, by the aid of memory and an awakened conscience, over the paths we have loved to tread, the secret delights that have charmed us most, the companionships we have cherished and most enjoyed, the kind of people whose society gave us the most intense and keenest enjoyment, and there, still gazing within ourselves, there rises before the mental eye a picture painted as truthfully as by the very hand of God Himself which with absolute faithfulness portrays the kind of heaven each worshipper is best fitted to inhabit and enjoy. We dare not always call it God's heaven or the Bible-lovers' heaven, but the realm or state which from that individual soul's past experience—he or she—is quite justified in believing would best secure the continuity of the kind of joy hitherto known on earth. There cannot be a moment's doubt in any one's mind that what has been so far said carries with it the emphasis of common sense and universal experience.

We must breathe heaven's atmosphere on earth. The radiance of heaven, whatever its final fulness, must fall upon the heart on earth *now*, and wherever there is a heart that is animated by a love of good and by the spirit of a hidden love of God, there heaven has in no dim or uncertain sense already been entered, and the land of promise, however far off at times it may seem, has actually proved to be within. The one golden word in this beautiful verse that gives the key as of heaven itself to every thoughtful inquirer after heaven is love—'things God hath prepared for them that love Him'. Where this blessed influence is unfeignedly existing, leavening the life, clarifying the spiritual vision, sorting out the soul's choicest delights, God is and Christ even now reigns, and in a certain sense heaven's atmosphere is already breathed, though its courts in the final sense are not yet fully won.

From all this there are reducible the following self-manifest deductions, which press themselves upon us all, and that in so solemn, so powerful and yet so persuasive a manner that they are unanswerable. First, *although no man knows where heaven is, every man knows the kind of heaven best suited to his secret tastes.* Next, *the heaven a heart secretly sighs after and most enjoys the foretaste of on earth is the only state best suited for that soul in the hereafter;* and finally, the state that affords most enjoyment on earth and which promises its continuity in the dread hereafter is the state that particular soul should inherit and no other. This might be cast into another set of words, viz., the sort of heaven best suited for a man is the sort of heaven he ought to have assigned him.—D. D. F. MAC-DONALD.

'The things which God hath prepared for them that love Him.'
—1 COR. II. 9.

HEREAFTER, and up there, above the clouds, you have been taught to think; until you were informed by your land-surveyors that there was neither up nor down; but only an axis of *x* and an axis of *y;* and by aspiring aeronauts that there was nothing in the blue but damp and azote. And now you don't believe these things are prepared *any*where? They are prepared just as much as ever, when and where they used to be: just now, and here, close at your hand All things are prepared,—come ye to the marriage.—RUSKIN, *Fors Clavigera* (III. 72).

REFERENCES.—II. 9.—*Expositor* (4th Series), vol. iii. pp. 350, 403; *ibid.* (6th Series), vol. v. p. 64; *ibid.* vol. viii. p. 454.

'Things which eye saw not, and ear heard not, and which entered not into the heart of man, whatsoever things God hath prepared for them that love Him. Unto us God revealed them through the Spirit.'—1 COR. II. 9, 10.

'THESE words,' says Miss Dora Greenwell in *The Covenant of Life* (p. 101), 'and those which follow in the twelfth verse, "now we have received of the Spirit which is of God, to know the things which have been freely given us of Him," and, indeed, the whole tenor of the chapter, make it evident that the Apostle is not looking beyond the time that now is. The mystery with which his thoughts are occupied is the life of God within the soul—that "preparation of the heart of man," wherein He reveals Himself after a manner not to be apprehended by outward sense, or recognised by natural perception. It is the heaven within us, and not the heaven above us, that the Apostle would here unfold to us; he is concerned, not with such things of God as we have yet to wait for, but with such as we have already received.'

REFERENCES.—II. 9.—C. Cuthbert Hall, *Christian World Pulpit*, vol. lxii. p. 12. Llewelyn Davies, *The Purpose of God*, p. 55.

THE THINGS WHICH GOD REVEALS TO THEM THAT LOVE HIM

'Eye hath not seen, nor ear heard, neither have entered into the heart of man, the things which God hath prepared for them that love Him. But God hath revealed them unto us by His Spirit.'—1 COR. II. 9, 10.

ST. PAUL claims for himself and his fellow-Christians a certain superior insight and receptiveness, an endowment peculiar and unique, an apprehension which others have not of the things which make up the higher and diviner life. 'Eye hath not seen, nor ear heard. . . . But God hath revealed them unto us by His Spirit.'

I. Now this truth has often provoked the wit of the satirist and the sneer of the infidel. They have laughed at the idea that anything could be revealed to the soul of faith which is not open to the eyes of the intellect. And sometimes, alas! their sneer has been not without provocation, for the truth itself has many times suffered in the hands of those who have abused and perverted it for their own ends. The priest has claimed it to silence the laity; the bigot and the persecutor have employed it to stop inquiry and quench the highest aspirations of men. And often the vulgar and self-confident preacher, talking the grossest absurdities, has denounced those who reasonably objected to his utterances as carnal, unspiritual, and incompetent to judge. It is open to anyone who is perhaps equally devoid of modesty and grace to use this as the cover of his own ignorance and arrogance, and to say, ' We know these things, and you do not'. All this is inevitable. You have read miserable parodies of the loftiest poems, and seen wretched caricatures of the noblest faces. So the sublimest truths may be easily turned into coarseness and buffoonery; but the truths remain great and immortal, in spite of that.

II. There is a spiritual faculty given to men which makes them wiser in the things of the spirit than all which the wisdom of this world knows, and the merest child in faith may feel and know what the intellectual giant has no perception of. There are simple things in everyday life which are close akin to this. You know people who are clever enough in their own department, and yet blind, deaf, unfeeling, and unappreciative concerning the things which are profoundly interesting to you; men who know fifty times more than you know about the world of books, yet have no more sensitiveness than a stone to the music which sets your heart beating with inexpressible raptures; men who could run up a column of figures whilst you are stumbling over the first of them, and who are no more affected by the most exquisite poetry than your favourite dog might be.

These differences run all through life. They determine whether a life shall be coarse and empty or refined and abounding with joy. There are perceptions which no training can give, which no schools can create: they are the endowment of nature, or rather the gift of God, and they are often in the possession of the child, or the untutored woman, and even of the unlearned preacher, whilst the most omnivorous reader and bookworm may be destitute of them.

And if you think of this you may well allow, if you do not understand, that the same truth holds in the life of faith and religious emotion.

III. It is simply impossible for the secrets of the Christian life to be revealed to those who have no Christian beliefs and sentiments. Plato draws a picture of the worshippers in the old pagan Mysteries. They are going through the sacred dance to the sound of sweet music which is being played in the midst of them. But there are spectators watching them from the hill-side afar off who say these dancers are mad. The spectators can see the movements of joy, but they cannot hear the music. And people outside the Christian life are like these spectators. They cannot hear the music, and all the rest is strange and inexplicable. They do not know the raptures which are felt when the load of sin is removed; when God, who has seemed far off, comes as near as a familiar friend; when life moves in heavenly places,

overshadowed by the love of Jesus, and there is a singing in the heart sweeter than all earthly music. They cannot know. They must taste before they can experience the things which God hath revealed to them that love Him.—J. G. GREENHOUGH, The Mind of Christ in St. Paul, p. 77.

REFERENCES.—II. 9, 10.—J. W. Houchin, The Vision of God, p. 132. T. Sadler, Sunday Thoughts, p. 101. Spurgeon, Sermons, vol. ii. No. 56. W. R. Inge, All Saints' Sermons, 1905-7, p. 92.

THE DEPTHS OF GOD

' But God hath revealed them unto us by His Spirit: for the Spirit searcheth all things, yea, the deep things of God.'—I COR. II. 10.

I. THE first suggestion of the passage is that as a man's own spirit alone knows the depths of his own nature, so the Spirit of God alone can know the depths of God, the mysteries of the Divine nature. A man also has depths within him; within him deep cries unto deep. The growth of a child is a series of revelations, but the development of life after childhood is hardly less surprising. Sir Walter Scott was a dull and wandering mind at school. It is no uncommon thing to find an unsuspected faculty emerging even late in life. The only personal knowledge of me that is in any sense full and inclusive is the knowledge acquired by my own spirit. In the same way the being of the Infinite is known only by the Spirit of God. The self-consciousness of the Being who made the universe, even as we know it, is as far beyond our thought as our human self-consciousness must be beyond the thought of the indistinguishable amœba, which floats in the ooze of the sea.

II. But now it is implied that the Spirit which is the self-consciousness of God can be and is imparted to the Christian, so that in some limited degree that self-consciousness of God, to which His own vast and unfathomable being lies revealed, produces, or reveals, in us a knowledge of His being. We must be careful here not to lapse into the vagueness and unrealities of Pantheism. And we can avoid the danger only by clinging close to the experience of the spiritual life. St. Paul is particular to say that this wisdom is only intelligible to the wise, or the full-grown, i.e. to those in whom the Spirit has been at work. What is it that occurs when by faith in Christ Jesus we receive the Holy Spirit? We can only say that we are introduced into the being and the life of God.

III. These depths of God are searched for us by the Spirit much as Hell, Purgatory, and Paradise were searched for Dante by Virgil and Beatrice. That is, we are taken into abysses, and round the spiral ledges of a mountain, and into the circles of heaven. No poet, not even Dante, could describe the experience. We shall not venture now to do more than enumerate a few of these unfathomable depths of God, and even in our fullest investigations later we shall not flatter ourselves that we have fathomed them. (1) There is, to begin with, the depth of the Divine nature, which is revealed by the Incarnation of the eternal Son, and the deep beyond the deep which is revealed by His suffering on the cross for us men and for our redemption. (2) Guided by the Spirit, we discover that the Incarnation implies the eternal being of God as Love; a relation between Father and Son which was before the world began and will be when the world has ended. The cross implies that the Love which is God is the love which goes out beyond, creating and redeeming; a love which makes men in His image, a love which will save them even by suffering and death. (3) In Romans XI. 33 Paul breaks into an exclamation as the great deeps become for a moment clear to him: 'O the depth of wealth and wisdom and knowledge of God!' It is by this initiation into the depths of the infinite God, and surely by this alone, that we can escape the terror of the infinite universe.—R. F. HORTON, *The Trinity*, p. 21.

THE DEEP THINGS OF GOD
I COR. II. 10.

WHAT do we understand by 'the deep things of God'? There are the depths of Godhead, but that is not what is intended in the text. It is not the depths of Godhead, but the deep things of God which the Holy Ghost wishes us to have and enjoy.

I. First of all, there is God's deep love. 'God *so* loved.' No plummet has ever been found capable of sounding the depths of that 'so'. We cannot learn God's love from Nature. Some people say that the Holy Ghost reveals God's love by the Incarnation of Christ. True, in the Lord Jesus we do see God's love, but we do not see its depths in the Incarnation. When the Holy Ghost wants us to know the great depth of God's love, He points us to Calvary.

II. Another deep thing that the Holy Ghost reveals is God's deep wisdom.

III. The Holy Ghost also reveals God's deep mercy.

IV. The Holy Ghost also reveals God's deep righteousness. 'Thy mercy, O Lord, is in the heavens; and Thy faithfulness reacheth unto the clouds. Thy righteousness is like the great mountains; Thy judgments are a great deep.' The deep things of God cannot be seen by the natural man —they can only be spiritually discerned.—A. G. BROWN, *The Baptist*, vol. LXIX. p. 812.

REFERENCES.—II. 10.—Bishop Bickersteth, *Sermons*, p. 77. *Expositor* (5th Series), vol. vii. p. 286; *ibid.* (6th Series), vol. iii. p. 416. II. 10-12.—*Ibid.* vol. iv. p. 187. II. 11.— J. Keble, *Sermons for Lent to Passion-tide*, p. 183. *Expositor* (4th Series), vol. x. p. 248. II. 12.—T. Arnold, *Sermons*, vol. iv. p. 125. J. Keble, *Sermons for Ascension Day to Trinity Sunday*, p. 209. Spurgeon, *Sermons*, vol. xxxv. No. 2087. W. T. Davison, *The Indwelling Spirit*, p. 59.

THE NATURAL MAN

'The natural man receiveth not the things of the Spirit of God; for they are foolishness unto him: neither can he know them, because they are spiritually discerned.'—I COR. II. 14.

'THE natural man.' The Greek is the 'psychical' man, the man in whom the soul is all, and the spirit

is like a dark untenanted chamber. The natural man is the man whose spirit is empty of God. In the third chapter of the same Epistle, Paul says: 'And I, brethren, could not speak unto you as unto spiritual, but as unto carnal, even as unto babes in Christ'. Now the 'carnal' man is a Christian, a babe in Christ. He is regenerate, he is in Christ, and Christ is in him; but instead of Christ being predominant, the carnal element is predominant.

I. There are Four Characteristics of the Carnal Life.—(1) The carnal life is a babe life. What is sweeter than a babe? But what is tender and beautiful in a babe for a few months is terrible at the end of twelve months, or ten years. And what is lovely in a young convert is terrible in a man of ten or twenty years of Christian life (2) And then the carnal man lives on milk. (3) A carnal Christian is also sectarian. 'I am of Paul, and I am of Apollos, and I of Cephas.' (4) 'Strong meat belongeth to them that are of full age, even those who by reason of use have their senses exercised to discern both good and evil' (Heb. v. 14). Here we have a fourth characteristic of the carnal Christian; such an one is unable to exercise his senses to discern good and evil.

II. How to get Rid of the Self-Life?—There are three steps: (1) The cross. Whenever the self-life obtrudes, reckon yourself dead to it; reckon that the cross stands between you and it. (2) The Holy Spirit. 'If ye through the Spirit do mortify the deeds of the body, ye shall live.' And again: 'The Spirit lusteth against the flesh'. It was by the Eternal Spirit that Christ offered Himself without spot to God, and it is by the Eternal Spirit that the cursed spirit of self is going to be antagonised in your life and mine. (3) This leads me to my third point, that whilst the Spirit of God in the depth of your heart is antagonising the self-life, He does it by making Jesus Christ a living bright reality. He fixes your thoughts upon Jesus.—F. B. MEYER, *The Soul's Ascent*, p. 75.

REFERENCES.—II. 14.—Bishop Bethell, *Sermons*, vol. i. p. 286. Spurgeon, *Sermons*, vol. vii. No. 407. *Expositor* (4th Series), vol. ii. p. 43; *ibid.* (6th Series), vol. iv. p. 164; *ibid.* vol. ix. p. 456.

'He that is spiritual judgeth all things.'—I COR. II. 15.

'HE that is spiritual judgeth all things'—if cleaned from fanaticism and presumption, and taken in connection with 'But yet I show unto you a more excellent way'—is at once, I think, our privilege and our duty.—DR. ARNOLD of Rugby.

REFERENCES.—II. 15.—Phillips Brooks, *The Law of Growth*, p. 294. II. 16.—J. Clifford, *The Christian Certainties*, p. 87. *Expositor* (6th Series), vol. i. p. 404. II. 31, 32.—F. D. Maurice, *Sermons*, vol. ii. p. 197. III. 1.—*Expositor* (4th Series), vol. i. p. 198.

'I could not speak to you as unto spiritual . . . I fed you with milk, not with meat, for ye were not able to bear it.— I COR. III. 1, 2.

A MAN always is to be himself the judge how much of his mind he will show to other men; even to those he would have work along with him.—CARLYLE, *Heroes*, VI.

'Nay, even now ye are not able.'—1 COR. III. 2.

IT is a fact, forced upon one by the whole experience of life, that almost all men are children, more or less, in their tastes and admirations.—DE QUINCEY, *Autobiographic Sketches*, XIII.

REFERENCES.—III. 1-8.—J. Bowstead, *Practical Sermons*, vol. i. p. 281. III. 2.—G. W. Brameld, *Practical Sermons*, p. 1.

'Whereas there is among you jealousy and strife, are ye not carnal?'—1 COR. III. 3.

SPEAKING of the spirit of jealousy, in his essay on *Modern Dissent*, Matthew Arnold observes that 'this temper is as much a spiritual hindrance—nay, in the view of Christianity it is even a more direct spiritual hindrance—than drunkenness or loose living. Christianity is, first and above all, a temper, a disposition; and a disposition just the opposite to "a spirit of watchful jealousy". Once admit a spirit of watchful jealousy, and Christianity has lost its virtue; it is impotent. All the other vices it was meant to keep out may rush in. Where there is jealousy and strife among you, asks St. Paul, *are ye not carnal?* are ye not still in bondage to your mere lower selves? But from this bondage Christianity was meant to free us; therefore, says he, get rid of what causes divisions, and strife, and "a spirit of watchful jealousy".

COMPARE the preface to Mazzini's essays on *Faith and the Future*, in which he asks, 'Why has *reaction* triumphed? The cause lies in ourselves; in our want of organisation, in the dismemberment of our ranks by *systems*, some absurd and dangerous, all imperfect and immature, and yet defended in a spirit of fierce and exclusive intolerance; in our ceaseless distrust, in our miserable little vanities, in our absolute want of that spirit of discipline and order which alone can achieve great results; in the scattering and dispersing of our forces in a multitude of small centres and sects, powerful to dissolve, impotent to found.'

REFERENCES.—III. 3.—W. M. Sinclair, *Difficulties of Our Day*, p. 109. T. Binney, *King's Weigh-House Chapel Sermons* (2nd Series), p. 341. III. 4-15.—*Expositor* (6th Series), vol. viii. p. 73.

'What then is Apollos? and what is Paul? Ministers through whom ye believed.'—1 COR. III. 5.

COMPARE Martineau's remark, in his review of Dr. Arnold's life: 'Above all, he wholly lost sight of *himself*, and never gave occasion for even the perversest spirit to suspect that his battle with school evils was a contest for personal dignity or power; in his dominance over wrong, he was himself but serving the *right*'.

REFERENCES.—III. 5.—Joseph Parker, *The Gospel of Jesus Christ*, p. 201. C. D. Bell, *The Name Above Every Name*, p. 51.

'I planted, Apollos watered; but God gave the increase.'—1 COR. III. 6.

'WE can look but a very little way into the connections and consequences of things: our duty is to spread the incorruptible seed as widely as we can, and leave it to *God to give the increase*,' says Butler in one of his sermons. 'Yet thus much we may be almost assured of, that the Gospel, wherever it is planted, will have its genuine effect upon some few, upon more perhaps than are taken notice of in the hurry of the world.'

REFERENCES.—III. 6.—S. Cox, *Expositions*, p. 377. III. 6-9.—Spurgeon, *Sermons*, vol. xxvii. No. 1602.

THE GUILD OF GOD

'For we are God's fellow-workers.'—1 COR. III. 9 (R.V.).

IT is a special feature of the Christian revelation that throughout it exhibits God as a Worker. Other systems represent Him as being eternally at rest; He is pictured as an infinite Dreamer; to impute to Him anything like personal action is considered derogatory to His glory. In a true sense the orbs of heaven, the forces of the earth, creeping things and flying fowl, are messengers and instruments of the Divine Will; but whilst they act involuntarily and unconsciously, we may co-operate with God intelligently, willingly, lovingly. In a sense altogether special it is our privilege to become His 'fellow-workers'.

I. Consider the great design and obligation of life. To what end does God work? To establish in the human heart and in human society the kingdom of justice and righteousness. If we are co-workers with God, let us often remind ourselves of His ideal, consult His plan and programme, and strive toward His purpose, which is altogether spiritual, holy, and beautiful. Men toil in a thousand different departments, at ten thousand differing tasks, and the result seems only a mass of isolated strivings; yet let us be sure that the unification of action is a fact also, that all kinds of social ministries are vitally related, and that one Divine co-ordinating Mind directs our divided and confused activities to a definite and an inexpressibly glorious end. (1) The workers must not despise or disparage one another, nor must any one thus treat himself or his task. (2) Let each in his place faithfully and industriously realise the splendid conception of the Master-Builder. 'I sing for God,' cried Jenny Lind, who did not always sing in cathedrals; 'I pray with my fingers,' said a celebrated organist; and the million toilers of the city working in the fear of God and the love of their neighbour make shrines of workshops and transform rough tools into sacred vessels of worship and blessing.

II. Remember the condition of success in the work of life. If 'God's fellow-workers,' we must do our part. Our infidelity, disloyalty, or sloth arrests the great Worker and His miracles of blessing. On the other hand, we must not forget our dependence. Do we not often pathetically fail because we forget the paramount Partner?

III. Here we find the grand encouragement in all our generous aspirations and effects. 'God's fellow-workers.' Then He will bring the work through. What an efficient coadjutor!—W. L. WATKINSON, *Inspiration in Common Life*, p. 40.

WORKERS WITH GOD

1 COR. III, 9.

IT is a bold claim to make, but facts correspond to it and justify it. There is a sense in which every man is a fellow-worker with God. St. Paul, of course, meant very much more than this when he described himself and his companions in service as 'fellow-workers with God.' His words speak of conscious and voluntary co-operation, a willing and intelligent oneness of purpose and effort with the will and work of God.

I. In creating the world we are called to be God's fellow-workers. Creation is not finished, but is always proceeding. In this continuous and never-ceasing work of creation man can help or hinder, develop or retard the creative purpose and process. The world into which he is born has all the material prepared to his hands; he is here to work it into more and better things. An eminent geologist has written a book that bears this title, *The Earth as Modified by Human Action*, and one has only to read it to see the wide range of human power, to see how closely man is in partnership with God in the work of creation, how much God needs man and man needs God.

II. And, in his own training and saving, in the work of developing, personal faculty and character, man is called to be God's fellow-worker. What he can do for the earth, and the creatures and things that live upon it, he can do for himself, fulfil and finish the Creator's purpose and plan. The statement in the Hebrew poem of creation, that man was made in the image of God, is prophecy, not history. It is the end seen from the beginning. Faith in what man can do and achieve does not mean any less faith in God. It includes God as the ground of all power, the inspiring Helper of all endeavour, the eternal life of all life. Real advance is only made when voluntary, purposeful efforts aid the unconscious strivings of Nature. It is an old saying that bids us pray as if God did everything, and work as if God did nothing. The will and work of God are identical not only with the moral regeneration of individuals, with the salvation and cultivation of the individual human soul, but with all work we respect and honour and rejoice in, with art, science, literature, politics, trade, with whatsoever activity works for the good of the community and the civilisation of nations.

III. In reconciling the world to Himself we are called to be fellow-workers with God. The work of atonement is in a peculiar sense the work of God. The Divine mission of Jesus Christ is not so much an interpolation in human history as the reflection and revelation in space and time of the universal and eternal labour and passion and sacrifice of God. It is the Father's work into which the Son enters. And if we have got the Spirit of Christ, if we are within the circle of His fellowship, then we cannot help sharing in that work of reconciliation which is most clearly set forth by Jesus Christ to be the work of God in our human world. Worse than the most hopeless pessimism is the optimism of the men who are content to repeat the creed, 'Truth and right are mighty, and must prevail'. But truth and right have never yet prevailed in this world without the help of true and righteous men. The only real failure in life, believe me, is to do less than our best.—JOHN HUNTER, *Christian World Pulpit*, vol. LX. p. 257.

REFERENCES. — III. 9. — H. H. Snell, *Christian World Pulpit*, vol. liv. p. 70. J. S. Boone, *Sermons*, p. 136. C. G. Finney, *Penny Pulpit*, No. 1570, p. 193. E. Armitage, *Christian World Pulpit*, vol. li. p. 364. A. Maclaren, *Expositions of Holy Scripture—Corinthians*, p. 30. III. 10.—*Expositor* (7th Series), vol. vi. p. 372. III. 11.—David Brook, *Preacher's Magazine*, vol. iv. p. 173. C. M. Betts, *Eight Sermons*, p. 3. H. Varley, *Christian World Pulpit*, vol. xlviii. p. 68. H. P. Liddon, *Sermons Preached on Special Occasions*, p. 220. F. D. Maurice, *Sermons*, vol. v. p. 237. Spurgeon, *Sermons*, vol. xxv. No. 1494. *Expositor* (6th Series), vol. iv. p. 293.

THE TRIAL BY FIRE

'For other foundation can no man lay than that is laid, which is Jesus Christ. Now if any man build upon this foundation gold, silver, precious stones, wood, hay, stubble; every man's work shall be made manifest: for the day shall declare it, because it shall be revealed by fire; and the fire shall try every man's work of what sort it is. If any man's work abide which he hath built thereupon, he shall receive a reward. If any man's work shall be burned, he shall suffer loss: but he himself shall be saved; yet so as by fire.'—1 COR. III. 11-15.

I. Let us ask, What is it we each build? The reply is, Character. What is character? It is the slow accretion of habits, acts, and impulses, of morality and emotion, tending toward a final mould, a fixed form. It is the accretion of habit, for we are so constituted that to do a thing once is to desire to do it again, and every act is the preface and preparation for a similar act. It is the work of impulse, for impulse is the glowing forge in which action is shaped. It is morality and emotion, for not more surely is the slenderest coloured thread gathered into the loom, or the lightest whisper chronicled on the wax tablet of the phonograph, than is each thrill of hope, each fear or prayer, recorded in the structure of character. Does it not follow, then, that character is everything to us: the one real possession which is imperishable? The whole worth of Christianity to the world is that it is the science of character, that it teaches men to build their lives up into a mould of moral beauty, and attain the stature of Christ. James Smetham said: 'It is of much more importance to preserve a fresh and tender love to God and man, than to turn the corner of an art career'.

II. But the Apostle strikes a subtler chord when he speaks of the mixed elements that exist in the best work, of things perfect and imperfect—the gold and the stubble—that jostle one another in human character. Who has not remarked the imperfections of religious men? Who has not seen, as St. Paul saw, that the same man has both gold and stubble in him, that his vision of truth is often limited and vitiated by some error of nature, that his flaws of temper exist side by side with a great apostolic passion for souls, or that his narrowness of sympathy spoils all the admirable grasp of truth which is his?

The whole history of the Church has been a record of these imperfections. The duty of charity towards others, which our own errors teach us, must not blind us to the main point of the passage, which is the testing of character which awaits us. Paul sees the fire that kindles for his trial, the purifying and avenging flame that is to test his work, and he would fain build only with such elements as the flames cannot consume.

III. What, then, is this flame? What does it mean for us? (1) Surely time is one of the flames by which all our work is to be tested. (2) Temptation also is the flame through which all character must pass. (3) But beyond time and temptation there lies the third trial, and it is of that St. Paul chiefly thinks: the last day—that day—the great assize. There is one final word of consolation. Nothing that is really good in us can ever perish, or need fear that flame.—W. J. DAWSON, *The Comrade Christ*, p. 261.

REFERENCE.—III. 11-15.—C. D. Bell, *The Name Above Every Name*, p. 165.

'If any man buildeth on the foundation gold, silver, costly stones, wood, hay, stubble; each man's work shall be made manifest: for the day shall declare it, because it is revealed in fire.'—I COR. III. 12, 13.

'THE more I think of the matter, and the more I read of the Scriptures themselves, and of the history of the Church,' Dr. Arnold wrote in 1827, 'the more intense is my wonder at the language of admiration with which some men speak of the Church of England, which certainly retains the foundation sure as all other Christian societies do, except the Unitarians, but has overlaid it with a very sufficient quantity of hay and stubble, which I devoutly hope to see burnt one day in the fire.'

THIS passage was often in Mrs. Oliphant's mind, not only on her death-bed, but earlier in her career as a novelist. 'What is the reputation of a circulating library to me?' she wrote in her autobiography. 'Nothing, and less than nothing—a thing the thought of which now makes me angry, that any one should for a moment imagine I cared for that, or that it made up for any loss. I am perhaps angry, less reasonably, when well-intentioned people tell me I have done good, or pious ones console me for being left behind by thoughts of the good I must yet be intended to do. God help us all! What is the good done by any such work as mine, or even better than mine? "If any man build upon this foundation . . . wood, hay, stubble; . . . if the work shall be burned, he shall suffer loss: but he himself shall be saved; yet so as by fire." An infinitude of pains and labour, and all to disappear like the stubble and the hay.'

REFERENCE.—III. 12, 13.—A. Maclaren, *Expositions of Holy Scripture—Corinthians*, p. 39.

'If any man's work shall be burned, he shall suffer loss: but he himself shall be saved; yet so as through fire.'—I COR. III. 15.

To Dominic, in allusion to his supposed share in the Albigensian crusade, and the foundation of the Inquisition, he used to apply St. Paul's words, 1 Cor. III. 15.—STANLEY'S *Life of Arnold* (ch. VIII.).

REFERENCES.—III. 13.—W. Redfern, *The Gospel of Redemption*, p. 135. R. W. Church, *Village Sermons* (3rd Series), p. 9. H. P. Liddon, *Sermons on Some Words of St. Paul*, p. 51. *Expositor* (4th Series), vol. ii. p. 66. III. 15.—C. D. Bell, *The Name Above Every Name*, p. 178. T. Binney, *King's Weigh-House Chapel Sermons*, p. 138.

THE COMING OF THE HOLY GHOST
(For Whit-Sunday)

'Know ye not that ye are the temple of God, and that the Spirit of God dwelleth in you?'—I COR. III. 16.

I. THE first visible fruit of the coming of the Holy Ghost was in the gift of tongues. Part of that gift of tongues seems undoubtedly to have been that certain of the number, where they were, could speak languages they were not able to speak before. They were able to sing the praises of God in a way that all kinds of different nations who had come to Jerusalem from all parts were able to understand. That was part of the gift, and a wonderful gift, and yet it was the least valued of the gifts of God. It was the extraordinary, and not the ordinary, gift of the Holy Ghost, and we make a great mistake when we think that the extraordinary must of necessity be of more value, of greater worth, than the ordinary. That is a mistake which people make in many other directions: for instance, despising the wild flowers of the wayside, because, as we say, they are common, and valuing more highly the flowers which are uncommon. So with the gifts of the Holy Spirit—there are those which are extraordinary, and which appear from time to time in the New Testament. They have passed; do not envy them. The ordinary gift of the Holy Ghost—that remains with us, and that is of much higher value than the extraordinary.

II. What is the ordinary gift? It is the gift of Spiritual power. 'Tarry ye in the city of Jerusalem, until ye be endued with power from on high.' That is the Master's promise, and they were to wait for it. Of this other gift of languages He said nothing—only of the more precious gift, the gift of the power from on high. It is the power of the Holy Spirit which enters into our own soul, into our own spiritual nature, and deals with it and strengthens it in every department. It takes hold of our understanding. The Holy Spirit entering into our soul, making the body and the soul His temple and dwelling within us, comes as an added strength to our understanding, raising our understanding, so that it can not only deal with the things that it sees, but rise to the height of faith, giving a new power of faith and opening our eyes to see the true bearing and meaning of the words of the Lord, and of the acts of the Lord. All that He has done and said for our own soul needs a key. There the words lie on the page, and they are like a locked room. It is the Holy Spirit Who can come and open those words for our understanding, according to the promise of the Lord: 'When He, the Spirit of truth, is come, He will guide you into all truth'. Remember, the words of the Lord are only to be understood by the help and by the power of the Holy Spirit.

III. The Holy Spirit comes and brings power, or brings strength to our own heart and to our own affections, and teaches a man, and helps a man to hate what is hateful and to love what is good and what is true. The Holy Spirit dwells within our hearts and puts in them that double faculty of the appreciation of what is good, the love of what is good, and the renunciation and hatred of what is evil.

And yet again, the Holy Spirit, entering into our hearts, finds His way into our will—our will which has been weakened by self-indulgence and self-pleasing—and puts new strength into that will, and gives to us what He gave to the Apostles at that time—new heart and new courage to face the difficulties before them. The coming of the Holy Ghost made of these men, who were cowards, heroes and martyrs. One after another, these men who had denied their Master, after the coming of the Holy Ghost, laid down their lives. The strength of the martyrs is the witness of the power of the Holy Ghost, just as all the most beautiful things which have been written and thought are the gifts of the Holy Ghost. And all true love of God and man is an outcome of that Holy Spirit Who has made the soul His temple and resting-place.

This gift of power to our understanding and our heart and our will—that represents the ordinary gift of the Holy Spirit; and that is at our disposal, and according to our goodwill and our earnestness and the use we make of God's gifts will be given to us of the fulness of the power of the Spirit.

CHRIST AND HIS HUMAN TEMPLES

'Know ye not that ye are the temple of God, and that the Spirit of God dwelleth in you?'—1 Cor. iii. 16.

This Epistle was written from the city of Ephesus where was that famous temple of Diana which was reputed to be the world's greatest work of art. It was addressed to Corinth, which city also was renowned for its splendid temples. Now we can imagine St. Paul writing in view of the Ephesian temple, or with his mind full of pictures which the sacred buildings of Corinth had impressed. He knew, at least, that these temples were always before the eyes and often in the thoughts of the Corinthian believers; and herein lies the point of such words as these: 'Know ye not that ye are the temple of God?' You poor, despised, scorned ones, cast out from society, are more and greater than these lofty fanes.

I. In these words there was the new Christ-given thought of the dignity of man. Man was more than stones and marble, and statuary and material splendour. Manhood with a bit of faith and goodness in it was more than wisdom and genius and wealth, and all that these things could produce. When Christ took upon Himself a human body, He made humanity Divine. The Incarnation was the real starting-point of human progress and elevation. Thrones and palaces and temples are not the glory

of the world, but men and women who reflect in their faces and conduct some of the majesty of the great King.

II. Think of the nearness and familiarity of the Divine presence. You have not to go in search of Him; you carry Him with you. Stones cannot be consecrated, but souls can: priests cannot introduce you to Him—He is nearer than the priest who whispers in your ears. He is part of you; your souls are the altar, your prayers are the incense, your aspirations are the painted windows and spires, your devout thoughts are the priests.

III. Now what a solemn thought of dedication and of holiness is suggested by these words. *Temple*—something detached, cut off, separated, taken out of the common, secular, corrupt world and marked out for other and higher uses; not to be employed again for any service that is low, vulgar, profane, for any service but what is pure and Divine; to be kept holy, undefiled, and perfumed with the incense of sweet thoughts and prayers. Keep the temple holy which He has made His own.

IV. And, finally, remember that the temple is a witness for God. And we are to be as living temples among the crowd of men, bearing witness of the Spirit of God that dwells within us, forcing upon their unbelieving minds thoughts of the Christ whom we love, showing in speech, temper, and conduct, the image of the Invisible, proving to the world that God is near and that Christ is living by the Divinity and Christ-likeness of our faces.—J. G. GREENHOUGH, *The Cross in Modern Life*, p. 192.

THE DIVINE INDWELLING

(*A Motive to Holiness*)

'Know ye not that ye are the temple of God, and that the Spirit of God dwelleth in you?'—1 Cor. iii. 16.

I. Let us consider the fact to which the Apostle appeals: 'Ye are the temple of God—the Spirit of God dwelleth in you'.

(1) This is not, first of all, merely a recognition of the presence of God in Nature. Doubtless, the sense of God's encompassing, all-pervading life must be one of the main factors in the thought of every thinking man who believes in the existence and spirituality of God. He conceives of God as the Being from Whom it is literally impossible to escape. 'Whither shall I go then from Thy Spirit? or whither shall I go then from Thy presence? if I climb up into heaven, Thou art there: if I go down to hell, Thou art there also. If I take the wings of the morning, and remain in the uttermost parts of the sea, even there also shall Thy hand lead me; and Thy right hand shall hold me.'

God, the everywhere present, enwrapping, upholding, penetrating through and through each creature of His hand, yet in His Uncreated Essence distinct from all, is before the Psalmist's soul. Man, if he would, cannot be where God is not, cannot place himself outside this all-pervading ubiquity of God

Thus the universe is the temple of God, and the Spirit of God dwells in it.

(2) Yet the Apostle does not mean that the Corinthian Christians were only God's temple as being a part of His universe. For, first of all, man, as man, is differently related to the Divine Omnipresence from anything else in Nature. Man alone can feel it, can acknowledge it, can respond to it. God is just as present with a plant or an animal as with man; but neither animal nor plant is conscious of the Divine contact; both animal and plant offer only the homage of an unconscious obedience to God's law. Man, however, can know and adore his God, by the homage of his intelligence and of his moral freedom; and thus the human soul is a temple of God, in a distinct sense from any of the lower forms of life. It is a living temple, whereof each wall, each pillar, each cornice, nay the arches and the very floor, are instinct with the life whether of thought or feeling, so designed and proportioned as even by their silent symmetry to show forth their Maker's praise. To those among Adam's children who are alive in Jesus Christ, God manifests His presence by His Spirit; and this manifestation makes them His temples in an altogether intenser sense than is possible for unregenerate man.

(3) For the presence referred to by the Apostle is not only the presence of the Holy Ghost in the Church. Primarily, indeed, the words imply that truth, 'Ye are the temple of God,' 'the Spirit of God dwelleth in' or 'among you'. It is indeed in the Church as a whole, and not in the individual, that the full majesty of the Spirit's presence is to be witnessed. The 'whole body of the Church is governed and sanctified' by the Spirit, in a deeper sense than any individual can be.

(4) The presence upon which he insists is ultimately a presence in the individual. It differs from the presence of the Spirit with saints and prophets under the Jewish Covenant, and still more from the occasional visits which He may have vouchsafed to heathens, in that, so far as the will of the Giver is concerned, it is normal and continuous. 'The Spirit of God dwelleth in you.' No passing visit is here, no sudden but transient illumination, no power, fitfully given and suddenly withdrawn. 'I will dwell in them, and walk in them; and I will be their God, and they shall be My people.' Such was to be the law of the Messianic kingdom: each of its subjects was to be gifted with an inward presence of the Holy One.

II. If we have difficulty in habitually realising such a truth, it is, I believe, because we fail to do justice in our ordinary thoughts to that higher side of our composite being, which is the seat of the Spirit's Presence within us. Man is not merely a perishing animal gifted with life, a $\psi v \chi \acute{\eta}$: he is an immortal spirit, a $\pi v \epsilon \hat{v} \mu a$.

III. Let us observe, in the substance of the Apostle's appeal, all the conditions of a really powerful religious motive.

(1) Of these the first is, that the truth or fact appealed to should not be an open question in the mind of the person to whom the appeal is made.

(2) A second condition of a strong religious motive is, that it shall rest upon a positive and not upon a merely negative conviction.

(3) A third condition of a strong working religious motive is, that it shall rest upon what is felt to be a present truth.

(4) A fourth condition of a strong religious motive is, that it shall appeal to the better side, to the more generous natural impulses of human nature.

IV. Lastly, be it observed that this conviction furnishes the true basis both for the moral training of children, and for real self-improvement in later life.—H. P. LIDDON.

REFERENCES.—III. 16.—C. Perren, *Outline Sermons*, p. 228. M. G. Glazebrook, *Prospice*, p. 182. Bishop Winnington-Ingram, *A Mission of the Spirit*, p. 123. A. Maclaren, *Expositions of Holy Scripture—Corinthians*, p. 47. III. 17.— *Expositor* (4th Series), vol. i. p. 202. III. 18.—Phillips Brooks, *The Mystery of Iniquity*, p. 153. *Expositor* (6th Series), vol. i. p. 93; *ibid.* vol. xii. p. 30.

TWO ESTIMATES OF FOOLISHNESS

'Let no man deceive himself. If any man among you seemeth to be wise in this world, let him become a fool, that he may be wise. For the wisdom of this world is foolishness with God.'—1 COR. III. 18, 19.

ST. PAUL touched a sensitive place when he talked in this way. If there was one thing which a Corinthian could not bear to have pricked it was his conceit in the matter of wisdom. To call that in question was the unpardonable insult. He was not particularly vain of his personal appearance, of his clothes, or his property; but he was always more than a little puffed up with intellectual pride. Of the two he would have much preferred an empty purse to a thinly furnished head, and he would almost rather be known as a criminal than be regarded as a fool. These words of St. Paul must have been like needles to him, unless he laughed them away as sheer stupidity. 'If any man among you seemeth to be wise, let him become a fool, that he may be wise.' The first point on which the Apostle insists here is—

I. That there are two estimates of folly—God's estimate and the world's estimate; and these two are often as contrary as light and darkness. 'The wisdom of this world is foolishness with God.' And if a man seems to be particularly wise in the eyes of the world, the best thing he can do is to become a fool in men's eyes in order to be called wise by God. That is St. Paul's extreme way of putting it, and it sounds extravagant. And yet it covers a profound and unquestionable truth.

'The wisdom of this world is foolishness with God.' And, on the contrary, what seems to the world folly is often, in God's sight, the highest and divinest wisdom. An honest life will not be always called wise; a life of purity will occasionally win cheap sneers. If you pursue great ideals, if you kneel often in prayer, if you spend your energies in self-denying labours, if you give freely to help your fellow-men if you often lift your eyes from the dust toward the heavenly crown, if you seek God's 'Well done!' rather than the praises of men, you are sure to be called by the baser sort, as all good men have been called—fools. Take it with a smile. Pin the name upon your breast, as a mark of honour. For it is an honour to have that name given by those who have no greatness of soul. You are in the way of God's wisdom, and it is of infinitely more consequence, both now and hereafter, that you should not be deemed a fool by Him, whatever you are in the eyes of men. For what He thinks folly now all lips will call folly some time, and the wisdom of this world is foolishness with God. The second thought which St. Paul gives us here is—

II. That a man is never wise until he feels himself a fool, and just trusts in that higher wisdom which is not his own. 'If any man seemeth to be wise in this world, let him become a fool, that he may be wise.' Some of us have had this grace given, to know that the human will is weak and the heart often prejudiced and darkened, that the most cultured mind cannot see a step before it, and the wisest mind stumbles unless God illumine, direct, and show the way. And we feel that we dare not take any important step in life until we have laid it before God in prayer. It is then that we become wise—then when we say—

An infant crying in the night,
An infant crying for the light;

'Show me Thy way, O Lord'; 'Take Thou my hand and lead me'. Then do we understand what St. Paul meant when he said, 'If any man among you seemeth to be wise in this world, let him become a fool, that he may be wise'.—J. G. GREENHOUGH, *The Mind of Christ in St. Paul*, p. 139.

REFERENCES.—III. 19.—E. A. Bray, *Sermons*, vol. i. p. 361, and vol. ii. p. 1. *Expositor* (4th Series), vol. xiii. p. 119; *ibid.* (5th Series), vol. viii. p. 308. III. 21.—Brooke Herford, *Courage and Cheer*, p. 235. T. Phillips, *Christian World Pulpit*, vol. xlvi. p. 307. *Expositor* (6th Series), vol. i. p. 94. III. 21, 22.—B. J. Snell, *The All-Enfolding Love*, p. 145. A. Maclaren, *Expositions of Holy Scripture—Corinthians*, p. 56.

'Wherefore let no man glory in men. For all things are yours; whether Paul, or Apollos, or Cephas, or the world, or life, or death, or things present, or things to come; all are yours, and ye are Christ's, and Christ is God's.'—1 Cor. III. 21-23.

'WHO,' asks R. H. Hutton in his review of Renan's *Paul*, 'who that has studied St. Paul at all has not noticed that bold, soaring, and—I might almost say by an audacious anachronism, if it did not give so false a conception of its intellectual motive—*Hegelian* dialectic, with which he rises from the forms of our finite and earthly thought to the infinite and the spiritual life embodied in them? . . . "Therefore let no man glory in men. *For all things are yours;* whether Paul, or Apollos, or Cephas, or the world, or life, or death, or things present, or things to come; all are yours, and ye are Christ's, and Christ is God's." What ease and swiftness, and power of wing in this indignant upward flight from the petty conflicts of the Corinthian Church; an upward flight which does not cease till the poor subjects of contention, though he himself was one of them, seem lost like grains of sand beneath the bending sky!'

REFERENCES.—III. 21-23.—Spurgeon, *Sermons*, vol. xliv. No. 2589. J. Caird, *Sermons*, p. 247. F. L. Goodspeed, *Christian World Pulpit*, vol. xlviii. p. 121. T. Arnold, *Sermons*, vol. iv. p. 47. W. L. Alexander, *Sermons*, p. 122. J. W. Boulding, *Sermons*, p. 21. A. Maclaren, *Expositions of Holy Scripture—Corinthians*, p. 65. III. 22.—C. Perren, *Revival Sermons in Outline*, p. 211. Spurgeon, *Sermons*, vol. xv. Nos. 870 and 875. *Expositor* (6th Series), vol. vi. p. 309. III. 23.—C. Perren, *Revival Sermons in Outline*, p. 335.

SECRETS MADE KNOWN
'Stewards of the mysteries of God.'—1 COR. IV. 1.

THE point for us is, 'What does the word "mystery" mean in the New Testament?' Mystery in the New Testament means one thing only, and that is something which has been kept secret for centuries, but has at last been revealed. And I am going to speak to you about five secrets—five mysteries if you like—five things which have been kept secret since the foundation of the world, but which have at last been told us.

Now what are those five secrets?

I. **What was there Behind that which we can See?**—It is a question which men have been trying to answer for thousands of years. What is behind it all? The answer has now been revealed, and it is astonishing to me the apathetic way in which thousands of men to-day regard this secret. The answer that has been given is that behind this puzzling universe of ours there is a living Person. He watches you with as much attention as if there were not another living person in the world. And when you pray, it is not as if you have one-forty-millionth part of God's attention, but you have His whole attention, because He is the living Person Who watches over all the world. It is a mystery of light, not a mystery of darkness.

II. **What is it all Tending to? What is the Object of Life?**—It has been divulged to us that the stream of life—the main stream—is a stream of love. With all its suffering, the happiness of human life outweighs the misery by ninety-nine to one. And therefore the Gospel that we have to preach is that you, and I, and all men move under a canopy of love.

III. **Can Sin be Forgiven?**—What we have to preach to-day is that sin can be forgiven. But can those be forgiven who lead the innocent astray? Not while they are impenitent. If they are penitent they will be forgiven. To those who believe in the crucifixion of our Lord, and still go on sinning and leading others to sin, I say that you are trampling the Son of God under foot and putting him to an open shame.

IV. **How is the Pardoned Felon to become a Holy Saint, to be Ready for Heaven?**—How is it that we find girls like pure lilies-of-the-valley in London living in houses which one would think can only produce the garbage of the streets, and boys standing firm under temptations to which some of the older men might succumb? The answer is, By the wonderful and extraordinary mystery of grace.

V. What is the Relation of God to this World? —God is using the outward world as a veil through which to teach and bless His children. Every sunrise is a sacrament of love and every sunset a sacrament of peace.

APOSTOLIC SUCCESSION

'Let a man so account of us, as of the ministers of Christ, and stewards of the mysteries of God.'—1 Cor. iv. 1.

APOSTOLIC succession, in the general usage of the phrase, stands for the theory of the origin of the episcopal ministry, which was developed in the conflicts with the heretics of the second and third centuries, which was formulated by the organising genius of St. Cyprian, and commended to the acceptance of the Church by his lofty character and masterful personality, and which was finally established in Christian thought and practice by the still greater authority of St. Augustine. Apostolic succession, as the titledeeds of an exclusive hierarchy, is a fiction, but as a doctrine of the Christian ministry, as such, it is profoundly true. And here we may distinguish three characteristics of the ministry, which attach to it by virtue of the fact that it perpetuates within the Christian society the ministry of the Apostles.

I. The Divine Commission.—We are warned away from low views of the ministerial vocation. We are reminded that the Christian ministry is no afterthought, no creature of policy, no temporary feature of the historic society, but, in and through all varieties of organisation, a Divinely ordained, Divinely commissioned, perpetually obligatory means of grace. It is no fiction, but blessed and momentous verity, that the Christian ministry stands in the succession of those Apostles to whom Christ's ordaining word was spoken: 'As the Father sent Me, even so send I you'.

II. The Sacerdotal Usurpation.—The Christian ministry, standing in the succession of the Apostles, has the same essential character. It is not, in the usual sense of the phrase, a sacerdotal ministry, and the most unfortunate results necessarily followed from the early and natural transference of Mosaic nomenclature to Christian ministers. Almost from the first the language implied and strengthened an utterly unchristian way of regarding the ministry. The conception of a ministry, succeeding to the sacrificial functions, and perpetuating the sacerdotal character of the Jewish priesthood, is obviously and utterly opposed to the apostolic conception.

III. The Pastoral Ministry.—Necessarily, in the wake of faithful preaching, follows the situation out of which the pastoral character of the Apostolic ministry arises. I need not remind you that in both its great branches, moral discipline and the administration of the sacraments, this pastoral ministry draws its authority from the Gospel. As a pastor, emphatic-

ally, the Christian minister answers to St. Paul's description. He is a 'minister of Christ and a steward of the mysteries of God'.—H. HENSLEY HENSON, *Christian World Pulpit*, vol. lx. p. 401.

REFERENCES.—IV. 1.—F. St. John Corbett, *The Preacher's Year*, p. 7. E. A. Stuart, *His Dear Son and other Sermons*, vol. v. p. 41. H. H. Henson, *Godly Union and Concord*, p. 239. IV. 1, 2.—*Expositor* (6th Series), vol. vii. p. 275. .

FAITHFULNESS AND FEAR

(For Advent)

'Let a man so account of us, as of the ministers of Christ, and stewards of the mysteries of God. . . . He that judgeth me is the Lord.'—1 Cor. iv. 1, 4.

I. Faithfulness to God.—The warning, 'It is required in stewards that a man be found faithful,' refers to all Christians. And the duty of faithfulness demands of all:—

(a) *That we do not despise the gifts with which God has entrusted to us.* These gifts are called 'mysteries'. The treasures of Divine truth and love are not indeed secrets—mysteries, in the sense that they remain completely hidden from us, or that they are only intended for a select circle. Still, every heavenly blessing is so far a secret that it is hidden to the natural man. Humanity with all its wisdom could not discover it. And it remains a mystery even now to the unspiritual. 'The natural man receiveth not the things of God.' It is when the heart feels its own natural weakness and poverty that these gifts are not despised, but greatly valued.

(b) *That we preserve these gifts pure and unadulterated.* Unbelief despises, superstition adulterates, the truth. The sacraments, the way of salvation, and many other truths of Scripture, have been obscured by errors. In the opposite direction, the superstition of the understanding has reduced our Lord Jesus to a Jewish Rabbi, and denied the Atonement.

(c) *That we diligently employ these gifts in the spirit of the Lord.* The Church must not be like the unprofitable servant who hid his Lord's talent in the earth. The Church of England, by its regular reading of God's Word, is a faithful steward of the mysteries of Christ.

II. Among other Qualities Necessary in a Steward, the fear of God occupies a large place. This is implied by the words: 'But with me it is a very small thing that I should be judged of you, or of man's judgment. . . . He that judgeth me is the Lord.' In this is included:—

(a) *Fearlessness of man's judgment of himself.* Many people boast, 'What do I care for men's opinion?' Such a boast is not often grounded in the fear of God, but in pride and self-will, or lightness of mind, or in a defiant spirit. St. Paul's freedom from that 'fear of man which brings a snare' was grounded on this: 'He that judgeth me is the Lord'. When we avoid all that, in the light of His Word, is displeasing to Him, we have a sure ground for disregarding the mere opinion of our fellows.

(b) *Mistrust of his own judgment of himself.* 'Yea, I judge not mine own self. For I know nothing against myself.' It is only Godless self-exaltation which says, 'I do not care for the judgment of others, I rely on my own'. St. Paul, on the other hand, has learnt how precarious his own judgment of himself really was. By it he was formerly led into the most dangerous courses. He who thinks more of God's judgment than either of his own or other men's will be likely to be led into right actions, and a right use of God's gifts, and will hesitate to pronounce judgment on others. He will leave such judgment to the Judge of all, the great trier of hearts. 'Therefore judge nothing before the time.' He will wait for the judgment and approbation of the Lord, 'Who will make manifest the counsels of the hearts : and then shall every man have praise of God.'

The great day comes when He comes.

References.—IV. 2.—W. R. Inge, *All Saints' Sermons*, 1905-7, p. 134. IV. 3.—J. M. Neale, *Sermons Preached in a Religious House*, vol. i. p. 190.

THE THREE TRIBUNALS

'With me it is a very small thing that I should be judged of you, or of man's judgment; yea, I judge not mine own self. For I know nothing against myself ; yet am I not hereby justified : but He that judgeth me is the Lord.'— 1 Cor. iv. 3, 4.

The Church at Corinth was honeycombed by the characteristic Greek vice of party spirit. The three great teachers, Paul, Peter, Apollos, were pitted against each other, and each was unduly exalted by those who swore by him, and unduly depreciated by the other two factions. So Paul, in the immediate context, associating Peter and Apollos with himself, bids the Corinthians think of '*us*' as being servants of Christ, and not therefore responsible to men ; and as stewards of the mysteries of God, that is, dispensers of truths long hidden but now revealed, and as therefore accountable for correct accounts and faithful dispensation only to the Lord of the household.

Here we have three tribunals, that of men's estimates, that of our own consciences, that of Jesus Christ. So let us look briefly at these three tribunals.

I. First, the lowest—men's judgment. Such a character as Paul's could not but be quick to feel the surrounding atmosphere, whether it was of love or of suspicion. So, he had to harden himself against what naturally had a great effect upon him, the estimate which he felt that people round him were making of him. I need not say a word about the power which that terrible court which is always sitting, and which passes judgment upon every one of us, though we do not always hear the sentences read, has upon us all. There is a power which it is meant to have. It is not good for a man to stand constantly in the attitude of defying whatever anybody else chooses to say or to think about him. But the danger to which we are all exposed, far more than that other extreme, is of deferring too completely and slavishly to, and being far too subtly influenced in all that we do by, the thought of what A, B, or C may

have to say or to think about it. 'The last infirmity of noble minds,' says Milton about the love of fame. It is an infirmity to love it, and long for it, and live by it.

(1) But not only in these higher forms of seeking after reputation, but in lower forms, this trembling before, and seeking to conciliate, the tribunal of what we call 'general opinion,' which means the voices of the half-dozen people that are beside us, and know about us, besets us all, and weakens us all in a thousand ways. (2) The direct tendency of Christian faith and principle is to dwindle into wholesome insignificance the multitudinous voice of men's judgments. (3) Cultivate more distinctly, as a plain Christian duty, this wholesome independence of men's judgment.

II. Note the higher court of conscience. The absolving by conscience is not infallible. I fancy that conscience is more reliable when it condemns than when it acquits. The inward judge needs to be stimulated, to be enlightened, to be corrected often.

III. Note the supreme court of final appeal. 'He that *judgeth* me'—not, 'will judge,' but *now* at this very moment. (1) The estimate will dwindle the sentences of the other two tribunals into nothingness. (2) That judgment, persistent all through each of our lives, is preliminary to the future tribunal and sentence.—A. Maclaren, *Triumphant Certainties*, p. 152.

References.—IV. 3, 4.—J. T. Bramston, *Fratribus*, p. 156. T. Arnold, *Sermons*, vol. i. p. 155. J. G. Greenhough, *The Mind of Christ in St. Paul*, p. 284. A. Maclaren, *Expositions of Holy Scripture—Corinthians*, p. 74.

SPIRITUAL CHARACTER

'For I know nothing by myself ; yet am I not hereby justified : but He that judgeth me is the Lord.'—1 Cor. iv. 4.

The Apostle has been talking of judgment, and he has plainly said, 'With me it is a very small thing that I should be judged of you, or of man's judgment : yea, I judge not mine own self. For I know nothing by myself'—against myself, as between man and man, 'yet am I not hereby,' through that simple fact, 'justified,' or made just ; the fact is we have nothing to do with judgment ; 'He that judgeth me is the Lord'. How calm he was, how almost defiant when face to face with social or hostile criticism ! How heart-searching he was ; how thoroughly this man grips every case that he deals with ! There is no escaping his iron handling. He is the kind of man to follow when we do not quite know what to do with some things. He is so courtly, so learned in the deepest laws, so profoundly human. Yet there is about him such mystery and gladness of unexplained divinity.

I. We are not to judge ourselves as others see us, but as we really, interiorly, spiritually are. Who then can stand ? None. That is the whole mystery ; if men would believe that one little sentence we should see new heavens and a new earth. if they acted upon the vision, and were obedient to the heavenly revelation. We see one another externally ; we think we are nice men. Oh the lie ! It is because we fail just there that we need no cross.

As to our own self-gratulation, boasting, and vain pride, we do everything conventionally well; we pay our debts, we exchange social courtesies, and we conduct ourselves generally so that our neighbours say about us we are nice, agreeable, respectable people. Oh if they knew, really knew!

We make ourselves coats and clothing of fig leaves, and we hide up all that is foul or unlovely in our sight and in the sight of other men. But no man can destroy his own sin. If any one could be persuaded to believe that—not merely to nod assent to that, but to believe it—there would go up out of this nation such a cry for the Gospel as would make a new nation of it. Concealment of sin is not destruction of sin; momentary forgetfulness of sin does not quench one cinder in hell. It is sin, sinful sin, the abominable thing which God hates, and which can only be really cleansed out of the soul by the hot heart-blood of the Priest of the universe.

II. So we are face to face with the great doctrine of spiritual character; what we are in motive, in purpose, in our heart of hearts, that is the question. O thou who dost boast of thy good reputation amongst neighbours, and empty thy pockets of testimonials to prove how respectable a man thou art, that is not the question. It is, What are we in the sight of white light, what are we in the sanctuary? Who can stand? None. What then? Penitence, self-renunciation, an earnest, piercing cry to the heavens for mercy, a clinging round the Cross. We are cursed by being satisfied with mere respectability. Respectability now takes the place of spiritual criticism. We do not refer to God, we refer to man. If a man with a thousand a year can testify that I am a respectable person, I care for nothing else; you know my referee, this is what he says about me. And socially, conventionally, that is true; spiritually and interiorly it is a lie; take it back, burn it.

III. Then we come face to face with the great doctrine of regeneration. Marvel not that I say unto you, Ye must be born again; except a man be born again he cannot enter into the kingdom of God. He must be born again without explanation, though he is a very intelligent creature. God is continually snubbing intelligence; God is often ordering mere knowledge off the doorstep of His palace. He does not want knowledge, intelligence, criticism, or anything of that kind, separately, independently, and by itself, so to say, but He wants the outgoing desire of the heart, the longing of the soul, the cry in the dark, Oh that I knew where I might find Him! The Gospel has a great broad, clear, trumpet-like answer to that inquiry. We see Jesus crucified, and we see Jesus crowned. That is God's answer. Then let us cease comparison with others and let us make every day a day of judgment upon ourselves. — Joseph Parker, *City Temple Pulpit*, vol. iv. p. 155.

'He that judgeth me is the Lord.'—1 Cor. iv. 4.

In the eighth chapter of her *Life of Charlotte Brontë*, Mrs. Gaskell quotes a friend who says that, 'One time I mentioned that some one had asked me what religion I was of (with the view of getting me for a partisan) and that I had said that that was between God and me; Emily (who was lying on the hearth-rug) exclaimed, "That's right". This was all I ever heard Emily say on religious subjects.'

REFERENCE.—IV. 4, 5.—J. M. Neale, *Sermons Preached in Sackville College Chapel*, vol. ii. p. 177.

THE INTERMEDIATE GOAL
'Until the Lord come.'—1 Cor. iv. 5.

I. WE may be certain that the thought of the coming of the Lord is meant to act as an incentive. When we feel tired and care-laden, when the way is steep and the lesson harder than usual, what a difference it might make to remind ourselves that it will not go on so for ever. After all, it is only 'until the Lord come'.

II. The thought of our Lord's coming will not only rouse and strengthen us to do things; it will also keep us from doing things, unnecessary things, and from one thing more especially. Let us listen to the Apostle as he describes it. Having spoken of the duty of faithfulness in the discharge of appointed duty, St. Paul goes on to say: 'But with me it is a very small thing that I should be judged of you, or of man's judgment; yea, I judge not mine own self. For I know nothing against myself, yet I am not hereby justified; but He that judgeth me is the Lord. Therefore judge nothing before the time, until the Lord come, who will both bring to light the hidden things of darkness, and will make manifest the counsels of the hearts: and then shall every man have praise of God.' You see what he means. The thought of the Lord's coming is to serve not only as an incentive to action, it is to be also a *restraint* upon criticism.—A. W. Robinson, *Church Family Newspaper*, vol. xiv. p. 1000.

JUDGMENT
'Therefore judge nothing before the time, until the Lord come, Who both will bring to light the hidden things of darkness, and will make manifest the counsels of the hearts: and then shall every man have praise of God.'—1 Cor. iv. 5.

THE rashness of hearers in pronouncing judgment upon ministers is no novelty. Such of the Corinthians as elected to prefer the teaching of Apollos or of Cephas to that of Paul, appear to have proceeded to charge the Apostle with having imperfectly instructed them in the Gospel. He does not submit to their tribunal; nor will he even trust to his own judgment. His appeal is to an infinitely higher Court. He announces—

I. That the Coming Lord will sit in Judgment.

(1) His 'day of judgment' will extend over a long period. (*a*) The term 'day' in Scripture is often used to express a considerable period. (*b*) The period of the judgment is not in the text expressly called a 'day,' but it is so described by implication. For it is here opposed to 'man's day' in the context (see v. 3, marg.). (*c*) In this view 'The Lord's day' will be opposed to a period of 6,000 years. It cannot, there-

fore, be limited to four-and-twenty hours, or to any inconsiderable period. It must extend through many ages.

(2) His day of judgment will be a day of ruling. (*a*) Such is 'man's day'—*viz.*, of judgment, to which it is opposed. This is the period in which man's opinions are current, his principles of action sanctioned, and his standards of truth, of morals and religion, admitted and approved. (*b*) Judgment in Scripture is not used exclusively, or even chiefly, in the forensic sense, but is another term for ruling. (*c*) Hence Christ comes to judgment in His quality as King (see Ps. ii. 6, 9; lxxii. 1, 2; St. Matt. xxv. 34-40). So the coming to judge and the coming to reign are the same thing (see Is. xxxii. 1; Jer. xxiii. 5; 2 Tim. iv. 1). There are not three personal advents of Christ.

(3) The reign will close with a great assize. (*a*) It will commence with military judgments. As God went forth in His Shechinah at the head of the armies of Israel, so in the latter days will He fight against the anti-Christian confederacy (see Joel iii. 9-17; Hag. ii. 6; Zech. xiv. 1, 2, 9; Rev. xix. 11-21). (*b*) These military judgments will introduce the reign of Christ. It will extend through the millennium. It will be distinguished by justice and truth. (*c*) At the close of this great period will be the great assize (Rev. xx. 11-15).

II. That Every Man then shall have Perfect Justice.

(1) Such a judgment is a necessity in equity. (*a*) The maxims of man's day will need to be reviewed. (*b*) The judgments of man's day will have to be reviewed. The fearful aggregate of wrongs perpetrated and suffered in the whole history of man's day will be adjusted in judgment. (*c*) The best human judgments are imperfect. Motives are misread by upright but fallible judges.

(2) In it shall every man have his meed of praise. (*a*) To this end all must appear before the Judge. (*b*) The Judge is competent to the task. He can 'bring to light the hidden things of darkness'. (*c*) The 'sons of God' will have the greater praise. The day of judgment will be the day of their 'manifestation,' or 'revealing' (Rom. viii. 19; 1 John iii. 2). Their grandeur will then come out to the day. (*d*) The 'servants of God' also will have His praise. (*e*) Even the pronouncedly wicked—the downright servants of the devil—will have any praise they can justly claim. But in reference to these it is to be feared praise is used euphemistically; the contrary of praise being implied (cf. 1 Sam. xxvi. 23). (*f*) The praise of God will be a true reward. If He says 'Well done,' the whole universe will re-echo the approbation. When He says, 'Well done,' it is the prelude to substantial and permanent promotion. The moral is that we should strive to merit this applause. The way is through the merits of Christ.

'The Lord will both bring to light the hidden things of darkness, and make manifest the counsels of the hearts.'—i Cor. iv. 5.

Is there record kept anywhere of fancies conceived, beautiful, unborn? Some day will they assume form in some undeveloped light? If our bad unspoken thoughts are registered against us, and are written in the awful account, will not the good thoughts unspoken, the love and tenderness, the pity, beauty, charity, which pass through the breast, and cause the heart to throb with silent good, find a remembrance too?—Thackeray, in *The Last Sketch.*

'The hidden things of darkness.'—i Cor. iv. 5.

But if I plan a little sin,
So small no eye can enter in?
Thou fool! if thine own soul can see,
What need for God to look at thee?
　　　　　—Evelyn Phinney.

References.—IV. 5.—T. F. Crosse, *Sermons*, p. 74. Bishop Wilberforce, *Sermons*, p. 57. R. W. Church, *Village Sermons*, p. 8. F. J. A. Hort, *Village Sermons in Outline*, p. 217. H. J. Wilmot-Buxton, *Notes of Sermons for the Year*, pt. i. p. 13. *Expositor* (6th Series), vol. ii. p. 390. IV. 6.—*Ibid.* (4th Series), vol. iii. p. 406. IV. 6-13.—*Ibid.* (6th Series), vol. i. p. 204.

THE GRACE OF RECEPTIVITY

'What hast thou that thou didst not receive?'—i Cor. iv. 7.

'Receptiveness,' George Eliot says, 'is a noble and massive virtue.'

I. There are two tendencies which are characteristic of the present time, and which make it hard to write our text upon our banner. (1) First, then, this is an inventive age. In every one of us, perhaps quite unconsciously, there is a touch of the inventor's and the discoverer's temper. That is to say, we are bred in the idea that all that is best and highest and most noble has to be won by human search and seeking. Does that then make us arrogant? Not so. But it makes it hard to remember that the things which count are after all not wages but are gifts. (2) Then this is a critical age. All of us, more or less, are touched with the critical spirit of the day, and the critical spirit even at its noblest is very far away from receptivity. When we are accustomed to get at truth by fine dissection, it is not easy to regard it as a gift.

II. Let us apply the text in different ways, and (1) let us think of the world of nature. We invent the telegraph, we do not invent the spring. We discover the power of steam, but not the dawn. These things find us, they are given freely; and I believe that the keenest intellect will fail to grasp the true value of this great creation, unless there come seasons when it can be let alone, and practice the great grace of receptivity. (2) Think again of our capacities and faculties. The possibility of all we do lies not in what we do but in what we get. Our gifts are the only basis of our gain. (3) What is heredity—that strange and awful fact—but the expansion by science of this inspired word? What motto for the text-books of heredity could match this motto, 'What have ye that ye did not receive?' Whence comes the bent and bias of my nature? The basis of all my strength and all my weakness, of all I battle with, of all I hope to be—the basis of it is the unsought-for gift of the generations who have passed and died. (4) Apply the text to the great gospel of the love of God. All love is a gift; you cannot compel or force it; it is only love when it is freely given; and if that is true of the love of man and woman it must be true of the love of God to me. The New Testament throbs and thrills with the glad thought that the Gospel is a gift. Therefore would I say to all who are longing and striving and toiling for the best: all that is best does not begin in striving; it comes as a gift from God and must be taken.—G. H. MORRISON, *The Unlighted Lustre*, p. 57.

'What hast thou that thou didst not receive?'—1 COR. IV. 7.

WHEN John Knox was dying, Doctor Preston demanded how he did. He replied : 'I have been tempted by Satan. When he saw that he could not prevail, he tempted me to have trusted in myself, or to have rejoiced or boasted of myself. But I repulsed him with this sentence, *Quid habes quod non accepisti?*' ('What hast thou which thou hast not received').

REFERENCES.—IV. 7.—Bishop Bethell, *Sermons*, vol. i. p. 221. H. P. Liddon, *University Sermons* (2nd Series), p. 18. Spurgeon, *Sermons*, vol. xxii. No. 1271, and vol. xxiv. No. 1392.

'Already are ye filled, already are ye become rich.'— 1 COR. IV. 8.

THOUGH there is no recorded instance of our Lord's making use of any of the weapons of wit, nor is it conceivable that He ever did so, a severe taunting irony is sanctioned by the example of the Hebrew prophets, as in Isaiah's sublime invective against idolatry, and in Elijah's controversy with the priests of Baal, and by that of St. Paul especially in the fourth chapter of the First Epistle to the Corinthians. Surely, too, we may say with Milton, in his *Animadversions on the Remonstrant*, that 'this vein of laughing hath oftimes a strong and sinewy force in teaching and confuting'.—JULIUS HARE, in *Guesses at Truth* (1st Series).

REFERENCES.—IV. 8.—H. Bonar, *Short Sermons for Family Reading*, p. 448. *Expositor* (6th Series), vol. i. p. 94. IV. 9.—*Ibid.* vol. viii. p. 74. IV. 9-14.—J. R. Legge, *Christian World Pulpit*, vol. lviii. p. 68.

'We are fools for Christ's sake. . . . Even to this present hour we both hunger, and thirst, and are naked, and are buffeted, . . . being reviled, we bless; being persecuted, we endure; being defamed, we entreat.'—1 COR. IV. 10 f.

COMPARE Cowper's famous lines on Whitefield (*Hope*, 574 f.):—

He loved the world that hated him: the tear
That dropped upon his Bible was sincere ;
Assailed by scandal and the tongue of strife,
His only answer was a blameless life ;
And he that forged, and he that threw the dart,
Had each a brother's interest in his heart.
Paul's love of Christ, and steadiness unbribed,
Were copied close in him, and well transcribed.
He followed Paul ; his zeal a kindred flame,
His apostolic charity the same.
Like him, crossed cheerfully, tempestuous seas,
Forsaking country, kindred, friends, and ease ;
Like him he laboured, and like him content
To bear it, suffered shame where'er he went.

'The speech of them which are puffed up.'—1 COR. IV. 19.

THE tongue of a man is very seldom sober.—MAXIM GORKY.

REFERENCES.—IV. 10.—David Brook, *Preacher's Magazine*, vol. v. p. 33. IV. 11-13.—*Expositor* (6th Series), vol. ix. p. 231. IV. 12.—*Ibid.* vol. x. p. 99 ; *ibid.* vol. xi. p. 293. IV. 16.—E. M. Geldart, *Echoes of Truth*, p. 247. IV. 17.—*Expositor* (6th Series), vol. ii. p. 259. IV. 18.—*Ibid.* vol. i. p. 204. IV. 19.—J. Bolton, *Selected Sermons* (2nd Series), p. 251. IV. 20.—Bishop Winnington-Ingram, *Christian World Pulpit*, vol. lx. p. 234. *Expositor* (7th Series), vol. v. p. 71.

'Shall I come to you with a rod, or in love and the spirit of meekness.'—1 COR. IV. 21.

'NOTHING moved her more,' says Charlotte Brontë of her sister Emily, 'than any insinuation that the faithfulness and clemency, the long-suffering and lovingkindness which are esteemed virtues in the daughters of Eve, became foibles in the sons of Adam.'

'A little leaven leaveneth the whole lump. Purge out the old leaven.'—1 COR. v. 6, 7.

THE 'eternal vigilance' required to maintain not only liberty but purity, should have for its guide a principle just opposite to the principle commonly followed. Most men, alike in public affairs and private business-affairs, assume that things are going right until it is proved they are going wrong ; whereas their assumption should be that things are going wrong until it is proved they are going right.—SPENCER, *Principles of Ethics* (§ 470).

REFERENCES.—IV. 21.—*Expositor* (5th Series), vol. vi. p. 296 ; *ibid.* vol. x. p. 426 ; *ibid.* (6th Series), vol. vii. p. 112 ; *ibid.* vol. ix. p. 73. V. 1.—J. D. Jones, *Elims of Life*, p. 220. V. 1, 2.—*Expositor* (5th Series), vol. vi. p. 203. V. 2. —*Ibid.* (4th Series), vol. ix. p. 15. V. 3-5.—*Ibid.* vol. ii. p. 385. V. 3-6.—F. D. Maurice, *Sermons*, vol. vi. p. 49. V. 5. —*Expositor* (4th Series), vol. i. p. 24 ; *ibid.* (5th Series), vol. ix. p. 351 ; *ibid.* (6th Series), p. 460. V. 6-8.—Spurgeon, *Sermons*, vol. xvi. No. 965. V. 7.—C. Perren, *Revival Sermons in Outline*, p. 169. Spurgeon, *Sermons*, vol. ii. No. 54. *Expositor* (4th Series), vol. vi. p. 29 ; *ibid.* vol. ix. p. 355 ; *ibid.* (5th Series), vol. iv. p. 277 ; *ibid.* (6th Series), vol. ii. p. 444. V. 7, 8.—F. D. Maurice, *Sermons*, vol. iii. p. 283. W. C. Wheeler, *Sermons and Addresses* (2nd Series), p. 202. R. M. Benson, *Redemption*, p. 308. J. Keble, *Sermons for Easter to Ascension Day*, p. 1. J. H. Holford, *Memorial Sermons*, p. 56. V. 8.—A. Maclaren, *Expositions of Holy Scripture—Corinthians*, p. 83. V. 9.—*Expositor* (5th Series), vol. vi. p. 236.

'I wrote to you to have no company with fornicators; not altogether with the fornicators of this world . . . for then must ye needs go out of the world.'—1 COR. V. 9, 10.

UNLESS above himself he can
Erect himself, how poor a thing is Man.

'Unless above himself, how poor a thing ; yet, if beyond and outside of his world, how useless and purposeless a thing. This also must be remembered. And I cannot help thinking,' says Clough, 'that there is in Wordsworth's poems something of a spirit of withdrawal and seclusion from, and even evasion of, the actual world'.

REFERENCES.—V. 9-11.—*Expositor* (6th Series), vol. v. p. 107. V. 9-13.—*Ibid.* vol. vi. p. 87. V. 10.—*Ibid.* vol. iii. p. 110 ; *ibid.* vol. x. pp. 57, 161.

'**I wrote to you not to keep company, if any man that is called a brother be a fornicator, or covetous, or an idolater, or a railer, or a drunkard, or an extortioner; with such an one no not to eat.**'—1 COR. V. 11.

IN *Fors Clavigera* (III. 49) Ruskin, after quoting some facts about the luxury of the wealthy and the violence of the lower classes, breaks out with an appeal to the clergy, and especially the bishops, to obey 'St. Paul's plain order in 1st Corinthians v. 11. Let them determine as distinctly what covetousness and extortion are in the rich, as what drunkenness is in the poor. Let them refuse, themselves, and order their clergy to refuse, to go out to dine with such persons; and still more positively to allow such persons to sup at God's table. And they would soon know what fighting wolves meant; and something more of their own pastoral duty than they learned in that Consecration Service, when they proceeded to follow the example of the Apostles in Prayer, but carefully left out the Fasting.'

REFERENCES.—V. 15.—*Expositor* (4th Series), vol. vi. p. 132. V. 19.—*Ibid.* (6th Series), vol. iv. p. 19. V. 21.—*Ibid.* vol. xi. p. 201. V. 23.—*Ibid.* (5th Series), vol. vii. p. 456. VI. 1.—*Ibid.* (6th Series), vol. x. p. 99. VI. 1-11.—*Ibid.* vol. i. p. 273. VI. 2.—W. H. Evans, *Sermons for the Church's Year*, p. 248. *Expositor* (6th Series), vol. vii. p. 113.

'**Know ye not that we shall judge angels?**'—1 COR. VI. 3.

ASTRONOMY without Christianity only reaches as far as—'Thou hast made him a little lower than the angels—and put all *things* under his feet'; —Christianity says beyond this—'Know ye not that we shall judge angels (as also the lower creatures shall judge us!)'—RUSKIN, *Mornings in Florence* (137).

REFERENCE.—VI. 3, 4.—*Expositor* (6th Series), vol. vii. p. 109.

'**Know ye not that the unrighteous shall not inherit the kingdom of God? Be not deceived.**'—1 COR. VI. 9.

RELIGION co-exists, as it were, in the mind of an Italian Catholic, with a faith in that of which all men have the most certain knowledge. It is interwoven with the whole fabric of life. It is adoration, faith, submission, penitence, blind admiration; not a rule for moral conduct. It has no necessary connection with any one virtue. The most atrocious villain may be rigidly devout, and without any shock to established faith, confess himself to be so. Religion pervades intensely the whole frame of society, and is according to the temper of the mind which it inhabits, a passion, a persuasion, an excuse, a refuge; never a check.—SHELLEY, Preface to *The Cenci*.

REFERENCES.—VI. 9.—*Expositor* (4th Series), vol. x. p. 200; *ibid.* (5th Series), vol. x. p. 108. VI. 9-11.—Spurgeon, *Sermons*, vol. xlvi. No. 2661. VI. 10.—J. Aspinall, *Parish Sermons* (1st Series), p. 162. VI. 11.—J. Keble, *Village Sermons on the Baptismal Service*, p. 86. *Expositor* (4th Series), vol. ix. p. 91. VI. 12.—H. M. Butler, *Harrow School Sermons* (2nd Series), p. 30. *Expositor* (6th Series), vol. xii. p. 275. VI. 12-20.—*Ibid.* vol. i. p. 280. VI. 13.—*Expositor* (4th Series), vol. ii. p. 42. VI. 15.—T. Arnold, *Christian Life: Its Hopes*, p. 147. *Expositor* (6th Series), vol. x. p. 366. VI. 17.—Spurgeon, *Sermons*, vol. xvi. No. 961. *Expositor* (4th Series), vol. ii. p. 49; *ibid.* (6th Series), vol. ix. pp. 63, 155.

THE BODY A TEMPLE

'**Know ye not that your body is the temple of the Holy Ghost?**'—1 COR. VI. 19.

LET us ask how as Christian people we ought to look upon our bodies, and what new light is shed upon their part in life through the redemption accomplished by Jesus Christ.

I. First note *the dignity of the body*. The text informs us what the Apostle believed about that. He has no hesitation in saying that these bodies of ours are temples of the Holy Ghost, or, as he puts it a verse or two before, 'members of Christ'. Think what that metaphor of the temple meant. There had been a temple in Israel before, all compact of ivory and gold and marble; and not many years were to pass, from the date of this letter, till its hour struck and it passed away. But, ere it fell, its place had been taken by the redeemed personalities in which Christ was dwelling. So St. Paul's argument is very simple—only this: God inhabits us; we inhabit our bodies; therefore our bodies are God's temple. Though he had laboured the point for page on page, he could have added nothing to the solemn emphasis of that one word—the body a Divine temple.

Let us lay the truth to heart, that Christ has redeemed both parts of our nature, and that His will for us covers both the material and the spiritual. The body has its own share in the great salvation. Certain ancient philosophers and some Christian thinkers who ought to have known better, have tended to despise the body; they have heaped abuse upon it, as the jail and prison of the soul; but the one fact of Christ's coming in the flesh has swept away all such shame and contempt and poured honour upon every member. Wherever His Gospel has penetrated, it has taught men a sweet and beautiful reverence even for the bodies of the dead. The nobility and sanctity of the human organism have been revealed in Jesus.

Moreover, if the body is redeemed, it is no longer our own, and has to be cared for as particularly as honesty bids us care for some one else's property. The guarding of health is a part of religion. To neglect or squander our bodily powers is to steal what belongs to God. As Charles Kingsley said once, and no man had a better right to speak: 'There has always seemed to me something impious in the neglect of personal health. . . . I could not do half the good I do do, if it were not for the strength and activity some consider coarse and degrading.'

II. Note, secondly, *the gravity of bodily sin*. Strictly speaking, this is the connection in which the text occurs. St. Paul is warning the Corinthians against the foul practices which made their city a by-word, and tainted every breath they drew. On that subject he does not argue. He simply bids them consider that their bodies are God's temples.

Where lies the gravity and guilt of sins like gluttony, intemperance, or lust in any form? In this, for one thing, that *they give the body the upper hand.*

The only right and safe thing is that the body shall always serve. Any attempt to reverse the Divine law of our nature, that that part of us which is akin to God must rule, means a loss of true manhood and inevitable suffering. Forget this, and the appetite which was but a means in the Divine plan comes to be an end it itself. 'Hold off from sensuality,' Cicero writes, 'for if you once give yourself to it, you will not be able to think of anything else.' The body ceases to be the soul's instrument or servant, and becomes its dungeon, then its tomb; so that the drunkard reeling down the street is, in too many cases, a man whose body has already become the grave of a lost spirit.

Then again, bodily sin is so heinous because it defiles what Christ has redeemed. The reason why Christ's atoning passion was endured, and followed by triumphant resurrection, lay in God's great purpose that our human nature, in both its parts, should be cleansed and restored in beauty and purity. For this He bore the shame, the grief, the scourging, the spitting, the awful desolation of the last hour. The aim and issue of it all was that we should become a habitation of God through the Spirit. Gross sin in the body thwarts and defeats that purpose. Therefore it is to be feared and avoided by men and women who have a stake in the Divine redemption, and know that God has called them unto holiness.

III. Lastly, note *the prospects of the body*. What is supremely important here also is to fix in our minds that truth, that the body has its own real share in the hopes and promises that cluster round the name of Jesus. The heathen said—our modern heathen say still—the body will perish like the animals; what matters it how we treat it? let us eat and drink, for to-morrow we die. Nay, replies Christian faith, there is a second and nobler chapter in the story even of this frail tenement we here inhabit, which sheds back its light upon the chapter we are living in now. God, who raised up Jesus, shall in due time also quicken your mortal bodies.—H. R. Mackintosh, *Life on God's Plan*, p. 129.

'Your body is a temple of the Holy Ghost.'—1 Cor. vi. 19.

'The body the temple of the living God,' Kingsley writes in one of his early letters. 'There has always seemed to me something impious in the neglect of personal health, strength, and beauty, which the religious, and sometimes clergymen of this day affect. It is very often a mere form of laziness.'

References.—VI. 19.—J. C. Hill, *Preacher's Magazine*, vol. v. p. 130. J. Stalker, *Christian World Pulpit*, vol. lv. p. 346. R. J. Wardell, *Preacher's Magazine*, vol. xvii. p. 266. W. Unsworth, *ibid.* vol. xix. p. 33. *Expositor* (4th Series), vol. ii. p. 42; *ibid.* (7th Series), vol. v. p. 498. VI. 19, 20.—Brooke Herford, *Courage and Cheer*, p. 191. D. W. Simon, *Twice Born and Other Sermons*, p. 141. T. Arnold, *Christian Life : Its Hopes*, p. 147. Spurgeon, *Sermons*, vol. xvii. No. 1004; vol. xxvi. No. 1554.

THE BODY IN THE LIGHT OF THE RESURRECTION

'Ye were bought with a price ; glorify God therefore in your body.'—1 Cor. vi. 20 (R.V.).

The Resurrection of Jesus, which we celebrate afresh at Easter-tide, is the witness not to the existence of a shadowy, unsubstantial life separated from these delightful shores by the untravelled sea, but to the largeness of a life that knows no death, and is as real, every bit of it, as the sky above us and the earth beneath our feet.

What a great thing it would be if people could be brought to see, as the Christians of whom we read in the New Testament most certainly saw, that it is a matter of supreme moment, not so much to what is sometimes understood by our eternal welfare, as to our whole view of what is meant by the life through which we are now passing, whether our conduct and conception of the world are really governed by our belief in Jesus' Resurrection.

I. It was no spirit from the vasty deep that first affrighted and then gladdened the eyes of those who had seen their Master die on the deserted cross of Calvary. Ghosts do not change the lives of men, inspiring the fearful with courage, the despairing with hope, the dying with life. 'Behold My hands and My feet, that it is I Myself.' It was no impalpable apparition that stood in the midst of those who had been the disciples of the crucified Nazarene, and said, 'Peace be unto you'. It was Jesus Himself in all the fulness, in all the reality of His rich, warm personality.

The sun shone with fairer light, as the old carol has it, on the morning when Jesus Christ arose. Many philosophers have taught that the soul is immortal; Christians believe in the resurrection of the flesh. Earth and sky seem more real to the sons of the Resurrection. We cannot picture to ourselves the garden of the Holy Sepulchre but as spread with a carpet of living green and decked with the fresh flowers of spring. The Christian falls in love afresh with the beauty of the world, as he is awakened by the joyous pealing of the bells in the dawn of Easter Day. If we meet a young man striding down the valley on his way to the early Communion, we find ourselves rejoicing in the strength of his limbs, in the glory of his manhood, in the dew of his youth, as from the womb of the morning. And the lithe form of a maiden tripping across the fields brings a new sympathy with the poet's fancy when he sings, 'her feet have touched the meadows and left the daisies rosy'.

This could never be, unless we felt instinctively that to the Christian the world meant infinitely more than it could ever mean to such as have never found that inexhaustible capacity for pure enjoyment which comes from drinking of the Well of Life. We who have been redeemed at the cost of God's own tears and blood, not from the body, but from the curse which has rested upon it, take our true place in universal nature, and amid the chorus of the birds, the hum of the bees, the sounding waves, the rushing winds, the breath of a living and life-giving earth, know how good it is to be alive as we offer the praise of redeemed lips, the thankful exercise of all our liberated forces to Him Who is the Father of our whole being.

II. St. Paul was a much greater Christian than those who came after him, and who emended the grand simplicity of his text until the shadow of that fatal distinction between body and soul, which in the history of the human race has again and again proved either the sanction of a maimed experience or the excuse for sinful indulgence, seems almost to rest upon one of the most magnificent passages in the whole Bible?

Do not let us mar the directness of this appeal by imitating the timidity of those later interpreters who read : 'Glorify God in your body and in your spirit'. We do not want to have our life divided up into body and spirit, secular and sacred, weekday and Sunday. The Devil likes to keep us talking about what we ought not to do on Sunday morning, because none knows better than he that our destinies are really determined by what we do on Saturday night. A few reserves which are labelled 'sacred' are the best guarantee that Beelzebub can have for undisturbed possession of the character. 'Give me the body' is the cry of every claimant for the citadel of Mansoul, 'and let who will have the spirit.'

Yes! there is but one problem in human life, and that is the problem of the body, the organ through which alone life manifests itself, the home of our activities, the seat of our desires. 'Glorify God in your body' was the straight appeal of one who knew what it was to stand fast in the liberty with which Christ had made him free. 'I beseech you,' he cries, 'by the mercies of God'—by the very form, that is, which your redemption has taken, by the manifestation of the Son of God in the likeness of sinful flesh, by the offering, not of the spirit, but of the body of Christ once for all, by the condemnation, the killing, the extermination of sin in the flesh, by the return of the Body which was crucified from the grave by which it could not be holden, and by the quickening of our mortal bodies of which that Resurrection is the pledge—'I beseech you by the mercies of God that you present your bodies a living sacrifice,' a holy offering, to the God Who has redeemed them. That, and that alone, is 'your spiritual service'.—J. G. SIMPSON, *The Church Times*, 19th May, 1911.

REFERENCES.—VI. 20.—E. M. Geldart, *Echoes of Truth*, p. 234. J. B. Lightfoot, *Cambridge Sermons*, p. 283. Spurgeon, *Sermons*, vol. xx. No. 1163. *Expositor* (4th Series), vol. vi. p. 29 ; *ibid.* (6th Series), vol. iv. p. 279 ; *ibid.* vol. ix. p. 44. VII.—*Ibid.* vol. i. p. 284. VII. 1.—*Ibid.* p. 253 ; *ibid.* (5th Series), vol. v. p. 142 ; *ibid.* vol. vi. p. 73 ; *ibid.* (6th Series), vol. i. p. 284. VII. 2.—*Ibid.* vol. x. p. 278. VII. 1-25.—*Ibid.* vol. vii. p. 117. VII. 5.—*Ibid.* (4th Series), vol. i. p. 350 ; *ibid.* (5th Series), vol. i. p. 15 ; *ibid.* (6th Series), vol. x. p. 372 ; *ibid.* (7th Series), vol. vi. pp. 20, 23. VII. 6.—*Ibid.* vol. i. p. 373 ; *ibid.* vol. iii. p. 277 ; *ibid.* vol. i. p. 373. VII. 7, 8.—*Ibid.* vol. v. p. 442.

'To the married I give charge, yea not I, but the Lord. . . . To the rest say I, not the Lord.'—1 COR. VII. 10, 12.

'HE can be nowise considered the disciple of Paul,' says Bacon in the *De Augmentis Scientiarum*, "who does not sometimes insert in his doctrines, "I, not the Lord," or again, "according to my counsel," which style is generally suited to inferences. Wherefore it appears to me that it would be of especial use and benefit if a temperate and careful treatise were instituted, which, as a kind of Divine logic, should lay down proper precepts touching the use of human reason in theology. For it would act as an opiate, not only to lull to sleep the vanity of curious speculations, wherewith sometimes the schools labour, but also in some degree to assuage the fury of controversies, wherewith the Church is troubled.' Again, in the *Advancement of Learning* (bk. II. xxv. 7), he observes that men, instead of saying, *ego, non dominus,* 'are now over-ready to usurp the style, *non ego, dominus ;* and not only so, but to bind it with the thunder and denunciations of curses and anathemas, to the terror of those which have not sufficiently learned out of Salomon that *the causeless curse shall not come.'*

REFERENCES.—VII. 10.—*Expositor* (4th Series), vol. ii. p. 70 ; *ibid.* (6th Series), vol. vi. p. 403. VII. 12, 25.—*Ibid.* p. 71. VII. 14.—*Ibid.* vol. ix. p. 13. VII. 16.—W. H. Hutchings, *Sermon Sketches*, p. 241. VII. 17.—*Expositor* (5th Series), vol. vii. p. 405 ; *ibid.* (6th Series), vol. ii. p. 299. VII. 19.—J. Iverach, *Christian World Pulpit*, vol. l. p. 262. Bishop Bethell, *Sermons*, vol. ii. p. 307. A. P. Stanley, *Canterbury Sermons*, p. 222. J. Iverach, *Christian World Pulpit*, vol. xlvii. p. 342. A. Maclaren, *Expositions of Holy Scripture—Corinthians*, p. 92.

'Let each man abide in that calling wherein he was called.'— 1 COR. VII. 20.

I AM for permanence in all things, at the earliest possible moment, and to the latest possible. Blessed is he that continueth where he is ! Here let us rest and lay out seed-fields ; here let us learn to dwell. Here, even here, the orchards that we plant will yield us fruit ; the acorns will be wood and pleasant umbrage, if we wait. How much grass everywhere, if we do but wait ! . . . Not a difficulty but can transfigure itself into a triumph ; not even a deformity, but, if our own soul have imprinted worth on it, will grow dear to us.—CARLYLE, *Past and Present* (II. ch. v.).

'IF there's anything our people want convincing of,' says Felix Holt, in chapter forty-five of George Eliot's novel, 'it is, that there's some dignity and happiness for a man other than changing his station.'

REFERENCE.—VII. 20-24.—*Expositor* (6th Series), vol. iv. p. 449.

'If thou canst become free, use it rather.'—1 COR. VII. 21.

'TRUE it is,' Dr. Arnold wrote in 1840, 'that St. Paul, expecting that the world was shortly to end, tells a man not to care even if he were in a state of personal slavery. That is an endurable evil which will shortly cease, not in itself only, but in its consequences. But even for the few years during which he supposed the world would exist, he says, " if thou mayst be made free, use it rather ". For true it is that a great part of the virtues of human nature can scarcely be developed in a state of slavery, whether personal or political. The passive virtues may exist, the active ones suffer.'

'Let each man, wherein he was called, therein abide with God.'—1 Cor. vii. 24.

THE worst feature of the rustic mind in our day, is not its ignorance or grossness, but its rebellious discontent. . . . The bucolic wants to 'better' himself. He is sick of feeding cows and horses; he imagines that, on the pavement of London, he would walk with a manlier tread. — GEORGE GISSING, *Private Papers of Henry Ryecroft*, p. 201.

'Do not despise your situation,' says Amiel. 'In it you must act, suffer, and conquer. From every point on earth we are equally near to heaven and the infinite.'

> THOU cam'st not to thy place by accident,
> It is the very place God meant for thee;
> And shouldst thou there small scope for action see,
> Do not for this give room to discontent;
> Nor let the time thou owest to God be spent
> In idly dreaming how thou mightest be,
> In what concerns thy spiritual life, more free
> From outward hindrance or impediment.
> —R. C. TRENCH.

WE continually hear it recommended by sagacious people to complaining neighbours (usually less well placed in the world than themselves), that they should 'remain content in the station in which Providence has placed them'. There are perhaps some circumstances of life in which Providence has no intention that people *should* be content. Nevertheless, the maxim is on the whole a good one; but it is particularly for home use. That your neighbour should, or should not, remain content with *his* position, is not your business; but it is very much your business to remain content with your own. What is chiefly needed in England at the present day, is to show the quantity of pleasure that may be obtained by a consistent, well-administered competence, modest, confessed, and laborious. We need examples of people who, leaving heaven to decide whether they are to rise in the world, decide for themselves that they will be happy in it, and have resolved to seek—not greater wealth but simpler pleasure, not higher fortune but deeper felicity.—RUSKIN, *Unto This Last* (iv.).

REFERENCES.—VII. 22.—C. S. Horne, *Relationships of Life*, p. 85. J. Martineau, *Endeavours After the Christian Life* (2nd Series), p. 58. *Expositor* (5th Series), vol. vii. p. 20. A. Maclaren, *Expositions of Holy Scripture—Corinthians*, p. 103. VII. 23.—Spurgeon, *Sermons*, vol. xx. No. 1163. *Expositor* (4th Series), vol. viii. p. 273. *Expositor* (5th Series), vol. vii. p. 374.

SERVICE IN A LOWLY SPHERE

'Brethren, let every man, wherein he is called, therein abide with God.'—1 Cor. vii. 24.

IT is not easy to every one to display the virtue of contentment. To be conscious of possessing powers which one never has an opportunity of exercising naturally arouses restlessness or despondency. The position of a slave, for example, in apostolic times must have been galling in the extreme. He might be, and often was, far superior to his owner in capacity and in culture, and yet had nothing he could call his own. But even he was exhorted, as a Christian, to serve the Lord Christ in the position he occupied, and to do so with cheerfulness and goodwill. Instead of struggling for his freedom, and so embittering his own lot, and that of other slaves, by a hopeless servile war, Paul urged that he should remain in the position he occupied when he was called to spiritual freedom. In his letter to the Church at Corinth, addressing slaves as well as citizens, the circumcised and the uncircumcised, Christians married and single, he said, 'Let every man abide in the same calling wherein he was called'. In other words, whether Christians are engaged in the doing of things great or small, they are to do them contentedly and devoutly, as part of their ministry unto the Lord. All is of His appointment, and all may be for His glory. He is glorified in us whenever and however our characters are developed and ennobled.

I. It may be well to confront the temptations which come to those who are only called to the ministry of little things, and to strip off the disguises of those spirits of evil who too often approach us as if they were angels of light.

Think of the temptation to indolence which assails a man whose work seems to him hardly worth the doing. Our Lord hinted at this in His well-known parable of the Talents, for it is the servant with only one talent who is represented as hiding it in the earth, instead of employing it for his master. The sin of neglecting one talent lay in the fact that the servant had one talent which he might either neglect or use.

Again, there are many who, in a commercial or professional career, are called to a post where drudgery is more obvious than recognition and reward. Unless they are able to accept their work as of God's appointment, and to believe that development of character may be as great a reward as an increase of income, they are likely to regard duty as hardly worth while, and do it carelessly, without heartiness or thoroughness. Thus the ideal becomes insensibly lowered from what it was at first, and the service of earth is no longer such a preparation for the service of heaven as it was meant to be.

II. How then can we resist these and other temptations? What encouragements can we think of which may help us to continue steadily and cheerfully in our ministry of little things?

(1) We may bethink ourselves of the value of unseen work in spheres outside our own.

(2) Think, too, of the effect of obscure and even menial work in preparing men for what is higher. We are all familiar with this in the spheres of human industry, and we have good reason to believe that the principle holds good in every sphere of Divine service;

and he that is faithful in a few things will, on account of his fidelity, become a ruler over many things, in a realm unseen and eternal.

(3) This reminds us that God Himself notices the ministry which man often shrinks from or despises.

(4) We may be helped still further if we reflect that the well-beloved Son, in Whom the Father was well pleased, of His own free will undertook precisely such duties, and thus made them sacred to us who are His followers.—ALFRED ROWLAND, *The Exchanged Crowns*, p. 97.

REFERENCE.—VII. 24.—A. Maclaren, *Expositions of Holy Scripture—Corinthians*, p. 112.

'It is good for a man to be as he is.'—I COR. VII. 26.

AMONG the countless problems presented to the mind, there is none more difficult than to distinguish clearly between the will of Providence and the accidents, to be surmounted, of daily life—to know when we should submit to circumstances, and when we should rise in rebellion against them.—JOHN OLIVER HOBBES, in *The School for Saints* (ch. XXI.).

MORE than half a century of existence has taught me that most of the wrong and folly which darken earth is due to those who cannot possess their souls in quiet; that most of the good which saves men from destruction comes of life that is led in thoughtful stillness.—GEORGE GISSING, in *The Private Papers of Harry Ryecroft*, pp. 13, 14.

'But I say, brethren, the time is shortened, that henceforth those that have wives may be as though they had none.'—I COR. VII. 29.

IN the fifth chapter of *Alton Locke*, Kingsley makes Crossthwaite, the sturdy Radical, thank God he has no children, whereupon young Locke asks him in surprise if he is a believer in Malthusian doctrines. 'I believe them,' Crossthwaite answered, 'to be an infernal lie. I believe there is room on English soil for twice the number there is now; and when we get the Charter we'll prove it; we'll show that God meant living human heads and hands to be blessings and not curses, tools and not burdens. But in such times as these, let those who have wives be as though they had none—as St. Paul said, when he told his people under the Roman Emperor to be above begetting slaves and martyrs. A man of the people should keep himself as free from encumbrances as he can just now. He will find it all the more easy to dare and suffer for the people when their turn comes.'

REFERENCES.—VII. 29.—O. Bronson, *Sermons*, p. 136. J. Edwards, *Preacher's Magazine*, vol. iv. p. 555. Spurgeon, *Sermons*, vol. xlix. No. 2861. VII. 29-31.—R. W. Church, *Village Sermons*, p. 305. J. H. Holford, *Memorial Sermons*, p. 232. J. Cumming, *Penny Pulpit*, No. 1504, p. 169. Spurgeon, *Sermons*, vol. viii. No. 481.

THE BREVITY OF TIME

I COR. VII. 29-32.

THE text supplies us with three thoughts for consideration :—

I. The fact of the constant passing away of time and all created things.

II. How the Christian should act in this transitory condition.

III. How such action brings blessed calmness in view of the fleeting time.—A. MACLAREN.

REFERENCE.—VII. 29, 31, 32.—J. Martineau, *Endeavours After the Christian Life* (2nd Series), p. 89.

ALGEBRAIC RELIGION

'As though.'—I COR. VII. 30.

WE are often challenged in Holy Writ to do a little spiritual algebra. The great teachers have called in an x.

Let us see how this works out in various ways. The subject is Algebraic Religion. 'As if,' 'As though'; it is not so, but take it as if it were so.

I. Let us look at creation in the light of this suggestion; by creation I mean this great wondrous system of things, even so far as it reveals itself to the naked eye, and let us go through it, or such portion of it as is accessible, as if it had been Divinely made, as if it throbbed with God. We do not say that it does so, but we ask ourselves to believe for the moment that it is so; and then we want to test the ideality by what we know of the fact. We are to assume that God made it all.

What is the other idea? The other x is that all came to be nobody knows how. I could believe the first theory sooner. The other lame and blind x is that somehow things—atoms, molecules, whatever the little things may be—got together, laid their heads together in counsel and finally came out in the shape of a universe. No, I am willing to oblige you, but I cannot; it would relieve me of some difficulty if I could oblige you, if I could say that the whole conception of things is confusion, a harum-scarum without policy, a great, marvellous display of nothingness. But the one man asks me to believe that the universe was made and is administered by a personal, living, loving God; and the other man asks me to believe that the whole thing called the universe is after all nothing at all but just a little film or species of expanded gas or magnified vapour that really means nothing and had no beginning, has no reality, and will have no ending. No! I think I will go to church. Now that you suggest the idea and ask me to look at the universe as if it were the expression of a great personality, I thank you for the idea; it does look as if it might be so; but to suggest that it is the expression of nothing leads me to say that credulity is even greater than faith.

II. Let us look at man as if—as though—he were obeying a Divine impulse. We do not say that he is obeying such an impulse, we are simply saying, Let us look at man in the light of the suggestion that he may be obeying a Divine impulse and working out a Divine purpose. I must say here, as I said a moment ago, that when I take in great breadths of human history it seems as if man, total man, were being machined, administered, and educated, and set to a great purpose by some living, mysterious, inscrutable Personality. What is the other x? The other x is: Man is a mere anecdote, a sort of crude and incoherent fact, generally a nuisance, not knowing whether he came from the east or from the west; a drunken kind of intoxicated and muddled dream of a thing. No; I will not walk one moment in company with that assumption. But when you ask me to look at man in great breadths of development and education and progress, as if he were working out a Divine purpose, you make a strong appeal to my reason.

There is order in all the development of life; God is ruling, directing. I might not myself have conceived that notion, but now that you suggest it, it seems to me wonderful that I never thought of it before. That is the way with all great discoveries, with all illuminated sayings and poems. The man who has been most with God speaks sentences that we ourselves would have spoken if they had occurred to us; we know their origin when we hear their music.—JOSEPH PARKER, *City Temple Pulpit*, vol. v. p. 88.

HOW TO USE THE WORLD

'And they that use this world, as not abusing it: for the fashion of this world passeth away.'—I COR. VII. 31.

IF St. Paul can give us guidance as to our relation to the world, it will indeed be opportune, for it is indeed a problem that is continually before us. And here is such guidance—'Use the world, as not abusing it'. Short and pregnant, but somewhat perplexing! It comes at the end of a passage which leads up to this. 'It remaineth, that both they that have wives be as though they had none; and they that weep, as though they wept not; and they that rejoice, as though they rejoiced not; and they that buy, as though they possessed not; and they that use this world, as not abusing it: for the fashion of this world passeth away.'

It comes, as you see, at the climax, after St. Paul has been discussing various departments of the world; and it is, therefore, a summary of men's attitude to the world as a whole. But that very word 'world' is so perplexing. What is meant? The word has so many uses. Is St. Paul thinking of that lurid world into which Faust went off to drown himself in a great sea of new and wild experiences? Or is he thinking of the world upon which the hermits turned their backs, not willing to touch it at all, but anxious only to escape into a wilderness, and to be far from the clamour of all the world? Or is he thinking of that more ordinary world such as faces you and me day after day, into which we peer with a good deal of uncertainty and perplexity—this world which we know we have renounced, and which yet is always close upon us, which presents such vast difficulty in front of us?

Well, certainly, 'the world' has many meanings of that sort; and equally certainly St. Paul is speaking here of the world, not necessarily in the sense of the evil world, but rather, may I not say? of a neutral world. Not the evil world, to which the word is so often applied in Holy Scripture, being that view of the universe which has left God out of account; but a neutral, and as yet ambiguous, world which may become to us that wrong world, if we go on looking upon it as a scheme wherein we may dispense with the thought of God; but may, on the other hand, if we will regard it aright, be to us God's world, indeed, nothing else but the kingdom of heaven. It is that world clearly; for St. Paul says we are to use it.

I. Given this world, we are to use it, but to use it as not abusing it; and there is our second difficulty. We are willing enough to do our best to use this world, but it is this limitation upon our use that is perplexing. Let me make to you two suggestions as to what this involves—'using the world as not abusing it, for the fashion of this world passeth away'. It means, then, in the first place, that we enter into the world, for it is the place that we cannot do without. The world is the familiar sphere that we know, and, therefore, our use of it does not involve a change of circumstances. It is not an appeal to us to leave our London and go into a desert if we can find one, or in any form to change our circumstances. What is wanted, if we are to use the world without abusing it, is not a change of position, change of climate, change of scene—not a change of circumstances in any shape, but a changed view, a view of the world as God's world.

II. Secondly, it involves also in us, not merely a change of view, but an attitude with regard to the world. We must be the conquerors of the world. There is no other alternative open to us. Either I must conquer the world or infallibly the world will conquer me. There is nothing intermediate between the two. And, therefore, if we are to use the world as not abusing it, it must be that we have obtained the position of mastery over it, that we have conquered the world. Unless we have done that, the world is our master; unless we attain that, then every single detail and item in our world has a supremacy over us instead of our having mastery over it: and that whole vast complex world, unless we have conquered it, becomes a conspiracy against us. I cannot use it without misuse unless I have, in some form or another, and somehow in some way, conquered it and made it my weapon, my means, my tool.

III. We have got to come back in detail to all those different departments of our world, and there, in the power of the cross, do our bits of renunciation. There are many steps that lead up to the cross of Calvary, and much of the way is uphill, and many steps are blood-stained; it is only by slow degrees and with great difficulty and halting footsteps and failing heart and courage that we can make our way there, or even take the pains—the pains! for it is that—of conquering the world. But as you do it step by step and day after day a transformation takes place as you know—a transformation of yourself and a transformation of your surroundings. Each bit of the renunciation that you make is a victory; each victory that you gain lets you into a larger sphere; each opening out of your sphere sets you in a more glorious fellowship with the Saints. And so as we go on day by day our world expands and victories increase; our knowledge of God is enhanced, our nearness to the Saviour is made more near. We ourselves wake up to find ourselves changed men in a changed universe—a universe that is for us no longer a mere conspiracy against us—no longer an evil world which we can only renounce, but, thank God, a kingdom of heaven of which, by His grace, we are the inheritors.—W. H. FRERE, *The Church Times*, 20th November, 1908.

FASHION

'The fashion of this world passeth away.'—1 COR. VII. 31.

WE all speak of the tyranny of fashion; and yet we most of us obey it. There are some people who seem to think that in regard to manners as well as habits and usages, all are sufficiently condemned if you call them old-fashioned; all are sufficiently recommended if you can only describe them as being in the very latest fashion, and the point that I want to emphasise is this, that if the Bible counts for anything, and if the Lord Jesus Christ, His character and His teaching, goes for anything, then all standards, all styles, all methods, all usages, be they fashionable or not, have got to be brought to the test of a certain fashion that He set—a fashion of thinking, a fashion of living and of attitude towards life, and that by that they shall be justified, or by that they shall be condemned.

I. Undue deference to fashion must result in a peril to your sincerity. What I want to urge upon you is this: that for the sake of something which after all is an artificial advantage you are sacrificing the substantial advantages of life. And what does it come to after all? To a matter of pretence, to a matter of hypocrisy, to an attempt to appear to be something that we are not: in point of fact it comes to the sin against which Jesus Christ waged His most ceaseless war, insincerity, hypocrisy, the ugly venomous poisonous fruit of the tree of the idolatry of fashion. If you believe for a single moment that by the use of any form or phrase you are either deceiving yourself, or deceiving another person, it is your bounden duty as a Christian to make yourself more explicit.

II. The peril to individuality and personality from the undue deference or idolatry of fashion is a very real peril in our time, and in all times the slave of fashion ceases to be himself or herself, becomes a mere mirror into which you look in order to see the reflection of their times. You look into their lives not to discover their own personal wealth and riches, but in order to see reflected there something which they have mirrored of the world outside. Dare to

be yourself. Resolve from the very first that you will not be slaves of any mere shibboleth, any mere formula, any mere usage of society. Think of the one and only Leader who is worthy of our homage, I mean the Lord Jesus Christ, of whom it was written in golden words that He was made in fashion as a man, and He made manhood the fashion, so that our late Laureate rose and said about Him, 'The highest holiest manhood Thou'. That is the only fashion worth having. Nothing is ever going to surpass it.—C. S. HORNE, *Christian World Pulpit*, vol. LXX. p. 273.

REFERENCES.—VII. 31.—George Adam Smith, *Christian World Pulpit*, vol. xliv. p. 44. E. A. Askew, *The Service of Perfect Freedom*, p. 13. J. Vaughan, *Fifty Sermons* (9th Series), p. 199. Spurgeon, *Sermons*, vol. liii. No. 3032. *Expositor* (4th Series), vol. ii. p. 261. VII. 32.—J. S. Maver, *Christian World Pulpit*, vol. lix. p. 46. Spurgeon, *Sermons*, vol. xxviii. No. 1692. *Expositor* (6th Series), vol. i. p. 372; *ibid.* vol. iv. p. 398; *ibid.* vol. vii. p. 372. VII. 33.—*Ibid.* (5th Series), vol. vi. p. 420.

'He that is married careth for the things of this world, how he may please his wife.'—1 COR. VII. 33.

'I'LL never marry,' says Felix Holt in George Eliot's novel of that name, 'though I should have to live on raw turnips to subdue my flesh. I'll never look back and say, "I had a fine purpose once—I meant to keep my hands clean, and my soul upright, and to look truth in the face; but pray excuse me, I have a wife and children—I must lie and simper a little, else they'll starve"; or, "My wife is nice, she must have her bread well buttered, and her feelings will be hurt if she is not thought genteel". That is the lot Miss Esther is preparing for some man or other.'

'She that is unmarried is careful for the things of the Lord, that she may be holy both in body and in spirit: but she that is married is careful for the things of the world, how she may please her husband.'—1 COR. VII. 34.

IN the third chapter of *Adam Bede*, George Eliot makes Seth plead thus with Dinah Morris: 'I know you think a husband 'ud be taking up too much o' your thoughts, because St. Paul says, "She that's married careth for the things of the world how she may please her husband"; and may happen you'll think me over-bold to speak to you about it again, after what you told me o' your mind last Saturday. But I've been thinking it over again by night and day, and I've prayed not to be blinded by my own desires, to think what's only good for me must be good for you too, and it seems to me there's more texts for your marrying than ever you can find against it.'

REFERENCES.—VII. 34, 35.—Bishop Gore, *Christian World Pulpit*, vol. lvi. p. 150. VII. 38.—*Expositor* (6th Series), vol. i. p. 285.

'Knowledge puffeth up, but love edifieth.'—1 COR. VIII. 1.

THIS was a favourite text of Bacon's. Thus, in *Valerius Terminus* he observes: 'Evermore it must be remembered that the least part of knowledge passed to man by this so large charter from God must be subject to that use for which God hath granted it; which is the benefit and relief of the state and society of man; for otherwise all manner of knowledge becometh malign and serpentine, and therefore as carrying the quality of the serpent's sting and malice it maketh the mind of man to swell; as the Scripture saith excellently, *knowledge floweth up, but charity buildeth up.*' A similar application occurs in *The Advancement of Learning* (I. 3). Curiously enough, F. W. Robertson, in one of his letters, connects this very text with Bacon himself. After quoting it, he remarks: 'Cultivated understanding has no necessary connection with strengthened, much less purified, will, in which moral excellence lies, and in which alone Bacon was—

> The wisest, greatest, meanest of mankind.'

COMPARE Froude's remarks (*Short Studies*, IV. pp. 268-269) upon Keble. If he 'had remained a quiet country clergyman, unconscious that he was a great man, and uncalled on to guide the opinions of his age, he would have commanded perhaps more enduring admiration. The knot of followers who specially attached themselves to him, show traces of his influence in a disposition not only to think the views which they hold sound in themselves, but to regard those who think differently as their intellectual inferiors.'

THIS then is the *prima-facie* advantage of the pursuit of knowledge; it is the drawing the mind off from things which will harm it to subjects which are worthy a rational being; and, though it does not raise it above nature, nor has any tendency to make us pleasing to our Maker, yet is it nothing to substitute what is in itself harmless for what is, to say the least, inexpressibly dangerous? is it a little thing to exchange a circle of ideas which are certainly sinful, for others which are certainly not so? You will say, perhaps, in the words of the Apostle, 'Knowledge puffeth up': and doubtless this mental cultivation . . . may be from the first nothing more than the substitution of pride for sensuality. I grant it; but this is not a necessary result, it is but an incidental evil, a danger which may be realised or may be averted.—NEWMAN, *Idea of a University*, p. 186.

THINKERS too often are apt to despise those who go through life without thinking. Thought is doubtless of high value; our first endeavour should be to think as often and as well as we can, but nevertheless we are wrong in believing that the possession, or the lack of a certain faculty for handling general ideas can actually separate men. After all, the difference between the greatest thinker and the humblest country yokel is often only the difference between a truth that at times finds expression, and another that never is able to crystallise into form.—MAETERLINCK.

REFERENCES.—VIII. 1.—W. Richmond, *A Lent in London*, p. 41. Archbishop Benson, *Christian World Pulpit*, vol. xlv. p. 136. Archbishop Magee, *The Gospel and the Age*, p. 241. Bishop Gore, *Christian World Pulpit*, vol. liv. p. 129. *Expositor* (6th Series), vol. i. p. 93.

KNOWLEDGE AND LOVE

'Knowledge puffeth up, but charity edifieth. And if any man think that he knoweth any thing, he knoweth nothing yet as he ought to know. But if any man love God, the same is known of Him.'—I COR. VIII. 1-3.

KNOWLEDGE puffeth up, charity edifieth. Knowledge passeth away, charity abides for ever. Knowledge sees through coloured glass darkly, love sees face to face. Knowledge may be greatest in devils, love makes angels and saints. Knowledge is temporal and earthly, ever changing with the fashions of earth; love is Godlike, heavenly, immortal, enduring like the mercy of the Lord for ever. Thus Paul sings in diverse tones to one clear harp.

I. Now, if any other of the Apostles had written in this way about knowledge, men would have been found ready to quote against him the old fable of Æsop about the grapes. Untutored peasants and fishermen lifting up their voices in disparagement of knowledge would have furnished the intellectual scorner with a convenient sarcasm. Ah, yes, these men were ignorant. Singularly enough, however, it is St. Paul, the one learned man in the apostolic band, who talks in this way.

II. Knowledge puffeth up. Yes, from the raw schoolgirl to the man of greatest literary attainments, this is the effect of knowledge when it is found without the warm and generous and tender emotions of the heart. Oh, how well did Paul express the jaunty airs and supercilious pride of loveless and unsanctified knowledge when he wrote these words, 'Knowledge puffeth up, but charity edifieth'.

III. We are always boasting that knowledge is power, that knowledge has enriched the world, that knowledge has done wonderful things for humanity. It is the idlest of delusions. Knowledge by itself has done very little. Heart rather than head has given to humanity its noble inheritance; love rather than knowledge.

IV. And who are doing the best work in the world now—its purifying, saving, uplifting work? Not the men who call themselves the cultured class. It is love, not knowledge, that generates all the power of sweet activities. It is to the pure, gentle, tender heart that God tells His secrets. And the loving heart, too, understands the mystery of sorrow and pain as the head does not and never can. The loving heart always knows what knowledge cannot tell it, that though the winter be here and the chill frosts of sorrow, yet behind the hills not far off are the flowers and fruits of an everlasting summer, and the sunny atmosphere of a love that can never die.—J. G. GREENHOUGH, *The Cross in Modern Life*, p. 31.

REFERENCES.—VIII. 1-9.—*Expositor* (5th Series), vol. vi. p. 65. VIII. 1-13.—*Ibid.* (6th Series), vol. ii. p. 374. A. Maclaren, *Expositions of Holy Scripture—Corinthians*, p. 125. VIII. 2.—W. M. Sinclair, *Christ and our Times*, p. 63. T. Arnold, *The Interpretation of Scripture*, p. 204. VIII. 2, 3.—*Expositor* (7th Series), vol. vi. p. 157. VIII. 4-6.—*Ibid.* (5th Series), vol. vii. p. 39. VIII. 5.—J. B. Lightfoot, *Cambridge Sermons*, p. 80. *Expositor* (5th Series), vol. vi. p. 227. VIII. 6.—*Expositor* (4th Series), vol. ii. p. 65; *ibid.* vol. x. p. 40;

ibid. (5th Series), vol. x. p. 425; *ibid.* (6th Series), p. 368. VIII. 9-13.—W. H. Parr, *Christian World Pulpit*, vol. xliv. p. 344. VIII. 10.—*Expositor* (6th Series), vol. ii. p. 431; *ibid.* vol. iii. p. 99. VIII. 11.—W. C. E. Newbolt, *Christian World Pulpit*, vol. xlvi. p. 13.

'If meat make my brother to stumble, I will eat no flesh for evermore, that I make not my brother to stumble.'—1 COR. VIII. 13.

ALL other requisites are unimportant compared with this primary requisite, that each shall so live as neither to burden his fellows nor injure his fellows.— SPENCER, *Sociology* (ch. XIV.).

REFERENCES.—VIII. 13.—Asa Mahan, *Penny Pulpit*, No. 1487, p. 33. VIII. 29.—J. Keble, *Sermons for Easter to Ascension Day*, p. 251. IX. 1.—*Expositor* (6th Series), vol. iii. p. 345; *ibid.* (7th Series), vol. v. p. 146. IX. 1-6.—*Ibid.* (4th Series), vol. vii. p. 269. IX. 5.—*Ibid.* (6th Series), vol. v. p. 413; *ibid.* vol. vi. p. 223; *ibid.* vol. viii. p. 74; *ibid.* (7th Series), vol. vi. pp. 20, 40, 181. IX. 7, 11, 13, 14.— W. M. Sinclair, *Christian World Pulpit*, vol. xlvii. p. 172. IX. 9.—*Expositor* (5th Series), vol. vi. p. 213. IX. 10.—G. L. Richardson, *Sermons for Harvest*, p. 40. IX. 11.—*Expositor* (5th Series), vol. x. p. 196. IX. 14.—F. W. Farrar, *Christian World Pulpit*, vol. lii. p. 356. *Expositor* (6th Series), vol. vii. p. 389; *ibid.* vol. xi. p. 45.

'It were better for me to die, than——.'—1 COR. IX. 15.

You find these heroic words in 1 Corinthians IX. 15. I purposely cut the text short here, and leave every man to fill up the concluding sentence for himself. Paul tells us the reason, but Paul's reason may not be ours. We have a great principle laid down here, and it is for each man in his own sphere and in his own way to apply that principle. I want every man who is here to take this as a motto, a living principle, a perpetual rule of life. 'It were better for me to die than that,' and let 'that' express every man's peculiar conviction and standard of integrity. Paul said, 'It were better for me to die than that any man should make my glorying void'. Then there are circumstances in which death is the preferable alternative. What are those circumstances? They must be very peculiar and very urgent. Yet here is the great principle laid down by the greatest man that ever lived as a servant of Jesus Christ, and that principle is that death is preferable to something else. 'It were better for me to die.' I wonder what the Apostle's point of glorying is. Well, he said, 'If we have sown unto you spiritual things, is it a great thing that we shall reap your carnal things?' If we have given you ideas, is it a great thing that you should clothe us and feed us and give us a pillow to rest our aching head upon? Nevertheless we have not used this power but suffer all things, lest we should hinder the Gospel of Christ. We are perfectly well aware that we have a right to this compensation; the Lord hath ordained that they who preach the Gospel should live of the Gospel. I know that I do not modify my right or claim, but I use none of these things. I would not be a burden to any man. This is my glorying, that I have done all this for nothing, and so much do I glory in it according to the measure of the grace of Christ, that it were better for me to

die than that I should lose my glorying. What we have to do with to-day is the principle or doctrine that there are circumstances in life in which death is the preferable alternative.

It would be difficult for me to get a hearer, I should almost have to beg for people to listen to me, if I preached this most monstrous doctrine that it is better to die than to do some things. The City says, No; let us fight now and conquer the god of this world in the spirit of the next.

I. It is better for me to die than to break my word. That is right. Does some man say that? He is a wise man and a hero. Why, certainly your word is yourself. That is the great doctrine of the Gospel, nobody believes it. But Jesus said, 'Let your yea be yea and your nay nay; whatsoever more cometh cometh of evil'. That one text would, if received with the heart and applied all day long, make a new world. Let your yea be yea and your nay let it be nay. That one little line would convert the world. The whole Gospel is in that one expression—the evangelical Gospel, all the blood which makes it evangelical, all the fire which makes it Divine. It were better for me to die than to break my word. I promised a dying friend that I would look after the boys, and he died in comfort when he received that assurance.

II. It were better for me to die than to deny the omnipotence of my Lord's grace. He said, 'My grace is sufficient for thee'. He said, 'I will be with thee in six troubles, and in seven I will not forsake thee'. Have I magnified this, and do men say, pointing to me, Behold what God's grace can do for the poorest creature? Or have I murmured and repined? have I rubbed off my baptismal seal, and am I now a Church-going Psalm-singing atheist? Oh, it were better for me to die.

III. 'It were better for Abraham to have died than to have told the king a lie.' He should have said, 'Yes, she is my wife'. 'But the king might have lifted a long sharp knife and taken my poor life away.' Well, it were better for you to have died than to have told that lie. But if so, who can live? Very few, but that is of no consequence. It is not necessary for any man to live, but it is necessary for every man to tell the truth. Ah me! what wonder if the Church is empty and her altars are forsaken by all but the giddy and the vain and the frivolous, who think that by dressing they can accomplish the will of God? It were better that David should have died than that he had put Uriah in the forefront and heat of the battle. Suppose he had died, he would have been a hero, one of God's heroes; he would have magnified God's grace, he would have illustrated the greatness of the Christian call, he would have been received up into heaven. But he did put the man in the front of the battle. In a sense he won; in God's own sense, he lost.

What have we done? Let that question be a sharp two-edged sword, though it cut the preacher in pieces and turn him into shed blood. What is this but saying in another form, 'What shall it profit a man if he gain the whole world and lose his own soul ? Or what shall a man give in exchange for his soul ?' It were better for him to die than that he should give his soul in exchange for the whole world, for all the worlds. That is the grand Christian doctrine, that is the tonic thought of the New Testament. We want enthusiasm for our faith, our love, our God, and Saviour Jesus Christ.—JOSEPH PARKER.

THE GOSPEL OF CHRIST AS AN OBLIGATION

'For though I preach the Gospel, I have nothing to glory of ; for necessity is laid upon me ; yea, woe is unto me, if I preach not the Gospel.'—I COR. IX. 16.

ST. PAUL often insists upon the fact that his main duty in life was to make known the Gospel of Jesus Christ. To save the souls of men was the one passion of his life. The obligation to preach the Gospel, and so to spread the kingdom, was enforced on Paul by several considerations, and as those ought to have weight with us also, I ask you to think of them.

I. This Divine impulse of his was partly due to the fact of his own redemption. You know how often reference is made in the New Testament to the sacrifice of Christ as the means of redemption, purchasing us, as it were, and giving God a new claim on our obedience. Thus Peter says: 'Ye were not redeemed with corruptible things, such as silver and gold, but with the precious blood of Christ'. Here lies a main distinction between the Christian and the unchristian man. The Bible proclaims that God is Lord over us ; and this not merely because He has made us for Himself, enduing us, as our Creator, with powers and possibilities we could never have acquired, and crowning us with His loving-kindness, but because when we had ignored this and gone astray like lost sheep, He in the person of His Son came to redeem us again to Himself. This should strengthen His claim indefinitely for service and inward devotion.

II. But, besides the fact of his redemption, Paul was always conscious of his position as a steward, holding in trust for another what he possessed and controlled. This is exactly in accordance with the teaching of our Lord, who, in His parables, often alludes to us as having been put in trust by an unseen Master who will at last demand of us an account of our stewardship. If that view be taken by us, it will no longer seem a hardship to give to His cause, or to spend our best energies in helping on His work.

III. Finally, a sense of gratitude for the mercies received in and through Christ was an element in the constraining force to which Paul alludes. Now the secret of our difficulties in regard to home and foreign missions lies just here. We ourselves do not realise the blessings of the Gospel sufficiently to fill us with an enthusiastic desire to enrich the world with them. The kingdom of Christ must be intensified in our own hearts before it can be extended among the heathen here and elsewhere. We want also to know more of the power of the Gospel in our own land in saving men from their sins and delivering us from the scandals which come from the unrighteousness and the unloveliness of those who profess to represent our Lord.—A. ROWLAND, *Open Windows and other Sermons*, p. 116.

'Woe is unto me, if I preach not the Gospel.'—I COR. IX. 16.

DESCRIBING the prostration into which grief for his wife's death plunged Dr. Donne, Izaak Walton observes that, with sighs and cries, 'he ended the restless night and began the weary day in lamentation, and thus he continued, till a consideration of his new engagement to God, and St. Paul's "woe is me, if I preach not the Gospel," dispersed those sad clouds that had thus blighted his hopes, and now forced him to behold the light'.

REFERENCES.—IX. 16.—E. A. Askew, *The Service of Perfect Freedom*, p. 197. Spurgeon, *Sermons*, vol. i. No. 34. *Expositor* (6th Series), vol. ix. p. 44. IX. 16, 17.—A. Maclaren, *Expositions of Holy Scripture—Corinthians*, p. 131. IX. 16, 26 and 27.—Bishop Gore, *Christian World Pulpit*, vol. lvii. p. 177. IX. 17.—F. D. Maurice, *Sermons*, vol. vi. p. 207. IX. 19-21.—*Expositor* (6th Series), vol. viii. p. 235. IX. 19-23.—A. Maclaren, *Expositions of Holy Scripture—Corinthians*, p. 142. IX. 20.—*Ibid.* (5th Series), vol. iv. p. 114. IX. 20, 21.—*Ibid.* vol. vii. p. 138. IX. 20-22.—J. Stalker, *Christian World Pulpit*, vol. li. p. 280. H. S. Holland, *ibid.* p. 65. IX. 21.—*Expositor* (5th Series), vol. ix. p. 347.

'I am become all things to all men, that I may by all means save some.'—I COR. IX. 22.

WE have the old *disciplina arcani* among us in as full force as in the primitive Church, but with an all-important difference. The Christian Fathers practised reserve for the sake of leading the acolyte the more surely to the fulness of truth. The modern economiser keeps back his opinions, or dissembles the grounds of them, for the sake of leaving his neighbours the more at their ease in the peaceful sloughs of prejudice and superstition and low ideals. We quote St. Paul when he talked of making himself all things to all men, and of becoming to the Jews a Jew, and as without the Law to the heathen. But then we do so with a view to justifying ourselves for leaving the Jew to remain a Jew, and the heathen to remain heathen.—JOHN MORLEY, *Compromise* (ch. III.).

'THE general spirit of Doddridge's advice,' says Sir Leslie Stephen (*English Thought in the Eighteenth Century*, ch. II. p. 387), 'was that the dissenting minister should try to please everybody. Doddridge wished the minister to become "all things to all men". That was rather too markedly the leading principle of his own life. The eminent dissenter was on friendly terms with the established clergy, and corresponded with bishops ; he had relations with Wesley and the Methodists ; he was a spiritual adviser of Lyttelton, and of the converted rake, Colonel Gardiner. His life was honourable, independent and laborious ; but we may perhaps surmise, without injustice to a good man.

that his emotions were rather facile, and that his temptation was to err on the side of complacency. There is a want in his writings of that piousness which is produced by the bracing air of more vigorous times; they show a tendency to flabbiness, and the enthusiasm has a hollow ring.'

HE prided himself upon his capacity for becoming *all things to all men*; but when he applied this maxim to his intercourse with the great, it always resulted in his becoming nothing but a flatterer or an obsequious adviser. . . . His employers never had any difficulty with him; they let him know their mind, and he went their way.—E. A. ABBOTT, *Francis Bacon*, pp. 327-328.

EVEN if Bacon had had the insight of a prophet, he could have done nothing with so pliant and self-seeking a nature. He wanted not only strength of convictions, but pertinacity in maintaining and imparting them. Like St. Paul if he could be all things to all men; but he had not the Pauline art of being instant in season and out of season for any policy except that which would commend him to the king.—E. A. ABBOTT, *Francis Bacon*, p. 151.

REFERENCES.—IX. 22.— H. Arnold Thomas, *Christian World Pulpit*, vol. li. p. 308. J. Keble, *Sermons for the Saints' Days*, p. 100. C. Perren, *Revival Sermons in Outline*, p. 317. H. P. Liddon, *Sermons Preached on Special Occasions*, p. 26. J. T. Bramston, *Fratribus*, p. 34. Spurgeon, *Sermons*, vol. xx. No. 1170, and vol. xxv. No. 1507. J. G. Greenhough, *The Mind of Christ in St. Paul*, p. 156.

ADVICE TO YOUNG ATHLETES

'Know ye not that they which run in a race run all, but one receiveth the prize? So run, that ye may obtain.'—1 COR. IX. 24.

I. ALWAYS play the game.

II. Learn to lose sometimes and yet keep your temper.

III. Let England attend to the weak and train them gently and carefully, and not devote all her attention to the mighty and the strong. May I also remind you that there is a race for which you were entered at your baptism, that there is training provided for you, that you may 'run well,' that a reward is offered, an incorruptible crown, and that Jesus Christ, who called upon you to enrol yourself, is Himself the judge.—C. H. GRUNDY, *Church Family Newspaper*, vol. xv. p. 672.

REFERENCES.—IX. 24.—R. W. Church, *Village Sermons*, p. 195. W. H. Hutchings, *Sermon Sketches* (2nd Series), p. 102. J. M. Neale, *Sermons for Some Feast Days in the Christian Year*, p. 36. Spurgeon, *Sermons*, vol. iv. No. 198. A. Maclaren, *Expositions of Holy Scripture—Corinthians*, p. 146.

HOW THE PRIZE WAS WON AT AN OLD ATHLETIC FESTIVAL

Know ye not that they which run in a race run all, but one receiveth the prize? Even so run, that ye may attain. And every man that striveth in the games is temperate in all things. Now they do it to receive a corruptible crown; but we an incorruptible. I therefore so run, as not uncertainly; so fight I, as not beating the air: but I buffet my body, and bring it into bondage: lest by any means, after that I have preached to others, I myself should be rejected.'—1 COR. IX. 24-27.

TIME has washed out much of the vivid colouring which these words had for those who first read them. The language and metaphors are borrowed from those ancient athletic festivals which date back from before the dawn of history, and which were counted among the chief glories of the Grecian people. The influence on Paul's thought of these great national gatherings is evident from all his writings. In the Epistle from which my text is taken, Paul is writing to Christians. They might be living amongst men who cared for nothing better than the poor perishing pine-wreaths of time, but *their* eyes were fixed upon ' the crown of glory which fadeth not away '. That was their faith; then says Paul, Live up to it.

I. But I must begin with a question, Is that true of us which Paul assumed to be true of these Corinthian Christians? The question is vital. Just as the racer must know where the goal lies, so we must settle the question, What I am going to live for? Is it for the things that will last, or for the things that will wither and die? The perishable pine-wreath or the unfading crown? Which?

II. Note, further, that if the true end of life is to be attained, it must be kept before us by a distinct effort of the mind. 'I so run,' said Paul, 'as not uncertainly.' Have you 'chosen your path—

Path to a clear-purposed goal,
Path of advance?'

For without that 'clear-purposed goal' life will end in failure.

III. But again—to return to the metaphor of my text—it is not enough even to keep the goal in view. To reach it there must be effort intense and prolonged, up to the very edge of our powers of endurance. If it is worth while to take pains to win a race, is it not to work out our own salvation? What makes your Samuel Budgetts, your 'successful merchants'? Tireless patience, unending toil; and do you think if getting 'on' is difficult, getting 'up' is easy? Like the racer that 'receiveth the prize,' so must we run if we would attain.

IV. Notice, in the last place, that 'every man that striveth in the games is temperate in all things'. Let no one mistake: this is no defence of asceticism as an end in itself, and for its own sake. It is only the affirmation of the great and true principle, that the lower must give way to the higher, wherever the two clash. 'If we would run well, we must run light.

Does anybody tell me I have forgotten the central truth of the Gospel? that I have been speaking of what man has to do for himself, and have said nothing of what God has done for him? There is no salvation by struggle, and there is none without it. Effort alone is vain, faith alone is equally vain.—G. JACKSON, *First Things First*, p. 115.

REFERENCE.—IX. 24-27.—G. Reith, *Christian World Pulpit*, vol. xlv. p. 52.

'They do it to receive a corruptible crown ; but we an incorruptible.'—1 Cor. ix. 25.

'THE question still recurs,' says Pater, in his *Plato and Platonism* (p. 233), when discussing the aims of Spartan education, '*To what purpose ?* Why, with no prospect of Israel's reward, are you as scrupulous, minute, and self-taxing, as he ? A tincture of asceticism in the Lacedæmonian rule may remind us again of the monasticism of the Middle Ages. But then, monastic severity was for the purging of a troubled conscience, or for the hope of an immense prize, neither of which conditions is to be supposed here. In fact the surprise of St. Paul, as a practical man, at the slightness of the reward for which a Greek spent himself, natural as it is about pagan perfection, is especially applicable about these Lacedæmonians, who indeed had actually invented that so "corruptible" and essentially worthless parsley crown in place of the more tangible prizes of an earlier age. Strange people ! Where, precisely, may be the spring of action in you, who are so serene to yourselves ?'

REFERENCES.—IX. 25.—S. Gregory, *How to Steer a Ship*, p. 136. *Expositor* (4th Series), vol. i. p. 202. A. Maclaren, *Expositions of Holy Scripture—Corinthians*, p. 153.

THE RACE AND THE FIGHT

'I therefore so run, not as uncertainly : so fight I, not as one that beateth the air.'—1 Cor. ix. 26.

WE have here two topics—first, the danger of running vaguely ; and, secondly, of fighting ineffectively.

I. I so run, St. Paul says, as not vaguely. There is a danger, then, of running vaguely ; and there are two modes of this error.

(1) We may fail to keep the goal in view. The Christian life is a precarious thing—in each one of us —on many accounts, especially because we are so apt to lose sight of our goal. If we do this we must run at hazard or go wrong. I greatly fear that many have (*a*) no definite goal at all. Every one, when asked, hopes to reach heaven. But what is heaven ? And what is reaching it ? Many of us have no real, no adequate notion, of heaven. A safe place, a place of rest, a place of meeting, a place of calm, a place where sorrow, and crying, and pain, and change will be no more. These are our more thoughtful ideas of heaven. I believe they are all true, but I am quite sure they do not make up, they scarcely touch, St. Paul's idea, for they are heaven without its foundation, heaven without its sun. St. Paul's heaven was briefly defined—where Christ is : ' I have a desire to depart, and to be with Christ'. It is impossible that we should desire this sort of heaven unless we know much of Christ here below. Many do without Him here ; they set Him aside in their daily life. Such cannot have the world or the eternity where Christ is, except in a very feeble sense, for their desire, their goal. But even those who know Christ may run vaguely in the same sense. They often (*b*) lose sight of the goal. Which of us keeps the goal always in view ? Be not hasty to answer. Think what it im-

plies. How unworldly, how heavenly-minded, how charitable, unselfish, and pure that man must be who is running thus, with his goal full in view, and that goal a right one !

(2) We may run vaguely by failing to keep within the course. There were very strict rules on this point in the Grecian games—every part was rigidly marked out ; the course must be all fairly traversed ; and there were perils awaiting the unskilful charioteer who took either a too circuitous or a too abrupt sweep at the turning-point. And a Christian in the spiritual race has not only to keep the goal in view, but he has also all along to keep within the course ; and that means he must live exactly by Christ's rules throughout his life on earth.

II. There is a second danger—that of fighting ineffectively. 'So fight I, as not beating the air.' This was an allusion to blows that fell short of the adversary by misdirection or by skilful evasion. Now we may beat the air in like manner—that is, fight ineffectively—in either of two ways :—

(1) We may mistake our real enemy. We may direct our attacks upon a wrong point. We have an enemy, but we do not always know who that enemy is. For example, there are those who are spending much of their strength upon what they deem errors of opinion. It is the duty, indeed, of Christian teachers to see that the truths of Revelation and the doctrines of the Gospel are carefully set forth, lest they mar the beauty of ' the faith once delivered to the saints '. But how different is all this from the practice of those who make men offenders for a word ; of hearers who sit in judgment on their teachers ; of those who fasten on slips of expression, often arising out of candour or fervour ! This is a mistaking of our adversary.

(2) We may mistake our adversary by a very common want of self-knowledge. We all take it for granted that we know our own faults. Where there is a very strong besetting sin in any of us, no doubt this is so ; but where the life has been more carefully regulated, and kept pure from gross stain, and the supremacy of conscience obeyed, it often happens that there is an almost entire ignorance of faults of spirit and temper patent to others. How often has some particular virtue been magnified into the whole of duty, such as, *e.g.*, the virtue of temperance or of purity, which has rendered us blind to other faults !

(3) We may ' beat the air' not by fighting with the wrong foe only, but by fighting with the real foe wrongly. Which of us has not done this ? Which of us has not regretted, resolved, yes, and prayed against, his besetting sin, and yet fallen again before it when it has assailed him ? This is sad indeed, and discouraging. We ought to have strength, considering the motive given us in Christ's death and the promised help of His Holy Spirit. It is all for want of faith, for want of accepting what is offered, for want of believing that there is a Holy Spirit given to all for the asking. If we did believe, we should use it ; but for want of faith we fall, even when ex-

perience of, and sorrow for, and resolve against, sin, and even prayer for victory, has not been wholly wanting.—C. J. VAUGHAN.

A CASTAWAY

'Lest that by any means, when I have preached to others, I myself should be a castaway.'—1 COR. IX. 27.

PAUL was too eager and too practical a man to dally with a bogy dread. After he had founded so many churches, written so many Epistles, and exercised so widespread an influence, in his quiet moments he was perpetually face to face with this awful nightmare, that the day might come when he would be a castaway; and the thought drove him almost to madness. Have you ever feared this? I am not sure that a man ever reaches his highest development without something of the element of fear.

I. Reverently, humbly, but most searchingly, I ask you whether it may not be possible that at this very moment you are already a castaway. 'A castaway' —in what sense? You must know that Paul lived to save men. It was the passion of his life; but he feared that unless he took good care, the hour might come in his life when Christ would say : 'Thou hast served Me well, but thou shalt serve Me no more. Of late thou hast become indolent, and choked with pride, and I have not secured thy whole obedience. I am now compelled to call upon some soul more alert, more obedient than thee; and that man I will use to do the work that thou mightest have done, but which thou didst fail to accomplish.'

II. Look for a moment upon the pages of Scripture, and see how they are littered with castaways! Let us then understand why men are cast away. (1) I take the first case, that of Esau. Is there not here some Christian, who in the past has had some steaming mess of pottage appealing to the senses? (2) I turn the page of Scripture, and come to the first King of Israel, Saul. A noble man in many respects, he was sent by God to fulfil His mission, but he put a reserve upon his obedience, and told Samuel : 'Blessed be thou of the Lord! I have performed the commandment of the Lord.' The old prophet at that moment detected the lowing of the herd and the bleating of the flock, and said very significantly : 'Performed the commandment of the Lord! What means then this bleating of the sheep in mine ears, and the lowing of the oxen which I hear?' I am not here to denounce special forms of sin. It is for you to determine if under the profession of obedience there are some flocks and herds that you are reserving for yourselves. Saul professed obedience, but kept back something for himself, and God rejected him.

III. This is very stern work. We must begin at the bottom; we must begin at the root of our self-confidence. The prime cause of all failure in private life as well as in public ministry is the assertion of self.—F. B. MEYER, *The Soul's Ascent*, p. 3.

REFERENCES.—IX. 27.—F. B. Cowl, *Preacher's Magazine*, vol. xvii. p. 526. F. J. A. Hort, *Village Sermons* (2nd Series), p. 99. J. Vaughan, *Fifty Sermons* (9th Series), p. 15. S. M. Taylor, *Church Family Newspaper*, vol. xv. p. 152. *Expositor* (4th Series), vol. ix. p. 196; *ibid.* (6th Series), vol. xii. p. 192. IX. 28.—*Ibid.* vol. ii. p. 376. X. 1, 2.—J. Keble, *Village Sermons on the Baptismal Service*, p. 65. X. 1-4.—*Expositor* (6th Series), vol. iii. p. 99. X. 1-11.—*Ibid.* vol. i. p. 214. X. 2.—*Ibid.* (5th Series), vol. vii. p. 398; *ibid.* (6th Series), vol. v. p. 48; *ibid.* vol. vi. p. 252.

'They were all baptised unto Moses in the cloud and in the sea.'—1 COR. X. 2.

'THEY were all baptised in the cloud and in the sea'; this is the register of all Christ's chosen ones. . . . It needs but a little consideration to perceive that devotion, self-sacrifice, all the higher moods and energies, even of natural feeling, are only *possible* to seasons of adversity.—DORA GREENWELL, in *The Patience of Hope*, p. 19 f.

BIBLICAL ROCKS

'That spiritual Rock.'—1 COR. X. 4.

THE people who are referred to in this argument of the Apostle's in the tenth chapter of First Corinthians did not know what was following them. Who knows what is following him? Who can draw a true picture of his own shadow? Who can talk to the shadow which he himself throws upon the ground in the sunlight? We may in a certain limited sense be men of intelligence, and we may have reserved for our own special use divers eulogistic and comforting terms; but herein we may have been acting foolishly. Who knows the ghost that is behind him? Who can interpret the spirits that are singing above him? We cannot tell anything as it really is; we make guesses, some of the guesses are clever and almost original, and give us a kind of fading fame in the esteem of our contemporaries; but if we come to central and essential matters, we must be taught, first of all, that we know nothing of the mystery of things, except as that mystery may be revealed to us by the superlative mystery known—and no other name will fit the personality—as the Holy Ghost. We are told by some persons that we ought not to read meanings into the Divine Word; I always retort, 'And we must be equally careful not to read meanings out of it'. Our fathers did not know what that Rock meant; not for hundreds of years was the world to know why the rock moved and the name of the rock and the purpose of the moving. We must for some meanings wait until the centuries have whispered the secret in the ear of our broken heart. If our fathers did not know the name of the Rock, the personality, so to say, of the Rock, so it is with us in many providences, in many deaths, in many cold, deep, cruel, keyless graves. Some day when the century has struck the right hour we shall know names and secrets and meanings which to-day simply constitute an impenetrable and lowering cloud, darkening the path along which our soul-life reluctantly moves.

I. In Exodus XVII. 6 : 'Behold, I will stand before thee there upon the rock in Horeb; and thou shalt smite the rock, and there shall come water out of it, that the people may drink'. It was a disastrous case; all the congregation of the children of Israel journeyed from the wilderness of Sin, and the people did chide with Moses, saying, Give us water, that we may drink. The reason you and I do not possess the water we really need and thirst for is that we think that we can find a well somewhere ourselves; the Lord says, Let it be so; go forth and find it. Not until we come back, with our self-conceit burned out of us, and with a tongue that can say nothing but Lord, save me! do we find the Horeb we need, the Rock that has in it fountains of unsuspected water.

II. And this case is not solitary. If we read Exodus XXXIII. 21, we shall come upon the same thought: 'Behold, there is a place for me, and thou shalt stand upon a rock'. What is the meaning of that rock? The meaning is, outside sanctuaries, so-called unconsecrated sanctuaries. Thou dost desire a vision which may not be granted unto mortal eyes in a mortal state; not until corruption has put on incorruption can thy prayer be answered: meanwhile make the rock a standing-place, stand there, wait there, and look, and behold My glory thou shalt not see, but My goodness, the hinder parts, the back of the glowing garment, not glory now, but goodness, and goodness as a pledge of glory. That is how it stands. We want to see the glory now, and we cannot do it; we want to be perfect now, and we cannot be perfect now; but we can struggle towards perfectness, we can cry out with a strong voice, and say, Lord, show me Thy glory! and if we only get goodness instead of glory, that is enough. Aim high.

III. In Numbers XXIV. 21 we read, 'Strong is thy dwelling-place, and thou puttest thy nest in a rock'. Secure refuges; it is not enough to have the nest, we must have the rock to put it in. There are some people that have a great nest, but they put it in the wrong bank, they put their gold in bad hands, and they never can find the gold any more. By nest, mean life, home, purpose, policy, fortune, whatever it may be that constitutes the true wealth of the soul; it is not enough to have it, thou must put thy nest in a rock. Not a strong rock only, but a high rock, right away so that the clouds are beneath it, and the stars all but stumble against it; a great strong rock.

IV. The Psalmist says, in Psalm XXVII., 'He shall set me up upon a rock'. The Psalmist had had a hard time of it, and then a joyous time. He spoke about the times of trouble, and he spoke about the time of destruction and his enemies, and he saw them in imagination all round about him; and then he said, in the midst of the whole survey, 'He shall set me up upon a rock'. Final triumphs, final deliverances. This is what it must come to in the end. Once, when Jesus Christ wanted to put His case with the greatest possible effect, He went back, as it were, to Exodus and Deuteronomy, to Numbers and the Psalms, where we have been this morning, and He said, 'Whosoever heareth these sayings of Mine, and doeth them, I will liken him unto a wise man, which built his house upon a rock'. I think we might translate the passage, His house upon *the* Rock. Was not the dear Saviour talking about Himself when He was talking about the Rock? Is there any other Rock but Christ? All else is sand.—JOSEPH PARKER, *City Temple Pulpit*, vol. VII. p. 251.

REFERENCES.—X. 4.—Basil Wilberforce, *Christian World Pulpit*, vol. xlviii. p. 113. *Expositor* (5th Series), vol. ix. p. 421; *ibid.* (6th Series), vol. vi. p. 412. X. 6.—J. M. Neale, *Sermons Preached in Sackville College Chapel*, vol. i. p. 8. *Expositor* (5th Series), vol. vi. p. 382. X. 9.—*Ibid.* (4th Series), vol. ii. p. 373.

HISTORY IN PERSPECTIVE

'Now all these things happened unto them for ensamples: and they are written for our admonition, upon whom the ends of the world are come.'—1 COR. X. 11.

ST. PAUL is here looking back over the long line of Hebrew history from the vantage-ground of the Cross. He knew it well, and was saturated with it, like so many other people, but formed his own opinions of it, and had been ready to hold to his estimate with a murderous tenacity which would make short work of opponents. He was at the same time no ignorant follower of the blindest Rabbinical tradition. And as he looks back over the chequered history of his race, he sees the hand of Christ in it all.

I. It is a Useful Thing for us to View History in Perspective from time to time; to look back and see how things which bulked so largely at the moment as to dwarf all else, and to shut out the true bearing of events upon our lives, take their places quite naturally in an ordered sequence tending to a due development. It is so when we find ourselves toiling along a dark road in some of those sunless days of disappointment which await us all. St. Paul himself was no stranger to the chilling influences of such times. We find him again and again moved to anger, to reproach, to scorn, to sorrow, to anything short of despair, by the broken road which, again here and there checks the progress of him who would prepare the way of Christ. In our own life, how sad it is to see around us the shattered ideals which strew the desert of unfulfilled hopes! We escaped the perils of fleshly Egypt. We have been sacramentally fed and nourished, but the Promised Land seems far off, and we are perplexed with the very monotony of our failures as we stumble on in the desert. When we doubt whether we are moving, when we seem to be slowly turning back on our own footsteps, look back and see—look across life and bring it into true perspective, and you will see by what you have passed on the march that there is some progress, and that even your falls may be written down under the head of experience.

II. We Must Never Despair.—There is one thing which the Apostle saw clearly, and we also may see in our retrospect—how much the purpose of God has been shaped by human sin. The passage to the Promised Land was not designed by God to be the gloomy thing it eventually proved to be. God's mercy prevented, that is went before, His people with a prospect of blessing, but it had also to follow them in order to adapt their life by correction and discipline to the alteration caused by their mistakes. As the Apostle looks back, what does he see as the main cause of the dark patch of failure which lies across the line of progress in which God still hastens to fulfil His promise? It is wilfulness, nothing else—wilfulness in one form or another: the wilfulness of those who find their human passions and desires too much for them. Directly an appetite is followed for its own sake apart from the purpose for which God implanted it, then there is confusion. The Promised Land is lost sight of; the desert is a desert to wander in, not a road to be passed, and here it is that the danger begins, and degradation speedily follows. Yet we know we are free.

III. Why do we go back to the Records of Rebellious Israel?—Here we have the reason. The Apostle tells us how to read these and how to read the records of all other Scripture given us by the inspiration of God. It is that we may find in them recorded on a large scale the history of our own dangers, and the remedy which God provides against them, that in learning to look back over life as a whole we may be less tempted by its dark hours, and may contemplate the resource of God in the face of man's wilfulness, and through patience and comfort of the Scriptures have hope.

References.—X. 11.—F. D. Maurice, *Sermons*, vol. i. p. 21. Bishop Alexander, *Verbum Crucis*, p. 145. *Expositor* (7th Series), vol. v. p. 134.

THE WEAKNESS OF STRENGTH

Let him that thinketh he standeth take heed lest he fall.'—
1 Cor. x. 12.

Take care of your strong points. I want to speak about the weakness of strength. It is customary to say that a chain is no stronger than its weakest link. It is quite right to direct our attention along that line, but there is another and completing line. Distrust yourselves when you are most conscious of your strength. Do not make too much an exhibition of your wonderful side; be very careful about your specialties; set a double watch over the pen of your pet graces; they may ruin you, they have ruined many: be self-distrustful, and in God's strength be self-confident. Paul speaks of the enabling Christ; the Christ that gives ability, and more ability, and still more ability as the days come and go until those who live nearest to Him cry by the end of the week, I can do all things through the Christ that enables me. We say in our English Version, 'Christ which strengtheneth me'; I like the other word, enableth me—feeds my ability, recruits my strength, waters the flower of my spiritual beauty, and sends all needful things to the oak of my power.

I. Let us see if we cannot establish the strange proposition that many men—not all—but many men have failed at the point of their supposed strength and fancied security. (1) You say that Moses was a man meek above all the men that dwelt on the face of the earth. It was just at the point of meekness that he became red-hot angry—the angriest man that the rocks of Sinai ever saw, and the angriest man that the rocks in the wilderness ever felt, for he lashed them as if, by some mighty thong, he could lacerate their backs and humble them to his will. Which is Moses—the meek man, so meek, so humble, so retiring; or the Moses that lifts up his arms and dashes the tables of stone to the earth, and that smites the rock, and calls in anger, as it were, for water? Whereas nature is not to be so solicited, but quite in another way, gentler, stiller, a way wholly sweeter and more obedient to the soft music of nature. You and I may fail at our meekness.

(2) How would you describe Abraham? 'The father of the faithful.' Is that his special grace? Probably so; he is called the father of the faithful, he is honoured for his faith; the word 'believed' occurs first in biblical history in connection with the name of Abraham; surely, therefore, there can be no stretch of imagination in saying that faith was Abraham's supreme virtue or grace. Well, it was just at that point that he told lies, and distrusted God, and turned his back upon the starry heavens that were meant to be an omen to him and to his seed for ever. He concocted lies, he turned his wife into his sister that he might escape a possible danger—he who held the charter of the stars and could read them into the history of his race, he indirectly, if not directly, told lies to a poor pagan hound that rebuked him for being false to his own faith and tradition. Let him that thinketh he standeth take heed at his strongest point. He may fall from the topmost pinnacle. He that is low need fear no fall, but what about him who touches the pinnacle-top gleaming in the sun? Lucifer, son of the morning—none fell so low as Lucifer, for none was ever quite so high.

(3) How would you describe Solomon? You would say that Solomon was noted for wisdom. That is so; 'As wise as Solomon' has become almost a proverbial expression. He had wisdom and understanding above all men upon the face of the earth. And what did he die of? Folly! Well for him if he had died when he had a renown for wisdom.

(4) We have heard of the patience of Job, brethren, and yet when patience does give way what can be so petulant? When the motion is in the other direction, self-accelerating every moment, who can stop the rushing wheels? Job was patient, his patience is historical; but he was the most impatient man in the world.

II. Take care of yourselves! is a voice that comes to us from all history, when you suppose you are strongest; let him that thinketh he standeth take heed lest he fall; if any man think that he knoweth anything, he knoweth nothing as it ought to be known. Oh for the larger love, the diviner pity, that takes in all souls. Better be deceived than rot away in some malignant and ungenerous suspicion of others. I have to keep under, in the grace and love of Christ, my own soul, and not to set up myself as a judge concerning other souls more than I can possibly help.—Joseph Parker, *City Temple Pulpit*, vol. IV. p. 31.

References.—X. 12.—J. T. Bramston, *Fratribus*, p. 18. J. Keble, *Sermons for Sundays After Trinity*. pt. i. pp. 293 and 303. Spurgeon, *Sermons*, vol. i. No. 22. *Expositor* (4th Series), vol. ix. p. 105.

'Wherefore let him that thinketh he standeth, take heed lest he fall.'—1 Cor. x. 12.

While there is life there is hope and there is fear. The most inveterate habits of vice still leave a power of self-recovery in the man, if he will but exert it; the most confirmed habits of virtue still leave the liability to a fall.—Mozley, *Augustinian Doctrine of Predestination*, p. 247.

TEMPTATION

'There hath no temptation taken you but such as man can bear; but God is faithful, who will not suffer you to be tempted above that ye are able; but will with the temptation make also the way of escape, that ye may be able to endure it.'—1 Cor. x. 13. (R.V.).

I. None of our temptations exceed our powers of endurance. This does not imply that we shall always overcome whenever we are tempted, but it does imply that we always may. In other words, it conveys the assurance that we shall never be placed where to sin will be a necessary or inevitable thing. God will so adjust our surroundings that we shall always be able to serve Him and do what is right in spite of all inducements to deny Him and do what is wrong. Not that it will ever cease to be an arduous thing to live as He would have us, or that temptation will be otherwise than a dangerous foe. But further, there will not only be hindrances without the Church, stubborn and unyielding enough if we be thoroughly in earnest, but there will also be obstacles within. The dust of conflict will never be laid. Checks and harassments will never disappear. But even where these abound the most, and do their best to overbear us, they shall never acquire such obstructive strength as to make it impossible to advance beyond them, and even by means of them, to better things.

II. The second ground of support furnished by my text is, that with every temptation God will also make a way of escape that we may be able to bear it. This is but an application of the general law that Christ's grace is sufficient for us, and covers the whole extent of our need. You will observe that He is said here to make the temptation as well as the way of escape. Nor is this without a purpose. He knows precisely the strength we need, because He has prepared the occasion on which we shall be called to use it. But how is it he makes a way of escape? He does not withdraw His temptation, or divest it of its force. For this would be to defeat the very purpose for which He has sent it. And this purpose is to develop by exercise the strength we possess, and train it into greater maturity, patience, and self-restraint.

III. We come now to the third ground of encourage-ment on which both the others rest. God is faithful. Therefore it follows that He not only controls the strength of temptation, but will also make us equal to the effort of sustaining it. (1) He cannot be true to His purpose of grace, and yet allow us to be over-come by the sheer weight and pressure of evil without a possibility of escape. (2) But not only would it be inconsistent with His purpose of grace were God to suffer overwhelming evil to assail us; it would also place Him in contradiction to Himself. And this cannot be. Let us, therefore, be of good courage.—C. Moinet, *The Great Alternative and other Sermons*, p. 105.

TEMPTATION

'There hath no temptation taken you but such as man can bear; but God is faithful, who will not suffer you to be tempted above that ye are able; but will with the temptation make also a way of escape, that ye may be able to endure it.'—1 Cor. x. 13.

There are two factors in every temptation, the sinful heart within, the evil world without, and they stand to one another much in the relation of the powder-magazine and the lighted match. Temptation originates in the heart, says James, and that is absolutely true. The heart is the powder-magazine. But for the lusts raging there, the allurements of the world would be absolutely powerless for harm. Temptation comes from the sinful world, says Paul; that is also true.

I. **Occasion to be Avoided.**—In face of the danger arising from temptation, what are we to do? First of all, and for this we have our Lord's authority and warrant, *we must avoid all possible occasion of temptation.*

We want above everything else a baptism of 'godly fear'. We want courage enough to be able to say, when invited to do this or that, 'I cannot—I am afraid'. Mr. Fearing, in John Bunyan's allegory, reached the Celestial City in safety; but the last view we have of Presumption is in that valley but a little beyond Interpreter's House, where he lies fast asleep and with fetters on his heels. Wherefore 'fear' lest we too, like that foolish Presumption, for the very same reason, fail of the promised rest. Remember your own weakness, I say, and *fear*. There are some things you had better never touch; there are some books you had better never read; there are some pictures you had better never see; there are some places you had better never visit; there are some people you had better never know. Your wisdom is to be afraid of them; to shun them; never to come near them. Listen to this sentence: 'The *fear* of God is the beginning of wisdom, and to depart from evil'—to give it a wide berth—'is understanding'.

II. **Temptation Common to Man.**—But supposing, as will of necessity happen, in spite of all our efforts, we find ourselves face to face with temptation, what then?

First of all remember this, and say it to your soul again and again, that no temptation has met you but such as is *common to men*. There is a difference in the meanings various commentators attach to the

Greek word ἀνθρώπινος in the text. Literally, it means 'of or belonging to man'. Our Revisers have translated it, 'such as man can bear'. But that seems to me to be reading into the word more than it really contains. I follow Dr. Charles Edwards, who has written, perhaps, the finest English commentary on this Epistle, and translate it ' common to men '. 'There hath no temptation taken you, but such as is common to man.'

That is the first thing to remember. For this is one of the pleas behind which men shelter themselves when asked to account for their failure. ' There never was such a temptation as mine,' they say. Men have a trick of salving their consciences and excusing their miserable collapses, on the ground that the temptations to which they were exposed were of quite unique and extraordinary force.

III. Temptation to be Conquered.—There is no positive comfort in the assertion that our temptations are common to men. When some one tried to comfort Tennyson in his grief for Hallam by reminding him that ' loss was common to the race,' the poet's retort, you remember, was this : ' That loss is common would not make my own less bitter, rather more '. And the knowledge that others are tempted in much the same way as we are, in itself does not bring much comfort and encouragement to our souls. But there is a truth which is of unspeakable comfort to those who are in the midst of manifold temptations, *viz.*, *every temptation is to be overcome.* Let me repeat it. *Every temptation is to be overcome.* You must make that belief your very own, if you are to emerge victorious out of your conflicts with temptation. To those who are down, who are dead beat, who are almost tempted to give up, we must say again and again, every temptation—without any exception—every temptation is to be overcome.

Henry Drummond tells, in one of his books, a story about the Duke of Wellington in the Peninsular campaign. He was trying to get his troops into a place of safety, and between him and their safety ran a deep and rapid river. Neither bridge nor ford could be seen, and it was a hostile country ; he sent his men up and down the side of the river to hunt for a bridge or a ford, and they found none. So the Duke himself went to the top of a hill near by, and looked through his telescope, and far away down the river-side he saw a town, and on the other side of the river he saw a straggling village, and he said, ' Now, between that town and that village there must be a bridge or a ford '. So when night came, he sent his soldiers in the silence and darkness to see, and they brought back the report : ' Yes, there is a ford '. He passed his army over that ford that night, and next morning they were all in the land of safety. The danger besetting us may be manifold and formidable, but remember this—*there is always a ford !* There is no occasion for despondency or despair. *Every temptation is to be conquered.*

IV. The Faithfulness of God.—And the ground and reason for our confidence that every temptation can be overcome is that *God is faithful.* 'God is faithful,' says the Apostle, 'who will not suffer you to be tempted above that ye are able, but will with the temptation make also the way of escape that ye may be able to endure it '.—J. D. Jones, *Elims of Life*, p. 92.

THE LIMITATIONS OF THE LAW OF ANTAGONISM

1 Cor. x. 13.

Very delightful is our text, showing how the Divine love tempers life's fierce tyranny. Nature is a sphere of darkness, life is a tragedy, into which revelation brings precious explanations and encouragements.

I. We observe that whilst discipline is essential to the perfecting of our nature, the struggle of life might be excessive and destructive. 'Tried above that ye are able.' How easily this might be ! We see in nature that the law of antagonism may become so severe and unremitting that it makes impossible those things of beauty and joy which prevail under normal conditions. The same is true of animal life. And this applies equally to man. He is all the better for a regulated conflict with his environment, but all the worse if the conflict attain undue severity. And this is just as true of our moral as it is of our physical and intellectual nature. It is truly comforting to recognise the hand of God limiting and regulating the severities of life, so that they may serve and not destroy us.

II. Let us observe some of the limitations which God has imposed on the severity of life. 'But will with the trial also make a way of escape.' (1) There are doors of escape in the direction of nature and intellect. It is not all conflict with nature. We have all gracious hours in which the discords of life are drowned in the music of the world. The door opening into the library, the picture-gallery, the observatory, the museum—all are doors of hope and salvation. (2) The Divine government softens the severity of life by the disposition and alternation of the trials by which we are exercised. We little know how much we owe to the vast variety and unceasing change which obtain in the disciple of human life. (3) The severity of life is broken by that law of reaction which God has established within our nature. Trials without discover forces within. Says Victor Hugo, 'There are instincts for all the crises of life'. A deep perplexity awakens a flash of insight ; a bitter opposition sets the soul on fire ; a grave peril opens our eyes to horses and chariots of fire ; a severe catastrophe evokes a heroism of which the sufferer had not thought himself capable. (4) The rigour of life is abated by the social law. What a royal gate is that of Charity ! How many welcome doors Sympathy opens ! What a grand door is Domesticity ! (5) Life is blessedly tempered by the religious hope. Victor Hugo says truly, 'The whole of existence resembles a letter modified in the postscript.' Marvellously in all kinds of ways does the grace of God assert itself in softening the severity that threatens utterly to overwhelm us.

—W. L. WATKINSON, *The Transfigured Sackcloth*, p. 207.

COMFORT IN TEMPTATION

I COR. X. 13.

TEMPTATION is our environment, as much with us as the air we breathe. They are the common lot of man, the fire through which the ore is purified from the dross. There is comfort in this thought.

I. But the comfort and strength of the thought is not that our trial is common to men and our temptations are the human temptations, but that other men have triumphed, and that we too by the same means can triumph.

II. There is this further comfort that temptation has its limits if a man be but true. 'God is faithful, Who will not suffer you to be tempted above that ye are able.' The finest commentary I know on this passage is a great sentence from one of Johnson's 'Essays,' which Boswell says he never read without feeling his frame thrill: 'I think there is some reason for questioning whether the body and mind are not so proportioned, that the one can bear all which can be inflicted on the other; whether virtue cannot stand its ground as long as life, and whether a soul well principled will not be sooner separated than subdued'. The first step to victory is to believe that the battle need not be lost at all. A man came to Sir Andrew Clark complaining of depression, inability to do his work, and that he was tempted to rely on stimulants. Sir Andrew saw the perilous state and forbade resort to stimulants, and when the patient declared that he would be unequal to his work and would sink, he replied, 'Then sink like a man'. Strength is got through the strain.

III. When we have a glimmering of the great and inspiring thought that this is the will of God for us, even our sanctification, we see how it must be, as St. Paul asserts, that 'God is faithful, Who will not suffer us to be tempted above that we are able, but will with the temptation also make a way of escape that we may be able to bear it'.

Faith does not remove the temptation altogether, which has still to be borne, but it makes a man able to bear it.

'The door is open,' said the Stoic, meaning that at the worst there was always suicide by which a man could cheat misfortune when it became too hard to bear. There is in every moral conflict a way of escape other than the way of dishonour or defeat.—HUGH BLACK, *Edinburgh Sermons*, p. 44.

REFERENCES.—X. 13.—*Christian World Pulpit*, vol. xlviii. p. 142. R. W. Dale, *Christian World Pulpit*, vol. xlix. p. 298. W. H. Evans, *Sermons for the Church's Year*, p. 190. F. de W. Lushington, *Sermons to Young Boys*, p. 9. Bishop Gore, *Christian World Pulpit*, vol. li. p. 217. C. A. J. Nibbs, *Preacher's Magazine*, vol x. p. 413. Spurgeon *Sermons*, vol. l. No. 2912; vol. xlv. No. 2603. X. 14-21.—*Expositor* (6th Series), vol. ii. p. 437. X. 14-22.—*Ibid.* (5th Series), vol. i. p. 238; *ibid.* (6th Series), vol. ii. p. 437; *ibid.* vol. iii. p. 29.

THE PERSONAL CHOICE

'I speak as to wise men; judge ye what I say.'—I COR. X. 15.

ST. PAUL is writing to Christians at Corinth. He knows well their circumstances; he has lived in their homes; he has worked as tent-maker there for two years and six months; he knows all their dangers, their difficulties, their embarrassments; he knows that it is impossible to move about in social life in Corinth without running up against idolatry. He knows that the idolatry there has availed itself of the natural passions of mankind and entwined itself with the social institutions of the city. He knows all this, and he writes sympathetically to the Corinthian Christians. He says to them—You cannot very well avoid idolatry if you enter into society at all. You will find yourself asked to dine with people whose banquets have an idolatrous significance; they will say to you abruptly at table, 'This meat has been offered to idols'. Then you stop eating. You will find, when you move freely among your fellow-men because you have an innate sense of fellowship, that that is embarrassed very often, prejudiced by the fact that they have already claimed those instincts for idolatry. You will find, that what is animal in you is evoked, elicited, and exaggerated too by the premium set upon animal passion in Corinth. But I need not go on, he says: I am not writing rules for you; that is not part of my work as a Christian teacher. I have only to tell you the doctrinal principle upon which you have to live. As for rules, I give you none. No Christian teacher, even an Apostle, has any authority to lay down rules for you. I leave that to yourself. I am writing to sensible men; argue it out for yourself. Judge ye what I say. I cannot lay down rules; that is no part of the Christian system. For it is always a fatal proposition of mankind to demand in the sphere of religion exact rules; and in the measure in which any religion is true it refuses to give men exact rules of conduct. Our Lord always refused to give men rules when they came after Him. And for this reason—the Christian character is formed not from without but from within: no formula can imprison the truth, no regulation can form character; and, after all, character is the chief thing. You must think for yourselves.

I. So St. Paul is a true follower of his Master when he says abruptly: But I am not going on with that matter; after all, there is no rule that will serve; I am speaking to sensible men, and you must judge for yourself; you must work it out for yourselves. You remember what St. Augustine said when some people asked for a rule of life. He replied: There is no rule of life but this, 'Love God and do what you like'. It is an extraordinary rule, and yet it is the only true one, 'Love God and do what you like'. But, you ask: Do you mean to say that if we love God it does not matter what we do? No, no; but I mean to tell you that if you love God you will not want to do what is wrong. 'Love God and do what you like,' will serve as a rule, for it means this—the love of God will purify your desires; and you will then only want to do what will please God. The love of God will illumine your understanding, will move your heart, will compel your obedience, will inspire your conduct, will shape your course. If you love God you will always will the will of God. That, after all, is the true rule of Christian conduct—to do the will of God.

II. As I move amongst business men very greatly I find that they commonly give me this verdict of their experience. They say: Well, the more I go on the more I realise that what is called my work is really my recreation; but my real work is at home; it is the formation of character, and above all things by the endurance of pains and sufferings and tribulations of this present life. When a man has got that secret he has learnt the whole secret of life—that the means by which he supports himself and family is only as it were incidental, it is by the way, that the true purpose of his being, his real work in life, is the formation of his own character as a Christian man, and the chief means to that end is the endurance of suffering and hardship and the troubles of this present life. St. Paul says that the troubles of the present life form our capacity to enjoy the glory that is eternal. He leaps to the conclusion in a moment, and he says: The troubles of the present life work out to glory; they form the capacity for attaining to the glory that is eternal.

III. So when we come to understand life aright we say the great task God has laid upon me is the formation of personal character; and if the way were cut and dried I should never form that character. The formation of character means at least independence; it means that we should weigh circumstances, realise alternatives, make a choice; that I should definitely set myself to follow a course that seems to be approved by judgment and conscience. Character is formed not from without but from within, not stamped out from a mould, but grown from a germ; and the germ of Christian character is the intense conviction, the personal faith that Jesus is God; and it has consequently that formative principle which expresses itself in the development of the Christian character. We must lay hold of the truth that there is no method can be offered to compel us into Christian conformity, but there is inspiration that can develop the Christian character. Not rules but a principle is what is given us. 'I speak as, to wise men; judge ye what I say.'—J. WAKEFORD, *Christian World Pulpit*, vol. LXXIX. p. 219.

REFERENCES.—X. 15.—*Expositor* (6th Series), vol. xi. p. 146. X. 16.—H. H. Henson, *Godly Union and Concord*, p. 254. E. A. Stuart, *His Dear Son and other Sermons*, p. 177. S. Pearson, *Christian World Pulpit*, vol. l. p. 97. R. Winterbotham, *Sermons on the Holy Communion*, p. 5. Spurgeon, *Sermons*, vol. xliv. No. 2572. *Expositor* (4th Series), vol. vi. p. 29; *ibid.* (5th Series), vol. viii. p. 47; *ibid.* (6th Series), vol. viii. p. 379. X. 16, 17.—Bishop Gore, *Christian World Pulpit*, vol. lvii. p. 225. X. 17.—Bishop Winnington-Ingram, *Christian World Pulpit*, vol. lii. p. 292. R. F.

Horton, *ibid.* vol. lv. p. 40. *Expositor* (6th Series), vol. i. p. 374. X. 21.—J. Denney, *Scottish Review*, vol. iv. p. 161. X. 23-33.—*Expositor* (6th Series), vol. ii. p. 300. A. Maclaren, *Expositions of Holy Scripture—Corinthians*, p. 146. X. 24.—C. S. Horne, *Christian World Pulpit*, vol. xlv. p. 115. X. 24-33.—*Expositor* (6th Series), vol. iii. p. 103. X. 27.—C. H. Grundy, *Luncheon Lectures at St. Paul's Cathedral*, p. 33. X. 29.—H. Varley, *Christian World Pulpit*, vol. lv. p. 374. *Expositor* (6th Series), vol. x. p. 276.

'Whether therefore ye eat, or drink, or whatsoever ye do, do all to the glory of God.'—1 COR. X. 31.

IF, instead of prescribing to ourselves indifferent Actions or Duties, we apply a good Intention to all our most indifferent Actions, we make our very existence one continued Act of Obedience, we turn our Diversions and Amusements to our eternal Advantage, and are pleasing Him (whom we are made to please) in all the Circumstances and Occurrences of life. It is this excellent Frame of Mind, this *holy officiousness* (if I may be allowed to call it such) which is recommended to us by the Apostle in that uncommon Precept, wherein He directs us to propose to ourselves the Glory of our Creator in all our most indifferent Actions, *whether we eat or drink, or whatsoever we do.*—ADDISON, in *The Spectator*, 3rd November, 1711.

To be a saint is always to make God our end.—F. W. FABER.

REFERENCES.—X. 31.—G. H. Morgan, *Christian World Pulpit*, vol. xliv. p. 124. Bishop Westcott, *The Incarnation and Common Life*, p. 125. R. F. Horton, *Christian World Pulpit*, vol. l. p. 353. H. R. Heywood, *Sermons and Addresses*, p. 150. W. H. Evans, *Short Sermons for the Seasons*, p. 114. C. G. Finney, *Penny Pulpit*, No. 1581, p. 41. *Expositor* (6th Series), vol. vii. p. 378. X. 32.—*Ibid.* (4th Series), vol. x. p. 203. X. 33.—T. Arnold, *Sermons*, vol. i. p. 173. XI.—*Expositor* (4th Series), vol. ii. p. 70; *ibid.* (5th Series), vol. x. p. 55. XI. 1.—H. Bailey, *The Gospel of the Kingdom*, p. 146. R. W. Church, *The Gifts of Civilisation*, p. 56. *Expositor* (6th Series), vol. ii. p. 259; *ibid.* vol. xi. p. 46.

THE DUTY OF PRAISING PEOPLE
'I praise you.'—1 COR. XI. 2.

WHAT is praise? There is all the difference in the world between praise and flattery. Praise is commendation of character, the expressed approval of conduct. Flattery is false or insincere praise. Flattery is essentially a lie; it is poisoned honey. The Bible utters most terrible denunciations against flattery. Yet the Book, which waxes fierce against flattery, enjoins praise; and in this text of mine Paul's voice rings out like a clarion in the gladdened ears of the Corinthian Church. 'Now I praise you.'

I. Praise is a Duty.—How Scripture illustrates this! *God* is ever praising man in this inspired history of humanity—now by direct message, now through human lips. *Christ* loved to praise. How He commended all who were in any degree commendable! (1) Conscience sanctions the duty of praising people. Conscience does not side with Epictetus when he says, 'We should not praise any one'. It confirms Paul when he cries, 'I praise you'. (2) Praise encourages effort towards higher good. 'Praise,' says

George Meredith, 'is our fructifying sun.' (3) Praise is a duty because it raises our appreciation of humanity. No pessimist can win man. (4) Praise of others discourages self-hood.

II. Praise is a Difficult Duty.—(1) The self-centred find it all but impossible. (2) The jealous cannot praise. (3) The unsympathetic feel it peculiarly difficult to praise. Many of us neglect the culture of our sympathies. We know men when we feel with them. As Smetham remarks in one of his letters, 'Pure love to every soul of man is the true standpoint from which to judge men'. He who allows himself to become unsympathetic freezes the fountain of praise. (4) The narrow-minded seldom praise.

III. Praise is a Much-Neglected Duty.—(1) Is it not neglected in the Church? If pastors and people praised with mutual love, if grumbling vanished and praises resounded, how happy and prosperous would the Churches be! (2) In the home this duty is glaringly neglected. (3) Praise is a duty much neglected in society.

IV. Praise is a Duty which requires Discrimination.—(1) It must not be excessive. (2) It must not exclude faithfulness. (3) Nor must we praise so as to arouse envy. (4) Beware of praising for the sake of popularity. Watch thy motive, O soul of mine!

V. Praise is a Duty which tests Character.—(1) You test yourself when you praise people. (2) You test the receiver of your praise when you eulogise him. J. M. Barrie, in one of his lovely books, says: 'The praise that comes of love does not make us vain, but humble rather'.

Be it ours to say, 'I praise you' often as we may! But let us be solicitous to give God the glory for all the praises we receive.—DINSDALE T. YOUNG, *Unfamiliar Texts*, p. 1.

REFERENCES.—XI. 2.—*Penny Pulpit*, No. 1492, p. 73. XI. 3.—*Expositor* (4th Series), vol. ii. p. 285; *ibid.* (6th Series), vol. ix. p. 152. XI. 7.—*Ibid.* vol. iii. pp. 139, 140; *ibid.* (5th Series), vol. iv. pp. 119, 164, 168. XI. 10.—*Ibid.* vol. x. p. 139.

THE RIGHTS OF WOMAN

'Nevertheless neither is the man without the woman, neither the woman without the man, in the Lord.'—I COR. XI. 11.

THERE were three great doctrines enunciated by Christ in the course of His earthly ministry which were in a marked degree 'revelations' to the human race. He taught the Fatherhood of God, the Brotherhood of Man, and the Dignity of Womanhood.

I. Consider the position of woman before the advent of Christ. It is acknowledged that in the *barbaric* nations woman was the abject slave of man. But even amongst the cultured and highly civilised nations of the earth, woman's position was very little higher than that of a slave.

II. Consider also woman as she exists in our own day in non-Christian lands. In Moslem countries women are at the mercy of the caprice and passion of men. The Zenanas of India and China are probably worse than the harem of the Turk; and as for

the poorer women, the low-caste women, they are the hewers of wood and drawers of water for the men. When we turn to darkest Africa there we find the 'lord of creation' sitting at his ease while his wives minister to his comfort, and provide for his household.

III. With the advent of Christ and His Gospel, and with the spread of Christianity, a new respect was born for woman. (1) There are her marriage rights. (2) There are the domestic rights of woman. (3) There are the spiritual rights of woman.—T. J. MADDEN, *Tombs or Temples*, p. 16.

REFERENCES.—XI. 11.—J. G. Rogers, *Christian World Pulpit*, vol. xliii. p. 75. *Expositor* (6th Series), vol. ii. p. 296. XI. 12.—*Expositor* (5th Series), vol. vi. p. 335. XI. 16.—*Ibid.* (6th Series), vol. xi. p. 461. XI. 18.—J. M. Neale, *Sermons Preached in Sackville College Chapel*, vol. ii. p. 79. XI. 18, 19.—*Expositor* (4th Series), vol. iii. p. 14; *ibid.* vol. ix. p. 9. XI. 18-34.—*Ibid.* (6th Series), vol. i. p. 214. XI. 20.—*Ibid.* vol. iii. p. 275.

'When ye come together.'—I COR. XI. 20.

COMPARE Charles Lamb's lines, *The Sabbath Bells* :—

> The cheerful Sabbath bells, wherever heard,
> Strike pleasant on the sense, most like the voice
> Of one, who from the far-off hills proclaims
> Tidings of good to Zion: chiefly when
> Their piercing tones fall *sudden* on the ear
> Of the contemplant, solitary man,
> Whom thoughts abstruse or high have chanced to lure
> Forth from the walks of men, revolving oft,
> And oft again, hard matter, which eludes
> And baffles his pursuit, thought-sick and tired
> Of controversy, where no end appears,
> No clue to his research, the lonely man
> Half wishes for society again.
> Him, thus engaged, the Sabbath bells salute
> *Sudden!* his heart awakes; his ears drink in
> The cheering music; his relenting soul
> Yearns after all the joys of social life,
> And softens with the love of human kind.

THERE was a little Roman Catholic church at the foot of the hill where his own was placed, which he always had to pass on Sundays. He could never look on the thronging multitudes that crowded its pews and aisles or knelt bare-headed on its steps, without a longing to get in among them and go down on his knees and enjoy that luxury of devotional contact which makes a worshipping throng as different from the same members praying apart as a bed of coals is from a trail of scattered cinders.—O. W. HOLMES, *Elsie Venner* (ch. v.).

THE SOCIAL VALUE OF THE LORD'S SUPPER

'When ye come together therefore into one place, this is not to eat the Lord's supper. For in eating every one taketh before other his own supper: and one is hungry, and another is drunken. What? have ye not houses to eat and to drink in? or despise ye the church of God, and shame them that have not? What shall I say to you? shall I praise you in this? I praise you not.'—I COR. XI. 20-22.

I. THE Lord's Supper is a new grouping of men—a new principle of classification, without any violent or revolutionary interference with the existing order of things. In the world, differences of rank, age, sex, grouped men and women in the usual way on the night in which Jesus was betrayed. At the supper tables of Pilate and Herod guests were arranged according to the relation they held to the Court, the Temple, the Sanhedrin, and the Exchange. But at one table a new order reigned. Jesus Himself was the centre. The greatest was he who rendered the best service in Christ's kingdom. And all division gave way to love. Now the trouble at Corinth was that they followed the old order of Pilate and Herod, not the new order of Jesus. Weekday differences were reproduced at the Supper. Well, the weekday differences are much the same now as they were in remote ages; and there is not the slightest probability that they will ever be otherwise. But in the Supper we have the means to neutralise differences, to break down the Chinese wall of prejudice, and blend all classes into a loving harmony.

II. But again, a certain measure of friction is inseparable from social life. When Paul heard of troubles in Corinth he did not whine, but accepted them as things not to be avoided, but to be overcome and sanctified. Our feelings are often hurt; bitterness creeps into our souls. Well, in our Lord's Supper we have a means wherewith to repair the ravages life makes in our affections, to heal the hearts' hurt, and make good all the damage done to our friendship by the gales and waves of life.

III. In the Supper, Christ sweetens earthly love with the promise of eternal life, and this should help to make all the relations of home and neighbourhood purer and sweeter. The thought of death is the bitter drop in our cup of love. Horace was moved to unwonted pathos as he thought of the end, and Huxley owned that as the years swept forward to the great cataract, the horror of extinction so possessed him that life, even in a hell, seemed preferable. Well, in the light of the upper room there is no death—only transition. Bring your friendship, your married life, bring all loves to feed at Christ's Table. For here the eternal side of things is shown.

IV. And at the same time that it feeds love it nourishes hope. As Christians we all engage, directly or indirectly, in some endeavour to better the world. But often the outlook is so hopeless. *Then* we relax in our efforts, or we curtail our gifts and starve the work. Well, Jesus foresaw it all. Here is a little festival of hope ordained by Christ. A Supper, not for the body, but solely for the heart. Here is the Bread of heavenly Hope. This is the wine of Assurance.—J. M. GIBBON, *Eden and Gethsemane*, p. 199.

REFERENCES.—XI. 20-34.—D. Martin, *Penny Pulpit*, No. 1603, p. 223. XI. 21.—*Expositor* (6th Series), vol. iii. p. 97.

THE CONTRASTS OF THE NIGHT OF BETRAYAL

'The Lord Jesus the same night in which He was betrayed took bread.'—1 COR. XI. 23.

THIS contrast may be distributed in three particulars. There is, in the first place, the contrast of grace with sin; in the second place, of faithfulness with treachery; and in the third place, of love with hate.

I. First: the *contrast of grace with sin*. The betrayal of Jesus by Judas was not a single act. It came to its climax in the kiss given in the garden. But it was a series of thoughts, resolves, decisions. All of them were known to Jesus. He had watched the tragedy in the heart of Judas as a chemist might watch a process, or a physician might watch the progress of a disease. On that last night He marked the final stage in the course of evil. He saw the fever rise to a burning flame. He heard the betrayal in the words on the lips of Judas. He saw it in the shifty glances of his eyes. He read it in the sullen anger of his heart. All that is hideous and repulsive and pitiless in sin sat down with Him at the feast. We know that it is not the most abandoned profligate who so fully incarnates sin as the man whose face and words are fair, and his cloaked malice inspired by hell. Jesus might have turned aside in loathing, and broken forth in exposing and withering rebuke. Yet with the hand of the betrayer dipping in the same dish with Him He sets up this Sacrament for sinful men. That is the contrast of grace with sin.

'On the same night in which He was betrayed, He took bread.'

II. Second: the *contrast of faithfulness with treachery*. Our Lord's last night was one of mingled joy and sorrow. It had hours of peace and exaltation, but towards its close the shadows deepened. The shadows of His shrinking from death, of His bewilderment at God's will and way, of His prevision of the cross, of His desertion by His own, and of the burden and shame of His last hour, quenched every joy but the joy set before Him. But the darkest shadow fell on Him from the treachery of Judas. 'Now is my soul troubled,' He cried, and we know where His eyes rested. They had caught sight of the face of Judas. There is no wrong baser than treachery. There is no pain so personal. It is the most execrated of crimes and the most difficult to forgive. In the annals of Scottish history there are two events which stand out as the blackest and foulest to people's minds. They are both deeds of treachery. For generations men have spoken of 'the fause Menteith who betrayed Wallace' with a strangely perpetuated resentment. No later indictment rouses the national feeling like the story of the massacre of Glencoe. Simple Scottish faces grow as dark as the gloomy glen itself when they tell the story to their children. It is due to the same moral reaction against treachery that in every army the traitor is punished with a swift and unrelenting stroke. The deserter from the ranks is treated as a felon. The coward's uniform is stripped from him and he is drummed out of the ranks. The traitor is set with his face to the wall, and the levelled muskets rain death upon him, and his body is cast into an unmarked grave. The man whom you find it difficult to forgive, whose name recalls a deed of falsehood, is the man whose words were fair, whose actions were secretly base. The Gospels reflect this instinctive resentment at the traitor's deed. The Evangelists never mention the name of Judas with compassion. The kindest word is that sombre sentence in Peter's prayer, 'that he might go to his own place'. To the Gospel writers he is always 'Judas Iscariot, which also betrayed Him'.

But the contrast Paul saw was not simply between a persistent treachery and the absence of resentment, but between that treachery and a persistent faithfulness. The night in which He was betrayed was not only the night of His patience but of His noblest loyalty. Without a murmur, without a bitter word, in faithfulness He goes forward to His cross, to be betrayed. 'On the night on which He was betrayed, Jesus took bread.'

III. Third : the *contrast of love with hate*. It is, I think, safe to say that this is the deepest contrast in Paul's mind. To Paul the most marvellous thing about Jesus was not His wisdom, nor His holiness, nor His meek endurance. It was His love ; that love which to Paul passed knowledge, and constrained him with its resistless force ; that love which had not been quenched by his own years of sin. Paul never speaks of Christ's love without seeing the heavens open. He becomes a poet with a poet's vision, and his rugged prose passes into a poet's music. On this night he sees love contrasted with hate. He sees love baffled by hate.

When we read that it was on the night in which He was betrayed that His grace triumphed over sin, His faithfulness over treachery, and His love, though baffled by one whose hate He could not expel, never failed, we can take new heart and find fresh comfort. With whatever disloyalty of heart, in whatever mood of alienation, with whatever lurking purpose of evil, we have come here to this table, we can now, in this moment, yield ourselves to Him whose love not even betrayal could quench.—W. M. Clow, *The Cross in Christian Experience*, p. 77.

References.—XI. 23.—F. St. John Corbett, *The Preacher's Year*, p. 155. *Expositor* (4th Series), vol. v. p. 434 ; *ibid*. (5th Series), vol. i. p. 337 ; *ibid*. (6th Series), vol. iv. p. 25. XI. 23-25.—*Ibid*. vol. x. p. 243.

THE SACRAMENTAL REMEMBRANCE AND TESTIMONY

I Cor. XI. 23-26.

I. If we are to reach the inner meaning of this many-sided mystery, we must consider the place and part of the Lord Himself in the upper room. Two symbolic acts and their interpreting words are brought before us. He appears in the midst of the Twelve as a priest, dedicating His own life in its outward form and its inner virtue to the will of the Father and the salvation of the world. At the beginning of His public ministry He had been described, by His own kinsman the Baptist, as the Lamb of God who beareth away the sin of the world ; and the Paschal significance of that utterance had perhaps never quite faded away from the minds of those who heard it. Has the Lord Jesus the same part and place in the sacramental celebrations of the future as He assumed in the upper room ? Does the first ministrant disappear from the rite, and is His personality merged with the emblems ? Of course, the emblems exchange their prophetic for a retrospective meaning, and the benign form, which stood before the disciples, passes out of view. But He is present in the power of His spiritual priesthood, and there is no room for a visible successor to His office.

II. Our Lord defines the motive which must rule disciples in their future celebration of this Covenant Feast. 'Do this in remembrance of Me.' This directing word fixes the standpoint of the participant, and puts the Sacrament into a realm of spiritual affection. Whatever else it may be, its practical value consists in the stimulus it affords to reflection, gratitude, and the homage of the soul. The test of a valid Sacrament is inward and practical. Does it summon up within us thoughts of the spotless offering, and bow our hearts to the love and law of the cross, so fulfilling the Master's hope ? Then, no matter what the form observed or the organisation of the church within which it is celebrated, it is just as valid as the sacramental act at which the Pope of Rome, or the Archbishop of Canterbury, officiates ; more so, if it melts the heart into a more plastic tenderness, and strengthens the faith into a loftier victory.

III. The Apostle reminds us that this sacred observance is a solemn corporate proclamation of the Lord's death, to be continued until the end of the world. 'As oft as ye eat this bread and drink this cup, ye do show the Lord's death till He come.' The object-lesson presented in the Holy Supper is the quintessence of all Gospel preaching. Wherever celebrated, the voice is heard proclaiming to the four winds that Christ gave Himself for our sins, according to the Scriptures. Whilst the disciples keep their Master's word, the world is compelled to reckon in some way or other with the cardinal doctrine of atonement.

Reference.—XI. 23-26. —Spurgeon, *Sermons*, vol. xlv. No. 2638.

THE LORD'S SUPPER AND PERSONAL FAITH

I Cor. XI. 24.

The Lord's Supper is a great symbol. The bread broken symbolises that Jesus Christ, dying for our sins, has become the bread of life. The eating of the bread symbolises the faith of the communicant. Faith thus unites us and Christ inseparably ; it gives us an inalienable possession of Christ. Faith then being on our side the great act of the Lord's Supper, let us note more particularly its action therein.

I. We in the Lord's Supper confess our faith. 'We make a confession,' many say, 'when we partake of the Lord's Supper.' They seem to mean that we profess a certain sanctity, or a certain superiority. No ; the Lord's Supper is not such a profession. It is rather the confession of our faith. He who partakes, confesses he is unable of himself to attain salvation. 'But,' say others, 'to partake of the Lord's Supper is to profess a great creed.' It is certainly to profess a certain faith. But it is a confession that is experimental, not dogmatic; practical, not theoretic.

II. But the confessing involves the exercising of our faith. In the Lord's Supper, Jesus Christ is most certainly present. His presence does not wait upon the consecrating word of priest. Christ is present as truly before as after the consecrating word of priest or minister. The communicant, discerning the Lord's presence and offer, does there and then receive his Saviour, His truth and grace, His love and spirit.

III. This being so, our third position follows, that in the Lord's Supper we receive nourishment to our faith. The silent impressive appeal of the symbols, the communion of saints, the presence of the Lord, quicken our faith to appropriate and assimilate Jesus Christ, so that our spiritual man is nourished, as our body is, by partaking of its appropriate food. This nourishment, it must be noted, depends upon the activity of the faith of the communicant.

IV. In the Lord's Supper our faith pledges us anew to Christ. If we confess, and exercise our faith in Christ, and receive spiritual nourishment in the Sacrament, our hearts involuntarily consecrate us anew to our blessed Lord. An act of consecration, therefore, should follow the partaking, and be a part of the communion.—A. GOODRICH, *Eden and Gethsemane*, p. 105.

REFERENCES.—XI. 24.—F. B. Cowl, *Preacher's Magazine*, vol. xvii. p. 525. Spurgeon, *Sermons*, vol. i. No. 2. *Expositor* (4th Series), vol. ii. pp. 77, 78. XI. 24, 25.—R. Winterbotham, *Sermons on the Holy Communion*, p. 26. XI. 24, 25.—*Expositor* (5th Series), vol. viii. p. 90. XI. 25.—*Ibid.* (4th Series), vol. v. p. 8; *ibid.* vol. vi. p. 138. XI. 26.—R. W. Church, *Village Sermons* (3rd Series), p. 101. F. D. Maurice, *Sermons*, vol. iv. p. 111. J. B. Brown, *Aids to the Development of the Divine Life*. J. Keble, *Sermons for Advent to Christmas Eve*, p. 469. J. Cumming, *Penny Pulpit*, No. 1511, p. 225. T. Arnold, *Sermons*, vol. iv. p. 228. D. C. A. Agnew, *The Soul's Business and Prospects*, p. 62. Bishop Wilberforce, *Sermons*, p. 209. Spurgeon, *Sermons*, vol. xxxix. No. 2307; vol. xliv. No. 2595; vol. l. No. 2872; and vol. li. No. 2942. G. H. Morrison, *Scottish Review*, vol. i. p. 422. *Expositor* (5th Series), vol. viii. p. 60. XI. 27.—*Ibid.* (7th Series), vol. v. p. 297.

FITNESS FOR THE LORD'S SUPPER

'But let a man examine himself, and so let him eat of that bread, and drink of that cup.'—1 COR. XI. 28.

I. WHAT constitutes fitness for communion? How shall a man prepare for the Lord's Table? Our text says: 'Let a man prove himself'. Exactly, but how? For this information we must consult the example and commandment of Jesus Christ Himself. The Supper was instituted by Him for purposes determined by Himself. Jesus, and Jesus only, is our teacher and standard in this matter.

II. And what does Jesus Himself say? 'This is My body which is for you.' The nerve of the whole lies in that emphatic 'My body,' says Weiss. My body, not My flesh, but My body, flesh, and blood, for you. Whatever that means, the Bread in the Sacra-

ment means. First and foremost, this table symbolises atonement, forgiving love.

III. In like manner also the cup, after supper, saying : This cup is the New Covenant in My blood, this do, as oft as ye drink it in remembrance of Me, for as often as ye eat this Bread and drink the cup, ye proclaim (ye evangelise) the Lord's death till He come. The bread stands for atonement, forgiveness, grace ; the cup for the new covenant, the new union of God with man, and man with his fellow, arising out of atonement.—J. M. GIBBON, *Eden and Gethsemane*, p. 23.

REFERENCES.—XI. 28.—T. F. Crosse, *Sermons*, p. 133. J. J. Blunt, *Plain Sermons* (3rd Series), p. 172. Spurgeon, *Sermons*, vol. xlv. No. 2647 ; vol. xlvi. No. 2699, and vol. l. No. 2865. XI. 28-30.—H. Bell, *Sermons on Holy Communion*, p. 11.

'He that eateth and drinketh, eateth and drinketh damnation to himself, if he discern not the Lord's body.'—1 COR. XI. 29.

'I HAVE known several men, who, though their manner of thinking and living was perfectly rational, could not free themselves from thinking about the sin against the Holy Ghost, and from the fear that they had committed it. A similar trouble threatened me,' says Goethe, in describing his early life, 'on the subject of the communion, for the text that one who unworthily partakes of the Sacrament *eateth and drinketh damnation to himself*, had, very early, already made a monstrous impression upon me. Every fearful thing that I had read in the histories of the Middle Ages, of the judgments of God, of those most strange ordeals, by red-hot iron, flaming fire, swelling water, and even what the Bible tells us of the draught which agrees well with the innocent, but puffs up and bursts the guilty—all this pictured itself to my imagination. . . . This gloomy scruple troubled me so much . . . that, as soon as I reached Leipzig, I tried to free myself altogether from my connection with the Church.'

DISCERNING THE LORD'S BODY

'He that eateth and drinketh unworthily, eateth and drinketh damnation to himself, not discerning the Lord's body.'—1 COR. XI. 29.

I. HE eats unworthily who does not discern the Lord's body.

II. He who does not discern the Lord's body is judged.

III. We are judged in order that we may not be condemned.—A. MACLAREN.

THE REAL PRESENCE

1 COR. XI. 29.

MANY have started frightened by the strong words of St. Paul, 'He that eateth and drinketh unworthily, eateth and drinketh damnation'. In very fear there are some who do not come at all to the table of the Lord. Better that our place be empty than that we eat and drink unworthily. Let this fear only drive us to seek for grace rightly to celebrate this holy ordinance. 'Not discerning the Lord's body.' One thing it cannot mean. It cannot mean that any priest can by any service or authority transform the bread and wine into the Body of Christ. He who takes it makes it the Sacrament; not he who gives it.

1. Let us consider devoutly what makes this Sacrament a fitting memorial of the Lord. Many have sought in other ways to recall that life and death—such ways as naturally suggest themselves. By many kinds of penance, by fasting, by humiliation, by gloom and grief men have sought to recall the Man of Sorrows. And they are right if the Church of to-day has but a cross and a grave. *But He is here.* Not a dead Christ or a departed Saviour is it that thus we celebrate, but One who saith, ' Lo, I am with you alway '.

II. See here a gracious provision for all time. This Sacrament means that for Him and for us the cruel limits of time and place are broken.

III. We discern herein the gracious brotherliness of our Lord. As He came of old so would He come to us, at home with us, sitting down at our tables. He would not be to us a stranger afar off, a mystery of awe too sacred for any place but the altar, too glorious for any moment but of worship. He would be one with us in the common round of life, teaching us that when we eat and drink we can do it to the highest glory of God.

IV. These very elements do help us to discern the Lord as the Saviour. The commonest and lowest of our wants is made to help our faith. By earth's poor bread He feeds our faith. He hath given Himself *for me* that He may give Himself *to me.*—M. G. Pearce, *The Preacher's Magazine,* vol. vi. p. 70.

References.—XI. 29.—J. Bolton, *Selected Sermons* (2nd Series), p. 84. J. Watson, *The Inspiration of Our Faith,* p. 274. XI. 30.—J. M. Whiton, *Christian World Pulpit,* vol. xlvi. p. 164. XI. 30-32.—*Expositor* (5th Series), vol. iv. p. 437. XI. 31.—H. P. Liddon, *Sermons on Some Words of St. Paul,* p. 65. XI. 31, 32.—J. Keble, *Sermons for Advent to Christmas Eve,* p. 458.

' We are chastened of the Lord, that we should not be condemned with the world.'—1 Cor. XI. 32.

There is nothing the body suffers that the soul may not profit by.—Meredith.

All sorrow is an enemy, but it carries within it a friend's message, too.—Carlyle.

References.—XI. 32.—Spurgeon, *Sermons,* vol. xlvii. No. 2746. XI. 42.—A. Maclaren, *Expositions of Holy Scripture—Corinthians,* p. 168. XII.—*Expositor* (4th Series), vol. ix. p. 82. XII. 1.—H. P. Liddon, *Sermons on Some Words of St. Paul,* p. 81. XII. 3.—R. F. Horton, *Christian World Pulpit,* vol. lii. p. 244. J. Baines, *Twenty Sermons,* p. 221. H. P. Liddon, *Sermons on Some Words of St. Paul,* p. 95. Phillips Brooks, *The Mystery of Iniquity,* p. 90. F. J. A. Hort, *Village Sermons* (2nd Series), p. 158. *Expositor* (6th Series), vol. v. pp. 45, 292.

' Now there are diversities of gifts, but the same Spirit.'—1 Cor. XII. 4.

In the *Iliad* (bk. XIII. 726 f.), Polydamas says to Hektor : ' Hektor, ill is it for thy counsellors to persuade thee. Since God has dowered thee with warlike

deeds, thou art fain to excel others in council as well. Yet by no means shalt thou be able to take all upon thyself. For to one God grants warlike deeds, to another the dance, to another the lute and song, and in the heart of another, farseeing Zeus hath set a goodly understanding to the profiting of many men.'

' Diversities of gifts.'—1 Cor. XII. 4.

Ruskin says : ' God appoints to every one of His creatures a separate mission; and if they discharge it honourably, if they quit themselves like men, and faithfully follow the light which is in them, withdrawing from it all cold and quenching influence, there will assuredly come of it such burning as in its appointed mode and measure shall shine before men, and be of service, constant and holy.'

References.—XII. 4.—J. S. Bartlett, *Sermons,* p. 97. Bishop Westcott, *Village Sermons,* p. 220. *Expositor* (5th Series), vol. iv. p. 51. XII. 4-6.—T. F. Crosse, *Sermons,* p. 27. Basil Wilberforce, *Christian World Pulpit,* vol. xlviii. p. 65. XII. 4-6, 13.—H. S. Holland, *ibid.* vol. liv. p. 8.

THE CHRISTIAN MINISTRY

' Now there are diversities of gifts, but the same Spirit. And there are diversities of ministrations, and the same Lord. And there are diversities of workings, but the same God, who worketh all things in all. But to each one is given the manifestation of the Spirit to profit withal.'—1 Cor. XII. 4-7.

Let me read the passage in Dr. Rutherford's rendering : ' There are gifts, each from each distinct, but the same Spirit; modes of service, each from each distinct, and the Master served the same; manifestations of energy, each from each distinct, and the same God, sole source of all energy whatsoever, in whomsoever manifested. None but has the opportunity offered him for revealing the Spirit for a beneficent end.'

I. When St. Paul wrote to the Corinthians the Christian Church was in its infancy. There was as yet no recognised ecclesiastical hierarchy, though already the necessity of maintaining order had created within the little communities of disciples a division of functions, which would inevitably lead on in due course to an official ministry. Assuredly there was nothing which could suggest the notion of an indispensable priesthood vested with sacerdotal functions by ordination, and holding these apart from the sanctions of the Christian congregation by an inherent and inalienable right. ' There is in the New Testament,' wrote Bishop Westcott, ' no trace of any rigid universal constitution of the Christian society. Of a primitive hierarchical ministry there is no record or tradition. And there is no provision for all time. The provision of a permanent and universal organisation of the Church was, in fact, wholly alien from the thought of the first age. The vision was closed by " the coming ". At the close of it the Lord was to come Himself.'[1]

II. What were the objects with which the primitive believers were originally formed into associations ? They desired to do two things : first, to set forward

[1] Additional note on ' The Christian Society and the Apostolic Ministry ' in ' Ephesians,' p. 169 f.

the kingdom of their Master, and, next, to keep themselves loyal to His discipleship. They existed therefore for two grand purposes—witness to the unconverted world, and mutual help in Christian living. They needed to organise themselves with that twofold end in view ; and, under the inspired leadership of the Apostles, we can see them even in the first age setting themselves to the task. Very soon they had to distinguish between the business of the community, 'the serving of tables,' and the more solemn ' ministry of the Word '. As the Christian missions were extended, and the number of converts increased, subordinate ministries were developed. St. Paul tells us that he did not usually administer baptism, but left that work to his companions. With the establishment of local churches there emerged the necessity of making provision for their instruction and good discipline. We find mention of ' presbyters,' and clear indications of a careful disciplinary dealing with scandalous Christians. Over everything the Apostles appear to have exercised an authoritative oversight, taking counsel together with the presbyters, and restraining the enthusiastic tendencies of the believers. Everything had a provisional aspect, for everybody expected the speedy return of the Lord, but with the passing away of that great illusion the provisional ministries inevitably began to take a more settled and permanent form. In the Pastoral Epistles we have the picture of an organised Church, with an official ministry, to which men and women were admitted by formal appointment. The close of the apostolic age was followed by an obscure period, of which the scanty literary memorials allow us to possess no certain knowledge ; but it is the case that, when the veil is lifted at the beginning of the second century, we find that the threefold ministry is already in existence.

III. The Christian minister is not a priest in any other sense than that in which every Christian man is a priest. He is appointed by public authority to serve his brethren in the office of a pastoral and teaching ministry, and so long as he labours honestly therein, he is justly entitled to their confidence, their sympathy, and their support. His ordination will do much for him. He will receive authority for his public ministry ; he will be given a sphere in which to work. A door of opportunity will be opened to him. But there is no grace in ordination to remedy the defects of education, or to make amends for the weakness of undisciplined habits of life. The ministerial commission adds nothing to personal qualifications, and grants no exemption from the Divinely ordained laws under which human effort must proceed. As a teacher his competence will necessarily depend in great part upon his knowledge ; as a pastor his success will turn on his courage and wisdom. Only hard work can secure the one ; only self-discipline and experience can secure the other. Let him not dream that ecstatic fervour can serve the turn of serious study or a facile sympathy do duty for thought and trouble. But when he has done his best to make himself efficient, let him remember that he has but prepared the altar. The fire which shall consume the sacrifice must descend from above. Self-dependence here will be a sterilising blunder. It is the hardest of all the lessons which the Christian minister has to learn. The strength of God moves with the efforts of a man, and the Christian minister ' by the manifestation of the truth commends himself to every man's conscience in the sight of God '. ' Love never faileth.'—H. HENSLEY HENSON, *Christian World Pulpit*, vol. LXXVIII. p. 305.

REFERENCES.—XII. 4-27.—Marcus Dods, *Christian World Pulpit*, vol. lv. p. 356. *Expositor* (6th Series), vol. iii. p. 25. XII. 6.—Ambrose Shepherd, *The Gospel and Social Questions*, p. 97. *Expositor* (5th Series), vol. vii. p. 254. XII. 7.—A. Maclaren, *Expositions of Holy Scripture*, p. 178. XII. 8-11. *Expositor* (4th Series), vol. ii. p. 103. XII. 9.—J. Bannerman, *Sermons*, p. 63. XII. 9, 10.—*Expositor* (4th Series), vol. v. p. 138. XII. 10.—*Ibid.* vol. iii. p. 362.

THE UNIVERSALITY OF THE SPIRIT

' All these worketh that one and the selfsame Spirit, dividing to every man severally as he will.'—I COR. XII. II.

I. ALL that is good in Christian men is the gift of the Spirit.

II. The universality of the Spirit ; or, each Christian man has it.

III. The endless variety in which the one Spirit manifests itself. Unity must needs express itself in infinite variety.—A. MACLAREN.

REFERENCES.—XII. 11.—J. Keble, *Sermons for Ascension Day to Trinity Sunday*, p. 281. Bishop Alexander, *Verbum Crucis*, p. 145.

' As the body is one and hath many members, and all the members of the body, being many, are one body ; so also is Christ.'—I COR. XII. 12.

' LIKE the flaming torches, the *lampada vitae*, which were passed from hand to hand, in the sacerdotal ceremonies of ancient Rome, this initiative,' says Mazzini, speaking of the moral initiative in Europe, ' has passed from one nation to another, consecrating each and all missionaries and prophets of Humanity. Were they not all destined hereafter to become brothers, fellow-labourers, equals ; each according to his especial capabilities, in the great common workshop of Humanity, towards a common end—collective perfection, the discovery and progressive application of the law of life ? '

REFERENCES.—XII. 12.—R. J. Campbell, *British Congregationalist*, 27th June, 1907, p. 633. Marcus Dods, *Christian World Pulpit*, vol. liv. p. 90. *Expositor* (6th Series), vol. viii. p. 379. XII. 12, 13.—Marcus Dods, *Christian World Pulpit*, vol. liv. p. 321. XII. 13-26.—*Expositor* (4th Series), vol. ii. p. 41. XII. 13.—*Ibid.* (6th Series), vol xii. p. 257.

' For the body is not one member but many.'—I COR. XII. 14.

' EVERY man would like to reproduce himself,' said Dr. John Duncan, ' and so turn God's beautiful variety into a hideous uniformity.'

REFERENCES.—XII. 14.—T. Arnold, *The Interpretation of Scripture*, p. 220. J. Stalker, *Christian World Pulpit*, vol.

xlviii. p. 376.　XII. 15.—H. S. Holland, *Vital Values*, p. 154. XII. 17.—A. P. Stanley, *Canterbury Sermons*, p. 397.　XII. 20.—S. Baring-Gould, *Village Preaching for a Year* (2nd Series), vol. ii. p. 251.　XII. 21.—A. P. Stanley, *Canterbury Sermons*, p. 397.　T. Barker, *Plain Sermons*, p. 257.　XII. 22.—G. Sarson, *A Lent in London*, p. 142.

'And whether one member suffereth, all the members suffer with it.'—1 COR. XII. 26.

THE simple truth is, that though it is one of the deepest laws of human society that we should bear each other's burdens—that when 'one member suffers all the members suffer with it'—that there is no such thing as the isolation of a sin, or even of the misery that proceeds in widening circles, though with slackening force, from every centre of sin—though it is a law of human fellowship that the good must suffer with the guilty (and the more willingly the higher they are in goodness), *as the price of that fellowship* —yet this is not a law of vicarious punishment, a law by which the penalty *proper to sin* is borne by one who has not committed that sin, but rather a law which intensifies a hundredfold instead of removing the sense of social responsibility, and consequently the burden of social guilt.—R. H. HUTTON, *Theological Essays*, p. 371.

REFERENCES.—XII. 26.—A. P. Stanley, *Canterbury Sermons*, p. 397.　F. D. Maurice, *Sermons*, vol. v. p. 263.　H. P. Liddon, *Sermons on Some Words of St. Paul*, p. 110.　XII. 27. —S. Baring-Gould, *Village Preaching for a Year*, vol. ii. p. 222.　XII. 28.—Spurgeon, *Sermons*, vol. xiii. No. 777.

THE BEST GIFTS

'But covet earnestly the best gifts: and yet shew I unto you a more excellent way.'—1 COR. XII. 31.

I. THINK of the manifold gifts which the Church owes to the Spirit.

II. The supremacy of Love.　In Paul's idea love to God is the one root of love to man.　It is the side of religion which is turned to the world and is the same as the side which is turned to God.　Love is the root and flower of everything.

III. This supreme Love is the Spirit's gift.—A. MACLAREN.

'But covet earnestly the greater gifts.　And a still more excellent way shew I unto you.'—1 COR. XII. 31.

I WOULD the great world grew like thee,
　Who grewest not alone in power
　And knowledge, but by year and hour
In reverence and charity.
　　　—TENNYSON, *In Memoriam* (cxiv.).

'NOT to all men is it given,' says Maeterlinck, 'to be a hero or a genius, to be victorious, always admirable, or even simply happy in external things; but it lies within the power of the least favoured of us to be loyal and gentle and just, to be generous and brotherly; he who has least gifts can learn to look on his fellows without envy or hatred, without malice or futile regret; he who has barely one talent can still learn to forgive an injury with an ever nobler forgiveness, can find more excuses for error, and more admiration for human words and deeds.'

REFERENCES.—XII. 31.—J. S. Boone, *Sermons*, p. 207. J. T. Bramston, *Fratribus*, p. 80.　R. W. Church, *The Gifts of Civilisation*, p. 3.　Spurgeon, *Sermons*, vol. xlvi. No. 2694.

1 COR. XIII.

THE pæan of love chanted at Ephesus under Nero for the poor saints of Corinth, has not perished with Corinth.　Annihilated for ever, the magnificence of Nero's Corinth lies buried to-day beneath silent rubbish-mounds and green vineyards on the terraces between the mass of the Acrocorinthus and the shore of the gulf; nothing but ruins, ghastly remnants, destruction.　The words of the pæan, however, have outlasted the marble and the bronzes of the Empire, because they had an unassailable refuge in the secret depths of the soul of the people.　The Corinthian Christians, who suffered other writings of St. Paul to be lost, preserved these ; copies were taken and circulated ; at the turning-point of the first and second century The Corinthians was already known at Rome, and probably St. Paul's other letters were also in circulation then in the Christian assemblies of the great Mediterranean coast cities, guarded with the gospels and other texts of the fathers as an heirloom and treasure.—ADOLF DEISSMANN, *Light from the Ancient East*, p. 399.

REFERENCE.—XIII.—*Expositor* (5th Series), vol. v. p. 135.

'If I speak with the tongues of men and of angels, but have not love, I am become sounding brass, or a clanging cymbal.'—1 COR. XIII. 1.

SPEAKING of an early friend, Joseph Fawcett, Hazlitt in his *Table-Talk* observes that 'he has made me feel (by contrast) the want of genuine sincerity and generous sentiment in some that I have listened to since, and convinced me (if practical proof were wanting) of the truth of that text of Scripture—"That had I all knowledge and could speak with the tongues of angels, yet without charity I were nothing !" I would rather be a man of disinterested taste and liberal feeling, to see and acknowledge truth and beauty wherever I found it, than a man of greater and more original genius, to hate, envy, and deny all excellence but my own—but that poor scanty pittance of it (compared with the whole) which I had myself produced !'

BUT was it thou—I think
Surely it was !—that bard
Unnamed, who Goethe said,
　Had every other gift, but wanted love;
Love, without which the tongue
Even of angels sounds amiss ?
　　　—M. ARNOLD, *Heine's Grave*.

BUT it was of Platen that Goethe spoke.　In his conversations with Eckermann (1825) he remarks : 'We cannot deny that he has many brilliant qualities, but he is wanting in—*love*.　He loves his readers and his fellow-poets as little as he loves himself, and thus we may apply to him the maxim of the Apostle— "Though I speak with the tongues of men and angels and have not love, I am become as sounding brass and a tinkling cymbal". . . . He is deficient in love, and therefore will never produce the effect which he ought.'

REFERENCES.—XIII. 1.—W. H. Brookfield, *Sermons*, p. 96. J. J. Blunt, *Plain Sermons*, p. 11. F. St. John Corbett, *The Preacher's Year*, p. 47.

' And if I know all mysteries and knowledge, but have not love, I am nothing.'—1 COR. XIII. 2.

'SOMEHOW,' says James Smetham, referring to De Quincey, 'there is a Divine instinct within us which decides that pre-eminence—using the term in its final sense—shall not be given to mere intellectual strength and prowess.'

REFERENCES.—XIII. 2.—H. M. Bate, *Church Family Newspaper*, vol. xiv. p. 776. *Expositor* (4th Series), vol. vii. p. 7 ; *ibid.* vol. x. p. 124 ; *ibid.* (5th Series), vol. i. p. 144.

ST. PAUL'S VIEW OF SACRIFICE

' Though I give my body to be burned, and have not charity, it profiteth me nothing.'—1 COR. XIII. 3.

IT has been pointed out that St. Paul, when he wrote, *Though I give my body to be burned, and have not love, it profiteth me nothing*, may have had an actual historical incident in view. A story is told by classical writers of an embassy sent to Augustus by Porus, an Indian king, attached to which was a fanatic who, under circumstances of which we have no information, publicly burnt himself at Athens. His tomb, according to Plutarch, was one of the sights of the city. It bore the inscription 'Zarmanochegas, the Indian from Bargosa, who after the fashion of his Indian forefathers made himself immortal, died here'. 'Now, Zarmanochegas is evidently the same word as Iramana-Karja, which means "teacher of the ascetics," and shows that its owner was not Braham, but Buddhist ; while Bargosa may be taken as identical with Barygoza, a city in which we know Buddhism flourished at the beginning of the Christian era. What more likely than that Paul, whose eye had been attracted by the inscription "To the unknown God," should have seen this also, and should have heard the story of the strange self-immolation which was still fresh in the minds of men ?'

Mr. Beard describes this as the only meeting-point that exists between Buddhism and Christianity, and it may well be that this exit by the gate of fire drew the thoughts of St. Paul. For the practice of suicide was hardly Greek, and took easier ways than through the flames. The death would thus be a wonder—a wonder apparently heroic, but on deeper reflection alike vain and cowardly.

St. Paul's devotion was unbroken ; but he testified that sacrifice by itself is nothing. The sacrifice which is the imitation of Christ must be moved by love, and must seek a worthy end. *Sacrifice and offering Thou wouldst not*, applies to all such purposeless and theatrical displays. The great oblation which is our example as well as our propitiation, and his own daily dying, were of another order.

I. Why did Christ die ? There is no difficulty in saying that He died for love. Trace the life-giving river to its fountain-head, and we see it spring in everlasting love. Though the deep human heart's first demand even in its fall is for justice ; though St. Paul declares that he is not ashamed of the Gospel of Christ, because first of all it reveals the righteousness of God from faith to faith, yet it is the love of the Atonement that draws us out of the dreary years of routine and of sin, and gives us power to become true sons of God.

II. And now that we have fairly entered the political period of Christianity, whose watchword is charity, it is well to consider what self-sacrifice really is. It is not lavish giving. Though, says the Apostle, I give all my goods to feed the poor, and have not love, it profiteth me nothing. A man whose whole income appears in subscription lists may or may not be charitable. In the war between the haves and the have-nots many will give lavishly to put off the day of reckoning. But what is surrendered from fear is not charity. Others, again, give from a sense of duty ; they understand that they ought to part with one-tenth of their incomes ; perhaps there is a lurking thought somewhere that God may prosper their business if they give Him some small share, but neither duty nor calculation is love. We believe there are in the Christian Church, that to-day looks so dead, so comfortable, so utterly deaf to its call, many thousand souls of the true Israel seeking to be led from the house of bondage. But their Moses will not put giving first. Love is first—that love which can be learned nowhere but at the Cross. The Gospel is the reinstatement of love, and love is maintained only by the sacrifice. Philanthropy is very popular, but it is only an outer energy, and it has been well said that a virtue which is fashionable is next door to being out of fashion. Love is the condition of the Christian disentanglement.

Neither is voluntary suffering the true self-sacrifice. Love will find the way to its own expression. There will be no need to seek occasions of sacrifice. If we but look where next to plant our foot, we shall in due time discover all the length and all the winding of the way.

III. We shall thus come to understand the life of St. Paul in its sweetness, in its greatness, in its pain —the life of constant suffering and constant triumph, the life that ever heard and never left unheeded the call to bonds and afflictions, the life that did not hurry to useless pains and unasked renunciations, the life that loved and was loved back, the life of a surrender that smoked day and night like the perfumes on the altar. And when all the years are full, when much has been attained, accomplished, foregone, we shall hear the last solemn call, *My son, give Me thine heart*, and go forth to our creating, redeeming, sanctifying God, to the church of the firstborn, whose names are written in heaven, and to Jesus.—W. ROBERTSON NICOLL, *Ten Minute Sermons*, p. 173.

REFERENCES.—XIII. 3.—H. Jones, *A Lent in London*, p. 134. *Expositor* (5th Series), vol. x. p. 325.

' Love suffereth long, and is kind.'—1 COR. XIII. 4.

TRYING to be kind and honest seems an affair too simple and too inconsequential for gentlemen of our heroic mould ; we had rather set ourselves to something bold, arduous, and conclusive ; we had rather found a schism or suppress a heresy, cut off a hand or mortify an appetite. But the task before us is rather one of microscopic fineness, and the heroism required is that of patience. To be honest, to be kind—to earn a little and to spend a little less, to make upon the whole a family happier for his presence, to renounce when that shall be necessary and not be embittered, to keep a few friends but these without capitulation—above all, on the same grim condition, to keep friends with himself—here is a task for all that a man has of fortitude and delicacy.—R. L. STEVENSON, in *A Christmas Sermon.*

'Love envieth not.'—I COR. XIII. 4.

'SWIFT,' says Dr. Johnson, 'seems to have wasted life in discontent, by the rage of neglected pride, and the languishment of unsatisfied desire. He is querulous and fastidious, arrogant and malignant ; he scarcely speaks of himself but with indignant lamentations, or of others but with insolent superiority when he is gay, and with angry contempt when he is gloomy.'

'Is not puffed up.'—I COR. XIII. 4.

THOSE whom their virtue restrains from deceiving others, are often disposed by their vanity to deceive themselves.—JOHNSON, *Life of Blackmore.*

REFERENCES.—XIII. 4.—C. Perren, *Sermon Outlines,* p. 333. F. Bourdillon, *Plain Sermons for Family Reading* (2nd Series), p. 84. *Expositor* (5th Series), vol. ix. p. 222. XIII. 4-7.—*Ibid.* (4th Series), vol. ix. p. 88. XIII. 4-8.—H. Elvet Lewis, *Preacher's Magazine,* vol. xix. p. 393. XIII. 4-13.— *Christian World Pulpit,* vol. lii. p. 36. D. L. Moody, *The Fulness of the Gospel,* p. 90.

'Is not easily provoked.'—I COR. XIII. 5.

'LOVE,' says George Eliot, 'has a habit of saying "never mind" to angry self, who, sitting down for the nonce in the lower place, by-and-by gets used to it.'

THERE is no safer test of greatness than the faculty of letting mortifying words and insults pass unheeded, and of ascribing them, like many other mistakes, to the weakness and ignorance of the speaker—merely, as it were, perceiving without feeling them.'—SCHOPENHAUER.

'Thinketh no evil.'—I COR. XIII. 5.

CHARITY is generous ; it runs a risk willingly, and in spite of a hundred successive experiences, it thinks no evil at the hundred-and-first. We must be knowingly rash, that we may not be like the clever ones of this world, who never forget their own interests.—AMIEL.

'Rejoiceth not in iniquity.'—I COR. XIII. 6.

'I HOLD it a crime,' says Caleb Garth in *Middlemarch,* 'to expose a man's sin, unless I'm clear it must be done to save the innocent.'

REFERENCES. — XIII. 5.—Archbishop Temple, *Christian World Pulpit,* vol. xlvi. p. 241. XIII. 6.—C. S. Horne, *Christian World Pulpit,* vol. lv. p. 408.

'Love . . . endureth all things.'—I COR. XIII. 7.

WRITING to a young friend on marriage, Henri Perreyve said : 'Love is not pleasure, it is not a mere selfish enjoyment, it is not the illusion of a coarse passion. He who loves gives himself above all ; in its final expression, love is sacrifice. Therefore he alone is the true lover who sacrifices his rest, his joys, his fortune and if need be, life itself, for the being whom he ought to love on earth or in heaven. Those who marry ought to surrender themselves as the priest does in his sacred office, with devotion, with self-abandonment—with joy, indeed, but with a solemn joy, which is closely akin to resignation, and which accepts suffering beforehand.' — LETTRES DE L'ABBÉ PERREYVE (edition of 1903), p. 98.

'Beareth all things . . . endureth all things.'—I COR. XIII. 7.

'THE many ties of acquaintance and friendship which I have, or think I have in life, I have felt along the lines, and they are almost all of them of such frail contexture, that I am sure they would not stand the breath of the least adverse breeze of fortune. But from you, my ever dear Sir,' writes Burns in 1787 to William Nicol, 'I look with confidence for the apostolic love that shall wait on me through good report and bad report.'

COLERIDGE makes the words 'beareth all things' the motto for the following lines on Forbearance :—

Gently I took that which ungently came,
And without scorn forgave :—Do thou the same.
A wrong done to thee think a cat's-eye spark
Thou wouldst not see, were not thine own heart dark.
Thine own keen sense of wrong that thirsts for sin,
Fear that.

'Believeth all things, hopeth all things.'—I COR. XIII. 7.

A FRIEND is one who incessantly pays us the compliment of expecting all the virtues from us, and who can appreciate them in us.—THOREAU.

COMPARE Cléante's outburst in *Tartuffe* (Act i. Scene 5) :—

Our age, my brother, has made plain to us
Some who may serve as glorious exemplars. . .
No trumpeters of virtue they ; you mark
No vaunt intolerable in their lives ; nay more,
Their piety is human, reasonable.
They blame not all we do, for that, they deem,
Smacks overmuch of arrogant pretence,
So, leaving proud words to the lips of others,
They make their actions a reproof to ours.
They build not on appearances of evil,
And quick are they to judge well of their neighbours.
No faction lurks in them, no sly intrigue,
Their only care is to live well and true.
They do not run the sinner harshly down,
But keep their hatred for the sin alone.
These, these the men for me ! That's the true life.
That's the example for us all to follow.

'Endureth all things.'—I COR. XIII. 7.

IT is not true that love makes all things easy ; it makes us choose what is difficult.—GEORGE ELIOT *Felix Holt,* ch. XLIX.

'Love never faileth.'—I COR. XIII. 8.

'IF you want a person's faults,' says Stevenson in his essay on Thoreau, 'go to those who love him. They will not tell you, but they know. And herein lies the magnanimous courage of love, that it endures this knowledge without change.'

References. — XIII. 7.—H. D. M. Spence, *Voices and Silences*, p. 197. Spurgeon, *Sermons*, vol. xxvii. No. 1617. *Expositor* (6th Series), vol. v. p. 218. XIII. 8.—T. F. Crosse, *Sermons*, p. 67. XIII. 8-10.—T. G. Bonney, *Sermons on Some of the Questions of the Day*, p. 56. XIII. 8-12.—J. Bowstead, *Practical Sermons*, vol. ii. p. 162.

WHAT LASTS

'Whether there be prophecies, they shall fail ; whether there be tongues, they shall cease ; whether there be knowledge, it shall vanish away. . . . And now abideth faith, hope, charity, these three. . . .'—i Cor. XIII. 8, 13.

We discern the run of the Apostle's thought best by thus omitting the intervening verses and connecting these two. The part omitted is but a buttress of what has been stated in the former of our two verses ; and when we thus unite them there is disclosed plainly the Apostle's intention of contrasting two sets of things, three in each. The point mainly intended by the contrast is the transiency of the one and the permanence of the other.

I. **What will Drop Away.**—Paul answers, 'prophecies, tongues, knowledge'. All our present modes of apprehension and of utterance are transient, and will be left behind. (1) Knowledge shall cease because the perfect will absorbs into itself the imperfect, as the inrushing tide will obliterate the little pools in the rocks on the seashore. (2) Knowledge will pass because here it is indirect, and there it will be immediate. 'We shall know face to face,' which is what philosophers call by intuition. (3) Modes of utterance will cease. With new experiences will come new methods of communication ; as a man can speak, and a beast can only growl or bark.

II. **What will Last ?**—'So then abideth these three, faith, hope, love.' The two latter come out of the former, and without it they are nought, and it without them is dead. (1) Faith breeds hope. *There* is the difference between earthly hopes and Christian people's hopes. The one basis on which men can rest is trust in Jesus Christ, His word, His love, His power, and for the heavenly future, in His Resurrection and present glory. (2) Faith, in like manner, is the parent of love. The abiding of all three is eternal abiding, and there is a heavenly as well as an earthly form of faith and hope as well as of love.

III. **What Follows from all this ?**—(1) Let us be quite sure that we understand what this abiding love is. Paul's notion of love is the response of the human love to the Divine, which Divine is received into the heart by simple faith in Jesus Christ. (2) Let us take this great thought of the permanence of faith, hope, and love as being the highest conception that we can form of our future condition. (3) Let us shape our lives in accordance with these certainties.—A. Maclaren, *Triumphant Certainties*, p. 162.

References.—XIII. 8 13.—A. Maclaren, *Expositions of Holy Scripture—Corinthians*, p. 186.

'For we know in part.'—i Cor. XIII. 9.
'Now I know in part.'—i Cor. XIII. 12.

Bishop King of Lincoln wrote, in his paper on Clerical Studies :—

'This conviction of our own ignorance is one of the most prominent and valuable features in the system of Bishop Butler.

'It is after all only what St. Paul has told us, that we know in part (ἐκ μέρους γὰρ γινώσκομεν). But it was the forgetfulness of this which led to the weakness of the great systems of the schoolmen in the Middle Ages. They were tempted by the desire for intellectual scientific completeness to add connecting pieces of their own invention, instead of, as Lord Bacon says, being content to have breaks and chasms in their system, and to cry out, "O the depth of the riches both of the wisdom and knowledge of God ! how unsearchable are His judgments, and His ways past finding out !" It is the forgetfulness of this condition of partial knowledge which has placed the modern Roman Church in such a perilous position, allowing herself to be led on by the popular desire to have everything defined and made plain, "howbeit," as Hooker said, "oftentimes more plain than true".

'This seems to me to be most important for us to remember in the Church of England at the present time, with the pressure of modern Romanism on the one side, and the desire for secular scientific knowledge on the other. We must not be afraid to say, ἄρτι γινώσκω ἐκ μέρους, and one of the best ways, I think, to be convinced of one's ignorance is to try to know.

'It is a matter not for pride but for thankfulness that hitherto the clergy of the Church of England have been better educated than the clergy of any other part of Christendom, but from different causes it is an obvious fact that men are now being ordained who have not had the same opportunities, which most of us had, of knowing how much there is that they do not know. It is more than ever, therefore, important that we should all continue reading, that we may preserve the condition so favourable to true humility and be ready for the gift of faith. Let this be a watchword for the Church of England, ἄρτι γινώσκω ἐκ μέρους.'—*The Love and Wisdom of God*, p. 337.

References.—XIII. 9.—R. W. Hiley, *A Year's Sermons*, vol. i. p. 106. A. Rowland, *Christian World Pulpit*, vol. xlix. p. 166. XIII. 10.—H. Windross, *The Life Victorious*, p. 65.

CHRISTIAN MANHOOD

'When I was a child, I spake as a child, etc.'—i Cor. XIII. 11.

If there be those among us, who, like the young ruler, 'worshipping Christ,' and 'loved' by Him, and obeying His commandments from their youth up, yet cannot but be 'sorrowful' at the thought of giving up their pleasant visions, their childish idolatries, and their bright hopes of earthly happiness, such I bid be of good cheer, and take courage. What is it your Saviour requires of you, more than will also be exacted from you by that hard and evil master, who desires your ruin? Christ bids you give up the world; but will not, at any rate, the world soon give up you? Can you keep it, by being its slave? Will not he, whose creature of temptation it is, the prince of the world, take it from you, whatever he at present promises? What does your Lord require of you, but to look at all things as they really are, to account them merely as His instruments, and to believe that good is good because He wills it, that He can bless as easily by hard stone as by bread, in the desert as in the fruitful field, if we have faith in Him who gives us the true bread from heaven? Daniel and his friends were princes of the royal house of David; they were ' children well favoured, and skilful in all wisdom, cunning in knowledge, and understanding science'; yet they had faith to refuse even the literal meat and drink given them, because it was an idol's sacrifice, and God sustained them without it. For ten days of trial they lived on pulse and water; yet ' at the end,' says the sacred record, ' their countenances appeared fairer and fatter in flesh than all the children which did eat the portion of the king's meat'. Doubt not, then, His power to bring you through any difficulties, who gives you the command to encounter them. He has showed you the way; He gave up the home of His mother Mary to ' be about His Father's business,' and now He but bids you take up after Him the cross which He bore for you, and ' fill up what is wanting of His afflictions in your flesh'. Be not afraid—it is but a pang now and then, and a struggle; a covenant with your eyes, and a fasting in the wilderness, some calm habitual watchfulness and the hearty effort to obey, and all will be well. Be not afraid. He is most gracious, and will bring you on by little and little. There is none like unto the God of Jeshurun, who rideth upon the heaven in thy help, and in His excellency on the sky. The Eternal God is thy refuge, and underneath are the everlasting arms. He knows no variableness, neither shadow of turning; and when we outgrow our childhood, we but approach, however feebly, to His likeness, who has no youth nor age, who has no passions, no hopes, nor fears, but who loves truth, purity, and mercy, and who is supremely blessed, because He is supremely holy.—J. H. NEWMAN, from the *Sermon on Christian Manhood.*

'When I was a child, I spake as a child, I felt as a child, I thought as a child.'—I COR. XIII. II.

O WHAT a wilderness were this sad world,
If man were always man, and never child.
　　　　　　　　　　—HARTLEY COLERIDGE.

HORACE WALPOLE used to say that Gray ' was never a boy,' and Coleridge confesses that at school ' I became a dreamer, and acquired an indisposition to all bodily activity; and I was fretful, and inordinately passionate; and as I could not play at anything, and was slothful, I was despised and hated by the boys; and because I could read and spell, and had, I may truly say, a memory and understanding forced into almost unnatural ripeness, I was flattered and wondered

at by the old women. . . . Alas! I had all the simplicity, all the docility of the little child, but none of the child's habits. I never thought as a child, never had the language of a child'.

COMPARE Wordsworth's lines written upon visiting Milton's rooms at Cambridge:—

> Yea, our blind Poet, who in his later day
> Stood almost single; uttering odious truth—
> Darkness before and danger's voice behind,
> Soul awful—if the earth has ever lodged
> An awful soul—I seemed to see him here
> Familiarly, and in his scholar's dress
> Bounding before me, yet a stripling youth—
> A boy, no better, with his rosy cheeks
> Angelical, keen eye, courageous look,
> And conscious step of purity and pride.

' LOOKING back upon all this period of his early years,' says Sainte-Beuve, ' Gibbon is careful to point out that the golden age of life's morning, which all praise, never existed for him, and that he "never knew the happiness of childhood". I have already noted the same thing with regard to Volney. Those who have lacked such maternal care, the early bloom and blossom of tender affection, the varied charm which imbues our early impressions, are more easily detached from the religious feeling than other people.'

'Now that I am become a man, I have put away childish things.'—I COR. XIII. II.

' Do as a child but when thou art a child,' says Sir Thomas Browne in his *Christian Morals,* ' and ride not on a reed at twenty. He who hath not taken leave of the follies of his youth, and in his maturer state scarce got out of that division, disproportionately divideth his days, crowds up the latter part of his life, and leaves too narrow a corner for the age of wisdom.' Again, in his *Religio Medici* (I. 42), he observes sadly: ' I find in my confirmed age the same sins I discovered in my youth; I committed many then because I was a child; and because I commit them still, I am yet an infant. Therefore I perceive a man may be twice a child, before the days of dotage.'

IN his *Walden,* Thoreau tells of a vigorous Canadian wood-chopper who came to him. ' But the intellectual and what is called spiritual man in him were slumbering as in an infant. He had been instructed only in that innocent and ineffectual way in which the Catholic priests teach the aborigines, by which the pupil is never educated to the degree of consciousness, but only to the degree of trust and reverence, and a child is not made a man, but kept a child.'

COMPARE also the account, quoted from Rousseau in Hazlitt's essay on ' A Sun-dial,' of how he sat up ' with his father reading romances, when a boy, till they were startled by the swallows twittering in their nests at daybreak, and the father cried out, half angry and ashamed—*allons, mon fils; je suis plus enfant que toi.*'

COMPARE Goldsmith's lines on Italy in *The Traveller:*—

Here may be seen, in bloodless pomp arrayed,
The paste-board triumph and the cavalcade ;
Processions form'd for piety and love,
A mistress or a saint in every grave.
By sports like these are all their cares beguiled,
The sports of children satisfy the child.

It were well if none remained boys all their lives ; but what is more common than the sight of grown men, talking on political or moral or religious subjects in that off-hand, idle way which we signify by the word *unreal?* 'That they simply do not know what they are talking of,' is the spontaneous, silent remark of any man of sense who hears them.—Newman, *The Idea of a University*, p. xvii.

References.—XIII. 11.—J. Martineau, *Endeavours After the Christian Life* (2nd Series), p. 78. Bishop Bethell, *Sermons*, vol. ii. p. 199. H. S. Holland, *Old and New*, p. 181. T. Arnold, *Sermons*, vol. iv. pp. 8 and 16. J. S. Maver, *Christian World Pulpit*, vol. liii. p. 318. T. Arnold, *Sermons*, vol. ii. p. 31. *Expositor* (5th Series), vol. vii. p. 470 ; *ibid.* (7th Series), vol. vi. p. 26.

THROUGH A GLASS DARKLY

'For now we see through a glass, darkly ; but then face to face: now I know in part ; but then shall I know even as also I am known.'—1 Cor. XIII. 12.

This fragment of Inspiration appears in the Revised Version thus : 'For now we see in a mirror, darkly ; but then face to face : now I know in part ; but then shall I know even as also I have been known'. Some critics, however, prefer another and fuller rendering : 'For now we see by means of a mirror, darkly, or in a riddle ; but then face to face : now I know in part ; then shall I fully know even as also I was fully known'. But it is an open question whether the reference made is to a medium of silver or polished metal which can only reflect objects, or to that of thin horn or pellucid stone used by the ancients. No matter, each figure admirably illustrates the thought of the writer.

I. The imperfection of the present is the first thought brought out in this passage. The medium of our vision is now defective. Nature is a mirror which reflects God ; but the primal transgression has shattered it, so that it now gives but misty or distorted views of Him. The Bible, too, is as full a revelation of God as it can be ; but its representations, albeit very sublime, are necessarily figurative, and therefore contain truth only in a relative form. So of nearly all the Divine facts. There is, however, one fact—'the faithful saying, worthy of all acceptation'—which shines brilliantly on its holy pages as noontide sun on cloudless skies (1 Tim. I. 15). The capacity of our mind is also now limited. Were the medium never so perfect, we could take but slight advantage of it, because we are, in a mental and moral sense, like the man whose blindness was only half healed, and who, when asked by Jesus what he saw, replied, 'I see men as trees walking'. Sin has so weakened and darkened our mind, that we often call good evil, and evil good. We now see by means of a piece of burnished metal, or through a plate of horn or translucent stone ; consequently, we know only in part ; and a child may ask a question which a philosopher could not answer.

II. But the perfection of the future is what we look forward to. The vision will then be unobstructed. It will be as immediate as the 'mouth to mouth' with which the I AM spoke to the leader of Israel (Num. XII. 8). 'Face to face.' 'This is,' as an eloquent divine remarks, 'the beatific vision'— absolutely clear and direct. A thick cloud necessarily intervened between Jehovah and Moses ; but how the latter yearned to see the face of the former ! (Exod. XXXIII. 18). To grant such a request would have proved fatal to the beholder. Not so in the great future. Oh what transporting views will then be had of God ! When the angels front His throne, they veil their faces with their wings ; but the redeemed and glorified have no wings. With God and them it is 'face to face' : no cloud on His face ; no veil on theirs ! And, if they see God thus in heaven, what can hinder them from seeing their friends 'face to face' there, and knowing them again ? The mind will then be perfected. 'Now,' we are known of God rather than He is known of us ; 'then,' God will be fully known by us ; yet not so fully as He knows us, because His knowledge of us is absolutely complete from the beginning, whereas our knowledge of Him will ever be progressive. We shall spend the golden ages of the great future in the rapt contemplation of His infinite perfections as exhibited in the face of Jesus Christ. There will be no mysteries then : the full-orbed light of eternity will illumine all worlds, all beings, and all things.

MYSTERY

1 Cor. XIII. 12.

I. It has ever been a mark of Christianity that it kept men alive to the mysteries around them. The souls that have drunk most deeply of the Christian doctrine are the souls who have most felt the mystery of life. And yet, perhaps, there never was a time in which the sense of mystery was less present than to-day. How far that dying out of the mysterious may be traced to the decline of living faith is a question that might admit of much discussion. But there are other causes which I should like to indicate. (1) One is the tyranny of facts under which we live. There is no man more apt to be blind to the great mysteries than the specialist, and this is pre-eminently the age of specialism. (2) And then again this is an age of machinery, and there is little mystery in a machine. 'So many hundred hands in this mill,' says Charles Dickens in *Hard Times*, 'so many hundred horse steam power. It is known, to the force of a single pound-weight, what the engine will do. . . . There is no mystery in it.' (3) And then this is an age of travel. The world is explored into its darkest corners. Knowledge has come, and perhaps a little wisdom with it ; but the older sense of the world's mystery has gone.

II. I think, then, that it is supremely important in these times that we should endeavour to keep alive the sense of mystery. And I am sure that the Lord Jesus Christ always meant it to have large room in His disciples' hearts. (1) Think, for example, of what our Lord meant by unbelief. 'Why are ye fearful, O ye of little faith?' Had they only felt the mystery of the Divine, touching and girding even the angry waters, they had been less disquieted out at sea. That was what Jesus meant by unbelief; not a mind that denies, but a spirit that disowns. (2) And then you remember that other declaration: 'Except ye become as little children'. You cannot even see the kingdom of God unless within you is the heart of childhood, and all things are mysterious to the child. III. It is notable, too, that Jesus deepened the mystery of everything He touched. (1) Take one of His leading words like *life*, for instance. When I think of what life meant in the old pagan world, how shallow it was, how sensuous and short, and when I compare that with the life that is in Christ I feel at once how the mystery of life is deepened in passing through the hands of Jesus Christ. (2) Or take the thought of *death*. Christ has illumined death; but has He banished its mystery? He hath taken away its sting, but deepened its mystery. (3) Take the thought of *God*. God was a Sovereign once, now He is Father, and there are more mysteries in Fatherhood than in Kingship. Christ has intensified the mystery of God.—G. H. MORRISON, *Sunrise: Addresses from a City Pulpit*, p. 12.

'For we now but see in a mirror, darkly.'—1 COR. XIII. 12.

IN his essay on Clough's poems, Bagehot describes how 'the best of us . . . strive, more or less, to "make the best of both worlds"'. We know that the invisible world cannot be duly discerned, or perfectly appreciated. We know that we see as in a glass darkly, but still we look on the glass. We frame to ourselves some image which we know to be incomplete, which probably is in part untrue, which we try to improve day by day, of which we do not deny the defects—but which nevertheless is our "all"; which we hope, when the accounts are taken, may be found not utterly *unlike* the unknown reality. This is, as it seems, the best religion for finite beings, living, if we may say so, on the very edge of two dissimilar worlds, on the very line of which the infinite, unfathomable sea surges up, and just where the queer little bay of this world ends, we count the pebbles on the shore, and image to ourselves as best we may the secrets of the great deep.'

MOST men's minds are dim mirrors, in which all truth is seen, as St. Paul tells us, darkly; this is the fault most common and most fatal; dulness of heart and mistiness of sight, increasing to utter hardness and blindness; Satan breathing upon the glass, so that if we do not sweep the mist laboriously away, it will take no image.—RUSKIN, *Stones of Venice* (III. 3).

TO be entirely just in our estimate of other ages is not difficult—it is impossible. Even what is passing in our presence we see but through a glass darkly. The mind as well as the eye adds something of its own, before an image, even of the clearest object, can be painted upon it.—FROUDE, on *The Dissolution of the Monasteries*.

NEWTON, Pascal, Bossuet, Racine, and Fénelon, that is to say, the most enlightened men on earth, in the most philosophical of all ages, and in the full vigour of their spirit and their age, have believed in Jesus Christ; while the great Condé, on his death-bed, repeated these noble words, 'Yes, we shall see God as He is, *face to face*'.—VAUVENARGUES.

'Now I know in part.'—1 COR. XIII. 12.

I WAIT and wonder: long ago
This wonder was my constant quest,
Wonder at our environing,
And at myself within the ring:
Still that abides with me, some quest
Before my footsteps seems to lie,
But quest of what I scarcely know,
Life itself makes no reply:
A quest for naught that earth supplies,
This is our life's last compromise.
                    —W. BELL SCOTT.

To the Minnow every cranny and pebble, and quality and accident, of its little native Creek may have become familiar: but does the Minnow understand the Ocean Tides and periodic Currents, the Trade-winds and Monsoons, and Moon's Eclipses; by all of which the condition of its little Creek is regulated, and may, from time to time (*un*miraculously enough) be quite overset and reversed? Such a minnow is Man; his Creek this planet Earth; his Ocean the immeasureable All; his Monsoons and periodic Currents the mysterious Course of Providence through Æons of Æons.—CARLYLE, *Sartor Resartus* (III. 8).

'MADAM,' Samuel Rutherford wrote once to Lady Kenmure, 'ye must go in at heaven's gates, and your book in your hand, still learning.'

REFERENCES.—XIII. 12.—Bishop Bickersteth, *Sermons*, p. 50. J. Cumming, *Penny Pulpit*, No. 1506, p. 185. J. Stalker, *Christian World Pulpit*, vol. liv. p. 10. J. C. M. Bellew, *Sermons*, vol. i. p. 164. Spurgeon, *Sermons*, vol. xvii. No. 1002. Llewelyn Davies, *The Purpose of God*, p. 80. *Expositor* (5th Series), vol. iv. p. 382; *ibid.* vol. i. p. 452; *ibid.* (6th Series), vol. x. p. 358.

THE GEOMETRY OF LIFE

'And now abideth faith, hope, charity, these three; but the greatest of these is charity.'—1 COR. XIII. 13.

IT is a deep saying of the Greek philosopher Plato that 'God geometrises'. And this means that God is the grand Geometrician of the Universe and has constructed it on geometrical principles.

A complete life is geometrical. It is a triangle, and its three sides are Work, Love, and Religion. They must all be there, and if one of them be lacking, the triangle is broken, the life is incomplete.

I. Work.—This is the base of the triangle. It is the foundation of life. Work is a necessity, and it is a sacred thing. Here I would specially address young men, and I would say to you : Recognise the sacredness of your work, whatever it may be, and accept it as God's appointment, as the work which He has given you to do. I know that you are often discouraged because it seems so trivial and common-place, because it has so little outcome and offers so little prospect of promotion. But recognise it as the will of God concerning you, and you will find it transfigured and invested with a new significance.

Quiet acceptance of the lot which God in His providence has appointed to us, and faithful perform-ance of the work, often so hard and distasteful, which He has given us to do—that is the way to a larger heritage and a loftier service.

II. Love.—Work alone is not enough. Even if it be not mere drudgery, it is a selfish thing, so we must bring in Love. Love carries us out of ourselves; it re-deems our lives from 'miserable aims that end with self,' and makes our work a gracious ministry. It lifts our horizon and broadens our world.

III. Religion.—This completes the triangle. If Work without Love be drudgery, Love without Re-ligion is tragedy. What is the use of loving if it must end with a green mound in the churchyard, with a tender memory and a vain regret ?

There comes to my remembrance here an incident of my own ministry. Death had suddenly visited a home and carried off a little child. It was a cruel blow to the poor mother. She was a widow, and the little maiden had been the light of her eyes and the gladness of her heart. I feared that the sorrow would crush her, but she bore up bravely ; and after-wards she said to me : 'I am sure that I would have lost my reason but for the promise of meeting my wee lassie again in the Father's House'.

This is the supreme blessing of Religion. It gives Love permanence. It teaches us that Death is, in St. Bernard's phrase, 'the Gate of Life'. It draws aside the veil and discovers to us the broad and beautiful world of Eternity, and the Holy City where the inhabitant never says, 'I am sick,' and no mourners go about the streets, and the Father's House where there are many mansions and where, by the mercy of Jesus, we shall all meet again on the eternal Sabbath morning.—DAVID SMITH, *Man's Need of God*, p. 15.

LOVE

'And now abideth faith, hope, love, these three ; but the greatest of these is love.'—1 COR. XIII. 13.

THE whole civilised world has come round—at any rate, in theory—to the teaching of St. Paul. The verdict of the popular magazine of to-day is, that cleverness may be a great thing, and learning a great thing, but a greater than these is Love. Pick up a philosophical treatise on ethics, and, in a more cum-brous style, you will find the same thing said. What comes out as the ultimate basis of conduct in such books ? Is it not Altruism ? But Altruism, after all, is but a cumbrous name for Love, and was taught the world by Christ, and therefore the verdict of the

ethical treatise is the verdict of St. Paul. Or take again practical life. Let a man be kind-hearted and generous, and there is nothing that he is not forgiven to-day. The popular verdict of the day is that sobriety is a great thing and honesty is a great thing, but 'a greater than these is Love'. And if this is so with regard to man's opinion of man, it is even more forcibly true with regard to man's opinion of God.

I. What has Love Done ?—The old-world stories of the Bible are but the beginning of all the stories of self-sacrifice endured by father for children, by children for father, by brother for brother, and friend for friend ; and a great chorus from all nations, and kindreds, and people, and tongues cries, 'This hath Love done'. Nor is it only the love of relatives and of friends. Who is this spare man with the stern, severe face who is searching the arches of London with his lantern ? This is Lord Shaftesbury. Again, what is this which comes looming up before us to-day ? Why do I speak of the Cross as it stands up clearer and clearer before our eyes ? Because what the Cross gives is the most overwhelming answer to our question, 'This hath Love done, this !'

II. If then Love hath done this, What is Love ? (1) The first answer which springs from its manifesta-tion in the Cross is, 'God is Love'. (2) And if the first thing about Love is that it is Godlike, the second follows from the first, and that is, it is inde-structible. (3) And thirdly, love is unselfish.

III. Have we got this Love ?—To be without Love is to be without God, and to be without God is to be lost. The old idea of the ancients was that fire was stolen from heaven ; but whether fire was stolen from heaven or not, Love only comes from heaven. Only by keeping our hearts throbbing with His can we truly love.—BISHOP WINNINGTON-INGRAM, *Banners of the Christian Faith*, p. 32.

IMPERISHABLE JEWELS

1 COR. XIII. 13.

THEIR order is instructive. Faith is the root. Hope springs out of faith, what faith believes hope expects. And love is the fruit produced by faith and hope. All three *abide* : faith abideth, hope abideth, love abideth.

I. Faith.—Our Lord taught St. Thomas the happiness of faith when He said : 'Happy are they that have not seen, and yet have believed' (St. John xx. 29). As to the origin of saving faith, it is of God. Its object is Christ and Christ only. Faith is the Yes of the heart to the promises and propositions of God.

II. Hope.—God is 'the God of hope' (Rom. xv. 13). 'We are saved in hope' (Rom. viii. 24), *i.e.*, hope is the element in which we are saved.

III. Love.—'Love is the crown of faith and hope.' There are two elements of earthly happiness. I mean, if you would be happy in your life you must have some one to love, and something to do. Apply this to spiritual things and you will see how true it is. Some One to love : Christ, Something to do : for

Him. Remember this : these three graces are *gifts*. Surely we may well add St. Augustine's prayer to our other prayers : 'Lord, give what Thou commandest, and command what Thou wilt'.—F. HARPER, *The Preacher's Magazine*, vol. x. p. 560.

'And now abideth faith, hope, charity.'—1 COR. XIII. 13.

THE Americans have many virtues, but they have not Faith and Hope. I know no two words whose meaning is more lost sight of. We use these words as if they were as obsolete as Selah and Amen.—EMERSON, on *Man the Reformer*.

'But the greatest of these is charity.'—1 COR. XIII. 13.

HOPE, Faith and Love at God's high altar shine,
Lamp triple-branched, and fed with oil divine.

Two of these triple-lights shall once grow pale,
They burn without, but Love within the veil.
　　　　　　　　　　　　—R. C. TRENCH.

'I SUPPOSE,' says George Eliot in a letter of 1862 to Miss Hennell, 'no wisdom the world will ever find out will make Paul's words obsolete,—"Now abideth faith, hope, charity, these three ; but the greatest of these is charity".'

A MAN's love is the measure of his fitness for good or bad company here or elsewhere.—O. W. HOLMES, *Elsie Venner* (ch.. XVII.).

REFERENCES.—XIII. 13.—W. R. Inge, *All Saints' Sermons*, 1905-7, p. 20. L. D. Bevan, *Sermons by Welshmen*, p. 266. T. H. Bell, *Persuasions*, p. 69. Bishop Winnington-Ingram, *Christian World Pulpit*, vol. liii. p. 124. Bishop Bethell, *Sermons*, vol. ii. p. 182. R. Higinbotham, *Sermons*, p. 193. H. Alford, *Quebec Chapel Sermons*, vol. i. p. 119. F. D. Maurice, *Sermons*, vol. i. p. 219. E. T. J. Marriner, *Sermons Preached at Lyme Regis*, p. 231. R. W. Church, *Village Sermons* (3rd Series), p. 74. A. J. Palmer, *Christian World Pulpit*, vol. lviii. p. 36. Alfred Rowland, *The Exchanged Crowns*, p. 29. R. J. Drummond, *Faith's Certainties*, p. 235. XIV.—*Expositor* (6th Series), vol. vi. p. 391.

'Follow after love ; and covet earnestly spiritual gifts, but rather that ye may prophesy.'—1 COR. XIV. 1.

IN his letter to the Governor of Edinburgh Castle (12th Sept. 1650), on the Scottish preachers' objections to lay preaching, Cromwell asks : 'Where do you find in the Scripture a ground to warrant such an assertion, That Preaching is exclusively your function ? Though an Approbation from men hath order in it, and may do well; yet he that hath no better warrant than that, hath none at all. I hope He that ascended up on high may give His gifts to whom He pleases. . . . You know who bids us *covet earnestly the best gifts*, but chiefly *that we may prophesy;* which the Apostle explains there to be a speaking to instruction and edification and comfort.'

REFERENCES.—XIV. 1.—J. S. Bartlett, *Sermons*, p. 156. A. J. Palmer, *Christian World Pulpit*, vol. lviii. p. 36. XIV. 2.—*Expositor* (4th Series), vol. ix. p. 83. XIV. 3.—*Ibid.* (6th Series), vol. ix. p. 271. XIV. 7.—H. S. Holland, *A Lent in London*, p. 230.

'If the trumpet give an uncertain sound, who shall prepare himself to the battle ?'—1 COR. XIV. 8.

THE eighth aphorism in the preface to Bacon's *De Augmentis Scientiarum* is : 'Certainty is so essential to law, that law cannot even be just without it. "For if the trumpet give an uncertain sound, who shall prepare himself to the battle ? " So if the law give an uncertain sound, who shall prepare to obey it ? It ought therefore to warn before it strikes.'

REFERENCES.—XIV. 8.—*Penny Pulpit*, No. 1653, p. 265. XIV. 10.—Bishop Boyd-Carpenter, *Christian World Pulpit*, vol. xlvi. p. 369. XIV. 11.—W. M. Sinclair, *Words from St. Paul's*, p. 69. *Expositor* (6th Series), vol. vii. p. 113. XIV. 12.—George Matheson, *Christian World Pulpit*, vol. lvi. p. 155. *Expositor* (5th Series), vol. ix. p. 437. XIV. 13.—H. S. Holland, *Vital Values*, p. 192.

'I will pray with the spirit, and I will pray with the understanding also ; I will sing with the spirit, and I will sing with the understanding also.'—1 COR. XIV. 15.

THE human mind stands ever in perplexity, demanding intellect, demanding sanctity, impatient equally of each without the other.—EMERSON.

REFERENCES.—XIV. 15.—W. C. Wheeler, *Sermons and Addresses* (2nd Series), p. 19. H. P. Liddon, *Sermons on Some Words of St. Paul*, p. 124. H. Alford, *Quebec Chapel Sermons*, vol. i. p. 34. XIV. 19.—J. M. Neale, *Sermons Preached in Sackville College Chapel*, vol. ii. p. 355.

THE CHILDLIKE CHARACTER

'Brethren, be not children in understanding : howbeit in malice be ye children, but in understanding be men.'—1 COR. XIV. 20.

'BE not children in understanding.' This text may seem by some of us to be not quite in key with a great many passages of Scripture with which we are familiar. The Apostle may even seem to be out of sympathy with his Master. Jesus said : 'I thank Thee, O Father, that Thou hast hid these things from the wise and prudent, and hast revealed them unto babes'. And He took a little child and set him in the midst of them as the type of the true Christian. 'Except ye turn, and become as little children, ye shall not enter into the kingdom of heaven.'
What is the reconciliation of the two instructions to be children and not to be children ?
I. Let us then begin by asking, What did Christ mean by saying that we are to become like children ? It is not the goodness of children which our Lord praises. It is certain natural qualities of children that have a sad way of vanishing as we grow older, but which, if they are lost, we must do our best to recover. What are those qualities ? If we recall the circumstances in which our Lord spoke about children, we shall at once see that the prayer, 'I thank Thee that Thou hast hid these things from the wise and prudent, and hast revealed them unto babes,' was uttered after His rejection by the chief priests and elders, and of His acceptance by the band of Apostles, and it must refer to that. And I would ask you, Is not one of the most characteristic and delightful qualities of children their habit of looking straight

at what is before them and judging it to the best of their power, without prejudice or fear of consequence, on its merits? A child's candour and simplicity sometimes, by clashing with our polite conventions, causes momentary annoyance, but it is, in essence, a most valuable quality, as we cannot deny even while we suffer from it. And it is this childlike quality in the Apostles which distinguishes them from the Pharisees and enables them to receive the new revelation of Christ.

Now this sincerity, this true thinking and plain speaking, which is natural to children, often tends to be worn away as we leave childhood behind us, by the proper and natural desire to stand well with the little world of society, politics, or religion in which we happen to move, and, if so, it must be recovered, and we have to set it before us as a virtue to be attained; we have to turn and become in this respect once more like little children.

II. And the second childlike quality which also we must labour to get back again is absence of self-importance. You will remember that our Lord's putting the little child in the midst followed upon the wrangling of the Apostles as to their order of precedence. Children are not, as a rule, concerned with themselves in such a way as that; they look away from themselves. And this self-importance brings in its train vices which are objectionable to others and excruciating to ourselves, one of which the Apostle notices in the text—Malice. Do not be malicious: children are not. Malice springs out of jealousy, and jealousy is the other side of self-importance.

III. And that word brings us back to the other part of our text—'In understanding be men'. Common sense, wisdom, comes as near as we can get to what St. Paul is here urging upon the Corinthians. He is not exhorting them to any great effort of intellect, nor to accept the foundations of the Gospel of Jesus Christ. St. Paul is always telling them that the Gospel appeals to the child more than to the grown man. In the apprehension of the message it is the child in us that comes into play—the frank outlook, the instinct for goodness, humility—all childlike qualities. It is to them the Gospel appeals. And so St. Paul is not contradicting his Master; he is urging that, when the Christian faith has been received, there is room in our religious life, as much as in any other life, for the exercise of a man's faculty of judgment, common sense. And, if you think about it, the child's virtue of sincerity and the man's faculty of judgment are very closely allied, and one is really the outgrowth of the other. I dare say you have often remarked the judgments of Christ. Those judgments of His which enraged the Pharisees, and almost His own disciples, were simple judgments of common sense, guided by sincerity. Is it not enough that we the clergy, or you the laity, should be as 'harmless as doves,' if we are not also as 'wise as serpents'. It is not enough to be children in malice; let us also 'in understanding be men'.

'Brethren, be not children in mind: howbeit in malice be ye babes, but in mind be men.'—1 COR. XIV. 20.

'WHEN, by what test, by what indication, does manhood commence?' De Quincey asks, in the thirteenth chapter of his *Autobiographic Sketches*. 'Physically by one criterion, legally by another, morally by a third, intellectually by a fourth—and all indefinite. Equator, absolute equator, there is none. Between the two spheres of youth and age, perfect and imperfect manhood, as in all analogous cases, there is no strict line of bisection. The change is a large process, accomplished within a large and corresponding space. . . . Intellectually speaking, a very large proportion of men *never* attain maturity. Nonage is their final destiny; and manhood, in this respect, is for them a pure idea.'

REFERENCES.—XIV. 20.—T. Arnold, *Sermons*, vol. iv. p. 258. T. Binney, *King's Weigh-House Chapel Sermons*, p. 96. *Expositor* (4th Series), vol. i. p. 268; *ibid.* (5th Series), vol. v. p. 31. XIV. 21.—*Ibid.* vol. iii. p. 406.

OUTSIDERS

'If . . . there come in those that are unlearned, or unbelievers.'
—1 COR. XIV. 23.

WHAT was the policy of the great-hearted Apostle? It was that everybody should at some point or other be able to come into the service of the Gospel, the worship of God, and should in some degree at least find the supreme blessing. There is a lesson to you, church leaders, preachers, and persons concerned as you suppose yourselves to be in the advancement of the kingdom of Christ. In the degree in which you are so concerned heaven's blessing cannot be withheld from you; but let us take care lest we become mere botanists or geologists or astronomers, lest we cultivate some favourite science of things, and lest, above all, we raise ourselves up and say, this place was not made for the unlearned; as for the unbelievers, turn them out. We must not do so. And the greatest man will be the first to say that in the Church of Christ there ought always to be at least one mouthful of bread for the very poorest soul that has crept into the Father's house.

I. The question which the Apostle put to the Corinthians is the question of all days. The Apostle Paul looks in upon the churches, and in the name of Christ says, What kind of preaching have you here? are you preaching to men, sinful, awful, shameful; or do you never refer to these things, but take the evil of the world for granted and leave it in the hands of the devil? That is poor preaching, poor praying, and poor singing. We are wrong, we are failing in duty, if we do not say in the construction of every service and the building up of every plan of operation, Now how will this fit the unlearned? what shall we say to the unbeliever if he challenge us at this point? We have made many churches, comfortable places, we know where we begin and how we continue and where we end, and if so much as a little child were to cry out in the middle of our perfunctory service we would be quite startled and wish the little angel to be cast out. You know nothing about the Church if that is your view ; the cross you have never touched if you despise the unlearned ; and if you cannot stop to explain your faith to the earnest, simple-minded inquirer or unbeliever you have not experienced the evangelising and redeeming spirit of the Cross.

II. We must, in thinking of the congregation, think of every one, of the great and the small ; and, blessed be God, I repeat that when a man is truly great he is always willing to wait for the slow and the crippled and the infirm.   He says, the preacher is now speaking to a class of persons of whom I am not one, but my not being one does not destroy the class of persons especially contemplated, and there must be something in the discourse for that class. So the sermon should be high as heaven and low as the ground we tread, balmy as the air we breathe, friendly as the sunlight that plays around us.

III. The great purpose of coming together in the church is edification, building up ; so we must have as much as possible of intelligence that can be appreciated ; not intelligence that moves itself right away from the tracks of the people, but that truer and more intelligent intelligence which says, Now where can we begin ? where are these people prepared to make an opening? let us bring the Gospel into their civilisation, into their language, classical or unclassical, and give them to feel that there is something in the Gospel for the building up of their hearts and lives.   That is right.   Heaven bless the thought.

There is one other aspect to be looked at, or the preacher would sit down without having completed his purpose.   We must not expect any one man to absorb the whole service to himself alone.   Even the unlearned man must not come into the church and say to the well-informed man, You have no business here, because all this church arrangement is for the unlearned and ignorant man ; so withdraw, if you please.   No ! A man is not bound at a great civic feast to eat up the whole banquet ; I do not know any law by which a man attending the great civic feast should be compelled to eat up the whole bill of fare.   I should recommend him not to do so ; let him take what suits him, let him take exactly what he wants or what he needs, and be content with that. But, remember, that the lines you omit may be the very lines that will suit some other man.   So it must be in the setting up of the religious service.   There should be something for everybody.   No man should find fault with the portion of another ; he should say, This is not the portion that I immediately care for, but my brother will relish it, his very soul will be in an ecstasy of thankfulness and delight.—JOSEPH PARKER, *City Temple Pulpit*, vol. IV. p. 107.

'If all speak with tongues, and there come in those that are unlearned, or unbelievers, will they not say that ye are mad ?'—1 COR. XIV. 23.

IN his essay on Unity in Religion, Bacon observes that the fruits of unity are towards those within and also towards those without the Church.   In the latter case, 'The Doctor of the Gentiles (the Propriety of whose Vocation drew him to have a speciall Care of those without) saith : *If an Heathen come in, and heare you speake with severall Tongues, will he not say that ye are mad ?* And certainly, it is little better, when Atheists and prophane Persons do heare of so many Discordant and Contrary Opinions in Religion ; it doth avert them from the Church and maketh them to sit downe in the Chaire of the Scorner.'

REFERENCES.—XIV. 24, 25.—T. Arnold, *The Interpretation of Scripture*, p. 212. XIV. 25.—Archbishop Benson, *Single-heart*, p. 1. XIV. 26.—W. M. Sinclair, *Simplicity in Christ*, p. 59. H. C. Beeching, *Church Family Newspaper*, vol. xiv. p. 444. *Expositor* (4th Series), vol. ii. p. 273 ; *ibid*. vol. ix. p. 87 ; *ibid*. (6th Series), vol. ii. p. 380. XIV. 28.—*Ibid*. (5th Series), vol. vi. p. 268. XIV. 29.—*Ibid*. (6th Series), vol. vi. pp. 395, 462.

'For God is not a God of confusion, but of peace ; as in all the churches of the saints.'—1 COR. XIV. 33.

IN men who have risen to wide-reaching power we generally observe an early preponderance of one of two instincts—the instinct of rule and order, or the instinct of sympathy.   The one instinct may degenerate into bureaucracy, the other into sentimentalism. Rightly ordered, they make the master or the leader of men.—F. W. H. MYERS, *Modern Essays*, p. 21.

REFERENCE.—XIV. 33.—J. Martineau, *Endeavours After the Christian Life* (2nd Series), p. 68.

THE RIGHTS OF WOMEN IN THE CHURCH

'Let your women keep silence in the churches : for it is not permitted unto them to speak.'—1 COR. XIV. 34.

Do the Scriptures forbid women to speak ? I have deliberately chosen for consideration the strongest text I could find in the Bible on this subject, which plainly settled the discussion so far as women in Corinth were concerned, and settles it for us, also, if the deliverance of the Apostle were final, and universal in its application.   No doubt there are those among us who are ready to say : 'We take God's word as our rule, and if we find a precept in it as plain as this we do not wish to go any further'.   But others lightly dismiss this view as being a private opinion of Paul's, which he would have been wiser to keep to himself.   I take neither of these views.   I believe that the Apostle spoke under the guidance of the Spirit of truth, and, therefore, with a Divine authority which his readers were bound to obey.   But while I accept the New Testament as my rule of faith and practice, I can only do so when its meaning is fairly interpreted—in the light which would naturally illumine it in the eyes of those who first read it.   And when I focus all the stray beams of that light, and concentrate them on this precept, I do not hesitate to say that as an absolute prohibition it was transient and local, that it was necessary for that time and place, but is neither necessary nor desirable as the final dictum of Christianity to the world at large, for all generations.   I will now give some reasons for this position.

I. First let me call your attention to the fact that

the New Testament does not attempt to regulate procedure for all ages and peoples. It lays down principles, but leaves procedure to be determined by the teaching of Him of whom Jesus said : 'He shall abide with you for ever, even the Spirit of truth'.

II. The condition of women under the old dispensation, and in the early Christian Church, was not one of universal silence. There is nothing in the Gospels, or the Acts, or in any Epistle addressed to Jewish Churches, which puts the smallest restriction on the rights and liberties of Christian womanhood.

III. There were good reasons for making this precept a distinct and definite rule in the Christian Churches which were found in Greek cities.

IV. There are other laws which, in their strict application, we regard as local and transient.

V. We hold, then, that inspired womanhood should not be debarred by artificial rules from Christian speech, or song, or prayer. We believe that woman is fit to take such part in the service of God as the result of Christianity itself, which has made many things natural and right which were formerly inexpedient or wrong.

VI. It need hardly be said that in the use of such liberty the Church must be guided by sanctified common sense.—A. ROWLAND, *The Burdens of Life*, p. 225.

REFERENCES.—XIV. 36.—*Expositor* (6th Series), vol. iii. p. 273. XIV. 37.—*Ibid.* (5th Series), vol. v. p. 253.

'Let all things be done decently and in order.'—1 COR. XIV. 40.

THE love of order—I the thing receive
From reverend men, and I in part believe—
Shows a clear mind and clean, and whoso needs
This love, but seldom in the world succeeds.
                                        —CRABBE.

REFERENCES.—XIV. 40.—F. C. Spurr, *Christian World Pulpit*, vol. xlviii. p. 92. J. S. Bartlett, *Sermons*, p. 165. H. C. Beeching, *Church Family Newspaper*, vol. xiv. p. 444. J. S. Maver, *Christian World Pulpit*, vol. liii. p. 126. XV.—*Expositor* (4th Series), vol. viii. p. 137 ; *ibid.* (7th Series), vol. v. pp. 403-416, 491-504.

WHAT IS THE GOSPEL

'Brethren, I declare unto you the Gospel.'—1 COR. XV. 1.

I. A Gospel of Mercy.—It is a Gospel of mercy. There are three points about it.

(a) *Its efficacy.* 'The Gospel which ye have received, and wherein ye stand.' The first Christians received this great message of God's truth as coming not from man. It was not St. Paul's Gospel ; he merely handed it on. It could not be improved by his own witness. This message the people received, and on the strength and truth of this message they stood. So the Christian to-day first receives this message unto himself, and then stands upon it as upon a foundation. That upon which we trust is not within us but outside of us. 'By which also ye are being saved.' If we treasure the Gospel we shall find it a source of ever necessary salvation. Remember that the Bible never tells us for a moment that our salvation is completed. It is going on all

the time we are here. God wants to save us not only from the past consequences, but from the daily contamination of sin. We are never really saved until body and soul are in their glorified state in heaven, temptation and sorrow are put away, and we live in an atmosphere where there is nothing to prevent the growth of holiness.

(b) *Its simplicity.* There are three chief points in the Gospel—that Christ died for our sins, was buried, and rose again. The death of Christ is of supreme importance. He came into the world in order that He might offer that mysterious sacrifice for the sins of the whole world. Then the burial of Christ certified His death. He really died. The Resurrection certified the sufficiency of that death. He triumphed over death and made it man's servant instead of his master. So you see the Gospel is not a matter of philosophy, but it is a simple declaration of fact.

(c) *Its trustworthiness.* These simple facts bear investigation, they can be proved. The Resurrection was witnessed to by all the disciples. Such is the Gospel of mercy—the great message of the redeeming work of our Saviour.

II. The Gospel of Grace.—The Gospel of mercy is outside us ; the Gospel of grace within us. And this Gospel of grace is the first source of Christian character. St. Paul was not all that he wished to be, but 'by the grace of God,' said he, 'I am what I am'. The grace of God had changed him, and he would no more have parted with the Gospel than with life, for it was his life. This great mystery of the grace of God passes our comprehension. The grace bestowed upon St. Paul was not in vain : it was the source of his usefulness.

'Now I make known to you, brethren, the Gospel which I preached unto you.'—1 COR. XV. 1.

'I MAY be thought bold,' says a writer in the *Spectator* (15th Dec., 1714), 'in my judgment by some ; but I must affirm that no one Orator has left us so visible Marks and Footsteps of his Eloquence as our Apostle. . . . His discourse on the Resurrection to the Corinthians, his harangue before Agrippa upon his own conversion and the necessity of that of others, are truly great and may serve as full examples to those excellent rules for the Sublime, which the best of criticks has left us.'

ABOUT three o'clock in the afternoon, one of his eyes failed, and his speech was considerably affected. He desired his wife to read the fifteenth chapter of first Corinthians. 'Is not that a comfortable chapter ?' said he, when it was finished. 'Oh what sweet and salutary consolation the Lord hath afforded me from that chapter !'—McCRIE's *Life of John Knox* (VIII.).

BY way of contrast, Matthew Arnold's remarks, in the fourth chapter of *Culture and Anarchy*, may be cited here : 'It surely must be perceived that the idea of immortality, as this idea rises in its generality before the human spirit, is something grander, truer, and more satisfying, than it is in the particular forms by which St. Paul, in the famous fifteenth chapter of the Epistle to the Corinthians, and Plato, in the *Phædo*, endeavours to develop and establish it. Surely we cannot but feel, that the argumentation with which the Hebrew Apostle goes about to expound this great idea is, after all, confused and inconclusive; and that the reasoning, drawn from analogies of likeness and equality, which is employed upon it by the Greek philosopher, is over-subtle and sterile. Above and beyond the inadequate solutions which Hebraism and Hellenism here attempt, extends the immense and august problem itself, and the human spirit which gave birth to it.'

References.—XV. 1.—R. W. Dale, *Christian World Pulpit*, vol. xliii. p. 257. J. C. M. Bellew, *Sermons*, vol. ii. p. 309. R. W. Dale, *The Epistle of James*, p. 204. *Expositor* (6th Series), vol. viii. p. 128.

THE GOSPEL OF CHRIST'S RESURRECTION

'Moreover, brethren, I declare unto you the Gospel which I preached unto you, which also ye have received, and wherein ye stand; by which also ye are saved.'—1 Cor. xv. 1 and 2.

I. Nothing can be more plain than that the Apostles, when they set themselves to obey their Lord's commands and to go forth preaching His Gospel, were content to rest their claim for belief on their knowledge of Christ's Resurrection.

II. The fact of Christ's Resurrection is the only explanation of the existence and power of Christ's Church. No delusion, no pious imagination or exaggeration could give the security on which faith builds.—W. H. Hutton, *Church Family Newspaper*, vol. xiv. p. 308.

References.—XV. 1, 2.—F. J. A. Hort, *Village Sermons in Outline*, p. 73. XV. 1-3.—*Expositor* (5th Series), vol. v. p. 13. XV. 2.—D. C. A. Agnew, *The Soul's Business and Prospects*, p. 145.

THE DEATH OF CHRIST

'For I delivered unto you first of all that which I also received, how that Christ died for our sins according to the Scriptures.'—1 Cor. xv. 3.

Let us attempt to gather up some of the main teachings of the New Testament about the meaning of the death of Christ.

I. Note the *central place the cross occupies in the New Testament*. 'All the light of sacred story,' says Sir John Bowring, 'gathers round its head sublime;' and so it does. It is the centre of gravity of the New Testament. For proof of what I say, you need but turn to the Gospels and notice the space the Evangelists devote to the account of our Lord's Passion; you need but turn to the Acts and the Epistles and read the account of the apostolic preaching. Look at my own text. 'I delivered unto you first of all that which also I received,' says the Apostle Paul, writing to his Corinthian converts, 'how that Christ *died for our sins* according to the Scriptures.' 'First of all.' This took first rank; this was Paul's primary and central message.

And it was not Paul alone who gave the cross this central and primary place. In doing this he was only following the example of the other Apostles who were in Christ before him. You have but to turn to the Epistles of Peter and John, and to the record of the apostolic preaching in the Book of the Acts, to see that the other Apostles placed the emphasis exactly where Paul placed it. Indeed, in this very paragraph from which my text is taken Paul asserts that identity in emphasis in set and definite terms. This was no message which he had himself invented, which Paul preached to the Corinthians. He delivered to them only what he had received. In preaching as he did he was at one with Peter, and John, and James, and the rest. 'Whether it be I or they—so we preached, and so ye believed.'

II. Now, what was it that the Apostles saw in the cross which led them to give it this supreme and central place in their preaching?

(1) They saw in it, first, *the final and consummate Revelation of the Divine Love*.

(2) And, secondly, the Apostles saw in the cross the *Divine judgment upon sin*.

(3) Thirdly, the Apostles see in the cross of Christ *the ground of pardon and forgiveness*.

The Gospel story seems to succeed or to fail very much as the vicarious suffering of Christ is present in it or absent from it. You have heard the story of the Moravian missionaries to Greenland. For years they toiled in Greenland teaching the natives about the Creation and the Fall, the Flood and the Dispersion, and so on, and all to no purpose. But one day John Beck read to a small company of them the old story of Christ's dying love. And one of them, Kayamak, with tears streaming down his face, said to him, 'Tell it me once more, for I too would be saved'. At last they had found the key to the Greenlanders' hearts.

And what happens in Greenland happens everywhere. In a little book entitled *Gospel Ethnology*, the author shows by a careful comparison of missionary enterprise for the past 170 years, that what has been most effective to pierce through the callousness and prejudices of heathenism has been the story of the cross, the sufferings of the sinless Saviour proclaimed to men as the means of their pardon and acceptance with God. And what is seen abroad in heathen lands is seen also here at home.

The vicarious sacrifice of Christ is the only thing that meets the deepest needs of the heart.—J. D. Jones, *Elims of Life*, p. 60.

References.—XV. 3.—J. D. Jones, *Sermons by Welshmen*, p. 284. R. W. Dale, *The Epistle of James*, p. 174. W. M. Clow, *The Cross in Christian Experience*, p. 306. W. B. Selbie, *The Servant of God*, p. 157. *Expositor* (4th Series), vol. iii. p. 402; *ibid.* (5th Series), vol. vii. p. 107. XV. 3, 4.—A. Maclaren, *The Wearied Christ*, p. 21; *ibid.* *Expositions of Holy Scripture—Corinthians*, p. 195. W. H. Evans, *Sermons for the Church's Year*, p. 107. T. Binney, *King's Weigh-House Chapel Sermons*, p. 307. *Expositor* (4th Series), vol. vii. p. 16; *ibid.* (6th Series), vol. ix. p. 123. XV. 3-5.—*Ibid.* (6th Series), vol. iv. p. 216; *ibid.* (7th Series), vol. v. p. 143. XV. 3-8.—*Ibid.* p. 510. XV.

3-9.—*Ibid.* p. 146. XV. 4.—*Ibid.* (6th Series), vol. x. p. 445. XV. 4-8.—*Ibid.* (7th Series), vol. v. p. 48. XV. 4-11.— *Expositor* (5th Series), vol. vii. p. 220. XV. 5.—W. H. Hutchings, *Sermon Sketches*, p. 117. T. V. Tymms, *Christian World Pulpit*, vol. lii. p. 276. *Expositor* (6th Series), vol. ii. p. 70; *ibid.* (7th Series), vol. vi. p. 100. XV. 5-8.—*Ibid.* (5th Series), vol. x. p. 66; *ibid.* (7th Series), vol. v. p. 316. XV. 6.—T. Arnold, *Christian Life: Its Hopes*, p. 1. Spurgeon, *Sermons*, vol. xlvi. No. 2659. A. Maclaren, *After the Resurrection*, p. 102. *Expositor* (7th Series), vol. vi. p. 109. A. Maclaren, *Expositions of Holy Scripture—Corinthians*, p. 205. XV. 7.—*Expositor* (7th Series), vol. v. p. 37. XV. 8.—Spurgeon, *Sermons*, vol. xlvi. No. 2663. *Expositor* (4th Series), vol. vii. p. 122; *ibid.* (5th Series), vol. iii. p. 423.

'For I am the least of the Apostles, that am not meet to be called an Apostle, because I persecuted the Church of God.'—1 Cor. xv. 9.

COMPARE the closing sentences of Matthew Arnold's essay on *St. Paul and Protestantism*. 'A theology, a scientific appreciation of the facts of religion, is wanted for religion; but a theology which is a true theology, not a false. Both these influences will work for Paul's re-emergence. The doctrine of Paul will arise out of the tomb where for centuries it has lain buried; it will edify the Church of the future. It will have the consent of happier generations, the applause of less superstitious ages. All will be too little to pay half the debt which the Church of God owes to this "least of the Apostles, who was not fit to be called an Apostle, because he persecuted the Church of God".'

REFERENCES.—XV. 9.—R. W. Hiley, *A Year's Sermons*, vol. ii. p. 89. J. S. Bartlett, *Sermons*, p. 22. *Expositor* (5th Series), vol. vi. p. 245. XV. 9, 10.—J. Keble, *Sermons for the Saints' Days*, p. 122.

'By the grace of God I am what I am.'—1 Cor. xv. 10.

DURING his last hours, John Knox woke from a slumber sighing, and told his friends that he had just been tempted to believe he had 'merited heaven and eternal blessedness, by the faithful discharge of my ministry. But blessed be God who has enabled me to beat down and quench the fiery dart, by suggesting to me such passages of Scripture as these: "What hast thou that thou has not received? By the grace of God I am what I am. Not I but the grace of God in me."'

REFERENCES.—XV. 10.—W. J. Dawson, *Christian World Pulpit*, vol. lii. p. 200. W. L. Watkinson, *ibid.* vol. lvii. p. 391. Spurgeon, *Sermons*, vol. xlix. No. 2833. *Expositor* (4th Series), vol. vii. p. 274; *ibid.* (6th Series), vol. viii. p. 230. A. Maclaren, *Expositions of Holy Scripture—Corinthians*, p. 216.

THE UNITY OF APOSTOLIC TEACHING

Whether it were I or they, so we preach, and so ye believed.'
1 Cor. xv. 11.

I. I ASK you to think of the fact itself—the unbroken unanimity of the whole body of apostolic teachers. I may take it all from the two clauses in the preceding context, 'how that Christ died for our sins according to the Scriptures, and that He was buried, and that He rose again the third day according to the Scriptures'. Now, what lies in it? (1) The Person of—the Christ. (2) They were unbrokenly consentient in regard to the facts of His life, His death, and His Resurrection. (3) The great meaning of the death, *viz.*, the expiation for the world's sins. There were limits to the unanimity. Paul and Peter had a great quarrel about circumcision and related subjects. The apostolic writings are wondrously diverse from one another. But in regard to the facts that I have signalised, they are absolutely one. The instruments in the orchestra are various, the tender flute, the ringing trumpet, and many another, but the note they strike is the same. 'Whether it were I or they, so we preach.'

II. Consider the only explanation of this unanimity. They were one, because their Gospel was the only possible statement of the principles that underlay, and the conclusion that flowed from, the plain facts of the life and the teaching of Jesus Christ.

III. Note the lesson from this unanimity. Let us distinctly apprehend where is the living heart of the Gospel—that it is the message of redemption by the Incarnation and sacrifice of the Son of God. There follows from that Incarnation and sacrifice all the great teaching about the work of the Divine Spirit in men dwelling in them for evermore. But the beginning of all is, 'Christ died for our sins according to the Scriptures'. And that message meets, as nothing else meets, the deepest needs of every human soul. Let this text teach us what we ourselves have to do with this unanimous testimony. 'So we preach, and so ye believed.'—A. MACLAREN, *Triumphant Certainties*, p. 140.

REFERENCES.—XV. 11.—J. Keble, *Sermons for Sundays After Trinity*, pt. i. p. 394. *Expositor* (5th Series), vol. ix. p. 13. A. Maclaren, *Expositions of Holy Scripture—Corinthians*, p. 225. XV. 12.—H. Alford, *Sermons on Christian Doctrine*, p. 242. T. Binney, *King's Weigh-House Chapel Sermons*, p. 340. *Expositor* (7th Series), vol. vi. p. 157. XV. 12-14.—H. Melvill, *Penny Pulpit*, No. 1502, p. 153. XV. 12-19.—Spurgeon, *Sermons*, vol. xxxviii. No. 2287. XV. 13.—A. G. Mortimer, *The Church's Lessons for the Christian Year*, pt. ii. p. 354. XV. 13-17.—*Expositor* (6th Series), vol. i. p. 391.

EVIDENCES FOR THE RESURRECTION

'And if Christ be not risen, then is our preaching vain, and your faith is also vain.'—1 Cor. xv. 14.
'That which we have seen and heard declare we unto you, that ye also may have fellowship with us: and truly our fellowship is with the Father, and with His Son Jesus Christ.'—1 John I. 3.

IT would be difficult to name two greater witnesses to the Resurrection than St. Paul and St. John. What is the evidence of the Resurrection? Open George Cornewall Lewis's book on the rules of historical criticism. He says the first rule you must put into operation is this, that you must have contemporary evidence.

I. The Evidence of Contemporary History.— Have we got contemporary evidence that Jesus Christ rose from the dead? Remember what you mean by contemporary evidence. Any evidence within a century is contemporary evidence. Remember that

that is accepted by every scholar in history. There is not to-day a scholar in Europe who has a reputation to lose who would challenge that the first three Gospels were written in the first century. I could not have said that in this pulpit twenty-five years ago. I should have been challenged by the most eminent scholars. That is what the Church has gained by criticism. We are more sure of the dates; they are further back than ever they were. What else have we got? Four letters written by St. Paul, one to the Romans, two to the Corinthians, one to the Galatians, admitted as genuine historical documents by sceptics like Strauss, or that eloquent French Free-thinker, Ernest Renan. Indeed Ernest Renan states that they possess every element of authenticity and genuineness.

II. Is the Evidence Intelligent?—Now George Cornewall Lewis says evidence must not only be contemporary but intelligent. Read St. Paul's Epistle to the Romans. There is not a book on theology in the language equal to St. Paul's Epistle to the Romans.

III. Is it Honest?—That is the next rule, says the great scholar. Is it honest? Now what had the Jews to gain in preaching this? In St. Paul's next verse he says, Yea, if Christ be not risen, we are false; the Apostle, the Church, the five hundred brethren, the women, are false witnesses. Now look at that. To me that is the biggest monument of its genuineness in the book. That you get Jews to go out and preach a lie, knowing it to be a lie, propagating a lie, and being persecuted for it, stoned, killed, isolated, shipwrecked, beaten, hungry, thirsty, all, what for? Preaching a lie? Why that in itself is almost a bigger miracle than one in the book. I cannot accept it; it is against all reason.

IV. The Evidence of the Memorial.—What else must you have? You must have a memorial established. Before this book was written, before one letter was written, they kept that memorial. Read contemporary history—Pliny's Letters to the Emperor Trajan. 'Who are the Christians?' said the Emperor. 'Who are those in Bithynia who have been persecuted?' Pliny wrote back and said: 'They are men who meet every Sunday morning, the first day of the week, to break bread, drink wine, sing a hymn, pray to One, a Nazarene, Who was crucified. They swear an oath to abstain from all evil, and after they have taken this simple feast, they pray again, and swear an oath to the Nazarene, that they will do all the good they can in the world.' That letter was written probably before St. John's Gospel was written. That memorial sweeps the world.

V. The Evidence of Easter.—Again the biggest feast in Christendom is Easter, the open grave. They say He did not die. This man—the best in the world—lent Himself to the biggest fraud ever perpetrated. Why even the enemies have given that up. They saw that would not account for the Church. They say the Apostles knew He was dead; that they stole the body and preached a lie. That

has been given up. It does not hold; it will not account for the enthusiasm, the hope, the courage, the self-sacrifice, the nobility. It has been given up. You must account for the Church. The Church did not come all at once, the Church with all its wonderful history, its splendid ritual, its glorious ceremonies, its magnificent liturgy and hymns. Where did it come from? To me it is a far more reasonable explanation to believe that He rose, than to account for it by some trickery of imagination, some imposture practised by some designing Jews. The miracle of the Resurrection is simplicity by the side of the complex and insidious reasons for the existence of the Christian Church.

THE RESURRECTION

(For Easter-tide)

'If Christ be not risen, then is our preaching vain.'—1 COR. XV. 14.

IT will be profitable for us to consider the triumphant tone of assured certainty on the part of St. Paul and of all the other Apostles upon the fact of the Resurrection. That note of certainty is very striking in the Second Lesson this morning. Let us then think of some of the grounds for that certainty.

I. The Resurrection not Expected.—First of all, we have this fact, and I do not think its importance can be overlooked, the belief in our Lord's Resurrection did not come with the Apostles. None of them were prepared for it. None of them in the least expected it. They did not even faintly hope that it might be. Their attitude of mind, after the awful tragedy of Good Friday, was simply one of blank despair, unillumined by any single ray of hope. We see the Apostles gathered together in their dumb despair, in that upper chamber, where they had gone for fear of the Jews, prepared for the very worst. The holy women, indeed, inspired with a woman's courage, made their way to the tomb in the early morning; but only to pay that last tribute of affection to the dead body of the Master they had loved, and that by completing the embalming of His body. Their only wonder as they went was, who should roll away the stone from the door of the sepulchre; and then, to their great astonishment, they found the stone rolled away. And then there is the vision of angels, who gave their message—the message of our Lord—to them, and they are convinced.

At once they make their way to the Apostles, where they are gathered together, and tell them the news. How was that news received? With absolute unbelief! 'Neither believed they them!' Everywhere, with all Christ's disciples, not only was there no expectation of His Resurrection, there was absolute disbelief until the truth was forced upon them by evidence that they could no longer resist.

For example; there were the two disciples on the afternoon of the day, sad and cast down. They had heard the rumour of the empty grave, that Christ had risen, but they did not for one moment credit it.

All they could say was : 'We had hoped that it would be so '. That hope had gone. The splendid vision of the future, which in Christ's life had appealed to their imaginations, seemed to them now to be merely a dream, and as a dream it had passed, leaving only sadness and darkness behind—not to these two only, but to all. 'Fools and slow of heart to believe.' This then is the state in which we see the Apostles and the disciples generally on the day of the Resurrection : weak, hopeless, truly unnerved.

II. The Resurrection a Fact.—But, after the Resurrection they have no longer any hesitation in believing in the reality of this stupendous miracle. Their conviction is firm and unshakable. It is the one subject of their teaching. It is the firm basis upon which all faith and teaching rests. It is a truth concerning which they cannot now keep silent ; for which they are now prepared to die. For this extraordinary change in their whole moral attitude there is only one possible explanation, namely, that they had sufficient evidence to convince them that what they had once thought to be not only improbable but impossible, had actually taken place, and that Christ had truly risen—the object of their worship.

III. The Foundation of the Christian Church.— Apart from the Resurrection of Christ, and from the Apostles' belief in it, how could they ever have attempted to do that which they did attempt, and which they succeeded in doing, namely, to found the Christian Church ? What object, what motive could they have had to do anything at all, if Christ had not risen ? To my mind, it is no exaggeration to say that, in these circumstances, the founding of the Christian Church and its marvellous growth, apart from the Resurrection, would have been an even greater miracle, greater even than the Resurrection itself, and more utterly inexplicable. But, given the Resurrection, given that absolute certainty concerning it, all that is inexplicable and impossible otherwise at once becomes possible and explicable.

The Resurrection of Christ is the sole reasonable explanation of the existence to this day of Christianity.

REFERENCES.—XV. 14.—F. B. Woodward, *Selected Sermons*, p. 157. A. Ainger, *Sermons Preached in the Temple Church*, p. 74. T. G. Bonney, *Sermons on Some of the Questions of the Day*, pp. 111, 122. *Expositor* (4th Series), vol. vi. p. 252 ; *ibid.* (6th Series), vol. viii. p. 345 ; *ibid.* (7th Series), vol. vi. p. 422. XV. 17.—T. G. Bonney, *Death and Life in Nations and Men*, p. 35. *Expositor* (4th Series), vol. viii. p. 467. XV. 18.—T. Arnold, *Sermons*, vol. iii. p. 103. *Expositor* (4th Series), vol. i. p. 29 ; *ibid.* (7th Series), vol. vi. p. 435.

THIS LIFE ONLY

' . . . this life only.'—I COR. xv. 19.

'IF in this life only we have hope in Christ, we are of all men most miserable.' In the Revised Version : 'If in this life only we have hoped in Christ, we are of all men most pitiable.' In the margin of the Revised Version : ' If we have only hoped in Christ in this life, we are of all men most pitiable.' The Versions and the margin say the same thing in other words. The truth admits of being variously stated ; there is no one unchanging formula. The truth comes in its own way, incarnates itself in its own flesh and shape, but it is always the same, as the Gospel is, whether preached on the high hill or in the deep dale, in thunder or in whispered love.

'This life only.' But that is an impossibility ; there is no 'life only'. We have made the little seas of language, the small pools, and islanded off the great continents of duration, continuity, and divinity. Always distinguish between what God did and what we have done.

I. 'If in this life only.' What is meant by that expression ? Sometimes what is meant is mistakenly called environment. That is not a scriptural expression ; that word has done a good deal of mischief in the Church. It sounds well, but there is nothing in it. If it were fuller of meaning it would be less resonant.

II. Take the expression 'this life only'. There is no such thing ; we cannot start an argument upon that basis. Sometimes we make large drafts upon the credulity of men, and say, Suppose for argument's sake—We cannot get even so far on this line. It is inconceivable and unthinkable. How far is it possible to dislodge the sophism that there is a lonely world, a cut-off life ? 'This life only.' Life cannot be so bisected ; no man has an instrument keen enough to cut life up into little pieces, allocate some of the pieces in this place and others in that place. It is not possible, it is not in the charter by which we hold our life. Unity is the sign of the universe. Sometimes for convenience sake we say, as the Apostle said, 'this life only'—here and now, in this place or in that place. In making such remarks we are taking great liberties with thought and with speech, we are showing our littleness and betraying our Master who has given us a kingdom to expound and to illustrate. When we break anything off from any other thing, the house is one. If we could grasp that idea in any approachably adequate degree there would follow mastery, a sense of rest, security, and ever-springing life and gratitude.

The Apostle says, 'hope in Christ'—an expression which renders the suggestion of there being a 'this life only' absolutely more and more, if the expression may be allowed, impossible. Christ never came with one world ; He belongs to all the world. The whole Christ-idea multiplies the worlds ; the Christ-idea even multiplies the life that is here and now around us. The Christ-idea makes the wilderness a banqueting palace, turns the stones into children of Abraham, makes the stars significant of many mansions in my Father's house. There you have the plural and the singular ; the mansions are many, the house is one. There are many stars at night visible to the naked eye : there is only one sky.—JOSEPH PARKER, *City Temple Pulpit*, vol. IV. p. 261.

REFERENCES.—XV. 19.—H. P. Liddon, *Sermons on Some Words of St. Paul*, p. 139. *Christian World Pulpit*, vol. xlix.

p. 119. T. Rhondda Williams, *ibid.* vol. li. p. 36. F. D. Maurice, *Sermons*, vol. v. p. 29. John Thomas, *Myrtle Street Pulpit*, vol. iii. p. 11. S. Baring-Gould, *Village Preaching for a Year*, vol. ii. p. 55. Spurgeon, *Sermons*, vol. x. No. 562. *Expositor* (6th Series), vol. iii. p. 371. XV. 20.—W. C. E. Newbolt, *Christian World Pulpit*, vol. xlvii. p. 257. J. Keble, *Sermons for Easter to Ascension Day*, p. 147. F. Bourdillon, *Plain Sermons for Family Reading*, p. 110. F. B. Cowl, *Preacher's Magazine*, vol. xviii. p. 143. H. Alford, *Sermons on Christian Doctrine*, p. 251. W. C. Wheeler, *Sermons and Addresses*, p. 162. T. F. Crosse, *Sermons* (2nd Series), p. 70. Spurgeon, *Sermons*, vol. viii. No. 445. *Expositor* (5th Series), vol. ii. p. 94. A. Maclaren, *Expositions of Holy Scripture—Corinthians*, p. 236. XV. 21.—*Ibid.* vol. iv. p. 257. XV. 20-22.—J. H. Holford, *Memorial Sermons*, p. 56. J. C. M. Bellew, *Sermons*, vol. iii. pp. 187, 201, and 213. XV. 21.—E. W. Attwood, *Sermons for Clergy and Laity*, p. 169. H. Bushnell, *Christ and His Salvation*, p. 240. XV. 22.—F. B. Cowl, *Preacher's Magazine*, vol. xviii. p. 46. *Expositor* (4th Series), vol. i. p. 130 ; *ibid.* (5th Series), vol. viii. p. 149 ; *ibid.* (6th Series), vol. ix. pp. 51, 151 ; *ibid.* vol. x. p. 359.

RANK

'But every man in his own order.'—1 COR. xv. 23.

THAT is a great and far-reaching principle. Paul declares it to be the principle of the Resurrection : the dead shall rise 'each in his own order' (R.V.) But the truth applies to-day as assuredly as in that final day ; and whilst it is conspicuously a law of the Resurrection, it is distinctly a law of present-day life.

I. This is a recognition of Variety. If God is to recognise human variety at last, surely we should do so now. Life is ranged in orders. The army of mankind is split up into regiments. And it is God who setteth men so. A great deal of injustice is done because we do not respect this great law of being. We must recognise individuality. We must recognise classes of men. Thank God for all the 'orders'. There is something noble and royal and Divine in all. (1) This is true of nations. Duty varies with endowment. (2) Churches are under this same law of variety—'Each in his own order'. Every Church has lessons for every other Church. (3) The same is true of Christians. All intolerance of our Christian brethren arises from our non-recognition of the great law of variety. (4) It would prevent much bitterness if we applied this ideal to Christian ministers. If there is a great variety there is also a great unity. 'The Head of every man is Christ.'

II. This is a determination of Destiny. Our 'rank' will determine our eternal estate. According to our Christian character shall our immortal portion be assigned. We are each now settling our final 'order'. Be ambitious to stand well at last.

III. This is a rule of Criticism. 'Every man in his own order.' If we are to be judged by that canon at last, we ought to judge one another by it now. It was said that the only poet Tennyson criticised roughly was himself. Charles Kingsley's widow said he was most stern toward himself. Be your own rigorous critic.

IV. This is a maxim of Service. God does not expect a kind of service from you for which you are constitutionally unfitted. God needs and asks all types of service. 'Only through each can all be gathered,' says Dean Vaughan.

V. This is also an inspiration to Holiness. To be content to be indifferent, mediocre Christians, when we are to be ranged at last according to our rank, is to commit eternal suicide. O believer, be thy best for thy Saviour's sake !—DINSDALE T. YOUNG, *The Enthusiasm of God*, p. 122.

REFERENCE.—XV. 23.—*Expositor* (4th Series), vol. x. p. 346.

THE COMING OF THE END

'Then cometh the end.'—1 COR. xv. 24.

IT is not possible to rule these words out of life. They are perpetually recurring. We contemplate a man's life from childhood to full manhood and old age ; all the works that he will do ; all the associations that he will form ; our eye runs along his whole course ; but, at last, we reach the point where, 'Then cometh the end,' sums up and closes all.

Beyond our own little sphere it is still true. Our text tells us of Christ and His finished work. Here is His great work, conquering death, redeeming men from sin, claiming the world for God ; but, even of His work, it is written, 'Then cometh the end, when He shall have delivered up the kingdom to God, even the Father ; when He shall have put down all rule and all authority and power'. Even the great redemptive work of Christ must some day be folded up and finished, and some new dispensation take its place.

Let us consider this strange characteristic of life— this constant recurrence of 'endings'; this law of perpetual perishing—or cessation of one man's work and its resumption by another—and re-starting, by which alone the perpetual motion of life is maintained.

I. The most striking thing about the whole matter is the way in which men's desire and dread are both called out by this constant coming of the ends of things ; this stopping and re-starting of the works of life.

(a) There is man's desire of the end. This partly arises from man's instinctive dread of monotony. 'I would not live always,' has been a true cry of the human soul. The wandering Jew, compelled to live on until his Saviour came again, has been one of the most pathetic and fearful figures which have ever haunted the imagination of mankind. Man's mere dread of monotony, his sense of the awful weariness of living on for ever, has made him rejoice that down the long avenues of life here, he could read the inscription of release, 'Then cometh the end'. Tell any man that he, out of all the mortals on earth, was to have no end here, and, whatever might be his first emotion, he would by-and-by be filled with dismay ; for every man has gathered something which he must get rid of, something he would not carry always ; and so he welcomes the prophecy, 'Then cometh the end'.

But it is not only the sense of the evil element in life that makes men desire the coming end. That is after all a poor and desperate reason. When life has been a success, and developed its better powers, then, for a man to say, 'This road is glorious, but I am glad to see it stops yonder; for beyond, without doubt, there is something yet more glorious'—that is a fine impatience. The noblest human natures are built thus. Let the life be filled with the spirit of the spring-time, and then 'cometh the end,' but not a cessation of life, but fuller life which the heart expects. The end which comes to the promise of spring-time shall be the luxuriance of summer. Thus, in many tones, some pathetic, some triumphant, yet all tones of satisfaction, do men desire the end. But there is that other point of view from which man regards the coming of the end in life.

(b) There is man's dread of the end. Undoubtedly the sense of the changefulness of things is what sends such a feeling of insecurity through all our ordinary living; a dread which haunts the very feature of life which, as we have seen, wakens also the almost enthusiastic desire of men's souls. And one reason is the soul shrinks from change; it shudders at the thought when it must reach, at last, the end of its journey here and embark on something new; and it is good in a way that the burden of proof should be on the side of change. Another reason is, that one shrinks from the thought of the coming end of the condition in which he is now living, in proportion, as he is aware, of how far he is from having fulfilled and exhausted the fulness and richness of this present life. But the strongest element in our dread of change is the great uncertainty which envelops every untried experience, the great mystery of the unlived. We dread the end even of our own imperfect condition.

Thus we recount our human lot and see man standing in desire and dread, at once, of this perpetual change, this perpetual coming of the end of things.

II. Fortunate, indeed, is it that the end of things does not depend upon man's choice, but comes by a will more large, more wise than his. If we, in such mingled mood, were at last compelled to give the sign when we thought the time had come for this mortal to put on immortality—how the desire and the dread would fight within us! We are spared all that. 'It comes of itself,' men say; the Christian man with perfect reverence and truth exclaims, 'God sends it'. Apart from this view of the changefulness of life, this perpetual hurrying of all things to an end, we can make nothing out of it all. But if around this instability of human life is wrapped the great permanence of the life of God; if no end comes which is not in His sight truly a beginning; then there is light shed upon it all, and everything is instinct with His spiritual design.—PHILLIPS BROOKS.

REFERENCES.—XV. 24.—*Expositor* (6th Series), vol. x. p. 5. XV. 24-28.—*Ibid.* (5th Series), vol. iv. p. 136. XV. 25.—W. Ross Taylor, *Christian World Pulpit*, vol. xlv. p. 45. Spurgeon, *Sermons*, vol. xiv. No. 807, and vol. li. No. 2940. *Expositor* (4th Series), vol. x. p. 324. XV. 26.—E. A. Bray,

Sermons, vol. i. p. 282. Spurgeon, *Sermons*, vol. xii. No. 721, and vol. xxii. No. 1329. XV. 27.—*Expositor* (4th Series), vol. vi. p. 251; *ibid.* vol. x. p. 40; *ibid.* (6th Series), vol. x. p. 370.

' Then shall the Son also Himself be subjected to Him that did subject all things to Him, that God may be all in all.'—I COR. XV. 28.

FOR a curious misapplication of this saying, see Emerson's essay on *Circles*, where he observes that 'Christianity is rightly dear to the best of mankind; yet was there never a young philosopher whose breeding had fallen into the Christian Church, by whom that brave text of Paul's was not specially prized: "Then shall also the Son be subject unto Him who put all things under Him, that God may be all in all". Let the claims and virtues of persons be never so great and welcome, the instinct of man presses eagerly onward to the impersonal and illimitable, and gladly arms itself against the dogmatism of bigots with this generous word out of the book itself.'

REFERENCES.—XV. 28.—Spurgeon, *Sermons*, vol. xliii. No. 2501. *Expositor* (4th Series), vol. i. p. 139; *ibid.* vol. x. p. 45. XV. 29.—J. Bunting, *Sermons*, vol. i. p. 71. J. G. Rogers, *Christian World Pulpit*, vol. liv. p. 249. J. M. Neale, *Sermons Preached in a Religious House*, vol. ii. p. 590. *Expositor* (4th Series), vol. i. p. 238. XV. 29-34.—*Ibid.* (6th Series), vol. iv. p. 185. XV. 30.—H. Howard, *The Raiment of the Soul*, p. 211. XV. 31.—Spurgeon, *Sermons*, vol. xiv. No. 828. H. J. Wilmot-Buxton, *Sunday Sermonettes for a Year*, p. 174. J. M. Neale, *Sermons for the Church Year*, vol. ii. p. 145. Dinsdale T. Young, *Unfamiliar Texts*, p. 42. *Expositor* (6th Series), vol. x. p. 359.

' If, after the manner of men, I fought with beasts at Ephesus, what doth it profit me?'—I COR. XV. 32.

CRITICISING, in his *Spirit of Modern Philosophy* (p. 452 f.) the optimistic idealism of Sidney Lanier and others, Professor Royce remarks that 'from every such half-hearted scheme of the moral order we return to the facts of life themselves. There they are, our ills and our sins—denying them does not destroy them, calling them illusions does not remove them, declaring them utterly insignificant only makes all the more hollow and empty the life of which they are an organic part. If, then, the only escape of our philosophy from the individual ills of life lies in denying their significance, and so the significance of this whole seeming world whereof they are a part, then indeed we are of all men most miserable. . . . Nay, what shall it profit us that after the manner of men we have fought wild beasts at Ephesus. There are no wild beasts, you see. It was all a dream, our morality.'

' If the dead are not raised, let us eat and drink, for to-morrow we die.'—I COR. XV. 32.

HIS loveless, cheerless boyhood was over, and the liberty of Oxford, which, even after the mild constraint of a public school, seems boundless, was to him the perfection of bliss. . . . He lived with the idle set in college, riding, boating, and playing tennis, frequenting wines and suppers. From vicious excess his intellect and temperament preserved him. Deep down in his nature there was a strong Puritan element, to which his senses were subdued. Nevertheless, for two years he lived at Oxford in contented idleness, saying with Isaiah, and more literally than the prophet, 'Let us eat and drink, for to-morrow we shall die'.—HERBERT PAUL's *Life of Froude*, pp. 20, 21.

REFERENCES.—XV. 32.—Bishop Gore, *Christian World Pulpit*, vol. lix. p. 382. R. W. Hiley, *A Year's Sermons*, vol. i. p. 198. J. B. Lightfoot, *Cambridge Sermons*, p. 109.

'Evil communications corrupt good manners.'—1 COR. XV. 33.

'WEDNESDAY 17.—I met the class of soldiers, eight of whom were Scotch Highlanders,' Wesley writes in his *Journal* for 1749, in Ireland. 'Most of these were brought up well; but evil communications had corrupted good manners. They all said, from the time they entered into the army, they had grown worse and worse.'

'OF all the painful things connected with my employment,' wrote Dr. Arnold of Rugby, 'nothing is equal to the grief of seeing a boy come to school innocent and promising, and tracing the corruption of his character from the influence of the temptations around him, in the very place which ought to have strengthened and improved it. But in most cases those who come with a character of positive good are benefited ; it is the neutral and indecisive characters which are apt to be decided for evil by schools, as they would be in fact by any other temptation.'

So many men are degraded by their sympathies. They have any amount of aspirations and would like to fly, but they have not the courage to fly alone. So they prefer to crawl—in company.—JOHN OLIVER HOBBES, in *The School for Saints* (ch. xxviii.).

'MANY a man's destiny,' says Stevenson in his essay on *Villon*, 'has been settled by nothing apparently more grave than a pretty face on the opposite side of the street and a couple of bad companions round the corner.'

REFERENCES.—XV. 33.—*Expositor* (4th Series), vol. i. p. 202 ; *ibid.* (5th Series), vol. iii. p. 383 ; *ibid.* (6th Series), vol. iii. p. 393 ; *ibid.* vol. vii. p. 296. XV. 34.—F. C. Spurr, *Christian World Pulpit*, vol. liii. p. 416. S. Gedge, *The Record*, vol. xxvii. p. 977.

THE RESURRECTION BODY

'With what body do they come ? '—1 COR. XV. 35.

OBSERVE here the contrast between other religious systems and Christianity. The most spiritual of Greek philosophers regarded man's body as a hopeless burden, a fatal clog on the soul ; Christianity recognises this as partly true of the body in its present state, but asserts that these imperfections are neither necessary nor permanent; it looks forward with absolute confidence to a future state, in which the whole man, spirit, soul, and body, shall be transfigured and glorified, on the ground of the Resurrection of Christ.

The fact of the Resurrection of Jesus Christ was not denied by the Corinthians; it made them Christians ; they knew the Church was founded, not simply on a Saviour Who had died, but upon one Who had been raised from the dead by the power of God.

St. Paul restates this fact; reaffirms two great truths involved—Christ died ; Christ had risen ; he marshals his evidence, and witnesses : Cephas, the Twelve, a surviving majority out of five hundred, St. James—all these had seen the risen Christ.

This is the Gospel which saves, awakens, and maintains the spiritual life. But, as he pressed home the issues of the Resurrection, doubts and difficulties arose ; questions asked by inquiring minds : 'How are the dead raised up ? With what manner of body do they come ? ' What the process, what the result of the Resurrection ?

The early belief in the Resurrection was not a stupid credulity. The Corinthians were intellectual, the objections natural then and natural now. As we have stood by the open grave we have known their force, and often asked ourselves, 'With what body do they come ? ' Will the child rise a child ? the old man an old man ? the cripple maimed ? the blind sightless ? Will the Resurrection body be of the same material and form, only reconstructed ? Is this the Christian faith ? If not, 'With what body do they come ? '

The Apostle meets these objections by analogy.

(Analogy does not, cannot demonstrate. This passage is not a proof of the Resurrection, nor intended to be so, but it meets certain difficulties impressively, powerfully ; it argues that the laws in Nature have their counterpart in the spiritual world ; that there is a unity throughout the system of the universe, and that the God of Grace and of Nature is one.)

I. 'Flesh and blood cannot inherit the kingdom of God.' There is no question, then, of re-gathering the particles of the dead body ; 'neither doth corruption inherit incorruption'. None of the particles composing a human body seven years ago exist in that body to-day ; they have passed into new combinations and forms.

St. Paul points us to the analogy of the seed and the plant : 'Thou foolish one ! that which thou sowest is not quickened, except it die : and that which thou sowest, thou sowest not that body that shall be, but bare grain, it may chance of wheat, or of some other grain, but God giveth it a body as it hath pleased Him, and to every seed his own body.'

Here we have a parable of wondrous force and beautiful simplicity. 'With what manner of body do they come ? '

Certainly not with the same body. The plant is entirely unlike the seed from which it sprang. The Resurrection body will not be the body which we now possess. The seed is not identical with the plant ; it is the parent of the organism, the form of which is determined by God.

'So also is the Resurrection of the dead.' The body is sown in corruption, liable to change, infirmity, dissolution ; but ' it is raised in incorruption '. Proof against sickness and death ; the glow of health throughout the ages. 'It is sown in dishonour,' in weakness—a natural body, frail and helpless, ruled by the senses; 'it is raised in power,' a spiritual body, a body fashioned anew.

II. Yet the Resurrection body will, in a real sense, be our own body. When clothed with it, we shall be the same persons that we are now. The Thames is the same river now that it was a hundred years ago, flowing from the same source, created by the same force, coursing in the same channel; it is still the Thames, though not a drop of its water to-day was there ten years ago.

The old man to-day says: 'I am the same person that I was twenty, fifty years ago; though not a single particle of my body is the same, yet I am the same'. So in the Resurrection, it will be our body, only the identity will not be that of form or of particles, but that of a permanent force and character which make it what it is and constitute its unity.

'God giveth it a body,' remember, not as it pleaseth Him, 'but as it pleased Him'—according to a certain law, which is His eternal will, that, through whatever changes the seed or germ of life should pass, something there shall be which shall connect its latest with its earliest stage.

III. The Resurrection body will be the manifested expression of ourselves. This, then, will be the Resurrection body—ourselves, essentially ourselves. We are perpetually judging men by what we have learned to call their 'expression'. We look into a face, and say, 'There is kindness, sympathy, tenderness'; or, 'There is pride, temper, passion, avarice'. But we often judge wrongly; for this self-expression is, at present, imperfect; in the Resurrection body it will be full, complete, the perfect expression of the inmost spirit. According to the lives we live now we shall be hereafter. The character formed here will determine our future expression. Our very bodies will be our condemnation or our glory in that day. We shall then wear the garb of holiness, or the livery of sin; and every man shall know, even as he is known.—J. STORRS.

REFERENCES.—XV. 35.—H. Bonner, *Sermons and Lectures*, p. 163. W. P. S. Bingham, *Sermons on Easter Subjects*, p. 88. T. G. Bonney, *Sermons on Some of the Questions of the Day*, p. 99. F. Hastings, *Christian World Pulpit*, vol. xlvii. p. 99. C. J. Ridgeway, *The King and His Kingdom*, p. 150. Dinsda T. Young, *Unfamiliar Texts*, p. 131. W L. Watkinson, *Th Fatal Barter*, p. 77. XV. 35, 36.—*Christian World Pulpit*, vol. xlviii. p. 295. XV. 35-37.—S. G. Fielding, *Christian World Pulpit*, vol. xlvii. p. 259.

ST. PAUL'S FOOL

'But some man will say, How are the dead raised up? And with what body do they come? Thou fool, that which thou sowest is not quickened, except it die. And that which thou sowest, thou sowest not that body that shall be, but bare grain, it may chance of wheat, or of some other grain. But God giveth it a body as it hath pleased Him, and to every seed his own body.'—1 COR. xv. 35-38.

ST. PAUL is here speaking of the Resurrection of the dead.

In this immortal chapter St. Paul asserts the doctrine and reasons about it, and in the text, he deals with a specific objection which was commonly urged against it. 'Some man will say, How are the dead raised up? and with what body—what manner of body—do they come?'

The objection, you observe, is twofold. It states two difficulties which were felt regarding the Resurrection in those days, and which are felt, perhaps no less acutely, still.

I. When these bodies of ours are laid in the grave, they are not preserved intact century after century, millennium after millennium, waiting until the resurrection morning shall break and the touch of God shall awaken them and His voice summon them forth from their secure abode. Nay, no sooner are they committed to the bosom of the earth than they are subjected to the mysterious processes of Nature's alchemy. They decay; they crumble; they vanish away. Open a grave where a dead body was laid only the other year, and do you find it still lying there, 'with meek hands folded on its breast,' awaiting the Resurrection? No, it has disappeared. It has disappeared, but it has not perished. It has been transmuted. The worn-out fabric has been taken down and re-made and woven by the deft hand of Nature, that skilful artificer, into new and diverse vestures. It has passed into other vital organisms— grass, flowers, trees, and animals. And how then are the dead raised up? How can the material which has undergone such dissolution and dispersion, be re-collected and re-fashioned. It belongs to the common store of matter which never increases and is never diminished through all its manifold transformations and adaptations; and the corporeal tabernacles which our souls inhabit now have served myriads before us during the long ages of the past, and will be theirs no less than ours at the Resurrection.

II. And suppose our bodies could be restored to us at the Resurrection: are they suited for the eternal world, which is so unlike the world that we inhabit now? It is a spiritual world, and shall we go thither, according to the coarse gibe of the Pagans in early days, with hair on our heads and nails on our fingers? What use will there be for material bodies with their carnal functions in that immaterial domain? This is the difficulty which vexed the mind of that believer in the city of Corinth when he asked: 'With what manner of body do they come?'

It is a hard question and a deep problem, and he was no frivolous sceptic who propounded it. He was an earnest man who would fain believe but found faith very difficult. And does it not seem as though the Apostle made a very bad beginning when he prefaced his answer to that distressed soul with an abusive epithet—'thou fool?'

No, look at the word and consider what it means. He listens to that difficulty about the Resurrection, and then he turns upon his questioner, not abusively but kindly and sympathetically, and says: 'Ah, you blind, unperceiving man! Look about you and see what is going on everywhere in this great, mysterious world; and you will never ask that question and never be troubled with that difficulty any more'.

And this is the lesson which I would bring home to you. Here is that transcendent mystery, the Resurrection of the dead, the awakening of our mortal bodies to a larger, fuller, more glorious life; and it seems a stark impossibility. But look around you, and you will see on every side innumerable prophecies, arguments, and evidences of this miraculous consummation. You observe, St. Paul points out two wonders which that troubled inquirer had never noticed, although they were continually being enacted before his eyes; for he was like the statue in the temple—senseless, unperceiving.

I. The first is the law that, in St. Bernard's phrase, 'Death is the Gate of Life'. 'That which thou sowest is not quickened, except it die.'

II. Death is not only the Gate of Life; it is the pathway to a larger, richer, and more beautiful life.

'Some man will say, How are the dead raised up? and with what manner of body do they come?' 'Ah, blind, unperceiving man!' answers the Apostle, 'look at the seed cast into the ground, quickened, and raised up to a new and more abundant life; and recognise what this betokens. So also is the Resurrection of the dead.'—DAVID SMITH, *Man's Need of God*, p. 109.

REFERENCES.—XV. 35-38.—Spurgeon, *Sermons*, vol. vi. No. 306. XV. 35-41.—*Expositor* (4th Series), vol. i. p. 161. XV. 36.—J. B. Lightfoot, *Cambridge Sermons*, p. 63. J. J. Blunt, *Plain Sermons*, p. 213. *Expositor* (4th Series), vol. i. p. 131. XV. 36, 37.—S. H. Fleming, *Fifteen Minute Sermons for the People*, p. 153. *Expositor* (5th Series), vol. v. p. 411.

THE RESURRECTION BODY

'Thou sowest not that body that shall be.'—1 COR. xv. 37.

I. THE body is essential to the complete idea of immortality.

II. The resurrection is not the resurrection of the present body, though it is in some way connected with it.

III. Men receive a glorious body not because of death, but because of life in Christ.—A. MACLAREN.

GOD AND THE BODY

'God giveth it a body.'—1 COR. xv. 38.

'GIVETH it a body as it hath pleased Him.' He must always be pleased; there cannot be two kings upon the throne of the universe; God never asks any man to share His throne with Him in the government of things: Providence is one, an integer that cannot be broken up into fractions or decimals: and we have to come to that conclusion; after all our wandering, we come back travel-stained and travel-worn, we put off our sandals and set our staff in its place in the corner.

What, then, is common to all these bodies and all these entities, what is the common denomination in which all these fractions stand? LIFE! Who has seen life? Nobody. Who can define life? No one. You never can define the truly great: you can define

living, but not life; loving, but not love; godliness but not God. There are some private chambers in the creation the doors of which we may not open. God is the creator of life, and in Christ Jesus He came to give man more life and life more abundantly, in wave upon wave, and billow upon billow, and ocean rolling over the shoulders of ocean; all life. There is no death in God.

I. God has given His own life a body. God always illustrates His own doctrine, and gives object-lessons in His own science. God has always been writing in white letters upon a black background. God has given Himself a body. Have we seen it? We have seen nothing else. Where is it? Everywhere. He who has seen only dust has not seen the very world he lives in; he who has seen only the surface of things has seen nothing, he can explain nothing, he can worship nothing, he has not seen enough to draw out his soul in religious adoration and expectancy. What is the body of God? Creation; all the things that are above us and around us and beneath us are endeavouring to express in visible form and symbol the It whose heart throbs and quivers through creation. I see God in all stars and flowers, in all angels and ravenous beasts, in all crystal temples and in all wild wildernesses and jungles; I see Him in the cultivated flower, on which He often smiles to see how poor a workman his little Adam is; and I see Him in the wild wayside flower, which bears more evidently, to the observing and religious eye, the signature of God. God comes to us in snow and in violets, in all colours, in all events; history is His tabernacle, providence His altar, life His throne: these are not Himself; the glove is not the hand, the house is not the occupant, the body is not the soul: creation is not God. God is within creation, and beyond it, outside it, above it, beneath it, around it: but creation is not God; God is a Spirit; God incarnated Himself in Adam; the whole Trinity was in that one Man, and that one man was a duality, 'male and female created He him'. How was Adam an incarnation of God? Because the Bible tells us that God created man in His own image, in the image of God created He him, in our image and likeness was Adam made. We have no explanation, we have only a fact; if we could accept facts, and let explanations alone, the Church would have next to nothing to do in the way of controversy, it would be reduced to the ministry of charity, to the holy apostleship of love and service.

II. God was supremely and gloriously incarnated, embodied in Christ. In Christ dwelt all the fulness of the Godhead bodily. God gave Himself a body when He caused Christ to be born of the Virgin, and to go forth that He might redeem with blood the self-enslaved and self-destroyed race of man. The Word was made flesh and dwelt among us; there is no other true and adequate explanation of Christ. Until you have come to His Deity—I speak now from the standpoint of my own conviction—you have not even begun to explain in any degree the mystery which goes through all the life of the world by the name of Christ. In Him was all fulness; all things are created by Him and for Him, and without Him was not anything made that is made. With these assurances, apostolically given, I can have no hesitation whatever in accepting Jesus Christ as God. He was the body of God, He was the impersonation of God, He did the work of God; He created by healing, He redeemed by sacrifice, He broke His heart that ours might not be broken. He died in the ineffable darkness that we might never know the meaning of such night as that which enshrouded His orphaned soul.—Joseph Parker, *City Temple Pulpit*, vol. VII. p. 12.

References.—XV. 38.—J. A. Alexander, *The Gospel of Jesus Christ*, p. 184. XV. 40.—F. Lawrence, *Christian World Pulpit*, vol. xliv. p. 285. *Expositor* (6th Series), vol. vi. p. 396. XV. 40, 48, 49.—*Ibid.* (4th Series), vol. i. p. 138. XV. 41.—C. S. Horne, *The Soul's Awakening*, p. 119.

'It is sown in corruption, it is raised in incorruption.'—I Cor. xv. 42.

Compare the closing words of Walton's Life of Donne, where he remarks : 'He was earnest and unwearied in the search of knowledge, with which his vigorous soul is now satisfied, and employed in a continual praise of that God that first breathed it into his active body ; that body, which once was a temple of the Holy Ghost ; and is now become a small quantity of Christian dust. But I shall see it re-animated.'

References.—XV. 42.—W. Alexander, *Primary Convictions*, p. 281. XV. 42-44.—*Expositor* (4th Series), vol. ii. p. 35.

THE NATURAL AND THE SPIRITUAL
'It is sown a natural body; it is raised a spiritual body.'—I Cor. xv. 44.

There is no more wonderful or impressive chapter in the Bible than this fifteenth chapter of the Epistle to the Corinthians, which deals with the transfiguration of this present life into its future state. Whenever we hear it read—as we often do on the saddest occasions of our lives—we are listening to the best explanation we shall ever get of the great change which will take place when we ourselves pass out of the present life.

I. Life Beyond the Grave.—In stating the fact of the future life St. Paul was, of course, not making a new statement, especially to the people of Greece. Their most ancient poets had written of a future life. They believed most thoroughly in a life beyond the grave. These Corinthians to whom St. Paul was writing had their own witnesses if they chose to call them. Indeed the Gentile world had shown in their past history an even clearer idea of immortality than had the chosen nation itself. They had obstinately clung to the instinctive belief that they must go on living— that the soul, whatever it was, wherever it was, would never be destroyed. But though there was this unmistakable certainty about the future, yet there was no glory in this certainty. Man would continue to live—that was the idea—but only in some shadowy state, some pale reflection of the life on earth. And so this letter of St. Paul to these clever Corinthians, these men of universal intelligence, had a very special message. It was not to prove that the soul was inde-

structible, but to prove by the Resurrection of Christ what sort of life awaited man beyond the grave. The value of human personality is the basis of St. Paul's letter.

II. A Spiritual Existence.—Our ideas of personality are so much bound up with the bodies that are so closely our own, that we shrink from the idea of a purely spiritual existence. It is so unintelligible ; we have not the slightest idea what pure spirit is like. We may say truly, of course, that our bodies are not ourselves—that, indeed, every particle of the body we see and feel undergoes some complete chemical change in the course of seven or eight years, while we remain the same, we continue the same personality. We admit logically and easily that our individuality—that mysterious something within us which is not imperilled by such changes as loss of limb or the chemical renewal of the flesh—is our true soul. Yet, though the thought is quite logical, we cannot separate the body from the soul, we cannot imagine a pure spiritual existence. St. Paul, however, distinctly encourages us to believe that the future life will not be that mere abstraction from which we recoil, will not be a merely spiritual existence ; but rather that the spirit will continue to have its body. We may be comforted by the hope that in the future life our friends, and we ourselves, shall possess some real distinction in form as well as in spirit. St. Paul speaks of another body, a spiritual body, yet a body bearing the closest relationship with the natural body. An analogy, he says, may be found in the growth of the seed—the seed which in its wonderful transformation to the flower loses none of its individuality. That suggests to us much that is comforting.

III. Recognition in Eternity.—It suggests to us the comfort of recognition. We shall not be lost to one another. The resurrection body will, we doubt not, in a way that we cannot yet conceive, present sufficient points of resemblance to the earthly body to make recognition possible. There is the consolation here that we all want—that we must have before we can ever take a calm view of death. All that is best in our life here has been sanctified by loving ties. Our spiritual growth has depended so largely on the way we have spent and used our life in the interests of others that we seem to demand the assurance that all this love will not be lost. Such an assurance is given us by St. Paul.

References.—XV. 44.—D. W. Simon, *Twice Born and other Sermons*, p. 220. J. M. Whiton, *Beyond the Shadow*, p. 51. B. J. Snell, *Sermons on Immortality*, p. 47. XV. 45.— Reuen Thomas, *Christian World Pulpit*, vol. xliv. p. 113. *Expositor* (4th Series), vol. x. p. 39. XV. 45, 46.—*Ibid.* vol. ii. p. 101. XV. 45, 47.—*Ibid.* (5th Series), vol. ii. pp. 175, 180 ; *ibid.* vol. iv. p. 399.

LIFE'S DEVELOPMENT
'Howbeit that was not first which is spiritual, but that which is natural, and afterward that which is spiritual.'—I Cor. xv. 46.

It is noteworthy that in the Hebrew Scriptures there is scarcely a hint of any belief in a Resurrection. The familiar verse from Job, so often read in the burial service, had not the meaning which Christians now attach to it, but referred only to the coming of a vindicator of justice and right, a living Redeemer who would justify a maligned man. Even the later prophets, Daniel and Ezekiel, give only faint suggestions of the future life. Yet when our Lord came some such expectations prevailed, though tinged with sensuous notions, which He earnestly sought to banish. The Sadducees alone among the Jews of His day denied both resurrection and immortality, but our Lord maintained the popular belief, developed and purified it, and based it on a sure foundation, for He built it on His own empty grave. By His Resurrection He gave the world the first indubitable evidence of the truth we rejoice in, so that when we depict on Easter cards, as we sometimes do, flowers of hope clustering round a cross, we suggest what is true as well as beautiful.

I. The doctrine of the Resurrection is based not on philosophic speculations, but on historic fact, and the doctrine is nowhere so fully set forth as in this wonderful and familiar chapter.

The Christian argument for our resurrection rests not on analogy, but on the fact of the Lord's Resurrection. He was the 'first-fruits' of them that sleep, and to any Jew that word first-fruits would have special significance. Every Jew had been accustomed to present the first-fruits of field and garden in the Temple, and when he presented them, or had them presented, he recognised in them pledges of what was unseen—fruit and corn in distant orchards and fields. Such then, says Paul, is the relation of Christ's Resurrection to ours, its promise and pledge.

The Apostle points us beyond what takes place at death, to what will be experienced after death. It is but a hint, yet the hint is unmistakable. The ransomed spirit passes at once into a state of felicity, but will subsequently be clothed with a glorified body like that of the risen Christ, and this will bring with it possibilities of heightened bliss and nobler service.

II. But my text may also be regarded as the assertion of a general law which prevails in the whole economy of God, for it is not only in the unseen future that the natural precedes the spiritual. In all God's dealings with men we see progressiveness and development, for He is ever pressing forward toward His own ideals, which men cannot mar nor demons destroy.

III. This truth is applicable to the revelations of God's will, which have always been progressive.

(1) The world was very gradually prepared for the manifestation of God in Jesus Christ. It was after long waiting that the spiritual followed the natural. In the earlier centuries simple lessons of dependence on God were taught. By the limitations of human power, and the interposition of Divine power, this lesson was enforced : 'Without Me ye can do nothing'. Still more clearly the patriarchs heard this truth, and by rewards, like Canaan, which were typical of the higher, they were helped heavenward.

Then the Mosaic economy proclaimed the penalty of sin, the separation caused by it between God and man, and the necessity for a Mediator. Still clearer views were granted to the prophets, and at last Christ appeared so that His disciples saw what prophets and kings had failed to see, that God is love, and he who dwells in love dwells in God, and God in him.

(2) If you contrast those two dispensations you will see their progressiveness yet more clearly. Christianity was to Judaism what manhood is to youth.

(3) And that dispensation became still higher when Christ disappeared as a human teacher, and became known and trusted as the exalted King of His people, ruling them and guiding them by His Spirit into all truth. Even in Christianity there was first the natural, then the spiritual, and this revelation is still growing, for the Lord hath yet more light and truth to break forth from His word.—ALFRED ROWLAND, *The Exchanged Crowns*, p. 15.

REFERENCES. — XV. 46. — *Christian World Pulpit*, vol. liii. p. 52. B. J. Snell, *Sermons on Immortality*, p. 9. J. Martineau, *Endeavours After the Christian Life*, p. 21. Phillips Brooks, *The Mystery of Iniquity*, p. 242. *Expositor* (5th Series), vol. ii. p. 164 ; *ibid.* (4th Series), vol. viii. p. 35. XV. 47.—*Ibid.* (6th Series), vol. ix. p. 58. XV. 47-49.—*Ibid.* vol. ii. p. 275. XV. 48.—J. Martineau, *Endeavours After the Christian Life*, p. 288. XV. 49.—*Expositor* (6th Series), vol. x. p. 191. XV. 49, 50.—*Ibid.* (5th Series), vol. v. p. 411.

'Flesh and blood cannot inherit the kingdom of God.'—1 COR. xv. 50.

'HE that resisteth pleasure crowneth his life' (Eccles. xiv. 5)—that is morality with the tone heightened, passing, or trying to pass, into religion. 'Flesh and blood cannot inherit the kingdom of God ;'—there the passage is made, and we have religion.—M. ARNOLD, *Literature and Dogma* (ch. I.).

REFERENCES.—XV. 50.—*Expositor* (4th Series), vol. x. p. 200 ; *ibid.* (6th Series), vol. viii. p. 360 ; *ibid.* vol. ix. p. 462. XV. 50-52.—*Ibid.* vol. iv. p. 15. XV. 51.—H. J. Wilmot-Buxton, *Sunday Sermonettes for a Year*, p. 186. J. M. Neale, *Sermons Preached in Sackville College Chapel*, vol. iv. p. 295. *Expositor* (4th Series), vol. x. pp. 106, 303 ; *ibid.* (6th Series), vol. x. pp. 153, 182. XV. 51, 52.—S. H. Fleming, *Fifteen Minute Sermons for the People*, p. 163.

THE LATEST TRUMPET OF THE SEVEN

'The trumpet shall sound.'—1 COR. xv. 52.

STRICTLY speaking, it is a military trumpet which is here referred to. War trumpets were greatly used in the old days for signals and for commands. But never was such a trumpet put to such a use as this. A final military summons is to be given. The latest of God's seven trumpets is to peal forth. Literally the words run, 'One shall blow a trumpet'. How solemn the announcement 'one shall blow a trumpet,' and that 'one' the Son of God !

I. This is a summons of farewell to earthly scenes. Probably such a message was never more distasteful to old and young than to-day. To think of the things which are seen as temporal is foreign to modern inclination, and repugnant to it. This text is a gospel ; good news of a truth ; for this trumpet blast means farewell to earth's painful scenes. Sir Thomas Browne wisely said, 'There is nothing strictly immortal but immortality'.

II. This is a summons to the immediate presence of God. (1) To 'God the *Judge* of all' will the last trumpet summon us. How shall we stand before Him? I pray you, familiarise yourselves with that ultimate point of view. (2) The God to whose immediate presence the trumpet will summon us will be 'the rewarder of all that seek Him'.

III. This is a summons to a glad assembly of saints. Who does not at times ache for such fellowship? And what reunions this will mean!

IV. This is a summons to wonderful revelations. God has his richest revelations yet to make. What glories are laid up in store! We shall never know how truly 'God is love' till we attain the beatific eminences. Lord Tennyson remarked to Bishop Lightfoot, and that saintly scholar endorsed it, that 'the cardinal point of Christianity is the life after death'.

V. This is a summons to unspeakable delights. The glory of Christ will make our cup overflow. We shall see Him as He is. And what a delight deathlessness will be! Sinlessness in ourselves and in all around us. To serve our God with flawless service and with ministry that cannot weary; this will heighten the high joys of glory.

VI. This is a summons of infallible certainty. 'The trumpet *shall* sound.' You cannot escape immortality, but you may lose eternal life.—DINSDALE T. YOUNG, *Messages for Home and Life*, p. 231.

REFERENCES.—XV. 52.—Archbishop Benson's Memorial Sermon for Bishop J. Prince Lee was preached from this text. The Bishop had wished to have upon his tombstone the single Greek word translated in our version "The trumpet shall sound". *Expositor* (4th Series), vol. **x.** p. 345. XV. 53, 54.—*Ibid.* (6th Series), vol. **x.** p. 199. XV. 53-58.—*Ibid.* vol. **iv.** p. 191.

VICTORY!

I COR. XV. 54.

THERE are very few who do not sometime think about the life beyond that which they are living now. It is an instinct of the human race. Death forces itself on us as a universal fact. No traveller but One has come back to describe to us this unknown country. But from the earliest days it pleased God to give to men glimpses of the unseen. It is Christ only Who 'has abolished death, and brought life and immortality to light'. Apart from Christ the future has no gleam of hope. No sure word comes from anywhere else. The world's greatest philosophers have nothing of their own to tell us. One of the best known of modern thinkers, Herbert Spencer, writing to an intimate friend, said: 'My own feeling respecting the ultimate mystery is such that of late years I cannot even try to think of ultimate space without some feeling of terror'. What a contrast to that triumphant cry, 'Death is swallowed up in victory!'

I. This is the hope, 'sure and certain,' with which we lay to rest those loved and cherished here, who have died in the Lord, whether it be some little one whose eyes have hardly opened upon this 'troublesome world,' or whether it be some honoured servant of God who has reached the ripeness of age, and spent many years in doing good. For them death has no sting, for sin in its strength has been conquered by Christ. The condemnation which the holy law adjudged He has borne. The power which sin exerted in us He has overcome, and the joyful chorus of the redeemed will rise : 'Thanks be to God, which giveth us the victory through our Lord Jesus Christ'.

II. The future for the Christian is all victory, but a victory which has had its anticipations here. The Christian's first step to heaven starts with the passage from death to life. He is already in possession of the triumphant life that will last for ever. For him dying is not death. He lives, he works, he hopes as one in sight of eternal victory. And this gives energy, stability, yea! perpetuity to all work that is done for God.—H. E. Fox, *The Record*, vol. xxvII. p. 476.

REFERENCE.—XV. 54.—*Expositor* (4th Series), vol. iii. p. 117.

CONCERNING THE COLLECTION

'O death, where is thy sting? O grave, where is thy victory? The sting of death is sin, and the strength of sin is the law : but thanks be to God which giveth us the victory through our Lord Jesus Christ. . . . Now concerning the collection.'—I COR. XV. 55 ; XVI. I.

THE fifteenth chapter of the Epistle to the Corinthians is the country of the springs; the sixteenth opens with a glimpse of the river. The fifteenth is the country of the truth, fundamental Christian truth, in which our personal hopes and triumphs have their birth; with the opening of the sixteenth I catch a glimpse of the shining graces which are the happy issue of the truth.

I. Look away for a moment to the springs. The Apostle is joyfully recounting our hopes and triumphs in Christ. 'O death, where is thy sting?' To those in Christ death has no poison, only honey; its burden is sweetness rather than pain. I may lift my tearful eyes in hope, and gaze along the 'living way' into the prepared palace of the ageless life. And what is the import of this? It means that the possibilities of the individual life have been raised to the powers of the infinite. That is the glorious burden of chapter fifteen, the emancipation and enlargement of life in the risen Christ. Now see the beautiful succession, taking its rise in the last verse of chapter fifteen and emerging clearly into view in the first verse of chapter sixteen. The larger life is succeeded, say rather accompanied, by larger living.

II. What was the occasion of this collection? There was a large body of poor Jews in Jerusalem who had eagerly received the Christ of God. For this they were excommunicated, outlawed, banned. But Christianity fostered humanity; faith evoked philanthropy; and from their fellow-believers in wider fields there flowed a steady stream of beneficence to alleviate their distress. The birth of Christianity was the birth of a new philanthropy.

III. It is this vital association that I desire to emphasise. Truth and activity are related as springs and rivers. If we want the one to be brimming, we must not ignore the other. That was the cardinal and all-determining weakness of Robert Elsmere. He denied the Resurrection, and all the specious and heartening truths which gather about it; and out of the dry, vacuous heart of its negation sought to educe a river of benevolent energy for the permanent enrichment of the race. 'I will open rivers in *high* places!' and only when we have the 'high places' in our life, the enthroned and sovereign truths of atonement and resurrection, and the sublime and awful prospect of an unveiled immortality, only then will our life be a land of springs, musical with the sound of many waters, flowing with gladsome rivers to cheer and refresh the children of men.—J. H. JOWETT, *Apostolic Optimism*, p. 156.

REFERENCES.—XV. 55.—J. Budgen, *Parochial Sermons*, vol. i. p. 50. J. Bolton, *Selected Sermons* (2nd Series), p. 23. H. S. Holland, *Vital Values*, p. 179. *Expositor* (4th Series), vol. iii. p. 120 ; *ibid.* (6th Series), vol. v. p. 87. XV. 55-58. —Spurgeon, *Sermons*, vol. li. No. 2929.

LAW, SIN, AND DEATH

'The sting of death is sin ; and the strength of sin is the law. But thanks to God, which giveth us the victory through our Lord Jesus Christ.'—1 COR. xv. 56, 57.

I. IT is sin that makes death terrible. 'The sting of death is sin.' We are all in a measure afraid of it. We try to forget it, but the endeavour is vain. I do not say, nor does the Apostle mean, that there is no bitterness at all in death save that which the sense of guilt brings. He means that the keenest torture of death, its poison, venom, sting, is found in the fact of sin. It is the guilty heart and the troubled conscience that clothe the last enemy with the garments of horror. We read that 'by one man sin entered into the world, and death by sin ; and so death passed upon all men, because all have sinned'. Does it mean that if we had known no sin we should have known no death, that we should have lived for ever upon this earth, and been spared what we call the final trial? No, it cannot mean that. It means that sin made death what it is to us—gave it its dread power and torture ; and that if we had known no guilt we should have faced it, and passed through it without fear—perhaps welcoming it as a weary man welcomes sleep.

II. The torturing power of sin is given by the law. 'The strength of sin is the law.' The Apostle does not mean here simply the Jewish law—the law embodied in Old Testament precepts and commandments—but that larger moral law of God which is written everywhere—that solemn, 'thou shalt not' and 'thou shalt,' which we hear continually in every speech and language, which is written in nature and history and all the books we read, which is stamped upon our very constitution and engraven on our heart of hearts.

III. The crowning fact, the sweet everlasting promise and assurance of the victory. 'Thanks be to God, which giveth us the victory through our Lord Jesus Christ.' What is this victory? (1) It is the lifting up of the awful weight of sin—the lightening and removal of all life's guilty and oppressive memories at the feet of a forgiving Father ; the deliverance, which comes from the cross ; the sweet, glad word of acceptance and pardon, which, like a burst of morning sunlight, sweeps all the vapours and darkness of our night away. (2) Then it is the bringing of the awful dreaded law into harmony with our will, or our will into harmony with the law. We can do it through Him who strengtheneth us. (3) And, lastly, it is the clearing of all doubt.—J. G. GREENHOUGH, *The Divine Artist*, p. 125.

'The sting of death is sin ; and the strength of sin is the law. But thanks be to God which giveth us the victory through our Lord Jesus Christ.'—1 COR. xv. 56, 57.

THESE are the words carved on the mural tablet in Haworth Church, below the name of Charlotte Brontë.

'WHEN the day that he must go hence was come,' says Bunyan, of *Mr. Valiant-for-Truth*, 'many accompanied him to the River-side, into which as he went he said, *Death, where is thy sting?* And as he went down deeper he said, *Grave, where is thy victory?* So he passed over, and all the Trumpets sounded for him on the other side.'

REFERENCES.—XV. 56, 57.—H. P. Liddon, *Sermons on Some Words of St. Paul*, p. 154. Spurgeon, *Sermons*, vol. i. No. 23.

VICTORY OVER SIN

'Victory through our Lord Jesus Christ.'—1 COR. xv. 57.

THIS fifteenth chapter of the First Epistle to the Corinthians was written to establish our faith in the resurrection of the body. But before the close of the chapter the Apostle recollects that there is another still more deadly foe, a foe which gives its sting to death itself, and that foe is sin. Sin, too, must be overcome. Now, we make no secret of the fact that life is a battle. The world, the flesh, and the devil are constantly assaulting us. We see our enemies advance against us in three battalions. But over them all we are told there is victory through our Lord Jesus Christ. Now how are we to gain the victory?

I. First of all, with regard to the devil, if you turn to the twelfth chapter of the Revelation of St. John, and the eleventh verse, you will see there how victory over him is won. There is a full-length portrait of him in the ninth verse. (1) How are you to overcome him as the tempter? You will see in the eleventh verse. 'They overcame him by the blood of the Lamb.' It is the only way in which you can really gain the victory over sin. (2) He is called 'the accuser of our brethren'. When he finds that his allurements will not cause us to fall, he will begin to accuse us, he will accuse us of sins which we have committed, and so he would try and keep us away from God. (3) When he finds that neither temptation nor accusation will drive them from God, he tries persecution. By the blood of the Lamb we put the great enemy to flight.

II. Then there is the world. How are we to overcome the world? In the First Epistle of St. John, the fifth chapter, and the fourth verse: 'Whatsoever is born of God overcometh the world: and this is the victory that overcometh the world, even our faith'. It is your faith which will overcome the world. The world comes and tries to tempt you by the things which are seen. How are you to overcome? You overcome by your faith, you overcome by seeing that the real things are the unseen things, not the things of time and sense.

III. And how are you to overcome the flesh, the third great enemy? In the First Epistle of St. Paul to the Corinthians, in the sixth chapter, and the nineteenth verse, speaking of those same sins of the flesh, he says: 'What, know ye not that your body is the temple of the Holy Ghost which is in you, which ye have of God? And ye are not your own.' This is the only power by which you can overcome the flesh—by realising the body as the temple of the Holy Ghost which dwells in you.—E. A. STUART, *The One Mediator and other Sermons*, p. 177.

THE VICTORY OVER SIN
(For Easter Even)

'Thanks be to God, which giveth us the victory through our Lord Jesus Christ.'—1 COR. xv. 57.

As we look to-day upon the empty cross and by faith anticipate the empty tomb of to-morrow we sing a note of triumph, for the Lord Jesus by His Death and Resurrection 'giveth us the victory' over sin.

I. **Sham Victories.**—Only let me here warn you not to mistake for a victory what is not one. It may be that a sin may be prevented or arrested only (a) *by some human consideration;* by a fear, for instance, of punishment, or of pain, or of earthly loss —without any higher motive. Then the amendment may be the result, again (b) *of a better education,* or a higher taste, or some change of outward association. Or, it may be, that a sin may be only (c) *driven in.* It may be as real before God in its latent condition, quite out of sight of man—perhaps, only in a thought—as it was in its overt act. Or it may be, that what appeared the subjugation of the sin is only (d) *the substituting of one sin for another.* It often occurs—and it never occurs without great danger of deception—it often occurs that a young man abandons the wicked indulgences of his passion, but it is only to take up the pride of position, and the display of circumstance, which all minister still to self, and become equal vices of his manhood. The fact is, the heart of a man, and the life of a man, has many phases; but if the love of God be not there, however man may judge, the one phase is not really nearer to God than the other; but in God's sight they are all equally dark. Call not such things as those victories.

II. **Real Victories.**—Real victories lie in a pro-

gression; the first must be within, over some spring of conduct within the mind. I do not say but that to conquer a wrong action will reflect upon the motive from which the action came. And the inner life is often affected by the outer. But no real victory is gained until there is a victory within the heart. The real place where the battle is fought, and the victory won, is within. It is in the deep places of the heart; it is in private exercise; it is in closet wrestlings; it is in ordered prayers; it is in the resolute struggles of the mind, put forth in the very moments of temptation; it is in communion with God. No victory that will stand—no victory worth the name—is ever gained without this. Then comes what meets the eye, what looks so great, what men talk about, and what men admire. Of all the rest they know nothing. But the true battle was fought before any man saw the victory.

III. **Aids to Victory.**—To help you to attain these victories let me suggest one or two things.

(a) *Make great use of the power of God's Word.* Our blessed Lord was pleased, each time, to foil and beat back the wicked one by 'It is written'. By His quotations from Deuteronomy, Christ brought the force of truth to countervail the moral evil. Hence the importance of the daily study of God's Word. No one ever conquered sin without it. You must be apt in the use of the Bible; and have ready to your hand, at the right moment, the right verse and the right thought. Before that light, properly brought to bear, darkness—and all sin is darkness—darkness will flee away.

(b) *Cherish the faintest whispers of the Spirit in your heart.* They are always coming. Honour them when they come—they will increase. Trifle with them—they will go away. When you have a better thought, then and there thank God for it. Turn it to some account. Do something. The enemy may be, and will be, more violent with you, because you do this; so also will the Spirit grow dominant. 'When the enemy cometh in like a flood the Spirit of the Lord shall lift up a standard against him.'

(c) *Realise that you are in Christ,* and Christ in you. Before the presence of Christ, when He walked this earth, the antagonism of all evil could never stand. It owned His higher power, and went into the very dust. Do not doubt, before the majesty of the Lord Jesus Christ in you, there will be the same effect; and that it will be strong and mighty, to the 'pulling down of the strongholds of sin and Satan'.

(d) *Never forget that 'this kind goes not forth but by prayer and fasting'.* It is the highest work which is given man to do—self-victory—for it is the basis of every other work in the world. And you must not wonder if the effort be a very severe one. But it is a matter in which God especially blesses great efforts. Have yours always in hand. Fight with your own heart, as with something that has to be mastered. Be particular about the little things, for there, indeed, the field is lost or won. Make each success the argument for another. Grapple with your besetting sin. And give God no rest till He lays it dead at your feet. It will then be in God's hand. He must do it. The means that you have may be very weak ; the pebble small, the sling simple, the arm young, but the prayer will go straight, and the giant will fall.

But these victories had never been except for a living union with Christ. The victory is His and His alone. By His Cross and Passion, and by His glorious Resurrection, He will deliver, and so with St. Paul we triumph and thank God for this glorious victory.

REFERENCES.—XV. 57.—F. D. Maurice, *Sermons*, vol. iii. p. 299. G. G. Bradley, *Christian World Pulpit*, vol. lvii. p. 266.

EASTER DAY
'Therefore, my beloved brethren, be ye stedfast, unmoveable, always abounding in the work of the Lord, forasmuch as ye know that your labour is not in vain in the Lord.'—1 COR. xv. 58.

ALL Christians, East and West, all those nearer to us at home from whom we have sometimes to deplore our unhappy division, agree in this great fundamental truth of the Christian religion—'Christ is risen indeed'.

I. And while all Christians agree that Christ is risen, so do they mean by this Resurrection that Christ had died for us, and by His Resurrection has proved that He was the Son of God, as He had said. So St. Paul understood the doctrine of the Resurrection. It proved Jesus to be the Son of God with power. To-day, when as Christians we keep the great festival of the Resurrection, we declare our belief that Jesus was the Son of God, that He died for us and rose again for our justification. What can we want more? 'If God be for us, who can be against us? If He spared not His own Son, but delivered Him up for us all, how shall He not, with Him, freely give us all things. It is God that justifieth, Who is he that condemneth? It is Christ that died, yea rather that is risen again, Who is even at the right hand of God, Who also maketh intercession for us.'

The Resurrection shows that Christ was the Son of God ; thus the Son of God died for us. Here, then, is pardon for all our sins. Here is pardon and peace for us all. But there is more. Christ not only died, but is risen again, and so there is new life and hope for us. 'Because I live,' the Saviour had said, 'ye shall live also.' Easter Day opens a new fountain of life for us. 'Christ is risen from the dead,' and not only so, but is 'become the first-fruits of them that slept. For as in Adam all die, even so in Christ shall all be made alive.'

II. By the Resurrection of Christ we are to receive new life from Him. As to-day we think of the risen, living Christ, we ought to see in Him the fulfilment of His own words. 'I am the vine, ye are the branches.' When we think of the risen Saviour to-day, we should try and picture Him to ourselves as the true Vine, and ourselves as the branches drawing our life from Him. We need not trouble ourselves by seeking to explain exactly the way in which this Christ-life lives in us. Some great facts we know, and a sufficiency of results has been given us to enable us to trust in hope. The whole effect of the Incarnation of the Son of God towards humanity is not to be seen in this life. Our life in this world down here now is but a very small and imperfect part of the whole results of the risen life of the Saviour. 'Our life is hid with Christ in God.' He is not where once He was, in the manger in the stable at Bethlehem. He is not now working in a little village shop at Nazareth. He is not now hanging on the cross on Calvary, but He is risen, He has ascended and is on the throne in the full enjoyment of the love and glory of the Father, angels, and archangels, and all the hosts of heaven worshipping Him. And that is where we are to be, in the place which the Saviour is preparing for us on the throne with Himself. That is the true end, the real flower and fruit of the Christ-life which we derive from the true Vine. But this world down here is, as it were, too cold a climate for us to see what the real beauty of the fruit of the Vine is. We can, as it were, only see the stem and the leaves. But on Easter Day we do well to reassure ourselves of the promise that we shall one day see Him as He is, and that we shall be like Him.

III. St. Paul, in the long chapter of which this text is the close, had been proving the fact of the Resurrection of Christ, and then he tells us what, in his mind, should be the practical conclusion.

'Therefore,' he says, 'therefore my beloved brethren, be ye stedfast, unmoveable, always abounding in the work of the Lord, forasmuch as ye know that your work is not in vain in the Lord.'

To be steadfast, unmoveable. This is the first great lesson for us to-day, to continue in this faith of our Lord's Resurrection, grounded and settled, and not to be moved away from the hope of the Gospel, which we have, as it were, heard again to-day in the words, 'The Lord is risen indeed'. To renew our act of faith, to stand firm, and abide its results. Our mental and spiritual attitude then should be one of trustfulness and hope. 'O Israel trust in the Lord, for with the Lord there is mercy and with Him is plenteous redemption.'

'ALWAYS'
'Always abounding in the work of the Lord.'—1 COR. xv. 58.

'ALWAYS' is a keyword of Christianity. Other religions make concessions to human nature. They allow periods of outbreak and unrestraint. If you will keep the law 360 days in the year, you can have five days to work your own will. You will be set free from one commandment if only you will obey the rest. Even in the corrupted forms of Christianity this tendency to allow some occasional relaxation may be found. No doubt it is very congenial to human nature. No doubt it helps to make the acceptance of a religion very much easier. We are not so unwilling to conform at times if times of license are given to us. But Christianity makes no exception, permits of no deviation. It takes its law and its power from the presence of Christ, Who is with us always, all the days, and all the hours of the days, through all the years of vivid experience, with their every grief and joy. Christ Himself is never absent, never leaves us alone, never loses us from His sight, never gives us leave to go astray even for an instant.

I. So confident of its power is Christianity that it carries its perpetual demands into every region of labour and thought. Yes, to every cave, every mountain height of every region. Thus we are to be 'always' abounding in the work of the Lord'. Has Christianity, then, no place for rest? If there is one thing above another in this weary world that we claim and crave, it is the privilege of rest. If six days of the week we labour and do our work, then does not the seventh belong to us? If we toil for eleven months of the year, do we not need the twelfth for play? Does Christ grudge us rest? No, verily, for it was as the Rest-giver that He came. Did He not preach His rest in the days of His flesh to a company of the poorest and most enslaved, wearied with labour, worn with sorrow? Did He not mercifully say to His disciples, 'Rest awhile'? Yes; but He bound together labour and rest as all the work of the Lord. When He rested Himself, He set the pattern of resting for His people. 'Jesus being wearied with His journey, sat thus on the well.' Sat *thus*. It may be, and it is sometimes, just as much the work of the Lord to rest as to labour. What is constant is our obligation to abound in the work of the Lord, to toil and to cease from toiling in His presence, by His strength, under His eye.

II. More than that, Christianity enters into the region of mood and feeling. It seems as if that world could never be brought under complete command. Our actions, our words we may recall; but who is to control emotion, who can answer for the moods that come and go, independently, as it seems, of our will? It is written, 'Rejoice in the Lord always, and again I say rejoice'. But how hard that is, hard for all, specially hard for us, for of all the emotions the emotion which our nation feels least is that of pure joy. It has almost died from us, save in the case of the very young. Christianity does not say that we are not to sorrow. What it forbids is the sorrow that is without hope. That sorrow is not to be indulged in for a moment. Christ says, Whoever comes and goes, I am with you —rejoice in Me.

III. Again, says the Apostle, we are always confident. Does this mean that the Apostle was a stranger to depression and fear? No servant of Christ has ever escaped these, has ever failed to know that strange sinking of the heart in the face of hostile powers, with which most of us are familiar. All our fathers passed under the cloud, and all passed through the sea. What he means is that he was confident, even as we are to be confident, about the issue. Even if his foes drove him away they sent him to the Lord.

If my bark sink, 'tis to another sea.

The wildest winds could but toss him to Christ's breast. We are never to lose this confidence for ourselves, nor ever to lose our assurance, nor ever to despair of the wonderful Church of Christ, nor falter in our faith that the Redeemer's victory is won and sure.—W. ROBERTSON NICOLL, *Sunday Evening*, p. 119.

HOPE AND SERVICE

'Therefore, my beloved brethren, be ye stedfast, unmoveable, always abounding in the work of the Lord, forasmuch as ye know that your labour is not in vain in the Lord.' —1 COR. xv. 58.

I. How does the Lord come to us in the matter of the revelation of the doctrine of rising again from the dead? The Lord has one great way of coming; the Lord comes by parable, by symbol, by little insufficient parallels and analogies; yet He always says to us, Do not make too much of these; there is falsehood in exaggeration; go no further than the parable invites you to go, for the parable simply indicates the direction and tells you to move along that high and ever-heightening line. This is the method of Jesus Christ; He cannot tell us poor finite struggling creatures the whole mystery of God and His purpose, but He says, the kingdom of God is like unto—— After that we have to study the symbol or picture, always taking care not to drive it with vehemence and feverish excitement, but to wait where it waits, and to look up where it looks up, and to avoid what it avoids, leaving the mystery, yet partially illuminating it. Are we in the Divine school, poor little infirm purblind scholars? Enough to be in it! The question is not how far we have got in our learning, but are we learning of the right teacher, are we in the right mood, and are we reading the right book? After that, I repeat, all matters of detail and mutability will arrange and adjust themselves to the main purpose of the revelation of the kingdom whose throne is an everlasting throne.

It is so that the Apostle deals with this doctrine of the Resurrection. He says, The Resurrection is like unto this little green bud in April. He does not say, This is the Resurrection, but, This is a parable of the rising-again; all these black branches have been sleeping under the snow for a month or two or more, but now there is a warmth in the air, there is a sense of awakening life, and the kingdom of the Resurrection is like this little green bud. But does one bud make the spring? Yes, it does. They say one swallow does not make a summer. They lie. The swallow makes no mistakes about the summer; if you have seen one, you have seen all; if you have seen one real living green blade, you have seen the spring, and he who has seen the spring has seen the summer with all her chaplet and all her flowing robe of beauty, and has felt on his cheek the soft breath of her mouth. We make a great mistake in not enlarging the parables. As the butterfly came out of that poor little home, so shall thy better self clothe its nakedness with a house that is from heaven. There is a natural beauty and there is a spiritual beauty, and all things are growing and growing to higher meanings and wider applications. O man, believe it, and stand up a host a thousand strong in the almightiness of God!

II. The Apostle, having lifted up our minds into these high figures and prophecies, says, Now let us return to our work: 'Therefore'. 'Therefore' in this instance is an emphatic word; it brings together lines and threads of reasoning and illustration, and it presents the whole argument in the form of business, activity, service. Therefore, because all these things shall be, because we shall triumph over the grave and taunt the enemy that we feared; therefore, up, work, serve, repeat all you have done for God through Christ with a heartier energy and a fuller sufficiency of strength and enthusiasm. Hope is to end in service, is to be the very inspiration of service, and is to be the guarantee of the reward of service. Christianity with its high levels, its great wide firmaments and great doctrine, has also its earthly duties, its domesticities, its neighbourliness, its willingness to help and bless all within reach. This is the test of all true religion.

III. The great inspiration of service is hope, and that hope we find in the great argument of the Apostle Paul in this very chapter. There is not one pessimistic tone in the whole argument. The Apostle faces his great subject and conquers it by the grace of Christ. He says, I am going to talk, not about death only, but about Resurrection; not about the law only, but about Christ; and I will show you how we have all the promises on our side, and I am going to sound a long rousing bugle note that will call men back from their pessimism and their distress and give them heart again. If you have no hope you cannot work with any real good and lasting effect. A preacher cannot do so if he is preaching to indifferent people. The merchantman cannot be his true and strongest self if he is always on the sunless side of the wall. Put into a man the spirit of hope, and you give him strength, nerve, assurance that all will be right by-and-by.—JOSEPH PARKER, *City Temple Pulpit*, vol. iv. p. 2.

THE STABILITY OF FAITH

'Wherefore, my beloved brethren, be ye stedfast, unmoveable, always abounding in the work of the Lord, forasmuch as ye know that your labour is not in vain in the Lord.'—1 COR. xv. 58.

STEDFAST *and unmoveable*. One is almost tempted to ask if these words have any application to present times and conditions. They seem rather to carry us back into a world which we have left far behind, a dull, old-fashioned, antiquated world in which all things were stationary, and the customs of each generation were handed down to its successor, and men were contented to follow the light which had guided their fathers, jogging on in the old paths, and setting their faces against all innovations and changes. There is little of that left now. The world in which we have our being is perpetually on the move. We are told that there is no longer any fixity in religious beliefs; that cloudy and obscure problems have taken the place of firm assurances; that men are drifting away from the moorings to which they were securely anchored, and that the very Church has been driven from its solid ground to shifting sands. Were this true, which I do not for a moment admit, save as an extravagant exaggeration, it would not be greatly surprising. It would only show that religion is affected by the temper of the times, and is feeling somewhat the spirit of restlessness and change which is heaving, wrestling, shaking, and disturbing all things.

I. You cannot point to any department or sphere of life in which there is stability of thought, unity of mind, and settled convictions. All questions are in a state of solution, all opinions are seething in a melting-pot ready to come out with a brand-new face. The air is thick with the sounds of clamour, dissensions, and debate. Old policies, old principles, old watchwords and shibboleths, are being tried in the fire and found wanting. Religion is bound to be touched and influenced by this deep and widespread unrest. It cannot be insensible to the heavings which are going on all around it, yet I venture to say that its vital faith and root-principles are less disturbed by them than any other region of human thought. People who are incessantly talking about the unsettlement in Christian beliefs forget the greater unsettlement which is everywhere else, and they make incomparably more of Christian divisions and uncertainties than the facts justify. The wish is often father to the thought. They see only what they desire to see. They are men whose own convictions are unsettled, and always have been, and they like to believe that their own minds represent the general mind. They are for the most part men who stand outside the Church, or hang on the extreme fringe of it. They see only its surface movements, and do not read its deeper heart and steadfast purpose. In fact, the great marching host of Christ's people knows very little about the unsettlement which is everywhere advertised. It is too busy in the Master's work to take heed to every changeful wind that blows, and too calmly confident of its faith to be made nervous by every shout and whisper of alarm. The bulk of real and earnest Christian people are steadfast, if not immovable.

II. We all move with the movements of the age; we cannot help it. We feel the pulse of the human throng, and throb with it. We move as an oak-tree moves when it grows and expands, and its branches are shaken and pruned by the storm, but the roots remain steadfast and unshaken. The whole Church has moved in the last twenty-five years, just as you have moved. But there is nothing in the range of modern things which has been so little shaken in its vital beliefs and foundations as Christ's Church and the Christian faith. All the grand certainties which are given in this chapter abide with us. There are few whole-hearted Christians who cannot say, with St. Paul, 'I have kept the faith'. There are few who cannot say, with Jesus, 'All that thou hast given Me I have kept, save that which had to be lost because untrue'. Where everything else has changed, the great Christian beliefs remain steadfast and immovable.

III. And really it is most desirable, and even imperative, that we should have a measure of steadfastness in these things, if we are stirred and shaken in all things else. The just man lives by his faith, he cannot afford to have it always in a state of transition. He cannot afford to have it always simmering in the melting-pot, and wondering how it will come out at the next stage. Life is not long enough for that business. It is crucifying to have the mind always on tenterhooks and to have the heart always unsettling itself to make a new settlement. Some people are always proclaiming the glory of uncertainty and the surpassing excellence of doubt. I do not covet that sort of glory, or aspire to that sort of excellence.

A man who would do life's work well and help others to do it must fix himself on certain great beliefs and regard them as steadfast and immovable. He cannot waste his energies in perpetual re-examination and re-testing and dissecting of them. We ought to be certain that there is an eternal future, a personal immortality, and a judgment to come which no man can escape. We should be assured that the great Christian verities cannot be shaken, and be determined that, so far as we are concerned, they shall not be shaken; that the Bible, on the whole, is to be trusted as God's revelation and our guide; that Christ is our Divine, unerring Master, whose words will abide though all things else dissolve, and that, following Him, we have clear light for the earthly journey and a safe Pilot through the dark unknown beyond.—J. G. GREENHOUGH, *The Mind of Christ in St. Paul*, p. 56.

REFERENCES.—XV. 58.—Spurgeon, *Sermons*, vol. xix. No. 1111. G. A. Sowter, *From Heart to Heart*, p. 186. H. Woodcock, *Sermon Outlines* (1st Series), p. 60. J. M. Neale, *Sermons Preached in Sackville College Chapel*, vol. iv. p. 156. Bishop Gore, *Christian World Pulpit*, vol. lvii. p. 377. Archbishop Davidson, *ibid.* vol. lix. p. 67. A. H. Moncur Sime, *ibid.* vol. liv. p. 38. XV. 63.—W. J. Knox-Little, *ibid.* vol. xlix. p. 267. XVI. 1.—*Expositor* (7th Series), vol. vi. p. 340. XVI. 1-8.—*Ibid.* (4th Series), vol. viii. p. 323; *ibid.* vol. ix. p. 259. XVI. 2.—*Ibid.* (6th Series), vol. ix. p. 367. XVI. 4.—*Ibid.* vol. i. p. 406. XVI. 5.—*Ibid.* (5th Series), vol. i. p. 387; *ibid.* (6th Series), vol. x. p. 441. XVI. 8, 9.—*Ibid.* vol. xi. p. 207.

'A great door and effectual is opened unto me.'—1 COR. XVI. 9.

In Wesley's *Journal* for 1st February, 1736, written as he approached the shores of Georgia, the following entry appears: 'We spoke with a ship of Carolina; and Wednesday 4, came within soundings. About noon, the trees were visible from the masts, and in the afternoon from the main deck. In the evening lesson were these words: "A great door and effectual is opened". O let no one shut it!'

REFERENCES.—XVI. 9.—*Expositor* (4th Series), vol. ii. p. 148; *ibid.* (7th Series), vol. vi. p. 278.

'Now if Timotheus come, see that he may be with you without fear.'—1 COR. XVI. 10, 11.

THIS was the passage from which John Angell James preached at Carr's Lane Meeting, Birmingham, on the Sunday before R. W. Dale became his colleague (1853). Writing to Dale, Mr. James said: 'There is little ground for the fear mentioned in the text, but I have thought it not unreasonable to require for you a warm-hearted, confidential reception'.

'Let no man therefore despise him.'—1 COR. XVI. 11.

'IT is of the nature of wisdom,' says Maeterlinck, 'to despise nothing; indeed, in this world, there is perhaps only one thing truly contemptible, and that thing is contempt itself.'

TRUE MANLINESS

'Quit you like men, be strong.'—1 COR. XVI. 13.

EMERSON says that the main enterprise of the world, both for splendour and extent, is the upbuilding of a *man*, and he is undoubtedly correct. The German philosopher Kant fully endorses the eloquent American's sentiments when he says to his students, 'Take humanity for an end'—that is, perfect yourselves, in order to be the better able to perfect mankind. The true man is the man likest Jesus and nearest God. Let us now study a few of the world's Ideals of Manliness.

I. For years the Athletic man was the Ideal. Ancient Sparta paid special attention to the growth of strong, sinewy, muscular men. But such an ideal was too animalistic, for it ignored the solemn fact that man was vastly more than a body of clay. Man is more than body. Man was not made for pleasure, but pleasure for man.

II. For years the Ascetic man, or Anchorite, was the Ideal. We are quite ready to believe that these anchorites meant well. They hoped to escape from their sins by escaping from the world; but you cannot get away from your soul by crossing the Atlantic or plunging into the Saharan desert. Your soul is ever with you! Have nothing to do with the anchorite style of religion. As Sydney Smith quaintly says: 'Never wear a face that is a breach of the peace'. The anchorite ideal is a failure, condemned by the unanimous voice of history.

III. For years the Patriot was the Ideal man. True manhood meant absolute consecration to one's country. Patriotism we admire; but it has its perils. Like sectarianism it may narrow our horizon, and it may degenerate into clannishness, and of all narrownesses, that is certainly one of the worst.

IV. For years the Intellectual man was the popular Ideal. Plato, Socrates, Homer, and others were considered the pattern-men. The mere intellectualist is not a full man, but a fragment. The true man is intellect *plus* heart-power and conscience-power. Byron, and Burns, and Shelley were intellectual stars of rare brightness; but who will dare say that they were ideal men?

V. For years the Civic man was the Ideal. The Roman ideal was true citizenship. The State was everything and the individual nothing ; and a system that crushes the individual can never produce the pattern-manhood. Citizenship, without moral principle at the root of it, is a hollow sham, and the subsequent decline and fall of Rome was the best evidence of the fact.

VI. For years the Judaic man was the Ideal. But the Jewish ideal was not the highest, for the Jews were too fond of *drilling* men into manhood. They paid too little attention to inwardness, and too much to circumcisions, and washings, and purifications. If you want to see the difference between the ideal Jew and the ideal Christian, just compare Mount Sinai with Mount Hattin, and the Decalogue with the Beatitudes.

VII. But we are proud to say that the Ideal man of to-day is the Christ's man, that is, the Christian. Diogenes could not find his man in Athens ; but we have discovered our Man in this old book, and His name is Jesus ! (1) Be magnanimous like Jesus. (2) Be courageous like Jesus. (3) Be sincere with Jesus. (4) Be pure like Jesus.—J. OSSIAN DAVIES, *The Dayspring from on High*, p. 145.

SPIRITUAL STRENGTH

' Watch ye, stand fast in the faith, quit you like men, be strong.'
                    I COR. XVI. 13.

WE are conscious of our weakness, our need is strength, but how shall we attain to it ? Elsewhere St. Paul, using the same military metaphors that we have seen here, tells his people how that strength is to be obtained. 'Be strong in the Lord, and in the power of His might.' From the words of the Apostle two things are clear.

I. The Struggle with Evil. — First he regards every man as engaged in a separate personal struggle with a real spiritual power of evil. It is not merely the evil that is inherent in his own nature. It is something more than that. It is an organised host of wickedness. It is, in fact, all that we mean when we say in the Catechism, 'The devil and all his works'. I know, of course, that the devil is often made, in the expression of Bishop Butler, a subject of mirth and ridicule ; but our Lord's language is utterly meaningless unless it signified that there is a real spiritual power of evil. He always seemed to find it hanging on the frontiers of His own life, tempting all along the way, especially in the hours of weakness and sorrow. May we not also appeal to the experience of spiritual people, of all those who have entered with all their power into the personal struggle against evil ? Is it not a fact that the more earnestly they have engaged in it the more they have been sensible of struggle with a real spiritual power, force, kingdom, method of evil ? Nay, may we not say of ourselves, is it not our own experience in the darkest hours of temptation, when the worst thoughts come, when the most awful strain is put upon us, do we then find it difficult to believe in the working of a personal power ? Nothing can be more foolish than to under-rate the power with which we are engaged, or may be engaged.

II. Sources of Spiritual Strength.—And then, secondly, after insisting upon the reality of this power, this kingdom of evil or of darkness, St. Paul insists upon every man's need of Divine strength. The Apostle would say, when he says here, 'Be strong,' as he says elsewhere, 'Be strong in the Lord'. Do not go unready, unprepared, unarmed, into the struggle against evil. Put on the whole armour of God, and remember that the putting on of the spiritual armour is not a matter for one or two occasions, however great they may be, in a lifetime ; it has to be continued from the beginning to the end.

Let me remind you of a few of the means by which we seek to attain that spiritual grace, that Divine help, without which the spiritual combat will certainly be a failure.

(*a*) *Prayer*. First of all, there is the weapon of prayer. Here we have always before us the example of our Lord Himself. What is prayer ? All of you know it is not a mere asking for something, above all it is a contact of spirit with spirit, of person with person ; it is the contact with God Himself, putting ourselves in touch with Him. If you doubt prayer, or the power of prayer, just remember for a moment, again in this instance also, what the experiences of spiritual men have been, how they have found prayer to be this very power in their lives, how they have proved it, how they have lived by it.

(*b*) *The devotional reading of the Scriptures.* Or, again, there is the devotional use of the Holy Scriptures. This use of the Holy Scriptures is much more rare than it used to be, and the Bible is much less read than it used to be, even by good, churchgoing, religious people. No doubt there are reasons for this. One reason is the enormous multiplication of every form of literature, especially ephemeral literature. People who read four or five newspapers a day have no time obviously to read the New or the Old Testament. Partly it may be caused by what is supposed to be the unsettlement of the basis of Holy Scripture. Most people hear something, if they know little, about Higher Criticism, but we may be sure that whatever has happened to the Holy Scriptures nothing has happened to make their devotional value less than it used to be. Questions of date or authorship do not really affect spiritual power. Experience shows still, as it used to show, that the Holy Scriptures can make men wise unto salvation.

(*c*) *The Holy Communion.* Or once more, there is the Supper of the Lord, or the Holy Communion. It ought not to be necessary now for one to say that the Holy Communion is not, what it used so often to be regarded as, a sort of mark or test of superiority. Believe me, it is not for strong men, but for weak men, for those who know and feel and realise their own weakness. Hesitate before you pass it by, before you let it go.

'Quit you like men.'—I COR. XVI. 13.

'IN Italy,' says Emerson, Napoleon 'sought for men, and found none. "Good God," he said, "how rare men are! There are eighteen millions in Italy, and I have with difficulty found two — Dandolo and Melzi."'

A DEPRESSION possessed him which he could not shake off. What had he to show, after all, for these fifty odd years of life granted to him? He feared his religion had walked in silver slippers, and would so walk to the end. Could it then, in any true and vital sense, be reckoned religion at all? Gross sins had never exercised any attraction over him? What virtue was there, then, in being innocent of gross sin? But to those other sins—sins of defective moral courage in speech and action, sins arising from over-fastidiousness—had he not yielded freely? Was he not a spiritual valetudinarian? He feared so. Offered, in the Eternal Mercy, endless precious opportunities of service, he had been too weak, too timorous, too slothful, to lay hold on them.—LUCAS MALET, in *Sir Richard Calmady* (bk. III. ch. IV.).

'ONE comes across human beings at times,' says Maxim Gorky, 'with complex characters, so that whatever name one applies to them seems a fitting one, only the one word "man" seems inapplicable to them.'

' Be strong.'—1 COR. XVI. 13.

CHARLES KINGSLEY wrote these two words once in answer to a question, 'What is your favourite motto or proverb?' And, when Dean Stanley preached his funeral sermon in Westminster Abbey, from this text, he observed that 'There were three main lessons of his character and career which may be summed up in the three parts of the apostolic farewell, "Watch ye; quit you like men and be strong; stand fast in the faith,"' adding that 'amidst all the wavering inconstancy of our time, he called upon the men of his generation with a steadfastness and assured conviction that of itself steadied and reassured the minds of those for whom he spoke, "to stand fast in the faith".'

REFERENCES.—XVI. 13.—J. Keble, *Miscellaneous Sermons*, p. 487. C. Neil, *Christian World Pulpit*, vol. xliv. p. 157. C. D. Bell, *The Name Above Every Name*, p. 111. F. W. Farrar, *Christian World Pulpit*, vol. xliv. p. 353, and vol. xlvi. p. 65. H. J. Wilmot-Buxton, *Sunday Sermonettes for a Year*, p. 210. W. J. Hills, *Sermons and Addresses*, p. 63. A. P. Stanley, *Sermons on Special Occasions*, p. 184. D. Macleod, *Christian World Pulpit*, vol. xlvi. p. 78. J. B. Brown, *Aids to the Development of the Divine Life*, No. iii. D. L. Moody, *The Fulness of the Gospel*, p. 72. *Expositor* (7th Series), vol. v. p. 270.

'Watch ye, stand fast in the faith . . . let all your things be done with charity.'—1 COR. XVI. 13, 14.

COLERIDGE concludes his first set of essays in the *Friend* with an appeal for moderation and forbearance in the prosecution of first reforms. 'A system of fundamental reform will scarcely be effected by massacres mechanised into revolution. We cannot therefore inculcate on the minds of each other too often or with too great earnestness the necessity of inculcating benevolent affections. . . . It is not

enough that we have once swallowed these truths— we must feed on them, as insects on a leaf, till the whole heart be coloured by their qualities, and show its food in even the minutest fibre.

'Finally, in the words of the Apostle!

'Watch you, stand fast in the principles of which ye have been convinced! Quit yourselves like men! Be strong! Yet let all things be done in the spirit of love.'

REFERENCE.—XVI. 13, 14.—A. Maclaren, *Expositions of Holy Scripture—Corinthians*, p. 252.

' Let all that ye do be done in love.'—1 COR. XVI. 14.

WHY does Paul add this word at this point? He has been exhorting the Corinthians to a manly, resolute religion : *stand fast in the faith, quit you like men, be strong*. Why speak of *love* in this connection? Because love is the atmosphere of a robust faith. There is a spurious or inferior type of strength which has firm convictions but insists upon its own opinions or methods without paying sufficient regard to the feelings of other people. This masterful temper is often confounded with true strength of character, and Paul seeks to guard against this misconception. A firm grasp of principle is always apt to be uncharitable. Its temptation is to grow impatient of any defects in the belief or conduct of others, and a trifle hard in its moral judgments. Resolute natures often say and do the right thing, but it is in the wrong spirit. Instead of edifying their fellows, they produce a feeling of irritation. They are difficult to work with. They want echoes, not colleagues, in the church. Their very tenacity of purpose develops an inconsiderateness which tends now and then to make trouble, instead of peace, in the community.

Paul suggests that forbearance and consideration, so far from being a mark of weakness, are an inseparable element of strength. A man who is strong in the faith, full of clear ideas and energy, ought to be strong *in love*, conciliatory, unselfish, forbearing.— JAMES MOFFATT.

'Now, I beseech you, brethren.'—1 COR. XVI. 15, 16.

I COULD not be content, unless I was found in the Exercise of my Gift, unto which also I was greatly animated, not only by the continual desires of the Godly, but also by that saying of Paul to the Corinthians, *I beseech you, Brethren (ye know the household of Stephanas, that it is the first fruits of Achaia, and that they have addicted themselves to the Ministry of the Saints) that ye submit yourselves unto such, and to everyone that helpeth with us, and laboureth*. By this text I was made to see that the Holy Ghost never intended that men who have Gifts and Abilities should bury them in the earth, but rather did command and stir up such to the Exercise of their Gift. . . . This Scripture, in these days, did continually run in my mind, to encourage me and strengthen me in this my work for God.— BUNYAN, *Grace Abounding*, pp. 269, 270.

'I am glad of the coming of Stephanas and Fortunatus and Achaicus . . . for they have refreshed my spirit and yours.'
—1 COR. XVI. 17, 18.

WHY are there men and women that while they are nigh me the sunlight expands my blood ?

Why when they leave me do my pennants of joy sink flat and lank ?—WALT WHITMAN, *Song of the Open Road.*

REFERENCES.—XVI. 17.—*Expositor* (4th Series), vol. x. p. 99. XVI. 21.—*Expositor* (5th Series), vol. x. p. 199 ; *ibid.* (6th Series), vol. ix. p. 450. XVI. 21, 22.—G. Campbell Morgan, *Christian World Pulpit*, vol. lix. p. 241. XVI. 21-24.—*Expositor* (5th Series), vol. x. p. 205. A. Maclaren, *Expositions of Holy Scripture—Corinthians*, p. 258.

'If any man loveth not the Lord, let him be Anathema.'—
1 COR. XVI. 22.

'IF there be any among you,' Samuel Rutherford wrote to his former parishioners at Anwoth, 'that take liberty to sin because I am removed from amongst you, and forget that word of truth which ye heard, and turn the grace of God into wantonness, I here, under my hand, in the name of Christ my Lord, write to such persons all the plagues of God, and the curses that ever I preached in the pulpit of Anwoth, against the children of disobedience.'

REFERENCES.—XVI. 22.—J. Bunting, *Sermons*, vol. i. p. 484. F. B. Woodward, *Sermons* (2nd Series), p. 56. H. J. Windross, *Preacher's Magazine*, vol. v. p. 179.

OUR LORD JESUS

'Our Lord Jesus Christ.'—1 COR. XVI. 23.

THE text is in the Epistle to the Romans ; the text is in both the Epistles to the Corinthians ; the text is in the Epistle to the Galatians, in the Epistle to the Ephesians, in the Epistle to the Philippians, in the First and Second Epistles to the Thessalonians. It is in the brief note to Philemon ; it is in the Epistles of Peter, and Jude could not write his little burning note without using it three times. The text is everywhere, in the heavens above and on the earth beneath, and in the waters under the earth. What is it ? It is short, but it is full as an acorn that holds all the oaks of Bashan in possibility.

The text is 'Our Lord Jesus Christ'. He was before all things ; He is above all things ; by Him all things consist, to Him they owe their cohesion and unity, their poetry and their purpose. It is the theme of every true ministry. He who has alighted upon this text need not turn a page, though he minister from jubilee to jubilee, and through all the coming, rising, falling, millenniums of time. He cannot be short of a subject ; the preacher's subject is fixed ; he is not dependent upon the journals of the day or upon the accident of the morning. His theme never changes ; it is the all-comprehensive theme ; there is nothing of monotony or sameness about it ; these seven notes have in them the greatest oratorios yet to be written.

I. It will be profitable to fix upon the keyword, so far as our special appropriation of the name is concerned. That personal, domestic, love-word is 'our' Lord Jesus Christ. It is in the word 'our' that the pathos palpitates and cries ; not Lord Jesus, not Lord Jesus with a grammatical article before it, but Lord Jesus with *our* in front of it—our Saviour; though the world despise Him, He is ours. We are pledged men ; we are not walking up and down amid a dozen Christs asking which we shall have, or shall we have any or none ; we represent a vow, an oath ; we carry about with us the brand, the stigma of the Lord Jesus. A wondrous little word is *our*.

(1) *Our* child ; he is not beautiful according to formal notions of beauty, he is not so precocious as other children are, he is not brilliant, he is by no means so shapely as if he were a trained athlete : but he is our child. Our eyes are blind to any possible deficiency ; our eyes cannot see what the eyes of cold criticism can perceive. The reason is that the child lives in the heart ; he is our child, and the house would be no house without him. If that little child were not to come home to-night nobody under our roof could go to bed. Why, he is only one. True, but he is ours. He is only little, fragile, puny. Quite true, but he is ours.

(2) So we speak of *our* country. I do not believe in a narrow patriotism. I could not accept any patriotism that was inconsistent with philanthropy ; and yet there is a sense in which the stones of our country, whatever it be, are more precious than the stones of any other country, though the stones of the other country be diamonds, and precious to the lapidary. It is an instinct, it is an inborn something, it is a mystery, but a mystery that is poetic, inspiring, comforting, ennobling. It is by the culture of such instincts that we become intellectually and morally rich and free.

(3) Where is there a man who does not say with natural pride 'our house' ? It is not a big one ; the garden, front and back, can hardly be called a garden ; the rooms are not large, there are few pictures on the walls, but we keep the window open, and he who keeps his window open may some day pray, for it is a long distance that man can see through his open window, and he may see in the clouds, where the first tabernacle was built, Jerusalem, the city of the great King ; it may come into his heart whilst he looks through the open window, to fall upon his knees and cry to the Invisible and the Almighty. Never obliterate or modify that word *our*, it is a personal pronoun that holds an entire grammar in itself.

II. And so, carrying the idea to its highest, widest application, we come upon 'our Lord Jesus Christ'. He may not be the Lord of some other man, but He is our Lord, we cannot dispute about Him. Who would bring his own wife into the market for a public opinion ? he wants no public criticism upon his larger life, his true grand heart ; he silences criticism. Alas ! we sometimes invite it upon the Man of God. Where we should knock a man down if he said words like that about our wife, we permit the fool to expectorate his contempt upon the name that we hold dearest of all. Remember, whatever He may be to other people, He is our Lord Jesus, our Saviour, our hope, and to stand by whilst He is being traduced is treachery; in such a case silence is blasphemy.

III. He is our Lord Jesus in example, in doctrine, in sorrow, in joy. How did He bear His sorrow?— even so must I bear mine, saith the Christian in every night-shadowed Gethsemane; I will listen to my Lord that I may know how to bear my sorrow; He delivered several sweet discourses upon grief and pain of heart, I will listen to Him, His voice is music; if I do not understand His words, I can kiss the lips that speak them: Let not your heart be troubled; ye believe in God, believe also in Me: Fear not, little flock; peace I leave with you, My peace I give unto you; not as the world giveth give I unto you. God help me, then! I will try to be a man. If the Lord Jesus spake such words, He did not speak them wastefully or idly, He spake them to a heart broken, helpless, hopeless; I do my Lord dishonour by letting His words lie outside the sanctuary of my heart; I will take them all in, and if I cannot sing my prayer, I will moan it.—JOSEPH PARKER, *City Temple Pulpit*, vol. VII. p. 156.

THE SECOND EPISTLE TO THE CORINTHIANS

2 CORINTHIANS

REFERENCES.—*Expositor* (4th Series), vol. ii. p. 69 ; *ibid.* vol. vi. p. 29 ; *ibid.* vol. vii. p. 278. I. 1.—*Ibid.* vol. x. p. 204 ; *ibid.* (5th Series), vol. vii. p. 21 ; *ibid.* vol. x. p. 158. I. 2.—*Ibid.* vol. 'vii. p. 65 ; *ibid.* (6th Series), vol. vii. p. 409.

COMFORT

'Blessed be God, even the Father of our Lord Jesus Christ, the Father of mercies, and the God of all comfort : who comforteth us in all our tribulation, that we may be able to comfort them which are in any trouble, by the comfort wherewith we ourselves are comforted of God.'—2 COR. I. 3, 4.

I. The Relation of Comfort to Trouble.—When we deal with sorrow, not merely as a practical but as a personal fact, no general considerations suffice ; speculation is powerless to assuage grief. We only know it is there, and we must either have it taken away or must be taught how to bear it ; in other words, we feel the pain, and we long after either happiness or comfort. And of the two it is not happiness but comfort that God has appointed for us. With Christ, comfort was the attendant and antidote of permitted sorrow ; and the two are inseparably associated in every Christian life.

II. Observe how the Apostle points us to the Source of Comfort.—' Blessed be God, even the Father of our Lord Jesus Christ, the Father of mercies, and God of all comfort, who comforteth us in all our tribulation.' God knows our need, and He has not left it unsupplied ; He knows that we have perplexity, trial, pain, and He has provided comfort.

III. Consider the Uses of Comfort in Affliction.— (1) Note how the sorrow he had endured deepened the Apostle's sense of the value of God's presence and love. (2) Note, further, that sorrow is made a means of spiritual training. (3) Affliction thus comforted bestows the power of sympathy. — ALEXANDER STEWART, *The Divine Artist*, p. 43.

REFERENCES.—I. 3, 4.—W. H. Harwood, *Christian World Pulpit*, vol. liii. p. 70 ; *Christianity in Daily Conduct*, p. 277. Spurgeon, *Sermons*, vol. xlv. No. 2640. I. 3-6.—G. Body. *Christian World Pulpit*, vol. lvii. p. 214.

2 COR. I. 4.

'IF he had sorrows,' says Lowell of Shakespeare, 'he has made them the woof of everlasting consolation to his kind.'

REFERENCES.—I. 5.—Spurgeon, *Sermons*, vol. i. No. 13. W. H. Hutchings, *Sermon Sketches*, p. 251. I. 7.—Bishop Creighton, *University and other Sermons*, p. 186.

'The answer of death.'—2 COR. I. 8-11.

HENRI PERREYVE wrote, a few months before his death, to his friend Charles Perraud : 'Dear friend, I send you a text which you know as well as I do, but I copy it out in full, because it has often been for my soul a truly wonderful recipe, bringing strength, comfort, and spiritual health. If we wish to make use of it, we must meditate deeply on every word.' [Then follows this passage in Latin.] " For we would not, brethren, have you ignorant of our trouble which came to us in Asia, that we were pressed out of measure, above strength, insomuch that we despaired even of life. But we had the sentence of death [responsum mortis] in ourselves, that we should not trust in ourselves, but in God which raiseth the dead, who delivered us from so great a death and doth deliver ; in whom we trust that He will yet deliver us." I know that each one ought to draw his life freely from the Holy Scripture, and that the words which save one do not seem to be written quite as specially for another. For myself, I have found, in repeated and varying circumstances of my life, such help from those words of St. Paul, that I cannot but repeat them to you at this moment. I know not whether any one has ever sounded more deeply the abyss of the weakness of a human heart, and the abyss of the saving help of the heart of God. What does all this mean, dear friend ? It means that you, by the will of God, are passing through a desolate region, because your soul must not rest in mediocrity, but must become *very holy*.'

REFERENCES.—I. 9.—J. Martineau, *Endeavours After the Christian Life*, p. 59. Spurgeon, *Sermons*, vol. xxvi. No. 1536. I. 10.—Spurgeon, *Sermons*, xlvii. No. 2718. I. 11.—R. W. Dale, *Fellowship With Christ*, p. 278. I. 11, 12.—Spurgeon, *Sermons*, vol. ix. No. 507.

A MINISTRY THAT SATISFIES THE CONSCIENCE

'Our glorying is this, the testimony of our conscience.'— 2 COR. I. 12.

'OUR glorying is this.' How would my hearers finish the sentence? When we have discovered the nature of a man's glorying we have got the real height of the man. Here is a man withdrawn from all carnal spheres, seeking no glory upon the public stage, placing no value upon transient fame ; but in the awful sanctuary of the conscience quietly glorying in its witness to the devotion and fidelity of his ministry. It is the only glorying which endures. The colours are fast colours ; they do not wash out in the drenching blast of life's tempestuous days. This man stands in the solemn presence of the great White Throne, and finds his glorying in the message which speaks from the Throne. 'Our glorying is this, the testimony of our conscience.' And yet this is no arrogant claim to perfection. His letters burn with the consciousness of his own defilement. In the latter part of our text the Apostle carefully describes the features of his ministry which brought him the restful witness of his conscience.

I. And first of all he had rejected the offers of 'fleshly wisdom'. He had been repeatedly advised to moderate the stringency of his message. It was the same temptation which assailed our Lord. But the Apostle was like his Master; he rejected the overtures. He would have no unclean ally in the ministry of holiness; he would accept no 'fleshly wisdom' in proclaiming the wisdom of the Highest. In this he found his glory.

II. And his conscience also testified to the holiness of his ministry. The Apostle claims that his ministry was absolutely separated unto God. Whatever he was doing the Lord dominated his purpose and work. And in this he gloried. He had not been led aside to minor purposes, and forgotten the primary aims of redeeming grace.

III. And his conscience testified to the simplicity of his ministry. I am using that word not in the degenerate sense in which it has fallen in these latter days, not in the sense of childishness, or even of lucidity, but in its great primary content of singleness of purpose, and of perfect openness and candour of life. 'I determined not to know anything among men save Jesus Christ and Him crucified.' And in this he gloried.

IV. And there is one other word he uses to describe his ministry among men. It is characterised by *sincerity*. The Apostle humbly boasts that his ministry among men is not condemned even in the searching light of God's countenance. He had sought his motives there! And therefore, even if he failed, he was calm and restful, for when he returned into the throne-chamber of his life he enjoyed the peace of God.—J. H. JOWETT, *British Congregationalist*, 13th February, 1908.

REFERENCES.—I. 12.—J. H. Jowett, *The Transfigured Church*, p. 229. D. C. A. Agnew, *The Soul's Business and Prospects*, p. 114. *Expositor* (4th Series), vol. iii. p. 93 ; *ibid.* (5th Series), vol. viii. p. 178. I. 15.—*Ibid.* (6th Series), vol. iii. p. 237. I. 15-17.—*Ibid.* vol. viii. p. 233. I. 16.—*Ibid.* (7th Series), vol. vi. p. 232. I. 17.—*Ibid.* (6th Series), vol. xii. p. 69. I. 19.—H. S. Seekings, *Preacher's Magazine*, vol. xvii. p. 224. *Expositor* (5th Series), vol. vi. p. 87. *Ibid.* (6th Series), vol. ix. p. 374. I. 20.—J. C. M. Bellew, *Sermons*, vol. i. p. 216. Spurgeon, *Sermons*, vol. xlvi. No. 2657. A. Maclaren, *Expositions of Holy Scripture—Corinthians*, p. 268. I. 21.—*Ibid.* p. 277. I. 22.—*Ibid.* p. 287. *Expositor* (5th Series), vol. vii. p. 301 ; *ibid.* (5th Series), vol. iv. p. 274. I. 23.—*Ibid.* (4th Series), vol. ix. p. 170.

THE EFFECT OF FAITH
'By faith ye stand.'—2 COR. I. 24.

FAITH is that by which men *stand*. I invite your attention to the effect of faith on the believing soul.

I. Faith as bowing us down before God. Faith is constantly associated with self-distrust.

II. Faith as making us stand erect before men. It sets us free from man's authority, from slavish submission to popular opinions and from all forms of ecclesiastical or social tyranny.

III. Faith as making us stand firm against sin. The truths of the Gospel in the mind weaken all temptation.—A. MACLAREN.

REFERENCES.—I. 24.—*Expositor* (6th Series), vol. xi. p. 146. II. 1.—*Ibid.* vol. i. p. 404 ; *ibid.* (7th Series), vol. vi. p. 81. II. 3.—*Ibid.* (5th Series), vol. vi. p. 238. II. 5-8.—*Ibid.* (4th Series), vol. ii. p. 385. II. 6-10.—*Ibid.* (6th Series), vol. i. p. 216. II. 10.—*Ibid.* (5th Series), vol. iv. p. 452.

FOREWARNED, FOREARMED
'We are not ignorant of his devices.'—2 COR. II. 11.

'KNOWLEDGE is power,' said Lord Bacon ; and to know some of the subtleties of that malevolent power that fights against us, is so far to be forearmed. Paul does not tell us what the devices were. But probably the devices of to-day are very much the same as in Paul's time. We are not ignorant of his devices—what, then, are some of these ?

I. Firstly, he labels evil things with pleasant names. There is a tendency in all language to do that. No man has ever loved to call the seamier side of things by its right name, or to look the darker facts of life straight in the face. It is this tendency of human speech that is caught up and wrested by the devil into an engine and instrument of ill.

II. He makes his onset on our strongest side. Our characters are complex products, and in every one of us strong elements and weak are strangely blended. The strongest Achilles has his defenceless heel. Thou hast a worst side, and generally men take thee on thy worst side. But thou hast a best side, and God takes thee on that. And Satan, transforming himself into an angel of light, assails on that side too. The Bible has many instances of that.

III. He uses tools. It is one mark of practical genius to choose the right instruments to do its work. Could you conceive a finer choice of instruments than Satan makes, when he is seeking to overthrow a human soul? Out of a hundred gates into your hearts and mine, he passes by those that are barred and chooses one that will open at a touch. His is the plan and his the whole device. But he gets other hands and other hearts to the work ; and the whole history of the tempted world, and the whole history of your tempted heart, tells the consummate genius of the choice.

IV. He shams defeat. To sham defeat is a well-known trick in warfare. Our unseen foe is a consummate strategist. Many a soul has been lost because it won—won in the first encounter, then said all's well, and laid its arms aside—till the old sin crept up again and sprang, and the last state was worse than the first.

V. He lays the emphasis upon to-morrow. We are always prone to put the accent there. In every life, for every start and every noble deed, God says, To-day. In every life, for every start and every noble deed, the devil says, To-morrow.—G. H. Morrison, *Flood-Tide*, p. 230.

References.—II. 12.—*Expositor* (5th Series), vol. i. p. 387 ; *ibid.* vol. ii. p. 275 ; *ibid.* (6th Series), vol. iii. p. 239 ; *ibid.* vol. ix. p. 21 ; *ibid.* vol. x. p. 344.

VICTORIES, NOT VICTORS

'Now thanks be unto God, which always causeth us to triumph in Christ, and maketh manifest the savour of His knowledge by us in every place.'—2 Cor. ii. 14.

The text has been read thus : ' But thanks be unto God, which always leadeth us in triumph in Christ, and maketh manifest through us the savour of His knowledge in every place '.

This is a beautiful picture. The subject ought to be treated pictorially. We should see a great king with a great procession of chariots behind him, and those chariots full of saved men, and the Captain of their salvation at the head pointing to these men as proofs of the reality and energy and beneficence of His redeeming and saving grace. Let the heart keep the picture vividly before its eyes : Christ at the head, miles of chariots, all golden, all filled with living hymns, all wounded men, but wounded to their own salvation ; and as they come along they say, We have been taken by Christ at the spear-point ; if you want to know what Christ can do, read the record of our experience.

I. This reading of the text does two things : first, it puts Christ in His right position, and, secondly, it puts Christians in their right position, and not Christians only, but Christian apostles and martyrs, the leaders and heads of the visible Church upon earth, appointed by Christ, clothed by Him with some mantle which is the truest honour of the soul. Christ is put in His right position by being put at the head of the great procession. Who is this that cometh up from Edom with dyed garments from Bozrah, this that is red in His apparel, travelling in the greatness of His strength? And who are these that follow Him, and sing as they follow? It is the army of the saved, it is the caravan of the blessed, it is the host on every member of which is sprinkled the saving blood, and by these grand trophies of His grace Christ spreads the news of His kingdom over all the waiting earth.

II. We are, then, to be specimens of Christ's victorious grace. What an honour, what a responsibility, yet what a danger! lest we should be self-deceived and be but half-subdued. The argument of Christ is, Believe Me for the work's sake ; here is the man, the man is the best argument ; personal character is the best defence ; remember what the man was, what the man is, to what energy he ascribes the change. He tells you it was the miracle of the grace of God ; believe the man. Why should you be keeping outside God's gracious kingdom, chaffering with some fellow-disputant, neither of you being able to discuss the mysteries of the kingdom of heaven with any adequacy of intellectual force or spiritual fitness ? why should you be asking hard questions in words ? There is the man, the soul, the publican, the thief,

the prodigal—there ! You have not to answer an argument in words, you have to destroy a logic in life, a grand syllogism in fact, in experience, in ascertainable consequence. Look at the instances you yourselves have known of the energy of the grace of Christ ; know that Jesus Christ calls you to consider what victories He has already won. Whatever your case or mine may be, there is an analogy, a parallel, an almost identical instance in the record of Christ's victories. Read it, and say, If Christ could conquer that man, He can conquer me.—Joseph Parker, *City Temple Pulpit*, vol. ii. p. 89.

References.—II. 14.—Bishop Doane, *Christian World Pulpit*, vol. lvii. p. 385. *Expositor* (4th Series), vol. iii. p. 93 ; *ibid.* vol. x. p. 274. A. Maclaren, *Expositions of Holy Scripture—Corinthians*, p. 296. II. 14-16.—C. Moinet, *The Great Alternative and other Sermons*, p. 279. W. Pulsford, *Trinity Church Sermons*, p. 198. II. 15.—J. G. Rogers, *Christian World Pulpit*, vol. xlvii. p. 52. II. 15, 16.—Spurgeon, *Sermons*, vol. i. No. 26. II. 16.—F. W. Farrar, *Christian World Pulpit*, vol. xliv. p. 233. H. M. Butler, *Harrow School Sermons* (2nd Series), p. 80. Morley Wright, *Christian World Pulpit*, vol. xlviii. p. 301. J. M. Neale, *Sermons on the Blessed Sacrament*, p. 1. A. Goodrich, *Christian World Pulpit*, vol. lvi. p. 248. J. G. Greenhough, *The Mind of Christ in St. Paul*, p. 293. II. 17.—*Expositor* (4th Series), vol. ii. p. 300 ; *ibid.* vol. iii. p. 94 ; *ibid.* (6th Series), vol. vii. p. 456 ; *ibid.* vol. viii. p. 75. II. 18.—G. Austen, *The Pulpit*, vol. i. p. 41. III.—*Expositor* (5th Series), vol. x. p. 260. III. 2, 3.—A. Rowland, *Christian World Pulpit*, vol. xliv. p. 299. H. Woodcock, *Sermon Outlines* (1st Series), p. 190.

2 Cor. iii. 3.

Dr. Deissmann speaks of ' the beautiful figure in 2 Cor. iii. 3, according to which St. Paul has a letter to write for Christ. This characteristic expression includes a parallel to the technical term " letter of Augustus," *i.e.*, Imperial letter, which is found in an inscription of the Imperial period at Ancyra.'—*Light from the Ancient East*, p. 379.

References.—III. 3.—J. G. Greenhough, *The Mind of Christ in St. Paul*, p. 194. *Expositor* (5th Series), vol. ix. p. 14.

OUR SUFFICIENCY

' Our sufficiency is of God.'—2 Cor. iii. 5.

The Apostle Paul occupied so peculiar a position that it cannot be doubted that he stood in need of peculiar assistance and guidance. His life was laborious, his duties were responsible, his difficulties were many, his influence was vast. He evidently felt that he was dependent upon the grace and sufficiency of God, and that whilst of himself he could do nothing, he could do all things through Christ Who strengthened him. Every true Christian, however slender his abilities, however obscure his position, feels in need of the grace which was sufficient for the Apostle of the Gentiles.

I. Insufficiency of Human Strength for Spiritual Service.—In the case of the Apostle, whose words are before us, this insufficiency was very conspicuous. It was his office to preach to civilised and barbarian, to Jews in the synagogue, to Gentiles in the market-place, to Christians in upper rooms ; to travel and to brave dangers by land and sea ; to endure imprisonment, stripes, and violence ; to defend himself and the Gospel before magistrates and before multitudes ; to expound the truth, to combat error, to oppose false teachers, to detect false brethren ; to write epistles both to fellow-labourers and to congregations ; to direct and control the actions of Christian communities. Well might he exclaim, Who is sufficient for these things ? This insufficiency is as real, if not as obvious, in the case of Christians in ordinary stations of life, and of Christian labourers called to ordinary service. To maintain a Christian character and to display a Christian spirit, to present a witness of power to the truth, to commend the Gospel by argument, by persuasion, by conduct—all this cannot be done by the use of resources merely human.

II. **Sufficiency of Divine Strength and Grace.**— This sufficiency is imparted by the clear *manifestation of Divine truth* on God's part, and by its clear apprehension on ours. Not by entrusting a secret, but by revealing great truths and principles, does the Lord qualify His servants for their work. Here was the instrument for Paul's work, the weapon for his warfare. And here all Christ's servants must seek their sufficiency. Pastors and evangelists, teachers and parents, should bear this in mind—that their competency for their several ministries depends first upon their grasping Christian truth, and embodying it in their spiritual life, and using it as their means of spiritual service. This sufficiency again is enjoyed by the *sympathetic reception on our part of the Holy Spirit's grace.* Strength, wisdom, forethought, gentleness, and patience are all needed in the service of the Redeemer. These are the fruits of the Spirit's presence and operation. Christian labourers need a heart open heavenwards to receive all sacred influences by prayer, by fellowship with God, by true receptiveness of attitude. A Divine, unseen, but mighty agency is provided for all true servants of Christ. And, assured of this, they may well lose sight of their personal weakness and ignorance and utter inadequacy, and be content and glad to be participators in the sufficiency which is of God.

REFERENCES.—III. 5.—F. W. Farrar, *Christian World Pulpit*, vol. xliv. p. 233. J. Keble, *Sermons for Sundays After Trinity*, pt. i. p. 457. A. Goodrich, *Christian World Pulpit*, vol. lvi. p. 248. *Expositor* (6th Series), vol. x. p. 373. III. 5, 6.—Spurgeon, *Sermons*, vol. xxxvi. No. 2160.

SPIRIT AND LETTER

'The letter killeth, but the spirit giveth life.'—2 COR. III. 6.

'THE letter killeth '—in all things. In merchandise, in the statute book, in the family, in reading, in literature, the letter killeth ; no man can live on cast iron : but the spirit giveth life—the poetry, the meaning, the purpose, the inmost intent and content ; there you have immortality. Let us see how far this can be simplified, and especially how far it can be applied ; because if we could get into the music of this text we should all be living Christians, ecstatic saints, glorious forerunners of the coming Lord.

I. We may have the right letters, but the wrong word. There is absolutely nothing in the letters except under certain conditions, and these conditions we are prone to overlook or to undervalue. Everything depends upon the letters being brought into the right relation. Every letter must not only be in the right place, but it must be uttered singly and collectively in the right tone. If people understood this the whole world, in the event of its being practically applied to conduct, would be full of light, full of music ; we should realise a new brotherhood, we should be almost in heaven. We may deliver the right words in a wrong tone. The soul gives the tone. We may deliver the right words, in the right order, but in the wrong tone ; and may preach the Evangelical Gospel without the Evangelical spirit : and a morning without dew is like a morning without a blessing.

II. Secondly. We may be correct in our letters and utterly wrong in our words. Can a man be both right and wrong at the same time ? Certainly ; that is what we are doing all the day. We must psychologically understand this if we would recover ourselves from the disease of heart-folly. Observe what the proposition is : We may have the right letters, and yet have the wrong word. The letter is nothing ; the letter is confusing ; the letter needs companionship, atmosphere, historical relationship, and, above all, a penetrating and uplifting, a redeeming and sanctifying spirit. Let us grope our way into the meaning of this strange paradox, that we may have the right letters and yet the wrong word ; the right letters, and yet the wrong sermon ; the right letters, and a doctrine degraded from a revelation to a profanity.

III. We know what this means in relation to work, to the common work of the common day. A workman may not do the work in the spirit, and therefore it is poorly or badly done. If a man shall take no pleasure in his work he cannot do it, except in a perfunctory and utterly unsatisfactory manner. Men who do the work only in the letter are liars and thieves and anything but patriots. When the right estimate of labour goes down, the country goes down. When men go to their work at the rate of three miles an hour and leave it at the rate of seven, they are not patriots, and they ought not to win any battles ; the God of order is against them, the spirit of the spring condemns their action and dismisses them from all holy and responsible relations. And this holds good in the pulpit and out of it. Unless a man really love his work and long for it, he cannot do it. We cannot live on painted fire. No man can continue the holy ministry of the cross for a lifetime and have as much joy in it at the end as at the beginning, except in the spirit of the cross that he preaches ; then he will be eternally young—an amaranth that no snow can chill into death. This holds good, therefore, in all sections, departments, and relations of life.

If we could receive these instructions we should have fewer Bible readers, but better ; we should know that the letter killeth, but that grace and truth give life and hope and music to the soul. We must get rid of the literalists, the men who only read the iron letter, and do not read the Bible in the Bible's own atmosphere. What do we want? I will tell you: the Holy Ghost; he only can read the book which he only wrote; we must become acquainted with the Author before we can read His writings with deep spiritual, lasting advantage. If any man lack wisdom, let him ask of God.—Joseph Parker, *City Temple Pulpit*, vol. ii. p. 185.

References.—III. 6.—C. Kingsley, *The Good News of God*, p. 124. J. Keble, *Sermons for Sundays After Trinity*, pt. i. p. 477. Llewelyn Davies, *The Purpose of God*, p. 16. *Expositor* (6th Series), vol. iv. p. 358; *ibid.* vol. xi. p. 63; *ibid.* (7th Series), vol. v. p. 497. III. 7-9.—J. Baines, *Twenty Sermons*, p. 255. III. 8.—J. Clifford, *The Christian Certainties*, p. 243.

FROM GLORY TO GLORY

'For if that which passeth away was with glory, much more that which remaineth is in glory.'—2 Cor. iii. 11.

It is of more than passing interest to note that the law of development, or, in modern scientific terminology, the law of evolution, was clearly grasped by the Apostle Paul, and applied by him with true philosophic breadth to that great department of thought to which he has so richly contributed, *viz.*, the sphere of spiritual truth, of the problems that deal with God's ethical relation to the world. The evolution of theology is no modern discovery. Let us then consider, How Paul related himself to the old theology, and, What he declared to be final and eternal in the new.

I. How Paul related himself to the old theology. (1) It is to be noted that Paul manifests a deep and sympathetic appreciation of the *glory* of the old. Renan says that before a man can give a true estimate and history of any faith, he must have once believed it, but now ceased to believe it. The former part of this statement is certainly true, but the latter part is either untrue or inaccurately expressed. There can be no true estimate without a *continued* belief, for the true value of any faith lies in *its living relation to the life*. It is impossible for us to estimate any religion or any creed except in as far as we discover in it elements such as have powerfully influenced our own lives, and in developed forms are still influencing them. No faith can be nobler save that which is deep rooted in the old, and has received birth from it. (2) Paul grasped clearly the permanent element in the old theology. He clearly distinguishes between the 'passing elements' and the permanent substratum.

II. But while Paul recognised the law of development in theology, he finds that, with the appearing of Christ, this law receives new and definite limits. The permanent factor is now manifested in such a form that it dwarfs the transient forms; so that, in an important sense, Paul finds himself already at the final stage of theological development. Paul presents this final and permanent factor in two forms, an abstract and a concrete. (1) The abstract form is the conception of Liberty, the Freedom of the Spirit.

There is no liberty in uncertainty and in detachment from the past. It is the eternal truth which we find in the past that makes us free. (2) That this was Paul's conception is made clear by the concrete form in which he presented this permanent element. The concrete and eternal heart of theology is Jesus Christ.—John Thomas, *Myrtle Street Pulpit*, vol. ii. p. 68.

SAVED BY HOPE

'Seeing then that we have such hope, we use great plainness of speech.'—2 Cor. iii. 12.

St. Paul says, 'we are saved by hope'. He puts in one sense a higher value on this than either on faith or love. He never says we are saved by faith, or we are saved by love.

I. Now, what does Hope say? It says, 'I know that there are certain rewards laid up in the kingdom of heaven for those that have fought the good fight and persevered to the end. I know that of my own self I cannot conquer in that fight, I cannot win in that race, I am nothing and can do nothing. But I also know that all the promises which I read in the Bible, promises of help, comfort, strength, are made to me, weak and sinful and miserable though I am; they are made to me if I will but lay hold on them; they are made to me as much as if there was not one other person besides me in the world. Therefore, in that confidence I will fight, because I know that if I do I shall conquer; I will run in the race, because I know that if I do I shall win the prize. I will fight and I will run cheerfully; what matter all little troubles, or inconveniences, or sorrows, if I have but such a hope to look forward to hereafter?'

II. But then, no one can really have such a hope who lets himself as a habit constantly be discontented, be dismayed, be put out, as we say, by the things of this world. How would it sound if we said, 'I know that whatever affliction I suffer here is but light, is but for a moment. I know that the crown laid up for me on high is imperishable and eternal; and yet, all the troubles of the world I *will* lay to heart; all its sorrows I *will* complain about; all its difficulties I *will* make the most of.' Whatever feeling this may be it is not hope. The feeling which comes nearest that which we ought to have is that we have in an inn, when we are on our way to a dear home. It may be full of inconveniences, but we match them directly with some of the delights of our own house. The people may be uncivil and surly: well, we shall be loved enough at home. The rooms may be inconvenient; that will matter little when we get home. We should reason thus in earthly matters, but when it comes to matters beyond this world, we reason so no longer. Then we think about the inconveniences of the way, the difficulties of the journey, the unkindness of our companions. And if ever we think of our future home, it is only as a kind of make-up for whatever difficulties we may find here.

If we believe that in our Father's house there are many mansions, that our Lord is gone to prepare a place for us ; that if our earthly house of this tabernacle were dissolved, we have a building of God, a house not made with hands, eternal in the heavens ; if, I say, faith teaches us these things, why cannot our hope lay hold on them and take them to ourselves, so as to despise and cast aside all earthly fear, yea, the very dread of death itself, and the terror of the judgment. For He that loved His own, loveth them unto the end, and ' Hope maketh not ashamed '.—J. M. NEALE, *Sermons Preached in Sackville College Chapel*, vol. II. p. 229.

REFERENCES.—III. 12.—*Expositor* (4th Series), vol. x. p. 211. III. 16.—T. F. Crosse, *Sermons*, p. 52. J. Keble, *Sermons for Sundays After Trinity*, pt. i. p. 442.

THE LIBERTY WHICH CHRIST GIVES
' Where the Spirit of the Lord is, there is liberty.'—
2 COR. III. 17.

I. THE soul of man pants for liberty as a hungry child cries for food. It is, indeed, the hunger of the soul. Every age and condition asks for it. The child's conception of manhood is a vision of freedom. He dreams of a time when he will be able to go his own way, and do his own pleasure, with no check or restraint imposed by parents and schoolmasters. Every youth clamours for freedom, to be his own guide and his own master, to follow his own bent, to employ himself and enjoy himself according to the dictates of his own will, with none to interfere. He asks for liberty to play, or work to do or leave undone, to walk in any path which seems desirable, to think his own thoughts and pursue his own ends, with no chains of authority to hold him back. We all feel the chains more or less. We are under *law*. And nobody loves law ; he only submits to it. Necessity drives, compulsion spurs. We go as we are ordered, but we go kicking. We have to do a thousand things which self-love resents, which pride and dignity recoil from. Not what we like, but what we must, is for all of us, more or less, the inevitable lot. And the human heart is always groaning under its limitations and bondage, and crying for more room, crying for liberty ! And here comes the Gospel answer to the cry : ' Where the Spirit of the Lord is, there is liberty '.

II. Now I do not suppose that any man will *leap up to embrace that answer* at once. We have to think twice, and many times, before we can understand that the Christian life is a life of liberty. If you look at it from the outside it does not seem to afford or promise any great amount of freedom. You are rather inclined to think that it forges a great many additional chains instead of breaking those which bind us already, and that it imposes new restrictions without sweeping away the old ones. Yes, it would never occur to you to come into the Christian life to gain your liberty. For its first appearance points all the other way. Yet it leads to higher freedom, and the only perfect freedom which man can have on earth. ' Where the Spirit of the Lord is, there is liberty.'

III. Look for a moment at *the Lord Himself.* You get in Him, and from Him, the first and most complete interpretation of these words. You get a vision of noble, beautiful, untrammelled liberty. He came not to do His own will, but the will of His Father. He was under authority, under orders. That was one side of His life. But the other side was one of perfect freedom, for His own will and the Father's will made one music.

IV. There is freedom in thought and freedom in conduct where the mind, or Spirit, of the Lord is. Where the Spirit of the Lord is, there comes, not bondage of mind, but glad, glorious liberty, freedom of thought and freedom of conduct. For in proportion as we have the mind of Christ we do all right and noble things, and we shun all base and degrading things, of our own free and deliberate choice.— J. G. GREENHOUGH, *The Mind of Christ in St. Paul*, p. 38.

TRUE FREEDOM
'Where the Spirit of the Lord is, there is liberty.'—
2 COR. III. 17.

CHRISTIANITY is a religion of liberty.

I. Where the Spirit of the Lord is, there is freedom from sin.

II. Where the Spirit of the Lord is, there is liberty in the service of God.

III. Where the Spirit of the Lord is, there is freedom from men. Where the Spirit is *not*, there is slavery like that of some nations where despotism has so long been the rule that men know not what freedom is. ' If the Son make you free ye shall be free indeed.'—A. MACLAREN.

REFERENCES.—III. 17.—J. M. Neale, *Sermons Preached in Sackville College Chapel*, p. 406. Spurgeon, *Sermons*, vol. i. No. 9. S. H. Fleming, *Fifteen Minute Sermons for the People*, pp. 30, 35. H. P. Liddon, *University Sermons*, p. 61. E. Bayley, *Sermons on the Work and Person of the Holy Spirit*, p. 119. III. 17, 18.—*Expositor* (4th Series), vol. viii. p. 277 ; *ibid.* (5th Series), vol. ii. pp. 174, 253 ; *ibid.* vol. iv. p. 425 ; *ibid.* (4th Series), vol. ii. p. 111 ; *ibid.* (5th Series), vol. ix. p. 350.

TRANSFORMATION INTO THE LORD'S IMAGE
' We all, with unveiled face beholding as in a mirror the glory of the Lord, are transformed into the same image from glory to glory, even as from the Lord the Spirit.'—2 COR. III. 18.
' Now we look into a mirror puzzlingly (literally ' in a riddle '), but then face to face.'—1 COR. XIII. 12.

OBSERVE the principle which St. Paul enunciates. The mirror is before you : look into it, look steadfastly, believingly, and lovingly ; and a miracle will be wrought. The glory of the Lord reflected there will be photographed upon you, and you will be transformed into the same image.

I. And this is no mere fancy. It is a spiritual law which, like every spiritual law, is just a natural law at its farthest reach. It is ever thus with the doctrines of Christianity. You find, when you consider those high mysteries and penetrate into the heart of them, that they are not mysteries at all, but familiar principles of daily experience operating beyond the domain of experience. And this, it seems to me, is not the least of the evidences of Christianity. It is rooted in the soil of earth; it is in line with the natural order, following its laws and carrying them to loftier issues.

Look at the principle which St. Paul here lays down, and do you not recognise it as a law of common experience? You know, for example, how one personality impresses itself upon another, if there be mutual trust and affection and admiration. Think of a revered teacher and his students—how they catch his spirit, assimilate his thought, and reproduce his teaching. He creates 'a school,' and you recognise its adherents by their likeness to the master. It is told of the later disciples of Pythagoras that they were accustomed to publish their books under his name, thereby confessing, with generous self-effacement, that they owed all to him. His teaching was the source of their wisdom. They simply reflected his glory. And you know how love transfigures, putting its imprint not simply on the soul but on the very flesh. Have you never noticed the miracle which is wrought upon a husband and wife who 'have lived and loved together through many changing years'—how they come to resemble each other, not merely in their habits and ways of thinking, but in their very look, as though a gentle hand had kept smoothing their faces day by day and transforming them into the same image? There is no kinship between them; it is Love that has wrought the miracle; and it almost startles you. It is all so much alike—the tone of the voice, the light in the eyes, the play of expression.

II. Our transformation into the Lord's image, St. Paul is careful to explain, is a gradual process. We are 'transformed from glory to glory'—first a little glory, then more, and at last the perfect likeness of our blessed Saviour. This is the final consummation, and we shall never attain it here; we shall never attain it until we get home and see His face. It is not His face that we see here, but only His reflection. The mirror is before us, and He is standing, as it were, behind us, and we see His image in the glass. But the mirror is often dim and uncertain, and the reflection obscure and broken, and we have to guess what He is like. 'Now we look in a mirror puzzlingly.' But one day we shall turn round and see Him 'face to face'; and then the transformation will be complete. 'We shall be like Him, for we shall see Him even as He is.'

III. Such is St. Paul's doctrine of Sanctification, and it is fraught with splendid encouragement. See how he emphasises a truth which we are apt to forget, thereby missing the way and disquieting our hearts—the truth that our transformation into the Lord's image is not our own work but the operation of the Holy Spirit. 'We are transformed into the same image from glory to glory, even as from the Lord the Spirit.' There is a crucifix known as the *Volto Santo* in the Cathedral of Lucca, and the story of it is a parable. It is said that Nicodemus was charged by an angel to fashion an image of the Lord; and he went to the forest and, hewing down a cedar, addressed himself to the task. It baffled his skill, and, wearied with his ineffectual labour, he fell asleep. And, when he awoke, behold, the work was done. The crucifix was before him, carved by angel hands.

And thus we are 'transformed into the Lord's image from glory to glory'. It is not our own work; it is the Holy Spirit's, and we do not further it by striving and fretting. Is it by its own effort that the earth is clothed with verdure? Ah, no! it is by the sweet influence of the sunshine and the rain and the dew from heaven, and the earth has only to spread its breast and receive the benediction.—DAVID SMITH, *Man's Need of God*, p. 199.

'Are changed.'—2 COR. III. 18.

CHANGE, the strongest son of Life,
Has the spirit here to wife.—MEREDITH.

REFERENCES.—III. 18.—Basil Wilberforce, *Christian World Pulpit*, vol. li. p. 136. A. E. Belch, *Preacher's Magazine*, vol. xvii. p. 359. E. W. Moore, *The Record*, vol. xxvii. p. 770. C. D. Bell, *The Saintly Calling*, p. 143. J. C. Nattrass, *Preacher's Magazine*, vol. xix. p. 219. E. Bayley, *Sermons on the Work and Person of the Holy Spirit*, p. 261. J. B. Lightfoot, *Cambridge Sermons*, p. 96. J. Laidlaw, *Studies in the Parables*, p. 243. *Expositor* (4th Series), vol. ii. pp. 49, 285; *ibid.* vol. iii. p. 93; *ibid.* vol. ix. pp. 91, 209; *ibid.* vol. x. pp. 210, 271; *ibid.* (5th Series), vol. iv. p. 119; *ibid.* vol. vi. p. 254; *ibid.* (6th Series), vol. x. pp. 194, 371. A. Maclaren, *Expositions of Holy Scripture*, p. 307.

THE TRIUMPH OF CONTINUANCE
'We faint not.'—2 COR. IV. 1.

'WE all, with unveiled face beholding as in a mirror the glory of the Lord, are changed into the same image from glory to glory, as from a Lord who is Spirit.' St. Paul follows these sublime words with a reference to his own life labour. 'Therefore seeing we have this ministry, as we have received mercy, we faint not.' 'We faint not.' We expect, perhaps, a clearer, prouder, more triumphant note. The word, for its place, seems tame and quiet. The Apostle is not stricken in spirit, but neither does he seem flushed with hope. When, however, we look closely at the expression, it yields us the truth that in the service of the Gospel continuance is triumph. The Christian has some humble task allotted to him—to teach in a Sunday school, to preach in a village church. The years pass; old associates depart, make their fortunes, return. They find their friend where he was—older, feebler perhaps, graver certainly, obscure and unmarked as before, but still at his post. They compassionately contrast his lot with more dazzling destinies, and he, too, may be inclined to self-pity. But to St. Paul the prophetic promise, 'They shall walk and not faint,' was the climax of Covenant grace. 'Having obtained help of God, I continue unto this day,' was to him the crown of mercies.

I. The thing was true, but the time appointed was long. For us the conditions are unaltered. Changes are superficial; all that is deepest remains unchanged. The elements of a soul's tragedy are still the same. What we have to remember is that we are dealing with a foe not affected by the progress of civilisation or the march of reason, not to be conciliated or disarmed. We are fighting the ancient enemies of God and man. This is not to daunt us from the wise and reasonable undertaking of hard things. It must not deepen our despondency over the work God wills us to do.

II. Next the Apostle reminds us that he had to meet his inveterate foes with an outward strength that was continually failing. In the ordinance of nature the physical force surely diminishes, whilst the calls on energy and courage grow more urgent. For St. Paul there was no respite. His place was ever in the front of battle. Yet his outward man was perishing. He was pressed on every side, perplexed, pursued, smitten down, always bearing about in the body the putting to death of Jesus.

The passing of youth takes something from us all—something of charm, ardour, venturesomeness, power over the minds of our fellows. The inroads of physical weakness take more. When we bid farewell to days of long, unwearied labour, to nights of sweet, unbroken sleep, something has gone from us never truly prized till it was lost. But the Apostle tells us that the inward man may be renewed from day to day. Whoever and whatever left him, he had staying power for his long struggle, and abode at the end of it in strength and hope. The bright visions did not forsake him ; he did not falter in his great task ; he was never sullen, never despondent, never rebellious ; in his darkest hours he was helped by that Spirit who is the restorer of energy and the quickener of hope.

III. Thus when St. Paul said, ' We faint not,' he claimed, and claimed truly, that he had mastered circumstances. He had not seen things go as he fain would. He had not been cheered by an experience of unbroken outward success. But he had not failed. Even when he had not succeeded, his soul had gathered strength and calm from the very arrest of progress. The energy of the spirit had not been foiled. Suffering had proved an annealing force by which he not only endured, but comprehended and believed while enduring. Every condition had in it the Divine spring of energy which left him unfainting—that is, neither apathetic nor supine. He had yielded to no dwindling tendencies ; there had been no shrinking or contracting of the heart. ' We faint not.' Again, was it a little thing ?

It is the triumph of all saints. We glory most not in their brilliant and victorious hours, but in their steadfast perseverance through light and shadow to the end. Remembering that, we bless God ' for their faith, their hope, their labour, their truth, their blood, their zeal, their diligence, their tears, their purity, their beauty.'—W. Robertson Nicoll, *Ten Minute Sermons*, p. 35 (see also pp. 43-50).

THE CHRISTIAN MINISTRY

'Therefore seeing we have this ministry, as we have received mercy, we faint not.'—2 Cor. iv. 1.

The word ' ministry ' has a general meaning, as it has, indeed, all through the New Testament. It applies to all God's people, as witnesses for the Lord Jesus and as bearers of the glorious Gospel of the grace of God. The text may be divided into three sections :—

I. There is a glorious ministry. (1) The ministry is a ministration of righteousness. The Gospel is based upon the righteousness of God, who is absolutely just in dealing with sin. (2) It is also a ministry of life and blessedness. (3) It is the true ministry of the spirit.

II. The text refers to a glorious experience, and that is the *sine qua non* for all Christian workers. Those who have not received God's mercy cannot by any means take the ministry of God to others.

III. There is a glorious optimism expressed—' We faint not.'—C. B. Sawday, *The Baptist*, vol. lxxi. p. 443.

References.—IV. 1.—T. Arnold, *Sermons*, vol. iii. p. 242. J. M. Neale, *Sermons Preached in a Religious House*, vol. i. p. 238. IV. 1-6.—*Expositor* (4th Series), vol. iii. p. 92. IV. 2.—W. P. Balfern, *Lessons from Jesus*, p. 285. J. Caird, *Sermons*, p. 1. Archbishop Magee, *The Gospel and the Age*, p. 295. *Christian World Pulpit*, vol. li. p. 79. H. Melvill, *Penny Pulpit*, No. 1674, p. 431. *Expositor* (7th Series), vol. vi. p. 90. IV. 3.—T. Arnold, *Christian Life ; Its Hopes*, p. 339. *Expositor* (4th Series), vol. i. p. 201. IV. 3, 4.—F. D. Maurice, *Sermons*, vol. i. p. 117. Spurgeon, *Sermons*, vol. xxviii. No. 1663. IV. 4.—W. H. Hutchings, *Sermon Sketches* (2nd Series), p. 114. *Penny Pulpit*, No. 1665, p. 359. Spurgeon, *Sermons*, vol. xxxv. No. 2077 ; and vol. xxxix. No. 2304. *Expositor* (4th Series), vol. ii. p. 285 ; *ibid.* vol. x. p. 42 ; *ibid.* (5th Series), vol. ii. p. 88 ; *ibid.* (6th Series), vol. vii. p. 278 ; *ibid.* vol. ix. p. 233. IV. 5.—J. G. Rogers, *Christian World Pulpit*, vol. xlvii. p. 52. H. H. Henson, *The Record*, vol. xxvii. p. 596. H. Harries, *Christian World Pulpit*, vol. xliv. p. 257. *Expositor* (6th Series), vol. ix. p. 272.

THE WORLD'S INDICTMENT OF CHRISTIANITY

'God, Who commanded the light to shine out of darkness, hath shined in our hearts, to give the light of the knowledge of the glory of God in the face of Jesus Christ.'—2 Cor. iv. 6.

I. There are in the Main Three Counts in the Indictment which the spirit of the age brings against Christianity.

(a) *In a tone of tolerant benevolence the educated man of the world says to us :* ' Your ethics on the whole are sound and good, but they are entangled in a mythology which has become incredible and almost barbarous. Keep the best of the Psalms, the Sermon on the Mount, and the mystical emotion of St. Paul and St. John, and let the rest go. Then we are prepared to accept you along with other teachers of enlightened morality. We can give you no exclusive place.'

(b) *There speaks the student of evolutionary science.* ' For my part,' he says, ' I do not altogether like Christian morality. It is founded on sentiment, not on reason. It thwarts the beneficent action of Nature by protecting the weak against the strong. It preaches forgiveness, whereas Nature never forgives. It encourages the good to sacrifice themselves for the bad, whereas the bad ought to be sacrificed for the good. In short, instead of furthering progress it obstructs it. It is a conspiracy of inferiority against strength.'

(c) *Much more clamorously, we hear all around us a very different complaint, couched in less academic language.* 'You sky pilots offer us a chance of another world in order that we may tamely submit to be trampled on in this. We do not want to hear about heaven and hell; we want better wages and shorter hours. If your religion will help us to get what we want here and now, well and good. Otherwise we have no use for it.'

II. The Conscious Weakness of the Church is Shown in the Way in which all these Attacks are met.—As for the first, we are in a state of genuine perplexity about the miracles. We have made a good many concessions, and are quietly preparing to make more.

III. The Faith cannot be Defended in this Timorous Fashion.—The only worthy defence of Christianity, as it seems to me, is, by essential principles of the religion of Christ as a faith and hope, involving a definite rule of life, without any anxiety as to whether such a presentation will satisfy the ambitions of the masses or assuage the fears of the classes. To the Christian the unseen world is the real world. Christ declared Himself to be the light of the world, Who was come that men might have life, and have it more abundantly.

IV. It is this Consciousness of a New Life and a New Light that is the Driving Force of Christianity.—How and why it came, who can say? But the new light was a fact, and a most potent fact. It lifted its possessor clean out of the ordinary ruts along which we plod and draw our burdens. It bore fruit at once in love, joy, and peace, that triad which gives us the Christian version of liberty, equality, and fraternity.

(a) *It bore fruit in love* through the spontaneous expansion of the sympathies.

(b) *It bore fruit in joy.* The Greek vocabulary had to be enriched with two almost new words for love and joy. Christian optimism is something quite distinct and peculiar. It does not say complacently with Robert Browning, 'God's in His heaven, all's right with the world'. It is inclined to say, 'God has come to us on earth because all was wrong with the world'. It is an optimism which has grappled with and overcome the deepest pessimism.

(c) *It bore fruit in peace.* As the Christian is sorrowful but always rejoicing, so he is at war but always at peace. His deepest life is hid with Christ in God. He does not fret himself concerning the ungodly. He does not doubt that good is stronger than evil, and therefore he is not tempted to be unscrupulous in his methods to do evil that good may come.

REFERENCES.—IV. 6.—Spurgeon, *Sermons*, vol. xxv. No. 1493. B. J. Snell, *The All-Enfolding Love*, p. 1. T. Phillips, *Preacher's Magazine*, vol. xviii. p. 202. E. M. Geldart, *Faith and Freedom*, p. 1. J. C. M. Bellew, *Sermons*, vol. ii. p. 348. H. Alford, *Quebec Chapel Sermons*, vol. i. p. 84. *Expositor* (4th Series), vol. ii. p. 321.

THE WEAPONS OF THE SAINTS

'For God, who commanded. . . . But we have this treasure in earthen vessels, that the excellency of the power may be of God, and not of us.'—2 COR. IV. 6, 7.

THE thought in the preceding verse is that God has made us light-bearers. The glory of God in the face of Jesus Christ has shined upon our hearts, filled our inner lives, spread thence to the outward life, and made us Divinely kindled lamps, mirrors to show Him to the world. Then, as the Apostle thinks of the feeble and unworthy instruments which are employed for this high purpose, he glides into another figure. The light is Divine, the light-holder is weakly human. The thing which holds has no intrinsic beauty and dignity; it derives them from the treasure entrusted to it.

I. We have here the lowly confession, the self-depreciatory language of all the saints, that they are the feeblest of instruments made strong and serviceable by the indwelling power of the Almighty. Left to ourselves we are among the creatures that crawl and grovel; united to the Holy One we receive power to become the sons of God. In that simple truth there is the casting down of every proud imagination, and the lifting up of the soul to a throne of power. There man loses himself, and finds his lost self again glorified. The secret of all religious strength lies in this profound conviction. It is to be conscious of a Divine power that raises us from the dust and upholds our feeble goings.

II. The second thought is that through these feeble instruments God manifests Himself to the world. Human souls irradiated with His light are the best and truest, and in one sense the only certain, witness of His presence and working on the earth. The Church does not win way in the world by her creeds and defences, but by her moral superiority. The real power of the Church has always been in the heroic, self-forgetting, saintly lives that it produced.

III. The human instrument is to forget itself in the work, to hide itself as far as possible that the Divine power may have full play, that God alone may be magnified, 'that the excellency of the power may be of God, and not of us'. Wherever the Divine fire burns, in the heart with purest flame, there the servant will most forget himself in the enthralling desire to make the Master all in all. The best of the old Greek vases, those which were fashioned with most delicate and exquisite skill, were so thin and transparent that they showed all the treasure within and could hardly be seen themselves. And surely those are Christ's best workmen who seek to make their own lives like that.—J. G. GREENHOUGH, *The Cross in Modern Life*, p. 134.

2 COR. IV. 6, 7.

FRA BARTOLOMEO, the great Italian painter, stole into a monastery to get away from the din and guilt of the world, and threw his paints and canvas away because he thought they were stealing his heart from God. But then his fellow-monks said to him, 'Why should you not paint again for the glory of God?' and he painted those charming, thrilling pictures of Gospel scenes and holy martyrs which are still seen in Italy to-day, and before which men stand, and even kneel, with tears in their eyes. Now, when his brother-monks bade him, as was the custom in those days, to write his name at the foot of each picture, he said : ' No ; I have not done it for my own glory, but to show forth Christ to men ' ; and so he just scratched on each work : 'Pray for the picture, or pray for the painter—for the painter that he may do his work in a better way, for the picture that it may more clearly show the Lord : and let the name of the artist be forgotten '.

REFERENCE.—IV. 6, 7.—J. G. Greenhough, *Christian World Pulpit*, vol. xlix. p. 307.

THE TREASURE IN EARTHEN VESSELS

'But we have this treasure in earthen vessels, that the excellency of the power may be of God and not of us.'—2 COR. IV. 7.

I. WHAT is the special treasure to which Paul refers? It is definitely mentioned in the preceding verse : 'The light of the knowledge of the glory of God in the face of Jesus Christ '. Knowledge of any kind has a certain value. But though in a broad sense 'knowledge is power,' many things we learn are of small account, and of transient advantage. Indeed, some knowledge we should be better without, for there is no fallacy more fatal than that which tempts a young man to 'know life,' which usually means to have experience of its doubtful or its wicked enjoyments. Whether in literature or in amusement it is infinitely better to remain, as far as possible, ignorant of evils which God hates, and sent His Son to put away. But as the heavens are high above the earth, so the knowledge of the glory of God in the face of Jesus Christ is exalted above all knowledge of that kind. This knowledge, supreme above all others, may come in glimpses to the student of nature with her marvels, or to the student of history with its evidences of Divine control; but it only shines radiantly and constantly in the face of Jesus Christ. Remember, we cannot carry the treasure unless we receive it. The light of the knowledge of the glory of God in the face of Jesus Christ must shine in our hearts; or else we shall never help to irradiate the world with it.

II. Let me now suggest a few thoughts on the earthen vessels which contain this treasure. Paul always acknowledged that the vessel existed for the treasure, not the treasure for the vessel. Therefore he recognised that it was of little consequence that he was personally frail, knowing as he did that the truth in him—the Christ in him—was not dependent on his life, nor on his eloquence, nor on his excellence. It is a lesson which it would be well for us all to learn, for self-abnegation is very rare, and very unpopular. It is the treasure, not the vessel, we are to be anxious about ; just as Aladdin cared much for the gold and jewels in his cavern and little for the earthen jars which contained them. (1) Now from this we may learn a lesson of humility. (2) Again, if it be true that the treasure is in earthen vessels, that the excellency of the power (the cause of success, and therefore the credit of it) may be of God and not of us, we may be hopeful as well as humble. God will take care of His own treasures, though the earthen vessels which hold them are exchanged for others, or are broken into fragments.—A. ROWLAND, *Open Windows and other Sermons*, p. 102.

THE MINISTERING VESSEL

2 COR. IV. 7.

LET us examine the passage as workers for Jesus Christ.

I. In the first place Paul thinks very humbly of himself. He calls himself a vessel, an earthen vessel. A *vessel*, something which is carried, carried by his Master, or else something which merely carries that which his Master puts into it. (1) In the first place, of course, it is necessary that the vessel shall be a clean vessel. The Master will not use dirty vessels. 'Be ye clean,' says Isaiah, 'that bear the vessels of the Lord.' (2) The second characteristic of these vessels is, that they are anointed vessels. Every power which we have should be reserved for Jesus, our lips to speak for Him, our lives to be used for Him. The anointing from the Holy One gives power. (3) And then, in the third place, they must be empty vessels. You must be empty of self, you must be empty of pride and of ambition, you must be willing to be nothing, only an empty vessel for the Master's use made meet. (4) And then the fourth characteristic of these vessels is that they must be filled. For this is the strange paradox : that it is only as we are empty that we can be filled. (5) They must be broken vessels. We must let our light shine before men, there must be nothing to hinder the shining of this light; we must be willing to be broken vessels. (6) The vessel must be at hand. I am more and more convinced that the reason why some men are more used by God than other men, is simply that they are living closer to God than other men. (7) Then, lastly, those vessels which are meet for the Master's use must be, as it were, *always at the pump*, so that they are always overflowing.

II. But if the Apostle thinks very humbly of himself, he thinks very highly of his message. It is *a treasure*. 'We have this treasure in earthen vessels.' Though it is only in earthen vessels, we have it. And what was the treasure? (1) It was, in the first place, the knowledge of God. St. Paul felt certainty about it. As Prof. Westcott says : 'The knowledge of God is not the acquaintance of certain facts as external to ourselves ; nor is it merely intellectual conviction of their truth and reality. But it is the appropriation of these facts as an influencing power into the very being of the man who knows them.' St. Paul's treasure was the knowledge of the glory of God. It was an all-round view of

God that St. Paul obtained, and this it was which made him so stable. (2) And where did he get it? 'In the face of Jesus Christ.' As he saw the character of Christ, as he followed the work of Christ, as he looked at the cross of Christ, he saw there a revelation of God as he had never seen elsewhere.— E. A. STUART, *The New Commandment and other Sermons*, vol. VII. p. 41.

REFERENCES.—IV. 7.—J. R. Cohn, *The Sermon on the Mount*, p. 166. *Expositor* (4th Series), vol. vii. p. 277. IV. 8, 9.—Hugh Price Hughes, *Christian World Pulpit*, vol. xliv. p. 397.

LIFE MANIFESTED THROUGH DEATH

'Always bearing about in the body the dying of the Lord Jesus, that the life also of Jesus might be made manifest in our body.'—2 COR. IV. 10.

THE modern Christian need not seek to make a martyr of himself, yet he may still bear about in the body the dying of the Lord Jesus in other ways.

I. Bearing about the Remembrance.—First of all by bearing about the remembrance of what the Lord Jesus did, and how He died for us, so that the thought of it may unconsciously affect our views of things, and may give a tone and colour to all our thoughts and ideas and opinions. Most of us know what it is to mourn over relatives and friends. Some of us can never quite forget father or mother, child or brother or sister who has gone. We always carry in our secret hearts a fond and loving remembrance of all that they were to us when they were here—a reverent and affectionate regard for the carrying out of their wishes. The old librarian at the Bodleian used every morning to look up at the portrait of John Bodley at the top of the staircase and say to himself, 'I will try to do to-day all that I am sure you would wish me to do'.

II. Bearing about its Transforming Power.— And then there is another way in which we may bear about the dying of the Lord Jesus. We may show in our daily life the transforming power of His death. Our whole life ought to be changed and affected by the fact that Christ died for us, so that all with whom we have any intercourse may see we have been affected and influenced by that death; may see upon us, in fact, the mark of the Christian, not outwardly, of course, but in the inward tone, in the general manner and demeanour of those who are so affected.

III. Bearing about its Victory over Sin.—And then, too, we will show the dying of the Lord Jesus in that daily dying to sin and living unto holiness, which is so essential to the Christian, and in the mortifying, killing, and extinguishing the evil thoughts, the bad desires, the crooked, perverse ways, and the aggravating temper, which are to-day our inheritance from the first Adam. In thus ruling and controlling ourselves we shall be carrying about in our body the dying of our Lord Jesus, we shall be showing to the world that His death has enabled us to have the victory over sin.

IV. Bearing it about Always.—Lastly, let us remember the word 'always'. Always bear it, never lay it down. Always bear it, not in discontent, but in humility.

FROM DEATH UNTO LIFE

'Always bearing about in the body the dying of the Lord Jesus, that the life also of Jesus might be made manifest in our body.'—2 COR. IV. 10.

THE greatest truth of the life and death and resurrection of Christ must be found in the lives of Christians. It always has been so and always will be so. The early Apostles realised this, and so they made it their aim not only to preach Christ but to live Christ. If Christianity is ever to be a power in the world it must first be seen to be such in the lives of those who profess it, and if this was necessary in the first century it is just as necessary in this twentieth century. The world does not ask so much for Christ to be preached as it does for Christ to be lived. That is the meaning of our text.

What does it mean, and how is it to be done? We must now die the death that Christ died in order that we may live again here and now, and be ourselves proofs of the truth of this resurrection.

Consider what the death of Christ means.

I. It was an Act of Complete Self-renunciation —the voluntary death of self. There was no thought of self in the death of Jesus. What a large place self occupies in our hearts. Self must die and Christ must reign in its place. That is one way in which we may bear about in the body the dying of the Lord Jesus, that His life may be made manifest, that men may know that self indeed is dead in us and that Jesus lives instead.

II. It was a Death to the World.—Christ might have been an earthly king surrounded with all pomp and power, but His kingdom was not on this earth. It is as hard to die to the world as it is to die to self, and yet if we are to bear about in our bodies the dying of the Lord Jesus we must die to the world as He did. It takes time for people to say that the business and pleasures of the world cannot satisfy, and yet it is perfectly plain that any man serving Jesus Christ properly must put Him first in all things.

III. The Death of Christ was an Act of Completion.—For some of us this struggle goes on through all our life, and is only ended with actual, physical death, yet this death to self and the world should take place now and here. Jesus Christ did not remain in death, and as He rose so we must rise to a new life altogether.

REFERENCES.—IV. 10.—*Expositor* (6th Series), vol. xii. p. 142. IV. 10-12.—*Ibid.* (5th Series), vol. iv. p. 119. IV. 13. —T. Arnold, *Sermons*, vol. i. p. 199. IV. 14.—*Expositor* (4th Series), vol. x. p. 107. IV. 15.—T. Binney, *King's Weigh-House Chapel Sermons*, p. 198.

PROGRESS THROUGH DECAY

'Though our outward man perish, yet the inward man is renewed day by day.'—2 COR. IV. 16.

IT will be well for us at once to set this triumphant utterance of the Apostle Paul in a wide and universal setting. He assures us of an experience in which decay and renewing go on together. It is surely of importance to know that this striking statement is not an isolated and unrelated fact; that it is not a peculiarity of Christian faith which is not repeated anywhere else in the wide world.

I. All progress must take place through change, all growth must be accompanied by decay. When we look deep enough, the antagonism between decay and renewal disappears, for the former is seen to be one of the necessary elements of progress. It is the superficial glance at decay that constitutes our danger, and is likely to lead us into grave mistakes and pessimistic fears. (1) To infer that the man is perishing because his body is decaying is not only a violation of Christian faith, but also an unjustifiable ignoring of all pervading principles of life and thought. (2) Turn to nature, and you find the principle in unceasing action. What is the real meaning of this continual change and decay? They are simply the external sheath of an unresting development. (3) In the world of human thought the same principle is written in characters so large that he that runs may read. The history of our race is strewn with the wrecks of human systems of thought. Can the wisdom of the wise and the visions of the good and great perish utterly? History supplies the answer with unmistakable clearness. By submitting to outward decay, they secure continuance, progress, and immortality. (4) Turning to the sphere of religion, and even that of the Divine revelation, we find the obvious manifestation of the same principle of development through decay. (5) Nor can we fail to discern the same process in the development of Christian thought. (6) In the general development of life, whether of nations or of individuals, the same law is in manifest operation.

II. No destruction of the outward form of things can injure the living spirit within. The greatest hindrance to the advancement of the inward life, whether in nature or in human progress, lies in the tardiness of that which is decaying to fall away, and to give room for the expansion of fresh life.

III. The Apostle's application of this principle now stands out in clear relief. The body perishes that we may be set free. When it falls asunder, we shall spread our wings like the chrysalis, and soar into the sun.—John Thomas, *Concerning the King*, p. 140.

DAILY PERFECTING
2 Cor. iv. 16 (R.V.).

The visible man feels the wear and weight of years; the friction of life gradually exhausts; the eye grows dim, the ear loses its sensitiveness, the limbs miss their firmness and flexibility, the feet their elasticity and fleetness; but the interior man need know no ageing. An unintermitting growth in inward strength and joy is the duty and privilege of every one of us. We are too apt to care for the soul by fits and starts, and against this error the text warns us. God does not perfect us at a stroke, but by constant and protracted discipline. Little by little does God by His spirit

bring out of us the infinite beauty and glory which He first put into us when we were made in His own image and likeness.

I. Let us daily instruct and uplift our mind through communion with the truth. Goethe said that we ought every day to see at least one fine work of art, to hear one sweet strain of music, to read one beautiful poem. Wherever such inspirations are practicable they are unquestionably most desirable. But far more than we need this bread of mental delight do we need daily bread for our spiritual imagination and reason, for the building up of our highest life in the glory and contentment of righteousness.

II. By daily fellowship with God let us preserve the soul pure and vigorous. We need daily cleansing. All reputable persons are ever solicitous concerning their physical purity; they scrupulously attend to their personal appearance many times a day; the satirist reproaches some of us for living between 'the comb and the glass'; and the cleansing of the soul must be maintained with the same system and ardour if it is to abide in strength and beauty.

III. Make the best of everyday discipline. Carefully improve life's routine and commonplace as well as study to improve its extraordinary occasions. The fullest sanctification of daily routine is one of the greatest secrets that the serious have to learn.

IV. Day by day let us do all the good we can. What a source of sanctification is the life of service! We clamour for large opportunities which are rarely, if ever, granted, missing meanwhile the little openings of daily life. 'No day without its line' was the canon of the great painter of antiquity; and thus, one by one, his masterpieces came to perfection. Let our motto be: 'No day without its helpful word and deed, however obscure our sphere'; and we too in the kingdom of souls shall turn out masterpieces which no artist in marble or colour may rival.—W. L. Watkinson, *Themes for Hours of Meditation*, p. 1.

CONSTANT RENEWAL
2 Cor. iv. 16.

I. Note that spiritual renewal is the demand and the gift of the Gospel.

II. This spiritual renewal is progressive and constant. Day by day. The fundamental idea is that this renewal does not accomplish itself at a bound, but by slow stages, by constant approximation to a goal far ahead.

III. This progressive renewal is continuous only while we adopt the means. (1) By the steady contemplation of Christ and eternal realities. (2) By the resolute excision and destruction of the old nature.—A. Maclaren.

References.—IV. 16-18.—Hugh Price Hughes, *Christian World Pulpit*, vol. liii. p. 337. IV. 17.—C. O. Eldridge, *Preacher's Magazine*, vol. xviii. p. 216. *Expositor* (4th Series), vol. i. p. 34. IV. 17, 18.—H. S. Holland, *Christian World Pulpit*, vol. lii. p. 248. G. Body, *ibid.* vol. lvii. p. 228. W. Page Roberts, *Reasonable Service*, p. 66.

SEEN . . . NOT SEEN

'While we look not at the things which are seen, but at the things which are not seen ; for the things which are seen are temporal, but the things which are not seen are eternal.' 2 Cor. iv. 18.

I HAVE been thinking much about words you will find in the Second Epistle of Paul to the Corinthians, chapter iv., verse 18. ' Seen . . . not seen ; temporal . . . eternal,'—the two languages each with a grammar of its own ; two styles of music, two gamuts, two different ranges altogether of utterance. Here is a new standard of proportion and a new light of colour and a new expression of life ; here, indeed, is a new language bigger and better than our mother tongue. 'Our light affliction'—of which we made so much and groaned so deeply ; we turned the summer into winter and the day into night : and, lo, a voice came to us suddenly, and found our hearts in a thrilling whisper saying, 'light affliction,' hardly anything worth mentioning, quite a matter of the surface ; there is no duration in it. You should look in the right direction if you would see your own self, O soul ; what is now accounted by you as a severe affliction is working out something beyond itself ; it is working out for you a far more exceeding and eternal weight of glory. What does 'eternal weight' mean ? I never heard these two words put together before ; what is the relation of 'eternal' to 'weight' or of 'weight' to 'eternal' ? It should be thus expressed : Weight upon weight of glory, dawn upon dawn of light, morning upon morning of blaze and radiance. And how does this wondrous vision come about ? It comes about whilst we look not at the things which are seen, but at the things which are not seen.

I. The creed is seen ; faith is unseen ; that is the distinction. You can alter a creed, you cannot alter faith.

Denominationalism is a thing seen ; worship is a thing not seen. Sectarianism is temporal, the Church is eternal.

We might apply the same thought in even the highest direction of all. The Bible in a certain sense is but a book ; it was written by men, copied by men, printed by men. We do not look at the merely mechanical book ; when we speak of the Bible in our highest moods we speak of the revelation. We do not ask the printer's permission to read it, we know it ; we do not ask the priest, the robed fraud, to read it for us, we claim to read it for ourselves, for it is the Father's speech to the son's heart, and between the Father and the son, meaning by son the whole human race, there is a confidence, subtle, impenetrable, all but omnipotent. All the controversy rages about the mechanical book : Who wrote it ? was this written in the Maccabean period ? can we trace this psalm to post-exilian sources or pre-exilic dates ? Hence the controversy and the expensive communication between man and man. The critic says that David could not have written the twenty-third psalm because he says he will dwell in the house of the Lord for ever, and David did not build the Temple. Oh, the folly, the madness ! Jacob, long before David was ever thought of, said in the rocky place where he slept, This is none other than the house of God—the unbuilt house, not built by hands ; not seen, but eternal ; the house in the clouds, in shadow, in outline ; the precursor of all the temples and altars yet to be reared by human hands. Why not look into the poetry, spirituality, and the true idealism of things, and catch the morning ere it dawns ?

II. Remember that the great things in life are all not seen. You cannot see love ; you can only see its incarnations. You cannot see faith ; you can only see its conduct, for it becomes a motive and turns the soul into action and into deeds of purity and charity. Thus would I rest. The little child can see the rosy-cheeked apple that its mother brought away from the orchard ; the child can see the apple, but not the love that plucked it. As a little child it must begin where it can ; the apple is an apple to the child, the metaphysical or penetrating force of the soul has not yet begun to assert itself, and therefore the little fingers and knuckles clutch the apple, and the little mouth shapes itself into an unspeakable doxology, and the whole earth is a beautiful place so long as that apple continues to exist. But the little child did not see the love that thought of it, the love that asked for it, the love that put it in a safe place, the love that dreamed for the child a sweet surprise ; the child does not see the love that folded the apple in the tissue paper, and the fingers that moved so deftly and opened the cotton wool in which the little prize lay snugly. All the little child could see was the rosy-cheeked apple ; all the ministry of preparation and love and forecast the little child knows nothing about. One day it will be explained in heaven !—JOSEPH PARKER, *City Temple Pulpit*, vol. ii. p. 128.

THE ETERNAL AND THE TEMPORAL

' For the things which are seen are temporal, but the things which are not seen are eternal.'—2 Cor. iv. 18.

EVERYTHING reminds us that what we see is short-lived, a passing show, a bit of stage scenery, a bird on the wing, perishable and perishing ; and yet, hidden in the midst of all that, and unseen, there is always something which abides, which outlasts time and decay, which speaks to us of immortality, which bears the mark of a changeless and eternal God.

I. There is decay and death in all things, and imperishable life in all things. God preaches a sermon to us on this text with the coming of every season, and it is but a sample of what He is teaching us every day. It is only the outside that perishes. The tree has life within itself, which will break into joyous beauty again when the spring-time comes ; the very flowers drop their seed and live again ; nature only casts its garments and sleeps awhile, and awakes again, when morning comes, as strong and beautiful as ever. Each human life reads the same lesson if we have only wisdom to receive it. We are always changing as we grow in years ; yet there is something deeper in us which changes not. We are always dying, yet behold we live. You get the same lesson if you look at human life on a larger scale. The fashions of the world change, and there is perpetual flux, waste, and decay. Humanity puts on new garments, takes up new thoughts, opinions, ambitions, and desires, yet there is something everlasting which abides. God has written eternity in the hidden heart of all things, not to mock us with vain dreams, but to make us certain that there is a happier and nobler life behind the veil.

II. If you would live well and sweetly, you must believe at every point that there are unseen eternal things beneath all that is temporal and seen ; you must believe it concerning your own moral endeavour. Look through your worrying weaknesses and failures to that deeper, nobler self which the Spirit of Christ is making for you—the man that is to be—the man of faith and love and goodness, meet to be partaker of the inheritance of the saints in light. You will need it, as St. Paul needed it, in the dark and cloudy days when the heart has its trouble and fears, when there is perhaps more pain than joy, and when one thing after another which has been dear to you slips away as the day fades into the night. Then you will be happy again, as he was, when you remember that it is only the outward man that perishes, and that all the deeper things remain; that, of all which God has given you, nothing will be permanently taken away which it is good for you to have ; and that the pain, whatever it may be, is the short night's discipline which prepares you for the joy in the morning.—J. G. Greenhough, *The Divine Artist*, p. 61.

References. — IV. 18. — Bishop Winnington-Ingram, *Under the Dome*, p. 186. F. D. Maurice, *Sermons*, vol. iv. p. 245. H. S. Lunn, *Christian World Pulpit*, vol. xlviii. p. 349. C. Vince, *The Unchanging Saviour*, p. 278. J. M. Neale, *Sermons for the Church Year*, vol. ii. p. 49. John Watson, *Christian World Pulpit*, vol. xlix. p. 316. C. Bradley, *The Christian Life*, p. 1. H. Drummond, *The Ideal Life*, p. 127. T. Jones, *Christian World Pulpit*, vol. li. p. 40. R. W. Church, *Village Sermons* (2nd Series), p. 171. E. M. Geldart, *Echoes of Truth*, p. 90. John Watson, *The Inspiration of our Faith*, p. 348. E. H. Bickersteth, *Thoughts on Past Years*, p. 59. F. W. Farrar, *Everyday Christian Life*, p. 70. Spurgeon, *Sermons*, vol. xxiii. No. 1380. Bishop Moule, *Christian World Pulpit*, vol. lxii. p. 9. *Expositor* (4th Series), vol. i. pp. 34, 208 ; *ibid*. (5th Series), vol. v. p. 383. A. Maclaren, *Expositions of Holy Scripture—Corinthians*, p. 323. V. 1.—R. Rainy, *Christian World Pulpit*, vol. liii. p. 387. Spurgeon, *Sermons*, vol. xxix. No. 1719. W. F. Shaw, *Sermon Sketches for the Christian Year*, p. 135. C. Cross, *Preacher's Magazine*, vol. v. p. 323. J. D. Jones, *Elims of Life*, p. 220. *Expositor* (4th Series), vol. i. pp. 34, 138 ; *ibid*. vol. x. p. 303. A. Maclaren, *Expositions of Holy Scripture—Corinthians*, p. 333. V. 1, 2.—R. Higinbotham, *Sermons*, p. 28. V. 1-3.—*Expositor* (4th Series), vol. i. p. 169. V. 2.—F. W. Farrar, *Christian World Pulpit*, vol. l. p. 195. V. 2-4.—*Expositor* (4th Series), vol. iv. p. 192. V. 3-5.—*Ibid*. (6th Series), vol. i. p. 210. V. 4.—T. Arnold, *Sermons*, vol. i. p. 237. J. S. Flynn, *Church Family Newspaper*, vol. xv. p. 1028. J. G. Greenhough, *The Mind of Christ in St. Paul*, p. 177. V. 5.—W. L. Alexander, *Sermons*, p. 168. Spurgeon, *Sermons*, vol. xvi. No. 912. *Expositor* (6th Series), vol. iv. pp. 187, 274. A. Maclaren, *Expositions of Holy Scripture*

—*Corinthians*, p. 343. V. 5-10.—Spurgeon, *Sermons*, vol. xxii. No. 1303. V. 7.—E. J. Boyce, *Parochial Sermons*, p. 1. C. S. Macfarland, *Christian World Pulpit*, vol. lix. p. 235. W. H. Evans, *Short Sermons for the Seasons*, p. 142. A. H. Bradford, *Christian World Pulpit*, vol. lvi. p. 136.—H. Woodcock, *Sermon Outlines* (1st Series), p. 214. C. Voysey, *Christian World Pulpit*, vol. lii. p. 43. Bishop Westcott, *The Incarnation and Common Life*, p. 263. Spurgeon, *Sermons*, vol. xii. No. 677. *Expositor* (5th Series), vol. i. p. 144. V. 8.—Spurgeon, *Sermons*, vol. vii. No. 413. A. Maclaren, *Expositions of Holy Scripture—Corinthians*, p. 353. V. 5.—J. M. Neale, *Sermons for the Church Year*, vol. ii. p. 35. R. Higinbotham, *Sermons*, p. 220. *Expositor* (4th Series), vol. ii. p. 59. A. Maclaren, *Expositions of Holy Scripture—Corinthians*, p. 361.

2 Cor. v. 10.

Carts go along the streets ; full of stript human corpses, thrown pell-mell ; limbs sticking up :—seest thou that cold Hand sticking up, through the heaped embrace of brother corpses, in its yellow paleness, in its cold rigour ; the palm opened towards Heaven, as if in dumb prayer, in expostulation *de profundis*, take pity on the Sons of men !—Mercier saw it, as he walked down 'the Rue Saint-Jacques from Montrouge, on the morrow of the Massacres': but not a Hand ; it was a Foot,—which he reckons still more significant, one understands not well why. Or was it as the Foot of one *spurning* Heaven ? Rushing, like a wild diver, in disgust and despair, towards the depths of annihilation ? Even there shall His hand find thee, and His right-hand hold thee,—surely for right not for wrong, for good not evil ! 'I saw that Foot,' says Mercier ; 'I shall know it again at the great Day of Judgment, when the Eternal, throned on His thunders, shall judge both kings and Septemberers.'—Carlyle, *The French Revolution*, vol. iii. bk. i. chap. vi.

2 Cor. v. 10.

The dying moment is the falling due of a bill. At this fatal instant one feels the coming home of a diffused responsibility. That which has been complicates that which will be. The past returns and enters into the future.—Victor Hugo.

References.—V. 10.—Spurgeon, *Sermons*, vol. xviii. No. 1076. Bishop Gore, *Christian World Pulpit*, vol. lvi. p. 406. C. Gutch, *Sermons*, p. 252. *Expositor* (4th Series), vol. i. p. 209 ; *ibid*. vol. iii. p. 274 ; *ibid*. vol. iv. pp. 61, 166 ; *ibid*. (6th Series), vol. x. p. 156. V. 13, 14.—J. G. Rogers, *Christian World Pulpit*, vol. xlv. p. 323. V. 13-15.—*Expositor* (5th Series), vol. v. p. 135. V. 13-17.—H. Smith, *Preacher's Magazine*, vol. xix. p. 31. V. 14.—H. Alford, *Quebec Chapel Sermons*, vol. i. p. 349. Spurgeon, *Sermons*, vol. xxiv. No. 1411. M. G. Glazebrook, *Prospice*, p. 58. Bishop Westcott, *Sermons*, 1901-2, p. 5. T. Arnold, *Sermons*, vol. iii. p. 1. S. G. Maclennan, *Christian World Pulpit*, vol. li. p. 54. Griffith John, *ibid*. vol. liv. p. 392. *Expositor* (5th Series), vol. ix. p. 51. A. Maclaren, *Expositions of Holy Scripture—Corinthians*, p. 371. V. 14, 15.—Bishop Gore, *Christian World Pulpit*, vol. li. p. 225. B. W. Noel, *Penny Pulpit*, No. 1657, p. 297.

HE DIED FOR ALL
'He died for all.'—2 Cor. v. 15.

The word 'death' is a cardinal word in the New Testament Scriptures. It enshrines a primary fact, out of which a great Gospel is born. 'Christ died for our sins.' But what is meant by 'to die'? Our conception is too commonly narrow and impoverished. Our emphasis is false, and false emphasis always means distorted truth.

I. We misinterpret death if we allow the body to determine our thought. Death is not primarily, but only very secondarily, an affair of the flesh. This is our Master's teaching. What we ordinarily call death, our Master insisted upon calling sleep.

II. The Master repeatedly declares that He came to save us from that which He calls death. 'If a man keep My word, he shall never see death.' Insert the common interpretation of the word death in that phrase, and the sentence becomes a dark confusion. We shall all sleep, saints and sinners alike; but we shall not all die; for if any man keep the word of the Christ, he shall never see death; he is passed from death unto life; he abideth for ever.

III. But my text tells me that 'Christ died'. He did more than sleep; He died. What, then, was the Saviour's death? Let us away into Gethsemane, at the midnight, that we may just touch the awful mystery. 'He began to be sorrowful and very heavy.' I think that marks the beginning of the dying. Go a little farther into the garden, and listen to the Master's agonised speech. 'My soul is exceeding sorrowful, even unto death;' exceeding desolate, 'even unto death'. He fears not the sleep, but, oh, He does shrink from the death! 'My God, My God, why hast Thou forsaken me?' That was death. What would follow would be only sleep. Christ Jesus walked that way of appalling darkness and alienation in place of His brethren.

IV. The Scriptures affirm that apart from Christ I am still under the dominion of 'the law of sin and death'; sin and abandonment, sin and homelessness, sin and forsakenness and terrible night. But the Scriptures further affirm that in Christ Jesus I come under the dominion of another law—the 'law of the Spirit of life'—and by this I am freed from the sovereignty of 'the law of sin and death'. Here, then, is the glory of the Gospel. It is declared that I, a poor struggling, self-wasted sinner, may by faith be so identified with Christ, that Christ and I become as 'one man'. This is the possible heritage of all men, made possible to all men by the Saviour's atoning death.—J. H. JOWETT, *Apostolic Optimism*, p. 171.

'He died for all.'—2 COR. v. 15.

TENNYSON tells of his visit to Mr. Wildman at Mablethorpe. The host and hostess were described by the poet as 'two perfectly honest Methodists'. He continues: 'When I came I asked her after the news, and she replied: "Why, Mr. Tennyson, there's only one piece of news I know, that Christ died for all men"'.

REFERENCES.—V. 15.—*Expositor* (4th Series), vol. i. p. 134; *ibid.* vol. vi. pp. 30, 347; *ibid.* vol. viii. p. 468; *ibid.* (6th Series), vol. ix. p. 45; *ibid.* vol. x. p. 31. V. 15-17.—*Ibid.* vol. ii. p. 208. V. 16.—R. W. Dale, *Christian World Pulpit*, vol. l. p. 330. T. Arnold, *Sermons*, vol. i. p. 129. W. G. Horder, *Christian World Pulpit*, vol. lv. p. 196. J. N. Bennie, *The Eternal Life*, p. 190. R. W. Dale, *Fellowship with Christ*, p. 31. *Expositor* (4th Series), vol. ix. p. 92; *ibid.* (6th Series), vol. iv. p. 216; *ibid.* vol. vi. p. 192; *ibid.* (7th Series), vol. v. p. 207. V. 17.—T. Arnold, *Sermons*, vol. i. p. 10. A. Bradley, *Sermons Chiefly on Character*, p. 77. Spurgeon, *Sermons*, vol. xv. No. 881; vol. xx. No. 1183, and vol. xxii. No. 1328. F. W. Farrar, *Truths to Live By*, p. 290. F. Ferguson, *Peace With God*, p. 191. T. V. Tymms, *Christian World Pulpit*, vol. lii. p. 187. H. Allen, *Penny Pulpit*, No. 1553, p. 61. H. Bonar, *Short Sermons for Family Reading*, p. 435. C. Perren, *Revival Sermons in Outline*, p. 253. W. Robertson Nicoll, *Sunday Evening*, p. 409. *Expositor* (7th Series), vol. v. p. 204. V. 17, 18.—T. Arnold, *Sermons*, vol. iv. p. 274. G. W. Brameld, *Practical Sermons* (2nd Series), p. 279. V. 18.—F. D. Maurice, *Sermons*, vol. i. p. 42. Spurgeon, *Sermons*, vol. vi. No. 318, and vol. xlix. No. 2837. H. P. Liddon, *University Sermons* (2nd Series), p. 183. *Expositor* (5th Series), vol. viii. p. 143. V. 18-20.—*Expositor* (4th Series), vol. v. p. 435. V. 18-21.—Spurgeon, *Sermons*, vol. xix. No. 1124. C. Perren, *Sermon Outlines*, p. 291. T. Binney, *King's Weigh-House Chapel Sermons* (2nd Series), p. 51.

RECONCILIATION IN CHRIST

'God was in Christ, reconciling the world unto Himself.'— 2 COR. v. 19.

I. 'GOD was in Christ.' This truth, which the Apostle Paul profoundly believed, and which was the starting-point of all his thought upon the things of God, is supposed to be of all others the one peculiarly acceptable to religious minds to-day. From the first dawn of the Christian era each age has had its special theological fashion; for good or for evil, men have laid emphasis on some one side of Christian doctrine to the exclusion or the minimising of others. And these latter days have witnessed a widespread revival of belief in the Incarnation, as the most fundamental of all Christian verities. 'That we only know God in Jesus Christ,' 'that Christ has for us the religious value of God,' have become the new shibboleths of a great body of religious thinkers. We need not seriously object to this. The Incarnation, *with its implications*, is the very foundation of the edifice of Christian truth. Apart from it Christian revelation would be a mystery and almost a fraud. The coming of God in Christ to dwell with the children of men was in the fulness of the times. All investigations into the history of the times immediately preceding and following the birth of Jesus show how marvellously a place was made for Him, and how He fitted into the place that had been made. Just as we find in the physical world that an organism is prepared by slow microcosmic stages for the performance of some higher function and entrance into some higher plane of being, so men had by the word of God been prepared for the new and higher spiritual possibilities which were to be made actual in Jesus Christ. The word became flesh when the world was capable of receiving the message which the Incarnation involved. In Christ man became created anew, for he then entered into the larger inheritance which had been prepared for him, and which he was of an age to receive.

That he did not enter upon it fully and at once was but of a piece with all God's action in the past.

II. 'Reconciling the world unto Himself.' Then the world needed to be reconciled. It was estranged, alienated from God. It is so still, though the fact is not always acknowledged. And if it is so, why? Why the need for reconciliation? How did it come about, it is often objected, that God so mismanaged affairs that men did not know Him and serve Him instinctively and needed to be reconciled? These are some of the difficulties that the very use of the word 'reconciliation' raises.

In the history of the race sin is independence of God. It has many forms, and manifests itself openly in a variety of ways. But in essence it is rebellion against God, impatience of His control, determination to be one's own master and to go one's own way. Sin may also be described as a disease—an unnatural and an unhealthy state that involves ceaseless and unavailing struggle. For this there can be no remedy save one which goes to the root of the mischief, and seeks to restore man once again to true and natural relations with God. This conclusion is confirmed not only by the history of revelation, but by man's own efforts to retrieve his position for himself.

III. We may say, in a word, that the supreme purpose of pre-Christian revelation is to vindicate the majesty of God's law and prove man to be a transgressor. But a very little study of this revelation serves to bring out its great educational purpose. The law is ever a schoolmaster. It does not exist for its own sake, nor is it an end in itself. It is the outcome of God's love and pity for the weakness of man; it serves to vindicate His righteousness and to bring transgressors to a better mind. The new law in Jesus Christ was a means of grace such as the old could never be, because it lifted man at once on to a higher plane in his relation with God. And it was made necessary not only by the insufficiency of the old order, but by the blunders and impotence of man. While we believe profoundly that man was made in God's image and has in him the spark of the Divine, we cannot but believe also in what theologians call his depravity. There is almost a perverse ingenuity in the way in which man has fallen short of his opportunities and wilfully turned light into darkness. The history of revelation, while on one side it is the story of God's love and willingness to save, is on the other a dismal tale of man's hostility to God and peevish aversion from His will.—W. B. SELBIE, *The Servant of God*, p. 8.

REFERENCE.—V. 19.—Marcus Dods, *Christ and Man*, p. 140.

RECONCILIATION AFTER CONVERSION

'Reconciling the world unto Himself. . . . Be ye reconciled to God.'—2 COR. v. 19, 20.

THERE are two reconciliations, if I may so put it, and I shall not be deterred by pedantry from so declaring my gospel. There is a reconciliation before conversion, necessary to conversion, and in itself a species of complete conversion; there is another reconciliation,

which seems to me oftentimes to be harder, deeper, as it were more exacting; a never-ceasing reconciliation; a reconciliation of growth, progress, advancement, perfectness. We have all, it is but reasonable to suppose, passed the first conversion or the first reconciliation; we carry no arms against God, no gun, or sabre or sword or cruel spear; we do not dare the Almighty to battle. I hear, as it were, the clash of falling arms, which, being interpreted, means, We fight no longer against our God; we say to Christ, Galilean, Thou hast conquered. We are no more scoundrels, ruffians. We may have passed into a still more dangerous state, and it is that second reconciliation which unmans and overpowers me. Have we received the second reconciliation? Some Christians do not hesitate about talking concerning the second blessing. It is a richly evangelical term; we have no need to be ashamed of it or to apologise for it. I will venture to ask, Have we received the second reconciliation? are we far away from the gate of Damascus, where our wrath was hot against the Lord and against His Christ? and have we passed into serener conditions, into a nobler and ampler, a saintlier and tenderer manhood? 'Be ye reconciled to God.'

I. We are reconciled to God in the matter of sin, through our Lord Jesus Christ, but are we reconciled to God in the matter of providence?

II. We are reconciled to God in the rougher sins and the initial sins, but what about God's discipline with our souls?

III. Are we reconciled to God in the distribution and in the allotment of talent and position and prize of a social kind? If so, we have got rid of the devil jealousy, envy. Are we reconciled to God when we see that the man standing next us has got five talents, and we have got but two?

When we enter into this blessing and security of the second reconciliation we shall have peace, we shall know that it is all right because God did it.

When we enter into this second reconciliation we shall get the best out of life, and until we enter the second reconciliation we shall not get the best out of life; it will be a mere scramble for existence, it will be a misreading of the Divine purpose, and it will be a great heat and unrest and irreligious tumult, until we get to the centre of things and know that God is bringing us into the second reconciliation, so that in the presence of the wilderness and the serpent and the great sea and deep river we shall be able to say, I can do all things through Christ which enableth me.—JOSEPH PARKER, *City Temple Pulpit*, vol. II. p. 280.

REFERENCES.—V. 20.—J. Watson, *Scottish Review*, vol. iii. p. 440. A. Maclaren, *Expositions of Holy Scripture—Corinthians*, p. 380.

AH, THE BITTER SHAME AND SORROW

'We are ambassadors therefore on behalf of Christ, as though God were intreating by us: we beseech you on behalf of Christ, be ye reconciled to God. Him who knew no sin He made to be sin on our behalf; that we might become the righteousness of God in Him.'—2 COR. v. 20, 21.

THERE is a fine Welsh poem in which the poet imagines that the Sun, and all the attendant planets and satellites in his sphere, passed before the Great White Throne of the Creator; and as each passed, He smiled; but when Earth came in her turn, He blushed. There appear to be five reasons in this text why man, the tenant of this world, may blush—why earth may blush—why we all, indeed, may blush.

I. Because we have never realised the awful character and nature of sin. That sin is heinous, black, and dreadful, we are all prepared to admit; but, probably, he who has *most* lamented sin has had but a very slight and superficial conception of its true nature and character. But after all, none could thoroughly understand how base and vile sin was until Jesus entered our world in the flesh, born of the pure Virgin. How often we only notice the real blackness of black when it is set against a white background; and we only know the real blackness of sin when we see it against the resplendent background of our Saviour's perfect character.

II. Let us remember how much sin cost God. 'God made Him to be sin.' How the nature of Jesus Christ must have shrunk from contact with sin! Martin Luther says that, 'For the time Jesus Christ was the greatest sinner that ever lived'. But this statement needs qualification. Still, Jesus became so closely identified with the sin of the race, that He stood before the universe as though it had all met in Him: 'He was made sin for us'.

III. Let us confess, with shame, our reluctance to believe in God's invitations. God beseeches men to be reconciled. The Greek word is most interesting. It might be rendered, God beseeches men to let His reconciliation have effect.

IV. God's ambassadors are sadly slack in His work. Here, surely, there is cause for shame.

V. We may be ashamed that we have not availed ourselves of the blessedness of the Divine righteousness. If it be asked how we may attain to this most blessed state, we may answer, take ten looks at Christ for one at self.—F. B. MEYER, *In the Beginning God*, p. 163.

REFERENCES.—V. 20, 21.—Spurgeon, *Sermons*, vol. xxxii. No. 1910. J. Budgen, *Parochial Sermons*, vol. i. p. 222.

SIN

'Him who knew no sin He made sin on our behalf.'—
2 COR. V. 21.

WHAT is sin? Sin is the difference between what I was meant to be and what I am. What were we meant to be? This we gather from observing what Jesus Christ was. Evidently each human being was intended to live the life of God, to carry out His will. to love Him, and to obey Him. That is what you and I were meant to be. What we are, we ourselves and God alone can know. But it is not that. It is very different from that. And the whole *margin*, in some cases very broad, in other cases narrower, but to the best of men always seeming much broader than to the worst—the margin between the man you are now, and the man that God meant you to be, is sin. There

is much sin in us for which we are not responsible; there is much also for which we are. That for which we are not responsible evokes the cry of horror; that for which we are, evokes the cry of guilt. But we shall get a clearer notion of what sin is if we endeavour to distinguish it from some other common ideas with which it is frequently confused; ideas like Crime, Vice, Wickedness.

I. Crime, for instance, is a breach of a human law, a gross offence against the constitution of civil society. But as there may be a great divergence between the law of a given society and the law of God, it by no means follows that a crime must be a sin. A crime is a sin only when and in so far as the human law against which it is a trespass is identical with the Divine law.

II. Vice and Immorality, as the most obvious illustrations of sin, are frequently treated as if they were co-extensive with sin. But it must be remembered that the notion of vice, and even the notion of immorality, is largely determined by the customs and the accidents of human society. Neither notion is like that of sin, definite and absolute.

III. Wickedness, which is a very vague term, comes much nearer to the idea of sin, because in Scripture the terms 'wicked' and 'sinners' are used almost interchangeably. But we fling about the word *wicked* in a wild fashion, and often declare a man is wicked because he has offended *us*, while the proper meaning of wickedness is that it offends God. Let us note one or two of the characteristics of sin as it appears in the practice of life. For one thing, note how sin works like a disease. Can the irreparable be repaired? And if so, how? Nothing in this universe can ever be undone. The question is not so much, Can God forgive? God can do anything. But it is rather, Can you forgive yourself?—R. F. HORTON, *Brief Sermons for Busy Men*, p. 15.

ATONEMENT

2 COR. V. 21.

IF we would bear in mind the definition of sin as the difference between what men are and what they were meant to be, we should readily perceive that the remission of sin involves nothing short of making men what they were meant to be. A humanity fulfilling the intention of God in its creation, and every individual filling the appointed place in such a restored humanity; that is the sublime dream which is suggested by the destruction of sin in the light of the definition of sin which we have derived from the New Testament. That such a result could only be effected by the Omnipotence of God is evident; but in the historical manifestation of Jesus Christ the Apostles saw the demonstration that the Divine Power was set upon that result; they saw also, and inwardly experienced, the potency and the process by which the splendid purpose was to be achieved.

I. For the removal of sin men had to learn what they were meant to be. That is given to the world in the person of the Divine Man, Jesus Christ; and it is expounded to men in that body of teaching which is preserved for us in the Four Evangelists. 'I am always amazed,' said Tennyson, 'when I read the New Testament, at the splendour of Christ's purity and holiness, and at His infinite pity.'

II. But the thought of what we should be only awakens us to a sense of our helplessness in the coils of sin which are round us from our birth. It was therefore the work of Christ to become the head of a new humanity, a second Adam, as St. Paul would say, or, in the simpler language of St. John: 'As many as received Him, to them gave He the power to become the children of God, to them that believe on His name, which were born not of blood nor of the will of the flesh, nor of the will of man, but of God'.

III. But when Christ came there were sinners inheriting the curse of nature and far gone in the corruption of the will, who needed to be re-made if they were to be freed from sin. And, because the Church has so imperfectly understood the evangel of the New Humanity in Christ, by far the larger proportion of persons even in a Christian country go so far in sin that their deliverance is a question of re-making. Jesus Christ announced the power which could thus re-make man in the simple but exalted language of John.

IV. 'Except a man be born again, he cannot see the kingdom of God.' It was Jesus 'lifted up' that was to be to sinful men what the serpent had been to the diseased Israelites. He who knew no sin was made sin on our behalf. Made sin! Yes, indeed, made sin in such a way that the law which condemned sin was fulfilled, and the sin it condemned was abolished.—R. F. HORTON, *Brief Sermons for Busy Men*, p. 29.

REFERENCES.—V. 21.—R. J. Campbell, *City Temple Sermons*, p. 61. Spurgeon, *Sermons*, vol. iii. Nos. 141 and 142; and vol. vi. No. 310. R. J. Campbell, *Christian World Pulpit*, vol. liv. p. 209. J. D. Thompson, *ibid.* vol. xlviii. p. 42. R. J. Campbell, *A Faith for To-day*, p. 255. W. L. Lee, *British Congregationalist*, 1st August, 1907, p. 93. *Expositor* (5th Series), vol. ii. p. 164; *ibid.* vol. vii. p. 281; *ibid.* (6th Series), vol. i. p. 376; *ibid.* vol. xi. p. 46. V. 25.—R. J. Campbell, *Christian World Pulpit*, vol. lvii. p. 20.

UNREALITY

'Receive not the grace of God in vain.'—2 COR. VI. 1.

THE Apostle is here warning us against what we fear is a very common fault in the present day. So many people seem to receive the grace of God, but it has no influence upon their lives, they receive that grace in vain. I want to say a word or two about the importance of sincerity and reality in religion. If we profess to have any religion at all, let us take great care that it is real. By 'real' I mean that which is not base, hollow, formal, counterfeit, sham, nominal; not mere show, pretence, skin-deep feeling, temporary profession, outside work; but, on the other hand, that which is genuine, sincere, honest, thorough; something inward, solid, intrinsic, lasting. Our religion may be weak, mingled with infirmities, but that is not the point now—is it real?

Epochs in a nation's history have been described as a golden age, a silver, a brazen, and an iron; if we measure the religion of the age in which we live by its quality rather than its quantity, it is an age of base metal and alloy. On every side we want more reality. Consider, then, the importance of reality in religion. The idea that this reality is common is a delusion, and the charge that it is uncharitable and censorious to question the assertion that 'all have good hearts at bottom' and are sincere in the main, is a false one.

I. What saith the Scriptures? Look at the parables of our Lord. The sower, the wheat and tares, the draw-net, the two sons, the wedding garment, the ten virgins, the talents, the great supper, the pounds, the two builders, contrast the true believer and the mere nominal disciple; all bring out in striking colours the difference between reality and unreality in religion, its uselessness and danger.

II. Look at our Lord's denunciation of the scribes and Pharisees; eight times in one chapter He denounces as hypocrites, in the most scathing words, men who, at any rate, were more moral and decent than the publicans and harlots. It was all intended to teach the abominableness of false profession and mere outward religion in God's sight. Open profligacy and sensuality are indeed ruinous sins, if not flung aside; but there seems nothing so distasteful to Christ as hypocrisy and unreality.

III. There is hardly a Christian grace or virtue which has not its counterfeit described in the Word of God.

(1) There is an unreal repentance. Saul, Ahab, Herod, Judas Iscariot, had feelings of sorrow for sin, but they never really repented unto salvation.

(2) There is an unreal faith. Simon Magus 'believed,' yet his heart was not right in the sight of God. So also the devils 'believe and tremble' (Acts VIII. 13; Jas. II. 19).

(3) There is an unreal holiness. Joash, King of Judah, became apparently very holy and good while Jehoiada lived, but at his death the king's religion vanished (2 Chron. XXIV. 2). Judas Iscariot's life resembled that of his fellow-Apostles until he betrayed his Master; nothing outwardly suspicious, yet he was a thief and a traitor.

(4) There is an unreal love and charity. There is a love which consists in tender expressions, and a show of affection in which the heart has no part. So St. John exhorts: 'Let us not love in word, neither in tongue; but in deed and in truth'; and St. Paul: 'Let love be without dissimulation' (1 John III. 18; Rom. XII. 19).

(5) There is an unreal humility. An affected lowliness of demeanour which covers a very proud heart (Col. II. 18, 23).

(6) There is unreal prayer. Our Lord denounced this as one of the sins of the Pharisees: 'for a pretence they made long prayers'. Their sin did not

consist in making no prayers, or short prayers, but unreal prayers.

(7) There is unreal worship. 'This people draw nigh unto Me with their mouth, and honour Me with their lips ; but their heart is far from Me' (St. Matt. xv. 8). The fatal defect of the Jewish worship was its want of heart and reality.

(8) There is unreal religious profession and talk. In Ezekiel's time some talked like God's people, 'while their hearts went after their covetousness' (Ezek. xxxiii. 31). St. Paul tells us that we may 'speak with the tongues of men and angels,' and yet be no better than sounding brass and tinkling cymbals (1 Cor. xiii. 1). These things show clearly the immense importance which Holy Scripture attaches to reality in religion.

IV. See to it that your Christianity be genuine, thorough, real, and true. Beware lest your Christianity consist of nothing but Churchmanship ; that you base all on membership, on the fact that you have been baptised, married, and will be buried, according to her formularies, but have never followed her doctrine or lived the life of a true Churchman.

HARVEST THANKSGIVING

'We then, as workers together with Him, beseech you also that ye receive not the grace of God in vain.'—
2 Cor. vi. i.

THE food of the world is the gift of God, the great All-Father who provides for us, His children ; and for the harvest, as year by year it comes, we have to thank Him. Yet there is this to remember, that God does not give this independently of ourselves.

I. Workers with God in the Harvest of Nature. —To get it we have to work for it ; to get it we have to be workers with Him. When St. Paul said, 'If a man will not work, neither shall he eat,' he was not merely emphasising a precept of social economy, or stating the law that ought to underlie the constitution of human society ; he was enforcing the Divine law that man must earn his food by the sweat of his brow. God gives us the seed, but He leaves us to sow it. Unless our part of the twofold work is done, our very sustenance will be withdrawn from us, and though this law came upon us as a punishment for sin, yet, like all God's judgments, it gives a blessing.

II. Workers with God in the Harvest of the World.—There is a second way in which we are to regard ourselves as workers with Him, for there is a second and a greater harvest—the harvest which will come at the end of the world when the reapers will be the angels. 'Lift up thine eyes,' said the Lord at the start of His ministry, 'and look at the fields, for they are white already unto the harvest.' 'Go ye into all the world,' He said at the end of that ministry, 'and preach the Gospel to every creature.' Those were wonderful words. We find Him constantly teaching that the seed is the word of God ; the field is the world ; the hearts of men the soil in which it is to be sown ; and, like the harvest of earthly grain, this harvest depends upon the power

of God. None but He can provide the soil ; none but He can cause it to bring forth. Yet even in this harvest God will not work alone.

III. Workers with God in the Harvest of the Soul.—There is a third way in which we must be workers together with God. There is the harvest of ourselves, our souls and bodies. What has God given us ? He has given us life and time, strength, power of body and soul and spirit. He has given us influence. He has given us much that we can use for ourselves and for other people, and has given us much that we may use for Him. It can bear fruit only by His power. Without Him we can do nothing, and God could, if He would, reap a rich harvest without any effort of our own. For every talent He has entrusted to us He can get tenfold, and from every one of us He can force fruit—some thirty, some a hundredfold. He could if He would. He could, but He will not. We have to work out our own salvation with fear and trembling with Him.

REFERENCES.—VI. 1.—C. Gutch, *Sermons*, p. 199. T. Binney, *King's Weigh-House Chapel Sermons* (2nd Series), p. 51. J. Keble, *Sermons for Lent to Passion-tide*, p. 12. J. C. M. Bellew, *Sermons*, vol. iii. p. 127. VI. 1, 2.—A. MacKennal, *Christian World Pulpit*, vol. xlix. p. 248. VI. 2.—C. O. Eldridge, *Preacher's Magazine*, vol. iv. p. 271. J. Aspinall, *Parish Sermons* (2nd Series), p. 20. C. Perren, *Revival Sermons in Outline*, p. 233. C. Bosanquet, *Blossoms from the King's Garden*, p. 1. R. W. Hiley, *A Year's Sermons*, vol. iii. p. 177. J. Keble, *Sermons for Lent to Passion-tide*, p. 53. Spurgeon, *Sermons*, vol. x. No. 603, and vol. xxiv. No. 1394. VI. 3.—*Expositor* (6th Series), vol. iii. p. 279.

2 Cor. vi. 4.

COMPARE Macaulay's description (*History of England*, ch. viii.) of the arrest of the seven bishops by James II. 'On the evening of the Black Friday, as it was called, on which they were committed, they reached their prison just at the hour of Divine Service. They instantly hastened to the chapel. It chanced that in the second lesson were these words : "In all things approving ourselves as the ministers of God, in much patience, in afflictions, in distresses, in stripes, in imprisonments". All zealous Churchmen were delighted by this coincidence.'

REFERENCES.—VI. 5. — *Expositor* (4th Series), vol. i. p. 350 ; *ibid.* (7th Series), vol. v. p. 57. VI. 6.—*Ibid.* (6th Series), vol. iii. p. 238. VI. 7.—*Ibid.* vol. x. p. 191.

'Through evil report and good report.'—2 Cor. vi. 8.

J. M. NEALE inscribed these words above his study door.

THE UNKNOWN APOSTLE
(For St. Matthias' Day)

'As unknown, and yet well known.'—2 Cor. vi. 9.

WHAT is the use of our thinking of an unknown Apostle who became an Apostle nineteen centuries ago ?

I. We may Learn from Him :—
(a) *About our Faith.* The election of St. Matthias is one of the proofs of the truth of the great central fact of our religion—namely, the Resurrection

of the Lord Jesus. He was chosen to be a witness of the Resurrection. He could not possibly be mistaken as to whether our Lord had risen, for he had seen Him. No doubt he laid down his life because he believed in the Resurrection of our Lord Jesus Christ.

(b) *About the Divine Origin of the Church.* Directly their Master was taken away from them, the Apostles chose one to fill the place of the traitor. They will not be called eleven any more, because our Lord called twelve and He promised that they should sit on twelve thrones, judging the twelve tribes of Israel. Theirs was not a diminishing body, not a Church likely to fail, but one which they know will go on increasing as a grain of mustard seed, until our Lord Jesus comes back again.

II. Unknown to Man.—There is not anyone who does not contemplate with some horror the thought that a century hence there will be nobody in the world who will remember him—who will recollect what he looked like, what he said. He passes away into utter darkness. There is a horror in being forgotten that we all of us feel, and many a man, to make his name known in the world, toils until he ruins his health through many busy days, sleeps not at night, devotes himself to thinking out that which will make him renowned. And yet, strive as he may, he does not win anything like the fame of that unknown Apostle St. Matthias.

III. Well Known to God.—St. Matthias may well be described as unknown and yet well known—unknown to us and yet well known to the Apostles and to Jesus Christ. Remember that in a way each one of us is unknown and yet well known too—unknown, perhaps, to our fellow-creatures, but known through and through to the angels and to God. In the Epistle for St. Matthias' Day, the Lord Jesus is spoken of as One Who 'knowest the hearts of all'. A thought like this may be of great use to us. He knows us better than we know ourselves. No man does thoroughly understand himself, but Almighty God knows us, and the angels know us. Let our one idea be that we may not be ashamed for the Lord Jesus to know us—our souls and our heart.

THE APOSTOLIC PARADOX

'As unknown, and yet well known.'—2 COR. VI. 9.

IT will at once occur to you how true this was of the Apostles. Wherever the Gospel of Jesus Christ is preached, and wherever the Word of God is read and loved, the names of Peter and of James, of John and Thomas, are familiar in our ears as household words— yet how little we know of any one of them! Nor does this hold only of the disciples. It is equally clear in the case of our Lord Himself. But if the words were true of the disciples and of Christ, they are not without truth for you and me. I wish to show how the Gospel, carried out in life, will make a man unknown and yet well known.

I. First, then, 'unknown'—I shall suggest some of the reasons that make the Christian life an unknown

life. (1) To begin with, Christianity lays its chief stress upon qualities that do not impress the imagination of the world. Our Lord deliberately laid His emphasis on the undramatic qualities of life. (2) Again the distinctive exercises of the Christian are exercises which he never can reveal. Among all the differences between the pagan faiths and the faith which is our treasure and our glory, none is more marked or more notable than the change from an outward to an inward worship. All that is most distinctive in the Christian—his prayer, his battle, his joy, his cross-bearing—takes place in the mystical room with the closed door. (3) Again, the distinctive service of the Christian life is not a service that attracts attention. There is no glitter and no glamour in it. There is none of the pomp and circumstance of war. (4) But I have yet to mention the deepest of all reasons, and I shall give it you in the Apostle's words. 'For ye are dead,' says Paul in a great passage, 'and your life is hid with Christ in God.'

II. 'Yet well known.' Spite of the obscurity of the Christian life, it is true that the Christian is well known. (1) He is well known when he little thinks of it. Some one is always helped or always hindered by the kind of life we lead from day to day. (2) The Christian is well known in heaven. In that great world where God the Father is, and where there is one like to the Son of man; in that eternal home where the angels are, and where they watch with profoundest interest this earthly drama, there is nothing of more absorbing interest than the struggle and the service of the saint. (3) The Christian may be unknown now, but he shall be well known in the last judgment. All that we ever strove to be and do, our secret hope, and cry, and struggle, and victory— all shall be written out and meet us again when we stand before the judgment seat of God.—G. H. MORRISON, *The Unlighted Lustre*, p. 268.

REFERENCES.—VI. 9.—H. J. Wilmot-Buxton, *Holy-tide Teaching*, p. 158. *Expositor* (6th Series), vol. x. p. 359.

THE UNLIMITED POSSESSIONS OF THE CHRISTIAN LIFE

'As poor, yet making many rich ; as having nothing, and yet possessing all things.'—2 COR. VI. 10.

WHAT means this apparently extravagant assertion that Christ's servants and witnesses are masters of unlimited wealth? Is it a flight of rhetoric, or a piece of sober truth? We must settle, first, what it is that makes a man rich. And here we may take either the lower or the higher ground ; we may be content with the superficial view, or we may grasp the deeper thought.

I. And, first, it may be asserted, without question, that a man's real wealth is not in anything outside, but in himself. It is what you are that makes you indisputable owners, and not what you have.

That is the true, grand idea of ownership to which every man comes who reads the problems of life aright. It is what he has within that constitutes his wealth : the mind enriched with the highest knowledge and the purest truth, and the heart inspired with goodness responding to all that is noble and Godlike, and beating with all the sweet, brave impulses of prayer, devotion, and love. Where that is, you may well say, 'As having nothing, yet possessing all things'. And if you start from that point you are led on to take a still larger account of your possessions.

II. All things belong to you which serve in any way to develop the inner life, and to make you rich in noble qualities and inspiring thoughts. We talk proudly about being heirs of all the ages, and in a surface sense it is true of every one who lives amid our modern civilisation; but in its deeper meaning it is only true of those who aspire to live the good and Divine life. The Christian of to-day is indeed the heir of all the ages; he enters into all their best legacies; he is in possession of all the highest things that they did, said, and thought. We have a real property in all the saints and martyrs, in all who fought the battle of faith and righteousness, in all the inspired men, all the Prophets, Psalmists, and Apostles, all the God-endowed men who have helped to illumine the human mind with heavenly truths and to stimulate the human will to fruitful endeavours. In a very true sense we own them and all that they did for us. 'Having nothing, yet possessing all things.'

III. If a man's wealth is what he is and what he hopes to be, then all the experiences of a Christian life should contribute to his possessions and make him richer in those treasures which are inalienable. They minister to the building-up of the Christlike man.

The past is ours, with all its hallowed traditions, its sacred memories, its beautiful legacies of truth, examples, and illustrious names. *The present is ours,* with all its trying experiences to establish our faith, its temptations to prove our integrity, its needs to teach us prayer, its griefs to purify our emotions, its great volume of human woes to draw out our pities, its innumerable calls for service to make us obedient and earnest men.

And *the future is ours,* to paint the prosaic dulness of the present with colours fetched from a more heavenly clime, and to fill whatever dreary hours we have with the golden pictures of hope, and to make us strong for all that labour to which we are called.—J. G. Greenhough, *The Mind of Christ in St. Paul,* p. 121.

THE JOY OF SUFFERING

'As sorrowful, yet always rejoicing.'—2 Cor. vi. 10.

Let me examine some of the constituents which go to form the joy of Christian suffering.

I. Why Times of Suffering should be also Times of Joy—His Sovereignty.—For God loves to show His power and inscrutability by 'crossing the hands' of our expectation, by doing that which we all thought, if not absolutely impossible, yet very improbable. It is simply—'God is not man,' and 'His

ways are not as our ways, nor His thoughts as our thoughts'. And 'He works after the counsel of His own will, and none can say, What doest Thou?'

II. And the Sovereign is the Father.—For, just as we sometimes have treasures, which we reserve for our children, and which we unlock and open for them only when they are sick, or in some particular trouble, so does our heavenly Father act with us. And in seasons of special need and sorrow, He has very pleasant things which we never saw or guessed in our brighter hours: thoughts, promises, secret communications, tokens of love and remembrance, kept back designedly—in His wise and just and loving economy—for this very purpose, for that very time.

III. When God opens our Minds to see it, every Suffering is an Argument of Confidence and Happiness.—Is not it part of the promise? See how St. Peter weaves it into the blessing: 'But the God of all grace, Who hath called us unto His eternal glory by Christ Jesus, after that ye have suffered awhile, make you perfect, stablish, strengthen, settle you'. It is the landmark of the way—as St. Paul pointed out to the Churches in Asia Minor. 'We must through'—that is the path—'we must through much tribulation enter into the kingdom of God'.

IV. It is the Badge of Fellowship with the whole Family of God.—'For the same afflictions are accomplished in your brethren which are in the world.' And it is the sequence of all the saints in heaven: for these 'all came out of great tribulation'. And it is the token of sonship: 'For what son is he whom the Father chasteneth not?' And it is the likeness of Him, the Great Sufferer of us all—when we humbly, at our immense distance, walk after Him, copy His wounds, bear His marks, drink His cup, share His grave, are 'planted with Him in the likeness of His death'.

Just put all these thoughts together, and is not there sunshine enough there, laid on the dark drops, to make a rainbow? and is not there background enough to reflect sorrow into love, and suffering into joy?

'As sorrowful, yet always rejoicing.'—2 Cor. vi. 10.

The time may come when, sobered and unmettled by age, Shibli Bagarag will no longer be as a war-horse neighing at the Call of Battle. The time may come when, broken and weary, the Musk-Ball may quite fail of its glamour, and work be mere drudgery. Even so he will not faint nor grow weary. The mark of the crescent, the seal of God, is on his spirit. 'As sorrowing yet always rejoicing' he can endure to the end.—James McKechnie, Meredith's Allegory, *The Shaving of Shagpat,* p. 86.

References.—VI. 10.—J. M. Neale, *Sermons Preached in a Religious House,* vol. i. p. 201. J. G. Adderley, *Christian World Pulpit,* vol. lix. p. 237. S. Bentley, *Parish Sermons,* p. 42. F. D. Maurice, *Sermons,* vol. v. p. 45. VI. 11.—*Expositor* (5th Series), vol. viii. p. 122.

ENLARGEMENT THROUGH SERVICE

'Our mouth is open unto you, O Corinthians, our heart is enlarged. Ye are not straitened in us, but ye are straitened in your own affections. Now for a recompence in like kind (I speak as unto my children) be ye also enlarged.'—2 COR. VI. 11-13.

As the Apostle himself had been. Coming into living personal contact with the living Christ had enlarged his heart, opened his lips, set his life in another key and made him the great missionary to the Gentiles.

I. When we study carefully the Old Hebrew Scriptures, especially the production of those most remarkable men, the Prophets of Israel, it is impossible to escape the recognition that Israel had a unique calling, involving a mission to the world. No study is more instructive than that which the late learned Hebraist, Dr. A. B. Davidson, enables us to make in his great book on *Old Testament Prophecy.* Under his guidance it is almost impossible to fail of the recognition that the Hebrew people were intended to be the great missionaries to the world at large, that their call was to evangelise the nations and to proclaim a kingdom of God whose characteristic elements should be justice and universality. Except in the persons of their poets and prophets they fall away from their high calling. The Jewish history as given in the Old Testament records, has in it something more than a hint or suggestion—a very palpable warning—that when God's people refuse to use the truth given them in a great human way for others, the stranger, the foreigner, and specially for those who need it most, they lose it.

II. This historical introduction is, of course, intended to have personal application. My next point is the influence of foreign missions on ourselves. Have they brought us enlargement? In a word, is our humanity of finer and nobler quality than it would or could have been but for our interest in foreign missions? (1) First of all, in enlarging our ideas, and deepening our emotions, as the *worship faculty* in human nature has been revealed to us everywhere existent. It is impossible to come upon the fact of the universal religiousness of humanity and not be so impressed by it that our thinking shall not be broadened and our feelings made more cosmopolitan. (2) In the second place, if foreign missions have expanded our intellect and deepened and mellowed our humanity, they have also tested our faith in the Divinity and consequent Sovereignty of Christ. We see as we have never seen before, that to confine the Sovereignty of Christ by any race-limit is to deny the essential unity of humanity. In a word, it is to deny the Divinity of our Lord. (3) In the third place, it is necessary to take a glance at foreign missions as attesting the growth-fulness of the faith faculty in the Christianised man. Growth-fulness is the only test of healthy life. We may test the sufficiency and ripeness of our faith by the sympathy we have for man *as man.*—REUEN THOMAS, *Enlargement Through Service*, p. 3.

REFERENCES.—VI. 12.—A. Jenkinson, *Christian World Pulpit*, vol. xliv. p. 116. VI. 14.—J. Keble, *Village Sermons*

on the Baptismal Service, p. 144. H. Bonar, *Short Sermons for Family Reading*, p. 263. *Expositor* (4th Series), vol. ii. p. 323; *ibid.* (6th Series), vol. xii. p. 55. VI. 14-16.—*Ibid.* (5th Series), vol. iii. p. 387. VI. 14-18.—*Ibid.* (6th Series), vol. i. p. 378. VI. 15.—*Ibid.* vol. i. p. 439. VI. 16.—S. Baring-Gould, *Village Preaching for a Year* (2nd Series), vol. i. p. 9. VI. 17.—A. Tucker, *Preacher's Magazine*, vol. xviii. p. 366. VI. 17, 18.—W. Brock, *Midsummer Morning Sermons*, p. 48. A. Tucker, *Preacher's Magazine*, vol. xviii. p. 275. VI. 21.—*Expositor* (5th Series), vol. ix. p. 86. VII. 1.—J. H. Jowett, *Christian World Pulpit*, vol. xlv. p. 120. Bishop Bickersteth, *Sermons*, p. 63. C. D. Bell, *The Name Above Every Name*, p. 99. F. Ballard, *Christian World Pulpit*, vol. lix. p. 113. *Expositor* (5th Series), vol. v. p. 137; *ibid.* vol. ix. p. 351. VII. 2.—*Ibid.* (4th Series), vol. i. p. 202. VII. 5.—*Ibid.* (5th Series), vol. ix. p. 421. VII. 7-11.—*Ibid.* (6th Series), vol. i. p. 216.

SORROW FOR SIN

'For godly sorrow worketh repentance to salvation not to be repented of: but the sorrow of the world worketh death.'—2 COR. VII. 10.

ALL sorrow for sin is not godly sorrow, and does not always work repentance. Sorrow for sin may issue either in spiritual life or in spiritual death.

I. Now there may be many reasons why men sorrow for sin. (1) Some men sorrow for sin because they look upon sin not so much as a crime as a ruin. They think of what they have lost through their sin, and as they look upon their ruin they hate the sin. (2) In the second place, some men grieve over sin because of the loss of character. (3) Other men grieve over sin because of the loss of self-esteem; they are the hot tears which flow from pride. There is a great difference, for instance, between Saul's 'I have played the fool,' and the poor publican's 'God be merciful to me a sinner'. Now it is quite true that even these sorrows for sin may produce a certain reformation, but the reformation is only temporary; it will only last so long as the emotion lasts; when the emotion evaporates the reformation will be at an end. No, as St. Paul tells you, the true sorrow is a godly sorrow; or, as the Greek word literally means, *a sorrow according to God*, a sorrow according to God's measure, a sorrow which He is working out.

II. Well then, how are we to get this godly sorrow? (1) It is produced by God the Holy Ghost; it is only the spirit of grace and supplication that can produce it, it is only the omnipotent power of the Holy Ghost that can bring water out of this flinty rock. (2) It is accompanied with prayer. (3) It is caused by looking at the Crucified. (4) This sorrow for sin is very individualising. Each has to go apart. We ought to sorrow for sin, we ought to sorrow for sin far more than we do, but, after all, it is not the sorrow which is going to atone—it is the blood of Jesus Christ God's Son.—E. A. STUART, *The One Mediator and other Sermons*, vol. xi. p. 145.

REFERENCES.—VII. 10.—Spurgeon, *Sermons*, vol. xlvi. No. 2691. D. L. Moody, *The Fulness of the Gospel*, p. 31. W. H. Evans, *Short Sermons for the Seasons*, p. 72. R. Allen, *The Words of Christ*, p. 28. *Expositor* (4th Series), vol. vi. p. 309; *ibid.* (5th Series), vol. vii. p. 276; *ibid.* vol. ix. p. 437. VII.

10, 11.—J. J. Blunt, *Plain Sermons*, p. 142. VII. 11.—J. S. Maver, *Christian World Pulpit*, vol. lix. p. 46. VII. 12.— *Expositor* (6th Series), vol. i. p. 108. VIII.—*Ibid.* (4th Series), vol. v. p. 343. VIII. 4.—*Ibid.* (6th Series), vol. viii. p. 390. VIII. 5.—Lyman Abbott, *Christian World Pulpit*, vol. xlviii. p. 119. W. Brock, *Midsummer Morning Sermons*, p. 12. A. Tucker, *Preacher's Magazine*, vol. x. p. 275. Spurgeon, *Sermons*, vol. xxxvii. No. 2234. VIII. 8.—W. H. Harwood, *Christian World Pulpit*, vol. xlv. p. 294. *Expositor* (6th Series), vol. iii. p. 277.

THE CHARM OF CHRIST

'For ye know the grace of our Lord Jesus Christ, that, though He was rich, yet for your sakes He became poor, that ye through His poverty might become rich.'—2 Cor. VIII. 9.

I would take the text as showing the God-nature in the self-giving of Christ.

I. The Divine Plenitude.—'He was rich' carries us up into the relation of the Son to the Father, and into the wealth He shared as Son with the Father. We have now to try and realise some of the great things which are of the essence of Deity, and to remember that they belonged to the riches of Christ as sharing in the nature of the Godhead. What, then, are the riches of God? (1) God is rich in omnipotence. In His pre-existence He was one with the Father in that eternal energy which is both the source and conservation of the things that are. (2) God is rich in omnipresence. It is an overwhelming thought that in all the vastness and in all the worlds there is no spot where God is not. (3) God is rich in wisdom. (4) God is rich in generosity. The whole of the life of God is a life of sacrifice. He is the blessed or happy God because He is the self-giving God. In nature He gives with surprising prodigality, and in grace with loving generosity.

II. The Divine Poverty.—He 'emptied Himself'. Now, if His riches consisted in sharing with the Father the attributes of Deity, surely His poverty must have consisted in the act of self-limitation in the Incarnation. He could no longer share with the Father in placing the seal of infinite wisdom on every flower that blooms and on every star that shines. He could no longer with the Father, out of plenitude of power, revel in the prodigality of Deity; He had 'emptied' Himself, and was poor; He had not lost His divinity, but it was circumscribed. Deity contracted itself in order to reveal itself, and the contraction is at once the shame and the glory of Jesus. Again—Jesus became poor as the Son of Man. He was poor socially. Isolation is the penalty of greatness.

III. The Divine Purpose.—There is a legend of Thomas Aquinas kneeling before the cross, when a voice said, 'Thomas, thou hast written and done much for Me. What reward shall I give thee?' Lowly he kneeled and said, 'Lord, give me Thyself!' When we possess Christ we get the true wealth, which is pure health of soul. That was the purpose of His coming and the grace of His poverty. By the charm of the condescension in which He became poor, He wins us to His wealth.—J. Oates, *The Sorrow of God*, p. 121.

References.—VIII. 9.—C. O. Eldridge, *Preacher's Magazine*, vol. x. p. 554. H. Woodcock, *Sermon Outlines* (1st Series), p. 40. G. W. Brameld, *Practical Sermons*, p. 26. W. H. Hutchings, *Sermon Sketches*, p. 257. A. Coote, *Twelve Sermons*, p. 1. F. D. Maurice, *Sermons*, vol. iii. p. 83. R. C. Trench, *Sermons New and Old*, p. 249. Spurgeon, *Sermons*, vol. iii. No. 151; vol. xxxvii. No. 2232; vol. xl. No. 2364; and vol. xlvii. No. 2716. *Expositor* (4th Series), vol. ii. p. 278; *ibid.* vol. v. p. 28; *ibid.* (5th Series), vol. ii. p. 248; *ibid.* vol. ix. p. 223; *ibid.* (6th Series), vol. iii. p. 411; *ibid.* vol. iv. p. 126.

2 Cor. VIII. 9.

In a small house beside the yard in front of City Road Chapel, John Wesley took his departure out of the world. In his wanderings he was always preaching or meeting classes. He seldom spoke; but once, in a wakeful interval, exclaimed, 'There is no way into the holiest but by the blood of Jesus. "Ye know the grace of our Lord Jesus Christ, that though He was rich, yet for your sakes He became poor, that ye through His poverty might be rich." That is the foundation, the only foundation; there is no other.'

References.—VIII. 9.—W. Pulsford, *Trinity Church Sermons*, p. 1. VIII. 10.—*Expositor* (4th Series), vol. viii. p. 323; *ibid.* (5th Series), vol. x. p. 426. VIII. 17.—*Ibid.* vol. iv. p. 164. VIII. 18.—*Ibid.* (4th Series), p. 334; *ibid.* (5th Series), vol. ii. p. 115; *ibid.* vol. vii. p. 405. VIII. 23.—*Expositor* (6th Series), vol. vii. p. 120. VIII. 24.—Spurgeon, *Sermons*, vol. xxvi. No. 1522. *Expositor* (4th Series), vol. v. p. 365. VIII. 25.—*Ibid.* (6th Series), vol. iii. p. 373. IX. 1.—*Expositor* (6th Series), vol. i. p. 209. IX. 5.—*Ibid.* p. 276. IX. 6.—F. D. Maurice, *Sermons*, vol. iv. p. 229. IX. 6, 7.—W. H. Evans, *Short Sermons for the Seasons*, p. 108. IX. 7.—J. S. Maver, *Christian World Pulpit*, vol. lvi. p. 127. J. H. Jowett, *Examiner*, 28th June, 1906, p. 628. Spurgeon, *Sermons*, vol. xiv. No. 835. *Expositor* (5th Series), vol. ix. p. 447. IX. 7-15.—*Expository Sermons on the New Testament*, p. 196. IX. 8.—*Expositor* (6th Series), vol. xi. p. 285. IX. 15.—J. Keble, *Miscellaneous Sermons*, p. 235. Spurgeon, *Sermons*, vol. xxvi. No. 1550; vol. xxxviii. No. 2247; vol. xxxix. No. 2290. J. M. Neale, *Sermons Preached in Sackville College Chapel*, vol. i. p. 101. J. Stuart Holden, *The Pre-Eminent Lord*, p. 225. X.—*Expositor* (6th Series), vol. vii. p. 107. X. 1.—John Watson, *The Inspiration of Our Faith*, p. 190. *Expositor* (5th Series), vol. vi. p. 66; *ibid.* (6th Series), vol. xi. p. 287. X. 1-10.—*Ibid.* p. 463. X. 2.—*Expositor* (4th Series), vol. iv. p. 298. X. 3, 4.—*Ibid.* (5th Series), vol. vii. p. 459. X. 3-5.—C. Bradley, *The Christian Life*, p. 362. X. 4.—W. G. Horder, *Christian World Pulpit*, vol. lix. p. 156.

SPIRITUAL GRAVITATION

'And bringing into captivity every thought to the obedience of Christ.'—2 Cor. x. 5.

The thought of the Apostle in this passage is a very simple and natural one; it is a contrast between the warfare of the hands and the warfare of the mind and soul. There were many things to remind him of the warfare of the hands. But, like all men of fine contemplative genius, he was aware of a force mightier than the force of armies which was always working in the world, viz., the force of ideas. If the world is hostile to Christ to-day, it is because Christians have not been obedient to Christ, because with us those staple thoughts and ideas, out of which temper and conduct grow, have not been brought into captivity to Him.

I. The first thing to observe, then, is that any conformity to Christ which does not include the thought—by which I mean the innermost intents of the mind and will—is vain and partial, and vain because it is partial. The reason for the comparative failure of Christianity is simply the failure of Christians to be Christians.

II. The second thing to be observed is, that the thought can be disciplined; and it is necessary to say this, and to insist on it, because many of us assume that there is something elusive in thought, something so wayward, subtle, and intractable, that it lies quite outside the control of the will. Professor Huxley once defined genius as a mind under perfect control—a servant always at heel, ready at any call to do its duty, and quick to respond to any demand that the will can legitimately make upon it. The process of education itself is nothing more or less than the art of controlling and disciplining the thought. And so it is in the Christian life: we must begin by the discipline of the thought.

III. But, thirdly, we need to ask by what means this captivity of thought may be gained? We may answer the question by asking another. What is the nature of that force which alone can control a man's thought with any adequacy, or can give him an impulse and mandate for its discipline? The only captivity which thought endures is the captivity of the ideal. Every man has some ideal, and his ideal is the governing factor in his thought. Three final suggestions we may think over at our leisure. First, goodness is a fine art, and is not a matter of magic. Secondly, the thought is not brought into captivity to Christianity, but to Christ. Lastly, learn to recognise the vast scope of the Christian religion.— W. J. Dawson, *The Comrade Christ*, p. 207.

'Bringing into captivity every thought to the obedience of Christ.'—2 Cor. x. 5.

Mr. Gladstone wrote at the age of twenty an account of his religious opinions in which the following prayer occurs: 'O heavenly and most merciful God, implant in me a godly fear of Thee, root out from me my ungodly fear of men; let the blessed Spirit, who despises not so humble an office, condescend to purge my unclean heart, to take away from it my own wavering and vacillating resolutions, and place in their stead a permanent and habitual sense of Thy presence, a lively faith, a love hearty and unconstrained, a looking unto Jesus for redemption, unto the Spirit for grace. May every thought be brought into the obedience of Christ, and may I walk in the footsteps of my beloved sister, my once suffering but now glorified sister, though in heaven still my sister.'

References.—X. 5.—Spurgeon, *Sermons*, vol. xxv. No. 1473. H. C. Beeching, *Seven Sermons to Schoolboys*, p. 64. Newman Smyth, *Christian World Pulpit*, vol. xliv. p. 245. H. P. Liddon, *Sermons Preached on Special Occasions*, p. 96. J. R. Illingworth, *University and Cathedral Sermons*, p. 144. H. P. Liddon, *University Sermons*, p. 156. W. Pulsford,

Trinity Church Sermons, p. 24. J. H. Jowett, *From Strength to Strength*, p. 103. *Expositor* (4th Series), vol. iii. p. 367; *ibid.* (5th Series), vol. vii. pp. 31, 142.

INDIVIDUALITY

'If any man trust to himself that he is Christ's, let him of himself think this again, that, as he is Christ's, even so are we Christ's.'—2 Cor. x. 7.

The intensity of human individuality is for ever surprising and shocking our anticipations. It overleaps all our categories; it refuses to conform to our conventions. Individuality is under obligation to declare and fulfil itself. It can no more be bound down by our schemes of classification than Samson by the withes of the Philistines. Try to tie it up to a beam of your own invention, and it will walk off with the beam and all. You can but accept the facts. By the same right by which you are what you are, he is what he is. Why should you wish to impress yourself upon him? Why should you require him to conform to your anticipation?

God alone can judge him, for God alone has made him for Himself. God has thrown into him a distinct and separate purpose of His own devising. God alone knows what the purpose is, and to God alone he answers for what he makes of it.

I. God has not exhausted His creative powers in creating us. He has new things in view, and here is one of them. The very certainty with which you yourself recognise the Divine intention in your own making ought to render you anxious to recognise the freedom and elasticity with which that same Divine intention expresses itself in others. They are so different from you, so strange, so odd, so incredible, so unintelligible, so incalculable, so funny. Yes, but you and they all witness to one God, who commits to each his special destiny. Each has his own equal right to exist. No one can override any other's claims.

So, gazing out at the endless swarms of individuals who pass before us, in infinite variety of surprise, unable to account for their peculiarity and diversity, we fall back, again and again, on this recognition by St. Paul of our common origin, and of the common authority to which we all lay our claim, and say: 'If any man trust to himself that he is God's, let him of himself think this again, that, as he is God's, so are all these'.

II. 'As he is God's, so are all these.' Is not this the only true democratic principle? Is not this what we mean by the equality of all men? We think that we have all arrived at this recognition of equality. It is a commonplace, a platitude. But, if so, do we also recognise the religious ground on which it rests, the spiritual assumption which justifies it? This equal right of every individual man to be himself has God for its background. How else is it explained? It is the Divine origin of each separate personality that endows it with this inalienable sanctity.

III. Belief in God, in and through Christ, has endowed every separate personality with this sacred right to be itself. Yet, it is just where we get to conscious belief in God that we find it most difficult to recognise this right. This is the exact point which my text brings out. It is because we are convinced of our own true relationship to Christ that we cannot but suppose that this relationship must be universal. In other and minor matters, in the rough and tumble of ordinary affairs, every individual may have his own strange way of saying things. We can allow, perhaps, for a mixed hubbub of voices in the world's business, or in politics, or in matters of sentiment; but when we come to the Eternal God, when we are dealing with loyalty to Jesus Christ, when we come to the realities of spiritual faith, then, surely, we must expect to find our own experiences verified in others.

Just as this man knows Christ for himself alone, so all may know Him. In this Christ shows Himself absolute and universal, not in the sameness of His manifestation, but in its utter diversity. He, the same Christ, can cover every individual difference. There is no one individuality for which He has not a special and individual disclosure of Himself to make. His revelations will be as varied as the individuals who receive them. His fertility of resource will be adequate to every new demand and level with every fresh variation in human nature. Therefore, let the true believer who trusts that he is Christ's own be perfectly prepared to find that others whom he cannot understand, with whom he inevitably collides, whose judgments he disputes, whose sentiments are wholly the reverse of his own, are, nevertheless, just as much Christ's as he is. There is no reason why this same loyalty to one Lord should not express itself in a thousand divergent ways through a multitude of differing characters. — H. Scott Holland, *Christian World Pulpit*, vol. LXXVII. p. 353.

References.—X. 10.—*Expositor* (4th Series), vol. x. p. 99; *ibid.* (5th Series), vol. iii. p. 384; *ibid.* vol. x. p. 20; *ibid.* (6th Series), vol. iv. p. 119; *ibid.* (7th Series), vol. vi. p. 226. X. 15.—*Ibid.* vol. viii. p. 75. X. 15, 16.—Archbishop Temple, *Christian World Pulpit*, vol. lviii. p. 321. X. 16.—*Expositor* (5th Series), vol. vi. p. 300. XI. 2.—*Expositor* (6th Series), vol. ii. p. 250; *ibid.* vol. x. p. 186; *ibid.* (7th Series), vol. vi. p. 278.

A PLEA FOR SIMPLICITY

'The simplicity that is in Christ.'—2 Cor. xi. 3.

There are some words that have a tragic history. To the hearing ear and to the understanding heart they whisper strange secrets about human progress. Now one of the words that has a pitiful history is that word simple. It has wandered far from the simplicity of Christ. It has so changed its dress, and lost its early character, that we are almost ashamed to keep it company.

I. If we have ever studied history at all, we must have been struck with a certain sweet simplicity about the characters of the very greatest men. There is something of the child about the greatest; a certain freshness, a kind of sweet unconsciousness; a happy taking of themselves on trust; a sort of play-element

throughout the drama. And all the time, powerfully, perhaps silently, they were swaying and steering this poor tossed world. Did you never feel that simplicity in Martin Luther? And did it never arrest you in George Washington? It is that simple element that has charmed the world. And I cannot think of any better witness to the abiding charm of true simplicity than the way in which vice has always tried to imitate it.

II. Now the most casual student of the life of Jesus must have noted the simplicity of Christ. (1) Think of His mode of life: was it not simple? It puts our artificial lives to shame. There is a music in it, not like the music of the orchestra, but like the music of the brook under the trees. (2) Think of His teaching: was not that simple too? It puts our sermons and our books to shame. Some cynic once said a very bitter thing about the style of Gibbon the historian. He said that the style of Gibbon was a style in which it was impossible to tell the truth. With the deepest reverence for our ascended Lord, I should venture to say just the opposite of Him—the style of Jesus the Teacher was a style in which it was impossible to tell a lie. It was so clear, so pure, so exquisitely truthful. (3) But the simplicity of Christ comes to its crown in the feast of the Lord's Supper. A cup of wine and a piece of broken bread—these are the seals and symbols of the Gospel. The cross is, as the greatest only are, in its simplicity sublime. I want you all then to feel again, still more I want you all to practise, the true simplicity that is in Jesus Christ. —G. H. Morrison, *Sunrise: Addresses from a City Pulpit*, p. 124.

References.—XI. 3.—Newman Smyth, *Christian World Pulpit*, vol. xliv. p. 120. A. Maclaren, *The Wearied Christ*, p. 148. F. Brown, *Christian World Pulpit*, vol. xlvi. p. 99. *Expositor* (6th Series), vol. vii. p. 393. XI. 4.—*Ibid.* (5th Series), vol. ii. p. 116; *ibid.* vol. vii. p. 107; *ibid.* (6th Series), vol. i. p. 30; *ibid.* vol. viii. p. 76. XI. 5.—*Christian World Pulpit*, vol. l. p. 303. *Expositor* (6th Series), vol. vii. p. 454. XI. 5, 13.—*Ibid.* vol. viii. p. 73. XI. 7.—G. W. Brameld, *Practical Sermons* (2nd Series), p. 163. *Expositor* (4th Series), vol. x. p. 298; *ibid.* (5th Series), vol. x. p. 196. XI. 9.—*Ibid.* (6th Series), vol. viii. p. 424. XI. 10.—*Ibid.* vol. viii. p. 31. XI. 12.—*Ibid.* vol. i. p. 395.

THE TRANSFORMATION OF EVIL

'For Satan himself is transformed into an angel of light.'— 2 Cor. xi. 14.

If the evil that assails us were as frightful in its aspect as it is in its essence, we should run little danger from its assaults; but too often it besets us in fair forms and in dazzling colours, and herein lies our peril. We now propose to distinguish several ways in which this transfiguration of evil is effected, and to indicate the path of safety amid these dangerous illusions.

I. The transfiguration of evil. (1) Evil is transfigured by imagination. Imagination is ever active in many ways and in many places, lending to evil things a fictitious splendour. Bates found on the Amazon a brilliant spider that spread itself out as a flower, and the insects lighting upon it seeking sweetness, found horrors, torment, death. Such transformations are common in human life; things of poison and blood are everywhere displaying themselves in forms of innocence, in dyes of beauty. (2) Evil is transformed by philosophy. *(a)* In matters of faith and worship we may be misled by philosophy. *(b)* In matters of conduct we may be misled by philosophy. (3) Evil is transfigured by society. Through ages society has gained an exquisite skill in enjoying the pleasures of sin whilst still stripping that sin of its grossness. Pride, lust, selfishness, indolence, gluttony, dishonesty, abound in the social circle, but the revolting features of these vices are lost under the paint and powder of fashion, the blandishments of taste, the lustre of gold, the affectations of courtesy, philanthropy, and piety.

II. We indicate the path of safety amid these dangerous illusions. (1) Let us not forget that the chief danger of life lies in this moral illusion. We need ever to be on the watch, seeing that Satan conceals his fell purposes under fair pretences, as the Greek assassins concealed their swords in myrtle branches. (2) Let us be sincere in soul. The single-hearted are clear-eyed, and without blindness, presumption, confusion, haste, they find and keep the pathway of life. (3) Let us respect the written law. The Bible is a wonderful book for destroying the glamour of sin, for exposing its sophistries and lies. Revelation makes palpable the *sophistry* of sin. Revelation makes palpable the *horror* of sin. Revelation makes palpable the *fruits* of sin. (4) Let us constantly behold the vision of God. And we are speaking of no abstract, mystical thing when we speak of the vision of God. We see the glory of God in the face of Jesus Christ, and to Jesus Christ must we bring whatever thing or theory may solicit us. In His light we shall know exactly what is true in riches, liberty, greatness, honour, pleasure. Oh, how the false and rotten shrivel in His presence! What a penetrating glance He has! What a revealing touch! What a convicting word! The eye that looks on Him cannot be deceived.—W. L. WATKINSON, *The Transfigured Sackcloth*, p. 67.

REFERENCES.—XI. 14.—C. D. Bell, *The Power of God*, p. 227. W. H. Evans, *Short Sermons for the Seasons*, p. 91. XI. 15.—*Expositor* (4th Series), vol. i. pp. 20, 35; *ibid.* vol. ii. pp. 66, 67, 382. XI. 20.—*Ibid.* (5th Series), vol. x. p. 149. XI. 22, 23.—J. Parker, *The Gospel of Jesus Christ*, p. 131. XI. 23.—*Expositor* (5th Series), vol. vii. p. 15. XI. 23-27.—*Ibid.* (6th Series), vol. xi. p. 205.

2 COR. XI. 24-28.

RAYMOND LULL thus reviewed his life: 'Once I was rich; I had a wife and children; I led a worldly life. All these I cheerfully resigned for the sake of promoting the common good and diffusing abroad the holy faith. I learned Arabic; I have gone abroad several times to preach the Gospel to the Saracens; I have, for the sake of the faith, been cast into prison; I have been scourged; I have laboured during forty-five years to win over the shepherds of the Church and the princes of Europe to the common good of Christendom. Now I am old and poor, but I am still intent on the same object, and I will persevere with it until death, if the Lord permit.'

REFERENCES.—XI. 25.—*Expositor* (4th Series), vol. ii. p. 324; *ibid.* (5th Series), vol. vi. p. 41. XI. 26.—G. G. Bradley, *Christian World Pulpit*, vol. xlix. p. 1. *Expositor* (6th Series), vol. viii. p. 76.

'Who is weak and I am not weak; who is offended and I burn not?'—2 COR. XI. 29.

CARDINAL VAUGHAN was only twenty-one when he wrote: 'Unless a priest's heart overflow how can he attend to any other's heart? Unless he be all on fire, how can he inflame the hearts of men? I fear that I am too much wrapped up in myself—I am not sufficiently "all to all". I cannot with sincerity exclaim, "Who is weak and I am not weak? Who is scandalised and I am not on fire? . . ." I do indeed feel these words—they go through me, they set me on fire. But when the moment, the cold, unsought-for moment comes for throwing myself into the weakness of others, for sympathising with them, for going with them, in a word, for assimilating myself to them—I do not, I cannot, do it. I am closed up in myself. I am simply Herbert Vaughan. O my sweetest Jesus, I have lost all patience with myself. When shall I put off the old man and clothe myself with the new? When shall I think and act with St. Paul?'

THE EDUCATIVE POWER OF WEAKNESS

'If I must needs glory, I will glory of the things which concern mine infirmities.'—2 COR. XI. 30.

I. Why does St. Paul Glory in the Things that Belong to his Weakness?—Not, I imagine, in themselves. But he gloried in his weakness, surely, because of the use, when it came to him in its different forms, he put it to. It is because all these things—poverty, distress, failure, sickness—throw the soul back upon God; they all demand and cry out for faith in God.

II. There are two Ways in which to Bear Trial and Weakness.—(1) The one is to let them drive us into ourselves, to dwell on our own sufferings, our own sorrows, the things that we have lost and the shadows that close slowly round us. That is the way to increase unhappiness, not to lighten it. (2) The one way to find happiness, however much you suffer, is always to look out for the good points in other people, always to think the best of them; for after all, if you are honest, you know the worst about yourself. That, indeed, is the second way in which we may bear trial and weakness, the way which St. Paul knew when he said that he was 'sorrowing, yet always rejoicing,' that if he gloried, it was his weakness which gave him the cause.

III. There is a Wonderful Power that comes with Weakness and Loss.—Your time of weakness may bring you to see clearly what is real goodness, real work, real duty. Only let your true desires be set on character, duty, goodness, and God wilbring you to them—through the weak things that are temporal to the things of power that are eternal. That is the lesson of the cross.—W. H. HUTTON, *Church Family Newspaper*, vol. XIII. p. 922.

REFERENCES.—XI. 30.—R. W. Hiley, *A Year's Sermons*, vol. i. p. 96. XI. 31.—J. Budgen, *Parochial Sermons*, vol. i. p. 150. XI. 32.—*Expositor* (5th Series), vol. ix. p. 118. *Expositor* (6th Series), vol. viii. p. 231. XI. 32, 33.—*Ibid.* vol. vii. p. 126. XII. 1-5.—*Expositor* (6th Series), vol. viii. p. 232. XII. 2.—*Ibid.* (4th Series), vol. v. p. 115. XII. 2-4. —W. H. Brookfield, *Sermons*, p. 13. *Expositor* (5th Series), vol. x. p. 268 ; *ibid.* (6th Series), vol. iv. p. 387. XII. 2-5. —*Ibid.* vol. iii. p. 340.

THE DIGNITY OF SUFFERING

'Of myself I will not glory, but in mine infirmities.'— 2 COR. XII. 5.

IT was a strange catalogue out of which St. Paul made his one solitary ' glory '—he, who could boast such learning, such teaching, such influence, such spiritual triumph as never, perhaps, fell to any other man! ' Thrice beaten,' ' stoned,' ' shipwrecked,' ' journeyings,' ' perils,' ' weariness,' ' painfulness,' ' watchings,' ' hunger,' ' thirst,' ' fastings,' ' nakedness,' ' weakness,' ' cares,' ' a thorn '. Never hero goes so low to gather all his laurels. He knew ' The Dignity of Suffering '—a truth good and great to know. God help us to learn the lesson.

I. At the Threshold.—The first thought which it is the duty and privilege of every Christian to think when he is passing into a trial is one full of dignity at the threshold : ' I am in the hands of God '. A man feels this—whether rightly or wrongly—more in his sorrows than he does in his joys. Sorrows generally drive us to our greatest thought. And strangely —though heaven is joy—we always feel nearer heaven when we are unhappy. I suppose it is because this world grows less—therefore the next grows greater. If you wish to elevate any pain or affliction, determine first that you will see nothing in it but the hand of God.

II. Suffering is always a Proof of Grace.—No skilful man ever puts a greater strain upon a machine than he knows it is able to bear. The severity of the stress is the proof of the excellence of the work. And, as Archbishop Leighton says, ' The pirate never attacks the empty vessel going out, but the rich argosy coming home '. The attack is the evidence of the good we carry. That man is worthy of all honour, and must command respect, who simply wears a calm aspect and a self-sustained deportment under all circumstances. But we go beyond that. It may have fallen to some of us to see—what is to my mind one of the most touching spectacles that any man can show—a person in great pain and sorrow and yet so sustained and ennobled by the Spirit in his own soul that he was not so much a receiver as an imparter of sympathy and the comforter and the guide and the helper of all about him.

III. The Dignity of our Lord's Bearing during His Last Agony.—Of all the noble spectacles man has ever seen, I know none to be compared for a moment with the grandness of our Saviour's bearing during His last agony—the last acts of that wonderful life.

(*a*) *Hear Him as He utters that awful passage*, in His unparalleled composure, in that pious argument with His own soul : ' Father, the hour is come ! . . . Father, glorify Thy name '.

(*b*) *And what dignity upon this earth was ever to be compared* with the washing of the disciples' feet !

(*c*) *And then that mandate* of the King of kings, that sovereignty, ordering His own betrayal—' That thou doest, do quickly '.

(*d*) *Or, see Him—that meek and oppressed* Man, standing in such an attitude of innocence and patient holiness that, before its fascination, a whole ruffian band goes back and falls to the ground !

(*e*) *And, when a prisoner at the bar*, before the proud representative of Rome, not using any but the language of pity to that proud potentate : ' Thou couldest have no power at all against Me '.

(*f*) *And who cannot but see, and wonder, and admire the dignity of the Son of Man* standing out against all the horrors of His cross in the strength of His one grand purpose ! Then He so disengaged Himself that He could offer up that exquisite prayer for His murderers.

It is not the endurance only, or the love, or the power, or the peace of our suffering Master we are to study and copy, but it is the dignity, the dignity of Jesus !

Be like Him. Never degrade your own or another's suffering. The sufferers are the great ones of the earth. Be dignified in misery. There is no glory like abasement. There is no strength so great as infirmities coming from God and borne for God ; and nothing more truly Christ-like, or dignified, than the struggles of a lifetime of sorrow and suffering for Jesus Christ's sake !

CUT TO THE QUICK

' And by reason of the exceeding greatness of the revelations —wherefore, that I should not be exalted overmuch, there was given to me a thorn in the flesh, a messenger of Satan to buffet me, that I should not be exalted overmuch.' —2 COR. XII. 7 (R.V.).

LET us consider :—

I. The Special Suffering of which the Apostle Complains.—(1) It was *acute*. Froude says that all Carlyle's troubles were imaginary ; and very many of our troubles are that, or little more. Yet we have real misfortunes and sorrows, and occasionally these are profound and acute. Many misfortunes scratch the surface ; a few times at least in life they search the depths and sting the soul. (2) It was *unutterable*. St. Paul does not disclose the character of his special sorrow, and commentators have sought in vain to pick the lock and reveal the hidden skeleton. But the great lesson to be learnt from the Apostle's silence is this, that there are sorrows in life which cannot be expressed. Superficial souls incapable of great grief will, upon the slightest provocation, fetch out their skeleton from its cupboard and dilate on its special features; but real griefs are sacred, and noble men are reticent. There is the silence of self-respect. There is the silence of delicacy. There is the silence of honour. There is the silence of affection. There is the silence of surprise and dismay. There is the silence of necessity. (3) It was *incurable*. Most troubles are forgotten with time, nay, time often gives them a tender grace, and it is not altogether sorrowful to recall them. But it is not thus with all our griefs: some of them are manifestly irremediable. (4) It was *malignant*. 'A messenger of Satan to buffet me.' We find most difficult to bear the sufferings which somehow make us most conscious of the presence and action of the powers of darkness.

II. The Design of the Apostle's Affliction.—(1) It contemplated his *safety*. 'Lest I should be exalted above measure.' Most subtle are the temptations of high spiritual estate; hard by are pitfalls and the valley of the shadow of death. (2) It designed his more complete *strength*. 'My grace is sufficient for thee.' 'When I am weak, then am I strong.' God takes away our natural strength, chastens the pride of our understanding and will, deprives us of worldly confidences and hopes, that He may reveal in us a new and Diviner strength. (3) It designed his larger *service*. We often see that through personal frailty and suffering men become more effective teachers of the highest truths —more pathetic painters, mightier poets, nobler preachers; and through his personal sorrows the Apostle was fitted for more effective service. Tens of thousands of God's people know that the blow which shattered them, and reduced them to what the world calls weakness, was the very providence that awoke in them a Diviner life, and fitted them for higher and holier service.—W. L. WATKINSON, *The Bane and the Antidote*, p. 247.

'A thorn in the flesh.'—2 COR. XII. 7.

GOD saw that the Apostle was a better man with the thorn than he would have been without it. The prayer was heard, and the answer was 'No'. Who knows what sins and failures St. Paul was saved from, by the constant pricking of the warning thorn? Was it not, indeed, a fairy thorn in his flesh touching him at risky moments, as though endued with some warning power, a mystic spike plucked from the very Crown of Thorns itself? Who knows?— E. E. HOLMES, *Prayer and Action*, p. 12.

REFERENCES.—XII. 7.—C. Bradley, *The Christian Life*, p. 393. *Expositor* (5th Series), vol. i. p. 238; *ibid*. vol. x. p. 118. XII. 7-9.—Brooke Herford, *Courage and Cheer*, p. 54. Spurgeon, *Sermons*, vol. xviii. No. 1084. R. C. Trench, *Sermons New and Old*, p. 86. XII. 8, 9.—*Expository Sermons on the New Testament*, p. 204. XII. 9.—Newman Smyth, *Christian World Pulpit*, vol. xlvii. p. 97. J. C. Wright, *The Record*, 7ol. xxvn. p. 3. Spurgeon, *Sermons*, vol. xxii. No. 1287: and vol. lii. No. 2974. *Expositor* (7th Series), vol. v. p. 494. XII. 9.—G. H. Morrison. *Christian World Pulpit*,

22nd June, 1910. XII. 10.—C. F. Aked, *The Courage of the Coward*, p. 47. H. M. Butler, *Harrow School Sermons*, p. 365. T. F. Crosse, *Sermons* (2nd Series), p. 139. S. H. Fleming, *Fifteen-minute Sermons for the People*, p. 190. Spurgeon, *Sermons*, vol. xxxiv. No. 2050. XII. 11.—Spurgeon, *Sermons*, vol. xxv. No. 1458. *Expositor* (6th Series), vol. viii. p. 73. XII. 14.—J. C. M. Bellew, *Sermons*, vol. ii. p. 269. *Expositor* (5th Series), vol. x. p. 184; *ibid*. (6th Series), vol. iii. p. 278.

'The children ought not to lay up for the parents, but the parents for the children.'—2 COR. XII. 14.

IN Luther's Table-Talk the following remarks are quoted under the heading 'Patres thesaurizent liberis:' Cordatus said: 'Many disapprove of this'. The Doctor [Luther] said: 'If our predecessors had left no treasures to us, what should we possess now? To-day we might live in idleness, if we were not obliged by God's commandment to leave something to our children" [E. Kroker, *Luther's Tischreden*, 1903, p. 183]. Luther's words are the more noteworthy as he was generous almost to a fault in his gifts to those outside his own family. Like his co-worker Melanchthon, he could never allow a beggar to knock in vain at his door. Unlike Melanchthon, Luther possessed a wife with keen business instincts, and a steady determination to increase her husband's property.

REFERENCES.—XII. 18.—*Expositor* (5th Series), vol. vii. p. 117. XIII. 1.—*Ibid*. vol. i. p. 401. XIII. 2-10.—*Ibid*. (5th Series), vol. v. p. 234. XIII. 3-5.—Spurgeon, *Sermons*, vol. xxx. No. 1788.

CRUCIFIED THROUGH WEAKNESS

'For though He was crucified through weakness, yet He liveth by the power of God. For we also are weak in Him, but we shall live with Him by the power of God toward you.' —2 COR. XIII. 4.

THOUGH He was crucified, yet He liveth, that is the whole sum and substance of the Bible. But this verse tells us much more; that He was crucified through weakness, that He liveth through power.

I. But how, crucified through weakness? Firstly, I know very well, it means that He submitted to become weak by taking our mortal nature, that He might be able to die for our sakes; that no man could have taken away His life, had He not laid it down of Himself; that He who said, 'The earth is weak, and all the inhabiters thereof; I bear up the pillars of it,' condescended to faint under the weight of the cross and to be helped by Simon of Cyrene. But it means a great deal more than this; else it could not join on to the latter part of the verse. 'Crucified through weakness' means, after a course, after a life, of weakness; and so indeed it was. And I know not but that these confessions of human weakness, so patiently borne, so openly confessed, do not above everything else show us the meaning of that saying of St. Paul, 'He emptied Himself'. Think—when His disciples went away into the city to buy food, He remained by the well; acknowledging thereby that He was not able, to speak after the manner of men, to do that which they could do. Think again— when they took Him, even as He was, in the ship, they were toiling in rowing, but He, as man, was so exhausted that He slept.

II. Never be ashamed to confess weakness either of body or mind. If you are told at any time to do anything which you feel to be above your strength, you will be much more like our Lord by saying so, than by making an effort which you ought not to make. For notice in these two remarkable proofs of our Lord's weakness how His perfect wisdom turned them both to be means of blessing. He sat on the well because He was weary, and thus the woman of Samaria and her fellow-townsmen were brought to His knowledge. He slept in the vessel because He was weary, and thus He proved Himself, sleeping as well as waking, to be Almighty.

III. 'For we also are weak in Him.' Hear what St. Bernard says: 'But as for me, Lord Jesus, my wonder is beyond all wonder that Thou shouldst call us weak in Thee, that Thou shouldst suffer us to lay all our weakness thus to Thy charge; that Thou shouldst give us Thy strength and take our infirmity. And is this, O Lord, the return that those Thy children ought to make? Is this all that Thou requirest of them, to be weak in Thee? Instead of urging them to give proofs of their strength, Thou only commandest them to lean their weakness on Thee; so that, saith the Bride, Thy left arm is under their head, drooping and bowed down by infirmity, and Thy right hand shall embrace them. Oh, wonderful superabundance of love. To love not strength only, but weakness; to accept, not only affection, but coldness! Who among the sons of men would thus act, save He only who is the Bridegroom of the Virgins, the true Lover of Souls?'

IV. 'We shall live with Him.' We could not live without Him. All the doctors of the Church agree in this, that if it were possible for His presence to be in hell, hell itself would become heaven. We *shall* live with Him where He is, if only we invite Him now to live with us where we are.—J. M. NEALE, *Sermons in Sackville College Chapel*, vol. i. p. 328.

REFERENCES.—XIII. 4.—J. M. Neale, *Sermons Preached in Sackville College Chapel*, vol. i. p. 328 ; *ibid. Readings for the Aged* (4th Series), p. 102. XIII. 5.—Spurgeon, *Sermons*, vol. iv. No. 218. Bishop Westcott, *Village Sermons*, p. 156. T. F. Crosse, *Sermons*, p. 133. E. W. Attwood, *Sermons for Clergy and Laity*, p. 125. D. C. A. Agnew, *The Soul's Business and Prospects*, p. 88. S. Baring-Gould, *Village Preaching for a Year* (2nd Series), vol. i. p. 151. F. D. Maurice, *Sermons*, vol. iii. p. 207. W. J. Brock, *Sermons*, p. 161. W. J. E. Bennett, *Sermons Preached at the London Mission*, 1869, p. 73. XIII. 8.—W. R. Harwood, *Christian World Pulpit*, vol. xlv. p. 294. XIII. 8, 9.—J. M. Neale, *Sermons for the Church Year*, vol. ii. p. 245.

CHRISTIAN PERFECTION

'This we also pray for, even your perfecting.'—2 COR. XIII. 9.

THERE is probably no subject Christian teachers touch so reluctantly as that of Christian Perfection. This is due partly to the difficulties of definition, and partly to the fact that it lays one open to misunderstanding. The Scriptures command perfection, promise perfection, and give examples of perfection. God does not mock us with impossible commands. There is an imperfect perfection. All perfection is relative except the perfection of God. Christian perfection does not indicate finality but fitness.

I. The meaning of perfection. To make perfect means to make fit, to put in order, adjust, adapt, arrange, and equip, so as to secure effectiveness and efficiency for the result to be achieved. The meaning is the same when applied to Christian life and experience. It is the adjustment, cleansing, and equipment of man's nature for all the purposes of the life in Christ. It is nothing more than making man fit in every part to do the will of God.

II. All the elements of Christian character are set forth in the Scriptures as capable of perfection. The elements that make up Christian character are Faith, Hope, Love ; and each of these may be perfect. (1) Faith. 'Night and day praying exceedingly that we may see your face, and may perfect that which is lacking in your faith' (1 Thess. III. 10). (2) Hope. 'Be sober and set your hope perfectly on the grace that is to be brought unto you at the revelation of Jesus Christ' (1 Peter I. 13). (3) Love. 'Above all things put on love, which is the bond of perfectness' (Col. III. 14).

III. Christian perfection experienced in the heart is manifest in the life. ' By their fruits ye shall know them.' (1) The first-fruit of the three-fold perfection of faith, hope, and love, is patience. (a) The Christian made perfect in faith, hope, and love will be perfect in his patience with God. (b) To many, patience with people is more difficult than patience with God. There is nothing can make us patient with trying people except faith in them, hope for them, and love of them. (2) Perfect obedience to the will of God. (3) A perfect tongue. (4) Perfect peace.

IV. 'If thou wouldst be perfect?' For such a life who among the redeemed has not sighed and prayed? How then may we attain unto a life so glorious? It is the work and gift of God, and can only become ours by consecration, cleansing, and indwelling.—S. CHADWICK, *Humanity and God*, p. 249.

REFERENCES.—XIII. 11.—*Expositor* (5th Series), vol. v. p. 38 ; *ibid.* (6th Series), vol. viii. p. 379.

VALEDICTION AND BENEDICTION

'The grace of the Lord Jesus Christ, and the love of God, and the communion of the Holy Ghost, be with you all.'— 2 COR. XIII. 14.

THE repetition of the text is the best sermon. 'The grace of the Lord Jesus Christ, and the love of God, and the communion of the Holy Ghost, be with you all.' What then? Then there will be no real separation. The true union is mystical, spiritual, Divine. We come to learn this by attending a costly and distressing school; we come to know this by experience. Disappearance does not violate union; not being able to see does not utterly impoverish the soul; there is an inward sight, there is a spiritual vision, there is a wondrous power of sympathy which can realise or put into body-forms all that is most sacred and healthful in human evolution.

I. What a wondrous argument is this benediction! It is a large theology; there is in this benediction a Trinity, a relation of persons, distinct and operative personalities, each member of the Trinity having something to do with the human soul. You cannot build your rhetoric without the Trinity; the poor sweltering rhetorician must have his three members in order to complete what he calls a climax—which nobody wants to hear. You cannot anywhere fail to see the threefold action, the threefold mystery of being, co-operation, and of development. Whatever may be the metaphysics of the Trinity, I know not, I cannot enter into that ineffable mystery; but I see a ladder rising from earth to heaven, and I see the angels of God descending and ascending, ascending and descending, holding continual and vital commerce with the uttermost parts of the great heaven. So it is with this Trinity; I meet it everywhere.

With what a wondrous instinct is the right word chosen by this speaker of the benediction! No poet can amend the phrase. 'The grace of our Lord Jesus Christ'—the favour, the pity, the daily care, the incessant solicitousness and love. 'The grace,' a word fit for the Cross, a word that is as the jewel syllable in the great literature crowded into the one pregnant word Atonement.

II. How, then, does the benediction proceed? 'And the communion of the Holy Ghost.' What fit words; what expert writing! If it were only a matter of the choice of words here is an instance of the finest bringing-together of the most exquisite terms; in a sense, the only terms that could fit the occasion. The Holy Spirit communes with the heart, speaks to it without words, hovers over it, breathes upon it, turns over the leaves when we read the words of Christ and annotates them with light. The Holy Ghost is the Spirit of companionship, filling all space, yet occupying no room; a contradiction in words, a verity and a music in experience. You cannot bless unless you have been blessed. Hypocrisy cannot pronounce a benediction; the words can be pronounced, but not the benediction itself in its innermost music and holy meaning. Only sincerity can produce the true music of the true heart.

III. 'I will not leave you comfortless.' 'The grace of the Lord Jesus Christ, and the love of God, and the communion of the Holy Ghost, be with you all.' I will change the text in one word. I have never throughout my long ministry been able to pronounce this benediction exactly as it is written. The change which I make is, I think, an amendment. 'Be with *us* all.' The minister has no right to stand apart as if he were dropping something upon others in an official and authoritative manner. I sit or stand with the smallest little child that God ever sent into the world; and I do not in pronouncing a benediction say, 'The benediction of God be with you,' I say, 'Be with us'—the little child, the poor cripple, the desolate soul—brother of the heart. We want a common blessing as we want a common atmosphere. —JOSEPH PARKER, *City Temple Pulpit*, vol. IV.

THE MYSTERY OF THE GODHEAD
2 COR. XIII. 14.

WHAT do men know of God? The Christian teaching about God is all that we, with our present very small powers, can know about that infinite and unseen Being, whose existence we infer, and Whom we call God, comes to us in one of three ways.

I. Nature, the existing world of things and men that we see. Every year teaches us more about Nature, and, therefore, more about God. If there is a veil that hides God in Nature from us, it is in our eyes, over our minds, and not in Nature.

II. But we learn about God in a second way. There is that marvellous figure in world-history, Jesus Christ. Christ reveals God to us. Just as Nature compels the recognition of a Cause behind it, and we name the Cause God, so Christ compels us to think how He came to be.

III. And there is the third revelation, nearer still to each of us, appealing not to our reason, not to our knowledge of Christ, which is limited to those who have learned about Him, but a voice speaking in the heart to every child of man. There is the survival of the brute in us all. It is awful. But there is also the light that shines amid it all—the light of God Himself in the human conscience.—J. M. WILSON, *Church Family Newspaper*, vol. XIV. p. 428.

REFERENCES.—XIII. 4.—A. Whyte, *Christian World Pulpit*, vol. I. p. 844. F. D. Maurice, *Sermons*, vol. iv. p. 147. C. D. Bell, *The Power of God*, p. 263. J. T. Stannard, *The Divine Humanity*, p. 165. S. P. Carey, *Christian World Pulpit*, vol. lvii. p. 262. J. Stuart Holden, *The Pre-eminent Lord*, p. 233; *ibid.* (6th Series), vol. viii. p. 372. XIII. 14, 15.—F. D. Maurice, *Sermons*, vol. iii. p. 223. XIII. 15.—*Expositor* (5th Series), vol. vi. p. 289. XIV. 2.—*Ibid.* vol. vii. p. 149. XV. 6.—*Ibid.* (6th Series), vol. vi. p. 243. XV. 27.—*Ibid.* vol. x. p. 192. XVI. *Expositor* (4th Series), vol. vii. p. 75. XVI. 1-16.—Spurgeon, *Sermons*, vol. xix. No. 1113.

GALATIANS

REFERENCES.—*Expositor* (4th Series), vol. ii. p. 69; *ibid.* vol. vii. p. 197; *ibid.* vol. ix. p. 254. I. 1.—*Ibid.* (6th Series), vol. i. p. 388. I. 2.—*Ibid.* (5th Series), vol. x. p. 159. I. 4. —F. D. Maurice, *Sermons*, vol. i. p. 279. *Expositor* (4th Series), vol. vi. p. 27; *ibid.* (6th Series), vol. vii. p. 278; *ibid.* vol. viii. p. 332. I. 4, 5.—Spurgeon, *Sermons*, vol. xlii. No. 2483. I. 6.—*Expositor* (5th Series), vol. vii. p. 118. I. 6, 7. —*Ibid.* (6th Series), vol. i. p. 29; *ibid.* vol. vi. p. 311. I. 6, 9.—*Ibid.* vol. iii. p. 232. I. 7.—J. Hall, *Christian World Pulpit*, vol. xlvi. p. 68.

THE UNALTERABLE GOSPEL

'But though we, or an angel from heaven, preach any other gospel than that which we have preached unto you, let him be accursed.'—GAL. I. 8.

I. IT is always the work of a critical stage in the history when the ways of escape are rigidly limited in number. The most appalling situations in life are not those from which we may flee through many doors. The graver the complications that face us, the fewer the feasible schemes of salvation from their cruel entanglement. And such common analogies have their special application to the subject of sin. If redemption is possible, it is inconceivable that it should be by a score of expedients, one equally good with another. If there be no Divine revelation, the problem is hopeless; and when the revelation of free mercy has once been made, the least departure from it is a sacrilege against God, and an offence against the hope and welfare of the race, for which crime is too light a name.

II. As Paul viewed this subject, an infinite and eternal wisdom was needed to design the process of escape, and an unheard-of munificence of love to carry it into effect. Again and again Paul affirms that this root-conception of the Gospel was hidden away in the deeps of the Godhead, that the angels could not explore the secret, and that it was only after many ages that the gracious redeeming mystery took efficacious shape in the work of Jesus Christ. If this be so, any alternative man may devise for himself must be a paltry, disappointing juggle. The Gospel is intolerant of either specious imitations or auxiliary rituals to eke out its virtues. It is all of a piece, and comes down from heaven.

III. This note of exclusiveness in the message of the Gospel is intended to make salvation sure for those who seek it. In travelling through thinly settled countries or amongst people of a strange language, we know how much easier progress is if there are no cross-roads. The ideal city of refuge is approached by one path in which the simple of heart cannot err. There is only one true way into the kingdom, one solitary method of salvation, one effectual remedy for human sin and woe; and it is in wisdom and mercy that God has stamped the Gospel as a thing apart to which there can be no rival.

IV. The tests of experience single out the Gospel for its place of unrivalled authority in dealing with the moral malady of human nature. Whilst in its first approaches to the human heart the Gospel is dependent for a time upon its advocates and witnesses, it soon becomes self-attesting truth and power. Its authority is intrinsic and ceases to be distinctively external. The words of the text imply that the Gospel is greater than its greatest witnesses. It bears its own credentials, and, in the end, depends upon neither human nor angelic authority to commend it.

'Though we, or an angel from heaven, preach any other gospel unto you than that which we have preached unto you, let him be accursed.'—GAL. I. 8.

BISHOP BRIÇONNET, the reforming prelate who was appointed in 1516 to the See of Meaux, was a timid and anxious man, who dreaded persecution. A Roman Catholic partisan has preserved the record of this significant warning given by the Bishop to his flock, and elicited either by the consciousness of his own moral feebleness, or by a certain vague premonition of danger, 'Even should I, your Bishop, change my speech and teaching, beware that you change not with me'. An early French authority gives a slightly different form to Briçonnet's caution. 'Formerly,' says a MS. fragment in the Library of Geneva, 'while he was preaching to them the Gospel, he said, as St. Paul wrote to the Galatians, that if he, or an angel from heaven preached to them any other doctrine than that which he was preaching, they should not receive him.' Briçonnet's courage broke down under the attack of the Sorbonne and he forsook the reformed faith.

REFERENCES.—I. 8.—*Expositor* (6th Series), vol. v. p. 469. I. 8, 9.—*Ibid.* vol. xi. p. 467. I. 8-12.—C. Perren, *Revival Sermons in Outline*, p. 223. I. 9.—*Expositor* (5th Series), vol. ix. p. 101; *ibid.* vol. x. p. 185. I. 10.—H. P. Liddon, *University Sermons* (2nd Series), p. 144. *Expositor* (5th Series), vol. ii. p. 76; *ibid.* vol. iii. p. 366; *ibid.* (6th Series), vol. iv. p. 119. I. 11.—Spurgeon, *Sermons*, vol. xxxvii. No. 2185. I. 11, 12.—J. Baines, *Sermons*, p. 44. I. 11-20.—*Expositor* (7th Series), vol. v. p. 206. I. 12.—*Ibid.* (4th Series), vol. iv. p. 118. I. 12-16.—*Ibid.* (6th Series), vol. ii. p. 209. I. 13.—*Ibid.* (5th Series), vol. vi. p. 245; *ibid.* (6th Series), vol. vii. p. 409. I. 13, 14.—*Ibid.* (4th Series), vol. vii. p. 119.

GAL. I. 14.

EVEN in quite intermediate stages, a dash of enthusiasm is not a thing to be ashamed of in the retrospect; if St. Paul had not been a very zealous Pharisee, he would have been a colder Christian. — R. L. STEVENSON.

REFERENCES.—I. 15.—Spurgeon, *Sermons*, vol. xi. No. 656. I. 15, 16.—H. S. Seekings, *Preacher's Magazine*, vol. xvii. p. 555. H. Melvill, *Penny Pulpit*, No. 1585, p. 75. *Expositor* (4th Series), vol. ii. p. 102 ; *ibid.* vol. vi. p. 374. I. 15-17.— R. W. Dale, *Fellowship with Christ*, p. 216. I. 16.—*Expositor* (4th Series), vol. viii. p. 138 ; *ibid.* (5th Series), vol. iv. p. 48.

'Immediately I conferred not with flesh and blood, neither went I up to Jerusalem, to them which were Apostles before me, but I went to Arabia.'—GAL. i. 16, 17.

WHEN Shibli Bagarag returned from the well of Paravid, with the brimming phial in his hand, Noorna said to him, ' Hadst thou a difficulty in obtaining the waters of the well ? '

He answered, ' Surely all was made smooth for me by thy aid. Now when I came to the well I marked not them by it, but plunged, and the depth of that well seemed to me the very depth of the earth itself, so went I ever downward ; and when I was near the bottom of the well I had forgotten life above, and lo ! no sooner had I touched the bottom of the well when my head emerged from the surface ! 'twas wondrous.'—GEORGE MEREDITH, *The Shaving of Shagpat*.

REFERENCES.—I. 17.—*Expositor* (5th Series), vol. x. p. 354; *ibid.* (6th Series), vol. i. p. 78 ; *ibid.* vol. viii. p. 231 ; *ibid.* vol. xi. p. 359. I. 18.—T. Vincent Tymms, *Christian World Pulpit*, vol. lxx. p. 356. I. 19.—H. A. Smith, *Preacher's Magazine*, vol. x. pp. 437, 505. *Expositor* (5th Series), vol. iv. p. 307. I. 21.—*Ibid.* vol. ii. p. 32. I. 23.—C. Parsons Reichel, *Sermons*, p. 60. I. 23, 24.—J. Keble, *Sermons for the Saints' Days*, p. 113. I. 24.—R. Allen, *The Words of Christ*, p. 41. J. G. Rogers, *Christian World Pulpit*, vol. xlvii. p. 194. II. 1.—John Watson, *Christian World Pulpit*, vol. lvi. p. 305. *Expositor* (6th Series), vol. viii. p. 332. II. 1-10. —*Ibid.* (5th Series), vol. ii. p. 104 ; *ibid.* vol. iii. pp. 84, 92, 175, 255, 262 ; *ibid.* vol. iv. pp. 43, 298 ; *ibid.* vol. vii. p. 327 ; *ibid.* vol. ix. p. 224 ; *ibid.* vol. x. p. 265.

BY REVELATION

'By revelation.'—GAL. II. 2.

PAUL was fond of the word revelation. ' When it pleased God to reveal His Son in me ' I ' went up by revelation ' ; ' If in anything ye be otherwise minded, God will reveal this also '. It is wonderful to see how this ministry of revelation penetrates the whole area and purpose of life. Sometimes we are startled into its use ; we find revelation where we did not expect to find it. We are so familiar with some things that we forget them ; we speak so fluently that we do not catch the emphasis of the music.

I. What could be a greater revelation according to the limitations of the case than the meaning of the alphabet ? We never think of that, because we use the alphabet mechanically ; it comes and goes just as we will it to come and go. But if you will take the mind right back to the beginning, and say to the little child, You have to learn all these poor curious-looking things, we call them letters, and you have to stamp them on your mind, and get them into your head, and know them every time you see them ; and then you may have to put two or three of them together, perhaps six or seven ; the alphabet means nothing, but it contains everything in the way of literature. Sometimes we learn by letters or by revelations made to us through the medium of letters, things that are symbolical, things that are quick with a great unrevealed and uncomprehended vitality and meaning.

II. Then again we change the ground of revelation, and we learn by experience. Through that gate God comes to man to bind up his wounds, and to take him more closely to His heart, showing him the vanity and transiency of the time-sphere and the space-world, and bathing him in the rivers of eternity. Some men can only learn by experience ; they learn nothing by spiritual revelation. Some men cannot understand anything unless they have experienced it. Want of sympathy often arises from want of knowledge. You have never had a headache, and therefore you cannot understand however anybody can be suffering from that complaint. You have never lost anyone, and you cannot understand the meaning of these hot rivers of tears, that awful eloquent silence, that expressive pregnant sigh of the soul. O, how poor is he who has never been desolated !

III. Then again comes the very highest phase of revelation, namely, the great spiritual communication between God the Spirit and man the spirit, the wondrous illumination, the sudden calling into light, the smiting down that there may be a great rising up. Then the whole enlightenment of the sphere of consciousness ; then the ghostly feeling that we have heard it all before ; then the mysterious feeling that we must have dreamed it. Then the book is put before us, the book which is called the Bible, and we feel that we have surely seen it somewhere ; that psalm is quite familiar, that going in the top of the mulberry trees is something we heard in the woods near our father's house at home. All these delineations and representations of character—why, we seem to know all the Bible folk ; we have met them ; not under their names as given on the written page, but there is not a man mentioned in the Bible or delineated with any completeness that we did not in some sort of way know. The people red-handed with murder, we know them, we have seen them, though they sell their souls for gold. Where did we see them ? They are quite familiar to us ; though they lie they are not strangers.

Let us get acquainted with the fact that revelation is going on round about us, and within us, and that revelation is not a church property. We should bring it into life, daily, experimental, practical life, and talk familiarly about it with tender reverence as a gift from heaven or some sheet of cloud let down fuller of stars than the sky.

IV. Sometimes a man is revealed to himself ; he says in blunt frankness that he would not have believed it of himself, it was quite a revelation to him. There he does not object to the word revelation, for it has not gathered around it its brightest robes. Sometimes we are revealed to one another; hence we often use such expressions as, It was quite a revelation to me. What do you mean by revelation? You simply mean, if you will be faithful to yourself, that you have seen the inside of things, that for a moment you have been at God's stand-point, and have seen realities, not appearances; philosophies, not phenomena.

How do we know certain things? By revelation. How do we know God? Only by revelation. How do we know about the forgiveness of sins? Only by revelation. This is not something found out in the schools; this is not a clever answer to a trying enigma; it is God's answer to the enigma of our own misery. That puts a new aspect on things. Certainly it does; but it puts the right aspect on them.

V. Then, finally, revelation comes and fits in all the gaps and all the strange places of life. Then revelation comes and says, Now let us walk together; O sweet, sweet heart, come with me, and let us walk together. Thou hast a cemetery in thine estate? Yea, I have. Come with me, and we will talk it out on the spot: this grave was for thy good, as well as for the good of the loved one ascended; it was fixed that this grave should be dug on the day mentioned on the marble, at the very moment—it was fixed that it should not be a moment later; this grave is a garden; see, thou canst plant upon this grave the flower of answered prayer; I will go home with thee—which is the worst part of the journey related to the cemetery. There is a kind of grim joy in going to it, but there is a bitter misery only in leaving it. I will go with thee, I will take thine arm, yea, the arm of thine heart. What thou knowest about death thou knowest only by revelation. Blessed, sweet bereaved one, blessed are the dead that die in the Lord. They have got it all over. The enemy can hurt them no more.—Joseph Parker, *City Temple Pulpit*, vol. iv. p. 136.

References.—II. 2.—*Expositor* (6th Series), vol. ii. p. 205. II. 3.—*Ibid.* (5th Series), vol. ii. p. 131; *ibid.* (6th Series), vol. i. p. 107. II. 4.—*Ibid.* (4th Series), vol. vii. p. 9; *ibid.* (6th Series), vol. vii. p. 457; *ibid.* vol. viii. p. 76.

'That the truth of the Gospel might continue with you.'—Gal. II. 5.

It seems to me that in every problem of moral conduct we confront, we really hold in trust an interest of all mankind. To solve that problem bravely and faithfully is to make life just so much easier for everybody; and to fail to do so is to make it just so much harder to solve by whoever has next to face it.—G. W. Cable, in *The Cavalier.*

References.—II. 6.—*Expositor* (4th Series), vol. vii. p. 204; *ibid.* (5th Series), vol. vii. p. 10. II. 6-9.—*Ibid.* vol. iv. p. 58. II. 7.—C. S. Robinson, *Simon Peter*, p. 9. *Expositor* (5th Series), vol. ix. p. 13. II. 7-9.—*Ibid.* vol. viii. p. 149. II. 7-10.—*Ibid.* (6th Series), vol. viii. p. 237. II. 8.—*Ibid.* p. 59. II. 8.—*Ibid.* (5th Series), vol. vii. p. 32; *ibid.* (6th Series), vol. v. p. 416.

'Only they would that we should remember the poor : the same which I also was forward to do.'—Gal. II. 10.

Is it fanciful to imagine that a touch of quiet irony lies in Paul's account of the last injunctions given to him at Jerusalem? As if he was likely to forget the claims of poor people, amid ecclesiastical and doctrinal discussions! Surely they might have taken that for granted. The authorities, no doubt, meant well. But, says Paul gravely, I did not need any prompting in that direction; ὃ καὶ ἐσπούδασα αὐτὸ τοῦτο ποιῆσαι. This does not mean that Paul then and there began to make it his object to collect for the poor, although doubtless he did use the 'collection for the poor saints in Judea' as a means of drawing together happily the two sides of the Church. He needed no official reminder of his Christian duty to the poor. Whoever might be lacking, he at least (so the change from μνημονεύωμεν to ἐσπούδασα may suggest) was not likely to be backward in this service.

One of the highest forms in which we can show our appreciation of a man's proved character is to take for granted that he will do some duty. We should assume that he will be ready for it. To remind him nervously of its obligation is, in one aspect, to indicate that we are not quite sure of him. Perhaps he may forget it, in the press of other interests! Let us charge him! Paul relates the exhortation, as he probably received it, with perfect courtesy. But one can imagine how he felt; not irritated—he was far too great a man for that—but half-amused, as many a person is who has to receive gratuitous advice, by mouth or letter, from well-meaning outsiders, upon the cardinal tasks which all the while lie closest to his own heart. He listens to the counsel, and then quietly goes his way, wondering what his friends take him for, after all; wondering whether they really thought that he needed at this time of day to be prodded to his duty.

'But when I saw.'—Gal. II. 14.
'As I beheld.'—Acts XVII. 23.

At Antioch and at Athens Paul's great, though perhaps not very welcome, service was that he detected the misdirection of religious energy. He believed in the charity which thought no evil, but he did not conceive this to mean an amiable habit of shutting one's eyes to inconsistencies and aberrations in human conduct. Things were going wrong at Antioch, although the local Christians either failed to realise it or were too timid to protest. Paul's keen penetration and courage saved the situation for Christendom. *When I saw . . . I said.* It was a time for plain speech, when issues had to be disentangled and principles cleared from any deviating practices. The Christians at Antioch were, like Christian and Hopeful in Bunyan's allegory, 'at a place where they saw a way put itself into their way, and seemed withal to lie as straight as the way which they should go'. They had been persuaded to deviate along this path, but no one realised it till Paul arrived. *I saw* ὅτι οὐκ ὀρθοποδοῦσιν—'that they were not on the straight path'. For the sake of their own peace as well as for the sake of their followers, he spoke out, impelled by the same motive as at Athens, where among the pagans he seems to have also felt urged by a sense, half of indignation, half of pity, at the misapplication of human reverence and earnestness. *I beheld . . . I now declare to you.* The sight of religious feeling running to waste, through confused and imperfect knowledge, always stirred Paul. Inside the Church and outside the Church, he was confronted with the pathos and mischief of this problem, and to it he brought the courage of his own convictions and the impact of his own practical sagacity, exposing the error ere it was too late.—James Moffatt.

References.—II. 10.—J. Keble, *Sermons for the Saints' Days*, p. 242. Spurgeon, *Sermons*, vol. ii. No. 99. *Expositor* (7th Series), vol. v. p. 279. II. 11.—H. M'Neile, *Penny Pulpit*, No. 1604, p. 231. *Expositor* (5th Series), vol. vii. p. 407 ; *ibid.* (6th Series), vol. iii. p. 351. II. 12.—*Ibid.* vol. v. p. 326 ; *ibid.* vol. vii. p. 139. II. 13.—*Ibid.* (7th Series), vol. v. p. 190. II. 14.—*Ibid.* (4th Series), vol. ii. p. 64 ; *ibid.* (5th Series), vol. iv. p. 164. II. 14-21.—*Ibid.* (4th Series), vol. vii. p. 10. II. 15.—*Ibid.* vol. i. p. 201. II. 16.—*Ibid.* vol. vii. p. 417 ; *ibid.* (5th Series), vol. vii. p. 284. II. 17.—*Ibid.* (6th Series), vol. ix. p. 64. II. 19.—C. Bradley, *The Christian Life*, p. 128. J. H. Holford, *Memorial Sermons*, p. 81. *Expositor* (6th Series), vol. vii. p. 265 ; *ibid.* (7th Series), vol. v. p. 524. II. 19, 20.—C. O. Eldridge, *The Preacher's Magazine*, vol. xix. p. 176.

ST. PAUL'S LOVE FOR CHRIST

'I live by the faith of the Son of God, Who loved me, and gave Himself for me.'—Gal. ii. 20.

It is a significant testimony to man's permanent need of Christ that the name of Christ is used and in a manner preached even where His unique Divinity is denied; even where the wonders of His life and death are rejected ; even where his sinlessness is questioned; even where He is resolved into some ghostly ideal never numbered among the sons of men. This is a proof of the paramount importance of keeping Christ and the emotions which Christ excites alive and supreme among the race. It is felt more or less dimly that the full claim of Christ to the passionate love of man must be made room for somehow if the preaching of religion in any form is to be continued.

I. But the question is whether such a love for Christ as St. Paul experienced can be severed from the Apostle's conception of his Redeemer's person and work. If we strip the life of Christ of its supernatural element ; if we deny the Virgin Birth and the bodily resurrection ; if we hesitate to accept His perfection ; if we deny that He proceeded forth and came from God, the Eternal Word, Who in the fulness of time became flesh that we might receive of His fulness, and therein be filled with all the fulness of God—can the preaching of Christ be maintained ? If we deny that He laid down His life for our sakes, having power to lay it down and to take it up; if we accept the theory that His death was no more

than a murder, that He perished as the feeble victim of an enormous wrong, can we still feel for Him what St. Paul felt?

II. Why did St. Paul love Christ with such an overwhelming passion ? To answer it aright would be to retrace the whole history. But first we say that St. Paul's love was the love of gratitude. 'He loved me and gave Himself for me'—that is the burning centre. Christ died for the ungodly. We are justified by faith in His blood. St. Paul knew the great desolation of the Victim of Love. Christ was made a curse for him on the tree of Calvary. Christ kept knocking by the voice of interior grace at the door of his heart till his heart opened. Then the soul that had been separated from the Author of Peace was restless and weary no longer. To him the meritorious death of Christ became the beautiful gate of the temple whereby he entered into the treasure-house of God. The full, finished, and perfect sacrifice and atonement for the sins of the whole world blotted out the transgressions that were past. More than that : if any man be in Christ there is a new creation. There is the stroke that ends him and the touch that begins him afresh. The faith of St. Paul apprehended the dying of the Lord Jesus, and the Spirit that raised up Christ from the dead quickened his mortal body. Mystically he died and rose again in Christ.

III. Then St. Paul knew himself to be in union and communion constant and intimate with the heavenly Saviour. His love was no mere gratitude for the past. It was a fervour of affection new every morning till his last day came.

St. Paul had no fear of light from any quarter. He was only afraid that there might be too little of it. But it was the illumination of the Spirit of Christ that he craved for and pursued. The world by wisdom knew not God. The darkness came down upon him sometimes, fell upon him sometimes as it falls on all believers. Now and again it seemed to bite into his very soul. Yet we can see now that the Lord Jesus was nearer him then than in times that seemed happier. And so it may be with us. The glory of Christ was St. Paul's first beginning and his last end.—W. Robertson Nicoll, *Sunday Evening*, p. 39.

CONVERSION OF ST. PAUL

'Nevertheless I live ; yet not I, but Christ liveth in me, and the life which I now live in the flesh I live by the faith of the Son of God, Who loved me and gave Himself for me.'—Gal. ii. 20.

Even after all these years we have not grasped yet all that the world owes to St. Paul. Indeed, in many ways it seems as if it had been reserved for our generation and for our special problems of the age to draw out all that in the providence of God we were meant to learn from that remarkable man whose conversion we commemorate to-day. What are the questions which are stirring men at the present day ?

First of all the demand for a man of strong intellect who at the same time is a humble and believing Christian. Again, do we not hear on all sides to-day the demand for the spiritual man who is at the same time a practical reformer? And if these demands come from without the Church, what demands do we hear rising within the Church? Men are getting tired to-day of these perpetual quarrels between one body and another body. The demand within the Church is for a man who answers to the ideal of the New Testament, who is at once a fervent Evangelist and a strong Churchman. And yet, beyond even those demands most pathetic and most pressing of all from all the hundreds who find the spiritual life difficult, who sometimes find Jesus Christ very far off from them, and the old, old story like a very distant bell, there is the demand for a man who has never seen Christ with the eye of the flesh, but to whom Jesus Christ is everything.

I. And in reply to those pathetic cries which rise from humanity to-day St. Paul is a living answer. He is a man of gigantic intellect, and yet one of the humblest Christians that ever lived. No man can sneer at St. Paul as a mere peasant or fisherman who would believe anything. In St. Paul we have an intellect that could form and write the Epistle to the Romans, and yet a man who was the humblest and most believing of Christians. We have a man who is deeply spiritual, who can say, ' I live ; yet not I, but Christ liveth in me'. Yet he left the most extraordinary work that ever man left behind him.

II. I put St. Paul before you as the breakwater that withstands sceptical attacks upon the faith, as the man who combines preaching with practice, as the rallying-point for all parties in the Church, and as the guide of all the wandering penitent souls into the haven where they would be.

We are growing in our Church to an understanding of the Gospel as St. Paul understood it. We believe in conversion, but we believe also in the gift that is given from heaven. We prepare our candidates for confirmation, for we read in the Bible, ' Then laid they their hands on them, and they received the Holy Ghost'. We have our preparation classes and our services to prepare our hearts for the Holy Communion. But, above all, we understand that when we come to that Holy Communion we receive a special gift which we can receive in no other way; and therefore try and take home the third lesson of St. Paul to-day—of toleration and understanding of those of a different school of thought from you, and the seeing how two sets of truths complement and supplement one another.

And lastly, and above all, are we taking home the fourth lesson—of what the Christian life really is? If not, let us look again at this wonderful man, who never felt alone, for his Master was with him, who feared no task that might be laid upon him because he was keen for the task, who had a thorn in the flesh but was not discouraged by it. ' My grace is sufficient for thee,' he was always hearing, and ' My strength is made perfect in weakness'.

WHAT IS IT TO BE A CHRISTIAN?

'That life which I now live in the flesh I live in faith, the faith which is in the Son of God, who loved me, and gave Himself up for me.'—GAL. II. 20.

HERE is Paul's answer, concise yet comprehensive, to our question, What is it to be a Christian? Mark then—to be a Christian is to be living by faith in personal union with Jesus Christ. The Christian life is a life of which Christ is 'motive, pattern, and power'. This is vital, essential ; all else is secondary.

I. To be a Christian does not mean simply to be what we call 'a good man'. While it may be true that a man may reject Christ and yet be possessed of many virtues—be, what we call, using the word in no very exact sense, a good man—nevertheless his life can never know the moral greatness, the repose, the triumph which are all possible to him whose life centres in Christ, who finds in His perfect example an ever-lifting ideal, in His Divine strength a never-changing stay.

II. To be a Christian does not mean necessarily to believe a certain creed. The holding of no number of opinions, accurate or inaccurate, biblical, theological, or what not, entitles a man to the Christian name. For here the vital point is not the relation of the intellect to a creed, but the attitude of the whole man—the will, the feelings, the intellect—to a person. He who thus with his whole being cleaves to Christ is a Christian, though he may be as yet in utter bewilderment as to the relation of his intellect to the various details of Christian doctrine.

III. To be a Christian is not the same thing as to have once experienced the change we call 'conversion'. Conversion is the first point in a series whose number is infinity. We are summoned not only to one supreme act of faith, but to a *life* of faith.

We may read our Bible and pray and worship till we are strapped hand and foot to the outward forms of religion ; but the love of the heart, the trust that is the outgoing of the whole soul—this is the one and only thing that can bind us to Christ Himself. Christ seeks our love, but He has first given His. He asks our trust ; but to win it, He laid down His life for us. Is He not the utterly loveworthy, the utterly trustworthy?—G. JACKSON, *First Things First*, p. 33.

THE PLACE AND POWER OF INDIVIDUALITY IN CHRISTIAN LIFE AND WORK

' I—yet not I.'—GAL. II. 20.

I. THERE is a distinct individuality in every man which knows itself as ' I ' and ' me '. It is no part of my present purpose to enter into a full metaphysical inquiry how we come to the consciousness of our own existence as distinct personalities. More akin to the object which we have in view, however, is it to get at the constituent elements of the 'self' that is in each of us. The germ of the whole, as it seems to me, is in the consciousness or experience of causation. Allied with this causation is free-will, which sits behind causation and directs it at its pleasure. Then, as the result of free-will, is responsibility. The 'I can' leads up to 'I ought,' and so consciousness develops into conscience. Then come in temperamental peculiarities which give their hue to all the rest, just as the stained glass in the window gives its own tint to the light which passes through it. To these must be added the influence of education, environment, experience, and the like, and the whole combine to form in a man that which we call his individuality.

II. When the Spirit of God regenerates a man, he does not destroy this individuality. Regeneration is not a change in the peculiarities by which a man is distinguished, but rather the purification and consecration of these, and of the man himself as a whole, to a new service. Thus it comes that in the Church of Christ we have not the dull monotony of uniformity, but the living beauty of variety.

III. When the Spirit of God works through a man, he uses the individuality of the man in all its features. He makes it largely determine the kind of service which the man is to render to his generation and to the Church, and it colours and qualifies that service itself. (1) For illustration of this we need not go beyond the limits of the Word of God itself. Thus take the case of inspiration, and you will see how truly each of the sacred writers might have said : ' I, yet not I, but the Spirit of God in me '. (2) But what is thus so markedly true in the matter of inspiration is equally conspicuous in the lower departments of spiritual effort.

IV. The actual result in all cases is to be traced to the operation of the Spirit of God through our individuality. The man is the instrument, but the Spirit is the hand that works with it ; and the glory is due not to the instrument, but to him who uses it and gives it efficacy. To sum up, then, let us distil the essence of our discourse into these two lessons : (1) Respect your own individuality. (2) Give God all the glory for what you are and have done.

GAL. II. 20.

WHAT is true of St. Paul is true of all those in whom the Christian faith has shown its highest genius in subsequent ages. These sayings of Christ as to being Himself the centre of human affections and the light of human lives, instead of repelling men, interpret their own highest experience, and seem but the voice of an interior truth and the assurance of an imperishable joy.—R. H. HUTTON, *Theological Essays*, p. 156.

IN the creation of art, or in the experience of religion, that which is the most perfect realisation of man's higher self abolishes this separate feeling ; and so it is with moral action and its concrete products. Thus when we wish to express the freedom of such creations or experiences from our lower selves, or to contrast their absoluteness with the results of our shifting desires, we are apt to use language which takes no notice of the share our will has had in them. It is not the poet who creates, but an inspiration of which

he is the mere vehicle ; it is not I who act but Christ that dwelleth in me.—A. C. BRADLEY, in *Hellenica*, p. 183.

WHEN our public service is done, then comes the time to meet ourselves alone. We have to meet ourselves in our weakness, in our ignorance, in our sin, in the awfulness and mystery of our separate existence. We hear voices speaking to us as if our personal fate were the one object of interest of the infinite compassion and the Eternal Love : ' Who loved me and gave Himself up for me '. . . . Let us not for any outward interest, tempted by the fascination of the widest thoughts and most absorbing aims, shrink from that contact with the inward discipline of our souls. —R. W. CHURCH, *Human Life and its Conditions*, p. 61.

REFERENCES.—II. 20.—J. Wright, *The Guarded Gate*, p. 105. J. Watson, *Christian World Pulpit*, vol. xlvi. p. 392. C. Perren, *Sermon Outlines*, p. 363. W. J. Knox-Little, *Christian World Pulpit*, vol. lix. p. 227. R. F. Horton, *The Hidden God*, p. 51. W. H. Hutchings, *Sermon Sketches*, p. 262. Bishop Nickson, *The Record*, vol. xxvii. p. 1124. H. P. Liddon, *University Sermons*, p. 217. T. Arnold, *Christian Life : Its Hopes*, p. 271. J. M. Neale, *Sermons Preached in Sackville College Chapel*, vol. ii. p. 235. R. W. Dale, *The Epistle of James*, p. 141. Spurgeon, *Sermons*, vol. xiii. No. 781 ; vol. xxvii. No. 1599 ; and vol. xl. No. 2370. J. Barlow, *Christian World Pulpit*, vol. lxx. p. 276. G. Campbell Morgan, *Mundesley Conference Report*, 1910, p. 358. J. H. Jowett, *The Transfigured Church*, p. 37. *Expositor* (4th Series), vol. ii. p. 102 ; *ibid.* vol. v. p. 434 ; *ibid.* vol. vi. p. 424 ; *ibid.* vol. viii. pp. 204, 435 ; *ibid.* (5th Series), vol. v. p. 5 ; *ibid.* vol. vi. p. 256 ; *ibid.* (6th Series), vol. iii. p. 340 ; *ibid.* vol. xi. p. 447. A. Maclaren, *Expositions of Holy Scripture—Galatians*, p. 91. II. 21.—Spurgeon, *Sermons*, vol. xxvi. No. 1534.

GAL. III. 1.

'How any man with clear head and honest heart,' wrote Sterling, 'and capable of seeing realities, and distinguishing them from scenic fancies, should, after living in a Romanist country, and especially at Rome, be inclined to side with Leo against Luther, I cannot understand.'

REFERENCES.—III. 1.—Bishop Winnington-Ingram, *The Men Who Crucify Christ*, p. 1. D. C. A. Agnew, *The Soul's Business and Prospects*, p. 1. T. Arnold, *Christian Life : Its Hopes*, p. 254. Spurgeon, *Sermons*, vol. xxvi. No. 1546. *Expositor* (4th Series), vol. vii. p. 129 ; *ibid.* (5th Series), vol. viii. p. 121 ; *ibid.* (6th Series), vol. ii. p. 371 ; *ibid.* vol. viii. p. 55. A. Maclaren, *Expositions of Holy Scripture—Galatians*, p. 100. III. 1-5.—*Ibid.* p. 192. 1-6.—*Ibid.* vol. x. p. 27. III. 2.—Spurgeon, *Sermons*, vol. xxix. No. 1705. *Expositor* (5th Series), vol. i. p. 230 ; *ibid.* (6th Series), vol. x. p. 362. III. 3.—Spurgeon, *Sermons*, vol. iv. No. 178. *Expositor* (5th Series), vol. v. p. 34.

GAL. III. 3, and v. 7.

WHEN the works of Millais were collected at the Grosvenor Gallery, an ardent appreciator of his genius Lady Constance Leslie, went early in the day to the exhibition. Ascending the stairs, she encountered the painter going out, with head bowed down. As she accosted him, and he looked up, she saw tears in his eyes. ' Ah, dear Lady Constance,' he said, ' you see me unmanned. Well, I'm not ashamed of averring that in looking at my earliest pictures I have been overcome with chagrin that I so far failed in my maturity to fulfil the full forecast of my youth.' He had cause to feel this disappointment.—W. HOLMAN HUNT, *History of Pre-Raphaelitism*, II. p. 392.

REFERENCES.—III. 4.—J. M. Neale, *Sermons Preached in Sackville College Chapel*, vol. iv. p. 185. A. Maclaren, *Expositions of Holy Scripture—Galatians*, p. 109. III. 6-9.—*Expositor* (4th Series), vol. vii. p. 208. III. 7, 9.—*Ibid.* (5th Series), vol. vii. p. 372. III. 8.—*Ibid.* vol. iv. p. 451 ; *ibid.* vol. vii. p. 23. III. 10.—Spurgeon, *Sermons*, vol. iv. No. 174. *Expositor* (5th Series), vol. ix. p. 61. III. 10-14.—Spurgeon, *Sermons*, vol. xxxv. No. 2093. III. 11.—*Ibid.* vol. xiv. No. 814, and vol. xlviii. No. 2809. III. 13.—*Ibid.* vol. xv. No. 873. *Expositor* (4th Series), vol. v. p. 441 ; *ibid.* vol. vi. p. 29 ; *ibid.* vol. viii. p. 193 ; *ibid.* (7th Series), vol. v. p. 203. III. 15-18.—*Ibid.* (5th Series), vol. viii. p. 299. III. 16. —*Ibid.* p. 330. III. 19.—Bishop Bethell, *Sermons*, vol. ii. pp. 358 and 374. Spurgeon, *Sermons*, vol. iii. No. 128. *Expositor* (5th Series), vol. x. p. 234 ; *ibid.* (6th Series), vol. iv. p. 385. III. 20.—Spurgeon, *Sermons*, vol. xxxvi. No. 2180. *Expositor* (5th Series), vol. iii. p. 98. III. 21.—F. W. Farrar, *Truths to Live By*, p. 274. *Expositor* (6th Series), vol. iii. p. 285 ; *ibid.* vol. iv. p. 428. III. 22.—Bishop Bethell, *Sermons*, vol. ii. pp. 323 and 341. Spurgeon, *Sermons*, vol. xix. No. 1145. A. Maclaren, *Expositions of Holy Scripture—Galatians*, p. 116. III. 23.—Spurgeon, *Sermons*, vol. xli. No. 2402.

THE LAW A SCHOOLMASTER

'But before faith came, we were kept under the law, shut up unto the faith which should afterwards be revealed. Wherefore the law was our schoolmaster to bring us unto Christ, that we might be justified by faith.'—GAL. III, 23, 24.

THE law a schoolmaster—a tutor! What law? There were two laws—the Ceremonial Law and the Moral Law ; the Levitical law and the law of the decalogue ; the law of symbol and the law of Sinai. There is an important sense in which it may be said that both these laws acted as schoolmasters to bring the Jews to Christ. The Ceremonial Law did this. But this is not the law that St. Paul specifically refers to in our text. The immediate direct reference is to the Moral Law, the law of Sinai. Two thoughts demand our attention:—

I. The Mission of the Law.—St. Paul in the text speaks of the law fulfilling two distinct offices—that of schoolmaster and that of jailer, shutting us up, imprisoning, leaving us no way of escape. Let us look (1) At the Law as Schoolmaster. What does the law teach? (*a*) The law reveals sin—its nature, baseness, and enormity. (*b*) The law accuses all men of sin. (*c*) The law denounces sin. (*d*) The law punishes sin. (2) St. Paul speaks of the Law as Jailer. Can we offer any compensation so as to claim freedom? Well, let us see. What have you to propose? (*a*) You may propose repentance as the condition of your release. Can the law accept this? Certainly not. The law has nothing whatever to do with repentance. (*b*) Suppose you go a step further and offer reformation. Can the law accept future obedience as an atonement for past disobedience? Certainly not. The claims of the law are absolute, sovereign, eternal. (*c*) If the law cannot release me

on condition of my repentance, nor yet on condition of reformation, may not the law forgive me without any condition? Certainly not. (*d*) May not the law by an act of sovereignty remit the penalty and free the transgressor? We must all feel that this would be an act of injustice. The law has solemnly declared that death is the penalty of transgression, and it cannot cancel its own sentence.

II. The Mission of the Lord Jesus Christ.—Jesus Christ in virtue of His sacrificial death becomes our redeemer, that is, our liberator, our setter-free. There are three aspects in our condition and character under which Jesus Christ becomes our setter-free. (1) As captives. We are in bondage as captives, prisoners of war, conquered by a foreign power. (2) As slaves. 'Sold under sin' is the humiliating description given of unregenerated men. (3) As criminals. This is the presiding thought of St. Paul in the text.

REFERENCES.—III. 23-25.—*Expositor* (5th Series), vol. viii. p. 433. III. 24.—H. P. Liddon, *Sermons on Some Words of St. Paul*, pp. 170, 185. T. Arnold, *Sermons*, vol. ii. p. 78. A. Barry, *The Doctrine of the Cross*, p. 19. R. J. Campbell, *The Examiner*, 21st June, 1906, p. 601. N. H. Marshall, *Christian World Pulpit*, vol. lxx. p. 363. III. 24, 25.— Spurgeon, *Sermons*, vol. xx. No. 1196. T. Binney, *King's Weigh-House Chapel Sermons*, p. 249. III. 26.—R. W. Dale, *The Epistle of James*, p. 227. R. J. Drummond, *Faith's Certainties*, p. 171. *Expositor* (4th Series), vol. viii. p. 279.

PROFESSION WITHOUT HYPOCRISY

'As many of you as have been baptised into Christ have put on Christ.'—GAL. III. 27.

IT is surely most necessary to beware, as our Lord solemnly bids us, of the leaven of the Pharisees, which is hypocrisy. We may be infected with it, even though we are not conscious of our insincerity ; for they did not *know* they were hypocrites. Nor need we have any definite bad object plainly before us, for they had none—only the vague desire to be seen and honoured by the world, such as may influence us. So it would seem that there are vast multitudes of Pharisaical hypocrites among baptised Christians ; *i.e.* men professing without practising. Nay, so far we may be called hypocritical, one and all ; for no Christian on earth altogether lives up to his profession.

No one is to be reckoned a Pharisee or hypocrite in his prayers who *tries* not to be one—who aims at knowing and correcting himself—and who is accustomed to pray, though not perfectly, yet not indolently or in a self-satisfied way ; however lamentable his actual wanderings of mind may be, or, again, however poorly he enters into the meaning of his prayers, even when he attends to them.

I. First take the case of not being *attentive* to the prayers. Men, it seems, are tempted to leave off prayers because they cannot follow them, because they find their thoughts wander when they repeat them. I answer, that to pray attentively is a *habit*. This must ever be kept in mind. No one *begins* with having his heart thoroughly in them ; but by trying, he is enabled to attend more and more, and at length, after many trials and a long schooling of himself, to fix his mind steadily on them. No one (I repeat) *begins* with being attentive. Novelty in prayers is the cause of persons being attentive in the outset, and novelty is out of the question in the Church prayers, for we have heard them from childhood, and knew them by heart long before we could understand them. No one, then, when he first turns his thoughts to religion, finds it easy to pray ; he is irregular in his religious feelings ; he prays more earnestly at some times than at others ; his devotional seasons come by fits and starts ; he cannot account for his state of mind, or reckon upon himself ; he frequently finds that he is more disposed for prayer at any time and place than those set apart for the purpose. All this is to be expected ; for no habit is formed at once ; and before the flame of religion in the heart is purified and strengthened by long practice and experience, of course it will be capricious in its motions, it will flare about (so to say) and flicker, and at times seem almost to go out.

Let a man once set his heart upon learning to pray, and strive to learn, and no failures he may continue to make in his manner of praying are sufficient to cast him from God's favour.

II. I proceed, secondly, to remark on the difficulty of *entering into* the meaning of prayers, when we *do* attend to them.

Here a tender conscience will ask, ' How is it possible I *can* rightly use the solemn words which occur in the prayers ? ' A tender conscience *alone* speaks thus. Those confident objectors whom I spoke of just now, who maintain that set prayer is necessarily a mere formal service in the generality of instances, a service in which the heart has no part,—they are silent here. They do not feel *this* difficulty, which is the real one ; they use the most serious and awful words lightly and without remorse, as if they really entered into the meaning of what is, in truth, beyond the intelligence of angels. But the humble and contrite believer, coming to Christ for pardon and help, perceives the great strait he is in, in having to address the God of heaven. This perplexity of mind it was which led convinced sinners in former times to seek refuge in beings short of God ; not as denying God's supremacy, or shunning Him, but discerning the vast distance between themselves and Him, and seeking some resting-places by the way, some Zoar, some little city near to flee unto, because of the height of God's mountain, up which the way of escape lay. And then gradually becoming devoted to those whom they trusted, saints, angels, or good men living, and copying them, their faith had a fall, and their virtue trailed upon the ground, for want of props to rear it heavenward. We Christians, sinners though we be like other men, are not allowed thus to debase our nature, or to defraud ourselves of God's mercy ; and though it be very terrible to speak to the living God, yet speak we must, or die ; tell our sorrows we must, or there is no hope ; for created mediators and patrons are forbidden us, and to trust in an arm of flesh is made a sin.

Let us but know our own ignorance and weakness and we are safe. God accepts those who thus come in faith, bringing nothing as their offering but a confession of sin. And this is the highest excellence to which we ordinarily attain ; to understand our own hypocrisy, insincerity, and shallowness of mind, to own, while we pray, that we cannot pray aright, to repent of our repentings, and to submit ourselves wholly to His judgment, who could indeed be extreme with us, but has already shown His loving-kindness in bidding us to pray. And, while we thus conduct ourselves, we must learn to feel that God knows all this before we say it, and far better than we do.

When we call God our Father Almighty, or own ourselves miserable offenders, and beg Him to spare us, let us recollect that, though we are using a strange language, yet Christ is pleading for us in the same words with full understanding of them, and availing power ; and that, though we know not what we should pray for as we ought, yet the Spirit itself maketh intercession for us with plaints unutterable. Thus feeling God to be around us and in us, and therefore keeping ourselves still and collect d, we shall serve Him acceptably, with reverence and godly fear ; and we shall take back with us to our common employments the assurance that He is still gracious to us, in spite of our sins, not willing we should perish, desirous of our perfection, and ready to form us day by day after the fashion of that Divine image which in baptism was outwardly stamped upon us.—J. H. NEWMAN.

REFERENCES.—III. 27.—F. W. Farrar, *Truths to Live By*, p. 304. R. W. Church, *Village Sermons* (2nd Series), p. 228. *Expositor* (6th Series), vol. iii. p. 411 ; *ibid.* vol. v. p. 48 ; *ibid.* vol. vi. p. 252 ; *ibid.* vol. x. p. 199 ; *ibid.* vol. xii. p. 257. III. 27, 28.—H. S. Holland, *Christian World Pulpit*, vol. xlv. p. 18. H. H. Snell, *ibid.* vol. xlv. p. 349. III. 28.— T. C. Fry, *A Lent in London*, p. 207. H. Alford, *Sermons on Christian Doctrine*, p. 68. *Expositor* (4th Series), vol. ix. p. 10. III. 29.—*Ibid.* vol. x. p. 37. IV. 1-7.—T. Barker, *Plain Sermons*, p. 71. IV. 1-13.—*Expositor* (4th Series), vol. ix. p. 262. IV. 3.—*Ibid.* (5th Series), vol. viii. p. 20. IV. 3-6.—Spurgeon, *Sermons*, vol. xxx. No. 1815.

THE INCARNATION

' But when the fulness of the time was come, God sent forth His Son, made of a woman, made under the law.'—GAL. IV. 4.

OF all births this Bethlehem birth was the most unique. A superhuman life *demands* a superhuman birth. Let us gaze reverently into the abyssmal depths of that manger-cradle in the Bethlehem-khan.

I. The first question that presents itself to us is this : ' Was it *necessary* that God should more fully reveal Himself to man ? ' We reply in the affirmative. Man had quarrelled with God ; and to a rebel sinner the dim light of Nature and Providence was wholly insufficient. Everywhere it was adamantine order, inflexible law, and iron sternness. ' Nature's infinite order was the poor sinner's infinite despair.'

II. Our next question is this : ' *Could* God favour

the human race with a fuller revelation of Himself?' He *could*, because His power was as infinite as His love. '*Would* He do so?' His love and righteousness enable us to reply : 'Yes, with all His heart'. The infinite is never so great as when He stoops down to the lowliest and minutest.

III. And now, we are met by another question : '*How* could the Infinite and Eternal best reveal Himself to humanity?' (1) It was necessary that He should reveal Himself through the *finite*. He must stand within the limits of our faculties before we can grasp Him. (2) It was not only necessary for God to reveal Himself through the finite, but also through the *familiar*.

IV. And now we come to another question : 'What was the best possible medium through which God the Infinite could reveal Himself to man the finite?' (1) Was physical nature the best medium, with its suns, and moons, and stars, and seas, and mountains? We take no jaundiced view of nature, but we think not ; for the religion of nature puts great questions which it cannot answer ; and the world keeps on crying with the dying German poet : '*Mehr licht!*' The moral cannot be fully revealed through the material. (2) Were books or written words the best of God's revealers? Words, whether spoken or written, constantly change in value and meaning. Carlyle in real life and Carlyle in his books were two very different men. A dogma has no heart. (3) Would an angel have better revealed God? Our reply is : 'To angel "Yes," but to man "No"'. 'How then could the Infinite and Eternal best reveal Himself to the human race?' Our unhesitating reply is : 'The Word must be made flesh'. God must reveal Himself to man through a life human 'at the red-ripe of the heart'.—J. Ossian Davies, *The Dayspring from on High*, p. 120.

References.—IV. 4.—R. J. Wardell, *Preacher's Magazine*, vol. xix. p. 222. *Expositor* (4th Series), vol. v. p. 28 ; *ibid.* vol. viii. p. 266 ; *ibid.* vol. x. p. 36 ; *ibid.* (5th Series), vol. ii. pp. 164, 181, 244 ; *ibid.* vol. iv. p. 399 ; *ibid.* vol. viii. p. 443 ; *ibid.* (7th Series), vol. vi. p. 382.

THE MISSION OF CHRIST

'But when the fulness of the time was come, God sent forth His Son, made of a woman, made under the law, to redeem them that were under the law, that we might receive the adoption of sons.'—Gal. IV. 4, 5.

I. The fact of Christ's mission into the world implies three things, as here stated : (1) His pre-existence as the Son. (2) The Divine origin of His Gospel. (3) The infinite preciousness of His salvation.

II. The time of His mission, as here described, implies : (1) That God had fixed a definite time for it, which had to be reached by the filling up of the period between the formation and the execution of the Divine decree. (2) Until the fulness of the time came Christ could not come, and the world was not ready for Him. (*a*) Man's inability to save himself had to be amply and variously shown. (*b*) Time had to be given to bring out the depths of depravity into which man could plunge. (*c*) God's long-suffering

had to be manifested. (*d*) The world had to be providentially prepared.

III. The condition under which His mission took place : (1) He was made, or 'born,' of a woman. (*a*) His proper Manhood. (*b*) Not created, like the first Adam, but born. Therefore like us in all things except sin ; therefore could take our responsibilities. (2) Born under the law. A true member of the Jewish race ; an Israelite indeed. The representative man belongs to the representative nation. The greatness of His condescension. His pledge to fulfil all righteousness for us.

IV. The object of His mission was : (1) To redeem them that were under the law. His primary purpose was to save the Jews, who were Abraham's seed, and who were under those obligations which He willingly took on Himself. (*a*) They were in bondage (ver. 3). (*b*) He redeemed, delivered by ransom ; gave Himself. (2) To give us the adoption of sons. His secondary purpose as regards both Jews and Gentiles. His being born under the law made Him peculiarly the Redeemer of them that were under the law. His being born of a woman gives His redemption a wider bearing, and opens up the adoption of sons to all men. The adoption of sons is not the condition of sons, for we are children ; but a formal and real adoption, which takes us, as it were, out of minority, and the bondage to tutors and governors ; the state in which though heirs, we differ practically little from slaves. It confers on us the rights, privileges, liberties, and dignities of full-grown sonship to God.

(1) Let us grasp, then, with faith the great fact of the mission of the Son of God.

(2) Let us adore the wisdom and power of God, which sent Him at the most fitting time, and had prepared the world for His coming.

(3) Let us realise the condescension of our Lord in humbling Himself to be born of woman, and to be subject to His own law.

(4) Let us accept His redemption from the curse and bondage of the law, and so enter upon the enjoyment of the adoption of sons.

THE COMING OF THE SAVIOUR

'But when the fulness of the time was come, God sent forth His Son, made of a woman, made under the law, to redeem them that were under the law, that we might receive the adoption of sons.'—Gal. IV. 4, 5.

The coming of Christ into the world on His saving mission is the grand central event of its history. The event is here presented in three aspects.

I. The Period at which Christ Came.—'The fulness of the time.' Men would have expected Christ's coming to follow closely on man's ruin ; but four thousand years were allowed to run their course. Christ came at the very period originally decreed by God—not a day later or earlier. Hence it is called 'the fulness,' or filling up, 'of the time'.

(*a*) *It was the fulness of prophecy.* The dying Jacob had predicted : 'The sceptre shall not depart from Judah, nor a lawgiver from between his feet, until Shiloh come'—Who was therefore to appear before Judea became merged in the Roman Empire (Gen. XLIX. 10). The glory of the second Temple was to exceed that of the first, built by Solomon, by the arrival in it of Jesus, 'the Desire of all nations,' implying that Christ was to come before the destruction of the Temple by the Romans under Titus (Hag. II. 6, 9).

(b) *It was the fulness of preparation.* Christ was ever ready to come, but man was not prepared to receive Him ; and the ages which intervened between the Fall and the Incarnation were tasked with the maturing of the necessary preparations. These corresponded in extent with the magnitude of the event.

(c) *It was also the fulness of expectation,* mankind being not only ready for Christ, but looking for Him. This was true of the Jews, as seen, not only in such saints as Simeon and Anna, but in the nation generally, a deputation being sent to John the Baptist to inquire : ' Who art thou ? Art thou the Christ ? '

II. The Manner in which Christ Came.—Now look at the manner in which Christ came. He came—

(a) *By Divine commission.*—'God *sent forth* His Son.' It was by the Father's will and good pleasure that Jesus came, no less than His own ; and the sacrifice which God made in sending His Son could not have been less than that of the Son in coming. Christ is God's Christmas gift, and the costliest He ever sent us.

(b) *In human nature.*—He was 'made of a woman'. By this we are to understand His assumption of our nature, His profession of true humanity. Man having sinned, it must be man who suffers. To win our confidence, Jesus must wear our nature, and take upon Him the heavy burdens of life, and drink its bitter cup, going down into the depths into which we had fallen to raise us out of them. Let woman gratefully hail the arrival of that Divine babe, for the distinction conferred on her in the person of Mary has more than wiped out the dishonour she inherited from Eve.

(c) *Under legal subjection.*—He was made under the law that He might endure its penalty and obey it for us, and fully satisfy all its claims. For the law was dear to God, and a sacred thing, as the transcript of His own holy image.

III. The End for which Christ Came.—Finally for what purposes did He come ?

(a) *Redemption.*—'To redeem them that were under the law.' And what is the essential element of law ? Not mere direction, or advice, or precept ; but *command enforced by penalty.*

(b) *Adoption.*—He came also to secure for us adoption, ' that we might receive the adoption of sons ' ; not only deliverance from the greatest evils, but the possession of the highest honour and blessedness.

IV. Two Personal Questions.—1. *Has Christ* *been received into our hearts ?* 2. *Do we yield Christ the gratitude and homage He claims ?*

THE HOUR, AND THE DIVINE DELIVERER

' But when the fulness of the time came, God sent forth His Son, born of a woman, born under the law, that He might redeem them which were under the law, that we might receive the adoption of sons.'—GAL. IV. 4, 5.

I. The Period of Christ's Manifestation.—It has often been pointed out that when certain characters are wanted they inevitably appear. When the hour strikes the man arrives, the man exactly suited to the hour. Christ is the centre of the history of the world, and there could be no error in the date of His appearance. The race had proved its inability to restore itself to lost truth, purity, and happiness. Nothing in nature is more wonderful than the way in which complementary things and creatures arrive together ; and in history the same phenomenon is repeated. ' God's trains never keep one another waiting ' ! The Incarnation is the crowning example of the dramatic unities of history.

II. The Nature of this Manifestation.—'God sent forth His Son.' ' Born of a woman .' God manifests Himself in nature, history, and conscience ; but here is a supreme, personal, and unique revelation of Himself—the Divine clothing Himself with the human that He might redeem the human. (1) There is nothing in this manifestation contrary to the Divine *greatness.* His greatness is that of supreme wisdom, righteousness, and love ; and with these perfections He is equally great, whether invested by the splendours of the heavens, or manifested in the simplicity of 'The man Christ Jesus '. (2) There is nothing contrary to the Divine *honour.* (3) There is nothing contrary to the Divine *purity.*

III. The Design of this Manifestation. — The purpose of the Incarnation was to convert the slaves of sin into the sons of God (Romans VIII. 3, 4). We once heard an Oriental relate that when he was converted to Christianity his old angry fellow-religionists treated him as a dead man, building his tomb, and following a bier to the graveyard. It was the glorious truth in a parable. He who is truly converted by the grace of Christ is dead to sin, and all the vices follow his bier. The devil follows as the chief mourner ; the rabble of the vices weep and blaspheme ; and the epitaph reads, ' How shall we who are dead to sin live any longer therein ' ? But out of this grave rises a new man in the power of Christ's resurrection.—W. L. WATKINSON, *The Ashes of Roses,* p. 268.

REFERENCES.—IV. 4, 5.—R. W. Church, *Village Sermons* (2nd Series), p. 29. *Expositor* (4th Series), vol. vii. p. 212. A. Maclaren, *Expositions of Holy Scripture—Galatians,* p. 126. IV. 6.—A. B. Bruce, *Christian World Pulpit,* vol. xliv. p. 131. H. M. Butler, *Harrow School Sermons,* p. 298. Spurgeon, *Sermons,* vol. xxiv. No. 1435. *Expositor* (4th Series), vol. vii. p. 429 ; *ibid.* vol. viii. p. 275 ; *ibid.* (6th Series), vol. ix. p. 71. IV. 6, 7.—H. Woodcock, *Sermon Outlines* (1st Series), p. 231. C. Bradley, *Faithful Teaching,* p. 158. C. Kingsley, *The Good News of God,* p. 61.

SON AND HEIR!

'Thou art no longer a bondservant, but a son : and if a son, then an heir through God.'—GAL. IV. 7.

I. WHAT shall we mention as the first of the ingredients in heavenly sonship? Will you be astonished if I begin with *Reverence?* That may appear to be a very grey element, but it is the groundwork of all the rest. There can be no true sonship when there is flippancy at the core of the life. At the very centre of the life there must be a little chapel, serene and untroubled, where the wings are quietly folded and the soul is prostrate in ceaseless adoration. In the great chapter which tells the story of a prophet's call and ordination, the seraphim are described as creatures with six wings ; ' with twain he covered his face, and with twain he covered his feet, and with twain he did fly '. I think we can claim kinship with the seraphim in that we are in possession of the pair of wings with which to fly! Never were Christian people more busy in flying about than they are to-day! I have said more than once that our popular vocabulary 1eeks with perspiration! We are for ever on the move, and busy doing this and doing that from morning until night. But I am not quite sure whether we could claim kinship with the seraphim in respect to the other wings. I think we are gravely lacking in those folded wings which suggest an amazed sense of the Highest, and which betoken reverence, awe, silence, and reserve. Reverence never hinders service —it enriches and perfects it. Perhaps if we had the folding, covering wings our very flying would have more serviceable results. Service which is devoid of reverence ever tends to run to superficial waste. If life has no holy of holies, then the whole of life is apt to become a mere shop, the sphere of common barter, or an entertainment house, the domain of flippant pleasures, or an open refreshment room, the place of a carnal feast. Henry Drummond once went out alone into the high Alps. He was there in the early morning. The stupendous heights encompassed him on every side. He was awed by their majesty. His soul was bowed in reverent worship. And then what happened? He broke out into loud and exuberant laughter! The succession was not accidental, it was the fruit of a hidden root. The man who begins with the reverent recognition of the holiness and majesty of God will rise into a buoyancy of spirit in which all the merry-making powers will have free course to be glorified. Our Lord's Prayer teaches us that before we can pass into the gracious liberty of forgiveness and conquest we must begin with the awed and reverent stoop: 'Our Father, which art in heaven, *hallowed be Thy name*'. In the heart of a laughing, exuberant, and healthy sonship there is a quiet and retired retreat where the incense of adoration rises both night and day.

II. Now look again into the casket of this wealthy and comprehensive sonship. Here is the second jewel which I would like to display to you. Surely one of the primary elements in sonship is the privilege of intimate communion with the Father. I was one of a party who visited Chatsworth the other day. We were allowed the privilege of going through the noble house. But our liberties were severely restricted. We were allowed to pass rapidly through what is called ' the show-rooms,' but we were rigidly excluded from the 'living-rooms '. In many places there were red cords stretched across inviting passages, and our progress was barred. If I had been a son of the house I could have passed into the living-rooms, the place of sweet and sacred fellowships, the home of genial intercourse, where secrets pass from lip to lip, and unspoken sentiments radiate from heart to heart. 'Thou art no longer a bondservant, but a son !' Then I, too, am privileged to enjoy the fellowships of the living-rooms, and no barrier blocks my way to the secret place. As a son I, too, am permitted to enter into a gracious intimacy with my God.

III. Sonship is not only distinguished by liberty of communion in the secret place, but by an emancipation from many kinds of bondage and restriction with which the world is burdened and oppressed. Sonship is conspicuously and radiantly free. The sons of God ought to fascinate and win the world by the range and grandeur of their freedom. Where others are bound they must reveal themselves to be free. 'But now thou art no longer a bondservant, but a son,' and because a son thou art free to defy the crowd and be alone! One with God is in the majority. And the real son is free from the fear of death. His life moves on, not to expected defeat but to ultimate triumph. The approaching shadow does not mark a terminus, but a point of transition into the larger and immortal life. In all these ways the son of the Almighty is 'called unto liberty '. Such is sonship, marked by reverence, distinguished by intimacy, and glorious in its liberty. By our lives do we placard this sonship before our fellows? By our very manner of life does this sonship flame before the world? Do we move about like those who constantly realise the Presence of the Infinite? Is every spot a piece of holy ground? Are we sharing confidences with the Father? Has the burden of the oppressor been loosed from our backs, and are we standing erect in joyful freedom? Then are we sons, and sons indeed! 'Now thou art . . . a son !' 'Behold what manner of love the Father hath bestowed upon us that we should be called the sons of God.'—J. H. JOWETT, *The Transfigured Church*, p. 73.

REFERENCES.—IV. 7.—T. Arnold, *Sermons*, vol. ii. p. 230. Bishop Westcott, *Village Sermons*, p. 49. *Expositor* (4th Series), vol. vi. p. 253 ; *ibid.* vol. viii. pp. 268, 280.

GAL. IV. 9.

IT is hard, we say, to have faith ; but do we realise what a task a man imposes on himself if he attempts to live without faith. . . . Instead of treating a religious faith as though it were a good thing to be added to life's capital, I would raise the question rather, whether a man will have capital enough for life left if he lets a Christian faith go ? . . . The hardest thing for the Apostle was, not to keep his faith in a risen Lord, but to conceive how anyone to whom the Gospel had come, should ever dream of doing again without it.—Newman Smyth, *The Reality of Faith*, pp. 45 f.

References.—IV. 9.—T. Sadler, *Sunday Thoughts*, p. 189. *Expositor* (4th Series), vol. ix. p. 342 ; *ibid.* (5th Series), vol. vi. p. 68. IV. 13.—*Ibid.* vol. vi. p. 379 ; *ibid.* vol. viii. p. 416 ; *ibid.* (5th Series), vol. i. pp. 131, 390 ; *ibid.* vol. vi. p. 302 ; *ibid.* vol. ix. p. 98. IV. 14.—*Ibid.* vol. ii. p. 373 ; *ibid.* vol. x. p. 2. IV. 15.—*Ibid.* vol. vi. p. 381.

'So then (ὥστε) am I become your enemy, because (ἀληθεύων ὑμῖν) I tell you the truth?'—Gal. iv. 16.

Both Blass (*Rhythmen der asianischen und römischen Kunstprosa*, 1905, p. 210) and Könnecke (*Emendationen zu Stellen des NT*, 1908, pp. 29-30) change ὥστε into ὡς δέ, and read the sentence as a statement, not as a rhetorical question. Zahn and Mr. Rendall, though retaining ὥστε, similarly refuse to take the sentence as interrogative. But the so-called consecutive ὥστε with the indicative offers no great difficulty, and the proposed alteration does not give any better sense to the passage. Taken as a reproachful question, it runs thus : 'After all our happy relations, my trust in you and your devotion to me, has it come to this, that I am (judged by you to be) your enemy because I have dealt faithfully and plainly with you (*i.e.* on my previous visit)?' Paul cannot reproach himself with any undue severity in this case. He had to point out the failings and errors of his friends for their own sakes, and he had done so in love (*cp.* Eph. iv. 15), without any trace of personal feeling. The Galatians could not plead the excuse of their friend having shown temper. They were guilty of a childish petulance in attributing hostile motives to the well-meant remonstrances of their Apostle. They could not conceive of a friend being obliged to differ from them for their own sake, and their wounded pride rebelled against any reflection being cast upon their conduct. Compare the preface to Baxter's *Reformed Pastor*, in which he observes : 'It is the sinful unhappiness of some men's minds that they can hardly think well of the best words or ways of those whom they disaffect ; and they usually disaffect those that cross them in their corrupt proceedings, and plainly tell them of their faults. They are ready to judge of the reprover's spirit by their own, and to think that all such sharp reproofs proceed from some disaffection to their persons or partial opposition to the opinions they hold. But plain-dealers are always approved in the end ; and the time is at hand when you shall confess that those were your truest friends.'[1]

'It is good to be affected at all times, and not only when I am with you.'—Gal. iv. 18.

The precise sense of the words is not quite certain, ζηλοῦσθαι being rather ambiguous. But they may fairly be taken, in general, as a protest against instability of character. The Galatians, Paul says,

---

[1] Zahn thinks that Isaiah lxiii. 7-9 was in Paul's mind. A better parallel would be 1 Kings xxi. 20.

---

were all right so long as they had their Apostle's strong influence bearing upon them. But when that was withdrawn, they relapsed. Their religion was too much a matter of association and companionship.

It is some credit to be influenced by a good man. Susceptibility to a fine character and admiration for a strong nature should count for much. But this ought to produce eventually a strength of personal conviction which can stand by itself, and such a result is the aim of every influential man. He seeks to create not adherents of his own opinion but continual followers of the truth. Genuine religion must be more than an enthusiastic devotion to the person of anyone who first impresses us with a sense of the reality of God. However powerful may be the impression he makes, faith must strike its roots deeper than personal admiration or the acceptance of another's lead. Otherwise our character simply becomes an echo of the last strong personality with whom we have been thrown in contact ; and as a strong influence is not always identical with a wise and sound impulse, the character lacks any steadfast and continuous principle. This, says Paul, is *not good* (Gal. vi. 3 and 7).

The twofold province of self-deception, in relation to the wrongdoing (*a*) of others, and (*b*) of oneself.

(*a*) After speaking of the duty of Christian forgiveness, Paul sharply adds a word against the danger of censoriousness. *If a man think himself to be something, when he is nothing, he deceives* (φρεναπατᾷ) *himself.* If he prides himself upon his own integrity, in contrast to the stained and broken character of a brother, he is making an immense mistake. He is the dupe of his own folly. It is self-deception to plume oneself upon being holier than one's neighbour. That is only to feed one's vanity, which is an empty nothing. It is an entire delusion, says Paul, for the religious man to entertain a lofty self-esteem, or to foster a sense of his own exceeding merit by dwelling censoriously upon the lapses of his brethren.

(*b*) Similarly, with regard to a man's own wrongdoing. *Be not deceived* (μὴ πλανᾶσθε), the Apostle insists ; no pretences will prevent the law of retribution overtaking a man, for all his fine words and position. *Whatsoever a man soweth, that shall he also reap.*—James Moffatt.

THE REINCARNATION OF CHRIST

'My little children, of whom I travail in birth again until Christ be formed in you.'—Gal. iv. 19.

In dealing with the Galatians, St. Paul was dealing with a distinct decline from the faith as he had preached it to them. The Apostle uses every means of persuasion in order to recall them to their allegiance, not to himself but to his Master and theirs, to whom they had plighted themselves. The very form of the sentence suggests mingled rebuke and appeal. There is a sting in that word 'again,' a sting of unavailing love for Paul, a sting of rebuke for them.

I. St. Paul's sorrow and panic of fear has had many subsequent illustrations in the history of the Church.

Many like Pliable have started with Christian in the new way, and turned back at the first obstacle. The passion of Christ and the passion of Christ's servants will not be over till there be evidence of perseverance unto the end, till Christ be formed in them, and they grow up into the full stature of Christ.

II. This is the great Christian task—

Though Christ a thousand times in Bethlehem be born
But not within thyself, thy soul shall be forlorn ;
The Cross of Golgotha thou lookest to in vain
Unless within thyself it be set up again.

This is the eternal truth of all mysticism. This is also the essential meaning of the great solemn act in Holy Communion. It stands for a far deeper mystery and a more wondrous miracle than transubstantiation, the changing of the bread into the actual body of our Lord. Not that the bread is changed into the body of Christ in the Real Presence, but that we who eat the flesh of the Son of Man are changed spiritually, and the very Christ is formed in us. This is the purpose of the Sacrament, and the purpose of the faith itself, till for each of us it is no longer I but Christ that liveth in me.

III. This is the goal, but it is not to be postponed and put away by us as some far-off event that may be looked for in the future. It is a *present* task. Would we know the method of attempting the task ? It is a simple secret. The practical working of it for us is that we bring every thought into subjection to the obedience of Christ. A practical implication of this high doctrine, and one which suggests duty, and responsibility, is that Christians are Christ's representatives on earth. Are we in any vital sense *stating the case* for the King ?—HUGH BLACK, *Edinburgh Sermons*, p. 22.

REFERENCES.—IV. 19.—S. A. Tipple, *The Admiring Guest*, p. 60. IV. 20.—*Expositor* (5th Series), vol. x. p. 278 ; *ibid.* (6th Series), vol. i. p. 205. IV. 21.—*Ibid.* vol. viii. p. 63. IV. 21-31.—*Ibid.* vol. x. p. 23. IV. 22-31.—*Ibid.* (4th Series), vol. ii. p. 96. IV. 24.—Spurgeon, *Sermons*, vol. ii. No. 69. IV. 25.—A. P. Stanley, *Canterbury Sermons*, p. 344. *Expositor* (5th Series), vol. ii. p. 154 ; *ibid.* (6th Series), vol. vii. p. 133. IV. 26.—John Hunter, *Christian World Pulpit*, vol. xliii. p. 24. R. F. Horton, *ibid.* vol. lxxviii. p. 225. IV. 28.—C. Bradley, *Faithful Teaching*, p. 1. IV. 29.—J. Keble, *Sermons for Lent to Passiontide*, p. 298. *Expositor* (5th Series), vol. i. p. 17 ; *ibid.* vol. vi. p. 335. IV. 30.—R. W. Church, *Village Sermons* (3rd Series), p. 93.

BONDAGE AND FREEDOM

'So then, brethren, we are not children of the bondwoman, but of the free.'—GAL. IV. 31.

IN this Epistle St. Paul carries our thoughts back to the pathetic scenes associated with the names of Hagar and Ishmael. It is a beautiful story, and St. Paul finds in it spiritual significance. The two women in the story are, he tells us, the two covenants, the old and the new. Hagar represents all that gathers round Mount Sinai, all that mass of Jewish law and ritual which had grown up in the course of centuries and upon which the Pharisaic mind laid such great and resolute emphasis. Sarah is symbolical

of all that comes by promise, all that takes the place of the first covenant, all that is after the Spirit and not after the flesh. In other words, Ishmael, the son of the handmaid, stood for Judaism ; Isaac, the son of the freewoman, stood for the Christian kingdom.

I. **Israel's Bondage.**—We know how the word 'bondage' grated on Jewish ears. 'We be Abraham's seed, and have never yet been in bondage to any man,' was the angry reply to our Lord on one memorable occasion. None the less, bondage there was, besides the worst and supreme bondage of sin— bondage which the Israelitish mind could not really forget or ignore, whatever Israelitish pride might pretend. There was the bondage of a foreign yoke. Roman soldiers had their garrison in Jerusalem. A Roman tribunal had power over life and death. Roman agents levied the imperial taxes, Roman penalties were inflicted on evildoers. Jerusalem was indeed 'in bondage with her children,' and in this passage St. Paul may well have been thinking of her political degradation in addition to her spiritual misery. And over against this bondage was the freedom of the city beyond the grave, the city into which the Messiah would gather all His elect, the city of which all believers were already citizens, the city which should hereafter be manifested in all her splendour. Yes ! the end was to be the victory of the Church of the Messiah, just as in old days Sarah had been successful in expelling Hagar, and Isaac had been preferred to Ishmael. But for awhile the antecedents of that victory must be borne with. Hagar in her exultation had insulted Sarah ; Judaism now persecuted Christianity. But this persecution should not last. Its issues were foretold in the fate of Hagar.

II. **Christian Freedom.** — 'Children . . . of the free.' 'Children of the freewoman'! That is the grand claim which St. Paul puts forward for Christian believers. That is the claim which the world so often refuses to admit. 'Leave your doctrinal imprisonment,' it says, 'and walk in the path of mental and spiritual liberty.' What shall we say in answer ? There is no doubt a sense in which we may all admit —may be thankful and proud to admit—our bondage. More than once does St. Paul himself express and testify to it. 'Paul a bondservant of Jesus Christ.' 'Paul a bondservant of God.' To such a bondage our Saviour Himself invites us. 'Take My yoke upon you and learn of Me.' But the acceptance of this bondage brought with it redemption from bitter and humiliating subjection. To be the servant of Christ—crucified, risen, ascended—was to be free indeed. The Apostle was thinking of the old dispensation. Yet what he says surely has its message for ourselves. The Gospel of Christian freedom never grows old. The Christian claim to bring freedom is as valid to-day as in the first century. The immediate application of St. Paul's phraseology is indeed to the past rather than to the present : but it is capable of application to the present. For what was, in its essence, the bondage which St. Paul feared, and from which the Gospel promised escape? Was it not the bondage which came from imperfect communion with God? Until a man was brought into the closest union with the Almighty and Eternal, he was not free with the liberty of an accepted and obedient son. He was till then in the position of Ishmael. He had till then not realised and appropriated the calling of Isaac. And we too—except we are in communion with God through the mediation of Christ—are children of bondage. It is the restoration of that communion through the Redeemer's cross which brings true emancipation. We ourselves could not have earned it. It is only by our unity with our Saviour that we gain it. In Christ we are of the lineage of the freewoman. Out of Him we are (as it were) of the family of Hagar the Egyptian.

III. The Tyranny of Evil.—We need to remember what a dread tyranny evil is, what an appalling curse it is, what fearful mischief it can do. It can effect our everlasting ruin. We need to bear in mind what it meant for the world in old days, before the Incarnation and Passion, before the price was paid and the ransom achieved. It meant nothing less than this— that there was a measure of severance between man and God, an awful fact separating in part the two, a terrible heritage preventing and forbidding the joy of perfect intercommunion. Man had fallen. Whatever the circumstances of that fall, there it was—and its issues were, humanly speaking, irremediable. But the Son of God came and, gathering all that life into Himself, made atonement. He broke the power of Satan and rescued man from a slavery which was binding him ever tighter and tighter, which was dragging him down ever lower and lower, which was crushing him ever more and more completely. Before Christ the history of the world is, broadly speaking, the history of a disaster culminating in a collapse which those who beheld it might well think to be irretrievable. After Christ the history of the human race is in the main the history of a gradual recovery, though of a recovery which has been broken into by periods of dark and hideous faithlessness. And the crucial question for us is, Are we the children of that disaster or of that recovery, of the handmaid or of the freewoman?

LIMITATIONS AND FREEDOM

'We are not children of the bondwoman, but of the free.'— Gal. iv. 31.

'Where the spirit of the Lord is, there is liberty.'—2 Cor. iii. 17.

CHRISTIAN liberty does not mean the right to do as we like. It is strictly limited. Bishop Westcott wrote, 'True freedom is not license to do what you like, but power to do what you ought'.

I. Limited by Want of Power.—Our freedom is limited by want of power. Whether it be in physical or temporal or spiritual power, the extent of our freedom is limited by the extent of our power. There is no such thing as real freedom without power. There is no such thing as absolute freedom without almighty power. What is the use of my being free

to do anything, if I have power to do nothing? Would it not be well for us to seek power rather than search fruitlessly for a false freedom? The power we need most is the power over our corrupt, sinful nature. 'I see another law in my members, warring against the law of my mind, and bringing me into captivity to the law of sin which is in my members,' is not the experience of one man only. Where are we to seek for power? 'Ye shall receive power from on high.' We need the power of the Holy Ghost within us. 'Where the spirit of the Lord is, there is liberty,' and nowhere else in the world is there true liberty.

II. By the Extent of our Knowledge.—But our freedom is also limited by the extent of our knowledge. No one can be absolutely free without perfect knowledge. What is the use of having the liberty to do what you like if you do not know whether you will like it when you have done it, and have scarcely any means of knowing what to choose to do? Where are we to get this knowledge? 'When He, the Spirit of Truth, is come, He will guide you into all truth . . . and He will show you things to come.' You shall know the truth, and the truth shall make you free. 'Where the Spirit of the Lord is, there is liberty.' When a man or woman is endowed with power from on high, when a man or woman is filled with the Spirit of Truth, He will guide him or her into all truth. Then you have something like real liberty. 'Not license to do what you like, but power to do what you ought.'

III. By the Strength of our Will.—There is another limitation—the strength and stability of our will. Even the powerful and the wise are limited in freedom by their wills. How many a man, for instance, has the power and the means of providing a happy home for himself, and knows full well the immense benefit of a happy home-life, and yet he does not have it because he has not control over his will. He has not the will to carry out what he has otherwise the power to do, and what he knows he would be the happier for doing. Under the same heading I may include the limitations of our desires.

It is only by doing God's will that we can accomplish anything, only by attuning our wills to His.

CHRISTIAN LIBERTY

'The liberty wherewith Christ hath made us free.'—Gal. v. 1.

WHAT is 'liberty?' Obedience to oneself; obedience to a law which is written in a man's own heart. If I obey myself, and myself is not a right self, it is, indeed, 'liberty,' but, being a bad liberty, it becomes 'licentiousness'. If I obey a law outside me, and the law within me is opposed to that outer law which I obey, the act I do may be quite right, and the only right one, but my obedience is not 'liberty,' it is compulsion; it is bondage. Liberty is when the outer law and the inner law are the same, and both are good. Christ made that agreement possible by His Cross. The Holy Ghost makes that agreement a fact by His operation in the heart. Self is never liberty, because self and God are two principles which must unite before a person can be free; and a sinful life never combines the two. Let us see how Christ gives 'liberty,' and what that 'liberty' is. We will look at it from three points of view.

I. Liberty from the Past.—Every one has a past which fetters him. There are things in your life which you can scarcely dare to look back upon, and when you do they shackle you. You feel that so long as those things are there, it is of little or no use to set about and try to live a better life. No future can undo them. Now, just to meet all this—the Cross of Christ having cancelled all the guilt, and paid all the penalty—the moment a man really believes, and accepts his pardon, he is cut off from all his sinful past! It is placed 'behind God's back'. It is 'cast into the depths of the sea'. It is as though it had never been. He may start quite afresh. No shadow, no fear, need come up from the years that are gone. He stands a liberated man! Now he can go—as Christ's freedman—with a spring—to better things to come. The God of his fear has been turned into the God of his love! And that is 'liberty' from the past 'wherewith Christ hath made us free'—the purchase of His cross, the gift of His throne.

II. Liberty from the Present.—Now look to the 'liberty' from the present. If I have received Christ into my heart, I am a pardoned man, I am a happy man, and I know and feel that I owe all my happiness to Him—therefore I love Him; I cannot choose but love Him; and my first desire is to please Him; to follow Him; to be like Him; to be with Him. And all the while there is a power working in me which is a great Liberator. He breaks chains for me. He opens doors for me. He emancipates me from the thraldom of the world—its habits, its opinions, its sneers, its judgments. He gives me an independence and a manliness which is my strength. And I know no other bond but His, which is the dearest to me in all the world, and that is liberty! And then see to what I am admitted. I can go into the presence of God. I can consult Him in every difficulty, and confess to Him every thought, and know it is forgiven then and there. I am free to His mercy-seat. I am free to His court. All the promises are mine. Oh, what a 'liberty' is this! What is all this earth can give, by the side of that blessed feeling? This is the present liberty wherewith Christ has made His people free.

III. Liberty from the Future.—And what of the future? A vista running up to glory! But are there no dark places? Chiefly in the anticipation. When they come they will bring their own escapes and their own balances. But my future—be it what it may—is all covenanted. Christ has told me not to be anxious about it. And I can never doubt Him. He has undertaken for me in everything. He will never leave me. He will be at my side all the way, and my path and my heart are both quite free! I am quite free from all my future. To die will be a very little thing. The grave cannot hold me. He has been through, and opened the door the other side. It is only a very short passage! quite light! all safe!

What a 'liberty' is here! The past—gone; the present—safety, peace, love; the future—sure!

References.—V. 1.—James Vaughan, *Fifty Sermons* (9th Series), p. 22. J. G. Rogers, *Christian World Pulpit*, vol. l. p. 8. E. M. Geldart, *Echoes of Truth*, p. 105. J. G. Rogers, *Christian World Pulpit*, vol. xlix. p. 406. H. Allen, *Penny Pulpit*, No. 1618, p. 339. B. J. Snell, *The Virtue of Gladness*, p. 153. H. Woodcock, *Sermon Outlines* (1st Series), p. 82. W. F. Taylor, *Christian World Pulpit*, vol. lix. p. 334. J. C. M. Bellew, *Sermons*, vol. iii. p. 274. G. A. Sowter, *From Heart to Heart*, p. 194. H. Wace, *Christian World Pulpit*, vol. lix. p. 338. V. 2-6.—*Expositor* (4th Series), vol. viii. p. 360. V. 5.—Spurgeon, *Sermons*, vol. xxi. No. 1228. Dinsdale T. Young, *The Gospel of the Left Hand*, p. 71. V. 6.—J. Iverach, *Christian World Pulpit*, vol. xlvii. p. 342. R. W. Hiley, *A Year's Sermons*, vol. iii. p. 55. A. P. Stanley, *Canterbury Sermons*, p. 205. W. P. Paterson, *Christian World Pulpit*, vol. liv. p. 316. Bishop Bethell, *Sermons*, vol. ii. p. 307. J. Iverach, *Christian World Pulpit*, vol. l. p. 262. Spurgeon, *Sermons*, vol. xxvi. No. 1553; vol. xxii. No. 1280, and vol. xxix. No. 1750. J. M. Gibbon, *Christian World Pulpit*, vol. lxx. p. 265. A. Maclaren, *Expositions of Holy Scripture—Galatians*, p. 136.

HINDRANCES

'Who did hinder you that ye should not obey the truth?'—
Gal. v. 7.

This text is a convenient motto for a sermon devoted to a discussion of some of the things that prevent and hinder men from embracing the Christian life to-day.

I. The Inconsistency of Christians.—There are objections raised on the score of other people; or, to put the matter quite bluntly, men find a genuine hindrance in the way of their acceptance of Christ and the Christian life in the inconsistent and unworthy lives that so many professing Christians live. Remember these two things:—

(1) If you wish to deal quite honestly by the Christian faith, you have no right to judge it by the unworthy lives of some who profess it; you must judge it by the account it gives of itself in the New Testament—you must judge it by Christ Himself.

(2) Considerations about other people ought not in any way to affect your personal relations to Jesus Christ. The relation between Christ and you is a purely personal and individual one. No third person can intervene. Christ makes a certain claim upon *you*. What are you going to do with Christ? Are you going to do *your* duty? This man's sins and that man's failures are quite beside the point. Religion is a personal business. Every man shall bear his own burden, whatsoever it be.

But, in addition to these difficulties caused by others, a great many people find hindrances in things personal to themselves.

II. Personal Unworthiness.—Many people find a terrible hindrance in *a vivid sense of personal unworthiness*. I am constantly meeting with people who, when urged to accept Christ and embrace the Christian life, object that '*they are not good enough*'. If you feel, like John Bunyan, that your heart is just a sink of iniquity, if the sense of your own guilt pinches you sore, then resolve to do what he did. 'My case being desperate,' he writes, 'I thought with myself, I can but die; and if it must be so, it shall once be said that such a one died at the foot of Christ in prayer.' Yes; if your case is so desperate, then make up your mind that if die you must, you will die at the foot of Christ's cross. But no sinner has yet died there.

III. Intellectual Difficulties.—Many find *intellectual difficulties* about points of Christian faith an almost *insuperable barrier*. I meet in the course of my ministry with many such. In olden days Churches laid considerable stress upon dogma and doctrine, and many found in these things a genuine hindrance to faith. But theological difficulties need no longer be a hindrance. For the most noteworthy difference between the Christianity of to-day and the Christianity of fifty years ago is the *change of emphasis*. Fifty years ago men felt that religion was bound up with belief in certain theological doctrines; since then there has been a movement back to Christ, and men to-day recognise that religion consists in the personal adhesion of the sinner to the Saviour.

IV. The Responsibility of Confession.—Others make a hindrance, or rather find a hindrance, in the sense of the *tremendous responsibility attaching to an open confession of Christ*. People say, 'I am afraid of undertaking the Christian life. My life will be scrutinised so closely, and I shrink from the possibility of bringing discredit upon the name of Christ.' Now, up to a point, that is a legitimate and healthy feeling. We do take upon ourselves a great responsibility when we confess the name of Christ. You say it is a serious thing confessing Christ. Yes, it is; but is it not a more serious thing *not* to confess Him?

And remember this—Christ never calls us to a duty without giving us the needed strength. 'My grace,' He says to every one who shrinks from the responsibility, 'My grace is sufficient for thee.' Do not therefore let the thought of the solemn responsibility that will rest upon you hinder you from accepting the Christian life.—J. D. Jones, *Elims of Life*, p. 107.

References.—V. 7.—F. B. Cowl, *Preacher's Magazine*, vol. xvii. p. 238. H. Melvill, *Penny Pulpit*, No. 1561, p. 121. V. 8.—A. Rees, *Christian World Pulpit*, vol. xliv. p. 140. *Expositor* (4th Series), vol. vii. p. 471. V. 10.—*Ibid.* (5th Series), vol. ix. p. 108.

THE OFFENCE OF THE CROSS

GAL. v. 11.

One thing which marks the ministry of Paul is how he lovingly yearned over the Jews. It is when we remember that deep longing that we realise what the cross meant for Paul. For the great stumbling-block of faith to the Jews—the offence that made the Gospel of Christ smell rank to them—was, as our text indicates, the cross. Now I want to make a little plainer to you why the cross was an offence to the Jews, and to put things in such a way that you may see at once that the same causes are operative still.

I. First, then, the cross was offensive to the Jews just because it blighted all their hopes. It shattered every dream they ever dreamed; every ideal that ever glimmered on them. They had prayed for and had dreamed of their Messiah, and He was to come in power as a conqueror. Then in the place of that triumph, there comes Calvary. In place of the Christ victorious, Christ crucified. If I know anything about the ideals men cherish now, and about the hopes that are regnant in ten thousand hearts, they are as antagonistic to the cross as was the Jewish ideal of Messiah. Written across Calvary is sacrifice; written across this age of ours is pleasure.

II. The cross was an offence to the Jew because it swept away much that they took a pride in. If there was any meaning in Calvary at all some of their most cherished things were valueless. The Jews were pre-eminently a religious people, and this is always one peril of religious people. It is to take the things that lead to God and let the heart grow centred upon them. And to-day has that offence of the cross ceased? I say that this is still the offence of Calvary, that it cuts at the root of so much that we are proud of.

III. But again, the cross was an offence to the Jews because it obliterated national distinctions. It levelled at one blow those social barriers that were of such untold worth in Jewish eyes. Now I would not have you imagine for a moment that Christ disregards all personal distinctions. There is always some touch, some word, some discipline, that tells of an individual understanding. But spite of all that, and recognising that, I say that this is the 'scandal' of the cross, that *there* every distinction is obliterated, and men must be saved at last or not at all.—G. H. Morrison, *The Wings of the Morning*, p. 277.

THE STUMBLING-BLOCK OF THE CROSS

GAL. v. 11 (R.V.).

What a favourite term of Paul's was this: 'the cross!' How he revelled in that phrase! Paul's conception of 'the cross' has perhaps never been better formulated than by the great and saintly Bishop Andrewes when he said memorably, 'Christ did nail with Himself on the cross the sins of the whole world'. By 'the cross' Paul ever means nothing less than the atoning death of our Lord Jesus Christ. 'Then hath the stumbling-block of the cross been done away,' he cried. A slanderous report had been raised concerning Paul's preaching. Paul's answer to the slander is that he is still bearing the opprobrium of the man who preaches 'the cross'. The stumbling-block of the cross is *not* done away.

I. What is 'the stumbling-block of the cross'? A stumbling-block is something which causes difficulty, creates irritation, evokes resentment. Dr. Best translates the expression 'the snare of the cross'. Now wherein lies the supreme difficulty, the snare, the scandal, of preaching Christ crucified as the one way of salvation? (1) 'The cross' is an awful manifestation of human sin. Sin is one of the words we must not drop out of our ecclesiastical speech. (2) The cross shows the cost of human redemption. Man was in bondage. What was the price of his release? Here is the answer 'the cross'. (3) The cross is so exclusive a method of salvation. That was a great part of the stumbling-block in Paul's preaching of the cross. Salvation in its largest definition is procured only by the cross of Christ. Still that truth is resented. (4) The cross saves apart from intellectuality. It is through the strait gate of intellectual renunciation that we must come to salvation. (5) The cross saves irrespective of human merit. (6) The cross is so incredible a mode of salvation. We hear much of the science of comparative religions, and it is in many respects a valuable science; but its studies never discover such a method of salvation as 'the cross'. This is the sole prerogative of Christianity. (7) The cross makes tremendous demands. It lays a terrific moral obligation upon us.

II. When is 'the stumbling-block of the cross' done away? (1) It is done away when we maintain other ways of salvation. (2) The stumbling-block of the cross is done away when we make the cross merely a ritualistic sign. (3) When we preach the cross without the atonement we do away with the stumbling-block of the cross. (4) They do away with the stumbling-block of the cross who ignore its claims. (5) The stumbling-block of the cross is gloriously done away when we accept its appeal. Say we with the saintly Leighton: 'The whole world in comparison with the cross of Christ is one grand impertinence.—Dinsdale T. Young, *The Enthusiasm of God*, p. 47.

References.—V. 11.—Spurgeon, *Sermons*, vol. lxiv. No. 2594. W. M. Clow, *The Cross in Christian Experience*, p. 115. V. 13.—Bishop Creighton, *University and Other Sermons*, p. 71. V. 14.—*Expositor* (4th Series), vol. ix. p. 343; *ibid.* (6th Series), vol. x. p. 277.

CHRISTIAN MORALITY

'This I say then, Walk in the Spirit, and ye shall not fulfil the lust of the flesh.'—Gal. v. 16.

I. The chief feature of St. Paul's teaching in reference to morality was its positiveness.

There are two ways to meet and deal with every vice: one is to set to work to destroy it; the other is to overwhelm and stifle it with its opposite virtue. The former is the negative, and the latter the positive method. There can be no doubt about St. Paul's way. To the poor Galatian, fighting with his fleshly lusts, he does not set a course of stern repression, but rather points him to a life of positive endeavour, to do something opposite: 'Walk in the Spirit, and—then—'. The Apostle laid hold on one of the noblest methods of the treatment of humanity —one that he had gained most directly from his Lord. These two methods of treatment, the negative and the positive, present themselves to us in all the other problems of life besides morality, and men choose between them. A man is beset with doubts,

perhaps about the very fundamental truths of Christianity. He may attack all objections in turn, and at last succeed in proving that Christianity is not false. That is negative. Or, he may gather about him the evidences of what his religion has done, and sweep away all his doubts, with the deep and complete conviction that Christianity is true. That is positive, and that is better. If you have a friend who believes an error, for his sake, and for your own, deal with him positively and not negatively. Do not try to disprove his error; rather try to make what you know to be Truth living and convincing; force it home upon his life; let him hear it in your voice, see it in your face, feel it in your whole life. Thus make it claim its true kinship with the truth.

II. Throughout the New Testament there is nothing more beautiful than the perfectly clear way in which the positive culture of human character is adopted and employed. The God of the New Testament, whose express image and glory we behold in the face of Jesus Christ, is not a God of repression, but a God whose Fatherhood is made so real that His holiness may be reproduced in His children; a God whose symbols are everything that is stimulating, everything that encourages and helps; Who leads on His children into that new life where sin becomes impossible, on an ever-ascending pathway of growing Christliness. And this character of the New Testament, of Christianity, is not in contradiction with the best aspirations of the human heart. Man is willing to exercise repression and self-sacrifice for a certain temporary purpose, to do some certain work—the world is full of self-sacrifice, of the suppression of desires, the restraint of natural inclinations; yet all the time there is a great human sense that not suppression but expression is the true life. Seek, then, to give expression to your true, your nobler self, to strive after purity and holiness, and these lower passions will lose their hold. You will not so much have crushed the carnal as embraced the spiritual. You will be 'walking in the Spirit,' and so you will 'not fulfil the lust of the flesh'. Is not this Christ's method? 'Whosoever committeth sin is the servant of sin'; but 'Ye shall know the truth, and the truth shall make you free'. It is the positive attainment, not the negative surrender; the self-indulgence of the highest, and not the self-surrender of the lowest—that is the great end of the Gospel.

III. And yet there arises much in the teachings of our Lord, and in the whole spirit of Christianity, which seems to contradict this conclusion. Has not the religion of Jesus always been called the very religion of self-sacrifice? Is not self-surrender exalted into a virtue and crowned with glory, as it never was in any other faith? That certainly is true. But in Christ's teaching self-sacrifice is always temporary and provisional, merely the clearing the way for the positive culture and manifestation of those great results of spiritual life which he loved: the right hand to be cut off, the right eye to be plucked out; mortification of the flesh, that the man may 'enter into life'. The self-sacrifice of the Christian is true in proportion as it copies the perfect pattern of the self-sacrifice of Christ. The Christian's self-surrender is called a being 'crucified to the world'; when, then, we turn to Christ's crucifixion we find the key to that of the Christian man. See how the positive power shines through that, the most heroic of all sacrifices. It is not simply the giving up of something, it is the laying hold of something too. He Who suffers is conquering fear by the power of a confident hope, a triumphant certainty. It is because He is walking in the Spirit that He is able so victoriously not to fulfil the lust of the flesh. It is because He clung to His Father that He came strong out of Gethsemane. He does no sin, because of the completeness of His infinite goodness. The way to get out of self-love is to love God. 'Walk in the Spirit, and ye shall not fulfil the lust of the flesh.'—Bishop Phillip Brooks.

References.—V. 16.—*Expositor* (5th Series), vol. v. p. 141 : *ibid.* (6th Series), vol. x. p. 362. A. Maclaren, *Expositions of Holy Scripture—Galatians*, p. 153. V. 16, 17.—F. D. Maurice, *Sermons*, vol. i. p. 263. T. Arnold, *Sermons*, vol. iv. p. 54. *Expositor* (4th Series), vol. ix. p. 189.

THE FRUIT OF THE SPIRIT
(*For Whit-Sunday*)

'This I say then, Walk in the Spirit, and ye shall not fulfil the lust of the flesh. . . . But the fruit of the Spirit is love, joy, peace, long-suffering, gentleness, goodness, faith, meekness, temperance.'—Gal. v. 16, 22, 23.

These words may well suggest to us thoughts for Whit-Sunday. We are reminded to-day of the spiritual life, and the Divine Author of it; we are reminded of the coming of the Holy Ghost, and of the grace, virtue, and power which He gave to those who received Him. We are reminded to-day that it is the abiding presence of the Holy Ghost in the Church and in the heart of each believer that makes the Christian life. The Christian life is something far more than morality: it is the planting of the Divine life—man, it is the infusion of another and spiritual nature; and St. Paul tells us here how that spiritual nature is shown and proved. He brings us to this simple test, which I wish briefly to emphasise.

I. That it is known by its fruits. It is never an easy thing to define spirituality or to say who is the spiritual man. You cannot tell how God joins Himself to the human soul and produces in what is naturally selfish, proud, pleasure-loving, greedy, and covetous the graces and feelings which are the very opposite of all these. It is of no use discussing the philosophy of it; it passeth understanding. The Apostle simply fastens us down to this : that it is known by its results. 'The fruit of the Spirit is love, joy, peace, long-suffering, gentleness, goodness,' and the rest. We are not on doubtful ground there. The spiritual man is one in whom the lusts of the flesh are held down by a higher power, who no longer loves with all the burning passion of his nature the things that can be seen, touched, and tasted, the things of the senses

and appetite, the glitter, show, and gains of the material world, but who loves best and desires most what Christ loved—goodness, purity, soul-beauty, and likeness to God. The spiritual man has the mind of Christ.

II. Where these fruits are the Spirit of God is. We sometimes say, with our short-sighted and foolish limitations, that the Spirit of God never works except in those who have believed exactly in our way. We say, 'They must have been convicted and regenerated, and brought into the acceptance of certain articles of belief, before they can have any part in the spiritual helps which God gives'. But we only show our ignorant presumption when we talk in that way. God refuses to be bound down by our little plans and schemes. The heart of the Eternal is larger than all the creeds. And though He only gives His spirit in all its fulness and power to those who cling to Christ in earnest faith, He does not withhold it altogether from others. Where you find in men and women something that is far higher than the sensual and animal; where there is courage and self-forgetfulness, and patience in sorrow, and compassion and tenderness towards others, and pure thoughts and striving after nobler things, *there* you may be sure that God has not left Himself without witness. These are the gifts of His good Spirit; they cannot come from any other. No more can all these graces grow where God is not than grapes can grow on thorn-bushes and figs on thistles. The fruits of the Spirit are these, and only the Spirit can produce them—love, joy, peace, long-suffering, gentleness, and goodness.

III. It is only where these fruits of the Spirit are that there is any real understanding of Divine things. St. Paul is always claiming for the Spiritual man superior discernments, claiming for him the power of judging all things, claiming for him joys which are unknown to others. But this power is not a thing of the intellect : it is a perception of the heart. It is where love, long-suffering, and gentleness are found that the things of God are understood.—J. G. Greenhough, *The Mind of Christ in St. Paul*, p. 212.

THE CONFLICT WITH SIN

'For the flesh lusteth against the Spirit, and the Spirit against the flesh : and these are contrary the one to the other ; so that ye cannot do the things that ye would.'—Gal. v. 17.

Whoever knows anything of the nature of his own heart would expect that the presence and the claim of good would immediately stir up the opposition and the virulence of evil. The fact is, that until there is some good, there can be no conflict at all. You, then, who feel your conflicts—you to whom the inner life is an agitation little guessed by those who see only the assumed calmness of a shallow surface—you, who wake up every morning to fight again and again the old battle of yesterday—you, who are to yourselves not as one nature, but two—not two, but many—and all arrayed against all—lift up your head out of the dust of that blinding fight, lift up your head, and rejoice ! And it will be a great help to you, if you thus lay down at once, with yourself, that

the conflict is not an accident, but a necessity—not exceptional in your case, but an universal rule, that it is the very condition of a Christian's calling, and a part of the Christian's inheritance; it is the badge of discipleship, it is the fellowship of Jesus.

I. In this Warfare there is, at least for a long time, a singular balance. Look, for instance, at the exact intention of the text, 'The flesh lusteth against the Spirit, and the Spirit against the flesh'—*i.e.* the natural or carnal part of a renewed man puts forth strong desires against the spiritual part, and the spiritual part puts forth strong desires against the natural and carnal part—and 'these are contrary'— lie, as the original Greek word is—'lie over against the other, so that ye cannot do the things that ye would'. Which way? Cannot do the good things you would, because of the carnal part? Or, cannot do the evil things you would, because of the spiritual part? Which? Certainly both. Chiefly the latter. You cannot do the bad things you would, because of the resistance or the prohibition of the spiritual taste that is in you. Whether you adopt this view or not —and it would not be well to view it thus always— you will certainly be right to recognise always, very plainly and very absolutely, the two distinct natures or powers which now are in you as a regenerate man. Do not extenuate the sin because of the grace, and do not disparage the grace because of the sin.

II. A Double Danger.—Here lies a double danger, and the path runs narrow between two precipices. A few say very presumptuously, and with awful speciousness, 'Because of the grace that is in me, I am no longer a sinner; I must not pray as a sinner, I must not feel as a sinner'. Very many more, with a most unfilial timidity, and a most unscriptural reason, say, 'Because I have so much sin in me, there can be no grace; I cannot believe that, being what I find myself, I am a child of God'. Admit both, confess to both, act upon both. There is a side—oh, how dark!—all blackness. That is earth's side. Now turn the portrait, and see it under the falling of another light. 'He that is born of God sinneth not; but he that is begotten of God keepeth himself, and that wicked one toucheth him not.' Christ in me— and that Christ in me is my being, I own no other, 'Christ in me the hope of glory'. 'Know ye not, brethren, every one of you, that Christ is in you, except ye be reprobate?' And Christ in you, the kingdom of heaven is in you. Now ye are 'light in the Lord,' now ye are holy, now ye are kings and priests, now ye are complete. How strange the paradox! How wide the contrast. Do you wonder at the awfulness of the conflict that goes on in a regenerate soul? And He stands very near in whom that warfare of yours is even now accomplished, and He says, 'Be thou faithful unto the death, and I will give thee a crown of life!'

REFERENCES.—V. 16-26.—*Expositor* (5th Series), vol. x. p. 106. V. 17.—R. W. Church, *Village Sermons* (3rd Series), p. 184. J. Keble, *Sermons for the Sundays After Trinity*, p. 31. *Expositor* (6th Series), vol. x. p. 369. V. 18.—H. R. Gamble, *The Ten Virgins*, p. 141. Bishop Bethell, *Sermons*, vol. ii. p. 390. *Expositor* (6th Series), vol. vii. p. 278. V. 18-25.— *Ibid.* vol. v. p. 300. V. 19.—*Ibid.* (4th Series), vol. ix. p. 193.

THE SPIRITUAL BATTLE

'The works of the flesh . . . the fruit of the Spirit.'—GAL. v. 19 and 22.

EVERY human heart is a battle-field whereon at some time or other flesh and spirit are locked in mortal strife, and the issues of the conflict are of the greatest importance. We see in the Epistle what are the results—whether flesh or spirit have the mastery. What a contrast there is presented to us in these few lines! The works of the flesh against the fruit of the Spirit! From the one the higher nature of man turns in utter abhorrence, while the other commends itself to God and man.

I. Present-day Sins.—I think we must be arrested by the solemn and awful fact that some of the sins of which the Apostle speaks are with us to-day. We must admit that there is amongst us much idolatry, many factions and divisions, hatred, heresies, and envyings. Now that is a consideration of the gravest importance. Why is it the Church in the course of its two thousand years of existence has not done more, for although we rejoice over the triumphs of the Gospel, as we look round there must be a note of sorrow. Look at the darkness of Africa! Look at the teeming millions of Asia still in the grip of heathenism! Nay, do not look so far. Look at Christendom itself, and one must admit that there is even in the Church of Christ much that makes the brain reel and the heart turn sick.

How is this? To answer this aright we must go back beyond the foundation of the Christian Church, and look at the life of the Founder. Jesus Christ was a Jew—a member of the most abhorred nation of antiquity; He never separated Himself from the nation to which He belonged; He worshipped in the synagogue and the Temple; He never wrote a volume of philosophy or a page of theology. What was the force that He put into the world? He never originated a party; He was not a master of a system; yet He set in motion a force that has stood for two thousand years through a storm of persecution, and through all the great advancements and changes of passing ages, and still to-day is the greatest moral force of the world. What was the secret of it all? His life was his theology; He came bringing a higher conception of manhood and the Godhead; a new reverence for God—the God of Love.

II. Christianity in the World.—If this is truly the secret of the power of Christ, so must it be the power of Christianity in the world to-day. It is not in the customs of the Church; the power of the Church is in the lives of the men and women who are living as Christ did. The Church is the casket, the men and women are the jewels; the Church is the body, the individual lives of the members of the Church are the soul. That is the thing we need to be reminded of. We are over-burdened with the idea of the desirability of great organisations, but it is the life that counts ; and as the life of the Christian is the power of the Church, so the lives of men and women should be the ultimate desire of the Church. Christianity is not the knowledge of Church history, but a true development of the joy and peace of the Christian spirit.

Organised Christianity has been considered better than individual Christianity. I do not say a word against organisations, but there is a danger lest we think that organisation is an end in itself instead of being only a means to an end. If I am shown a wonderful machine, and, asking what does this machine produce, am told that it does not produce anything, but it works, I should say what a wonderful waste of energy.

'They that are of Christ Jesus have crucified the flesh.' Ah, Paul, that is a cruel word ! Yes, it is a cruel process this weeding out of the flesh that the Spirit may enter. I am thankful for that word. It seems to me that it has a great meaning for us. The death on the cross was a long, lingering agony, and I believe that the death of the flesh is a long, lingering agony also. What I plead for is that we should take a definite step towards self-abnegation ; put self on the cross and let it die there. If we do not do so, are we wholly yielded to Christ ? That is the process which is the beginning of fruit-bearing—the fruit of the Spirit.

ENVYING
GAL. V. 21.

BION asked an envious man that was very sad : *What harm had befallen to him, or what good had befallen to another man.*—BACON.

REFERENCE.—V. 21.—*Expositor* (4th Series), vol. x. p. 200.

JOY THE FRUIT OF THE SPIRIT

'But the fruit of the Spirit is love, joy, peace, long-suffering, gentleness, goodness, faith, meekness, temperance.'—GAL. V. 22.

HERE you have a rich cluster of the grapes of Eshcol, truly an earnest of our inheritance, a foretaste of heaven itself. We can but pluck one from the cluster to-day, for I want to speak to you upon this : the fruit of the Spirit is joy.

I. In the first place, we must insist that joy is the fruit of the Holy Spirit. It is quite true that joy is not the first-fruit of the Holy Spirit. The first-fruit of the Holy Spirit is sorrow. But this is not the ultimate end of the Holy Spirit : this is only like the cleansing of the cup before the wine is poured into it. The sorrow may endure for a night, but in the morning, the glad resurrection morning, the joy appeareth. Now many of us can witness to the truth of this. We have found out that His ways are ways of pleasantness, our religion is our recreation, our duty is our delight. As an old writer has said : 'Joy is one of those birds of paradise which, when man fell, was about to fly back to its native heaven, but God caught it in the silken nets of promise, and retained it to sing in the cage of a broken and a contrite heart '.

II. How is this fruit of the Spirit to be cultivated ? Because this fruit of the Spirit is a hot-house plant ; it does not flourish in the biting cold of indifference, nor amidst the howling winds of unbelief. How am I to have this fruit of the Spirit ? (1) It ripens under the hearing of God's Word. It has something substantial to rest upon, it is a fruit which has a root to it, it goes deep down into the revelation of God's truth. (2) But there is another way in which that joy is produced. It becomes even sweeter as you see others receiving the blessing. (3) Again, this joy is increased by prayer.

III. There are some things which hinder this joy. (1) Sometimes the Christian loses his joy because his taste has been vitiated with other joys. (2) Directly you attempt to seek your own way, you lose this joy ; directly you are filled with self-ambition, self-thought, you lose this joy.

IV. Mark where this joy abides. It dwells between peace and love. You can have no joy unless you have true love to God. And there must be peace with your brother man.

V. What is the result of having this joy ? In the eighth chapter of Nehemiah, and in the tenth verse, you read : 'The joy of the Lord is your strength.' (1) It is your strength in time of temptation. (2) It is a strength to you also in your work.—E. A. STUART, *The Communion of the Holy Ghost and other Sermons*, vol. x. p. 41.

REFERENCES.—V. 22.—T. F. Crosse, *Sermons*, p. 67. B. J. Snell, *The Virtue of Gladness*, p. 73. Spurgeon, *Sermons*, vol. xxvii. No. 1582, and vol. xxx. No. 1782. Bishop Winnington-Ingram, *A Mission of the Spirit*, pp. 31, 52, 104, 135, and 171. *Expositor* (4th Series), vol. ix. p. 88 ; *ibid.* vol. x. pp. 120, 125 ; *ibid.* (5th Series), vol. ix. p. 221 ; *ibid.* (6th Series), vol. iv. p. 8 ; *ibid.* vol. v. p. 295.

THE FRUIT OF THE SPIRIT

'But the fruit of the Spirit is love, joy, peace, long-suffering, kindness, goodness, faithfulness, meekness, temperance.'—GAL. v. 22, 23 (R.V.).

FRUIT is the spontaneous outcome of the life of the tree—its finished product. Given a tree, one may confidently forecast the nature of the fruit. In like manner, the Spirit has its natural product : it yields fruit. And its fruit after its kind is in the graces of Christian character here set forth. If a man fail here, whatever else he may possess, he has no right to believe that he has the Spirit of God ; and if anyone have not the Spirit of Christ, he is none of His. On the other hand, if those qualities are being produced in him, he need not mourn the absence of the more showy and attractive gifts, or desire any further assurance of the presence of the Spirit with him.

I. But a little reflection makes clear that the Apostle's words, far from being forbidding, are actually most welcome and inspiring. This is the message they bring to us: The life of a good man is through the Gospel, within the reach of all ; and that not as a more or less uncertain issue, but as a quite natural, one would say, inevitable result. We are not saying that none of these virtues are produced in the life of them who know not, or who deny Christ. The names of scores of whom we have heard or read, of some perchance whom we know, rise up as witnesses to the contrary. The great moral systems of the ancient world had profound influence. Among non-Christian peoples many virtues flourish. *Their moral system lacks a dynamic.*

II. Moreover, the number of the virtues recited, and their seeming contrariety, must not dismay. To possess the nine were to be a moral prodigy indeed! It is just this, however, which St. Paul says is the natural consequence of the life of the Spirit. He produces in us not one grace only, but all together. He says not 'fruits,' as of many, as though the Tree of Life bore nine manner of fruits, appearing in nine different forms; but 'fruit,' as of one, of which these nine qualities are the constituent elements. Singly they may be found elsewhere, but in union one with another they form the fruit of the Spirit, the ripe product of the Gospel of Christ.

III. Just in the manifestation of these characteristic virtues in their union does the world recognise the supremacy of the Christian religion. Do what it will, it cannot produce the like.—F. L. WISEMAN, *God's Garden*, p. 273.

THE CHRISTIAN IDEA OF TEMPERANCE

'The fruit of the Spirit is . . . temperance.'—GAL. v. 22, 23.

'TEMPERANCE' is a much misconceived term. It greatly needs re-definition. It specially requires to be expounded in the light of God. Let us engage ourselves with the distinctively Christian idea of temperance. Christian temperance is the only adequate and excellent temperance.

I. 'Temperance' is a most inclusive quality. The Greek word means literally 'self-control' or 'self-mastery'. In five New Testament instances out of six the word refers to the restraint of natural impulses. The Fathers limited the idea of the word far too much in one direction. Certainly moderns perpetrate similarly unfortunate limitation in another direction. The elders unduly restricted the reference of the word to sensual lusts; we to-day too much refer it to strong drink. But 'temperate *in all things*' is the inspired word of Paul—yes, '*in all things*'. (1) This temperance must be applied to pleasures. Pleasures are choice gifts of God. But what many forget is that these are to be pruned and delimited, else they wreck the soul. (2) Duties should be subjected to the great Christian law of temperance. Self-control is required in regard to all duties. The end of life is not duty, but character. (3) So in the matter of *gain*. Manmonism is a nation's deadly foe, and we need the remonstrance of Ruskin, in his *Crown of Wild Olives*, when he says: 'Only the nation gains true territory who gains itself'. (4) To temper this sublime rule of 'temperance' applies. An old Buddhist adage runs: 'One may conquer myriads of men in battle, but he who conquers him-

self is the greatest victor'. (5) 'Temperance' must pervade speech. (6) Food is to be brought always under this great rule. (7) 'The fruit of the Spirit is . . . temperance' in respect of strong drink. The great question for Christians is as to the point to which self-control in this matter must be carried. Each conscience must determine this for itself, and no man has a right to determine it for you.

II. 'Temperance' is the inspiration of God alone. 'The fruit of the Spirit' it is. God only can give man self-mastery. (1) If 'temperance' be a Divine inspiration, then it should be admired and encouraged because of its high and holy origin. (2) 'Temperance' being God's impartation, we should recognise Him whenever and wherever we see it. (3) As 'temperance' is the work of God, we should deplore its absence as a grief and dishonour to Him. (4) Seeing 'temperance' is of God and of God only, do not attempt to separate it from Him. (5) Every form of self control is 'the fruit' of the Spirit. Then of the Spirit let us seek it.

III. The 'Spirit' works 'temperance' by many agencies. (1) Not seldom He does it by our realisation of the evil of intemperance. (2) By the study of Scripture the Spirit constantly imparts this lofty grace. (3) The Spirit uses the instrumentality of general literature to create 'temperance'. (4) The pulpit is a powerful agency of the Holy Spirit in this matter. (5) How wonderfully the Spirit uses prayer for the creation and development of this 'fruit'! Private and public intercession are the greatest of all moral forces.—DINSDALE T. YOUNG, *The Enthusiasm of God*, p. 217.

REFERENCES.—V. 22, 23.—Lyman Abbott, *Christian World Pulpit*, vol. lii. p. 105. A. Maclaren, *Expositions of Holy Scripture—Galatians*, p. 162.

'Temperance.'—GAL. v. 23.

MELANCHTHON told his students in his Postilla that his father, George Schwartzerd, was so extremely temperate that he ate of only one dish at table. Melanchthon used also to praise the temperance of his grand-uncle, the famous Reuchlin, who drank habitually in his later years not wine or beer, but a kind of grape-water called *lora*. He thought that Reuchlin's good health in advancing years was largely due to his moderation in food and drink.—*C. R.* vol. xxiv. pp. 22 and 517.

REFERENCES.—V. 23.—*Expositor* (4th Series), vol. x. p. 115; *ibid.* (6th Series), vol. xii. p. 191. V. 24.—F. J. A. Hort, *Village Sermons* (2nd Series), p. 108. Spurgeon, *Sermons*, vol. xxi. No. 1239. V. 25.—T. Binney, *Penny Pulpit*, No. 1582, p. 49. J. Keble, *Sermons for the Sundays After Trinity*, p. 41. E. Bayley, *Sermons on the Work and Person of the Holy Spirit*, p. 38. *Expositor* (6th Series), vol. ix. p. 43. VI. 1.—H. Woodcock, *Sermon Outlines* (1st Series), p. 30. *Expositor* (4th Series), vol. ix. p. 95; *ibid.* (6th Series), vol. iv. p. 207; *ibid.* vol. viii. p. 78. VI. 1-2. —J. Berry, *Christian World Pulpit*, vol. xlvi. p. 348. B. J. Snell, *The Virtue of Gladness*, p. 9. VI. 1-5.—*Expositor* (5th Series), vol. x. p. 115.

BEARING ONE ANOTHER'S BURDENS

'Bear ye one another's burdens, and so fulfil the law of Christ.'
—GAL. VI. 2.

WE sometimes read that in shipwrecks, and the like times of great danger, the cry is 'Every man for himself, and God for us all'. It cannot be so in reality. If every man be for himself and himself alone, then God will not be for any of us.

I. We read in the Collect for Michaelmas Day that God has constituted the services of men as well as angels in a wonderful order. He has made us all to lean on one another; He has so ordered the world that in something the weakest may help the strongest. There is a certain amount of suffering, known only to God, which the whole Church has to go through, and when that shall have been borne, then the warfare of the Church will be accomplished, then her iniquity will be pardoned, then we shall be received into the land of the living, and all tears will be wiped from all faces. Therefore the more any single person bears, the less he leaves to be borne by others. I should not have dared to say it unless the Holy Ghost, who cannot lie, had spoken it by the mouth of Paul. But now I say it boldly that in all our sufferings, in a certain sense, we are suffering for others, and therefore so far we are like Christ.

II. But this is not the bearing of one another's burdens which St. Paul here speaks of. He means that every day, yes, and every hour, we must all help and all be helped. None of us must be too selfish to help, none of us must be too proud to be helped. You have all noticed in great buildings how cunningly and wisely the stones of the arches are fitted in together; take out one and they all come to the ground; but let them thus hang on one another, and they bear up a huge mass of buildings, the weight of which one cannot reckon.

III. It is by being helped that we help; it is by being comforted that we comfort. We know how St. Paul comforted the feeble-minded, supported the weak, consoled the afflicted. But did he obtain no help and comfort himself in his turn. Certainly. 'Ye are our glory and joy,' he says. And again, 'For I know that this shall turn to my salvation through your prayers'. And so yet again, 'Ye are our hope and joy, a crown of rejoicing'.

So let us have no more to do with that saying, 'Every man for himself, and God for us all'. Let it rather be, 'Every man for his neighbour, and God for us all'. That would be a true saying—that would be a prophecy as well as a proverb. Everyone of us can give something; none of us is above receiving something.—J. M. NEALE, Sermons in Sackville College Chapel, vol. II. p. 139.

GAL. VI. 2.

'BEAR ye one another's burdens, and so fulfil the law of Christ.' That is the formula of the religious life earthwards. And the reason which creates the necessity for the canon is not far off—'For every man shall bear his own burden'. No one may break the moral law—every one shall bear his own burden; but, the law once broken, or the special need once created, the work of self-sacrificing love begins, and the law of Christ must be fulfilled in mutual sympathy and helpfulness.—Memoirs of Henry Holbeach, vol. II. pp. 58, 59.

REFERENCES.—VI. 2.—R. C. Trench, Sermons New and Old, p. 50. J. H. Jowett, British Congregationalist, 4th October, 1906, p. 229. I. Hartill, Christian World Pulpit, vol. l. p. 186. R. J. Wardell, Preacher's Magazine, vol. xix. p. 269. F. D. Maurice, Sermons, vol. iii. p. 253. H. S. Lunn, Christian World Pulpit, vol. liv. p. 267. C. S. Macfarland, The Spirit Christlike, p. 115. W. J. Knox-Little, Christian World Pulpit, vol. lvii. p. 248. VI. 2-5.— M. G. Glazebrook, Prospice, p. 191. Spurgeon, Sermons, vol. xlix. No. 2831. T. B. McCorkindale, Christian World Pulpit, vol. lxx. p. 298. A. Maclaren, Expositions of Holy Scripture—Galatians, p. 171. VI. 3.—Expositor (4th Series), vol. ix. p. 89.

PERSONAL RESPONSIBILITY

'For every (each, R.V.) man shall bear his own burden.'—GAL. VI. 4, 5.

THE direct reference is to the burden of temptation, but the words of the Apostle allow a larger interpretation, and we may justly regard him as implying here the burden of personal responsibility. The text reminds us of the universality of responsibility. 'Every man,' 'each man'. The text reminds us also of the individuality of responsibility. 'His own burden.' There is something singular and incommunicable in each individual lot. We must help others because we have a burden of our own, is the touching argument of the Apostle; but it is also implied that we must not shirk our personal burden. Let us notice several ways by which the sense of individual responsibility may be injured, and the serious consequences of such injury.

I. See how the sense of responsibility is threatened by the philosophy of our day. Much of our modern science and philosophy strives to show that we are, one way or other, the victims of necessity. The teachings of this philosophy we must steadily resist. Physical laws do not explain our character, our conduct, our experience, our graces and vices, our consciousness of innocence or guilt. There is something in us that there is not in nature. If we exert aright our energy of will nature enters into league with us, and her richest outcome will be the noble men and women who knew how to use without abusing her.

II. Let us note how the sense of responsibility is endangered by ecclesiasticism. If revelation teaches any one doctrine with perfect clearness, it is that of our personal relation to God, our personal accountability to God, and really everything in character and practical life seems to depend upon the full recognition of this fundamental truth. When the Church takes upon itself to see to the salvation of my soul, it has done its best to ruin me for time and for eternity. Whatever ecclesiasticism assumes or promises, we must bravely bear our burden. Anatole France says: 'An education which does not exercise the will is an education which depraves the soul'.

III. Let us mark the sense of personal responsibility *as it is endangered by legislation*. In our day there is a strong tendency to put more and more responsibility upon the State, that is, to make the multitude responsible for the individual. So far from the State taking our burdens, we must regard the State as part of our burden. In a spirit of noble patriotism loyally bear your share of the burden of civic and national life.

IV. Finally, note the sense of personal responsibility *as it is affected by business and domestic life.* In our business life let us realise our obligation. In domestic life realise individual responsibility. Respect your individuality. Do not confound yourself with other people, do not lean upon other people, stand on your feet. We may not put our burden on our brother, but we may lean on God.—W. L. WATKINSON, *The Blind Spot*, p. 167.

INDIVIDUAL RESPONSIBILITY

'Every man shall bear his own burden.'—GAL. VI. 5.

THESE words embody one of the most rudimentary and yet one of the weightiest truths of the Gospel, the individual responsibility of each man to God. Without a distinct perception of this our religion must necessarily be vague and feeble in its practical effects, but let it be firmly grasped and consistently acted upon, and it will sink into the very foundations of our life, and shape its whole character and growth.

I. To this sense of responsibility, then, there are two things that are requisite. (1) There must be a clear and authoritative definition of duty. This is provided for us by revelation. It is primarily a disclosure of the character of God, and consequently of what that character requires. It lays down firmly the great landmarks of morality, and calls upon us to shape our course accordingly. (2) The second condition of responsibility is freedom to act upon the directions which God has thus given to us. This is not provided by revelation, but is an integral part of our nature, which revelation everywhere recognises and appeals to. It is, in fact, our highest and crowning prerogative, for all our powers are entrusted to its keeping, and absolutely lie at its mercy. It places our destiny in our own hands.

II. These, then, being the two conditions essential to our responsibility to God, and conditions that are present in the case of each of us, let us see how the sense of it gradually develops and grows up between them. (1) In childhood and early youth it makes itself but feebly felt, its pressure being wisely relieved and adjusted to our strength. This is accomplished by that abridgment of our freedom which our own ignorance and incapacity necessitate. Because we cannot provide for ourselves, and know little or nothing of the world beyond our own homes, we are

placed under the care and guidance of others. (2) But, while the parental thus, to a large extent and for a considerable period, supersedes the Divine authority, other competitors soon come in to dispute the ground. Now against, or at least above, the influence of all other rivals and claimants for our respect, Christianity sets up continually a counter claim which it presses persistently upon us. It says with an imperative voice: 'Honour thy father and mother'; but it never says, 'Honour society, or fashion, or professional or public opinion'. It sanctions only one transference of our allegiance, and that is from our parents to God. And the time when this transference ought to take place is the next critical time in our lives. The question comes to be whether we shall put ourselves under guidance now of our free and deliberate will. But it is plain you will not consider, or consent to, God's offer unless His authority assumes a commanding position in your thoughts and becomes definite and even irresistible in its appeals. There are two ways in which Scripture endeavours to bring this about. (a) The first of these is by throwing a clear light on the personality of God, as the ultimate ground of right and wrong. (b) Besides this revelation which Scripture gives us of God it asserts with solemn reiteration the great fact of retribution.—C. MOINET, *The Great Alternative and other Sermons*, p. 155.

REFERENCES.—VI. 5.—G. H. Morrison, *The Scottish Review*, vol. ii. p. 215. VI. 6.—*Expositor* (6th Series), vol. iv. p. 24. VI. 7.—J. Learmount, *The Examiner*, 3rd May, 1906, p. 418. F. W. Farrar, *Everyday Christian Life*, p. 248. W. R. Inge, *All Saints' Sermons*, 1905-7, p. 124.

SOWING AND REAPING

'Be not deceived ; God is not mocked : for whatsoever a man soweth, that shall he also reap. For he that soweth to his flesh shall of the flesh reap corruption ; but he that soweth to the Spirit shall of the Spirit reap life everlasting.'—GAL. VI. 7, 8.

WE have here a great and important law of human life. We might indeed call it *the* law of human life. Let us spend a little time in looking at the law, so that, if possible, we may see clearly what we have to do with it, and what it has to do with us.

I. First, there is the *fact* that underlies the law. It is this: human life is a sowing and reaping. It is not a succession of isolated experiences. It is a closely compacted whole. The sowing and reaping are not separated from each other in time, as in the natural harvest. Every day of our life we are sowing something for the future, and reaping something from the past. The sowing and reaping thus go on contemporaneously and continually.

II. Now for the law. 'Whatsoever a man soweth, that shall he also reap.' A most simple and natural law, necessary, one would think, in the nature of things; yet men live on, and sow on, and hope to find it otherwise in their case. We reap what we sow in kind; but the quantity is largely increased. Sow one sin, and you may have a horrible harvest of ten or more. On the other hand, each act of obedience or self-denial or kindness prepares the way for many more.

III. We come now to the *application* of the law; and evidently there might be an endlessly varied application of it. But while there may be endless varieties, there are two great kinds; so that we can, looking at the subject broadly, have a twofold application of the law, as in the text. (1) 'He that soweth to his flesh'—what does that mean? Immediately we think perhaps of those whose hearts are set on pampering their baser lusts and passions. But does 'the flesh' mean only the baser lusts and passions? Certainly not. Selfishness belongs to the flesh just as undoubtedly as lust does. And the same kind of harvest is in store in the end. Not at first. There was a difference in the sowing, and there will be a difference in the reaping. (2) If you expect to reap the harvest of a rich and blessed eternity, you must sow to the Spirit. This does not mean the giving up of all the things of the flesh. But it does mean that all our lower desires are to be regulated, subordinated, and controlled by the higher life of the Spirit.—J. MONRO GIBSON, *A Strong City*, p. 229.

SOWING AND REAPING
GAL. VI. 7, 8.

THERE are certain lessons both of seed-time and harvest which should never be forgotten by the preacher—in fact, they never can be quite forgotten by him, because they enter so largely into Bible teaching, and always form part of his message to man. Everything has been said about them that can be said, and yet it is helpful to stir up the mind by way of remembrance.

I. We always divide and classify human lives by these three terms—spring, summer, and autumn: or, if you prefer it, seed-time, waiting-time, and harvest. Those three times are represented in every congregation. Some of you have done very little reaping yet; your young hands and minds are busily sowing, and you can only guess what the harvest will be. Others of you have done a great deal of labour and thought, and may be of sin, which have not yet brought forth their fruits—the time has not come. You will only understand the outcome of it all when the ripening and mellowing years are upon you. And a few of us have begun to reap. We are gathering what we sowed in earlier years. And it is not until you reach that time of life when the sowing is mainly over and the daily reaping has begun that you fully understand and believe these words of St. Paul. You believe them then because every day brings you a new proof of them.

II. A great many people, especially in youth, but more or less all through life, believe that God can be mocked. No one ever makes that mistake about Nature, which is really only another name for God— only a portion of His ways and thoughts. Every one knows that as you deal with Nature so she will deal with you. The sort of life you live in your youth

inevitably determines the kind and quality of man and woman that you will be further on, unless there is some complete and fundamental change wrought by God just as you pass into the fuller years, and even then the ill sowing which you have done will have its harvest. If you begin by having no faith in God, you end by losing faith in nearly everything. The greater part of this harvest, be it good or bad, is never reaped on earth. There is a hell about which we know nothing, save that it is too terrible for words to describe. And there is a heaven of perfect peace and glad reward, which far exceeds all that our imagination can picture.—J. G. GREENHOUGH, *Jesus in the Cornfield*, p. 167.

REFERENCES. — VI. 7, 8. — J. B. Lightfoot, *Cambridge Sermons*, p. 48. *Expositor* (6th Series), vol. iii. p. 129. VI. 7-9.—W. Robertson Nicoll, *Sunday Evening*, p. 127. VI. 8. —R. F. Horton, *Christian World Pulpit*, vol. xlvii. p. 36. *Expositor* (4th Series), vol. i. pp. 202, 203.

THE CURE FOR WEARINESS
'Let us not be weary in well-doing.'—GAL. VI. 9.

I. The Keynote of Hope.—St. Paul gives us in our text the keynote of hope and perseverance. 'Let us not be weary in well-doing, for in due season we shall reap if we faint not.' He reminds us of the need of energy and courage and hope, and tells us of the certainty of final victory if only we go steadily on, trusting less in self and more in the grace of God. A great power for good is lost by that sort of reserve which leads a man to hide away all that is best in his life and character. There is amongst us, and especially amongst men, far more religious feeling than is allowed to appear on the surface; a deeper love of truth, a more reverent spirit of prayer, but this is too often concealed beneath a careless manner and a flippant habit of speech. Many men, active in business or official life, brilliant in social gifts, have a deep sense of their duty to God and man, and a very real desire to know and to do what is right; and yet this higher side of their character is hidden, whereas if it was more apparent it would be a great help and encouragement to others, and especially to the young who are growing up around them. St. Paul once said that he bore in his body the marks of the Lord Jesus. That may perhaps mean that at the time he wrote he had still the actual scars of scourging and ill-usage in his Master's service; but there is another sense, and a very real one, in which we should all of us bear about the dying of the Lord Jesus, and especially in this season of Lent. This is the secret of that kind of influence which is most useful; this is the power common to all true workers for God; they have imprinted on their hearts, and so shining forth in their daily life, the lessons of Gethsemane and Calvary, the great constraining power of self-sacrifice.

II. The Cure for Weariness.—It is the lot of all mankind to be weary. Even our Lord bore for us this weariness and heaviness; not only physical suffering which made Him rest by the well, and sleep in the fishing-boat, but He knew also the weariness of disappointment, the heaviness of heart which made Him weep over Jerusalem. There is surely comfort in this thought, for by it we know that it is not wrong to be weary sometimes.

> Well I know thy trouble,
>   O my servant true ;
> Thou art very weary,
>   I was weary too.

But if there be sometimes depression and disappointment in the spiritual life, it is the lot still more of those who live without God in the world. The question is, What sort of weariness will you have? The fatigue of work well done, which has its reward in rest, or that weariness which comes from the pursuit of vanity? Surely it is well to be weary if it brings us to rest beneath the cross, if it makes us listen to the voice of love. But there is a kind of weariness which is hard to bear, a weariness in which we can claim the sympathy of our Lord, when our efforts for others seem to fail, when the harder we try the less we seem to succeed. If there be a mother here who has often poured out her heart to God in prayer for a wandering child, if there be a wife who has striven hard to win her husband to God, or a man who has prayed for his friend, you must not give it up, you must not suppose that your prayers are lost. Behind that cloud of silence and uncertainty there is the boundless love of God waiting to bless you for your efforts and to give you the answer for which you long, or it may be something better still. Be not weary in well-doing.

III. Another more Personal Form of Weariness and disappointment is when we find that the evil within us is still strong, that the old temptations have still a power to allure, that we have still the root of an old besetting sin. We must not expect that an evil habit which has perhaps been growing for years can be shaken off at once by one impulsive effort or by the strength of one resolution. Remember the expression used in the New Testament to describe the process by which we gain self-mastery; it is a very strong and significant one; we are to crucify the flesh. Now crucifixion was a slow, lingering, painful death. And the figure seems to tell us that our battle with sin must be a long one, and will not soon be over. But, thank God, the final issue is certain if only we are faithful and true.

GAL. VI. 9.

IT is not the fever of superficial impulse that can remove the deep fixed barriers of centuries of ignorance and crime.—BEACONSFIELD, in *Sybil*.

REFERENCES.—VI. 9.—D. Burns, *Christian World Pulpit*, vol. xliii. p. 83. J. Keble, *Sermons for Easter to Ascension Day*, p. 211. G. G. Bradley, *Christian World Pulpit*, vol. xlvii. p. 3. Archbishop Benson, *Singleheart*, p. 17 ; *Christian World Pulpit*, vol. li. p. 199. T. Arnold, *Sermons*, vol. iii. p. 234. Bishop Gore, *Christian World Pulpit*, vol. lv. p. 265. Archbishop Benson, *Living Theology*, p. 129 ; Spurgeon, *Sermons*, vol. xxiii. No. 1383. A. H. Moncur Sime, *Christian World Pulpit*, vol. lviii. p. 250. VI. 9-10.—S. R. Hole, *ibid.* p. 231.

GAL. VI. 10.

DARWIN added to his *Autobiography* these words : ' I feel no remorse from having committed any great sin, but have often and often regretted that I have not done more direct good to my fellow-creatures.'

REFERENCES.—VI. 10.—J. Budgen, *Parochial Sermons*, vol. ii. p. 204. C. Garrett, *Christian World Pulpit*, vol. lv. p. 331. A. Maclaren, *Expositions of Holy Scripture—Galatians*, p. 180. VI. 11.—*Expositor* (6th Series), vol. xii. p. 294 ; *ibid.* (7th Series), vol. vi. p. 383. VI. 11-17.—*Ibid.* (4th Series), vol. vii. p. 215 ; *ibid.* (5th Series), vol. x. p. 199. VI. 11-18.—*Ibid.* vol. i. p. 437. VI. 12.—*Ibid.* vol. vi. p. 27. VI. 13.—*Ibid.* (6th Series), vol. viii. p. 78.

THE INCOMPARABLE GLORY OF THE CROSS

' But God forbid that I should glory, save in the cross of our Lord Jesus Christ, by whom the world is crucified unto me, and I unto the world.'—GAL. VI. 14.

LET us try to understand what Paul means by the cross, and not put too narrow a limitation upon it. He was not using the word in any vulgar sense. He meant by the cross all that was included in the Incarnation mystery—the manifestation of God in the flesh, the spotless and holy manhood, the life of sympathy and healing, the heavenly wisdom of the teachings, the great condescension, the great love, the great sacrifice, and the great redemption : they were all summed up in the one word ' the cross '.

I. He thought there was nothing within the range of human vision or human imagination worth glorying in, worth boasting of, save that alone ; nothing of which the world had any reason to be proud but that. The world of which Paul spoke has melted away. The glory of all that world is little more than a handful of dust, while the cross is still the greatest power in the world—the ever-increasing power ; the object of its purest devotion ; the source of its richest thoughts and sentiments in art, poetry, music, and worship ; the inspiration of all its finest energies and hopes ; the fountain which supplies all its grandest ideals. Truly, time has vindicated the foolish dreamer ; the foolishness of God has been proved wiser than men.

II. But that is history. That belongs to the past. How does the saying stand in our own times? Is there nothing in this age which gives us cause for unqualified boasting, nothing which should lift up and expand with pride and flatter the human heart, save that one thing in which the Apostle gloried? There are a thousand things in our modern life and surroundings which we cannot help regarding with delight and a measure of admiration and pride. Great are the triumphs of civilisation. Ah, yes! you can fill books with the wonder and glamour of it all, and you might well be elated with pride as you think of it, if there were not always some offset to every part of it—some dark background, some painful accompaniment which suggests humiliation and even tears. What, then, may we glory in? Well, in every exhibition of the cross and its power. All the real radiance of our times comes from the cross. It is the cross which saves our civilisation from corruption. The cross is the gathering-point, the focus, the source, of all that elevates the thought and preserves the hopes of this present time ; and therefore we may say with all the emphasis of the Apostle : 'God forbid that I should glory, save in the cross of our Lord Jesus Christ'.

III. Finally, bring it home to yourselves. If the cross is in your lives, in your thoughts, in your hopes, there is a radiance which nothing can dim ; there is the splendour of an inspiring and lovely promise thrown over all the paths you tread.—J. G. GREEN-HOUGH, *The Cross in Modern Life*, p. 1.

GLORYING IN THE CROSS

'But God forbid that I should glory, save in the Cross of our Lord Jesus Christ.'—GAL. VI. 14.

WE cannot accustom ourselves to meditate too seriously upon the holiness of the All-pure God. Intrinsically holiness is not terrific, but lovely. It is terrific to unholy creatures, because they have a sense to know that the approach of the Holy One is destruction to all that is unholy.

I. See how the case stands. It pleased God in His wisdom to create man, and to endow him with freedom of will. But freedom of will implies a power to disobey. Man did disobey. But disobedience is unholiness. Man became unholy, and begat an unholy race. But unholiness is alienation from God, and alienation from God is misery. Reconciliation without atonement is, in the nature of things Divinely constituted, impossible. The annihilation of our race would, therefore, have been mercy. Annihilation would have been better than everlasting misery. But, blessed be God, He has in His mercy devised the means by which an exception may be made to that which He has constituted as the rule to all creation, by which an unholy race may be brought back into communion with the Holy God without impeachment of His Holiness ; and where the cross of Christ is planted, the misery of those who shall be miserable will be the result merely of their own individual acts.

You see, then, the design of God in the redemption of man. It is to remove the barrier which rendered our approach to the Godhead impossible ; to reconcile what, without the interference of Omnipotence, would be irreconcilable ; to prove that God can continue holy, and yet bring back to communion with Him, the Holy One, a race of beings by nature unholy.

II. Now, there is in the Deity, with respect to man, one will ; that will being that man, though unholy, shall be rendered capable of communion with the Holy One. For the accomplishment of that one Divine Will, each of the Persons in the One Essence has a peculiar office. As in the creation of man you will find a consultation, so to speak, held by the Three Persons in the Godhead—'Let Us make man in our image' ; as, also, after the fall—'Behold, man is become as one of Us' ; so we find that They acted, as it were, by Covenant, in respect to man's redemption. In this Covenant we find the Everlasting

Father set before us as the Person to Whom satisfaction shall be paid, the Person exacting justice, and yet in mercy sending His only begotten Son, preparing a body for Him, appointing Him a Mediatorial Kingdom, giving Him for a Covenant to the people. Hence we find the Lord Jesus Christ represented as the Mediator of a better covenant, and His blood called the blood of the everlasting Covenant (2 Tim. I. 9 ; 1 Pet. I. 20 ; Rev. XIII. 8).

III. This mystery of mercy, then, is all dependent upon the Cross of Christ. Are we not, then, one and all, ready to exclaim with the Apostle, 'God forbid that I should glory, save in the Cross of the Lord Jesus Christ'? For in what else should we glory ? Except for the Cross of Christ, what are we ? What, but unholy creatures, and, as such, miserable, perishing creatures ? Worldly wealth and power, mental endowments, talents, learning : these things, which are merely the means lent us by God by which we are to work out what He hath begun for us, our own salvation, and for the use of which we shall be responsible, are not subjects in which to glory ; they soon perish with our perishing selves. There are certain privileges in which we may rejoice—the privileges of Grace, of our election ; and, as it was lawful for the Israelites to glory in being of the Circumcision, it is lawful for us, in a higher degree, to glory in having been baptized into the Church, and made the children of God. We may, indeed, rejoice in these privileges, but we may not forget on what those privileges rest—we may not overlook the Cross of Christ ; that which is our shame, because it proclaims the unholiness of our race ; but which is, nevertheless, our glory, since it brings us back to God.—DEAN HOOK.

THE CROSS OF JESUS

'God forbid that I should glory, save in the cross of our Lord Jesus Christ.'—GAL. VI. 14.

THE first and the second crosses are easily understood, easily explained. They were the consequences of crime, of offences against the law of God and of man. But the third cross, the cross of Jesus, there comes the difficulty ! How shall we understand that ? What is its chief mark and character ? You can understand it at all, you can give it meaning, only by thinking of it as a sacrificial cross, as atoning, redemptive suffering for sin. Shame and pain and sin meet there, as in the other two crosses, but while His was the pain, His was not the sin. It is not like the other crosses ; it is separate from them entirely.

I. Mistakes about the Cross.—As you know, all men nowadays, even many that would call themselves Christians, do not regard the cross in the way that you and I do. Let us just for a minute or two see where mistakes can be made on this matter.

(a) *A judicial murder.*—Think, for instance, what it would mean if the cross of Jesus was only a judicial murder. What awful confusion it brings into the world ! The like we know would be done again in similar circumstances. It is quite possible that such a thing should take place again, but that would only make the confusion thrice confounded, and we should only have to mourn in the case of the death of a man by judicial murder for the wrong that was perpetrated on a sinless or unoffending man. It would do us no good, nobody any good.

(*b*) *The death of a good man.*—Or if the cross of Jesus, the death of Jesus on the cross, be only the death of a good man, what is that to you and me? It serves no good purpose. No one in the world can attach a good purpose to such a thing. It will not help you in sorrow, it will not help me or anyone in sin; it only deepens the sorrows of humanity profoundly, and makes the blackness of human history a darker thing than ever.

(*c*) *The death of the greatest martyr.*—Or if the death of Jesus, the cross of Jesus, be only that of the greatest martyr that has ever lived, again, I ask, what good is there in that? He may witness to righteousness, He may witness to purity, but where is the good of that? What good is it to you and to me? The world has been very, very slow to follow mere witnesses. Men may weep over the awful wrong done to the great martyr, but why should we go on saddening the world year by year, telling the story of His awful death, and making the world and the hearts of men and women sadder than they need be? Rather, far better, take the cross down from every church, banish it from every ornament, take it away, and beg men to forget the awful thing, the horrid mischance of the death of the greatest martyr that ever lived.

These things will not account for the cross of Jesus as it is now judged by those who love Him, nor will it put any meaning into it that is worth talking about to you or anyone. It will not account for anything that now gathers around the cross. We have to account for men glorying in the cross of their Lord Jesus Christ. We have to find an explanation for men and women and little children dying gladly for the Crucified.

II. The Cross explained:—

(*a*) *It represents God's sorrow for sin.*

(*b*) *It shows us God's love.*—The cross of Jesus shows us God's love, bringing pardon and righteousness to the sinner.

(*c*) *It represents God's sacrifice.*—The cross of Jesus shows us God's love, sacrificing itself in order to do this for you and for me. There is how the possibility becomes actual. It is God's self, it is God's very love, sacrificing itself in order to do this. It is a sacrifice of God or it is nothing. The death of a man, a mere man, can be nothing for you and for me; but if there be the life of God bound up in it, if it be God in a way in which no man can adequately explain, if it be God actually sacrificing Himself, taking the sinners' place, sharing the sinners' sin, bearing the sinners' penalty, then you can see how it is possible for pardon to be given, for righteousness to be ours, and for everlasting glory to be ours also. God has done this, and this is what the cross means.

REFERENCES.—VI. 14.—Spurgeon, *Sermons*, vol. xxxi. No 1859. H. Bonar, *Short Sermons for Family Reading*, pp. 138, and 148. H. P. Wright, *Preacher's Magazine*, vol. xvii. p. 460. W. B. Selbie, *The Servant of God*, p. 179. R. J Drummond, *Faith's Certainties*, p. 125. VI. 15.—J. Iverach *Christian World Pulpit*, vol. xlvii. p. 342. A. P. Stanley, *Canterbury Sermons*, p. 190. F. D. Maurice, *Sermons*, vol. iv. p. 49. Bishop Bethell, *Sermons*, vol. ii. p. 307. J. Iverach. *Christian World Pulpit*, vol. l. p. 262. *Expositor* (4th Series), vol. x. p. 112; *ibid.* (7th Series), vol. v. p. 204. VI. 16.—*Ibid.* (5th Series), vol. vi. p. 385.

APOSTOLIC ANGER

'From henceforth let no man trouble me; for I bear in my body the marks of the Lord Jesus.'—GAL. VI. 17.

THE Epistle to the Galatians is the one letter of St. Paul which is full of expressions of almost unmixed indignation. St. Paul's letters are generally full of gentleness and tenderness, but in this letter to the Galatians his tenderness seems for once to be laid aside. It is a striking and a solemn picture of Apostolic anger.

I. If you will Compare this Letter ever so Hastily with St. Paul's other Letters, you will see how displeased he must have been. To begin with, it opens without a trace of that kindly and affectionate introduction with which all St. Paul's other letters commence. Even when he has much to find fault with, it is St. Paul's manner to begin his letters with the pleasantest and most cheering topic he can think of. In most cases there would be something to commend in his converts; and therefore before he proceeds to correct them he begins by praising them where he could do so truthfully. You see this in the cases of the Epistles to the Romans and the Corinthians, even though in the latter case there was so much to find fault with. It is not so here. After the very briefest salutation, he plunges at once in verse 6 of Chapter I. into the severest rebuke. 'I marvel that ye are so soon removed from Him that called you.' And then he goes on to pronounce that solemn and awful curse on any who had taught a different Gospel from his own. Read the letter straight through without stopping for the chapter divisions, and you will find that it bears you on like an impetuous torrent. Usually St. Paul writes long sentences. Here they are short and incisive—short, terse, and impetuous, bearing the stamp of the eager earnestness with which they were written. Only when, as we may say, the first vehemence of the composition is beginning to be spent, about the middle of the third chapter, does a word of returning kindness show itself. 'My little children,' at last he calls them, and tells them that he would be glad 'to change his voice' towards them; *i.e.* not to speak so harshly. But for all his wishes that he might change his voice, still he does not, so far as this letter is concerned. It ends as sternly as it began. No kind messages, no tender greetings, such as are common in the other letters. All is abrupt and severe.

II. What does this Mean?—The meaning of the word is easy to explain, and the fact that St. Paul *could* say this of himself was just the thing which enabled him to be thus angry and sin not, in the way which the whole letter has shown. St. Paul *did* bear about him abundant marks which showed that he belonged indeed to Christ. In other places St. Paul is fond of calling himself the servant of Jesus Christ, or even the *slave* of Jesus Christ. Now, in those days it was the custom frequently to mark or brand slaves with some mark or letter to show to whom they belonged. St. Paul then here alludes to the scars of the wounds he had received in the service of his master, the scars of the stonings and the scourgings which he describes in 2 Cor. xi. 23, 25. These scars he says are as the marks or brands which prove him to be Christ's property. A free man acts on his own account, and on his own responsibility. A slave does what his Master orders him, and nothing else. St. Paul means to say that in all that he has done and taught, he has *not* been acting on his own responsibility. He has *not* taught out of his own mind. He has *not* considered himself free to teach just whatever he pleased. Quite the contrary. He has acted throughout as Christ's slave. He has given up his freewill to Christ. He has done and taught nothing but what Christ has bidden him. The responsibility is not with him, but with Christ. Thus, then, what St. Paul means to say is this : Whatever I have said and done, has been said and done by me as Christ's slave. Whoever resists me resists Him whose property I am. These scars and wounds with which I am branded are the marks which show that I am His. Therefore let all men beware how they resist me.

III. To Apply all this to Ourselves :—

(*a*) *St. Paul was Christ's slave.* You may sum up the whole of the Christian religion in the one word, self-subdual.

(*b*) *The more His servants come up to the true standard of perfect self-surrender* to their Master, the more they will bear the marks of Him Whose property and servants they are. And what are the brands or marks which are stamped and burned into those who are not their own, but Christ's? Surely these marks will consist in the similarity of their lot to what was Christ's lot, or rather in the similarity of *some portion* of their lot to what was Christ's.

References.—VI. 17.—H. R. Haywood, *Sermons and Addresses*, p. 227. H. D. Rawnsley, *Church Family Newspaper*, vol. xiv. p. 68. F. W. Farrar, *Everyday Christian Life*, p. 282. J. M. Neale, *Sermons Preached in a Religious House*, vol. ii. p. 467. *Expositor* (4th Series), vol. vii. pp. 201, 278 ; *ibid.* vol. ix. p. 264 ; *ibid.* (6th Series), vol. iii. p. 139. A. Maclaren, *Expositions of Holy Scripture—Galatians*, p. 189.

THE EPISTLE TO THE EPHESIANS

EPHESIANS

REFERENCES.—I. i.—A. Maclaren, *Expositions of Holy Scripture—Ephesians*, p. 1. I. 2.—E. J. Kennedy, *Old Theology Re-Stated*, p. 11. *Expositor* (5th Series), vol. vii. p. 65. I. 3.—H. S. B., *Expository Sermons on the New Testament*, p. 213. A. Maclaren, *Expositions of Holy Scripture—Ephesians*, p. 8. I. 3, 4.—Spurgeon, *Sermons*, vol. xxix. No. 1738 ; vol. xxxviii. No. 2266. I. 3-6.—E. J. Kennedy, *Old Theology Re-Stated*, p. 2. I. 3, 20.—*Expositor* (4th Series), vol. i. p. 138. I. 4.—*Ibid.* (5th Series), vol. v. p. 137. I. 4, 5.—*Ibid.* (6th Series), vol. x. p. 178. I. 5.—Spurgeon, *Sermons*, vol. vii. No. 360. *Expositor* (5th Series), vol. viii. p. 144. I. 5, 7.—A. Maclaren, *Expositions of Holy Scripture—Ephesians*, p. 18. I. 6.—*Christian World Pulpit*, vol. lvi. p. 79. Spurgeon, *Sermons*, vol. viii. No. 471 ; vol. xvi. No. 958 ; vol. xxix. No. 1731 ; vol. xlviii. No. 2763.

'In Whom we have . . . the forgiveness of sin.'—EPH. I. 7.

FORGIVENESS of sins lies at the very heart of the Christian religion. That title of our Lord which appeals most to the heart of mankind is the title which is His as Saviour. It is proclaimed in that fact which of all facts in history has most impressed itself upon the imagination of mankind, the Sacrifice of Christ. In the Apostles' Creed we say, 'I believe in the forgiveness of sins'. It is a petition in that prayer which is the model of all prayer—the Lord's Prayer, we pray, 'Forgive us our trespasses'. And it is the experience of a multitude of souls fallen into sin, but raised from the dust of sin to new life, endowed with new spirit, inspired with new hopes, and all because they believe in the forgiveness of sins.

I. What is Forgiveness ?—What does it mean, this forgiveness of sins ? It is easy to see that forgiveness is something more than the remission of penalties. A great French writer, Victor Hugo, tells a story of a convict who had been doing penal servitude for nineteen years, and who was released on ticket of leave, and he found on every hand that men's doors were closed to him ; how he comes to the door of a French bishop, and there he begs for food and shelter. And the food and the shelter are granted him ; but he sees the bishop's silver plate and when he cannot sleep at night the temptation comes to him, and he yields to it, to take the silver, and he goes. A few hours afterwards he is brought back by the police, and they are admitted into the presence of the bishop. 'Ah,' he says, 'I am glad to see you. I gave you the candlesticks too. They are worth ten pounds. Why did you not take them with the rest ?' And he turns to the police, explains that a mistake has been made, that the captive must be let go free. The police go, and then the bishop turns to the man and says to him, 'My brother, never forget that you have promised to employ this money in learning to be an honest man. You no longer belong to evil, but to good. I withdraw your heart from the spirit of perdition, and I give you to God.' Now to treat a guilty man as though he were not guilty, is that forgiveness ? Certainly in some cases to do so would be an intolerable wrong. Here is a man who makes a livelihood out of vice. To treat that man as innocent would be sinful. But here is this man treated by his friend just as though he was innocent, and to the onlookers such action seems to be what someone has called an inspiration of wisdom, the surpassing wisdom of love which is like the love of God. Where does the principle come in ? It lies in the possibility of restoring the man to righteousness. But it is only so long as this restoration is a possibility that such forgiveness can be said to be really forgiveness, and find justification.

II. The Justification of Forgiveness.—But there must be something in the man which justifies the treatment. The consciousness of guilt, the turning away from sin, the self-identification once more with righteousness—there must be these things in the man. And then forgiveness is the embrace of Divine love, the receiving back again into favour, the return of the penitent. Let me ask how is this possible ? Men are so far below the ideal of righteousness by which God purposes they should live ; again and again they fall ; and the best of men, the saints, are just men and women who are most tormented with the consciousness of sin. It is St. Paul who sets himself down as the chief of sinners. The cry of Job is the pathetic cry of mankind, How should man be just with God ? and the answer to that cry came from God. It is proclaimed in the life and death and resurrection of Him Who is the Lamb of God that taketh away the sin of the world. The mind of man can see but a little way into these secrets, but he sees that there is a close bond of union between Christ and the men that He came to save ; mankind is made one with Him by His Incarnation. He came, and what by His Incarnation was made possible to mankind is made actual by baptism. Then we are made members of the Body of Christ, then we are made one in Him and He in us. It is this oneness with Christ, this union of humanity with Him, which inspires St. Paul's words, 'There is neither Jew nor Greek, there is neither bond nor free, there is neither male nor female : for ye are all one in Christ Jesus'.

III. The Essentials of Forgiveness.—The first thing in penitence is the consciousness of guilt, and the guilt of sin is manifested in its penalties, and its

651

penalties are suffering and sorrow and death. Man never knew the greatness of the guilt which attached to sin until he saw our Lord accept it and bear its burdens. That suffering of the body, that darkness, that cry of desolation, 'My God, My God, why hast thou forsaken Me?'—these things taught men as no words uttered by the most eloquent lips could ever have taught these things, taught men as no experience of their own dull natures could ever have taught, God's detestation of sin. As men learned God's estimate of it, so the realisation of His indignation against sin was forced upon their hearts. Then the second essential to true penitence is contrition. There must be genuine sorrow for sin, and that contrition our Lord offered for us. He is the Beloved in Whom we have our redemption through His blood, the forgiveness of our trespasses. He is the propitiation for our sins. Our oneness with Christ, the infinite potency of sacrifice, the fulfilment by our Lord on man's behalf of the necessary conditions of forgiveness—from these things a little light is thrown on that deep enigma, how sinful man can be made just before God.

REFERENCES.—I. 7.—D. L. Moody, *The Fulness of the Gospel*, p. 11. Spurgeon, *Sermons*, vol. vi. No. 295; vol. xxvi. No. 1555; vol. xxxvii. No. 2207; vol. xlix. No. 2363. G. Campbell Morgan, *The Bible and the Cross*, p. 57. James Orr, *Mundesley Conference Report*, 1910, p. 342. A. Maclaren, *Expositions of Holy Scripture—Ephesians*, p. 26.

THE ENERGY OF GRACE

'In whom we have redemption through His blood, the forgiveness of sins, according to the riches of His grace, wherein He hath abounded towards us in all wisdom and prudence.'—EPH. I. 7, 8.

GRACE is too commonly regarded as a pleasing sentiment, a welcome feeling of cosy favour entertained toward us by our God. The interpretation is ineffective, and inevitably cripples the life in which it prevails. Grace is more than a smile of good nature. It is not the shimmering of an illumined lake; it is the sun-lit majesty of an advancing sea. It is a transcendant and ineffable force, the outgoing energies of the redeeming personality of God washing against the polluted shores of human need.

I. In the text the energies of grace are more particularly discovered in their relationship to sin. 'Forgiveness of sins according to the riches of His grace.' The word 'grace' is not a prevalent word in modern speech, and its rare occurrence may be explained by the partial disappearance of the word 'sin' from our vocabulary. If we exile the one we shall not long retain the other. What philosophy and personal inclination are disposed to extenuate, the Christian religion seeks to deepen and revive.

II. What is the ministry of the heavenly energy? The inspiring evangel of the text gathers itself round about three emphases. Let us feast our eyes on the wealthy programme. (1) Grace flows round about the life in powers of liberation. It sets itself to deal both with the guilt and the power of sin, and it removes the one, and subdues the other. (2) The grace that liberates also illuminates. The grace that

brings 'redemption' also confers 'wisdom'. (3) Grace brings 'prudence,' power of fruitful application; power to apply the eternal to the transient; power to bring the vision to the task, the revelation to the duty, the truth to the trifle.

III. How do we come into the sweep of the marvellous effluence of the grace of God? 'In whom we have.' That is the standing ground. To be in Him, in the Christ, is to be in the abiding-place of this superlative energy.—J. H. JOWETT, *Apostolic Optimism*, p. 111.

REFERENCES.—I. 7-10.—E. J. Kennedy, *Old Theology Restated*, p. 34. I. 9, 10.—*Expositor* (4th Series), vol. i. p. 140; *ibid.* vol. vi. p. 421; *ibid.* (5th Series), vol. iv. p. 136. I. 9, 20.—*Ibid.* (7th Series), vol. v. p. 148. I. 10.—*Ibid.* vol. ii. p. 181; *ibid.* (6th Series), vol. xi. p. 347. I. 11-14.—A. Maclaren, *Expositions of Holy Scripture—Ephesians*, p. 35. I. 12, 13.—Spurgeon, *Sermons*, vol. xxxiii. No. 1978. I. 13.—*Ibid.* vol. x. No. 592. W. H. Hutchings, *Sermon Sketches*, p. 268. *Expositor* (5th Series), vol. vi. p. 10. I. 14.—*Ibid.* (6th Series), vol. iv. p. 274. A. Maclaren, *Expositions of Holy Scripture—Ephesians*, p. 43. I. 13, 14.—Spurgeon, *Sermons*, vol. vii. No. 358; vol. xxii. No. 1284. H. R. Mackintosh, *Life on God's Plan*, p. 87. I. 15.—*Expositor* (4th Series), vol. v. p. 363; *ibid.* (5th Series), vol. viii. p. 407. I. 15-23.—E. J. Kennedy, *Old Theology Re-stated*, p. 55. I. 16.—*Expositor* (5th Series), vol. viii. p. 165.

PROGRESSIVE REVELATION

'That the God of our Lord Jesus Christ, the Father of glory, may give unto you a spirit of wisdom and revelation in the knowledge of Him; having the eyes of your heart enlightened, that ye may know what is the hope of His calling, what the riches of the glory of His inheritance in the saints, and what the exceeding greatness of His power to reward who believe.'—EPH. I. 17-19.

THE Apostle prays that the Ephesians may have supernatural light shed upon the gold of their supernatural wealth.

I. It is our great privilege to grow in clearness of understanding, beholding with more open vision the beauty and preciousness of the truth as it is in Jesus. The first light that falls upon our spiritual understanding is marvellous light; but whilst we continue obedient unto the heavenly vision, it will shine ever more brightly. The vision of a faithful soul grows in comprehensiveness and penetration, realising with infinite delight the great and beautiful doctrines of the spiritual universe. The biographer of the late Dr. Dale, of Birmingham, says of him: 'He lived under the benignant sway of a succession of great truths, following one another like the constellations of the heavens'. In successive periods of his life familiar truths in succession became extraordinary, captivating him, filling him with wonder, thrilling him with delight. Is not this the ideal life? First one and then another article of the creed glowing into light, dawning on the soul, seizing it, occupying it, delighting it, leaving it with special enrichment and perfection! A true course is one of progressive illumination. No Christian life is altogether right and satisfactory except more light, and more, is shining upon it out of God's Word —except uninteresting bits of the raiment of the truth are continually being transfigured; except passages which resemble darkened glass are becoming telescopic; unless commonplace chapters of historian, Prophet, and Apostle suffer a strange change into streets of gold whose stones are like unto a stone most precious, as it were a jasper stone, clear as crystal; and unless starless spaces in the firmament of revelation are being sown with galaxies, and irradiated with the glory of the Lord.

II. Note that the sources of illumination are within. 'Having the eyes of your heart enlightened.' It is insight rather than reflected light; it springs up in the depths of the soul. This is not the instruction gained by intellectual study; it is rather experimental, coming through the inner powers of affection, thought, and will.—W. L. WATKINSON, *The Ashes of Roses*, p. 79.

REFERENCES.—I. 17-23.—Bishop Stubbs, *Christian World Pulpit*, vol. xlvi. p. 358. *Expositor* (5th Series), vol. v. p. 251, I. 18.—J. G. Greenhough, *The Mind of Christ in St. Paul*, p. 148. A. Maclaren, *Expositions of Holy Scripture—Ephesians*, p. 52; *ibid.* p. 62.

IN THE HEAVENLY PLACES
EPH. I. 18-20.

THE phrase 'in the heavenly places' is peculiar to the Epistle to the Ephesians, where it occurs no less than five times. It is one of many marks of the unique character of this Epistle, in which St. Paul again and again employs it; and yet never once does the expression seem to occur to him in that other letter which Tychicus carried—the letter to Colossæ—which (as we have seen) is so closely bound, by ties of subject-matter, time, and place, to this Epistle.

The word translated 'heavenly' occurs about twenty times in the New Testament, including other Epistles of St. Paul, but the expression 'in the heavenly (places)' is found in no other known writing. No substantive is attached to the adjective, and we might render it 'among the heavenly things (or blessings),' if that gave a better meaning. But it does not do so; the familiar phrase 'in the heavenly (places)' is best, and brings us into relation with that unseen world where the risen Master is, where we are blessed 'in Him,' and in which lie those spiritual powers which on the one hand oppose us, and on the other hand rejoice to learn the mysteries of man's redemption. We shall find that it is impossible too severely to *locate* the phrase; 'it is a region of ideas, rather than a locality,' says Dean Armitage Robinson; although the thought of *place* cannot, as we shall see, be wholly eliminated from it.

I. There can be no doubt that chapter I. 20 comes first in order of thought. It brings us face to face with the common theme of both Epistles—the supremacy of Christ over all rivals. In the spiritual realm, here described as 'the heavenlies,' lie all the forces that rule the universe. There is the throne of God; there Christ sits 'at the right hand of God, in the glory of the Father'; thither He has been raised, above every conceivable rank and order of celestial beings, the sharer of the throne of God.

II. The next context (II. 6) takes us a step farther. This verse states a fresh truth, and reveals the almost startling fact that, our Lord being thus 'raised' and 'seated' 'in the heavenly places,' *we* too are raised and seated there 'with Him'. In other words, the present abode of Christ (I. 20) is the present abode of the Church (II. 6). All who 'believe that Jesus Christ hath suffered death upon the cross for them, and shed His blood for their redemption, earnestly remembering the benefits they have thereby, and giving Him hearty thanks therefore,' are in actual present possession of these blessings, because they are '*in Christ*'. In other words, this *life in the heavenlies* is a present reality, an anticipation, as well as a pledge, of future glory. The Christian can even here on earth 'lay hold on the life which is life indeed'.

III. In chapter I. 3 a still further stage is reached. Every spiritual blessing which we receive depends upon the first two stages of the argument. Our Lord is 'in the heavenly places'; we are 'in Him' in a real and present sense, and so are ourselves in the same 'heavenly places'. What follows? Being thus united to Him, all His fulness flows to us, we are in contact with the sole fount of every blessing, so that we have thus reached the very summit of St. Paul's great argument. We are 'blessed with every spiritual blessing in the heavenly places'; but mark how all this is so! —'IN HIM.'

Our standing 'in the heavenly places' depends upon our union with 'the Lord,' and every conceivable blessing that we can enjoy depends upon this contact there with Him.

IV. In chapter III. 10 St. Paul is speaking of the great 'mystery' or secret, once hidden but now revealed, of 'preaching unto the Gentiles the unsearchable riches of Christ.' All men are destined in this Gospel age to learn God's purpose in history, which is, in St. Paul's language, 'the dispensation of the mystery'. But not only are all *men* to understand this progress of the Divine purpose; there are celestial intelligences who love to learn more of the gracious outcomes of God's love. 'Which things,' says St. Peter, 'angels desire to look into' (1 Pet. I. 12).

V. The last context in which we find the words (VI. 12) is a surprising and a startling one. The same words which are used to describe the abode of Christ, our own position of blessing in Him, and the home of the holy angels, are here used to describe the scene of our conflict with 'the spiritual hosts of wickedness'. 'Our wrestling' with them is described as taking place 'in the heavenly places,' just as in this same Epistle Satan is described as 'the prince of the power of the air'. The common use of this word 'air' in Scripture is of the atmosphere which surrounds the earth; and we must remember that the word 'heaven' has a wide range of meaning, for there is 'the heaven of heavens,' and St. Paul speaks of being caught up into 'the third heaven'. We may, therefore, think of 'a heavenly place' which corresponds to the region of 'the air,' no less than of one which is the abode of the holy angels and of God Himself. But it is foolish to attempt to localise too closely; the term is designedly vague, so as to include the realm and abode of *all spiritual forces and powers.* There reigns the Father in His supreme majesty, there the Son of God reigns in His mediatorial kingdom, there the Holy Spirit pours 'blessed unction from above,' and there we are the object, not only of watchful interest to those ministers that do God's pleasure, but also of never-ceasing attack from the ministers of Satan.

Thus, if our life 'in the heavenly places' involves great privileges, it also involves serious conflict. *We are 'in the heavenly places,' but so too are our foes;* or, at least, they can reach us there and disturb our peace. But, thank God, we can face the fact without fear.—Bishop Drury, *The Prison Ministry of St. Paul,* p. 157.

THE STANDARD MIRACLE

'That we may know . . . the exceeding greatness of His power to us-ward who believe, according to that working of the strength of His might which He wrought in Christ, when He raised Him from the dead.'—Eph. i. 18, 19, 20.

The resurrection of Jesus Christ from the dead is the New Testament standard of power. It is the sample and pledge of what God can do for man.

I. The uniqueness of Christ's resurrection. The resurrection of Jesus Christ from the dead reveals the might of God working at the fulness of its strength. When we want to know what God is able to do, we go back to the Resurrection of His Son. This crowning miracle is inclusive of all others. It demonstrates conquest over every dominion that affects human life. Of the unique significance of the resurrection the Scriptures leave no room for doubt. It is God's crowning testimony to His Son, and the essential witness of the Christian Church. Spiritual identification is the end for which Christ died and rose again. Salvation becomes a personal possession to all who, by personal faith, accept Jesus as their Representative and Lord.

II. Spiritual Resurrection. Regeneration is the spiritual counterpart of the resurrection. It is a birth out of death. Conversion is the standing miracle of the power of God. Like the resurrection, the miracle of conversion includes in one act the salvation of the whole man. Regeneration secures all elements of reform. The spiritual resurrection inaugurates a new life. The man who lives in the power of Christ's resurrection is raised to a plane of life beyond the imitations of the natural man. The life which began in a miracle is miraculously sustained.

III. The power of the Spirit. (1) This resurrection power is the power of the spirit, which is the efficient course in all Christian service. 'Ye shall receive power, when the Holy Ghost is come upon you.' The spirit of Pentecost is the spirit of power. (2) Christ's resurrection is the pattern and pledge of our own final resurrection. The ultimate demonstration of this power 'will fashion anew the body of our humiliation, that it may be conformed to the body of His glory, according to the working whereby He is

able to subject all things unto Himself'.—S. Chadwick, *Humanity and God,* p. 137.

References.—I. 18, 20.—Spurgeon, *Sermons,* vol. xxv. No. 1466. I. 19.—*Expositor* (7th Series), vol. v. p. 157. I. 19, 20.—Bishop Alexander, *The Great Question,* p. 129. A. Maclaren, *Expositions of Holy Scripture—Ephesians,* p. 72. I. 19-23.—Spurgeon, *Sermons,* vol. ix. No. 534. F. D. Maurice, *ibid.* vol. ii. p. 85. I. 20.—*Expositor* (5th Series), vol. vii. p. 297; *ibid.* (6th Series), vol. vi. p. 248. I. 20, 21.—*Ibid.* vol. vi. p. 249. I. 23.—*Ibid.* (4th Series), vol. v. p. 31. I. 22, 23.—G. Packer, *Christian World Pulpit,* vol. xlix. p. 392. *Expositor* (5th Series), vol. iv. p. 136.

'The Christ which is His body.'—Eph. i. 22, 23.

Anthony Froude ' is as delighted with Arnold as I am; on his remarking to Dr. Pusey on the beauty of Arnold's comparing the Church and State to the Soul and Body, Pusey quietly but most solemnly said, "I consider the Church belongs to a much higher Body".'—Caroline Fox's *Journals.*

Reference.—I. 23.—*Expositor* (5th Series), vol. vii. p. 241.

EPH. II.

The Apostle Paul is not always just the same. He is consistent, but never monotonous. He is a sevenfold man; his Epistles are his truest photograph. Have you ever read the Epistles in the light of that suggestion?—not only to find out what the Epistles are, but what their author was. He never wearies us, because he has a great gift of escaping monotony. He is rugged, incoherent, sometimes almost verbally self-contradictory; he is full of parentheses, he makes great use of bracketings and asides and literary diversions, yet all the while there is a wholeness which eyes that love him can perfectly discern. In some Epistles he is argumentative, almost contentious; he is pushing a point upon the attention of his correspondents, and he wants to establish a plea. He is not so enjoyable in such Epistles. He sometimes elicits pity for the other man. He is heroic in his logic and destructive in his conclusions; then I sometimes prefer to turn over a page. To the Colossians, the Ephesians, he is as it were in another sense more vividly and tenderly and approachably the Apostle of the grace of God. In the Galatians he talks to the Galatians; in the Corinthians he talks to the Corinthians; they have their local disputes and matters to adjust and to determine. But to the Ephesians and Colossians he speaks universals, he reveals solar systems; his strides are constellations; they are infinitely wondrous in intellectual conception, in imaginative and ideal colour and emphasis—Catholic Epistles in very deed; addressed to one church, but meant for all men and all ages.

I. Take the first verse of this chapter: 'And you hath He quickened, who were dead in trespasses and sins'. That verse is theology in one sentence; you need no more. As we found in Genesis i. 1 all the Bible, so we find in Ephesians ii. 1, the whole scheme of God and the whole revelation of human history. You—dead, quickened; you alive, brought from the dead. There are moral resurrections as well as physical.

II. 'Wherein in time past ye walked according to the course of this world, according to the prince of the power of the air, the spirit that now worketh in the children of disobedience' (ver. 2). There is the world for you in one gloomy sentence. This is Paul's reading of moral history. Paul was no fancy lecturer; Paul did not write out a course of dreams and call them a course of lectures: Paul recognised that the air is full of the devil. The devil has hardly left room for the summer in all that air which he breathes and poisons. He would edge out the summer if he could; he tempts the spring; he says to that sweet young thing, the vernal spirit, Blight, O blossoms! Arise, O East Wind, and kill the buds! choke those little birds in their homely nests! It is the devil. Do not attempt to argue him out of existence. Never under-value the enemy; never under-estimate his resources; take it for granted that, whether you are fighting spiritually or physically, you have a great enemy to meet, and prepare yourselves accordingly, or you will lose the battle, and you will deserve to lose it.

III. 'Among whom also we all had our conversation in times past in the lusts of our flesh, fulfilling the desires of the flesh and of the mind; and were by nature the children of wrath, even as others' (ver. 3). That is not modern talk. We have schooled ourselves by false schooling out of these great solemn, bedrock verities. The Apostle never would have suffered for our poor superficial theories; the Apostle would not have endured suffering and gloried in tribulation because he had received into his fancy some cobweb theory of creation, its evolution and its destiny. Not for such things did men preach in sorrow and seal in blood. If we have little conceptions about man and God, we shall have a little crumbling church, always at war with itself, and always losing the sham fights which it challenges and invites. Marvellous master was Paul! What deftness! what magnanimity! what wondrous subtlety of persuasiveness! 'We all had our conversation.'

IV. 'But God, who is rich in mercy, for His great love wherewith He loved us, even when we were dead in sins, hath quickened us together with Christ (by grace ye are saved); and hath raised us up together, and made us sit together in heavenly places in Christ Jesus' (ver. 4-6). 'Us,' 'us,' always 'us'—a priest who invokes a benediction upon himself as well as his people. That is brotherhood, that is holy masonry. 'God, who is rich in mercy'—not rich in thunderbolts only, not rich in lightnings and tempests and great whirlwinds. Mercy is the greater part of Him, if we could but see it. It was 'when we were dead in sins' that God showed the richness of His mercy. It was not when we were partly recovering ourselves, it was actually when we were dead in sins, and, being dead, helpless, lost; it was then that the Sun of Righteousness arose with healing in His wings. God makes us now sit in heavenly places; that is, in the heavenlies, in the world above the world, in the unseen kingdom.

V. 'That in the ages to come He might shew the exceeding riches of His grace in His kindness toward us through Christ Jesus. For by grace are ye saved through faith; and that not of yourselves: it is the gift of God' (vers. 7, 8). Salvation is not by intellect, knowledge; because then heaven would be full, if full at all, of grammarians. 'Grace,' 'faith,' that is a foreign tongue. It is! it is heaven's tongue; it is the tongue of the Infinite Love. Grace means favour, pleasure, kindness, pure simple love, appreciation; it is a gift, not a bargain; it has no equivalent; the number stands alone, and the sign of equal-to never follows it. It is above algebra, above grammar.

VI. 'Not of works lest any man should boast' (ver. 9). That is the very point. There must be no boasting; we must simply stand out, and say, It is the Lord's doing, and marvellous in our eyes. 'Not by works of righteousness which we have done, but according to His mercy hath He saved us, by the washing of regeneration, and the renewing of the Holy Ghost.' We have nothing to do with our own making. We had nothing to do with our physical birth, we have nothing to do with our superior or spiritual birth. For the next verse says:—

VII. 'For we are His workmanship, created in Christ Jesus unto good works, which God hath before ordained that we should walk in them' (ver. 10). Into what beautiful English might this be rendered! Instead of saying 'workmanship,' speak the word that is almost Greek in its very form—'we are God's poems'. God is the Poet, we are the poems.—JOSEPH PARKER, *City Temple Pulpit*, vol. II. p. 176.

REFERENCES.—II. 1.—Spurgeon, *Sermons*, vol. iii. No. 127; vol. xxxviii. No. 2267, and vol. xl. No. 2388. *Expositor* (4th Series), vol. i. p. 205. II. 2.—*Ibid.* (6th Series), vol. viii. p. 36. II. 3.—Bishop Stubbs, *Christian World Pulpit*, vol. xlv. p. 385. S. Cox, *Expositions*, p. 40. J. Johns, *Preacher's Magazine*, vol. xix. p. 409. *Expositor* (5th Series), vol. vii. p. 149; *ibid.* vol. ix. p. 12. II. 4.—C. Perren, *Revival Sermons in Outline*, p. 141. II. 4, 5.—Spurgeon, *Sermons*, vol. xiv. No. 805, and vol. lii. No. 2968. A. Maclaren, *Expositions of Holy Scripture—Ephesians*, p. 81. II. 5.—Spurgeon, *Sermons*, vol. xlvii. No. 2741. *Expositor* (4th Series), vol. i. pp. 201, 203; *ibid.* vol. x. p. 297.

ASCENDING WITH HIM

(For Ascension Day)

'And hath raised us up together, and made us sit together in heavenly places in Christ Jesus.'—EPH. II. 6.

THE great Forty Days of our Lord's Resurrection Life on earth are ended. These days have been a season of waiting, a time of rest and preparation for the great work of the future. Our Lord has appeared again and again to His own, but His appearings have been fitful and mysterious, as though to prepare them little by little for His final farewell. And now He and His Apostles meet together for the last time. How little did they realise that it was so! The veil was still lying on their hearts, and although He had told them plainly that after 'the little while' He would be leaving them to go to the Father, yet the very last question they asked Him a few moments before His Ascension shows us clearly how wide they were still of the mark. 'Lord, wilt Thou at this time restore again the kingdom to Israel?' They felt that they were standing on the threshold of some tremendous change. The news of Easter Day, and the Resurrection of their Master, had raised their hopes once more of seeing the kingdom established, but our Lord's answer gives no encouragement to such thoughts; 'it is not for them to know the times or seasons.' the poor brain would reel had He drawn but an outline of one century's history of that spiritual kingdom which he was then founding. No! Lift up your hearts, He seems to say—the Father Himself loves you, leave the future in His hands—you shall receive power when the Holy Ghost is come upon you. And then, 'while they beheld,' in the act of blessing them, He was parted from them. There is no grief, strange to say, at what appears to be His final departure from them. They return to Jerusalem with great joy.

I. What was the Secret of this Great Joy?—Was there a lingering feeling that this was only a further manifestation of His glory—that He had not really left them, but only withdrawn from sight for awhile? Death they knew could not separate them; He had spoiled principalities and powers and triumphed over the long-cherished victory of the grave, and all power is now given unto Him in heaven and earth. Perhaps He has gone to muster His legions of angels and to restore again the kingdom to Israel. Is this the cause of their joy? Nay, but even then an earnest of the Spirit was given them; another Comforter unseen stood near, and their deep but unexplained joy was the fruit of that Spirit which was poured upon them on the Feast of Pentecost without measure; the Divine light of those streams of fire penetrated the darkness of their understanding and showed them the things of God in their due proportion; they walked about Zion and beheld her battlements rising on every side; they saw the living stones hewn and shaped with unseen hands coming from all parts and filling their places in the Spiritual Temple; they counted the towers of that city, which hath the twelve foundations, whose Maker and Builder is God. From that day old things had for ever passed away with them.

II. This is Our Joy too.—Little by little the Apostles learnt the full significance of the Lord's Ascension, that in Him and by virtue of His Ascension they were also sitting in the heavenly places; in His Ascension they saw the first-fruits of our race passing beyond angels and archangels, and established on the right hand of God's throne on high. The Lord had gone up with the sound of the trump, and once more the trumpet should sound, and the waiting Church would be caught up to meet Him in the air. This was the comforting thought of those early days, and it shall be ours too. In the hour of trial let us lift up our hearts to our home beyond. On Good Friday, as we gazed on His bleeding figure nailed to the Cross, we smote our breasts and said: 'There I

see myself, it is my place'. To-day the veil is lifted, and we see heaven open and behold ourselves sitting with Him in the heavenly places. The cross has won for us the throne and crown of glory. Lift up your hearts in praise and thanksgiving for His glorious Resurrection and Ascension, and for the coming of the Holy Ghost!

III. Our Life here must be a Life of Heavenliness.—In the East the first-fruits of the early figs were called forerunners, they were pledges of the coming harvest; so Christ is our Forerunner, and we must grow up into Him in all things, we must be like Him, our affections must be set on things above, our hearts must be weaned from the world and prepared by self-discipline and by the grace of the Holy Spirit for the life of the world to come.

HIGH LATITUDES

'God hath raised us up together, and made us sit together in heavenly places in Christ Jesus.'—EPH. II. 6.

THE text does not speak of a future exaltation, but of one that has already taken place; it does not refer to a rare mood or passing ecstasy, but to a permanent loftiness of soul: it teaches that in the power of the Spirit the Christian habitually realises an ideal life in Christ Jesus. Let no one in the name of the practical despise the mysticism of the text. What would become of literature if a transcendentalist like Emerson or Maeterlinck did not appear every now and then? What would become of art if an idealist like Watts did not occasionally excite our wonder? What would become of ethics if it were not for the intermittent visitation of poets, mystics, and saints fluttering the utilitarians? What we now propose is to insist on the splendid gain of realising to the full this heavenly life, the vital advantage of living with a vivid consciousness of God, in the rich experience of His grace, in the clear, commanding hope of immortality.

I. In heavenly places in Christ Jesus we are most exempt from error. If we mind only earthly things, we must necessarily become the victims of manifold misconceptions, prejudices, superstitions, and illusions. What, then, shall we do that we may retain the sanity of our nature, the truth of vision, and that our verdicts may be reliable? Mount into 'God's own climate, beyond fog, dust, and cloud, beyond the causes and occasions of disturbance and aberration; see life in God's light; test all by the spirit and teaching of the Christ: so shall you "be filled with the knowledge of His will in all wisdom and spiritual understanding"'.

II. In heavenly places in Christ Jesus we are safest from contamination and peril. Already to many of us certain forms of moral besetment are as though they were not; if we mount to higher ranges, other possibilities of evil of which we are conscious will similarly cease; whilst on the highest summits of all we best deal with whatever assaults of the soul are still inevitable. Yet, live high as we may, we cannot get beyond the range of temptation. 'Heavenly places' are the best places in which to fight the foes of the soul, the choicest coigns of vantage.

III. In heavenly places we realise fulness of peace and blessedness. These radiant altitudes mean perfected felicity. Whymper, the Alpine climber, said of one of his guides that 'he was happy only when upwards of ten thousand feet high'; and no one knows the pure joy of life until he leaves beneath him the eagle's nest and finds the mystic edelweiss of snow-white purity in the blue depths of 'God's own climate' of infinite holiness and love.—W. L. WATKINSON, *Inspiration in Common Life*, p. 23.

REFERENCES.—II. 6.—C. Perren, *Sermon Outlines*, p. 159. *Expositor* (4th Series), vol. i. p. 138; *ibid.* vol. x. p. 340. II. 7.—H. Bonar, *Short Sermons for Family Reading*, pp. 273 and 282. Spurgeon, *Sermons*, vol. xxviii. No. 1665. A. Maclaren, *Expositions of Holy Scripture—Ephesians*, p. 91. II. 8. —W. M. Sinclair, *Simplicity in Christ*, p. 83. J. Stalker, *Christian World Pulpit*, vol. xlvii. p. 221. Spurgeon, *Sermons*, vol. xviii. No. 1064, and vol. xxvii. No. 1609. *Expositor* (5th Series), vol. i. p. 143. A. Maclaren, *Expositions of Holy Scripture—Ephesians*, p. 98. II. 8, 9.—C. Perren, *Revival Sermons in Outline*, p. 327. J. Johns, *Preacher's Magazine*, vol. xvii. p. 324. II. 8-10.—H. S. Holland, *Church Times*, vol. lix. p. 624. J. J. Blunt, *Plain Sermons*, p. 195. J. Hannah, *Preacher's Magazine*, vol. xix. p. 324. G. W. Brameld, *Practical Sermons*, p. 291. II. 9.—*Expositor* (7th Series), vol. v. p. 338. II. 9, 10.—Spurgeon, *Sermons*, vol. xxxvii. No. 2210.

THE REDEEMED LIFE GOD'S WORKMAN-SHIP

'For we are His workmanship, created in Christ Jesus unto good works, which God hath before ordained that we should walk in them.'—EPH. II. 10.

I. NOTE, first, **The Christian's New Nature.**—'We are His workmanship, created in Christ Jesus.' The idea that in believing men a change has been wrought which amounts to a reconstituting of their nature, is here expressed twice over, for the sake of emphasis. To begin with, the word translated 'workmanship' implies that a Christian owes his character and standing to God precisely as a *poem* owes its conception to the singer's intellect and fancy. The dramas he produced we call the works of Shakespeare, and in like manner men and women are the works of God. God is the author of what they now are. A believer's soul is the Divine poem. Elsewhere in the physical world we may read the Divine prose, but when God writes His name in a human heart, that is His poetry.

Then besides that, the same idea is underlined by the use of a second cognate term; we are *created*, says the Apostle, in Christ Jesus. Creation is one of those words which distinguish, and form the special glory of, the Bible. Doubtless in other religious books you will find cosmogonies and cosmologies of the most varied kind; half-noble, half-fantastic attempts to explain the origin and genesis of all that is. But it was left for the Bible, as some one has said, 'to inscribe the name of God on all things visible and invisible, and append to it the word *create*'. The note is struck in its first sentence. 'In the beginning God created.'

II. Note, **The Purpose for which the New Nature is Bestowed.** We are 'created in Christ Jesus unto good works'.

St. Paul indicates in one brief phrase the right relation of good works to the Christian life. It is 'unto good works' that we are created in Christ. Or, to put it otherwise, good works, holiness, Godlike character, is the aim of God in creating us afresh: it is His ultimate goal; accordingly it cannot be the cause of our being saved, but must be its issue and consequence. It is the fruit of the good tree, not its root or vital sap; and we are said to be created for good works just as a tree is created, or exists, for its fruit. Hence the true relation is altogether distorted and reversed when character and conduct are made preconditions of our obtaining Divine grace, instead of the joyous result of our having accepted it.

III. Note, **The Pre-ordained Divine Ideal.**—These good works, the Apostle adds, 'God has prepared that we should walk in them'. In other words, for each of us a path of spiritual development has been prepared beforehand, our travelling by which will be the realisation of that Divine ideal of our life which has hovered before the mind of God from the beginning. H. R. MACKINTOSH, *Life on God's Plan*, p. 43.

REFERENCES.—II. 10.—Spurgeon, *Sermons*, vol. xxxi. No. 1829. Bishop Sheepshanks, *Christian World Pulpit*, vol. liv. p. 295. E. H. Bickersteth, *Thoughts in Past Years*, p. 215. A. Maclaren, *Expositions of Holy Scripture—Ephesians*, p. 108. II. 11, 12.—J. Stalker, *Christian World Pulpit*, vol. xlviii. p. 184.

SIN AS ALIENATION FROM GOD

'Having no hope, and without God in the world.'—EPH. II. 12.

THESE terrible words form part of the description given by St. Paul of the state of his heathen converts before they accepted the Gospel of Christ. But though they were thus originally applied, it is, I think, quite allowable to see in them a description of the effect of sin generally. For the words are used of the heathen because they were sinners; it was as sinners, and in consequence of their sinful state, indeed we might say, as the essence of that state, that they 'had no hope, and were without God in the world'. I take them, therefore, as my text, when I consider the final and most fearful aspect of sin, its power of alienating us from God. 'Without God in the world.' The word translated 'without God,' ἄθεοι, is capable, indeed, of other explanation. It might be taken to mean, as in our word 'atheist,' unbelievers in God. But this rendering is excluded by the qualification ἐν τῷ κόσμῳ—in the world, which clearly points to a contrast between the relation of the sinner to God and his relation to the world. He is in the world, and subject to all the influences of the world, and is 'without God'. Not merely forgetful of God, or without belief in Him, but withdrawn from His life, without knowledge of Him, without His help in the dangers of the worldly life, without any hope of His mercy and love. They had 'no hope, and were without God in the world'.

I. This, then, is the effect of sin on the soul; it alienates the sinner from God, it leaves him in the world and without God. It is not, of course, meant that any man while yet alive on earth is altogether separate from the God 'in whom we live and move and have our being'. He upholds the whole order of creation; not a sparrow falls, and therefore not a man breathes without His will, His help. Withdrawn from God the world would cease to be; there can be no such thing as absolute alienation from God in this life.

Sinners are 'without God' because they lose the power of communing with Him, of 'feeling after Him and finding Him'; and, further, they are 'without God,' because He is hostile to their sin, and to themselves so far as they are identified with their sin. Man is alienated from God, and God is alienated from man by man's sin. That is the twofold aspect of this final result of sin which we have to consider.

II. Man loses by sin the power of communing with God, of relying on His help, of realising His love.

This communion is destroyed by sin. I do not mean repented sin, for that, though it weakens and clouds the soul, is by God's mercy in Christ forgiven, and the sinner is restored to his lost union with God; but I mean sin which the soul will not give up, sin entertained and delighted in, sin which dwells in the memory and controls the will. Whenever a man is living in sin and finds pleasure in it, the thought of God is no comfort or rest, but bitterness and disquiet, and He flies from communion with Him. For sin takes away the very conditions which make the thought of God the stay of the soul. When external troubles or anxieties come upon a man, troubles uncaused by anything he has done, but none the less oppressive, there is no consolation or rest like that of laying the whole before God, and leaving the solution of it in His hands. It is not our own doing, its causes are independent of us; God will accept the burden we lay upon Him, and sooner or later 'unto the godly there ariseth up light in the darkness'. But when our own sin has caused it, and we will not cease from the sin, there is no comfort in appealing to God. The first condition of His help is wanting; we dare not give up the very cause of the trouble that is weighing us down. So the sinner shrinks from the one source of comfort, and cuts himself off from communion with God. For he trembles before the wide and unyielding claims of God on the soul. He wants to keep something back, to retain one 'bosom sin,' to hide a part of himself from the Divine eyes; and God claims the whole or will have none.

III. God Himself is not, cannot by His very nature be passive while man is forsaking Him. He is always hostile to sin, and must therefore hate that which is sinful, in so far as it is identified with sin. The sinner chooses his own pleasure, his own will instead of God's will. He has turned from God, and has chosen himself, and in the pursuit of his own ends has forsaken his Master and Friend; and then when he would return, he finds that his rebellion is also banishment,

that God has forsaken *him*, that sin, which is man's desertion of God, is also punishment, which is God's departure from man. He has preferred himself to God, and God's punishment is to leave him with himself. 'Ephraim has joined himself to idols; let him alone.' Yes, even in this world we see that punishment beginning, as the sinner wakes up to find himself far from the abiding source of happiness, cut off from communion with God, estranged from the Divine life; and yet he cannot forsake his sin, for it has enthralled his will, and has become itself his sharpest penalty. But this is only the partial anticipation of the 'last state of that man,' in that condition which is only conceivable to us as 'eternal sin,' eternal 'alienation from the life of God'.—A. T. LYTTELTON.—*College and University Sermons*, p. 100.

REFERENCES.—II. 12.—O. Bronson, *Sermons*, p. 107. *Expositor* (6th Series), vol. ix. p. 57. II. 12, 13.—H. W. Webb-Peploe, *Christian World Pulpit*, vol. liii. p. 396. II. 13.—Spurgeon, *Sermons*, vol. xv. No. 851. *Expositor* (4th Series), vol. vi. p. 31; *ibid.* (5th Series), vol. vi. p. 223. II. 13-17.—*Ibid.* (6th Series), vol. vi. p. 461. II. 14, 15.—*Ibid.* vol. iii. p. 135. II. 15.—F. D. Maurice, *Sermons*, vol. i. p. 137. II. 16.—*Expositor* (4th Series), vol. v. p. 436; *ibid.* (6th Series), vol. x. p. 31. II. 17.—C. S. Horne, *Daily News*, 23rd December, 1907, p. 3. *Expositor* (4th Series), vol. iii. p. 373; *ibid.* (6th Series), vol. ix. p. 104. II. 18.—W. P. Du Bose, *The Gospel According to St. Paul*, p. 143. II. 19.—H. S. Holland, *God's City*, p. 29. S. H. Fleming, *Fifteen Minute Sermons for the People*, p. 123. F. J. A. Hort, *Village Sermons in Outline*, p. 103. J. Martineau, *Endeavours After the Christian Life*, p. 65. II. 20.—Spurgeon, *Sermons*, vol. xxiii. No. 1388. R. Vaughan Pryce, *Christian World Pulpit*, vol. lii. p. 401. *Expositor* (5th Series), vol. ii. p. 27. A. Maclaren, *Expositions of Holy Scripture—Ephesians*, p. 118. II. 22.—C. Gutch, *Sermons*, p. 124. T. Arnold, *Sermons*, vol. i. p. 255. Bishop Westcott, *Disciplined Life*, No. ix. Spurgeon, *Sermons*, vol. v. No. 267. III. 1-12.—*Expositor* (6th Series), vol. viii. p. 235. III. 3-6. G. F. Pentecost, *Christian World Pulpit*, vol. xlviii. p. 259. III. 4.—A. W. Robinson, *The Mystery of Christ*, No. xi. *Expositor* (5th Series), vol. x. p. 269; *ibid.* (6th Series), vol. x. p. 362.

CHRISTIANITY A REVELATION

'The mystery of Christ . . . in other ages was not made known to the sons of men, as it is now revealed unto His holy Apostles and prophets by the Spirit.'—EPH. III. 4, 5.

I. FIRST of all, let us notice what is implied in this, when we say that Christianity is a revelation.

For one thing, there is implied a contrast. When we say that Christianity is a revelation, we mean that it is not an induction or an invention.

Every religion purports to be a revelation. Ay and more, every religion in so far as it is true—and there is an element of truth in every religion—is what it purports to be, a revelation. We need not be surprised at the statement that there is an element of true self-revelation by God Himself to the hearts of men in even the crudest religions. Not only are the ideas of religion and revelation, as Sabatier says, 'correlative and religiously inseparable,' but it is in line with Scripture. 'God left not Himself without a witness.' The Old and New Testaments are both full of this thought. The sun in the heavens is His herald. The recurring seasons, the gifts of harvest-tide, are His messengers. Conscience and the sense of right and wrong are His witness within. And when the Parsee worships the sun he has caught one ray, and reflected it, from the light Divine. The Greek worshipping Demeter, the great Earth-Mother, has caught and reflected another. Confucius heard a voice Divine in the call of duty. And the Furies with their lash for the transgressor were held in holy reverence because to their worshippers they seemed the vindicators of a law which, men discerned, had come into their hearts from God. It is where and when God shows Himself that men fall down and worship. Till then they are seekers with a void in their hearts which nothing earth-born can satisfy. But God appears; God reveals Himself; and they recognise Him and reverence and adore. A revelation alone can satisfy the religious instinct which is an essential element in our human nature.

II. Being satisfied that our religion is and must be a revelation if it is a religion at all, the second point for us to consider is the way in which the revelation has been made. How has God shown Himself?

(a) For one thing, God has revealed Himself progressively. He has come like the 'sun shining more and more unto the perfect day'. The history of Christianity is the history of a steadily enlarging understanding of the wealth of the revelation which there is in Jesus Christ our Lord.

(b) For a second thing, God's revelation of Himself is not intellectual only, but personal.

(c) A third point to be noted about God's method of revealing Himself is that He has revealed Himself first to individuals, and then through them to their fellows.—R. J. DRUMMOND, Faith's Certainties, p. 3.

REFERENCES.—III. 6.—F. St. John Corbett, The Preacher's Year, p. 19. III. 7.—Expositor (5th Series), vol. ix. p. 375.

WEALTH THAT NEVER FAILS

'The unsearchable riches of Christ.'—EPH. III. 8.

'THE unsearchable riches.' The inexorable wealth, ranging vein beyond vein, mine beyond mine, in land beyond land, in continent beyond continent! And, then, side by side with this immeasurable glory, the Apostle puts himself. 'Unto me, who am less than the least of all saints, is this grace given!' What an arresting and daring conjunction! Let us turn our contemplation to one or two aspects of this 'unsearchable' wealth.

I. The Lord Jesus Christ has created so exacting a conception of Himself in the minds of men that no ministry of man can satisfy it. No human ministry can express it. In all our best representations of the Lord there is always a missing something, an 'unsearchable' something, which the most masterly figures cannot span.

II. But it is not only that our Saviour has created an exacting conception of Himself, He has also, by

His 'unsearchable riches,' created an exacting ideal of human possibility. Every summit brings a new revelation, the reward of every attainment is a vision of further glory.

III. We cannot exhaust their powers of application to the ever-changing conditions in human life and destiny. In the Christian life new conditions never find us resourceless. Our wealth is inexhaustible, and always manifests itself as current coin.

IV. But it is not only that 'the unsearchable riches of Christ adapt themselves, and reveal the wealth, to the changing condition of our years, it is, that in our personal crises, when life suddenly leaps into fierce emergency, their resources are all available, and never leave us in the lurch. There are three great crises in human life—the crisis of sin, the crisis of sorrow, and the crisis of death—and by its ability to cope with these crises every philosophy and every ministry must be finally determined and tried. We can never get to the end of 'the unsearchable riches of Christ'. They are our glory in time, they will be our endless surprise in eternity.—J. H. JOWETT, The British Congregationalist, 24th January 1907, p. 84.

EPH. III. 8.

CHRIST gives us to possess not God only, but men also as our riches, the unsearchable riches which we have in Him.—McLEOD CAMPBELL.

REFERENCES.—III. 8.—Spurgeon, Sermons, vol. xiii. No. 745, and vol. xx. No. 1209. Bishop Westcott, Christian World Pulpit, vol. xlv. p. 360. F. E. Paget, Helps and Hindrances to the Christian Life, vol. i. p. 60. J. G. Rogers, Christian World Pulpit, vol. lxi. p. 398. III. 8-11.—J. Clifford, Christian World Pulpit, vol. lviii. p. 209. III. 9.—Expositor (4th Series), vol. i. p. 32. III. 10.—Spurgeon, Sermons, vol. viii. No. 448, and vol. xvi. No. 933. Expositor (4th Series), vol. i. pp. 138, 153; ibid. vol. vi. p. 77. III. 11.—Ibid. vol. i. p. 32. III. 11, 20.—Llewelyn Davies, The Purpose of God, p. 28. III. 12.—W. P. Du Bose, The Gospel According to St. Paul, p. 143.

PATRIOTISM AND INTERCESSION

'For this cause I bow my knees unto the Father of our Lord Jesus Christ, of Whom the whole family in heaven and earth is named, that He would grant unto you . . . to know the love of Christ, which passeth knowledge, that ye might be filled with all the fulness of God.'—EPH. III. 14, 15, 16, 19.

ALL great missionary pioneers, founders, and leaders seem to come to a time in their lives when God's purposes and plans become unveiled to their vision, and, as in a moment, the future unfolds itself to their spiritual gaze. So it was with Noah after that great crisis in the world's history at the Flood. By faith, in the spirit of simple obedience and holy, far-seeing awe, he had prepared the Ark and entered it with his family. He had passed reverently through the discipline of his strange retreat, and was ready, after his sacrifice of thanksgiving, for the vision of God's providential government and the future expansion of the race of man. So with Abraham, strong in the faith that boldly faces the unknown and 'waits on the Lord to renew its strength'. Step by step he approaches the crucial and unexpected trial of his belief. But the discipline of faith had prepared him. He offers his son in sacrifice, but stays his hand immediately at the Divine call. Then it is that the whole vision of the purpose of God in the family and tribal and national life of Israel opens before his mind. Think, too, of Moses and his training, all preparatory to that magnificent vision of God on Mount Sinai as a Moral Being having personal moral relations with mankind.

I. And St. Paul, the greatest of missionary pioneers, steeped in all the visions and hopes of Judaism, burning with zeal for its glorious revelation, its secure privileges, and its inspired claims—when the eyes of his soul were opened on the Damascus road to see the glimmerings of a world-wide significance in the religion and history of his people, and see it all focussed in the incarnate personality of Jesus, immediately he 'confers not with flesh and blood,' but bursts through all conventional bonds and cautions and expediencies. He takes the yoke of Christ, becomes the Lord's slave, submits his whole being, is led by the hand of Ananias, is healed, taught, and baptised. Then he goes into his retreat in the wilderness, hears unspeakable words, sees the meaning of the call to 'go far hence unto the Gentiles,' and simply goes. He founds Church after Church, leaving with each the Divine gifts of the Faith, the Ministry, and the Sacraments, with powers of self-government, self-support, and self-expansion. And he does this work, too, if in all simple joy of soul, yet in 'much trembling,' in much depression, in bodily infirmity, amidst the scorn of philosophers, the hatred of his own people, 'fightings within and fears without,' in 'prisons frequent and deaths oft'. He sees the incarnate life of Jesus becoming incarnate in all humanity. For God's purposes there is one race, the human race; but one Saviour, His Son; one family, the Church; 'one Lord, one Faith, one Baptism,' as there is and can be but 'one God and father of us all'. And within sound and sight of Cæsar's Palace, where was focussed, in the person of the Emperor, Rome's Imperial and imperious world-wide sway, St. Paul sees and feels in it all a parable of the universal Kingship of Jesus, the universal brotherhood of mankind, in the one universal family of His Holy Catholic Church; and as the glorious vision lays hold of and enthrals his soul he 'bows his knees unto the Father of our Lord Jesus Christ, of Whom the whole family in heaven and earth is named, that He would grant unto the world to know the love of Christ which passeth knowledge, that it might be filled with all the fulness of God.'

II. In the second chapter of this Epistle to the Ephesian and other Churches of Asia St. Paul passes quite naturally from the fact and idea of the Fatherhood of all humanity to the idea of the family and then to the home, the house itself, the temple of the Triune God. 'Through Christ we both have access by one Spirit unto the Father, and are built upon the foundation of the Apostles and Prophets,

Jesus Christ Himself being the Chief Corner-stone, in Whom all the building, fitly framed together, groweth into a holy temple in the Lord.' Then suddenly his prison-chamber expands and becomes to his soul like some vast cathedral temple, and, as though ministering at its high altar, he lifts his hands and bows his knees unto the Father in heaven and raises the great intercession as the Imperial vision of Christ's universal sovereignty holds him and claims and proclaims the Real Presence of God in, to, and for humanity in the Sacramental efficacy of the Incarnation, Death, and Resurrection of the Son of God and Son of Man, 'in Whom ye also are builded together for an habitation of God through the Spirit'. No wonder that it has been said of this Epistle that 'in it St. Paul has given to his teaching a new centre, that of the Church of God'. It is eucharistic in its visions and ideals and practical exhortations. It begins with thanksgiving and ends in a benediction, and its core and centre in the text is like a consecration prayer. There is the unity of all Creation, and the restored unity of humanity in Christ the Head of the Body —the Church. Christ, the Great High Priest of humanity, ministers the great salvation in and through His own Body, prepared from all eternity in and within the mystical Body which He was forming out of universal humanity, and wherein, as far as salvation or 'saving health' was concerned, there was to be no individual privilege or preference, neither Jew nor Gentile, and yet wherein all differences of race, language, or circumstance, all varieties of genius, talent, or experience would find themselves unified, strengthened, perfected, and glorified in the manifold (many-coloured) 'unity of the Spirit, which is the bond of peace'.

Am I wrong in thinking of this Epistle to the Asian Churches as the account of a great Sacramental vision which had germinated and grown in the soul of the Apostle, and became incarnated in his life as the years went on? Again and again you can feel the heart of the great missionary pulsating to bursting-point as the thrill and throb of the infinite movement and purpose of the Blessed Trinity in Creation, Providence, and Grace, like some great drama set to music, possesses him, lightens and brightens his spiritual vision, enthrals and compels his will, inspires and inflames his soul, so that he could even 'wish himself accursed from God' if only the Israel of Abraham could but see the vision and accept its destiny as the Israel of God, and if only Rome and the nations in their worship of force, and Greece in its worship of beauty and wisdom, could and would but see revealed as in a Sacrament, in the Incarnate Word, 'Christ the Power of God and the Wisdom of God'. 'For this cause I bow my knees unto the Father of our Lord Jesus Christ, that ye might be filled with the fulness of God.'

He sees in Jesus Christ, the God-man, the one and only principle of a universal brotherhood, a universal citizenship, and a universal Empire, demanding faith in the eternal justice of God, hope in His eternal mercy, and an all-embracing love shown in mutual service——

Each for his brethren, all for God.

BISHOP W. T. GAUL, *The Guardian*, 16th September, 1910.

REFERENCES.—III. 14.—Bishop Westcott, *The Incarnation and Common Life*, p. 161.   III. 14, 15.—J. Martineau, *Endeavours After the Christian Life* (2nd Series), p. 95.   III. 14-16.—J. Bowstead, *Practical Sermons*, vol. ii. p. 148.

THE LOVE OF GOD

'For this cause I bow my knees unto the Father of our Lord Jesus Christ, of Whom the whole family in heaven and earth is named, that He would grant you, according to the riches of His glory, to be strengthened with might by His Spirit in the inner man ; that Christ may dwell in your hearts by faith ; that ye, being rooted and grounded in love, may be able to comprehend with all saints what is the breadth, and length, and depth, and height ; and to know the love of Christ, which passeth knowledge, that ye might be filled with all the fulness of God.'—EPH. III. 14-19.

I. THE fact that God feels a deep love for men is one hard to contemplate, still harder to realise. Yet it is the starting-point of Christianity. It is the very core of the revelation of Jesus. The inspired declaration that 'God is Love' (1 John IV. 8, 16) has changed the temper and life of every man and every community which has come to believe that the statement is true. It has been a thousand times more potent to produce right living than had been the previous belief that God is power. Therefore love is more potent than law, and love is the essence of the Gospel. It is true that in the case of an earthly ruler affection may be thrown away upon unworthy subjects, and that legal compulsion alone will produce results. Nevertheless, Jesus insists that God Himself is so constituted that He can never rest content until He has won for Himself the love of all His creatures. Jesus uncovers the love of God for men, and allows it to work. It may work by sharp methods, for love can be 'cruel to be kind'. But, we are taught, the object which God sets before Himself is not to break a recalcitrant will, or compel a sullen obedience to His laws, but to draw all men to Himself. But the fact that God loves men, though it may gain a certain amount of assent in the abstract, becomes difficult to realise, and raises grave doubts in the human mind, when men reflect on what the statement involves.

(1) The sense of one's own individual insignificance in the universe of Existence—this thought presents one difficulty. That God should entertain affection towards humanity as a whole does not seem unreasonable, but we cannot realise the fact that God has a distinct and separate love for each single human soul which has ever lived. Yet, if this be not the truth, then His love for men becomes a mere phrase not worth contending about.

(2) Another difficulty is the fact of human unloveliness. Men, taking them as a whole, are not very lovable. Comparatively few inspire real affection. Alas! it is but too true that those who come personally into contact with multitudes, and have to deal with them officially or commercially, come to have a sort of contempt for humanity ; they see too much of the foibles and petty faults of character to feel any general sentiment of affection ; they have discovered the unloveliness of men.

(3) There is one other difficulty, and that the most formidable—the fact of human suffering.

If it be true that God loves His children, why does He leave them to suffer so? This has been the dark mystery of the ages ; it is the difficulty with many still. It has led men to atheism. It has led them to attribute to God the qualities of the devil. It has driven them, in frantic despair, to curse God and die. It has led others to grovel before God as abject slaves before an Oriental despot. It has led others, again, to throw their children into the flames and the waters as propitiatory sacrifices to angry deities. It has led many among us to think of a Law, instead of a Person, as the Centre of things—has this apparent Divine indifference to the cries of human agony.

II. Now St. Paul looks these facts squarely in the face, and yet bursts out in praise of the goodness and lovingkindness of God. Why does he do so? What new light has he upon the 'painful riddle of life'? He is not hazarding a mere opinion ; it is not a conclusion thought out or discovered by any method common among men. Jesus had said not long before that any one who saw Him would see the Father. Now many beheld Him, but comparatively few recognised Him for what He was. In this minority was St. Paul. (The Apostle Paul claimed for Himself an equal authority with the other Apostles, because he had seen the Lord, not in a mere vision, but 'objectively'—after His Ascension—in glory). This sight of God in the Person of Jesus Christ changed his estimate of his fellow-men by changing his notion about God. It set all the facts of life with which he was familiar in a new light. They remained the same, but they no longer meant the same. As he learned from the Master what is the real disposition of God towards men—that all men are the sons of God, and that God has a personal interest in each individual soul, because of this relationship—this kindled in him that 'enthusiasm of humanity' which is the great mark of Christianity. Real love for men is only possible in the Presence of God. So absolute is the Christian conviction of God's lovingkindness that from it he educes an explanation of human pain, and he does it clearly : 'My son, despise not thou the chastening of the Lord ; for whom the Lord loveth He chasteneth, and scourgeth every son whom He receiveth . . . (*et seq.*)' (Heb. XII. 5-11). The Apostle's assertion amounts to this—that the ills which assault men, and sometimes take the zest out of living, are no meaningless accidents, nor purposeless agonies caused by the crampings of a soulless 'law,' but that they are the smartings from the stripes of a rod laid on reluctantly, but intentionally by a Father. It is true that we see many an ill which we find it hard to account for on this theory ; that we see sufferings which teach no lesson to the victim, because they do not leave the victim alive to learn, so terrible and swift are they. Nevertheless, while the theory of suffering must remain in some cases partly shrouded in mystery, as a trial of our faith, no other theories of life bring the same intellectual relief and moral uplifting as does the great Christian doctrine that God is love, and that He is slowly bringing His children by this mysterious discipline, among other things, into a recognition of their relationship to Him.—S. D. M'Connell.

References.—III. 14-19. H. S. Holland, *Christian World Pulpit*, vol. lviii. p. 216. A. M. Fairbairn, *ibid.* vol. lviii. p. 19.

GOD'S FAMILY

'Of Whom the whole family in Heaven and earth is named.'
—Eph. iii. 15.

There are many illustrations used in Holy Scripture to set forth the relationship in which the people of God stand to each other and to Him, but the most expressive of these is taken from domestic life. It is the one presented in our text, and under its familiar imagery the Church of God is described as one great family, the members of which are bound to each other by the possession of one common life, the distinction of one common name, and the union with the same parental head. It is a family, the members of which, though sundered by time and space, and divided into two great sections, the one in heaven and the other here on earth, are all bound together in one blessed bond, and linked to each other by special sympathies, and are looking forward to dwell together in one happy and eternal home.

I. Relationship with God.—It is only through that relationship that they can have communion with each other. To be united to each other they must first be united to Him. Just as in a family it is the possession of a common life, derived from the same parental source, which constitutes the bond of union, so in the family of God it is the spiritual life, derived from Him, which forms the basis of communion. St. John puts this beyond question when he says, 'That which we have seen and heard declare we unto you, that ye also may have fellowship with us, and truly our fellowship is with the Father, and with His Son Jesus Christ' (1 St. John i. 3). In another place he testifies that this fellowship of Christians with God as their common Father is through faith in His dear Son; for 'as many as received Him to them gave He power to become the Sons of God, even to them that believe in His name' (St. John i. 12). Elsewhere we are clearly taught that the impartation of this Divine life is wrought through the Holy Spirit, 'for as many as are led by the Spirit of God, they are the sons of God,' and the contrast is very solemn —'If any man have not the Spirit of Christ he is none of His' (Rom. viii. 9, 14). All true believers, then, are members of this family, and in that respect are designated 'saints'—not only on account of their separation from the rest of the world, and the holy service to which they are called, but on account of the Divine life of which they are partakers.

II. The Ideal of the Christian Church.—To us who are not gifted with omniscience or discerning of spirits, the visible Church is the body of those who profess His truth, are baptised into His name, and observe His ordinances; but all who belong to it do not necessarily belong to that spiritual communion to which properly the name of Saints belongs. A visible Church with its external ordinances and terms of communion is, from the very nature of the case, indispensable in our present state; and the commands concerning our union with the visible Church and our observance of its appointed ordinances are clearly laid down in Scripture; but still we must not forget that this is not enough for our salvation. In order to that there must be vital union with Christ Himself; there must be forgiveness of sin through faith in His precious blood; there must be renewal of heart by His Holy Spirit; there must be willing and faithful service, which springs from love to Him. The judicious Hooker, who is so distinct and copious in speaking of the Church as a visible body, is equally clear in speaking of the Church as the mystical body of Christ. He says: 'That Church of Christ, which we properly term His Body Mystical, can be but one; neither can that one be sensibly discerned by any man, inasmuch as parts thereof are some in heaven already with Christ, and the rest that are on earth (albeit their natural persons are visible) we do not discern under this property, whether they are truly and infallibly of that body. . . . They who are of this society have such marks and notes of distinction from all others, as are not objects of our sense: only unto God, who seeth their hearts, and understandeth all their secret cogitations, unto Him they are clear and manifest. . . . If we profess, as Peter did, that we love the Lord, and profess it in the hearing of men, charity is prone to believe all things, and therefore charitable men are likely to think we do so, as long as they see no proof to the contrary. But that our love is sound and sincere, that it cometh from 'a pure heart, and a good conscience, and a faith unfeigned,' who can pronounce saving alone the Searcher of all men's hearts, who alone intuitively knows in this kind who are His?' So that while there is, and must be, a visible Church on earth, and in it a visible communion of saints, there is within that Church a still more sacred shrine, and a still more holy fellowship. There is a Church as seen of men; there is a Church as seen of God. We cannot ignore the one without a breach of duty and of charity. We cannot overlook the other without a forgetfulness of truth, and of our own salvation. We must beware, on the one hand, of that easy and fashionable but deceptive religion which contents itself with the profession of orthodox doctrines, or the observance of appointed ordinances; we must beware, on the other, of that arrogant and selfish spirit which, relying on its own strength or spirituality, considers itself independent of those visible means of grace which have been appointed by God for the personal and mutual benefit of all His children.

III. This twofold view of the Church of God, if it seem on the one hand to narrow our view as to its extent, will help to widen and deepen our ideas as to 'the communion of saints,' for it will show us how manifold and how real that communion is. But does it really narrow our views as to the extent of the Church of God? Does it not rather expand them? Are we not too prone to ask, with the querulous disciples, 'Lord, are there few that shall be saved?' Are we not too apt to exclude from our ideal of the Church those who do not belong to our own communion, or to include in it only those who agree with us in certain views concerning the doctrines or ordinances of religion? And do not our ideas enlarge when we come to think of all the saints of God who lived in all the ages before Christ's birth, and of all who have lived in all the centuries ever since? Do they not take a wider range when we remember the great multitude which 'no man can number, of all nations and kindreds and people and tongues,' who shall stand at the last before the throne of God, having 'washed their robes and made them white in the blood of the Lamb'? It is when we dwell on thoughts like these that we begin to realise that outside our own communions there are and have been saints of God, with whom perhaps we cannot sympathise in respect of all their views, but with whom we can and ought to sympathise in the best of bonds as members of the one great family of God. We come to recognise the family likeness even where we cannot trace the ecclesiastical genealogy, and gladly admit the spiritual relationship even where we cannot verify the mode of admission to it. And we can do all this without prejudice to our convictions or surrender of our principles.

THE CHURCH A FAMILY

'Of Whom the whole family in heaven and earth is named.'—
Eph. iii. 15.

The name of the Church in the text I have selected is 'the family'. There are many names for the Church in the Bible; the family represents perhaps the sweetest.

I. What is the Church?—When the Church began, it was a family, with the love of a family, the cohesion of a family, the economy of a family, and very soon there came the quarrels that so often happen in a family. Yet a family that sometimes has moments of discord still is full of love. St. Paul calls the Church a brotherhood; it is the development of the idea of the family, for the Church, increasing in ever-widening circles, has names corresponding to that increase. The brotherhood is a wider term than family, it is a uniting of certain people from many families. And, as the Church grows, you find another name for the family in the Epistle to the Hebrews. It is now more than a family, more than a brotherhood; it has become a city, with all the complications of a city, all the varied interest of a city, with its business, its pleasure, and sometimes its vices. But the Church is more than a family, more than a brotherhood, more than a city; it is a commonwealth, and that is the name I like the best. The commonwealth. Every member of it is bound to kill selfishness, to work for the good of the community. 'What is best for the people?' is the question of the Church, and the individual must always make his own interest subservient to the good of the whole community. But the Church is more than a family, more than a brotherhood, more than a city, more than a commonwealth; it becomes in the Bible a nation, a collection of nations, until the idea of the Catholic Church is the world converted.

II. The Foundation of the Church.—What is the Church founded on? What have we got? Now notice. We have a Person—Jesus Christ; we have a Book—this Bible; we have an Institution—the Church of God. A Person, a Book, an Institution—the world killed the Person, Jesus Christ, yet to-day He is alive and more at work than ever; the world tries to kill the Book, yet here it is in your pulpit to-day as strong as ever; the world has tried to kill the Church, yet, after two thousand years, it is getting larger than ever. Why do they not kill the Book, Why do they not kill the Church? Because they cannot. Institutions that are not wanted, die. The Church lives because it is wanted. You want it, you know that. Your home wants it. That boy of yours in business wants it; that girl of yours, who is just getting married, she wants it. The poor children in the slums, they want it. The institution is wanted. The Church lives because it is wanted. The immortal part of man wants the Church, and so the Divine foundation fits the Divine need in man, lays hold of your soul, and that is the reason that it lives. You cannot kill it. Churches have died, or in the language of the Book of the Revelation, their candlestick has been removed out of its place—churches, but not the Church. The Church lives.

References.—III. 15.—Spurgeon, *Sermons*, vol. xxi. No. 1249. F. D. Maurice, *Sermons*, vol. vi. p. 75. C. H. Grundy, *Luncheon Lectures at St. Paul's Cathedral*, p. 45. *Expositor* (4th Series), vol. ix. p. 100. A. Maclaren, *Expositions of Holy Scripture—Ephesians*, p. 128.

THE INNER LIFE OF A NATION

'Strengthened with might by His Spirit in the inner man.'—
Eph. iii. 16.

Who would not desire to possess a strength as invincible as that which was the secret of St. Paul's faith and hope and life? There is an inner and there is an outer man in every one of us. There is an inner and there is an outer life in the nation, in the family, and in the individual. In the nation the inner life is not always recognised, even by its own people, until some grave necessity sets the heart of the nation beating and throbbing, and the people are roused by a common feeling hitherto unsuspected.

I wish to point out four of the great characteristics that ought to mark the inner life of our nation.

I. No One ought to Forget that in whatever Position he has to Live he ought to be dominated by such a sense of responsibility that he never forgets that the people around him will judge not only his religion but will judge his nationality by the example and evidence which they have in him.

II. The Love of Duty must ever characterise every individual among us. It is well known that when Napoleon wrote his despatches he never forgot to mention the glory that he said attached to the achievements of his troops ; it is equally well known that when the Duke of Wellington wrote his despatches he never mentioned the word *glory*, but he never failed to call attention to the *duty* which his men performed.

III. There must be Sympathy with those over whom we have any Authority and those among whom our lot is cast. If India is maintained for long as our great trust and the sphere of our beneficent rule, it will be due not only to the excellence of the rule but to the exhibition of the spirit of sympathy. And that which is true of that nation you may depend upon it is characteristic and true of all those over whom England has any rule.

IV. There must be Self-sacrifice.—We may thank God for the noble examples given of self-sacrifice by our troops, by our blue-jackets, by men who have done signal and noble service to the Empire. Whether standing, like Lord Cromer, almost alone in Egypt ; whether standing like those great Viceroys of India who have maintained our rule and been loyal for our crown ; whether it be the lonely hearts or whether it be in the most active spheres of operation ; it has been by self-sacrifice, by not seeking their own but by seeking the good of others, that the name and the fame have been obtained.

It is the inner life of the family which begets the inner life of the nation.

References.—III. 16.—A. Maclaren, *Expositions of Holy Scripture—Ephesians*, p. 132. III. 16-19. Spurgeon, *Sermons*, vol. xii. No. 707.

THE INDWELLING CHRIST

'That Christ may dwell in your hearts by faith.'—Eph. iii. 17.

There is no religion in the whole world, except the religion of the Gospel, that hints even at such an idea as this—God, Christ, in my own self. It is the most wonderful and unexpected thought in the whole inspiration of God. The question that starts in our minds is this—'is this promise to be accepted, to be fulfilled, in anything like its literal meaning'? The answer is this—It is a personal and real fact. Jesus Christ dwells in our hearts and rules them, if we are children of God by faith. In proportion as simple faith takes hold of the living Christ, He becomes a real Person and a real Life. If we approach Jesus Christ critically, He will look another way ; if we approach Jesus Christ doubtfully, He will look the other way, too ; if we approach Jesus Christ sympathetically, the Holy Spirit will help us to know, and to see, and to feel that He is the Friend of our life.

I. The thought of Christ dwelling in our heart ought not to be a very difficult one for people like ourselves to grasp its conception. Let us think of an analogy. A widowed mother, with no child but one single boy. This boy, as he grows up, becomes increasingly dear to her heart. As he grows up, to her great sorrow he is overwhelmed with a passionate love of the sea. For years and years that poor lonely widowed soul never hears of him, and wonders whether he is living or dead. She never will leave his name out of her prayers. Is it very difficult for you to understand what is meant when it is said of such a person, ' Her boy dwells in her heart ? ' Is it more difficult to think of Jesus Christ as the object of religious love dwelling in our hearts also ?

II. But then Jesus dwells in our hearts in a much more real way than this. Jesus Christ in the believer's heart not only as the object of his affection, but as the very life of his soul. You know, perhaps, the process of grafting, by which a little twig, with no root, is grafted into a tree till it becomes part of the tree, and the life of the tree flows into the twig, and the life of the tree becomes that of the twig. Is it difficult for you, with that analogy, to realise the conception of one person dwelling in another person's heart as the power of that person's soul and life ? So the believer appropriates the life of Jesus, and the conception of Christ dwelling in your heart as the life of your soul is not a very difficult one for you to understand.

III. Another question arises to one to ask and to answer, which is this, How does Jesus Christ get admission into our hearts in such a way that He may be said to dwell in them ? Is that a very difficult question to answer ? Is it necessary even to ask the question ? How does anybody get admission into our houses so as to dwell in them or to stay in them ? By our consent, not otherwise, by no other way. How does Jesus Christ get admission into men's hearts so as to rule and dwell in them ? The answer is the same, by men's consent, not otherwise, and in no other way possible or conceivable.

Jesus Christ gains admission to our hearts by our own consent, but how does He enter ? What is the opening through which, when you have invited your friends to your house, or given them permission to come, they enter ? It is the door, and there must be some similar opening through which Jesus Christ enters the heart. What is the opening ? What is the means ? The opening, the means is this : it is our faith, our simple acceptance of the Lord and Saviour Jesus Christ as the sinner's substitute and the believer's Light.

It is the beginning of everything that is good to let Jesus into the heart. You cannot go far wrong when you do that. It only requires a little faith just to open the door. He will bring the Light with Him, pardon, strength for service, and hope, and glory.

The way to keep Christ is the way in which we get Him to come. He keeps in our hearts by continual acts of faith on the part of believers. That is the sum and substance of Christianity, of the Gospel of Jesus Christ, Christ in the soul of the child of God.

REFERENCES.—III. 17.—C. Brown, *God and Man*, p. 54. H. S. Holland, *God's City*, p. 86. Bishop Bethell, *Sermons*, vol. i. p. 138. H. M. Butler, *Harrow School Sermons*, p. 120. A. Maclaren, *Expositions of Holy Scripture—Ephesians*, p. 142.

THE CHURCH'S CONCEPTION OF CHRIST

' To the end that ye, being rooted and grounded in love, may be strong to apprehend with all the saints what is the breadth, and length, and height and depth, and to know the love of Christ which passeth knowledge, that ye may be filled unto all the fulness of God.'—EPH. III. 17-19 (R.V.).

THE true man desires to know, to understand, to apprehend. Paul was a man who wanted to *know* —to know the highest things. He made it his business in life, next to knowing for himself, to make others know, to be their teacher. At the same time, he was willing to know from others. Paul's desire for these Ephesians was that they might be strong to apprehend with *all* saints the love of Christ in its breadth, and length, and height, and depth : that is, in its wholeness and fulness.

I. It has been said that Paul's thought was something like this. From that old captivity of his in Rome, his mind went away, carried him to the Ægean Sea, whose blue waters lay in beauty about the yellow sand of the Ephesian shore ; and, looking in thought upon the land, he seemed to see a mighty castle, a splendid fortress. There it was, beautiful, strong, capacious, majestic. But would all men look at it alike ? Paul thought that every one looking upon it would not give the same judgment about it ; not that they would disagree about any part of it, but each would be so struck by one part of it as almost to neglect the rest.

II. To Paul there was in history one Form, one Existence, one Personality, upon whom many men had been lavishing their thought after His appearance. That Form, that Person was Jesus Christ. He was Love. (1) Some saw the breadth of that love ; they thought of ' the nations lying beside each other on the earth, over all of whom the love of Christ would extend itself'. (2) Others saw the length of it ; they could not forget ' the successive ages during which it will reach '. (3) Others thought of the height of it, of ' the glory at God's throne and near His heart to which it could elevate all '. (4) But others thought of the depth of it ; they thought of ' the misery and corruption of sin, into which it will descend '.

III. And to-day in considering Christ, His character and work, men in various ways grasp special aspects of it. Now, it is well for us that we should, therefore, consider the belief of the saints *as a whole*. As a body, they preserve the symmetry of truth.

IV. What was Paul's desire for these Ephesians, and for himself also ? It was this—that they might be able to apprehend with all the saints, what is the breadth, and length, and height, and depth of the love of Christ. He did not desire them to see aspects only of that love, but the whole of it.

V. The conception of Christ by *the* Church is larger than that of any specific Church. He is in each, but is fuller and finer than any *one* of them represents Him to be.—J. ALFORD DAVIES, *Seven Words of Love*, p. 134.

REFERENCES.—III. 17-19.—R. W. Church, *Village Sermons*, (2nd Series), p. 287. F. de W. Lushington, *Sermons to Young Boys*, p. 94. *Expositor* (5th Series), vol. ix. p. 95.

THE DEPTH OF LOVE

' May be able to comprehend with all saints what is the breadth, and length, and depth, and height.'—EPH. III. 18.

THE love of Christ is the love of God. What we find in the heart of Christ, in His character, in His words and actions, is to be regarded as a revelation of the Invisible God. That indeed is the whole significance of Christ's manifestation—' He that hath seen Me hath seen the Father '. This manifestation was made, we may believe, because apart from it we were incapable of gazing into the heart of God. The aspect of things speaks with sufficient clearness of Law, of Intelligence, of Power working to an end ; but it can hardly be said to bear on it the legend of love. Apart from Christ it is open to any man to maintain that God is an unknown Force, inexorable, indifferent to human suffering, regardless of human life, a concatenation of awful uniformities which move like a car of juggernaut over prostrate human beings to some unknown goal. Remembering, then, this incontestable fact, we shall examine with eager interest the evidences of the Love of Christ, and seek to know it, though it passes knowledge.

I. First of all there is the human life of Jesus, as it is recorded in the Gospels. However fragmentary the reports, however difficult the attempt may be to harmonise them into a consistent record of facts, or a harmonious combination of features, there can be no question that the records give us an unexampled impression of a heart of love. Not only is the love of Christ indisputable in the Gospel narrative ; but it stands out as a passion of a new type. Compare it with the love of which Plato's Symposium treats, that love, not wholly free from sensual passion, and when free from sensual passion, losing itself in a cold intellectual atmosphere.

II. But the impression of His love, made by the course of His earthly life, is wrought to an extraordinary fulness and intensity by the cross. Whenever the cross is allowed to give its own witness, undisturbed by imperfect theories and dogmas, whenever Christ is evidently crucified before the eyes of men, a great appeal proceeds from the unique spectacle.

III. And yet, when we have made all allowance for the portrait of love, unexampled and affecting in the story of Christ's life and death, can we say that these historic facts fully explain the language of the text ? Surely not. This passion which echoes in the language of Paul and re-echoes with undiminished force in the hymns of Bernard, and again, with even increased fulness and feeling in the letters of Samuel

Rutherford; this passion, which is known at the present time, and rises beyond the power of language in millions of Christian hearts, is only to be explained by the interior movements of the Spirit.—R. F. Horton, *The Trinity*, p. 133.

References.—III. 18, 19.—C. Kingsley, *The Good News of God*, p. 146. Archbishop Benson, *Living Theology*, p. 3. A. Maclaren, *Expositions of Holy Scripture—Ephesians*, p. 151.

THE FULNESS OF GOD

'That ye might be filled with all the fulness of God.'—Eph. III. 19.

These words form the conclusion of St. Paul's prayer on behalf of the Ephesian Church. It is a very wonderful, one might almost say a very awful prayer. And what St. Paul prayed for on behalf of his Ephesian converts, that we too ought to seek for ourselves.

I. St. Paul takes for granted that a Real Christian is a Man who has been Made Over Again, and not merely a man of this world who is a little more moral, or a little more decent, or a little more outwardly attentive to his religious duties than other men of the world. Quite the contrary. According to this mighty prayer, the Christian is one upon whom all the powers of the Godhead have been brought to bear, so as to make him what may be termed a *Divine* man, not a worldly man. See the orderly progression of the Divine work as thus prayed for by St. Paul. First of all St. Paul prays that God the Holy Ghost will give him strength; then that God the Son may dwell in him, giving him first the grace of love, and then the grace of knowledge of Divine things—that knowledge which passes or exceeds the comprehension of other men. And then, when the man has been thus prepared by the strengthening which the Spirit brings, and by the Divine love and the Divine knowledge which Christ brings—then St. Paul prays for the final grace of all —namely, that he may be filled with all the fulness of God the Father. None of us can fully enter into all that these words convey. Perhaps even those who come nearest to being filled with that fulness would be least able to speak about it or to explain it. But still we may try to set forth a little of what it must mean.

II. For a Person to be filled with anything, it is Plain that, first of all, he must be emptied of all Else.—Hence it is absurd for any of us to think of being filled with God's fulness so long as he is under the dominion of any purely earthly or temporal wishes, or desires, or ambitions, or passions, or tastes. The words imply a totality of self-surrender to God. In praying to be filled with God the Father's fulness, we pray that all our powers and faculties and desires and energies and likes and dislikes may be just what they would be if all our merely earthly desires were taken out of us, all that is selfish and mean and bad were emptied out of us, and the vacant space filled up by a pouring in of the character of God our Father. It is the same as praying that we may be just what God would be if we could imagine God to be put in our place.

III. This, then, is what St. Paul Prays for:— (1) That each Christian man upon earth may be, each in his own way and in his own sphere, an 'Image of God'; and (2) that each of us may have God's approbation and God's service as his chief end and aim, as an ever-present motive, as a thought never absent from our minds. After all, Christianity consists not so much in what we do as what we are, or rather what we become. Faith in God and Christ; faith in Christ and in the Holy Ghost raises us to a good hope that, if we will but empty ourselves of all that is earthly and selfish, and cling to Him in whatever walk of life He points out to us, God will take care of the growth of our Christian character; He will fill us with His own fulness.

References.—III. 19.—Spurgeon, *Sermons*, vol. viii. No. 455, and vol. xxix. No. 1755. *Expositor* (5th Series), vol. vii. p. 256. A. Maclaren, *Expositions of Holy Scripture—Ephesians*, p. 171.

The Power of Prayer.—Eph. III. 20.

Luther said : 'No one believes how great is the force and efficacy of prayer, unless he has learned it from experience. It is a great thing when anyone feels a mighty need and then can lay hold on prayer. I know this, that as often as I have prayed with earnestness—with real earnestness—I have without doubt been abundantly answered, and have obtained more than I asked. Our Lord God may sometimes have delayed, but yet He heard me.'—E. Kroker, *Luther's Tischreden* (1903), p. 338, No. 646.

References.—III. 20.—W. F. Shaw, *Sermon-Sketches for the Christian Year*, p. 87. III. 20, 21.—Bishop Gore, *Christian World Pulpit*, vol. xlix. p. 273. Spurgeon, *Sermons*, vol. xxi. No. 1266. A. Maclaren, *Expositions of Holy Scripture—Ephesians*, p. 180. III. 21.—*Expositor* (6th Series), vol. vii. p. 278.

Eph. IV.

In the *Memorials of Dr. McLeod Campbell* (vol. I. p. 127), he observes, apropos of Edward Irving's dying conversations, 'I was finding no trace of the subject of the Church in anything she (*i.e.* Mrs. Irving) was mentioning, until she said that in the course of that same last day he had asked her to read to him "the testament of the Lord to his Church—the neglected testament"; when she read to him the fourth of Ephesians'.

THE HEAVENLY CALLING

'I therefore, the prisoner of the Lord, beseech you that ye walk worthy of the vocation wherewith ye are called.'— Eph. IV. 1.

When St. Paul bids us 'walk worthy of our calling,' he bids us do a great thing, and perhaps his words make little impression on many of us. For, in truth, our Christian calling seems a long way off from many of us, and almost out of sight. For the most part we left it behind at our baptism, and have made no further inquiry about it; other callings occupy our time and thoughts. And these lower motives do us injury; they are apt to shut out and overpower the higher. Indeed, this is the rule which the world itself sets up for us. If we keep up to its standard it is enough. And if we were to live here always this might be enough. We might go on buying and selling, and not trouble ourselves about anything further. But, you know, we are not to live here always, and this makes all the difference.

There is another and a higher world to be taken into account, and the calling which will suffice for this present world will not suffice for that other world, which is our true home, and whither we are bound. And, what is more than this, God has given us a calling which alone, if we follow it faithfully, will enable us to attain it.

I. God has given us His only begotten Son to be our Pattern and Guide. He has come down for this end—first of all, to put away our sin by the sacrifice of Himself, and then to guide us in the way which He has trodden before us to Heaven. To this, then, we are called—to the imitation of our Lord Jesus Christ—to nothing less than this. The world's rule and calling will not carry us far; we must not trust to it, it will break off and fail us when we need it most—in the hour of death and in the day of judgment.

II. The Ephesians, to whom these words were written, doubtless understood them better than we, for they had been called from being heathens, and all around them were heathens still. Now, we can only understand clearly by way of judgment or comparison, and so, when all around us are professing Christians, it is difficult to understand what our Christian calling is. We do not see, as the Ephesians, the light of Christianity and the darkness of heathenism side by side. And, moreover, what we do see tends to confuse us, for we see men who have been baptised and plainly called to be Christians living in many ways like heathens, though not openly or in the same degree. Thus our views of our Christian calling become indistinct and confused; the Church and the world become one; we cannot tell what our calling is, or how we may walk worthy of it. Yet—

III. There are certain marks of our calling which cannot be mistaken.

(1) There are the sure outward marks which distinguish us Christians from heathens and make up our calling.

God has called us through His Church, and by a Sacrament, and has bidden us serve Him in it. By the Sacrament of Baptism we were admitted into His Church, otherwise we could not be Christians at all. This is what really separates us from the heathen: we are made by our baptism members of Christ, children of God, and inheritors of the kingdom of heaven. These are privileges which Christian men have, and the heathen have not. They are not joined to Christ by His ordinances, they have not the remission of sins, or the gift of the Holy Ghost, which come by Christian baptism, and in no other way. They are not made partakers of the Divine Nature, they have no share in the blessings which are given through the Church in Confirmation of holy matri-

mony, in sickness, or in death—above all, they cannot be partakers of the Body and Blood of Christ in the Holy Communion.

(2) Again. There are certain other marks, of which St. Paul here tells us. There is the mark of Unity. After having exhorted us to walk worthy of our vocation, the Apostle thus explains what he means: 'With all lowliness and meekness, and longsuffering, forbearing one another in love, endeavouring to keep the unity of the Spirit in the bond of peace'; for, he adds, 'there is one Body and One Spirit, even as ye are called in one hope of your calling, One God and Father of all, Who is above all, and through all, and in you all'. Here, then, is a plain mark—we must be lovers of unity; this is the end of our calling, that we may all be one in Christ Jesus. He came to make us one, to take away the ancient curse, to join men together once more in Himself, to be Himself the centre of their unity, to join them to Himself, and make them one in His Body, which is the Church.

(3) There is the mark of Christian love. 'Love,' says the Apostle, 'is the fulfilling of the law.' 'Thou shalt love thy neighbour as thyself, for love worketh no ill to his neighbour.' So that Christian love or charity is the very bond and foundation of this unity. It does no ill to its neighbour—it does the very contrary, its seeks out all means of doing him good; and so, as injuries divide men, and cause them to hate each other and separate from each other, so does love, by doing good, unite and bind together in one.

(4) There are those graces which are the grounds of Christian love, the only condition of its existence. So when the Apostle bids us to 'walk worthy of our vocation,' it is 'with all lowliness, and meekness, and long-suffering, forbearing one another in love'. And for the same cause he bids us put away 'lying, and wrath, and theft, and filthy speaking, and bitterness, and clamour, and evil speaking,' because these things tend to separate men and destroy the unity which Christ has appointed for them.

These, surely, are plain marks of our calling. Unless we have these marks in some good measure we cannot be His. We must be joined to Him by the Sacraments which He hath ordained for that purpose—first by Baptism and then by Holy Communion—and by being partakers of the Church's offices and prayers; that, thus being made one with Him, we may be one also, by this outward union in His Body, and by the grace of charity which is its life, with all our brethren.

References.—IV. 1.—W. J. Hills, *Sermons and Addresses*, p. 137. J. T. Bramston, *Fratribus*, p. 170. F. de W. Lushington, *Sermons to Young Boys*, p. 15. A. Maclaren, *Expositions of Holy Scripture—Ephesians*, p. 194.

GOD'S MILD CURFEW

'I therefore, the prisoner of the Lord, beseech you that ye walk worthy of the vocation wherewith ye are called, with all lowliness and meekness.'—Eph. iv. 1, 2.

We are all familiar with Mrs. Browning's beautiful words:—

Nor seek to leave thy tending of the vines
For all the heat of the day, till it declines
And death's mild curfew shall from work assoil.

Should we not rather say God's mild curfew? If life is long, that curfew comes before death. Between the hour of curfew and the hour of the last rest there is a blessed and solemn pause. We are assoiled from labour before we die, if only we keep our ears open. If we really pray for guidance to the Most High, we shall hear the curfew and hail it when it comes. It is because we do not hear and obey the signal of release that with so many of us the last act is tragedy.

I. In how many cases this is so! Laborious, honoured, and powerful lives have again and again ended in frustration and stress. Men would not hear the mild curfew of God, and they have tried to ignore or to battle with the unkindly summons of man. They have purposed that more than the full lustre that beamed in the days of their meridian triumph should glorify their last years. And the result has been that gloom has come upon them at the last and lain upon them like a pall. The statesman has lived to the extreme limit of human life to sit among the ruins of the tower which he built, and which he has thrown down with his own hand. Even when this destiny has been devoutly endured, it has been full of sadness and of warning. Another has been expelled from his kingdom and has spent his closing days in bitter and chafing thoughts, in cruel, scornful, impotent protests and complaints. The great preacher who stayed beyond his hour has died shattered in soul and body upon the field. The ambition to sit too long at life's imperial banquet has brought the proudest to sup off the broken meats in the end, and to eat their bread in tears. It may be said, and it is sometimes true, that these humiliations have subdued the spirit, and that it had to be subdued thus before there could be worked upon it the last miracle of spiritual change. It may be said that sometimes unchequered success has blinded and hardened, and that a new nobility of soul has sprung from the new discipline of sorrow and failure. It may be so, but this must mean that the moral nature was partly stunted and partly diseased.

II. They are right, we believe, who think that the last stage of a long life ought to be its glory and its crown. John Bunyan was inspired to speak of the land of Beulah as bordering the Jordan on this side. Yet how few of our greatest and noblest visibly tarry there at last and pass away in the splendour of its peace. A famous Swedenborgian was wont to speak of the progress towards perfection as made by the removal of present happiness. If happiness were continuous there would be no advance. So happiness is taken from us, and we pass on to a new stage, day succeeding day through the six stages of regeneration till the evening and the morning of the sixth day, and then the finished work and the day of rest. The dream of the mystics was not all a dream. They imagined that there was a land to be reached before death, secluded from the tumult and the pain of time,

and before which the tempests might blow their challenging horns in vain. The Middle Age imagined the famous temple, Sangreal, with its dome of sapphire, its six-and-thirty towers, its crystal crosses, and its hangings of green samite, guarded by its knights, girded by impenetrable forests, glittering on the onyx summit of Mount Salvage, invisible to the impure, inaccessible to the faithless, but giving to the simple the immediate presence of the Infinite. There before dying it is granted to gaze, to love, and to know. There is a spiritual reality which corresponds to this. For years and years on to old age men dream that there is only one kind of happiness, the happiness of their wills gratified and their ambitions realised and the little idols they have set up smiling down upon them. When they are made wise in the communion of the Holy Ghost, they understand that the true blessedness is quite other than that, that it comes to those who have died to the anarchy of inordinate desire and live the life that is hidden with Christ in God. The mood of intense and simple blessedness, which is so much higher than the happiness that comes from prosperous and prominent and well-rewarded work, rises from our faster attachment to Christ, from our completer detachment from the things of earth and time, from our clearer realisation of the Mystical Union. The Christian realises the height of his peace, not in the company of admiring and applauding crowds, not in seeing the spirits subject to him, but in the company of that Love which has chosen him, and found him, and carried him away. It is to that profounder blessedness God's mild curfew calls us.—W. ROBERTSON NICOLL, *Sunday Evening*, p. 45.

REFERENCES.—IV. 1-3.—J. Bowstead, *Practical Sermons*, vol. ii. p. 132. IV. 1-6.—*Expositor* (5th Series), vol. vi. p. 148. IV. 1-16.—E. J. Kennedy, *Old Theology Re-stated*, p. 97.

A PLEA FOR UNITY

'Forbearing one another in love; endeavouring to keep the unity of the Spirit in the bond of peace.'—EPH. IV. 2, 3.

MUCH is heard about Christian unity and the paralysing effect that our divisions inevitably produce on various Christian bodies. We may well consider this question on the Sunday after Ascension Day, and our text is certainly appropriate.

I. **Why has there been Failure?**—'Endeavouring' suggests failure, does it not? 'Endeavouring to keep the unity of the Spirit in the bond of peace,' that is the lesson which comes home to us in this season. Surely Ascension time should strongly develop our appreciation of the living Christ Who is at our very hand. When we think of the growth of wealth and the influence that is exerted by it, it is easy to see that material things attain a great hold over the thoughts and the imaginations of men, and the result is a weakening of our spiritual capacity. The announcement was made to the Apostles that Jesus Christ would come again. It was graven deep in their memory. Jesus was gone, but they felt that He was very near, and they felt that that unseen Presence might at any moment come to them again. But to us Christ is hidden. He is, as it were, far off behind the veil which hides Him from us. Is it not so? We have not the sublime faith of the Apostles, who thought that at any moment He might be with them again; and it is this which separates us from those who do not agree with us; it is this want of spiritual force which prevents unity. We must pray that the Holy Spirit may operate with all Christians, and it is this operation which leads to unity.

II. The Qualities of the Holy Ghost.—What are the qualities of the world-restraining, world-uniting Holy Spirit? Do not these qualities make for peace and the bond of love? We cannot wonder that the Lord Jesus Christ made it His last prayer that His Church might be one when we know what has occurred, what is always occurring by the lack of unity. Yet this unity which has always been desired has never yet been realised. How do we account for our Lord's Prayer that His Church may be one? He knew that dissension was bound to come into the Church, and that there was bound to be disagreement between it and the world—bound to be disputes between the kingdom of heaven and the kingdom of man. Did unity exist in the days of St. Paul? No, it never did exist within the Church; and when we read of the differences in the early Church, and of those differences of opinion, of course there must be a feeling of bewilderment on all those who have prayed for unity when they think that there has never yet been that blessed peace which we have all hoped for, and which we will try to pray for more earnestly than ever. We should do our best to heal our divisions, and we should seek after that unity of the spirit of which St. Paul speaks in our text.

III. Unity is Strength.—Let us be united. Above all, let us be united in prayer. We may surely hope that if our hearts be opened to let in the influence of the Holy Spirit, the day will come when we are united in peace because we have endeavoured to keep the unity of the spirit in the bond of peace.

REFERENCES.—IV. 2.—J. Keble, *Sermons for the Sundays After Trinity*, p. 129. IV. 2, 3.—Bishop Creighton, *The Heritage of the Spirit*, p. 201.

UNITY, NOT UNIFORMITY

'Endeavouring to keep the unity of the Spirit in the bond of peace.'—EPH. IV. 3.

THESE words of St. Paul find their place in the letter which has justly been called a treatise on the ideal Church. Its constitution, its ministry, and its aims show themselves in indwelling, vital force. Much needed as they were, no doubt, to those to whom they were at the time addressed, they have had their application in all the ages of the world-wide Church, and they come home to us with a special force in these later days. Let us try to arrive at their real meaning.

I. The Oneness of the Spirit.—Let us get away from the time-honoured and beautiful language of our Authorised Version, and let us make for ourselves a clearer and more literally plain version of the words as St. Paul wrote them. 'Eagerly striving to guard the oneness of the Spirit in all,' that is in the bond of peace. The oneness of the Spirit! The Apostle is inspired by that glorious conception of the one holy apostolic Church which has ever been the cherished dream of all the noblest and best Christian teachers and leaders of all shades of opinion in every age, yet which has never been realised since the first few years of the infant Church's life in Jerusalem. It seems that, if we look at the whole body of professing and baptised Christians throughout the world, or if we narrow our horizon and confine our scrutiny to our own branch of the Church, this ideal is farther from us than even in the most controversial and troublous times of the past.

II. The Dawn of a Brighter Era.—In spite of all this, however, there are many signs around us which herald the dawn of a new era and a better time. The day has gone by—and thank God for it—when men treated unity as if it were uniformity, and endeavoured to procure it by physical torture or the penal clauses of Acts of Parliament. We have learnt by experience that men cannot be coerced by human and material means to think alike, and that carnal weapons will never promote the spiritual kingdom of our dear Lord and Master; and if we have learnt so much, we have surely advanced towards a right comprehension of what St. Paul in his text begs us seriously to strive for. Even in his days grievous party faction had arisen in many of the newly formed Christian communities, and yet he could write, in spite of these divisions and factions, 'guard the oneness of the Spirit,' as if it were a treasure which had not been lost.

III. The Treasure not Lost.—Let us who now read his words lay them to heart, and take heart and thank God. Let us remember, while we naturally lament the bitterness of party jealousy and sectarian strife, that, paradoxical as it may seem, it was the Prince of Peace Himself Who said of His own mission, 'I am not come to bring peace, but a sword'. For you and for me, then, it seems that the message of God is this: let us hold fast that form of sound words which we have received as our most precious heritage. 'One Lord, one faith, one baptism, one hope of our calling,' let these be our watchwords in the battle; but let us remember that we are called upon to be in charity with all men; let us fight the unfair and sneering judgment of our fellows who cannot see our aspect of the truth; let us remember the words of Him Who said, 'Forbid him not, for he that is not against us is for us'. But let us also rejoice in the success of any endeavour to win souls for our dear Master's kingdom; so we, by zealously trying to guard the oneness of the Spirit by means of the bond of peace, and having continued faithful to our trust here, may be counted worthy of entering into the home of perfect peace hereafter, where all who love the Lord Jesus in sincerity shall be finally united in Him, and shall be made partakers in the glory of the Trinity in unity.

THE UNITY OF THE SPIRIT

'To keep the unity of the Spirit.'—EPH. IV. 3.

THE world upon which St. Paul looked out was divided by most serious divisions, although outwardly it appeared more united than ever it had been before, in the unity of the great Roman Empire. To the Jew the Gentile was a dog, and no words could express the contempt of the Gentile for the Jew. Here was one of the great divisions of the world. Another was the division between slaves and freemen. A slave was hardly accounted a man. Besides this, there were the divisions which we ourselves look out upon to-day—rich and poor, noble and baseborn, educated and ignorant, cultured and rude. Yet St. Paul could speak of a unity, a oneness which could bind men together.

I. Let us try then to understand what this unity was. The Jews had always been looking forward to a great Prince Who should come from God to draw them together as a nation, and make them victorious over the heathen world. And the Messiah had come, but in so different a guise that they disowned and rejected Him. St. Paul had learned to see in Christ the Son of God, Who had become Man, as the One who had shown to men what is the true human life, and had lifted our humanity to the very throne of the universe. Here was a hope for all mankind. Those who accepted Christ as their Lord received a new life. They were made and kept one in Him. In Christ's name they were placed on a level of perfect equality. It did not matter whether they were slaves or freemen, they were lifted up by their baptism into a position of equal spiritual privilege. The slave, St. Paul says, was Christ's freeman, and the master was Christ's slave. It did not matter whether they were rich or poor, high or low, wise or unlearned, they were lifted by their baptism to an equal wealth and nobility of spiritual riches and Divine sonship. This was the unity which St. Paul so prized. Here was, to his view, the hope of the world.

II. As St. Paul looked into the future he saw the vision of a splendid hope. The Body of Christ was growing as new members were being perpetually baptised into it. If only the unity could be preserved, that was the essential point. The conception of the body must be grasped and lived up to. The Christian life must be above all things a life of membership in the body.

What has been the result to the world of that little seed of unity which was planted in apostolic days? First, the fierce controversy between Jew and Gentile as to their rights and privileges within the Christian society has disappeared. Next, after many centuries the great curse of slavery has been removed from all Christian countries, and men are no longer bought and sold like cows and horses. Further, the provision of education for the very poorest has begun to do something to bridge the gulf which for so long divided those who could read from those who could not, and a way is opened for the workman's clever boy to reach the university. Something has been done, and we do well to take account of it. It is slow work, indeed, but yet the world moves, and this in spite of the fact that the Christian society has fallen so short of the Apostle's ideal, and has failed so conspicuously to keep the unity. If the unity had been kept, how great would the progress have been ! As we look round to-day we are tempted to despair in view of the division among the Christians themselves. Where, we ask, is the humility that delights in lowly service, where is the mutual forbearance that makes quarrels impossible? What has become of the unity of the one body and the one Spirit? Must we sadly despair of the one hope of mankind? Has Christianity failed? If it has failed, or so far as it has failed, it has been because it has lost sight of its early ideal. It has forgotten to keep the unity. If it is to recover its ancient power, and to continue its sacred work, we must recover the lost ideal, we must realise the truth of the body and its members, we must cultivate the life of fellowship.

REFERENCES.—IV. 3.—Spurgeon, *Sermons*, vol. xi. No. 607. J. G. Rogers, *Christian World Pulpit*, vol. xliv. p. 248. J. Keble, *Sermons for the Sundays After Trinity*, p. 140. Archbishop Maclagan, *Christian World Pulpit*, vol. xlviii. p. 241. T. Arnold, *Sermons*, vol. i. p. 56. R. Kemp, *Christian World Pulpit*, vol. li. p. 340. F. D. Maurice, *Sermons*, vol. ii. p. 155. Bishop Wilberforce, *Sermons*, p. 116. Basil Wilberforce, *Sanctification by the Truth*, p. 85. *Expositor* (5th Series), vol. ii. p. 112.

' Endeavouring to keep the unity of the Spirit in the bond of peace. There is one body, and one Spirit, even as ye are called in one hope of your calling ; one Lord, one faith, one baptism, one God and Father of all, Who is above all, and through all, and in you all.'—EPH. IV. 3-6.

THE call for unity is always attractive to the social instincts of mankind, and in times of danger it becomes a stirring cry. No one, I suppose, but a misanthrope, would desire, if it could be avoided, to remain at variance with his neighbour. And there are times when religion is threatened, or when evil seems to loom large, when we turn instinctively to others for sympathy and help. Unity, whether of outward organisation or inward spirit, always stands for some kind of strength.

I. Our Unhappy Divisions.—At the bottom, I suppose, of all our Christianity lies the one object that the whole world should be converted to Jesus Christ; and nothing, surely, can be more contrary to the mind of Him we call our Master, and by Whose name we are called, than the unhappy divisions of Christendom. St. Paul comprises in the unity of the Spirit nine sources of oneness. When we have so much in common, how is it that we cannot forget the points on which we are not alike? We are bound to ask ourselves sometimes, What is the reason for this discordant element? Why is it that there has been hostility even to some of the historic survivals of primitive Christianity? St. Paul would not force unity into uniformity. He recognises that under the operation of the same Spirit there are diversity of gifts. But all are to be parts of the same body, joined together in Jesus Christ. We think, perhaps, of the sins of the official Church in the past; but I think it was not merely the unwisdom of the Church in those times towards those bodies or men who had new ideas which seemed to be contrary to the spirit of Christianity, but which have often proved to be merely a reinterpretation of its creeds. It was not merely the grasp of temporal power. It was not merely the un-Christian and careless lives of those who have at different times represented the Church. There must be some stronger reason than this why men who claim to be animated by the Spirit of Christ are yet very widely separated from each other. I suppose the dividing line is often found in the very primary conception of what the Church is.

II. The Basis of Unity.—Unity, if it is something more than a mere philosophic dream, if it is to have something more than an abstract value, is bound to have some outward expression. It would seem from the first that the Church which was to be Christ's representative in the world must have some rules, some outward organisation, some officers who should be held responsible, and some form of belief which it could hand on as descriptive of the religion it maintained. History has brought to us certain wide divergencies of opinion as to the character of the essence of Church organisation. On the one side a great deal has been sacrificed to this ideal; while, on the other, liberty of conscience and opinion has become a sort of fetish. The Church of England holds a middle way between these two ideas. But surely the great thing for us when we aim at the unity of the Spirit, is to recognise that there is a great deal for the Church, and, while we hold fast our own interpretation of the best way to reach it, to recognise that others sincerely believe that there is a different interpretation of the facts.

III. A False Unity.—At the same time, in religion, which demands the very highest exercise of all man's faculties, the truth is of the utmost importance, and for a man to acquiesce in anything which appears to him not to be the highest form of truth is for him to be a traitor to his nature which was made in the image of God. There can be, perhaps, no unity of the Spirit between a man who holds firmly the Divinity of Christ, and another who is entirely doubtful about Christ being God at all. Surely it is not compromise of this kind that is asked for. We believe that God has appointed the Church to convert the world through certain means of salvation; this is His way, and we have no right to choose another. Again and again we are implored in the New Testament to hold fast the form of sound words. We are warned against thinking that it does not matter what belief we have or how we express it in worship. These things, we are bound to remember, have really the closest relationship to practical life. But when we have put before ourselves this ideal of Christ's Church, when we have sincerely looked into our hearts and examined what our belief is, then we may go on to be charitable towards other people whom we may also sincerely believe have a different conception of the ideal.

ONE SPIRIT
'One Spirit.'—EPH. IV. 4.

'ONE Spirit' means that, just as in the fulness of time, the Eternal Son, Who had from all eternity been in the secrets of the Father's counsels, Who had been the agent in creation, Who had made all things, and without Whom was nothing made that was made, came forth to carry out their joint plan of Redemption with the cry, 'Lo! I am come to do Thy will, O God'; so also in the fulness of time from the heart of the same Godhead came forth God the Holy Spirit; and with the sound of a rushing mighty wind and with tongues of fire He came forth and tabernacled on earth as God the Son had done. This and nothing less is the awful truth, that He is as really on earth now as Jesus was in the home of Bethany, that He has never gone back, that there is an Ascension Day for God the Son, but that there is no Ascension Day for God the Holy Ghost.

I. What then is it that the Christian Church believes? (1) First, that He is a Person—that He comforts, strengthens, guides, loves—as only a Person can. (2) That He is a distinct Person; at the baptism of Jesus Christ, God the Father says: 'This is My beloved Son'. God the Son is in the water; but God the Holy Ghost descends in bodily form as a dove, distinct from the other two Persons of the Godhead. (3) That we live under His dispensation now; that these are the times of the Holy Spirit; and that we might as well describe a home and leave out the mother's love, as describe religion and leave out the 'One Spirit'.

II. How is 'One Spirit' the secret of a peaceful, loving, and progressive religious life? We see in a moment by looking at the functions the Spirit came into the world to fulfil. (1) He came first, we are told, 'to take of Christ and show Him to us'; He was to make Christianity real to us; He was to take of the cross and bring its meaning home to us, and so convict the world of sin, and righteousness, and judgment; He was so to work upon our hearts as to make us cry each to ourselves as we look at the cross: 'He loved me and gave Himself for me'. (2) He was to give us the sense of the Fatherhood of God and help our infirmities in prayer. (3) The express object and aim of the One Spirit was to draw us together, to make the world good and to make it one.

III. What, then, are we to do in order to put ourselves in connection with the moving Power of the Spiritual world? (1) We are told to ask for Him to come. To pray for the Holy Spirit means to put yourself in a frame of mind to which the Holy Spirit can come. It means (a) Self-examination. (b) Surrender. (c) Obedience.

IV. But suppose you do all this, and pray for guidance to the 'One Spirit,' and then apparently are guided wrong? What are we to say? (1) There is no promise at all that the immediate results of the guidance will appear. We must hear what the years and centuries may say against the hours.—BISHOP

WINNINGTON-INGRAM, *Banners of the Christian Faith*, p. 133.

REFERENCES.— IV. 4.— W. H. Evans, *Sermons for the Church's Year*, p. 207. *Expositor* (7th Series), vol. v. p. 498. IV. 4-6.—J. Budgen, *Parochial Sermons*, vol. ii. p. 212. IV. 5.—J. Keble, *Village Sermons on the Baptismal Service*, p. 19. *Expositor* (5th Series), vol. vii. p. 39. A. Maclaren, *Expositions of Holy Scripture—Ephesians*, p. 203. IV. 5, 6.—F. D. Maurice, *Sermons*, vol. vi. p. 111. IV. 6.—J. Vaughan, *Fifty Sermons* (9th Series), p. 173. W. M. Sinclair, *Church Family Newspaper*, vol. xiv. p. 240. *Expositor* (5th Series), vol. vi. p. 334.

'Unto every one of us is given grace according to the measure of the gift of Christ.'—EPH. IV. 7.

HENRI PERREYVE writes : 'We must indeed admire that flexibility of the Christian faith, which makes it accessible, even in the practice of perfection, to souls of very different kinds. Thus the same faith, the same worship, the same morality lead to heaven the soul of a profound philosopher like Thomas of Aquinas and the soul of a poor village child.'— *Lettres de Henri Perreyve à un Ami d'Enfance*, p. 252.

REFERENCES.—IV. 7.—H. P. Liddon, *Sermons on Some Words of St. Paul*, p. 199. A. Maclaren, *Expositions of Holy Scripture—Ephesians*, p. 207. IV. 7-12.—Spurgeon, *Sermons*, vol. xvii. No. 982. IV. 8.—F. D. Maurice, *Sermons*, vol. ii. p. 103. W. Knight Chaplin, *Christian World Pulpit*, vol. lviii. p. 70. H. J. C. Knight, *The Record*, vol. xxvii. p. 2. Bishop Westcott, *Village Sermons*, p. 195. *Expositor* (5th Series), vol. vii. p. 271. IV. 8-10.—*Ibid.* (4th Series), vol. iii. pp. 242, 361. IV. 8-12.—J. Clifford, *Christian World Pulpit*, vol. lv. p. 88. IV. 8-13.—T. H. Ball, *Persuasions*, p. 195. IV. 9.—*Expositor* (5th Series), vol. ii. p. 85 ; *ibid.* vol. vi. pp. 145, 334 ; *ibid.* vol. vii. p. 222. IV. 9-10.—G. Bellett, *Parochial Sermons*, p. 197. IV. 10.—W. F. Shaw, *Sermon Sketches for the Christian Year*, p. 108. J. Keble, *Sermons for Ascension Day to Trinity Sunday*, p. 114. IV. 11. —*Expositor* (6th Series), vol. v. p. 16. IV. 11, 12.—J. B. Brown, *Aids to the Development of the Divine Life*, No. vi. W. G. Horder, *Christian World Pulpit*, vol. lix. p. 110. J. Parker, *The Gospel of Jesus Christ*, p. 201. IV. 11-13.—J. Bowstead, *Practical Sermons*, vol. ii. p. 195. *Preacher's Magazine*, vol. xix. p. 35. IV. 12.—Bishop Creighton, *University and other Sermons*, p. 138.

TILL AND UNTIL

'Till we all come——.'—EPH. IV. 13.

THE immediate point is not what we are coming to, but the fact that we are coming, and that something is coming to us, and that this double action is the secret of the inspiration, the culture, the strengthening of our innermost life. The text therefore is 'till . . . until,'—the something that says, You have not finished yet ; there is another hill to climb, and then you will see it ; there is another stream to ford, and on the other bank of that stream you will see what flowers can grow, and how mean are all the plants on this side the river. Till the sunshine comes, till the heavenly band appears and sends its thundering anthem through the quivering sky ; till then, hope on ! You have not yet arrived, but you are proceeding, you are on the right road, and you have this little

singing word to cheer you in all your climbing and in all your descending and in all your fighting and in all your sorrow, 'until— !'

The keyword is till or until ; the same word, the same idea, and that idea an idea of encouragement and assurance, a word to hide in the heart and to listen to in the darkness when there seems to be no 'until,' when there seems to be but one settled frown on the brow of time. Yet the custodians of God's decrees, the Divinely appointed priests of the eternal ark, are enabled to hear the sweet word 'until,' and such men, unknown, mayhap despised, have kept the world alive.

I. Where does this word 'till' or 'until' occur ? Where all the great words occur, as I have told you a thousand times. Where do all the great words occur ? In the Book of Genesis ; and you have never read it ! I speak not to the few who are familiar with the Divine Word, but to the many who never read it. You do not read the Divine Word when you only read it in the letter. The Divine Word is not a letter, but a spirit ; it is not written music, but music sung and music brayed out from brass and throbbed as it were on living drums. We must go to Genesis for our first grand 'until' (chapter XLIX. 10). Jacob is dying, he knows that his life is slowly but certainly trickling away ; he calls all his sons around him, and makes such speeches as mortal man never made either before or since ; and most of you have never read them ! Never was such eloquence heard before ; there are no forged climaxes, no mechanically built periods, no half-forgotten and hesitant recitations ; but great, grand, flowing eloquence. When the patriarch came to his son Judah he waxed almost as eloquent as when he came to his son Joseph, but not altogether as eloquent. The old man was at his best when his hands as it were groped for the head of Joseph, but he was beautiful when he spake to Judah—Judah who bore an awful scar of unfaithfulness and badness, but which was much covered up, if not wholly healed, by processes of grace which only experienced souls understand. Said Jacob, 'The sceptre shall not depart from Judah, nor a lawgiver from between his feet, until Shiloh come'. There is the 'till' or the 'until,' the word of promise, the gleam of hope, the pledged morning. No man can tell us what 'Shiloh' means ; we have had the word in Hebrew and in Greek, and we have called around it a whole market-place of expositors, a whole gallery and sanhedrin of learned men, but they can make nothing really final out concerning all the wells and fountains and springs that are hidden in this word Shiloh. But there is a Christian acceptation of the term, which is sufficient for us. The ancient Jews, indeed, associated the name Messiah with the word Shiloh, and regarded them as practically interchangeable terms ; but the ancient Jews did not know Messiah as we know Him ; therefore we must attach a Christian interpretation to Shiloh, and find him in Bethlehem, and on Calvary, and on Olivet, and away yonder in the midst of the temple of intercession.

II. Another 'until' we find in Psalm LXXIII. 17, 'Until I went into the sanctuary'. Then I saw all about it. The sanctuary is the only place where you can see everything, Church or State, just as it is. You see nothing really until you see it from the point of the altar. The religious soul, the soul that bathes itself in the stream of the Divine wisdom and the Divine light, is the greatest soul under heaven.

III. We might call on our way in the house of Canticles, the house of the love-dreams, and there in chapter II. 17 we shall read, 'Until the day break and the shadows flee away'. That is a grand 'until'. Is it possible that the sun can find his way through all the grey cold clouds of December? Is there a day promised? Will the day break? Who ever heard the gates of the morning creak as they swung 'ack on their golden hinges? Who ever heard a cramping army bringing up the sun as if by strength of muscle? Who ever heard the stars make a noise? Yet through all this wondrous process of the suns there is a silent march, a silent incoming of the Messianic period, and when the day breaks upon the grave, the grave shall be as a cradle; and when the day breaks on sorrow and sickness, failure, disappointment, and manifold misery, we shall see the whole sphere of life in its proper colours, relations, and proportions, and find that God has been busy in the darkness. God does wonderful things in the night time; what He has done in the sanctuary of densest darkness we shall never know till the shadows flee away; then we shall find that all the while He has been building a palace for us, a right glorious and royal house, and making things ready for our souls away beyond the humble paths of the stars which now we think a long way off, but we shall think them a longer way off still when we get above them and look down on them with a kind of gracious contempt of their twinkling and quivering lamps. Hope on! There is a word in the wintry air, a song in the wintry night—'Until!'

IV. Paul's idea of 'until' was a coming to the measure of the stature of perfect men in Christ Jesus. Perfect does not mean what it is often supposed to mean and what people get up more or less futile and senseless meetings for the purpose of promoting. There are no perfect men in that narrow sense. There is probably no sin greater in its possible implications than sinlessness as it is narrowly and imperfectly understood. Not until resurrection has done for the body what regeneration has done for the soul shall we know the meaning of 'perfect' in its moral and spiritual sense. Meanwhile, it may signify the culmination of a new period, the advancement, chapter after chapter, of a new book, promotion after promotion to school after school in the higher academies of creation; it may mean as much as can be done here and now, but not perfection except as the end is the beginning of another period. The Bible ends, Revelation can only begin.—JOSEPH PARKER, *City Temple Pulpit*, vol. II. p. 252.

THE PERFECT MAN

'Till we all come in the unity of the faith, and of the knowledge of the Son of God, unto a perfect man, unto the measure of the stature of the fulness of Christ.'—EPH. IV. 13.

CHRIST gave His gifts to men that they might grow up to be men, and reach that perfect manhood in which there is no error or infirmity.

I. The body has to be seen to if we would be perfect men; an unhealthy body is a great hindrance.

II. The full and free use of all our intellectual powers, whatever they may be, is necessary to the attainment of the perfect manhood.

III. Above all, we must see to the complete development of our moral nature.—W. C. SMITH, *The Scottish Review*, vol. VII. p. 443.

REFERENCES.—IV. 13.—C. Perren, *Sermon Outlines*, p. 313. H. J. C. Knight, *The Record*, vol. xxvii. p. 2. T. G. Bonney, *Church Family Newspaper*, vol. xv. p. 940. Bishop King, *The Love and Wisdom of God (A Sermon for Railway Men)*, p. 186. R. J. Drummond, *Faith's Certainties*, p. 275. W. L. Watkinson, *The Fatal Barter*, p. 177. *Expositor* (6th Series), vol. xi. p. 148. A. Maclaren, *Expositions of Holy Scripture—Ephesians*, p. 216. IV. 13, 14.—*Ibid.* (5th Series), vol. v. p. 31. IV. 13-15.—*Ibid.* (4th Series), vol. i. p. 198.

DOCTRINAL FICKLENESS

'That we henceforth be no more children tossed to and fro, and carried about with every wind of doctrine.'—EPH. IV. 14.

I. THE Apostle suggests to us a grave impediment to religious growth. 'That we henceforth be no more children.' (1) The words before us imply that doctrinal fickleness is inconsistent with advanced religious life. It is the symptom of childishness, a state that must be outgrown before the standard of Christ can be in any sense reached. We smile at the tastes of those eccentric orientals who have brought themselves to admire a cramped foot and tottering gait in their women, and yet there is a sphere in which some of us show a taste as perverted as that. We praise faith in proportion to the crippled daintiness of its foothold and the diameter of the oscillations it describes in its clumsy effort at progress. With some people, doctrinal fickleness is the fashionable trick that stamps a man a member of the higher coteries of culture. (2) The Apostle traces back the diverse teaching that issues in doctrinal inconstancy to the loose moral conditions of the society in which his readers lived.

II. The conditions of religious growth are suggested in the words before us. 'But speaking the truth in love.' Alford translates, 'Being followers of the truth'; and Ellicott, 'Holding the truth in love'. It is only in the sphere of the renewed affections that the perception of truth in its ultimate certainties is possible. Do not hanker too anxiously after scientific verification for the highest religious truth. The highest spiritual truth can only be known through spiritualised affections. The touchstone of truth is its power of promoting moral growth, and little moral growth seems possible to us away from the atmosphere of Divine love diffused through the ministries of the Church.

III. The standard of Christian growth. 'May grow up into Him in all things which is the Head, even Christ.' His life was spotless, and the sacrifice unwavering and absolute—a continuous daily carrying of the cross on which He died, because the faith was unclouded and steadfast. And this unclouded vision of God and of the world for which He gave Himself was received and sustained through the Spirit that descended upon Him in visible witness at His baptism, when the heavens were opened to His humanity, and the glory of the far-off wonders streamed into the nature He had received of the Virgin. The standard is put up for us in Jesus Christ. And it is this same Spirit which prepared this humanity and then inhabited it with constant light, which proceeds from Him to us, which works through the true Christian ministry in all its forms, and will, if we are followers of the truth in love, take us up even into the measure of the stature of the fulness of Christ.

EPH. IV. 14.

IN some of the typhoons that sweep the coasts of Eastern Asia, trees that are torn up by the roots not infrequently suffer less permanent injury than trees to which no visible damage has been done. I have seen a tree, blown down after it had attained a height of ten or fifteen feet, strike a new root at the summit of the old growth, and thrive again for years. Trees, on the other hand, from which scarcely a bough has been snapped, die from the mere shock their sensitive fibres receive in the storm. I have seen men who were my contemporaries in theological study turn their backs upon the Christian ministry and become leading sceptics. The hurtling storm broke, and they were plucked up by the roots. I am not so sure that their destiny is so sad as that of other men I know, who have retained every separate article of their creed intact, but the sensitive fibres of whose faith have been so agitated by the passing controversies, that their beliefs, whilst retaining the old logical completeness, have almost ceased to be vital and operative.—T. G. SELBY, *The Imperfect Angel*, p. 119.

REFERENCES.—IV. 14.—W. B. Selbie, *Christian World Pulpit*, vol. lii. p. 294. J. Keble, *Sermons for the Saints' Days*, p. 207.

EPH. IV. 14-23.

WE are reading in Paul's Epistle to the Ephesians. It is more like walking through a forest than dallying in a garden. We must in many a case give up his grammar and acquaint ourselves with the music of his soul. Paul did not write much; when he did write he wrote as a blind man might be supposed to write, in large capital letters, saying, 'Ye see how large a letter I have written unto you with mine own hand'. Poor weak-eyed man, he could hardly see the boldest capitals which he inscribed upon his paper; and as a tired man he thought he had done more than he really had done; he thought it was

a large letter because it took so much out of him. There are many standards of measurement.

I. We have come to the fourteenth verse of the fourth chapter : 'That we henceforth be no more children, tossed to and fro, and carried about with every wind of doctrine, by the sleight of men, and cunning craftiness, whereby they lie in wait to deceive.'

Yet we must always be children. Children are so good that we baptise them; we receive them into our arms with this certificate, written in light and perfumed in the incense of the morning, 'Of such is the kingdom of God,' and we baptise them with the dew of the morning. Yet we must in another sense no longer be children, we must not tarry in the cradle; he would be a monster, not a man, who at thirty years of age still needed to be rocked to sleep in his cradle. It is in these things that we are not to be children; not in the child-sense, the childlike sense, the little clinging, trustful child-sense; always that; in that sense the heavens are full of cradles. To God we must always be beginning; to the Infinite we must always be little sparklets, mere specks and blossoms of things, holding within us great and solemn possibilities. In another sense we are not to be childish, foolish, receiving instruction and letting it fall out of the mind as soon as it gets into it; in that sense let us be no more children, tossed to and fro, carried about by every wind; that is the children's little game, and for children it is natural and it is pleasant.

II. Look what an image of human nature is given in these words—'alienated from the life of God.' The whole of the eighteenth verse is a great nocturne, it is a picture struck out of a cloud, it is a statue hewn out of sevenfold midnight. 'Having the understanding darkened, being alienated from the life of God through the ignorance that is in them.' 'Alienated from the life of God'—O how shall we represent that isolation, that desolated orphanage? Shall we imagine a tree taking its roots out of the earth and placing itself upon the face of a rock that it may have no more connection with the soil?—for the soil is full of light, the soil is full of dew; though there be no rain on the surface, there is dew at the core. We dig down to dew, and in all the strata through which we dig we are cutting sunshine to pieces; the earth is a store of morning, a gallery piled with sunshine. Shall we imagine the poor tree saying, I will have none of it, I will tear myself out of this place, and instead of seeking to plant myself in another part of the soil I will lay myself down on the rock and turn my roots to the morning sun? It cannot be; for a day or two it may seem as though it were a possibility and even a fact, but only for a day or two; the tree must be rooted in the earth as the earth is rooted in God, where all things grow harmonically, proportionately, sympathetically, and tree waves to tree as hymn might sing to hymn. There is a dread possibility of a man taking himself out of the current of things

The soul that takes itself out of the appointed currents shall die. Many persons are trying to live without God; they are alienated from the life of God through the ignorance that is in them. They do not know that other people are praying for them, they do not understand the philosophy of intercession. We know not who may be praying for us in the general assembly and Church of the firstborn; but we know that Jesus Christ Himself ever liveth to make intercession for us.

In the nineteenth verse there is an expression more terrible, if possible, than we have yet come upon. 'Past feeling.' Read the whole verse: 'Who being past feeling have given themselves over unto lasciviousness, to work all uncleanness with greediness'. 'Past feeling.' Is not he past feeling who for thirty years has heard the Gospel preached with simplicity and pathos and power, and is to-day a worm of the earth, a groveller in the mud? 'Past feeling': the spring comes without being hailed and saluted, and the summer is allowed to pass by without a smile of recognition, and the golden autumn is only regarded as a contribution to the market-place, and all the jewellery of frost and all the spotless linen of the mountain snow go for nothing, because he who was made in the image and likeness of God has lost sensibility and power of response to all poetic and ideal and spiritual appeals.

III. In all this magnificent portrayal of human nature there are top-lights, half-lights, bright lights, gleamings above the brightness of the sun. For example, Paul talks about coming 'into a perfect man'. He will not despair at all the rubbish which he has been portraying and pathetically describing; he sees the possibility of growth. A perfect man means a mature man, a full-grown man who has reached the highest inch of his possible stature, not a perfect man in any merely sentimental and pietistic sense, but full grown. The orchard is perfect when the apples are ready for plucking; the acres are perfect when the golden grain swings in the gentle breeze, and says without words, I am ready to be cut down and to be turned into bread.

And what a beautiful expression we find in the fifteenth verse—'speaking the truth in love': truthing it in love, doing everything in love; growing up into Him in all things in love; finding our duty in love. If we lose this power of love we cannot do any duty, we cannot be our best selves. It is motive that gives a man the true self-possession.—JOSEPH PARKER, *City Temple Pulpit*, vol. II. p. 210.

'Speaking the truth in love.'—EPH. IV. 15.

AFTER Macaulay had published his article in the *Edinburgh Review* on Gladstone's ecclesiastical views, the latter wrote a letter to him, containing the following words: 'In those lacerating times one clings to everything of personal kindness in the past, to husband it for the future; and, if you will allow me, I shall earnestly desire to carry with me such a recollection of your mode of dealing with a subject upon which the attainment of truth, we shall agree, so materially depends upon the temper in which the search for it is instituted and conducted'.

'May grow up into Him.'—EPH. IV. 15.

IN his *Apologia* (ch. I.), speaking of Thomas Scott's writings, Newman says that for years he used 'almost as proverbs what I considered to be the scope and issue of his doctrine, "Holiness rather than peace," and "growth the only evidence of life"'.

REFERENCES.—IV. 15.—A. S. Ray, *Penny Pulpit*, No. 1679, p. 471. W. P. Balfern, *Lessons from Jesus*, p. 143. W. M. Sinclair, *Simplicity in Christ*, p. 27. H. P. Liddon, *Sermons on Some Words of St. Paul*, p. 215. W. G. Horder, *Christian World Pulpit*, vol. xlviii. p. 365. W. G. Rutherford, *The Key of Knowledge*, p. 40. IV. 15, 16.—Spurgeon, *Sermons*, vol. xlv. No. 2653. J. Denney, *Christian World Pulpit*, vol. lii. p. 312. J. Barker, *Plain Sermons*, p. 1. J. B. Lightfoot, *Cambridge Sermons*, p. 172.

THE CHURCH, THE BODY OF CHRIST

'Christ: from whom the whole body fitly joined together and compacted by that which every joint supplieth, according to the effectual working in the measure of every part, maketh increase of the body unto the edifying of itself in love.'—EPH. IV. 16.

I. THE Church itself is spoken of in terms that suggest both the inter-adaptation and cohesion of its parts. As in the natural body there is no friction between the several members, but all work smoothly together, so it is in the body of Christ. Different gifts are not to be ranged in rivalry, as though each existed irrespectively of the rest, and with a view to independent ends. Each contributes in its own way to the efficiency of the whole, so that none can be suppressed or unduly discouraged without the general good being a sufferer thereby. Moreover, each in itself is incomplete, and depends upon others for producing its full and appropriate effect, as musical notes only attain their maximum of expression in harmonious combinations.

II. The sole source of the Church's life is Christ. All Christians admit that from Christ originally every gift and quickening influence proceeds. The points of difference appear when you begin to ask about the means through which these are conveyed. The great thing is to keep in mind that it is to Christ Himself in the last resort we must be indebted, and that anything connected with the Church is serviceable to us just in so far as it brings us into connection with Him. For what is true of the whole Church is also true of its individual members; and, indeed, only becomes true of her by being true of them. It is by that which every joint supplies, by the contact of souls each with its living Lord, that she is fitly joined together and compacted.

III. St. Paul here describes the manner of the Church's growth. It is harmonious, according to the working in due measure of each several part. As the excessive growth of any one limb disfigures the body and impairs its general usefulness, so the undue cultivation of any special gift, or the over-accentuation of any particular doctrines, will lead to a one-sided development of the Church's activity and life. In order to advance there must be some sort of equilibrium and unity of movement. Growth is not growth when, in a complex organism, it only involves a part of the whole. It is simply a process of malformation. In like manner extreme developments of ritualism or extreme protests against it : exclusive devotion to one favourite truth, without paying attention to others that counterbalance and correct it ; an absorbing pursuit of one kind of excellence or usefulness—contribute not to the strength but to the weakness of the Church. Lastly, St. Paul sets before us the god or aim of the Church's growth : that it may edify itself in love. But remember that the love to which St. Paul refers is not merely a sentiment or feeling of fervour. He speaks of that grace which is the fulfilling of the law, and synonymous with the bearing of one another's burdens.—C. MOINET, *The Great Alternative and Other Sermons*, p. 247.

REFERENCES.—IV. 16.—W. M. Sinclair, *Words from St. Paul's*, p. 113. *Expositor* (4th Series), vol. ii. p. 41.

THE CHRISTIAN LIFE

'Walk not as other Gentiles walk.'—EPH. IV. 17.
'I . . . beseech you that ye walk worthy of the vocation wherewith ye are called.'—EPH. IV. 1.

I. WHO is it that makes this appeal ? It is St. Paul, one of the most majestic figures in the history of God's work in the world, who has heard the call and made himself a faithful answer to it. We must remember that St. Paul was now in prison, and so far from his condition of imprisonment, so far from that withholding him or checking him in the mighty work to which he had been called, and in his faithfulness to that call, indeed, we may say that, as a matter of history, it only emboldened him, made him more brave, made him persevere, made him cling the more, made him full of living, earnest zeal and charity towards his fellow-men. Yes, we see that, if we look below the surface, God's power does not work in the tossing of the storm, or in the devouring power of fire, or in the violence of earthquakes; it is rather in the still small Voice. And so it was in that small Voice, so to speak, within his state of imprisonment, that St. Paul's power was increased, and it was from that state of imprisonment in Rome that he, as it were, captured the whole world for Christ at all times.

II. 'I beseech you.' There is his earnest appeal. He has done it himself ; he has listened to the call and obeyed it to the utmost, to the abandoning of everything in the world which his lower ambitions pointed to. Everything he sacrificed to this great call of Heaven, and he lived the life afterwards in entire obedience to the Lord. Well, there is the one who appeals to us, and to this appeal we all ought to listen. What is it he points to ? It is the calling of the Christians to God's service. He remembered that call from Heaven—'Saul, Saul, why persecutest thou Me ?' First of all, that call from above comes

home to every soul who listens to Heaven's inspiration ; and then the life which follows that call, the obedience for which that call asks. 'Follow Me,' not merely 'Listen to Me,' but 'Follow Me'. There is the calling of the Christian first, and then his life, the life of service, the life of unselfishness, the life of the love of heavenly things, the life of faith, of true purity and self-abandonment, following Jesus Christ, following on in the way of your own salvation, following on in the noble work of uplifting man from his state of sin and death, helping God in the great cause of the regeneration of the world—this is the calling of the Christian, this is what God wants. Every one of us, old and young, rich and poor, has to go to Him, and live His life, and join in His splendid work for the salvation of mankind.

III. Then St. Paul follows on to give some marks of the Christian life. 'With all lowliness and meekness.' Are not these two of the Beatitudes ? 'Blessed are the poor in spirit.' What is that but lowliness and humbleness of mind, the conquest and the putting out of our hearts of all boastful intentions, all envy and jealousy of others ? And then, again, meekness. Is not that another of the Beatitudes ? 'Blessed are the meek ; for they shall inherit the earth.' The quiet ones, who do not use the sword, who turn from fleshly weapons to the weapons of the Spirit—these are the ones who win the world and inherit the world. St. Paul has another mark of the Christian soul, 'longsuffering,' the longsuffering which is the virtue contrary to impatience, putting up with things which are contrary, crosses which have to be borne, difficulties which have to be met, temptations which have to be fought, going on perseveringly, unyieldingly, putting faith in God and going on with the battle for God's sake, because God can never fail, and if you belong to God He will not let you finally be vanquished. 'Forbearing one another in love.' Instead of these impatient and quick condemnations of others, these quick and hard judgments bestowed upon others, these unkind thoughts which spring so readily into our minds, this forbearance, forbearing one another, holding yourself in, checking yourself when some angry or unkind and uncharitable thought arises— here is another mark of the Christian soldier, of him or her who is true to the vocation and calling. 'Forbearing one another in love,' because we are all one body. Then he passes to that fifth mark of the Christian — faithfulness to the Christian calling, charity, the Spirit of unity. Then he ends by reminding us what is the real underlying bond to which we are called, and to which we in duty ought to try to be true—our Lord, because we are all one. So he ends this part of the appeal by speaking of the great unities of God.

IV. Look over the world, look above the world into the millions of the stars of the Heavens, look back over the centuries which have passed, and there seems sometimes to be an enormous, endless variety of change. But it all goes back to the One great Author, and Creator, and Lord of all. Or, look again at the different human beings, their different talents, tastes, and places of living, and ages of living. How different they all are, what an individuality! And yet God calls all men into the mystical body. You ought to be one in spirit, full of love, charity, and forbearance, and humble towards all men because you belong to one body, comprising different conditions, gifts, works, states of life, but one body.

REFERENCES.—IV. 17.—H. J. Wilmot-Buxton, *Sunday Sermonettes for a Year*, p. 196. IV. 17-19. *Expositor* (6th Series), vol. xi. p. 201. IV. 17-32.—E. J. Kennedy, *Old Theology Re-stated*, p. 111. IV. 19.—O. Bronson, *Sermons*, p. 149. *Expositor* (5th Series), vol. vi. p. 203 ; *ibid.* (6th Series), vol. v. p. 218. IV. 20.—J. Vaughan, *Fifty Sermons* (9th Series), p. 145. *Expositor* (6th Series), vol. iii. p. 118.

CHRIST OUR LESSON AND OUR TEACHER

' But ye have not so learned Christ : if so be that ye have heard Him, and have been taught in Him.'—EPH. IV. 20, 21.

THE words which I have selected as my text are but a fragment of a closely concatenated whole, but I may deal with them separately. They lay, as it seems to me, the basis for all Christian conduct.

I. Christ our Lesson and Christ our Teacher. The relation of the person of Jesus Christ to all that He has to teach and reveal to the world is altogether different from that of all other teachers of all sorts of truths, to the truth which they proclaim. You can accept the truths and dismiss into oblivion the men from whom you got them. But you cannot reject Christ and take Christianity. (1) Christ our Lesson—The sum of all duty, the height of all moral perfectness, the realised ideal of humanity is in Christ, and the true way to know what a man or a nation is to do is to study Him. (2) Christ our Teacher—The conception of Christ as a teacher which is held by many who deny His redeeming work and dismiss as incredible His Divinity seems to me altogether inadequate, unless it be supplemented by the belief that He now has and exercises the power of communicating wisdom and knowledge and warning and stimulus to waiting hearts. Reverence the inward monitor.

II. The Condition of Learning the Lesson and Hearing the Teacher. Unless we keep ourselves in union with Jesus Christ His voice will not be heard in our hearts, and the lesson will pass unlearned. If we would keep ourselves, by faith, by love, by meditation, by aspiration, by the submission of the will, and by practical obedience, in Jesus Christ, enclosed in Him, as it were—then, and then only, shall we hear Him speak. What does a student in a school of design do? He puts his feeble copy of some great picture beside the original, and compares it touch for touch, line for line, shade for shade, and so corrects its errors. Take your lines to the Exemplar in that fashion, and go over them bit by bit.

III. The Test and Result of having Learned the Lesson and Listened to the Teacher is Unlikeness to Surrounding Corruption. It is just as needful as ever it was, though in different ways, for Christians to exhibit unlikeness to the world. I do not want you to make yourselves singular. A Christian man's unlikeness to the world consists a great deal more in doing or being what it does not do and is not, than in not doing or being what it does and is.—A. MAClAREN, *Christ's Musts*, p. 137.

REFERENCES.—IV. 20, 21.—Spurgeon, *Sermons*, vol. xlvii. No. 2719. A. Maclaren, *Expositions of Holy Scripture—Ephesians*, p. 224. IV. 20-24.—J. J. Blunt, *Plain Sermons*, p. 64. J. Budgen, *Parochial Sermons*, vol. ii. p. 1. IV. 21.—W. F. Adeney, *Christian World Pulpit*, vol. lii. p. 84. A. P. Stanley, *Canterbury Sermons*, p. 45. *Penny Pulpit*, No. 1573, p. 215. IV. 22.—*Expositor* (4th Series), vol. i. p. 202 ; *ibid.* vol. iii. p. 138. A. Maclaren, *Expositions of Holy Scripture—Ephesians*, p. 233.

UNCLOTHED AND CLOTHED UPON
EPH. IV. 22, 24.

THE great lesson for Christian people, which tests the reality of their discipleship, is this double exhortation, ' put off the old . . . put on the new '.

I. The actual self, which must be got rid of. This old self has for its characteristic that it is governed by, shaped by lust. Paul's notion of 'the lusts of the flesh' includes not only gluttony and drunkenness and uncleanness of other sorts, but also the most purely mental desires ; such as ambition and love of fame. (1) The Apostle's next thought is : these desires are liars. And is not that true? What does it mean that men have got two names for almost all sorts of vices ; one of which they apply to their own sins, one which they keep for other people's? Why is licentiousness called ' sowing wild oats '? why is miserliness called ' prudence '? (2) And then, says the Apostle, these desires which lie make the man that obeys them steadily progressive in corruption. So many a life very fair in external appearance is really in its depths rotting away by self-indulgence, corrupting with ' lusts of deceit '.

II. The new self which may be put on. As deceit is the characteristic of the one, so truth is the origin and source of the other. The Apostle suggests by these characteristics the motives for, and the possibility of realising this magnificent ideal, and being renewed in ourselves by a new self. So then here are the thoughts which he thus packs together. (1) A Divine creative act in Jesus Christ is ready to give to every one of us a real new self and a new life straight from God. (2) This possible new life will be fashioned after the Divine likeness. It is created after God, instead of being moulded by the pressure of these earth-born and earth-desiring lusts. The true likeness of man to God, which is lost in man's sin, lies in his moral nature, his love of good, his hatred of evil.

III. Our double task—put off, put on. We must daily not only be thwarting our inclinations, for that is a poor affair, but be getting rid of the inclinations themselves. You cannot destroy the desires, but you can divert them. Make a new bed for the river, and the old bed will soon be left dry.—A. MACLAREN, *Christ's Musts*, p. 148.

REFERENCES.—IV. 22-24.—F. J. A. Hort, *Village Sermons* (2nd Series), p. 89. IV. 23, 24.—*Expositor* (5th Series), vol.

x. p. 200.　IV. 24.—W. H. Evans, *Sermons for the Church's Year*, p. 212.　*Expositor* (6th Series), vol. iii. p. 122.　A. Maclaren, *Expositions of Holy Scripture—Ephesians*, p. 247.

THE GREAT HUMAN BROTHERHOOD

'For we are members one of another.'—EPH. IV. 25.

THE words mean that each individual of the human race is related to every other, just as the several organs and limbs of our body are related.　The assertion is usually made of those who are united to Christ by faith, as if they were one, the connected parts of one body.　Here, however, the truth is given a wider range.　It is applied to every man's neighbour, and if we ask 'Who is my neighbour'? the answer is given in a certain parable which we are not likely to forget.　The Apostle is repeating here one of his favourite thoughts, a thought insisted upon in one Epistle after another, and expressed in a variety of ways : 'None of us liveth to himself'; 'There is one family in heaven and earth'.　Each life is part and parcel of the larger universal life.　Humanity is one bundle strung together by its Creator.

Now this was one of the greatest strides which human thought ever made.　When St. Paul saw and announced this truth he lifted himself two thousand years and more ahead of his own generation.　Let me remind you of some of its applications—how it is true both in the particular and the universal, affecting us in things near and in things remote. 'We are members one of another.'

I. It is exemplified in the home circle.　*There* we get our elementary lessons in it, and learn to understand its wider applications in the world outside.　God teaches us all the rudiments of religion in that primary school.　A well-ordered Christian home gives us the truest picture that we can find on earth of the heaven above.　In the tender love of parents we get our first and best conceptions of the Divine Fatherhood, and in the pains and burdens which a mother suffers for her child is the everlasting type of that vicarious principle which is seated and enthroned in the very heart and government of God.　Around the fireside, on the domestic hearth, we are for ever unconsciously weaving the 'pattern of things in the mount'.

II. This principle is enforced in every aspect of Church life.

The Church is the household of God, subject to the same common impulses, movements, and conditions as an ordinary home.　In moral and spiritual things, especially, we are bound intimately together.　We share out our gifts, and he who climbs to the mountain-tops of faith draws others after him.　Everywhere in the religious life there are these mighty currents of sympathetic feeling and action.　We are carried forward and backward together on the same flowing and ebbing waves.

III. And now I ask you to take the words in their widest range.　They are true of the greater world outside the Church, true of the nation and of the whole human family.　We are constantly having the fact brought home to us that all souls are God's, and therefore ours ; that humanity is one, that all sections, classes, communities, and races are governed, swayed, or affected in varying degrees by the same forces, influences, agencies, and movements.　The world is joined by sympathetic cords.　Railways, ships, and electric cables are all helping to reveal to us God's thought of His one family.　He maketh the winds His angels, His messengers flaming fire, and all events, when rightly understood, enforce the Gospel truth that 'He hath made of one blood all nations of men'.　'We are members one of another.'—J. G. GREENHOUGH, *The Mind of Christ in St. Paul*, p. 107.

REFERENCES.—IV. 25.—E. McClure, *A Lent in London*, p. 10.　J. G. Greenhough, *Christian World Pulpit*, vol. liii. p. 154.　J. J. Blunt, *Plain Sermons* (3rd Series), p. 146.　*Expositor* (6th Series), vol. x. p. 366 ; *ibid.* vol. xi. p. 282.

EPH. IV. 26.

ANGER kept till the next morning, with manna, doth putrefy and corrupt. . . . St. Paul saith *Let not the sun go down upon your wrath*, to carry news to the antipodes in another world of thy revengeful nature.　Yet let us take the Apostle's meaning rather than his words, with all possible speed to depose our passion ; not understanding him literally, so that we may take leave to be angry till sunset ; then might our wrath lengthen with the days, and even in Greenland, where day lasts above a quarter of a year, have plentiful scope for revenge.　And as the English ; by command from William the Conqueror, always raked up their fires and put out their candles, when the curfew-bell was rung, let us then also quench all sparks of anger and heat of passion.—THOS. FULLER.

THE falling of a tea-cup puts us out of temper for a day ; and a quarrel that commenced about the pattern of a gown may end only with our lives.—HAZLITT, *Winterslow* (ch. VII.).

EPH. IV. 26.

'CALL for the grandest of all earthly spectacles,' says de Quincey (*Confessions of an Opium-Eater*), 'what is *that*?　It is the sun going to his rest.　Call for the grandest of all human sentiments, what is *that*?　It is, that man should forget his anger before he lies down to sleep.'

REFERENCES.—IV. 26.—*Christianity in Daily Conduct*, p. 89.　A. Ainger, *Sermons Preached in the Temple Church*, p. 166.　*Expositor* (4th Series), vol. ix. p. 100 ; *ibid.* (5th Series), vol. ix. p. 442 ; *ibid.* (6th Series), vol. i. p. 197 ; *ibid.* vol. xi. p. 142.　IV. 28.—*Ibid.* vol. iii. p. 277.　IV. 29.—A. Bradley, *Sermons Chiefly on Character*, p. 20.　*Expositor* (6th Series), vol. xii. p. 63.

GRIEVE NOT THE SPIRIT

'Grieve not the Holy Spirit of God.'—EPH. IV. 30.

How sad it is to grieve a friend !　But to grieve the best of friends, Who never, never has misrepresented to us the love of God and the possibility of our own lives, but Whom we so often grieve in ways that must not be forgotten, this indeed seems more than sad, more than culpable. I speak then of three simple ways that we are to avoid by which we might be grieving the Holy Spirit of God.

I. By Lack of Christian Charity.—We do so often forget that through want of love to the brethren we are grieving that Spirit of God Who is the Spirit of love. Selfishness no doubt is at the root of our want of love to the brethren. And not only selfishness but that narrowness of spirit which prevents one seeing the good in others and from realising that Christ is leading them on perhaps quite as much as He is leading us on, and therefore that love to the brethren ought to be extended far wider than we are accustomed to allow it to extend; we are to take care that we love others no less than we believe God the Father, God the Son, and God the Holy Ghost must love them. Beware, then, of want of love to the brethren.

II. By Wilfully Indulged Sin.—'If any man defile the temple of God, him shall God destroy.' And can we forget that any wilfully indulged sin, any allowance of ourselves in ways that we know instinctively, intuitively, must grieve the Spirit of God, ought *never* to be followed for a single instant. Loyalty to the laws of God, loyalty and obedience to those plain laws written upon our hearts, which God has implanted within us, must necessarily be obeyed. Beware, then, that no word of yours ever is allowed to raise evil thoughts in the minds of others or to do them harm. Beware that no thoughts are allowed to be cherished for a moment in your breast which might lead you in any way to defile the temple of God and to grieve that gracious Spirit; but rather determine that in sincerity and openness of heart and mind, in singleness of aim, with a clear purpose to do that which is right in the sight of God, you are indeed pure-hearted and striving to do that which Christ has taught you to do in all things.

III. By Distrust of the Love of God.—He calls us His children; He has done all things on purpose to bring us into union and harmony with Himself; He bids us by the Spirit that He gives us look up to Him and call Him, 'Abba, Father'; and how it must grieve Him when after all we distrust that love of God, when we think that somehow things must be wrong with God, and that He is not watching over and caring for us, instead of feeling that our own hearts are out of gear, that the machinery will not work because we have allowed it to become clogged with evil or have not in any way used it aright. And the same gracious Spirit brings us back to God, and therefore must there be the constant prayer from us that He would return to us if we have driven Him away, so that we by His power may return again to our God.

'Grieve not the Holy Spirit of God, whereby ye are sealed unto the day of redemption.'—EPH. IV. 30.

THE Church at Ephesus was regarded by St. Paul as a model of the Church universal. But he does not lose sight of its failures. The world, and Satan, and the flesh are opposed to it, and therefore abuses and disorders arose in it. St. Paul warns its members against these evils, and then reminds them of their duties and privileges.

I. A Strict Prohibition.—'Grieve not the Holy Spirit of God.' The Holy Spirit is the crown of Divine gifts; and His high office is to take of the things of Christ and show them unto His redeemed. For these reasons He must not be grieved by them; but, alas! they do grieve Him. How?

(a) *By neglecting the monitions of conscience.*—The conscience is God's vicegerent and our monitor—the light within us, just as the sun is the light without us. If the conscience then is unheeded or silenced, the Holy Spirit, Who works immediately and necessarily with it, is disappointed and grieved, because it is no longer available to His blessed influence and power.

(b) *By substituting material for spiritual religion.* Many were guilty of this in apostolic days, and St. Paul had often to guard the spiritually minded against this evil. Witness his Epistles to Timothy. Does the same necessity exist now? Professing Christians are found everywhere departing from the simplicity of the Christian faith. What follows? Doubts, declensions, falls. Such turning away from the faith, with all its accompanying mischiefs, must grieve the Holy Spirit.

(c) *By trifling with the sacred things of God.* The Bible is sacred, so is the Sabbath, so is the temple, and so are Divinely-appointed ordinances. If the Book of books is left unread, or read with indifference, as if it were only a human composition or a fable; if the Sabbath—'the pearl of days'—is devoted to carnal pleasure instead of the glory of 'the Lord of the Sabbath'; if the sanctuary is entered with irreverence instead of awe; and if religious ordinances are performed without 'the unction of the Holy One'—all this is trifling with the sacred things of God, and the Holy Spirit is grieved.

II. A Gracious Privilege.—'Whereby'—or in Whom—'ye were sealed unto the day of redemption.' All Christians are sealed with an immovable royal seal, which bears on it the image and superscription of Christ, and this seal is none other than the Holy Spirit Himself.

(a) *His sealing declares Christians to be the property of God.* Christ redeemed them for Himself, and God has accepted them from Him.

(b) *His sealing consecrates them for the service of God.* 'For ye are bought with a price,' says St. Paul; 'therefore glorify God in your body and spirit, which are God's.' We may always be serving God, and this service of God is the sole thing which makes life desirable and momentous. Business is weariness; pleasure is vanity; ambition is disappointment; but the service of God is blessedness.

(c) *His sealing makes them sure for the day of God.* It is not for this life only, but for that which is to come. It expands to the day when God Himself will display His glory in noontide splendour: the day of days, which will never be darkened by night.

GRIEVING THE SPIRIT

'Grieve not the Holy Spirit, whereby ye are sealed unto the day of redemption.'—EPH. IV. 30.

THERE seems to be something touching in the exhortation, because, you know, you can only grieve a friend; you cannot grieve an enemy. You may anger an enemy, but it is only our friend that we grieve. Therefore, remember that this exhortation reminds you of the love of the spirit. 'Grieve not the Holy Spirit of God.'

I. Why is He Grieved?—(1) Because of His own character, because He is holy. Can you imagine what it is for the Holy Spirit to live in a sin-stained world? We can understand how, when our Lord Jesus Christ was upon earth enduring that contradiction of sinners against Himself, He must often have sighed as he saw the sin and suffering round about Him. So the Holy Spirit is grieved because He is holy. (2) And then the Holy Spirit is grieved for our sins. (3) The Holy Spirit is grieved because every sin on the part of the Christian is a stumbling-block to others.

II. How do You Grieve Him?—Well, here in this chapter he suggests four ways. (1) In the first place, in the nineteenth verse, by acts of sins. O Christian, remember, your body is the temple of the Holy Ghost. What a sanctifying influence that should have! (2) Then, in the twenty-fifth verse, by untruthfulness. Put away all lying, and grieve not the Holy Spirit of God. (3) Lastly, by sins of the tongue. All evil speaking is hateful to the spirit of God. If there is one prayer which you ought to pray with all your soul, it should be this: 'O God, take not Thy Holy Presence from me!'—E. A. STUART, *The Divine Presence and other Sermons*, vol. VI. p. 89.

REFERENCES.—IV. 30.—Spurgeon, *Sermons*, vol. v. No. 278, and vol. xiii. No. 738. W. F. Shaw, *Sermon Sketches for the Christian Year*, p. 86. F. V. Dodgson, *The Record*, vol. xxvii. p. 1228. J. Martineau, *Christian World Pulpit*, vol. lii. p. 129. T. Arnold, *Christian Life: Its Hopes*, p. 193. R. W. Church, *Village Sermons* (2nd Series), p. 307. *Expositor* (6th Series), vol. iv. pp. 274, 279. A. Maclaren, *Expositions of Holy Scripture—Ephesians*, p. 262.

EPH. IV. 31.

IT is difficult to understand how some people can have the courage to be unforgiving, day after day, week after week. They go to sleep, they wake up again; they hear the birds sing; they see the sun shine upon the just and the unjust; a thousand blessings are theirs; but still they hold out and refuse their own blessing to the offenders. They hear of sorrows that can never be healed; they hear of joys befalling their fellow-men; they realise life and death, and it does not occur to them that there is no death like that of coldness and estrangement.—MISS THACKERAY.

REFERENCE.—IV. 31.—W. H. Evans, *Sermons for the Church's Year*, p. 287.

BAD TEMPER

'Let all bitterness, and wrath, and anger, and clamour, and evil speaking, be put away from you, with all malice; and be ye kind one to another, tender-hearted, forgiving one to another, even as God for Christ's sake hath forgiven you.'—EPH. IV. 31, 32.

BAD temper is a serious factor in the misery of this sombre, suffering world; and yet it is a subject to which scanty allusion is made. There is no region of human life in which bad temper does not leave its trail of unhappiness. It works quite as much pain and disaster as the graver delinquencies for which we reserve a stern reprobation.

I. Bad temper sometimes manifests itself as chronic querulousness, inbred disability for being pleased, an inclination to blame others for the mischances and mortifications of life, big and little alike. Every thorn in the wilderness becomes a grievance against the pilgrim companion, a mememto of Paradise Lost, which at once suggests the idea of making others do penance for the inferior environment which frets us. Again, it shows itself in rasping, dictatorial aggressiveness of speech and manner.

II. This unhappy frailty is often the product of a temperament highly refined and sensitised, and men and women who are the very elect of their generation are most subject to it. Slow, practical, unimaginative people escape these temptations to nervous distress and impatient outbreak. The Latin writer was dealing with a fact of common knowledge when he spoke of 'the irritable race of poets'. And the description applies to every type of the æsthetic temperament, and to every man or woman who is in any sense an idealist.

III. Hasty and ungracious temper is sometimes caused by inordinate fatigue and physical weariness. Men and women often wear themselves out, and bring their tempers to danger-point by toil, drudgery, over-pressure out of all proportion to the reserve of strength. The laws of nature should be sacred in our eyes, and bad temper is often a penalty of their infraction.

IV. Another cause of this disquieting infirmity is the impatience into which men are goaded in times of rush and urgency.

V. The deepest root of this evil is the exaggerated estimate we have of ourselves and of what is due to us. The besetment is no passing agitation of the mere surface of the life, but takes its rise in a fixed idea that we are entitled to special consideration from the world around us.

VI. The most discouraging aspect of this question is that conversion does not always effect the change in the tempers of those who are the subjects of it which we are taught to look for. The main current and thought of life is turned into right channels, but in too many cases back-eddies occur in which danger lurks, momentary retrogressions of feeling, a spasmodic upsurging of the old Adam.

VII. If this blemish is to be removed from the character, there must be the frank admission that it is sinful, and that it will yield to the methods of grace.

VIII. The Apostle teaches the remedy for every temper into which haste, bitterness, or unholy anger enters. 'And be ye kind one to another, tender-hearted, forgiving one another, even as God for Christ's sake hath forgiven you.'

THE EVANGELICAL GRACE OF TENDER-HEARTEDNESS

'Be ye kind one to another, tender-hearted.'—EPH. IV. 32.

I. THERE are several causes working in the world which make it a hard thing to keep the tender heart. (1) One of the commonest of all is custom. What open hearts we had when heaven lay about us in our infancy ! But now, we are dulled down a little ; we are less sensitive, less eager, less receptive ; and one inevitable peril of all that is the peril of ceasing to be tender-hearted.

(2) Another enemy of this same grace is the fierce struggle which many have to live. Men say it is difficult to be true to-day ; it is equally difficult to be tender. You could hardly expect a soldier on the field to be a perfect pattern of gentleness. At home he might be that—with his own children—scarcely amid the rigours of the war. And in that city-battle of to-day which we disguise with the name of competition, a man must be in deadly peril of losing the genius of the tender heart. In simpler communities it was not so. Life was easier in simpler communities. And time was longer, and men had larger leisure, and the sense of brotherhood was not quite lost. But in the city with its stress and strain, with its pressure at every point, and with its crowd, life may have the joy of growing keen, but it has also the risk of growing cruel. It is not often that the successful man is what you would call the tender-hearted man. The battle has been too terrible for that : there has been too much crushing underfoot ; and always when a man tramples upon *others*, he tramples in that hour on his own heart. Now I want you to remember that when Paul wrote to Ephesus, he wrote to a city like Glasgow or like Liverpool. He was not addressing a handful of quiet villagers. He was writing to a commercial metropolis. And that, I take it, just means this, that Paul was alive to the dangers of the city, and knew how supremely difficult it was there to keep the secret of the tender heart.

(3) But the greatest enemy of tender-heartedness is the old sad fact of sin. Sin hardens a man's heart towards his wife. It hardens a man's heart towards his children. It hardens him to the touch of human need and to the call which the world makes upon his sympathy. And that is why the grace of tender-heartedness is so conspicuously a Christian virtue—

because it betrays that conquest over sin which has been won for us in Jesus Christ.

II. I know no virtue that is oftener disguised than the virtue of which I am speaking. It is not one of the qualities of which men are proud as they are proud of courage or endurance. On the contrary, they are a little ashamed, should one suspect them of being tender-hearted. And so very often they hide it out of sight, and wrap it up in the most strange disguises, and assume a manner that is so far from gentle that it takes a little while to guess the truth. It is not always those of gentle manners who really possess the gentlest hearts. Some of the tenderest men I ever knew have had a rough, even a boisterous, exterior. They were like Mr. Boythorn in *Bleak House*, who was always for hanging somebody or other, and all the time was feeding the canary that nestled without a tremor in his hand.

III. The great secret of the tender heart lies in the fellowship of Jesus Christ. It is the continual wonder about Jesus, that He was so strong and yet so tender-hearted. No authority could make Him quail: no array of power could ever daunt Him ; and yet a bruised reed He would not break, and smoking flax He would not quench. When that mind of Christ is given by the Spirit to you and me, then whatever happens, however we are treated, we shall be kind one to another, tender-hearted.—G. H. MORRISON, *The Return of the Angels*, p. 190.

REFERENCES.—IV. 32.—Spurgeon, *Sermons*, vol. xi. No. 614, and vol. xxiv. No. 1448. J. Watson, *Christian World Pulpit*, vol. li. p. 193. F. B. Cowl, *Preacher s Magazine*, vol. xviii. p. 238. G. B. F. Hallock, *Christian World Pulpit*, vol. lv. p. 366. H. Bushnell, *Christ and His Salvation*, p. 333. J. Learmount, *British Congregationalist*, 11th July, 1907, p. 42.

THE LESSONS OF CHILDLINESS

'Be ye therefore followers of God, as dear children.'—EPH. V. I.

IT is the great mark of the Gospel that its deepest truths are presented to us in forms taken from our daily life. The cleansing water and the simple meal are made sacraments—revelations—of Divine mysteries. The ties of family are the chosen emblems of our heavenly fellowship. One of these relations is set before us in the words which I have taken for my text. We all are as children in His household, heirs, indeed of a glorious inheritance, but yet children and then nearest Him when we realise most fully our childly duties at His feet. Let us then dwell on three lessons of childliness.

I. The Lesson of Dependence.—A child never forgets his dependence. He sees before him the image of a noble future, but he makes no haste to escape from the bonds of grateful service. For he, too, has a service to render. Effort, vigour, patience, are included in all action, and the child's reward is that his work is like his father's work, or in harmony with it. And this is a just description of our position with regard to our heavenly Father.

II. The Lesson of Trustfulness.—A child has no doubts, no misgivings. It is enough that his father has spoken. He examines not the message but the credentials of the bearer. There is something sublime in such a faith, which in later years is wholly unattainable. But all human powers fall below the claims which it makes. It can be satisfied only in its spiritual aspect. There, indeed, the childly heart will find no rude disappointment. The Christian will not yet see all, but all which he sees will strengthen his trust.

III. For the lessons of dependence and trustfulness are completed in **The Lesson of Partial Knowledge.** The Christian professes that he knows in part. At present his Father knoweth all things, and when that which is in part is done away, then will he know even as he is known.—BISHOP WESTCOTT, *Village Sermons,* p. 101.

REFERENCES.—V. 1.—Spurgeon, *Sermons,* vol. xxix. No. 1725. F. Bourdillon, *Plain Sermons for Family Reading* (2nd Series), p. 45. Bishop Westcott, *Village Sermons,* p. 101. A. Maclaren, *Expositions of Holy Scripture—Ephesians,* p. 270.

TO THE DEAR CHILDREN

'Be ye therefore followers of God as dear children, and walk in love, as Christ also hath loved us.'—EPH. v. 1, 2.

THE text calls on all of us, as God's dear children, to try to follow, not our own pleasures and our own tastes, but to walk in the footsteps of Christ our Saviour. And we cannot do this without some care, and pains, and watchfulness over ourselves.

I. What are the faults, the temptations, to which you feel yourselves most liable? (1) There is, first of all, selfishness, the caring much, or the caring only for your own comfort and pleasure, and the caring not in the least, or very little for that of others. (2) Again, there is meanness; the readiness to tell an untruth, a lie, plain and direct, in order to gain something for which you wish. (3) Boastfulness. It is not the attempt to get everything for yourself, but it is the constant making yourself, not other persons, or other things—but yourself, and yourself only, the subject of all your thoughts and words. (4) Faults of temper. (5) Fits of sullenness.

II. Let me add one or two words on two different kinds of unselfishness. 'Love as brethren, be pitiful, be courteous,' says St. Peter. (1) Let me take the last first. Remember that by politeness or courtesy we mean nothing more than the showing in our outward manners, and often in little things, that we think of others, not merely of ourselves. It is not a very hard task if you go to the root of the matter—strive to be glad to make those around you happy, and you will soon learn the welcome secret of true politeness, true courtesy, and find in it no sham piece of artificial polish, but a means of making yourself near and dear, not only to others, but to your Saviour and your God. (2) And lastly, be pitiful. Never, never, let your after memory, when you grow up, be stained with recollections of cruelty. Learn to find a joy and pleasure in kindness and tender-heartedness, in making others happy, in obeying the royal law that

bids us do to others as we would have them do to us.—G. G. BRADLEY, *Christian World Pulpit,* vol. LXI. p. 20.

REFERENCES.—V. 1, 2.—J. J. Blunt, *Plain Sermons,* p. 18. Marcus Dods, *Christ and Man,* p. 25. *Expositor* (6th Series), vol. ix. p. 45. V. 1-7.—*Ibid.* vol. xii. p. 131. V. 1-14.—E. J. Kennedy, *Old Theology Re-stated,* p. 128. V. 2.—C. S. Horne, *The Soul's Awakening,* p. 83. A. Tucker, *Preacher's Magazine,* vol. xvii. p. 176. W. H. Evans, *Sermons for the Church's Year,* p. 287. W. J. Brock, *Sermons,* p. 225. *Expositor* (4th Series), vol. i. p. 230. V. 4.—A. Ainger, *Sermons Preached in the Temple Church,* p. 296. *Expositor* (6th Series), vol. xii. p. 63. V. 6.—*Expositor* (4th Series), vol. i. p. 23.

DARKNESS AND LIGHT.

'For ye were sometimes darkness, but now are ye light in the Lord: walk as children of light.'—EPH. v. 8.

I. THIS word 'darkness' is not indicative of mere dim or transient fog or inconvenient grading of light; it is a deeper, severer, ghastlier word. 'Ye were sometimes darkness,' not dark, but darkness itself, sevenfold night, yea, more than night ever was; for surely every night must have somewhere and somehow its relieving star. It was not so with you in your former state; you were living darkness, without ray or glint or beam of light, as far away from light as it is possible to be. That is a wonderful conception of human nature and of human condition before the Father of lights. You were not merely broken lights, scattered beams, that it was impossible to put together; there was no beam in you, you had never been illumined, you had never been warmed, you had never even heard of the summer of holiness; ye were simply incarnate, embodied darkness. Who could call us out of that state? What matchmaker could strike a little flash that would drive away such gloom? Where the darkness is so dense God Himself must handle the occasion, or there is nothing for it but fatal night. Sometimes we have said of a great singer, he is not musical, he is music; that is to say, he is not a merely mechanical player, a man who has got into his memory what is written in a book, but the music is in him, a well of water springing up into everlasting melody. So, reversing the picture, the Gentiles were not dark, they were darkness; unpenetrated, and but for the Divine mercy, impenetrable clouds. Occasionally we say of a man, He is not eloquent, he is eloquence, embodied, incarnate, breathing, walking, living eloquence; he has not learned something by rote, he has not recited something of which his memory is in charge, but the holy gift is moving in him like a spirit, a genius, a heavenly choir. Reverse the picture, and you have the Apostle's idea: Ye were not dark, you were darkness, the thing itself, sevenfold night; no imagination could conceive the intensity of the darkness of your condition.

II. Then the contrastive 'but'—'but now . . . light'; not partial light, not a grey light, not a mere hint of light, but as truly as you were once darkness, so truly are you now light. 'Walk as children of light.' The miracle is as great on the one side as on the other. Chaos was not partial chaos; chaos was not a mere mood or transient phase of disorder; it was utter confusion, without date, without measure, without figure, a tumultuousness and disorderliness not to be spoken of in words in any adequate sense or with any adequate fitness. Chaos is not partly order and partly confusion; the old chaos on which the Holy Spirit brooded was utter chaos, shapelessness, amorphousness, that which could not be ruled into order by any skill created; but now, since the beginning, chaos has given place to order, proportion, music, perspective, and all the apocalypse and summer of colour. That is the difference. Chaos has no history. People want to know when the creation began. They can never know it. All depends upon what you mean by creation. The thing upon which creation operated may be calculable, but the thing out of which creation took its materials may lie back, so to say, in the memory of God alone. Transfer the figure to the Christian life, and then you have first the darkness, utter dense darkness, on which moon and star never shone, not to speak of dawning light and wakening morning. Then you have light, glory, midday, points of extreme. Unless we recognise the extremity of the points we shall lose the whole movement of the miracle. Let us keep our memories well refreshed with the fact that once we were darkness; let us pity those who are in darkness still. Do not imagine for a moment that the man on the street can come into the sanctuary of God and partake of it and be as one of the called saints of heaven all in a moment. He cannot; nor can he hear the Gospel, much less understand it. He is darkness. A great mystery of movement must take place in his soul by the power of the Holy Ghost. We want again Genesis first chapter and first few verses; we want especially the Spirit brooding over the infinite night, the infinite disorder, with a view to having brought out of it proportion and harmony and rest.—Joseph Parker, *City Temple Pulpit*, vol. II. p. 220.

Reference.—V. 8.—A. Maclaren, *Expositions of Holy Scripture—Ephesians*, p. 277.

THE FRUITION OF FULLER LIFE
' The fruit of the Spirit.'—Eph. v. 9.

Abundant fruit-bearing, whether it appear in character or in service, depends on the quickening of spiritual life. Everything else is subordinate to this, although much else is to be desired. It may not seem to outsiders that success in religious work depends on this. They may attribute it to social or intellectual influences, but in so far as success is spiritual (and that alone abides) its source is not in us. Spiritual power only passes through us from above to enrich the world. We believe that spiritual life in the soul of man depends on the quickening power of the Holy Spirit, who both initiates and intensifies it. Our enjoyment of it simply depends on our fulfilling the condition laid down by the risen Christ. ' If any man open the door, we will come in to him.'

I. We are often reminded in Scripture that fruit is expected of us. I will point out a few specimens of those fruits we too seldom see in the debilitated Christian life with which we are sadly familiar. (1) Zeal for the salvation of souls has become with some professing Christians an unmeaning phrase, or at least an unpopular one, although sinners never needed more than now a Saviour from sin, from self, from pessimism, and from hell here and hereafter. Let us never forget that the world will test us by the presence or absence of this Divine fire. (2) Amid the fruitage of a fuller Christian life will be found that *love* which our Lord makes much of, and of which some of His followers think so little.

II. It remains that we should notice certain conditions on which fuller spiritual life depends. (1) Like all other life, it requires nourishment, and this we are to take, not with fitful infrequency, but constantly, as those who have been taught to pray, ' Give us this day our daily bread'. (2) Atmosphere is as important as nourishment. Children require fresh air as well as food. Even the strongest man becomes depressed and his vitality lowered if he remains long in a vitiated atmosphere; but he becomes exhilarated, shaking off gloom and brooding, when he strides onward in the bracing air of a sunny hill-side. And that is the idea suggested to my mind by the declaration of the Psalmist about the happy ' people who know the joyful sound, they shall walk all day in the light of Thy countenance'.—A. Rowland, *The Burdens of Life*, p. 157.

THE FRUIT OF THE LIGHT
' The fruit of the light is in all goodness and righteousness and. truth.'—Eph. v. 9.

I. The Light which is Fruitful.—The light of which my text speaks is not natural to men, but is the result of the entrance into their darkness of a new element. Now I do not suppose that we should be entitled to say that Paul here is formally anticipating the deep teaching of the Apostle John that Jesus Christ is 'the Light of men,' and especially of Christian men. He is here asserting that the only way by which any man can cease to be in the doleful depths of his nature, darkness in its saddest sense, is by opening his heart through faith, that into it may rush, as the light ever does where there is an opening—be it only a single tiny cranny—is made, the light which is Christ, and without Whom is darkness.

II. The Fruitfulness of this Indwelling Light.— Fruit is generally used in Scripture in a good sense. It conveys the notion of something which is the natural outcome of a vital power. And so when we talk about the light being fruitful, we are setting in a striking image the great Christian thought that if you want to get right conduct you must have renewed character.

III. The Specific Fruits which the Apostle here Dwells Upon.—They consist, says he, in all goodness and righteousness and truth. Now all these three types of excellence are apt to be separated. For the first of them—amiability, kindliness, gentleness—is apt to become too soft, to lose its grip of righteousness. Righteousness, on the other hand, is apt to become stern, and needs the softening of goodness to make it human and attractive. Truth needs kindliness and righteousness, and they need truth. He desires that each of us should try to make our own a fully developed, all-round perfection—*all* goodness and righteousness and truth. We should seek to appropriate types of excellence to which we are least inclined, as well as those which are most in harmony with our natural dispositions.—A. MACLAREN, *Christ's Musts*, p. 239.

REFERENCES.—V. 9.— R. C. Lewis, *Sermons by Welshmen*, p. 296. *Expositor* (6th Series), vol. vii. p. 279. A. Maclaren, *Expositions of Holy Scripture—Ephesians*, p. 286.

PLEASING CHRIST

' Proving what is acceptable unto the Lord.'—EPH. v. 10.

WHAT pleases Christ is the Christian's highest duty.

I. The only attitude which corresponds to our relations to Christ. How remarkable it is that this Apostle should go on the assumption that our conduct affects Him, that it is possible for us to please or displease Jesus Christ now. That loving Lord, not merely by the omniscience of His Divinity but by the perpetual knowledge and sympathy of His perfect manhood is not only cognisant of but is affected by the conduct of His professed followers here on earth. Then, surely, the only thing that corresponds to such a relationship as at present subsists between the Christian soul and the Lord is that we should take as our supreme and continual aim that ' whether present or absent, we should be well-pleasing to Him '.

II. We have here the all-sufficient guide for practical life. What is it that pleases Jesus Christ? His own likeness. And what is the likeness to Jesus Christ which it is thus our supreme obligation and our truest wisdom and perfection to bear? Well, we can put it all into two words—self-suppression and continual consciousness of obedience to the Divine will—crucify self and commune with God. But not only does this guide prove its sufficiency by reason of its comprehensiveness, but also because there is no difficulty in ascertaining what at each moment it prescribes. If a man wants to know Christ's will, and takes the way of knowing it which Christ has appointed, he shall not be left in darkness, but shall have the light of life.

III. We have here an all-powerful motive for Christian life. No motive which can be brought to bear upon men is stronger when there are loving hearts concerned than this simple one, ' Do it to please me'. And that is what Jesus Christ really says. So we have the secret of blessedness in these words. For self-submission and suppression are blessedness.—A. MACLAREN, *Christ's Musts*, p. 249.

REFERENCES.—V. 10.—A. Maclaren, *Expositions of Holy Scripture—Ephesians*, p. 295. V. 11.—*Ibid.* p. 303. Spurgeon, *Sermons*, vol. xli. No. 2401. *Expositor* (6th Series),

vol. iv. p. 205. V. 11-21.—A. Maclaren, *Expositions of Holy Scripture—Ephesians*, p. 313. V. 13, 14.—F. D. Maurice, *Sermons*, vol. iii. p. 163.

SLEEPERS, WAKE

(For Advent Sunday)

'Wherefore He saith, Awake, thou that sleepest.'— EPH. v. 14.

No eye but a man's own can gaze, almost as the eye of God, on the unveiled human heart. But when men's eyes are opened, and they have been brought to look fairly and fully on themselves; when they have entered that awful solitude in which the soul is alone with God; when they have been brought to connect their own personality with the shame and guilt of sin; when the voluble spirit of excuse is at last dumb—what follows? I know no word which will describe the result of self-revelation so briefly as 'awakenment'. The ordinary moral and spiritual condition of most men, in their common life, can only be pictured by the metaphor of sleep. There are many degrees and forms of this spiritual sleep. There is that of human feebleness, that venial imperfection to which our Lord referred when He said, 'The spirit indeed is willing, but the flesh is weak'. Then deeper and worse is the sleep of those who, though not guilty of flagrant sin, are yet absorbed in the worldly life; given up to its dissipations and trivialities; losing, for the sake of living, all that constitutes a true life. But deepest and deadliest of all is the slumber of those who have sold themselves to do evil; who work all uncleanness with greediness; who have abandoned themselves to a life of falsehood, or avarice, or drink, or sensualism, or crime. Yet so common is this sleep, in one or other of its forms, that the Scriptures are constantly striving to arouse men from its fatal torpor.

This sleep, in any of its forms, cannot and will not last for ever. In vain men may fold their hands; in vain they may cry, 'A little more sleep, a little more slumber'—they must be awakened. Either in this world or the next must come the awakenment which results from seeing ourselves as we are. Thus, then, to each one of us—either by our own repentance or with penal retribution, either here or in the world hereafter—awakenment will come.

I. It comes in different ways. 'There are those to whom it comes in storms and tempests; others it has summoned in hours of revelry and idle vanity; others have heard its "still small voice" in leisure and placid contentment; and others during seasons of sorrow and affliction, to whom tears have been the softening showers which caused the seed of heaven to take root, and spring up in the human heart.' But when it comes penally, and in the way of catastrophe, it is then an awful moment.

(1) Awakenment has its awfulness even for the best of men. 'Behold,' cried David, 'I was shapen in iniquity; and in sin did my mother conceive me' (see Job ix. 30, 31). And Peter: 'Depart from

me, for I am a sinful man, O Lord'. And Paul: 'Wretched man that I am, who shall deliver me from the body of this death?' And Augustine: 'Liberate me from a bad man—myself!' And so many others. Such are the confessions of the holiest; yet so ignorant is the world of the depth of the true soul's contrition when it sees its own sinfulness, that it has interpreted these confessions as a proof of unusual personal vileness, and not the self-reproach of souls who longed only to be pure as He is pure.

(2) But if awakenment has its awfulness for the holiest and best, what must it be to the man who, in spite of the self-revelation, still loves, and refuses to forsake, his sins? It is a tremendous moment which first reveals to a man that he, too, is hitherto a lost soul. What must be the feelings of a man who for twenty, thirty, forty, fifty years has been outwardly honest and moral, but who, suddenly held by the accelerating impulse of sins secretly cherished, forced to own to the bond to which he has set his own seal, commits a crime, and is forced to sit down amid the ruins of his own life? The man who first deviates from rectitude takes a first step toward a precipice; and he soon finds that to stand still is impossible, that to retreat would be ruin, and that to advance is destruction.

II. How terrible the awakenment when nothing of the sin is left but the ruin it has wrought; when the man realises that the beautiful life God gave him has been lost and wasted; that he has been an utter and inexcusable fool; that it had been better for him that he had not been born—in that moment the man must know what Christ meant by the 'outer darkness,' the 'worm that dieth not,' and the 'fire that is not quenched'. And yet it is a most blessed thing for any man if that awakenment—so he neglect it not—comes during life; yea, even if it comes in the very hour of death. But remember how much more often death ends not in contrition, therefore not in repentance, but in dull torpor or hard defiance.

III. Has not Christ died for us?—died to save us and all mankind? He offers us peace here and beyond the grave; and not to us only, but to all who believe in His name. All that we have to do is to trust Him; to seek Him now—now—in the accepted time; to love one another; to work for Him; to obey His laws; to spread His kingdom. If, happily for us, the awakenment from the dream of sin have come, not in terror and as with the thunder-clap, but through 'still small voices,' let us seek to make those voices heard by others. And let us, while there is yet time, pray: 'God be merciful to me a sinner'; 'That it may please Thee to have mercy upon all men; we beseech Thee to hear us, good Lord'.—F. W. Farrar, *Sermons in America*.

CHRIST THE LIGHT-GIVER

'Wherefore He saith, Awake, thou that sleepest, and arise from the dead, and Christ shall give thee light.'—Eph. v. 14.

The progress of thought in later times has resulted in our becoming more alive to the seriousness and difficulty of questions concerning our very existence and destiny. In all ages there have been some who have asked these questions anxiously, and at times indeed they have convulsed the world. But now (more than ever) we are sent straight to nature and to fact, and we are told to be real; to think of what our words mean; and these questions of the whence and whither of mankind are felt by us more than by our forefathers to be formidable ones. Eyes have been opened to see the wonders and the mysteries of the most familiar things of life: the triple mystery of certain inexplicable facts; the mystery of sin; of pain, of will. Whence and why do I come into life? What is to become of me? What am I on the way to? These questions carry with them to those in the street, and by the domestic hearth, happiness or distress, hope or darkness, life or death. And one thing further has been brought home to our consciousness, and that is, that Nature by itself cannot give the answer. Nature does indeed speak of God, of duty, of immortality. 'The heavens declare the glory of God.' Conscience cannot escape from Right and Wrong. The human soul in the face of death believes that it is not to die. But though Nature does teach us of God and hope, of justice, purity, and prayer, its answers to our questions are dark and imperfect. The gainsayer declares that it is silent; the doubter that it is ambiguous. It hardly helps man to understand himself.

I. Whence come we? Where are we? Whither are we going? Who can help asking? It is impossible to measure the hopelessness of such an answer as science only gives us. Have we indeed nothing besides? Ah, yes! Encompassed in mystery as we are, little as we know of the infinite, yet that dreadful sense of not knowing what we are, and why we are, of being fatherless, uncared for, has passed away from the world. 'The dayspring from on high hath visited us, to give light to them that sit in darkness, and in the shadow of death; and to guide our feet into the way of peace.' But whatever we know or do not know, we know this—that One has come, as no one ever came to the world before, Who came to make quite certain questions on which men have been in the deepest perplexity; Who came to tell us whence and why we are, and what we have before us in the after-time. He came to tell us, once for all, that we are not orphans and castaways; He came to tell us of our Father in heaven, even God. We know that He is come, we know that He died, we know that He is risen from the dead. Some one among the sons of men has conquered death; and we know that this tremendous event has changed, not only the course, but the aspects of the world and human life. Neither are, nor can be, what they were before it—what they would be without it. 'Awake, thou that sleepest, and arise from the dead, and Christ shall give thee light.' He has come, and He has spoken. He has given light by His victory over the grave, and in that light all that He was, and said, and promised stands before us in the illumination of a Divine unveiling: 'God manifest in the flesh'. 'We beheld His glory, the glory as of the only begotten of the Father, full of grace and truth.'

II. The answer, as far as it goes, is as clear, as real, as the question. It is given in terms of which we can measure the meaning and the force. For we know what death is, and we know what must be meant by 'One being alive from the dead'. We ask—what Nature cannot tell us—from whose hands we came? One from the dead tells us that we come from, and are ever in, our Father's hand. We grope in darkness among the tremendous problems of moral evil. One from the dead has come, and tells us that sin indeed is a reality; that He died for the sin of men, and that its forgiveness and cure are in His hands. We ask, What is death? He is come from the grave itself, and He tells us, and shows us in His own Person, that death is but an incident, an appearance; that there is life beyond it—life with its purpose fulfilled; life and righteousness; life and immortality. We stand silent when the sufferers ask us why they suffer. What is the meaning, or justice, or use of those tremendous dispensations of agony which seem to visit without distinction the innocent and guilty— the misery of the helpless child, the pangs of the brute creation? Pain and its phenomena are ultimate facts, insoluble as they are awful. But this we know, that He Who was the conqueror of death and the Redeemer of His creatures drank together with them the cup of pain.

III. And we know more. We know that He is come, and has conversed with men. We know that He has promised, though He went away, yet still to be with us in our course through the storms and pains of life. 'Lo, I am with you all the days, even to the end of the world.' 'Where two or three are gathered together in My name, there am I in the midst of them.' We have Him Who once appeared among us; who was dead, and is alive for evermore. We have Him, the King and Master of all living men, to our comfort and blessing and guidance, if we will. He is here unseen, watching us, judging us. He is here, though they know it not, to the proud and insolent; He is here, to the humble and meek.

REFERENCES.—V. 14.—Spurgeon, *Sermons*, vol. xii. No. 716. Basil Wilberforce, *Sanctification by the Truth*, p. 25. T. J. Madden, *Tombs or Temples?* p. 69. J. A. Alexander, *The Gospel of Jesus Christ*, p. 289. G. W. Brameld, *Practical Sermons*, p. 143. T. Rhondda Williams, *Christian World Pulpit*, vol. lvi. p. 189. C. Perren, *Revival Sermons in Outline*, p. 126. J. Keble, *Sermons for Easter to Ascension Day*, p. 87. *Expositor* (4th Series), vol. iii. p. 351. A. Maclaren, *Expositions of Holy Scripture—Ephesians*, p. 318. V. 14, 15. —*Ibid.* (6th Series), vol. vi. p. 396.

NOT AS FOOLS, BUT AS WISE

EPH. v. 15.

I. 'NOT as fools, but as wise.' St. Paul appeals to us as reasonable creatures; he appeals to our common sense—to what must be clear to our mind and judgment as soon as we give the subject serious thought.

Judge for yourselves, he seems to say; the things which you know and believe of yourself and the world around you must make a difference to your way of living. A fool is he who will take no count of his circumstances. Consider your real circumstances; think of what you have learned to believe without any kind of doubt of what this life is, what it was given you for, and what is to come after it. Think of the part God has taken in it to help and save you; what Christ has done, given, and promised; and then, consider how 'wise men' ought to shape their lives. But—

II. Suppose it had been different. Suppose, for a moment, that all we know and believe had never been; that we had never heard of God; that we found ourselves here on earth, not knowing how we came, why we were living, or what we were meant for; and that all we knew of life were that there it was. Or suppose that we had only heard of God, our Maker and Ruler, by dim and uncertain report, as the heathen may, but that He had never had any dealings with us, and that we knew not where to find Him, or what He was. Imagine this to be our state —passing through life without the faintest notion of what life is, where it comes from, and whither it goes; having no light to guide us but what we could get for ourselves; no help out of this world, no comfort, no refuge, no prospects, nothing but the dark, unknown, hopeless grave. Suppose this were the condition of things in which we were living. Then there would be no prayer, for there would be no God to pray to, or to hope in. There would be no faith, no love of God, no obedience. There might be a certain sense of right and wrong, but there would be nothing to support right and condemn wrong. We should be in the world as forlorn outcasts, knowing their own bitterness, pain, heartache, and death—all the evils of the world—and knowing, too, all the evils of the world and of our own hearts, but without anyone above to look up to; without redemption, without remedy, without hope.

III. And now consider what is, in fact, the case with us. We cannot imagine, without difficulty, what we have been supposing. Even the very heathen dimly see the awful Power and Godhead amid their foul idolatries.

Not we only, but the whole world, knows God. The heathen know something of Him; forgetful Jews know more; but we Christians have a knowledge which leaves all this behind. We know that God has been with men, spoken to them, made them know something of His mind. We believe in Jesus Christ, the Everlasting Son of the Father, the Maker, the Light and Life of men. We believe that He took upon Him to deliver man, and that, for this purpose, He did not abhor the Virgin's womb. We believe more—that He died for our sins, that He overcame the sharpness of death, and did open the kingdom of heaven to all believers. We believe that He ascended into heaven, and sitteth at the right hand of God, in the glory of the Father, and that He shall come to be our Judge. And we believe that we now have in Him One who hears all prayers, heals all wrongs, and can bind up every broken heart. Men may now appeal to a love which has made God's world look new. 'We therefore pray Thee help Thy servants, whom Thou hast redeemed with Thy precious blood.' Look where we will, our eyes ever encounter something which reminds us of the cross of Christ.

IV. Put these two pictures side by side : life as we supposed it without knowing anything of God, or our origin or destiny; and, on the other side, life in which man throws himself on the love of God, as His servant, redeemed by the precious blood of Christ. Then 'walk not as fools, but as wise'. St. Paul appeals to us as men of common sense. Would any man of sense, who knew and believed the facts last stated, think of living as if all that we knew were depicted in the first picture? And yet it is one of the commonest sights of our experience to see men living a life which they would live just as well if they were absolutely without God in the world. Many still live as those who, in their ignorance, said : 'Let us eat and drink, for to-morrow we die'. Are not St. Paul's words the words of truth and soberness when he calls us 'not as fools, but as wise'—knowing and believing what we do—not to live as if we knew it not; as if we had nothing but this life and this world before us, but to live as Christian men and women ought to live—doing the will and fulfilling the purposes of the God with Whom they have so much to do ?

REFERENCES.—V. 15.—Bishop Westcott, *Disciplined Life*, No. ix. V. 15, 16.—C. M. Betts, *Eight Sermons*, p. 19. J. J. Blunt, *Plain Sermons*, p. 259. A. Maclaren, *Expositions of Holy Scripture—Ephesians*, p. 327.

WATCH—YOURSELVES, YOUR OPPORTUNITIES

'See then that ye walk circumspectly, not as fools, but as wise, redeeming the time, because the days are evil. Wherefore be ye not unwise, but understanding what the will of the Lord is.'—EPH. v. 15-17.

THESE are admonitions addressed to Christian people by an inspired Apostle; not only to Christian people as individuals, but to Christian people organised into communities. The passage might be compressed into two lines :—

Look diligently to yourselves,
. . . and your opportunities.

I. Yourselves first. There are two kinds of temper to be steadfastly guarded against. The temper of levity, which turns everything into a jest. And the other temper to be guarded against is sleepy self-satisfaction. (1) A Christian man needs to make constant and fresh effort to remember who he is and Whose he is. That He is the property of Christ—redeemed by the agony of the Son of God. (2) And then he is to realise clearly and sharply where he is. Do not let us make any mistake on this point; he is in an unfriendly world, a world, that, to say the least

of it, cares nothing for the things which most interest him. (3) The Christian man must remember that the world is hostile to God. (4) We are not only in an unfriendly world; we are in a world that is to be won to God, and won by us. (5) We are not only surrounded by an unfriendly world—we are still more closely surrounded by an unfavourable spiritual atmosphere; by invisible agents whose aim is to weaken and destroy the finest fruits of the spiritual life.

II. We need to look carefully to our work. There is no reason why there should be any folly in Christian work. Enthusiasm does not mean irrationalism. (1) 'Understand,' the Apostle says; use that faculty, and understand what the will of the Lord is. (2) And having understood it, we are to do it, and to do it promptly. That is the meaning of the phrase, 'Buying up the opportunity'. The psychological moment comes, and you must act, or it goes, and carries the opportunity with it. Every department of life abounds in illustrations of the importance of this precept—of the fatality of neglecting it. Why does the Apostle speak about *buying up* the opportunity? Because the embracing of it means cost. You yourself were not redeemed without sacrifice. You will never carry out the will of God without cost to yourself.—CHARLES BROWN, *Light and Life*, p. 91.

REFERENCES.—V. 15-17.—A. P. Stanley, *Sermons on Special Occasions*, p. 118. V. 15-33.—E. J. Kennedy, *Old Theology Re-stated*, p. 140. V. 16.—Bishop Westcott, *Village Sermons*, p. 314. Archbishop Maclagan, *Christian World Pulpit*, vol. li. p. 248. W. Baird, *The Hallowing of our Common Life*, p. 6. R. Appleton, *The Pulpit*, vol. i. p. 31. J. S. Bartlett, *Sermons*, p. 172. J. Budgen, *Parochial Sermons*, vol. i. p. 115. S. Cox, *Expositions*, p. 1. W. J. Brock, *Sermons*, p. 335. S. Baring-Gould, *Village Preaching for a Year* (2nd Series), vol. i. p. 50. H. Bonner, *Sermons and Lectures*, p. 206. G. W. Brameld, *Practical Sermons* (2nd Series), p. 176. V. 17.—T. Arnold, *Sermons*, vol. ii. p. 190.

THE PLENITUDE OF THE SPIRIT

'Be filled with the Spirit.'—EPH. v. 18.

WHAT is meant by the Plenitude of the Spirit?

I. The phrase occurs in a command or exhortation; the Apostle makes use of the imperative mood. We are bidden to do, or to be—a demand is made upon us. Yet the verb is passive in form, and it is natural to object that the process described is God's work, not ours. That august Breath of God blows when and where He lists; we can neither originate nor control Divine influence. The 'baptism of the Spirit,' the 'outpouring of the Spirit,' the 'descent of the Spirit,' do not denote action on our part, but the reception of an essentially Divine gift. When we read of the Primitive Church that they were 'all filled with the Holy Ghost,' or that Stephen or Barnabas was 'full of the Holy Ghost,' the impression conveyed is one of supernatural power resting on these men. Self-inspiration is absurd. To issue a command that men should acquire what God alone can confer might seem to imply either a blunder or a blasphemy.

II. The injunction 'be filled' means that we may, we can, and therefore we ought to play our part.

'Ye must be born again' implies that we can be so born, and then a glorious possibility of privilege becomes a sacred duty. The relation between the Divine and the human is not that of an alien supernatural power energising passive clay into fresh life. That is a heathenish notion of inspiration which would regard the Holy Spirit as a magical, external power which must be invoked in the fashion of the prophets of Baal, who cut themselves with knives to procure the boon of supernatural fire from heaven. The Spirit is here, waiting—oh, how He waits! He is unspeakably near to every heart of man—longing, wooing, drawing, striving, filling each soul as far as He can whenever there is room to receive Him, quickening when the faintest movement of response makes it possible for Him to infuse new life; or as a favouring wind to fill the sails of the soul still further, and carry the frail vessel on its forward, homeward way.

But that is not precisely the thought of the text. It is addressed not to mankind at large, but to the Church. It refers not to the vague indefinable Divine Spirit of the Pantheist or the Mystic, but to the Spirit of Christ. The Spirit who is known, loved, understood, and obeyed; the Spirit who originated the new life in the heart of every member, and made each man who is in Christ a new creation; the Spirit who operates in us every moment, though in scanty measure because of our meagre faith and lukewarm love; the Spirit who at every moment—at this moment—waits, longing to raise, inspire, purify, and empower us as He has never done before.

We are directed to find our fulness in Him, and in Him alone. That does not mean the cessation of effort till a Higher Power shall quicken us. Nor does it mean a feverish and anxious occupation in good works and religious ordinances, as if we could kindle loftier affection by sedulous attention to detailed duties. It means that we are to go back to the Fountain-head at once, and always with a directness and immediacy that takes no denial; that every Church and every member is to be in his own place an organ of a Higher Will, intelligently and earnestly co-operating with a Power which informs and sustains and animates the whole. The work that was done at first was not done by us, but by a Higher Power in us and through us; decline begins when men forget this and concentrate attention upon their own efforts. Renewal implies a requickening from the primal source—the love of God in Christ poured abroad in the heart of the Holy Spirit given unto us.

III. The heart that would be Spirit-filled must first be empty. Empty, that is, of everything that would prevent the Spirit from doing His characteristic work. For there is no necessary antagonism between the operation of the Spirit of God and a thousand varied aims for which the Church legitimately strives, a thousand interests in the world which she seeks to promote. Distinguish between a true and a false spirituality. Not by withdrawing the leaven from the mass of meal can the lump be leavened, but by

the potency of a ferment mighty enough to quicken the whole. Still it is clear that the Holy Spirit of God cannot fill as He would an already full vessel, and there simply is not room enough for the Spirit to work in some churches that are calling loudly for His presence, in many hearts that are praying earnestly for His indwelling. Apart from subtle forms of sin, with which we are not now concerned, the pathways of the soul may be blocked, the Divine channel may be obstructed, the soil of the heart choked with a tangle of thorns and weeds, and thus not the entrance, but the plenary work of the Spirit be effectually hindered.—W. T. DAVISON, *The Indwelling Spirit*, p. 235.

THE SPIRIT-FILLED LIFE
'Be filled with the Spirit.'—EPH. v. 18.

THE Spirit dwells in the believer, and the believer lives in the Spirit. The Spirit finds in the believer His home, medium, and means; and the believer finds in the Spirit his sphere and element. Every need of spiritual life and Christian service is supplied in the fulness of the Spirit. To be filled with the Spirit is every believer's birthright, but there are many Esaus. Fleshly desires hinder the work of the Spirit, and the inheritance is bartered for the things of earth. Jesus Christ is the supreme example of the spirit-filled life. To Him the Spirit was given without measure. His life was lived in abiding surrender to the will of the Spirit. He is the ideal and pattern of the life made possible to all by the coming of the Spirit. The leading features of the Spirit's work in Him are marked by special mention of the Spirit as directly connected with them, and in the study of them we may find the distinctive marks of the Spirit-filled life.

I. The Spirit-filled life is a life of conquest over temptation. Being full of the Spirit does not bring immunity from temptation but exposure to it. I Jesus was tempted like as we are. it follows we shall be tempted as He was. Every man's Pentecost is the signal for Satan to gird himself. Temptation comes to the spiritual man in its intensest and most subtle forms. (1) The first temptation in the Spirit-filled life is the temptation of bread. The temptation is to use the gift of God for self-gratification. Satan urges the use of the power for selfish ends: to make it a means of getting bread. (2) The second temptation deals at the root with the same question as the first. It is still self, only at the other extreme. The first appeal was to give self the first care, the second to give it no care at all. (3) The third temptation is also a question of adjustment. The Spirit is given for ministering, and to the Spirit-called and Spirit-filled worker there comes the problem of the relative positions of the human and the Divine, the natural and the spiritual, in the work of God. In his zeal there is urged upon him the use of carnal weapons for spiritual ends.

II. The Spirit-filled life is a life of service. The preparation, the call, and the equipment for Christian service is of the Holy Ghost. Our need is not more churches and better appliances, but a universal baptism of the Spirit of God.

III. The Spirit-filled life is full of joy. We cannot be gladsome by resolution. Joy is a fruit, the natural product of an inner life. How does the fulness of the Spirit open a fountain of joy? The Spirit makes men glad with the consciousness of God, and a God-like enthusiasm for out-flowing. There is no life like the life filled with the Spirit.—S. CHADWICK, *Humanity and God*, p. 227.

THE ENTHUSIASM OF THE SPIRIT

'Be not drunk with wine, but be filled with the Spirit.'—EPH. v. 18.

I. THE enthusiasm of the Spirit takes a man out of himself. A man hampered by circumstances is like a bird in a cage. He continually strikes against the cruel iron bars; he frets with impatience at his stern limitations, and he wants to escape somewhere. Well, he can escape into the forgetfulness of sleep, or the madness of intoxication, but it is the wrong way of dodging his limitations. The right way is to seek refuge in God. There is an escape from self, there is an actual transfiguration of a man's personality. There is such a thing as being lifted up out of the drudgery and routine of life. There is such a thing as being possessed by a power nobler than ourselves, and it is to be filled with the Spirit.

II. The enthusiasm of the Spirit, instead of destroying a man's personality, ennobles it and builds it up. Wine makes me forget my troubles, but it dissolves my character, makes my personality fall into pieces, spoils and mars and destroys my manhood. But when the Spirit of God comes, He simply finds my nobler self, and causes it to blossom and to fructify. You can be your worst self by being filled with the Spirit of greed and selfishness and wine, but you can only be your higher self, the self that you are intended to be, by being filled with the Spirit of God.

III. The enthusiasm of the Spirit produces harmony and order and joy. One of its manifestations is to speak to each other in psalms and hymns, and 'making melody in our hearts'. This is in striking contrast to the intoxication that comes from wine, which agitates and upsets the life, and engenders wretchedness and misery. We are possessed of a great number of faculties, and each faculty under proper stimulation yields joy and pleasure. But the joys resulting from the exercise of the lower faculties are more tumultuous and transient and less satisfying and wholesome, while the joys that ring forth from what is noblest in our nature are calm and deep and permanent.

IV. The enthusiasm of the Spirit leads a man to a right relationship with his fellow-men, 'subjecting yourself one to another in the fear of God'. False excitement leads into the exaggeration of a man's self-importance. But the Spirit of God leads to service and self-denial, to patience and humility, to the obliteration of self, and the appreciation and

helpfulness of others. The Holy Ghost is ethical and social. Whatever the Pentecost means, it means a baptism of humility and love.—T. PHILLIPS, *Baptist Times and Freemen*, vol. LIV. p. 447.

EPH. v. 18.

AFTER being drunk at Corrichatachin, Boswell rose next morning and 'went into Dr. Johnson's room, and taking up Mrs. McKinnon's Prayer-book, I opened it at the twentieth Sunday after Trinity, in the Epistle for which I read, "and be not drunk with wine, wherein is excess". Some would have taken this as a Divine interposition.

EPH. v. 18.

'THE energy natural to the English race degenerates to savage brutality,' wrote Cobden, in one of his letters, 'under the influence of habitual drunkenness; and one of the worst effects of intemperate habits is to destroy that self-respect which lies at the bottom of all virtuous ambition.'

REFERENCES.—V. 18.—W. F. Adeney, *Christian World Pulpit*, vol. li. p. 59. J. Binney, *King's Weigh-House Chapel Sermons*, p. 218. Spurgeon, *Sermons*, vol. xxxv. No. 2111. Bishop Winnington-Ingram, *A Mission of the Spirit*, p. 111. *Expositor* (6th Series), vol. viii. p. 57. V. 18, 19.—J. Arnold, *The Interpretation of Scripture*, p. 228. E. H. Bickersteth, *Thoughts in Past Years*, p. 137. V. 19.—E. Griffith-Jones, *Christian World Pulpit*, vol. lviii. p. 387. R. Moffat Gautrey, *ibid.* vol. lxxviii. p. 294. R. W. Hiley, *A Year's Sermons*, vol. ii. p. 202. *Expositor* (4th Series), vol. ii. p. 27. *Ibid.* vol. iii. p. 402. V. 19, 20.—F. J. A. Hort, *Village Sermons in Outline*, p. 63.

THE THANKFUL LIFE

'Speaking to yourselves in psalms and hymns and spiritual songs, singing and making melody in your heart to the Lord; Giving thanks always for all things unto God and the Father in the name of our Lord Jesus Christ.'—EPH. v. 19-22.

I. LIVE the thankful life. Let us have no more groaning and complaining, but let us have music and psalm and hymn and spiritual song, an inward and outward melody. The Church has forgotten all its exhortations to thankfulness and to music; it has made for itself a series of threnodies very depressing and soul-enslaving, services and tests of discipline and standards of heartless and often hypocritical solemnity. The Apostle says, Let us have no more of this; there is a sunny side even to Christian faith; there are whole days, long bright summer days, in which it becomes us to sing one to another in psalm and hymn and spiritual song and to match the summer with a human melody. Let a cheerful life be added to the evidences of the truth of the Christian religion. Paul was never ashamed of his overflowings of joy; he mingled the cup of life so dexterously and with so sweet and sacred a cunning that no man ever drank such a cup as Paul drank; he said, Yea, we glory in tribulations also. Nothing could repress him or depress him; his religion forced its way through fog and smoke and storm and pain and loss; he took tribulation with a strong man's hand, and added it to his wealth. This is the victory that overcometh the world, even our faith. Always hear the music that is in everything. There is fire in ice; there is music in silence, there is music in the radiance of the face.

II. If we have had our psalm and hymn and spiritual song, what then, thou great disciplinarian of the Church? I will tell you, says Paul; after the song must come the discipline. You will find all along the Christian line that song and discipline alternate; they seem to balance one another; in that, as in the record of Genesis, the evening balances the morning, and the evening and the morning are the whole day. Discipline succeeds melody: 'Submitting yourselves one to another in the fear of God. Wives, submit yourselves unto your own husbands, as unto the Lord.' We shall miss the whole point of this if we take it out of its connection and make a jest of it. There are no jests in the Bible. The buffoon can find them on the altar, almost on the Cross, but the wise man finds no such blots. Observe the atmosphere in which the Apostle is now writing; take note of the atmosphere which he has created around these Gentile converts. Do not place the Ephesian converts on a level with Christian and experienced nations. When the temperature is at the highest, when joy is at the zenith, when all the summer fruits are growing and all the summer birds are singing, he says, Submit yourselves one to another in the fear of God. And in that atmosphere it is easy to do so; in any other atmosphere it is impossible. That is the exposition. Where the atmosphere is right there will be no difficulty. 'Submitting yourselves one to another.' That is the key of all that follows. The submission is never to be on one side only; and where there is submission on both sides there is no humiliation, there is sympathy, there is union, there is a mysterious kin.

III. You cannot lay down little rules upon any matters of personal or household discipline. What then can we do? The Apostle has already told us— 'Be filled with the Spirit'. To rule without ruling, to lead without leading, to drive without cracking the whip, to be a man without being a fool; that is only possible when we are filled with the Spirit, when we are breathing the vital atmosphere, when we are one with Christ.—JOSEPH PARKER, *City Temple Pulpit*, vol. II. p. 242.

THE ROYAL DEBT

'Giving thanks always for all things in the name of our Lord Jesus Christ to God, even the Father.'—EPH. v. 20 (R.V.).

I. THE Spirit of Thankfulness ought to be the temper of our whole life—'giving thanks always for all things'. (1) God *merits* our thanks, if such an expression may be allowed. Our very being is His wondrous gift. The things which gladden and go to the enrichment and perfecting of life are His gifts. And as He is the supreme giver, so is He the source of all our blessing. (2) God expects our thanks. We cannot believe that the living God is indifferent to the Spirit in which His boons are accepted. Our nature teaches us better. He whom we worship is

not the great machinist, chemist, or artist—such a being might be insensible to gratitude; but we give thanks 'to God, even the Father,' and it is impossible to think that love and gratitude have no place in our relation to Him.

II. This spirit of thankfulness is possible only in the grace and power of Jesus Christ. The name of Christ is that general and holy element, as it were, in which everything is to be received, to be enjoined, to be done, and to be suffered. The Spirit of the natural man is the spirit of criticism and depreciation. Dowered with treasures of light and darkness, inheriting a large and wealthy place, the language of discontent is our native speech. Let us see, then, how in the Christian life these infinite repinings are changed into praise. (1) The truth and grace of Jesus Christ make thankfulness possible by convincing us of our true position before God. Ingratitude, in the main, arises out of infinite and inveterate conceit. Satisfied that we are worthy of the greatest of God's gifts, we really appreciate none. Here the truth of the Gospel effects a fundamental change; it convinces us that we are sinners, without merit and rights; and in doing this, gives a new standpoint whence we view the whole field of life. (2) Christ makes thankfulness possible through restoring in us the spiritual faculty by which we discern the greatness and sweetness of all things. Genius shows itself and its transcendence by discerning the grandeur, romance, and joy of all things great or small. The Spirit of Christ creates in us a faculty of spiritual appreciation corresponding to genius in the mental realm. (3) Christ makes the habit of thankfulness possible by assuring us that the painful things of life serve equally with the brightest. The 'all things' must not be limited to agreeable things. 'Forget not all His benefits.' We cannot recall all the treasures of the deep along whose shore we have travelled; but we can keep a few pearly shells which retain the echoes of the vast music of the ocean of the eternal love.—W. L. WATKINSON, *Themes for Hours of Meditation*, p. 20.

EPH. v. 20.

IF we had to name any one thing which seems unaccountably to have fallen out of most men's practical religion altogether, it would be the duty of thanksgiving. It is not easy to exaggerate the common neglect of this duty. There is little enough of prayer; but there is still less of thanksgiving. . . . Alas! it is not hard to find the reason of this. Our own interests drive us obviously to prayer; but it is love alone which leads to thanksgiving.—FABER, *All for Jesus*, pp. 208, 209.

REFERENCES.—V. 20.—Spurgeon, *Sermons*, vol. xix. No. 1094. G. A. Sowter, *Sowing and Reaping*, p. 96.

THE GLORY OF SUBMISSION

'Submitting yourselves one to another in the fear of God.'— EPH. v. 21.

THESE words set before us the spirit of unselfish devotion in which as Christians we are directed to regard the relations of life. And if we consider the words attentively, I believe that we shall find in them one of the very central rules of Christian action. Here if anywhere the contrast between the promptings of our natural spirit and the teaching of our Lord is sharp and decisive. The impulse of benevolence leads to noble acts of devotion ; but that devotion which the Holy Spirit teaches is ever present in all the commonest details of our life, converting all into one great sacrifice to God. And it is in this that we have the full account of that submission of which St. Paul speaks.

I. It is a sacrifice of ourselves. Submission in the Christian sense is an act of strength and not of weakness ; a victory and not a defeat ; a victory over self, felt and realised. This is the first characteristic of that submission to one another by which we must each endeavour to fulfil St. Paul's words. It is not the easy, thoughtless, indifferent acquiescence of a mind which is alike incapable of resolution and resistance ; but the calm, steady, deliberate denial of his own wishes by one who knows well the value of that which he forgoes, and knowing still forgoes it.

II. It is also a sacrifice for others—not for one only, but for all among whom God's providence may place us. As Christians we are simply told to submit one to another ; and thus we have opened to us a boundless field for the trial of our faith. Every act of our daily business may furnish us with a test whereby we may know whether we are indeed serving God.

III. Thus we come to the third work of Christian submission ; it is in the fear of God. This fear is at once the motive and the limit of our submission. Our submission is a sacrifice for Christ, and offered in the fear of Christ. There can be no submission where His honour is endangered ; and then only is submission true when His will is its final object. At last submission will be crowned by sovereignty.—BISHOP WESTCOTT, *Village Sermons*, p. 304.

REFERENCES.—V. 21.—W. G. Horder, *Christian World Pulpit*, vol. lvii. p. 235. F. J. A. Hort, *Village Sermons in Outline*, p. 107, 118, 123, 134, 140 and 145. V. 22, 23.—A. Brown, *British Congregationalist*, 16th August, 1906, p. 57. *Expositor* (6th Series), vol. ii. p. 292. V. 22-25.—C. S. Horne, *Christian World Pulpit*, vol. lix. p. 121. V. 22-33, B. J. Snell, *The All-Enfolding Love*, p. 65. F. J. A. Hort, *Village Sermons in Outline*, p. 123. V. 23.—E. T. J. Marriner, *Sermons Preached at Lyme Regis*, p. 123. *Expositor* (6th Series), vol. i. p. 281. V. 25.—Spurgeon, *Sermons*, vol. xlii. No. 2488. *Expositor* (4th Series), vol. vi. p. 423. V. 25-27. —Spurgeon, *Sermons*, vol. xi. No. 628. V. 27.—*Expositor* (4th Series), vol. ii. p. 302. V. 28.—F. B. Cowl, *Preacher's Magazine*, vol. xvii. p. 239.

THE NOURISHED AND CHERISHED CHURCH

'. . . nourisheth and cherisheth it, even as the Lord the Church.' —EPH. v. 29.

NOTHING in St. Paul's conception of the wonderful Church of Christ is more startling than his undoubting faith in the work she was to do, and in the tender, unslumbering love that would for ever guard her.

The great Gospel is itself the great paradox, and we need not wonder that it is surrounded by companion paradoxes. Few can be more astonishing than these : the apparent abandonment, which is nevertheless a constant tending of the Church, and the apparent overcoming by world-powers which is nevertheless a victory.

I. As to the first, let us remember that the saints have never misdoubted Christ and His promises, nor the interest of the Church in these, however they may have misdoubted their own. Alexander Peden is represented by a poet as taking counsel with God whether he should be able to keep true—

So I sought the Lord when we met
At the black Moffat Water to get
　Just a blink of light on the way,
　And to know whether I should play
The man in the dark times yet.

But He said, ' Content you now,
You shall be where I think best;'
' Yea, Lord,' I said, ' but Thou
Knowest I never did bow
To Baal with the rest,
Nor take the black false test ;'
But He said, ' Content you now '.

But even Peden, the gloomiest of all the great witnesses, never feared that the Lord would forsake His Church. 'There shall be brave days such as the Church of Scotland never saw the like; but I shall not see them, though you may.' 'Lord, I die in faith,' said another, 'that Thou wilt not leave Scotland, but that Thou wilt make the blood of Thy witnesses the seed of Thy Church, and return again and be glorious in Thine own land.' Warriston recorded his 'sure hope that the Church would be visited and freed'. In his last moments James Guthrie, too, foresaw the good of God's chosen, the gladness of His nation, the glory of His inheritance. In the very height of their extremity these men never questioned the present nourishing, cherishing love of Christ to His Church and the glory that was to be. If persecution sifted the Church, it was well, for her great danger had ever been that of becoming a bit of the world under another name. An eminent preacher has said, 'I do not myself feel any regret at the departure of monied people. In some places there is such a dependence on a little oligarchy of wealthy people that there seems no alternative for the Lord of the Churches but to send the rich away.' That is pure New Testament doctrine.

II. The strength of the Church appears in her persecution as clearly as her faithfulness. When the shock strikes the slumbering land, men discover that they have to reckon with a power which the world did not originate and cannot subdue. In the darkest and weariest hour of overthrow and pain the Church has wings folded at her side. They will unfold, and then she is free. The strength of the Church is altogether supernatural, and she is mighty just as she knows it. All the Church's trial is that the word may be fulfilled, 'Thou shalt call thy walls Salvation'.

And then the world knows her, and seeks her for what she is. The world has long since discovered that in the natural there is no redemption. No fibre of its heart is stirred by Gospels which cannot promise deliverance from the prison-house of law. When we touch the illimitable world—unknown, and yet well known—when we tear up our calculations, when we forget the circumstances that are so dead against us, when we regard no more the chains that bind the weakening limbs, the hour of release is at hand. The Church of Christ rises girt for her task, and the world perceives that she is not so weak as she seemed to be. No, nor yet so poor.—W. Robertson Nicoll, *Ten-Minute Sermons*, p. 283.

ASPECTS OF THE MYSTICAL UNION

'We are members of His body, of His flesh, and of His bones.'
—Eph. v. 30.

The depth and intimacy of the mystical union between our Lord and His believers are nowhere more boldly expressed than in the words of the Epistle to the Ephesians, ' We are members of His body, of His flesh, and of His bones '.

Let us see how this great and ruling truth helps us to confront the problems of life.

I. Consider its relation to the social work of the Church. Many of us remember the time when a very sharp line was drawn between the spiritual and the secular, and the spiritual was exalted. The preacher's business was to work for the salvation of souls. The Church was a building for the worship of God and the preaching of the Gospel. It was occupied two or three times a week, and for the rest quite useless. Philanthropy was held to be distinct from Christianity. It was inspired by Christianity, no doubt, and was good in itself, but it was not allowed to invade the sphere of the Church's true activity. As for recreation, it was thought outside the Church's mission, and was even regarded in some quarters as hostile to the spiritual energies of the faithful. By and by there came menaces and reproaches from the leaders of the working people. Worse than that, we became aware of the fact that the people were drifting away from organised Christianity. Many of us well remember that we were irritated by these challenges. We had been brought up to believe that our business was to bring souls to Christ, and that if we could do that, other problems would gradually solve themselves. We forgot that the Church once made it her special business to care for the poor, and that when this became the function of the State, a true and precious link was broken. Now we perceive that the Christ, Who is Incarnate and Supreme, is united to the bodies and the souls of His people, and we are members of His body, of His flesh, and of His bones. So we perceive that His work of redemption has gone wider than we thought, and that it extends to the bodies as well as to the souls of men. What is done merely for the body is a step towards salvation. Looking round his great congregation one Sunday night, Mr. Spurgeon spoke of the extremities to which some were reduced. 'Some of you,' he said, 'are hungry, and do not know where to turn for a morsel of bread. Has it even come to this?' Whoever fed the hungry, worked

towards the Christian salvation. All social work takes a new colour and a happy radiance when it is done in the thought of the union—in the remembrance that Christ died for the body as well as for the soul, and that He means to have with Him the whole man, body and soul, in the House not made with hands.

II. It is the thought of the mystical union that helps us to understand the resurrection of the body. When we realise that Christ took for our sakes the body as the temple of the Holy Ghost, we know that the body cannot really die. Christ did not take our flesh as a garment to be laid aside. He took it as part of Himself. We have been taught the doctrine of the literal resurrection of the flesh. St. Paul asserted the continuity of the body, and he denied explicitly the *literal* resurrection of the flesh. In his view, the body is united to Christ as well as the soul. There is an interdependence between the two in Him even when they are separated by death. Body and soul remain in union with Christ, and, in a day to be, body and soul will be united to make the one man in Christ Jesus before the throne of the Incarnate God. St. Paul teaches us that the body which shall be, is not the body that is. Nevertheless, it is not a new creation, but, in some sense known to God, a resurrection of the body in which we are at present. The body which we shall wear in glory is as truly the same body as we are wearing now, as the body we are wearing now is the same body with which we were born. These risen bodies will be like the body of the risen Lord. Changes unthinkable will have passed over them, but they will be the same. When He smote the gates of brass and snapped the bars of iron in sunder, and returned to His disciples from the dead, they did not know Him at first, but after a little time they knew Him. It was as when friends part and go out into foreign lands, and come back after years of toil and separation, and do not know those whose faces they had gazed on from the beginning. But by and by something—a tone of voice, a look of love—brings recognition, and gradually the past is traced in the present. So death comes and separates the body from the soul for a time, but neither from Christ, and we look forward by faith to the ending of separations. A great citizen of Birmingham used to comfort himself very much with this Greek word, σαλπίσει, 'the trumpet shall sound '. Yes, the trumpet *shall* sound. All the New Testament is meaningless unless it teaches the coming of a day of days, when the old order shall end, and the new everlasting order begin.—W. Robertson Nicoll, *The Lamp of Sacrifice*, p. 261.

References.—V. 30.—Spurgeon, *Sermons*, vol. xx. No. 1153, and vol. xxxviii. No. 2244. V. 32.—H. S. Holland, *Christian World Pulpit*, vol. xlv. p. 177.

THE CANON OF CONDUCT

'For this is right.'—Eph. vi. i.

I. The Standard of Christianity. 'Right' is a law of conduct not based on accident or convenience; it arises out of the depths of eternity, and is comprehended in the depths of our nature. Duty is sublime, founded on eternal relationships; conscience is the index of the Divine and supernatural; right differs essentially from might; justice and convenience are terms wide asunder by the breadth of the heavens; righteousness is the law of the unchanging universe, the will of Him in whom is no variableness, neither shadow of turning. If, then, the rule of right is the declared will of God, where must we look for that declaration? (1) Partially it is expressed in Nature. (2) The revelation of the Divine will is further disclosed in the law of Sinai. (3) The rule of conduct finds complete expression in Jesus Christ. The application of the rule of right to individual acts and special situations requires the utmost carefulness. '*This* is right.' Miss Martineau has a story of Carlyle setting forth on horseback to seek a fresh house, with a map of the world in his pocket; after this fashion, by reference to universal ideas we consider ourselves competent to resolve our personal, local, current difficulties. Much, however, comes between the general sense of righteousness and any specific act of moral judgment. We must take infinite pains to acquaint ourselves with facts, and to know how the rule of right applies. 'Human progress means, before all things, the education of conscience.' Here, then, is the criterion of conduct. 'For this is right.' With a sincere mind, seconded by diligence, determine what is the noblest act or course of conduct in any given circumstances, then adopt it at any cost or hazard.

II. The Standards of the World. Here we get into the plural. By what tests, then, do men of the world decide their course of action? (1) For this is customary. Great is the power of tradition. Great is the power of opinion. Great is the power of fashion. (2) For this is popular. (3) For this is profitable. Georges Sand bears this testimony: 'I have witnessed revolutions and closely seen the actors in them; I have fathomed the bottom of their souls—I should rather say of their bags'. (4) For this is pleasant. Diderot gave this quaint instruction to artists. 'Be the disciple of the rainbow, do not be its slave.' But is not the epigram of Diderot also an instruction for life? Be the disciple of the pleasant, do not be its slave. (5) For this is clever.

If you desire to live in peace and pure felicity, make the text your star. It sounds hard and harsh, it does not seem to contain a grain of poetry or note of music, yet it yields the secret of blessedness, the poetry of life, the flowers of the soul, the music of heaven.—W. L. WATKINSON, *Inspiration in Common Life*, p. 92.

REFERENCES.—VI. 1.—*Expositor* (5th Series), vol. i. p. 238. VI. 1-4.—F. J. A. Hort, *Village Sermons in Outline*, p. 118. VI. 1-9.—E. J. Kennedy, *Old Theology Re-stated*, p. 155. VI. 4.— M. G. Glazebrook, *Christian World Pulpit*, vol. liv. p. 28. T. Barker, *Plain Sermons*, p. 191. VI. 5-8.—J. Fleming, *Christian World Pulpit*, vol. lvi. p. 69. VI. 5-9.—C. S. Horne, *Relationships of Life*, p. 85. F. J. A. Hort, *Village Sermons in Outline*, p. 140. VI. 6.—H. M. Butler, *Harrow School Sermons* (2nd Series), p. 218. VI. 7.—Spurgeon, *Sermons*, vol. xxv. No. 1484. VI. 8.—*Expositor* (5th Series), vol. vii. p. 20.

THE QUIET MIND

'My brethren, be strong in the Lord, in the power of His might.'—EPH. VI. 10.

QUIETNESS is really an expression of strength. Look into almost all the language of the Scriptures and you find people with secure minds because they were secure in quiet. There is nothing dull about that quietness conducive to sleep. It is not like a stone with moss all over it. It is the grandest feature of the human and spiritual life. It is a sort of quietness, only it takes a lot of learning with many people. It is easy to be busy, and get hot thoughts, and have differences, but the grand word 'quietness' is the best sense of power. It is a mind worth having. It is the grandest mind.

I. Why is it many of us cannot have a quiet mind? We say there are so many things to keep us restless. It may be a house to manage, or a difficult bit of work, or the difficulty of getting work—things are so hard. My friends, a quiet mind is not built on things. There is no secure mind on a foundation of circumstances. You may drive the circumstances under and try to build it on them, but it will not rest there. It is a world of continuity; a world in which things will keep shifting, in which people keep moving one another along. You cannot fix yourselves in a comfortable income and a snug berth, and say: 'I have a quiet mind because I am safe for ever'. You can't do it. There is no such security to be had. Often people who come to the Church of God ask us to put things right. If you have Christian hearts we shall do our best. They are down on their luck, or something disastrous is coming. Not by any amount of skill, of readjustment or warmheartedness, to help your wisdom, can we give to any one of our fellowmen a foundation on which a quiet, strong mind can rest. You can see people shaking with both hands in the park, saying: 'If only we could alter all these things, we should make people happy'. It is a libel on human nature to say happiness can be built on a construction of things. It cannot. There is no rock on which the fabric of man's happiness can rest secure. It is the sand fabric of this world's good things. No life can rest on it.

II. What is a secure mind? How do we get it? I am sure many of you have it. It would be music in your ears to be reminded once again what it really is. You may take from the sixth of Ephesians a very good illustration of the secure mind. What is the picture presented to us? There you see an old, not a very old, but he looks an old, man in a narrow Roman lodging. His face is worn with the pain men put upon him, and with the anguish of much physical trouble which has come to him in long travellings among the bandits of Asia Minor, and the storms of the sea, and the scourgings often repeated. There he stands, or sits, in his room. With him is a Roman soldier, to whom he is chained by the wrists. Here in this prison, this lofty spirit, with a life of so severe pain, is writing a letter of cheer, and some of the words of his letter I read as my text. What are his words? 'My brethren, be strong in the Lord, and in the power of His might; put on the whole armour of God,' and so on. Why did he say that? What was there to make him feel in that courageous mood? Look at the things about him. The thing most obvious was a Roman soldier. If you have read anything about those people, you would know they were a very unpoetical, unsympathetic people indeed. They were cold-blooded; their business was to take the world by force of arms, crush out all finer feeling. That was the person who suggested to him this. Instead of being depressed by that cold, forbidding presence, that spoke of captivity and the death not very far off, he takes that soldier to pieces, he literally takes him to pieces. Crushed by the thought of his unsympathetic presence? No. He can take every bit of that man's armour and treat it as an illustration of something. 'Look at his armour,' he says. 'There is his helmet, look at his sword, his sandals, his breastplate.' Why, every bit of it, instead of being something to crush the mind into coldness, only gives him something to remind him of glorious service for the living Christ. He had the soldier and the Lord Jesus Christ with him as well. So he was strong, not in his circumstances. He had not the good luck to be resting on some social structure. He had not happiness on an economic basis; but he had happiness resting on the living Christ, who was with him in the Roman prison. Presently, when he stood before the Cæsar, the Lord stood by.

III. The busiest of us can find a little time to lift up our hearts unto the Lord. Those saints were not the people to manage things wonderfully, they were not workers of miracles, or different from you and me. Yet they were saints. Why were they saints? If you were to make this a perfect world you would not make any more saints. Saints cannot be made perfect by things. They are the people who stand up as soldiers—I don't believe in any other saints but the soldier-saints. There is no sainthood without fighting a good fight. It cannot be had. They are not fighting in Nebuchadnezzar's strength, or Goliath's, or David's, but in the power and might of the Lord. Let us remember that. We have an inheritance incorruptible, undefiled, that fadeth not away. This world will take our bodies into its earth some day, but we cannot be held by this world. God has made us. He is our Father, and to Him our spirits shall go at the last, I hope, having been made strong in the Lord and the power of His might. Having fought a good fight and finished our course, we shall hear those words: 'Well done, thou good and faithful servant; thou hast stood up as a soldier!'—A. W. GOUGH, *Christian World Pulpit*, vol. LXXVI. p. 359.

THE POWER OF THE WILL

'Finally, my brethren, be strong in the Lord, and in the power of His might.'—EPH. VI. 10.

I. LET us ask ourselves, why is it that we so often wish to do right and cannot? why is it that we are so frail, feeble, languid, wayward, dim-sighted, fluctuating, perverse? why is it that we cannot 'do the things that we would?' why is it that, day after day, we remain irresolute, that we serve God so poorly, that we govern ourselves so weakly and so variably, that we cannot command our thoughts, that we are so slothful, so cowardly, so discontented, so sensual, so ignorant? Why is it that we, who trust that we are not by wilful sin thrown out of grace (for of such I am all along speaking) why is it that we, who are ruled by no evil masters and bent upon no earthly ends, who are not covetous, or profligate livers, or worldly-minded, or ambitious, or envious, or proud, or unforgiving, or desirous of name—why is it that we, in the very kingdom of grace, surrounded by angels, and preceded by saints, nevertheless can do so little, and instead of mounting with wings like eagles, grovel in the dust, and do but sin, and confess sin, alternately? Is it that the *power* of God is not within us? Is it literally that we are *not able* to perform God's commandments? God forbid! We are able. We have that given us which makes us able. We are not in a state of nature. We have had the gift of grace implanted in us. We have a power within us to do what we are commanded to do. What is it we lack? The power? No; the will. What we lack is the real, simple, earnest, sincere inclination and aim to use what God has given us, and what we have in us.

A man, for instance, cannot attend to his prayers; his mind wanders; other thoughts intrude; time after time passes, and it is the same. Shall we say, this arises from want of power? Of course it may be so; but before he says so, let him consider whether he has ever roused himself, shaken himself, awakened himself, got himself to will, if I may so say, attention. We know the feeling in unpleasant dreams, when we say to ourselves, 'This is a dream,' and yet cannot exert ourselves to will to be free from it; and how at length by an effort we will to move, and the spell at once is broken; we wake. So it is with sloth and indolence; the Evil One lies heavy on us, but he has no power over us except in our unwillingness to get rid of him. He cannot battle with us; he flies; he can do no more, as soon as we propose to fight with him.

There is a famous instance of a holy man of old time, who, before his conversion, felt indeed the excellence of purity, but could not get himself to say more in prayer than 'Give me chastity, but not yet'. I will not be inconsiderate enough to make light of the power of temptation of any kind, nor will I presume to say that Almighty God will certainly shield a man from temptation for his wishing it; but whenever men complain, as they often do, of the arduousness of a high virtue, at least it were well that they should first ask themselves the question, whether they desire to have it.

II. I would have every one carefully consider whether he has ever found God fail him in trial, when his own heart had not failed him; and whether he has not found strength greater and greater given him according to his day; whether he has not gained clear proof on trial that he *has* a Divine power lodged within him, and a certain conviction withal that he has not made the extreme trial of it, or reached its limits. Grace ever outstrips prayer. Abraham ceased interceding ere God stayed from granting. Joash smote upon the ground but thrice, when he might have gained five victories or six. All have the gift, many do not use it at all, none expend it. One wraps it in a napkin, another gains five pounds, another ten. It will bear thirty-fold, or sixty, or a hundred. We know not what we are, or might be. As the seed has a tree within it, so men have within them angels.

Hence the great stress laid in Scripture on growing in grace. Seeds are intended to grow into trees. We are regenerated in order that we may be renewed daily after the image of Him who has regenerated us. In the text and verses following, we have our calling set forth, in order to 'stir up our pure minds, by way of remembrance,' to the pursuit of it. 'Be strong in the Lord,' says the Apostle, 'and in the power of His might. Put on the whole armour of God,' with your loins girt about with truth, the breastplate of righteousness, your feet shod with the preparation of the Gospel of peace, the shield of faith, the helmet of salvation, the sword of the Spirit. One grace and then another is to be perfected in us. Each day is to bring forth its own treasure, till we stand, like blessed spirits, able and waiting to do the will of God.—J. H. NEWMAN.

REFERENCES.—VI. 10.—T. Parr, *Christian World Pulpit*, vol. lviii. p. 74. F. B. Cowl, *Preacher's Magazine*, vol. xviii. p. 570. H. M. Butler, *Harrow School Sermons* (2nd Series), p. 106. S. Baring-Gould, *Village Preaching for a Year* (2nd Series), vol. ii. p. 175. C. Parsons Reichel, *Sermons*, p. 170. *Expositor* (6th Series), vol. vi. p. 119. VI. 10-14.—E. J. Kennedy, *Old Theology Re-stated*, p. 169.

THE ARMOUR OF GOD

'Put on the whole armour of God, that ye may be able to stand against the wiles of the devil.'—EPH. VI. 11.

IN his immortal allegory Bunyan represents Christian as arrived in his pilgrimage at the stately palace Beautiful; and, after rest and refreshment, conversation and devotion, some grave and comely damsels led him into the armoury where they showed him all manner of furniture which the Lord had prepared, sufficient indeed to equip as many pilgrims as there are stars in the firmament. They then harnassed him from head to foot with what was of proof, as he would surely meet with many antagonists on his way to Mount Zion. St. Paul desired the Christians at Ephesus to be as perfectly mailed as Christian in the palace Beautiful. So he leads them into the Temple

of Divine Truth, and shows them the armour God has prepared for them; but he leaves them to furnish themselves; nevertheless, he repeatedly enjoins them to do so without delay, as their need was great. Our need is as great and imperative.

I. **The Armour to be Worn.**—There are six pieces; but not one for the back, because we must alway face the foe, and never flee from him. But we must not mistake the figure employed. This armour is for the soul, and not for the body; and it is to defend us from our great spiritual adversary, who, with his legions, would decoy us to slay us. Moreover, it is Divine: it has been thoroughly tested, and never once battered through, but has shielded myriads of souls, till they exchanged the shout of battle for the pæan of victory. There is, first, the girdle. The girdle is very strong; it not only binds together what is loose, but, fastened tightly round the loins, it so braces the warrior that he can throw his whole force against his enemy. Even thus the truth of God must girdle our souls, binding well together our wandering thoughts and affections, and so uniting all our inner powers that we can dash against Satan with a might he cannot withstand. There is also the breastplate. This, in armour, is the metal vest which envelops the lungs and other vital parts, reaching from the neck to the thighs. This part is indispensably requisite. So is the Divine breastplate, which is Christ's righteousness upon us, and Christ's righteousness within us. Then there are the sandals. These save the extremities, and are lashed to them with sound thongs. Without them the warrior could neither plant himself firmly, nor fly on a commission received. Thus finely is the Christian pictured as acting alway under the peaceful motives of the Gospel. Furthermore, there is the shield. The ancient champion would ever have his shield, whether made of skin, or steel, or more precious metal; it was a miniature rampart, behind which he cleverly sheltered himself. Our shield is our faith; and, when skilfully used, it quenches the fiery darts of the wicked one, turns to flight the armies of the aliens, and defies the combined powers of death and the grave. Next, there is the helmet. This protects and adorns the head. So does the hope of salvation cover and beautify the Christian champion. Heavy blows may fall upon it, yet he lifts up his head in the day of battle, and cherishes in his heart the hope that will never render him cowardly nor ashamed. And, lastly, there is the sword. The sword is offensive and aggressive. If a Damascus blade, it will not snap, but pierce between the joints of the finest and strongest harness. How like to this is the Word of God! It is verily a keen two-edged weapon. What slaughter it makes of the ignorances and reasonings of the natural mind, and the passion and lusts which war against the soul! Jesus wielded it triumphantly when contending with Satan in the wilderness; and the feeblest saint, with this instrument in his hands, can do exploits.

II. **The Reason for Wearing this Armour.**—We have to 'stand against the wiles of the devil'. And who is he that we must be fully equipped to meet him? He is a spirit; hence invisible, and thus the more able to damage us. He once ranked with the princes of heaven; but he fell from his first estate through pride and daring, and dragged down with him a host of celestials. And ever since then—long ages ago—he has been pursuing the same dreadful course on earth. Now, how shall we stand against his wiles? Not clad in our own armour, or that of others, as was David in that of Saul, but in God's armour, and in the whole of God's armour. And even then we must not face him in our own strength, for that would be to war with him to our own hurt, as in the instance of Eve; but we must meet him as the stripling shepherd met the giant of Gath—'in the name of the Lord'.

DEFENCE AND DEFIANCE

'Put on the whole armour of God.'—EPH. VI. 11.

THE motto of our volunteers is 'Defence, not Defiance,' but in the war with evil we must adopt the title 'Defence and Defiance'. 'The whole armour of God,' or what is called elsewhere 'the armour of light,' is the sanctification of our whole nature through the grace of our Lord Jesus Christ. This is the only panoply invulnerable by evil.

I. Defence against the sins which beset us is implied in our text. The faithful disciple of Christ is secure in fidelity to the truth, in the power of purity, in the peace which garrisons his heart, in the love of God and goodness, in his pervasive righteousness, in his fellowship with heaven, in his faith and hope laying hold of eternal life. The grosser temptations fail to deprave one who is clothed in the shining mail of holiness. The more subtle forms of sin are equally innocuous to the pure in heart. There is no gross tangibility in the temptations to which many good people are subject; the enemy attacks with unseen array and smokeless powder.

II. The Defiance of Evil.—It is not enough to defend ourselves from the assaults of evil; we must challenge and fight it at every step, even when it does not decisively challenge us. To 'let sleeping dogs lie' is not sound policy in the moral life. Our attitude must be aggressive, whether evil is palpable or obscure. We must deal with evil in an uncompromising spirit, allowing no truce, granting no quarter. It is an axiom with the military that a purely defensive war must end in defeat; and certainly we often fail in spiritual warfare because we do not press the battle to the gate, and thoroughly subjugate the enemy when God gives us his neck. We must deal with evil in the spirit of abounding courage and confidence. We must also struggle against evil in the full assurance of final victory. 'When Immanuel,' says John Bunyan, 'had driven Diabolus and all his forces out of the city of Mansoul, Diabolus preferred a petition to Immanuel, that he might have only a small part of the city. When this was rejected, he begged to have only a little room within the walls; but Immanuel answered: 'He should have no place in it at all, no, not to rest the sole of his foot'. To this end and in this confidence we must pursue the struggle.—W. L. WATKINSON, The Ashes of Roses, p. 93.

REFERENCE.—VI. 11.—W. F. Shaw, Sermon Sketches for the Christian Year, p. 44.

EPH. VI. 12.

I LOVE the brave! But it is not enough to be a swordsman, one must also know against whom to use the sword.—NIETZSCHE.

THE CHRISTIAN WARFARE

'For we wrestle not against flesh and blood, but against principalities, against powers, against the rulers of the darkness of this world, against spiritual wickedness in high places.'—EPH. VI. 12.

As life goes on there comes to most of us a clearer view of its meaning and of its intense importance. The words, 'This is not your rest,' gain fresh meaning as the years go by. And another truth, also, is borne in upon us—namely, that we are surrounded by strange, hidden forces, harassed by unseen foes, that the more deliberately we try to live with a high aim in view the more surely are we battered and assaulted; the more we realise that even now we are fellow-citizens with the saints of the household of God the more we find war and strife to be our portion. The life you and I have to live belongs only in part to this visible sphere. 'The things that are seen are temporal, but the things which are not seen are eternal.' And as it is with the spiritual blessing, so it is with the spiritual forces of evil that are against us.

In the account of our Lord's temptation we are allowed to see a glimpse of what the battles with those unseen hosts meant to Him, and to learn by His example the methods by which to meet them. And we need to learn them, for if it is true that the battle has to be fought, if our foes are as vigilant as they ever were in the olden days, we must look to our weapons. The important thing is that we should each of us for himself make the warfare a reality; and I would suggest just two practical points.

I. First, we must be given to prayer. The conflict, as we have seen, must be waged in the heavenly places, in the world of unseen reality, and so our weapons, if they are to be effective, must penetrate to that hidden sphere. We must push past the visible to the invisible world; we must get through the things of sense to the deeper realities which lie behind; and we shall do this in no other way but by prayer. We should set ourselves quite deliberately and very patiently to find out more fully than before what prayer means, and what it involves. Prayer has been very well and simply defined as the lifting up of the mind and heart to God. Words, you see, are not of the essence of prayer, though of course prayer usually will find its way out on to the lips, because out of the abundance of the heart the mouth speaketh.

II. But prayer in its essence is the contact of the human soul with the living God. We lift up our hearts unto the Lord. Prayer takes us through into the heavenly places; we penetrate to the throne of grace. Now if this is true, we see why prayer needs so great an effort. It is the exercise of the very best and highest powers that God has given to us. It is the putting forth, or it ought to be the putting forth, of the whole inner force of the man. Prayer which makes little or no demands on our energies is not prayer at all in any real sense of the word. It is only playing at prayer. And never was there a day when the effort was more needed than it is now. The world is so full of a number of things—the rush and the whirl of life, the eager haste, the keen competition, the absorbing and numberless interests, the fret and anxiety, the wear and tear of an unquiet, busy age. All those things make prayer very difficult. We must learn where we ourselves are to gain the needed strength for our conflict. We shall never learn it in the midst of the full rush of life if we have not first gone quietly into the desert with our Lord.

III. And there is one more duty which none of us must dare to neglect if we are to wrestle with any effect against the powers of evil. If it is necessary to lift up our hearts to God, it is necessary also to keep under our bodies. 'The flesh lusteth against the spirit.' To give full licence to the body, even in what is lawful, is fatal to true living. We are not, most of us, I suppose, called to an ascetic life. We are called to live as busy, active men and women in the world. But we cannot ignore facts, and there is no more certain fact than this—that owing to the strange enfeeblement of our wills, which is due to sin, we have not any of us that complete control over our bodies that we ought to have.

God forbid that we should ever make the mistake of imagining that our bodies are in themselves evil. The essence of sin lies not in the body, but in the weak, disordered will which fails to control it. It is because this is so that the need of fasting in some shape or form has never passed away, and never will so long as man is what he is. Yet fasting, like other spiritual exercises, may be an utter unreality. It may be practised as if it were an end in itself, a thing to be used for its own sake. So used, it will minister to nothing but folly, and pride, and self-will. Used as God means it to be, in a humble spirit, as a means to higher things, it will bring the blessing that always comes to those who obey. By prayer, then, which is prayer indeed, and by self-discipline, we shall be enabled in the power of Christ our Lord effectively to carry on the conflict in the heavenly places—that conflict to which we, as Christians, are committed.

REFERENCES.—VI. 12.—Phillips Brooks, *The Mystery of Iniquity*, p. 71. F. D. Maurice, *Sermons*, vol. vi. p. 289. Phillips Brooks, *The Law of Growth*, p. 61. *Expositor* (4th Series), vol. i. p. 138; *ibid.* (6th Series), vol. vi. p. 212. VI. 12, 13.—H. P. Liddon, *Sermons on Some Words of St. Paul*, p. 230.

THE TRINITY OF TEMPTATION
'The evil day.'—EPH. VI. 13.

IN dealing with temptation we must remember that a man may be tempted either of God or he may be tempted of Satan. In Hebrews XI. 17 we are told that God did 'tempt' or 'try' Abraham. God tries us that we may rise; Satan tries us that we may fall.

I. There are three trinities in the world. The trinity in unity above us, the Father, Son, and Spirit—one God; the trinity within us, spirit, soul, and body—one man; and the trinity beneath us, the world, the flesh, and the devil. The world, the flesh, and the devil are present in every temptation that comes to man. (1) What is the world? In 1 John II. 26 we are told what is in the world: 'The lust of the flesh, the lust of the eyes, and the pride of life'. These were the lines along which Christ's three temptations came. These the Apostle shows are *in* the world, but he does not give a definition of the world. The world really is the appearance or semblance of things, a mirage! (2) As for the flesh, there is no better definition than that given in Romans VII. 18, where the Apostle says : 'In me, that is, in my flesh'. 'Flesh' is 'me-ism,' egotism. What is the centre letter of the word 'sin'? 'I'; and the centre of egotism is 'I'. (3) The devil. The nearer you live to Christ, the more certain you are there is a personal devil. Of course, I do not think that the devil has the attributes of God. If you say that the devil tempts everybody you make him omnipresent and omniscient, which are attributes of God alone. Our wrestling is not against flesh and blood, but against principalities, against powers, against the rulers of the darkness of this world, against the hosts of spirits of wickedness in the heavenly places (Eph. VI. 12, Revised Version). Why should Satan tempt man to fall? The whole gist of the fall is that Satan should rule, should take from the brow of man the crown that the Creator put there.

II. The temptation of our Lord. When Satan had made man his subject, God's plan seemed thwarted; but God, in the person of His Son, became man and encountered Satan, not in the exercise of His Deity, but 'He emptied Himself'.

III. The succour for tempted souls. We must remember that on the cross Jesus Christ became the representative man, and met the world, the flesh, and the devil in the hour of His weakness. If He could overcome them then, what can He not do now He is strong in resurrection glory? If we are linked to Christ by faith, we shall keep our standing, in spite of temptations, and Christ will bring Satan under our feet.—F. B. MEYER, *The Soul's Ascent*, p. 123.

THE ARMOUR OF GOD
'Wherefore take unto you the whole armour of God, that ye may be able to withstand in the evil day, and having done all, to stand.'—EPH. VI. 13.

PREPARATION—that is the first note of Advent—preparation for a struggle which must last while life lasts. No thinking man would deny that the be-all and end-all of our early years is preparation for the life that we are to live when we go out into the world. And Christianity advances its claim: What preparation have you made, and what preparation are you now making, for the moral and spiritual struggles of after-life?

Let us then speak of what St. Paul considers to be the preparation of the Christian warrior. Twice he speaks of the whole armour : 'Put on the whole armour of God' ; 'Take up the whole armour'. In the Greek it is one word, the 'panoply' of God. This 'panoply,' or complete equipment, consists of six parts—the girdle, the breastplate, the sandals, the shield, the helmet, and the sword. Of these, one only is an offensive weapon ; the rest are for the protection of the soldier. But all of them are God's gifts to those who are to fight His battle ; all belong to the supernatural order, and they are parts of a whole. I am not speaking to those who, to the best of their natural powers, are fighting on the side of right ; I am speaking, as St. Paul is, to those who have been admitted to the supernatural life by the Sacrament of Baptism, and received their armour in Confirmation—the 'Sacrament of warriors'. St. Paul speaks of—

I. The Girdle of Truth About the Loins.—Now, we read constantly in the Bible of girding up the loins, and it is always in preparation for some active work. It was the gathering of the long flowing robe close round the body, so as to leave the limbs at liberty. The custom of the Hebrews was to wear the girdle, the sword-belt, round the waist, as our soldiers wear it now. And the Christian's girdle is to be Truth—not mere conscientiousness, but Truth. Your loins are to be girt about with Truth. Without that, the soldier will be impeded by his flowing robe. And the Truth is the Truth revealed by God, the deposit of the faith committed to the Church, which is the pillar and ground of the Truth. Did you ever see a Christian soldier fight at odds without his girdle ? I know few sadder sights. He is fighting against the powers of sin and unbelief ; but all his movements are impeded. He is fighting without his girdle. He is a Christian still, a soldier still, but he has given up or lost his rule of faith—the Truth of God. Laxness of religious belief is as inconsistent with real freedom as a loose ungirdled robe is inconsistent with a soldier's active life.

II. The Breastplate.—Elsewhere St. Paul calls it the breastplate of faith and love ; here he follows Isaiah and speaks of it as the breastplate of righteousness. And righteousness means simply a good life lived in the strength of God. That which belongs to the Christian is the power to do in God's strength that which man by nature longs, yet fails, to do. There have been men who have thought lightly of the holy life, and put a transient emotion in place of the hold on Truth, and lost their hold on that in which a hold on Truth results—a holy life. Yet, where sin is present in the life, where the breastplate of righteousness is pierced, though the girdle of Truth be on our loins and the shield of Faith before us, our armour is incomplete. The darts will pierce where they have pierced before. The soul that carries a secret sin will never stand before the assaults of Satan.

III. The Sandals : 'Have your feet shod with the preparation of the Gospel of peace'. That is, I think, the readiness to proclaim to others the good news of God. A religion which shows no missionary enthusi-

asm is a dead or dying religion ; a personal faith, which begins at home and stays there, is not a belief in the Gospel of Christ. The sandals of readiness to work for God are part of the equipment of the soldier of Christ.

IV. The Shield of Faith.—Faith is the correlative of Truth. It is the Divine virtue which corresponds to that which God has told us about Himself. Strictly, all faith has God and the revelation of God for its object. How many forget to hold the shield of Faith over the body armour, to let it meet the first brunt of the enemy's attack ! Many an arrow might have been rendered harmless had it been met by the shield of Faith—yes, even by a battered shield, like his who cried, 'Lord, I believe ; help Thou mine unbelief'.

V. The Helmet of Salvation ; or, as it is called elsewhere, the Hope of Salvation. Hope is not that sanguine disposition which is but little removed from ignorance : it is a grace of God, and yet it becomes more and more a rational power. Faith and hope were the two presuppositions of the early Christian efforts. Six hundred against the world, and the Church went forth conquering and to conquer, because it believed and hoped. If for a moment we lose hope, or if that hope is a mere emotional thing which fails us when all seems dark, then we feel our want of power ; the enemy finds us out, and it is a forlorn hope. We are fighting without our helmet ; and he who has lost his helmet is ready to throw away his shield, for to lose hope is to lose faith too.

VI. The Sword of the Spirit, which is the Word of God. All else is for defence ; this is for attack. The Christian cannot win the battle simply by avoiding wounds ; he must drive the enemy from the field. The phrase is not necessarily to be restricted to the Holy Bible ; and yet, when I look back to that great battle fought and won in the wilderness, I see how the Tempter again and again recoiled from the sword of the Spirit, and shrank away before the invincible answer, 'It is written '.—AUBREY MOORE.

MELANCHTHON'S LAST PUBLIC MESSAGE

'Wherefore take unto you the whole armour of God.'—
EPH. VI. 13.

IN his last public lecture, delivered in the early morning of Good Friday, 1560, Melanchthon used these words, referring to the need for a new obedience in the believer, 'Necessaria est et nostra Panoplia,' with an evident allusion to Ephesians VI. 13, 'Take unto you the whole armour of God'. The Latin narrative adds that these were the last words he uttered in public, as the lecture he desired to give on Easter Sunday morning was omitted on account of his increasing weakness. These words, 'Necessaria est et nostra Panoplia,' were therefore the last public message of the Præceptor Germaniæ to his generation. During his illness Melanchthon quoted two verses from Psalm cxx. which to us seem to express the chief sorrow of his life : 'My soul hath long dwelt with him that hateth peace. I am for peace but when I speak they are for war.' Yet the man of peace left behind him a soldier's instruction :—

> Take to arm you for the fight
> The panoply of God.

The old German version translates his words : ' Es ist auch unser vleis und Ritterschaft von nöten' ['We need also diligence and knightly courage '], and the narrative suggests that these qualities had been conspicuously displayed in Melanchthon's own career.

[See the text of the original in Dr. N. Müller's revised and annotated edition (1910), pp. 11 and 62.]

' Take unto you the whole armour of God.'—Eph. vi. 13.

A NOBLE thought is the soul's defensive armour; encased in it a man may suffer bombardment from life's pollutions and take no stain. ' The whole armour of God '—if in the urgency of battle you forget its details, take it just as the 'pearly shell' of a noble thought.—JAMES McKECHNIE, MEREDITH's Allegory, *The Shaving of Shagpat*, p. 124.

' Having done all, to stand.'—Eph. vi. 13.

DR. EUGENE STOCK tells us that as far back as 1833 William Jowett concluded the instructions to John Tucker on his departure for Madras with some words found in the letter of Ignatius to Polycarp on the latter's position in Smyrna, 'Stand steady as an anvil when it is struck'. Tucker in after years often recalled them, saying, 'Be an anvil and not a hammer'.

REFERENCES.—VI. 13.—R. C. Trench, *Sermons New and Old*, p. 71. J. Hunter, *Christian World Pulpit*, vol. xliii. p. 42. G. W. Brameld, *Practical Sermons* (2nd Series), p. 47. A. Maclaren, *Expositions of Holy Scripture—Ephesians*, p. 337.

THE WHOLE ARMOUR OF GOD

EPH. VI. 13-18.

No man could have invented this expression. It brings with it some sign and token of its Divine origin. The most of things that are in the Scriptures are things that never would have occurred to the mind of man. Hence I stand by the old argument that the Bible is a book which no man could have written if he would, or would have written if he could. The uniqueness is part of the argument. 'The whole armour of God.' Is there any mere poetry in the word whole? Is it employed or introduced in order to perfect a rhetorical climax? or is there great weight of meaning in the word whole? Is it the emphatic word in the exhortation? or are all the words on one high level?—the monotony not of weakness or weariness, but of completeness. We must revert to our own spiritual experience if we would receive a sufficing answer to these inquiries. Could we do without the word whole? What does the word whole stand for in this connection? It stands for completeness; there must not be one piece of the panoply overlooked, nor must the places and arrangements of the armour be for a moment changed or otherwise related. The provision of the Divine grace is complete; we are armed from the head to the foot, there is no unprovided place or spot in all this Divine clothing with spiritual steel.

I. Many persons are armed in places. If nine points out of ten are attended to, these people suppose that they are very well provided for, but they are not. You have shut up all your castle, every window, every door, except the postern gate, the little gate behind, the small door that a small burglar may pass through. All that is wanted is not an army of burglars, but one little child-burglar that can creep through an unguarded pane of glass. Enough ! the castle is in the hands of the thief. How noticeable it is that people are very fond of pet graces and favourite virtues, and how they dangle these before the eyes of these poor creatures who are not similarly created or provided for at those special points. Do not let us who are not tempted in some directions hold ourselves up as stupendous models of behaviour in some other direction. A man may not be drunk, but his soul may be steeped in covetousness, which is worse than drunkenness. A man may not be led away by his passions, but he may be greedy, selfish, self-considering, proud, and pride is worse than any sin that stalks about the city in the night-time. We condemn sin at wrong points, or we exaggerate some sins and practise others. Hence the beauty, the force, the necessity, of the expression or commandment, ' Put on the whole armour '. Every inch of it, be equally strong at every point ; ay, and it will take thee all thy time to panoply thyself in the steel of God.

II. It is wonderful in reading over this panoply to discover how much of it is meant for defensive purposes. It is not all meant for aggression. Christianity is both aggressive and defensive. It is astonishing, I repeat, how much of the Christian armour is for purposes defensive. The helmet does not fight, it protects ; the shield does not aggress, it secures, defends, protects the very heart of the warrior. We need a great deal of defensive armour. The devil is wily. If there is one little heel-spot missed in the Christian Achilles that little vulnerable heel will be found out, and some great assault will be made upon it ; mayhap the injection of some deadly poison ; and injections are not accompanied with noise or with an uproar that is supposed to betoken heroism and angry strife ; injection may be silent. The morphia is inserted with hardly any sense of pain, the digitalis makes no noise when it gets into the life and helps the poor labouring breath. So there are many noiseless temptations, there are many assaults that are not suspected ; and therefore this saying is true. What I say unto one I say unto all. Watch ; resist the devil, and he will flee from you. But to be called to all this arming and watching and fighting and agonising expectancy, is this the way to life eternal ? Yes, and other way there is none.

III. It is very noticeable that a great deal of this combat is what may be called hand-to-hand strife. It is not a discharge of ball and other missile over a space of miles ; it is wrestling. Two men do not wrestle when they are standing five miles apart, nor a mile apart, nor a yard apart. It is when they are grappling, one with the other, seeking for the tightest place, watching every movement of the antagonist, anticipating and discounting it; the uplifting that there may be the downcasting. Sometimes the Christian warfare is just as hand-to-hand and arm-to-arm as this. Jacob wrestled; we speak and sing of wrestling Jacob. The record says, 'Now there wrestled with him,' and the wrestlers were so near to one another that the one touched the thigh of the other, and it shrank, and the muscle shrunken abides there till this day to tell what angel tussles there have been in the dark nights of spiritual experience.

IV. Is this armour all to be turned against the enemy? No; it is to be turned, so to say, but to say it with tenderest reverence, sometimes against God. How so? The proof is here: Having equipped yourselves, then follows the command or exhortation, 'Praying always with all prayer and supplication in the Spirit, and watching thereunto with all perseverance and supplication for all saints'. Does the Lord make an armoury that can be employed against Himself? Yes, in a certain sense, but that sense must be very carefully and even tenderly distinguished and discriminated. The action is this: 'The kingdom of heaven suffereth violence, and the violent take it by force'. And God, having armed the men, says, Now come and take My kingdom. God is willing to be overthrown. The angel was willing that Jacob should throw him as it were in some great struggle. No man can ever take the celestial fort; it must be surrendered by God in answer to prayer.—JOSEPH PARKER, *City Temple Pulpit*, vol. III. p. 22.

EPH. VI. 14.

LET us keep a brave heart and clear armour. What beautiful armour for a Christian lady that 'armour of light,' 'having on the breastplate of righteousness'. I was talking of that at our prayer meeting an hour since. It was suggested by going into my study late last night. The windows were open—shutters not to; but as I looked out into the moonlight I saw there was a fine defence of snow round the house; for no robber would venture to come and leave his footmarks there. Think of the angel of snow defending our homes, *i.e.* pure, white, new-fallen snow, for if the snow is trampled on and turned into slush, it is no longer of use that way. It is only in its purity that it is a guard and a defence.—DR. ROBERTSON of Irvine, to Mrs. Maxwell.

REFERENCES.—VI. 14.—E. J. Kennedy, *Old Theology Restated*, p. 180. T. S. Herrick, *Preacher's Magazine*, vol. xvii. p. 168. Brooke Herford, *Courage and Cheer*, p. 68. *Expositor* (6th Series), vol. xi. p. 362. A. Maclaren, *Expositions of Holy Scripture—Ephesians*, p. 343; *ibid.* p. 350.

THE READINESS OF THE GOSPEL OF PEACE

'And your feet shod with the preparation of the gospel of peace.'—EPH. VI. 15.

THE great Apostle was much given to the use of illustrations. Like his Divine Master, he clearly saw the analogy between things external and things internal and spiritual, and employed the one for the purpose of making the other more easily intelligible.

I. We must be ready for service. The believer is not saved by his works: but he is saved that he may work, and the genuineness of his new life is to be manifested by service. Now the possession of peace with God, much more the assurance of the possession of the peace of God within us, will give us readiness for the performance of the service which is required of us by the will of God, and defined for us by the necessities of our own generation. For where there is peace there is whole-souledness: there is nothing to disturb the attention, divide the heart, or divert the mind; and so he who possesses it can give himself wholly to that to which he gives himself at all. The possession of this peace will keep him also from being fastidious about the place in which he serves.

II. But in the second place the Christian must be always ready for sacrifice, and the possession of the peace of God will give him that readiness. He is not to go out of his way seeking for a cross, for that would be to make himself a 'martyr by mistake'; but if, while moving on his appointed path of duty, he is confronted with a cross, then he is to take up that and humbly and bravely bear the suffering and sacrifice which it imposes, for Christ's sake. Then, as he never can tell when precisely he will be met by such a cross, he must hold himself always in readiness for it.

III. The Christian should be always ready for sorrow, and the gospel of peace will give him that readiness. The believer does not escape sorrow in the world, and he ought to be ready for its coming. But where shall he get that readiness? Not from philosophy: that may make a Stoic of him, and lead him to submit, somewhat haughtily, to the inevitable, but it will give him neither the resignation nor the consolation of the Christian. Pride will not give it to him, for that will only wrap him in the mantle of seclusion, and make him discontented and irritable with God and all around him. But the Gospel of peace will give it to him, for that assures him that everything that comes to him is under the supervision and control of God.

IV. The Christian should be ready for death, and the gospel of peace will give him that readiness. That which we most of all need in the prospect of our leaving the world is readiness to go. Nay, that readiness, rightly understood, is all we need. And in what does that readiness consist? Not in any special occupation at the moment, but in the habitual character of the soul; not in the performance of any rite, such as the observance of the supper, or the reception of extreme unction; no, but in the faith which rests on Jesus Christ, and in the possession of that peace which He bestows.

REFERENCES.—VI. 15.—E. J. Kennedy, *Old Theology Restated*, p. 192. A. Maclaren, *Expositions of Holy Scripture—Ephesians*, p. 353. VI. 16.—*Ibid.* p. 361. Spurgeon, *Sermons*, vol. vii. No. 416. E. J. Kennedy, *Old Theology Restated*, p. 204. VI. 17.—H. Allen, *Penny Pulpit*, No. 1577, pp. 1, 21. E. J. Kennedy, *Old Theology Re-stated*, pp. 216, 229. Spurgeon, *Sermons*, vol. xxxvii. No. 2201. A. Maclaren, *Expositions of Holy Scripture—Ephesians*, p. 367.

INTERCESSION

' Praying always with all prayer and supplication in the Spirit, and watching thereunto with all perseverance and supplication for all saints.'—EPH. VI. 18.

INTERCESSION is the characteristic of Christian worship, the privilege of the heavenly adoption, the exercise of the perfect and spiritual mind.

I. First, let us turn to the express injunctions of Scripture. For instance, the text itself : ' Praying in every season with all prayer and supplication in the Spirit, and abstaining from sleep for the purpose, with all perseverance and supplication for all saints.' Observe the earnestness of the intercession here inculcated ; ' in every season,' ' with all supplication,' and ' to the loss of sleep'. Again, in the Epistle to the Colossians ; ' Persevere in prayer, watching in it with thanksgiving, withal praying for us also '. Again, ' Brethren, pray for us '. And again in detail ; ' I exhort that, first of all, supplications, prayers, intercessions, and giving of thanks, be made for all men ; for kings, and all that are in authority. I will therefore that men pray in every place.' On the other hand, go through the Epistles, and reckon up how many exhortations occur therein to pray merely for self. You will find there are few, or rather none at all. Even those which seem at first sight to be such, will be found really to have in view the good of the Church.

II. Such is the lesson taught us by the words and deeds of the Apostles and their brethren. Nor could it be otherwise, if Christianity be a social religion, as it is pre-eminently. If Christians are to live together, they will pray together ; and united prayer is necessarily of an intercessory character, as being offered for each other and for the whole, and for self as one of the whole. In proportion, then, as unity is an especial Gospel-duty, so does Gospel-prayer partake of a social character ; and intercession becomes a token of the existence of a Church Catholic.

III. Intercession is the especial observance of the Christian, because he alone is in a condition to offer it. It is the function of the justified and obedient, of the sons of God, ' who walk not after the flesh but after the spirit ; ' not of the carnal and unregenerate. This is plain even to natural reason. The blind man, who was cured, said of Christ, ' We know that God heareth not sinners ; but, if any man *be a worshipper of God and doeth His will*, him He heareth '. Saul the persecutor obviously could not intercede like St. Paul the Apostle. Our first prayers ever must be for ourselves. Our own salvation is our personal concern ; till we labour to secure it, till we try to live religiously, and pray to be enabled to do so, nay, and have made progress, it is but hypocrisy, or at best it is overbold, to busy ourselves with others. I do not mean that prayer for self always comes first in order of time, and intercession second. Blessed be God, we were all made His children before we had actually sinned ; we began life in purity and innocence. Intercession is never more appropriate than when sin had been utterly abolished, and the heart was most affectionate and least selfish. Nor would I deny, that a care for the souls of other men may be the first symptom of a man's beginning to think about his own ; or that persons, who are conscious to themselves of much guilt, often pray for those whom they revere and love, when under the influence of fear, or in agony, or other strong emotion, and, perhaps, at other times. Still it is true, that there is something incongruous and inconsistent in a man's presuming to intercede, who is an habitual and deliberate sinner. Also it is true, that most men do, more or less, fall away from God, sully their baptismal robe, need the grace of repentance, and have to be awakened to the necessity of prayer for self, as the first step in observing prayer of any kind.

The privilege of intercession is a trust committed to all Christians who have a clear conscience and are in full communion with the Church. We leave secret things to God—what each man's real advancement is in holy things, and what his real power in the unseen world. Two things alone concern us, to exercise our gift and make ourselves more and more worthy of it. —J. H. NEWMAN.

REFERENCES.—VI. 18.—S. G. Maclennan, *Christian World Pulpit*, vol. xliii. p. 170. Brooke Herford, *Courage and Cheer*, p. 1. J. Chambers, *Christian World Pulpit*, vol. liv. p. 158. H. Melville, *Penny Pulpit*, No. 1622, p. 25. VI. 18-24.— E. J. Kennedy, *Old Theology Re-stated*, p. 242. VI. 19.— Archbishop Magee, *Christ the Light of all Scripture*, p. 129. VI. 19, 20.—*Expositor* (6th Series), vol. xi. p. 207. VI. 23.—A. Maclaren, *Expositions of Holy Scripture—Ephesians*, p. 381. VI. 23 and 24.—J. H. Holford, *Memorial Sermons*, p. 114. VI. 24.—A. Maclaren, *Expositions of Holy Scripture —Ephesians*, p. 391.

THE EPISTLE TO THE PHILIPPIANS

THE SAINTS OF GOD

(*For All Saints' Eve*)

'The Saints who are at Philippi.'—PHIL. I. I.

To-morrow is the day of All Saints. For quite a thousand years the churches of the West have given the first of November to this great commemoration, illuminating the declining and darkening year with the spiritual splendour of the thought of these exalted multitudes who have outsoared our shadows into the light of God. For it is with the holy ones departed that the festival, beyond a doubt, was primarily from the first concerned. It contemplated the saints in that reference of the word which is often its distinctive reference in the Bible, as where the Old Testament seer beholds 'the Lord our God coming, and all the saints with him,' and where the Christian Apostle hails the same supreme prospect in its clearer and more articulate glory, 'the coming of the Lord Jesus Christ, with all His saints'.

That reference passed into current language and normal use, as we find it largely illustrated in Shakespeare for example and in Milton. And so the noble Collect of our Book, a prayer of the Reformation age, lifts us up to remember and to emulate the immortals ; 'Grant that we may follow Thy blessed saints in all virtuous and godly living'.

I. Let us remember that the word saint, when we follow it through the Bible, above all through the New Testament, by no means most frequently connects itself with the holy dead in 'those heavenly habitations,' where (to use the words of the tenderest supplication of the Prayer Book) 'the souls of them that sleep in the Lord Jesus enjoy perpetual rest and felicity'. Rather the word gravitates by Scriptural usage towards the seen and the temporal for its setting. By a saint the Apostle commonly means a being altogether, as to conditions and surroundings, like ourselves. We read of 'poor saints,' who need pecuniary relief by church collections, of 'saints' whose feet, tired and bemired with travel, the pious widow washes ; 'saints' resident and busy in town and city life, saints of Rome, and specially of Cæsar's household, saints of Colossæ, of Thessalonica, and, as in the text, saints of Philippi. Not the Garden of God was the place of life for the latter, but the Roman military town, with its vices and superstitions, and its angry rabble, its shops and market, its courthouse, and its inner prison. One of these Philippian saints was a merchant-woman, another was governor of the gaol, another a recent victim of demoniacal possession, still very likely the chattel of the slave-owner. Yet to this whole company St. Paul gives without reserve the glorious name. There and then, in the thick of their Philippian life, they were all the saints of God.

II. 'The saints who are at Philippi,' the ἅγιοι there. What does the word ἅγιος mean ? Taking together its etymology and its use, we find it conveying a blended and elevating notion of religious awe, and of a Divine ownership. Kindred to ἅγος, it casts round its bearer the solemn halo or *aura* of a mysterious presence, a contact with the Eternal. The invisible world has touched the man, and sympathised with him, and breathed itself into him. God has called him, and drawn him near, into a personal connexion.

Then, also, ἅγιος, by its usage, as well as in the light of the Hebrew word which in Scripture it represents, lends itself to the thought of separation, of detachment, to an ownership sovereign and supreme. The Lord has not only spoken to the man, but has annexed him. The person not only worships, but belongs. The presence around him and above him imposes an absolute claim upon him. It bids him live no longer to himself but to his God, to his Redeemer, Who has bought him, to his Sanctifier, Who occupies his soul.

III. Thus interpreted, the word saint, as in its other and heavenly reference, is indeed a great word and uplifting. It carries in it the powers of the world invisible, and the grandeur of the fact that the redeemed man's life is lived always and in the whole of it within the possessing hands of God. No lower significance satisfies the truth of the designation. Nothing can be more wide of that truth than to explain saint as a conventional synonym for the baptised Christian and no more. To be sure, it is applied impartially to all the baptised ; the Apostle here indicates by it evidently the whole membership of the missionary Church. But this he does, as James Mozley long ago convincingly reasoned, not as if the word saint admitted into itself a secondary and inferior sense, a sense, as Pearson puts it, of 'outward vocation' and charitable presumption'. Rather the 'presumption' of the usage is that the people addressed are all what they all are called, that they are Christians indeed to a man and to a woman, that they are redeemed beings who have all responded to their redemption, that they have all felt, in fact, the power of the Eternal Presence, and its overawing love, that without exception they have yielded themselves to the Divine Possessor, and are appropriated to Him.

Yet meanwhile the word, thus exacting and exalted, is no remote and intangible term of an imaginative devotion. The Apostle means by it manifestly, as we have seen, something which can live, and labour, and suffer, in the common walk of life. He applies it without an effort to their modern mortal lives.

Such homely saintship, as we know, was the traditional habit of the primeval Church. Some seventy years later than the date of our text, it was the strange sunlight of a celestial life shed upon the common path, which moved the soul of Aristides and prompted his appeal to Antonine. In his wonderful sketch of the Christians of the second century I find no allusion whatever to ascetic rigours and seclusions, nor again to supernatural displays, to unknown tongues, and sudden healing miracles. But the observer stood awed and magnetically attracted before the people, who without pretension, without self-consciousness, but with the large facility of a new nature, were always true, and always pure, and always kind in ordinary intercourse, glad and thankful before their God. In everything, faultlessly faithful in each relative duty of life, ready every day for a happy death, by nature or by martyrdom.

The apostolic succession of the saints is the same still in its idea, and it can be the same still in its realisation.

'The saints of God, their conflict past!' It is good for us to salute them, some of them dear unspeakably to ourselves, gathered together in their glorious rest on high. But they all were first the saints of some Philippi here below as we are called to be to-day. They were all once true men and true women hallowed by the Eternal Presence here, and separated and surrendered here to the possession and the uses of their King.—Bishop H. C. G. Moule, *Church Family Newspaper*, 5th November, 1909.

THE COURTESY BORN OF JESUS
'Paul and Timothy.'—Phil. i. i, 2.

How beautiful is the conjunction of the aged Apostle and the young disciple in sacred league and covenant! I wonder how much each owed to the other in the ministry of the Spirit? How far was it Timothy's ministry to keep the old man young, and to warm his soul continually with the kindling influence of youthful enthusiasm? It is a gracious remembrance, that, in these latter days of limitation and suspicion, Paul could drink at the fountain of a young man's love. He had the inexpressible privilege of scenting the perfumes of love's springtime, and feasting upon the first sweet fruits in the garden of a young and grace-filled soul. Beautiful must have been their companionship—youth revering age, and age having no contempt or suspicion of youth, but each ministering to the other of the flowers and fruits of his own season. 'Paul and Timothy.' It is the union of springtime and autumn; of enthusiasm and experience; of impulse and wisdom; of tender hope and quiet and rich assurance.

I. Servants of Jesus Christ.—The early Apostles gloried in exhibiting the brand-marks of their Lord. Here, in this letter, the first thing the Apostle shows us is the mark of the branding   A little while ago

I was present at a sheep-shearing in the very heart of the Highlands, and I noticed that when the heavy, burdensome fleece had been shorn from the affrighted sheep, the liberated beast was branded with the owner's initials and went bounding away, prominently exhibiting these signs of its owner's name. And Paul and Timothy had been delivered from a heavy burden : the vesture of oppressive habits had been removed by the power of a crucified Lord, and on their emancipated lives they bore the marks of their owner—the 'brands' of the Lord Jesus. *Whose I am.* They belonged to Him who had redeemed them with a heavy price, and they counted it to be their glory, and their crown of rejoicing, that they were not their own, but the branded 'bond-servants' of the Lord Jesus Christ.

II. To all the Saints in Christ Jesus which are at Philippi. The saints are reared in unlikely neighbourhoods. It was at Philippi that the multitude was so hostile and violent. It was at Philippi that Paul had 'many stripes' laid upon him, and that he was 'thrust into prison,' and his feet 'made fast in the stocks'. One would have thought that in this fierce persecution the little Church would have been destroyed, and that in these scorching antagonisms the early, tender leaves of Christian faith and hope would have withered away. But ' He maketh grass to grow upon the mountains'—even in those unlikely places—and He reared His saints amid the threatening decimations of Philippi. For let it be remembered that, though Philippi was the sphere of their living, it did not provide the rootage of their life. The saints were '*at* Philippi,' but they were '*in* Christ Jesus,' and that is the secret of their endurance 'when the sun was up' and the hot beams of hostility blazed upon their unoffending heads.

III. With the Bishops and Deacons.—'Honour to whom honour is due.' These men had done the work of collecting the help which had been sent to the needy Apostle, and they must receive special and generous recognition. St. Paul was a prince of courtesy. Courtesy is not the creation of effort, it is the product of grace : it is born, not made. Paul was born of grace, and therefore he was gracious, and instinctively his courtesy fitted itself to all the changing requirements of the day.

IV. Grace to You.—Behind graciousness was grace, and the courtesy broadened into a prayer for the supreme gift. Get grace, and all gifts are gained. Grace is the bountiful mother of all the graces.

V. And Peace.—Where grace abides peace will dwell. They are inseparable companions. Grace is the native element in which all our powers awake and work in happy service. Now peace is not the absence of movement : it is the absence of friction. The real symbol of peace is not to be found in some secluded motionless mountain tarn, but in the majestic progress of some quiet brimming river. Peace is not symbolised in the death chamber, but in the rhythmic, smooth movements of the engine-house. When grace reigns, man moves in God in perfect unison, man co-operates with man in fellowship without strain, and 'all that is within us praise and bless' God's 'holy name'. When grace reigns, life loses all its 'strain and stress,' and, in the absence of friction, 'all things work together for good'.—J. H. JOWETT, *The High Calling*, p. 1.

REFERENCES.—I. 1 —*Expositor* (6th Series), vol. iv. p. 46. I. 2.—*Ibid.* (5th Series), vol. vii. p. 65. I. 3.—W. Wynn, *Christian World Pulpit*, vol. xlvi. p. 338. I. 3-5.—W. Baird, *The Hallowing of our Common Life*, p. 84. I. 3-7.—Spurgeon, *Sermons*, vol. xxxvi. No. 2154. I. 3-8.—J. H. Jowett, *The High Calling*, p. 9. I. 5, 6.—*Expositor* (5th Series), vol. v. p. 139. I. 6.—Spurgeon, *Sermons*, vol. xv. No. 872. J. Keble, *Sermons for the Sundays after Trinity*, p. 308. Spurgeon, *Christian World Pulpit*, vol. lix. p. 133. W. H. Hutchings, *Sermon Sketches*, p. 274. A. Connell, *Scottish Review*, vol. iii. p. 161. I. 7.—Bishop Creighton, *University and Other Sermons*, p. 124. *Expositor* (4th Series), vol. v. p. 343. I. 9.—H. P. Liddon, *Sermons Preached on Special Occasions*, p. 286. A. P. Stanley, *Canterbury Sermons*, p. 328. I. 9, 10.—T. Arnold, *Christian Life: Its Hopes*, p. 208. I. 9-11.—Bishop Westcott, *Village Sermons*, p. 289. I. 9-14.—J. H. Jowett, *The High Calling*, p. 17. A. Maclaren, *Expositions of Holy Scripture—Philippians*, p. 206.

THE MORE EXCELLENT WAY

'That ye may approve things that are excellent.'—PHIL. i. 10.

IN this very remarkable prayer, St. Paul is guided by a conception of Christianity as it really is, and he is expressing successive aspects of the world into which it introduces men. The text describes one such aspect, and an extremely important one, *viz.*, the approvals of a life, its unforced choices, instinctive preferences, and habitual consents. There are a thousand little points of manner, speech, thought, and action, in which both of two possible courses are justifiable, but one is the finer course, and belongs to the things which are excellent. This prayer is for a type of character founded upon the habitual choice of such things.

I. Obviously this first of all requires *appreciation* —to know what one desires and to desire rightly. If it be important to learn how to say No, it is still more important to learn how to say Yes, and to say it emphatically. For, even in so unsatisfactory a world as this, there are some things which are excellent—things that are 'true, honest, just, pure, lovely, and of good report'. There is a certain number of such things round about us all. Some people are turning over large heaps of them, to find the unpleasant things below, but that does not alter the fact. If your world of thought and choice is ugly and second-rate, that is neither God's fault nor the world's. It is your own fault, who have approved these things for emphasis. The world is strewn with the good gifts of God. 'Here is God's plenty,' as Dryden says of Chaucer: and the opulence of the world is the heartening message of many others who have found 'power each side, perfection every turn'. It is a great and wise thing to look around us with chaste desire and loving eye, and to see and appreciate the choicest excellence.

II. Yet appreciation must be balanced with *criticism*, for in a world like this there is a very manifest limit to approval, and criticism, no less than appreciation, is a distinctively Christian duty. Marius the Epicurean recognised in his Christian friend, 'some inward standard of distinction, selection, refusal, amid the various elements of the fervid and corrupt life' around them. Even in literature, as Pater elsewhere insists, the choicest work depends upon the art of cutting off surplusage; and all finest things, like the diamond, gain their beauty by sacrifice of precious dust. 'Excellence is not common and abundant,' says Matthew Arnold, 'whoever talks of excellence as common and abundant is on the way to lose all right standard of excellence.'

III. Thus Christian character also involves *selection*, not only of obvious right in contrast with wrong, but of the finest kind of right and that which is fittest for the special occasion. To reject open immorality and to accept all the rest without discrimination, is respectability, the religion of the Pharisees. But every respectable Pharisee proves the truth of the saying that 'the good is the enemy of the best'. There is a scale of fineness among things respectable, and Christ insists that we shall not be content with a second-best, though it be good. In this way He has produced a special type of man, more delicately sensitive in choices than the rest. Such men, whose spirit habitually dwells among the highest things, show a rare spiritual culture, an exclusiveness, an aristocracy of spirit, which partly explains Christ's insistence on the narrow way and the straight gate, and the few that find it.

Yet that is not so true as it seems. Instincts may be acquired and tastes rectified within a lifetime. These are the last results of certain ways of dealing with life which are open to all. Those who live worthily among plain and ordinary issues, who train their minds to think accurately and dispassionately, who keep their eyes open and gain experience of the world, come in the end to a spontaneous and immediate discernment of the lower and the higher ways.— JOHN KELMAN, *Ephemera Eternitatis*, p. 104.

REFERENCES.—I. 10.—H. J. Wilmot-Buxton, *Sunday Sermonettes for a Year*, p. 206. F. D. Maurice, *Sermons*, vol. iv. p. 67. J. Kelman, *Scottish Review*, vol. iii. p. 243. I. 12.— L. D. Bevan, *Christian World Pulpit*, vol. li. p. 283. I. 12-14.—D. J. Weller, *ibid.* vol. l. p. 52. I. 12-20.—A. Maclaren, *Expositions of Holy Scripture—Philippians*, p. 211. I. 14-18.—*Expositor* (5th Series), vol. vii. p. 107. I. 15-18.— J. C. Lees, *Christian World Pulpit*, vol. liv. p. 36. *Expositor* (6th Series), vol. xi. p. 467. I. 15-19.—J. H. Jowett, *The High Calling*, p. 25. I. 18.—Spurgeon, *Sermons*, vol. vii. No. 370; *Ibid.* vol. xix. No. 1139.

MAGNIFYING CHRIST

'According to my earnest expectation and my hope, that in nothing I shall be ashamed, but that with all boldness, as always, so now also Christ shall be magnified in my body, whether it be by life, or by death.'—PHIL. i. 20.

YOU have in those words a picture, a portrait of a minister of Jesus Christ. You have a portrait of St.

Paul drawn by the hands of Paul himself. As he dictates the words, he is hardly thinking of himself at all. He is just opening his heart after his manner to those whom he loved in the Church at Philippi, and he tells them what they know well enough, that his earnest expectation and hope was that in nothing he should be ashamed, but that, as always, so now also Christ should be magnified in his body, whether it were by life or by death. Was St. Paul's expectation realised, or was his confidence ultimately disappointed? Did he fail in that position in which God had put him, or did he actually and really magnify Jesus Christ his Lord in his body whether by life or by death?

I. St. Paul's Confidence justified.—I would have you notice first of all that St. Paul's confidence, his expectation, of which he speaks here, was tested, and tested to the uttermost. St. Paul never knew from one day to another which would be his last. That prison door might any moment open, and the executioner enter who would take him to a shameful punishment, a public execution, and I ask you to think again what that must have meant to St. Paul. He faces the alternatives here in this letter. He looks at life and he looks at death. He puts them both into his scales and weighs them. He looks at death. It meant the cessation of all that pain and travail, all that persecution, these bonds and imprisonment. It meant deliverance from that party at Rome and similar parties elsewhere. This on the negative side. Positively, it meant to be with Jesus Christ ; and St. Paul, as you see in this letter, is just glancing in at the gate of heaven, and as he does so the whole soul of the man goes out in these words, 'I desire to depart and to be with Christ, which is far better'. And then he looks at life ; and what did life mean? I have said life meant a continuance of all that he was going on with day by day, and year by year. He could hardly suffer more, but he was not likely to suffer less, and that to St. Paul meant life at its best. Do not forget that. St. Paul would not exchange that life for any other that man could give him in the world. As he looks at these two things, life and death, each is so excellent that he says, 'I am in a strait betwixt two'. 'I know not which to choose.' And then, as he thinks of the needs of the little Philippian Church, and when he remembers how essential he is as yet for their guidance and help, he says, 'I am confident that I shall abide in the flesh for your sakes, and I am content that it should be so.' Is not this wonderful? I ask you to think of this living man—with our temptations, our weaknesses, and our trials, and far more, and I ask you to think how he met them as we have it depicted here. St. Paul's confidence was not misplaced, St. Paul's expectation was not disappointed.

II. St. Paul's Secret.—Now as to his secret. Remember, this is the picture in our text, not merely of an Apostle, but of every Christian man and woman. To you he would say, as he said to one of the Churches, 'Be ye Ambassador for Him'. You and I want to know, we who call ourselves Christians, what St. Paul's secret was, and you have it here in the words adjoining my text, 'To me to live is Christ'. These words may be peculiarly useful to any of us. There are a great many persons in Christian England who do not see why they personally need what is termed conversion. They do not see, when they look at their own lives, that there is any particular difference between themselves and some who profess to have been truly born again and brought into the service of Christ. Their lives are respectable, their conduct is upright, their standards are Christian, they do not see that there is any particular need of change. These words of the Apostle may be a test to one and to another. Will you say them in your heart as I speak them, 'To live is——'. What word will you put in there? Remember the alternative of Christ is self. Let me ask you again to say these words in your hearts, and to put in what actually represents the main ambition of your life, 'To me to live is——' Now you know where you are. I can imagine one saying something like this, 'Yes, but I want to be honest ; I do not want to be a hypocrite. If I take Jesus Christ as the New Testament bids me, I am not sure that I shall continue, and I do not want to fail.' Did St. Paul fail? We have good reason for knowing that he did not. He never did fail, and his behaviour in these trying conditions was his witness to these soldiers day by day, and they knew and felt the power of it.

III. Can there be any Higher Ambition?—Whether you be a minister of Jesus Christ like St. Paul, or whether you be what we term a layman—man or woman—can there be any higher ambition in life than this set before us, now to magnify Christ in our bodies, whether by life or by death? 'Magnify Christ,' you say. 'How can I magnify Him Who is infinitely great?' You cannot make Christ any greater than He is, but you can magnify Him, your life may become a magnifying lens, and men shall look at Jesus Christ through your conduct as they looked at Jesus Christ through the conduct of his servant St. Paul. You may make Him appear infinitely greater than He does in the eyes of the men and women who live at home with you, whom you meet in your business and in your social circle. 'My earnest expectation and my hope is,' said the Apostle 'that in nothing I shall be ashamed, but that with all boldness, as always, so now also Christ shall be magnified in my body, whether it be by life, or by death.'

THE CHRISTIAN IDEA OF DEATH.

'To die is gain.'—PHIL. I. 21.

I THINK the text would read more strongly if we were to omit that intruded 'is' in both cases. Let us delete this intrusive verb, and look at the text in this naked English : 'For me to live—Christ, and to die—gain'. That is nobler poetry, that is a better scansion of the poem. O Death, thy sting? Strike out the 'where is'. Grave, thy victory? It is a giant's taunt, and terrific and derisive challenge and rebuke.

I. A most curious mind is this of the Apostle Paul. He thinks aloud whilst he is apparently only writing with his hand or with the hand of another man. This is a monologue, this is the soul over-heard, caught in its most secret and sacred whispers; what a privilege that we may hear the greatest soul that ever lived in the Christian Church talking! 'For me to live is Christ, and to die is gain:' I am in a strait betwixt two, having a desire to depart and be with Christ—that is what I want, it is far better —nevertheless, to abide in the flesh is more needful for you; I know that; I am in a strait betwixt the two; to die might be gain, not to me, a poor dying man, but to the cause. Some promote the cause by dying for it; it was so Christ lifted up His cross, until its magnitude turned the firmament into a cloud, and its glory abashed the sun. We think our work is done when we die; probably in this matter, as in many other matters, we are quite wrong; it may be that by dying in harness, being brave to the last, and working the furrow only half-way through or wholly through, we are doing more by dying than we could do by living. Let our ignorance hold its breath, let our impiety dismiss its crude and often blasphemous dreams and anticipations, and let God have His own way in His own Church among His own people. It might be a cowardly thing to desire to die if by dying we mean getting out of it, shaking it off, having nothing more to do with it, with its anxiety and its burdensomeness and its agony; that would be cowardice, and we should put Christ to a blushing shame if we talked so and yet professed to be the followers of His cross. To die may be the greatest contribution we can make to the faith which we have endeavoured to express in words, and which now we must in one gigantic final effort endeavour to express in sacrifice.

II. The religion of Christ is a grand religion to die in. It is so fearless, it is familiar with the spirit of eternity; it has grown the soul into a reverent familiarity with things big as infinity and glorious as incarnated light. This is the sign of our growth, that the things which once affrighted us now exercise upon us all the subtle power and fascination of a charm or spiritual enchantment. Once we feared to look upon a dead body; in the England that I can remember the poor dead flesh was set in a dark room, with a few dim-lighted candles just to mitigate the darkness; and there were watchers, people who sat up all night near the dead or near the chamber where the dead was coffined; everything was in a sad, hopeless hush; few dare go near the dead. We have not so learned the Christ; the death-chamber has been turned into the centre of the house, the only bright spot in the whole habitation. What may we not learn from that image of triumph and that image of rest? That is the natural fruition of true faith in Christ, who 'both died, and rose,'—as if the dying and the rising were part of the same act, hardly

a pause between the going and the coming, the departing and the return. So the literature of experience has undergone a new punctuation.

III. Christian death is full of brightness that living eyes cannot see, and full of hope that this poor, struggling, hesitating, self-contradicting experience of ours cannot adequately spell or interpret as one interprets who has the gift of telling what a dream is. We must be very careful therefore how we interpret the experience of those who die. Blessed are they that die in the Lord; for they rest, and their interpretation follows them, and we, too late, see meanings in things we did not understand and in actions which we were ignorantly inclined to resent. When we know all we shall forgive all and ask that all may be forgiven. The history of Christian dying would be the most thrilling history in literature. But it cannot be written, we can only see a verse or a chapter here and there, and from these broken fragments we may infer somewhat of the dignity and the restfulness and the triumph of dying in Christ. Weep for yourselves, do not weep for the Christian dying. It is quite right for you to weep, because you are still in the body, you are still environed by the world, the flesh, and the devil, your nerves are exposed to rough winds and to touches that have no gentleness in them; cry, relieving your misery by the rivers of your grief, but do not grieve for those who have gone. They are not the authors of misery, they are the inspirers of wisdom and confidence and hope.—Joseph Parker, *City Temple Pulpit*, vol. III. p. 146.

THE SECRET OF ST. PAUL'S LIFE
'To me to live is Christ.'—Phil. i. 21.

What was the secret of St. Paul's life, that secret which made him the greatest of all missionaries to the Gentile world? We have not to go far in our search, for he himself has revealed it in the words of my text. The secret of St. Paul's life was the power and the presence of a living Christ.

I. **Christ in Life.**—We are Christians in proportion as we possess the spirit of Christ, in proportion as we identify ourselves with Him, in proportion as we are able to say, with something of the bold, transcendent phrase of St. Paul, 'To me to live is Christ'. With St. Paul this was no mere exaggeration or figure of speech. He had so far lost himself in Christ that he had made a practical surrender of his own personality. You know, in the ordinary affairs of life, how a man will become so absorbed in a great love, a great ambition, a great art, that he can pay no real heed to anything else. His very self seems merged in the idea or the person that has thus entranced him. It was so, and more than so, with St. Paul and Jesus Christ. The old Paul with all his interest, hopes, enthusiasms, and ideals had practically ceased to exist. ' I live no longer,' he says. The old Paul was dead, and in his place had arisen not a new Paul, but, as he elsewhere expresses it, ' Christ liveth in me '. The thought of Christ, the service of Christ, the

Spirit of Christ, the judgment and presence of Christ, these have become the one supreme, overpowering, all-pervading, dominating fact in the Apostle's consciousness of life. He draws the fact of all his real existence, of all his higher being, all that made him what he now was, simply from the life which Christ Himself inspired, and which could not last one hour without Him.

II. The Power of Growth.—Life has the power of growth or expansion. A dead thing, such as a crystal, may change under chemical laws, but it cannot be said to grow. Growth means a vital and organic change; it is never seen, therefore, except where there is life. The converse is equally true, that wherever you find life you find also growth, or expansion. The plant shows its life by its development. Apply that to the Christian's life within the soul, and you will find that you have a very practical test of its reality. The spiritual life, like life in other forms, has this expansive power, this quality of growth. If we would understand the value of our own Christianity, we cannot do better than look into our hearts and compare what we are to-day with what we used to me. Are our faces turned to the sunrise or to the twilight? Are we hoping, struggling, aspiring; are we alive in Christ?

III. The Power of Resistance.—Then, again, life has the power of resistance. Every creature that lives is beset by all sorts of powerful forces that seem to aim at destruction. Life has even been defined as the 'successful resistance of death'. And the more vigorous a life is, the more numerous and the more terrible, often, are its enemies. And so we, if we have this life of Christ within us, must cultivate this power of resistance. We shall have to resist selfish desires, we shall have to resist the spirit of the world. We have to resist self because we have, as Christians, a higher law than that of self to walk by, and because self is a very subtle being, very ready to lead us astray even under the pretence of having good intentions, even under the pretence of doing God's service. 'I have written to you, young men,' says St. John, 'because you are strong,' and he goes on to explain why they are strong. 'Because ye have overcome the wicked one.' That is the secret of greater strength: resistance to the thoughts and pleasures and seductions of the world.

IV. The Power of Production.—And, then, all life has the power of production. The plant realises the end of its existence by turning to flowers and fruit. Flowers and fruit of a true, noble, unselfish nature are the inevitable results of the Christ-life in the soul. He Himself has said it in one word: 'The tree is known by its fruit'—known to be vigorous, known to be growing or decaying, known to be dying or dead. Show by the earnestness with which you labour to overcome your besetting sin, and struggle for truth and for virtue, that your repentance is real, that you are sincere when you claim for yourself this great name of Christian. Spiritual life must be productive as well as progressive and strong. It must

grow, it must resist, it must bear fruit, and, glorifying our Father Who is in heaven, we shall realise Who it is that lives in us and by Whom and in Whom we live.

THE CHRISTIAN METAMORPHOSIS

'To me to live is Christ, and to die is gain.'—PHIL. I. 21.

THIS text describes the Christian metamorphosis, that complete subjection to Christ, involved in discipleship, which displaces, as it were, the original Ego, and puts Him in its place, ranging under Him all the activities which it formerly ruled. 'To me to live is Christ,' says the Apostle. So completely was his whole life taken up and concerned with his Lord, so entirely was it dictated and determined by Him, that it really was Christ's life. To bring out the nature of this life a little more clearly, there are one or two things to be noticed regarding it.

I. First of all, St. Paul was indebted to Christ for it. If he traced it back he found it went no farther than his journey to Damascus. Wherever he went behind that, even by a step, Christ was not to be found. Now, the question is, how are you to account for so sudden and total a change? For as to its suddenness no one can doubt. Then few, I suppose, will dispute the completeness of the change. St. Paul was indebted for the life he lived, not to any happy combination of circumstances, nor to the sudden awaking into energy of any dormant element in his nature, but to Christ Himself, with whom for the first time it had come into direct and open contact, and from whom it took its new and triumphant departure. Nothing can communicate life but a living person—neither sacraments, nor worship, nor any orthodoxy, however pure. Are you, then, indebted for your life to Christ? What has been the use of His death upon the cross so far as you are concerned?

II. When St. Paul said: 'To me to live is Christ,' he meant that Christ was not only the beginning and perennial source of his life, but also its terminus and goal. Christ in His perfect manhood was that into which he would grow. And so it is with every Christian's life. Christ is what it naturally tends to become. We may know whether our life has come from Christ by seeing whether or not it is making towards Him. 'To die is gain.' . . . If to us to live is Christ there need be no fear that death will deprive us of anything which we really prize. For it is not Christ that dies, nor the life we have received from Him; but only that in which it resides, its temporary tabernacle and home. In short, death will lead to the perfection of our identity with Him, bringing about the end of that which is here begun. But remember that all this is only on the supposition that to us now to live is Christ.—C. MOINET, *The Great Alternative and other Sermons*, p. 53.

REFERENCES.—I. 21.—Spurgeon, *Sermons*, vol. iii. No. 146. R. J. Campbell, *New Theology Sermons*, p. 1. J. Martineau, *Endeavours After the Christian Life*, p. 277. R. E. Bartlett,

Christian World Pulpit, vol. xlv. p. 342. W. P. Balfern, *Lessons from Jesus*, p. 321. H. Drummond, *The Ideal Life*, p. 107. A. L. N., *Christian World Pulpit*, vol. xlix. p. 119. W. C. Wheeler, *Sermons and Addresses*, p. 1. W. B. Selbie, *Christian World Pulpit*, vol. l. p. 328. J. W. Houchin, *The Vision of God*, p. 149. A. E. Hutchinson, *Christian World Pulpit*, vol. liii. p. 77. A. P. Stanley, *Sermons on Special Occasions*, p. 71. A. W. Williamson, *Christian World Pulpit*, vol. liv. p. 390. *Expositor* (4th Series), vol. ii. p. 102. I. 21-24.— C. Bradley, *The Christian Life*, p. 317. I. 21-25.—A. Maclaren, *Epositions of Holy Scripture—Philippians*, p. 219. I. 21-26.—J. H. Jowett, *The High Calling*, p. 32.

HOW TO BE IN A STRAIT

'For I am in a strait betwixt two, having a desire to depart and to be with Christ; which is far better.'—PHIL. I. 23.

WHEN St. Paul wrote this Epistle to the Philippians, he was in prison, and in a strait betwixt two— between the desire for fellowship with Christ in sufferings while doing God's work *here*, on the one hand, and fellowship with Christ in the glory which shall be revealed, on the other. But St. Paul was not the only one who is in a strait. Many are conscious of being so; but not like Paul. Was the great Apostle of the Gentiles weary of His service? No. 'And He said unto me, My grace is sufficient for thee; for My strength is made perfect in weakness. Most gladly, therefore, will I rather glory in my infirmities, that the power of Christ may rest upon me' (2 Cor. XII. 9).

I. **What, then, did He mean?**—Did he think it was necessary to depart in order to have Christ with him? Oh, no. The word which is here translated 'depart' is a peculiar word, and it only occurs in one other place in the New Testament, in Luke XII. 36, where it is translated *return* from the wedding. The allusion is to a ship leaving one coast to make for another on the return voyage, taking up its anchor, loosing its hold, and setting sail for the opposite shore. It describes the position of a man standing upon such a ship looking out to the brighter shore and longing for the ship's cable to be let go, and the anchor taken up, that he may go *home*. It is '*far better*'.

II. **What was it Paul Wanted?**—*More* of his Christ; to see Him as He is; not as he saw Him here, 'through a glass, darkly'; he wanted to know as he was known, to know all about his precious Christ, to be with Him without interruption from within or without; to see the hands that were pierced; the brow that was crowned with thorns for him; to hear the voice that had once said, 'Saul, Saul, why persecutest thou Me?'

III. **What was the Ground of St. Paul's Assurance?**—For he had not one particle, not a shadow of warrant which may not be the portion of any child of God. He tells us; 'I know whom I have believed, and am persuaded that He is able to keep that which I have committed unto Him against that day'. (2 Tim. I. 12).—MARCUS RAINSFORD, *The Fulness of God*, p. 174.

A STRAIT BETWIXT TWO
PHIL. I. 23. (R.V.).

I. THE first thing to be especially marked is the way in which the Apostle regarded death, the death of the body, the passing away of the spirit. As a great gain, a blessing, a thing to be coveted. There are not many Christian people who have found their work in the world, who are beloved and loving, who feel Paul's desire. Death is still, in perhaps the majority of cases, regarded as a calamity, a time of unrelieved gloom, and it is to be feared that we have lost the conception of death which prevailed among the early Christians, and very often concerning those who have gone from us we sorrow even as do others who have no hope.

II. The happy conception of death which Paul cherished, so happy that his soul had a desire and a longing for it, is to be traced to his conception of that which lay beyond. There are two considerations which make death unwelcome to us. One is the enjoyments we have here, the other is the uncertainty of what the future contains; we dread the mysterious, we people an unknown land with terrors. There was nothing negative about Paul's conception; it was not to be out of the hurly-burly, away from sorrow, disappointment, strife, care. It was to be with Christ. What appeared entirely clear to Paul was that it was not a matter of speculation, but of revelation. Death was going to Christ; it was not a departure merely, it was an arrival.

III. It is clear that if departure means being with Christ, all Christian life should be a preparation for it, a progress towards Christ, a discipline to fit us to be with Christ; we have to learn to talk with Him, to be like Him, to be made fit to dwell with Him, to learn the habits of His life.

IV. And another thing becomes clear from this passage, viz., that no joy that any of us may experience in the way of going to Christ can for a moment be compared with the joy of being with Him.

V. Finally, it has become clear through our meditation that everything depends on our relationship to Christ.—CHARLES BROWN, *Light and Life*, p. 205.

'Having a desire to depart.'—PHIL. I. 23.

PRINCIPAL RAINY said on this passage: 'The prospect of departing in God's good time, to us unknown, should be a great and bright hope before us—the refuge of our hearts in trouble, the retreat into which we go when we would soothe and cheer our souls, a great element of the cheerfulness and patience of our lives—while we assure ourselves that the best of all we find here is by and by to give place to that which is far better.'

DR. RAINY also said: 'Do not make dying a separate thing from living; let the one and the other be continuous parts of one unbroken fellowship with Christ, so that you may die at last departing to that which is far better, on the self-same principles and grounds on which you have gone about any day's or any hour's avocations.'

'Having a desire to depart and to be with Christ, which is far better.'—PHIL. I. 23.

WHEN Luther was living at the Wartburg, and suffering from ill-health, Melanchthon wrote from Wittenberg to Spalatin (July, 1521): 'One anxiety remains, with regard to his health. I fear lest he should wear himself out with grief of mind, not for his own sake, but for ours, that is to say, for the Church. For I am not wholly ignorant of what he suffers. You know with what anxious care we must preserve the frail vessel which holds such a treasure. Should we lose him, I doubt not that God's wrath would be implacable. Through him a lamp has been kindled in Israel. If that were to go out, what other hope would remain for us? So leave nothing undone that you may find out what treatment is best in his case, and how help may be given not to him only, but to us also—yes, to us alone. For I know how he desires to depart and to be with Christ. . . . O would that with this worthless life of mine I could purchase the life of him than whom the world to-day holds no diviner being.'—*Corpus Reformatorum*, vol. I. cols. 417, 418.

DR. DODS wrote in 1863 to his sister Marcia: 'I was reading in one of the Puritans (you mind Goodwin) on Sunday and came upon this: "Death parts two old friends (body and soul) but it joins two better friends, the soul and Christ"'.—*Early Letters*, p. 291.

GEILER of Kaysersberg quoted the words 'cupio dissolvi' as one of the proofs of spiritual progress. 'If a little bird,' he said, 'is kept captive in a room, it stretches out its little neck when it comes near a window, and would like to escape. . . . If the window is opened even a little, it finds a way to slip out.'

WHEN Archbishop Laud was on the scaffold, Sir John Clotworthy asked him what special text of Scripture he found most comfortable. He replied, '*Cupio dissolvi et esse cum Christo*'. 'A good desire,' answered the knight, who added, 'there must be a foundation for that desire and assurance.' Laud rejoined, 'No man can express it, it is to be found within'. 'The Archbishop's last prayer,' says Dr. Stoughton, 'is the most beautiful thing connected with his history, and reminds us of Shakespeare's words:

> Nothing in life
> Became him like the leaving it'.

'Lord, I am coming as fast as I can, I know I must pass through the Shadow of Death before I can come to see Thee, but it is but *umbra mortis*, a mere shadow of death, a little darkness upon Nature, but Thou, by Thy merits and passion, hast broke through the jaws of death; so Lord, receive my soul, and have mercy upon me, and bless this kingdom in peace and plenty, and with brotherly love and charity, that there may not be this effusion of Christian blood amongst them, for Jesus Christ's sake, if it be Thy will.'

REFERENCES.—I. 23.—Spurgeon, *Sermons*, vol. v. No. 274, and vol. xix. No. 1136. R. Higinbotham, *Sermons*, p. 1. *Expositor* (4th Series), vol. x. pp. 302, 447. I. 27.—Spurgeon, *Sermons*, vol. xi. No. 640. J. M. Neale, *Sermons for the Church Year*, vol. ii. p. 67. F. B. Woodward, *Sermons* (2nd Series), p. 207. Bishop Gore, *Christian World Pulpit*, vol. liii. p. 409. F. B. Woodward, *Selected Sermons*, p. 92. W. Jay, *Penny Pulpit*, No. 1708, p. 703. F. W. Farrar, *Christian World Pulpit*, vol. lvii. p. 337. *Expositor* (7th Series), vol. vi. pp. 85, 548. I. 27, 28.—C. Perren, *Revival Sermons in Outline*, p. 342. J. H. Jowett, *The High Calling*, p. 38. A. Maclaren, *Expositions of Holy Scripture—Philippians*, p. 233. I. 28.—*Expositor* (4th Series), vol. v. p. 365. I. 29, 30.—J. H. Jowett, *The High Calling*, p. 43. II. 1.—Spurgeon, *Sermons*, vol. vii. No. 348. II. 1-4.—A. Maclaren, *Expositions of Holy Scripture—Philippians*, p. 244. II. 1-11.—*Expositor* (6th Series), vol. iv. p. 125. II. 3.—J. S. Boone, *Sermons*, p. 245. J. H. Jowett, *From Strength to Strength*, p. 3. *Expositor* (6th Series), vol. xi. p. 283. II. 3, 4.—J. H. Jowett, *The High Calling*, p. 56.

AGAINST CONTROVERSY

'Let nothing be done through strife or vainglory ; but in lowliness of mind let each esteem other better than themselves. Look not every man on his own things, but every man also on the things of others. Let this mind be in you, which was also in Christ Jesus.'—PHIL. II. 3-5.

THERE are two great notes in St. Paul's Epistle to the Philippians :—

I. The Note of Joy.—The first the note of joy: 'Rejoice,' he is always crying, and this is the more noble because, as you remember, he wrote as a prisoner and as one in chains. And the point reminds us once more that no chain can ever fetter the free spirit :—

> Stone walls do not a prison make,
> Nor iron bars a cage.

Even so one thinks of Bunyan with his body indeed in Bedford gaol, and with his spirit in the House Beautiful, or treading the Delectable Mountains, for in spite of circumstances he finds more in Christ to make him glad than in the world to make him sad.

II. The Note of Love.—And, secondly, there is the note of love. There is no Epistle in which the fire of love burns more brightly. We can see quite early that it is an anxious love that he has for his Philippian converts. The serious faults he notes in some other Churches are absent here. He commends their faith and purity and charity; and yet even here it is not all perfect: he has heard of discord and differences; he has noted the growth of party spirit and personal rivalry. We have sometimes seen something of this sort in the Modern Church, and indeed this warning of St. Paul's may very well save us from the common danger of idealising the past. There are still some who speak as if there were a time when all Christians loved one another in the golden ages of the Church, but little by little we are compelled to learn that there never was a golden age of the Church. Perhaps there is no more dangerous infidelity than that which is always looking to the past: that infidelity which denies the presence and power of the Holy Spirit the Sanctifier, and which in the present day never looks for the voice of God. If the virtues of the early Church are to be found to-day, so in other forms we find those weaknesses which once grieved the hearts of the Apostles.

III. A Warning Note.—Here is one instance before us now ; the forming of the Church of Philippi in the presence of the elements of personal self-assertion and party spirit. St. Paul urges on the converts as a remedy for this the cultivation of the spirit of humility. 'Let nothing be done in the spirit of strife or vainglory,' he says. It is, I think, beyond dispute that we are in need of some such warning. There are not wanting certain signs of the rekindling of party spirit. The English Church, in spite of the service she has done for the nation, has been vexed and troubled by matters of little importance. I do not say they are of no importance, for every matter which affects the worship of Almighty God must be of some importance. The Founder of Christianity declared the heart of all good lay in the worship of God in spirit and in truth.

IV. A Plea for Comprehensiveness.—I would at this time entreat you as individuals and as a body to use and exercise all your influence to preserve the comprehensiveness of the English Church. By that I do not mean the lax tolerance of all opinion, for a Church without a creed would be a Church ready to perish. I mean rather that spirit which will consist of loyalty to the great central truths of our religion, but which is still anxious to allow a wide latitude in what we might call inferential theology. The English Church stands by and in certain eternal verities. Her faith is expressed in the ancient baptism, but there are a large number of questions in which differences of opinion and practice are inevitable, and must be tolerated. So it may be well for us to take and hear the words of the Apostle : 'Let nothing be done in strife or vainglory'. He exhorts us to that lowliness of mind so far removed from party spirit and self-assertion. There are two things which will help us here :—

(*a*) *Religion will present itself in different fashions to different classes of minds.* St. Paul, St. John, and St. James held the same faith, but hardly in the same fashion, and through all the centuries of Christian history we are told how different men adopted different attitudes of mind towards faith.

(*b*) *We must consider the incompleteness of our knowledge.* Human knowledge widens every year, and the more it widens the more it brings home to us our ignorance. A few centuries ago it might have been said that a single man might know all that there was to know. It is different now. We live in an age of specialists! One man studies stars, another insects. We are only at the beginning of many studies which must more or less affect religion. Take the case of the study of the myths and religions of the world. Only now is the archæologist really revealing the treasures of the past. No doubt it does seem easy at times to take a strong line—it seems bolder and more courageous than to look all round a question—but surely the spirit of self-assertion is singularly unbecoming in us who are the little children of the day.

CHRISTIAN ALTRUISM

'Look not every man on his own things, but every man also on the things of others.'—PHIL. II. 4.

IT is necessary to fix our attention, to begin with, on one little word—the little words are often of great importance—'also'. You are not to neglect your own things, you are not to despise them. There are two possibilities open to us. The first is that of our thinking that other people's affairs are more important and more interesting than our own. That is one extreme to be avoided, and it is indicated by this word 'also'. The opposite and more probable danger for most of us is that of becoming entirely and exclusively absorbed in our own things, of imagining that they are the only things worthy of serious and sympathetic consideration, so that we never seriously contemplate the affairs of other people, but fall into that thoroughly unchristian and detestable spirit of 'Every man for himself,' which mars the beauty and strength of life. So we will remember that little conjunction 'also,' and remember that no one is fit to take care of his neighbours until he has learned to take care of himself; and then, having fixed that idea in our minds, we will go on to emphasise the apostolic injunction, 'Every man *also*'.

I. And first let us begin with the Church, which is where the writer began. There are two dangers arising out of Christian work in the Church. The one is, that when one undertakes a certain piece of work, he should be left to struggle alone with his difficulties, without sympathy from those in whose name he undertakes it. The other is that he should think that his work is the only important work, and that his fellow-Christians whose sympathies are not warmly exercised in his particular office are not Christian workers, they are scarcely Christians at all, or worthy to be called members of the Church. It is necessary to feel that no work is unimportant—to be depreciated, none to be allowed to lapse into slovenliness, for if it be, the whole body will suffer.

II. If you look at the context you will judge that 'things' may include the excellences and the trials of others. You can picture instantly how undesirable a companion, how useless a member of society, that person must be who is principally occupied in contemplating his own virtues or his own trials, and who cannot be brought to exercise his imagination for an hour upon the virtues and trials of his neighbours.

III. You might also apply this injunction to the convictions and tastes of others. It is vitally important for the goodwill and usefulness of a community that we should realise that other people have these as well as ourselves.

IV. I would venture to apply the principle of the text to our home relations. We can never have the harmony of the Christian home unless this precept be practised, and if the home is not Christian the Church can never truly be.

V. And I would go a step further, and cast the light of this precept upon our commercial relations, as employees and employers, and I think you may safely say that if a man is not a Christian in these relations he is not a Christian at all.—CHARLES BROWN, *Light and Life*, p. 167.

LOOKING ON THE OTHER SIDE
PHIL. II. 4.

THAT is a fine piece of advice if we take it in the right way. Read it as St. Paul intended, and it is one of the wisest and noblest things we can do. It was what our Lord Jesus Christ was always doing, and what every person does who shows any likeness to Jesus Christ.

I. We are to endeavour as far as we can to look at things with our brother's eyes as well as with our own. It is not always easy. We all look at things from a different point of view; we all see them in a different light. Still we may, by taking a little kindly trouble, get some fair understanding of our brother's thoughts and feelings. Nine-tenths of our quarrels and disputes would be prevented, or they would be speedily healed, if we took as much pains to read our brother's view of the question as we do to insist upon our own. How much more considerate we should be, how much more lenient in our judgments, if we tried to understand the circumstances of others, their difficulties, their temptations, as we understand our own.

II. Further, we are advised to do this for the sake of our own happiness, cheerfulness, and peace of mind. The most unhappy people you can find are those who move and live and have their being in the little world of their own troubles and grievances. They talk and feel as if there were no sorrows like unto theirs. And it is just because they take no interest in other people's sorrows, because they do not care to think of them or know of them. Yet all around them, perhaps in the very next house, hearts are breaking with a grief compared with which theirs is but child's play. We must have pities, sympathies, and affections which go out on every side, hearts that compassionate the wretched, hands eager to help the needy, hearts that bleed for human wrongs, hands which are always ready to soothe human pain.—J. G. GREENHOUGH, *The Cross and the Dice-Box*, p. 263.

OTHERNESS
PHIL. II. 4.

OTHERNESS is simply altruism translated into the vernacular. The Apostle does not endeavour to wind us up to that height of fantastic sentiment where a man shall be concerned alone with the things of other people and of no concern whatever about his own. When a man proposes to help his neighbour and yet cannot take care of himself then it is a spectacle for gods and men.

I. And now when I plead for otherness I would plead that you take an interest in the affairs of other people because they are your own affairs. A word about that man who is sometimes very difficult to deal with and sometimes very discouraging. 'Why,' says this man, 'should I trouble with the affairs of my neighbour? I receive no help; I do not see why I should give help.' No help? Did no man lend a hand to you when you were beginning business? 'Well, there was one.' Think of the people who have helped you; think of the people who have encouraged you, and pass it on, for you have been dependent on other men's things. Ah! we are all tied up together in this mysterious unity of human life, and I charge you therefore to regard the things of the man next you because they are your own things.

II. Look on the things of this man next you because your things are better. What of the hundreds of people who are decent and hard-working, but who have very poor homes, hardly any pleasure, a narrow horizon, and a heavy burden of care? What of them? Yes! And what of the hundreds who are not more amiable than other people, and not harder working than other people, who have got ample homes, endless pleasures, luxuries more than are good for them, and, what is better, all abroad an open horizon? What of them? If that man has the better things so notoriously, and this man the poorer things so undeniably, then is it not according to the highest law that this man here hold his better things in wise and charitable trust for the man who is the poorer? That at any rate is practical.

III. We should have regard of the things of other people because if we have our own things they will be a great deal sweeter to us.

IV. Think of the things of other people because One thought of our things. This argument is written in the lives of philanthropists and saints, the lives of our own homes, the lives of Christian friends, but it issues in resplendent and eternal character from the cross of Jesus Christ.—JOHN WATSON, *Christian World Pulpit*, vol. lx. p. 265.

REFERENCES.—II. 4.—A. H. Moncur Sime, *Christian World Pulpit*, vol. liii. p. 85. W. J. Hills, *Sermons and Addresses*, p. 149. *Baptist Times and Freeman*, vol. liv. p. 431. J. G. Simpson, *Christus Crucifixus*, p. 3. II. 4, 5.—H. S. Holland, *Christian World Pulpit*, vol. xlix. p. 12. J. Keble, *Sermons for Easter to Ascension Day*, p. 282. R. C. Trench, *Sermons New and Old*, p. 112. *Expositor* (6th Series), vol. xi. p. 142.

THE MEEKNESS OF THE CROSS
'Not looking each of you to his own things, but each of you also to the things of others.'—PHIL. II. 4.

I. CHRISTIAN humility is not an alternative to greatness of soul. It is a protest against the limitations by which it is too often hedged. The spirit, aware of its high capacities, but scarce daring to trust itself, seeks command of manifold resources whereby it may manipulate the world for the benefit of mankind. 'What is the use,' said Cecil Rhodes in one of his published speeches, 'what is the use of having big ideas if you have not the cash to carry them out?' That is the way in which the man who knows his power expresses the requirement of an adequate opportunity in terms intelligible to the average mind. Give me the sphere appropriate to my personal powers and I will use it, not for the purpose of vulgar acquisition, but for the accomplishment of a great task, for the realisation of a magnificent idea. This is the spirit that year by year is filling, with the best intelligence which the country can command, all those posts and offices of public service in which men may gratify the noble ambition of working for the common weal with benefit to the State and credit to themselves. But what if Christ should apply to any such the supreme test, 'Sell all that thou hast,' what then would be the answer? You would be perfect—then renounce the opportunity. You seek a real adventure—forgo your vantage-ground of wealth, station, official responsibility; take up your cross and follow Me.' How many would be ready to court the tragedy which such a choice would all but inevitably bring?

II. Humility was not first brought to the birth in the stable at Bethlehem, nor was the cross the earliest throne where it received the crown. Its reign was already from of old when the morning stars sang together. It was as the sword in the hand of St. Michael when Lucifer was thrust down from heaven. It is the spirit in which from creation's earliest dawn the Divine finger has wakened all things into life; the spirit in which a bounteous Providence, beholding the things that are in heaven and earth, has crowned the year with His goodness; the spirit in which the Father has wistfully sought the love and friendship of His children. Humility is not the creation of God's hand. It lives in the beating of His heart. As He loves so He humbles Himself. And the death of His Son was no benefaction with which, out of the riches of an infinite liberality, He endowed the poor, but the offering with which He pressed His suit upon a reluctant people, saying to each one of us, 'My son, give Me thy heart'.

III. This is the consideration which gives to humility its true dignity and value in the character of the Christian man. It is for this reason that many of the definitions—or, we had better say, descriptions—by which men endeavour to express it fall infinitely short of its true proportions. It is doubtless true that 'God is in heaven and thou upon earth,' and that therefore it becomes the children of men to refrain their souls and keep them low. But just as many a man will talk bravely of the rights of property who is yet careful to add that 'Of course, we are only stewards,' so the infinite distance which separates the creature from the Creator may encourage rather than repress a spirit which is the reverse of humility in the narrower sphere where comparison is not impossible, but inevitable. Nor can that lay claim to rank as a Christian virtue which depends for its realisation upon the chasm that separates human personality from Divine. Rather may it be expected to flourish among those who say that God is great and Mohammed is His prophet. If it be true that, as the Hebrew prophet bids us, we are to walk humbly with our God, or as the Christian Apostle puts it, to humble ourselves beneath His

mighty hand, we must seek the principle of this self-abasement elsewhere than in the infinite distance which separates our little lives from His august Eternity.

Humility, like every aspect of the character that is truly and properly Christian, must find its spring no less than its goal in the character of God. For it is from Him that Christ comes forth, as it is to Him that He returns.—J. G. Simpson, *Christus Crucifixus*, p. 3.

THE MIND OF CHRIST

'Let this mind be in you, which was also in Christ Jesus.'—Phil. ii. 5.

St. Paul tells us that we ought to have the mind of Jesus Christ; to think as He did, to have something of His Spirit and feeling, at all times. But especially should we desire to understand and share that mind at this time, when His cross and Passion fill our thoughts. We cannot believe in the cross, we cannot understand it, without having something of the Spirit which led to the cross.

I. The mind of Jesus Christ, as St. Paul speaks of it here, was His Infinite Compassion and His Infinite Humility.

(1) His Infinite Compassion. We want no one to tell us the fact that sin is in the world, and that it brings on men unhappiness and ruin in every shape; we want no one to tell us what sickness is, and pain and weakness; what it is to have great hopes, and see them fail; and that, though there is much happiness blended with our sorrow, there comes at last one thing that there is no getting rid of—a man must die. Such is man's condition, and, to make it worse, he tears himself and others, and makes all more miserable, by his sins, his selfishness, cruelty, greediness, and wrong-dealing—a condition which, without the hope and salvation brought by Jesus Christ, is indeed dark and dreadful. Truly says the Apostle, 'There is none other name under heaven given among men, whereby we must be saved'. His name opens to us hopes beyond all thought. Take away that name, and there is nothing left. This condition of man He knew, and He looked down on us, and had compassion on us. He beheld us in all our sorrows and sins—and He loved us. He, perfect in Holiness, in Glory, He beheld our suffering life, and His heart yearned towards us. He Himself would be our Deliverer. There was a sacrifice to be made; a great price to be paid; great pain to be suffered. But the sorrows and evils of the world filled His thoughts, and over against them He set His Infinite Compassion. But there was something more in the mind of Christ.

(2) His Infinite Humility. This leads us to think at once of the nature of His coming among us: His humiliation; what He came to do; how He was received; His sufferings and sacrifice; and His victory.

He, the Everlasting God, left the Throne of His Glory in heaven and came down that He might live with men, and live with them not as their earthly king; not to rule, but to minister; to live with us as our Brother; born among us only to be poor and to suffer; and He humbled Himself even to the death on the cross. And why?

(a) Because the sins of men had made life hopeless, and without remedy. He came to heal the diseases of the soul, to take away sin, to reclaim men. He came to bring the great remedy, because sinners had provoked God's righteousness, and brought such danger on the world. And—

(b) How did His creatures receive Him? 'He was in the world, and the world was made by Him, and the world knew Him not. He came unto His own, and His own received Him not.' This was the great refusal and rejection. He met with 'the daily contradiction of sinners,' and at last He, the Judge of all men, the Sinless and True, submitted to stand before the judgment-seat of fools and hypocrites, to have sentence passed on His claims by blind and wicked judges, charged with blasphemy by His own high priests. Thus He submitted to the fate of any ordinary just man, unjustly accused. We can only partly measure what such humiliation means.

II. This was the mind of Jesus, with which He wrought out that sacrifice by which our sins have been taken away, by which the hope of eternal bliss has been opened out amid the perplexities and sorrows of this mortal life. The sacrifice began when He came to share our nature, it went on all through His tempted life, and it was completed when He cried 'It is finished,' and bowed His Head, and gave up the ghost. 'Wherefore God also hath given Him a name which is above every name: that at the name of Jesus every knee should bow.'

THE MIND OF CHRIST

'Let this mind be in you, which was also in Christ Jesus.'— PHIL. II. 5.

THE historic Christ is for us the power of God and the wisdom of God. There have been numberless books written on this subject in the last few years. Has any fresh light been thrown upon it? The character of Christ in some ways is better known to us than to the Christians who lived before the labours of modern New Testament scholars.

Let me call attention to two or three salient points which to me have become clearer as the result of reading some of these recent studies.

I. We have been too much inclined to Picture our Saviour as before all Things Calm, serene, and gentle. The conventional face of Christ in art expresses benign dignity and little else, but there are several indications in the Gospels that His was a strongly emotional and deeply stirred nature. His family, St. Mark tells us, said He was beside Himself. The Spirit drove Him into the wilderness, surely under the influence of intense agitation. The agony in the Garden of Gethsemane was the result of a tremendous inward struggle. The calm, the serenity, the dignity and sweet reasonableness, were all there, but beneath the surface glowed fires of which we may not guess the tremendous energy. He must have impressed those who met Him with a sense of awful power under restraint. His disciples were constrained to treat Him with utter reverence. No one ever dared to pity Him. Only twice do we read of advice being offered Him, and on each occasion the dearly-loved counsellors, His mother and St. Peter, received a withering rebuke; and yet this awe-inspiring personality was full of gentleness and tenderness for the sick, the sorry, and the sinful. This union of strength and tenderness must have given the character of Jesus a unique charm and attractiveness.

II. What was the Source of this Temper, so wonderfully compounded of Strength and Sweetness?— The Gospels answer this question very plainly. It was the unique intensity with which our Saviour realised the presence of God, the perfect spontaneousness of His life in the eternal world. With what simple and natural love and confidence He lifted up His heart to His heavenly Father and communed with Him day and night! How this life in God's presence turned all His joy into thanksgiving and all His pain into submission! St. Paul, who entered the secret of His life and teaching as few if any have done, puts into maxims the mind of Christ. 'Pray without ceasing.' 'In everything give thanks.' 'Whether, therefore, ye eat or drink, or whatsoever ye do, do all to the glory of God.' If He felt the burden of civilisation in that comparatively simple state of society, what would He have said to us? Would He not have advised us earnestly to try a simpler life for our souls' health? 'What shall it profit a man if he gain the whole world and lose his own soul?'

III. The Sins which our Lord hated were Three —hypocrisy, selfishness, and worldliness. The hypocrite, or actor, is one whose outward conduct is not the true expression of his heart and soul, and the hypocrite ends in deceiving himself. The double heart makes the double head. Want of sympathy is a cardinal sin in Christianity as it is in no other religion. When St. Augustine said that he desired to know nothing save God and his own soul, he was misled by his love of rhetoric into stating, in epigrammatic form, a view of religion which, though not ignoble, is precisely not that of the religion of Christ. If the world contained only God and self there would be no Christianity. Lastly, worldliness is based on a radically wrong standard of values. The world—that is to say, human society, as it organises itself apart from God—assigns tasks and pays wages which have no necessary connection with the work which God intends us to do, or the reward which He intends us to receive.

REFERENCES.—II. 5.—J. M. Neale, *Readings for the Aged* (4th Series), p. 53. F. B. Meyer, *Christian World Pulpit*, vol. lix. p. 318. G. Bellett, *Parochial Sermons*, p. 240. F. St. John Corbett, *The Preacher's Year*, p. 67. R. W. Church, *Village Sermons*, p. 77. W. M. Sinclair, *Difficulties of our Day*, p. 123. C. Kingsley, *The Good News of God*, p. 302. R. J. Wardell, *Preacher's Magazine*, vol. xviii. p. 34. J. M. Neale, *Sermons Preached in Sackville College Chapel*, vol. i. p. 187. II. 5-7.—J. W. Burgon, *Servants of Scripture*, p. 112.

OUR EXAMPLE

'Let this mind be in you, which was also in Christ Jesus: Who, being in the form of God, thought it not robbery to be equal with God; but made Himself of no reputation, and took upon Him the form of a servant, and was made in the likeness of men: and being found in fashion as a man, He humbled Himself, and became obedient unto death, even the death of the cross.'—PHIL. II. 5-8.

THESE words are the most sublime, the most important, perhaps, in the writings of St. Paul—indeed, I had almost said in all Scripture. For they reveal to us with singular distinctness the foundation truth of the Christian religion—the incarnation. They tell us Who it was that became incarnate, and what His incarnation involved. They carry us up to the very heights of His glory as God, they carry us down to the depths of His humiliation as Man; and they propose for our example nothing less than Christ in all His fulness as God and Man.

I. The passage has been called the ladder of our Lord's humiliation, since it describes the steps by which He descended to the lowest depths of human need, in His work of redeeming our fallen race. There are clearly three stages or steps indicated by the finite verbs with which the other clauses of the sentence are grouped. (1) In regard to the first stage of the ladder. 'He emptied Himself,' we find associated with the verb 'emptied Himself' two clauses. 'He took upon Him the form of a servant,' and 'He was made in the likeness of man'. We have, therefore, in this first stage of the ladder a statement that the incarnation was an 'emptying' and this emptying is explained as being equivalent to the taking of the form of a servant and becoming man. (2) The second stage speaks of a further humiliation, that being found in fashion as a man, He humbled Himself. He not only assumed human nature, but accepted the penalty which belonged to fallen nature. (3) The third and last stage of the ladder is found in the clause, 'He became obedient, even to the death of the cross'. That is, that having chosen to die, of all the modes of death possible, He accepted that which was most painful, most humiliating.

II. How wonderful is the power and pathos of the story of our Lord's death! St. Paul tells us that He Who assumed human nature—was God What marvellous condescension! It is not only that the just suffers for the unjust; it is not only that the sufferer Himself is sinless, but He is God!

III. What is the lesson we are to learn from it? It is summed up in the Collect for to-day, in which we pray that we may follow the example of our Lord's humility and of His patience.

IV. Now we are able to understand the injunction with which St. Paul begins the passage, 'Let this mind be in you, which was also in Christ Jesus'. What did He surrender? (1) His rights. (2) His liberty.

And then again, in His sacrifice He chose the hardest way. And we, when we realise that a duty must be done, how often we choose the easiest way. —A. G. MORTIMER, Lenten Preaching, p. 63.

REFERENCES.—II. 5-8.—P. T. Forsyth, Christian World Pulpit, vol. xlvii. p. 276. C. H. Robinson, Church Family Newspaper, vol. xv. p. 340. A. Maclaren, Expositions of Holy Scripture—Philippians, p. 253. II. 5-11.—J. N. Bennie, The Eternal Life, p. 68. J. H. Jowett, The High Calling, p. 62. Expositor (5th Series), vol. iv. pp. 161, 241. II. 6.— H. Woodcock, Sermon Outlines (1st Series), p. 121. Expositor (4th Series), vol. iii. p. 368; ibid. (5th Series), vol. ii. pp. 82, 248. II. 6-8.—R. W. Hiley, A Year's Sermons, vol. i. p. 178.

THE FORM OF A SERVANT

'He took upon Him the form of a servant.'—PHIL. II. 7.

I. IN order that we may be followers of Christ, and that our life and character should be like His, we must freely surrender our wills to God. If you read the Gospels there are two convictions that infallibly impose themselves upon you. (1) The first of these is that none has ever loved man so wisely and faithfully as Christ. Ingratitude did not repel Him, nor cold and pitiless scorn freeze the fountains of His pity. (2) How was it Jesus loved, and loved so loyally to the end? It was because He was doing the will of His Father who sent Him, a will that He knew could never be defeated, and would rise triumphant from its apparent wreck. And so it must be with all who would truly wear the form of a servant.

II. We must wear the form of a servant always and everywhere. Christ never laid it aside from the moment He assumed it at Bethlehem till He had said 'It is finished'. So it ought to be with us. Worship is the highest act of service. Yet to be genuine it must be the crown and expression of a life of obedience. But how often we renounce and refuse the form of a servant! We like to assume it in some things, and to discard it in others. But they that are Christ's have crucified the flesh with its affections and lusts. It is no longer ours to question or dispute, to murmur or rebel.

III. The strength of service lies in our sonship. We saw that the spring of Christ's enthusiasm lay in His relation to God. So also our service must rest on filial fellowship with God. If it be not sustained and upheld by this it is rendered in our own strength, and is simply the assertion of our self-will. Moreover it will lack what alone can make it truly acceptable to God. For it will lack freedom, and be burdened with the spirit of bondage, or inspired by a pride that will strip it of the character of service and change it into the form of a favour. Nor, on the other hand, will it be profitable to men, for though it may relieve their surface wants, and dry their tears for a time, it will not stanch their deepest wounds nor carry with it the power of an endless life.—C. MOINET, The Great Alternative and other Sermons, p. 201.

REFERENCES.—II. 7.—Expositor (4th Series), vol. ii. p. 278. II. 7, 8.—Ibid. vol. x. p. 36. II. 7-9.—S. Baring-Gould, Village Preaching for a Year, p. 75. II. 8.—Spurgeon, Sermons, vol. xxxviii. No. 2281. S. H. Fleming, Fifteen-minute Sermons for the People, p. 1. Expositor (4th Series), vol. vi. p. 30; ibid. (5th Series), vol. viii. p. 156. II. 8, 9.—Ibid. (4th Series), vol. i. p. 144. II. 9.—H. S. Holland, Vital Values,

p. 13. *Expositor* (5th Series), vol. vii. p. 297 ; *ibid.* (6th Series), vol. vi. p. 248. II. 9, 10.—J. G. Greenhough, *Christian World Pulpit*, vol. liii. p. 314. H. S. Holland, *ibid.* vol. lxvii. p. 1. *Expositor* (4th Series), vol. i. pp. 138, 139. II. 9-11.—Spurgeon, *Sermons*, vol. ii. No. 101. *Expositor* (5th Series), vol. vi. p. 249. A. Maclaren, *Expositions of Holy Scripture—Philippians*, p. 260. II. 10, 11.—*Expositor* (4th Series), vol. vi. p. 420. II. 11.—*Ibid.* (6th Series), vol. v. p. 45.

'Work out your own salvation with fear and trembling.'—
                  PHIL. II. 12.

WILLIAM BLAKE said to a student who came to him for advice : ' Do you work in fear and trembling ? ' ' Indeed I do, sir,' ' *Then you'll do,*' was the reply.

REFERENCE.—II. 12.—*Expositor* (4th Series), vol. x. pp. 99, 119.

DELIVERANCE FROM THE POWER OF SIN

'Work out your own salvation with fear and trembling.'—
                  PHIL. II. 12, 13.

I. 'WORK out your own salvation.' There is a sense in which salvation is finished. There is another sense in which it is in process. Finished by Christ when He died, and yet in process by the Holy Ghost in our heart. (1) Remember that sin is a parasite. The day will come when I shall stand up before my God without a trace or freckle of sin. (2) God comes into your heart to take your side against the parasite sin. (3) Remember further that His purpose is to deliver from the power of sin. The guilt is gone, but the power remains, and He can only deliver from this gradually. To-day you see things to be wrong which five years ago you permitted, and five years from to-day you will see things wrong which you now permit. Evidently the work is progressive. (4) We may be saved from known sin—but not from temptation.

II. Work out what God works in. ' Work out your own salvation with fear and trembling, for it is God that worketh in you.' How careful you ought to be ! Be very fearful lest by a word or act of yours you spoil and thwart and put back God's work in your life. God in you will work to will, and then God in you will work to do what He wills. He does not work to make you feel, because feeling ends in smoke so often. God does not work in you to think, because you think and think again. But God works in you to *will*. That is, there rises up in your heart a *desire* which becomes at last a *purpose* to be free. No one knows it, no one guesses it ; but in your soul there rises up the will. The willing and the doing are from Him, and by faith you look to Him to do for you what you cannot do for yourself.—F. B. MEYER, *The Soul's Ascent*, p. 107.

REFERENCES.—II. 12.—W. Smith. *Christian World Pulpit*, vol. xlvi. p. 116. A. Shepherd, *The Gospel and Social Questions*, p. 25. J. C. Lees, *Christian World Pulpit*, vol. xlvii. p. 27. R. J. Wardell, *Preacher's Magazine* vol. xix. p. 77. *Christian World Pulpit*, vol. lv. p. 102. Spurgeon, *Sermons*, vol. xvii. No. 1003. II. 12, 13.—J. H. Jowett, *The High Calling*, p. 68. J. Stalker, *Christian World Pulpit*, vol. xlvii. p. 221. C. Perren, *Revival Sermons in Outline*, p. 342. D. E. Irons, *Christian World Pulpit*, vol. liii. p. 398. J. M. Whiton,

Summer Sermons, p. 177. J. Keble, *Sermons for Sundays after Trinity*, pt. i. p. 313. R. Allen, *The Words of Christ*, p. 203. F. B. Woodward, *Sermons* (1st Series), p. 1. W. C. Smith, *Christian World Pulpit*, vol. lvi. p. 364. Spurgeon, *Sermons*, vol. xiv. No. 820. A. Maclaren, *Expositions of Holy Scripture—Philippians*, p. 268. II. 14-16.—Spurgeon, *Sermons*, vol. viii. No. 472. J. H. Jowett, *The High Calling*, p. 74. A. Maclaren, *Expositions of Holy Scripture—Philippians*, p. 281. II. 16.—*Ex ositor* (4th Series), vol. i. p. 203. II. 16-18.—A. Maclaren, *Expositions of Holy Scripture—Philippians*, p. 287. II. 17.—*Ibid.* (6th Series), vol. i. p. 139. II. 17, 18.—J. H. Jowett, *The High Calling*, p. 81. *Christian World Pulpit*, vol. lv. p. 81. II. 19-24.—J. H. Jowett, *The High Calling*, p. 86. II. 19-24.—A. Maclaren, *Expositions of Holy Scripture—Philippians*, p. 295.

PHIL. II. 20, 21.

WHEN we are most earnest ourselves, we are surest to feel the lack of earnestness in others ; sincerity stirred to its depths will tolerate nothing less. It then becomes a new test of a companion. So a weak solution may not reveal a poison when a strong one will.—JAMES LANE ALLEN.

REFERENCES.—II. 21.—W. H. Evans, *Sermons for the Church's Year*, p. 282. *Expositor* (6th Series), vol. iv. p. 276. II. 22.—*Ibid.* (5th Series), vol. ii. p. 227 ; *ibid.* vol. vi. p. 86.

EPAPHRAS : 'A HEART AT LEISURE FROM ITSELF '

' He longed after you all and was full of heaviness, because ye had heard that he had been sick.'—PHIL. II. 26.
' Epaphras, who is one of you, a servant of Christ, saluteth you, always labouring fervently for you in prayers, that ye may stand perfect and complete in all the will of God.'
                 —COL. IV. 12.

THE identification of Epaphroditus mentioned in the Epistle to the Philippians with Epaphras the minister to the Colossians is precarious. The names are the same, but there is difficulty in supposing that one person is meant. Still, put together, the descriptions make up a harmonious and singularly beautiful type of Christian character—of ' a heart at leisure from itself '. In Philippians, Epaphras is represented as sorrowful even to agony, because his friends had heard of his illness. He had been sick—sick almost to death—but he would fain have had no one burdened by his trouble. In Colossians we have the servant of Christ always striving for the saints in prayer, that they may stand perfect and fully assured in all the will of God. This was a heart of gold.

I. Few examples are more timely than that of Epaphras in his unwillingness to have his sickness published abroad. Of all trouble, it is perhaps true that it is best even for ourselves not to speak much of it. This is so true of the greater griefs that an almost certain gauge of the depth to which pain has sunk is the measure of its repression. The more real the pain, the greater is the anxiety the world should ignore it. Only inexperienced sufferers are voluble. Those familiar with the secrets of anguish are silent. They do their best to hide from the outer world the consciousness, the memory, and the expectation of their suffering. They make much of alleviations, and eagerly welcome whatever soothes and distracts. They know that expression reacts upon emotion, and makes the burden heavier. This is even truer about lesser sorrows. The mortifications of wounded vanity make a more or less appreciable element in the discipline of life, and they are always intensified by being proclaimed. Even while he suffers, one may doubt whether there is any just cause for pain, and the memory of the slight or disappointment fades away if it is not cherished. Once tell it, and it becomes objective, with an independent existence—a living minister of misery.

II. But in the mind of Epaphras there was a nobler feeling. He knew that the Philippians were hardly bearing up under the weight of their own sorrows. Life was difficult to them as to him, and its troubles were perhaps growing day by day. With the generosity of a great nature, he believed that they loved him well—that his illness would sadden them deeply—and it lay with a double weight on his heart because it had burdened theirs. The 'importunate canvass for sympathy' often wears affection out, and sufferers die unlamented because they have exhausted the resources of compassion. Nor even should the claim be urged through looks that are silent pleas for pity; as far as possible, Christians must divest themselves even of the air of sorrow. We read in Marie Bashkirtseff's life that when she heard she was attacked by consumption, she exclaimed, 'Is it I ? O God ! I ! I !! I !!!' Many will remember Robert Hall's words on recovering from a keen paroxysm of anguish, 'But I have not complained, have I, sir ? No, and I will not complain.'

III. For we have a hiding-place, a refuge, in One whose patience we can never tire, whose sympathy never fails. Epaphras is found 'always striving in prayer'. Perhaps our faithlessness is shown in nothing so much as in the current limitations of Scriptural teaching on prayer. We are to go to God with all —'Pour out your hearts before Him, ye people'. There we are to begin, and we shall end with Christ. He offered up prayers and supplications with strong crying and tears, and the issue was peace. God loves so well to hear us that it is almost a treachery to Him that we should go with our trials to any other. He knows that we must have sympathy—lively and complete. But is not His sympathy—the sympathy of God in Christ—sufficient for us ? The true guerdon of pain faithfully borne is the assurance that it has put God to trial—that we can now be sure of His grace—that He has given the victory to what in us is higher and diviner—and that, having done this, He will bring us through all that awaits us, and not see us cast away. This is the witness of exercised spirits. They have entered an abiding serenity, for they know that there is that in them which has survived the worst that time can do, and which must conquer at the last.

IV. Epaphras could not have prayed with such tender warmth unless he had sought directly to bless and help his friends. Prayer is a suggesting grace, and it is answered often by guidance to him who offers it. We are not only forbidden to burden others needlessly ; we are to be kind. There are people who make conscientious provision for those who depend on them, by unceasing toil and much sacrifice. That is not enough ; the heart must be refreshed. Lacordaire wrote : 'Above all other things be kind. Kindness is the one thing through which we can the most resemble God and the most disarm men. Kindness in mutual relations is the principal charm of life.' What are we doing to increase the innocent happiness of others, to gladden the weary, to lift the worn spirit from the dust ? Every day we should resolve to do something—were it but to speak a word or write a letter—to bring some brightness into another's life.—W. ROBERTSON NICOLL, *Ten-Minute Sermons*, p. 11.

REFERENCES.—II. 25.—J. H. Jowett, *The High Calling*, p. 92. *Expositor* (5th Series), vol. x. p. 158 ; *ibid.* (6th Series), vol. i. p. 132 ; *ibid.* vol. iii. p. 235. II. 25-30.—A. Maclaren, *Expositions of Holy Scripture—Philippians*, p. 305. II. 29, 30.—J. H. Jowett, *The High Calling*, p. 100. III. 1.—*Ibid.* p. 106. III. 1-3.—A. Maclaren, *Expositions of Holy Scripture—Philippians*, p. 311. III. 2, 3.—*Ibid.* p. 112. III. 2. —*Christianity in Daily Conduct*, p. 293.

BEWARE OF THE DOGS

'Beware of the dogs, beware of the evil workers, beware of the concision : for we are the circumcision, which worship God in the Spirit, and rejoice in Christ Jesus, and have no confidence in the flesh. —PHIL. III. 2, 3.

THE text enshrines the presentation of a contrast— on one side dark, forbidding, and revolting ; on the other side radiant and alluring, 'Beware of the dogs : beware of the evil workers ; beware of the concision'. What is all this but a solemn and urgent warning against externalism, against all dependence upon outward ordinance and form ? What are the marks of true religion ? Paul enumerates three, and they appear to me to be full and all-sufficient.

I. The first characteristic of true religion is worship. Yes, but what kind of worship ? 'Worship in the Spirit.' Not a ceremonial act, not the curbing of the flesh, not the eating of a wafer. These may be the signs and symbols of worship ; they do not constitute the worship itself. Worship is in the spirit. I know the kind of service which was observed in Paul's temple. 'We give thanks without ceasing.' 'We pray without ceasing.' 'I am poured out upon the altar.' Thanksgiving ! Supplication ! Sacrifice ! This is the nature of true religion.

II. The second characteristic of true religion is exultation. 'We glory,' we rejoice, we boast ! 'We glory in Christ Jesus.' In Him we find our crown of rejoicing. In Him we make our boast. Not in forms ; not in ordinances ; not in privileged exclusiveness ; not in remote descent, and in distinguished succession ; we glory, directly and immediately in Christ Jesus our Lord. 'God forbid that I should glory save in the cross of our Lord and Saviour Jesus Christ.' When anything else is exalted to the throne of glory, the spaciousness of religious life is contracted, and the soul is imprisoned in a carnal bondage.

III. The third mark of true religion is spiritual assurance. 'We have confidence, but not in the flesh.' But where shall we gain our confidence? Back in the Christ! 'We know that our sins are forgiven us for His name's sake.' Our confidence is born out of our fellowship with the Lord.—J. H. Jowett, *Apostolic Optimism*, p. 36.

References.—III. 4-8.—A. Maclaren, *Expositions of Holy Scripture—Philippians*, p. 321. III.—4-17.—*Expositor* (6th Series), vol. iv. p. 288. III. 6.—*Ibid*. vol. ii. p. 301. III. 7.—N. Smyth, *Christian World Pulpit*, vol. xliv. p. 40. *Expositor* (5th Series), vol. vi. p. 382.

THE GOOD THE ENEMY OF THE BEST

'But what things were gain to me, those I counted loss for Christ. Yea, doubtless, and I count all things but loss, for the excellency of the knowledge of Christ Jesus my Lord, for whom I have suffered the loss of all things, and do count them but dung, that I may win Christ, and be found in Him.'—Phil. iii. 7, 8.

What things? What are the things that he estimates as loss—birth, lineage, rank, education, social standing, even moral attainment, the very things that men usually count precious, and some of which they pursue with greedy desire? These are the things which the Apostle says he counts but rubbish, that he may win Christ, and be found in Him. These things are good in themselves; the difficulty is that unless kept in their proper places, and rightly estimated at their own value, especially as compared with the incomparable blessings of the kingdom of Christ, these good things may become the enemy of what is better, yea, even of that best—knowing Christ and being found in Him. That is the Apostle's thought, and to it attention cannot be too closely given. The good may be, and often is, the enemy of the best, as the French proverb puts it.

I. Let us see How it Applies.—First, in regard to the great and fundamental truth of the New Birth. Even a careless reader of the New Testament cannot miss the fact that to be a Christian means passing somehow through a great experience and having a great soul's history. Now, in regard to this great truth in the world, and especially in the Christian Church of to-day, among Christian families, and in nominally Christian circles, how often is the good permitted to become the enemy of the best. Respectability, good breeding, education, culture, the influence of a good home, social status are permitted to take the place of the thrilling experience of personal knowledge of Christ, and many seem to think that among people so born and reared such a thing as conversion is unnecessary. Men forget to put first things first.

II. Weakness in the Church.—This great truth is just as applicable to the Christian life and to Christian people. How many are content with laying the foundation instead of rearing the temple of a devoted and holy life, how many are satisfied with

striking the first blow instead of winning the battle, how many are satisfied to show bud instead of bringing forth fruit! Contentment with present experience is permitted to be the enemy of the greater things that God has prepared for all those that love Him.

III. The Problems of Life.—This great truth is just as applicable, and certainly it may be very helpful when we apply it to the varied experiences of life. A burden of woe is the undertone of all the world's joy. May not the meaning of it be this, that God the Father, who has a purpose in every life, does not and will not permit the good to become the enemy of the best. It is good to have child or husband, to be rich in the good things which God gives; it is better to cherish them when we have them, and even to think of them with fond memory when they are gone; but there *is a best*, and our Father wants us to have that too.—D. L. Ritchie, *Peace the Umpire and other Sermons*, p. 110.

References.—III. 7, 8.—G. W. Brameld, *Practical Sermons*, p. 278. III. 7-9.—Spurgeon, *Sermons*, vol. xxiii. No. 1357. J. H. Jowett, *The High Calling*, p. 118.

ST. PAUL'S SACRIFICES

'Christ Jesus my Lord, for Whom I have suffered the loss of all things.'—Phil. iii. 8.

I. These words of St. Paul seem very definite when we begin to think about them. They appear to contain an allusion to some definite circumstance in his past life, of which we hear nothing, or next to nothing, elsewhere. What loss had St. Paul suffered? Let us try to put together all that we know or can infer about Paul's position in life before his conversion. We know, for instance, that he was a Roman citizen, and this fact alone tells us a good deal. He speaks of this with pride, saying he is a citizen of no mean city. And this citizenship implies that his family had been long settled in Tarsus, and probably that members of it served the office of magistrate. What we know, too, about St. Paul's education, his being sent to Jerusalem apparently for the express purpose of being taught by Gamaliel, tends also to prove that his family was well-to-do. How comes it, then, that during the greater part of his apostolic career he is evidently a poor man? The conclusion is irresistible; St. Paul must have been disowned by his family. He had become one of those of whom our Lord speaks, who had left home, and brethren, and father, and mother, and lands for His name. St. Paul's family, we are reminded in this chapter, was of pure Jewish descent. There must have been great rejoicing in the home at Tarsus when the news came of Paul's zealous persecution of the new sect. All the greater, therefore, must have been the shock of the news of his conversion. Perhaps the final rupture did not take place immediately. Not long after his conversion St. Paul went back to Tarsus, and seems to have stayed there for several years. We learn from the Epistle to the Galatians that he preached the faith there, so that his relations with his family during that time must, to say the least, have been strained and painful ; but when he finally decided to preach the Gospel to the Gentiles the estrangement must have been complete. It was impossible for a strict Pharisee to condone such an offence as that. The only member of the family of whom we hear definitely was Paul's nephew, his sister's son, who betrayed the conspiracy of the Jews to murder Paul after his arrest at Jerusalem. The Jews evidently believed that any member of St. Paul's family would be willing to go any length in order to stop his preaching. Not long after this there is evidence that St. Paul must have been in possession of some means. By appealing to Cæsar he would probably have incurred expense. He could not have lived in the hired house at Rome without private means. Whether there had been a reconciliation, or whether on his father's death some portion of the estate naturally and unavoidably devolved on him, we have no means of knowing. St. Paul counted these things as refuse provided that he might gain Christ.

II. The delicate reticence of St. Paul about these money matters gives us a high idea of the refinement of his nature. It is only on indirect evidence that we are able to trace the allusion involved in the words of the text. St. Paul stands, in this respect, on a far higher level than St. Peter. He does not remind his Lord of the sacrifices he has made. He does not say with St. Peter, 'Lord, we have left all and followed Thee'. Still less does he incur the imputation which St. Peter does not altogether escape, of trying to bargain with Christ when he says, 'What shall we have therefore?' St. Paul feels a generous and lofty disdain for these so-called losses and sacrifices. They were not a loss ; they were gain, since they led to Christ. Even the breach with his family is regarded by him in this spirit, and yet we cannot doubt that his sensitive nature felt it acutely.

The Jews attached great importance to the Fifth Commandment, and St. Paul tells us that as to the righteousness which is in the law he had been found blameless. Like St. Francis of Assisi in similar circumstances, he probably did not resist his father's will until it was clear to him that compliance would be a sin.

III. Christianity does not make any appeal to the mass of mankind to sell all that they have and follow Christ. It is only in exceptional cases that this appeal is made, and sometimes those to whom the suggestion comes cannot rise to the height of this counsel of perfection. Like the young man with great possessions, they go away sorrowful. Yet if one reads the obituary notices in the newspapers, it is almost startling, I think, to see how many men and women nowadays do give up their fortune, their lifetime, sometimes even their life itself, to the service of Christ and the good of their fellow-men. Little is known of their lives by the world at large, but they have heard their Master's call, and have left all and followed Him. These are the chosen few, spiritual natures, gifted with an exceptional enthusiasm.

To the mass of men the appeal which Christianity makes is something different. It bids us do our duty, follow our conscience, take our stand on our moral and religious principles without counting the cost. We must be ready with St. Paul to suffer the loss of all things for the sake of Christ—we must be ready, I mean, to risk losing much that we value for the sake of what we hold sacred. The man of high principle differs from the unprincipled man in that he would do this unhesitatingly. The perfect Christian differs from the imperfect Christian in that he would do it willingly and gladly for the sake of the love that he bears to Christ. We are not, I dare say, called upon to give up our inheritance or to break entirely with those nearest and dearest to us, as was St. Paul ; but, none the less, the claim which Christianity makes on our religious life is an exacting one.

REFERENCES.—III. 8.—Bishop Creighton, *The Heritage of the Spirit*, p. 91. T. Arnold, *Sermons*, vol. i. p. 28. W. M. Sinclair, *Words from St. Paul's* (2nd Series), p. 138. Reuen Thomas, *Christian World Pulpit*, vol. l. p. 137. C. S. Horne, *The Soul's Awakening*, p. 191. J. H. Jowett, *Christian World Pulpit*, vol. liv. p. 241. III. 9.—W. Robertson Nicoll, *Ten Minute Sermons*, p. 109. H. W. Webb-Peploe, *Christian World Pulpit*, vol. liii. p. 389. *Expositor* (4th Series), vol. iv. p. 186 ; *ibid.* vol. viii. p. 81 ; *ibid.* (5th Series), vol. iv. p. 135 ; *ibid.* vol. vii. p. 281 ; *ibid.* (6th Series), vol. x. p. 367.

THE POWER OF CHRIST'S RESURRECTION

'That I may know Him, and the power of His resurrection.'
—PHIL. III. 10.

WHAT is the sense of this word 'power'? There is no room for mistake as to its general import. By the power of a fact we mean the bearing of the consequences, as distinct from the existence of the fact ; we mean the inferences which may be drawn from it, or the influence which it will naturally exert.

I. The power of the Resurrection is to be seen first of all in a Christian's *thought*. It is the fundamental fact which satisfies him of the absolute truth of the religion of Christ.

Now here, first, it is abundantly clear that the Apostles felt certain of their facts. They did not merely whisper in assemblies of the faithful that Jesus was risen, as a private topic of comfort for Christian souls ; they carried their bold assertion of the Resurrection before tribunals, which were filled by their keen, bitter, and contemptuous enemies, and challenged them to gainsay it if they could. If, after the fashion of modern times, the ruling Sadducees had appointed a scientific commission to investigate the matter, nobody would have been better pleased than the Apostles. They had nothing to lose, they had everything to gain, by a thorough searching inquiry. 'We have not followed,' one of them wrote in after years, 'cunningly devised fables,' 'we cannot,' they said a few weeks after the event—'we cannot but speak the things which we have seen and heard'. They trusted their senses sufficiently to believe One who revealed to them a world higher and greater than the world of sense ; and in doing this, certainly, they could say with the Psalmist, that He had 'set their feet upon the rock, and ordered their goings, and had put a new song in their mouth, even a thanksgiving unto our God'. For them the Resurrection warranted the truth of Christ's mission, the truth of Christianity. All that Christ had said, all that He had promised and foretold, was raised by it to the high level of undisputed certainty. With the mighty power of such a miracle, so certified, impelling and sustaining them, they went forward, they could not but go forward, to win the attention, the acquiescence, the faith of men in the truths which it attested. What became of them personally it mattered not. If they succeeded, it would be in the strength of the risen Jesus. If they failed, the mighty risen One would yet succeed. There it was, ever before them, the imperious, the invigorating fact that He had broken forth from His grave as He said He would ; and it only remained for them, as it remains for us at this hour, to do justice to the evidential power of His Resurrection. St. Paul maintains the Resurrection of Christ to be so bound up with Christianity, that to deny it is not simply to cut its most important incident right out of the heart of the Christian creed, but that it is to part with Christianity as a whole. 'If Christ be not risen, then is our preaching vain, and your faith is also vain.' 'If Christ be not raised, your faith is vain ; ye are yet in your sins ; then they also which are fallen asleep in Christ are perished.' Deny the Resurrection, and Christianity collapses altogether, as certainly as does an arch when its keystone is removed ; and in place of the Conqueror of death and the Redeemer of souls, there remains only a Jewish rabbi, whose story has been curiously encrusted with legend, and some of whose sayings are still undoubtedly entitled to attention. But conversely, admit the Resurrection, and you must confess the Creed. In admitting the truth of the Resurrection, you make an admission which, if you are a thinking man, must govern, colour, impregnate your whole thought, must make faith intellectually easy, and doubt unwelcome. For the Resurrection guarantees the absolute truth of Christ's teaching and mission ; it converts His death into the transient preliminary of an eternal triumph ; it leads on to the Ascension and the Perpetual Intercession in heaven ; it is the warrant that He will come to judgment.

II. But it is in the conduct of the Christian, in his moral and spiritual life, that the power of the Resurrection may chiefly be felt. This was the main scope of the Apostle's prayer. He had no doubt about the truth of the Gospel. But to know the risen Christ in his own heart and will—this was a field wherein boundless improvement was possible, even for St. Paul; it was a field of improvement, moreover, in which, on this side the grave, perfect satisfaction was unattainable. What, then, are the necessary conditions of an effective moral power, of a power which shall stimulate and control feeling, resolution, action? There are, I apprehend, two main conditions which

must be satisfied by any such power ; and which are satisfied, and that amply, by the Resurrection of Jesus Christ.

(1) In the first place, it opens out before the eye of the soul its one adequate aim in all action and in all endurance ; that is to say, a union of the whole man with God, extending through the vast perspectives of a boundless eternity.

(2) But the Resurrection of our Lord Jesus Christ also satisfies the second condition of an effective moral power ; it assures to us the continuous presence of help from on high. To have revealed a future life to us in our unaided weakness would have been to abandon us to despair ; but, as it is, the revelation of our eternal home is also the assurance of our being enabled, if we are willing, to secure it.—H. P. LIDDON.

THE RESURRECTION AND PERSONAL EXPERIENCE

'That I may know Him, and the power of His resurrection.'— PHIL. III. 10.

I. THE Apostle implies in these words that the Lord's Resurrection was the channel through which power was conveyed for the redemption of His people from the condemnation of sin. And this was to be an experience of ever-growing depth and certainty. Its energies were to effect the release of believing disciples from the impending threats of the law. Cross and blood, thorn-crown and furrowed flesh from which life has sped, could never assure rebels of the grace of the great God whose laws have been despised. But the Resurrection is a witness that Divine favour is bestowed again upon the new humanity, of which Jesus was the beginning, the type, and the living advocate.

II. The Apostle thought of Christ's Resurrection as the centre from which the new manifestations of a Divine life in man derived their animating and upholding forces. The death of the Holy One of God was only a part of the satisfaction made for the sinful race. The putting right of those who had got woefully wrong must be completed by vital processes emanating from the indwelling presence of the risen Lord.

III. The Apostle Paul thought also of the power of the Resurrection as a triumphant counteractive to the perils and death-risks of a hostile world. If we make proof of the Resurrection power which justifies from sin and renews into righteousness, we shall have fresh assurances against hazard and death. Water has no power to generate electrical energy as it lies in the still, tideless lake, the sluggish river which moves placidly through a flowered landscape, or in the dikes and canals of Holland, the land of tulips and dairy farms. The engineer puts his turbines and his dynamos where torrents come thundering through the frowning chasms and rushing out of the gloomy valleys. And the power of the Resurrection, the glory of its unknown forces, its mystic possibilities are not always known in the quiet scenes of life and amidst its pastoral serenities. It is through stress and danger, through turmoil and conflict that the glory of Him who raised up Jesus from the dead manifests itself afresh.

IV. The Apostle regards those processes of grace and providence which issue from the glorified humanity of the Lord, to repel the evils of the earthly lot, as reaching their climax in the believer's victory over the ravage and terror of death. The power of the Resurrection working within and around us ought to nerve with the fortitude of an unflinching faith and change the associations of the tomb. He who is alive to all the influences emanating from the person of the risen Lord loses his dread of the unknown hereafter, and his tears for the departed are disburdened of selfish repining and despair.

PAUL'S STRANGE AMBITION

'That I may know . . . the fellowship of His sufferings.'—
PHIL. III. 10.

THE Apostle Paul is expressing here the intense longing of his heart. It is a little bit of spiritual autobiography. He uncovers his secret desires to the Philippian Christians, opens the chamber of his inner life, and we see what is working there. You often wonder what is moving in some prominent personality, what is the secret and predominating purpose of his life. It is well to turn that curious inquiry in upon ourselves. Supposing every man's heart were unveiled, and this were a kind of Palace of Truth, one wonders what would be discovered as the ruling passion of each man's life—with one to be rich, with another to have some sort of position, with another to be approved and loved, with another to get pleasure, with another to be useful, or to be free from some besetting sin.

Would there be any one who would confess to this peculiar passion of Paul?

We would all like to know the peace of Christ, the joy and comfort of Christ, His thankful trust in the Father's love. We would some of us brace ourselves to bear some shadow of His experience of suffering, if it pleased God to lay it upon us, but to long for it is quite another thing. A bold, brave spirit must his be, who can pray and long to share the sufferings of Christ. Can we understand the feeling out of which this desire sprang? And can we see the reasonableness of the desire, and whether it is a desire that ought to be in us and cherished by us? Let us see.

I. First, as to *the feeling out of which this desire sprang*; if we can see that, we shall see the reasonableness of it. And indeed it is very easy to see; it shines out and breaks out in all the words and writings of Paul. It was his intense and consuming love for Christ, a love reverent, worshipful, grateful, the love of one who felt that Christ had done everything for him, and was more to him than all the glory of the world. At any moment he would not only have suffered anything, he would have died for the love that he bore to Christ; and he never lost it, as some of us do, it never abated in its fervour, it grew more and more intense as life went on.

And inasmuch as Christ was still reviled and mocked among men in the days of Paul, as He still grieved over the sins and follies of the sons of men, and still carried their sins upon His heart, we can understand how out of his vast love for the Lord, Paul longed for fellowship in His sufferings.

II. Further, we can understand the longing of the Apostle, if we *remember what caused the sufferings of Christ*. It was the sin and misery of the world; and what he longed for was that he might feel towards the sin and misery of men as Christ felt towards it. We are not fit to deal with the sin of our fellow-men until we can share the feeling of Christ as He wept over Jerusalem.—CHARLES BROWN, *Light and Life*, p. 63.

THE POWER OF CHRIST'S RESURRECTION

(*For Easter*)

'That I may know Him, and the power of His resurrection.'—
PHIL. III. 10.

THE thought of the Resurrection is with us still, and what can be more appropriate for a few thoughts this morning than our text? The power of His Resurrection! What is that? Who can fathom the depth of those mysterious words?

I. **Power over Temptation and Sin.**—The power of His Resurrection means a steady rise over temptation and sin. In some parts of England on Easter Day they have a strange but beautiful superstition that the bright sun dances for very joy, and surely we may excuse that superstition when we remember that on Easter Day we begin to know something of the power of His Resurrection.

II. **Power over Conscience.**—The Resurrection of our Lord and Saviour Jesus Christ has a wonderful power over conscience. If Christ had died, and only died, we should have been grateful for the unparalleled sacrifice; but it would end there. There are many men who would teach us and tell us that the character of Christ was beautiful and sublime—that He was an Apostle, the flower of perfect humanity, and that there, suspended on the cross, He represents to all ages a witness of all human goodness and self-sacrifice. If Christ died upon the cross merely to exemplify human goodness, He has no power to heal our consciences, to give us rest and peace. The Resurrection of Jesus Christ teaches us that the sacrifice which was made by the Lord on Calvary has been accepted by God, so that Jesus Christ did not merely die as the exemplar of all that was human and good, He died there as the Passover offering for the sins of the world; and so, when we stand before His open grave we see that this conscience of ours can be healed, because the sacrifice that Christ made upon Calvary has been accepted by God. The Resurrection is, as it were, the letter which tells us that God is willing to forgive the past because the sacrifice of Jesus Christ has been accepted.

III. **A Life Worth Living.**—There are some who talk in sombre tones about life being 'short'. They say, 'I am weary to-night, and I feel that my life will soon be at an end'. Again, when people become very old they feel that they are in the way of other people. These old people say, 'I shall not be sorry when my time comes to go away'; but when the time does come they do not want to die, they are going to have a good struggle for life. But what is there in this world to live for if there is no resurrection or no salvation? When, however, you realise that there is a resurrection, life is not hopeless; then we see that life is worth living.

IV. Even Life for Evermore.—This morning, look once again into the empty tomb of our Saviour Jesus Christ. He has risen from the dead. We have strange ideas of death! We think of it in quite a wrong way; but the resurrection shows us that death is a phase of life, and not an abrupt close of life. Death is merely a passage, and we pass into the other world to live for ever and ever. In that other life there will be ample leisure. All the good we have sown in our hearts in this world will develop through the long days of eternity. There will be by-and-by a reunion of body, soul, and spirit, and our life will be carried on in that other world under conditions of perfection and glory. Do you remember in the story of the Resurrection that we are told there was an angel standing at the head of the place where the body of Jesus lay? We are told that he was a young man, and what do we learn from that? Simply that angels must be hundreds and hundreds of years old, and yet he is spoken of as a 'young man'. We learn from this fact that when we get to that other world we shall never grow old, or be weary, or carry about care; but in that other world there will be youthful perfection and an enthusiasm which will never be killed.

Easter has a number of thoughts for each one of us. Some of us lay flowers on the graves of those who have been dear to us; but our thoughts should not be sad—all the sadness should go when we think of the day of resurrection.

REFERENCES.—III. 10.—Spurgeon, *Sermons*, vol. x. No. 552, and vol. xxxv. No. 2080. J. A. Davies, *Sermons by Welshmen*, p. 308. C. D. Bell, *The Power of God*, p. 96. E. Griffith Jones, *Christian World Pulpit*, vol. lvii. p. 120. R. W. Hiley, *A Year's Sermons*, vol. iii. p. 145. T. F. Crosse, *Sermons* (2nd Series), p. 213. J. T. Bramston, *Fratribus*, pp. 141, 149. F. D. Maurice, *Sermons*, vol. vi. p. 1. Bishop Wilberforce, *Sermons*, p. 129. G. Campbell Morgan, *The Bible and the Cross*, p. 79. W. Robertson Nicoll, *Ten Minute Sermons*, p. 118. *Expositor* (6th Series), vol. iii. p. 121; *ibid.* (7th Series), vol. vi. p. 236. III. 10, 11.—H. Alford, *Quebec Chapel Sermons*, vol. iii. pp. 160, 173, 187. A. B. Davidson, *Waiting Upon God*, p. 277. J. H. Jowett, *The High Calling*, p. 124. A. Maclaren, *Expositions of Holy Scripture—Philippians*, p. 336. III. 12.—Spurgeon, *Sermons*, vol. xxxix. No. 2315. F. W. Farrar, *Truths to Live By*, p. 352. R. C. Trench, *Sermons New and Old*, p. 207. J. H. Jowett, *The Examiner*, 17th May, 1906, p. 478. C. Cuthbert Hall, *Christian World Pulpit*, vol. lxii. p. 12. *Expositor* (4th Series), vol. iii. p. 415; *ibid.* (5th Series), vol. v. p. 34. A. Maclaren, *Expositions of Holy Scripture—Philippians*, p. 348. III. 12-14 J. H. Jowett, *The High Calling*, p. 130.

SPIRITUAL CONCENTRATION

'This one thing I do.'—PHIL. III. 13.

IF it were asked what, under God's grace, was the secret of St. Paul's power—his power of writing, his power of preaching, his power of argument—I should not hesitate to say, concentration. He had singularly attained the habit of taking a distinct aim, and then making everything bear to that 'one' desired point. No one is ever very great, very useful, very happy, who has not this quality in his character. Let me strongly here urge upon every one, as a general rule—especially the young — to cultivate concentration. Have a work to do—know what it is—and do it. Know your end, and keep to it. Fix your aim steadily, and then bring your whole being to the attainment of that end. Decision is energy; energy is power; power is confidence; and confidence is success. If you fail in anything, the probability is that it was not for want of ability, but simply because there was not sufficient 'oneness' in your mind about it, and therefore not sufficient decision—which nothing but 'oneness' gives. Life, with most of us, loses its 'oneness' just because its aims are too many.

I. The Supremacy of Christianity.—What a mere insignificance are all things else besides! What else I do—how I dress, how I fare, how I eat, how I drink, how I get on, what people think of me, what this world is to me—what a mere trifle! What is it compared for a single moment with my soul and my eternity, the gospel of my salvation, the consent of God to all I ask and all I have, and that judgment to which I am to be summoned? Yet, are men living —are you living—as if these things were so? Religion takes its place, and where? It ranges one in a hundred, one in ten, one in two. And where is its place? What is it? A very quiet, commonplace thing, and very plain, very diluted, with a great deal of routine in it. It has its decencies—and you are here. It has its properties—and you are here. It has its degrees of interest and feeling. But if you measure by earnestness, and compare the intensity we put into religion with the intensity we throw into other things, is it one in two, is it one in ten, is it one in a hundred?

II. The Work of Grace in a Man's Heart should be the Happiest of all Things.—It is the only thing that ever gives to man any real satisfaction in the world. It gives peace; and in this sense it is easy and light. It becomes easy and light by the joyousness of that elastic spirit which bears man up. But to get this heart of ours—this dull, stubborn, wicked heart, changed, and to love God, and to please God, and to get to heaven, is very hard work. And unless you go to it intently, and embracingly, and determinately, you will not do it. I know it is the work of the Holy Ghost in a man, without which no man can desire or take one step. But, nevertheless, to be a Christian is a hard work. It demands all a man's power—his intellect, his memory, his judgment, his affections, his courage. It will tax them to the uttermost. It is a struggle and a battle; and at the very best it has to be fought not only in the visible, but invisible world. It is a work not to be done in a given period, but a work life-long. All other enterprises— the approbation of the world, the achievements of instruction, the accumulation of business—are nothing in comparison with it. 'The kingdom of heaven suffereth violence, and the violent take it by force.' 'Many shall seek to enter in, and shall not be able.' It is done by whole-heartedness. It is only done by positive striving, by that spirit which goes to it honouringly, reservedly, as to the highest work that is ever given man to do. 'This one thing I do.'

III. God Must See His own Reflection in Your Soul.—Now, God is 'one'. God was 'one' when He came to the great work of your salvation. The Father, the Son, and the Holy Ghost, in all their threefold office. He brought His whole power, His whole love, His whole wisdom, His whole justice, to effect your redemption. Therefore, God must see the 'oneness' of the way in which you deal with your redemption.

PHIL. III. 13.

Miss Caroline Fox gives the following note of a conversation with Sterling. 'Thorwaldsen was one of the greatest geniuses and clearest intellects in Europe. When engaged over his Vulcan, one of his friends said to him, "Now, you must be satisfied with this production". "Alas," said the artist, "I am." "Why should you regret it?" asked his friend. "Because I must be going down-hill when I find my works equal to my aspirations."'

'An ingenious artist of our own time,' says Hazlitt (*Table-Talk*, 'On the Past and Future'), 'has been heard to declare that if ever the Devil got him into his clutches, he would set him to copy his own pictures. Thus the secure self-complacent retrospect to what is done is nothing, while the anxious, uneasy looking forward to what is to come is everything. We are afraid to dwell on the past, lest it should retard our future progress; the indulgence of ease is fatal to excellence.'

References.—III. 13.—H. H. Henson, *Godly Union and Concord*, p. 30. G. H. Morrison, *Scottish Review*, vol. ii. p. 25. P. Wyatt, *Christian World Pulpit*, vol. xlvi. p. 342. T. F. Crosse, *Sermons*, p. 193. J. H. Jellett, *The Elder Son*, pp. 278, 291. J. M. Neale, *Sermons for the Church Year*, vol. ii. p. 180. R. Flint, *Sermons and Addresses*, p. 123. H. C. Beeching, *Church Family Newspaper*, vol. xiv. p. 112. F. E. Gardiner, *ibid.* vol. xv. p. 112.

PERFECT BUT NOT PERFECTED

'Brethren, I count not myself to have apprehended; but this one thing I do, forgetting those things which are behind, and reaching forth unto those things which are before, I press toward the mark for the prize of the high calling of God in Christ Jesus.'—Phil. III. 13, 14.

Let us examine the elements that constitute the criterion of Christian perfection as here laid down.

I. First of all, Christian perfection has done with the past, 'Forgetting those things which are behind'. What does the Apostle mean by forgetting the past?

If you carefully consider the chapter, you will discover the thought connection which the Apostle has in his mind. He has been telling the Philippians what he has sacrificed for the sake of the knowledge of Jesus Christ. But now he is able to say: Whatever pangs I then endured, however my heart may then have bled for the past, now I stand above it. I have forgotten it. And so he implies that for the Philippian converts also the same criterion holds good. And we also must apply the criterion to ourselves. Has that from which we have escaped any power now to make us halt on our way? If we can stand this test then we have attained to a strength and power of Christian life which is called in the New Testament Christian perfection.

II. Christian perfection according to the Apostle reaches forth into a higher goal in the future. There are some people that define Christian perfection in this life as a rounded and complete thing, as the reaching of the goal; the very thing Paul declared he had not attained. Such a conception must of necessity lead to self-complacency, and close the vision of a higher goal in the present life. But that is not the meaning of this passage. According to Paul, as many as be perfect have the vision of a far away goal. Christian perfection, according to this criterion, is that stage of life that realises most intensely its imperfection. Observe that this attitude involves a certainty of mind with respect to future glory. No man ever did well in the present if he had no vision of the future.

III. We note that Christian perfection recognises its ground, its goal, and its inspiration in Jesus Christ. 'I press toward the mark for the prize of the high calling of God in Christ Jesus.' (1) 'In Christ Jesus.' The Apostle knows of nothing beyond that limit. (2) 'The high calling.' 'The *high* calling' is called in the Epistle to the Hebrews 'the *heavenly* calling'. The phrase implies that this calling comes from, and leads to, the highest sphere to which man can attain. (3) Then the passage leads us in the last place to the Christian anticipation of a *perfected* life in a fuller and completer sense, when the goal shall be reached, and the prize shall be obtained.—John Thomas, *Myrtle Street Pulpit*, vol. III. p. 193.

FORGETTING THE THINGS BEHIND

PHIL. III. 13, 14.

To apprehend is to lay hold of; and what is that of which St. Paul does not account himself to have laid hold of? He that had been so tried by temptations, he that had so suffered for the name of Christ, he that had laboured more abundantly than the rest of the Apostles, even he did not feel that he had done enough for his own salvation.

I. 'Forgetting the things that are behind.' We have fallen into sin, again and again and again, when we thought to do good. As the same St. Paul says evil was present with us. What then? We are to forget all that, so far as it may discourage us; we are to keep it out of our sight, so far as it may hinder us from running with patience the race that is set before us. What should we say to any general, who, when speaking to his men, were to say, 'Remember, soldiers, that you were beaten at such a time, that you lost courage at such a time, that the enemy stole a march upon you at such a time?' Would he not rather say, 'Remember, soldiers, that then you conquered, that then you did such and such a valiant action, that then your praise was in all mouths?' And if they had suffered a great defeat, he would say, 'It is true that at such a time you failed, but then there were such and such reasons for it; we have put all that to rights; and now we shall go on in the certain assurance of victory'.

II. But those words of St. Paul's are true in another sense. That of which I have already spoken rather belongs to God's true servants, who may fall sometimes, but who are fighting His battles still. This is for those who are idle, who are careless, who think that heaven may be gained with less than all their heart and all their strength. 'Why am I always to be struggling? I remember when I was much worse than I am now. I have done a great deal. I have done enough. You cannot expect me always to be trying, always to be persevering.' And I should answer, 'But I do expect you to be always trying. But you must persevere to the end. Forget everything that you have done. Now begin anew. As they say, make a fresh start. Imagine that this were the very beginning of your Christian life. Set out again and try as hard as if you had never tried before.'

III. 'I press towards the mark.' The great mark, the one mark, the mark which we always ought to have before our eyes, the prize to which we are called. Ought not we who really believe that there is such a kingdom, that there is such a crown, that there are such companions, that there is such a reward, to be ashamed that we care for the little troubles and vexations of this world? Ought not anyone who is going home to be ashamed if he made much of the troubles of the journey, heat, or dust, or crowd?—J. M. NEALE, *Sermons in Sackville College Chapel*, vol. II. p. 163.

THE MARKS OF A CHRISTIAN

PHIL. III. 13, 14.

I WISH to enumerate some of the marks of Christian progress.

I. **Faith.**—'We live,' says Wordsworth, 'by hope, by admiration, and by love.' We also live by faith; but faith without hope, admiration, and love would be nothing more than a cold corpse.

II. **Self-sacrifice.**—The value of our faith is measured by our self-sacrifice. This mark of Christian progress is seen not only in what it takes up but what it gives up.

III. **Self-control.**—Remember the power for good

or evil of the tongue.—*Church Family Newspaper*, vol. XIV. p. 464.

REFERENCES.—III. 13, 14.—R. Flint, *Sermons and Addresses*, p. 1. J. G. Greenhough, *Christian World Pulpit*, vol. lvii. p. 92. H. P. Liddon, *Sermons on Some Words of St. Paul*, p. 246. H. S. Seekings, *Preacher's Magazine*, vol. xvii. p. 466. J. A. Alexander, *The Gospel of Jesus Christ*, p. 371. A. Maclaren, *The Wearied Christ*, p. 158. H. P. Liddon, *University Sermons*, p. 28. J. M. Neale, *Readings for the Aged* (3rd Series), p. 218. C. D. Bell, *The Saintly Calling*, p. 183. J. J. Blunt, *Plain Sermons* (3rd Series), p. 129. Spurgeon, *Sermons*, vol. xix. No. 1114. A. Maclaren, *Expositions of Holy Scripture—Philippians*, p. 359. III. 14.—B. J. Snell, *The All-Enfolding Love*, p. 49. J. W. Boulding, *Sermons*, p. 41. R. Allen, *The Words of Christ*, p. 285. III. 15.—Archbishop Maclagan, *Christian World Pulpit*, vol. liv. p. 216. A. Maclaren, *Expositions of Holy Scripture—Philippians*, p. 369. III. 15, 16.—J. H. Jowett, *The High Calling*, p. 137. III. 16.—A. Maclaren, *Expositions of Holy Scripture—Philippians*, p. 381. III. 17.—T. F. Crosse, *Sermons* (2nd Series), p. 122. III. 17-19.—J. H. Jowett, *The High Calling*, p. 143; *Expositor* (6th Series), vol. ii. p. 259.

PHIL. III. 18.

THE artist, except when he rises to the height of a Blake, does not get beyond irritation and annoyance; the philosopher smites them with cold sarcasm; the moralist, or he whom in the narrower sense we call religious, assails them by turns with solemn denunciation and pathetic entreaty. This last alone, when it crosses his mind, and he realises for a moment what is to him so incredible, that there are those who 'mind earthly things,' says it '*even weeping*.'--SIR JOHN SEELEY, *Natural Religion* (pt. II. ch. I).

REFERENCES.—III. 18.—H. Melvill, *Penny Pulpit*, No. 1691, p. 567. III. 18, 19.—Spurgeon, *Sermons*, vol. ii. No. 102, and vol. xliv. No. 2553. J. Keble, *Sermons for the Sundays After Trinity*, p. 352. III. 19.—J. Keble, *Sermons for the Sundays After Trinity*, p. 363. *Expositor* (4th Series), vol. i. pp. 24, 35, 138, 210; *ibid.* vol. ii. pp. 66, 295, 382; *ibid.* (5th Series), vol. ix. p. 190.

HEAVEN

'For our conversation is in heaven, from whence also we look for the Saviour, the Lord Jesus Christ.'—PHIL. III. 20.

WHAT is heaven? That is a question to which the Church can give a partial, though as yet necessarily an incomplete, answer. It is manifest that the Church must depend upon the revelation of her Divine Founder Himself. For heaven lies beyond the range of human intuitions or discoveries. 'No man hath seen God at any time;' and no man hath seen heaven.

I. We turn, then, to the words of Jesus Christ. And here it is important to remark that, when He spoke of heaven, He was careful to use such language as is figurative or analogical. It is impossible in human words to give an exact account of a supernatural existence. Yet human words must be employed, and such as will convey the best idea which the audience is capable of apprehending. The words of our Lord relating to heaven need to be accepted under the limiting condition that 'eye hath not seen, nor ear heard, neither have entered into the heart of man' the things of heaven; and that revelation of them is not literal, but spiritual. But while it is true that our Lord's words respecting heaven must be regarded as adumbrations of an inexpressible and inconceivable reality, it is not impossible to draw certain inferences from His teaching and from His life.

(1) Thus He taught, beyond doubt, the existence of heaven. He did not prove it; He took it for granted. To Him, as to all who have learnt the secret of the Gospel, the life of earth is the shadow, the life of heaven is the substance; the one is transient, the other is real, enduring, absolute, true.

(2) Jesus Christ then taught the reality of heaven; and, in His teaching, He spoke of it with complete knowledge, with complete certainty. He professed and claimed to know all about heaven. As being the Son of God, as having descended to earth from God, He could, if He would, afford to mankind a full revelation of the celestial city, wherein His Father dwelt. 'No man hath seen God at any time; the only Begotten Son, which is in the bosom of the Father, He hath declared Him.' This is the substance of His revelation.

(3) Whether it was His will or not to reveal the character of heaven, He declared explicitly that it was within His power to reveal it. 'In My Father's house are many mansions. If it were not so, I would have told you. I go to prepare a place for you.' It is remarkable, then, that our Lord should have observed in all His teaching so great a reticence in speaking of heaven. Heaven was clearly one of those subjects upon which it was impossible for Him to tell, as a Man to men, all He knew.

(4) There is, however, a manifest intention not to exaggerate the awfulness of the invisible world. It may be said of Jesus Christ that, while He laid a powerful emphasis on the reality and significance of that world, He intended it to be a hope, a solace, a motive to holiness, and not to exercise a paralysing influence upon human action, as was the case in the year A.D. 1000, when the anticipation of the world's end as imminent impoverished and impaired human action. The will of God is that we should prepare ourselves in this life for the next, not that we should sacrifice this life and its endeavours as though they were practically worthless.

II. Among the lessons of Christ's teaching upon heaven there are two which seem to stand out in relief—He taught that the enjoyment of the heavenly life depended upon character and conduct in this life; and also, that the access to the heavenly life lay in the method and revelation of His hid Gospel. It is not in man to merit heaven.

III. Heaven is not a place, or a period, but a state. Is it possible to understand that existence? The soul of man is the seat of personality or identity; and it is the soul which is immortal and enters heaven. But, if we know what it is that is immortal, we may hope to know what it is that the immortal being is capable of being or doing. The intellectual, moral, and spiritual faculties of man continue eternally. No merely negative conception of heaven can be just. To regard it simply as a state of immunity from sin and sorrow and suffering is to mistake its character altogether. The death of saints is an emancipation from limiting conditions. It is a progress and exaltation. It is the entrance into a sublime existence, into the perfect state and perfect exercise of the intellectual, moral, and spiritual faculties—in a word, into heaven.

IV. It is asked by many an anxious, yearning heart if they who have known and loved on earth will regain such mutual knowledge in eternity? Can it be doubted that this knowledge will be theirs? Continuity, it has been said, is by death broken; identity remains; personality survives the grave. And if it be so, then it may be permitted to hope—nay, indeed, to believe intensely—that in heaven we shall enjoy the society of those who have been nearest and dearest upon earth. We shall know them, and they us. We shall live with them in full and free communion; we shall participate in their joy, their gratitude, their adoration; the saddest of all earthly fears, the fear of separation, will be wanting. There will be no more parting for ever.—BISHOP WELLDON.

THE EARTHLY AND THE HEAVENLY CITIZENSHIP

'Our conversation is in heaven.'—PHIL. III. 20.

'CONVERSATION' in this passage, as indeed the Revised Version shows, means 'citizenship'; and so to take it is the only way of entering fully into the strong and solemn purport of St. Paul's words. For he knew what citizenship was. He was himself, as he says, 'a citizen of no mean city,' but not of Tarsus only; he was a citizen of the Roman Empire, the greatest confederation of races and peoples which the world had ever known until the British Empire attained its pre-eminent position; he was the inheritor of an imperial franchise so august that an English statesman, speaking on a memorable occasion in the House of Commons, could find no better emblem of the safety and the dignity guaranteed to all subjects of the late Queen by their British citizenship than the ancient phrase consecrated to the ears and the hearts of all citizens of Rome, *Civis Romanus Sum*.

I. The Christian possesses a double franchise—a franchise of earth, and a franchise of heaven. But these are not incompatible, nor even separable. St. Paul knows nothing of the modern conventional distinction between the secular and the sacred sides of human life. In his eyes the State may be less sacred, but it is not less truly sacred, than the Church. He would almost as soon allow that the State has no concern with religion as that the Church has no concern with civic duty or social reform. Whatever may be the equitable relation of different religious bodies living side by side in the same political community, it would, I think, seem to him a paradox to maintain that, at a time when the State is interested, as it never was before, in the amelioration of the physical and moral conditions under which the mass of the people, in the great cities especially, live, it should deliberately discard the most efficacious and energetic of all motives to philanthropy—religion, or the love of God, which is the one unfailing warrant for the love of man.

II. A good citizen, and still more a good Christian, is not two beings, but one. There is no possibility of dividing his life into water-tight compartments. He is not a religious man in church and an irreligious man outside. He cannot be honourable in public life if in private he is fraudulent or untrustworthy. It is for this reason that the people have been led in recent years by a sound and sure instinct to demand of their public men throughout the constituencies an obedience to those moral laws upon which all societies and communities ultimately depend. They have silently argued that a statesman or a politician cannot make a worse beginning of elevating his fellow-citizens than by debasing himself. Men are tempted to essay the task of making others better ; but the one infallible service which they can render the State is to make themselves better. Political schools, parties, administrations, cabinets, rise and fall, and it is often difficult to appraise the good or the evil they have done ; but there is no one, not the poorest or humblest citizen, who may not, if he will, enrich the State with the treasure which is most enduring and ennobling—his own sincere, honest, upright, virtuous Christian life.

III. We all need to be raised day by day, in thought and character, from the citizenship of earth to the citizenship of heaven. We need to live more and more not as worldly men and women, whose souls are bounded by the range of mere temporal and terrestrial aspirations, but as the citizens of an eternal commonwealth, the sons and daughters of the Lord Almighty, redeemed and consecrated by the Passion of the Saviour Jesus Christ. So, but so only, shall we live on earth the life of heaven ; so shall we lift the society in which we move to ourselves, by lifting ourselves to God.

THE CHURCH AND SOCIAL QUESTIONS

'Our citizenship is in heaven.'—PHIL. III. 20.

AMONG all the changes which have come over religious and theological teaching within living memory none seems to me so momentous as the acute secularising of the Christian hope, as shown by the practical disappearance of 'the other world' from the sermons and writings of those who are most in touch with the thoughts and aspirations of our contemporaries. You may look through a whole book of modern sermons and find hardly a reference to what used to be called the Four Last Things, except perhaps in a rhetorical peroration at the end of a discourse. The modern clergyman certainly need not be afraid of being nicknamed a 'Sky-pilot'. The New Jerusalem which fills his thoughts is a revolutionised London.

As for the old appeals to hopes and fears beyond the grave—the scheme of government by rewards and punishments on which Bishop Butler dilates—they are gone. Our generation will not listen to them. 'Give us something to help us here and now,' is the cry. 'Tell us how to remedy social evils, and especially how to reduce the amount of physical suffering. Show us how the toiling masses may be made more comfortable. Listen to what the working-man is saying, and you will find that he wants no cheques upon the bank of heaven. No ; he is saying, like Jacob, ' If God will keep me in this way that I go, and will give me bread to eat and raiment to put on, then shall the Lord be my God '. Show the poor fellow that this is exactly what the Church wishes to do for him ; explain to him that now at last, after eighteen centuries, we are beginning to understand what Christianity really means—that it is an engine of social reform, a crusade against unfair distribution : and the Church may yet justify her existence.'

I. Now, whether you sympathise with this sort of language or not, you must admit that the change is a momentous one. The Gospel has never been so preached before. From the time of the first martyrs to our own day the Christian has always felt that this world is not his home. His eyes have been fixed on the curtain which hangs between us and the Beyond, through which, as he believed, stream forth broken rays of a purer light than ever came from the sun. In all the changes and chances of mortal life he has looked for the city that hath foundations, whose builder and maker is God. He has enriched his mental pictures of this glorious home with all the fairest and noblest images that he could find in the world of time and space, and he has prayed every day that he may at last be admitted to the never-ending companionship of saints and angels in that eternal world, and to the beatific vision of God Himself, Whom those only can see who have been made like Him in holiness. And along with these hopes he has been haunted by the horror of perpetual exile from the presence of God—a doom so dreadful that not even by recalling all the ingenuities of human cruelty can we realise one tithe of the suffering that the soul must endure when it knows what it has lost. However pictured, the eternal world has been hitherto for Christians the real world.

II. What was the message of Jesus Christ to mankind ? How did he judge human life, and how would He have us judge it ? We have been told to distinguish between judgments of fact and judgments of value. The two cannot, indeed, be held apart, for a fact which has no value is not even a fact, but an unrelated and meaningless accident, if such a thing were possible, and assuredly that which has no existence has also no value. But the distinction is sometimes useful, and we may apply it here by saying that the revelation of Jesus Christ was a revaluation of human life based on certain eternal objective facts. The essence of Christianity is a transvaluation of all values in the light of our Divine sonship and heavenly citizenship. The first Christians were accused of turning the world upside down ; and this is just what the teaching of Christ does, if the average man sees the world right side up. The things that are seen are temporal, fugitive, relatively unreal ; the things that are not seen are eternal, real in their changeless activity and inexhaustible fulness of meaning. Our Saviour lived Himself in the presence of these timeless realities ; He was ' in heaven,' as St. John seems to say, even after He 'came down' to earth ; He communed continually with His Heavenly Father ; every joy was for Him a thanksgiving, every wish a prayer. And, so living, He knew that the only thing that matters in this world is the life or soul, which is here on its trial, passing through its earthly pilgrimage towards weal or woe.

III. Jesus Christ's standard of value—His transvaluation of all values in the light of our Divine sonship and heavenly citizenship—is the standard for all Christians. Give yourselves time to think and pray. Ask God to show you what things are really valuable and worth striving for, and what things are not. Bring your whole scheme of life into His presence. Try hard and earnestly to make the eternal world real to you. It will never be real to you unless you try hard to see it. The spiritual eye needs training and exercise as much as the physical organ. Creatures who live in the dark end by losing their eyes. And do not live softly. Luxury is bad from every point of view. Learn to endure hardness as good soldiers of Jesus Christ. The cross has to be borne by all of us, and, believe me, it is only the thought of our heavenly home, where Christ has gone before to prepare a place for us, that can make that yoke easy and that burden light.—W. R. INGE, *The Guardian*, 18th Nov. 1908.

THE HEAVENLY CITIZENSHIP

' For our conversation is in heaven ; from whence also we look for the Saviour, the Lord Jesus Christ : Who shall change our vile body, that it may be fashioned like unto His glorious body, according to the working whereby He is able even to subdue all things unto Himself.'—PHIL. III. 20, 21.

THERE are many important truths which concern us all contained in these words of St. Paul. Just notice what we have in these words.

I. **Heaven is where Christ is.**—First it is implied that there *is* a heaven, ' for our conversation is in heaven'. It is clearly stated that Christ dwells in that heaven, wherever it may be. It may be, as the scientists tell us, above or below ; but wherever it is these words plainly state that Christ is there. This Apostle tells us we are to look for Him from heaven. That was what St. Paul said to the Philippians—if he were here he would say the same to you, he would say we are to look for Jesus Christ from heaven. You know whether in your daily life, in your work and play as Christian men and women, you are looking for the Lord Jesus Christ from heaven.

II. **The Purpose of our Looking.**—And then we are told in the words of the text what is the purpose of our looking for Him. When we look for a person we expect him to come to us, and so, if the Philippians were looking for the Lord Jesus Christ, they would have a certain purpose in view. The purpose is stated here. It is to change our vile or worthless bodies, our poor corruptible bodies, of which St. Paul spoke in 1 Corinthians xv. It is to change these bodies of ours, or transform them so as to alter their character altogether, not to take away their identity, but to make a real change—a change that will make them like unto the glorious body of our Lord. His glorious body is His resurrected body.

III. **The Power of His Appearing.**—Then we are told of the power which is one of the most important points in this passage, 'The working whereby He is able even to subdue all things unto Himself'. Now take this passage in connection with what we read in 1 Corinthians xv., where we are told that the last enemy that shall be destroyed is death, so that when we talk of death, or when we pass a cemetery or place where the dead are laid, we should be very solemn indeed. I take it that by the last enemy is also meant the worst enemy, and I think you will all agree that death is an awful enemy indeed. He levels all, whatever their class may be—the statesman, the philanthropist, the actor, the sailor, the soldier. ' Then cometh the end, when He shall have delivered up the kingdom to God, even the Father ; when He shall have put down all rule and all authority, and power.' There shall be no more grieving, no more crying ; both God and the Lamb shall be in that new place which is created for us after the enemies are destroyed, and ' His servants shall serve Him '. There shall be no light needed there, the Lord God giveth them light, and they shall reign for ever and ever. There is to be a new state of things. It is that men shall be so spiritualised in some marvellous way— filled with the Spirit of God, filled even more deeply than the Apostles were on the day of Pentecost. Man will receive his life from God Himself, because his life will be the new life of Jesus Christ flowing into all the redeemed, and they will be united by Him to God the Father. In this thought death loseth its bitterness, for sin is destroyed, so that it will never be possible for another fall of man to take place, because there will be no more possibility of sin, no more temptations, none of those trials to which man is subjected in this present world. Man's vile body shall be assimilated to the body of Jesus Christ by an irresistible power.

And the purpose of all this is that God may be all in all. God the Father is to predominate ; and so we can see that the manhood or womanhood that we possess in this world will all be subjected to God the Father. And can we wish it to be subjected to anyone else ? Can you desire anyone to have perfect power over you except that God Who has made you, that God Who takes care of you and loves you, and Who has assigned you a place in this world, and promised to have a place prepared for you in heaven ? Can you commit yourselves in life or death to anyone with such faith as to God the Father? May that God take care of us, may He Who gave us existence here find us a far happier life hereafter, and bring us to that blessed place where Christ Himself is, and where He shall be all in all.

REFERENCES.—III. 20.—Spurgeon, *Sermons*, vol. viii. No. 476. F. J. A. Hort, *Village Sermons* (2nd Series), p. 149. J. B. Scott, *Christian World Pulpit*, vol. xlvi. p. 220. E. Bersier, *Sermons in Paris*, p. 255. R. F. Horton, *Christian World Pulpit*, vol. xlvi. p. 273. J. J. Blunt, *Plain Sermons* (2nd Series), p. 132. W. M. Sinclair, *Christian World Pulpit*, vol. liii. p. 181. Basil Wilberforce, *Christian World Pulpit*, vol. liii. p. 334. J. H. Jowett, *The High Calling*, p. 149. *Expositor* (7th Series), vol. v. p. 503. III. 20, 21.—Spurgeon, *Sermons*, vol. xvii. No. 973; vol. xxxiii. No. 1959. F. D. Maurice, *Sermons*, vol. i. p. 235. Bishop Gore, *Christian World Pulpit*, vol. liii. p. 400. R. W. Church, *Village Sermons* (3rd Series), p. 141. J. Bunting, *Sermons*, vol. ii. p. 153. III. 21.—Bishop Creighton, *Christian World Pulpit*, vol. liv. p. 307. *Expositor* (4th Series), vol. viii. p. 145 ; *ibid.* vol. x. p. 105 ; *ibid.* (5th Series), vol. i. p. 180 ; *ibid.* vol. ii. p. 135 ; *ibid.* (7th Series), vol. vi. p. 114. IV. 1. Spurgeon, *Sermons*, vol. xxxiii. No. 1959. J. H. Jowett, *The High Calling*, p. 156. A. Maclaren, *Expositions of Holy Scripture—Philippians*, p. 1.

EUODIA AND SYNTYCHE

'I beseech Euodia, and beseech Syntyche, that they be of one mind in the Lord.'—PHIL. IV. 2.

THIS is a dual biography in a nutshell. These persons are nowhere else referred to. The outline is faint enough ; yet on thoughtful consideration it reveals not a few interesting facts.

I. The persons here mentioned were women. They were members of the Philippian Church, which is often spoken of as a 'woman's church'. It is frequently said by way of criticism that two-thirds of the members of the entire Christian Church are of the gentler sex. But shall the fact be regarded as a reflection on the character of the church? Before we leap to that conclusion, let us yoke with it another fact ; to wit, seven-eighths of the inmates of our prisons and penitentiaries are men. A fair deduction from both these premises can place no discredit upon the Church for her preponderance of female membership. Indeed, it speaks eloquently for her thoughtfulness and purity of character.

II. We are given to understand that Euodia and Syntyche were good women. There is much in a name. Euodia means 'fragrance' ; Syntyche means 'happiness'. We are informed that they were 'labourers in the Gospel'. We have a further intimation as to the character of Euodia and Syntyche in the statement that their names were written 'in the Book of Life'.

III. These good women were not of one mind.

IV. The quarrel was about a trifle. We infer this from the fact that Paul asked for no investigation of their case. Indeed, the whole affair would appear to have been much ado about nothing. It may have originated in a bit of gossip, a flash of temper, or an inadvertent word. Is it not true that most disagreements have a slight origin? We should find it

difficult to account for most of our likes and dislikes ; and as for our bitter disagreements, it would be quite impossible to justify them.

V. It would appear that both women were to blame. This may be inferred from their having an equal interest in the message : 'I beseech Euodia, and beseech Syntyche'. It takes two to make a quarrel.

VI. The results of this quarrel were far-reaching. It has come down through nineteen hundred years.

VII. We do not know that Euodia and Syntyche were ever reconciled on earth. The women who were parties to this Philippian quarrel are generic types. And the practical application is plain. If there are bitternesses to be healed or differences to compose, let us not wait until the shadows enfold us.—D. J. BURRELL, *The Gospel of Certainty*, p. 73.

PHIL. IV. 2.

'IT has been justly observed,' says Dr. Johnson in *The Rambler* (99), 'that discord generally operates in little things ; it is inflamed to its utmost vehemence by contrariety of tests, oftener than of principles.'

REFERENCES.—IV. 2.—*Expositor* (6th Series), vol. x. p. 45. IV. 2, 3.—J. H. Jowett, *The High Calling*, p. 162.

'Whose names are in the Book of Life.'—PHIL. IV. 3.

IN his *Specimen Days in America*, describing the cases of the soldiers he visited in hospital during the Civil War, Walt Whitman writes : 'No formal general's report, nor book in library, nor column in the paper, embalms the bravest, north or south, east or west. Unnamed, unknown, remain and still remain, the bravest soldiers.'

REFERENCES.—IV. 3.—S. K. Hocking, *Christian World Pulpit*, vol. xlvii. p. 102. J. G. Greenhough, *ibid.* vol. liii. p. 264. A. Maclaren, *Expositions of Holy Scripture—Philippians*, p. 11.

PHIL. IV. 4.

DR. MARCUS DODS wrote at the age of twenty-six to his sister Marcia : 'If you are going to send texts I'll send you one that will last you all the year and more—χαίρετε ἐν κυρίῳ πάντοτε· πάλιν ἐρῶ, χαίρετε, Rejoice in the Lord always : again I say, rejoice : then notice the connections on to the end of the paragraph'.—*Early Letters*, p. 165 (see also p. 257).

EQUANIMITY

(*Christmas*)

'Rejoice in the Lord alway, and again I say, Rejoice.'—PHIL. IV. 4.

IN other parts of Scripture the prospect of Christ's coming is made a reason for solemn fear and awe, and a call for watching and prayer, but in the verses connected with the text a distinct view of the Christian character is set before us, and distinct duties urged on us. 'The Lord is at hand,' and what then? —why, if so, we must 'rejoice in the Lord' ; we must be conspicuous for 'moderation' ; we must be 'careful for nothing' ; we must seek from God's bounty, and not from man, whatever we need ; we must abound in 'thanksgiving' ; and we must cherish, or rather we must pray for, and we shall receive from above, 'the peace of God which passeth all understanding,' to 'keep our hearts and minds through Christ Jesus'.

Now this is a view of the Christian character definite and complete enough to admit of commenting on, and it may be useful to show that the thought of Christ's coming not only leads to fear, but to a calm and cheerful frame of mind.

I. Nothing perhaps is more remarkable than that an Apostle—a man of toil and blood, a man combating with powers unseen, and a spectacle for men and Angels, and much more that St. Paul, a man whose natural temper was so zealous, so severe, and so vehement—I say, nothing is more striking and significant than that St. Paul should have given us this view of what a Christian should be. It would be nothing wonderful, it *is* nothing wonderful, that writers in a day like this should speak of peace, quiet, sobriety, and cheerfulness, as being the tone of mind that becomes a Christian; but considering that St. Paul was by birth a Jew, and by education a Pharisee; that he wrote at a time when, if at any time, Christians were in lively and incessant agitation of mind; when persecution and rumours of persecution abounded; when all things seemed in commotion around them; when there was nothing fixed; when there were no churches to soothe them, no course of worship to sober them, no homes to refresh them; and, again, considering that the Gospel is full of high and noble, and what may be called even romantic, principles and motives, and deep mysteries; and, further, considering the very topic which the Apostle combines with his admonitions is that awful subject, the coming of Christ; it is well worthy of notice that, in such a time, under such a covenant, and with such a prospect, he should draw a picture of the Christian character as free from excitement and effort, as full of repose, as still and as equable, as if the great Apostle wrote in some monastery of the desert or some country parsonage. Here surely is the finger of God; here is the evidence of supernatural influences, making the mind of man independent of circumstances! This is the thought that first suggests itself; and the second is this, how deep and refined is the true Christian spirit!—how difficult to enter into, how vast to embrace, how impossible to exhaust! Who would expect such composure and equanimity from the fervent Apostle of the Gentiles? We know St. Paul could do great things; could suffer and achieve, could preach and confess, could be high and could be low; but we might have thought that all this was the limit and the perfection of the Christian temper, as he viewed it; and that no room was left him for the feelings which the text and following verses lead us to ascribe to him.

And yet he who 'laboured more abundantly than all' his brethren, is also a pattern of simplicity, meekness, cheerfulness, thankfulness, and serenity of mind.

II. It is observable, too, that it was foretold as the peculiarity of Gospel times by the Prophet Isaiah:

'The work of righteousness shall be peace; and the effect of righteousness, quietness and assurance for ever. And My people shall dwell in a peaceable habitation, and in sure dwellings, and in quiet resting-places.'

'But this I say, brethren, the time is short.' What matters it what we eat, what we drink, how we are clothed, where we lodge, what is thought of us, what becomes of us, since we are not at home? It is felt every day, even as regards this world, that when we leave home for a while we are unsettled. This, then, is the kind of feeling which a belief in Christ's coming will create within us. It is not worth while establishing ourselves here; it is not worth while spending time and thought on such an object. We shall hardly have got settled when we shall have to move.

'Be careful for nothing,' St. Paul says, or, as St. Peter, 'casting all your care upon Him,' or, as He Himself, 'Take no thought' or care 'for the morrow, for the morrow will take thought for the things of itself'. This of course is the state of mind which is directly consequent on the belief, that 'the Lord is at hand'. Who would care for any loss or gain to-day, if he knew for certain that Christ would show Himself to-morrow? no one. Well, then, the true Christian feels as he would feel, did he know for certain that Christ would be here to-morrow.

III. The Christian has a deep, silent, hidden peace, which the world sees not,—like some well in a retired and shady place, difficult of access. He is the greater part of his time by himself, and when he is in solitude, that is his real state. What he is when left to himself and to his God, that is his true life. He can bear himself; he can (as it were) joy in himself, for it is the grace of God within him, it is the presence of the Eternal Comforter, in which he joys. He can bear, he finds it pleasant, to be with himself at all times,—'never less alone than when alone'. He can lay his head on his pillow at night, and own in God's sight, with overflowing heart, that he wants nothing, that he 'is full and abounds,' that God has been all things to him, and that nothing is not his which God could give him. More thankfulness, more holiness, more of heaven he needs indeed, but the thought that he can have more is not a thought of trouble, but of joy. It does not interfere with his peace to know that he may grow nearer God. Such is the Christian's peace, when, with a single heart and the Cross in his eye, he addresses and commends himself to Him with whom the night is as clear as the day. St. Paul says that 'the peace of God shall *keep* our hearts and minds'. By 'keep' is meant 'guard,' or 'garrison,' our hearts; so as to keep out enemies. And he says, our 'hearts and minds' in contrast to what the world sees of us. Many hard things may be said of the Christian, and done against him, but he has a secret preservative or charm, and minds them not.—J. H. NEWMAN.

REFERENCES.—IV. 4.—Spurgeon, *Sermons*, vol. xli. No. 2405. B. J. Snell, *The Virtue of Gladness*, p. 73. W. H.

Evans, *Sermons for the Church's Year*, p. 15. J. T. Bramston, *Fratribus*, p. 66. J. H. Jowett, *The High Calling*, p. 168. A. Maclaren, *Expositions of Holy Scripture—Philippians*, p. 21. IV. 4-7.—F. J. A. Hort, *Village Sermons in Outline*, p. 221.

THE GOLDEN MEAN

'Let your moderation be known unto all men. The Lord is at hand.'—PHIL. IV. 5.

'YOUR moderation,' forbearance, conciliatoriness, yieldingness.

I. Note this admonition as it applies to matters of faith. The Apostle designed to put the Philippians on their guard against treating coldly or harshly those of another creed; the text is a warning against bigotry and dogmatism. The danger was lest they should exhibit an intolerant spirit in dealing with their unconverted neighbours. This admonition is by no means out of date; the modern Christian needs to give it most prayerful consideration, for he also is in danger of haughtiness and exclusiveness. (1) There is a pride of orthodoxy. (2) There is the pride of denominationalism.

II. The admonition of the text applies to matters of character. We are tempted to judge our brethren harshly; some of them are not like us in certain particulars, and we conclude that they are inferior in wisdom or devotion. (1) We must beware how we deal offensively with any whom we may imagine to be inferior to ourselves. (2) And let us be careful lest we grieve those who are different from ourselves.

III. This admonition applies to matters of conduct. We are to display our reasonableness in daily life, and not severely to judge our fellows. It is not always easy to say what is exactly right and fitting to be done; we must, therefore, watch against illiberality and painful dogmatism. 'Reasonableness of dealing, not strictness of legal right, but consideration for one another,' is the lesson of the text and the high duty of the Christian life. The earth itself is not a rigid body; it yields to stress, it displays a certain plasticity for which the astronomer allows; and such is the character of living goodness. Just as the mighty ocean softly adjusts itself to all the articulations of the shore without any sacrifice of majesty; as the rock-ribbed earth is tremblingly sensitive, yielding to stress whilst delicately true to its orbit; so the strong, sincere, pure soul has a quick sense of the essential and non-essential —is ready within well-understood lines to give and take, and so preserves that aspect of ease and beauty which belongs to whatever is strong and free.— W. L. WATKINSON, *Themes for Hours of Meditation*, p. 113.

REFERENCES.—IV. 5.—W. M. Sinclair, *Christ and Our Times*, p. 231. R. W. Hiley, *A Year's Sermons*, vol. ii. p. 346. F. St. John Corbett, *The Preacher's Year*, p. 7. W. H. Evans, *Short Sermons for the Seasons*, p. 20. J. Keble, *Sermons or Advent to Christmas Eve*, p. 391. J. Jefferis, *Christian World Pulpit*, vol. xliv. p. 403. J. H. Jowett, *The High Calling*, p. 174. IV. 6.—*Ibid.* p. 180. Spurgeon, *Sermons*, vol. xxv. No. 1469. A. Maclaren, *Expositions of Holy Scripture—Philippians*, p. 31.

MAN'S CARE CONQUERED BY GOD'S PEACE

'Be careful for nothing; but in every thing by prayer and supplication with thanksgiving let your requests be made known unto God. And the peace of God, which passeth all understanding, shall keep your hearts and minds through Christ Jesus.'—PHIL. IV. 6, 7.

LET us see whether this exhortation against anxiety is as impracticable and visionary as some assume it to be; whether, on the contrary, it is not one of the wisest and kindest precepts God ever gave to His children; whether fuller obedience to it would not relieve us of our burdens and wipe away our tears, giving smiles in the place of sadness and peace in the midst of storms.

I. In distinguishing between various kinds of care, there are some which are evidently right, others as evidently wrong, and some which require thought before we can determine whether they are lawful or unlawful. (1) It is clear that some cares are perfectly justifiable. The injunction to pray about them implies this, and our obedience to Divine precepts necessitates them. (2) There are some cares which are as certainly wrong, because they flow from an evil source which taints them. Envy, suspicion, ambition, consciousness of guilt, pride, ill-temper may originate them and often do. (3) But, besides these, there are cares about which it is by no means easy to say whether they are lawful or unlawful. Can we find any touchstone to which we can bring a doubtful care, to test whether it be right or wrong? I think we can, and that it lies before us in my text, where we are pointed to prayer. Any care you can confidently pray about is lawful. (4) But some cares, lawful enough in themselves, become unlawful through their excess.

II. To let in the light of heaven on anxieties and cares—in other words, to pray over them—is to expel the evils in them. (1) Those evils are manifold. Even the body suffers from over-anxiety, as sleepless nights, a care-worn face, and shattered nerves often testify. Our mental faculties are affected too. (2) How is this to be averted? We want a power put within us which will drive out the strong man armed, being stronger than he. And this is brought in by prayer.

III. The effect of obedience to this precept is set forth in the words: 'And the peace of God, which passeth all understanding, shall keep your hearts and minds through Christ Jesus. This peace is not a passive possession but an active power which 'keeps the heart'; or, as Paul says to the Colossians, 'rules the heart'.—A. ROWLAND, *Open Windows and other Sermons*, p. 130.

REFERENCES.—IV. 6, 7.—Spurgeon, *Sermons*, vol. xl. No. 2351. J. A. Beet, *Christian World Pulpit*, vol. xliv. p. 273. E. Armitage, *ibid.* vol. xlviii. p. 149.

'The peace of God which passeth all understanding, shall keep your heart and mind.'—PHIL. IV. 7.

IN the letters of J. M. Neale, an account is given of the death of the Rev. Charles Simeon. It is from the pen of Mr. Carus. 'I went in to him after chapel this morning, and he was then lying with his eyes closed. I thought he was asleep, but after standing there a little while he put out his hand to me. I said, 'The peace of God, which passeth all understanding, shall keep your heart and mind'. He said nothing. I said again, 'They washed their robes, dear sir, and made them white in the Blood of the Lamb ; *therefore* they are before the throne of God'. 'I have, I have !' he said. 'I have washed my robes in the Blood of the Lamb ; they are clean, quite clean—I know it.' He shut his eyes for a few minutes, and when he again opened them I said, 'Well, dear sir, you will soon comprehend with all saints what is the breadth, and length, and depth, and height, and know the love of Christ, which passeth knowledge, that ye may——' He tried to raise himself, and said, after his quick manner, 'Stop ! stop ! you don't understand a bit about that text ; don't go on with it—I won't hear it—I shall understand it soon !' After a little while he said, 'Forty years ago I blessed God because I met one man in the street who spoke to me, and, oh, what a change there is now' !

REFERENCES.—IV. 7.—Spurgeon, *Sermons*, vol. iv. No. 180 and vol. xxiv. No. 1397. Bishop Creighton, *University and other Sermons*, p. 1. T. Arnold, *Christian Life : Its Hopes*, p. 238. Archbishop Benson, *Living Theology*, p. 211. E. J. Boyce, *Parochial Sermons*, p. 188. Phillips Brooks, *The Law of Growth*, p. 219. T. Binney, *King's Weigh-House Chapel Sermons* (2nd Series), p. 79, 94, 106, 121. J. H. Jowett, *The High Calling*, p. 186. A. Maclaren, *Expositions of Holy Scripture—Philippians*, p. 39.

PROTECTED THOUGHTS

'The peace of God ... shall guard your hearts and thoughts.'
—PHIL. IV. 7, 8.

IN the Christian life the thought-realm is the seat of the greatest difficulty with which a man is confronted. Our thoughts are so elusive, so difficult to control, and so entirely independent of any known law, that to order them arightly seems an impossibility. It is characteristic of the Gospel that such a difficulty is not ignored, but is honestly faced and frankly dealt with. It proposes a solution of the problem of the thought-life the worth of which can only be known by personal test, and the man who would know the fulness of the Evangel must seek the fulfilment of its promises here. Indeed, in its ultimate analysis the adequacy of the Gospel as a scheme of salvation depends upon its power in this hidden realm of our being, for our thoughts are by far the largest parts of our lives. We think far more than we speak or act, and it is a matter of common experience that our thoughts are the springs of both speech and action.

I. The power of thought is the strongest force in the life of any one of us, as witness its annihilation of distance and time, and its disregard of circumstances. Our holiest moments are often invaded by our unholiest imaginations, and uncontrolled thought at such times makes vivid to us things long since past.

On this account it is that thought manifests its greatest strength as an avenue of temptation. Our temptations come to us mainly by our thoughts, which gather strength in this respect from their own past victories.

II. The fact, that our thoughts have a direct and powerful influence upon others is an added emphasis upon the necessity of our endeavouring to apprehend the fulness of Christ's salvation in this respect. It is quite impossible to disregard what is now known as the power of thought-communication and transference, a misapprehension of which has led not a few into a regular cult of thought-power, from which a right understanding of the Gospel in its fulness would have saved them. Now we may understand something of its reality and influence by looking at it inversely. We all know the power of thoughtlessness and the strength which it has to wound and to hurt. We all know that nothing cuts us so deeply as thoughtless treatment on the part of those from whom we expected something better. And by introversion we may understand something also of the influence of holy, pure, and loving thought.

III. Along with the creation of personal self-discovery, the Gospel proclaims an inward emancipation, promising to the surrendered heart a guardianship of thought which liberates from moral bondage, and a communication of power which brings 'every thought into captivity to the obedience of Christ'. And these words are not expressive of an unattainable ideal, spoken to mock us with the sense of shortcoming which they create, but are rather a call to us to enter into the joy of our Lord.

The Gospel does not call us to a life of mere passivity, which would be, to say the least, of but questionable morality. We are to co-operate with Him, and it is always within our own power to keep ourselves in the love of God. Hence it is that the Gospel imposes a rigid self-discipline with regard to thoughts, and lays upon us the responsibility for thought-selection. Assuming that we have learned our own helplessness, that we have yielded ourselves to the Lord, and are now relying upon His promise to undertake the responsibility of guarding our hearts and our thoughts, it enjoins 'Whatsoever things are true, honest, lovely, of good report think on these things'. Christ does not supersede our own activities but rather strengthens them, and to us is committed the task of crowding out the evil by the good, always in reliance upon His imparted strength.—J. STUART HOLDEN, *The Pre-Eminent Lord*, p. 131.

RIGHT THOUGHTS

'Finally, brethren, whatsoever things are true, whatsoever things are honest, whatsoever things are just, whatsoever things are pure, whatsoever things are lovely, whatsoever things are of good report ; if there be any virtue, and if there be any praise, think on these things.'—PHIL. IV. 8.

ST. PAUL here tells the beloved Philippians what things to think of, what to value, what to practise in their lives ; if they do this, he says that the 'God of Peace' will certainly be with them. Let us look at the things which he suggests for their meditation and practice a little more closely.

I. Whatsoever Things are True.—The word has a fuller and deeper meaning in the Bible than it now has. Truth with us means the opposite of falsity in speech, but in Scripture it means the opposite of all unreality, all sham. St. Paul bids them think habitually of all that is real; on the substance, not on the shadow; on the eternal, not on the transitory; on God, not on the world. 'Whatsoever things are real'—God, the Soul, Eternity, the Gospel of Jesus Christ—'think on these things.'

II. Whatsoever Things are Honest.—The word in the original means 'noble,' 'grave,' 'reverend,' 'seemly'. It is an exhortation to dignity of thought as opposite to meanness of thought. It invites to the gravity of self-respect. Nothing becomes too bad for men who have lost their self-respect. Why is this sea of life strewn with hopeless wrecks? Could the unmanly man, the unwomanly woman, have sunk to such depths of loathsome degradation if they had ever thought of whatsoever things are honest? There are no words of counsel more deep-reaching th n these, especially to young men and women.

III. Whatsoever Things are Just.—Justice is one of the most elementary of human duties, and one of the rarest. Try to be, what so few are, habitually fair.

IV. Whatsoever Things are Pure.—Ah! that this warning might reach the heart of every one of you, and inspire you with the resolve to banish from your minds everything that defileth. Impure thoughts encouraged lead inevitably to fatal deeds and blasted lives.

V. Whatsoever Things are Lovely.—Winning and attractive thoughts that live and are radiant in the light. If you think of such things, the baser and viler will have no charm for you. Try then, above all, 'the expulsive power of good affections'. Empty by filling—empty of what is mean and impure by filling with what is noble and lovely.

VI. Whatsoever Things are of Good Report.—The world delights in whatsoever things are of ill report—base stories, vile innuendoes, evil surmisings, scandalous hints; it revels in envy, hatred, malice, and all uncharitableness. If you would be noble, if you would be a Christian man, have nothing to do with such things.

VII. Then, if there be any Virtue, and if there be any Praise, think on these Things.—The words do not imply the least doubt that there is virtue, and that there is praise, but they mean, whatever virtue and praise there be, think on these. There is no nobler character than the man who knows the awful reverence which is due from himself to his own soul; who loveth the thing that is just and doeth that which is lawful and right, in singleness of heart; who keeps the temple of his soul pure and bright with the presence of the Holy One; who hates all that is ignoble and loves his neighbour as himself. What has such a man to fear? The eternal forces are with

him. His heart, his hope, his treasure, are beyond the grave; and ever and anon he is permitted to see the heavens open, and 'the angels of God ascending and descending upon the Son of Man'.—DEAN FARRAR.

WHAT TO THINK ABOUT

'Finally, brethren, whatsoever things are true, whatsoever things are honourable, whatsoever things are just, whatsoever things are pure, whatsoever things are lovely, whatsoever things are of good report; if there be any virtue, and if there be any praise, think on these things.'—PHIL. IV. 8.

'THINK on these things.' 'These things' constitute the prescribed liberty of Christian manhood. They are a kind of inventory of the mental furnishings of the Christian life. And I think everybody will readily grant that the furnishings are not cheap and stingy, not bare and monotonous, but liberal and varied, graceful and refined.

Now let me review these glorious possibilities, this authorised dominion in Christian freedom of thought.

I. Whatsoever Things are True.—True, not simply veracious. The word 'true' is not used by the Apostle as we use it in a court of law, when we enjoin a witness to 'speak the truth, the whole truth, and nothing but the truth'. The things described in a police court as true are usually ugly and repulsive; truth is always beautiful. Truth in a police court is correspondence with fact. Truth as used in the New Testament is correspondence with God. An unclean story may be accurate; an unclean story can never be true. A story is true when in very substance it shares the likeness of Him who is the truth. Veracity accurately describes a happening, truth describes a particular happening. We are therefore enjoined not to think about merely accurate things, but about accurate things which unveil the face of God.

II. Whatsoever Things are Honourable.—Things that are worthy of honour, worthy of reverence, the august and the venerable. The Authorised Version uses the old English word 'honest,' which is suggestive of gravity, seemliness, dignity. There is a certain fine stateliness in the word, recalling the impressive grandeur of a cathedral pile. Whatsoever things make the character of men and women to resemble the imposing proportions of a cathedral, 'think on these things'.

III. Whatsoever Things are Just.—And yet our word 'just' does not convey the Apostle's mind and meaning. Justice can be very cold and steely, like the justice of a Shylock. It may mean only superficial exactitude as between man and man. But to be really just is to be right with God. No man is really just until he is adjusted to his Maker. Whatsoever things satisfy the standards of the Almighty, 'think on these things'.

IV. Whatsoever Things are Pure.—But to be pure is to be more than just. It is to be stainless, blameless, and unblemished.

V. Whatsoever Things are Lovely.—We are to bring the amiable and the lovable within the circle of our regard. John Calvin gives the meaning as 'morally agreeable and pleasant'. I am glad that juicy word came from the lips of that austere prophet. Dr. Matheson tells of a young woman who came to him in great distress over her failure to fulfil the religious duties of life. He was aware that at this very time she was living a life of sacrificial devotion to a blind father. 'I asked if this service of hers was not a religious duty. She answered, "Oh no, it cannot be, because that brings me such joy, and it is the delight of my heart to serve my father".' It is a most common and perilous mistake. There are tens of thousands of duties and liberties which are juicy and delicious, and they are the portion of those who sit down at the Lord's feast.

VI. Whatsoever Things are of Good Report.—Not merely things that are well reported of, but things which themselves have a fine voice, things that are fair speaking, and therefore gracious, winsome, winning, and attractive. And then, as though he were afraid that the vast enclosure was not yet wide enough, and that some fair and beautiful thing might still be outside its comprehensive pale, the Apostle adds still more inclusive terms, and says, '*If there be any virtue*,' whatever is merely excellent; '*and if there be any praise*,' whatever is in any degree commendable—take account of them, bring them within the circle of your commendation and delight, 'think on these things'. Fasten your eyes upon the lovely wheresoever the lovely may be found.—J. H. JOWETT, *The High Calling*, p. 192.

TIME TO THINK

'Think on these things.'—PHIL. IV. 8.

THIS age has been called an age of growth, and so in many ways it is—growth of empire, of commerce, of wealth, of population, and an improvement in physique.

But what of spiritual growth? There is a growth in organisations, in spiritual activities, in spiritual fuss, but this is only the scaffolding; the building itself grows but little. What is the remedy? We find it in the first word of our text, 'Think'.

I. Get Time to Think.—It is more necessary than many realise; it is indeed absolutely necessary, for without time to think our spiritual life cannot grow. We hear too much of the voice of man. Get time to hear the voice of God.

II. Acquire the Habit of Thinking.—The mind quickly forms habits just as the body does, and if those habits are habits of idleness or day-dreams or vanity, the mind will soon become useless for thinking. Discipline your mind! Keep still and think. Think deeply, and so become deep. Think regularly, and so acquire the habit of thinking.

III. What shall we Think?—It is a good thing to drive out wrong and impure thoughts from our hearts —we must do so; but unless we obtain good thoughts to fill their place the evil thoughts will return with sevenfold force. What, then, shall we think? 'Whatsoever things are true, honest, just, pure, lovely, of good report, if there be any virtue, any praise, think

on these things.' That is the great remedy for our lack of spiritual growth. The scaffolding is here; let us build up the spiritual building.

THE REGULATION OF THOUGHTS

'Whatsoever things are true, whatsoever things are honourable, whatsoever things are just, whatsoever things are pure, whatsoever things are lovely, whatsoever things are of good report; if there be any virtue, and if there be any praise, think on these things.'—PHIL. IV. 8.

WHAT a vast and varied domain there is spread out before man in which his thought may expatiate! Have we not in this itself an intimation of our immortality? It has been said that 'art is long, and life is short'. The truth is that life is long too, as long as art—long even to infinity. He who has given the eternal faculties and the eternal longing will also give the eternal life. 'As a man thinketh in his heart, so is he.' A man can never be better than his thoughts. Everything good and everything evil originates in thought. And herein we are greatly helped or hindered, as the case may be, by the power of habit. What you want is carefully—painfully, if necessary—to cultivate the habit of choosing those things which are good and pure and honourable and lovely and of good report. It may be a slow process, but it is a sure one, if only, by the grace of God, you persevere. For you must remember that interest in a particular subject is, to a very large extent, a matter of habit. Bearing in mind that what is necessary is not simply a good resolution such as one might make at the close of a sermon, or in one of his better moods, but a steady and persevering course of training and culture, let us see more precisely what it is we have to do.

I. The first thing clearly is to select that which is good (as opposed to that which is evil) to think about. Here comes in the weighty truth that 'to the pure all things are pure, but unto them that are defiled and unbelieving is nothing pure; but even their mind and conscience is defiled'. It is not so much the things at which we look as the way in which we look at them, which makes the great difference.

II. Not only, however, is it our duty to select that which is good as opposed to that which is bad, but to choose that which is best in preference to that which is inferior, to think about. God made us to soar. He has given us atmosphere enough to soar in, and heaven enough to soar to; and it is a shame that so many of us should be content to think such paltry thoughts as we do. There is one theme which is loftier and more inspiring than all others, which we neglect at the peril of all that is highest and best, and most hopeful in us—the great theme of the Gospel—'Jesus Christ and Him crucified'.

III. While the greatest theme of all which can engage our attention is the truth as it is in Jesus, there is no disposition to narrow the range of our thinking. There is only one thing narrow in Christianity, and that is the gate—the entrance.—J. M. GIBSON, *A Strong City*, p. 165.

THE DISCIPLINE OF THOUGHT
PHIL. IV. 8.

WHEN we speak of unseen things, we commonly refer to things that are eternal. We associate the unseen with the world beyond the veil, where the angels of God, innumerable, are around the throne. But the world of thought, of feeling, of passion, and of desire —that world still baffles the finest powers of vision : as surely as there is an unseen heaven above us, there is an unseen universe within. I wish, then, to turn to the world within. I believe that most of us give far too little heed to what I might call the discipline of thought. First, I shall speak on the vital need there is of governing our thoughts. Next, on how the Gospel helps man to this government.

I. First, then, on the government of our thoughts —and at the outset I would recognise the difficulty of it. I question if there is a harder task in all the world than that of bringing our thoughts into subjection to our will. And yet there are one or two considerations I can bring before you, that will show you how, in the whole circle of self-mastery, there is nothing more vital than the mastery of thought. (1) Think, for example, how much of our happiness—our common happiness—depends on thought. Our common happiness does not hang on what we view. Our common happiness hangs on our point of view. Largely, it is not things themselves ; it is our thoughts about them, that constitute the gentle art of being happy. (2) Again, how much of our unconscious influence lies in our thoughts. That very suggestive and spiritual writer, Maeterlinck, puts the matter in his own poetic way. He says : 'Though you assume the face of a saint, a hero, or a martyr, the eye of the passing child will not greet you with the same unapproachable smile if there lurk within you an evil thought'. (3) There is only one other consideration I would mention, and that is the power of thought in our temptations. In the government of thought—in the power to bring thought to heel—lies one of our greatest moral safeguards against sin.

II. How does the Gospel help us to govern our thoughts ? To some of you the mastery of thought may seem impossible—it is never viewed as impossible in Scripture, and the secret of that Gospel-power lies in the three great words—light, love, life. (1) Think first of light as a power for thought-mastery. In twilight or darkness what sad thoughts come thronging which the glory of sunlight instantly dispels. The glory of Christ is that by His life and death He has shed a light where before there was only darkness. The light of Christ, for the man who lives in it, is an untold help in the government of thought. (2) Then think of love—is it not one mark of love that our thoughts always follow in its train ? (3) Then think of life—are not our thoughts affected by the largeness and abundance of our life ? Christ's great tide of life, like the tide of the sea that covers up the mudbanks, is the greatest power in the moral world for submerging every base and bitter thought.—G. H. MORRISON, *The Unlighted Lustre*, p. 1.

THINGS THAT ARE LOVELY
PHIL. IV. 8.

AND 'these things' constitute the prescribed liberty of Christian manhood. They are a sort of inventory of the mental furnishings of the Christian life. If we are to find our mental furnishings among things that are lovely, where shall we make our explorations ? We can find them in humanity, in nature, and in God as revealed to us of Jesus Christ our Lord.

I. Turn, then, to *humanity*, and whatsoever things are lovely think on these things. And do not be surprised if I counsel you to begin with yourselves. Steadily seek and contemplate the true and the gracious, and the better side of your own self. Do you imagine that this will foster self-conceit ? It will only nourish a healthy self-respect. In the most barren wastes of life solitary blooms are blowing. They may be weak and fragile and sickly, but 'think on these things'. And we must busy ourselves in diligently seeking hidden beauties in the lives of others. It is a very chivalrous and manly guest, and it receives a rich reward.

II. And turn to *nature*, and 'whatsoever things are lovely think on these things'. We need to 'get back to the land' in more senses than the political one of which we are so helpfully hearing to-day. We want to get back to its poetic significance, its mystic interpretations, its subtle influences upon the spirit by its ministry of light, and shade, and colour, and fragrance, its delicate graces, and its awful austerity. We need a refreshed communion with God's beautiful world. It is a most neglected side of modern education.

III. And lastly—and surely firstly, too—turn to the Lord Jesus, and contemplate 'the chief among ten thousand, the altogether lovely'. Is it not relevant counsel to our age to advise men to sometimes lay down their apparatus of criticism, and just bask in the contemplation of the moral glory of our Lord ? I am not disparaging criticism, but I am advising that criticism be not allowed to suffocate devotion. I once saw an eminent professor of physics who was so intent upon watching the disturbance effected in a cup of coffee by allowing the bowl of his spoon to rest upon it that he took no breakfast at all ! It is possible to be so occupied with critical problems concerning the Bread of Life that we altogether forget to eat. And so I say it is well at times, and very frequently too, to lay all critical questions on one side, and just absorbently contemplate the spiritual glory of our Redeemer.—J. H. JOWETT, *The British Congregationalist*, p. 252.

REFERENCES.—IV. 8.—F. W. Farrar, *Everyday Christian Life*, p. 46. H. Howard, *The Raiment of the Soul*, p. 44. T. Sadler, *Sunday Thoughts*, p. 139. W. J. Hocking, *Christian World Pulpit*, vol. xlv. p. 59. F. W. Farrar, *ibid.* vol. xlviii. pp. 49, 52. A. P. Stanley, *Canterbury Sermons*, p. 291. A. L. Lilley, *Christian World Pulpit*, vol. liii. p. 202. *Church Family Newspaper*, vol. xv. p. 564. R. J. Drummond, *Faith's Certainties*, p. 215. *Expositor* (5th Series), vol. ix. p. 437 ; *ibid.* (6th Series), vol. xi. p. 147. A. Maclaren, *Expositions of Holy Scripture—Philippians*, p. 48.

THERE may be something more finely sensitive in the modern humour that tends more and more to withdraw a man's personality from the lessons he inculcates, or the cause that he has espoused ; but there is a loss herewith of wholesome responsibility ; and when we find in the works of Knox, as in the Epistles of Paul, the man himself standing nakedly forward, courting and anticipating criticism, putting his character, as it were, in pledge for the sincerity of his doctrine, we had best waive the question of delicacy, and make our acknowledgment for a lesson of courage, not unnecessary in these days of anonymous criticism, and much light, otherwise unattainable, in the spirit in which great movements were initiated and carried forward.—R. L. STEVENSON, in *Men and Books*.

REFERENCES.—IV. 9.—J. H. Jowett, *The High Calling*, p. 198. IV. 10.—*Expositor* (5th Series), vol. viii. p. 409 ; *ibid*. vol. x. p. 196. IV. 10-14.—A. Maclaren, *Expositions of Holy Scripture—Philippians*, p. 58. IV. 10-23.—W. C. Smith, *Scottish Review*, vol. vi. p. 248. IV. 11.—Spurgeon, *Sermons*, vol. vi. No. 320. T. F. Crosse, *Sermons* (2nd Series), p. 122. H. P. Liddon, *Sermons on Some Words of St. Paul*, p. 262. J. Keble, *Sermons for the Sundays After Trinity*, p. 86. J. H. Jowett, *The High Calling*, p. 204. *Expositor* (6th Series), vol. xi. p. 285.

CONCURRENT ADAPTATION

'Not that I speak in respect of want ; for I have learned, in whatsoever state I am, therein to be content. I know how to be abased, and I know also how to abound ; in everything and in all things have I learned the secret both to be filled and to be hungry, both to abound and to be in want, I can do all things in Him that strengtheneth me.' —PHIL. IV. 11, 12 (R.V.).

TRUE life with serene acquiescence accommodates itself to things as they are, and, whilst still pursuing its highest ideals, finds in its surroundings the conditions of its unfolding and satisfaction. All inward irritation and revolt on the score of circumstance mean so much defect of life.

I. Note the wide range of the Apostle's experience. We are naturally curious as to the history of a teacher who declares that he has found the secret of perennial content. If the circumstances of such a man were narrow and monotonous, if his life were cloistered and uneventful, we should not be greatly impressed by his avowal ; he who is to witness with effect on this subject must have a history. This the Apostle had. He had ranged all climes from the south to the north pole of human circumstance and sentiment. He assures us, however, that no change found him unprepared. From none did he shrink, and by none did he suffer loss. Those who have not mastered the secret of adjusting themselves to the incidence of the perpetual unsettlements of life are liable to suffer terribly in spirit and faith, temper and character.

II. Mark the process by which the Apostle arrived at this perfect contentment. Whatever may be the aspect of his lot to the carnal eye, he accepts it with gratitude and expectation : 'I can do all things in

Him that strengtheneth me '. How, then, is the Christian thoroughly reconciled to a life which occasions the natural man such deep discomfort, and which involves him in dire peril ? (1) Christ restores the inner harmony of our nature upon which the interpretation of the outer world depends. In the sovereign power of redeeming and sanctifying grace the conscience is sprinkled from guilt, the passions are purified, the heart glows with love, the will is sceptred, and with peace, patience, and power dwelling within there is no longer any reason or temptation to quarrel with things outside. (2) By rendering us self-sufficing, Christ renders us largely independent of the outer world. To the natural man the world of circumstance is the whole of life. But he who lives in the Spirit, and walks in the Spirit, has an altogether different conception of the place and power of circumstance. He knows of another world than that which meets the carnal eye—of a kingdom within him having marvellous interests, treasures, dignities, sciences, and delights of its own. Within his own heart he carries the summer, the fountain, the nightingale, and the rose, therefore the palace does not mock nor the prison paralyse. (3) By strengthening us in the inner man Christ makes us masters of circumstance.—W. L. WATKINSON, *Themes for Hours of Meditation*, p. 72.

REFERENCE.—IV. 11, 12.—E. Armitage, *Christian World Pulpit*, vol. lii. p. 202.

OLIVER CROMWELL, a few days after the death of his daughter, Lady Elizabeth Claypole, 'called for his Bible, and desired an honourable and godly person there (with others) present to read to him Philippians IV. 11-13—"Not that I speak in respect of want, for I have learned, in whatsoever state I am, therewith to be content. I know both how to be abased, and I know how to abound. Everywhere and in all things I am instructed, both to be full and to be hungry, both to abound and to suffer need. I can do all things, through Christ which strengtheneth me," which read, saith he : to use his own word, "This Scripture did once save my life, when my eldest son died, which went as a dagger to my heart, indeed it did". And then, repeating the words of the text himself, declared his then thoughts to this purpose, reading the tenth and eleventh verses of Paul's contentation, and submission to the will of God in all conditions (said he) : "'Tis true, Paul, *you* have learned this, and attained to this measure of grace : but what shall *I* do ? Ah, poor creature, it is a hard lesson for me to take out ! I find it so !" But reading on to the thirteenth verse, where Paul saith, "I can do all things through Christ that strengtheneth me "—then faith began to work, and his heart to find support and comfort, and he said thus to himself : "He that was Paul's Christ is my Christ too," and so drew water out of the wells of salvation, Christ in the covenant of grace.'

ADVERSITY is sometimes hard upon a man ; but for

one man who can stand prosperity, there are a hundred that will stand adversity.—CARLYLE, *Heroes* (v.).

ACCLIMATISATION OF CHARACTER

'I know how to be abased, and I know also how to abound ; in everything and in all things have I learned the secret both to be filled and to be hungry, both to abound and to be in want. I can do all things in Him that strengtheneth me.'—PHIL. IV. 12. 13 (R.V.).

I. THE vicissitudes of our life, especially when they are sudden and unexpected, are always attended by serious peril. Artificial acclimatisation in Nature is possible only when effected with great care, and even then it is often followed by disappointment. Said a tourist to a famous Swiss guide : 'You have been in all weathers, and all changes of weather'. 'The changes are worse than the weather,' replied the guide. The alternations of circumstance and experience in human life are repeatedly more dangerous to faith and principle than the most trying settled conditions to which time and habit have reconciled us.

II. And this ordeal of change was never more incessant and sharp than it is to-day. In the simple times of the past things were more stereotyped and existence more sluggish than we now know them to be. Every hour we see and feel the ebb and flow of things, and without swift handling of the helm we may easily make shipwreck.

III. Yet this acclimatisation of character is happily possible, as we learn from our text. With a patience and skill that science cannot rival, with subtle and inexhaustible resources, Nature effects marvellous acclimatisations in plants and flowers, creating in regions intermediate between hot and cold climates a profuse vegetation of a tropical character which can, nevertheless, sustain almost an arctic severity. Grace effects much the same thing for human nature. 'I can do all things in Him that strengtheneth me'. What is entirely impossible in artificial acclimatisation is effected by Nature ; and that which is unattainable in character through any artifice of our own becomes delightfully actual and experimental through the grace of Christ. In a high and sincere spirituality of life we attain perfect liberty touching the outside world, drawing wisdom and blessing from all surroundings and sensations, as the bee sips honey from flowers of all shapes and colours.—W. L. WATKINSON, *Inspiration in Common Life*, p. 108.

THE POWER OF THE CROSS

'I can do all things in Him that strengtheneth me.'— PHIL. IV. 13.

'CRUCIFIED with Christ.' Such is the language in which the author of the Epistle to the Philippians elsewhere describes his relation to Calvary. But is there any life which, unless we are admitted to its secret history, seems less like crucifixion than the career of the stout Apostle Paul ? There is no paleness in its presentation. Its hours are crowded with glorious life. It is romantic, adventurous, and vivid. If happiness indeed consist in the unimpeded exercise of function there is abundance of this quality in the missionary journeys which the Acts records. St. Paul is perhaps the most vigorous, efficient, self-realising character in the pages of the New Testament. He who bids the Christian imitate the humility of Him who took upon Him the form of a slave is himself one of the world's masters. He would withstand you to the face as soon as look at you. He knows his mind and carries through his purpose. No doubt he was impatient of dull wits, and was, it may be, too ready to call the tiresome unbeliever a fool, the priestly bully a whited wall. None can deny him the honour of the strong man, who leaves his mark, creates ideals, and makes history. 'I can do all things' seems to portray the man more faithfully than 'I am crucified'.

His missionary journeys rival in interest the travels of Odysseus. They impress us by the fulness of their experience rather than by the greatness of their self-sacrifice. The strong man delights in dangers, in hair-breadth escapes, in critical situations. The adventurous lad who first hears the celebrated catalogue of Pauline perils hardly pities the man who encountered them. These are all in the day's work of him who would earn the reward of efficiency.

I. The Christian, then, according to the type which is presented to us in the New Testament, is the man that can do all things, or, to borrow a striking phrase from the Lord's own teaching, who through faith can remove mountains. The characteristic note of the Gospel is not sacrifice but salvation. 'In hoc signo vinces' is the legend inscribed upon the banner of the cross. Calvary is the symbol not of renunciation but of life. It is very easy to get a distorted view of the real message which the Gospel brings to human needs if we go for our ideals outside the range of the Apostolic Church, if we seek for the pattern of Christian manhood whether in mediæval or modern times. We need not hesitate to acknowledge the witness of the saints in every age to the manifoldness of Christ if we look rather to the New Testament for the due proportions of Christian discipleship.

The gospel of the cross was no apotheosis of pain, but the proclamation of power. It presents to our gaze a spectacle of Divine tenderness only because it is the message of victorious life. And for St. Paul it is the Gospel which is the fixed thing in Christianity ; the inviolable unchangeable centre of authority ; the standard presentation of the fact of Christ which gives unity, cohesion, and solidity to all the riches of wisdom and knowledge which are hid in Him.

II. In Jesus pain is transmuted into power, only because to Him is given all authority in heaven and in earth, and in His hands He bears the keys of hell. In Him we behold no servile submission of the creature to the Law of the God who made it. He is Himself the very son and substance of the Everlasting Will, enthroning the humanity which He assumes, manifested as the goal and destiny of all creation. How near to every age and to each human life He seems—how near and yet how far !

As, when some traveller among the mountains has climbed the shoulder of a westward hill and almost thinks his journey at an end, the scene expands; the perspective widens; ridge behind ridge, alp behind alp, peak behind peak appears, rising in stairs and terraces to meet the horizon now almost lost in dreamy distances of dazzling light; so Christ the end of human life becomes a vaster Christ the nearer we attain.

But with God all things are possible. This is no formal acknowledgment of an omnipotence which, if it have concrete existence, is a fact too general and remote to have any real bearing upon the practical concerns of life, but a great experience which has made men strong. 'Ye shall receive power' was the form in which the risen Master renewed the promise of an energising influence, an inward presence, a controlling Personality, which entering into His elect should make them sons of God. 'Repent ye and be baptised every one of you in the name of Jesus Christ unto the remission of your sins,' such was the burthen of St. Peter's witness on the Day of Pentecost, 'and ye shall receive the gift of the Holy Spirit'.—J. G. SIMPSON, *Christus Crucifixus*, p. 25.

'I can do all things through Christ which strengtheneth me.'
—PHIL. IV. 13.

CARDINAL VAUGHAN wrote in the spring of 1882: 'I am fifty years old. It is said that no man becomes a saint after fifty. I am determined to give no peace to myself or to my Holy Patrons, or indeed to our dear Lord Himself. By prayer even this miracle can be performed, and a dry, hard, stupid old stick like me can reach great sanctity *in eo qui me confortat.* St. Francis of Sales died at fifty-six: St. Francis of Assisi, Xavier, and St. Charles were dead and saints about ten years earlier. What a grace to have *spatium pœnitentiœ.* I am determined to use the remaining time better than the last, God helping.'—J. G. SNEAD-COX, *Life of Cardinal Vaughan*, vol. I. p. 452.

REFERENCES.—IV. 13.—Spurgeon, *Sermons*, vol. vi. No. 346. J. B. Lightfoot, *Cambridge Sermons*, p. 317. J. M. Neale, *Sermons Preached in Sackville College Chapel*, vol. i. p. 400. F. A. Noble, *Christian World Pulpit*, vol. l. p. 152. T. F. Crosse, *Sermons* (2nd Series), p. 122. J. A. Alexander, *The Gospel of Jesus Christ*, p. 410. J. H. Jowett, *The High Calling*. D. 210. J. G. Simpson, *Christus Crucifixus*, p. 25. IV. 14.—*Ibid.* p. 216.

PHIL. IV. 15.

NOTHING is harder to manage, on either side, than the sense of an obligation conferred or received.—MORLEY's, *Life of Cobden* (ch. I.).

THE law of benefit is a difficult channel, which requires careful sailing or rude boats.—EMERSON.

REFERENCES.—IV. 15.—*Expositor* (5th Series), vol. viii. pp. 122, 135; *ibid.* (7th Series), vol. vi. p. 371. IV. 16.—*Ibid.* (4th Series), vol. x. p. 333. IV. 17.—Bishop Westcott, *The Incarnation and Common Life*, p. 195. IV. 18.—*Expositor* (4th Series), vol. vi. p. 194. IV. 19.—Spurgeon, *Sermons*, vol. xxix. No. 1712. H. J. Bevis, *Sermons*, p. 131. IV. 19,

20.—J. H. Jowett, *The High Calling*, p. 222. IV. 20-23.—A. Maclaren, *Expositions of Holy Scripture—Philippians*, p. 74.

THE SAINTS OF CAESAR'S HOUSEHOLD

'All the saints salute you, chiefly they that are of Cæsar's household.'—PHIL. IV. 22.

IT is the *chiefly* upon which I want to lay the stress—that the warmest and most loving salutation should have come from the unlikeliest place. St. Paul is sending a letter to the Church at Philippi. He sits in all the rude discomforts of a prison, writing amidst much difficulty, secured by a coupling chain to a soldier. Is this life wasted? He is preaching in this prison to a greater congregation than could ever be gathered in the market place or on Mars' Hill. At that hour, when time seemed to stand still, he was preaching to all the ages. And this day this word is ours because Paul was in prison. But of this ministry in the dungeon the fruit was not only afar off in the future, *it was immediate.*

I. Let us think of those of whom St. Paul writes, 'the saints of Cæsar's household'—certainly the last place to which we should go to look for saints. Rome at that time was the most unlikely place in the world to look for a saint. No language could utter the depth of abomination to which it had sunk. And of all its people the most miserable was the lot of the slave. So many of these were there that they could only be kept in subjection by the most terrible severity. To complete it all they were slaves in *Cæsar's household.* This Cæsar was Nero—a very monster in iniquity. Here it is, then, where the example and influence of this monster had poisoned the very atmosphere—within the walls of Nero's palace—that a little company of his own slaves gather in loving fellowship around Paul the prisoner, and send their loving greeting to the Church at Philippi.

II. To us, too, the saints of Cæsar's household send their greetings. (1) There are those whose position seems to make Christianity a difficulty—they may think sometimes, perhaps, almost an impossibility. My brother, my sister, these saints of Cæsar's household salute you. What think you would *they* count those hindrances of which you make so much? (2) And yet again, others shrink in fear of themselves. Surely, again, these saints of Cæsar's household salute you! (3) Does it seem to some that their sphere is so little, so narrow, so lowly, that there is no room for any service for God? Again the saints of Cæsar's household salute you.—M. G. PEARSE, *The Gentleness of Jesus*, p. 125.

SAINTS IN THE HOUSEHOLD OF CÆSAR

'All the saints salute you, chiefly they that are of Cæsar's household.'—PHIL. IV. 22.

THERE are few contrasts so startling as that which is suggested by this Epistle to the Philippians. We read our pagan history and we read our Bible, but it is not often that the two come so close together and that the lines of both histories touch for one moment to separate again. Here we have for the first time that union of sacred and profane history. Here seems to commence that long struggle between the religion of Christ and the Empire of Rome, which ended by establishing the Gospel upon the ruins of the Eternal City. Here we read of Philippi, the advanced guard of the ambition of Macedonian kings, but now the seat of a Christian Church. Philippi, on whose battlefield the future of the world was decided just a hundred years before, now sending Epaphroditus to bear comfort and help to the Apostle in his Roman prison. Everything seems to point to the same contrast between the inspired word of Christian advice as written in this Epistle and the Roman Prætorian command, between the purity and piety of the writer and that golden palace of sin and shame outside the walls of which he wrote, between the preaching of St. Paul, Apostle of Christ, and Nero, Emperor of Rome, tyrant, matricide, and anti-Christ. There, for two years, as we know, waiting for his trial, the Apostle abode, and thither came many of his friends, Timotheus, Luke, Aristarchus, Marcus, Demas—their names are familiar to the whole Christian world; but who are these of whom the text speaks, 'saints of Cæsar's household'? We do not know. The Bible is silent. The history of the world has passed them over, the history of the Church knows them not. By chance, indeed, in the dark recesses of the Catacombs, amid the quaint symbols of the hope of immortality, their names may even now be deciphered, but beyond that we know them not.

I. Christians under Adverse Circumstances.—It is about them that I would fain say to you just two words. One is that if we can conceive of any place in the world more unlikely than another at that day in which to find a Christian man it was Nero's palace. If we had been asked where we should expect to hear of a Christian in Rome, Nero's gilded palace would be the very last place which would be mentioned. A friend of Paul, a follower of Jesus Christ in that palace of bastard art, and lust, and murder! What sins he must have witnessed, what temptations must have beset his path, what responsibility, what difficulties, I had almost said what impossibilities, in the way of a Christian life. Well, then, the encouragement to us is this, that, if there, then anywhere it is possible to be a follower of our Blessed Lord. The encouragement is, that there must surely be no difficulties of life, no post of duty, no situation of temptation, in which a Christian man, by the grace of God, may not work his life unharmed. All may learn by this example the sufficiency of the Grace of God to sustain and strengthen them in the most adverse circumstances.

II. Our Real Danger.—The world in which we live, our domestic, professional, social, political world, it is to us Cæsar's household. We have to live there, work there, wait there for our Blessed Master, and, though of course superficially the world has changed, there is no arena, there is no garment of flaming pitch, there is no fierce cry, of 'Christians to the lions!' nothing that could tempt to apostasy in our case, or offer excuse to weak human nature to compromise with sin and infidelity, yet our dangers are no less real. The world is, after all, though softer and gentler, no less dangerous to Christian men, because day by day they are brought in contact with those who neither serve nor know our Divine Master, and then zeal in duty brings its own temptation, earthly labour has its own peril. Our foes are really not so much the foes that we find in the world, but the foe we bear about with us wherever we go. But a heart right with God, a mind directed by His Spirit, a habit of dependence on His grace and of prayer, a habit of close walking with our Lord and Saviour, these will keep a man safe anywhere, and the more difficult it is to make profession of faith in our own individual circumstances, so much the more distinct and decided by the grace of God may that profession be.

III. Never Despair of Finding Good Men Anywhere.—Moreover, I think that from these unknown saints in Cæsar's household we may all of us, men and women, learn a lesson of charity, never to despair of finding good men anywhere. God sees not as we see, sufficient if He knows His own, and will one day bring them into the light. Depend upon it there will be many in heaven whom we did not expect to meet. For God's servants are often hidden sometimes from pure unobtrusiveness, sometimes from a shrinking fear lest they should after profession fall and bring dishonour on the cause, sometimes again from circumstances which have not brought out their character before those with whom they live. But let us comfort ourselves with the assurance that God knows them and will declare them one day. We ourselves are blind and err in our judgment, and we have no right to pass sentence on one another. Let it be enough for us that our heavenly Father allots to all His children the post that they are to take in life, and when the pressure is too strong or the temptation too great for their strength, then the same loving Father will assuredly call them from it, or if not then, He can by His grace sustain them in it and hold up their goings that they slip not, for if there could be saints in the golden palace of Nero it is incongruous and illogical to suppose that there is any post of earthly duty or difficulty or temptation to which we could be subjected, in which we could plead that it is impossible to do right.

REFERENCES.—IV. 22.—J. H. Jowett, *The High Calling*, p. 234. J. Tolefree Parr, *The White Life*, p. 106. J. Thew, *Broken Ideals*, p. 97. IV. 23.—J. H. Jowett, *The High Calling*, p. 239.

THE EPISTLE TO THE COLOSSIANS

COLOSSIANS

REFERENCE.—I. 1, 2.—T. F. Crosse, *Sermons* (2nd Series), p. 219.

TEMPORAL AND SPIRITUAL HABITATIONS

'To the saints and faithful brethren in Christ at Colossæ.'—
COL. I. 2.

FOCUSSED together, as by the lenses of a double lantern, we see at once the actual and ideal condition of these Asiatic Christians. They were in Colossæ, a small town in a Phrygian valley, much decayed from its former greatness, overshadowed by its more important neighbours. Of all the places to which the Apostle directed his letters it was of the least significance to the world, yet of supreme importance to itself. Turn to the other picture. These Christians were in Christ. There is a circle within a circle here; they were in Christ in Colossæ. It became a different place as they looked at it from the shelter of Christ.

I. Wherever our Colossæ is we rarely look out upon it with quite clear and unprejudiced eyes. Our vision is coloured by our moods and fancies; we see it through the medium of our thoughts, passing tempers, and abiding purposes, and our reaction upon it largely depends upon the quality of this inward thought world, the faith that is the spiritual home of the soul. Although the outward facts seem terribly hard and set, it is surprising how small a difference in our hearts it takes to transform them. We write 'home' upon one house in a monotonous red brick row, and it becomes a living poem to us. We do our daily walk to the accompaniment of some thrilling thought, and it sets our feet to music where they have often dragged wearily.

II. It is only the inward wealth of life that can transform our world. As it is not what enters into the man, but what comes out from him, that defiles him, so it is what comes out from us that saves and redeems our daily living. Our inward faith does not simply make the world look differently, it actually changes it. The purity of the home cleanses the city. The soul that dwells in the secret place of the Most High reshapes its Colossæ, and all things are new because of its inward renewing.—W. CHARTER PIGGOTT, *Sunday School Chronicle*, XXXVI. p. 300.

REFERENCES.—I. 2.—*Expositor* (5th Series), vol. vi. p. 2; *ibid.* vol. vii. p. 65. I. 3.—R. W. Riley, *A Year's Sermons*, vol. ii. p. 257. I. 5.—Spurgeon, *Sermons*, vol. xxiv. No. 1438. I. 5, 6.—*Penny Pulpit*, vol. vii. p. 145. I. 9.—Bishop Creighton, *Christian World Pulpit*, vol. lvi. p. 243. H. P. Wright, *Preacher's Magazine*, vol. xviii. p. 277. T. Arnold, *Sermons*, vol. iv. p. 23, 31. *Expositor* (5th Series), vol. viii. p. 404. I. 9, 10.—Spurgeon, *Sermons*, vol. xxix. No. 1742. I. 9-11.—E. A. Stuart, *Christian World Pulpit*, vol. lxi. p. 305. I. 10.—J. Weller, *Christian World Pulpit*, vol. xlvii. p. 190. F. St. John Corbett, *The Preacher's Year*, p. 173. *Expositor* (7th Series), vol. vi. p. 275. I. 11.—*Ibid.* (6th Series), vol. xi. p. 292. I. 12.—J. Cumming, *Penny Pulpit*, No. 1510, p. 217. R. Higinbotham, *Sermons*, p. 57. W. J. Brock, *Sermons*, p. 61. Spurgeon, *Sermons*, vol. xlvii. No. 2751. *Expositor* (5th Series), vol. x. p. 156. I. 12, 13.—Spurgeon, *Sermons*, vol. vi. No. 319. I. 13.—E. A. Stuart, *His Dear Son and Other Sermons*, vol. v. p. 1. F. Bourdillon, *Plain Sermons for Family Reading* (2nd Series), p. 173. *Expositor* (5th Series), vol. vi. p. 158; *ibid.* (6th Series), vol. viii. p. 155. I. 14.—W. Redfern, *The Gospel of Redemption*, p. 83. R. J. Campbell, *Christian World Pulpit*, vol. lvii. p. 6. W. R. Evans, *Sermons for the Church's Year*, p. 271. R. J. Campbell, *A Faith for To-day*, p. 227. Marcus Dods, *Christ and Man*, p. 140. I. 15.—*Expositor* (4th Series), vol. x. p. 39; *ibid.* (5th Series), vol. ii. p. 86; *ibid.* (6th Series), vol. x. p. 198. I. 15, 16.—*Ibid.* vol. i. p. 399. I. 15-17.—*Ibid.* vol. iv. p. 119. I. 15-21.—*Ibid.* p. 136.

CHRIST AND THE CREATION

'For by Him were all things created, that are in heaven, and that are in earth, visible and invisible, whether they be thrones, or dominions, or principalities, or powers: all things were created by Him, and for Him.'—COL. I. 16.

A VERY narrow notion of the functions of Christ is afloat in the atmosphere of popular religious thought, though not perhaps formulated into dogmatic phrases. According to this, our Lord is virtually regarded as limited in work, and even in nature, to the mission of redemption. Such an idea implies that the existence of Christ is dependent on the existence of sin; that if there had been no evil there would have been no Saviour; that the very being of the Son of God is but an expedient required for the deliverance of man. So stated, the doctrine must be considered by all Christians as monstrous. In the Bible an infinitely larger range is given to the work and nature of Christ. If there had been no sin, Christ would still have visited the world in some way of Divine goodness. He came in the creation before the birth of sin.

I. The Relation of Christ to Creation.—The relation of Christ to creation is threefold:—

(a) In Christ is the *fundamental basis* of creation. All things were made 'in' Him, *i.e.* His thoughts are the archetypes of the worlds and their contents, and the genesis of them follows the principles of His nature.

(b) Christ is the *instrumental agent* of creation. All things were made 'through' Him. He is the Mediator in creation as well as in redemption.

(c) Christ is the *end* of creation. All things were made 'unto' Him, *i.e.* they grow into His likeness, they move upwards towards the realisation of His life (Christ in His human earthly nature was the highest development of the upward movement of creation), they are destined to serve and glorify Him.

II. The Scope and Range of Christ's Work.—The scope and range of the work of Christ was universal in creation. It included (*a*) all things, visible and invisible, *i.e.* physical and spiritual existences, or things within our observation and the infinite population of the regions of space beyond ; (*b*) all orders of beings, thrones, etc., none too great for His power, none too small for His care ; (*c*) every variety and every individual. Different classes are specified. Creation is not a work merely of general laws, it implies individual formation under them. All this vast and varied work is ascribed to Christ as its foundation, its efficient instrument, and its end.

III. We Learn :—

1. *As regards Christ.*—(*a*) His *pre-existence*. This does not involve the eternity of His human nature, which surely began to be when 'the Word was made flesh'. That which was Divine in Christ was before all things. The Christ-side of God, all that is so touching and so winning in the marvellous revelation of God in Jesus, is no new phase of His character. It was before the sterner revelation of Sinai. It is eternal (Heb. xiii. 8). (*b*) His *glory*. All that is great and beautiful in creation glorifies Him through Whom it came into existence.

2. *As regards the Creation.*—(*a*) This must be in harmony with Christ. Therefore we must interpret its darker phases by what we know of the spirit and character of Christ : and we must expect that ultimately its laws and forces will make for Christianity, breathing benedictions on the faithful followers of Christ, and bringing natural penalties on those who rebel against His rule. (*b*) We should endeavour to trace indications of the spirit and presence of Christ in nature.

References.—I. 16.—*Expositor* (4th Series), vol. iv. p. 428 ; *ibid.* vol. vi. p. 252; *ibid.* (5th Series), vol. vii. pp. 31, 146. I. 16-18.—Bishop Stubbs, *Christian World Pulpit*, vol. xlvii. p. 86. J. Budgen, *Parochial Sermons*, vol. ii. p. 8. I. 17.—*Expositor* (6th Series), vol. xi. p. 447.

THE PRE-EMINENT LORD

'That in all things He might have the pre-eminence.'—Col.
i. 18.

This is characteristically Paul's doctrine. The supremacy of Christ is to his mind the only possible outcome of His Saviourhood. In his consciousness the cross is the foundation of the throne, and he is jealous that all who share in the saving benefits of Christ's death should give Him that place in heart and life to which He is rightly entitled. For himself this has long been the secret of his life's strength and explanation of the fruitfulness of his service. Christ is to him the 'Lord of all'. He is 'before all things,' and over all things exercises His beneficent control. 'For Jesus' sake,' expresses the governing motive of his whole life. 'The Man Christ Jesus' comprehends his entire message, and to be well-pleasing unto Him is his supreme aim. In the light of His pre-eminence he interprets all the providences of life, and even when

fettered he is but 'the prisoner of Jesus Christ'. His outlook, too, is bounded by the pre-eminent Lord, for 'we look for the Saviour—the Lord Jesus Christ,' is the triumphant expectancy with which he both encourages himself and his fellows. Past, present, and future hold alike for him nothing which is not directly related to the Lord, Whose he is and Whom he serves. And it is this same pre-eminence to which Christ is entitled on the part of all who call Him Saviour that is the Apostle's keen desire. He would enthrone Him in the life of the congregation and the individual alike, recognising Him as the Master of assemblies and as the King of the heart.

I. It is chiefly in regard to its personal significance that this desire of the Apostle needs to be laid to heart, for after all the Church is but an aggregation of individuals. If the life of the unit be right, the life of the congregation will not long be deficient. Hence the most important consideration is as to the securing of the pre-eminence of Jesus in the lives of individual believers, and nothing is more heart-searching and wholesome than the personal query as to the relative position which He occupies in our lives. For Christians are mainly divisible into three classes—those who give Him place, those who give Him prominence, and those who give Him pre-eminence.

II. The importance of giving to Christ this His rightful place is attested by the fact of common experience that that which is pre-eminent in thought and affection exercises the strongest formative influence in the cultivation of character. This is seen when men make money, pleasure, ambition, or success the pre-eminent thing in life, and devote to it their best strength of thought and energy. Character deteriorates, powers of vision become dim, and holier impulses are killed at the birth, until that to which pre-eminence has been voluntarily given becomes the absolute master. It is a man's own safety and highest good, as well as the honour of Christ, which is determined by the place he assigns to the Son of God.

III. The pre-eminence of the Saviour affords us too an explanation of many of the mysteries of life which, apart from His supremacy, are hard and indeed almost impossible to understand.

But let it not be thought that the actual pre-eminence of Jesus in any life is a mere inference from truth, a mere philosophic acceptance of doctrine, or a mere prospect of faith and hope. Let it never be forgotten that it is rather a definite consecration in expression of personal indebtedness—the response of a love which constrains. Professor Drummond used to tell of an invalid girl whose life, so unruffled in its peace and fragrant with the beauty of holiness, was a constant source of wonderment to those who knew her pain and were acquainted with her circumstances. After her death the secret was discovered. A small locket which had hung about her neck was found to contain the words, 'Whom having not seen I love!' The pre-eminence of Jesus Christ is the pre-eminence which love will ever give to the One of its choice, however costly it proves.—J. STUART HOLDEN, *The Pre-eminent Lord*, p. 3.

COL. I. 18.

MANY years ago the late Dr. Howson, then Dean of Chester, one of Simeon's latest hearers, gave me a vivid reminiscence of his own. Trinity Church was crowded as usual, aisles as well as pews. . . . The text was Colossians I. 18: 'That in all things He might have the pre-eminence'. One passage was written for ever on the listener's heart by the prophetic fire of the utterance, as the old man seemed to rise and dilate under the impression of the Master's glory: 'That He might have the pre-eminence! And He *will* have it! And He *must* have it! And He *shall* have it!'—BISHOP MOULE, *Life of Simeon*, pp. 94, 95.

COL. I. 18.

THE Christian will never call it religion to keep, like Septimius Severus, a bust of Christ in his private chapel, 'along with Virgil, Orpheus, Abraham, and other persons of the same kind'. He claims to address himself to a Being made human enough to give our love a place to cling, but remaining Divine in His perfection, in His illuminating and responsive power.—F. W. H. MYERS, *Modern Essays*, p. 303.

REFERENCES.—I. 18.—Spurgeon, *Sermons*, vol. xiv. No. 839. F. B. Proctor, *Preacher's Magazine*, vol. xix. p. 320. R. J. Drummond, *Faith's Certainties*, p. 81. *Expositor* (6th Series), vol. x. p. 113. I. 19.—C. O. Eldridge, *Preacher's Magazine*, vol. xvii. p. 222. Spurgeon, *Sermons*, vol. xvii. No. 978. A. Whyte, *The Scottish Review*, vol. iii. p. 525. Spurgeon, *Sermons*, vol. xx. No. 1169. I. 19, 20.—*Expositor* (4th Series), vol. i. p. 140 ; *ibid.* vol. vi. pp. 31, 420. I. 20.—G. Campbell Morgan, *The Bible and the Cross*, p. 101. *Expositor* (4th Series), vol. v. p. 436 ; *ibid.* (5th Series), vol. viii. pp. 136, 144 ; *ibid.* (6th Series), vol. vi. p. 248. I. 21.—W. H. Griffith Thomas, *The Record*, vol. xxvii. p. 300. A. Berry, *The Doctrine of the Cross*, p. 83. I. 21, 22.—G. Campbell Morgan, *The Bible and the Cross*, p. 37. I. 22, 28.—*Expositor* (5th Series), vol. vi. p. 69. I. 23.—H. Allen, *Penny Pulpit*, No. 1763, p. 423. Spurgeon, *Sermons*, vol. xxviii. No. 1688. J. Keble, *Village Sermons on the Baptismal Service*, p. 189.

COL. I. 24.

IT has been said that the one infallible note of all false Christs and of all anti-Christs, of all and indeed the only false Gods, however they may be disguised by trappings of royalty, is the absence of a crown of thorns. And certainly the men who have, above all other men, set God before the eyes of an unwilling world, have shared that crown.—W. S. PALMER, *The Diary of a Modernist*, p. 16.

'THAT WHICH IS BEHIND OF THE AFFLIC-TIONS OF CHRIST'

'Who now rejoice in my sufferings for you, and fill up that which is behind of the afflictions of Christ in my flesh for His body's sake, which is the Church.'—COL. I. 24.

ST. PAUL was accustomed to urge upon his converts, men and women, who would all in one way or another experience the fulfilment of the Lord's words, 'In the world ye shall have tribulation,' that they should nevertheless be of good cheer. 'Rejoice in the Lord always,' so he taught, and like Chaucer's poor parson, he followed it himself. When we speak about sufferers that we know, we think it high praise to say, 'How perfectly patient they were'! Here is a higher note, not patience, but joy. There were personal reasons for this, no doubt. He knew well that his sufferings had been the means of his receiving a fuller measure of that life of grace which strengthens the soul. That was a cause for rejoicing, but it was not the chief, not the uppermost in his mind. It is a quite unselfish delight that we have here in these difficult words, difficult because does it not come upon us with a shock to hear that there was anything lacking in the afflictions of Christ? Yet 'I fill up on my part that which is behind of the afflictions of Christ'. The words are quite plain, they clearly state that there is something wanting in the afflictions borne by Christ. How can that be so? And, if so, can any man's be counted with His to fill up the deficiencies? We may nevertheless make a distinction in the Saviour's sufferings. There were those which no man could share when He trod the wine-press alone, and of the people there was none with Him ; but the Greek word that is used in the text is not the word in the New Testament in connection with the atoning work of Christ. It tells of afflictions of body and of mind which came upon Him as a holy and self-denying Person, in the midst of a corrupt and selfish world, born as one of the great human family, and to these there was something left to add. Yes, it is for us to say, 'I fill up on my part that which is behind of the afflictions of Christ for His body's sake, which is the Church'.

I. Our Relation to Christ.—But, then, what I bear for the sake of others, these are my afflictions. How can they fill up His? Can they be mine without being His? Depend upon it, unless being a member of His body is but a phrase, is but a metaphor, your sufferings are His. To understand that we must understand our oneness with Jesus Christ our Lord. There are different kinds of unions.

(*a*) *External union.*—There is a merely external union, as when you add one more stone to the fabric which rises from the ground. It is an integral part, one with the whole, but what is that unity compared with the unity which takes place when you graft upon a stock a living shoot, that becomes part of the tree?

(*b*) *Vital union.*—There is union, not local, but vital, and the sap circulates through the new limb. You injure it now and you injure it not alone, you injure the tree itself. This is a union of that kind, vital, that the baptised believer has with the Saviour. 'I am the Vine, and ye are the branches. Cut off from Me, you wither ; abiding in Me, you bear much fruit.'

And so, because we are one with Christ in that living way, He truly shares in our sufferings. Can the body be injured and the head suffer nothing? Wound a limb and the brain quivers with pain. In all our afflictions He is afflicted. What a different aspect our troubles would wear if that was realised!

II. St. Paul's Sufferings.

II. St. Paul's Sufferings.—How and when did St. Paul learn to identify himself so confidently with Christ that he could speak of his own sufferings for the Church as actually Christ's sufferings? I think we know—in the blinding splendour of that revelation on the road to Damascus, when he lay, proud Pharisee as he was, prostrate on the earth in the midst of his astonished train. There stood before him, seen by him alone, the majestic, reproachful Christ the Lord. 'Saul, why persecutest thou Me'? He never had done so literally; still the sad voice said, 'Saul, why persecutest thou Me'? It was because he gloried in persecuting the Church, gloried in a pitiless harrowing of the poor souls who clung to the Lord, that Christ could never forget that they were members of the Lord and their sufferings were His, for 'Inasmuch as ye did it to the least of these My brethren, ye did it unto Me'. That was a crushing thought to Saul the persecutor; it was joy to Paul the Apostle. 'Now I rejoice in my sufferings for your sake, and fill up on my part that which is behind of the afflictions of Christ in my flesh.' Poor flesh it was, so weary and weatherbeaten, so scarred with the rough handling of the world; but the great, brave heart, so fixed on God, so full of enthusiasm for the Master, cried, 'I rejoice for His body's sake, the Church'. So you see it was an unselfish joy. His afflictions were for the sake of the brethren.

BODILY SUFFERING

'I fill up that which is behind of the afflictions of Christ in my flesh for His body's sake, which is the Church.'—Col. I. 24.

Our Lord and Saviour Jesus Christ came by blood as well as by water, not only as a fount of grace and truth—the source of spiritual light, joy, and salvation —but as a combatant with sin and Satan, who was 'consecrated through suffering'. He was, as prophecy had marked Him out, 'red in His apparel, and His garments like Him that treadeth in the wine-fat'; or, in the words of the Apostle, 'He was clothed with a vesture dipped in blood'. It was the untold sufferings of the Eternal Word in our nature. His body dislocated and torn, His blood poured out, His soul violently separated by a painful death, which has put away from us the wrath of Him whose love sent Him for that very purpose. This only was our atonement; no one shared in the work. He 'trod the wine-press alone, and of the people there was none with Him'. When lifted up upon the cursed tree, He fought with all the hosts of evil, and conquered by suffering.

Thus, in a most mysterious way, all that is needful for this sinful world, the life of our souls, the regeneration of our nature, all that is most joyful and glorious, hope, light, peace, spiritual freedom, holy influences, religious knowledge and strength, all flow from a fount of blood. A work of blood is our salvation; and we, as we would be saved, must draw near and gaze upon it in faith, and accept it as the way to heaven. We must take Him, who thus suffered, as our guide; we must embrace His sacred feet, and

follow Him. No wonder, then, should we receive on ourselves some drops of the sacred agony which bedewed His garments; no wonder, should we be sprinkled with the sorrows which He bore in expiation of our sins!

And so it has ever been in very deed; to approach Him has been, from the first, to be partaker, more or less, in His sufferings; I do not say in the case of every individual who believes in Him, but as regards the more conspicuous, the more favoured, His choice instruments, and His most active servants; that is, it has been the lot of the Church, on the whole, and of those, on the whole, who had been most like Him, as Rulers, Intercessors, and Teachers of the Church. He, indeed, alone meritoriously; they, because they have been near Him. Thus, immediately upon His birth, He brought the sword upon the infants of His own age at Bethlehem. His very shadow, cast upon a city, where He did not abide, was stained with blood. His blessed mother had not clasped Him to her breast for many weeks, ere she was warned of the penalty of that fearful privilege: 'Yea, a sword shall pierce through thy own soul also'. Virtue went out of Him; but the water and the blood flowed together as afterwards from His pierced side. From among the infants He took up in His arms to bless, is said to have gone forth a chief martyr of the generation after Him. Most of His Apostles passed through life-long sufferings to a violent death. In particular, when the favoured brothers, James and John, came to Him with a request that they might sit beside Him in His kingdom, He plainly stated this connection between nearness to Him and affliction. 'Are ye able,' He said, 'to drink of the cup that I shall drink of, and to be baptised with the baptism that I am baptised with?' As if He said, 'Ye cannot have the sacraments of grace without the painful figures of them. The cross, when imprinted on your foreheads, will draw blood. You shall receive, indeed, the baptism of the Spirit, and the cup of My communion, but it shall be with the attendant pledges of My cup of agony, and My baptism of blood.' Elsewhere He speaks the same language to all who would partake the benefits of His death and passion: 'Whosoever doth not bear his cross, and come after Me, cannot be My disciple'.—J. H. Newman.

References.—I. 24.—Bishop Gore, *Christian World Pulpit*, vol. liii. p. 372. J. H. Jowett, *Christian World Pulpit*, vol. lxi. p. 324. *Expositor* (6th Series), vol. iii. p. 377; *ibid.* vol. iv. p. 13; *ibid.* vol. viii. p. 265. I. 24-27.—*Ibid.* vol. viii. p. 235. I. 26.—*Ibid.* (4th Series), vol. i. p. 32; *ibid.* (6th Series), vol. iv. p. 394.

THE HOPE OF GLORY

'To whom God was pleased to make known what is the riches of the glory of this mystery among the Gentiles, which is Christ in you, the hope of glory.'—Col. I. 27.

Christ in you the hope! Now why does St. Paul say that of the secrets of God. And remember the mysteries of God are the revealed secrets that He has stooped down and whispered to our ears. 'God stooping shows sufficient of His light for us in the dark to rise by,' the poet Browning said. But why does St. Paul say that this is a gloriously rich mystery?

I. First of all, it is the hope of what all men want and few men get, and that is Power.

Do you want the first thing that everyone who understands life really wants, and that is power? Then have Christ in you, Christ *in* you, not outside you, that is not enough. You may respect Christ, you may think well of religion, you may speak well of the clergy because they do so much good social work in your district; but that is not power. If you have been brought by the Holy Spirit here, it is that Christ without you may be changed into Christ within you, and that you, too, may be strong like those people, you, too, may no longer be a useless person in your district making, very likely, your home miserable by your temper, or your friends miserable by your weakness, and useless in the Church down here by your sloth and want of power to witness. All that may be changed to-night and you may flame away down here for years, one of the brilliant hopes of the Church, but it will not be unless Christ without you becomes Christ within you—Christ in you the hope of power.

II. But that is not all. Not only is Christ within you—and this is the second reason why this secret is worth knowing—not only is it that Christ within you is the secret of power, but also the secret of growth. It is like the blazing sun coming down upon a rather unsatisfactory field of corn; and the blazing sun brings out the ripeness and the richness of the corn; it brings on the whole crop in the field— the blaze of the sun does the work.

III. Again, I am going to use a word now which has a very distasteful sound in some people's ears, and that is the word 'holiness'. I believe if you were offered, some of you, the choice of whether you would prefer to have said of you, He is the holiest man or holiest woman in Willesden, or the most attractive and the most agreeable, nine out of ten would choose the second at the bottom of their souls, because they do not understand this: that holiness, if you can get it pure, is the most winning thing in the world; that goodness, when it is unalloyed, simply draws like a magnet, and that when we are put off a holy man or holy woman it is because of the dross and not the gold; because the gold is mixed up with some dross of manner, of self-centredness, or priggishness which puts us off the holiness. But get the holiness and goodness pure, and it wins the world.

How are we 'to get to glory?'—to use an old expression which has rather died out now. Christ in you the hope of glory; Christ in you the secret of holiness. And because the secret of power and progress and holiness, therefore the hope of glory. Christ in you the hope of glory!—BISHOP WINNING-TON INGRAM, *Christian World Pulpit*, vol. LXXVII. p. 120.

REFERENCES.—I. 27.—H. Bell, *Sermons on the Holy Communion*, p. 55. Spurgeon, *Sermons*, vol. xxix. No. 1720.

L. D. Bevan, *Christ and the Age*, p. 3. A. Whyte, *The Scottish Review Sunday Supplement*, vol. iv. p. 82. *Expositor* (5th Series), vol. ii. p. 254.

COL. I. 27.

IT is not for nothing that it is said, 'Christ in you the hope of glory'. I will be content of no pawn of heaven but Christ Himself; for Christ, possessed by faith here, is young heaven and glory in the bud.—SAMUEL RUTHERFORD.

THE JUSTIFICATION OF CHRISTIAN PREACHING

'Christ . . . whom we preach.'—COL. I. 27, 28.

THE aim of Christian preaching is personal, social, universal. And the theme of it is Christ. Is the theme, is the message, adequate to the aim? Judge for yourselves by those three considerations.

I. We assert that the message is adequate because Christ, whom we preach, is able by many manifest proofs to make the life of the individual a positive force.

II. We assert that the preaching of Christ justifies itself, and is adequate because He reconciles the duality, the contrast, apparent contradiction, which runs through all our life. I mean the duality which you have between the inner life of the soul and the outward demands of duty, between spiritual life and practical conduct, between faith and works.

III. We assert that the message of the evangel justifies itself, and is adequate to its end because Christ is co-extensive with human life.—A. CONNELL, *Scottish Review*, vol. III. p. 439.

REFERENCES.—I. 27, 28.—E. H. Bickersteth, *Thoughts in Past Years*, p. 85. W. Scrymgeour, *Christian World Pulpit*, vol. xliv. p. 314. H. S. Seekings, *Preacher's Magazine*, vol. xviii. p. 560. I. 28.—J. Thew, *Christian World Pulpit*, vol. l. p. 246. Spurgeon, *Sermons*, vol. xliv. No. 2581. J. Keble, *Sermons for Advent to Christmas Eve*, p. 352. T. Arnold, *Christian Life: Its Hopes*, p. 200. J. Edwards, *Preacher's Magazine*, vol. xix. p. 173. *Expositor* (5th Series), vol. v. p. 34; *ibid.* (6th Series), vol. xi. p. 147. I. 29.—Spurgeon, *Sermons*, vol. xvi. No. 914.

THE ABOUNDING ASSURANCE

'Unto all riches of the full assurance of understanding.'—COL. II. 2.

THE Apostle has just been speaking of an intense spiritual struggle through which he has passed on behalf of the Churches at Colossæ and Laodicea, to most of whose members he was personally unknown. The purpose of his supplication was that they might be comforted, bound together into a compact fellowship, and enriched with sure and all-sufficing spiritual knowledge—three blessings vitally connected with each other. Failing of such attainments, they could not hope to rise above that fickleness which left them the prey of wandering sophists. The subject-matter of this assurance is the mystery of God's purpose towards us in Christ Jesus.

I. It is through our union with Christ that the treasures hidden in His mysterious nature are conveyed to us, and become 'the riches of the full assurance of understanding'. If the mysteries, of which He is the steward, can gladden, purify, and consecrate the heart and awaken songs of praise to a pardoning God, we may boldly claim the revelation of these mysteries. When we are honestly contrite, and with all our hearts trust His Son for salvation, it cannot be God's will that we should be tormented by uncertainty. He has given power to His Son to declare our absolution, the grace and wisdom of the Son are never at fault in the exercise of this ministry, and the presence of the infinite love in the central consciousness is the highest form of assurance. This assurance, inasmuch as it corresponds to the treasures of wisdom in Christ, ought not to be meagre, stinted, precarious. The Apostle is emphatic, almost to the point of redundancy. 'The riches of the full assurance of understanding.'

II. The Apostle speaks of this exalted experience as one of the blessed consummations of Christian fellowship. ' Knit together in love unto all riches of the full assurance of understanding.' It is through mutual sympathy and helpfulness that the blessing is retained, and others are led into participation with it. Civilisation itself begins in brotherhood and co-operation, and man's ascent into the heights of religious life follows the same order. This full assurance of knowledge is vital to spiritual prosperity. Assurance makes all the difference between a spiritual and an unspiritual man, a weakling and a champion, an inglorious mute and a great confessor. It is the appointed province of evangelical religion to diminish the area of haze, unsettlement, dubiousness, and to understay the spirit with strong bed-rock convictions.

REFERENCE.—II. 2, 3.—Bishop Westcott, *Christian World Pulpit*, vol. xlvii. p. 292.

THE CROSS AND CULTURE

'In whom are hid all the treasures of wisdom and knowledge.' —COL. II. 3.

EVERY one can see that these words contain a great truth, but what the Apostle meant is not so easy to define. In one sense Christ has little to do with wisdom and knowledge. We do not sit at His feet to be made men of culture ; we do not go to Him direct for lessons in history, politics, science, literature. And yet, though it is no business of His to supply knowledge, there is profound truth in these words of St. Paul, that the treasures of wisdom and knowledge are in Him. Without Him wisdom and knowledge are hardly worth having. If there be not a spirit of love and human brotherhood, and something of the cross, working amid the intellectual forces, it is doubtful whether the world will be any better off for all its boasted acquirements.

I. The mind which simply gathers stores of knowledge may be as full as a dictionary and as unfeeling ; as cold as a piece of flint and as hard ; as inhuman as a fossil and as useless. There is a pharisaism of culture, and there is no pharisaism so hard and proud and unmerciful as the pharisaism of culture. There is a science which has no emotion, no pity, no tears, no soft places in its heart, if indeed it has a heart, and no thought of hope for humanity at large. What better is the world for wisdom and knowledge of that kind ?

II. Moreover, it is a matter of common observation, and one of the most certain teachings of history, that wisdom without faith at the heart of it, intellect without profound religious feeling, tends not to righteousness and purity and unselfishness, but to moral lawlessness, self-indulgence, and splendid vice. The cross is the one vein of precious heavenly gold that runs through the mass of intellectual forces.

III. It is the light which He sheds that makes much of our knowledge and wisdom bearable. Were it not for the spirit of hopefulness which He breathes into all problems, our knowledge would only add to our pain, and our wisdom would only teach us despair. But with Christ to illumine these dark problems they cease to be hopeless.

IV. Finally, and most truly, that one field of knowledge which He opens out is incomparably better than all the rest. Let the world's wise men be silent, that He may speak to us, for in Him only are hid all the treasures of wisdom and knowledge.— J. G. GREENOUGH, *The Cross in Modern Life*, p. 23.

REFERENCE.—II. 3.—J. G. Greenhough, *Christian World Pulpit*, vol. xlvii. p. 136.

ORDER AND STEADFASTNESS

' Joying and beholding your order and the stedfastness of your faith in Christ.'—COL. II. 5.

A SCENE in which the virtues of order and steadfastness are presented to the eye always awakens some throb of pleasure in the observer, whatever the ends to which they may be made to contribute. To produce order in a community of men and women distinctive in their personalities and including the utmost diversity of taste and temperament is a surpassing triumph of Divine skill and power.

I. Order implies four things: (1) Order presupposes submission to a common centre of authority. Its worth and quality will be determined by the kind of authority which calls it forth. (2) Order implies the suppression of lawless and capricious personal tastes, and the art of possessing our souls in patience at all times. (3) Order implies an intuition of the part each has to play in a common scheme of life and work. (4) Order implies not only the discovery of the part each has to play in a common scheme but the fulfilment of that special part by methods which will help and not hinder the work of others.

II. Success is measured by the spirit of order which animates men and the communities into which they are grouped. In an age which is unfriendly to human prerogative it may perhaps be our temptation to depreciate order and cry out for guerilla evangelism. Order, it must be admitted, is too often a synonym for frigidity, red tape, servile mechanism, punctiliousness in trifles, death. But in the Apostle's vocabulary it means the tramp of Christ's conquering hosts in perfect time to God's music.

III. Order helps that steadfastness of faith which is the second great quality commanded by the Apostle. The lack of it brings panic, disorganisation, abasement, defeat.

IV. Quiet and undisturbed conditions of life are sometimes attended by a specious show of steadfastness lacking all inherent reality. Unless the foundations be deeply laid, faith may prove itself a fair-weather virtue that can only survive under circumstances of indulgent tenderness. Sooner or later the crisis of trial comes, and proves how superficial was the profession.

V. The foundations of our faith must be well and deeply laid if we are to attain this ideal of steadfastness. For us at least religion must be the best demonstrated of all truths, the most central of all realities, the most imperial of all obligations.

VI. The steadfastness of faith is not inconsistent with freedom, mental flexibility, an all-round power of self-adjustment when the great emergency comes.

REFERENCES.—II. 5.—T. G. Selby, *Preacher's Magazine*, vol. iv. p. 385. Archbishop Temple, *Christian World Pulpit*, vol. l. p. 422. *Expositor* (5th Series), vol. vii. p. 459.

AN ADDRESS FOR THE NEW YEAR

' As ye have therefore received Jesus Christ the Lord, so walk ye in Him.'—COL. II. 6.

I. HERE is expressed the undoubted privilege and portion of every real child of God. 'Ye have . . . received Jesus Christ the Lord.' Remember the Apostle is addressing himself to men and women of like passions with ourselves. Called by a faithful God into the fellowship of His Son Christ Jesus the Lord, ye have received Him.

II. Our text implies the means whereby this great grace had been bestowed upon them, and realised by them, as well as the evidence and proof by which the Apostle was enabled to conclude concerning the Colossians, that they had 'received Christ Jesus the Lord'. If Christ Jesus the Lord be received by any of us, it must be in the reception of God's Word and testimony concerning Him. If we are to be made partakers of the Holy Ghost, if ever God the Comforter takes possession of our souls, or ministers to our hearts, it must be by the means and agency of God's testimony concerning the Lord Jesus Christ. And if ever we are to have faith, either in its beginning or its increase — faith whereby we lay hold on Christ, and rest in Christ—faith whereby we enter into the comforts of the Holy Ghost, and take possession of His blessed Person—faith must come by hearing, and hearing by the Word of God.

III. The text contains an exhortation and command, founded upon this fact of their having received 'Christ Jesus the Lord': 'Walk ye in Him'. Observe the order. We cannot walk in Christ until we have received Christ. The testimony of God concerning the patriarchs, Enoch and Noah, of old, was this, 'They walked *with* God'. Here is an exhortation from your Father and your Friend, a command by the Holy Ghost, sent down from heaven. 'Walk

ye *in* Him.' The man that walks in God 'walks in the light !' he 'walks in the truth !' he 'walks at liberty !' he 'walks in strength !' he 'walks in fulness !' he 'walks in love !'

IV. Lastly, our text implies that there is a proportion and analogy between the faith that receiveth 'Jesus the Lord,' and the fruitfulness, joyousness, happiness, as well as the reality of our walk in Him. —MARCUS RAINSFORD, *The Fulness of God*, p. 181.

REFERENCES.—II. 6.—H. Woodcock, *Sermon Outlines* (1st Series), p. 68. Spurgeon, *Sermons*, vol. viii. No. 483.

THE BEGINNING AND DEVELOPMENT OF THE CHRISTIAN LIFE

' As ye have therefore received Jesus Christ the Lord, so walk ye in Him ; rooted and builded up in Him.'—COL. II. 6, 7.

YOU may call the subject of the passage before us the beginning and the development of the Christian life ; the latter is to be, in the heart of it, all of a piece and consistency with the former, of the same complexion and the same character. 'As ye receive the Lord Jesus so walk in Him.'

I. Now, what is the beginning ? 'Ye received the Lord Jesus.' That is the conception of the Christian life. I do not know that we have not got away from it a little. You think the Christian life begins in giving. It begins in receiving. You think it goes on in giving. It goes on in receiving. Of course you give yourselves to Christ to begin with, but first of all you receive, and the ground of all your service and of your acceptance is your receiving. You surrender the citadel of your life to God. Quite right, but in that very act of surrender you welcome the King, with His authority and His rule. What is absolutely necessary to-day to be proclaimed upon the housetops is this—the Christian life begins not in an ordinance which a man observes either for himself or for another ; not in works, but in faith, and faith is primarily receiving, believing is receiving.

II. Now, go another step ; what do you receive ? *Whom* did you receive ? That is the way to put it. Ye received the Lord Jesus, ye received Christ as Lord. Mark that ! Ye received a Person, and with Him forgiveness of sins, and with Him comfort, and with Him rest, and with Him joy, and with Him the strength to do the will of God.

In one of his last and most beautiful sermons in the last days of his ministry, Dr. Dale, one of the greatest theologians that ever lived, tells us that in a time of great prostration and suffering and nervous breakdown, in the very extremity of mortal weakness, when he sorely needed consolation and support, he endeavoured to draw strength from the wonderful truth that Christ the Eternal Son of God is our brother, that He clings to man with all a brother's affection. But somehow, says Dr. Dale, that thought failed to bring me the comfort that I wanted. Then, he says, I remembered that Christ was my Lord, and it steadied me at once, gave me rest of heart, and courage and strength. And that truly great theologian and great Christian goes on to say : 'It was not sympathy I needed, so much as the consciousness of being in the strong hands of One who was my Lord, who was responsible for me'. 'And,' says Dr. Dale, 'this is the truth for times of health and strength as well as for times of sickness. Christ is not only my friend—it is wonderful condescension if I keep His commandments ; but He is my Lord ; He owns me, He possesses me, and I am at rest from usurping tyrants if the King is on the Throne.'—CHARLES BROWN, *God and Man*, p. 16.

REFERENCE. — II. 7. — H. Macmillan, *Christian World Pulpit*, vol. lvi. p. 100.

COL. II. 8.

STAND up, O heart, and yield not one inch of thy rightful territory to the usurping intellect. Hold fast to God in spite of logic, and yet not quite blindly. Be not torn from thy grasp upon the skirts of His garments by any wrench of atheistic hypothesis that seeks only to lure thee into utter darkness ; but refuse not to let thy hands be gently unclasped by that loving and pious philosophy which seeks to draw thee from the feet of God only to place thee in His bosom. Trustfully though tremblingly let go the robe, and thou shalt rest upon the heart and clasp the very living soul of God.—JAMES HINTON.

REFERENCES.—II. 8.—*Expositor* (6th Series), vol. iv. p. 410 ; *ibid.* vol. x. p. 268. II. 9.—*Ibid.* vol. iv. p. 389. II. 9, 10.—A. Whyte, *The Scottish Review*, vol. iii. p. 525.

THE PERFECT TYPE IN CHRIST

'Ye are complete in Him.'—COL. II. 10.

I. THIS means, to begin with, that the Ideal Man, towards whom the race is blindly striving and stumbling, of whom poets have sung, and seers had visions, and prophets uttered strange things, and towards whom human aspiration has longingly strained its vision, crying out in the agony of its desire, 'Oh, that I might know where I might find Him !' is not, as some would have us believe, a dim cloud of beauty on the far horizon of the future, nor a 'complex' of generalised qualities, as yet unrealised ; it means that this eternal Word has become 'flesh,' has 'tabernacled among us,' 'and we have beheld His glory, the glory as of the Only Begotten of the Father, full of grace and truth'. It means that once in the course of the ages God has sent a Man into the world, complete and flawless in His perfections of character, pure as the snow on Alpine heights, touched to finest issues in all His activities, free from stain and frailty, so that men gazing at this Son of Man, this 'first-born of all creatures,' can say, 'Yes, that is what God meant when He said, Let us make man in Our image, and after Our likeness'. That is what Jesus is on His human side. He is the typical Man. 'We are complete in Him.'

II. When with a kindling eye, and a humbled heart, we try to analyse the impression made upon us by the typical humanity of Jesus, we are struck with three sublime features in His character. (1) The first is the scope of His nature. Here in the Gospels is no merely local or racial or temporary ideal, but a picture of glorious breadth, and amplitude, and reality. Here is a personality which, while it is splendidly individual, rises above its environment of time and nationality into that region in which every human peculiarity, every limitation of sex and age, passes away, and in that fadeless countenance we see mirrored the grandeur of a full complete manhood. (2) The second supreme quality in the personality of Jesus is its intensity. It stands forth from the written page with sublime boldness and strength. Its very serenity is the outcome of a boundless spiritual vitality. (3) The third quality that stands out in this Divine personality is its perfect poise and balance. He is Man, 'fulled-summed in all His powers'.

III. It would be a tempting subject to pursue this general train of thought into the details supplied to us by the Gospels, but a very few hints must suffice. (1) This combined scope, intensity, and poise of nature are very clearly visible if we consider the Christ as the ideal Thinker of the world. (2) The same is true of the *heart* of Christ. His inner life, as we have glimpses of it in the Gospels, how large, how deep, how intense it shows ! (3) And what soul ever gave itself to the service and saving of man, with a scope so vast, with a love so intense, with a vision so serene, of human sorrow and limitation, as did the Christ ?— E. GRIFFITH JONES, *Types of Christian Life*, p. 93.

REFERENCES.—II. 10.—T. Nicholson, *Sermons by Welshmen*, p. 320. W. Adamson, *Christian World Pulpit*, vol. lii. p. 359. J. Vaughan, *Fifty Sermons* (9th Series), p. 285. II. 11, 12.—C. Gutch, *Sermons*, p. 151. II. 12.—J. Keble, *Village Sermons on the Baptismal Service*, p. 181. II. 13.— Spurgeon, *Sermons*, vol. xxxv. No. 2101. *Expositor* (4th Series), vol. i. p. 205 ; *ibid.* vol. v. p. 441. II. 13, 14.— Spurgeon, *Sermons*, vol. xlv. No. 2605. II. 15.—*Ibid.* vol. v. No. 273. *Expositor* (4th Series), vol. iii. pp. 246, 362 ; *ibid.* (5th Series), vol. vi. p. 378 ; *ibid.* (6th Series), vol. x. pp. 193, 198, 370, 374. II. 17.—F. E. Ridgeway, *Plain Sermons on Sunday Observance*, p. 19. II. 18.—*Expositor* (4th Series), vol. iv. p. 400 ; *ibid.* (5th Series), vol. ii. p. 133 ; *ibid.* vol. v. p. 464 ; *ibid.* (6th Series), vol. i. p. 203 ; *ibid.* vol. viii. p. 429. II. 20.—*Ibid.* (5th Series), vol. vi. p. 28. II. 22.—*Ibid.* vol. i. p. 202 ; *ibid.* (7th Series), vol. vi. p. 360. II. 23.—*Ibid.* (6th Series), vol. i. p. 373.

ON THE HEIGHTS

'Seek those things which are above, where Christ sitteth on the right hand of God.'—COL. III. 1.

WHAT are the things that are above ? Does the Apostle mean the things that belong to the future life ? Well, they do belong to the future life, and it is well for us to think of that life, and to think that we shall live in it, and that these things are the things that are current coin there. But he means the present life, for he exhorts us to seek these things, and to have them *now*, the things that abide, of which death cannot rob us, the things which belong to the spirit and character of men. They are too many to enumerate. Some of them are mentioned in the latter part of this chapter, but there is one in Whom they are all embodied. Seek the things that are above 'where *Christ* is'. Seek *character*, the Christ-like character, purity, truth, love to God and men, reached through faith and fellowship. These are the highest things a man can seek.

Now, what about them? This: you must seek them—they do not come without seeking—and seek them with resolute and set purpose. Set your mind or your heart on them, they may be yours, though it be only by almost desperate endeavour, and they are worth more than all the glory and honour and wealth of all the world. The greatest achievement on earth is the achievement of character in yourself and in others.

I. Now, nothing is more certain than that it is one of the easiest things in the world to be called off from this quest, and that people often give it up as life goes on and as cares and possessions accumulate. There is a tremendous downward pull which is constantly exerted, and which increases as life goes on. There is an awful glamour cast over physical pleasure and material gain, and there are seasons in the life of the best of us when it seems as if character were nothing in comparison with money or pleasure.

Life, the high life in a man, the life that links him to God, is wrought upon and worn away by so many influences, that it requires a vast amount of attention to keep it in repair.

II. Where shall we begin? Begin with the Church. It is possible for a Church to lose its tone, to be carrying on things on the lower level.

The message of the text comes to us all with great force. 'Seek, set your mind on the things that are above where Christ sitteth.' Lift up your eyes to Him. Take your directions from Him. Ask what He would do and what He would have you do. Be content with nothing short of the highest.

There is the region into which St. Paul brings our motto. There may it be steadfastly adopted. It would mean a new beginning for some of us, a return to forsaken ways for others. Our inheritance is in the things that are above. He who seeks them shall have them. They are within our reach, and he who has them shall be fitted for the everlasting fellowship of the saints in light. For that we were made. To bring us to that Christ both lived and died and rose again.—CHARLES BROWN, *God and Man*, p. 106.

RISEN WITH CHRIST

'If ye then be risen with Christ, seek those things which are above, where Christ sitteth on the right hand of God.'—COL. III. I.

THIS exhortation is based on a fact and a principle. The fact is, that Jesus Christ has risen from the dead, and is now at the right hand of God; the principle is, that faith in that fact ought to affect the estimate which we form of the relative value of things on earth and things in heaven. Accepting it as a fact that Jesus Christ died and rose again from the dead, what ought to be the practical outcome of our belief in it on our present earthly life?

I. Now, in answer to this inquiry, I remark that an intelligent belief in the Resurrection of Christ ought to give us a new ambition in life. If the Resurrection

revealed only the fact of future existence, without showing us that there is any intimate relation between the life that now is and that which is to come, it is conceivable that a belief in it might not operate much in changing or moulding our present character. But when we view it in connection with the ascension of Christ into heaven and with the statements which He and His Apostles have made upon the subject, we become convinced that the position which we are to occupy hereafter will be fixed, not in any arbitrary and capricious manner, but by the character which we have formed and the work which we have done here. The cross was the precursor of the crown ; and just in so far as we approach to the likeness of our Lord Jesus here, we shall attain to the measure of His glory hereafter. Here, then, is an ambition worthy of immortal beings.

II. An intelligent belief in the fact that Christ has risen from the dead ought to give us a new support through life. One writes of these 'dead but sceptred sovrans whose spirits rule us from their urns'; and it is to be feared that multitudes place Jesus simply at the head of these. But to think of Him thus is not to believe in and realise His Resurrection. He does not rule us from an *urn*. He rules us from a *throne*, whereon He sits endowed with 'the power of an endless life'. Ah! if we but dwelt on this aspect of the matter, what a power would come from the risen Lord to vitalise and ennoble all our conduct, and to sustain us under all difficulty and trial !

III. An intelligent belief in the fact of the Resurrection of Christ ought to give us comfort when we are bereaved of Christian friends, and to give us calmness in the contemplation of our own departure from the world. That victory over death achieved by Christ has changed the relation of death to all Christ's people.

RAISED WITH CHRIST

'If then ye were raised together with Christ, seek the things which are above.'—COL. III. I.

YOU see where the 'if' comes in. It is not 'if Christ be risen from the dead'. That is certain fact. St. Paul was sure of it. The evidence was so widespread. It is not if Christ be raised, but if ye then were raised with Christ. And yet, so far as these Christians at Colossæ were concerned, St. Paul did not wish to express any doubt. It is the argumentative 'if'. It might be rendered 'since'. Since ye then were raised together with Christ. Assuming that your conversion is as real, your faith as genuine as that of these Colossians, this tremendous fact is true of you : 'ye were raised with Christ'. What does it mean ? The New Testament teaching concerning the Resurrection of Christ passes through three stages. In the first the dominant thought is the bearing of the fact of the Resurrection on the Person of Christ, that it is the seal of all His teaching, the Divine endorsement of His claim to be the Messiah, the Son of God. The second stage is the bearing of the fact of the Resurrection upon our view of a future life, that it is the pledge to us of our resurrection, the assurance of the certainty and reality of the life of the world to come. The third stage is in the bearing of the fact of the Resurrection upon the present spiritual and moral condition of the believer. Mark, then, these points of correspondence between Christ's Resurrection and our spiritual and moral quickening.

I. Both are the result of the working of a Divine and supernatural power. Every true conversion, all real conquest of self and sin, is as much the outcome of the power of God as the Resurrection of Jesus Christ from the dead. All true holiness is supernatural.

II. Again, both imply the passing through real death. So we have it in Romans vi : 'If we have been planted together in the likeness of His death, we shall be also in the likeness of His Resurrection'. Christ died for our sins that we might not have to die for them. If you died with Christ you have passed through a real death ; you are dead to things to which formerly you were alive, you are alive to things to which formerly you were dead.

III. Once more, both imply the entering into a new life. In a real sense you live unto God. You begin to know the power of Christ's Resurrection. The world-conquering, self-crucifying, sin-subduing power of the risen Christ enters your life.—F. S. Webster, *Church Family Newspaper*, vol. xv. p. 438.

Col. III. 1.

I have often applied to idiots in my own mind, that sublime expression of Scripture that *their life is hidden with God.*—Wordsworth to Prof. Wilson.

References.—III. 1.—W. Pierce, *Christian World Pulpit*, vol. xlv. p. 222. C. Brown, *God and Man*, p. 16. B. J. Snell, *Sermons on Immortality*, p. 56. H. Bonar, *Short Sermons for Family Reading*, pp. 185, 194. S. A. Tipple, *The Admiring Guest*, p. 30. H. P. Liddon, *University Sermons*, p. 250. J. R. Illingworth, *University and Cathedral Sermons*, p. 208. *Expositor* (5th Series), vol. vii. p. 297 ; *ibid.* (7th Series), vol. vi. p. 152.

THE UPWARD LOOK

' If then ye were raised together with Christ, seek the things that are above, where Christ is, seated on the right hand of God. Set your mind on the things that are above, not on the things that are upon the earth.'—Col. III. 1, 2 (R. V.).

Inquire into—

I. The Nature of this Higher Life.—'Seek the things that are above, where Christ is, seated on the right hand of God.' Everywhere in nature is found a certain upward gaze and striving. Apart from all revelation, we find in ourselves instincts seeking upward aspirations towards things higher than those of time and sense ; we look beyond the physical life, we conceive ideas and hopes touching the unseen and the eternal. Now what has the faith of Christ to say to this inner striving, to these glances, longings, dreams, aspirations after the spiritual and abiding? (1) Most frankly and emphatically does Christianity *accept* the upward-seeking instinct. (2) Christianity *stimulates* the upward-seeking instinct. It not only sanctions otherworldliness, it sets itself steadily to develop to the utmost the spiritual instinct. (3) Christianity *defines* the upward-seeking impulse. There is confessedly deep mystery about the nature and design of this instinct ; the profoundest philosophers have been perplexed by it, wondering as to its precise signification. But in Christ the mystery is practically solved, the vague splendour after which we blindly grope becomes definite. ' Seek the things that are above, where Christ is, seated on the right hand of God.' That is, contemplate all the higher truths in the light of the risen Christ, and in the strength that He gives work up to those truths.

II. Why we should Live this Higher Life.—(1) It is only thus that we attain personal perfection. A star cannot be imprisoned in a shed, it demands a sky ; and to attain perfection and fully display its glory the soul demands a sky. There is no supreme character except through a supernatural creed. (2) We should live this higher life because if we do not we shall not get this world. The astronomer is a ready example of the fact that very frequently the condition of getting a thing is that you look away from it. What perhaps strikes us most when inspecting a telescope is that it shuts out so much. The astronomer shuts the earth from his sight, not because he does not care for it but that he may better understand it and realise its possibilities. The Apostle withdraws our eyes from earth and fixes them on the eternal world, not that he is indifferent to human circumstance and happiness, but because he knows that only thus are we fitted to inherit all things.

It is in the power of Christ alone that we can live this higher life. The Death and Resurrection of Christ have not only a moral signification, they have also an inspiring and transforming power. All is impracticable without the grace of God in Christ Jesus ; all is possible with it.—W. L. Watkinson, *The Bane and the Antidote*, p. 95.

References.—III. 1, 2.—H. Alford, *Quebec Chapel Sermons*, vol. iii. p. 294. A. Maclaren, *After the Resurrection*, p. 130.

THE RISEN LIFE

' If ye then be risen with Christ, seek those things which are above, where Christ sitteth on the right hand of God. Set your affection on things above, not on things on the earth. For ye are dead, and your life is hid with Christ in God.'—Col. III. 1-3.

I. You must have remarked, in studying the Epistles of St. Paul, how he identifies the Christian with his Lord, in His Crucifixion, His Death, and His Resurrection. He sees in these great events figures of that moral and spiritual revolution which has taken place in the heart and soul of every believer, of every one born of God.

(a) He identifies the Christian with the Crucifixion of Christ. Referring to his old self-life, he says, 'I am crucified with Christ' ; he also uses the peculiar phrase ' the old man' in reference to his former self, and speaks of it as being crucified. This ' old man,' meaning the old corrupt sinful self, is to be crucified, so that it can no longer dominate the ' new man'. The believer must so identify himself with his Lord's Crucifixion that he is to reckon the old corrupt body of sin, the old evil life, as crucified with Christ.

(b) He identifies the true man of God with the Death of Christ. 'Ye died' (Col. III. 3); 'Planted together in the likeness of His Death'; 'Reckon yourselves dead indeed unto sin' (Rom. VI. 5, 11). In Colossians III. 5 you have the word 'mortify,' showing continuity of teaching on this point. This is the Apostolic doctrine as regards the believer's attitude to sin: he is dead to it.

(c) He identifies the Christian with the Resurrection of Christ: he is risen with Christ. Buried with Christ, and raised with Him too—this is the teaching of the text. The life which we now live in the power of the Son of God is equivalent to a resurrection from the dead—it is a 'risen' life.

Alive unto God—that is to be our position. Pray that you may indeed 'know Him, and the power of His Resurrection,' as He ought to be known by all His saints. But—

II. The 'power of His Resurrection' suggests further wholesome doctrine.

(a) If we are 'risen with Christ' we have left our graveclothes behind us, as Jesus left His in the tomb. He did not go about during His risen life with the garments of death clinging to Him. Christ calls upon us to show forth to the world that we have done with the grave, that we are walking 'in newness of life,' in the power of His Resurrection.

(b) During our Lord's forty days post-resurrection sojourn He appeared ten times only to His followers. The inference is that the 'risen life' of Christ was spent chiefly in communion with God. And the spiritual life of His people will suffer because of the stress of earthly things, unless they get more into contact with heaven and God, unless they, like Him, anticipate the Ascension, and 'in heart and mind thither ascend'. In this busy age, especially, we have need to restore our souls by communion with God.

(c) This 'risen life' ought to be practically manifest in its blessed activities. 'Seek those things which are above.' In that one word 'Seek' we have expressed the outward life of Christian effort; we have expressed also the true aim of a consecrated life—'those things which are above'. But this risen life is not only seen in the outward life of earnest service, but also in—

(d) The inward life of strenuous thought. 'Set your mind on the things that are above.' The mind, the affection, must be centred upon God. You are called to be heavenly-minded. Brethren, 'as a man thinketh in his heart' so will he become. Our thoughts, if they are heavenly thoughts are weaving for us a robe of purity, of charity, of holiness unto the Lord. As a man thinketh now so is he, and so shall he be hereafter. See that your mind is set upon things above, not on things on the earth.

But, in speaking of these things pertaining unto the higher life of the soul, some may say: 'This is all very beautiful, but it is not very practical; I do not see how I can live this "resurrection life"'. Yet surely it is a very practical thing for you and for me to seek and pray that the whole bent of our being, until the end of our days, be Godward. The bent of our life decides our eternal destiny. The tree not only lies as it falls, but it falls as it leans. Set your mind—i.e. the whole bent of your mind—upon things above.

If this 'resurrection life' is worth anything it will influence life in the home, in business, in society. The heavenly minded man is not a saint on a pedestal to be gazed at, nor a man altogether separate from earthly affairs. He will interest himself in all that makes for righteousness and peace and joy; he will 'act the citizen,' and do good unto all men. And all this he will do in the power of the 'new life' which has made him alive unto God and unto men.—ARCHDEACON MADDEN.

REFERENCES.—III. 1-3.—T. J. Madden, *Tombs or Temples?* p. 69. J. J. Blunt, *Plain Sermons* (2nd Series), p. 75. *Expositor* (7th Series), vol. vi. p. 431. III. 1-4.—H. S. Seekings, *Preacher's Magazine*, vol. xvii. p. 270. III. 1, 10.—*Expositor* (5th Series), vol. vii. p. 254.

NATIONAL REPENTANCE: MATERIALISM

'Set your affection on things above, not on things on the earth.'—COL. III. 2.

THE idea of the present, the material, the visible, the tangible, the sensuous, has taken possession of the minds and hearts of a great many men and women of all ranks and classes, to the exclusion of the future, the spiritual, the invisible, the ideal; and the change in the conduct of people who put aside all thoughts of things higher than the things of earth is very great indeed.

I. Materialism is the attempt to account for every development of the creation as we see it, even the mind of man, without God. Even thought itself, even the consciousness of thought, is supposed to be merely the movement of material atoms in the brain. It is an old and clumsy theory, and really accounts for nothing. It is briefly that matter existed originally in countless minute particles or atoms all over space; that these touched each other; that then there grew a wider and wider movement among the whole mass; and that consequently all the complexities of the universe began to grow. Such a theory needs only to be stated in order to see that it bristles with difficulties for which it offers no apology.

II. Once more: and this difficulty is most serious. Materialism does away with the immortality of the soul, as well as denying the existence of God. But if there is no God, and if your soul utterly perishes at death, where do you get any sanction for morality? The vast majority of mankind believe in the great truths of the Being of God and the immortality of the soul in some sort of way and in varying degrees; and the standard of moral conduct is raised in accordance with such deep and far-reaching truths; once take them away, and there would be no difference between right and wrong, except merely what was held to be useful, nothing to protect the honour of your wives and daughters, no check on universal selfishness.

III. The result of this unthinking complaisance, so largely prevalent in the world of to-day, is this : The great mass of men and women who are not religious treat material prosperity as the great thing to be aimed at. I need hardly remind you that this is a most enervating and degrading pursuit. It is well symbolised in *The Pilgrim's Progress* as the occupation of the man with the muck rake. It tends to obscure and finally to exclude all the ideas that make life noble and truly enjoyable.—W. M. SINCLAIR, *Difficulties of Our Day*, p. 83.

'Set your affection on things above.'—COL. III. 2.

THE things above are not precisely those of another world, but of another sphere than the habitual one of our thoughts. They are not the things above our heads, but those which are above our natural sentiments. To set our affections on things above is to set our affections on God Himself ; it is to subordinate our life to Him ; it is to seek and find God in everything.—VINET.

IT is not *we* that set the lights before us at which we aim ; they gleam upon us from beyond us ; if but by the immediate gift of God ; and our part is complete if we keep our eye intent to see them, and our foot resolute to climb whither they show us the way. The beacon aloft is given, the path to reach it alone is found.—MARTINEAU.

THE HIGHER PREFERENCES

'Set your affection on things above, not on things on the earth.'—COL. III. 2.

THE affections have been defined as the faculty or power which regulates or determines all our likes or dislikes for persons or things, our tastes, our friendships, our loves. This faculty or power ought to be brought under control by every reasonable man and every reasonable woman. People sometimes say that there is no accounting for tastes, and to a certain extent that is quite true. We cannot always account for our own tastes, our own likes or dislikes, much less can we for those of other people. Sometimes they are instinctive, we cannot always give a reason for them; and here there is a danger. For instinct surely may be inspired by the devil just as it may be by God. You may allow your instincts to become debased, you may allow your tastes to became vitiated and mean ; you may spoil your judgment so that you prefer what is ignoble and small and petty to what is great and good and noble. Now here comes in the use of a little discipline. You ought to check your preference, you must guard your instinct by choosing only what is really worthy of esteem. You must refuse to grow attached to what is unworthy of your affections, what is unworthy of your consideration.

I. Choose the Best Things.—First of all, to deal with things and subjects, you can cultivate good taste, whether it be in the matter of literature or art or conversation, or any other such thing. It is a duty to choose always the best that is within our reach. It seems obvious, it seems easy in theory ; in practice it is really very difficult. Self-culture always means a good deal of effort. It is such a temptation to read always the least serious books, for instance, or the books that appeal to the lighter side of our nature, even the books that appeal to our lower side. It is so tempting in the matter of conversation to indulge in the flippant, thoughtless, and even harmful talk ; it is very easy to grow very fond of it. It is so easy in behaviour to allow the passions or the temper to regulate our actions, instead of our calmer and much truer judgment. You must choose the beautiful, choose the pure, choose the refined.

II. Choose the Best Friends.—Then, in the matter of persons, how is one to choose one's friends ? This is somewhat an important point. A bad friend very often means one's ruin. Again you must choose what is noble and what is true. Fix your eyes upon such qualities as honour, courage, duty, unselfishness, purity. Do not allow your preference to rest upon the mean, the cowardly, the selfish, the dishonest, the impure ; and then slowly and surely your affections will fix themselves upon the better traits of character. You will become naturally disposed to make good friends instead of bad ones. And still further we must be ourselves pure, ourselves unselfish. We must not choose friends simply with a view to position, or wealth, or personal advantage ; choose them unselfishly, bravely, honourably, choose them for their goodness and holiness. Often that means the sacrifice of pride, position, or wealth. Do not let affection run wild, or it may choose the bad, and that bad choice may mean your ruin.

III. The Control of the Affections.—And, lastly, our affections must be controlled as regards those that we love most. Remember that there is a selfish, inconsiderate kind of love. There is a love that proceeds from passion and impurity, there is a love not founded upon sympathy and upon self-sacrifice : there is also an uncurbed, unrestrained love, which regards its object as belonging absolutely to itself rather than as a trust from God. People very often, under the cover of love, will allow those they love all kinds of indulgence, all kinds of laxity. They seem to think that love is an excuse for many things that would be otherwise inadmissible. Whether in regard to things or persons, our affections need strict discipline ; you may easily grow fond of what is ignoble, unworthy of respect. Let us in our prayers ask God to send His Holy Spirit into our hearts that we may follow the advice of the great Apostle to the Gentiles : 'Set your affection on things above, not on things on the earth'.

REFERENCES.—III. 2.—J. Stalker, *Christian World Pulpit*, vol. l. p. 56. W. L. Alexander, *Sermons*, p. 309. H. M. Butler, *Harrow School Sermons* (2nd Series), p. 54. E. A. Bray, *Sermons*, vol. i. p. 240.

LIFE HID WITH CHRIST

(*Before Communion*)

' Ye are dead, and your life is hid with Christ in God.'—COL.
III. 3.

WORDS like these, it is obvious, are not addressed indiscriminately to the world at large. They describe a class of people, and demand an audience, which, if fit, is also few. Not that the text is in any sense obscure, although it belongs to an age far from our own. Not that it raises needless barriers. Only, it takes for granted that we have undergone a great peculiar experience, which has brought us into a new world. In short, as very few sayings even in the New Testament do, it touches the centre and focus of personal Christianity. It tells the open secret of discipleship.

Three aspects of truth are here, I think, which may help us as we approach the Table of Christ.

I. First, note *the old life left behind*. ' Ye are dead,' St. Paul writes, or even, as in stricter accuracy we may render, ' ye died '. He is indicating a definite occasion in the past. Sometimes the passage of a soul into God's kingdom is a very sudden thing. It may even be as the flight of a bird for swiftness. We lie down one night our old selves, and ere we sleep again the revolution has occurred. In this text, however, suddenness of that kind is not necessarily implied. Men may die swiftly, or they may die slowly ; it matters nothing, once they have wakened on the immortal side of death. At the equator no visible line is stretched round the world for all to see ; nevertheless, the line is actually crossed ; at some definite point the ship leaves one hemisphere and enters on the other. Just so, when God's eye reads our past, many circumstances may take on a bold prominence and fixity of outline that were concealed, or only half-displayed, to our feebler gaze. Where we saw nothing but an unbroken, imperceptible advance, He, it is possible, may discern a cleavage, sharp as though effected by a scimitar-stroke, between the old existence and the new. And the fittest metaphor to illustrate the transition that St. Paul can think of is that passage from one world to another which we call *death*.

II. Note, secondly, *the hidden life now possessed*. ' Your life is hid with Christ.' In other words, there is something about each genuine believer, however simple, which will more than tax the keenest intelligence to explain. Christian character is not to be accounted for by mere surface phenomena. To unveil the secret, you must go down into the buried regions beneath ordinary thoughts and avocations, down into the unseen depths of personality. As you cross a highland moor you may come upon a curious bright streak of green, winding in and out among the heather, its pure and shining verdure clearly marked against the dull brown of its immediate surroundings. What is it, and how came it there? Whence rises the sap to feed this soft elastic ribband of turf? There is a tiny stream below, a runnel of sweet water flowing down there out of sight, only hinting

its presence by the green beauty above. So the springs of Christian life are hid, hid with Christ in God.

III. Note, lastly, *the life yet to be revealed*. In the New Testament men's eyes and thoughts are ever bent forward, as they wait for the voice and footfall of a returning Lord, when that which is hid now will be so no longer. It *is* hidden now, just because we are here and Christ is yonder. But like the bud sleeping within its swelling sheath, the Christian's present lot is big with promise. One day the secret will be out. ' When Christ, who is our life, shall appear, then shall we also appear with Him in glory.'

Our life is hid now, because Christ also is hid, not in darkness unsearchable, but in the light undimmed and excelling where God dwells.—H. R. MACKINTOSH, *Life on God's Plan*, p. 143.

THE RESURRECTION

(*For Easter Day*)

' For ye are dead, and your life is hid with Christ in God.'—
COL. III. 3.

THE Resurrection of Jesus Christ has always been in the Church of God its chiefest note of glory. If the Church of God were to meet every single one of its doctrines without alluding to the subject, it would be the same, for it is not only written on parchment, but on the fleshly tablets of the heart. The Church of God is older than any one of these books, and from heart to heart, throughout Christendom, from the Day of Resurrection to this Easter Sunday, has passed the truth ' The Lord is risen,' and the answer to the truth, ' He is risen indeed '.

We are told by St. Paul that Twelve Apostles were chosen for this purpose : to witness to the Resurrection, and we know for certain that the Twelve Apostles were protected from being destroyed, when Christ suffered His Passion, because they were kept alive by God to witness the Resurrection. The first sermon the first Ministers of Christ preached was the Resurrection. We know from Holy Scripture they went out and preached this sermon, Jesus and the Resurrection. They were stoned, beaten, and imprisoned, and killed for preaching it. To-day, we are not stoned, or killed, or imprisoned, but we are laughed at. Of the Apostles we read, the more they were maltreated, the more they preached it ; and the more we are laughed at, the more we assert it, and preach it.

I. ' Christ is risen—He is risen indeed.' The Greek Church asserts the fact popularly, not only in the Church but in the street. The Czar of all the Russias comes out of his palace, and, seeing the sentinel, kisses him and says, ' The Lord is risen,' and the soldier says, ' He is risen indeed '. One cabman in the street gets off his stand, and another gets off his sleigh, they embrace, and the one says to the other, ' Christ is risen,' and the other answers, ' He is risen indeed '. There the man in the street has only one thing to say that Easter morning, that Christ is risen. Now we Westerns are not so minded, but I hope this Easter morning you sing up the old song in your hearts. It is not only assertion, it is something more, it is a hymn of joy, and I hope that every one of you will sing up in your heart this morning the old song of the Church, 'Christ is risen—He is risen indeed'.

II. And this was the motive principle of the early martyrs. And when they were persecuted, the martyrs were simply splendid. They all of them went into the amphitheatre with this light in their souls, immortality in Christ. Perpetua—matron, mother, martyr—entered into the amphitheatre, and they were astonished at her look. They tell us that there was a light in her eyes, supernal, before which her persecutors quailed, and the beasts that were to tear her to pieces drew back. It was the light of immortality. She knew Christ had said, 'Because I live, ye shall live also'. So too it has been with all the martyrs all down the ages. It has been said that, after the bit of Latin which was put on the Cross, the first bit of Latin which stole into the Church was 'Deo gratias,' 'Thanks to God,' which the martyrs said when they were condemned to death, for they knew that through the grave and gate of death they should pass to a joyful resurrection.

III. Revive your poor faith on the altar of Easter. The Christian's hope is, has been, and ever shall be immortality in Christ. Now is that lamp burning in your sanctuary? Ask yourselves, could you die happy in Christ? Have you overcome death in yourselves? See to it then, men, that you die like men, and see to it, women, that you die like Christ, that the light of immortality burns steady within your souls. Relight the light at the altar.

REFERENCES.—III. 3.—Bishop Boyd-Carpenter, *Christian World Pulpit*, vol. lv. p. 129. J. W. Houchin, *The Vision of God*, p. 149. T. Arnold, *Sermons*, vol. iv. p. 39. H. M. Butler, *Harrow School Sermons*, p. 344. Bishop Bethell, *Sermons*, vol. ii. p. 263. *Expositor* (6th Series), vol. i. p. 379; *ibid.* vol. vii. p. 265.

CHRIST OUR LIFE
COL. III. 4.

'CHRIST, who is our life;' name all-sacred and all-beautiful, 'Holiest of holies, Jesus Christ our Lord'; tenderly and intimately near to us, transcendently above us, higher than the heavens.

To rest awhile before the revelation of His greatness and His fulness, His unsearchable riches, His love passing knowledge, will only the better prepare the believer for the simpler and larger reception of His gift of life. To apprehend the glory of the Fountain will make credible the freedom and the virtues of the stream. The earthen vessel may be as rough and poor as possible. But let it be opened to receive that water, and what may not be the bliss of purity and power within it?

He then, this same Lord Jesus Christ, is here affirmed to be our life. The phrase, we remember, is strictly Scriptural. To the recent converts at Colossæ (Col. III. 4) St. Paul uses it, as about a fact

already confessed and familiar: 'When Christ who is our life shall appear, then shall ye also appear with Him in glory'. This is the precise authority for our phrase. But it is only the central point, as we well know, of a large mass of New Testament language which sets out the same idea. Close at hand, in the same Colossian passage (ver. 3), we have a specimen: 'Your life is hid with Christ in God'. We have it in a form yet more vivid in the Galatian Epistle (II. 20): 'I live, yet not I, but Christ liveth in me'. And in that to the Ephesians the thought is carried to the inmost recess of expression, when we read (III. 17) of 'Christ dwelling in the heart,' as a fact of experience intended to be the portion not of a select few but of every true disciple. St. John is as emphatic as St. Paul (I. 11, 12): 'God hath given us eternal life; this life is in His Son; he that hath the Son hath the life'.

We need not recall at length how amply the Lord's own words (John XIV. 6, 19) seal the language of His Apostles: 'I am the life'; 'Because I live ye shall live also'.

I. What does it mean? In vain shall we try to answer the question to its depths, to analyse its whole secret, to explore its perfect issues. We may indeed say with reverent confidence what it does *not* mean. It implies no absorption of our personality into His, no identity of our self with His, such that it should ever be true to say, as has been said, and by pious teachers, that 'our deepest self is God'. For my own part, I cannot too earnestly deprecate such words, which I take to express conceptions alien to the whole spirit of Biblical theology, words which betray an unbalanced insistence on that great truth of Divine immanence, which needs, like all great truths, its counterpoise if it is not to sink into an error proportionally great. 'Christ is our life' is a statement wholly, remotely, other than 'Christ is our self'. He is the Indweller, but He is not the shrine. It is written, 'Christ liveth in me'. But this is not to displace me but to occupy me; to be near to me with a nearness deeper and tenderer than can be thought, but all the while to be eternally and transcendently distinct and above. He is Maker, Redeemer, sovereign Lord. I am the being enabled, freely, in my personality, to respond in worshipping love to Him.

But now, within the humble limits of our perception, what does the phrase mean? It means, let us be perfectly sure, no mere figure of speech, however warm and vivid. It means no mere potency of His influence upon us, by way of precept or even of supreme example, as when the believer, pondering the Passion, feels himself 'inspired,' in the words of the hymn, 'to suffer and to die'. It means an unspeakably spiritual, and therefore unspeakably genuine, union and presence. It means the living Son of God so dwelling and moving in the inner world of the man who is united to Him by the Holy Ghost, in the bond of faith, that nothing less can be said than that the Christ of God is there. In the will He is personally and presently working. In the affections He is breathing the Divine love into the human faculty. In thoughts and purposes His presence and His motions are a living power to prompt and to guide. The man is so charged, may we dare to say, with Him that the familiar prayer, whose wonder so easily escapes us as we sing, receives an ever-developing fulfilment :—

　　　　Guard my first springs of thought and will
　　　　And with Thyself my spirit fill.

'He that is joined to the Lord is one spirit,' says the Apostle in a passage (1 Cor. VI. 17) of surprising depth and power, and as practical as possible all the while. For the context there, what is it ? It is the case of a recent Corinthian convert, tempted to return to the foulest sins of the wicked city. And the Divine antidote for him, not for a cloistered and contemplative devotee, but for him, what is it to be ? Just when vice smiles in his face and whispers its deadly sweetness to his soul, he is to recollect that he is 'joined to the Lord, one spirit'; 'Christ is his life'.

II. That allusion brings us already to the question, What will be the issues and results of a believing recollection that Christ to the believer is nothing less than life? Issues practical indeed will come to him who recalls the spiritual fact and, using it, turns it into power. It was his by covenant in his baptism. It became his in fruition when, by living faith in Christ his Head, he responded to his baptism and actualised its blessings. But now, the more he uses his possession, the more he possesses it. And in that possession what can it not do for him, what can he not do in it ? Rather let us say, what can he not do, not in it but in Him who is his life, in whom he lives, who lives in him ?

'Christ my life' will be the talisman of power on the one hand to detach him from the bondage of the world over his will, and on the other to attach him to the world in sympathetic service. He who is his life, alike and at once overcame the world and gave Himself for it. So did the Head. And the limb, surrendered to the Head, will in his measure do the same, because that life is in him, and in power.

Sin and sickness are facts lying upon wholly different planes. But I for one cannot doubt that normally the soul's health is at least friendly to that of the body which, glorified at last, is to be its inseparable partner and vehicle for ever. It is most creditable that, in untold instances, the maladies and the fatigues of this tabernacle, however truly we do often 'groan in it, being burdened,' are mysteriously affected for relief by the remembrance that Christ is our life. And what will it not be to recite that password of immortality, true for our whole being, when we commit ourselves to Him in the act of death ? It assures to the spirit an unbroken life and a present bliss with Him. It assures equally to the body the radiant wonder of resurrection after a little while.

III. Come, then, and let us 'possess our possession'. Let us take our Redeemer at His word, and be quite sure that for us, so doing, He is life. To live out

that wonderful fact shall be our ambition, always new and supremely innocent ; to 'run with it, and not be weary ; to walk with it, and not faint'.

That great Christian, Henry Venn the elder, Simeon's early friend and guide, writes thus in a letter to his father-in-law, Charles Elliott, April, 1787 :—

'I had in past days a family very dear to me, and not enough for their maintenance from year to year ; and in case of my death they were to be destitute. I was, however, wonderfully free and cheerful in my heart. And my preservative was wholly this, " He that hath the Son hath life ".'

A long century later lived and died my late dear friend in God, George H. C. Macgregor, son of a parish minister in the north of Scotland. He once told me how came to him his first strong grasp on this same secret, Christ our life. One summer night (he was then a young probationer for the ministry) he had addressed a cottage congregation on Col. III. 4. As he walked home in the twilight over the heather his text still sounded in his mind, and suddenly (such things do happen) its doctrine flashed and burned into a Divine reality for himself. 'What, is Christ indeed my life ?' And within five steps on the moorland, so he said to me with solemn emphasis, the young man passed into a new life—a life that shone unwavering with holy light and fire till, some twelve years later, still in his splendid youth, he passed upwards, only to live more perfectly and for ever by Christ who is our life.—H. C. G. MOULE (Bishop of Durham), *Christian World Pulpit*, vol. LXXVIII. p. 231.

REFERENCES.—III. 4.—Spurgeon, *Sermons*, vol. xi. No. 617. J. Bunting, *Sermons*, vol. ii. p. 484. III. 5.—*Expositor* (5th Series), vol. x. p. 108 ; *ibid.* (6th Series), vol. i. p. 276 ; *ibid.* vol. xii. p. 191. III. 6.—*Ibid.* (4th Series), vol. i. p. 23 ; *ibid.* (6th Series), vol. viii. p. 36. III. 9.—S. Baring-Gould, *Village Preaching for Saints' Days*, p. 161. *Expositor* (6th Series), vol. xii. p. 69. III. 9, 10.—*Ibid.* (4th Series), vol. iii. pp. 138, 141. III. 10.—*Ibid.* vol. ii. p. 285.

THE DIVINE GLORY OF CHRIST

'Christ is all and in all.'—COL. III. II.

THESE sublime words no more fit man than Saul's armour fitted the stripling David. Of Christ alone can we say that ' He is all things in all things '.

I. Christ's pre-existence proves His Divinity. It cannot be said of any man that he lived for thirty centuries before his birth ; but as for Jesus, He was high before He became so low, He was rich before He became so poor, He was God before He became Man. As Irving well puts it : ' Tell me now, ye wise men, who deprive Him of His Divinity, how was Christ rich before He became poor if He were not God before He became man ?'

II. His Divine titles teach His Divinity. In the Old Testament He is often styled 'Lord' in the same sense as Jehovah. The Father styles Him His Son— not *a* Son, but *the* Son, the only begotten—His unique Son, because of the same essence as Himself. These sublime titles convince us that the brow of the Son of Mary was radiant with the Godhead's diadem.

III. The Divine attributes given to Christ teach His Divinity. All through the Bible He is spoken of as Eternal, Omnipotent, Omniscient, Omnipresent, and Unchangeable.

IV. Homage was rendered unto Him which by right belonged only to the Divine. Gabriel styled Him the 'Son of the Highest'. A centurion said of Him: 'Truly this was the Son of God'. Even the Devil styled Him 'the Holy One of God,' and no truer Gospel was ever preached by an archangel!

V. The sublimity of His character, and teachings, and works prove His Divinity. (1) He passed through the world as unpolluted as a sunbeam passes through a foul atmosphere. (2) Never was there anything more pure than His teaching except it was His example. As a teacher He was unrivalled, 'Never man spake like this Man'. He spoke of heaven as if from its very throne, and He spoke of God as if from His very heart. (3) His miracles were marvels of power. When Jesus slept, the Galilean storm awoke; but when Jesus awoke, the storm slept in peace.—J. Ossian Davies, *The Dayspring from on High*, p. 201.

'Where there is neither . . . bond nor free; but Christ is all, and in all.'—Col. iii. 11.

Some of the greatest leaders of the Church have been slow to accept St. Paul's teaching as to the equality of bond and free in Christ. St. Leo the Great, as Bishop Gore reminds us, held that the condition of a slave was a bar to orders. 'He bases his refusal to allow the ordination of slaves on the ground that their condition does not leave them the liberty and leisure requisite for a priest; but it is couched in language which breathes the spirit of a Roman patrician much more than the feeling that in "Christ Jesus there is neither bond nor free". He talks of the "dignity of birth" being wanting to them, and he speaks scornfully of the "mean estate (vilitas) of a slave polluting the Christian ministry".'—Bishop Gore, *Leo the Great*, p. 142.

'There is neither Greek nor Jew,' etc.—Col. iii. 11.

Dr. Eugene Stock, in his history of the C.M.S., tells us that when Bishop Wilson went out to India, he was at once confronted with the caste question in the native Church. 'He took a strong line at once. Basing his decision on the grand New Testament principle that in Christianity "there is neither Greek nor Jew, circumcision nor uncircumcision, Barbarian, Scythian, bond nor free, but Christ is all, and in all," he directed that as regards Church usages, "caste must be abandoned, decidedly, immediately, finally". . . . 'In 1835 Bishop Wilson visited the South and dealt earnestly and lovingly with the disaffected Christians, pleading with them the example of the Good Samaritan, who did not stop to ask who the "certain man" was, nor dreamed of being defiled by touching him. "And what," exclaimed the Bishop, rising from his seat in the crowded church, "did our blessed Master say to this? *Go and do thou likewise.*" A long pause,' says his biographer, 'of motionless and breath-less silence followed, broken only when he besought every one present to offer up this prayer, "Lord give me a broken heart to receive the love of Christ and obey His commands". Whilst the whole congregation were repeating this in Tamil, he bowed upon the cushion, doubtless entreating help from God, and then dismissed them with his blessing.'

CHRIST IS ALL, AND IN ALL
Col. iii. 11.

How little can we see of Christ but a bare and faint outline! Why, it will take all eternity to exhaust that subject; it will take all eternity to learn how good, how wise, how great, how holy, how merciful is Christ. And you observe that the Apostle seems to have got that idea here in the words of our text, for he gives us a description of Christ; but it is a remarkable description. He does not say, 'You see Christ is good, Christ is loving, Christ is patient with us, Christ is tender'. He does not go on to His other attributes and say, 'Christ is wise, and Christ is great,' but he gathers them all up into one cluster, and in six monosyllables he tells us 'Christ is all, and in all'.

I. Christ is all, and in all in the Bible. Wherever you open it I care not, you will come to Christ in the Bible. You will find as you read that Book that everywhere, if we look for Him, everywhere we shall find the Christ. We go back, for instance, to the Old Testament, and there in the heart of the Jewish administration we see the Lamb, the offering appointed by God and by Moses through God, smoking upon the altar, the Lamb of sacrifice for sin offered to God, and we say, 'Behold the Lamb of God, which taketh away the sin of the world'. We go on, and turn over any page, and we are sure to encounter Christ. We come on to Isaiah, the Evangelical prophet, and we find him declaring, 'For unto us a child is born, unto us a Son is given, and the government shall be upon His shoulder; and His name shall be called Wonderful, Counsellor, The Mighty God, The Everlasting Father, The Prince of Peace'. I go back to the first book in the Bible, and there I find in Genesis that Jacob with his last breath tells us, 'Unto Him shall the gathering of the people be'. I come to the last chapter of the Old Testament in Malachi, and find it declared, 'Unto you that fear My name shall the Sun of Righteousness arise with healing in His wings'. I come into the New Testament, and there of course I expect to find Him. Christ in the Gospels; every miracle, Christ in the miracle; every parable, Christ in the parable; and afterwards in the Acts of the Apostles, the early story of Christianity—Christ in them all. I go on and find Christ in all the Epistles. I am just going to close the Book, and I find Christ in the Apocalypse, and the last word which He speaks to us after, shall I say, His Ascension, through His inspired and loving Apostle John, is 'Behold, I come quickly'. Christ is everything, then, in the Bible, all and in all.

But there are some people who read the Bible as historians. Well, read it as a history. It is the most wonderful history in the world. But if a man only looks at it as a historian he may be absorbed in the history, yet he will not read the story or find the history of Christ for his own salvation.

The fact is that no one will find Christ in this Book without looking for Him; but the soul that comes to this Book and opens it to find Christ will not be disappointed. Christ will step out from behind the pages of this Book, and He will reveal His love, and mercy, and His friendship to your heart and to your soul, and Christ will reveal Himself more and more to those who seek Him. But I do not believe that any others are likely to find Christ. I believe that if a man stands outside the Truth until something has satisfied him, he will remain there. But it is the man who comes to this Bible and says, 'Sir, I would see Jesus,' it is that man to whom the gate is opened. He finds Christ, and in finding Christ he finds peace, and pardon, and comfort, and life, and salvation, and heaven, for Christ is all and in all in the Bible.

II. Secondly, and briefly, Christ is all and in all in redemption. We were under condemnation through sin. It was Christ Who came down from heaven to earth and said, 'Deliver him from going down to the pit: I have found a ransom'. We are slaves through sin. It was Christ Who came and gave deliverance to the captives and opened the prison doors. We were in darkness: it is Christ Who says, 'I am the Light of the World'. And when we come to Him He gives us of the Bread of Life. But more than this, we want to know as sinners how we can be justified before God. Well, here we have it, through redemption, 'being justified freely by His grace through the redemption that is in Christ Jesus'. But we want to know more than this. We want to know that we shall never be overtaken by the consequences of this sin. How do I know that I shall never come into condemnation? 'There is therefore now no condemnation to them which are in Christ Jesus.' Wherever you look for redemption you will find an answer to your fears, and a clearing of all your sins through Christ, if you just look up to Him Who achieved this great redemption for us. Is there a tear that He did not shed? Is there a burden that He did not bear? Is there a sorrow that He did not share? Is there a battle that He did not fight? Is there a victory that He did not win? The hand of sorrow may push you down, the hand of disappointment may fling you back; but that hand which is so patient, and so gentle, and so tender will at last wipe away all tears from our eyes. For in the story of redemption Christ is all, and in all.

REFERENCES.—III. 11.—Spurgeon, *Sermons*, vol. xvii. No. 1006. J. Stalker, *Christian World Pulpit*, vol. li. p. 280. Spurgeon, *Sermons*, vol. xliii. No. 2501. *Preacher's Magazine*, vol. xvii. p. 468. J. Keble, *Sermons for Ascension Day to Trinity Sunday*, p. 249. Spurgeon, *Sermons*, vol. l. No. 2888. Dinsdale T. Young, *The Gospel of the Left Hand*, p. 85. Alfred Rowland, *The Exchanged Crowns*, p. 151. *Expositor* (5th Series), vol. vi. p. 256; *ibid.* vol. vii. pp. 20, 277.

COL. III. 12.

COMPARE Mrs. Carlyle's description of Father Mathew administering the pledge in London to a crowd of unfortunate and dissipated paupers. 'In the face of Father Mathew, when one looked from them to him, the mercy of heaven seemed to be laid bare.'

'Humbleness of mind.'—COL. III. 12.

HUMILITY is the altar on which God wishes to offer our sacrifices to Him.—LA ROCHEFOUCAULD.

REFERENCES.—III. 12.—J. M. Whiton, *Summer Sermons*, p. 193. III. 12, 13.—S. Baring-Gould, *Village Preaching for a Year*, vol. i. p. 136. *Expositor* (6th Series), vol. xi. p. 283.

FORGIVENESS
'Forgiving one another.'—COL. III. 13.

IN the last hour of that last day, when the silent morning light has glimmered through the window for the very last time before our failing eyes, and we feel the burden of our many sins pressing heavily upon us, there will be nothing that can give the trembling mind of the strongest man of us any comfort unless he can say with truth: 'And now, Lord, what is my hope? Truly my hope is even in Thee.' Nothing, unless he can receive back through the familiar voice of the Spirit of God, speaking by a pure conscience, the same message which the Lord gave to the man sick of the palsy, 'Son, be of good cheer; thy sins be forgiven thee'.

And surely it will be well, while as yet we are in the full vigour of both mind and body, 'and the evil days come not, nor the years draw nigh, when we shall say, We have no pleasure in them,' that we consider what grounds we can have for this assurance.

I. There is a temper from which no improvement could ever come. If at any time we were so inflamed with conceit that we thought God was unjust in not giving us more good things than we had already received; if we supposed that we owed nothing to Him, and He everything to us; if we pretended that He had no law which we ought to obey, but was only an indulgent benefactor, to spoil us with the favours of His omnipotence—then should we not say 'farewell to our consciences'? Following the rule of our own ruinous impulses without check, we should feel no restraint upon even the most disastrous of our passions. Owing no duty to God or man, we should be hideous monsters of selfishness; with no inspiring thoughts to purify our affections, and no ideas of right, wrong, and responsibility to guide us, we should be greedily given to everything evil.

II. To save us from setting out on our career in a spirit so mistaken and fatal, our Lord has mercifully put into our daily prayer a reminder of how the case really stands. There is no happiness apart from God. God is that essence of goodness and perfection apart from Whom there is no life; Who keeps everything in safety; Whose perfect Will is the law of the universe. To Him we owe everything. To the goodness of His Being belong the ideals of our homes, friendships, and affections. To His pervading loving-kindness we attribute our enjoyments in the present, our hopes for the future, our knowledge of Him, our understanding of His revelation, our salvation in Jesus Christ, our instruction in the way of peace and happiness.

III. We owe all this to God; but we owe Him much more. These are the things He has done for us, and given us, or which He can do and give. Is there no duty we owe Him in return? More than that, can we have these things without owing Him any duty at all? Some come to us by nature, and we can spoil them by neglecting our duty to God; some we cannot have at all without recognising this duty and acting upon it. We owe God love, gratitude, reverence, trust, obedience. We find His laws for us in our consciences, in His Word, in the revelation of His Son. We must resign our wills into His hands, our lives, thoughts, principles, affections—all to be guided and ruled by Him. When a heart is so willingly given up to Him, He sends His Spirit, His grace, His power, and does so guide and rule it. He makes the sacrifice easy. He alone can govern the unruly wills and affections of sinful men. That is what we owe to God in order to be what we are intended to be; we have to yield up to Him all that we have and are.

Therefore it is with the precious promises of God's Word before us, and with all the bitter remembrance of our shortcomings behind us, our Lord bids us bend daily before our gracious Father, and say, in penitence and humility, in love, trust, and hope, 'Forgive us our debts'.—W. M. SINCLAIR.

THE VIRTUE OF FORBEARANCE
'Forbearing one another.'—COL. III. 13.

IF a man is to live with any joy and fulness, and to find what a noble abode this world may prove, there are three virtues which he must steadily pursue. The first is faith in God, for without faith existence will always be a tangled skein : the second is courage, for every life has its hills, and we breast them but poorly if our heart is faint; and the third is forbearance—forbearing one another.

I. Some of the evils of the unforbearing spirit. (1) One of the first of them to arrest me is that it makes life a constant disappointment. There is only one highway to the world's true comradeship—it is the road of forbearing one another. (2) Another evil of the unforbearing spirit is this, that it presses hardest on life's tenderest relationships. There are some worms that are content to gnaw green leaves, and to spend their lives on the branches of the tree. But there are others that are never satisfied with leaves, they must eat their way into the red heart of the rose. That is the curse of the unforbearing spirit—it gnaws at the very heart of the rose of life. (3) But there is another evil of the unforbearing temper—it reacts with certainty upon the man himself. For with what judgment we judge we shall be judged, and with what measure we mete it shall be measured unto us.

II. I wish to indicate the character of true forbearance. (1) True forbearance begins in a man's thought. It is a good thing to be forbearing in our acts, a great thing to be so in our speech, yet I question if we have begun to practise rightly this pre-eminently Christian virtue, till we are habitually forbearing in our thought. (2) Again true forbearance is independent of our moods. It is a mock forbearance that comes and goes with every variation in the day. (3) There is one other mark on which I would insist, and it is this, that true forbearance helps to better things. It is like the sunshine which brings the summer nearer; it is part of that gentleness which makes men great.

III. Let me suggest some thoughts that may help to make us more forbearing. (1) Think how little we know of one another. We know far too little to be censorious or harsh. (2) Think how greatly we ourselves need forbearance. Even if we do not give it, we all want it. (3) Think how God has forborne us. The forbearance of God is a perpetual wonder. It is a great example : shall we not copy it? Days will be golden, and silenced birds will sing, when we revive the grace of forbearing one another.—G. H. MORRISON, *The Unlighted Lustre*, p. 170.

REFERENCE.—III. 13.—Spurgeon, *Sermons*, vol. xxxi. No. 1841.

THE PERFECTING POWER OF LOVE
'Above all these things put on love, which is the bond of perfectness.'—COL. III. 14.

A WORD or two will explain to us the figure which the Apostle uses to convey his meaning : 'Above all these things put on love, which is the bond of perfectness'. The picture in the Apostle's mind is that of one who is putting on his raiment. He sees a man throwing around his body the loose and flowing garments of antiquity. And then it occurs to him that these loose garments, no matter how fine or beautiful they be, can never be worn with comfort or with grace unless they are clasped together with a girdle. Without that girdle, drawing all together, they hamper and hinder a man at every turn. *It* is the perfect bond of robe and tunic, the final touch that makes them serviceable. And so, says Paul, is it with love; it is the girdle of every other grace; it is the final touch that beautifies the whole, and makes every garment of the spirit perfect. Under the figure, then, there lies one thought—it is the thought of the perfecting of love.

I. In the first place, let us consider how love is needed for the perfecting of gifts.

(1) How true this is of *spiritual* gifts we learn from the first Epistle to the Corinthians. That Church at Corinth was very rich in gifts; so rich, that there was trouble over them. What was the counsel which the Apostle gave? First, he said, Covet earnestly the *best* gifts. Remember, he means, that though all gifts are of God, yet all are not equal in spiritual value. But then immediately he turns from that, as though it were too hard for these Corinthians, and he says 'but yet I show you a more excellent way'—and that more excellent way is love.

It is thus that Paul introduces that great chapter in which he glorifies the powers of love.

(2) Not only is this true of spiritual gifts; it is true of artistic and intellectual gifts. Over them all a man must put on love, for love is the final touch that perfects them. Whatever be your gift, over that gift put on the belt of love.

II. Once more, I ask you to **observe that** love is needed for the perfecting of service.

Something is wanting to make **service** perfect; to make it a thing of beauty and a joy for ever; and what it lacks to crown it with delight is the final touch of love. It is love that makes every service perfect. It is love that turns the task into delight. Love never asks how little can I do. Love always asks how much. And that is why in all the range of service there is no service like that inspired by love, whether the love of a mother for her children, or that of Jesus Christ for all mankind.

III. Once more, I want you to observe that love is needed for the perfecting of relationships.

Now when you come to think of it, you find there are three great enemies of sweet relationship. The first is selfishness, the second pride, and the third destroyer of life's ties is fear.

Love is the sworn enemy of selfishness, for it sets a crown upon the other-self. Love is the sworn enemy of pride, for love is ever warm and ever humble. And as for fear, there is no fear in love, but perfect love casteth out fear, for fear hath torment. It is thus that love is imperatively needed for the perfecting of every human tie. Like a girdle you must clasp it on if you would wear the garment of relationship. It and it only is the bond of perfectness between one life and every other life. Without it we may eat and drink and sleep. But with it, in our common life, we live.

IV. Love is needed for the perfecting of religion.—G. H. MORRISON, *The Return of the Angels*, p. 130.

PEACE THE UMPIRE

'And let the peace of God rule in your hearts.'—COL. III. 15.

To receive this peace and to keep it is to abide in blessedness. It is the peace behind which the heart of man entrenched can be at rest 'when all without tumultuous seems'; the deep peace of the deep sea, though the surface of life be storm-tossed and tempest-driven.

I. It is this peace, this heavenly dove, which murmurs joy, that is to rule, to arbitrate, to be referee, to be umpire in our hearts. Men need such an umpire. The important matter, however, is to see this Divine arbitrator at work. Our judgments ofttimes hesitate in their verdicts, for life is a tangled skein, and the path of duty often winds through a labyrinth of the false and true, of good and evil, and the apparently neutral. God's peace is our greatest treasure, the preservation of it our first duty. Its decision must be final, and whatever other men may do, however right a certain course may be or them, anything that robs us of God's peace is wrong for us.

II. But there are other and very important applications of this great truth. Let peace be the umpire not only of the heart but also of the home. The preservation of home's peace ought to be the first concern of all who belong to it. Let us make peace the ruling goddess of the home life, the umpire from whose verdict there can be no appeal. It is necessary to the growth of all that is beautiful, fragrant, and holy in human relationships.

III. Peace, God's peace, must also be made the umpire in the Church. Where strife is Christ is not. How powerfully that truth has been portrayed by the Belgian artist, Wiertz, in his great pictures, in which he always represents Jesus as turning away in pain and horror from scenes of hatred and strife. The only conflict in which the Church can engage is its holy war against the world. In the Church all must lay aside self-will, and live seeking and enjoying the peace of the household of God.

IV. Has the time not come when all good men must pray and strive to make peace the umpire between nations, and hasten the day when men will lay aside 'reeking tube and iron shard,' and learn to study war no more. Certainly peace must be the attitude, and the preservation of it the endeavour of all Christians, for the kingdom of God which they seek is righteousness and peace.—D. L. RITCHIE, *Peace the Umpire and other Sermons*, p. 9.

THANKFULNESS

'And be ye thankful.'—COL. III. 15.

THIS is an abrupt appeal. Dr. Maclaren calls it 'a jet of praise'. When Paul's heart was fullest his speech was abruptest. The adjective 'thankful' is only used this once in the New Testament. But thankfulness is a duty and delight greatly prominent in the holy pages. To be unthankful is to be unscriptural. May we so reflect upon this jet of praise that our speech and our lives shall plash with melodious fountains of thanksgiving.

I. Thankfulness is a spiritual possibility. 'Be ye thankful' is not uttered to mock us. Nothing is commanded which is not possible to man through grace. (1) Note that this grace of thankfulness is a climacteric grace: '*And* be ye thankful'. Thankfulness is the crown of the graces. Your conquering brow lacks its garland if you are wanting this celestial quality. (2) Thankfulness is recognised as in some degree already existing. Paul said literally 'Become ye thankful'. It is as if he said, 'Become *more* thankful'. (3) As Paul uttered this word it was a great endeavour after a grand ideal. The idea which hides in that 'become' is a constant striving after an unreached standard. But this becoming thankful is no easy task. Constant prayer and ceaseless vigilance are needed if we are to attain this grace. What a noble ideal of thankfulness Paul always sets before us! In II. 7 of this Epistle he presents an aspect of this ideal, '*abounding* in thanksgiving' (R.V.). Sing far more eloquent and far louder songs. In Ephesians v. 20 we have another illustration of the standard of gratitude, 'Giving thanks *always* for *all things*'. Is there 'always' some cause for thanksgiving? Yes. Praise must be perennial. (4) This grand ideal has a sure secret of attainment. After the lapse of but one verse Paul says : 'Giving thanks to God the Father *through Him*'. Gratitude is evangelically achieved. All ethics are evangelically realised.

II. Thankfulness is a spiritual blessedness. How rich they are who are thankful! Ingratitude is impoverishment. Thankfulness glorifies God. Thankfulness is a great spiritualising force. What a check upon gloom is gratitude! Thankfulness as it destroys the base elements of our nature develops all the higher. Thankfulness is not least a blessedness because it brings us into fellowship with the hosts of heaven.—DINSDALE T. YOUNG, *The Enthusiasm of God*, p. 161.

REFERENCES.—III. 15. — Hugh Black, *Christian World Pulpit*, vol. l. p. 139. F. D. Maurice, *Sermons*, vol. i. p. 19. Spurgeon, *Sermons*, vol. xxviii. No. 1693. G. Body, *Christian World Pulpit*, vol. liii. p. 184. W. H. Evans, *Short Sermons for the Seasons*, p. 151. Bishop Alexander, *Verbum Crucis*, p. 177. A. Connell, *Christian World Pulpit*, vol. lxi. p. 386. III. 16.—W. T. Davison, *Christian World Pulpit*, vol. l. p. 218. C. J. Ridgeway, *The King and His Kingdom*, p. 101. T. Sadler, *Sermons for Children*, p. 113. Spurgeon, *Sermons*, vol. xlvi. No. 2679. T. Binney, *King's Weigh-House Chapel Sermons*, p. 231. J. Bolton, *Selected Sermons* (2nd Series), p. 108. W. Robertson Nicoll, *Ten Minute Sermons*, pp. 251, 259. *Expositor* (4th Series), vol. ii. p. 27. III. 17.—F. St. John Corbett, *The Preacher's Year*, p. 34. Spurgeon, *Sermons*, vol. xvi. No. 913. Bishop Westcott, *The Incarnation and Common Life*, p. 125. W. H. Evans, *Sermons for the Church's Year*, p. 56. T. Arnold, *The Interpretation of Scripture*, p. 236. H. Alford, *Quebec Chapel Sermons*, vol. i. p. 67. T. Arnold, *Sermons*, vol. iv. p. 302. F. Bourdillon, *Plain Sermons for Family Reading* (2nd Series), p. 24. S. Pearson, *Christian World Pulpit*, vol. xxv. p. 289.

COL. III. 20.

I OBEYED word, or lifted finger, of father or mother, simply as a ship her helm; not only without idea of resistance, but receiving the direction as a part of my own life and force, a helpful law, as necessary to me in every moral action as the law of gravity in my leaping.—RUSKIN, *Præterita*, § 49.

REFERENCE.—III. 20, 21.—C. S. Horne, *Relationships of Life*, p. 13.

COL. III. 21.

HIS father's severity was such, that once the boy cried out, 'Kill me, father, kill me at once'; and in his indignation at parental injustice, he made a will in these laconic terms, 'omne matri, nihil patri.'—PROF. KNIGHT's memoir of Dr. John Duncan (*Colloquia Peripatetica*, p. xxxvi).

'To my deep mortification,' says Darwin, 'my father once said to me, "You care for nothing but shooting, dogs, and rat-catching, and you will be a disgrace to yourself and all your family". But my father, who was the kindest man I ever knew, and whose memory I love with all my heart, must have been angry and somewhat unjust when he used such words.'

'Not with eye-service.'—COL. III. 22.

BISMARCK attributed the Germans' victories over the French to the fact that 'I know that there is Some One who sees me when the lieutenant does not see me'. 'Do you believe, your Excellency, that they really reflect on this?' asked Fürstenstein. 'Reflect, no; it is an instinct, a feeling, a tone, I believe.'

TO THE HALF-HEARTED

'Whatsoever ye do, do it heartily, as to the Lord.'—COL. III. 23.

NOTE how our text is introduced : it has a very suggestive and illuminative context. 'Servants, obey in all things your masters according to the flesh,' that is verse twenty-two; and then, 'Whatsoever ye do, do it heartily, as to the Lord,' that is verse twenty-three. Now the servants of whom Paul speaks are not domestic servants in our sense. They were slaves, bought for a little money: the property and the chattels of their master. Yet even to slaves, who got no wages and who had no rights, clear and imperious comes the command of God, 'Whatsoever ye do, do it heartily'. I want you to note, too, that this text was never better illustrated than in the life of the man who was inspired to pen it. It is, then, of this whole-heartedness, of this fine concentration or enthusiasm, that I want to speak.

I. True enthusiasm is not a noisy thing. Whenever we think of an enthusiastic crowd, we think of uproar, tumult, wild excitement. And I grant you that in the life of congregated thousands, touched into unity by some great emotion, there seems to be some call for loud expression. But just as there is a sorrow that lies too deep for tears, there is an enthusiasm far too deep for words; and the intense purpose of the whole-hearted man is never noisy. There is a certain silence, as of an under-purpose, wherever a man is working heartily.

II. But if whole-heartedness be not noisy, this at least is true of it; it is one condition of the best success. Could we trace the history of failure—that long, sad story of the world—I think we should find that for one who went to the wall through want of intellect, there were a score who reached that pass through want of heart.

III. But the virtue of whole-heartedness is more than that. It is one of the conditions of the truest happiness. When we are half-hearted, the hours have leaden feet. But when, subduing feeling, we turn with our whole energy of soul to grapple with our duty or with our cross, it is wonderful how under the long shadows we hear unexpectedly a sound of music.

IV. And there can be little question that the more heartily we do our humble duty, the more we feel we are doing it for God. To be whole-hearted is to be facing heavenward. And the great loss of all half-hearted men and women is this, that above the dust, and the stress and strain of life, above the fret and weariness of things, they catch no glimpse of the eternal purpose, nor of the love, nor of the joy of

God. Indeed, if that old saying 'like to like' be true, the men who are half-hearted must be blind. For if there is one demonstrable fact, I think it is this : we are the creatures of a whole-hearted God. It is the pity of all half-hearted men that they are out of harmony with God.

V. Note how the writer lays his hand on the real secret of all the large enthusiasms. He centres his appeal upon a person.—G. H. MORRISON, *Sunrise : Addresses from a City Pulpit*, p. 230.

COL. III. 23.

IN his sixteenth year he [Bismarck] was confirmed by Schleiermacher in the little Trinity Church at Berlin, and one interesting reminder of this event remains. The text then placed in his hands by the great theologian was from the Epistle to the Colossians, 'whatsoever ye do, do it heartily as unto the Lord and not unto men '. There are various evidences that this mandate impressed him. It survived the roystering, the doubts, the cynicism, which at various times eclipsed it, and it is now written in golden letters above his tomb at Friedrichsruh.—A. D. WHITE, *Seven Great Statesmen* (1910), p. 403.

REFERENCES.—III. 23. — R. G. Soans, *Sermons for the Young*, p. 63. J. Clifford, *Christian World Pulpit*, vol. liii. p. 324. H. M. Butler, *Harrow School Sermons*, p. 398. J. M. Neale, *Sermons Preached in Sackville College Chapel*, vol. iv. p. 190. III. 23, 24.—H. P. Liddon, *Sermons Preached on Special Occasions*, p. 193. III. 24.—Spurgeon, *Sermons*, vol. xx. No. 1205. W. H. Evans, *Sermons for the Church's Year*, p. 126. IV. 2.—Spurgeon, *Sermons*, vol. vii. No. 354. John Kelman, *Ephemera Eternitatis*, p. 266. IV. 3.—*Expositor* (6th Series), vol. vii. p. 398 ; *ibid.* vol. x. p. 344.

THE CLAIM OF THE OUTSIDER

'Walk in wisdom towards them that are without, redeeming the time.'—COL. IV. 5.

I. NOTE the distinction here assumed, 'them that are without,' which necessarily implies them that are within. This distinction is assumed throughout the New Testament. (1) The reality of this division. We serve one master : on the best of authority we affirm this. We obey one law ; the higher law of the mind, or the lower of the flesh. We develop one character. Our character is the outcome of one dominant idea, one reigning purpose, one master-passion. We are within or without. (2) The determination of this distinction. Who are the within, who the without? In the New Testament this momentous question is decided by our relation to Christ. To be within is to be in Him. (3) The infinite significance of this distinction. The glory of Christianity must be seen from within. We do not know the glory of a garden by a glimpse through the hedge, the glory of a cathedral by walking about it, and looking up at its dark windows, or the glory of a country by sailing round its shores ; the garden, shrine, or country must be judged from within, and from within must we judge the Lord Jesus and all that pertains to His faith and service. It is from the standpoint of personal trust, sympathy, and experience that we realise

the reality and preciousness of all that is comprehended by the Church of God.

II. The duty of the within to the without. Christians must act judiciously toward all men. To this end —(1) We must maintain high character. 'Walk in wisdom.' That is, when you possess the essential elements of the Christian character be on your guard against technical defects which hide or diminish the full effect of that character. Oh ! let us take care of character. So long as the Church stands out in the beauty of holiness, in acts of love, in ministries of blessing, it attracts, grows, triumphs ; but all is over on the day that there are finer characters out of it than there are in it. (2) We must cherish a gracious spirit. (a) The without may be alienated by rigidness. (b) We alienate by roughness. (c) We repel by hardness. (d) We alienate by gloominess. As Robert Louis Stevenson protests to a correspondent : 'I do not call that by the name of religion which fills a man with bile'. Yet how many of us are habitually austere and sad ! Let us be filled with Christ's spirit and emulate His example.—W. L. WATKINSON, *Themes for Hours of Meditation*, p. 96.

REFERENCES.—IV. 5.—H. Woodcock, *Sermon Outlines* (1st Series), p. 261. *Expositor* (6th Series), vol. viii. p. 421. IV. 7-9.—*Ibid.* vol. iii. p. 235. I. 9.—R. W. Riley, *A Year's Sermons*, vol. iii. p. 305. IV. 10.—*Expositor* (4th Series), vol. iii. p. 229 ; *ibid.* (5th Series), vol. vi. p. 81 ; *ibid.* vol. x. p. 319. IV. 2.—T. Arnold, *Sermons*, vol. iii. p. 226. IV. 13. —*Expositor* (5th Series), vol. ix. p. 437 ; *ibid.* (6th Series), vol. ix. p. 22.

ST. LUKE THE EVANGELIST

(For St. Luke's Day)

'Luke, the beloved physician.'—COL. IV. 14.

ST. LUKE is said to have been born at Antioch ; the probability, therefore, is that he was, as Jerome says, a Syrian, and thus a Gentile. If so, then he was a proselyte to the Jewish religion. According to his Gospel and the Acts, he was well acquainted with Jewish rites, customs, opinions, and prejudices. The date of his conversion to Christianity is unknown ; but of his conversion, as a blessed reality, there is not the shadow of a doubt. Epiphanius and others have supposed him to have been one of the Seventy commissioned by our Lord. It has been said that ultimately he suffered martyrdom when eighty-four years of age.

I. He is described in the text as 'the beloved physician,' and the tradition that he was a skilful painter is due probably to a confusion of names, for there was an early Greek painter of the same name. As a physician he was of essential service to St. Paul, not only in his own personal needs, but in his missionary enterprises, as the healing art was then, as it is now, of great advantage to the furtherance of the Gospel among the heathen. Through attending to the body the modern medical missionary may reach the soul, and by saving the one may, under the Divine blessing, save the other.

II. St. Paul and he were great friends, as the text

clearly shows. The appellation of 'the beloved physician' signifies that St. Luke, apart from his professional services, possessed certain amiable and holy characteristics which had won St. Paul's admiration and affection. He loved his physician ; and his physician reciprocated his love. 'Only Luke is with me,' he says. There is a tone of deep sadness in this avowal, but it magnifies the friendship of both of them.

III. St. Luke was evidently a well-educated man. His learning is proved by his Gospel to have been great ; for it stands out from the others in its evidences of a higher education, its peculiar beauty and pathos, its didactic style and graphic descriptiveness. Universality is its predominant feature. The author presents Jesus not only as the Messiah of Israel and the Incarnate Son of God, but as the Divine Son of Man ; and he principally records those sayings and deeds of our Lord by which the Divine mercy was shown to the Gentile world. The Acts of the Apostles, which St. Luke also wrote, is a supplementary composition. It begins where the Gospel ends, so that united, the two form one history anent the life of Christ on earth, and the establishment of His Church in the world. In no part of the Bible have we such models of preaching, such tender, eloquent, and powerful appeals to the understanding and the heart.

LUKE, THE BELOVED PHYSICIAN
(*For St. Luke's Day*)
COL. IV. 14.

I. IT is as the author of the Gospel that the Church is most interested in St. Luke. That book is one of the four golden columns on which rests the Christian history. It is one of the four golden trumpets which have sent forth the summons of Christ to the sons of men. It has, moreover, its own peculiar character. It was not so Jewish as the others ; there is a peculiar human breadth and richness in it. It gives the fullest account of our Lord's Nativity, and relates the parable of the 'Prodigal Son'. But it is not only as the writer of the Gospel that we know St. Luke. He was also the author of 'The Acts of the Apostles,' and was the fellow-labourer of St. Paul, who is the central figure of the larger portion of the book. St. Paul, in his Epistles, thrice mentions him, and twice he styles him 'the beloved physician'. That is almost all. By early tradition, and from some incidental indications, we gather that Lucanus was a Gentile and a citizen of Antioch, that he was a physician by profession, that he travelled with St. Paul, and that before he died he wrote, at St. Paul's suggestion, the Gospel which bears his name. And yet there is something more. It seems clear that St. Luke's character as a physician remained an influential fact, even after he became a missionary. His style, the events of our Lord's life which he selects for his narration, bear marks of the physician's habits of thought and speech. St. Paul's allusion to him as 'the beloved physician,' and the fact that Luke appears to have joined Paul on several occasions when that Apostle's strength broke down under one of those recurrent attacks of prostration, all seem to imply that he continued to practise the art of healing, and that it was as a physician also that he travelled with St. Paul from place to place. In St. Luke, then, we see, what since his time has been the natural and normal type of Christian life, the inspiration by a new spiritual power of an earthly vocation, so that it continued to be exercised, and, moreover, fulfilled its true ideal. This suggests certain thoughts with reference to—

II. The general relation of the Christian life to men's occupations and professions.

The disposition to find the simplicity of motive under the variety of action is familiar enough now, and it is right in its aim. The world of human action, like the world of Nature, is a scene of endless superficial variety which, by and by, we learn to gather into unity under some common force, under the power of some central inspiration. To the shallow observer each profession and calling is a life by itself; it will have its own thoughts, standards, principles, and passions ; nothing in common with others. But that is only the superficial aspect. Very soon he who lives begins to discover some deeper forces working underneath, and giving a real unity to all this seemingly incoherent life. How will it be, then, if you can reach one point which is the genuine centre of the whole mass—one supreme force, of which they are all only modifications and manifestations, issuing from the very heart of all—and this one central fountain of force, the soul's love for God as its Father ; so that everything which a man had a right to do at all upon earth might be ideally done as an expression of this central force—the love of man for God ? Consider what effects the warm fire of the love of God must have upon the life, in certain arts and professions, of which the world must necessarily be full. It must—

(1) Purify all the professions. It melts away the dross and leaves the gold. It makes the man purely the thing he means to be, without any admixture of baseness or corruption.

(2) It makes the professions to be no longer means of separation but of sympathy and union between men. If you and I feel always beating through our diverse callings and methods of activity the common purpose of the love of God, then the harder we work in different ways the more our lives are one.

(3) It will sanctify the secular work of your life. No thoughtful man has failed to feel that the division of labour represented by the many and various occupations of life has its dangers—corruption, narrowness, loss of human sympathy, and such like. Where is the safeguard against these things ? Not by deserting your profession, but by deepening it ; by seeking a new life under it ; by praying for, and never resting until you find regeneration, the new life lived by the faith of the Son of God. So only can your life of trade, or art, or profession be redeemed ; so only can it become for you and for the world a blessed thing.

This is the lesson taught us by the lives and comradeship of St. Paul and St. Luke. We see the figures of Paul and Luke walking together as ministers of Christ—theology and medicine labouring in harmony for the redemption of man, for the saving of body, soul, and spirit—and the picture is very sacred and impressive. Thus may these two professions, and every other 'calling' in life, in fellowship with religion, working together as if they were one, grow to be more and more a worthy channel through which the helpfulness of God may flow forth to the neediness of man.—The late BISHOP PHILLIPS BROOKS, *The Light of the World.*

REFERENCES.—IV. 14.—W. G. Horder, *Christian World Pulpit*, vol. xlii. p. 245. F. D. Maurice, *Sermons*, vol. ii. p. 270. S. Baring-Gould, *Village Preaching for Saints' Days*, p. 190. IV. 15.—*Expositor* (6th Series), vol. v. p. 95. IV. 17.—I. E. Page, *Preacher's Magazine*, vol. xviii. p. 308. J. Bunting, *Sermons*, vol. ii. p. 368. IV. 18.—*Expositor* (5th Series), vol. x. p. 199.

THE FIRST EPISTLE TO THE THESSALONIANS

I THESSALONIANS

REFERENCES.—I.—*Expositor* (4th Series), vol. ii. p. 256. I. 1-5.—C. Perren, *Revival Sermons in Outline*, p. 336. I. 2. —*Expositor* (5th Series), vol. vi. p. 87 ; *ibid.* vol. viii. p. 165. I. 2-4.—M. Gardner, *Christian World Pulpit*, vol. lxxii. p. 35.

THREE GREAT CHRISTIAN GRACES

'Your work of faith, and labour of love, and patience of hope in our Lord Jesus Christ.'—1 THESS. I. 3.

NOTICE the characteristics which the Apostle attached to these three graces when he says practically that faith is a *work*, love is a *labour*, hope an *enduring patience*.

I. First of all with regard to work as a characteristic feature of faith. In the work of salvation there are two parties concerned—God and man, Giver and receiver, a Saviour and saved. (1) Faith has work as its distinctive feature, because it is not solely belief, not an abstract proposition of truth, but a personal trust in a living person. (2) Work must be the characteristic feature of all true faith, inasmuch as from its very nature it involves a hearty compliance with the will of Him who is the object of it.

II. What holds true of the great Christian grace of faith holds equally true of love. ' Your labour of love,' says the Apostle—that is, your love of which labour is the characteristic feature, although it is more than a labour. This love has (1) Christ for its object, and (2) our fellow-men. The love of man for man must be rooted in the love of man for God first.

III. Lastly, says the Apostle, 'Your patience of hope in our Lord Jesus Christ'. In the grammatical Greek it means that Christ is the great object of the Christian's hope. The grand characteristic of this hope is here said to be patience. The word in Greek is very strong—implying bravery, manliness, facing dangers, the discharge of difficult and painful duties with a calm mind ; bearing up under trial and discouragements ; constancy in faith under the most adverse circumstances.—J. MACGREGOR, *Scottish Review*, vol. IV. p. 105.

REFERENCES. — I. 3. — A. Maclaren, *Expositions of Holy Scripture—Thessalonians*, p. 155. *Expositor* (4th Series), vol. ii. p. 258. I. 4.—*Ibid.* vol. vii. p. 12 ; *ibid.* (7th Series), vol. v. p. 58. I. 4-6.—Spurgeon, *Sermons*, vol. li. No. 2920.

POWER MANIFESTED

'Our Gospel came not unto you in word only, but also in power.'—1 THESS. I. 5.

THE Gospel can come to members of the Church in word only.

I. To the Church at Thessalonica it came in.—
(a) *Power*—*i.e.* with a compelling and urging force ;
(b) *The Holy Ghost*—*i.e.* the hearts were receptive and willing to receive Him ;
(c) *With much assurance*—much trust, confidence, and faith.

II. Power Manifested.
(a) *They became followers* (ver. 6), Greek mimics or imitators of the Lord.
(b) *Ensamples* (ver. 7)—*i.e.* bearing the impression of the Lord. *Ill.*—The die used in the Royal Mint for stamping the coins and medals leaves an impression. The Gospel, when received in power, causes all our actions and words to bear the impression of Christ.
(c) *Sounded out the word* (ver. 8), or as Greek echoed forth. As they received, so they gave forth.
(d) *Turned from idols* (ver. 9) to serve the living God. Christian England is full of idolatry. Here is one of the results when the Gospel comes in power.

REFERENCES.—I. 5.—Spurgeon, *Sermons*, vol. xi. No. 648. *Expositor* (6th Series), vol. iii. p. 415 ; *ibid.* vol. xi. p. 46. I. 6, 7.—*Ibid.* (4th Series), vol. ii. p. 262. I. 7.—*Ibid.* (5th Series), vol. vi. p. 382. I. 8.—Spurgeon, *Sermons*, vol. xxxv. No. 2076. A. Maclaren, *Expositions of Holy Scripture—Thessalonians*, p. 164. I. 9.—*Expositor* (4th Series), vol. ii. p. 257. I. 9, 10.—Spurgeon, *Sermons*, vol. xxx. No. 1806. *Expositor* (4th Series), vol. i. p. 23 ; *ibid.* vol. ii. pp. 258, 259 ; *ibid.* vol. vii. p. 15 ; *ibid.* vol. x. p. 98. I. 10.—*Ibid.* (5th Series), vol. viii. p. 146 ; *ibid.* vol. ix. p. 94. I. 14, 15. —*Ibid.* vol. iv. p. 369. II. 2.—John Watson, *Christian World Pulpit*, vol. xlvi. p. 228. II. 2-9.—*Expositor* (4th Series), vol. vii. p. 14. II. 3.—*Ibid.* (6th Series), vol. xi. p. 363. II. 6.—*Ibid.* vol. viii. p. 74. II. 6, 9.—*Ibid.* (5th Series), vol. x. p. 196. II. 7.—*Ibid.* (7th Series), vol. vi. p. 226. II. 11, 12.—H. W. Webb-Peploe, *The Record*, vol. xxvii. p. 798. II. 12.—A. Maclaren, *Expositions of Holy Scripture — Thessalonians*, p. 170. II. 13. — W. Sanday, *Christian World Pulpit*, vol. lii. p. 193. *Expositor* (5th Series), vol. viii. p. 404. II. 13, 14.—Spurgeon, *Sermons*, vol. xxxiii. No. 1979. II. 15.—*Expositor* (5th Series), vol. x. p. 354. II. 16.—*Ibid.* (4th Series), vol. i. p. 23 ; *ibid.* (6th Series), vol. xii. p. 108 ; *ibid.* (7th Series), vol. vi. p. 486.

ORPHANED FOR AN HOUR

' Taken from you for a short time in presence, not in heart.'— 1 THESS. II. 17.

ONLY a great heart could have said this. Such glowing sentences are amongst the most vivid and positive evidences of inspiration. Paul was a great father mother, a great brother-sister, a woman and a man There is nothing like the Pauline affection ; there is so much reason under it, around it, above it; it is so complete and cogent and intense in logic; it is a great flower whose roots go down to the rock. Paul loved the society of the believing Church; he was at home amongst his own folks; they knew one another, and when they did not speak they could translate the very silence into eloquence.

I. 'Being taken from you:' literally, Being orphaned. In the English language we limit the word orphan to a certain set of circumstances; we say that a child who has lost father or mother is in that degree an orphan. In the Greek language there was more licence of application of the term; in that language men spoke of themselves as being orphaned when they were bereaved of their children; not only were the children orphans, but the bereaved parents were orphans; thus the eloquence and the music of this glorious declaration. 'Being orphaned from you,' feeling the loneliness and the cold and the desolation and the miserableness of being away from you. That is a nobler use of the term: blessed are they who, feeling the pain of orphanage, have hope that pain may be taken away. 'Being orphaned from you for a short time': literally, for one little hour; sixty minutes and no more: a vanishing orphanage, a desolation that is being consumed by its own agony. 'Being orphaned from you for an hour in presence:' literally, in face, that is all; it is only the face that is wanting, and that not wholly wanting, for there is a vision in the air, an outline on the background of the darkness. Now we seem to enter into the very sanctuary of the Apostle's meaning: 'Brethren, being orphaned from you for the season of a little transient hour, in face, not in heart, we endeavoured the more abundantly to see your face with great desire'. After all, the face may be part of the soul; do not despise the visible presence. No two visible presences are exactly alike; one face cannot take the place of another; but, after all, it is the face and not the soul, and the face that owes everything to the soul behind it. Ah me! there are faces behind whose formal beauty there is no throbbing and surgent soul.

II. A most tender expression is this of the text, 'taken from you'; that is a common experience; 'not in heart,' that is a special experience. They are separated who have no heart-fellowship. Proximity is not brotherhood; the man sitting next you is separated from you maybe by the diameter of the universe; to be near is not necessarily to be identical. Separation of hearts; that is woe; where there is no kinship in love; that is orphanage that endures through all the hours, through all the duration of eternity.

III. Is there any experience in the life of Christ kindred to the experience of the text? I think the experience of the Master and the experience of the disciple are often identical, each being taken in its own degree. 'Yet a little while, and ye shall not see Me.' But we can always see the soul we have loved? True, but not the face, which is the outward and visible symbol of that soul. 'A little while ye shall not see Me; and again a little while, being orphaned from you for one short hour, and ye shall see Me'—the other face, the inner face, the vision face. Our friends come back to us in vision. They do not need the face of flesh; that was rough and temporary, exposed to all the cruelty of the wind and storm and all the plague of insidious disease; but, having shuffled off the mortal and the visible, they come back with new life and a new visibleness. Has the soul no eyes? are eyes only instruments on which the optician operates? is there no vision of the heart, no sight of the soul, no perception of the immortality that throbs in every human heart? 'A little while, and ye shall not see Me, and again a little while and ye shall see Me'—from another point of view, in another light; and you will pass from the body to the spirit, away from the body to the Holy Spirit. That is the mystery of Providence, that is the wonderful part of our spiritual education, so that loss may be gain, and having lost you may possess for ever in an imperishable relation, almost in an imperishable form: for there is a spiritual body and there is a natural body; when this corruptible shall have put on incorruption, and the heavens shall be alive with new presences, then shall be brought to pass the saying that is written, Death is swallowed up in victory! We must attain to this higher fellowship, to this clearer vision, to this surer realisation of the things which God intended to remain.

REFERENCES.—II. 17.—*Expositor* (5th Series), vol. i. p. 223. II. 18.—Spurgeon, *Sermons*, vol. xi. No. 657. II. 19.—*Expositor* (4th Series), vol. x. p. 99. III. 2.—*Expositor* (5th Series), vol. x. p. 158. III. 8.—Spurgeon, *Sermons*, vol. xxx. No. 1758. III. 11.—T. H. Ball, *Persuasions*, p. 272. III. 11-13.—*Expositor* (4th Series), vol. ii. p. 258. III. 12.—*Ibid.* (5th Series), vol. x. p. 324. III. 12, 13.—J. G. Greenhough, *Christian World Pulpit*, vol. li. p. 88. IV. 1.—R. Allen, *The Words of Christ*, p. 216. J. Keble, *Sermons for Lent to Passion-tide*, p. 127.

THE TRUE END OF MAN

'This is the will of God, even your sanctification.'—1 THESS. IV. 3.

THE will of God called all things into being, and conserves all things in existence by its power. And the message to our fainting souls to-day, is that this Almighty will is on our side in the great battle with evil; that this will is concerned in our salvation.

I. Before we proceed to a further consideration of the text, there are two words in it which we must examine carefully. The words 'will' and 'sanctification'. To take the latter first, what precisely is meant by our sanctification? If we open our Bibles we shall find that it is applied both to things and persons. In the very second chapter of Genesis we have the word applied to the seventh day. 'And God blessed the seventh day, and sanctified it.' We find our Lord saying of Himself, 'For their sakes I sanctify Myself'. This is the will of God, that you should be separated from the world; that instead of having the world as your master and your end, you should be consecrated to God, having Him for your

Lord, belonging to Him, being children of God, walking as children of light. The other word which we must notice is the word 'will'. God *wills* all men to be saved. God wills your salvation, and in that will provides for each one *sufficient* grace to enable him to attain salvation.

II. 'This is the will of God, even your sanctification.' From this it follows that God's providence will order the circumstances of our life, with an end to our sanctification. (1) By supplying us with opportunities of grace sufficient to enable us to work out our salvation. God gives all that we need. (2) By opportunities of discipline. Consider some of the opportunities of discipline which come to us by God's will, for the purpose of sanctifying us. (a) The discipline of pain. How differently pain works in souls. (b) The discipline of sorrow. What opposite results sorrow produces in different souls! (c) The discipline of temptation. (d) The discipline of work.

III. 'This is the will of God, even your sanctification.' What courage this thought arouses in the fainting soul! I have on my side the mightiest force, the force which called this world into being. Though all things and men and the powers of evil were against me, if God were on my side I need not fear what they can do unto me.—A. G. MORTIMER, *Lenten Preaching*, p. 14.

REFERENCES.—IV. 3.—H. Drummond, *The Ideal Life*, p. 279. R. W. Church, *Village Sermons* (2nd Series), p. 53. C. D. Bell, *The Saintly Calling*, p. 23. W. H. Evans, *Sermons for the Church's Year*, p. 252. C. Gutch, *Sermons*, p. 1. F. D. Maurice, *Sermons*, vol. i. p. 101. IV. 7.—H. W. Webb-Peploe, *The Record*, vol. xxvii. p. 770. IV. 8.—E. W. Attwood, *Sermons for Clergy and Laity*, p. 107. IV. 9-18.—A. Maclaren, *Expositions of Holy Scripture—Thessalonians*, p. 183. IV. 10.—F. W. Farrar, *Sin and its Conquerors*, p. 74. IV. 10-12.—*Expositor* (4th Series), vol. ii. p. 202.

RELIGION IN BUSINESS

'Study to be quiet, and to do your own business, and to work with your hands.'—1 THESS. IV. 11.

IT is no uncommon thing to hear business men declare that they have no time to attend to religion. But such a statement reveals a complete ignorance of the very nature of religion, and especially of the peculiar traits which distinguish the Christian religion. Too busy with life to attend to the claims of religion! That is like the famous complaint of one who could not see the forest for the trees, or of that other who could not see London for the houses. The trees are the forest. The houses are London. This active, eager, business life is your religion. Too busy to be religious! God's answer would be, 'If you cannot be religious when you are busy, how could you be if you were at leisure? If you cannot make bricks of clay, how could you make them of straw?' It is a new note that is struck in the New Testament, where business, the buying and selling, the work by which the daily bread is earned, is enjoined as the means of realising the kingdom of heaven. The amazing change seems to be produced almost in-

sensibly by the mere facts of the Incarnation. And because this was the distinctive element of the Gospel at its inception, it was also the new discovery of the Reformers at the beginning of the sixteenth century.

I. Your handicraft, or business, or profession, is before all things the service which you have to render to God, the means by which your religion is to be exercised. The biographer of Michelangelo says, in speaking of his designs: 'Incomplete as they are, they reveal Michelangelo's loftiest dreams and purest visions . . . there is an air of meditation and of rapt devotion. The drawings for the Passion might be called the prayers and pious thoughts of the stern Master.' Every lawful and honest calling is a service rendered to the community and to Christ. I imagine no one can be in doubt whether a calling is of this character or not. If it is, whether making or distributing, whether feeding or clothing, whether instructing or amusing or recreating, you may do it as the agent of Christ.

II. There is then no distinction between our religion and our daily business. The one is the Spirit, the other is the body which the Spirit is to animate. I will hazard one suggestion on the mode of breathing the Spirit into the body. See that you begin the busy day by definitely commending it to Christ, and committing yourself to His care and direction. But you say, The very nature of my employment is contrary to my conscience. I cannot ask God's blessing on the things I have to do. But if you cannot ask God's blessing on your business, you can ask Him to deliver you from it. Have faith in God. It is a question of a right *will* and of a simple faith. Tennyson beautifully described a living poet as 'a reed through which all things blow into music'. You, as a Christian, in the world, busy with its duties and even to all appearance submerged beneath its concerns, become 'a reed through which all things blow into religion'.—R. F. HORTON, *Brief Sermons for Busy Men*, p. 1.

THE AMBITION OF QUIETNESS

1 THESS. IV. 11.

The Church at Thessalonica, to which Paul wrote the letter, was in an unsettled and distracted state. The Gospel had come to it in such reality that it was tempted to be untrue to duty. Paul was not speaking to philosophic students. He was speaking to handicraftsmen, many of them weavers. And he said: 'Make it your ambition to be quiet, and to do your own work as we commanded you, that you may walk honourably towards them who are without'.

I. Now the truth which unites the clauses of our text is that quietness is needed for true work. Study to be quiet and to do your business; you will never do the one without the other. In a measure that is true of outward quiet, at least when we reach the higher kinds of labour. Every man who is earnest about the highest work makes it his ambition to be quiet. Of course there is a certain type of man that is largely impervious to outward tumult. Mr. Gladstone could read and write in Downing Street in total oblivion of the marching of the Horse Guards. But that does not mean that he did not require quietude ; it means that he could command an inward quietude, and that he was master of such concentration as visits most of us only in rare moments.

II. But the words of our text have a far deeper meaning than can ever be exhausted by quietness of circumstances. They tell us that the best work is never possible unless there be a quietness of the heart. It is one of the legends of our Saviour's childhood that in Joseph's workshop He was a perfect worker. It is only a legend, and yet, like every legend, it leans for its secret of beauty on a truth, and the truth is that here was perfect peace, and perfect peace produced the perfect work. (1) Think, for example, of the disquiet of despondency ; does not that tangle all that we put our hand to? (2) The same is true of the unrest of the passions ; work becomes drudgery in their disquiet. (3) Again, the need of inward quiet for toil is seen in the working of an uneasy conscience. There is not a thing you do, not a task or duty you can set your hand to, which is not adversely and evilly affected if at the back of all there be an unquiet conscience. Study to be quiet, then, and do your business. Make it your ambition to have the rest of Christ.—G. H. MORRISON, *The Wings of the Morning*, p. 310.

ASLEEP IN JESUS

(*For All Saints' Day*)

'But I would not have you to be ignorant, brethren, concerning them which are asleep, that ye sorrow not, even as others which have no hope.'—1 THESS. iv. 13.

I. The Communion of Saints.—All Saints' Day is a day on which we show whether those words that some of us say every day have any meaning at all. 'I believe in the Communion of Saints.' I cannot conceive that anyone in this Church is not interested in the worship, the praise, and the prayer that the Church offers on All Saints' Day, because there is probably not one of us who has not somebody beyond the veil, some one in Paradise, some one we strive, though but with a feeble longing, to get into closer communion with, some we have 'loved long since and lost awhile'. Surely there is no person with any feeling of sympathy in his or her soul who can think at all about All Saints' Day and be as if he or she had not thought.

II. Life After Death.—Where is the soul ? Where shall I go when I die ? I know I shall not merely sleep. I have heard the text ' where the tree falls there shall it lie,' but God has spoken louder than that : He has said He is not the God of the dead, but of the living. And my Lord and Master, when He came down to earth to reveal my Father's mind to me, knew I should want to know something of the life after death. He did not tell me much, but He told that little very clearly. You remember the parable of Dives and Lazarus, you remember the

conversation which Jesus represented as taking place between two men. There is not only a conversation, which of course means life, but there is an appeal to memory of the things in this world. And then we know that our Lord did not go to heaven on His death, ' but to preach to the spirits in prison '—in a place of safe keeping. You do not preach to people who are incapable of hearing—who are asleep. So you see our Lord would have us clearly understand that those loved ones whom we think of individually and collectively on All Saints' Day are alive in the full sense of the word.

III. In God's Safe Keeping.—How then shall we deal with those who are dead ? You know that a family never gets smaller. It has some of its members behind the veil, but all are to be joined together again. Scripture does not reveal very much, but we have very sound ground to go on. Surely we may understand this : the very word life means progress, development in one direction or another. Those in Paradise gain a clearer knowledge, a closer communion with God. I love to think—and my Lord has given me a right to think it—that if I strive after Him here, hindered by all that is summed up in the word ' flesh,' I shall gain Him more closely there. We do not know what the saints are doing, we know nothing about Paradise, but we know that God has them in safe keeping. And one day we hope to join them, and what are you and I doing to prepare for the fuller life beyond the veil ?

"THEM THAT SLEEP IN HIM"

1 THESSALONIANS iv. 13 is quoted in these words from the last Collect in the Burial Service : ' Who also hath taught us, by His holy Apostle St. Paul, not to be sorry, as men without hope, for them that sleep in Him '.

J. H. NEWMAN writes :—

' There are, who have not the comfort of a peaceful burial. They die in battle, or on the sea, or in strange lands, or, as the early believers, under the hands of persecutors. Horrible tortures, or the mouths of wild beasts, have ere now dishonoured the sacred bodies of those who had fed upon Christ ; and diseases corrupt them still. This is Satan's work, the expiring efforts of his fury, after his overthrow by Christ. Still, as far as we can, *we* repair these insults of our Enemy, and tend honourably and piously those tabernacles in which Christ has dwelt. And in this view, what a venerable and fearful place is a Church, in and around which the dead are deposited ! Truly it is chiefly sacred, as being the spot where God has for ages manifested Himself to His servants ; but add to this the thought, that it is the actual resting-place of those very servants, through successive times, who still live unto Him. The dust around us will one day become animate. We may ourselves be dead long before, and not see it. We ourselves may elsewhere be buried, and, should it be our exceeding blessedness to rise to life eternal, we may rise in other places, far in the east or west. But, as God's word is sure, what is sown is raised; the earth to earth, ashes to ashes, dust to dust, shall become glory to glory, and life to the living God, and a true incorruptible image of the spirit made perfect. Here the saints sleep, here they shall rise. A great sight will a Christian country then be, if earth remains what it is; when holy places pour out the worshippers who have for generations kept vigil therein, waiting through the long night for the bright coming of Christ! And if this be so, what pious composed thoughts should be ours when we enter churches! God indeed is everywhere, and His angels go to and fro; yet can they be more worthily employed in their condescending care of man, than where good men sleep?'—*Sermon on the Resurrection of the Body.*

References.—IV. 13.—C. D. Bell, *The Name Above Every Name*, p. 220. *Expositor* (4th Series), vol. x. p. 304. IV. 13, 14.—T. H. Ball, *Persuasions*, p. 156. IV. 13-17.—*Expositor* (7th Series), vol. v. p. 148.

SLEEPING THROUGH JESUS

'. . . them also which sleep in Jesus.'—1 Thess. iv. 14.

Accurately rendered the words run, 'them which sleep *through* Jesus'. There are two thoughts that I wish to dwell upon as suggested by these words.

I. The Softened Aspect of Death, and of the State of the Christian Dead.—It is to Jesus primarily that the New Testament writers owe their use of this gracious emblem of sleep. But Jesus was not the originator of the expression. You find it in the Old Testament, where the Prophet Daniel, speaking of the end of the days and the bodily resurrection, designates those who share in it as 'them that sleep in the dust of the earth'. And the Old Testament was not the sole origin of the phrase. Many an inscription of Greek and Roman date speaks of death under this figure: but almost always it is with the added, deepened note of despair, that it is a sleep which knows no waking, but lasts through eternal night. Now, the Christian thought associated with this emblem is the precise opposite of the pagan one. It is profoundly significant that throughout the whole of the New Testament the plain, naked word 'death' is usually applied, not to the physical fact which we ordinarily designate by the name, but to the grim thing of which that physical fact is only the emblem and the parable—*viz*, the true death which lies in the separation of the soul from God; whilst predominantly the New Testament usage calls the physical fact by some other gentler form of expression, because the gentleness has passed over the thing to be designated. What, then, does this metaphor say to us? (1) It speaks first of rest. But let us remember that this repose, deep and blessed as it is, is not, as some would say, the repose of unconsciousness. However limited and imperfect may be the present connection of the disembodied dead, who sleep in Christ, with eternal things, they

know themselves, they know their home and their Companion, and they know the blessedness in which they are lapped. (2) But another thought which is suggested by this emblem is most certainly the idea of awaking. The pagans said, as indeed one of their poets has it: 'Suns can sink and return, but for us, when our brief light sinks, there is but one perpetual night of slumber'. The Christian idea of death is that it is transitory as a sleep in the morning, and sure to end. As St. Augustine says somewhere: 'Wherefore are they called sleepers, but because in the day of the Lord they will be re-awakened'.

II. Note the Ground of this Softened Aspect.—They 'sleep through Him'. In order to grasp the full meaning of such words as these of the Apostle, we must draw a broad distinction between the physical fact of the ending of corporeal life, and the mental condition which is associated with it by us. What we call death is a complex thing—a bodily phenomenon *plus* conscience, the sense of sin, the certainty of retribution in the dim beyond. The mere physical fact is a trifle. Jesus Christ has abolished death, leaving the mere shell, but taking all the substance out of it. It has become a different thing to men, because in that death of His He has exhausted the bitterness, and has made it possible that we should pass into the shadow, and not fear either conscience or sin or judgment.—A. Maclaren, *Triumphant Certainties*, p. 232.

References.—IV. 14.—*Expositor* (4th Series), vol. v. p. 137; *ibid.* (5th Series), vol. iv. p. 362. A. Maclaren, *Expositions of Holy Scripture—Thessalonians*, p. 190. IV. 15.—*Ibid.* (4th Series), vol. x. pp. 105, 449; *ibid.* (6th Series), vol. x. p. 153. IV. 16.—Spurgeon, *Sermons*, vol. xxxii. No. 1900. *Expositor* (4th Series), vol. x. p. 99; *ibid.* (6th Series), vol. x. p. 184. IV. 16, 17.—J. M. Whiton, *Beyond the Shadow*, p. 195.

A FUNERAL SERVICE

'So shall we ever be with the Lord.'—1 Thess. iv. 17.

These words come to us as words of comfort, words of hope, in our hours of bereavement. They emphasise one of the great lessons taught us by the Resurrection, that because Christ rose from the dead the future of the believer is assured. We are often puzzled about the state of our blessed dead, but God's Holy Word tells us all we need to know about them. No doubt it leaves much to be revealed at that great day when all secrets shall be disclosed; but the Apostle tells us clearly (verses 13 and 14) that the soul which has passed away in the faith of Christ is with Jesus. 'Them also which sleep in Jesus' is the phrase used, and there could not be a more beautiful description of the faithful departed. Truly St. Paul had ground for rebuking unseemly grief. *We* are not to sorrow as those who have no hope; *we* have a sure and certain hope, and it is fixed upon the risen Saviour. It was this great doctrine of Jesus and the Resurrection that St. Paul first preached to the Thessalonians (Acts xvii. 3);

and now, when he is writing to them calling them to sanctification, he reminds them again that it is Jesus and the Resurrection which is their one hope for this world, the world to come, and through all eternity.

Let us learn some practical lessons for our own comfort from these words of the Apostle.

I. **The Chief Joy of Heaven.**—To us the chief joy of heaven will be that we shall be in the presence of Jesus. 'Father, I will that they also, whom Thou hast given Me, be with Me where I am' (John XVII. 24). To be with Christ, that is the deepest aspiration of the Christian heart.

And when we think of that supreme joy of heaven we cannot wish our friend back again in this troublesome world. We cannot doubt but that he has already seen the King in His beauty.

II. **The Union of Christ and the Believer.**—Do not these words of St. Paul to the Thessalonians emphasise the closeness of the union which exists between Christ and the believer? 'In Jesus' (ver. 14), 'In Christ' (ver. 16)—could anything be closer? This beautiful idea sends us back to the words of the Master Himself. 'I go to prepare a place for you. . . . I will come again and receive you unto Myself, that where I am, there ye may be also.' No separation; absolute identity; and, 'for ever with the Lord'. And as the believer is, and will be, one with Christ, so in that great Resurrection Day shall we be one with each other. That will be the great reunion—

> Father, sister, child, and mother
> Meet once more.

We are looking forward to that day. At every Eucharist when we thank God for His servants departed this life in His faith and fear, we pray that 'with them we may be partakers of the heavenly Kingdom'.

III. **Do we find Comfort in these Words?**—St. Paul, having spoken to the Thessalonians of this glorious hope, bade them 'comfort one another with these words'. Do they bring comfort to us? They may heal the sorrow caused by the departure of our loved one, but is it a source of comfort to *us* to know that the chief joy of heaven is the presence of Jesus?

REFERENCES.—IV. 17.—Spurgeon, *Sermons*, vol. xxiii. No. 1374. *Expositor* (4th Series), vol. iv. p. 33. IV. 18.—*Ibid.* (5th Series), vol. i. p. 451. V. 1-8.—*Ibid.* vol. ii. p. 73. V. 2.—*Ibid.* (5th Series), vol. v. p. 243; *ibid.* (6th Series), vol. xii. p. 102. V. 3.—*Ibid.* vol. ii. p. 259.

I THESS. V. 4.

SOME injustice has been done to the Christian creed of immortality as an influence in determining men's conduct. Paul preached the imminent advent of Christ and besought his disciples therefore to watch, and we ask ourselves what is the moral value to us of such an admonition. But surely if we are to have any reasons for being virtuous, this is as good as any

other. It is just as respectable to believe that we ought to abstain from iniquity because Christ is at hand, and we expect to meet Him, as to abstain from it because by our abstention we shall be healthier or more prosperous. Paul had a dream—an absurd dream, let us call it—of an immediate millennium, and of the return of his Master surrounded with Divine splendour, judging mankind, and adjusting the balance between good and evil. It was a baseless dream, and the enlightened may call it ridiculous. It is anything but that, it is the very opposite of that. Putting aside its temporary mode of expression, it is the hope and the prophecy of all noble hearts, a sign of their inability to concur in the present condition of things.—MARK RUTHERFORD, *The Deliverance*, pp. 59, 60.

REFERENCES.—V. 4.—*Expositor* (5th Series), vol. ix. p. 304. V. 5.—L. De Beaumont Klein, *Christian World Pulpit*, vol. liii. p. 379. V. 6.—C. S. Horne, *The Soul's Awakening*, p. 143. Spurgeon, *Sermons*, vol. ii. No. 64; vol. iii. No. 163, and vol. xvii. No. 1022. *Expositor* (6th Series), vol. iv. p. 190.

'Putting on the breastplate (or rather, the coat-of-mail) of faith and love.'—I THESS. v. 8.

FAITH and love are the coat-of-mail. They cannot be protected by anything external to themselves. Trust in God is its own defence in an age of doubt and temptation. Love to men carries with it an invincible power which is of itself sufficient to overcome harshness and cynicism. All that faith and love require is to be *put on*. Their vitality depends upon their exercise. If worn daily, they will protect the believing man against indifference to the claims of God and men; they will produce a sensitiveness to God and an alertness to the needs of others which safeguard the soul against the deadly wounds of apathy. To exercise a vigilant faith in God, to practise consideration, unselfish help, and self-sacrifice, these, Paul would suggest, are the one safe attitude for a Christian to assume. Occupied with these, he cannot be surprised or overthrown.

Faith is, in fact, its own security, if it is a living faith. It may and does gain support from the fellowship of those who are like-minded. That is one reason why Paul combines here as elsewhere *faith and love*. But this brotherhood or fellowship is in its turn an expression of vital faith in God, so that in the last resort it holds true that 'faith is not to be saved by anything that would supersede faith, but only by its faithfulness' (T. H. Green) to the tasks which God reveals to its inner vision. Paul freely recognises the immense help afforded to Christian faith and love by reliable historical tradition, organisation, and definite statements. But he proposes no coat-of-mail *for* faith. He has absolute confidence in its inherent power of maintaining itself, furnishing its own evidence, and supplying its own vital energy. JAMES MOFFATT.

REFERENCES.—V. 8.—*Expositor* (7th Series), vol. v. p. 565. A. Maclaren, *Expositions of Holy Scripture—Thessalonians*, p. 198. V. 8-10.—*Ibid.* (4th Series) vol. ii. p. 257.

V. 9, 10.—N. H. Marshall, *Christian World Pulpit*, vol. lxxiii. p. 85. V. 10.—A. Maclaren, *Expositions of Holy Scripture—Thessalonians*, p. 210. V. 11.—*Ibid.* p. 220. V. 12.—*Expositor* (6th Series), vol. i. p. 207. V. 12, 13.—F. C. Davies, *The Record*, vol. xxvii. p. 1260. V. 13.—*Expositor* (4th Series), vol. ix. p. 196.

1 Thess. v. 14.

EVERY one should consider himself as entrusted, not only with his own conduct, but with that of others. and as accountable, not only for the duties which he neglects, or the crimes he commits, but for that negligence and irregularity which he may encourage or inculcate.—DR. JOHNSON.

REFERENCES.—V. 14.—W. H. Evans, *Short Sermons for the Seasons*, p. 124. A. L. N., *Christian World Pulpit*, vol. xlviii. p. 287. V. 15.—T. Sadler, *Sunday Thoughts*, p. 52. *Expositor* (6th Series), vol. x. p. 99; *ibid.* (7th Series), vol. vi. p. 184.

THE OBLIGATION OF JOY
'Rejoice alway.'—1 THESS. v. 16.

WE have our moments of joy, but to rejoice alway is a great and at first sight an impossible demand. And yet you find the Apostle Paul, as in the first letter that has come down to us from his pen, so in the last undisputed letter from his pen, saying to the Philippians, 'Rejoice, and again I say rejoice'. Now, why this insistence upon the obligation of joy? Is it not because the Christian Gospel has furnished us with an enduring ground for joy, so that if anyone ceases to rejoice it is an argument that he has fallen from Christ? Naturally, the question comes to us, How is it to be done? Now, to get the answer to that question we must see how St. Paul himself answered it. It is evident in the third chapter and the third verse of this Epistle to the Philippians that he had an answer, for he there says that 'We are the circumcision, which rejoice in Christ Jesus,' and that at once shows us that he did not think we could find a permanent ground of rejoicing in our own narrow and troubled lives. Life, then, is not to be lived in yourself, but it is to be lived in Christ. Now, to bring this out as clearly as possible, I will call your attention to the ethical aspect, the spiritual aspect, and the cosmic aspect of Christ.

I. The Ethical Aspect of Christ.—What is the ethical aspect of Christ? It is that, once in the history of the world, there is the perfect character, the man as man should be; and it means, therefore, that every human being can so fix his thought upon the perfection of human life and conduct that he is able to correct the sorrowful impressions of the world by the ideal in the person of Jesus.

II. The Spiritual Aspect of Christ.—This spiritual aspect of Christ means that in Him as He was and as He is, in Him as a working power in the world, you have God fulfilling His purpose among men; and, evidently, the purpose of God is that out of men He should make the sons of God.

III. The Cosmic Aspect of Christ.—St. Paul caught a glimpse of it when he tells us that in Christ Jesus the whole creation was made and consists. The

idea seems to be that Christ is not only significant for human life, that He is not only the Redeemer of men, but that He is significant for the universe, that He is the Redeemer of this great system of things, and that in Him it all consists because He is the first-born of all creation, for in Him are all things created, through Him and unto Him are all things. Now, if this cosmic idea of Christ once gets possession of you, see what it means and what it brings to you, because it would signify that Christ is not only the Redeemer of your soul, but is the secret and the meaning in this unmanageable universe—which often oppresses you by its magnitude and disturbs you by its unintelligibility.—R. F. HORTON, *Christian World Pulpit*, vol. lx. p. 273.

REFERENCES.—V. 16.—T. C. Finlayson, *Christian World Pulpit*, vol. xlviii. p. 401. T. D. Barlow, *Rays from the Sun of Righteousness*, p. 188. V. 16-18.—A. Maclaren, *Expositions of Holy Scripture—Thessalonians*, p. 229.

PRAY WITHOUT CEASING
1 THESS. v. 17.

ST. BASIL believed that we may in real truth pray without ceasing. 'Not in syllables, but rather in the intention of the soul and in acts of virtue, which extend to all the life, is the power of prayer. . . . When thou sittest down to table, pray; when thou takest food, give thanks to Him that gave it thee; when thou supportest thy weakness with wine, remember Him that gave thee that gift to make glad thy heart. When the time of taking food has passed, let not the memory of the merciful Giver pass too. When thou puttest on thy coat, thank Him that gave it thee: and when thy cloak, increase thy love to God, who provided us with garments fit for both winter and summer. Is the day over? Thank Him who gave us the sun for the service of our daily work, and gave another fire to lighten the night and serve the rest of the needs of life. Let night afford other suggestions of prayer. When thou lookest up to heaven, and seest the beauty of the stars, pray to the Lord of all things seen, and adore the all-merciful Artist of the whole, who in wisdom hath made them all. And when thou seest all living things buried in sleep, then again worship Him who even against our will breaks off by sleep the stress of our toil, and, by a short respite, restores our strength. . . . Thus mayest thou pray without ceasing, not in words, but by the whole conduct of thy life, so uniting thyself to God that thy existence is an unceasing prayer.' —R. TRAVERS SMITH, *St. Basil the Great*, p. 146.

A CHRISTIAN'S DUTY
'Pray without ceasing.'—1 THESS. v. 17.

CONSIDER :—

I. What Prayer is.—Intercourse between God and man.

II. The Dignity of Prayer.—It brings us into the very presence of God.

III. The Power of Prayer.—It can rule the world.

IV. The Duty of Constancy in Prayer.—For supplication must be constant as well as persevering, therefore 'Pray without ceasing'.

'Pray without ceasing.'—1 Thess. v. 17.

Luther said : 'I have to drive myself on every day to prayer. I count it sufficient if, when I lie down to rest, I can say the Ten Commandments, the Lord's Prayer, and after that a text or two. Meditating upon these I fall asleep.'—E. Kroker, *Luther's Tisch-reden*, p. 294, No. 584.

References.—V. 17.—H. E. Brierley, *British Congregationalist*, 26th July, 1906, p. 721. Spurgeon, *Sermons*, vol. xviii. No. 1039. Bishop Creighton, *University and Other Sermons*, p. 34. J. R. Illingworth, *University and Cathedral Sermons*, p. 164. T. G. Bonney, *Sermons on Some of the Questions of the Day*, p. 88. David Smith, *Man's Need of God*, p. 187. V. 17, 18.—J. Keble, *Sermons for the Sundays After Trinity*, p. 407. V. 17-25.—Bishop Westcott, *Village Sermons*, p. 324.

THANKFULNESS

'In everything give thanks ; for this is the will of God in Christ Jesus concerning you.'—1 Thess. v. 18.

The duty of thankfulness is a duty which God Himself has laid upon us. It is a duty that has been hallowed for us by the example of our Lord Himself. 'Having given thanks,' we read, He distributed the loaves to the hungry multitude in the wilderness (John vi. 11) ; and similarly, at the institution of the supper, 'He took bread, and when He had given thanks, He brake it' (Luke xxii. 19). It is a duty, moreover, which in our own hearts we cannot but feel to be both right and fitting, in view of the blessings with which on all sides God has surrounded us.

I. Think of the bounties of God's providence. How numerous they are ! What self-evident proofs of the loving-kindness and goodness of God ! What have we that does not come to us from God ? In all that concerns our natural, no less than our spiritual, lives we are dependent upon Him. And, consequently, He demands from us, as He is entitled to do, the sacrifice of thanksgiving and praise. In saying this I do not, of course, for a moment forget that this thankful spirit may not always be easy. In the struggle with poverty, in the sorrows and trials of life, which fall to the lot of some, it may be hard to find place for a feeling of thankfulness. Even in the darkest lot some streak of light, the herald of the coming day, may be found. 'I am being taught,' said Bishop Hannington, who triumphed over no ordinary difficulties, who never lost heart when most men would have despaired, 'never to be disappointed, but *to praise.*' Let us only strive to make the best of what we have ; let us only look on the bright side even of our disappointments and failures—believing that they too will work together for good to them that love God ; and gradually we shall find that it is possible in *everything to give thanks.*

II. In this attitude we are confirmed when, passing from the bounties of God's providence, we think of the exceeding riches of His grace. When man sinned

and fell God spared not His own Son, that the work of redemption might be complete. But not to dwell further upon that *unspeakable gift of love* itself, let us not forget how clearly and how freely the knowledge of that gift is brought within our reach. (1) We have an open Bible. (2) Or what, again, of our weekly day of rest? (3) The Sacraments of His Church.

III. We give God thanks for the promise not only of the life that now is, but also of the life that is to come. 'Some people,' says Mrs. Browning, 'also sigh in thanking God.' The thankfulness which God desires is unrestrained, willing thankfulness, in the very uttering of which we not only gather its true blessing from the past, but are strengthened and encouraged for the future.—G. Milligan, *God's Garden*, p. 127.

1 Thess. v. 18.

The last piece of public service which he performed at their [the General Assembly's] request, was examining and approving a sermon which had been lately preached by David Ferguson, minister of Dunfermline. His subscription to this sermon, like everything which proceeded from his mouth or pen about this time, is uncommonly striking. 'John Knox, with my dead hand but glad heart, praising God that of His mercy He leaves such light to His kirk in this desolation.'—McCrie's *Life of John Knox*.

1 Thess. v. 18.

We found my father standing before us, erect, his hands clenched in his black hair, his eyes full of misery and amazement, his face white as that of the dead. He frightened us. He saw this, or else his intense will had mastered his agony, for, taking his hands from his head, he said, slowly and gently, 'Let us give thanks,' and turned to a little sofa in the room ; there lay our mother dead. . . . Then were seen in full action his keen, passionate nature, his sense of mental pain, and his supreme will, instant and unsparing, making himself and his terrified household give thanks in the midst of such a desolation—and for it.—Dr. John Brown, *Horæ Subsecivæ*.

References.—V. 18.—J. C. Lees, *Christian World Pulpit*, vol. xlvi. p. 316. Alfred Rowland, *The Exchanged Crowns*, p. 56.

THE FIRE OF THE SPIRIT
(For Whit-Sunday)

'Quench not the Spirit.'—1 Thess. v. 19.

I. 'Quench not the Spirit.' What is it that you and I generally try to quench, or, as the Greek word may be translated, to extinguish ? You say at once it is fire. Is there, then, any connection between the Holy Spirit and fire ? Just reflect. To-day is Whit-Sunday. If you were in church this morning at the Holy Communion, you must have heard the following passage read as part of the Epistle : 'When the day of Pentecost,' *i.e.* Whit-Sunday as it is now called, 'was fully come,' the Apostles 'were all with one accord in one place. And suddenly there came a sound from heaven, as of a rushing mighty wind, and it filled all the house where they were sitting. And there appeared unto them cloven tongues like as of fire, and it,' *i.e.* the fire, 'sat upon each of them. And they were all filled with the Holy Ghost,' or Holy Spirit, 'and began to speak with other tongues as the Spirit gave them utterance.' Here, then, in the Epistle of to-day is the Spirit; here, too, is the fire; the Spirit and the fire are most intimately connected. Remember, too, how John the Baptist said of the One mightier than himself Who should come after him, 'He shall baptise you with the Holy Ghost,' or Holy Spirit, 'and with fire'.

In the light of these passages it is possible, I think, to interpret my text as follows : The Holy Spirit is as fire ; He descends upon human nature ; He glows in human hearts ; do not quench, do not extinguish the fire of the Spirit ; rather fan it into such a flame that it may penetrate and illuminate all your lives.

'Quench not the Spirit.'

It is the solemn responsibility of man that he can either fan or quench, as he will, the Spirit of God.

II. The fire of the Spirit burns in societies as well as individuals ; yet there, too, the fire may be fanned or it may be quenched. Upon the pages of Christian history are inscribed as in letters of gold the high resolves which men and women, acting under the inspiration of the Holy Spirit, have solemnly formed and deliberately executed for the amelioration of the world.

III. There is yet a third atmosphere in which the Holy Spirit burns as a fire, and in which He may be fanned or quenched by the operation of human lives. I speak of the Holy Spirit in the Church.

There is a movement for drawing the forces of Christendom—too long sundered and too often opposed—nearer together. It is the policy of Christian Reunion. It is authoritatively commended to the interest and intercession of the Church on this Sunday. It cannot but be dear to the heart of Him who prayed for His disciples that they might be one even as He and His Father in heaven were one.—BISHOP WELLDON, *The Gospel in a Great City*, p. 129.

SUPPRESSED VOCATIONS

'Quench not the Spirit. Despise not prophesyings.'—
I THESS. V. 19.

ONE of the saddest chapters in the chequered history of the Church is that which recites the tragedy of suppressed vocations—a chapter, alas ! still unfinished. A suppressed vocation involves an arrest of benign purifying revival within the Church, and a humiliating postponement of God's merciful purpose towards the world.

I. The gifts and callings of our fellow-believers are often sterilised by the frigid censorious tempers which creep into church life. Criticism has important services to fulfil, for it tests principles, sifts out sagacious from unprofitable methods, tunes to more perfect music the speech through which men are swayed ; but when criticism dominates the heart, and becomes a pitiless and gagging censorship, it works untold mis-

chief. Every church is a storehouse of unknown aptitudes and endowments. Great apostleships may slumber in some of the commonplace souls around us, ungrown helpers of human need and healers of social sores are at our side, young men and maidens encircle us, in whom the Divine Spirit has already quickened the earnest and promise of fitness for the work the new century is bringing ; and if we could only make our church life brotherly, electric, intensely stimulating, these dawning gifts and potencies would come to perfection in a far higher ratio than in the past.

II. A temper of covert and unconfessed envy often leads men to disparage the gifts of others, and to put stumbling-blocks in the path of their enterprise. Tempers of envy and ambition, of jealousy and strife, of insolent prerogative and self-vaunting power, not only quench the sacred light within our own souls, but obscure gifts and oppose vocations in the elect souls through whom the Spirit seeks to illuminate and sanctify the world.

III. It is to be feared that gifts and callings which come down from above are sometimes stifled by the high-handedness and misrule of those who account themselves lords over God's heritage. The work of the Spirit may be thwarted by the pride of officialism or by the exigencies which arise in the pursuit of party schemes. Next to his personal salvation, the thing most precious to a Christian believer is the vocation he has received from God. And it should be precious to others also, for it is only by 'that which every joint supplieth, through the effectual working in every part,' that the best ideals of edification and prosperity are reached.

I THESS. v. 19.

THE great malady of the soul is cold.—DE TOCQUE-VILLE.

I THESS. v. 19.

WHO does not know this temper of the man of the world ? that worst enemy of the world ? His inexhaustible patience of abuses that only torment others ; his apologetic word for beliefs that may perhaps not be so precisely true as one might wish, and institutions that are not altogether so useful as some might think possible ; his cordiality towards progress and improvement in a general way, and his coldness or antipathy to each progressive proposal in particular ; his pygmy hope that life will one day become somewhat better, punily shivering by the side of his gigantic conviction that it might well be infinitely worse.—JOHN MORLEY's *Voltaire*, pp. 12, 13.

REFERENCES.—V. 19.—S. A. Tipple, *The Admiring Guest*, p. 151. C. Perren, *Revival Sermons in Outline*, p. 250. F. Bourdillon, *Plain Sermons for Family Reading* (2nd Series), p. 166. *Expositor* (5th Series), vol. vii. p. 301 ; *ibid.* (7th Series), vol. v. p. 496. V. 21.—S. K. Hocking, *Christian World Pulpit*, vol. xliv. p. 90. J. B. Hastings, *ibid.* vol. xlviii. p. 333. J. Burnet, *Penny Pulpit*, No. 1623, p. 33. Archbishop Maclagan, *Christian World Pulpit*, vol. l. p. 241. E. J. Hardy, *ibid.* vol. liv. p. 395, and vol. xlvii. p. 390. A. T. Lyttelton, *College and University Sermons*, p. 114. *Exposi-*

tor (4th Series), vol. iii. p. 415 ; *ibid.* vol. ix. p. 101 ; *ibid.* (6th Series), vol. xi. p. 146. V. 21, 22.—F. D. Maurice, *Sermons*, vol. iii. p. 193. V. 22.—J. Eames, *Sermons to Boys and Girls*, p. 185.

COMPLETE SANCTIFICATION

'And the very God of peace sanctify you wholly ; and I pray God your whole spirit and soul and body be preserved blameless unto the coming of our Lord Jesus Christ.'— I THESS. v. 23.

IT may be thought that Paul prayed here for what he was never likely to see ; that his ideal of character was altogether too high to be practical. This complete consecration was surely altogether out of the range of these ordinary Thessalonians, who were busy amid the traffic and trade of that great centre of commerce. Paul did not think thus. He did not regard it as at all impossible that men who are fully occupied in ordinary work at home, or in the city, should be sanctified wholly and made blameless unto the coming of the Lord. In fact the New Testament teaching generally goes to show that unless we are being sanctified altogether, we are not being truly sanctified at all. For good Matthew Henry was quite right when he said of true holiness, 'it is symmetry of soul' ; and surely that is possible to anyone who is a new creature in Christ Jesus.

I. We will first remind ourselves that in this remarkable phraseology Paul specifically includes the whole nature of man as that which should be, and may be, sanctified. Not only here, but elsewhere in Scripture, a man is spoken of as consisting of body, soul, and spirit ; and these three are one, the man himself is one in three.

II. What then is this sanctifying? To 'sanctify' is to set something apart for a holy purpose, so that it may be regarded as holy, and as being profaned if used for a lower purpose. If you would see what it is to be 'sanctified,' look to Jesus. (1) His body was sanctified ; for all its powers were used in absolute accordance with the will of God. To be sanctified is to be like Him. (2) Again, the soul is to be sanctified. In other words, your mental powers, your capacities of hoping and loving, are all to be sacred. (3) Similarly with the affections. (4) It may seem strange to speak about sanctifying the spirit ; for if that be the highest part of man, it would seem to follow that it is essentially holy. But it is not. We need to be cleansed from secret faults and kept back from presumptuous sins.

III. This complete sanctification is a necessity if we would be conformed to the likeness of our Lord. Any part of our nature may become a channel of temptation unless the whole be sanctified.

IV. But whence is it to come? Our text, especially in the original, where emphasis is strong on 'God Himself,' suggests that it is in Him, not in ourselves, that we have hope.

V. There is a special motive for desiring this hinted at in the text. It is the coming of the Lord Jesus.— A. ROWLAND, *The Burdens of Life*, p. 141.

I THESS. v. 23.

EXACTLY in proportion as the Christian religion became less vital, and as the various corruptions which time and Satan brought into it were able to manifest themselves, the person and offices of Christ were less dwelt upon, and the virtues of Christians more. . . . Gradually as the thoughts of men were withdrawn from their Redeemer, and fixed upon themselves, the virtues began to be squared, and counted, and classified, and put into separate heaps of firsts and seconds ; some things being virtuous cardinally, and other things virtuous only north-west. It is very curious to put in close juxta-position the words of the Apostles and some of the writers of the fifteenth century touching sanctification. For instance, hear first St. Paul to the Thessalonians : 'The very God of peace sanctify you wholly ; and I pray God your whole spirit and soul and body be preserved blameless unto the coming of our Lord Jesus Christ. Faithful is He that calleth you, who also will do it'. And then the following part of a prayer which I translate from a MS. of the fifteenth century : 'May He (the Holy Spirit) govern the five senses of my body ; may He cause me to embrace the Seven Works of Mercy, and piously to believe and observe the Twelve Articles of the Faith and the Ten Commandments of the Law, and defend me from the Seven Mortal Sins, even to the end.'—RUSKIN, *Stones of Venice* (vol. II. § viii.).

REFERENCES.—V. 23.—T. Arnold, *Sermons*, vol. i. p. 227. J. Stalker, *Christian World Pulpit*, vol. xlviii. p. 292. *Expositor* (5th Series), vol. i. p. 147 ; *ibid.* vol. iv. p. 121 ; *ibid.* vol. v. p. 136 ; *ibid.* vol. ix. pp. 71, 351. V. 23, 24.—J. Keble, *Village Sermons on the Baptismal Service*, p. 282. V. 25.—J. A. Alexander, *The Gospel of Jesus Christ*, p. 473. J. Bowstead, *Practical Sermons*, vol. i. p. 1. Bishop Westcott, *The Incarnation and Common Life*, p. 3. V. 27.—A. Maclaren, *Expositions of Holy Scripture—Thessalonians*, p. 237.

THE SECOND EPISTLE TO THE THESSALONIANS

2 THESSALONIANS

REFERENCES.—*Expositor* (4th Series), vol. ii. p. 256. I. 1.
···*Ibid.* (5th Series), vol. vi. pp. 2, 87; *ibid.* vol. vii. p. 65.
I. 3.—Spurgeon, *Sermons*, vol. iv. No. 205, and vol. xxxi. No.
1857. I. 3-10.—S. Cox, *Expositions*, p. 301. I. 4.—C. S.
Horne, *The Soul's Awakening*, p. 95. I. 8.—*Expositor* (4th
Series), vol. i. p. 23; *ibid.* vol. ii. p. 257; vol. x. p. 104. I.
9.—*Ibid.* vol. i. pp. 24, 29, 30, 34, 132, 201. I. 9, 10.—F. E.
Paget, *Helps and Hindrances to the Christian Life*, vol. i. p. 8.
I. 10.—Spurgeon, *Sermons*, vol. xxv. No. 1477. *Expositor*
(4th Series), vol. x. pp. 109, 190. A. Maclaren, *Expositions
of Holy Scripture—Thessalonians*, p. 248.

THE SECOND ADVENT

'Now we beseech you, brethren, by the coming of our Lord
Jesus Christ and by our gathering together unto Him.'—
2 THESS. II. I.

'OUR gathering together!' These words touch a
note which ought to find a response in every part
of the world. Man is a social being; and, go where
you will, people as a rule like 'gathering together'.
Christmas, *e.g.*, is peculiarly a time when English
people like to 'gather together'; it is the season when
family meetings have become a national institution,
in town and country, among rich and poor. It is indeed the one time in the twelvemonth, with many,
for seeing their friends. Business is at a standstill for
a space. Poor and shallow the philosophy, hard and
cold the religion, which sneers at Christmas gatherings.

Anything that helps to keep up family affection
and brotherly love is a positive good to a country.
Long may the custom last, and never end. But
earthly gatherings have their sad side; death makes
painful gaps in the family circle; and in the happiest
gatherings we ofttimes miss some dear familiar face
and voice.

I. There is a better 'gathering' yet to come!
There shall be hereafter an 'assembly' which will far
outshine any earthly 'gatherings'; where there shall
be joy without sorrow, mirth without tears.

(1) When will this 'gathering' be? It will be at
the end of the world, when Christ returns to earth the
second time. Visibly He went away, visibly in the
body He will return; and the very first thing that
He will do will be to 'gather together' His people
(Matt. XXIV. 31).

(2) What will be the manner of this 'gathering'?
This is plainly revealed in Holy Scripture. The dead
saints shall be raised, and the living saints shall all be
changed (Rev. xx. 13; 1 Thess. IV. 16, 17; 1 Cor.
xv. 51, 52). And this 'gathering' will be great,
wonderful, humbling :—

(*a*) Great—because all the people of God, from the
first saint of God's to the last born at the time of
His coming, out of every nation, all shall be assembled
together; His saints now scattered seem a little flock;
but hereafter, when gathered together, they will be
'a multitude which no man can number'.

(*b*) Wonderful—because His saints in different
ages and from different climes, who have never seen
each other in the flesh, nor known each other's native
tongues, shall form one harmonious throng; the confusion of tongues shall cease (Rev. v. 13; VII. 9, 10).
Moreover, many will be there whom we might never
have expected to see at all (Matt. XIX. 30).

(*c*) Humbling—because an end will then be made
of all that disfigured and hampered the 'Church' on
earth—an end to bigotry, party spirit, religious
jealousy, and pride. They will meet there in perfect
agreement who refused to meet on earth; all differences will be sunk, for at last all will be completely
'clothed with humility' (1 Pet. v. 5).

(3) What will be the object of this 'gathering'?
For the safety and reward of Christ's people. However fearful the signs of the impending judgment,
His saints will have no cause to tremble, or to dread
the great day of their 'gathering together'; they
shall be hidden in the secret place of the Most High.
And this 'gathering together' will mark the inauguration of their exceeding great and final reward;
complete justification from all guilt will be declared
to all; each will receive that 'crown of glory which
fadeth not away,' and 'the kingdom prepared before
the foundation of the world'; and the great throng
will be admitted publicly into the joy of their Lord.

II. Why is this 'gathering together' of His people
a thing to be desired?

Because, (*a*) it will be a state totally unlike their
present condition. To be scattered rather than
gathered seems to be the rule on earth. Few continue
long together even during their lives here. Children,
parents, friends, fellow-workers fellow-Christians, are
being continually forced asunder from various causes;
and, as life draws to its close, many a one is left
almost alone. The hour is coming when there shall
be no such thing as separation and loneliness. There
will be no lack of company in that great 'gathering together'.

(*b*) It will be an assembly of one mind and one
heart. There are none such now. Mixture, hypocrisy, disunion, false profession, discord, creep in
everywhere here. The tares grow together with the
wheat. The foolish virgins tarry along with the

wise. There is a Judas and a Demas in every Christian congregation; and wherever the 'sons of God' come together, Satan is sure to appear among them. But this will cease on that day, when our Lord shall present to the Father a perfect Church 'having neither spot nor wrinkle, nor any such thing' (Eph. v. 27).

(c) It will be a 'gathering' at which none shall be absent. The weakest lamb will not be left behind in the wilderness. We shall hold communion with all the saints of God who have fought the good fight before us, from the beginning of the world. We shall once more see our dear ones who fell asleep in Jesus, better, more beautiful, than we knew them on earth.

(d) It will be a 'meeting' without a 'parting'. There are no such meetings now. 'Good-bye' is ever treading on the heels of 'How are you?' The cares and duties of life seem to eat up all our days and to make any appreciable period of inter-communion impossible. But the hour cometh when 'farewell' shall be buried for ever; when we shall meet in that endless state of 'blessedness' to part no more. No wonder the Apostle Paul bids us look up and look forward.—The late BISHOP RYLE.

REFERENCES.—II. 1.—F. D. Maurice, Sermons, vol. iii. p. 53. Expositor (5th Series), vol. x. p. 150. II. 1, 2.—Ibid. (4th Series), vol. ii. pp. 75, 259. II. 1-12.—Ibid. (6th Series), vol. ii. p. 257; ibid. vol. xii. p. 99. II. 2.—Ibid. (5th Series), vol. x. p. 273; ibid. (6th Series), vol. ii. pp. 253, 260; ibid. vol. xi. p. 366. II. 3.—Ibid. vol. iv. p. 121. W. F. Shaw, Sermon Sketches for the Christian Year, p. 10. II. 3, 4.—A. Rowland, Christian World Pulpit, vol. l. p. 346. II. 3-11.—Expositor (4th Series), vol. ii. p. 261; ibid. vol. x. p. 353. II. 5.—Ibid. (6th Series), vol. xii. p. 118. II. 7.—Ibid. vol. ix. p. 95. Phillips Brooks, The Mystery of Iniquity, p. 1. II. 8.—D. Heagle, That Blessed Hope, p. 90. Expositor (4th Series), vol. x. pp. 109, 291. II. 9.—Ibid. vol. i. pp. 36, 296. II. 10.—Ibid. p. 201. C. H. Grundy, Luncheon Lectures at St. Paul's Cathedral, p. 23. II. 10-12.—Bishop Gore, Christian World Pulpit, vol. lvi. p. 129. II. 13.—E. Bayley, Sermons on the Work and Person of the Holy Spirit, p. 105. R. F. Horton, Christian World Pulpit, vol. lxxiii. p. 88. Expositor (4th Series), vol. vi. p. 250; ibid. (5th Series), vol. vii. p. 285. II. 13, 14.—Spurgeon, Sermons, vol. i. Nos. 41 and 42.

CALLED UNTO GLORY

'He called you . . . to the obtaining of the glory of our Lord Jesus Christ.'—2 THESS. II. 14.

I. OF all the statements regarding the high calling of the Gospel, this is perhaps the most profound. It expresses as the purpose of God not merely that His people should be enriched, illuminated, and uplifted by the gifts which He bestows upon them through Christ, but that they should be identified with Him in that which was the distinctive glory of His life. For the glory of Christ is not merely to be seen in His present dignity and power in heavenly places, but comprehends also the obscure life which He lived on earth, and which was the pathway to the throne. His was not the glory of position, of wealth, or of material power, but of character. And since God 'looks not upon the outward appearance' and does

not estimate worth in the same scale and with the same judgment as obtains amongst men, the obscure life of the Saviour is to be understood as the true illustration of glory. The glory of character, of sincerity, of obedience, of self-effacement is that which is seen in Him and which, in the sight of God, is of greatest worth and beauty. And this is the glory which the Gospel calls us to share, and this the beauty with which our lives are to be constantly irradiated.

II. The glory of service is the secret of the Saviour's influence over the hearts of His followers. He conquered them by stooping. And we who are called unto the obtaining of the same glory will find opportunity for the acquisition and exertion of true and helpful influence only as we serve. For this all life's common duties will afford us occasion, for life in all its complexity of duty and responsibility is a man's God-given chance for realising to the fullest degree the glory which is to be found alone in following the footsteps of the Master.—J. STUART HOLDEN, The Pre-eminent Lord, p. 61.

REFERENCE.—II. 14.—Expositor (5th Series) vol. vii. p. 32.

2 THESS. II. 15.

SHE fully understood what St. Paul means when he tells the Thessalonians that because they were called, therefore they were to stand fast. She thought with Paul that being called; having a duty plainly laid upon her; being bidden as if by a general to do something, she ought to stand fast; and she stood fast, supported against all pressure by the consciousness of fulfilling the special orders of One who was her superior.—MARK RUTHERFORD, The Deliverance, pp. 62, 63.

REFERENCES.—II. 15.—H. H. Henson, Godly Union and Concord, p. 45. Expositor (5th Series), vol. vi. p. 91. II. 16.—Ibid. (4th Series), vol. i. p. 34; ibid. vol. ii. p. 258. II. 16, 17.—Spurgeon, Sermons, vol. xix. No. 1096; vol. xxvi. No. 1542; vol. xl. No. 2363; vol. lii. No. 2991. A. Maclaren, Expositions of Holy Scripture—Thessalonians, p. 267. III. 1.—J. B. Meharry, Christian World Pulpit, vol. xlvii. p. 329. W. Unsworth, Preacher's Magazine, vol. xix. p. 178. Bishop Cabrera, Christian World Pulpit, vol. liii. p. 298. Bishop Oluwole, Church Family Newspaper, vol. xv. p. 672. Bishop Westcott, Christian World Pulpit, vol. lv. p. 369. III. 1, 2.—A. Lamont, Christian World Pulpit, vol. lxxiii. p. 219. John Thomas, Myrtle Street Pulpit, vol. ii. p. 73. III. 3.—J. Keble, Sermons for Septuagesima to Ash-Wednesday, p. 381.

PATIENCE

'The patience of Christ.—2 THESS. III. 5.

'THE patience of Christ.' It is so the phrase runs in our R.V. as also in the margin of the A.V., in place of the A.V. 'patient waiting for Christ'. The phrase once spoken is felt to be inevitable; Paul could not have written otherwise. Patience is so truly the word of the Christ life. We have all traced, as St. John does, in the features of the Christ before High Priest or Pilate and on the cross, the likeness of the suffering Servant of Jehovah, who bore our griefs, carried our sorrows; the Sufferer as a lamb brought to the slaughter, a sheep before the shearers, dumb and opening not his mouth. Such an one has lived out by His own patience to the end His precept of patience to His followers. With His example there we can believe it true that 'he that endureth (has patience) unto the end shall be saved,' and that 'in your patience ye shall win your souls'.

I. If patience is a word of the Christ life, if part at least of the secret of Christ is divulged in its syllables, we shall be sure it will be a part of the secret of a ministry in His name. By enduring, being patient, unto the end, we shall be saved, not only as Christians, but as pastors of the flock of Christ : by our patience we shall win our souls, and by our patience shall we win the souls of others. If we must 'in all things approve ourselves as the ministers of God,' first in that list of all things must stand, as with Paul, the 'much patience'.

II. Why is such a patience a victorious quality ? I suppose, first and last, because it is a special form of the quality which wins all victories everywhere; it is a form of selflessness; it gains life by losing life. When patience fails us, it is a preference of self to something worthier than self; we break out on an opponent or a fellow-worker because pride is brushed against or our personal activity is checked; we throw up a task because we want ease or because the strain will not be rewarded. The patience of saints is their effacement of their personal interests and likings in the interest of the Great Will. But if that Will *is* the Great Will, and the things that are done upon earth, It doeth them, then to be patient, that is, to be at one with the power which 'doeth them,' must be to succeed, must be a victory which overcomes the world.

III. But also (though we shall be praising the same truth in the language of the secular) patience is success because it is the true adjustment of the soul of man to the world of fact which environs him, it is the apt correspondence by which we live and survive. The moral laws of the universe, like the physical, work very slowly ; human nature moves as the glaciers, scarce measurably ; human character is built as the coral reefs, during æons; religious faith is shaped by a discipline as deliberate as that which moulds through ages the types of animal life. Therefore the shepherding of men is an industry which must be plied with no hope of quick returns and a contentment with the smallest profits. Clearly patience is the correlative in the worker to the vastness of scale and the tardiness of movement in the work. In a slow world the man who can wait is the man who wins, for it is he who is the fittest and survives. In a vast world the man whose mind is wide enough to mirror that vastness, the man who (to invert a historic saying in politics) studies God's universe with a small-scale map and so is not daunted by its distances, this man has the intelligence which enables him to be Θεοῦ συνεργὸς, a labourer together with God.

But lastly (and still I believe we are but phrasing anew the thing first said, though we give it now the highest name we know), is not Patience in work just another word for Faith ? We can be patient because we know Whom we have believed, and that we are patient is the proof that we have believed. Patience is faith not in the activity of a moment, but the activity which goes on ; it is faith, might one not say, in its dimension not of intensity, but of time. No wonder, then, if patience is faith, that it should be the victory that overcometh the world.—J. HUNTLEY SKRINE, *Sermons to Pastors and Masters*, p. 151.

PATIENT WAITING FOR CHRIST

'And the Lord direct your hearts . . . into the patient waiting for Christ.'—2 THESS. III. 5.

ALL life is a mystery. The loftiest archangel cannot himself create the lowliest living organism. All creation confesses to her God, 'With Thee is the fountain of life'. But how much more impenetrable is the veil spread over that highest conceivable vitality, which we call spiritual life ? This, of all mysteries, is the most profound. It is an effluence from the essential life of God ; the breath of the Holy Spirit in the heart of man ; it is Christ living in us, the hope of glory.

I. God has provided the means for the deepening and strengthening of this higher life in His people, by which He is pleased to act upon them individually, and, through them, upon the world ; to meet their present needs in the conflict which is upon them. We want grace in our time of need. That time is now, and the promised supply is at hand, and ready for our use. Thank God ! that needful present grace is ours in Christ ; we have the Father's footstool at which to kneel ; we have a High Priest Who is with us always ; we have the promised Comforter, who abides with us for ever ; we have the holy Communion of Saints in the Church of God ; and we have the means of refreshment which God has provided for us on our pilgrim way. The Great Householder has provided abundantly for His servants during His absence. But this does not embrace the whole provision made for our spiritual training and education. We are being disciplined for eternity ; we are heirs of an everlasting kingdom ; children of a Father Who hath made us meet to be partakers of the inheritance of the Saints in light ; and it is not worthy of our heavenly calling that our thoughts, desires, and joys should be bounded by our present needs and their supply, although these needs concern our immortal souls, as well as our mortal bodies, and that supply comes from the ever-living God.

II. We must look not only inward and upward, but onward—onward to the 'glory that shall be revealed'. The heirs of God and joint-heirs with Christ must not be absorbed in 'this present,' however lofty and noble its responsibilities may be. We shall see greater things than these. 'Our life is hid with Christ in God.' But it will not always be so. 'When Christ, Who is our life, shall appear, then shall we also appear with Him in glory.' This passage affords a clue to one of the truest helps, and unmasks one of the greatest hindrances, of spiritual life. What if this life, which is of Divine origin, like a bulb which fails to pierce some uncongenial clay, ceases to struggle upward ; it is the partial paralysis of life. Our highest privilege is this—'We have the mind of Christ'; but He is Himself expecting until His enemies be made His footstool. The Great Husbandman has watched every blossom and ripening cluster of the mystic Vine. The ultimate design of our Great Advocate, who prayed, 'Father, I will that those whom Thou hast given Me be with Me where I am,' has never been for one moment absent from His mind. For this final triumph He is waiting and working. Nor will He rest until His latest promise to the seventh Church is fulfilled—'To him that overcometh will I grant to sit with Me in My Throne. . . .'

III. Now, only as our hearts beat truly with His, only as our most real desires are in unison with His, can we live that spiritual life which to live is Christ.

Our Lord's earthly life was lived, and His ministry fulfilled, in the light of His Return to Judgment. In His Sermon on the Mount, in His charge to His Apostles, in His private discourses, in His most impressive parables, in His farewell converse, in His good confession before the Sanhedrin — he pointed to That Day. After His Ascension, the promise of His Return was the consolation which angels poured into the bereaved hearts of the Apostles. Thus it runs as a golden thread through all the Epistles. St. Paul never wearies of it; St. James urges patience in contemplating it; St. Peter reminds the elders of the Advent of the Chief Shepherd; St. John comforts by the assurance, 'When He shall appear, we shall be like Him'; St. Jude re-echoes Enoch's warning, 'The Lord cometh'. And the last book of the inspired canon bears on its forefront, 'Behold, He cometh with clouds,' and closes with the threefold watchword, 'I come quickly'.

IV. As we drink in the spirit of these Scriptures, we are tempted to exclaim, 'Surely there will not be one laggard heart : all will watch and wait and long for the return of their absent Lord'. But has it been so? Looking broadly over the history of the Church of God, have the servants of the Householder been watching for His return? Has not the parable of the Ten Virgins been continually repeated— 'While the Bridegroom tarried they all slumbered and slept'?

From one cause or another, the Church has relaxed her vigil. There are, indeed, those who watch for the faintest sound of the footfall of their returning Lord. But they are few and far between. Perhaps of all hindrances to spiritual life none is more insidious than the answer to the ringing Advent call, 'Yet a little sleep, a little slumber, a little folding of the hands to sleep'. But if slothfulness hinders His return, watchfulness helps the spiritual life (in the exercise of faith and patience) more than words can say. This lifts the heart to that which is imperishable and eternal. This cheers us on in our patient work for Him at home, for we hear His voice, 'Occupy till I come'. This, too, is the mainspring of missionary work. The time is short, the Master near. —Bishop Bickersteth, late of Exeter, *Church Congress*, 1878.

References.—III. 5.—Archbishop Magee, *Sermons at Bath*, p. 271. I. E. Page, *Preacher's Magazine*, vol. xviii. p. 133. S. H. Fleming, *Fifteen Minute Sermons for the People*, p. 133. Spurgeon, *Sermons*, vol. xxxiv. No. 2028. A. Maclaren, *Expositions of Holy Scripture—Thessalonians*, p. 277. III. 7-12.—*Expositor* (6th Series), vol. xii. p. 102. III. 9.— *Ibid.* (5th Series), vol. vi. p. 382. III. 10.—W. Richmond, *Christian World Pulpit*, vol. xlv. p. 188. H. H. Almond, *Sermons by a Lay Headmaster*, p. 149. F. S. Root, *Christian World Pulpit*, vol. xlviii. p. 198. III. 10-12.—*Expositor* (6th Series), vol. xi. p. 282. III. 13.—Spurgeon, *Sermons*, vol. li. No. 2918. III. 14.—*Expositor* (6th Series), vol. iv. p. 207. III. 15.—*Ibid.* vol. ii. p. 257. III. 16.—F. D. Maurice, *Sermons*, vol. v. p. 321. Spurgeon, *Sermons*, vol. xxiii. No. 1343. W. H. Griffith-Thomas, *The Record*, vol. xxvii. p. 799. A. Maclaren, *Expositions of Holy Scripture—Thessalonians*, p. 288. III. 17.—*Expositor* (5th Series), vol. x. p. 199 ; *ibid.* (6th Series), vol. ii. p. 253 ; *ibid.* vol. x. p. 75. III. 17, 18.—*Ibid.* vol. viii. p. 372.

THE FIRST EPISTLE TO TIMOTHY

I TIMOTHY

REFERENCES.—I. 1.—*Expositor* (6th Series), vol. iv. p. 410 ; *ibid.* vol. v. p. 220. I. 2.—*Ibid.* (5th Series), vol. ii. p. 224 ; *ibid.* vol. vi. p. 86. I. 4.—*Ibid.* (4th Series), vol. vi. p. 253.

CHRISTIAN LOVE

'Now the end of the commandment is charity out of a pure heart, and of a good conscience, and of faith unfeigned.'
I TIM. I. 5.

IT is quite a popular thing to glorify love. A great many people say, 'Love is the one thing needful ; what does it matter what a man believes, or where he worships, so long as he loves God and his brother man?' Well, that seems to be going a good deal too far the other way. It is quite true love is most precious, but it is not the only precious thing, and there are plenty of texts telling us that the truth is also a most precious thing. If religion has its emotional side, it has no less its intellectual and its practical side. Guard against the mistake of making love everything. Yet, if love be not everything, it is a great deal. The Bible speaks of love to God and love to man ; and there are terribly high standards of love given us. To love the Lord thy God with all thy heart and thy neighbour as thyself is a sufficiently high standard to daunt any one ; and we can fancy many a plain, sensible, honest man saying, 'Impossible ; no one can reach that height'. Yes, it is nearly impossible ; but not quite. I have read of holy men and women who have seemed to love God with all their hearts. What do you think of Father Damien, who, knowing perfectly well what it meant, went and lived in Leper Island, till he took the complaint and died ? I could name men of high promise and prospects in this world who have, for pure love, given up all to live and labour among the poor and outcasts. Such characters may be rare, but they are not impossible ; but, even were they rarer, remember there is God's ideal given us. The standard is high, that we all may have something to work up to. No one can rightly complain of love being unpractical ; 'love is the fulfilling of the law'. If we love God with all our hearts, we shall certainly do all we can to please and obey Him ; and if we love our neighbour as ourselves, we shall certainly never injure or wrong him. Moreover, God asks for love ; He makes it a part, a large part, of religion ; and certainly a religion without love would be a terribly dry, cold, dreary sort of thing.

St. Paul tells us there are three sources of the true and blessed love which God asks for.

(1) It must flow out of 'a pure heart'.

(2) Love must issue out of 'a good conscience'.

(3) Love is the outgrowth of 'faith unfeigned'.

Faith is the power in the soul which makes real the unseen, which lives for another world ; it is the realising faculty. Surely this faith in the unseen lies at the root of all religion. But it must be 'unfeigned'. It must be real—no mere words, no mere profession. It must set the soul in the presence of God. Above all it must make real to the soul the living Saviour. It must be faith in Jesus Christ. It must realise Him as the Atonement for sin, as the example of the Perfect Man, as the living Intercessor. Faith shows us One infinitely lovable, and the sight kindles love. 'We love Him, because He first loved us.' It is thus that faith worketh by love. Well may we take up the anxious cry, 'Lord, I believe ; help Thou mine unbelief' !—BISHOP WALSHAM HOW.

REFERENCES.—I. 5.—J. Keble, *Sermons for Septuagesima to Ash Wednesday*, p. 54. R. Flint, *Sermons and Addresses*, p. 176. E. W. Attwood, *Sermons for Clergy and Laity*, p. 285. J. H. Jowett, *British Congregationalist*, 19th September, 1907, p. 238. *Expositor* (5th Series), vol. v. p. 31. A. Maclaren, *Expositions of Holy Scripture—Timothy*, p. 298. I. 5-7.— E. W. Attwood, *Sermons for Clergy and Laity*, p. 1. I. 6.— *Expositor* (7th Series), vol. vi. p. 373. I. 8.—L. D. Bevan, *Sermons to Students*, p. 65. *Expositor* (5th Series), vol. vi. p. 69. I. 9.—T. Arnold, *Sermons*, vol. iv. p. 69.

THE GOSPEL OF THE GLORY

'. . . The Gospel of the glory of the blessed God.'—I TIM. I. 11 (R.V.).

WE define the Gospel as 'good news,' and the etymology is, doubtless, correct. But 'good news' of whom and of what? We must get a larger definition in the sweep of this word 'glory'.

I. **The Source of the Gospel.**—It is certainly the most wonderful thing on earth and the most fascinating. I compare it with the other religions, and, while they are silent, it tells me things about God which I long to know—things which answer and satisfy the clamorous voices within. Paul says the source of the Gospel is the 'blessed God'. God ! Then that is to claim a supernatural origin for the Gospel. Precisely. God alone can account for the Christian ethic. The effects in human character are supernatural, and as the effect must partake of the nature of its cause, the cause must be supernatural. The Christian Gospel was not born on earth of flesh and of blood, but in heaven of spirit and of life. There are many religions, and they are all the evolutions of man ; but there is only one Gospel, and it is the speech of God in Christ. The proof of its Divine origin lies in its perfect adaptation to the complex life of man. The Gospel is more than a 'body of truth' —it is a spirit, a life.

II. **The Nature of the Gospel.**—The 'glory of the blessed God' is the goodness of His Fatherhood, and

775

the Gospel is the showing of such a Father. Its glory lies in the new face of God—the goodness of the Father—which it reveals. The essential feature of the Gospel is the Fatherhood of God. It includes, and it makes possible, all the facts and the truths of historic Christianity.

III. The Medium of the Gospel.—Christ was the medium for the showing of the Father to us. Now in this lies the fascination of the Gospel—*in a person.* The other religions are all ethical frames ; but the ' Gospel of the glory ' puts a face into the frame, and it is Jesus—the face of God revealed ! The personality of Christ is the portrait of God. ' I have swept the heavens with my telescope, and have not seen God ! ' said Lalande. Precisely. Because he was looking only for stars ; he saw what he searched for. The face is the face of God in Christ, and ' blessed are the eyes that see '. If you have the Christ you have the Father, and everything in God becomes your property.—J. OATES, *The Sorrow of God,* p. 28.

THE HAPPINESS OF GOD

' The blessed God.'—i TIM. i. 11.

WE all recognise that God is ' blessed,' as being the object of praise and adoration ; but He is more than this, for Paul means that God is the Possessor of personal happiness, just as truly as of wisdom, power, and love. Nothing is more likely to inspire us with hope than the knowledge of this fact—that our God is infinitely happy, and longs that all His creatures should be happy too. Such a Gospel can be found nowhere else.

I. Let us inquire where through Scripture, or apart from it, we are to find revelations of the inmost character of the God we adore? Surely not in the material world, however magnificent its splendour and resistless its forces, but in *man,* and most clearly of all in the Divine Man. It is a false theology which would lead us to forget that to a certain extent, and in some respects, we bear a likeness to God. Hence what we know of ourselves gives us conceptions of Him which are true as far as they go ; although beyond these there are heights of happiness and depths of love in the Infinite nature, which must remain utterly out of our reach. ' The Gospel of the glory of the happy God is in *Jesus Christ.*'

II. Let us try to discover wherein this Divine happiness consists. What makes our happiness fitful and transient can never limit the bliss of Him whom we adore. (1) For example, we are often troubled by our ignorance. We are liable to mistakes, and are perplexed by uncertainty. But the happy God is ' clothed with light as with a garment,' invested with the radiance of perfect knowledge. (2) Remember how our happiness is marred by inability to do what we gladly would ; but what do we read of Him ? ' He works all things according to the counsel of His own will.' (3) But the happiness of God consists not only in perfect knowledge, and tireless, fault-

less activity, but also, and chiefly in this, that He is absolutely good ; as our Lord reminded us when He said to the young ruler, ' there is none good but One, that is God '.

III. But, it may be asked, What has all this to do with us ? The revelation we have here is not of a God lapped in ease, serenely contemplating from afar the struggles and sorrows of His creatures, but of God in Christ reconciling the world unto Himself, redeeming it from sin and misery at an infinite cost. Himself supremely happy, because supremely good, He seeks and strives to make us good, that we may be happy too. Sin is the one thing in the universe which affects the happiness of God, and it is this fact which makes credible to some of us the intervention of God to deliver us from it, as seen in the Incarnation, the Atonement, the Resurrection, and the Ascension of our Lord Jesus Christ.—A. ROWLAND, *The Burdens of Life,* p. 21.

REFERENCES.—I. 11.—J. G. Greenhough, *Christian World Pulpit,* vol. li. p. 305. Spurgeon, *Sermons,* vol. xiii. No. 758. W. J. Brock, *Sermons,* p. 47. C. Perren, *Sermon Outlines,* p. 318. E. H. Bickersteth, *Thoughts in Past Years,* p. 171. T. Binney, *King's Weigh-House Chapel Sermons,* p. 77. *Expositor* (5th Series), vol. ix. p. 13. A. Maclaren, *Expositions of Holy Scripture—Timothy,* p. 308. I. 12, 13.—F. W. Macdonald, *Christian World Pulpit,* vol. liv. p. 180.

INJURIOUS

' Injurious.'—i TIM. i. 13.

THERE is something subtler than blasphemy, less vulgar than persecution ; there is injuriousness. This is true of all things.

I. There are quiet, simple-looking, innocent-looking things that are the instruments of death. Some of them are in a bottle, in a very small bottle, in a bottle with a label, in an almost ornamental bottle ; but there is death in every drain the bottle holds. These poisons do not kill by axe and fire and vulgar block and chain ; these destroyers are very quiet, they are dumb destroyers ; the sting has no voice—only death. About these things who cares ? What we care about is the blasphemy, the persecutor, the wild man who can only understand the gospel of a strait-jacket ; there we could get up a demonstration a million and a half strong, if due time for advertisement were given. But who will get up a demonstration against injuriousness, about these quiet little globules in the spiritual or moral bottle ? Why, the globules would be astounded if they heard that there was to be a great demonstration against them—spicules, globules, atoms, nothings. But they are doing more deadly work in the world than soldiers can do.

II. ' Injurious.' This is true not only of things, but, secondly, it is true of habits. You understand something of the action of the imperceptible ?—understand it more. We read in the prophet that grey hairs are here and there upon him, and he knoweth it not. There is an imperceptible decay. Sometimes the old man stretches himself to his full inches, and says, ' I am as strong as ever '. He does not see his own occasional stoop. Who ever saw really and truly his own stoop? Other men see it, and yet, whilst the stooping, kindly old friend says, 'I feel in back and in limb and in brain just as strong as I ever was,' his friends simply turn round and look somewhere else. This is a great gift, and is well meant. The young are also subject to this form of injuriousness when they are told, as they always are told by the devil, that there is no harm in it; I can show you the very pick and cream of the land who all do this; there is really no harm; you can have enjoyment, you can spend a very joyous hour, and I will defy the acutest dialectician to prove that there is the slightest harm in this thing: now you try it for yourself and see if my words be not true.

III. This is illustrated, in the third place, by social influences. There are injurious persons about all the time, and they nearly all go to church, and complain of the singing if it is not loud enough to give them an opportunity of showing that they cannot sing. The Apostle called such people, in another passage, 'backbiters'. They never swear; that would be too large an order to make upon their energy; but they can do a world of mischief by dodging behind the back.

IV. Let us beware of mean sins, of spreading social contagion. What but the Gospel can get at that sort of iniquity? You could make a programme of six pages for getting clear of drunkenness and swearing and uncleanness and gambling, but you never have yet produced a programme for getting clear of these inner and apparently smaller things. I have never seen a programme for cleansing the soul, except in the New Testament.—JOSEPH PARKER, *City Temple Pulpit*, vol. IV. p. 21.

REFERENCES.—I. 13.—Spurgeon, *Sermons*, vol. xxvi. No. 1574. W. M. Clow, *The Cross in Christian Experience*, p. 219. *Expositor* (5th Series), vol. ix. p. 48; *ibid.* vol. x. p. 275. I. 14.—*Ibid.* (6th Series), vol. viii. p. 352.

SALVATION FOR THE CHIEF OF SINNERS

'This is a faithful saying, and worthy of all acceptation, that Christ Jesus came into the world to save sinners: of whom I am chief.'—1 TIM. I. 15.

PAUL had passed through and lived his own keen and intense human life in them: he had been a point of refuge in the last resort for many a heart-broken and paralysed sinner; creatures with scarce a remnant of human nature discernible in them had come to him and told him their sins, and had shown him in their hopeless soul, their weakened mind, their scarcely living body, the greatness of their sins, and yet he looks at them all and says, 'Sinners, of whom I am chief'.

I. What does Paul mean? If it is neither a mere form of speech he uses, nor the utterance of ignorance; if he neither thought it proper to assume a 'graceful humility,' nor spoke in ignorance of the ordinary sins of men, what did he mean? If in good faith he judged himself to be a greater sinner than any of those foul wretches he had seen in Corinth or in Rome, on what did he ground this judgment?

Now, it is a commonplace of religion that in proportion as a man is himself good, he is quick and severe in dealing with his own unrighteousness, and charitable towards other men; admitting all conceivable apology for them, 'hoping all things, believing all things' in their exculpation, but condemning himself without a hearing. And this fact, in the first place, must be taken into account in explaining Paul's words. His own sins were his immediate concern, on them the weight of God's law had first manifested itself in his conscience; and in connection with them, and not with the sins of other men, had God's holiness first revealed to him its reality, its penetrative truth, its power, its relation to human life.

II. To all persons, then, who feel that theirs has been a very shameful career; to all who have taken so little interest in Christ that they cannot conceive what interest He can have in them; to all who know that they are not the kind of people that do much good in the world; to all who are ashamed to hope for much, or to claim boldly to be heirs of God, and attempt a thoroughly Christian life; to all conscious of great sin, Paul says, 'The grace that saved me is sufficient for you'. Your sins are great, greater than you think, but not greater than Paul's. More polluting to the character, more debasing, more selfish and silly, they may be; but certainly not greater in the sense of needing more grace and love in Christ to pardon them. You may have tried every kind of sin that was open to you; you may have yielded to every form of self-indulgence that ever tempted you; you may have continued in shameful sin long after you knew something of God's nearness to you, and love for you; you may have carried your sin far on with you into a would-be Christian life, and mixed in your own soul things holy and profane, Christ's purity and your own impurity, until you are horrified at yourself, and cannot but think that exceptional punishment must fall upon you; but Paul says, and says truly, that you have not sinned as he sinned, and that as he found mercy so may you.

III. To those who have believed on Christ, a very serious difficulty may have arisen about the manner in which this salvation is practically effected. You have believed, you say, for ten or twenty years, and you seem to be yet as much a sinner as ever. It is replied that this is your own fault, that you must remember very many occasions on which, so far from watching against temptation you have courted sin. Well, but, you answer, it was for this very reason I gave myself to Christ, that this instability of mine might be obviated. I knew I could not keep myself from sin, and therefore I gave myself to Him, expecting that He would save me, and it seems I am little better than if I had been in my own hands. If there is any meaning in being saved by another, any reality in this salvation from sin by Christ, must it not mean that He secures that those who believe in Him be not left to themselves? If Christ does not secure that I pray, that I entertain holy thoughts and dispositions, that I watch against temptation; if, in short, He does not take me wholly into His hand, with all my sin, and save me from my own carelessness and folly, can I in any real sense call Him my Saviour?

Every man is conscious that it does in quite a true sense depend on himself whether he become holy or no; not on himself alone, but none the less on himself. And were Christ to give us such help as should not only move and support, but quite supersede our own efforts, He would thereby destroy and not save us; He would keep us for ever weak. And because He truly saves us, He inspires us to work out our own salvation. He might interfere more manifestly in our life, He might take us in His arms at a rough or slippery place, and we might thus arrive cleaner and fresher, but certainly weaker, at our destination. The aid He gives is like life itself, deep and hidden, but the spring of all else; not superseding, but giving energy to all our own feelings and actings.—Marcus Dods, *Christ and Man*, p. 176.

THE FAITHFUL SAYING

'This is a faithful saying, and worthy of all acceptation, that Christ Jesus came into the world to save sinners: of whom I am chief.'—1 Tim. i. 15.

I. Why did St. Paul call himself the chief of sinners? It is a mere truism to say that the success of a religion depends to a large extent upon the personal veracity and goodness of its founders. Now, St. Paul was practically the founder of Christianity over a large area of the heathen world. It was he who had told them almost everything they knew of Christ. And he frequently declared that he himself was the style of man a Christian ought to be. 'Be ye followers of me,' he said, 'as I also am of Christ.' How, then, were they to understand him when he asserted himself to be the chief of sinners? What did he really mean? The truth is that St. Paul had a very rare and exceptional insight into his own heart, and also into the nature of sin. He knew how terrible were the passions that once strove in his own heart, and still slumbered there. And above all his bright vision of the holiness of God, his sublime conception of Christ's purity, threw a white light that beat upon his sin and exposed its every line and feature, and movement. And so Paul the aged, the Apostle of Jesus Christ, still stood, at the end of his warfare, chief of sinners in his own esteem.

II. Let us consider now why St. Paul appended this remark about himself to the statement in the verse. The drift of the passage leads us to believe that he meant it to confirm the faithfulness of the saying. It was equivalent to putting his subscription at the foot of it, as one who endorsed it or attested its truth. In proof of the assertion that Christ Jesus had come into the world to save sinners, he appealed to his own case as specially to the point. I should say that the most desperate man is he who is neither careless, nor a profligate, nor a formalist, but one who, earnest and correct in conduct, is conscientiously attached to a false or defective creed and bent en-

thusiastically on pushing its claims. Was not St. Paul very much such a character as this? Christ saved the man who of all men in the world seemed the least likely, and the most difficult, to be saved.

III. We come now to the statement that Christ Jesus came into the world to save sinners. Sinners were the object of His mission, and sinners without any distinction. He makes the same offer, and promises to do the same thing, for every one of us—that thing being to save us. Christ saves us by enabling us to beat our sin in fair fight, by making us so strong and hopeful that whereas before we were overrun at its pleasure, and carried captive at its chariot wheels, now we stand up against it, and bruise Satan under our feet.—C. Moinet, *The Great Alternative and other Sermons*, p. 35.

THE DIVINE SOURCE OF REDEMPTION

1 Tim. i. 15.

'Christ Jesus came into the world.' The salvation of man—that is, his deliverance from the debasing element, the destroying element—is from above; it is directly Divine and supernatural.

I. Man cannot save himself. God never does anything for us that we can do for ourselves. What we are capable of doing God leaves us to do, although we may serve a long apprenticeship of thought and suffering before we attain the necessary proficiency. But we could not save ourselves, and therefore God has stepped in to deliver us by a mighty act of extraordinary grace. The Incarnation was the stoop of God to do for mankind what it could not do for itself.

II. There is no power of redemption within the race. In the street we see an acrobat stand upright, another instantly leaps upon his shoulders, another on his, perhaps a fourth mounts higher still on the human ladder, and one might think that they meant to scale the heavens; but this kind of thing comes to an end long before they touch the morning star. Some think that a similar trick may be tried in another sphere, and accomplish the elevation of the race. The schoolmaster is to mount the sturdy shoulders of the tradesman, the politician is to support himself on both, the scientist is to carry upward the imposing column, and lastly the æsthete must crown it with his light, graceful figure, and together they will raise society into the seventh heaven of perfection. But these admirable combinations go no further in the moral world than they do in physics. If society is to be lifted to high levels, it will be by a hand out of heaven.

III. There is no law of salvation operative in the world. The fact that Christ came into the world proves that there is no natural redemption. Whenever men are saved it is by the intervention of superior strength and goodness. (1) It is so with the individual sinner. He is helpless, often painfully helpless, until directed, encouraged, and assisted by noble friends. (2) It is the same with the debased classes: if they are saved, help must come from without. (3) It is the same with fallen nations—they never raise themselves. The higher nations must save the lapsed nations. (4) It is the same with the race. The salvation of humanity depended upon a superior Power coming to its rescue and working out its redemption.—W. L. WATKINSON, *The Ashes of Roses*, p. 15.

A FAITHFUL SAYING
1 Tim. i. 15.

HERE is a wonderful saying. No such wonderful saying was ever heard in the world before or since. The Jew was willing to believe that the God of Israel could admit into His High Presence the holy men to whom He had entrusted some great enterprise, and who had proved themselves worthy of such great honour. The Greeks believed that for the gifted and the great, for splendid heroes who had wrought prodigies of valour in the battle-field or in the games, the gods might stoop to give some token of their favour and protection. But that God should care so much for men who have slighted Him—and forgotten Him, and insulted Him, and rebelled against Him! To the Greeks such an idea was a folly, to the Jews an offence. Yet still more wonderful was the saying—that the Son of God should come down as a man, taking upon Him not only our nature but our curse—the awful load of the world's sin; and that He should bear for us all shame and agony! Surely it is the most wonderful saying that the world ever heard, so wonderful that it could only have come down from heaven.

I. Experience has proved it a faithful saying. There is nothing in the world to-day that has such testimonies to commend it as this Gospel of our salvation.

II. If this is a faithful saying, then there are three things that do greatly concern us every one. (1) If Jesus Christ has come into the world to save us, then we must be in great danger. (2) Then surely none but Jesus Christ can save me. (3) Then he has come to save *me*.—M. G. PEARSE, *The Preacher's Magazine*, vol. xi. p. 354.

1 Tim. i. 15.

I DON'T think one talks of things that are absolutely part of one. 'This is a true saying, and worthy of all men to be received, that Christ Jesus came into the world to save sinners.' Does my heart beat? Do I put one foot in front of another as I walk? I don't talk to you about these things. I suppose—yes, I suppose that is why I never talked to you about the other. Just because it is so natural to me.—E. F. BENSON, *Paul* (ch. XIX.).

REFERENCES.—I. 15.—Spurgeon, *Sermons*, vol. iv. No 184. W. Redfern, *The Gospel of Redemption*, p. 11. F. D. Maurice, *Sermons*, vol. ii. p. 185. Spurgeon, *Sermons*, vol. ix. No. 530. T. L. Cuyler, *Christian World Pulpit*, vol. xlviii. p. 127. F. B. Woodward, *Sermons* (2nd Series), p. 92. Spurgeon, *Sermons*, vol. xxiii. No. 1345. W. H. Hutchings, *Sermon Sketches* (2nd Series), p. 148. F. B. Woodward, *Selected Sermons*, p. 75. Spurgeon, *Sermons*, vol. xxiv. No. 1416.

R. W. Riley, *A Year's Sermons*, vol. iii. p. 45. E. A. Bray, *Sermons*, vol. ii. p. 119. W. H. Evans, *Sermons for the Seasons*, p. 88. G. W. Brameld, *Practical Sermons* (2nd Series), p. 1. Spurgeon, *Sermons*, vol. xxxix. No. 2300. W. Page Roberts, *Reasonable Service*, p. 91. *Expositor* (5th Series), vol. ix. p. 441. A. Maclaren, *Expositions of Holy Scripture—Timothy*, p. 316; *ibid.* p. 326. I. 15-17.—Spurgeon, *Sermons*, vol. xxxi. No. 1837. I. 16.—A. Maclaren, *Expositions of Holy Scripture—Timothy*, p. 335. I. 17.—*Ibid.* p. 344. L. D. Bevan, *Sermons to Students*, p. 157. I. 18.—E Holyoake, *Christian World Pulpit*, vol. lii. p. 58. *Expositor* (5th Series), vol. viii. p. 123.

CHRISTIAN CRUSADERS
'Holding faith and a good conscience.'—1 Tim. i. 19.

IN this chapter we are privileged to gaze upon the early stages in the making of a young crusader. The veteran soldier is giving a commission to a young and brave recruit.

I. Let us first look at the nature of the crusade. 'The end of the commandment, which is love.' And so that is the purpose of the commission, the coronation and enshrinement of love in the hearts of men. But of what kind of love does the Apostle speak? It is 'love out of a pure heart, and a good conscience, and faith unfeigned'. The words remind me of the River Leven, which empties its waters on the northern shores of Morecambe Bay. If we trace it back from the open sea we shall come to Lake Windermere, and then Rydal Water, and then Grasmere, and then away up to the springs, and to the mists on the hills. And here is the river of love, and if we trace it back we shall find it flowing through a pure heart, and further back through a good conscience, and further back through faith unfeigned, and away to the high hills of the eternal God.

II. And who are to be the crusaders? Look at the young fellow before us. The Divine hand had been placed upon him in mystic ordination. And this, not because he was an exception, but because he was the type. Prophecies have gone before on all of us, Who are they who are outside the circle of vocation? Everybody is called to the holy warfare.

III. And what is to be the crusader's equipment? (1) 'Holding faith.' And what is faith? Faith is loyalty to a hero, and Christian faith is loyalty to the Christ. That kind of faith not only substantiates the eternal but appropriates it. (2) 'And a good conscience.' I am to fight with a clean, sweet life. What is the use of fighting with anything else? What quality of cleaning can we do with a dirty duster? If I myself am impure I shall lose the perception of the crusade.

IV. But my text points out a peril which besets the crusader, to which we shall do well to pay heed. (1) The Apostle warns his young companion that the thrusting aside of a good conscience would make shipwreck of the faith. (2) And it is not only that a defiled conscience paralyses the faith; it works most palpable ravages upon the temperament. We lose the fine mood of chivalry, and we become impatient, and irritable, and unfitted for noble crusades.

—J. H. JOWETT, *British Congregationalist*, 3rd September, 1908, p. 202.

REFERENCES.—I. 19.—W. F. Shaw, *Sermon Sketches for the Christian Year*, p. 123. G. A. Sowter, *From Heart to Heart*, p. 202. I. 20.—*Expositor* (4th Series), vol. i. p. 408.

'Prayers . . . for all men.'—1 TIM. II. 1.

ST. PAUL says somewhere, 'I exhort that first of all prayers . . . be made for all men'. Few souls are capable of that wide and deep prayer which embraces the interests of all the earth and all the Church of God. We limit ourselves too much ; we look at our own concerns too closely ; souls remain as it were folded back upon themselves, saddened by the monotonous view of their own imperfections and discouraged by their weakness. We must know sometimes how to shut our eyes to ourselves, to lose ourselves from sight, to forsake the sad and wearisome care for our own interests, to look higher and farther, to see God's work in the world and to pray for the coming of His kingdom.—*Lettres de l'Abbé Perreyve*, p. 393.

REFERENCES.—II. 1.—W. F. Shaw, *Sermon Sketches for the Christian Year*, p. 131. W. M. Sinclair, *The New Law*, p. 55. E. W. Attwood, *Sermons for Clergy and Laity*, p. 529. *Expositor* (6th Series), vol. xii. p. 57. II. 1, 2.—P. M'Adam Muir, *Christian World Pulpit*, vol. lii. p. 10. J. Keble, *Sermons for Septuagesima to Ash Wednesday*, p. 402. G. C. Lorimer, *Christian World Pulpit*, vol. liv. p. 259. Bishop Frodsham, *Church Family Newspaper*, vol. xv. p. 632. II. 1-4.—F. J. A. Hort, *Village Sermons in Outline*, p. 58. II. 1-5.—*Expositor* (4th Series), vol. i. p. 140 ; *ibid.* vol. vi. p. 421.

1 TIM. II. 2.

THE duty of princes is not to save souls but to preserve peace.—THOMASIUS.

1 TIM. II. 2.

'IN Church to-day,' Dr. Arnold writes from Paris, in 1827, 'there was a prayer for the king and the royal family of France, but they were prayed for simply in their personal capacity, and not as the rulers of a great nation, nor was there any prayer for the French people. St. Paul's exhortation is to pray, not for kings, *and their families*, but for kings and *all who are in authority*, "that we may lead a peaceable life in all godliness and honesty". So for ever is this most pure command corrupted by servility and courtliness.' See further J. A. Froude's *Bunyan* ('English Men of Letters'), pp. 88, 89.

REFERENCES.—II. 2.—*Expositor* (5th Series), vol. vii. p. 459. II. 3, 4.—R. F. Horton, *Christian World Pulpit*, vol. lvii. p. 312. Spurgeon, *Sermons*, vol. xxvi. No. 1516. II. 4.—W. H. Harwood, *Christian World Pulpit*, vol. xlv. p. 294. J. Vaughan, *Fifty Sermons* (9th Series), p. 205. J. Keble, *Sermons for Easter to Ascension Day*, p. 171.

THE MAN WHO IS BEST WORTH TALKING ABOUT

'The Man Christ Jesus.'—1 TIM. II. 5.

THERE is surely nothing in the world so well worth thinking of as this Man ; and most of us believe that there will be nothing in the future world so well worth looking at as His face. He is the only human form on which the thoughts can dwell and the eyes can gaze for ever without growing weary.

I. This Man is our religion. If you want to find out what Christianity is in its simplest and largest meaning, you have only to find out what this Man said and did and was. A Christian is one who believes thoroughly in the Man Christ Jesus, who makes this Man Christ Jesus the Master of his thoughts, the guide of his actions, the judge of his daily life, who loves and obeys and adores this Man above everything else, and who tries in his own poor way to make his own life a little like that of his Master. There is no definition of a Christian which will bear examination except that.

II. I would remind you that it was the simple unadorned manhood of this Man that makes Him beautiful and worth looking at. The Man Himself, and not His belongings. When we are speaking of the great ones of the earth, we say, Look at his throne, his elevated position, his noble birth, his splendid surroundings, palace, servants, wealth, or his gifts, talents, and genius. But when we are speaking of Jesus, we say, Look at the Man. He needs no setting off, no gilded framework. He had nothing but His own sweet goodness to win for Him the reverence of the world. And it teaches us all this lesson, that goodness and qualities of heart are the only really beautiful things in the world.

III. He brings the great unseen God down to us, and makes the unseen, far-off God near. For truly no man could have lived a life like that if He had been *only* man. In His face is a glass, through which we see Him who governs all things—the great eternal Father. It is our only way of learning what God is like. For no mortal man has ever seen Him. Where is He and what is He like, we say? and there is no clear answer but this : 'The Man Christ Jesus'. All that we know of God is there, and it is all we need to know.

IV. I would point you to this Man, because the thought of Him and the sight of Him give us hope and promise concerning ourselves. His manhood lifts our own nature up—our own nature. It proves that we have something in us akin to the Divine ; something that can become Godlike. By the help of God we can each become in a measure Christlike, and therefore Godlike. Now that is what makes it so stimulating to look at this Man.—J. G. GREENHOUGH, *The Cross and the Dice-Box*, p. 177.

REFERENCES.—II. 5.—W. M. Sinclair, *Christian World Pulpit*, vol. xliv. p. 17. Bishop Gore, *ibid.* vol. xlix. p. 257. T. F. Crosse, *Sermons* (2nd Series), p. 64. H. Allen, *Penny Pulpit*, No. 1558, p. 93. *Expositor* (5th Series), vol. iv. p. 257.

1 TIM. II. 5, 6.

'FOR there is one God' (a Mohammedan could go thus far : but the Christian confession is completed by the further testimony), 'one mediator also between God and men, Himself man, Christ Jesus, who gave Himself a ransom for all.' This might serve as a text for a sermon upon the exclusiveness of Jesus Christ. Dr. Theodor Kaftan has published an address, in the fourth series of the *Biblischen Zeit- und Streitfragen* (1908), which discusses it in this light. All truth, as he points out, is exclusive. If there is one correct method in an inquiry, it is mistaken kindness to talk as though the question of method were still debatable. The man who knows the true road to knowledge in any province, will not amiably let beginners try vain experiments along lines of their own, to the inevitable and sometimes irreparable loss of time and money. He will insist upon attention to the proper method. Dr. Kaftan applies this to the modern attitude towards comparative religion. 'Nowadays, "religions" not religion is the clue : or, to put it otherwise, "religion" not "the religion". The claim of Christianity to be *the* religion—a claim based on this very fact that there is but *one* mediator between God and man— this claim is felt by many to be an unjustifiable reflection upon all other religions, and a highly suspicious isolation of the Christian religion.' As he proceeds to show, it is in reality neither. One can recognise with perfect sympathy and gratitude the moral and religious aspirations voiced outside Christianity. One can and one must ; for Christianity is no partisan religion, nor does it lie outside all historical relations to the other movements of religion among men. But it is exclusive none the less, inasmuch as Jesus Christ for the first time made fellowship between God and man a reality ; through the knowledge of God, which he revealed, this fellowship became possible, and through the reign of God, which he incorporated, it is perfected. The pre-eminent and distinctive place of Jesus Christ must be conserved. 'To allow Him to fall into the background in the religious life of the soul ; to let Him disappear, as it were, behind God ; to seek in this direction the solution of our Christological difficulties—is practically the same as if we were to recognise that the purity and soundness of our bodily condition lay in as anæmic a condition as possible.' The *one God* implies *one mediator*. —JAMES MOFFATT.

REFERENCES.—II. 5, 6.—W. M. Clow, *The Cross in Christian Experience*, p. 101. II. 6.—*Expositor* (4th Series), vol. v. p. 434. II. 7.—*Ibid.* (6th Series), vol. viii. p. 235. II. 8.— Lyman Abbott, *Christian World Pulpit*, vol. lvi. p. 49. M. G. Glazebrook, *Prospice*, p. 164. G. C. Lorimer, *Christian World Pulpit*, vol. liv. p. 259. A. Maclaren, *Expositions of Holy Scripture—Timothy*, p. 353. II. 20.—*Expositor* (6th Series), vol. i. p. 211. III. 5.—*Ibid.* vol. vii. p. 275.

MODERN SNARES

'The snare of the devil.'—1 TIM. III. 7.

I. THE snares are always about our feet. They vary in their guise, but their purpose remains unchanged. I want to look at a few of the perils which thus beset the youth of our modern life. (1) There is the snare of materialism. I speak of it not as a theory, but as a life. In Watts' 'Mammon' there is a great pompous figure in heavy scarlet and gold. His face is fat and sightless. Brutal hands and feet are resting carelessly on the Godlike figures of the young. The bloated materialistic presence has the ears of an ass, indicating that he is powerful but imbecile. That is the materialistic life, the worship of naked gain, the pursuit of carnal power, and the unconsidered crushing of all the ethereal elements in our richly dowered being. It is one of the most insidious snares of the devil in our time. (2) And there is the snare of cynicism. In our childhood we live and move in an atmosphere of happy confidence and trust. But this is how the cynic is made. First of all, we discover our own duplicity. There comes a momentous day when I discover that I am putting in the shop window of my life goods of a different quality from what I keep in my warehouse. It dawns upon me that I am leading a double life, that appearances say one thing when the reality is quite another. And then I begin to wonder if others are the same. I read myself into them, and at last I discover a man in some duplicity. Now a double discovery of this kind is apt to embitter a man, and he becomes a cynic. The man who fosters the cynical spirit converts his world into a charnel house. It is the very opposite of the Christian spirit. 'Don't bark against the bad, but chant the beauty of the good.' (3) And there is the snare of superficialism. There is the peril of moving and abiding upon the superficies, of being contented with the surface waters, the shallow but by no means crystal pools which lie here and there in the common ways.

II. How can we be lifted above these modern perils ? (1) Seek height of fellowship, and begin with the highest of the heights, even with the Lord Himself. (2) Seek the fellowship of the saints. If you cannot find them in actual life, then seek their companionship in noble books. (3) Seek breadth of outlook. Read the best books. Take notes of the best books, and incarnate their best teachings. (4) Seek depths of noble service. The indolent are never safe.—J. H. JOWETT, *The British Congregationalist*, p. 228.

REFERENCES.—III. 9.—Bishop Bickersteth, *Sermons*, p. 33. *Expositor* (5th Series), vol. ii. p. 168. III. 13.—C. Parsons Reichel, *Sermons*, p. 382. *Expositor* (4th Series), vol. v. p. 184. III. 14-16.—H. S. Holland, *Christian World Pulpit*, vol. lvii. p. 72. III. 15.—Spurgeon, *Sermons*, vol. vii. No. 393. Bishop Jayne, *Christian World Pulpit*, vol. lii. p. 369. F. W. Farrar, *ibid.* vol. liv. p. 247. J. B. Mozley, *University Sermons*, p. 332. Spurgeon, *Sermons*, vol. xxiv. No. 1436. W. J. Hills, *Sermons and Addresses*, p. 1. H. Allen, *Penny Pulpit*, No. 1611, p. 287. S. Baring-Gould, *Village Preaching for a Year* (2nd Series), vol. i. p. 17.

GOD MADE VISIBLE

'God was made manifest in the flesh.'—1 TIM. III. 16.

WE are taught that there is a great scheme of providence at work round about us. It is a very mysterious providence ; if you look at it in the wrong light, it is so mysterious as to be painful and destructive in its expression and energy. If I would study the providence of God, I would read all that Jesus Christ did. What shall I get from such a perusal of His record ? A clear vision of what at present is regarded as the invisible providence. We talk about a providence within a providence; we speak thus almost atheistically. The providence of God is as plain as the sunlight, as beautiful as the summer landscape. How can we approach it? By studying Jesus Christ; the daily life of Christ was the daily life of God. Then why tear the clouds asunder to see some at present invisible providence? It is needless, it may soon become impious. We need not batter the cloud-door, and say, Admit us to see the machinery of the universe. No need of that; read the life of Jesus Christ, and you will see what God is doing, what God can do, and what God has been doing all the undated and uncalendared ages.

This brings the matter very closely to us. The kingdom of God is amongst us, the kingdom of God is within you. Why stretch your necks to see something beyond the horizon when God Himself is standing in your midst and manifesting Himself in your own flesh? Then we will study Jesus, and see what He thought about the people and about life, and how He sought comfort for all the persons that trusted to Him, how He made the orchards grow and the wheat-fields and the vineyards and the yards of olives. That is right; now you are becoming religious.

I. How does God Deal with the Poor?—Ask Jesus. What does Jesus say? He says to His disciples when they mention the necessities of the people to Him, Give ye them to eat. Yet we are the men who want to know what God does for the poor in His providence! He gives to me that I may give to the man sitting next me. He has made the man sitting next me rich in gold that he may hand some of it over to me. He sets up the great doctrine of mutual interdependence; not the bastard socialism of a card-up-the-sleeve with which some swindler may seek to win the game, but the true socialism and masonry of brotherhood. That is too simple a plan for many persons; they like something more intricate, something that needs to be explained in long and resounding words; whereas God in Christ says to every man who has a loaf, Give some of it to the man who has no bread; I gave you the loaf, not that you might keep it, but that you might distribute it, and I have so arranged the economy of life that distribution is multiplication, and that whoso gives the bread most freely will be surprised at the last to find that he had more to end with than he had to begin with.

II. What does the Invisible and Unthinkable God do in the Matter of the Prodigality and Sinfulness of the World?—Read Jesus Christ's life and you will get the answer at once. What is God's plan about a lapsed and ruined world? 'The Son of man is come to seek and to save that which is lost.' That is what God is doing all the time; He is seeking and saving the lost; He is keeping the door of His own heart open that the very least and worst of His children may enter in and be saved. We have a pleading God, a self-humbling God, a God we keep standing out in the dews of the midnight and amid

all its boisterous winds; and we are asking profound or foolish questions about God's method of dealing with the world He made and loved and redeemed.

III. What is God's Method of Judgment?—We read of a great white throne, we read of a day of final audit and trial. We need not wonder about that; Jesus Christ has gone through the whole process; if we study Him we know all about it; and the day of judgment may be no longer than one flash of light, than the twinkling of an eye. What is God's plan of judgment as shown by Jesus Christ? He said, Where much is given much will be required; where little is given little will be expected. Where there is poverty and difficulty about doing certain things, yet there sounds this sweet music, She hath done what she could. Let us go to Jesus when we would know about God. Let us study His example when we would apprehend somewhat of Divine metaphysics. With Christ at hand no man need be at a loss for God.—JOSEPH PARKER, *City Temple Pulpit*, vol. II. p. 137.

REFERENCES.—III. 16.—Spurgeon, *Sermons*, vol. xiii. No. 786. Lyman Abbott, *Christian World Pulpit*, vol. xlvii. P. 75. Spurgeon, *Sermons*, vol. xviii. No. 1087. T. Arnold, *Sermons*, vol. ii. p. 70. S. Bentley, *Parish Sermons*, p. 1. E. A. Bray, *Sermons*, vol. ii. p. 296. O. Bronson, *Sermons*, p. 48. *Expositor* (5th Series), vol. vi. pp. 151, 330, 380; *ibid.* vol. vii. p. 297; *ibid.* (6th Series), vol. iv. p. 153; *ibid.* vol. xii. p. 105. III. 17.—*Ibid.* vol. ii. p. 378. IV. 1.—*Ibid.* p. 296. IV. 1-5.—*Ibid.* vol. xii. p. 182.

I TIM. IV. 2.

IT is not the suffering, and mutilation, and death of man's body that most needs to be diminished—it is the mutilation and death of his soul. Not the *Red Cross* is needed, but the simple *Cross of Christ* to destroy falsehood and deception.—TOLSTOY (preface to *Sevastopol*).

REFERENCES.—IV. 3.—*Expositor* (7th Series), vol. vi. p. 177. IV. 6.—*Ibid.* (5th Series), vol. i. p. 337. IV. 7.—W. J. Hocking, *Christian World Pulpit*, vol. xliv. p. 187. A. Maclaren, *Expositions of Holy Scripture—Timothy*, p. 361. IV. 7, 8.—C. J. Ridgeway, *Christian World Pulpit*, vol. xlvi. p. 403.

THE PROMISE OF THE LIFE WHICH IS TO COME

'Godliness is profitable for all things, having promise of the life which now is, and of that which is to come.'—I TIM. IV. 8.

ST. PAUL assumes that there *is* a life to come; and he asserts that, of this life, godliness has the 'promise'. In other words, men live after they die; and the life *after* death depends upon the life *before* death. No living man is in a position to say that, when we die, we have done with the life that now is, and that there is no life of any sort to come. And be it borne in mind that the life which is to come is not starting anew; it is simply *going on*. It is not a second life begun; it is the first life continued. There *is* a life which is to come; that life is *bound to come;* and of *it*, godliness has the promise.

I. This promise is twofold; and in two places we read it. (1) In the letter of Holy Scripture, Romans,

ii. 7 : 'To them who by patient continuance in well-doing, seek for glory and honour and immortality,' God will give 'eternal life'. In plain words, God has made eternal life to follow loving obedience. (2) We read the promise, not only in the letter of Holy Scripture, but in the spirit of vital godliness. Evangelical religion is an earnest and pledge of the blessedness of the life which is to come, because it actually consists in that life *already begun* in the soul of the true believer. To a good man there is, strictly speaking, only *one life*. I hold it fatal to any worthy standard of Christian living to think of death as a miracle, and to think that *dying* will work some marvellous change in ourselves—that is, in our nature. Death is but a circumstance. Life in the better land will be present Christian experience *developed, broadened, matured ;* and at the same time *purged* of certain incidents which now are apt to disturb our peace and mar our joy.

II. Of the 'life which is to come,' godliness has the 'promise'. But I beg you to see to it that *your* godliness has these five marks : (1) Godliness personal, not hereditary. (2) Godliness possessed, not simply desired. (3) Godliness vital, not formal. (4) Godliness evangelical, not ritualistic. (5) Godliness kept as well as got.—*Joseph Bush : A Memorial*, p. 163.

References.—IV. 8.—T. Stephens, *Christian World Pulpit*, vol. liv. p. 151. Spurgeon, *Sermons*, vol. xvi. No. 946. James Baldwin Brown, *The Divine Life in Man*, p. 167. R. F. Horton, *This Do*, p. 133. IV. 8, 9.—Spurgeon, *Sermons*, vol. xvi. No. 937. IV. 10.—*Christian World Pulpit*, vol. xlix. p. 175. Spurgeon, *Sermons*, vol. li. No. 2964. John Watson, *The Inspiration of Our Faith*, p. 203.

INFLUENCE : IS IT GOOD OR IS IT BAD ?

'Be thou an example.'—1 Tim. iv. 12.

Our subject is 'Influence : Is it good or bad ?' It must be the one or the other, and for a text I cannot choose a better than the words I have just read, taken from the First Epistle to Timothy, which is appointed for our Second Lesson at Evening during one of the days of the past week.

I. Example Tells.—In one sense we are alone. We are individuals, we personally live, we personally die, and we must personally appear in the judgment of God. Every man shall give account of himself before God. But in another sense we are not alone. We are not and we cannot be alone. No man liveth to himself. He must influence those who are about him by speech, by conduct, by the whole tenor of his life. Supposing you tell lies ; some one hears and and knows. Supposing you talk against religion and sneer at sacred things, and disparage Christ's Church and Sacrament and Bible-reading and devotion, cognisance is taken of what you say. Live for the world, for its pleasures and lusts, for self, some one is influenced. Children watch you and copy your ways and speeches.

II. If Influence be for Good there must be Certain Characteristics.

(a) *There must be a holy disposition.* The heart within must be right with God, or else the external conduct will be unsatisfactory.

(b) *You must also have peace of mind*, that peace which God gives, that legacy, that grand legacy, that Christ the Prince of Peace left to His followers in all ages.

(c) *There must also be absolute integrity.* Wrong principles and deviation from anything that is right essentially is detrimental.

(d) *There must also be likeness to Christ.* Men must be able to take knowledge of you that you have been with Jesus.

Reference.—IV. 12.—*Expositor* (5th Series), vol. vi. p. 382.

'Give attendance to reading.'—1 Tim. iv. 13.

Bishop King of Lincoln wrote in his paper on Clerical Study :—

'It is because in all true knowledge we draw near to God that reading and study have such an alluring and refreshing pleasure. This exercise of the mind in the discovery of the truth has its own alluring delights, and reward ; but we, with the light of Christian revelation, can see more clearly what the cause of that high pleasure is, it is the drawing near of the mind to God ; the knowing more of His ways that we may know Him more, and knowing Him more that we may love Him more ; for so our minds and hearts will be at rest.

'It is this which made Lord Acton in his inaugural lecture say : " I hope that even this narrow and disedifying section of history [*i.e.* modern history] will aid you to see that the action of Christ, Who is risen, upon mankind, whom He redeemed, fails not, but increases ".'—*The Love and Wisdom of God*, pp. 347, 348.

Reference.—IV. 13.—F. J. A. Hort, *Village Sermons in Outline*, p. 78.

THE CHARISMA

(An Ordination Sermon)

'Neglect not the gift that is in thee, which was given thee by prophecy, with the laying on of the hands of the presbytery.'
1 Tim. iv. 14.

The history of the Church of God in the past and her existence to-day attest that she possesses a Divine presence and is instinct with the life of her risen Lord. Nations have risen and flourished, have decayed, fallen, and disappeared, but the Church has remained. 'Every power has touched it, every science has scrutinised it, every blasphemy has cursed it,' but the gates of hell have never prevailed against the Church because her Lord who was dead is alive for evermore. She saw the last days of the Roman Empire ; she stood at its grave, and bestowed upon it a parting blessing. She stood at the cradle of the English nation, fostered its infancy and youth, and has preceded every national advance as the pillar of fire before the host of Israel. Her forms have changed, her appearance is altered, but her nature has ever been the same. Her creed is what it was in the days of the Apostles.

I. 'Lo, I am with you all the days, even unto the

end of the world.' This all-important truth is the secret of the perpetuity of the Church's life, and lies at the very foundation of the solemn service of this morning. The Great High Priest still walks amidst the golden candlesticks. To-day the children of Christ and members of His kingdom take up the strains of the hymns of victory of the ancient Church : '*Christus vincit, Christus regnat, Christus imperat*'. Whatever may be our qualification, natural or acquired, one thing is absolutely essential to make a man an efficient minister of Christ—it is that earnestness of purpose, that persistent and single-hearted energy, which can only be described as life, and which can only be communicated by the 'Lord and Giver of Life' Himself. It is in the combined manifestation of Divine and human authority that we are enabled to 'serve God with one spirit in the Gospel of His Son'.

In such an hour as this I would, with God's help, give you comfort. Your hearts must not be cast down to-day, but lifted up to the Lord with the holy joy and with the ardent courage of soldiers of the cross, who are to receive from the hands of your Prince in heaven, through His deputed agent, the golden spurs of knightly service, and that which no earthly prince can give—the strength to wear the armour which He Himself supplies to meet those special conflicts which lie before you.

II. I have chosen my text because in it St. Paul distinctly states that in Ordination a gift is bestowed which meets this sense of need which doubtless you are keenly feeling at this present time. 'Neglect not the gift that is in thee, which was given thee by prophecy, with the laying on of the hands of the presbytery.' The Apostle says that the gift came to Timothy through the concurrent means of prophecy and of the laying on of hands. I cannot enter into any question of Church government. I would simply remind you that in his second Epistle to Timothy St. Paul writes, 'Stir up the gift of God which is in thee by the putting on of *my* hands'. To-day, in the words of the Rubric, 'The Bishop with the priests present shall lay their hands upon every one that receiveth the order of priesthood'. As certainly as, in answer to the prayer of faith in the rite of Confirmation, the candidate, in the laying on of hands, in the words of the catechism of the Eastern Church, 'receives the gift of the Holy Ghost for growth and strength in the spiritual life,' so certainly does the candidate for Ordination, who is Divinely called, receive the power of the Holy Ghost in the laying on of hands. The word χάρισμα, which occurs fourteen times in the Pauline Epistles and nowhere else in the New Testament, excepting 1 Peter IV. 10, always means an endowment, or gift of grace, bestowed by the Holy Spirit for some *special ministration* or *official service*. In the text before us the call of the Spirit was through prophecy, *i.e.* through inspired preachers, who declared the Spirit's will to invest Timothy with the χάρισμα for the work. The laying on of hands was the act which formed, with the

prophecy, 'an appropriation of the Spirit in prayer, through the instrumentality of others, for a definite object'.

III. '*Neglect* not the gift.' In the verses before the text St. Paul writes to Timothy, 'Be thou an example of believers, in word, in conversation, in charity, in spirit, in faith, in purity—give attendance to reading, to exhortation, to doctrine,' and thus 'neglect not the gift'. The life which God gives, spiritual as well as physical, is dependent upon human effort, and the employment of the means which He Himself supplies. Be 'wholly in these things'. 'Give heed to thyself and the teaching'—to the culture of thine own spiritual life, and of the function and duties of religious instruction. 'Continue in them.' Habitual, not fitful and spasmodic service will meet with reward. 'In doing this thou shalt save both thyself and them that hear thee.' What does the Apostle mean? The traveller who stands on the shore of the Dead Sea near the mouth of the Jordan wonders why this inland lake should be so salt that no animal life can exist in it, as he looks upon the volume of sweet water which is ever entering in. He has the chief answer to the enigma in the fact that this sea receives but never gives. It has no outlet. Let a river flow into a lake whose waters flow out, and not only does it irrigate and fertilise the barren lands beyond, but the lake itself is enlivened and purified. 'Neglect not the gift that is in thee.'—J. W. BARDSLEY, *Many Mansions*, p. 118.

REFERENCE.—IV. 14.—*Expositor* (6th Series), vol. vi. p. 396.

THE MAN AND THE TEACHER

'Take heed to thyself, and to thy teaching. Continue in these things : for in doing this thou shalt save both thyself and them that hear thee.'—1 TIM. IV. 16.

THERE is an intimate relation between the preacher's 'self' and his 'teaching'. This relation is of two kinds : (*a*) The preacher's 'self' largely determines the force and influence of his teaching. (*b*) It largely determines the contents of his faith. It is clear that, if our message be one of infinite importance—*and it is*—then in virtue of that message the person of the true preacher becomes of very great importance also, and such a one must not lightly esteem the significance of his own life.

I. Let me enumerate the moral qualities which appear to me fundamentally necessary to give force to our preaching. (1) The first is, Manliness. This general idea of manliness may be summed up in four qualities : (*a*) Sincerity. Preachers have great temptations to become actors, imitators, and copyists. But, depend upon it, if God has singled you out to be a prophet, He has given you an individuality of your own, which you should strenuously preserve. As sincere men, too, we should have a horror of *cant*, whether new or old. (*b*) Manliness includes Generosity. Meanness is execrable in a preacher. His heart should be large, his sympathies wide and warm. (*c*) You may think it strange that I should include Humility in the qualities of manliness. Yet humility is both strong and lovable; pride and arrogance are both unlovable and weak. (d) Further, the Fearlessness which is an attribute of complete Manliness, gives unquestionably great force to the utterances of the preacher. (2) The Christian preacher should earnestly cultivate personal holiness. If we would fire the world, our spiritual life must burn brightly.

II. Yet, notwithstanding this great influence of the 'self' upon the 'teaching,' the injunction, 'Take heed to yourself' needs to be supplemented with 'Take heed to your teaching'. (1) Without entering into the controversy concerning the nature of inspiration, there are certain facts that must be absolutely final for the Christian preacher. 'Jesus is God incarnate, and the Expiator of sin.' For him that denies these truths Christianity ceases to be. (2) Need I put in a plea for the diligent study of the Bible, for an agony of wrestling with its great truths? (3) Don't, for the sake of God and men, lower the holy standard of the kingdom of God. Our message will have power in proportion as our own power is renewed; it will inspire others in proportion as it inspires us.—JOHN THOMAS, *Myrtle Street Pulpit*, vol. II. p. 169.

REFERENCES.—IV. 16.—C. G. Finney, *Penny Pulpit*, No. 1578, p. 13. J. Caird, *Sermons*, p. 301. V. 1, 2.—R. F. Horton, *Christian World Pulpit*, vol. lvi. p. 392. V. 4.— J. Stalker, *ibid.* vol. liv. p. 275. T. Sadler, *Sermons for Children*, p. 69. V. 6.—J. Bolton, *Selected Sermons* (2nd Series), p. 68. *Expositor* (4th Series), vol. i. p. 205; *ibid.* vol. ii. p. 424. V. 8.—*Ibid.* (5th Series), vol. i. p. 144. V. 17.—*Ibid.* vol. iv. p. 378. V. 18.—*Ibid.* (4th Series), vol. ii. pp. 71, 76; *ibid.* vol. iii. p. 305. V. 20.—*Ibid.* (6th Series), vol. iv. p. 205. V. 21.—H. D. M. Spence, *Voices and Silences*, p. 127.

'Some men's sins are open beforehand, going before to judgment; and some they follow after.'—1 TIM. v. 24.

PROF. RICHARD MOULTON quotes this text in his exposition of 'The Merchant of Venice'. He says that 'the story contains a double Nemesis, attaching to the Jew himself and to his victim. The two moreover represent the different conceptions of Nemesis in the ancient and modern world: Antonio's excess of moral confidence suffers a nemesis of reaction in his humiliation, and Shylock's sin of judicial murder finds a nemesis of retribution in his ruin by process of law. The nemesis, it will be observed, is not merely twofold, but double in the way that a double flower is distinct from two flowers; it is a nemesis *on* a nemesis; the nemesis which visits Antonio's fault is the crime for which Shylock suffers *his* nemesis. Again, in that which gives artistic character to the reaction and the retribution the two nemeses differ. Let St. Paul put the difference for us. "Some men's sins are evident, going before unto judgment; and some they follow after." So in cases like that of Shylock the nemesis is interesting from its very obviousness and the impatience with which we look for it; in the case of Antonio the nemesis is striking for the very opposite reason, that he of all men seemed most secure against it.'—RICHARD MOULTON, *Shakespeare as a Dramatic Artist*, pp. 46, 47.

REFERENCES.—V. 24.—J. Baines, *Sermons*, p. 15. J. C. M. Bellew, *Sermons*, vol. iii. p. 96.

'Some men's sins are open beforehand, going before to judgment; and some men they follow after. Likewise also the good works of some are manifest beforehand; and they that are otherwise cannot be hid.'—1 TIM. v. 24, 25.

MOST editors take these verses, in connection with what precedes, as a reminder to Timothy that human character is not easy to read, and that the outward life of men requires careful scrutiny before it is passed or rejected by any one who has to make appointments or administer affairs within the society. Men are not always what they seem. They may be either worse or better than a superficial reading of their actions might suggest.

Wohlenberg, in his edition of the Epistles (Zahn's *Kommentar zum Neuem Testament*, XIII. pp. 187 f.) ingeniously proposes on the other hand to connect these verses with the following injunction to Christian slaves (VI. 1, 2): 'Let as many servants as are under the yoke count their own masters worthy of all honour, that the name of God and of His doctrine be not blasphemed. And they that have believing masters, let them not despise them, because they are brethren.' The connection is as follows, according to Wohlenberg: 'Slaves occupy a position in which their misdeeds become quickly known and receive immediate punishment, whereas their good actions are usually allowed to pass unnoticed. On the other hand, when their masters sin, the wrong-doing gets hushed up and palliated, while any praiseworthy action on the part of masters is at once made public and honoured, thanks to their conspicuous position.'

This exegesis makes the Apostle side with the slaves rather than with their masters, or at least dwell more on the faults of the latter. The former must not bring discredit on the Gospel by impertinence or laziness, nor must they presume on the kindness of such masters as happen to be Christians themselves, by insubordination. Let them not fear that their own virtues will go for nothing. And let them not imagine that their masters' injustice and cruelty will escape the judgment of God.

With the general sentiment we may compare Mr. Yorke's method in *Shirley*, ch. iv.), when he got vexed with successful evil in this world. He 'believed fully that there was such a thing as judgment to come. If it were otherwise, it would be difficult to imagine how all the scoundrels who seemed triumphant in this world, who broke innocent hearts with impunity, abused unmerited privileges, were a scandal to honourable callings, took the bread out of the mouths of the poor, browbeat the humble, and truckled meanly to the rich and proud—were to be properly paid off, in such coin as they had earned. But,' he added, 'whenever he got low-spirited about such like goings-on and their seeming success in this mucky lump of a planet, he just reached down t'owd book' (pointing to a great Bible in the book-case), 'opened it like at a chance, and he was sure to light of a verse blazing wi' a blue brimstone glow that set all straight. He knew,' he said, 'where some folk was bound for, just as weel as if an angel wi' great white wings had come in ower t' door-stone and told him.'—James Moffatt.

References.—V. 24, 25.—*Expositor* (7th Series), vol. v. p. 566. VI. 1.—*Ibid.* (6th Series), vol. ii. p. 398. VI. 2.—J. S. Boone, *Sermons*, p. 1. VI. 3.—*Expositor* (6th Series), vol. xi. p. 45.

1 Tim. vi. 4.

'I cannot bring myself to take much interest in all the controversies that are going on,' Max Müller wrote in 1865, 'in the Church of England. No doubt the points at issue are great, and appeal to our hearts and minds, but the spirit in which they are treated seems to me so very small. How few men on either side give you the impression that they write face to face with God, and not face to face with men and the small powers that be.'

FALSE SUPPOSITIONS IN LIFE

'Supposing that gain is godliness.'—1 Tim. vi. 5.

'Supposing that gain is godliness.' You never need go to any other text for the remainder of your pulpit lives. 'Supposing that gain is godliness'—false suppositions in life; twisted, crooked, awkward minds that are always getting hold of things by the wrong end. You know them? Yes, I do—getting into a corkscrew kind of mind, out of which a straightforward answer never came. There is no straight line in a corkscrew. 'Supposing that gain is godliness,' or that godliness is gain—getting confused. What was he preaching about to-day? 'The text was, I think, "Supposing that godliness was gain," or, "supposing that gain is godliness," or something of that kind.' You will never make a Christian out of such people, they do not know what they are talking about. They have no clear ideas, no straightforward thought. Well, I do not know, I am sure, whether to blame them; for what can a man do if he has been born with a mind that has no centre and with a mind that has no circumference, a corkscrew mind, a twisting, perverting, half-forgetting, confusing mind? That is the difficulty. Why, perhaps there are not more than two people who will know what the text was when the sermon is done. 'Oh, yes, something about —well if'—no, no, there is no if in it—'that godliness is gain, that gain is godliness'. They have no straightforward ideas, they are living in confusion. Better have only two ideas and know what they are than have a dozen and hold them chaotically, confusedly, and absurdly. Now that is where so many people get wrong. They know fifty things in a half sort of way. They begin a sentence, and expect you to finish it—the most tormenting company I ever go into. They know half a proverb, and say, 'Now, you see, that proverb—"a bird in the bush—a bird in the bush"—you know what I mean'. No, I don't, and you don't. Why don't people get some clear idea of what Jesus Christ wants to be at? 'The Son of Man is come into the world to seek and to save that which is lost.' Why not do that, hold to that, keep that as the pure jewel, the very jewel of the Divine heart?

No, I can't get on with you; you want to know about evolution, which no man can tell you much about, and you want to know about heredity, and you want to know the whole pack of cards, and a pack of nonsense. Why don't you stick to the Gospel, the one grand eternal line—salvation by the Cross? Don't be clever, don't be too clever; there will be no living with you if you become much cleverer in your own estimation.

I. Now, the Apostle says, they have got the true words, gain and godliness, godliness and gain, whether to put the one first or the other first, they do not know. They must therefore make up their minds; they must be right in the first line, and then they may be right in the last line. But godliness—who can define it? Nobody. What is the full word? Godlikeness. Ah, that makes a new word, not only a new orthography, but a new grammar. Godlikeness. Now the Apostle says, 'Bodily exercise'—counting things, putting things back again, hanging them up, taking them down, rubbing, scrubbing, lacerations; he says, 'Now, dear friends, I have been watching you, hear me, "Bodily exercise profiteth"'—what does the New Testament say?—'profiteth little'? No, no; it does say that, but that is not right. 'Bodily exercise profiteth a little.' See, there is something in it, it profiteth a little, it is a kind of beginning, a kind of pledge and earnest; but you must go further, you have got a little profit, but godliness—the rising of God over the whole character, the brooding and throbbing of God in the whole soul —that makes men and guarantees heaven.

II. False suppositions are vicious arguments; false suppositions turn men away from the right point of view, from the right goal, and torture and confuse the mind. Have you got that idea? The elders in Christ know it well, but I want all the young souls, and groping, fumbling people, to get hold of that, and having got hold of it, keep it; it will serve you in all your discussions, controversies, and misunderstandings.

Now shall I give you an instance or two of these false suppositions? I will, if you please.

(1) A woman was crying, sobbing, looking round, and, seeing a man, was afraid; and she, 'supposing him to be the gardener'. False suppositions in life again; they meet you at every turn. Yet no gardener ever looked quite like that. No. But I suppose he is the gardener. Well, what will you say to him? 'Oh, Sir, if thou have borne Him hence, tell me where. They have taken away my Lord, and I know not where they have laid Him. Oh, Sir, if thou have borne Him hence, tell me where thou hast laid Him, and I will go to Him, and if He cannot speak to me, I will speak to Him.' Ah, there are always people who are seeking dead Christs. Only paint them a Christ, and you have no idea how far they will travel to see the painting. They cannot imagine that the Christ of God is alive for evermore. Now you must get a right idea of life. Why, a man once said to us in my house, 'You know, the idea, the

bare idea, of worshipping the Virgin Mary, worshipping a dead woman!' 'No,' said my wife, 'the Virgin Mary is not dead.' That is right—grand. Christ is not dead; Abraham, Isaac, and Jacob are not dead. God is the God of the living, and not of the dead. You can get wrong by limiting and narrowing things, and supposing that thirty or forty or seventy years terminate a man's life. There is no dead Christ. When we seek Him, we must seek Him as a living Christ, and so seeking Him we shall find Him.

(2) There comes another false supposition, which I have always thought very curious and preached about it twenty times or more. There was a great commotion on the hill-side, or in the city or elsewhere, and there was the usual comment upon it—ever since the days when Samuel was about to be born, ever since the day when Hannah did this—[silently moving the lips], 'You see Hannah, she is drunk, you see how it is, look at her lips'. And so they said on this occasion 'They are drunk'. And one said, 'No, no, these are not drunken, as ye suppose'—the same word, 'suppose'—'seeing it is but the third hour of the day'. No, you must go deeper, you must find a larger and fuller explanation of this; this is nothing less than the Spirit of God working in its wonderful way. Now, believe that, and you will cover the whole ground. Oh, it is so easy to say people are drunk, it comes naturally to beautiful, innocent, guileless human nature. Oh, when shall we have the man that comes with broad interpretations, grand definitions, and that lifts up the occasion to its right level? When will that man come? He will himself be counted drunk. Until the Church gets drunk in that way, that particular special way, the Church will make no impression upon the world. So long as the Church is one of a number of institutions, she will be respectable, and she will have her little day and cease to be. She must be drunk, not with wine, wherein is excess, but be filled with the Spirit, and then she will come into close grips with the devil, and fling him to the dust and trample on him. Be earnest, be alive.

III. Then what have we to do, preacher? I tell you what we have to do : you have got to cleanse the mind of all false suppositions. Now I must get into every corner of your mind, and get these suppositions out—out! It is so difficult to get a supposition out; a supposition is like a prejudice. No man ever really got hold of a prejudice and pulled it and threw it into the fire. Now you must get rid of all these false suppositions. When you came into the Church what was your motive? 'Well, of course, I have been very much disappointed, you know; I thought that if I entered the Church in any of its communions, I should have peace and joy, and get rid of the enemy.' Oh, no! he never was such an enemy as when you prayed your last, greatest prayer; he hated you then. Some of the great Apostles have said, they that will live godly shall suffer persecution, expect persecution. What persecution have I endured for Christ's sake? None; I have worked on the sunny side of the wall; my shame is reserved for the day of judgment.—Joseph Parker.

Reference.—VI. 5.—*Expositor* (4th Series), vol. i. p. 202.

1 Tim. vi. 6, etc.

In an age when fortunes are made, either by pleasing vast numbers of persons, and those for the most part half-taught and rude of habit, or else by pleasing those who have amassed fortunes and nothing else—the pursuit of fortune is the ruin of art. I may be asked, what practical measures I would advocate to remedy this state of things, a state of things which seems but another illustration of the old saying—that 'the love of money is the root of all evil'. . . . The only true remedy is that contained in the Apostle's words to Timothy : 'They that will be rich fall into temptation and a snare, and into many foolish and hurtful lusts, which drown men in destruction and perdition'. And it is as true for the artist or the poet to-day as it was for the divine and the disciple, as it was true for the Apostle's own son in the faith, whom he had left in Ephesus : 'But then, flee these things; and follow after righteousness, godliness, faith, love, patience, meekness'. Men hear these words in church on Sunday, and for the next six days in the week they go to 'change and to their office, and contend for the turn of the market like hungry tigers at the hour of meal. 'They that will be rich fall into temptation and a snare, and into many foolish and hurtful lusts.' And no snare is so cunning as that spread for those that will be rich in fame and money by their skill in art.—Frederic Harrison, *Realities and Ideals*, pp. 332 f.

Reference.—VI. 6.—R. G. Soans, *Sermons for the Young*, p. 30.

1 Tim. vi. 7.

'Constantine,' says Dean Stanley (*History of Eastern Church*, vi.), 'usually preached on the general system of the Christian revelation; the follies of paganism; the unity and providence of God; the scheme of redemption; the judgment; and then attacked fiercely the avarice and rapacity of the courtiers, who cheered lustily, but did nothing of what he had told them. On one occasion he caught hold of one of them and drawing on the ground with his spear the figure of a man, said: "In this space is contained all that you will carry with you after death".'

1 Tim. vi. 7-10.

The way to visit a palace is to take your Testament and read the Epistles as you walk about. Never does the insignificance of all human splendours diminish to such a degree at such a time.—B. R. Haydon.

Reference.—VI. 8.—J. S. Boone, *Sermons*, p. 265.

1 Tim. vi. 9.

Where you are, remember that you are in the very centre of the barbaric mercantile system of England, whose rule is, 'They that make haste to be rich,' instead of 'piercing themselves through with many sorrows,' do their best as wise and prudent citizens.

Remember that *that* is a lie; and without offending any one (and the most solemn truths can be spoken without offence, for men in England are very kind-hearted and reasonable), tell them so, and fight against the sins of a commercial city.—KINGSLEY, *to a Liverpool Clergyman.*

REFERENCES.—VI. 9.—*Expositor* (4th Series), vol. i. p. 24; *ibid.* (7th Series), vol. vi. p. 381. VI. 9, 10.—T. Barker, *Plain Sermons*, p. 26. VI. 9-11.—A. Jenkinson, *Christian World Pulpit*, vol. liv. p. 156. VI. 10.—E. A. Bray, *Sermons*, vol. i. p. 262. R. C. Trench, *Sermons New and Old*, p. 60. VI. 12.—Spurgeon, *Sermons*, vol. xxxvii. No. 2226. F. W. Farrar, *Christian World Pulpit*, vol. liv. p. 305. D. W. Whittle, *ibid.* vol. lvi. p. 254. Spurgeon, *Sermons*, vol. xxxiii. No. 1946. C. Perren, *Revival Sermons in Outline*, p. 248. T. F. Crosse, *Sermons*, p. 114. O. Bronson, *Sermons*, p. 245. J. H. Jowett, *British Congregationalist* (New Series), No. 106, p. 122. VI. 12-14.—A. Maclaren, *Expositions of Holy Scripture—Timothy*, p. 370. VI. 12-19.—*Expositor* (4th Series), vol. i. p. 203. VI. 13.—*Ibid.* vol. ii. p. 261; *ibid.* (5th Series), vol. vii. p. 218; *ibid.* (6th Series), vol. ix. p. 267. VI. 14.—*Ibid.* (4th Series), vol. x. p. 109. VI. 16. —*Ibid.* vol. i. p. 34; *ibid.* vol. iii. p. 402.

SPIRITUALITY AND CIVILISATION

'God, who giveth us richly all things to enjoy.'—1 TIM. VI. 17.

IN a time of abounding wealth, of leisure and opportunity, of manifold luxury and fashion, novelty and pleasure, it is of the first importance that we understand our relation to the opulent civilisation which marks our age.

I. Let us then observe that the Christian life is a comprehensive and catholic life. The Christian is free to enter into all possible relations with the world : seeing everything, using everything, enjoying everything. It is not the genius of our spiritual faith to narrow the earthly life, but to make it as wide as possible. Some teachers maintain that it is the highest wisdom to narrow life as much as possible, to bring into it as few things and interests as possible, to reduce it to as few sensations as possible. I venture to say that this is exactly contrary to the genius of the Christian faith. The world is accustomed to regard spiritually minded men as specially narrow, as fanatically morbid and exclusive. Let us not be misunderstood. We are as broad as nature ; all her pipes are in our organ, all her strings are in our harp.

II. But the catholic life can be realised only through the limitations laid down in the context : 'Charge them that are rich in this world, that they be not high-minded, nor trust in uncertain riches, but in the living God, who giveth us richly all things to enjoy ; that they do good, that they be rich in good works, ready to distribute, willing to communicate ; laying up in store for themselves a good foundation against the time to come, that they may hold on eternal life'. (1) Note how this applies to the *physical life.* Nothing is more common than the notion that a spiritual faith does injustice to our animal nature, and discourages us in relation to the whole range of carnal pleasure. But in truth it is only through the discipline of our corporeal life, such a discipline as the text suggests, that we can enjoy the fulness of the possibilities of our physique. (2) Note how the higher law applies to wealth, fashion, and luxury. Let us clearly and fully recognise the legitimacy of the affluence of the times. Let us not proscribe these things of taste and splendour, but insist that they shall be conditioned by godliness, righteousness, and disinterestedness. (3) Finally, a word as to the bearing of our text upon our intellectual, æsthetic, and sentimental life. Here, once again, we recognise that God 'giveth us all things richly to enjoy'.

But whilst Christianity sanctions this glowing and delightful universe, it insists upon the supremacy of the spiritual and ethical elements.—W. L. WATKINSON, *The Blind Spot*, p. 135.

REFERENCES.—VI. 17.—*Expositor* (6th Series), vol. iii. p. 390. VI. 18, 19.—James Vaughan, *Fifty Sermons* (9th Series), p. 9.

THE REALITY OF THE SPIRITUAL LIFE

' The life which is life indeed.'—1 TIM. VI. 19 (R.V.).

IN speaking of a life that is 'life indeed,' St. Paul implies that all life is not such, but that many live a false life. In the conviction of the Apostle, the true life, the life indeed, is the spiritual life. Can we, in this perplexing pilgrimage of life, distinguish between the true and the false ? Several tests will demonstrate the reality of the spiritual life.

I. The Persistence of the Spiritual Instinct.—Despite the most frantic efforts we cannot rid ourselves of the consciousness of the spiritual universe. If our faith in the spiritual world were a mere hallucination, a perception without an object, it would of necessity ever become more attenuated and less influential. The scientist assures us of this. Creatures never retain organs of any sort that are useless. The spiritual instinct is the most inveterate and influential of all our instincts.

II. The Irrationality of Human Life without the Spiritual Idea.—If we are to regard the universe as rational, and human life as serious and satisfactory, the spiritual idea is essential. There is no logic in life except we give it the larger interpretation ; it is a melancholy enigma, and only that, until we recognise its spiritual ideas and laws, its transcendent ideals and hopes.

III. The Deep Satisfaction of those who Cherish the Spiritual Hope.—It has been said by a cynical philosopher that man is simply a lucky bubble on the protoplasmic pot. But if he is nothing more than a bubble, blown by the breath of blind chance and pricked by the hand of blind death, he will steadily and reasonably refuse to believe that he is a 'lucky' bubble. It is altogether another thing with the spiritual man. (1) We may affirm that in the truest sense the Lord Jesus revealed to us the spiritual world. Christ, by flashing upon us the great vision of the Divine, the perfect and the eternal, awoke in us the latent spiritual instinct ; it is He who founded that active, passionate, fruitful, spirituality which created the modern world, and in which lies the hope of the race. (2) In Christ alone do we find ability to live the spiritual life. A Jewish legend affirms that if an angel spends seven days on the earth it becomes gross and opaque and loses the use of its wings. We all know the debasing power of the worldly environment. The heavenly virtue is our supreme salvation against the whole treacherous, debasing environment.—W. L. WATKINSON, *The Bane and the Antidote*, p. 57.

REFERENCES.—VI. 19.—G. S. Barrett, *Christian World Pulpit*, vol. xlvi. p. 312. Spurgeon, *Sermons*, vol. xxxiii. No. 1946. W. L. Watkinson, *Christian World Pulpit*, vol. xlviii. p. 214. R. F. Horton, *The Hidden God*, p. 145. W. L. Watkinson, *Christian World Pulpit*, vol. lviii. p. 228. A. Maclaren, *Expositions of Holy Scripture—Timothy*, p. 379.

TIMOTHY'S LIFE AND MISSION

' O Timothy, keep that which is committed to thy trust.'—
I TIM. VI. 20.

THE text comes to us in one of the Epistles written by St. Paul to his tried friend and companion Timothy, and what do we know about that apostolic man ?

I. His Infancy.—He was the son, like the great St. Augustine, of a religious mother and a heathen father, and by the care of his mother, Eunice, he was trained from a child in the knowledge of ' the Holy Scriptures, which are able to make thee wise unto salvation through faith which is in Christ Jesus '. Now, St. Paul, of course, there is speaking of the Old Testament, because the New Testament did not as yet exist. It is a very familiar and a very charming picture, that of Timothy at his mother's knee learning his first lessons in the Book of Life. But we ought not to think only of the grace and the tenderness of this little vignette of an old-world family party. See rather what it has to teach us.

(a) *It is the right and the duty of parents* to instil into their children that fear of God which is the beginning of wisdom according to the dictates of their consciences. But there is another point and much more important. What Timothy read with his mother was the Old Testament Scriptures, and we see what St. Paul says of those.

(b) *The ancient Hebrew Scriptures are able to make men wise unto salvation* through faith in Christ Jesus. Through faith, the Apostle says, and he means that in themselves they are not adequate because they were written long before the coming of the Gospel and to prepare the way of the Gospel, and that they are therefore inferior to the Gospel, just as the twilight of the dawning is inferior to the full splendour of the sun ; but if a man have faith, if the spirit of Christ Jesus is in his heart, if, therefore, he knows already Him towards Whom the Jews were being led through shadows and through symbols, then

he can see the finger of God in every page. He can see that these old Scriptures are imperfect, and he can see where they are imperfect, and yet at the same time he can see how they are instinct with the growing light of God, while at the same time he blesses God for the fuller light in which he stands. Now is not that what St. Paul means, and does it not answer a great number of questions that are perpetually asked, and that trouble men's minds ? Look upon the Old Testament as the Gospel of the infancy, and you will find that many a perplexity dies away quite of its own accord.

II. His Ordination.—Timothy became the friend and the companion of St. Paul, and finally he was selected to be one of the great officers of the Church, or, as we say, he was ordained. It is important to recall the text which tells us about that fact to your memory. 'Neglect,' the Apostle says, 'neglect not the gift that is in thee, which was given thee by prophesy, with the laying on of the hands of the presbytery ' ; and in another notable passage which we may couple with this—whether it refers to the same incident or to that later time when he was specially set in charge of the Church of Ephesus—St. Paul says, ' Wherefore I put thee in remembrance that thou stir up the gift of God, which is in thee by the putting on of my hands '. Well, there you have first of all the prophet, the inspired layman, the representative of the Church whose voice was the voice of God, and through whom the Holy Ghost spoke, saying, 'Separate unto Me this man or that for the work of My ministry '. Prophecy, in the narrower sense of the word at any rate, has ceased, but in the place of the prophets stand all good Christian people. It has always been their part, and should be more emphatically and confessedly their part to bear their testimony.

III. His Work.—The reason why Timothy was sent to Ephesus was that the Church there was torn by idle and profane questions. A question is idle when it cannot be answered, and therefore ought not to be asked, and it is profane when it causes strife instead of ministering to godliness, when it leads men to think more of their own devices and less of the sovereign grace of God. There were many such questions in the primitive Church. Timothy was despatched to that scene of contention not to plunge joyously into the fray, but to preach that there is one God and one Mediator between God and man. In that simple Gospel St. Paul knew that there was grace and mercy and peace.

REFERENCES.—VI. 20.—G. Body, *Christian World Pulpit*, vol. lviii. p. 233. W. M. Sinclair, *Difficulties of our Day*, p. 13. VI. 20, 21.—*Expositor* (6th Series), vol. iv. p. 21.

THE SECOND EPISTLE TO TIMOTHY

2 TIMOTHY

REFERENCES.—I. 1.—*Expositor* (4th Series), vol. i. p. 203. I. 1-7.—A. Maclaren, *Expositions of Holy Scripture—Timothy*, p. 1.

'When I call to remembrance the unfeigned faith that is in thee, which dwelt first in thy grandmother Lois.'—2 TIM. I. 5.

ST. BASIL the Great owed his earliest religious education to his grandmother Macrina, who brought him up with his brothers, and formed them upon the doctrine of the great Origenist and saint of Pontus, Gregory Thaumaturgus. Canon Travers Smith wrote in his *Life of St. Basil* :—

'Macrina had not only been taught by the best Christian instructors, but had herself with her husband suffered for the faith. In the persecutions of Maximin she and her family were driven from their home and forced with a few companions to take refuge in a forest among the mountains of Pontus, where they spent nearly seven years, and were wont to attribute to the special interposition of God the supplies of food by which they were maintained at a distance from all civilisation.

'It must not be supposed that the charge of Basil's childhood thus committed to his grandmother indicated any deficiency in love or piety on the part of his mother. Her name was Emmelia, and Gregory describes her as fitly matched with her husband. They had ten children. Of the five sons three became bishops—Basil, Gregory of Nyssa, and Peter of Sebaste.'

REFERENCES.—I. 6.—J. Keble, *Sermons for Septuagesima to Ash Wednesday*, p. 323. Spurgeon, *Sermons*, vol. xviii. No. 1080.

A CALL TO CHRISTIAN COURAGE

'God hath not given us the spirit of fear ; but of power, and of love, and of a sound mind.'—2 TIM. I. 7.

HERE we have the true Spirit of a Christian set forth in three particulars, and each of these is an antidote to timidity.

I. God has given us the Spirit of power. Herein lies our fitness for whatsoever form our witness-bearing ought to take. The consciousness of inward strength removes all fear. It is said, 'The world belongs to those who have courage'; then the saints ought to possess it, and it is because of their cowardice, if they do not.

II. God has given us the Spirit of love. Thus He has brought us into sympathy and fellowship with Himself, for God is love. If conscience make cowards of us all, a good conscience should make us fearless.

III. God has given us the Spirit of a sound mind. As opposed to the madness and folly of sin, religion is a return to the true reason, sound judgment, and right action. (1) A sound mind is a mind evenly balanced. (2) A sound mind is candid, open to all the truth and eager to gather it from all quarters. (3) A sound mind controls the life, and thus ensures true Christian temperance. (4) A sound mind gains, often quite imperceptibly, a great influence over other minds.—C. O. ELDRIDGE, *The Preacher's Magazine*, vol. VI. p. 81.

2 TIM. I. 7.

THE last words written by Lady Dilke, which close her *Book of the Spiritual Life*, run thus : 'To their solemn music, the fateful years unroll the great chart in which we may trace the hidden mysteries of the days, and behold those foreshadowings of things to come towards which we know ourselves to be carried by inevitable steps—not gladly, indeed, but with that full and determined consent with which the brave accept unflinchingly the fulfilment of law and fate. "For God hath not given us the Spirit of fear ; but of power, and of love, and of a sound mind."'

REFERENCES.—I. 7.—F. D. Maurice, *Sermons*, vol. vi. p. 93. *Expositor* (6th Series), vol. xi. p. 204. I. 8.—J. Baines, *Sermons*, p. 168.

2 TIM. I. 9.

WHAT needs admitting, or rather proclaiming, by agnostics who would be just is, that the Christian doctrine has a power of cultivating and developing saintliness which has had no equal in any other creed or philosophy.—J. COTTER MORISON, in *The Service of Man* (ch. VII.).

REFERENCES.—I. 9.—Spurgeon, *Sermons*, vol. xii. No. 703. *Expositor* (4th Series), vol. i. p. 33.

THE PROMISE OF LIFE

'Life and immortality brought to light through the Gospel.'—2 TIM. I. 10.

I PRESUME most of you either own or have seen a print of Millet's picture, 'L'Angelus,' which represents a French peasant and his wife resting momentarily from their work in the field to join in prayer at the sound of the vesper bell, and some of you may know the exquisite use to which the late Henry Drummond put this picture in his address on work and love and worship. I shall take these three elements of life—though there is a fourth at which the picture hints but faintly, and of which Drummond said nothing—the element of suffering. And I shall try to remind you how, under a Christian interpretation, these drive our minds toward the life that is life indeed.

I. Let us look first at work, which for most of us

means three-quarters of our life, the returning toil of each new day, much of it sordid and monotonous; can it possibly be made to speak to us of the eternal life?

Work, when it is Christianly interpreted, drives our minds toward the thought of the life essentially continuous with this, while in its accidents different. It is this thought that is the climax of St. Paul's reason in his famous resurrection chapter, 1 Cor. xv., for after his triumphant hymn of praise because of our victory over death, he brings the whole argument to a climax in reminding us that it is now worth while our working if our work be in line with God's work, for our work here leads into life beyond, 'wherefore, my beloved brethren, be ye stedfast, immovable always, abounding in the work of the Lord; for as much as ye know that your labour is not in vain in the Lord'—*i.e.* such work as you do here show forth God must have its crown of fulfilment in the land where His glory specially rests.

II. It is in the attachment of heart to heart that men have found the most powerful presage of immortality, and poets in all ages have with almost frenzied certitude proclaimed their conviction that love is stronger than death. Where love is, God is; and where God is, life must ever be. If our love be drawn from Christ's there may be sacrifice before it, but never separation. For if our love be baptised into the spirit of Christ, it is taken up into His life and cannot die. This is not subjective conviction: this is not mysticism, this is New Testament doctrine, the very essence and foundation of the last writings of St. John, the final interpreter to us in point of time of the incarnation of Jesus Christ our Lord.

III. It is, however, only when we pass to worship that the promise of eternal life becomes irresistible. For consider what worship is. Worship is a reciprocal movement between the human spirit and God; it consists, that is to say, of our upward aspirations and God's stooping responses. Worship is friendship between God and man; but think for a moment what it means for the Eternal God to enter into friendly relations with any one. His friendships are not capricious, but partake of His own eternal nature; in other words, they endow those who are the subjects of this friendship with His own immortality.

Now consider how Jesus Christ interpreted and transfigured this experience of worship; through Him it becomes possessed of certain characteristics that emphasise the certitude of the eternal life; for example, it becomes through Him a *life of filial intimacy;* and sonship carries with it the promise of home. Our filial aspirations, as has been said, are the earliest part of us; there is a sequence of thought which it is almost impossible to escape in the sentences: 'Now are we the sons of God,' and 'It doth not yet appear what we shall be'. As we experience it here, the adoption of sons involves the certain hope of a home-coming to God.

Work, love, worship—these, then, Christianly understood, are promises, of eternal life.

IV. And what of suffering? Without its Christian interpretation it is but an emphasis on life's transiency. When we suffer, it is all that binds us to the physical, that is, that comes to the front of our thoughts—the pains and disabilities of the body, prospect of dissolution and bereavement.

As sufferers we are the subject of change, and so Buddha read the fact of suffering; it was to him one of the facts that pointed to the desirability of escape from the terrors of self-conscious life. So far from containing within itself any promise of immortality, it was one of the facts that made him long for the cessation of consciousness and of desire. But Christ has transformed all that. He interpreted suffering and so moulded the sufferers who believe in Him that often it is Christian sufferers for whom the veil is worn the thinnest between this life and the life that is to be, so that they become preachers of the land of far distances, and bring the eternal order within our view. It is, of course, Christ's own sufferings that have thus suffused all other pain with the heavenly glow; it is in Him that suffering supremely bears the promise and potency of immortality.—G. A. JOHNSTON Ross, *Christian World Pulpit*, vol. LXXVII. p. 257.

2 TIM. I. 10.

'I MYSELF,' says Thomas Boston in his *Memoirs*, 'have been several times, on this occasion, taking a view of death; and I have found that faith in God through Christ makes another world not quite strange.'

REFERENCES.—I. 10.—Eynon Davies, *Sermons by Welshmen*, p. 327. *The Record*, vol. xxvii. p. 756. E. Bersier, *Sermons in Paris*, p. 230. J. C. M. Bellew, *Sermons*, vol. i. p. 351. J. H. Holford, *Memorial Sermons*, p. 37. T. Binney, *King's Weigh-House Chapel Sermons*, p. 41. *Expositor* (5th Series), vol. v. p. 389.

DOCTRINE AND LIFE

'I know Whom I have believed.'—2 TIM. I. 12.

I. The Importance of Right Doctrine.—The most living Christian experience, if it is to be better than unauthorised, unverifiable fancy or feeling, is in its essence connected with revealed doctrine. Without that warrant, the warmest emotions about God, or Christ, may have no solidity of fact beneath them. Not that every believer must, or can, enter into the same fulness of doctrinal truth. But some doctrine the little believing child must have, and the old believing cottager who cannot read. To know Whom they trust they must know about Him; they must know something of the doctrine of the Son of God. We *may* carry our advocacy of the claims of doctrine too far, but our present risk is the very opposite. It is to regard persons more than truths, teachers than teaching. It is to make moral earnestness the first thing and the last. It is to look for the glory of God somewhere else than in the face of Jesus Christ, as that face is seen in the mirror of the Word, in the light of the Spirit. I plead, then, for the supreme importance of sound and solid doctrine, of clear views, of what is revealed about Christ—

(a) *His person and His work.*
(b) *His sacrificial blood.*
(c) *His indwelling life.*
(d) *His intercession above.*

II. We Turn to the Necessity, the Bliss, of a Personal Acquaintance with the Living Lord Jesus Christ.—We have looked awhile on what some may call the 'dry bones' of doctrine, but which are in fact the *vertebræ* of the backbone of life. But now we look again at St. Paul's words, and we embrace the blessedness of a personal knowledge of—not it, but Him. If we would live, if our Christianity is not to be a synonym for barren mental speculation, or somewhat commonplace philanthropy, or merely carnal contentiousness, or, worst of all, a cloak for a life of entire and complacent selfishness, then we must know Him and abide in Him. Among the doctrines of the faith is this, that if I know all mysteries, and have not holy love, I am nothing; and that, on the other hand, Christ can dwell in my heart by faith, by the work of the strengthening Spirit. Who shall describe the happiness of direct personal acquaintance with Him, as it were behind (not without) all thinking, and all work, which thought and work He yet can fill and can use? It is the reality of realities.

(a) *In it the most advanced and instructed believer*, and the most timid beginner in the life of faith, alike have part and lot.

(b) *It gives wings of light* to the highest musings and most accurate studies of the believing theologian.

(c) *It warms and sweetens the arduous tasks* of the believing toiler for the souls and bodies and homes of men.

(d) *It smiles on the dying bed* of the little child, and refuses to fall out of the aged mind, which drops everything else in its palsy.

A few years ago, in India, died a little native boy, of twelve years old. Almost unawares he had learned the doctrine, and had found the Lord. Too weak to converse, almost too weak apparently to think, he twice over, at the last, folded his skeleton hands, and slowly repeated those unfathomable words, 'The Lord Jesus Christ, the Lord Jesus Christ'.

THE ASSURED KNOWLEDGE OF THE PERSONAL SAVIOUR

'I know Him.'—2 Tim. i. 12 (R.V.).

I. This Knowledge is Personal in its Object.—Evidently the Apostle intended to emphasise the actual personality of the Object of his faith. Christianity is not creed, not document, not church, not Sacrament; Christianity is Christ, Christ is Christianity. But you ask, 'Is it possible for me to know Christ in this positive manner? He is no longer on earth. How, then, may I know Him?' Probably the Apostle Paul had never seen Christ in the flesh; he had seen Him in vision only. True knowledge of persons is never obtained through the organs of outward sense. (1) Paul knew Christ through the organ of faith. The margin reads, 'I know Him whom

I have trusted'. (2) By love. Paul gave his heart to Christ. It is the lover always who knows. (3) By obedience. As Robertson long ago remarked: 'Obedience is an organ of spiritual knowledge'. He who will do the will of God shall know. (4) By suffering. Evermore there is a knowledge of Christ sweeter, deeper, more blessed than all other which comes to the believer when he suffers with Christ and for Christ.

II. This Knowledge Inspires at once a Noble Character and Life.—As the generations pass the character of the Apostle Paul shines out with ever-increasing glory. The secret of that wonderful character was, according to his own testimony, his faith in Jesus Christ. Thus to know Christ in this positive manner, to wrap the roots of the heart around Him, to draw the sap of life from Him, is to have life cut off from all that is sordid, earthly, and selfish, and transfigured with the glory of the Lord.

III. This Knowledge Inspires Calmness in Trial and Confidence in Death.—Amid the shocks of temporal disaster, or when fierce fires of persecution burn around us—or when cruel wrongs oppress the soul, or when the heart is wrung with parting pangs, and we have to kiss cold lips, and bid the long goodbye; or when fell diseases smite us low, and blot out all the hope of life—we are kept in perfect peace if only we know Him. When we come to the mystery of death, the only thing which will give us calmness and confidence is the assured knowledge of Him who is evermore the Resurrection and the Life.—J. TOLEFREE PARR, *The White Life*, p. 59.

2 Tim. i. 12.

IF you have had trials, sickness, and the approach of death, the alienation of friends, poverty at the heels, and have not felt your soul turn round upon these very things and spurn them under—you must be very differently made from me, and, I earnestly believe, from the majority of men.—R. L. STEVENSON.

REFERENCES.—I. 12.—Spurgeon, *Sermons*, vol. v. No. 271. J. Stalker, *Christian World Pulpit*, vol. lvi. p. 171. S. H. Fleming, *Fifteen Minute Sermons for the People*, p. 194. Spurgeon, *Sermons*, vol. xvi. No. 908. John Watson, *Christian World Pulpit*, vol. lix. p. 299. T. A. Cox, *Penny Pulpit*, No. 1484, p. 9. W. M. Sinclair, *Difficulties of our Day*, p. 158. H. P. Liddon, *Sermons on Some Words of St. Paul*, p. 276. J. D. Jones, *Elims of Life*, p. 220. John Watson, *The Inspiration of our Faith*, p. 214. W. H. Brookfield, *Sermons*, p. 36. A. W. Hutton, *Christian World Pulpit*, vol. lxx. p. 328. *Expositor* (4th Series), vol. x. p. 190. A. Maclaren, *Expositions of Holy Scripture—Timothy*, p. 16.

THE TWO TRUSTS

'I am persuaded that He is able to keep that which I have committed unto Him. That good thing which was committed unto thee keep by the Holy Ghost which dwelleth in us.'—2 Tim. i. 12, 14.

You will observe that these two sayings are in one point identical. They express the one great thought of the Christian life, in its twofold aspect—the thought of Christ's faithfulness to us, and of our answering fidelity to Him. In both there is the idea of a weighty and solemn trust—of something that has unspeakable value committed to the keeping of another, left under his watchful guard, which he is pledged to defend at all cost. Let me set it briefly before you : Christ's loving demand that we shall keep that which He has committed to us ; our joyous certainty that He will guard for evermore that which we have committed to Him.

I. First, let us think of what He has entrusted to us. Paul calls it that good or that beautiful thing ; and we say in brief that it is twofold—the name of Jesus and the faith of Jesus. (1) He has left His pure, undefiled name in our keeping. When the crusader went off to the holy war, he left some sworn friend to fill his place—to do what he would have done, to shield those whom he would have defended, and especially to answer all slanders that were uttered against the absent one, and maintain unsullied his pure reputation. In some such way the great Master has left us in charge. The whole Church is made responsible for the honour of her Lord, and every single disciple shares in the sacred trust. (2) He has committed to us what we call 'The Faith,' the body of truth and doctrine which He gave as His message from the Father, and which constitutes the heritage of the Church—'the faith,' to quote the saying which is often misused, but which we are never weary of repeating, 'the faith once for all delivered to the Saints'. And how are we to keep it ? To keep the faith is to live it. We cannot be fairly said to hold any doctrine until we make it a part of our every-day life.

II. And now I speak of the other side of the Christian life, of that which relates to our trust in the King's promise, and of His pledge to keep that which we have committed unto Him. There are certain things which we can do. We can defend the faith, we can maintain the honour of His name, we can preserve our own lives unspotted from the world. But then there remains a large province of things which enter into our deepest life, over which we have no power whatever, which we can but leave with blind, helpless, childlike trust in His loving, mighty hands. There is the future of the Church. There is our own and its results, its rewards. Then, further, there is our own immortality. And, finally, there are our beautiful affections, the friendships which we have cultivated with so much care and cherished with such ardent solicitude, which we have woven about our souls until they have become an inseparable part of our souls. Let us keep our trust, and be assured that He will keep His.—J. G. GREENHOUGH, *The Cross in Modern Life*, p. 178.

REFERENCES.—I. 12-14.—Spurgeon, *Sermons*, vol. xxxii. No. 1913. I. 13.—A. H. Sayce, *Christian World Pulpit*. vol. lviii. p. 241. Spurgeon, *Sermons*, vol. ii. No. 79. R. W. Hiley, *A Year's Sermons*, vol. iii. p. 314. *Expositor* (5th Series), vol. vi. p. 385. A. Maclaren, *Expositions of Holy Scripture—Timothy*, p. 26. I. 13, 14.—G. Body, *Christian World Pulpit*, vol. lviii. p. 233. I. 14.—H. S. Holland, *ibid.* vol. lix. p. 380.

A FRIEND IN NEED

' The Lord give mercy unto the house of Onesiphorus ; for he oft refreshed me, and was not ashamed of my chain.'—2 TIM. I. 16.

THIS letter, many scholars think, may have been penned on the very eve of the great Apostle's death. We seem to have a premonition of the end in that brave verse of the fourth chapter : 'I have fought the good fight, I have finished the course, I have kept the faith '. Our text, therefore, has in it something of the peculiar weight and intensity that oft-times characterise parting words of the dying. St. Paul was never prone to indiscriminate praise or blame. He had greater matters in hand than the strewing of compliments even upon his coadjutors in the proclamation of the Christian Gospel. Hence we may assume that the singularly cordial words he speaks of Onesiphorus are the product of deep and manly feeling.

Onesiphorus means bringer of help; so that in this instance 'at least name and nature coincide ; for it was the promptness and the richness of the help he brought that went to Paul's heart.

I. First, then, consider Onesiphorus *in the rôle of a Christian friend*. One of the qualities in him which these verses specially underline is, you will note, the consistency of his helpfulness.

(1) Two features, I imagine, in Onesiphorus' conduct at Rome touched St. Paul with peculiar gratitude. In the first place, he took pains to help his friend. ' He sought me out very diligently, and found me.'

The main thing required to make us helpful is not sentiment, but action.

(2) Then besides that, Onesiphorus was not ashamed of Paul ; and *that* memory the Apostle treasured with a rare depth of gratitude. Evidently he was used to having people ashamed of him. It was all part of being a Christian. But to treat him so never crossed the other's mind. To know St. Paul was the pride of Onesiphorus' life. So far from being ashamed or afraid to be seen in his cell, I have no doubt he grew positively elated over his success in finding him.

II. Note secondly, *how much this kindness meant to Paul*. No one had ever lived more completely human than the Apostle to the Gentiles. The desire for friendship became at times with him almost a physical craving. It is not to be imagined that he always lived upon the heights, on the blue altitudes, for example, to which he soars in Colossians or Ephesians. No ; there were hours of loneliness and sorrow, when in his dejection he would have given all he had for the voice of a loved friend, and a look from his kindly eyes. So think of the shock of pleasure that came to the solitary captive when one day his cell-door swung back, and in strode this trusty henchman, all the way from Asia. A friend in need is a friend indeed.

III. Lastly, note *how St. Paul repaid the other's kindness*. In one word, he prayed for him ; he took his name in love to the throne of God ; and this is the best recompense any of us can make for sympathy or help. Says a saint of the seventeenth century, writing to an acquaintance who lived by habit in fellowship with God : 'When you have the King's ear, remember me' ; and surely each of us has at least one friend from whom we also might beg this kindness.—H. R. MACKINTOSH, *Life on God's Plan*, p. 73.

REFERENCE.—I. 18.—*Expositor* (6th Series), vol. vi. p. 388.

THE CHRISTIAN SOLDIER

'Thou therefore, my son, be strong in the grace that is in Christ Jesus. . . . Thou therefore endure hardness, as a good soldier of Jesus Christ. No man that warreth entangleth himself with the affairs of this life ; that he may please Him Who hath chosen him to be a soldier.'—2 TIM. II. I, 3, 4.

ST. PAUL's admiration of soldiers, and his choice of a soldier to be the type of one who belongs to Jesus Christ, the Lamb of God, meek and gentle—all this is quite easily explained, and has been very often explained, but nevertheless it ought to challenge much more attention and thought than we usually give it. When St. Paul says, 'My son, endure hardness as a good soldier of Jesus Christ,' it seems to us a commonplace ; but we have to consider what the word meant when St. Paul uttered it. What are the qualities of the soldier that we ought to be able to show in our religion, in our penitence, and in our gratitude to our Saviour ?

I. St. Paul loved soldiers, and owed much to them ; and, seeing their frank and brave carriage, he says, This also is what the Christian is to be : let him be the good soldier of Christ, and keep himself from all entanglements of civil life, the ordinary affairs of this life, which he must use but not be used by, in order that he may give satisfaction to Him Who has chosen him to be, not His darling, but His soldier.

II. What has the soldier, then (side by side, no doubt, with many faults like other men, with special faults belonging to his condition), which is purely good ? St. Paul would point us to two things, Discipline and Endurance. He is a man of discipline, who has taken, in the Roman phrase, a sacrament, or oath. He has chosen his side and has his Master. It is that which our dear Lord Himself praises in the first centurion of the Gospel (St. Matt. VIII.). He knew his master and his place ; he knew the great principles of authority, which, whether one exercises it or subjects oneself to it, depends upon something deeper still—fidelity. It is not a mere pride which brings hearts down by the reverberation of its claim, it is not an influence which sways a crowd by its attraction ; it is a reference to something lying behind, it is a claim upon a past account, it rests upon something agreed upon beforehand. The soldier, as disciplined, knows his master, and is servant because he knows to whom he has committed himself.

III. And we Christians need that lesson very much. There are Christians who all their life long are wondering on which side they shall stand, and who are ever learning and never coming to the knowledge of the

truth. Let us pray our Captain, our Lord and Saviour, that we may not fall into the awful curse of those who deny Him, their Master, who shrink back from a yoke which is no voluntary yoke, because it forms part of that great compact which is all our salvation. If Christ saves us He commands us ; if Christ pardons us He claims us. Discipline, obedience, fidelity, a clear recognition of the Masterhood under which we serve, are wrought in and with the most secret, the most delicate, the most tender hopes of the penitent : if we hope that our tears will not be in vain we must see that our minds are set firm ; if we hope that our penitence will not be rejected we must see that our feet walk along the path traced for us by Jesus, Who is not only our Saviour, but our Lord. Let us know our own side, let us grasp the great faith and go forward, that we may prove the strength of Him Who hath chosen us to be His soldiers.

IV. But I long to say a word about the hardness, the endurance, of the military life. That also is a lesson to us as a nation and a Church. In the nation there is a perilous seeking after softness, pleasure, satisfaction, ease, a longing to avoid what is hard ; I speak not of luxury, I speak not of eating and drinking, of 'lying soft and rolling swift' : those are mere specks upon the stream of our life. I speak of that general and widespread longing to avoid all that is unpleasant, to avoid the word that costs us or our neighbour pain, to avoid the manly course when we are in an awkward situation, to replace the Christian ideal of suffering and conflict by another ideal of mere release from bodily pain, of an earthly and passing peace of mind, of a health and bodily development which subjects all other interests to its own. That is what we must indeed recoil from, lest we be found, searching after what is soft, to have lost our Saviour. The man who is trying to find a soft place in the world will never find one soft enough. It is from those given up to pleasure, and longing for what they call happiness, that we hear words which come near to rebellion against God Himself when they have met with one of the common troubles of life. They see endless losses in losses which are indeed real, but in which braver souls find encouragement. Fighting people find the world tolerable and joyful ; it is those who recognise it as a battle who are optimists. The soft theory means a bitter heart, and the bold acceptance of God's call to arms means a heart at peace, knowing peace under the banner of a King at war.

REFERENCE.—II. 2.—Archbishop Benson, *Living Theology*, p. 109.

2 TIM. II. 3.

A DEPRESSING and difficult passage has prefaced every new page I have turned in life.—CHARLOTTE BRONTË, in *Villette*.

2 TIM. II. 3.

GARIBALDI told his Sicilian volunteers : 'Men who follow me must learn to live without food, and to fight without ammunition'.

REFERENCES.—II. 3.—Spurgeon, *Sermons*, vol. xvi. No 938. R. Primrose, *Christian World Pulpit*, vol. xlvi. p 27.

C. Perren, *Revival Sermons in Outline*, p. 308. H. P. Liddon, *Sermons Preached on Special Occasions*. p. 342. S. Spink, *Penny Pulpit*, No. 1689, p. 551. J. Aspinall, *Parish Sermons* (2nd Series), p. 182. *Expositor* (5th Series), vol. vii. p. 459. II. 4.—A. Maclaren, *Expositions of Holy Scripture—Timothy*, p. 45. II. 5.—J. Martineau, *Endeavours After the Christian Life* (2nd Series), p. 62. *Expositor* (5th Series), vol. x. p. 240. II. 8.—Spurgeon, *Sermons*, vol. xxviii. No. 1653. *Expositor* (5th Series), vol. iii. p. 450 ; *ibid.* vol. ix. p. 13. II. 9.—Basil Wilberforce, *Christian World Pulpit*, vol. li. p. 81 ; *ibid.* vol. li. p. 294. Spurgeon, *Sermons*, vol. xxxiii. No. 1998. W. T. Davison, *Christian World Pulpit*, vol. lv. p. 262. J. A. Alexander, *The Gospel of Jesus Christ*, p. 499. *Expositor* (4th Series), vol. viii. pp. 115, 116. II. 10.—*Ibid.* vol. i. p. 34. II. 12.—Bishop Gore, *Christian World Pulpit*, vol. xlvii. p. 263. W. J. Knox Little, *Christian World Pulpit*, vol. li. p. 278. Spurgeon, *Sermons*, vol. x. No. 547.

'He abideth faithful.'—2 Tim. ii. 13.

AMONG the cavaliers who fought at Edgehill was Sir Jacob Astley, whose prayer and charge, says Dr. Stoughton, were characteristic of the bluff piety of the best of his class. 'O Lord, Thou knowest how busy I must be this day. If I forget Thee do not forget me. March on, boys ! '

REFERENCES.—II. 13.—G. Bellett, *Parochial Sermons*, p. 32. Spurgeon, *Sermons*, vol. xxv. No. 1453. A. Maclaren, *Expositions of Holy Scripture—Timothy*, p. 58.

2 Tim. ii. 14-16.

I REMEMBER no discussion on religion in which religion was not a sufferer by it.—LANDOR.

THE WORKMAN AND HIS OVERSEER
'Study to shew thyself approved unto God, a workman that needeth not to be ashamed.'—2 Tim. ii. 15.

THESE are words that you might write anywhere : on the bishop's palace, on the magistrate's bench, on the king's throne, on the editor's office, on the factory door, on the gardener's spade, on the maid-servant's broom, on the schoolboy's satchel.

I. God expects us all to be workmen. Our Lord Jesus has told us that God Himself has never ceased to work from the beginning, and His will is that we should all be co-workers with Him. Christianity is a divine workshop, and all who seek for admittance at its door must come with their loins girded for service. Christ expects every man to do his duty, and duty means hard, honest work of some kind. Our religion tells us all that labour and not pleasure should form the main substance of life, and that manhood loses all its dignity if it does not play a workman's part in the world. Everywhere the Christian idea is gaining ground, that rank and nobility are determined by service ; that there can be no greatness in indolence, but that there is something great in all honest work.

II. We are to do our work and live our lives as under the eyes of the Great Overseer, remembering that we are seen of Him whom we cannot see, and that each day's work is submitted to His inspection. That is what the Apostle means by ' Study to show thyself approved unto God '. For it is not likely that we shall do our work well without an overseer. It is well for all of us that our brother-men take account of our doings. That is good, but there is something better. For if we recognise no judges of our work, and no overseer except our fellow-men, we lose the highest motives, and the most constant spur.

III. We are to work and live in such a way that we shall not be ashamed of ourselves. I know it is a hard task. It is all but impossible for a man to live and work in such a manner that he is never ashamed of himself. One of the noblest men I ever knew, the Hon. Baptist Noel as he was called, who had given up family prospects and position for conscience and Christ's sake, said tremblingly, just as he was dying, to some one who whispered to him, ' You will soon see Jesus,' ' Yes ; I shall be very glad, but very much ashamed '. There is no escape from that with the best of us. But we can endeavour by the help of God to make each day's shame less, and to stand before God at last with something that will bear thinking of as well as much that we would thankfully forget. —J. G. GREENHOUGH, *The Cross and the Dice-Box*, p. 99.

REFERENCES. — II. 15. — G. Lester, *Preacher's Magazine*, vol. x. p. 359. Spurgeon, *Sermons*, vol. xxi. No. 1217. J. Baldwin Brown, *Aids to the Development of the Divine Life*, No. xi. *Expositor* (5th Series), vol. vi. p. 69.

THE LAW OF MORAL ENVIRONMENT
' Shun profane babblings : for they will proceed further in ungodliness, and their word will eat (or spread) as doth a gangrene.'—2 Tim. ii. 17 (R.V.).

ONE subject suggested by the text is the deep social and religious truth of the influence of environment. Timothy is asked to shun, and to do what he can to make others shun the evil doctrine and ungodly life of their environment, which have crept into the Church also. It is because the Apostle realises the tremendous power of environment that he warns with such impressive solemnity. He knew that a little leaven leaveneth the whole lump.

I. We usually take an outside and surface view of what environment means. We think of it as our outward surroundings, conditions of work, and conditions of home life. But the law of environment is a far subtler thing than all that, and cuts much deeper into our lives. After all is said about material conditions, it has to be remembered that the chief environment of a human life does not consist of things but of *persons*. There is a moral and spiritual climate as well as a physical. The people make the homes and the workshops and the towns, which have such influence over our lives.

II. When we think of it, we see that all the permanent influences of life come from persons. Home is not the walls where furniture is stored, but the place where others exercise their weird influence over us. The real environment, the mighty forces that play upon life and mould character, are thus spiritual ; and this is where we have power over our environment. We can submit to what is evil in that environment, or we can shun it.

III. In all human intercourse influence permeates ceaselessly the whole circle from centre to circumference—your influence on others, their influence on you. It is not a plea for a hermit life, but a plea for serious consideration of the conditions of social life. The consideration should be twofold, the sense of your duty towards others, the sense of a necessary duty towards yourself in this matter.—HUGH BLACK, *Edinburgh Sermons*, p. 113.

REFERENCES.—II. 17.—Bishop Magee, *Sermons at Bath*, p. 124. II. 18.—*Expositor* (6th Series), vol. v. p. 468 ; *ibid.* (7th Series), vol. vi. p. 151.

THE FOUNDATION OF GOD

'Nevertheless the foundation of God standeth sure, having this seal, The Lord knoweth them that are His. And, let everyone that nameth the name of Christ depart from iniquity. But in a great house there are not only vessels of gold and of silver, but also of wood and of earth, and some to honour, and some to dishonour. If a man therefore purge himself from these, he shall be a vessel unto honour, sanctified, and meet for the Master's use, and prepared unto every good work.'—2 TIM. II. 19-21.

You will remember that the closing pages of the Bible are made glorious with a vision of the New Jerusalem, that is, a vision of the perfected Christian Church, and that that vision was seen by St. John from the heights of a great mountain. I am never surprised to hear that men see wonderful things from the heights of the mountains. Are you not surprised, however, to find that a similar vision appeared to St. Paul, when he was in his prison-house at Rome? In that narrow, dark prison he looked out and saw God's great house - the New Jerusalem, the perfected Christian Church. The eye sees what it brings the power to see. I want us to see the vision that appeared, then, to St. Paul.

I. And, first of all, I want us to gather the impression that was produced upon St. Paul when he looked upon the great house of the Lord. When St. Paul looked upon the house of the Lord he said it was a great house, and had been built by a mighty workman ; that it had stood steadfast in the midst of all the turmoils of time, and that is the impression that ought to be produced upon us when we gaze upon the Christian Church.

II. I want you to pass upward and look upon these inscriptions : (1) 'The Lord knoweth them that are His'. There are a great many people to whom God says that, to whom you never say that. And one of the greatest surprises will be to find so many people in heaven that we never expected to meet. (2) 'Let everyone that nameth the name of Christ depart from iniquity.' Let us have great sympathy with doubt, and hesitation, and becloudment of mind, but a very stern voice for all iniquity. We must have a pure Church.

III. But now we must get inside. Go into the banqueting hall. Look ! See ! It is ready for the King. The vessels of silver and gold as they stand upon the festal table seem to suggest one question to me. It is : How may I be a vessel of honour in the house of the Lord ? Paul says : 'If a man, therefore,

purge himself from these he shall be a vessel unto honour'. And it is supposed that the reference there is to such men as Hymenæus and Philetus. We have light upon the character of one of these men who troubled the Early Church. He made 'shipwreck of faith and of a good conscience '. If you want to be a vessel of honour in the house of God, get very near to your Master.—J. S. SIMON, *Christian World Pulpit*, vol. LXXIII. p. 198.

REFERENCES.—II. 19.—T. Jones, *Christian World Pulpit*, vol. lii. p. 408. C. D. Bell, *The Name Above Every Name*, p. 67. Spurgeon, *Sermons*, vol. xxxi. No. 1854. J. Bowstead, *Practical Sermons*, vol. ii. p. 99. *Expositor* (6th Series), vol. x. p. 358. A. Maclaren, *Expositions of Holy Scripture—Timothy*, p. 68. II. 20.—*Ibid.* (4th Series), vol. ii. p. 39 ; *ibid.* (7th Series), vol. vi. p. 275. II. 20, 21.—Spurgeon, *Sermons*, vol. xxiii. No. 1348. A. Maclaren, *Expositions of Holy Scripture—Timothy*, p. 77. II. 26.—*Expositor* (4th Series), vol. vi. p. 22. III. 1.—T. Arnold, *The Interpretation of Scripture*, p. 245. *Expositor* (6th Series), vol. v. p. 468.

' Unthankful.'—2 TIM. III. 2.

INGRATITUDE is always a form of weakness. I have never known men of ability to be ungrateful.—GOETHE.

THE USE AND ABUSE OF PLEASURE

'Lovers of pleasure more than lovers of God.'—2 TIM. III. 4.

I SUPPOSE we should say, taking a general view of humanity, that while man has to work, and work is essential, man also needs pleasure and recreation. But then this recreation or pleasure will depend very much upon two things for its beneficent results : first, the kind of pleasure, and secondly, the degree in which we indulge in it. We may all have too much of a good thing ; we may all indulge in that which is adverse to our advantage.

I. There are different kinds of pleasure, and a man may abuse pleasure in two ways. If you would judge pleasure, you must judge it from the standpoints of degree and kind. (1) If a man gives up too much time to pleasure, you know what happens ; it weakens his moral fibres ; it introduces a disinclination for work ; it impairs his power and capacity for usefulness. (2) The wholesomeness of pleasure will depend upon the character of the pleasure itself. There are some pleasures which are unwholesome ; there are some pleasures which are wholesome. I take it that that pleasure which takes the form merely of frivolity at least does the man no good ; and by doing the man no good, that frivolous pleasure does him harm, for it makes no demand upon the mind, no demand upon the heart, no demand upon the spiritual energies. Then there are pleasures which are distinctly harmful, and as such are to be avoided. (a) There are the pleasures of over-eating and over-drinking. (b) But there are worse pleasures—pleasures of self-indulgence, pleasures of distinct immorality, which degrade a man and bring him to the animal state. (c) And there are pleasures, which turn upon money —the chink of money.

II. What, then, is pleasure for ? Pleasure is intended for recreation—the recreating of the man. And, mark you, there are splendid, wholesome recreations in the world. But pleasure, like everything else, may be used and may be abused ; and it is a law of our higher nature that we must be for ever making choice.

III. Now, what is the attitude of Christ towards pleasure ? There never was a more natural teacher than Jesus Christ ; there never was a more natural life than the life of Jesus Christ. The Master never would say : 'Turn your back upon pleasure as an evil thing,' but He would say : 'Judge your pleasures ; judge them from the standpoint of your moral elevation, your moral characters, and the work you have to do for men and for God '.—BISHOP BOYD-CARPENTER, *Christian World Pulpit*, vol. LXXIII. p. 215.

'Lovers of pleasure more than lovers of God.'—2 TIM. III. 4.

HIS guide was not duty ; it was not even ambition ; but his guide was self ; it was ease and amusement and lust. The cup of pleasure was filled deep for him, and he grasped it with both hands. But pleasure is not happiness. There is no happiness for him who lives and dies without beliefs, without enthusiasm, and without love.—OSMUND AIRY, *Charles II.*, p. 416.

'High-minded.'—2 TIM. III. 4.

MOST men seem rather inclined to confess the want of virtue than of importance.—DR. JOHNSON.

REFERENCES.—III. 4.—W. Brock, *Midsummer Morning Sermons*, p. 146. III. 5.—F. C. Spurr, *Christian World Pulpit*, vol. li. p. 86. Spurgeon, *Sermons*, vol. xxxv. No. 2088. A. Maclaren, *Expositions of Holy Scripture—Timothy*, p. 86. III. 6.—*Expositor* (4th Series), vol. iii. p. 367. III. 8.—*Ibid.* vol. i. p. 202. III. 10.—*Ibid.* (5th Series), vol. i. p. 337. III. 10-12.—*Ibid.* (4th Series), vol. viii. p. 15. III. 11.—*Ibid.* (5th Series), vol. x. p. 274.

THE EVOLUTION OF EVIL

'But evil men and impostors shall wax worse and worse, deceiving and being deceived.'—2 TIM. III. 13.

LET us consider, first, the law of evolution in regard to several aspects of evil ; and, secondly, the principle on which this evolution depends.

I. The Evolution of Evil.—(1) The evolution of evil in relation to faith. The development of error is the matter immediately before the Apostle in this place ; he is speaking of those who go from one heresy to another. Men begin by questioning the great articles of their creed ; they commence the process in no specially offensive temper, they seem only to obey the necessity and follow the methods of an independent mind. Gradually, like as when a moth fretteth a garment, the criticism becomes more antagonistic and destructive, until ere long the critic finds himself renouncing all the great inspiring articles of his faith ; what began in an apparently laudable inquiry into the truth of religion ends in universal scepticism. Are we, then, to be afraid of testing our belief, afraid of a life of intelligence, knowledge, reflection ? We ought to turn with scorn from any such ignoble intellectual surrender. The point of the

Apostle's admonition is, we must take care in what spirit we begin and prosecute our criticism. (2) The evolution of evil in relation to character. Evil possesses wonderful capabilities of expansion, multiplication, transformation, transmigration, exaggeration. Notice specially three points in the susceptibility to development and increase. (*a*) One evil contains within itself the possibilities of all evil. (*b*) The mildest form of evil contains within itself the possibility of the most extreme evil. (*c*) The development of evil is peculiarly rapid. (3) The evolution of evil in relation to destiny. Men in this life often go a long way in the development of evil ; they become dead to truth, to decency, to hope. But we have no reason to suppose that this degeneration ends here. Revelation fixes no limit to the evolution of good. But at the same time revelation fixes no limit to the evolution of evil. It propounds the awful doctrine of a 'bottomless pit,' which in the language of our day, signifies unarrested, limitless degradation.

II. The Principle on which the Evolution of Evil Proceeds.—'Deceiving and being deceived.' Man may be made worse as well as better by association.

III. The Lessons Suggested by our Theme.—(1) Avoid the beginnings of evil. (2) Cultivate purity of heart. (3) Loyally keep the social law.—W. L. WATKINSON, *The Transfigured Sackcloth*, p. 111.

REFERENCES.—III. 14.—H. D. M. Spence, *Voices and Silences*, pp. 81, 97. III. 14, 15.—Archbishop Temple, *Christian World Pulpit*, vol. lxi. p. 262. III. 14-17.—R. F. Horton, *Christian World Pulpit*, vol. liii. p. 241. W. H. Griffith Thomas, *Mundesley Conference Report*, 1910, p. 287. III. 15.—W. F. Shaw, *Sermon Sketches for the Christian Year*, p. 4. Spurgeon, *Sermons*, vol. xxxi. No. 1866. J. J. Blunt, *Plain Sermons* (3rd Series), p. 243. W. M. Sinclair, *Words from St. Paul's*, p. 164. Bishop Ryle, *Christian World Pulpit*, vol. xlvii. p. 309. S. Pearson, *Christian World Pulpit*, vol. lv. p. 218. A. Maclaren, *The Wearied Christ*, p. 191. R. F. Horton, *Christian World Pulpit*, vol. lvii. p. 276. *Expositor* (6th Series), vol. v. p. 55. III. 16.—W. M. Sinclair, *Christ and Our Times*, p. 49. F. W. Farrar, *Everyday Christian Life*, p. 143. C. Perren, *Sermon Outlines*, p. 202. C. Gutch, *Sermons*, p. 214. *Expositor* (4th Series), vol. iii. p. 253 ; *ibid.* vol. viii. p. 468 ; *ibid.* vol. x. 250. III. 16, 17.—D. M. Ross, *Christian World Pulpit*, vol. lv. p. 27. C. Perren, *Sermon Outlines*, p. 331. T. G. Bonney, *Sermons on Some of the Questions of the Day*, p. 34. Page Roberts, *Church Family Newspaper*, vol. xiii. p. 970. *Expositor* (5th Series), vol. viii. p. 111.

THE MAN OF GOD

'The man of God.'—2 TIM. III. 17.

LET us look at the detached sentence—'the man of God '. There are some men well known to us, it may be, with whose name we never would think of associating the name of God. They are the miracles, they are the outstanding wonders and monsters of history. I say there are men well known to us with whom we could not associate the name of God, we should be conscious of a revulsion ; nay, we might go further still and consider in cool reason that to associate the name of God with some men, or some men with the name of God, would be a kind of profane comedy.

Are not all men men of God? In one sense, the lowest, are not all men men of God? Yes, in the Divine purpose. Then why does not the Divine purpose effect itself, establish itself in a great fact? Because so mysterious is human nature that a man can say No to God.

If any man be in Christ Jesus he is a new creature; he started from a new point, he passed through a new Eden, he is on a new and higher road, he is on the road to the true manhood. O thou drooping and half-despairing soul, the door of mercy stands open, and on it is written in red flame and as it were in red blood struggling with the flame, Jesus Christ, the true Man, the God-Man, the saving Man.

I. Who is this man of God? It is the man who has been born again. God met him in a far country, in a wild, wild land, known for hunger and desolateness and misery; and God made great proposals to him in the name of Jesus Christ, told him that he might return from the land of desolation into the land of plenteousness and long nightless summer. We have all to be born again. Man was made in Genesis, he is born in the Gospel. Before, he had but a kind of foothold on the earth out of which he was raised, but now in Christ Jesus he is a soul held of God, and in Him he lives and moves and has his being.

II. And who is this man of God? The man whose supreme thought is God Himself, who longs to see God with the eyes of faith and love. He misses God if He be gone but for an hour. We know what this is in the house. The individual makes the house, the one person makes the other persons tolerable. There are people who if they were to go out of the house would take everything with them. Whenever I see a little toddling child on the streets, I say, sometimes loudly: 'If that little two-feet-long thing were not to go home to-night, nobody else would go'. But does the house depend on that little toddling creature? It does. Of course the father and mother will say: 'Baby has not come home, but she will turn up in the morning; if she is not close at hand she is safe in the police-station, so we will lie down and get what sleep we can, and we shall see her in the morning'. Is it so? Answer! It is thus that some people miss God. 'Why standest Thou afar off, O God?' 'Oh if I knew where I might find Him!' Hear that voice—lonely, hollow, crying voice, appealing as it were to the very wind, that the soul so lonely might be taken into the presence of the Father. A soul thus yearning may be well entitled to be described as a 'man of God'.

III. Who is this man of God? He would take supreme delight in the service of God. It is no burden to him; everything else is comparatively burdensome; he is a truly religious man. There are many religions that are not religious; there is many a sermon that is not religious. Religiousness is a peculiar quality of thinking, a special and incommunicable quality of desire; true religion or religiousness is—we can find no better name for it, we have searched all the vocabularies—prayer, a living cry to

a living God.—Joseph Parker, *City Temple Pulpit*, vol. vi. p. 10.

2 TIM. IV. 2.

Observe, he puts longsuffering before doctrine, and that because nothing except patience answers with those who are hard to win. Patience enables us to possess not only our own souls but those of others also.—St. Francis de Sales.

2 TIM. IV. 2.

In the ninth chapter of *The Saints' Everlasting Rest*, Baxter observes that 'we are commanded to "exhort one another daily," and "with all longsuffering" (2 Tim. iv. 2). The fire is not always brought out of the flint at one stroke; nor men's affections kindled at the first exhortation; and if they were, yet if they be not followed, they will soon grow cold again. . . . If you reprove a sin, cease not till the sinner promise you to leave it, and avoid the occasions of it. If you are exhorting to a duty, urge for a promise to set upon it presently.'

Reference.—IV. 3.—H. D. M. Spence, *Voices and Silences*, p. 33.

ST. LUKE THE EVANGELIST

'Be thou sober in all things, suffer hardship, do the work of an Evangelist, fulfil thy ministry.'—2 Tim. iv. 5 (R.V.).

Here are four distinct thoughts. They are thoughts of St. Paul the friend of St. Luke, whom we commemorate to-day, and they form the opening words of the Epistle for this day. They are nearly his last thoughts. He was nearing the end; he was forsaken by his friends—'Only Luke,' he wrote in this chapter, 'is with me'. Each thought comes straight and warm from one of the largest hearts ever given to man. Further, each is not only a thought but a charge—a charge countersigned, we cannot doubt it, by the sign-manual of the Divine Master Himself.

I. Sobriety in all Things.—'Be thou sober.' Be temperate, calm, collected. Keep your heart warm, but your head cool. To each matter that comes to be dealt with, whether to cheer or to trouble, give its due proportion, neither more nor less. Do not let the heat, the headiness, the wild outcries of others make you lose your own balance. Be on the alert against surprises. Be on the watch alike against your own drowsiness and against the midnight assaults of others, and in all that calls for judgment, counsel, doctrine, action, 'keep a temperate brain'. Whatever others may be, 'Be thou sober'.

II. Suffer Hardship.—Clearly the word had a special force for St. Paul and for those whom St. Paul sent forth to battle. In our day it has a special force for some of the clergy, not least those whose work lies in foreign lands, and whose dangers are not only dangers of the soul, but also of the body. We cannot hear the name of China, we can scarcely hear the name of India, or Uganda, or Nyassa, without being reminded that to 'suffer hardship,' even in the most literal sense, may at any time become the lot—shall we not say the glorious privilege?—'before they taste of death,' or even in the hour of death itself, of some of those devoted brothers who are representing us in the mission field. But, apart from this, there is surely a meaning for us all, clergy alike and laity, in this emphatic word, which might well be the motto of a great life—'Suffer hardship'. In every human life, and at many stages of each life, there is always, seen or unseen, some eventful 'parting of the ways'. There is the level, smooth path of ease, and there is the steep rough path of difficulty; the path of 'least resistance' and the path of trenchant daring; the path of tactful—if you will, kindly—compromise and the path, always of outspoken resolve, sometimes of outspoken leadership. No man who weighs his words, and knows something of the complications of modern life, can doubt that again and again the easier path will be also the path of wisdom and of charity. But there are a hundred voices always ready to advise the softness of compromise. There is not always ready a voice to recall the old soldierly word of command, 'Suffer hardship'. There are times when the sterner voice is truly the present voice of God, 'Suffer hardship'. Speak out. Say the word that must offend. Be content to be for a season misunderstood, misconstrued, misliked, and even denounced, if by any means you may gain a hearing for some eternal truth of God which in your heart and intellect you know to be vital.

III. The Work of an Evangelist.—I sometimes think that this part of our ministry, which should surely be the most delightful, is the one which in practice we clergy find the hardest. Judge us, but judge us generously, by the history of nineteen hundred years. What is the character which we have made for ourselves? Are we outwardly spoken of, as we inwardly thought of, as bringers of 'good news'? Do men single out this as one of the services for which they thank us? Do they expect from us some thought, some word, some comment, on what is passing in human souls, or on the words of Christ in Scripture, or on the works of God in Nature—something which will brighten their homes, add to their sense of being happy, and breathe the freshness of what is known both to poetry and to religion as 'newness of life'? We can hardly put the question without a seeming touch of self-accusing irony. And yet, if we know anything of the history of the Christian Church; if we have followed the life of any of her first-rate evangelists; if we have observed how men and women hung on the lips of any of the greater thinkers and preachers and writers—whether Fathers, or Bishops, or monks, or friars, or Reformers, or translators of the Bible, or scholars and teachers in Universities, or missionaries at home like Whitefield and the Wesleys, or missionaries abroad like Boniface, or Xavier, or Duff, or Swartz, or Marsden, or the two Selwyns, or Patteson, or Whipple, or Mackay, or Hannington—if, I say, we have noted the spell which these men cast over those to whom they offered their message, it was, we must all admit, because they were felt to be bringing 'good news'. They had something fresh to tell about God

and about the Saviour, and about the Eternal indwelling Spirit, and about the brotherhood of the Christian society, and about man's life and man's death. They had something to say which made for gladness of heart, which left the burden of life brighter, which threw over it the rainbow of hope, which was the breaking of some yoke, and was the unveiler and herald of some 'power from on high'.—H. M. BUTLER.

REFERENCES.—IV. 5.—W. H. M. H. Aitken, *Christian World Pulpit*, vol. xlvi. p. 251. W. G. Rutherford, *The Key of Knowledge*, p. 142. W. J. Adams, *Christian World Pulpit*, vol. lxi. p. 268. IV. 5, 6.—G. Trevor, *Types and the Antitype*, p. 253.

THE BACKWATER OF LIFE

'The time of my departure is come.'—2 TIM. IV. 6.

PAUL knew that his work was done. How does this man, the servant of Jesus Christ, bear himself in these closing days? With what thoughts of the friends about him, of the years that lie behind, of the few fleeting days that still remain, and above all, of the great Beyond that is now so near to him? It is a testing day in a man's life when he comes to know what he has long secretly feared, that the prizes he has coveted and toiled for are not for him, that already he has done the best he is capable of, and that henceforth his influence will be within less and everlessening circles. Perhaps there is nothing that some of us so much dread as the coming of the days whereof we shall say that we have no pleasure in them. May it not help us if we listen to the last words of the Apostle Paul?

I. And in the first place, mark the Apostle's quiet confidence and joy. 'Youth,' some one has said, 'is a blunder, manhood a struggle, old age a regret.' Paul might have called his youth a blunder, and his manhood a struggle, but his old age a regret—no! a thousand times no! Long ago it had been his desire that he might finish his course with joy; and now his prayer is being answered.

II. The Apostle's life-convictions remain with him still in unshaken strength. Nor are the old interests of his life dead and gone from him. He gives manifold directions to Timothy: 'The clothes that I left at Troas with Carpus bring when thou comest, and the books, especially the parchments'.

III. Very beautiful also is Paul's attitude towards those who were near him in these last days. There is, too, if I mistake not, a new note of tenderness in Paul's voice.

IV. Need I say Paul did not fear to die? Paul welcomed death because he saw beyond death. 'There is the Mainstream,' writes Mr. James Payn, 'the Backwater and the Weir, and there ends the River of Life.' What is after that he does not know; with him it is from death to dark. But with Paul it is from death to day. To Paul death was but as 'the lifting of a latch'; to us, perhaps, who are young and strong, 'the thought of death is terrible, having such hold on life'. But if our work is done, if we are in the backwater and the end is near, God grant that in deepening peace and with ever-growing tenderness we may do the things that remain, till the soft mellow light of evening fade into that last darkness that brings the swift dawn of the eternal day !—G. Jackson, *Table Talk of Jesus*, p. 239.

References.—IV. 6.—Spurgeon, *Sermons*, vol. xvii. No. 989. C. Perren, *Revival Sermons in Outline*, p. 191. IV. 6, 7.—H. Woodcock, *Sermon Outlines* (1st Series), p. 219. IV. 6-8.—J. W. Boulding, *Sermons*, p. 153. A. Maclaren, *Expositions of Holy Scripture—Timothy*, p. 100.

2 TIM. IV. 7.

I MAY not boast with the Apostle that I have fought a good fight, but I can say that I have fought a hard one. For be my success small or great, it has been won without wilful wrong of a single human being and without inner compromise or other form of self-abasement.—James Lane Allen, in *The Choir Invisible*.

References.—IV. 7.—G. Dawes Hicks, *Christian World Pulpit*, vol. lvii. p. 40. J. G. Greenhough, *ibid.* vol. xlix. p. 202; *ibid. The Cross in Modern Life*, p. 219. R. J. Wardell, *Preacher's Magazine*, vol. xviii. p. 178. *Expositor* (5th Series), vol. i. p. 144; *ibid.* (7th Series), vol. vi. p. 370.

THE CHRISTIAN LIFE : A FIGHT, A RACE, A TRUST

' I have fought the good fight, I have finished the course, I have kept the faith ; henceforth there is laid up for me the crown of righteousness, which the Lord, the righteous Judge, shall give me at that day.'—2 Tim. IV. 7, 8.

I. First of all, Paul says, Christian life and Christian service are a conflict, a battle. ' I have fought.' Any conception of the Christian life that leaves out this side of it is a soft, inadequate and misleading conception. There is no Christian life apart from conflict. Paul says that it is not only *a* fight but it is *the* good fight. No sight is fairer than that of the man making war on the base within and the base without, fighting with self, sin, the devil, and the world, and in God's strength overcoming.

II. The second metaphor, ' I have finished my course'. When Paul says here, ' I have finished my course,' he does not mean the sands of life have run out, but I have run along the appointed track. He means. I have fulfilled the Divine destiny. Henry Drummond said, ' God has a will concerning a man's character, and then He has a will concerning a man's career'. Find out God's will for you and go straight on whatever comes.

III. Now the last metaphor, ' I have kept the faith'. The Christian life is a great entrustment, a great stewardship. Your Christian life begins in your trusting Jesus. But that is only half. The other half is that Christ is trusting you. Supposing we are true soldiers of Christ, what is the end ? Not death. There is ' a crown of righteousness '.—Charles Brown, *The Preacher's Magazine*, vol. XVII. p. 439.

References.—IV. 7, 8.—J. H. Holford, *Memorial Sermons*, p. 192. J. M. Neale, *Sermons Preached in Sackville College Chapel*, vol. iii. p. 415. H. Woodcock, *Sermon Outlines* (1st Series), p. 225. F. B. Woodward, *Selected Sermons*, p.

42. Bishop Bethell, *Sermons*, vol. ii. pp. 1, 16. F. B. Woodward, *Sermons* (1st Series), p. 190.

THE LOVE OF CHRIST'S APPEARING

' And not to me only, but unto all them also that love His appearing.'—2 Tim. IV. 8.

Do you notice where St. Paul places a ' love' of the Second Advent ? He was writing as ' Paul, the aged,' with his own ' crown of righteousness ' now full in view. But that does not at all prevent him keeping his eye upon the coming of Christ. And I conceive that however close death may be to a man, the right point of contemplation is still the Advent. There are four attitudes of mind in which we may stand respecting the ' appearing' of Christ. By far the worst is ' indifference '; and that indifference may be either the dulness of ignorance, or the apathy or the deadness of the moral feelings. The next state is, ' fear '. There is always something very good when there is ' fear '. It requires faith to ' fear '. But above ' fear ' is ' hope '. ' Hope' is expectation with desire : knowledge enough to be able to anticipate and grace enough to be able to wish it. And here the ladder is generally cut off; but God carries it one step higher—' love'. ' Love' is as much above ' hope' as ' hope' is above ' fear '—for ' hope' may be selfish, ' love' cannot be ; ' hope' may be for what a person gives, ' love' must be for the person himself. Therefore a man might deceive himself, by thinking all was right in his soul, because he ' hoped' for the Second Advent; but he might, after all, be set upon the pageant, and the rest, and the reward. But to the individual that ' loves' it, there must be something infinitely dear in it ; and that one dear thing is the Lord Jesus Christ.

The ' love of Christ's appearing' is not a simple idea, but one composed of many parts. I would separate four, which four at least go to make it.

I. Manifestation of the Saints.—The moment of the manifestation of Christ will be the moment of the manifestation of all His followers. Then, perhaps, for the first time, in their united strength and beauty—declared and exhibited, and vindicated, and admired, in the presence of the universe. And, oh, what a subject of ' love' is there ! Some we shall see selecting and individualising us, as they come, with the well-remembered glances of their loving smiles. But all sunny in their sacred sweetness' and their joyous comeliness. Never be afraid to ' love' the saints too much. Some speak as if to ' love' Christ were one thing, but to ' love' the saints were another thing ; and they almost place them in rivalry ! But the saints are Christ. They are His mystical body, without which Christ Himself is not perfect.

II. The Manifestation of Christ's Kingdom.—Another part of the ' appearing'—very pleasant and very lovable to every Christian—will be the exhibition that will then be made of the kingdom and the glory of Jesus. If you are a child of God, every day it is a very happy thought to you, that Christ gains some honour. If you yourselves get a victory—ever so little a one—over some sin—if you make the very smallest attainment in some grace—you would like to feel, 'This pleases Christ. This magnifies Christ. Not I, He is higher.' And if you chance any day to hear of or see any advance of the empire of God's truth the very fact has drawn out the deepest feelings of your heart. Only think what it will be to look all around, as far as the eye can stretch, and all is His! 'On His head are many crowns!' His sceptre supreme over a willing world! Every creature at His feet! To behold that Saviour—your Saviour—everything to all—and still not a whit the less yours. He everything to you; and you everything to Him!

III. The Manifestation of Christ.—But there is another thing after which you are always panting. I mean the image of Christ upon your soul. 'Why am I not more like Him?' But now you stand before Him, in His unveiled perfections, and you are like Him, for you 'see Him as He is!' And if 'His appearing' is to appear in you, is not that cause to love Him? It is difficult for any who have not known quiet hours of holy meditation to realise what it will be to see Him—'Whom having not seen, they love'.

References.—IV. 8.—A. Coote, *Twelve Sermons*, p. 99. D. C. A. Agnew, *The Soul's Business and Prospects*, p. 30. *Expositor* (4th Series), vol. ix. p. 4; *ibid.* vol. x. p. 109; *ibid.* (5th Series), vol. vii. p. 278. IV. 9, 10.—J. M. Neale, *Sermons for the Feast Days in the Christian Year*, p. 309.

DEMAS

'Demas forsook me, having loved this present world.'—
2 Tim. iv. 10.

Among all the portraits of the New Testament there is none more arresting, more solemn in its suggestiveness, more eloquent in its appeal, than this of Demas. 'Demas forsook me, having loved this present age.' These words were written by the Apostle of the Gentiles in circumstances of trials and loneliness. Almost certainly they are among the last words that he wrote or dictated. He was in prison, expecting the end. The words almost immediately preceding those of my text reveal this fact: 'I am already being offered, and the time of my departure is come'.

Paul was alone, save for the companionship of Luke, waiting the final act: Crescens away, Titus away, Timothy away, and Mark away. But they were all away upon the business of the King, and even though he missed them he thought of them with gladness. There was one whose absence filled his heart with sorrow: 'Demas forsook me,' not on the King's business, but 'having loved the present age'. Now, we have seen Demas before. At the close of the Colossian letter, a letter of the first imprisonment in all probability, Paul wrote, 'Luke, the beloved physician, and Demas salute you'. There was a time, then, when Demas was by the side of Paul, in company with Luke, ministering to him in the need of the hour. At the close of his letter to Philemon he referred to him as a fellow-worker. But now he had to write, 'Demas forsook me, having loved the present age'. That in a sentence is the story of a spiritual

tragedy. A man who had been in closest fellowship with the Apostle, both in ministry and in suffering, had left him.

I. No man who has once known our Lord Christ, and been in fellowship with Him, immediately forsakes Him. The devil never wins such a man by frontal attack. There is always an insidious flank movement upon Man-soul ere Man-soul is captured. There is always heart-backsliding before there is definite and open backsliding. I take up my newspaper one day, and I see that which, alas! the newspaper is all too ready to publish, that some minister or prominent Christian worker has been arrested for fraud, or has fallen into vulgar sin; and I know that preceding that open fall such minister or worker has been drifting. Always first the subtle, insidious force, alluring the soul; always next definite choice, decision, a volitional yielding to the alluring force; then some day, inexorably, suddenly, Demas has gone, and the world finds out that which God knew long before.

Let us consider these things a little more fully for our warning. The alluring forces. It is a very noticeable fact that this text is constantly misquoted: 'Demas forsook me, having loved this present *evil* world'. The word 'evil' was not used by the Apostle. Why is it that it is so constantly used in quotation? Is it not because there is a subconscious sense that it is so insufficient to say, 'having loved this present age'; that there is nothing to be afraid of in 'this present age'; that there must have been some quality of evil in the age, seducing Demas, ere he could be lured from his loyalty to Christ? Now, as a matter of fact, when we introduce the word 'evil,' we rob the text of its keenest edge. The sharpness of the sword is in the adjective, rather than in the substantive: 'Demas forsook me, having loved this *present* age'.

How did the age allure Demas? First, by the enticement of its nearness; secondly, by the enticement of its method; and finally, by the enticement of its gifts.

II. This love that took Demas away was that of deliberate choice. If we would really understand the meaning of the solemn warning, let us take the word of Paul when Demas was yet with him, and helping him. He wrote to the Colossians, 'Set your affection, your mind, on the things that are above'. In this high and holy mystery of the spiritual life let no man say that he cannot help what he loves. Religion is of the will. Set your affection upon the things that are above—that is the great word, and it is a command. Demas set his affection deliberately upon the present; came to some hour of crisis in which he said, I have been comparing these things, and I have come to the deliberate conclusion that I will take no risk on an uncertain eternity. I will make sure of the thing that is right here, under my eyes.

Following that deliberate decision Demas went from Paul. He left the prison, he left the difficulties; he went from fellowship with the little band of souls who still loved His appearing; he left Luke, and Crescens, and Tychicus, and Timothy, and Titus; he left Christ.—G. Campbell Morgan, *Mundesley Conference Report*, 1910.

References.—IV. 10.—Phillips Brooks, *The Mystery of Iniquity*, p. 224. C. Brown, *God and Man*, p. 210. J. Stuart Holden, *The Pre-Eminent Lord*, p. 187.

PAUL UNDER DEPRESSION

'Only Luke is with me.'—2 Tim. iv. 11.

We have affinity with Paul in the mood in which these words discover him. He is in the depths. We have been there. When he sings we cannot always accompany him, but he is sure of our fellowship when he sighs. We are unable to soar with him to the seventh heaven, but when he moans, 'Only Luke is with me,' he becomes our brother and companion in tribulation. We cannot range with him the mystic uplands, but we can take his hand in the dreary prison-house. When he philosophises he gets away from us, but he is close to us when his bitter tears overflow. Let us observe this royal soul under depression. It will cheer us in our forlorn seasons.

I. The Depression of a Noble Soul.—How faithfully is Paul's drear depression reflected in this plaintive memorandum, 'Only Luke is with me!' And it was a justifiable depression. There is an *accidie* which is atheism. There are glooms which are the pestiferous exhalations of unbelief. Moreover, there is a frequent depression which is the result of thoughtless and selfish indulgence. The extravagant supper of the night leaves stupid depression next morning. We need not waste sympathy upon such retributive sadness.

But how different is the depression of this faithful Apostle! His dejection arises from painful circumstances.

Paul's depression arose from *impaired health*. The thorn in the flesh had always a cruel sting, but its edge was sharpened in the dismal prison. Strong pain became ferocious pain. Paul had ever borne this cross, but it pressed overwhelmingly upon him now.

Paul's depression sprang from his *excessive labours*. The bow of Ulysses was unstrung. Its horn was worm-eaten and its string was mildewed. And what a conquering bow it had been!

Then Paul's depression was the *depression of age*. He was an old man now. He felt old, and that constitutes real old age. He subscribed himself 'Paul the aged' And evening hours bring evening shades. He was darkened by the fogs which often fall heavy on the banks of the Jordan. I would call for warm sympathy with all such. We may all require that sympathy ourselves in a little while. Speak your kindest words to such depressed souls. Seek to irradiate their darkness. Pray much that unto these loyal souls there may arise light in the darkness.

II. A Pathetic Spectacle of Loneliness.—Paul's loneliness was intensified by the fact that living friends had become unfriendly. He had not only to bear the grief of friends fallen on sleep, but the tragedy of the unfaithful friend.

III. Great Compensation in a Distressing Lot.—If Paul was depressed and lonely, his compensation was rich. 'Only Luke is with me.' It is a sign of his despondency that he projects that 'only' upon the statement. Had he not been whelmed with all God's waves and billows, he would not have used that limiting word. The 'only' is a little window through which we can see his forlornness. 'Only Luke is with me.' Matthew Henry inquires, 'And was not this enough?' It is a natural inquiry. But depression and loneliness have to fight hard against querulousness.

'Only Luke is with me!' Nay, Paul! Luke's Lord and yours is with you! John Wesley makes Paul say, 'But God is with me and it is enough'.

'Only Luke is with me.' And he had enriching fellowship with this choice servant of God amid disquieting surroundings. What medical relief the beloved physician would afford him! It was a great thing to have a doctor as his friend in such extremity. Intellectual stimulus he would also gather from Luke, the man of lovely mind. Paul's vocabulary and his store of metaphor were notably augmented by his fellowship with Luke. Students of these latest letters of Paul do not fail to notice medical words and ideas which Paul had never employed before.

IV. A Saint Verging on the End of Life.—'Only Luke is with me,' he writes, and he is very near his rough and hazardous journey's end. Frequently trials multiply as the end of life approaches. It is the final test of faith and hope and love. The cross grows heavier as faith's journey ends, and the crown of life flashes on our view. And verily the crown shines on Paul's tear-dimmed eyes. 'Henceforth there is laid up for me the crown' (ver. 8): he has just written. And the very crown he has all his life been panting for—'the crown of righteousness'.

We shall not fare badly at the last if 'only Luke' is with us. Keble calls Luke 'the sick soul's guide'. The Anglican Collect for St. Luke's Day runs thus: 'Almighty God, who calledst Luke the Physician, whose praise is in the Gospel, to be an Evangelist and Physician of the soul: may it please Thee, that, by the wholesome medicines of the doctrine delivered by him, all the diseases of our souls may be healed, through the merits of Thy Son, Jesus Christ our Lord'.

When Richard Jefferies lay on his dying bed he and his wife read much together in the Gospel of Luke. It will be well with each of us at the last if we can say, 'Only Luke is with me'.—Dinsdale T. Young, *The Gospel of the Left Hand*, p. 59.

ST. LUKE THE EVANGELIST

'Only Luke is with me.'—2 Tim. iv. 11.

St. Luke is known to us as 'the beloved Physician'. We think of him, too, as the writer of the Gospel which bears his name, and also of that wonderful book in which are recorded the triumphs of the early Church, the Acts of the Apostles. He is not very frequently mentioned in the Scriptures, but such references as there are present him to us in a beautiful light. 'The Physician'—surely it is a happy thing for us to know that thus early in the Christian Church there was so close a connection between the ministry of medicine and the ministry of the Gospel. 'The Evangelist'—how delightful to think of this cultured and refined man being the bearer of the Evangel, the good news which his writings have given to the world, that 'unto us is born a Saviour, Which is Christ the Lord!' 'The Faithful Friend'—no, he is not specifically called so in the New Testament, but our text states it in sufficiently eloquent terms. May we think of him in this threefold capacity.

I. The Faithful Friend.—St. Paul was writing his second letter to Timothy from his prison in Rome. He was ready to be offered, and the time of his departure was at hand. He had no fear, no misgiving about himself, for he had fought a good fight, and he knew that there was laid up for him a crown of righteousness. But he was saddened and depressed by the defection of friends, particularly by that of Demas, who, having put his hand to the plough, had turned back, because he 'loved this present world'. Other friends were absent from necessity, but St. Luke was by his side, and his presence would be congenial not only because they had much in common intellectually, but also for the reason that they were united in the bonds of holy love to their common Lord. 'Only Luke is with me.'

II. The Evangelist.—St. Luke has laid us all under a debt of gratitude for his beautiful record of our Lord's life. 'His superior education is proved by the philological excellence of his writings (viz., the Gospel and the Acts of the Apostles, which are but two volumes of one work). His preface, in pure Greek, implies previous careful study of documentary and other evidence. He speaks of other attempts to write a "Life of Christ," which were unsatisfactory. Though it is the same Gospel, it is narrated with peculiar independence, containing additional matter, more accuracy in preserving the chronological order of events, and complying with the requirements of history. He tested tradition with documentary records (e.g., i. 5; ii. 2; iii. 1); by comparing the oral testimony of living witnesses (i. 2, 3); and only when he had "perfect understanding of all things from the very first" ventured to compile a "Life of Christ" as a perfect *man*, restoring human nature and offering Himself a sacrifice for all mankind. To him we are indebted for the history of the birth and childhood of Jesus and the Baptist, for those liturgical hymns, and the scene in the synagogue at Nazareth (iv.), which were probably communicated by the Virgin Mary.'

III. The Beloved Physician.—The name is familiar to us all, and what a depth of sympathy and love and patience it conjures up! His gifts as a doctor were consecrated to the Lord's service, and do not we know in our own experience how great a work can be done by the modern doctor who recognises that he is a steward of the Great Physician of the soul? The medical man can be, if he will, a very real missionary of the Gospel, and he can always do much to make easy the visits of the parish clergyman to the sick room. It is a blessed thing to know that doctors and clergy are to-day acting together to a far greater extent than they have ever done before, and such unity of action cannot but conduce to the eternal comfort and happiness of the patient. The Church honours the healing art as the gift of God.

A HOLY ALLIANCE

'Only Luke is with me.'—2 Tim. iv. 11.

THERE is a note of pathos in this word 'only' which is not to be interpreted as a belittling of Luke. It is rather a revelation of the Apostle Paul. These two have much to give to each other, and the ministry of each will be vitally enriched by the ministry of the other.

I. I remark, first, what a natural alliance this is. 'Luke is with me,' says the Apostle of the spiritual. A colleagueship of such a kind is not likely to miss a certain plain fact which good people have found it possible to overlook, namely, that men have bodies as well as souls. The beloved physician, in his calling, is as much within the sphere of religion as the Apostle. (1) How finely this comradeship suggests a ministry which squares with the great facts of human need. Sin and disease are the two great ravagers of human life, and next to sin disease works the tragedy and pathos of human history. (2) It is a natural comradeship if you consider how helpless one of these ministries must often find itself without the other. The world expects that what Paul and Luke represent should go together.

II. The second remark which suggests itself is what a supreme and compelling precedent there is for this association. I will read one verse of the New Testament, for it recalls One in whom the ministry of Paul and Luke, and every other gracious ministry, either to the souls or the bodies of men, finds both its example and its benediction: 'And they brought unto Him all that were sick and diseased, and blind and leprous, and He healed them'. This is the great compelling precedent behind the mutual ministries of the Apostle of grace and the man of healing.

III. Last of all, what a permanent mutual ministry this comradeship suggests and its compelling precedent enjoins. The first friends of Jesus recognised this. They did not look askance at sorrow and suffering, they went to meet it as something their Lord had taught them to claim as an opportunity for love and service. The social wing of the early Church is the earliest phase of the Institutional Church. The sick and the afflicted are ours because they are His. Only the infinite pity is adequate to the infinite pathos of human suffering. But the infinite Divine pity has its human mediators.—T. YATES, *Christian World Pulpit*, vol. LXVIII. p. 4.

REFERENCES.—IV. 11.—H. J. Wilmot-Buxton, *Holy-tide Teaching*, p. 180. J. D. Jones, *Elims of Life*, p. 239. James

Moffatt, *The Second Things of Life*, p. 1. *Expositor* (4th Series), vol. iii. p. 229 ; *ibid.* (5th Series), vol. vi. p. 81 ; *ibid.* vol. x. p. 319.

'The Books.'—2 TIM. IV. 13.

MR. SPURGEON says, in his sermon entitled 'Paul—his Cloak and his Books':—

'We do not know what the books were about, and we can only form some guess as to what the parchments were. Paul had a few books which were left, perhaps wrapped up in the cloak, and Timothy was to be careful to bring them. *Even an Apostle must read.* Some of our very ultra-Calvinistic brethren think that a minister who reads books and studies his sermon must be a very deplorable specimen of a preacher. A man who comes up into the pulpit, professes to take his text on the spot, and talks any quantity of nonsense, is the idol of many. If he will speak without premeditation, or pretend to do so, and never produce what they call a dish of dead men's brains—oh! that is the preacher. How rebuked are they by the Apostle! He is inspired, and yet he wants books! He has been preaching at least for thirty years, and yet he wants books! He had seen the Lord, and yet he wants books! He had had a wider experience than most men, and yet he wants books! He had been caught up into the third heaven, and had heard things which it was unlawful for a man to utter, yet he wants books! He had written the major part of the New Testament, and yet he wants books! The Apostle says to Timothy and so he says to every preacher, "Give thyself unto reading". The man who never reads will never be read; he who never quotes will never be quoted. He who will not use the thoughts of other men's brains, proves that he has no brains of his own.'

REFERENCES.—IV. 13.—Spurgeon, *Sermons*, vol. ix. No. 542. F. Hastings, *Christian World Pulpit*, vol. liv. p. 140. J. Stalker, *ibid.* vol. lv. p. 406. Dinsdale T. Young, *Messages for Home and Life*, p. 61. *Expositor* (6th Series), vol. v. p. 55. IV. 14.—*Ibid.* (4th Series), vol. i. p. 408.

A STUDY IN UNSELFISHNESS
2 TIM. IV. 16, 17.

IT is especially difficult to avoid egotism when one has to speak of one's own experiences, but Paul's unselfish spirit comes out with remarkable clearness in this passage at three points. (1) In his references to the Roman Christians who seemed to have failed him at the critical moment. *At my first defence no one took my part, but all forsook me: may it not be laid to their charge.* He does not blame them for their gross cowardice. It is not their desertion of him which weighs on his mind, so much as their failure to seize an opportunity for serving Christ. *May it not be laid to their charge!* The tone is magnanimous pity. Paul forgives and prays that God may forgive them. He entertains no personal resentment. (2) In his references to his own courage. That was due to Divine aid ; he claims no credit for it, and does not draw attention to his own virtues. *The Lord stood by me and strengthened me.* Paul got power to stand firm and give a ready answer to the judge's queries. He does not plume himself upon his ready wit and bravery, but acknowledges the hand of his Lord in the matter. If he was not intimidated, the glory was God's. (3) The object of his personal deliverance was wider than his own comfort. The aim of God's intervention, in sparing his life for the meantime, was *that through me the message might be fully proclaimed, and that all the Gentiles might hear.* Even the postponement of the trial served, in his judgment, to promote the greater ends of the Gospel. He regarded himself consistently as the agent of the cause, not as the main object on which all other considerations should hinge. This absence of pretension forms the third and highest note of unselfishness in the passage. He would not pose as a victim or as a hero in the cause of Christianity.—JAMES MOFFATT.

REFERENCES.—IV. 16-18.—J. Edwards, *Preacher's Magazine*, vol. xviii. p. 414. IV. 18.—*Expositor* (5th Series), vol. viii. p. 146. A. Maclaren, *Expositions of Holy Scripture—Timothy*, p. 124. IV. 20.—Spurgeon, *Sermons*, vol. xxv. No. 1453.

THE EPISTLE TO TITUS

TITUS

REFERENCES.—I. 1.—*Expositor* (5th Series), vol. i. p. 143; *ibid.* vol. vi. p. 3. I. 2.—Spurgeon, *Sermons*, vol. x. No. 568. W. H. Hutchings, *Sermon Sketches*, p. 301. *Expositor* (4th Series), vol. i. pp. 33, 204; *ibid.* (5th Series), vol. ix. p. 77. I. 4.—*Ibid.* vol. vi. p. 86. Spurgeon *Sermons*, vol. xli. No. 2439. R. C. C., *Preacher's Magazine*, vol. xvii. p. 183. I. 5.—T. Barker, *Plain Sermons*, p. 271. I. 5-7.—*Expositor* (6th Series), vol. ii. p. 376. I. 9.—*Ibid.* vol. iv. p. 205. I. 12.—*Ibid.* (5th Series), vol. iii. p. 384. I. 13.—Archbishop Magee, *Sermons at Bath*, p. 242. I. 15.—C. F. Aked, *Christian World Pulpit*, vol. xliv. p. 171. C. Kingsley, *The Good News of God*, p. 154. G. Caird, *Lay Sermons*, p. 205. II. 1, 7, 8.—H. S. Holland, *Christian World Pulpit*, vol. xlvii. p. 72.

SOUND IN PATIENCE

'Sound in patience.'—TITUS II. 2.

THE Apostle Paul has himself been described by a great Biblical student as ' Paul the undiscourageable '. And, indeed, he is worthy of the name, and there is no better way of studying the significance of his teaching than by watching his own life. He is his own best commentary on his own counsels. His purposes were frequently broken by tumultuous shocks. His plans were destroyed by hatred and violence. His course was twisted here, diverted there, and wrenched a hundred times from its appointed goings by the mischievous plots of wicked men. The little Churches he had founded were in chronic disturbance and unrest. They were often infested with puerilities, and sometimes they were honeycombed by heresies which consumed their very life. And yet how sound and noble his patience ! With what fruitful tenderness he waits for his lagging pupils ! His very reproofs are given, not with the blind, clumsy blows of a street mob, but with the quiet, discriminating hand of a surgeon. This man, more than most men, had proved the hygienic value of endurance, and he, more than most men, was competent to counsel his fellow-believers to discipline themselves to the 'soundness of patience'.

I. Let us, therefore, look a little more closely at the virtue. This virtue of patience is to be exercised in seasons of waiting. This is certainly the hardest and most exacting exercise. I suppose that the rarest form of courage is displayed when we are compelled to sit still, and things are happening in which we can take no part. Action would reduce the tension and bring relief, but action is impossible. The acutest strain is not in the fighting, but in perilous waiting when fighting is impossible. It is in seasons like these that the finest courage and the ripest patience display their superlative glory. ' Although the fig-tree shall not blossom, neither shall fruit be in the vines : the labour of the olive shall fail, and the fields shall yield no meat ; the flocks shall be cut off from the fold, and there shall be no herd in the stalls ; yet will I rejoice in the Lord, I will joy in the God of my salvation.' This is surely a supreme instance of the virtue of being ' sound in patience '.

II. But the virtue of patience is also to be exercised in seasons of activity. The army needs patience in waiting ; it also needs patience in fighting. Impatience can spoil the waiting, and impatience can spoil the fighting. Impatient action defeats its own ends. An impatient shot registers a very erratic mark. An impatient batsman throws away the game. Yes, we require patience in the field as well as in the pavilion. And so it is a general principle in life ; patience is not something to be called up merely in hours of enforced indolence ; it is not a stand-by in emergencies ; it is the virtue which endows every moment with promise, and which makes the most commonplace action healthily effective.

Now let me mention two or three conditions in life in which this ' sound patience ' would operate with splendid effectiveness.

(1) First of all, then, we need a ' sound patience ' when we are *in the presence of oppressive mysteries*.

(2) We need a ' sound patience ' *in the presence of burdensome disappointment*.

(3) We need a ' sound patience ' *in the presence of a loitering progress*.—J. H. JOWETT, *The Transfigured Church*, p. 149.

TITUS II. 2.

IN my very young years I had a gravity and stayedness of mind and spirit, not usual in children ; insomuch that when I saw old men behave lightly and wantonly towards each other, I had a dislike thereof raised in my heart.'—GEORGE Fox's *Journal*.

A SCHOOL FOR WOMANHOOD

' That they may teach the young women.'—TITUS II. 4.

THE suggestion of my text is 'that they may teach'. That is characteristic of the Bible. It is eminently a teaching book. The word rendered ' teach ' is rendered in the Revised Version ' train '. But perhaps its most literal translation would be ' school '—' that they may *school* '. This sacred book would put us all to school, and it would keep us there. Are young women the only ones who need instruction ? The first verse bids Titus, the Bishop of Crete, ' speak the things which become sound doctrine,' or ' healthful teaching,' and instead of this being required only for young women it is imparted also to old men, aged women, young men and servants. But, in the instance before us, we are interested to know who are to be the instructors, 'That *they* may teach the young women'. Who are the 'they'? The reply is found in the previous verse. It is 'the aged women'. Women are best taught by women. Nor must we fail to notice the *method* of this teaching. It is to be the teaching of example, which is so proverbially better than precept. There must, however, be verbal instruction, and God's Apostles to-day must not forget in teaching all to 'teach the young women'.

I. Has not the Church too often forgotten to teach such? And yet the influence of women is incalculable. In view of the multiplied and multiplying influence of their sex, it is indeed right that the Christian pulpit should 'teach the young women'.

II. Let me remind you also that woman owes her influence to Christ That woman's nature was equally honourable with man's nobody believed in the pagan world; but as Augustine well said : 'The Saviour gave abundant proof of this in being born of a woman'. He, and He alone, has placed woman on the crowning slope of honour.

III. Consider the elements of character which give to young women their highest influence. (1) To brighten home with love—this is what the Apostle would first teach the young women. (2) Another lesson Paul would have young women taught is 'to be discreet'. The R.V. renders this 'to be sober-minded'. It might be read 'self-restrained'. In another place the original word is translated 'temperate'. Sober-mindedness is certainly a lesson which young women need to-day. Does not the age demand that the other meaning of this word, 'temperate,' be urged upon young women? The life of woman is often blasted through lack of self-restraint. (3) A further apostolic lesson for young women is to be 'chaste'. (4) 'Keepers at home' is again an indoctrination of St. Paul. The R.V. gives it as 'workers at home'. Home duties are the first of duties. (5) The next quality urged is 'good,' or as the R.V. has it 'kind'.

What if young women who name the name of Christ and profess His hallowed service omit or forget these homely duties? 'The word of God' will be 'blasphemed' or evil spoken of.—DINSDALE T. YOUNG, *Messages for Home and Life*, p. 17.

TITUS II. 6.

'I HAVE delivered up my son to you,' Cromwell wrote in 1649 to the Mayor of Hursley; 'and I hope you will counsel him; he will need it; and indeed I believe he likes well what you say and will be advised by you. I wish he may be serious; the times require it.' In the next year (1650) he again wrote to the same friend : 'I hope you give my son good counsel; I believe he needs it. He is in the dangerous time of his age; and it's a very vain world. O how good it is to close with Christ betimes!—there is nothing else worth the looking after.'

REFERENCE.—II. 7.—*Expositor* (5th. Series), vol. vi. p. 382.

ADORNING THE DOCTRINE

'Adorn the doctrine of God our Saviour in all things.'—TITUS II. 10.

THE universal test of religion is character, and that standard of judgment is a just standard. If the world is to be won for Christ it must be won by the unconscious evangelism of homely virtues and the upright, generous lives of the followers of Christ. Where you have a good life going out in the inspiration and power of Christianity you have an evidence of Christianity. As a sceptic once said : 'There is not an argument for Christianity that I do not see through except one. I cannot make out how it was my mother was so good a woman.'

I. The life that adorns the Gospel is the real evidence of Christianity Christ implicitly rested the demonstration of His religion on the conduct of His disciples. The only evidence for Christ is that of Christians. We may treat that thought with effortless familiarity; but it is a wonderfully important thought full of thrust and moment. It means this, that Christians *must* be better than other men; if not, Christianity breaks down. Most of us are advocates for Christianity without being Christians. 'Christian is that Christian does.' You may know the truth of Christ, you may feel at times rapturously ecstatic. But what is it all for? All for this, to make us like Christ. Your religious life is not across the seas of far ideals and undiscovered truths—your religious life consists in putting goodness into homely outward shape. There are still men like Bulstrode in *Middlemarch*, who could not conceive that there was any relation between his business and religion, who thought that 'the Lord's cause' had no connection with his shop at all.

II. How are we to be *induced* to adorn the Gospel of God? A preacher may stand up and say to his congregation 'Be good,' until the crack of doom. There is nothing more futile. It is not good advice that we need; it is good motive, or momentum to carry us past the place of danger. We need some principle of life, some flow of inspiration, that is large enough to influence the whole nature. And that, as I understand it, is the crux of our holy religion. To be a Christian means to be in touch with Christ, to let Christ help us. Live so near to Christ that He has some chance of beautifying your life; submit yourself to the power of His Spirit. He means to be your comrade, your Saviour. But He cannot unless you will. When the Gospel of Christ grips a man's soul it entails the saving of a man's whole life.—B. J. SNELL, *The All-Enfolding Love*, p. 129.

REFERENCES.—II. 10.—Spurgeon, *Sermons*, vol. xli. No. 2416. W. L. Watkinson, *Christian World Pulpit*, vol. xlix. p. 284. A. Maclaren, *Expositions of Holy Scripture—Titus*, p. 132. II. 11.—*Expositor* (4th Series), vol. i. p. 140; *ibid.* vol. vi. p. 421. II. 11-14.—Spurgeon, *Sermons*, vol. xxxii. No. 1894. II. 11-15.—J. A. Alexander, *The Gospel of Jesus Christ*, p. 221. II. 17.—A. Maclaren, *Expositions of Holy Scripture—Titus*, p. 149.

THAT BLESSED HOPE

(An Advent Sermon)

'Looking for that blessed hope and the glorious appearing of the great God and our Saviour Jesus Christ.'—TITUS II. 13.

I FEAR that this great truth—the coming again of the Lord—is largely a neglected truth.

Since the Lord Jesus Christ departed into the heavens, and men are really touched by matters spiritual, you will find, if you study the history of the great majority of the professing Christians, that they have almost entirely, if not quite, ignored the coming of the Lord Jesus Christ as a Person to fulfil a great historical event. They think of that as a merely emotional dream of certain enthusiasts; and if they do admit that He is coming again in glory, they simply think of it as a general idea—that there will be some day a manifestation of judgment and glory; but with the details they have not the slightest possible interest.

I. The Second Advent as a Matter of Reason.—I ask you, as a matter of reason, is it likely that the Great High God, Who has, as we are told in the opening of the Epistle to the Hebrews, appointed His Son to be Heir of all things, would allow His retirement from the earth as if defeated, and never see to it that His purpose was completely fulfilled? When the Lord Jesus Christ left this world, He passed up from the Mount of Olives and from the sight of a few humble followers, who claimed Him in their hearts as King. But the world at large ignored Him entirely, and Satan might well have been said to have gained a magnificent victory, if nothing further took place historically with regard to the Jesus of Nazareth. Consequently, we may expect, on the very ground of reason, that there must be a further return of Christ in majesty and glory to claim the kingdoms of this world for Himself and His father. Otherwise, throughout the hosts of hell there might be an acclamation cry, 'We have beaten the Lord, that God of your heaven'. They have not beaten Him! They never can! And it is because we believe the Word of the living God, and expect our God is to have a triumphant victory in all matters connected with the history of this world, that we, some of us at least, are now 'looking for that blessed hope,' and we seem to see the dawn of that wondrous day when Christ shall take to Himself His great power and reign, when the kingdoms of this world shall become the Kingdom of our Lord and of His Christ.

II. What Saith the Scripture?—We must inquire what is revealed to us in the Scripture with regard to this historical fact, of which we are expecting the fulfilment. In what manner will the Lord Jesus Christ return? Our text speaks of it as 'the glorious appearing of our Saviour Jesus Christ'. He is to come 'in like manner' as He went up. And the Lord Jesus Christ, our Blessed Saviour, who went up to heaven as Jesus, the Perfect Man, to claim our places there and prepare them for us, in the presence of God and the angels, is coming back to 'receive the kingdom' according to His own parable. He comes to be King, and His title is to be 'the Lord Himself'.

III. Christ and the Church.—What will it be to Christ when He looks upon His Church, and says, 'My beloved, My beloved!' That is my Saviour's joy, my Saviour's reward for all His pains. 'For the joy that was set before Him, He endured the cross, despising the shame, and is set down at the right hand of the throne of God,' henceforth waiting till His enemies are crushed, and His saints are ready to meet Him, and the cry goes up from earth as well as from heaven above: 'My Lord, my God'. Not only will it be a satisfaction to His own soul; He will see God satisfied, too. When He was upon earth, there was one thought in His mind. 'I have glorified Thee upon the earth . . . I came not to seek my own glory, but the glory of Him that sent Me.' I can imagine (oh, so feebly!) the wondrous feeling of my Lord and Master as He looks upon that perfected Bride—gathered in all ages from earth—how He turns back for a moment to His Father's throne, and says, 'Father, I have glorified Thee; I have glorified Thee!'

IV. What Shall we Say to these Things?—I ask you to think that we are to get ready. A little child said to its mother, 'Hadn't we better begin to pack up for heaven?' Are you beginning to pack up for glory? Are you getting ready, for that wondrous moment when all our beloved ones shall meet us—not only our own beloved on earth, but our dearly beloved Lord—to meet Him in the air and be like Him, because we see Him as He is. I beseech you to be getting ready, 'for in such an hour as ye think not the Son of Man cometh'. Get ready, and help others. It is an honour to be called of God to go out and hasten the time when the Bride shall be ready to meet her Lord. Work your work while yet it is day; you will not have long to win souls for Jesus. Are we ready to receive Him? He will come in a moment, in the twinkling of an eye. May our prayer be, 'Come, Lord Jesus; come quickly!'

REFERENCES.—II. 13.—H. Alford, *Sermons on Christian Doctrine*, p. 266. D. L. Moody, *The Fulness of the Gospel*, p. 82. C. D. Bell, *The Power of God*, p. 197. *Expositor* (4th Series), vol. x. p. 109. II. 13, 14.—J. Keble, *Sermons for the Sundays After Trinity*, p. 372. II. 14.—Spurgeon, *Sermons*, vol. ii. No. 70. A. Maclaren, *After the Resurrection*, p. 241. G. A. Sowter, *From Heart to Heart*, p. 212. *Expositor* (5th Series), vol. ix. p. 437; *ibid.* (6th Series), vol. i. p. 367. A. Maclaren, *Expositions of Holy Scripture—Titus*, p. 171; *ibid.* p. 180.

TITUS II. 15.

'I MET the society [at Norwich] at seven,' says Wesley, in his journal for September, 1759, 'and told them in plain terms, that they were the most ignorant, self-conceited, self-willed, fickle, untractable, disorderly, disjointed society, that I knew in the three kingdoms. And God applied it to their hearts: so that many were profited; but I do not find that one was offended.'

REFERENCE.—II. 15.—H. D. M. Spence, *Voices and Silences* p. 9.

OUR MOTTO

'Ready to every good work.'—TITUS III. I.

PRIMARILY these words refer to our duty as Christian citizens. But I think we may very well enlarge the scope of the words, so that we may take them as our motto for our whole life, and not only for our lives as Christian citizens.

I. What do we Mean by Good Work?—The Christian is to be ready for every beautiful work, because the work of God is always beautiful. Good works are beautiful, and they call forth the admiration of all true beholders. It requires a certain amount of courage to do good works. There are many men who are not men enough to do good works, cowardly men, men who just follow the multitude to do evil. And therefore the good works are not only those that are beautiful in themselves, but that require a certain amount of courage and manliness on the part of Christian men to engage in them.

II. Well, then, why should we be Ready for every Good Work?—(1) Because we were created for good works by God in Christ Jesus. (2) We must be ready for good works because in the fifth chapter of the Gospel of St. Matthew, and in the sixteenth verse, it is these good works that glorify God. 'Let your light so shine before men, that they may see your good works,' your beautiful works, 'and glorify your Father which is in heaven'. (3) By doing these good works we follow the example of our Lord Jesus Christ. (4) In order to provoke one another to good works (Heb. x. 23), in order that we may be thus a pattern to other men. (5) These good works are your best adornment.

III. You must be Ready to every Good Work.— Well, now, how are you to do it? (1) You must be consecrated to Him, you must be ready to do whatever He appoints. (2) You must be cleansed, sanctified, meet for the Master's use. (3) In the thirteenth chapter of the Epistle to the Hebrews : 'That great Shepherd of the sheep, through the blood of the everlasting covenant, make you perfect in every good work to do His will, working in you that which is well-pleasing in His sight, through Jesus Christ'. The Greek word there means, to set a dislocated arm, to put something right which has got wrong. When this dislocation is set right, then there will be the prospect of our being ready for every good work. (4) In the third chapter of the second Epistle to Timothy, and in the seventeenth verse : 'That the man of God may be perfect, throughly furnished unto all good works'. Furnished for all good works. (5) There must be a real keen anxiety to do them. (6) You want to be stablished for every good work if you are to fulfil the purpose for which God has called you. (7) In the first chapter of the Epistle to the Colossians, and in the tenth verse, 'Fruitful in every good work'. Because after all it is not so much how much we do, but what we do in the doing of it.—E. A. STUART, The True Citizen and other Sermons, vol. IX. p. 65.

EQUIPPED FOR WELL-DOING

TITUS III. I.

THESE words describe the normal attitude of mind which the Christian believers in the island of Crete were to maintain with steadfast resolution. Calls to service, like the Lord's coming to judgment, may sometimes be upon us when we are not looking for them. 'Ready unto every good work.' It is much more likely that we shall miss the pregnant occasion than that the occasion will fail to arrive. The history of failure is the story of unreadiness. This malady sometimes shows itself in a disabling sense of personal unfitness for the task which solicits us. This infirmity which hampers our life-work sometimes arises from the fact that we project our own unfitness into the minds of others, and assume that they are not ready to improve by the good works we are sent to do.

I. The first condition of this habitual fitness for service is a mind attuned to the Divine kindness, and in constant agreement with the goodwill of God. We shall never falter in good works, or miss the great opportunities which lie in our providential pathway, if we are possessed by the remembrance of God and His mercy to just and unjust alike. It is but another way of stating the same truth to affirm that Christ and His Word must be in us as the foundation of this fitness. In sending Marconigraphs across the sea, it is necessary that the instruments should be 'syntonised' with each other. Unless receiver and transmitter are keyed into a fine correspondence the message will be lost, and the electric vibrations which indicate it will wander unread through the wide spaces of the air. The Bible 'syntonises' us with the mind of God, making us sensitive subjects of His fine commands.

II. A further essential of this daily fitness for service is a firm assurance that since God has made it the chief function of the new life that it should abound in good works, He cannot possibly put us under conditions where this high function will be thwarted. He has so ordained the world into which we are sent, that it is a meet sphere for this Christlike vocation.

III. This fitness for every kind of gracious service must be maintained by diligent daily exercise. A French writer has said : 'If Paganini, who uttered his soul through the strings of his violin, spent three days without practising, he lost what he called the stops of his instrument, meaning the sympathy between the wooden frame, the strings, the bow, and himself. If he had lost this alliance, he would have been no more than an ordinary player.' And that sympathy between the soul of the worker, the written word, the stricken race and the God who redeemed it, which is the mainspring of all great achievement, may be lost by neglect. Nothing can make up for the lack of this inward readiness. If we are ready for every good work we are ready for the coming of the King.

REFERENCES.—III. 1, 2.—H. Bonner, Sermons and Lectures, p. 172. III. 1-4.—Expository Sermons on the New

Testament, p. 248.   III. 3-8.—Spurgeon, *Sermons*, vol. xxxiv. No. 2042.

THE PHILANTHROPY OF GOD
(*For Christmas Day*)

'The kindness of God our Saviour and His love toward man.'
—Titus iii. 4.

THE message of Christmas affects each of us in different ways at different times, for it deeply concerns our whole humanity. It never loses its power. Men and women whose hearts are untouched by other great facts of Divine revelation feel strangely thrilled as their ears catch the angels' tidings of the birth of the Virgin's Son. Christmas appeals to the primary instincts of humanity; it meets man's deepest needs; and if those without the Church feel a new glow at this season, surely we who are accustomed to meet here must be more deeply moved still. We pass beyond the outward expressions of the joy to the inner meaning of which everything else is but a sign. 'The Word was made Flesh and dwelt among us.' The Incarnation is the making of God poor that we may be made rich.

I. The Philanthropy of God.—In what does wealth consist? Not surely in money, not even in knowledge. What are the most precious things, the things we hold most dear? We think of home, and we realise the glory of motherhood and the dignity of childhood, and we understand that through the Incarnation we have become inestimably wealthy in the power of home which binds hearts together indestructibly. We think of the riches of Christian literature and art springing through the centuries from that humble home at Bethlehem. We think of the new spirit which helps us in that work which is so trying to body and brain, for the whole routine of life is known to God Who became a labourer in the city of Nazareth. And if all this true wealth is ours in this world through the Incarnation, what shall we say of the treasure and Divine riches given to us for the sustenance of our spiritual life, of the grace of Jesus Christ in His Church and in His Sacrament, of the knowledge of His will in His inspired Word and through His ministers, of the hope of everlasting life which binds earth and heaven? The kindness and philanthropy of God! In all parts of the world men are even now gleaning these riches of Christ's poverty, the riches of an inheritance which is incorruptible and fadeth not away.

II. 'Let this Mind be in You.'—Surely, as we consider the message of Christmas and realise all that that means, we find in it not only a gospel of infinite joy but also a challenge to imitate the example of Him Who has made this wealth ours. 'Let this mind be in you which was also in Christ Jesus'—the mind of true philanthropy. Christmas is the festival of kindness. Through the Incarnation philanthropy has acquired a new meaning. It is not to be asserted indeed that there were no efforts to alleviate poverty and suffering before the Incarnation. The sympathies of humanity have had some expression at every period of the world's history, and we know that the Roman noble gloried in giving alms to the beggar. But still there was nothing like the Christian conviction of the obligation resting upon each man to do all in his power wisely to alleviate misery. The example of Christ in His Incarnation is followed again and again by His disciples, for the true Christian realises that the unfortunate have around them the halo of the suffering of Christ. But at the same time it must be remembered that there is nothing in Christ's teaching, or in the teaching of His Apostles, which approves of indiscriminate almsgiving. We must give ourselves trouble to see that our charity is always well advised, and that it is not a generous giving to comfort ourselves independently of the result of our bounty. The kindness and philanthropy exhibited in the Incarnation is our pattern.

REFERENCES.—III. 4.—Archbishop Alexander, *Christian World Pulpit*, vol. liv. p. 20.   III. 5.—J. C. Lees, *Christian World Pulpit*, vol. xlii. p. 27.   D. L. Moody, *The Fulness of the Gospel*, p. 52.   T. Binney, *King's Weigh-House Chapel Sermons*, p. 198.   *Expositor* (5th Series), vol. x. p. 60.   III. 7.—B. J. Snell, *Sermons on Immortality*, p. 20.   *Expositor* (4th Series), vol. i. p. 204.   III. 8.—A. Maclaren, *Expositions of Holy Scripture—Titus*, p. 189.   III. 9.—*Ibid.* (5th Series), vol. x. p. 371.   III. 15.—*Ibid.* vol. viii. p. 167.

THE EPISTLE TO PHILEMON

PHILEMON

REFERENCES.—I. 9.—J. Martineau, *Endeavours After the Christian Life*, p. 105. I. 10.—R. W. Hiley, *A Year's Sermons*, vol. iii. p. 305. *Expositor* (5th Series), vol. vi. p. 86.

THE UNPROFITABLE MADE PROFITABLE

'Onesimus . . . aforetime unprofitable . . . now profitable.'—PHILEM. 10, 11.

THIS is graphic portraiture; two pictures of one man, and each picture presented by a word ; one man, Onesimus, unprofitable, profitable. And immediately we see a contrast. Mark most carefully these preliminary matters. The contrast is not a contrast in the accidentals, of material things. I believe that such a contrast would have been permissible ; I believe that such a contrast did exist. I have seen a picture of contrast on that level of some Salvation Army warrior in this district, of what he was and what he is. I am not sure of the wisdom of that kind of thing, but I am of the truth of it. But this is not a picture of Onesimus, a runaway slave, and Onesimus clothed and in his right mind going back to his duty. Neither is this a contrast in the essentials of spiritual experience save as that spiritual experience of the man does actually shine through the actual contrast suggested. It is not Onesimus aforetime carnal and now spiritual. That also is true, but that is not the picture drawn. If we are to look at these two pictures to observe this contrast and deduce the values suggested, we must notice exactly to what the Apostle is drawing attention.

I. What, then, is the contrast ? It is a contrast in the matter of this man's relationship to his fellow-men. I repeat, not a contrast as to the accidentals, of material things ; not as to the essentials of spiritual experience, but of relationship to his fellow-men—'aforetime unprofitable, now profitable to thee and me'. While, therefore, on this page we have all these portraits, and every one of them reveals some triumph of Christ, in each one some new glory shining as the result of life in Christ, here in the very centre of the things that Paul prominently desired to draw attention to is the figure of Onesimus as he was with regard to his fellow-men before he was begotten by the Apostle in his bonds, and Onesimus as he was with regard to his fellow-men after he was begotten by this Apostle in his bonds.

Notice the real value of this letter and this text. The declaration of Paul to Philemon concerning Onesimus is the making of this claim for Christianity —that Christianity takes hold of the unprofitable man and makes him profitable ; that the mission of Christianity is that of the transformation of waste into wealth ; that by what Christ works in the life of a man all those ancient and symbolic words of ancient prophecy are fulfilled. The touch of Christ on the life of a man transmutes the man from base metal to precious metal, and consequently changes the man from base coinage and unprofitable into current coinage of the very realm of heaven, which is profitable. There is the supreme miracle of Christianity, the supreme wonder that is for ever working, taking hold of the waste materials of life, and making them into wealth for time and eternity.

II. What is the secret of this transformation wrought in the life of the man ? In one word, almost incidentally written and yet fundamental to our understanding of the story, 'Onesimus, my beloved, begotten in my bonds'.

If you would understand the Apostle's use of the word begotten in the letter to Philemon, let me direct your attention to the same use of another word in another letter. In writing to the Corinthian Christians Paul says : 'Though you have ten thousand tutors in Christ you have not many fathers, for in Christ Jesus I begat you through the Gospel'. And when in chains Paul wrote of a runaway slave he begat in his bonds.

He preached the Gospel of that risen Christ and by that preaching in faith that man was apprehended, changed, and the waste was transmuted into wealth, and the unprofitable was made profitable. This is the secret of Christianity flashed upon this page in one word.

And what are the evidences of such transmutation ? Recognition of such responsibility and surrender thereto by the man who has robbed his master and fled. Some of you will remember how Dean Farrar has woven the story into beautiful fiction, *Darkness and Dawn*. The man who had wandered here and there at last found himself in Rome, in contact with that great Apostle, and was begotten. What is the evidence he was begotten ? His willingness to go back to responsibility, to pay the debt he owes, to become profitable rather than unprofitable.

So in that little verse there stand before us those tremendous facts about Christianity. Christ takes hold of the unprofitable man and makes him profitable. There are other planes upon which men may discuss that important matter of the commonwealth of human relations. I only referred to them to say this, that Christ alone confronts Onesimus and changes him from the unprofitable to the profitable. That is the central wonder, and the perpetual victory and the supreme glory of the Christian fact.—

G. Campbell Morgan, *Christian World Pulpit*, vol. LXXVII. p. 177.

GOD'S SECRET STAIRS

'Perhaps he therefore departed for a season, that thou shouldest receive him for ever.'—Philem. 15.

Writing to Philemon about Onesimus, the servant who had treated him so wrongfully, but in whom old things had passed away, St. Paul says: 'Perhaps he therefore departed for a season, that thou shouldest receive him for ever'. The words have meanings beyond their first application.

I. The gain of uncertainty . there is one thought which they bring. Now, it is a blessed thing that all the heavenly Father's intentions and doings are not clear as noonday, but that the twilight hangs about many of them. (1) It is a lesson in humility. (2) It is a lesson, too, in faith. The Christian is puzzled. The Christian has to say, 'Perhaps' (3) And it is a lesson in His many-sidedness. We have to tell ourselves, 'Perhaps this is His design,' or 'Perhaps that is the purpose of His great and unfathomable soul'.

II. The presence of God : it is a second truth which the words convey. Onesimus 'departed,' foolishly, wickedly; that is the human side. Onesimus 'was parted' from Philemon by the hand of the Lord ? that is the Divine side. Our life, short as it is, is full of partings. (1) Some of us are parted from our plans. (2) We are parted, moreover, from our possessions.

III. The lastingness of love : it is a final lesson which I glean. Onesimus was coming back, never to be separated from Philemon any more at all. He had gone away a heathen; he was returning a disciple. The love of God in Christ Jesus their Lord had drawn them into unity, had fused them into a single spirit, not for this world only, but for the next world as well. There are bonds which it is hard to break. (1) There is the bond of country (2) There is the bond of Church. (3) There is the bond of home. Yet none of these bonds is eternal. The one love which endures is the love of Christ. When our friends are His, they are ours so long as His heaven abides and He Himself lives. So 'there is nothing out of love hath perpetual worth'. 'All things flag but only love, all things fail and flee.'—A. Smellie, *Scottish Review*, vol. v. p. 418.

References.—I. 15.—C. D. Bell, *The Power of God*, p. 82. J. M. Neale, *Readings for the Aged* (3rd Series), p. 62. Spurgeon, *Sermons*, vol. xxi. No. 1268. *Expositor* (4th Series), vol. i. p. 34. I. 15, 16.—R. W. Hiley, *A Year's Sermons*, vol. iii. p. 305. J. M. Neale, *Sermons Preached in Sackville College Chapel*, vol. i. p. 350. I. 16.—J. W. Burgon, *Servants of Scripture*, p. 99. J. Eames, *Sermons to Boys and Girls*, p. 11. I. 19.—A. Maclaren, *Expositions of Holy Scripture—Philemon*, p. 196.

PHILEM. 22.

Lord, I read how Paul, writing from Rome, spake to Philemon to prepare him a lodging, hoping to make use thereof, yet we find not that he ever did use it, being martyred not long after. However, he was no loser, whom Thou didst lodge in a higher mansion in heaven. Let me always be thus deceived to my advantage. I shall have no occasion to complain, though I never wear the new clothes fitted for me, if, before I put them on, death clothe me with glorious immortality.—Thos. Fuller.

WHAT WE OWE TO ST. LUKE

(For St. Luke's Day)

'Luke, my fellow-worker.'—Philem. 24.

What is the debt which the Church owes to St. Luke ? This cultivated Gentile, with his scientific training, his literary and artistic gifts, his cosmopolitan sympathies, his romantic delight in adventure—what message does he bring to us, what elements does he contribute to our conception of religion ? It will be found, I believe, that St. Paul's 'fellow-worker' (particularly when we consider him in his character of third Evangelist) has lessons to convey to us—lessons not so clearly and emphatically taught elsewhere in the New Testament—lessons of peculiar and imperishable value; lessons, moreover, which at the present time seem to have a special claim upon our reverent attention. Let me set before you briefly three examples of such lessons. They will serve at least to indicate the nature of the obligation which every Christian owes to the Evangelist St. Luke.

I. First, then, we are principally indebted to St. Luke for our insight into the pardoning love of God in Christ for sinners. The 'beloved physician' clearly had a large heart himself; he was filled with profoundest pity for the sorrows and sins of men. It was natural, therefore, that in setting forth our Lord he should seek to present Him primarily as the large-hearted Saviour of the human race, the Revelation to each and all of God's boundless charity. How many magnificent passages expressive of the greatness of this Divine redeeming love are found in St. Luke alone! He only preserves that inimitable parable of the prodigal welcomed home, the recital of which would always bring tears into the eyes of St. Augustine; he only relates the stories of the sinner in Simon's house who loved much and was much forgiven, and of the robber to whom Paradise was promised on the cross; he first records the most wonderful saying in the whole of the Gospels—'The Son of Man came to seek and to save that which was lost'. And these are but few of the instances. Again and again, more fully and persistently than any of the Evangelists, St. Luke reveals and illustrates the Saviour's pitying love—the 'passion of compassion' which impelled Him to the rescue of the fallen and perishing. This is a theme on which he never tires of dwelling, and Dante was true to the facts of the case when he characterised our Evangelist as supremely 'the historian of the gentleness of Christ'.

II. Turn now to another lesson that is taught us by St. Luke. Just as this writer, more than any of the Evangelists, enables us to realise God's saving love for sinners, so more than any does he accentuate the dangers which lie about the path of those whom God would save. Particularly he is the preacher of the perils of prosperity. The perils of wealth, the perils of pleasure, the perils of the easy life of comfort and security—this is the subject of his repeated warnings. The most radical teachings concerning the good things of this world are to be found in the third Gospel. Here only are woes pronounced on the rich and the satisfied and the merry and the popular; here only we read the parable of Dives damned, and that of the Fool who heaped up treasure for himself, but was not ' rich toward God ' ; here possessions are personified as a demon of unrighteousness,' and the solemn word is heard, ' Whosoever he be of you that renounceth not all that he hath, he cannot be My disciple '. So determined, indeed, is the hostility of St. Luke towards property and prosperity that one scholar has described him, not without some show of reason, as ' the Socialist-Evangelist '.

III. Let us note just one other lesson that is taught us by St. Luke. He stands, it seems to me, as the type and representative of Christian humanism and culture. Not only was he a traveller and a man of science and a scholar; as an historian his merits have been proved beyond . dispute, while as a literary genius he is probably unequalled by any early Christian writer. Renan declares that his Gospel is the most beautiful book in the world, and a recent German critic aptly designates the author as ' the poet-painter among the Evangelists '. A tradition, which is apparently as old as the sixth century, claims him literally as a painter ; and, though this may not be accepted, there is still a real sense in which St. Luke may be regarded as ' the father of Christian art '. For from him, in larger measure than from any other Evangelist, the great religious painters have derived their inspiration. You have only to visit one of the famed European Galleries and mark the subjects of the pictures to perceive that this is so. There you find reproduced with an almost wearisome reiteration such scenes as the Annunciation, or the Presentation, or the Ascension ; as Christ among the Doctors, or at the supper-table of Emmaus. There in room after room you light upon the same familiar figures—Martha who serves, and Mary who listens, the Shepherds adoring the Babe in the manger, the white-haired Anna and the small Zacchæus ; or, again, the Pharisee and the Publican, the Unjust Steward, the Good Samaritan, and the Prodigal Son. Not all of you may realise that for the wonderful originals of these favourite scenes and portraits we are indebted exclusively to the superb artistic skill of the Greek ' poet-painter ' St. Luke.

Shall we not, then, be justified if we look upon St. Luke as teaching us by example the profound and weighty lesson that all that is best in culture, all the treasures of knowledge and imagination and emotion, should be sought out and used for Christ ?—F. HOMES-DUDDEN, *The Guardian*, 28th October, 1910.

REFERENCE.—I. 24.—*Expositor* (5th Series), vol. vi. p. 81.

THE EPISTLE TO THE HEBREWS

HEBREWS

The Epistle to the Hebrews is just such a performance as might naturally have come from an eloquent man and mighty in the Scriptures; in whom the intelligence, and the powers of combining, type-finding, and expounding, somewhat dominated the religious perceptions. The Epistle to the Hebrews is full of beauty and power; and what may be called the exterior conduct of its argument is as able and satisfying as Paul's exterior conduct of his argument is generally embarrassed. Its details are full of what is edifying.—MATTHEW ARNOLD, in *St. Paul and Protestantism*.

The object of the Epistle to the Hebrews was to prove the *superiority* of the Christian religion; the object of the Epistle to the Romans to prove its *necessity*.—COLERIDGE.

I CHERISH the thought of the richness there was in the first days of the Church, when even the writer of such an Epistle as this should be a forgotten man.—WESTCOTT.

'God who at sundry times and in divers manners, spake in time past unto the fathers by the prophets.'—HEB. I. I.

IN the fulness of time both Judaism and Paganism had come to nought; the outward framework, which concealed yet suggested the Living Truth, had never been intended to last, and it was dissolving under the beams of the Sun of Justice which shone behind it and through it. The process of change had been slow; it had been done not rashly, but by rule and measure, 'at sundry times and in divers manners'; first one disclosure and then another, till the whole evangelical doctrine was brought into full manifestation.—NEWMAN, *Apologia Pro Vita Sua* (ch. I.).

'HERE,' Mr. Gladstone writes in his introduction to Sheppard's Pictorial Bible, 'we perceive one of the high prerogatives of the Scriptures which helps to explain their close and elastic adaptation to the progressive needs of our race. No other sacred books are so minutely and exactly divided by periods and by authorship. No others cover so vast a range of time and of diversified human history. They began for a family, and they ended for a world. Not given at once and in stereotype, but "at sundry times and in divers manners".'

A GREAT number who chose to write on subjects that came within the relations of the Christian system, as on the various views of morals, the distinctions and judgments of human character, and the theory of happiness, with almost unavoidable references sometimes to our connection with Deity, to death, and to a future state, ought to have written every page under the recollection that these subjects are not left free for careless or arbitrary sentiment since the time that 'God has spoken to us by His Son'; and that the finest composition would be only so much eloquent impiety, if essentially discordant with the dictates of the New Testament.—JOHN FOSTER, *On the Aversion of Men of Taste to Evangelical Religion* (ch. VII.).

REFERENCES.—I. 1.—H. Martin, *Preacher's Magazine*, vol. xviii. p. 159. Bishop Westcott, *The Incarnation and Common Life*, p. 277. *Expositor* (6th Series), vol. iii. p. 39; *ibid.* vol. vi. p. 409; *ibid.* vol. vii. p. 86. I. 1, 2.—E. J. Hardy, *Christian World Pulpit*, vol. lvi. p. 203. T. F. Crosse, *Sermons* (2nd Series), p. 1. R. J. Campbell, *City Temple Sermons*, p. 1.

CHRISTIANITY AND JUDAISM

'God, having of old time spoken unto the fathers in the prophets by divers portions and in divers manners, hath at the end of these days spoken to us in His Son, whom He appointed heir of all things, through whom also He made the worlds; who being the effulgence of His glory, and the very image of His substance, and upholding all things by the word of His power, when He had made purification of sins, sat down on the right hand of the Majesty on high.'—HEB. I. 1-3 (R.V.).

THESE verses contain two main divisions of thought:—

I. A contrast between the Old Revelation and the New.

II. The Nature and Work of the Son of God.

I. A Contrast between the Old Revelation and the New.—Bishop Westcott writes: 'The contrast between the Old Revelation and the New is marked in three particulars. There is a contrast (*a*) in the method, and (*b*) in the time, and (*c*) in the agent of the two revelations.' 'God, having of old time spoken to the fathers in the prophets, in many portions and in divers manners, hath spoken in these last days in His Son.' The law of progression, which is stamped on creation, seen in God's providential government of the world, and experienced in the work of the Spirit in the individual soul, is clearly evidenced in Divine revelation. God did not at once open up the fulness of His mind, and unfold to view the treasures of His grace. His revelation was given 'piecemeal'—in numerous portions (πολυμερῶς). Each fragment is in advance of that which went before.

'God, having of old times spoken unto the fathers in the prophets by divers portions and in divers manners, hath at the end of these days spoken unto us in His Son.' The same voice spoke in both; but in the utterances of the prophets there were but partial gleams, glances, aspects, and scattered fragments of revelation. In the Son there was unparalleled fulness. This stage of revelation is in vast advance of earlier stages of Divine communications. 'The perfect manifestation takes up into itself the broken and imperfect voices. The dream fades in the reality, the vision melts in the tangible image, the type is lost in the antitype, the historical event is merged in One who professes to be the source of all history.[1] The prophets were the chords through which the heavenly music sounded ; the Incarnate Son of God was the complete instrument which gave to man the perfect melody of heaven. 'Every prophet added his own touch to the glorious picture of the days of the New Covenant, until, after sufficient elaboration of the main figure, the painters all withdrew, and let fall the curtain for awhile. The Person is already depicted, who shall raise this curtain again, and with His own hand trace for His contemporaries the fulfilment of the prophecy.'[2] The Son of God unites in Himself the whole of God's revelation.

II. The Nature and Work of the Son of God.— I can only comment on the grand sentences, 'Who being the effulgence of His glory, and the very image of His substance,' with great brevity. Dr. Newman, in his *Arians*, says that the word 'effulgence' expresses 'the essentially ministrative character of the person of the Son'. Dr. Owen writes : 'The words denote the Divine nature of Christ ; yet not absolutely, yet as God the Father in Him doth manifest Himself to us'. A luminous body is perceived by the splendour which streams forth from it. The Son is 'the brightness of the Father's glory'.

The verse which we are now considering is an epitome of the first two chapters of this Epistle. The first chapter is one continued argument for the Deity of Christ ; the second chapter for His humanity ; and then in the first verse of the third chapter the writer bids us consider how by reason of His twofold nature He is fitted to be the 'High Priest of our profession, Christ Jesus'. He is human, and can suffer in the same nature that sinned. He is Divine, and therefore He is able to meet the requirements of a law promulgated by an infinite Being, and to offer a sacrifice of an infinite value. Christ, in His twofold nature, is a bridge which spans the abyss which separates a holy God from sinful man. The ultimate reason for the Incarnation is to be found in the sin of man The effulgence of 'God's glory' and 'the very image of His substance' in our nature 'put away sin by the sacrifice of Himself'. He 'Himself purged our sins'. In this passage we are standing on the mountain-summit of the Incarnation, and we see around us seven mighty peaks in this Alpine region of thought. Let us gaze upon the first group of four. (1) The God-man is the end of all history. He 'is appointed heir of all things'. (2) He is the beginning of all history. In Him and for Him God made 'the world'—the ages—all that exists and moves in time. He is the spring from which all the streams of time have risen, as well as the sea into which they flow. He is the final cause of all human life. He is not only the goal of Judaism, but the climax of the world's history. (3) He is before all

[1] *Expositor*, vol. x. p. 279.
[2] Van Oosterzee, *The Image of Christ*, p. 104.

history. He is from everlasting, 'the brightness of God's glory, the express image of His person'. The Son is co-eternal with the Father. ' In order to the being of a Son there must be a Father ; but it is no less true that in order to the being of a Father there must be a Son. Fatherhood is no older than Sonship, the one is only as the other is.' (4) He is throughout all history. He 'upholdeth all things by the word of His power'.—J. W. BARDSLEY, *Many Mansions*, p. 45.

' His Son, Whom He made heir of all things, . . . who being the brightness of His glory, and the express image of His person, and upholding all things by the word of His power, when He had by Himself purged our sins, sat down on the right hand of the Majesty on high.'—HEB. I. 2 f.

WHERE can you find the mind of the Christian theologian of that early day better set forth than in the Epistle to the Hebrews, whoever may be the writer ? And what position does he take up ? He begins by stating that the Son of God is the 'heir of all things, through Whom also He made the worlds' ; 'Who being the effulgence of His glory, and the express image of His person, and upholding all things by the word of His power, when He had made purification of sins, sat down on the right hand of the Majesty on high ; having become so much better than the angels, as He hath inherited a more excellent name than they' ; and then he goes on to argue at length that whereas the higher spiritual orders of being whom the Jews called angels, and who were God's ministers, though not bound by earthly conditions, all rank beneath the Son of God, this Son of God nevertheless manifested Himself in this petty world of ours to purify us from sin, and obtain for us the blessedness which sin forfeits. Of course I do not dream of attributing to any writer of the first century speculations like Professor Whewell's on *The Plurality of Worlds*. But I do say that such writers had gathered, probably from the time of the Babylonian exile, a very steadfast belief in a vast hierarchy of beings in power far superior to man, and that their belief in this hierarchy of superior beings in no degree affected their conviction that the redemption of man from sin is a work worthy of the Divine Incarnation, and of that Divine suffering to which the Incarnation led and in which it was fulfilled.—R. H. HUTTON, *Contemporary Thought and Thinkers*, vol. I. pp. 293, 294.

REFERENCES.—I. 2.—H. Wace, *Christian World Pulpit*, vol. lviii. p. 140. I. 2, 3.—Spurgeon, *Sermons*, vol. xlv. No. 2635. I. 3.—W. H. Hutchings, *Sermon Sketches* (2nd Series), p. 162. *Expositor* (4th Series), vol. vi. p. 77 ; *ibid.* (6th Series), vol. viii. p. 201 ; *ibid.* vol. x. p. 198 ; *ibid.* vol. xi. p. 447. I. 5.—F. St. John Corbett, *The Preacher's Year*, p. 13. *Expositor* (5th Series), vol. ii. p. 82 ; *ibid.* (6th Series), vol. v. p. 150 ; *ibid.* vol. x. p. 113.

'Who maketh His angels spirits, and His ministers a flame of fire.'—HEB. I. 7.

THERE comes a terrible moment to many souls when the great movements of the world, the larger destinies of mankind, which have lain aloof in newspapers and other neglected reading, enter like an earthquake into their own lives—when the slow urgency of growing generations turns into the tread of an invading army or the dire clash of civil war, and grey fathers know nothing to seek for but the corpses of their blooming sons, and girls forget all vanity to make lint and bandages which may serve for the shattered limbs of their betrothed husbands. Then it is as if the Invisible Power that has been the object of lip-worship and lip-resignation became visible, according to the imagery of the Hebrew poet, making the flames his chariot and riding on the wings of the wind. . . . Then it is that the submission of the soul to the Highest is tested, and even in the eyes of frivolity life looks out from the scene of human struggle with the awful face of duty, and a religion shows itself which is something else than a private consolation.—GEORGE ELIOT, in *Daniel Deronda*.

REFERENCES.—I. 9.—*Expositor* (6th Series), vol. xii. p. 55. I. 10.—*Ibid.* (4th Series), vol. ii. p. 248. 1. 10-12.—H. S. Holland, *Christian World Pulpit*, vol. lix. p. 69.

'But Thou remainest.'—HEB. I. 11.

IN Dr. Andrew Bonar's study hung the text he was so fond of, and had had printed for himself, *But Thou remainest*. A lady called to see him one day in great sorrow and depression of mind. Nothing seemed to bring her any comfort. All at once, as they talked together, Dr. Bonar saw her face light up, and she said, 'You don't need to say anything more, I have got what I need,' and she pointed to the words of the text which had caught her eye, *But Thou remainest.*—*Reminiscences*, p. 93.

REFERENCE.—I. 11.—J. W. Whiton, *Beyond the Shadow*, p. 3.

'They shall perish, but Thou remainest; and they all shall wax old as doth a garment; and as a vesture shalt Thou fold them up, and they shall be changed.'—HEB. I. 11, 12.

THE generations of man are but the hours of a season, a little longer than a single year. The memory of them is trampled in by the million feet of their successors, themselves in turn to be trampled in as swiftly and cared for no more. But the stars which we see are the stars which they saw. Time has not dimmed their brilliance, or age made them loiter on their course. Time for them is not. They are themselves the measurers and the creators of time. Have they too their appointed end? 'They shall perish, but Thou shalt endure. They all shall wax old like a garment; as a vesture shalt Thou change them, and they shall be changed. But Thou art the same, and Thy years shall not fail.' Is this true? No answer peals to us out of the abysses of space. No evidence can be alleged to satisfy a British jury.—FROUDE, *Oceana* (ch. II.).

REFERENCES.—I. 12.—W. Richmond, *Church Family Newspaper*, vol. xiv. p. 12. *Expositor* (6th Series), vol. vii. p. 280.

ST. MICHAEL AND ALL ANGELS

'Are they not all ministering spirits, sent forth to minister for them who shall be heirs of salvation?'—HEB. I. 14.

THE attitude of the average Christian towards the angels is usually that of indifference. They do not much care whether they exist or not! They do not take their Bibles to find out the facts God has told them about the angels. They take little or no pains to establish relations with them, they are careless about the blessings which God intends to send us through them. So the Church, trying to rescue us from our persistent blindness, has established this festival of St. Michael and All Angels' Day, and it should act as a reminder of their ministry to us.

That God has given to us in the holy angels a great means of grace we cannot afford to ignore.

I. **The Ministry of Angels.**—I would ask you to think whether the angels are not designed to have great power over us, for what I should call the service of the Invisible Altar of Trust. Yes, there is an Invisible Altar of Trust, and there is not a person in this church that has not been made better at some time or other in their lives, and who has not known what it is to be strengthened by somebody's power of belief in them. Possibly the belief is in no way justified, yet the fact alone that the belief was held by somebody has stirred many a man and woman up to better things. There is always somebody who thinks well of us, and hopes well for us, and if we do not care much about ourselves (not well enough to do or be our best for very long together), that fact may always serve to consecrate us afresh. Now if we can once get it into our minds and imaginations that the angels think well of us, always see the best of us, always grieve for anything that is less than the best for us, that the angels are always thinking the best for us, and working the best for us, there is a whole world of consecration in the realisation of this thought.

II. **God's Messengers.**—The angels always can choose, because they see our Father's face, perfectly catching His expression and those suggestions for our good which the Father sends for us in that way through them. How wonderful to think of the angels always observing the Father's face with such understanding of every shade of expression of it; always able to decipher the meaning of every alteration in that expression; always able to catch the Father's Will for the salvation of some poor wayward child of His on earth. It makes all life different if we try to learn about, and to put into practical use, our belief in such things as these. They are worth thinking about; they are based upon what is revealed!

III. **Treasures of God's Love.**—The Bible will help us to work out more and more the problems which God has brought within our reach, and within the sphere of our experience if we choose to read and pray and to work and believe about them. On the other hand, if we shut our eyes to all these mysterious truths what is life for? Is life given to us that we go on missing every day all the treasures of His ingenuity and love? I suppose, when we get beyond death, and see more clearly than we can see here, and understand more widely than we can understand now, all that God has planned for our salvation from the beginning of eternity—I suggest, I say, there will be nothing more absolutely painful, nothing that will make a more complete hell, than the consciousness of all we have missed, the conviction beyond death of the value of all we have ignored this side of the grave. Do not let it go on until it is too late! Why should we miss, and go on missing, these treasures of God's love? From to-day let us just register the fact that God is reminding us that this is irreparably lost for those who have no eye open to the glory of the angels, and no ear open to the wisdom of the angels, and no willing response to the loyalty of the angels, and no co-operation with the ministry of the angels.

'Are they not all ministering spirits, sent forth to minister for them who shall be heirs of salvation?'—HEB. I. 14.

AND is there care in heaven? And is there love
In heavenly spirits to these creatures bace,
That may compassion of their evilles move?
There is: else much more wretched were the cace
Of men then beasts. But O! th' exceeding grace
Of highest God that loves his creatures so,
And all His workes with mercy doth embrace,
That blessed Angels he sends to and fro,
To serve to wicked men, to serve his wicked foe.

How oft do they their silves bowers leave,
To come to succour us that succour want!
How oft do they with golden pineons cleave
The flitting skyes, like flying Pursuivant,
Against fowle feendes to ayd us militant!
They for us fight, they watch and dewly ward,
And their bright Squadrons round about us plant;
And all for love, and nothing for reward.
O! why should heavenly God to men have such regard?
　　　　　SPENSER'S *Faerie Queene* (II. VIII. 1, 2).

'Are they not all ministering spirits.'—HEB. I. 14.

CARDINAL VAUGHAN says: 'We are touched by the love of our God as shown towards us in the ministry of His hidden angels, but I think the exhibition of His love is even more touching as vouchsafed through those who are our fellow-travellers along the road of life.'

REFERENCES.—I. 14.—R. F. Horton, *The Hidden God*, p. 183. W. P. S. Bingham, *Sermons on Easter Subjects*, p. 134. I. 31.—*Expositor* (4th Series), vol. vi. p. 132.

'Lest haply we drift away from them.'—HEB. II. 1.

THERE is nothing I so hardly beleeve to be in man as constancie, and nothing so easie to be found in him, as inconstancy. . . . Our ordinary manner is to follow the inclination of our appetite this way and that way, on the left or on the right hand; upward and downeward, according as the winde of occasions doth transport us; we never thinke on what we would have, but at the instant we would have it: and change as that beast that takes the colour of the place wherein it is laid. What we even now purposed we alter by and by, and presently returne to our former biase. We goe not, but we are carried: as things that flote, now sliding gently, now pulling violently, according

as the water is, either stormy or calme.—MONTAIGNE (*Florio*), II. 1.

DRIFTING FROM CHRIST

'Therefore we ought to give the more earnest heed to the things which we have heard, lest haply we let them slip.' —HEB. II. I.

THE counsel is one to Christian men to beware of drifting from Christ. Such is our theme—Drifting from Christ. But perhaps it is natural we should speak of another thing first.

I. It must be a long while now since men began to speak of their life as a running stream. It was inevitable the figure should suggest itself to them as soon as they began to think; we all feel its aptness as often as we reflect upon the ceaseless vicissitude that laps our lives round. Of course, it would be a mistake, and worse than a mistake, to think of this ceaseless movement in which we are all involved as if it were a mere brute fate to which simply we must perforce submit. 'Life,' says the Apostle to Christian believers, 'life,' with all its elements and conditions, 'is *yours*'. This continual change to which we are all committed is for one thing the condition of progress. And besides, how flat and stale life would otherwise be! And yet I believe every one will feel that were there nothing but ceaseless change in our earthly lot, no anchor sure and steadfast for us anywhere, life would be terrible indeed! Ah, it is everything for us to have attached ourselves to Jesus Christ! everything that by strong cords of trust and loyalty we should be fast moored to Him!

II. But it is time to speak now, in the second place, of what is meant by *drifting from Christ*. Of those who once were alongside Jesus Christ, how many that we could name have drifted very far! It is not easy even for Christian people always to have the Lord Jesus Christ for the fixed centre of their lives. Too often their relations to Him grow relaxed somehow, and His sublime Figure recedes into the distance, threatening to pass out of view—an unhappy process which comes about in very various ways. Thus for example (1) A storm may have broken out in their life and driven them away from Christ. It may have been a storm of doubt, or a storm of trouble. (2) Or again, it may be an influence less obvious that does it. (3) When neither of these influences succeeds in detaching us from our Lord, there is another influence that may—an influence more slow and subtle and secret still. A thousand varying cares and moods and occupations agitate the surface of our lives. And with this there comes a chafing and a fretting which may by slow degrees wear out the strands of loyalty that bind us to our Lord.

III. How can a Christian who has drifted away from Christ regain his moorings once more? It is by no violent efforts, no strong beating up against the adverse forces of his life, still less by any weak complaining of them, that any man will regain his old attachment to Jesus Christ; but just by giving 'earnest heed—the more earnest heed to the things which he has heard about Him'.—A. Martin, *Winning the Soul*, p. 31.

DRIFTING

Heb. ii. 1 (R.V.).

There is as much need for this exhortation to-day as when it was first written. There are many signs of religious decadence which we shall be wise to heed, lest we ourselves, caught in the prevailing current, drift away from the truth of God, from the day of God, and from the Christ of God. John Ruskin was not far wrong when he said that a Red Indian, or an Otaheitian savage, had a surer sense of Divine existence round him, the God over him, than the plurality of refined Londoners and Parisians. Allowing that there is some exaggeration in this, I fear that there is too much truth in it.

I. With a view to our spiritual help, let us see what those things are which we have heard, and then glance at the danger of losing them and the means of holding them fast. (1) Among the new truths these Hebrews had heard was the readiness of God to receive all who came to Him. (2) Take another example of what this writer alluded to—the truth that suffering is often as much a sign of God's love as success. (3) Think also of Christ's revelation of the spiritual nature of acceptable worship. (4) But all this resolves itself into the possibility of losing our hold on the living God, for it is the fact of His Fatherhood which constitutes the brotherhood; it is because He is a God of Love that we are sure our troubles are over-ruled for good; and it is because He is a Spirit that we must worship Him in spirit and in truth.

II. The danger of loosening our grip on spiritual realities is serious. The nature of spiritual truths and things is such as to make them elusive. They are not evident to our senses.

III. How, then, shall we safeguard ourselves against this peril? The answer is here—by taking more earnest heed to the things we have heard. (1) Could you not give more time to the study of God's Word? (2) Again, you will be taking more earnest heed to things you have heard when you live as if you believed them. (3) Above all, strive to keep up in prayer, here and alone, such personal communion with God in Christ that your affection as well as your intellect may grasp Him.—A. Rowland, *Open Windows and other Sermons*, p. 88.

References.—II. 1.—J. H. Jowett, *Christian World Pulpit*, vol. xliii. p. 150. C. Perren, *Sermon Outlines*, p. 336. S. A. Selwyn, *Church Family Newspaper*, vol. xiv. p. 52. E. Griffith-Jones, *Christian World Pulpit*, vol. lvi. p. 408, and vol. lviii. p. 292. J. Bowstead, *Practical Sermons*, vol. ii. p. 15. A. Maclaren, *Expositions of Holy Scripture—Hebrews*, p. 205. II. 2-4.—J. Bunting, *Sermons*, vol. i. p. 133.

NEGLECTING THE GREAT SALVATION

'How shall we escape, if we neglect so great salvation; which at the first began to be spoken by the Lord, and was confirmed unto us by them that heard Him?'—Heb. ii. 3.

The object of the writer of this Epistle was to show to the Jews how much *better* the Gospel dispensation was as compared with the old covenant. The keynote of the Epistle is the word *better*—a *better* priest, a *better* tabernacle, a *better* sacrifice, are to be found in the new covenant. There are two points to which I wish to direct your attention.

I. Why this salvation is called *great*. (1) It is called great on account of its great author. It was the conception of the great heart of the great God of heaven and earth. Think of the greatness of our God. Take the telescope and sweep the heavens with it on some clear, starry night. What a revelation of God's greatness we have there! Let us turn to the microscope and there we see the perfection of God's workmanship, how the tiniest of His created things (unlike man's workmanship) will bear the minutest inspection. I turn from God the Creator to God the Ruler of the earth, and there too in the pages of history I see His might and His power. (2) It is a great salvation because of its subject—a lost world. The loving arms of God seem to enclasp this sinful, this rebellious world, and we hear His voice of love saying, 'Not one of these sons and daughters of Mine shall perish' so God loved the world. (3) It is a great salvation because of the great object it has in view. It is not only to redeem a world lost, ruined, and cursed, but to redeem *man* in that world. (4) It is a great salvation because of the great price paid for it. There is no arithmetic, no numbers, by which we can *calculate* the great *price* of this great salvation. (5) And the *end* makes it great, even eternal glory. The purpose and plan was to bring many sons to glory. To be in His presence, to behold His glory, to be transformed into His image—this is the great salvation.

II. The serious consequences that follow from neglecting it. If the Jew perished with less light and fewer privileges, *how shall we escape!* Alas! we are busy about everything but the one thing needful. How shall we escape if we *neglect*? There is nowhere in this universe where we may escape to. We cannot hide from God.—T. J. Madden, *Tombs or Temples* p. 119.

References.—II. 3.—H. Allen, *Penny Pulpit*, No. 1584, p. 65. II. 4.—*Expositor* (5th Series), vol. vii. p. 141.

'For not unto angels did he subject the world to come, whereof we speak.'—Heb. ii. 5.

In a letter to Lady Elgin, written in 1833, Erskine of Linlathen points out the distinction 'between the dispensation of Christ and the dispensation of ἄγγελοι (Heb. i. and ii.). The dispensation of Christ embraces in it a oneness with the mind of God—not merely a readiness to do His will, when we know it, but a participation in His mind, so that, by a participation in the Divine nature, we enter into the reasons of His will, and do not merely obey the authority of His will'.

References—II. 5-9.—*Expositor* (5th Series), vol. ii. p. 184. II. 6.—J. N. Friend, *Preacher's Magazine*, vol. xvii. p. 458. II. 7.—*Expositor* (4th Series), vol. ii. p. 435 ; *ibid.* (6th Series), vol. iv. p. 385.

'Not yet.'—Heb. ii. 8.

You can remember that text, you have not ability enough to forget it. But we remember many things intellectually which we forget morally and sympathetically. 'Not yet'—why it sounds like a song of hope; there is no despair in this strain. The meaning is, We shall by and by—perhaps round the next mountain shoulder—we shall see the holy land, the garden of God. 'Not yet;' we are waiting for it; the night is cold and long, but it will expire, and then we shall see the morning and feel its friendly warmth. 'Not yet,' but after a while; a few more struggles, and then the victory. We fight in the hope of the triumph. In mere fighting there is nothing but heartache and disappointment, but in the things that are beyond the morning is the smile.

Let us see if we can paraphrase and amplify this most beautiful thought.

I. 'Not yet, but'—broken music, but God's music. All things we know of God are broken. Oh, the broken instruments that are lying on the floor of this orchestra, broken trumpets, broken organs, broken lives—broken, all broken; they shall all be gathered up and put together again, and God's band shall be one loud sweet anthem-song. We do not see the whole world converted to the faith. They say it would be, but it is not. There are atheists, there are cannibals, there are heathen, there are pagans, there are savages, who would dine off you if they could. You promised the earth should be green, and behold it lies in waste lands. Hold on! What do you see? Why, we see one man, and he only of the poor sort, believing. That is enough; why speak scornfully of the solitary specimen? He is an instance, he grows in the soil of his soul the plant of faith—enough! Why do you lose heart in missions foreign and home? Is there only one man in all the world who believes? then the cause of Christ must be in a bad way. Not at all; that one man does believe, he keeps up the continuity of faith, he comes out of the secret places of the Most High, he is walking back to the sanctuary that is invisible, and in his tarrying here for a moment, he irradiates the planet with a strange mystic glory. We do not yet see all the land covered with summer flowers; it is but February, and cold icy February, and the very devil's in the air blackening it with his unholy blight. Talk about summer! Yes, we do. We do not yet see the spring and the summer in all their full blossoming, but this little girl was out this morning, and she found this little blue violet. She did? Yes. In the open air? Yes. Sure? Quite. Not grown under glass? No, in the open air. Then the spring is here in that violet; that is enough, it took the whole solar system to grow that violet. You are taking a poetical view of things. Not at all, I am taking a prosaic view of things; because that violet is here in the open air the whole land shall glow with summer. There is a proverb—like most of the proverbs, half a truth or a whole lie—which says that one swallow does not make a summer. Yes, it does; that one swallow is the

prophet of the Lord: He cannot come alone, you do not see his following.

II. If these things be so, what follows? Patience is one of the things which follow. God always takes time. I do not know how long it was before He came to look upon chaos. Chaos has no history, chaos keeps no archives, no records. But in due time, called by the prophet-poet, 'The beginning,' the dateless date, He came and looked and shaped the universe into music and meaning. I do not wonder at our being impatient. We have but a handful of years at our disposal, some seventy—a few more or a few less, what matters? We want everything done in our day and generation, and the Lord never hurries Himself. He who breathes eternity need not be worried and fretted by feverish time. Patience! I never ask any man to join the Church, I never urge any man to come to the communion of the Lord's Supper; I never dig up the seed I have sown to see how it is getting on. Foolish man who takes up the roots to know whether they are growing and how fast they are growing. Son of man, go forth and preach the preaching that I bid thee; whether the people hear or forbear is no business of thine. You want to see immediate results. That is a sign of impatience: fall into the music of the universe, fall into the solemnity and the peacefulness of God's intention. The earth is redeemed, that fact is accomplished, and one day He will come to claim his redemption, and it will be all there. Confidence is another of the things which well becometh us under the inspiration of this meditation. It will all come to pass; we cannot even hinder the truth in any permanent or enduring sense. We can hinder it for a time and in a place, but a very limited hindering is the hindering that is possible to man. 'We can do nothing against the truth but for the truth.' It hath pleased God that His economy shall work in that way. He has made us fellow-labourers in His great husbandry, and at the last He will credit us with the whole; He will say, 'Thy faith hath made thee whole'. His harvest is the fruition of thy faith. Condescending God, merciful God, Person of the dear Jesus, He told the cripples that came to Him in the days of His flesh that they had made themselves whole by their faith—a wondrous co-operation of pity and love.

Participation is another of the things which belongs to this series of thoughts. We shall be partakers of His glory. We shall reap where He has sown, His furrows shall be our harvest, and we shall have great delight together. Oh for that harvest day, that day of the laden wains, and the merry singing—Harvest Home! Every one of us credited with having grown some of the corn, so big, so overflowing is the Divine love. Have you seen the resurrection? No. Yes, you have. No, I have not seen the resurrection. You have, you have seen these flowers: this is the resurrection. If these things, so shapely, comely, beautiful, and fragrant, came out of the cold black earth, the argument for the resurrection is complete. I have not seen the resurrection, you say. No, but you have seen one white lily out of the black earth. It is enough; if He brought that lily out of the earth, He can bring your child up too. I have not seen the resurrection. Yes, you have. Where? Why, in that arum lily that you pointed out to me the other day, that beautiful arum lily, so graceful, so spotless, that I said to it, Whence comest thou? Out of the earth—almost into heaven. The text is—I saw some persons come in late who ought to have been here in time—the text is, 'Not yet, but '.—JOSEPH PARKER.

REFERENCE.—II. 8.—H. Alford, *Quebec Chapel Sermons*, vol. iii. p. 84.

MAN AS KING

'Thou didst put all things in subjection under his feet. For in that He subjected all things unto him, He left nothing that is not subject to him. But now we see not yet all things subjected to him. But we behold Him . . . even Jesus.'—HEB. II. 8, 9.

I. 'WE see not yet all things in subjection to man.' 'Not yet,' but we are to see it. This supremacy is the final goal of humanity. The threads of the ages have been woven in the great loom of Time with the weft of the Divine purpose and the warp of human experience, and on the web is traceable in clear characters the God-given sovereignty of man.

II. 'Not unto angels has God subjected the coming world.' Not to them, but to men like ourselves, who have to do with sheep and oxen and the beasts of the field, with cotton and calicoes, with science and art; whose life is as 'fragile as the dewdrop on its perilous way from a tree's summit,' and yet so strong that it destroys itself by sin; man, 'made a little lower than God, and crowned with the glory' of a present participation in His nature, and therefore by and by to be invested with the 'honour' of sharing His rule.

III. But if to man, to what man is this sceptre of dominion finally granted? The conquering race is the godly race, of any colour, or country, or time. Not 'the great white race,' but the great Christian race, rises to joint-heirship with Christ Jesus in the salvation and service, and sovereignty of the future of humanity.

IV. Though eighteen centuries have elapsed since that forecast of the destiny of man was quoted, endorsed, and explained by the writer to the Hebrews, amid the wreck and overthrow of Judaism, we have, alas! to adopt the writer's lament, and say, as we look on man and his world to-day, 'not yet do we see all things subjected unto him'. He is only slowly learning that he is a spirit, and is for large breadths of his time and in wide areas of his life the slave of 'things'.

V. But surely, that is not all we see! Recognise fully the prodigious loss due to man's forfeiture of his predestined royalty; tabulate the miseries he owes due to his falls; omit no item in the tale of the poorness of his life, the selfishness of his spirit, and the fecundity of his sin; yet that is not all the whole human fact. On this earth and amongst men —'we see Jesus,' and though, in seeing Him, the

first glimpse may only confirm the impression that man has not yet fully entered on his inheritance, yet the deeper look assures us that he is on his way to it, has already been anointed with the oil of joy above his predecessors and contemporaries, and, though suffering, is really ascending by suffering to the throne from which he shall rule for evermore. In what ways do men come to sovereign spiritual power? The Epistle to the Hebrews is the full and inspiring answer. The rule of life comes to the builders of the city of God; the men who, in glorious succession, work out the Divine purpose of redemption on the earth, and find the Author and Finisher of their work in the Christ. Authority is in the revelation of God, and it increases till in the 'new covenant' it is at its maximum of light and power. World-rulers are men of ethical glow and passion, who believe in the invisible, and work for righteousness with self-sacrificing devotion. Seeing Jesus, we see these four paths to the sovereignty of the Christian race, and of the Christian religion through that race; the path of history; of Divine revelation; of saintly character; and of self-suppressing enthusiasm for the welfare of the world.—J. CLIFFORD, *The Secret of Jesus*, p. 199.

THE CROWNED CHRIST

HEB. II. 8, 9.

WE have in these words a contrast between the greatness of man and the supremacy of Christ. The writer of the Epistle admits the greatness of man, but suggests that he had fallen short of the ideal— he had not yet realised his dominion : 'We see not yet all things subjected to him '. Then he proceeds, on this alleged greatness, to suggest an argument for the supremacy of Christ. Man, though great, had failed, but 'we see . . . Jesus . . . crowned'. We find the writer asserting two things :—

I. That Man has not yet Realised Universal Dominion.—See how true this is—(1) In the realm of matter. Since the Epistle was written, how great has been the progress of Science! The dominion of man over matter is vast and most wonderful. A Kepler has traced the orbit of a planet, and with awe exclaimed, 'I thought over again the thought of God!' A Franklin has drawn lightning from the clouds, and directed its course. A Young has suggested the wave theory of light. A Newton has discovered the force of gravitation. A Harvey has revealed the circulation of the blood. A Darwin has collected the facts on which the theory of natural evolution became possible. And yet, with all these wonderful discoveries of man in the realm of matter, how true it is, 'We see not yet all things subjected to him'. (2) In the sphere of life. (3) In the sphere of mind. (4) In the sphere of the spiritual.

II. That Christ is Destined to Realise this Universal Dominion.—The writer sees clearly that the coming of Christ makes possible for man the heights of life—that now he may win a closer fellowship with God, and, defying evil, march to the great future as a

Son of God. He sees Christ crowned on the heights because He made all this possible for man, and in Him he sees the ultimate victory of the race. But on what does this splendid vision rest? The vision rests on the three granite pillars of the Christian Gospel—(1) The Incarnation. (2) The Redemption. (3) The Priesthood. Though we see not yet 'all things subjected to him,' we see Jesus crowned, and the crowning of Christ involves the ultimate making and crowning of man. On these three pillars of the faith we may build our great hope and win the vision of man complete in Him. If redemption were a failure, Christ would lose His crown. The crown of man as a returning Son of God *is* the crown of Christ.—J. Oates, *The Sorrow of God*, p. 108.

'We see not yet all things put under his feet, . . . but we see Jesus.'—Heb. ii. 8, 9.

It is this which gives such terrible, even blighting power to the words and writings of unbelievers, which barbs and sends home many a dull scoff that would otherwise fall harmless ; that they touch a conscious, ever-rankling wound. *What they urge against Christianity is true.* The believer knows, already knows, all that the infidel can tell him ; the eye of love can see as clearly as that of hate, and it has already warmed over all the other exults in ; has seen springs sink down suddenly among the sands of the desert ; has looked upon bare and stony channels, now ghastly with the wreck and drift of ages, yet showing where once a full, fair river bore down life and gladness to the ocean. The Christian would fain explain, account for these long delays, this partial efficacy, this intermittent working. He feels that he is in possession of the key which is to open all these intricacies, but at present he finds that, like that of the pilgrims, 'it grinds hard in the lock'. He sees Jesus, but he sees not yet all things put under Him.—Dora Greenwell, in *The Patience of Hope*.

THE TASTE OF DEATH AND THE LIFE OF GRACE

'That He by the grace of God should taste death for every man.'—Heb. ii. 9.

I. Jesus Christ not only died, but He tasted death as incredible bitterness and penury of soul.

II. He did so because He died for every man. He experienced in a Divine life the universal death.

III. Yet this desertion and agony of death was a gift and grace of God not only to us but to Him. And He knew it was so. And that faith was His victory and our redemption.—P. T. Forsyth, *Christian World Pulpit*, vol. lviii. p. 296.

ASCENSION DAY

'But we see Jesus, who was made a little lower than the angels for the suffering of death, crowned with glory and honour.'—Heb. ii. 9.

Thoughts of joy and gladness mingle with all our meditations of Ascension-tide. Christ is now seen to have all things put under Him. In this Jubilee of the Saviour's coronation, we may forget for a moment all our preceding commemorations. Bethlehem, Gethsemane, Calvary, the manger, the wilderness, the cross, the grave, they are only so many beautiful memories —stages in that triumphant progress by which the Holy One ascends to the Throne. Our eyes 'see the King in His beauty,' and they can fix their gaze on nothing else : ' We see Jesus, Who was made a little lower than the angels for the suffering of death, crowned with glory and honour'.

I. What was the glory here spoken of? First, there was the glory of a great salvation for the lost children of men. The anticipation of this honour entered into that intercessory prayer recorded in the seventeenth chapter of St. John. Now this joint glory of the Father and the Son consisted in bringing many sons into glory. And in order thereto, Christ was to be set as a King upon His holy hill of Zion. 'The government was to be upon His shoulder.' He was to become the centre of ten thousand times ten thousand redeemed and happy beings who had been washed from their sins in His own Blood, and who should live only to cast their crowns at His feet. And there were means and agencies for carrying out these objects to be employed upon the Throne. No sooner had Christ ceased to drink of the brook by the way, and had sat down on the right hand of the Majesty on high, than the sun of His Godhead shone forth with all the effulgence of its original and eternal brightness. Men were to see the glory, both of the Father and of Christ. The triumphs of the cross shall be made manifest. The victories of the Holy Spirit shall begin. The work of the all-prevailing intercession shall go on within the veil. There shall be, as it were, a mighty revival in heaven, all the powers therein wondering at the extending reign of righteousness and the fruits of the outpoured gifts of the Ascension on the hearts of the sons of men. ' Thy Throne, O God, is for ever and ever : the sceptre of Thy Kingdom is a right sceptre : Thy people shall be willing in the day of Thy power.'

II. ' Crowned with glory and honour,' in that, all things, both in heaven and earth, shall be subject to the kingdom of mediation (see Eph. i. 20-23) ; and again, ' All things were made by Him and for Him '. ' For Him,' observe, that is, in His character as Mediator. The kingdom of mediation embraces the visible and the invisible ; the whole of our present mundane system was constructed with a view to afford a theatre magnificent enough for the work of Christ, and for the training of suitable instruments for the accomplishment of His great purposes. The Saviour's exaltation reminds us then that we are subjects of the Mediator's world ; that the earth is the platform of an achieved redemption ; that all things were made for, and put under the dominion of the Crucified : ' All power is given to Him in heaven and in earth '. All power to seal pardons ; to impart gifts ; to quicken, sanctify, redeem, save. It was needful that in all things He should have the pre-eminence. All beings, all worlds must see Him ' crowned with glory and honour '.

'Crowned with glory and honour,' in that on the ascended Saviour should be concentrated all the homage and adoration of the heavenly world (Phil. II. 10), plainly affirms the dominion of Christ over all worlds, intelligences, and kingdoms. He is ' God over all, blessed for ever '.—D. Moore.

HEB. II. 9.

WHEN I think of our Lord as tasting death it seems to me as if He alone ever truly tasted death. And this, indeed, may be received as a part of the larger truth that He alone ever lived in humanity in the conscious truth of humanity. But when I think of death as tasted by our Lord, how little help to conceiving of His experience in dying do any of our own thoughts or anticipated experiences seem fitted to yield! What men shrink from when they shrink from death, is either the disruption of the ties that connect them with a present world, or the terrors with which an accusing conscience fills the world to come. The last had no existence for Him who was without sin : neither had the world, as the present evil world, any place in His heart.—McLeod Campbell, *The Nature of the Atonement*, pp. 259 f.

'We see Jesus.'—HEB. II. 9.

BISHOP KING of Lincoln wrote : ' We cannot understand the mystery of sorrow. We can "see Jesus" the "Man of Sorrows" and see how His earthly ministry apparently was a failure. They did not care for Him —wonderful and purifying example for us all, warning us against the dangers of popularity and apparent success.'—*Spiritual Letters*, p. 64.

REFERENCES.—II. 9.—Spurgeon, *Sermons*, vol. xiii. No. 771, and vol. xxv. No. 1509. J. T. Parr, *Christian World Pulpit*, vol. lvi. p. 4. R. W. Church, *Village Sermons* (3rd Series), p. 85. *Expositor* (4th Series), vol. vi. p. 132 ; *ibid.* (5th Series), vol. vi. p. 375 ; *ibid.* vol. ix. p. 472 ; *ibid.* (6th Series), vol. xii. p. 45. II. 9, 10.—C. Kingsley, *The Good News of God*, p. 340.

'Perfect through sufferings.'—HEB. II. 10.

THOUGHT, true labour of any kind, highest virtue itself, is it not the daughter of Pain? Born as out of the black whirlwind ;—true *effort*, in fact, as of a captive struggling to free himself : that is Thought. In all ways we are ' to become perfect through *suffering* '.—CARLYLE, *Heroes* (lecture III.).

REFERENCES.—II. 10.—J. G. Binney, *Christian World Pulpit*, vol. liii. p. 22. Spurgeon, *Sermons*, vol. viii. No. 478, and vol. xlv. No. 2619. J. Bunting, *Sermons*, vol. i. p. 51. C. S. Macfarland, *The Spirit Christlike*, p. 127. Archbishop Cosmo Lang, *Christian World Pulpit*, vol. lv. p. 235. *Expository Sermons on the New Testament*, p. 256. G. Body, *Christian World Pulpit*, vol. lvii. p. 200. H. Bushnell, *Christ and His Salvation*, p. 219. J. Farquhar, *The Schools and Schoolmasters of Christ*, p. 145. *Expositor* (4th Series), vol. i. p. 143 ; *ibid.* vol. iii. p. 370 ; *ibid.* vol. iv. p. 34 ; *ibid.* (6th Series), vol. viii. p. 386. A. Maclaren, *Expositions of Holy Scripture—Hebrews*, p. 229. II. 10-18.—*Ibid.* (4th Series), vol. iv. p. 428. II. 11.—J. Keble, *Sermons for Lent to Passion-tide*, p. 288. C. D. Bell, *The Power of God*, p. 40. J. Bowstead, *Practical Sermons*, vol. i. p. 298. J. Bunting, *Sermons*, vol. ii. p. 124. II. 11-13.—Spurgeon, *Sermons*, vol. xli. No. 2418. A. Mac-laren, *Expositions of Holy Scripture—Hebrews*, p. 239. II. 11-17.—*Expositor* (6th Series), vol. ix. p. 59. II. 12.—*Expositor* (4th Series), vol. iii. p. 118 ; *ibid.* (5th Series), vol. vii. p. 197. A. Martin, *Winning the Soul*, p. 319. II. 13.—H. Varley, *Christian World Pulpit*, vol. lvii. p. 237. II. 14.—Spurgeon, *Sermons*, vol. iv. No. 166. F. J. A. Hort, *Village Sermons* (2nd Series), p. 37. S. Baring-Gould, *Village Preaching for Saints' Days*, p. 181. *Expositor* (4th Series), vol. ii. p. 47 ; *ibid.* (5th Series), vol. vii. p. 222.

EMANCIPATION FROM THE FEAR OF DEATH

' That through death He might destroy him that had the power of death, that is, the devil ; and deliver them who through fear of death were all their lifetime subject to bondage.'—HEB. II. 14, 15.

DEATH is a subject which may at present be remote from our thoughts, but it is an experience in which we shall all one day or other be interested. To be frequently in the contemplation of death is perhaps the mark of a feeble rather than of a robust spirit, yet we ought not to refuse the calls which in God's providence invite us to consider death. And, if it be extravagant to demand that a large part of our life should be consumed in contemplating its end, we may, like Nelson, while fighting on deck yet keep our coffin in our cabin.

It is well to be assured that one of the purposes served by the mission of Christ was to dispel the fear of death by destroying that which gave it power to terrify. The fear of death is here represented as a bondage, a condition of slavery out of which every child of God must be emancipated.

I. If we analyse this fear we find that there are various causes producing it. First of all there is the bodily pain, which frequently precedes death, and may in our own case do so. Dread of pain increases with age, as we learn more of the capacity for suffering which our body possesses, and as we see more of the terrible forms of disease by which life is slowly worn out. It is human nature to shrink from long-continued and hopeless weakness, from months of uselessness and slow decay, from the gradual extinction of all the functions of life, and the constantly renewed misery of the medical or surgical appliances which we know can but prolong for a short time a life that has become torture. But this cause of fear may be left to be dealt with by common sense and nature. For it is unreasonable to distress ourselves with prospects of such a kind. For all we know, death may find us in sleep or may have passed before we were conscious of its approach, or in our case it may come with none of these attendant horrors. Dr. Hunter, in his last moments, grieved that he ' could not write how easy and delightful it is to die '. The late Archbishop of Canterbury quietly remarked, ' It is really nothing much after all '.

II. A second cause of this fear is a more reasonable one. We fear death because it brings to an end the only life we know experimentally.

But if we believe what both nature and Christ teach us, that this life is but the training-ground for another, that the powers here cultivated and the tools here whetted are for use in a larger and intenser existence ; if we consider that once *this* life was as strange and new to us as any other can be, and that death is really the bursting of the shell that hinders us from entering the ampler air of our true and eternal life, we have surely cause enough to throw such regrets and fears to the winds, and even long, as some have longed, to learn what the true life of God and God's children is.

III. But this leads us to the most fruitful cause of fear, the consciousness that after death comes the judgment. Whatever men hold regarding the last judgment or the mode of it, all men feel that at death there *is* a judgment, that death ushers them into a fixed, final, eternal state. This is the instinctive apprehension of untaught men as well as the warning of revelation.

The natural boldness which confronts death cheerfully, or sullenly submits to the inevitable, disappears when this added knowledge of the significance of death enters in. Mere natural courage is irrelevant in facing judgment. This letter was written 'to the Hebrews,' to men who had lived under a legal religion, and who could expect to escape punishment only if they had complied with all that the law commanded. But to be sure of this was impossible, and the result was that we find them exclaiming, 'In this life death never suffers a man to be glad '.

Our emancipation from bondage to this fear is accomplished by ' the destruction of him that had the power of death, that is, the devil '. The devil was considered to be the counsel for the prosecution, the embodiment of an accusing conscience. Death was looked upon as the result of the primal curse, as separation from God and from all good on account of sin ; a just and true view. The devil had the power of death in the sense in which the state has the power of the sword to inflict punishment on evil-doers. The devil used the common idea of death to terrify and appal and separate from all hope in God. The Jew was haunted with such visions as Zechariah had when he saw the high priest himself clothed in filthy garments. This was the sting of the serpent ; but in Christ the primeval promise was fulfilled, the serpent's head was crushed. The devil's weapon is struck from his hand. He can no longer persuade the children of God that death means separation from God and entrance upon a life of suffering.—MARCUS DODS, *Christ and Man*, p. 238.

' Forasmuch then as the children are partakers of flesh and blood, He also Himself likewise took part of the same ; that through death He might destroy him that had the power of death, that is, the devil ; and deliver them who through fear of death were all their lifetime subject to bondage.'— HEB. II. 14, 15.

' AT another time,' says Bunyan in *Grace Abounding* (116), ' as I was set by the fire in my House, and musing on my Wretchedness, the Lord made that also a precious word unto me, *Forasmuch then as the children* are partakers of flesh and blood, He also Himself likewise took part of the same ; that through death He might destroy him that had the power of death, that is, the devil ; and deliver them who

through fear of death *were all their lifetime subject to bondage*. I thought that the glory of these words was then so weighty on me that I was, both once and twice, ready to swoon as I sat ; yet not with grief and trouble, but with solid joy and peace.'

' Who through fear of death were all their lifetime subject to bondage.'—HEB. II. 15.

IN the preface to *Colloquia Peripatetica* (p. lxxv.), Prof. Knight remarks that, for all the genuineness of Dr. John Duncan's faith, 'nevertheless, it is true that he was " all his lifetime subject unto bondage ". His spirit did not live in the sunshine. Though he would have appreciated Luther's saying, ' I sit and sing, like a bird on a tree, and let God think for me," he never entered into the core of that experience.'

' O ! WHO will deliver me from this fear of death ? What shall I do ? Where shall I fly from it ? Should I fight against it by thinking, or by not thinking of it ? A wise man advised me some time since, ' Be still and go on '. Perhaps this is best, to look upon it as my cross ; when it comes, to let it humble me, and quicken all my good resolutions, especially that of praying without ceasing ; and at other times, to take no thought about it, but quietly to go on ' in the work of the Lord '.—WESLEY's *Journal* (January, 1738).

REFERENCES.—II. 14, 15.—A. Ainger, *Sermons Preached in the Temple Church*, p. 87. J. Keble, *Sermons for Septuagesima to Ash Wednesday*, p. 391.

' Through fear of death.'—HEB. II. 15.

IN 1518 Erasmus lay dangerously ill at Louvain. After his recovery he wrote to Beatus Rhenanus : ' When the disease was at its height I neither felt distressed with desire of life, nor did I tremble at the fear of death. All my hope was in Christ alone, and I prayed for nothing to Him except that He would do what He thought best for me. Formerly, when a youth, I remember I used to tremble at the very name of death.'

' He taketh hold of the seed of Abraham.'—HEB. II. 16.

HE does not forsake the world,
But stands before it modelling in the clay,
And moulding there His image. Age by age
The clay wars with His fingers and pleads hard
For its old, heavy, dull, and shapeless ease.
          —W. B. YEATS.

REFERENCES.—II. 16.—Spurgeon, *Sermons*, vol. ii. No. 90. II. 17.—R. M. Benson, *Redemption*, p. 86. *Expositor* (5th Series), vol. vii. p. 369 ; *ibid.* (6th Series), vol. v. p. 155 ; *ibid.* vol. x. p. 182. A. Maclaren, *Expositions of Holy Scripture—Hebrews*, p. 249.

' In all things it behoved Him to be made like unto His brethren. . . . For in that He Himself hath suffered being tempted, He is able to succour them that are tempted.'—HEB. II. 17, 18.

IN a letter, written during May, 1851, F. W. Robertson tells a correspondent that, ' except in feeling a fellowship and oneness with that Life, and recognising parallel feelings and parallel struggles, triumphantly sometimes, I do not see how life could be tolerable at all. He was Humanity, and in Him alone my humanity becomes intelligible. . . . Was not *He* alone in this world?—unfelt, uncomprehended, suspected, spoken against? and before Him was the cross. Before us, a little tea-table gossip, and hands uplifted in holy horror. Alas! and we call that a cross to bear. Shame! Yet still I do admit, that for a loving heart to lack sympathy is worse than pain.'

REFERENCES.—II. 18.—J. C. M. Bellew, *Sermons*, vol. i. p. 331. Spurgeon, *Sermons*, vol. ix. No. 487 ; vol. xxxiii. No. 1974, and vol. l. No. 2885. Marcus Dods, *Christ and Man*, p. 1. *Expositor* (4th Series), vol. ii. p. 373. II. 26.— A. Tucker, *Preacher's Magazine*, vol. xix. p. 230.

REVELATION IN A SON

HEB. III. I.

THE text of the Epistle to the Hebrews will be found in the first verse of the third chapter, 'Consider the Apostle and High Priest of our confession, *even* Jesus'. Like all Christian teaching, it finds its centre in the historic Personality and Life, which is the constant element because it is the Divine Fact.

I. It is of the utmost importance to make clear to ourselves the fact that the work of Christ is essentially a unity, that He is not at one time concerned with making known the name of God, at another with fulfilling His Will in the redemption of mankind. He manifests the love of God, as He could not fail to do, in fulfilling the Father's loving purpose of reconciliation through death. The Fact of Christ crucified, the work of Calvary, the Death of the cross is itself God's word, God's message. It is this position, established in the first two chapters, that justifies the author in proceeding to his theme. 'Wherefore, holy brethren, partakers of the heavenly calling, consider the Apostle and High Priest of our confession.'

II. When God speaks in the prophets, He does so indirectly, mediately, through the interposition of the human voice. When God speaks in a Son, He does so directly, immediately, through the facts themselves, which the human voice more or less imperfectly represents. It is the difference between nature and science, between reality and representation, between the actual world and the lesson-books which describe its processes. Prophecy interprets God's purposes : facts realise them.

III. It is important to remember that the union of the messenger and the priest was already portrayed in the pages of that Old Testament prophet the fulfilment of whose ideal in Jesus the Messiah was the characteristic discovery of the Apostolic Church. The second Isaiah is the great anticipator of the Epistle to the Hebrews. It is he who fixes for ever the sacrificial idea as the only adequate expression of the deliverance, the opening of the prison to them that are bound, which the Messenger and Servant should preach as a gospel to the poor. For this elect and beloved representative of Jehovah was to be, not like the prophets a preacher of righteousness, but a bringer of salvation, and as such a man of sorrows, led as the sacrificial lamb to the slaughter, bearing the iniquity of His people, and, because He had poured out His soul unto death, dividing the spoil with the strong. I think we shall best represent the difference between the work of the Servant and the work of that long line of 'servants in the house,' from Moses onwards, who had preceded Him, if we say that, while the prophets declared the righteousness of God, in the Suffering Servant that righteousness was to become redemptive.

IV. The priestly mediation of Jesus, of which His death is the embodiment, and His exaltation the Divine acceptance, is not only the subject of the Epistle to the Hebrews, but is itself the message of the Gospel. He is God's Apostle in His capacity as priest. This means an entirely different view of the proportions of the Christian Faith from that with which we have been made familiar by the teaching, for example, of the late Bishop Westcott, whose interpretation of this Epistle is, if my view be correct, prejudicially affected by the general point of sight which he adopts. There is, as I believe, in the New Testament no Gospel of the Incarnation as such, far less a Gospel of creation. The Scriptures give us no warrant for speculation as to whether the Word would have become flesh independently of the actual conditions under which God intervened in human life. Christ is not presented as the necessary consummator of a development which, apart from the fact of sin, would have been incomplete without Him. We simply do not know what such a development would have meant. But He is the reconciler, His death being the essential feature in this historical manifestation : 'I am the living one, and I became dead'. To acknowledge this is of the highest importance if we are to appreciate the self-surrender and voluntary love of God, the debt we owe Him, and the dependence in which we stand towards His Christ, who for our sakes became poor, took upon Him (the exact expression which follows should be noticed) 'the form of a slave,' and endured the cross. And it enables us to understand what the writer of Hebrews means by God speaking to us in a Son. He does not mean us to dwell upon the Incarnate Son as an object of contemplation, His personality, His teaching, His self-expression as a revelation of the Eternal Father, and then to go on to consider His redeeming work. He has not really omitted to develop in detail the work of the Son as the Apostle, referring us, as it were, to the Gospel according to St. John for a fuller treatment of the subject. No, God's speech is nothing else but the facts of the sufferings of Christ and the glory in which they issued. 'When He had made purification of sins, He sat down on the right hand of the majesty on high.'—J. G. SIMPSON, *Christus Crucifixus*, p. 51.

REFERENCES.—III. 1.—G. Trevor, *Types and the Antitype*, p. 206. A. Maclaren, *Expositions of Holy Scripture—Hebrews*, p. 258.

CONSIDER

, ABOVE all, Romanes,' said Darwin to G. T. Romanes, , cultivate the habit of meditation.'

'He that built all things in God . . . Whose house are we.'—
HEB. III. 4, 6.

'LIFE,' says George Macdonald, 'is no series of chances with a few providences sprinkled between to keep up a justly failing belief, but one providence of God.'

REFERENCE.—III. 5, 6.—*Expositor* (5th Series), vol. vii. p. 28.

'If we hold fast the confidence and the rejoicing of our hope firm unto the end.'—HEB. III. 6.

HAD we fast-hold on God by the interposition of a lively faith; had we hold-fast on God by Himselfe, and not by us; had we a divine foundation; then should not humane and worldly occasions have the power so to shake and litter us, as they have. Our hold would not then yeelde to so weake a batterie: The love of noveltie; the constrainte of Princes; the good success of one partie; the rash and casuall changing of our opinions, should not then have the power to shake and alter our beleefe. We should not suffer the same to be troubled at the wit and pleasure of a new argument, and at the perswasion, no, not of all the rhetorike that ever was: we should withstand these boistrous billowes with an inflexible and unmoveable constancie.—MONTAIGNE (*Florio*), II. 12.

REFERENCES.—III. 6.—*Expositor* (6th Series), vol. vii. p. 410. A. Maclaren, *Expositions of Holy Scripture—Hebrews*, p. 268. III. 7.—Spurgeon, *Sermons*, vol. xx. No. 1160. III. 7, 8.—John Watson, *Christian World Pulpit*, vol. lviii. p. 81. C. Perren, *Sermon Outlines*, p. 305. A. Maclaren, *Expositions of Holy Scripture—Hebrews*, p. 275. III. 8.—H. D. M. Spence, *Voices and Silences*, p. 247. H. Woodcock, *Sermon Outlines* (1st Series), p. 52.

'Take heed, brethren, lest there be in any of you an evil heart of unbelief.'—HEB. III. 12.

THE commonest sort of fortitude prevents us from becoming criminals in a legal sense; it is from weakness unknown, but perhaps suspected, as in some parts of the world you suspect a deadly snake in every bush,—from weakness that may lie hidden, watched or unwatched, prayed against or manfully scorned, repressed or maybe ignored more than half a lifetime, not one of us is safe.—JOSEPH CONRAD, *Lord Jim* (ch. v.).

THE parting of Life's road at Doubt and Faith! How many pilgrim feet throughout the ages, toiling devoutly thus far, have shrunk back before that unexpected and appalling sign! Disciples of the living Lord, saints, philosophers, scholars, priests, knights, statesmen—what a throng! What thoughts there born, prayers there ended, vows there broken, light there breaking, hearts there torn in twain! Mighty mountain rock! rising full in the road of journeying humanity!—JAS. LANE ALLEN.

'Take heed lest there be in any of you an evil heart of unbelief, in departing from the living God. But exhort one another daily . . . lest any of you be hardened through the deceitfulness of sin.'—HEB. III. 12, 13.

A PROPER sense of public duty will prompt endeavours to stop abuses the moment they become visible, without waiting for them to become serious. The misdoings which, in course of time, make useless or mischievous this or that administration, begin with trivial derelictions of duty, which no one thinks it worth while to protest against. Each increment of mischief, similarly small, is passed over as unimportant; until at length the evil is found to have grown great and perhaps incurable.—SPENCER, *Principles of Ethics* (§ 470).

REFERENCES.—III. 12.—Spurgeon, *Sermons*, xliv. No. 2552. *Expositor* (6th Series), vol. x. p. 128. III. 13.—H. Alford, *Sermons on Christian Doctrine*, p. 13. J. J. Blunt, *Plain Sermons* (3rd Series), p. 87. Spurgeon, *Sermons*, vol. xi. No. 620, and vol. xxxvi. No. 2130. A. Maclaren, *Expositions of Holy Scripture—Hebrews*, p. 285. III. 14.—*Ibid.* p. 295. Spurgeon, *Sermons*, vol. xviii. No. 1042. III. 15.—H. Windross, *Preacher's Magazine*, vol. x. p. 272. III. 16.—T. Arnold, *Sermons*, vol. iv. p. 157.

'They could not enter in because of unbelief.'—HEB. III. 19.

IN the first chapter of *The Saints' Everlasting Rest*, which is based on Heb. IV. 9, as its text, Baxter observes: 'When God would give the Israelites His Sabbaths of rest, in a land of rest, He had more ado to make them believe it than to overcome their enemies, and procure it for them'.

REFERENCE.—III. 19.—G. H. Morrison, *Scottish Review*, vol. i. p. 130.

A BIBLE READING
HEB. IV. etc.

I WANT to conduct, so to say, a Bible reading, and to fix upon one or two special and pregnant words which invite us to the larger light, to the fuller opportunity, to the diviner joy. The writer of the Epistle to the Hebrews is an eloquent man; I do not know his name, I do not care to inquire into it, but he is a man of marked power of expression: he uses words uniquely, and with a personal accent, and he surrounds us with a radiant, most exhilarating atmosphere. His favourite word in this chapter, and in one or two other places that I shall quote presently, is 'Let us'. Here is something for ourselves to do; let us pull ourselves together, and do it; now is your opportunity, seize it. These imperatives are not stern as all imperatives would appear of necessity to be; they are persuasive, gentle, full of hope; they give the very courage which they invite. How much depends upon how a thing is said! I have often taken occasion to say that the word 'woe' as pronounced by Jesus Christ might have a tear in it. We always associate the word 'woe' with some snowstorm, some bolt of fire, some cloudy look that has anger in it. But that might not be so necessarily; Jesus might be simply revealing the results of certain sowings and preparations, and He might say in a gentle whisper, 'Woe is in that act; I warn you of it, do not do it, refrain from repeating it; even you, scribes and Pharisees, hypocrites, actors, may be warned in time; this woe is so pronounced as to invite you to escape it'. I always try to read the New Testament with tears; it is a book whose music only yields itself to gentle entreaty. When Jesus seems the most severe He may be most gentle: take that as a hint, and write it upon your New Testaments, and in your studies, and in the market place and on the highway ; read the New Testament in the light of that suggestion.

'Now let us therefore fear,' because some people did not enter into rest and they might have done so (Heb. IV. 1). He was grieved forty years with them ; their carcases whitened the wilderness. They could not enter in because of unbelief ; let us therefore fear, let us learn something from history. All these carcases rotting in the wilderness are appeals ; on each of them is written the word Beware, take care, do not let history pour its waters upon barren rocks or barren sands. Let us fear lest a promise being left us we should permit it to escape our attention. You see the very ground written all over with promises ; they hang upon the fruit trees in the orchard, they drop from the little breasts of the birds as they sing their morning psalms. Let us look out for promises ; they are filling the air. Promises are where we least expect them ; turn over that leaf that seems to be hiding nothing, but simply seems to be lying on the ground, and under it you may find a blossom of a promise. Blessed are they who expect God ; blessed are they who have appointments with Christ ; O ! thrice blessed and heavenly their estate who can find Him even at the grave. Why, methinks He is more at the grave than He is at the feast. One of His great forerunners said : 'The house of mourning is better than the house of feasting'. I wonder what he meant ; he was not delivering an opinion, he was laying down and inculcating by example and experience a profound philosophy. You are better after you have cried than after you have laughed. The fool will tell you differently, the fool will tell you that your tears are vain, it is no use grieving needlessly, you cannot do anything, the event is past and gone, and therefore be up and doing and follow the band. O thou swollen fool ! 'Let us therefore fear,' lest a promise should escape us ; take care, those bushes in the heavenly gardens are full of birds, little birds, that one day will be great birds ; let us go a-birding, and see what we can catch in the hedges of the promises. Do you keep your Bible close to your heart ? do you keep your memory in your heart rather than in your intellect ? is yours a memory that clings to promises, prophecies, poetries ? is yours a spiritual power that can raise up out of the stones children unto Abraham ? is yours an anthem-music that can make the stone walls dance as if in merriment ?

I. 'Let us fear therefore.' Fear is wonder, expectation. Let us be covetous, economical—see, there is a crumb, gather it, put it into the great basket. Our hunger will need it some day. There is not a promise in all the Bible that we do not at some time or another want. We need all the promises of God, and they are described as exceeding great and precious. Have you ever written upon a long card all the promises ? Why, there is a promise for every mental mood, there is a promise that exactly fits the ever-changing experience of the day. God's jewellery fits every finger, and looks well, for it is the jewellery of love.

II. Now, thus saith the Apostle, 'Let us labour therefore ' (Heb. IV. 11). He is as fond of the word 'therefore' as he is fond of the word 'let us'. In the first verse, 'Let us therefore,' in the eleventh verse, 'Let us labour therefore'. What would he have us labour for ? Why, he says in a very remarkable form of expression, 'Let us labour therefore to enter into that rest'. Rest can only be entered into by labour. No man enjoys himself who does not labour. Any man who resigns all labour gives himself up into the hands of the devil. Why, it is your work that keeps you alive. Work is wine, medicine, food, stimulus, joy. 'Well, but,' say you, 'I could do with a little less work.' That is perfectly possible ; some people are overworked, some hearts are overborne. When we speak thus we speak a human language and with human limitations. Even here is a great promise. Now the Apostle says, 'Fall not and be not too much discouraged and overborne, for there hath no temptation or trial happened unto you but God will make a way of escape.' He will enable you to bear your burden ; then it will not be too much ; if the burden cannot be lessened, the grace can be increased, and the increase of grace is a lightening of the load.

III. Let us hear how this wonderful logician goes on. 'Let us hold fast our profession.' 'Seeing then that we have a great high priest, that is passed into the heavens, Jesus the Son of God, let us hold fast our profession'—let us get hold of Him with both arms, both hands, all fingers, and hang on to Him if we can do nothing better. The writer said in the first verse, 'Let us therefore fear ' ; in the sixteenth verse he says, 'Let us therefore come boldly unto the throne of grace'. 'Let us therefore fear,' 'Let us therefore labour,' 'Let us therefore come boldly unto the throne of grace'. Christianity is logic, Christianity is not sentiment ; Christianity has a great chain of reasoning, persuasion, conviction behind it and along with it. The Apostle Paul was fond of the word 'Therefore'. He could not have written any of these Epistles if he had not employed that logical term, and Apollos, if Apollos wrote the Epistle to the Hebrews, has the same formula ; he was credited with being an eloquent man, but he was a logician as well. Some people cannot imagine that any man can be more than one thing. You never can get into their heads ideas in couples, they are stupid themselves, and therefore they think everybody else must be stupid : all lunatics think all men mad ; it is a sign of insanity. The Apostle who wrote this Epistle is described as an eloquent man and mighty in the Scriptures. He mightily persuaded men that he had got hold of the living Christ. So I will ask you to go through this fourth chapter of the Epistle to the Hebrews, and say whether you are not in the hands of a man who uses the word 'Therefore,'—for this reason, on this account, obey. He is a soldier and a general who gives the reasons for his orders.

IV. And then in the twenty-eighth verse of the twelfth chapter the Apostle says, 'Let us have grace, whereby we may serve God acceptably with reverence and Godly fear'. 'Let us'—always 'let us' ; because the Apostle says in effect, 'This is possible, you can do it, but you can only do it by doing it'. Ah, it is hard to teach that lesson! You can only swim by swimming; you will never learn to swim standing shivering on the river-brink, you must fling yourself into a river or sea as into a mother's arms, and the sea is a great nurse, and a most gentle monster. 'Let us have grace, whereby we may serve God acceptably with reverence and Godly fear'—in a better way with more refinement, with more meaning, with more reality. O let us, brethren, let us—let us enter into this covenant, let us say, This year shall be the very best year in our lives, God helping us. But then we shall have to pay (ch. XIII. 13). This is the final stroke. 'Let us go forth therefore.' I thought he was an eloquent man, but he is a logician, he has got me in his grip, he is a master; I thought we should have tropes and flowers and music and pictures and dancing sunshine making pictures for us on the wall or on the meadow, and with this man it is always, 'Therefore, therefore, therefore; because you did this thing, therefore do that'. I went to him because they told me he was an eloquent man, and a mighty orator, and with a great gift of musical expression. I find that he is a disciplinarian, a logician, a reasoner. I like my preacher to be rich in anecdotes that never happened. I like illustrations that I can throw off. Why does the preacher not give us such illustrations? This Apollos, if he were Apollos, is eternally saying, 'Therefore, therefore, therefore'; I cannot get rid of these 'therefores'. One of two things must be done; I must get rid of this man, or I must wisely accept logic set to music, music strengthening into logic.

Christianity is a great argument. Do not make any mistake about this matter. It means all you can give it; it will never rest until it has taken from you all your strength and all your devotion, and having given God all, then, says this same man, do not give up your confidence, which hath great recompense of reward: for God is not unfaithful to forget your work and labour of love; He knows every strain you have made, every effort, and He says to you in the time of your apparent exhaustion and sinking depletion, 'Gather up the fragments'. What fragments? These. Why, I never saw them until now. Gather them up against the next day of hunger, and you will find that you have more at the end than you had at the beginning. A paradox, but a most glorious fact! —JOSEPH PARKER.

REFERENCES.—IV. 1, 2.—Spurgeon, Sermons, vol. xx. No. 1177. IV. 2.—Ibid. vol. xxxv. No. 2089. IV. 3.—T. Arnold, Christian Life: Its Hopes, p. 223. Spurgeon, Sermons, vol. xv. No. 866, and vol. xxxv. No. 2090. A. Maclaren, Expositions of Holy Scripture—Hebrews, p. 303. IV. 3, 7.—Expositor (5th Series), vol. v. p. 386. IV. 3-9.—G. Body, Christian World Pulpit, vol. liv. p. 87. IV. 7.—John Watson, Christian World Pulpit, vol. li. p. 241. C. Perren, Revival Sermons in Outline, p. 280. C. G. Finney, Penny Pulpit, No. 1636, p. 133.

'There remaineth a rest to the people of God.'—HEB. IV. 9.

NOTWITHSTANDING fair prospects and outward distinction, he clung more and more passionately to his quiet country home; the 'far off look,' the longing for rest and reality, and for the unfolding of the mystery of life, grew stronger upon him, and, though always bright and cheerful with his children, he said more frequently to his wife, 'How blessed it will be when it is all over, to lie down in that dear churchyard together!'—CHARLES KINGSLEY's Life (ch. XVIII.).

REFERENCES.—IV. 9.—R. C. Trench, Sermons New and Old, p. 279. Spurgeon, Sermons, vol. iii. No. 133. Hugh Price Hughes, Christian World Pulpit, vol. lvii. p. 184. A. Coote, Twelve Sermons, p. 116. T. Arnold, Sermons, vol. i. p. 112. Expositor (4th Series), vol. iii. p. 134; ibid. (5th Series), vol. vi. pp. 229, 325. IV. 9, 10.—A. Maclaren, Expositions of Holy Scripture—Hebrews, p. 312.

THE SABBATH OF THE SON

'He that is entered into His rest, He also hath ceased from His own works, as God did from His.'—HEB. IV. 10.

THERE are three great Sabbaths. There is the Sabbath of the Father, when His work of creation is completed, and He rests on the seventh day from all His works. There is the Sabbath of the Son, when His state of humiliation is ended, when His work of travail and redemption is complete, when He dieth no more, when He also hath ceased from His own works, as God did from His. There is, lastly, the Sabbath of the Holy Ghost, when the Son has delivered up the kingdom to God, even the Father, when He has put down all rule and all authority and power, when death is destroyed, when the Son Himself is made subject unto Him that did subject all things unto Him, that in the unity of the Eternal and Adorable Trinity God may be all in all.

Our subject is the Sabbath of the Son.

I. Through these chapters in Hebrews we hear continually the sweet chimes of rest. Those to whom the words were spoken lived, as we are living in the twentieth century, in an age of care and change. It was a time of upheaval, a time of distress, a time when men's hearts failed them for fear of what was coming. So the inspired writer speaks continually of rest, rest passing from one stillness to another yet more calm, of a peace becoming steadily more golden and more glowing till the last rest is reached. The First Rest is the rest that comes to those who hear Christ saying, 'Hither to Me,' who in faith obey Him as He calls them. 'Come unto Me all ye that labour and are heavy laden, and I will give you rest.' This is the rest of faith. In this Rest are received, no matter how broken it may be, the remission of sins and the gift of eternal life.

II. There is the Rest of those who hear Him out to the end of His promise, and obey Him when He says, 'Take My yoke upon you and learn of Me, for I am meek and lowly in heart: and ye shall find rest unto your souls. For My yoke is easy and My burden is light.' These are they who enter into the Second Rest, the rest after rest, 'the rest of the man who is already at rest, the repose of a man who has received a given rest, and now discovers the found rest'. Spurgeon says: 'The Lord Jesus gives to His people a priceless casket called the gift of rest; it is set with brilliants and inlaid with gems, and the substance thereof is of wrought gold ; whosoever possesses it feels and knows that his warfare is accomplished, and his sin is pardoned. After a while the happy owner begins to examine his treasure. It is all his own, but he has not yet seen it all, for one day he detects a secret drawer, he touches a hidden spring, and, lo! before him lies a priceless Kohinoor, surpassing all the rest. It had been given him, it is certain, but he had not seen it at first, and therefore he finds it. Jesus Christ gives us in the gift of Himself all the rest we can ever enjoy, even heaven's rest lies in Him. But after we have received Him we have to learn His value, and to find out by the teaching of the Spirit the fulness of the rest which He bestows.' The Second Rest is a rest in service. It is the rest of those who take Christ's yoke and burden upon them.

III. But beyond that rest is the rest, or rather the Sabbath Rest of the Son. I have taken the text, with Alford and Maclaren, as referring to Him. In a sense His redeeming work is over. Never again can men smite Him. Never again can death touch Him. He has entered into His rest, into His Sabbath, and has ceased from His own works, as God did from His. But of Christ it is true that He is united to His people, and that they share His destinies. Professor Bruce has remarked that the key-word of this Epistle to the Hebrews is 'forerunner'. He shares in our experiences, and He draws us on by His grace to share in His. As He has entered His Sabbath, so perhaps even on earth may we.

If we have borne the cross in patience, may there not come to us one day a new lightsomeness, when we are aware of no yoke and of no burden? May we not awake in that day and think out the hours before us in a quite different fashion? May we not long to penetrate farther into the mystery of the Divine revelation, to go to our books with eagerness and with rapture, counting all other interests secondary or dead? May we not be so full of the Spirit of God and so conscious of His power that we shall long to go to those people who have tried us and to bring them the sympathy, the patience, the warning, the encouragements that they need? May not our hearts come to be so wrapped up in the progress of the kingdom that we shall hear eagerly of its news, hardly thinking about the way in which it is communicated? May we not come to be above law, above plans, and above rulers, and bring forth fruit naturally and unconsciously and in due season? In other words, may we not cease from our own works, as God did from His, and as Christ did from His when He fell asleep on the cross?

I think that there is much in the recorded experience of believers which encourages this hope. Was it not true of John Wesley that for many years he abode in this Sabbath of the Son? As I read his Journals, and especially the later volumes, I seem to see that he was not any longer a worker, but simply a fruit-bearer. From all his many journeys he carried and wore the white rose of rest. Nothing irked him, nothing disturbed him. He was at peace. Even here he had entered the Sabbath Rest that remaineth for the people of God. And I may venture to say that Dr. Andrew Bonar, both in his life and in his printed words, left on my mind the same impression. He was dead to the solicitations and even to the weariness of the flesh. He had ceased from his own works, and men gazed on him and marvelled at the fruit-bearing Tree of God.

I am encouraged still further to believe in it by the remainder of this chapter, for the note is taken up unmistakably in its closing verses. 'He is a priest *for ever.*' How precious is that 'for ever!' 'He that is entered into His rest, He also hath ceased from His own works, as God did from His. . . . Seeing, then, that we have a great high priest, that is passed into the heavens, Jesus, the Son of God, let us hold fast our profession. For we have not an high priest which cannot be touched with the feeling of our infirmities ; but was in all points tempted like as we are, yet without sin. Let us therefore come boldly unto the Throne of Grace, that we may obtain mercy, and find grace to help in time of need.' Let us come boldly unto the Throne of Grace, for He hath ceased from His own works. He has, as it were, nothing else to do but to hear us and to bless us. In the day of His flesh, when He was in the fiercest trial of His own works, there was one who sought Him while He might be found, and called upon Him while He was near. This was the thief on the cross, and the thief, coming boldly unto the Throne of Grace, was heard. But now how much more may we come boldly, for though the cross was His Throne, He hangs on the cross no longer. He is on the Throne. He Who knows our infirmities, Who was in all points tempted like as we are, to Whose eyes all things are naked and open, is calling to us. He is on the Throne, unwearied, unwounded, all-knowing, all-pitying—that He may give us rest.

IV. There is next the Rest of Heaven. However few and feeble and short our steps have been in the Kingdom of Grace, we pass from it to the Kingdom of Glory. By faith and by death we attain the perfect rest. We become very full of rest. We are at rest in the Lord. We are among the people who have clean passed over Jordan, and our enemies have no more that they can do, and Satan is bruised under our feet. Of that rest we can only speak as the Scripture teaches us, but we know that it is not a rest of inactivity.

V. Then there is the Sabbath of the Holy Ghost beyond the Sabbath of the Son, when the number of the elect is accomplished, when the kingdom is fully come, when the deep and wide Sabbath of eternity breaks, never to change or end.

Let us labour therefore to enter into that rest. The desire for the final rest of God is no ignoble craving for immunity and repose. It is a search after God's deepest bosom.

And I would be where no storms come,
Where the green swell is in the havens dumb,
And out of the swing of the sea.

—W. ROBERTSON NICOLL, *Sunday Evening*, p 1.

REFERENCES.—IV. 11.—J. Bannerman, *Sermons*, p. 343.
A. Maclaren, *Expositions of Holy Scripture—Hebrews*, p. 323.

THE DUTY OF STUDYING THE BIBLE

'For the word of God is quick, and powerful, and sharper than
any two-edged sword, piercing even to the dividing asunder
of soul and spirit, and of the joints and marrow, and is a
discerner of the thoughts and intents of the heart.'—HEB.
IV. 12.

BELIEVE me, nothing can be a substitute for the study
of the Bible. Our own meditation will show us something of Divine truth, the written and spoken words
of others will show us more, but the immediate revelation of the Divine character and methods and
purposes is given us in the Bible alone. I believe we
do not realise sufficiently that we must always be
very patient, and at times simply passive, in our
devotional use of the Bible. Take the short sayings
of Christ, such as that you have heard interpreted
this term, ' Where the body is thither shall the eagles
be gathered together'; or the mysterious vision of
the prophet, such as that of Ezekiel in the valley of
dry bones; or the historical narrative, such as the
perplexing story of the old prophet who misled his
brother prophet—whatever it may be, take it and
saturate your mind with it, leaving aside all commen-
taries and human explanations, and then wait till
the light comes to you, and the message which God
means to send you through His teachers or through
His Son. Patience is the first requisite, and humility
is the second. You must be content to learn, and in
learning to forget yourself. The Bible has so much
that is strange at first sight and unlike our own circumstances, that we are tempted to turn from it and
choose what specially suits ourselves, or that in which
our own preconceived ideas seem to be reflected and
corroborated. Rather beware of your favourite books,
and passages, and texts in the Bible; the others which
you do not care for have probably a more vital and a
more humbling message for your soul, just because it
is distasteful to you. Therefore regularity is a third
requisite, lest you should leave out any part that
does not specially appeal to you, and so keep back
some of the counsel of God to your own soul. And
above all, read with prayer: prayer before for the
guidance of the Holy Spirit of truth, prayer after for
strength to do what God has shown us by His Word.
There is nothing that so helps to fix and impress a
truth upon the mind as the resolute translation of it
into practice; and every period of such devotional
study as I have tried to describe should, if it is to
leave a permanent mark behind it, end with prayer
that you may carry out the sacred teaching in your
daily life. Patience, humility, regularity, prayer:
thus aided and prepared you will, though it may at
first seem dark and hard, come to feel all that the
saints, all that the Psalmists found in God's Word.
It will be to you 'a lantern unto your feet, and a
light unto your eyes': it will show you your 'secret

faults': by the love of it you will be led into 'great
peace'.—A. T. LYTTELTON, *College and University
Sermons*, p. 290.

THE RULE OF OUR THOUGHTS

'Quick to discern the thoughts and intents of the heart.'—
HEB. IV. 12.

IF you desire to be kept from yielding to temptation,
you must be very careful of your thoughts.

I. Keep thy heart clean. You keep your wealth,
you keep your home, you keep your health, you keep
your character, but above all these things keep your
heart. Why? Because out of it are the issues of life.
When Bunyan depicted the character of Ignorance, he
made him say: 'I think my heart is as good as anybody's heart, and as for my thoughts, I take no notice of
them'. He shows at once that he does not know
himself, and that he is exposed to every temptation
that crosses his path. 'As a man thinketh in his
heart, so is he' (Prov. XXIII. 7). The thoughts lay
down the tram-lines upon which presently the tram-
car makes its way. Just as the tram-car will pass up
and down the rails in a great city, so does the act
follow along the track of the thought. Butler in his
Analogy says there are three steps in the formation
of character—act, habit, character. Thackeray ampli-
fied this saying thus: 'Sow a thought, reap an
act; sow an act, reap a habit; sow a habit, reap
character; sow character, reap destiny'.

II. In dealing with our thoughts, two things are
necessary: (1) We need to be able to sift out bad
thoughts from good thoughts; to know the traitor,
however well he is dressed, and keep him out. We
need discernment. Why? Because 'the god of this
world hath blinded the minds,' that is, the thoughts,
'of them that believe not,' that is, the unregenerate
(2 Cor. IV. 4). Man is blind. Next, we find the
understanding darkened, being alienated from the
life of God through ignorance (Eph. IV. 18). 'He
that is spiritual judgeth all things, yet he himself is
judged of no man,' or, as the Revised Version has it,
'he who is spiritual *discerneth* all things' (1 Cor.
II. 15). (2) We need keeping power. Just as Jesus
commended His spirit to His Father, so do you, when
you leave your room in the morning, commit the
keeping of the gateway of your soul to Him.—F. B.
MEYER, *The Soul's Ascent*, p. 139.

'For the word of God is quick, and powerful, and sharper than
any two-edged sword, piercing even to the dividing
asunder of soul and spirit.'—HEB. IV. 12.

How 'quick and piercing' is the word in itself! Yet
many times it never enters, being managed by a feeble
arm. What weight and worth is there in every
passage of the blessed Gospel! Enough, we would
think, to enter and force the dullest soul, and wholly
possess its thoughts and affections; and yet how often
does it fall as water upon a stone! The things of
God which we handle are Divine; but our manner of
handling is human. There is little we touch, but we
leave the print of our fingers behind.—BAXTER, *The
Saints' Everlasting Rest* (ch. III.).

References.—IV. 12.—Spurgeon, *Sermons*, vol. xxxiv. No. 2010. J. Stalker, *Christian World Pulpit*, vol. xliv. p. 203. E. M. Geldart, *Echoes of Truth*, p. 79. IV. 12, 13. —G. A. Bennetts, *Preacher's Magazine*, vol. xviii. p. 263. J. B. Lightfoot, *Cambridge Sermons*, p. 150. *Expositor* (4th Series), vol. vi. p. 68.

HIM WITH WHOM WE HAVE TO DO

' Him with whom we have to do.'—Heb. iv. 13.

I. We have to do with God in the operations of nature. It is true, indeed, that the advance of science has revealed order, regularity, and law in the physical universe; but that is only what we might have anticipated, if, as the Bible declares and we believe, the world was called into being at the first, and is still sustained by the power and wisdom of the Most High, for God is not the author of confusion. We are not surprised, therefore, to find that He proceeds upon fixed principles; but we must beware of allowing that which we call a law to hide from us the ever active agency of Him whose orderly method of operation that law is.

II. We have to do with God in the overtures of the Gospel. If we want to avail ourselves of the force which God has put into and maintains in electricity, we must comply with the conditions on which it is generated and becomes operative. The man of science investigates by patient research the methods of its operation, and then sets himself in conformity with these to avail himself of its help. Now, in the same way, if the Gospel is God's power for a certain purpose, and we wish to take advantage of it for that purpose, we must comply with its conditions and laws. These are faith in Jesus Christ, as the only Mediator, Redeemer, Sacrifice, and Lord, and repentance unto life. If you have to do with God in the overtures of the Gospel, then the bearing of its proclamations assumes a very serious character indeed. For in such a case you have to answer not the herald, but God.

III. We have to do with God in the dispensations of Providence. By Providence I understand God's overruling care over all events in nature and all the actions and circumstances of men. Now if we assent to the doctrine that God's Providence is in and over all events, it will give a new importance in our view to every occurrence. Ah! if we only had more faith in the truth that it is with God we have to do in the losses and crosses of our lives, there would be less of worry and despondency in our hearts.

IV. We have to do with God in the duties of daily life. Our responsibilities in society and business are not to each other merely, or to the laws of the State alone, but to God. We are under obligation to our fellows, indeed; but we are so because God has laid these obligations on us.

V. We shall have to do with God in the awards of final judgment. The judgment is absolutely certain; for ' it is appointed unto men once to die, and after death the judgment'. It is to be universal; for before the judge shall be 'gathered all nations'. The judge is to be the Omniscient One who is acquainted with the secret things of each man's heart and life, and the righteous one who shall render to every man according to his works. And His awards are to be eternal; for the wicked 'shall go away into everlasting punishment, but the righteous into life everlasting'.

' All things are naked and open to the eyes of Him with whom we have to do.'—Heb. iv. 13.

' Lastly,' says Butler in his sermon before the House of Lords, ' the consideration that we are the servants of God reminds us, that we are accountable to Him for our behaviour in those respects in which it is out of the reach of all human authority; and is the strongest enforcement of sincerity, as *all things are naked and opened unto the eyes of Him with whom we have to do*. Artificial behaviour might perhaps avail much towards quieting our consciences, and making our part good in the short competitions of this world; but what will it avail us considered as under the government of God?'

References.—IV. 13.—J. M. Whiton, *Summer Sermons*, p. 143. R. W. Church, *Village Sermons*, p. 242. G. Bellett, *Parochial Sermons*, p. 297. *Expositor* (6th Series), vol. viii. p. 437.

' We have a great high priest, that is passed into the heavens, Jesus the Son of God.'—Heb. iv. 14.

At first, one's conceptions of Him are abstract to a large extent; they ought to become more and more concrete. To find ourselves any nearer the belief that we *have* an High Priest, once a man, now passed into the heavens, and whom the heavens will contain till the restitution of all things, ought to be a glad thought. We feel His workings, His efficacies. —James Smetham, *Letters* (pp. 85, 86).

' A great High Priest.'—Heb. iv. 14.

The word ἀρχιερεύς, ' high priest,' to which the Epistle to the Hebrews gave currency as a worshipful term applied to Christ, shows how a cult-word that was certainly developed within Primitive Christianity from Jewish premises entered spontaneously into the usual parallelism as soon as it found itself in the world. It was by this word, as numerous inscriptions have shown, that the title *pontifex maximus*, borne by the emperors, was translated in the East.—Adolf Deissmann, *Light from the Ancient East*, pp. 369, 370.

Reference.—IV. 14.—J. Bunting, *Sermons*, vol. i. p. 187.

ASCENSION DAY

' Seeing then that we have a great High Priest, that is passed into the heavens, Jesus the Son of God, let us hold fast our profession. For we have not an High Priest which cannot be touched with the feeling of our infirmities; but was in all points tempted like as we are, yet without sin. Let us therefore come boldly unto the throne of grace, that we may obtain mercy, and find grace to help in time of need.'—Heb. iv. 14-16.

In His Ascension our Lord entered heaven, not only as a King of Glory, but He entered the highest heaven on our behalf as our great High Priest. Almost the whole of the book of the Epistle to the Hebrews deals with this matter—the entrance of our

Blessed Saviour into the highest heaven. And writing to the Hebrew people, as we should expect, the Apostle goes on to show in a good deal of detail how all the old sacrifices found their fulfilment in and their perfection in His Sacrifice upon the cross. And in the Epistle you will note that we find there a sketch of the perfect priest, and how our Lord represents to us the Perfect Priest. The priesthood of our Lord Jesus Christ began with the beginning of His earthly life. The Holy Child in the manger at Bethlehem was our great High Priest, and the manger of Bethlehem was like the altar of His sacrifice, and all the way through His life there went up on our behalf the priestly offering of a perfect sacrifice. The sacrifice appears in its greatest and highest and most perfect form upon the cross, where once for all He gave His life and shed His precious Blood for us, and as at this time He entered heaven to present on our behalf that great sacrifice of His life, and of His death upon the cross. Again and again, in the Epistle to the Hebrews and in the Epistle to the Romans, we read of the priestly work of intercession.

The word 'intercession' means to go between ; our Lord's intercession is a going between man and God, between man who has sinned and God against Whom man has sinned. And He stands there between the living and the dead, between God and His sinful creatures, that He may bring us back to God, and may obtain from the Father our pardon and our healing.

I. So at this time we think of our Lord entering into heaven to continue for ever a work on our behalf, His work of endless intercession. That intercession is of two kinds : There is the intercession of His simple presence, the fact that in heaven He bears our own nature, the nature of those who have sinned against the Eternal Father, that in His own hands, and feet, and side He bears the mark of that which He has endured for our salvation. The simple presence of His wounded human nature is a perpetual intercession on our behalf. Beyond that there is the actual pleading for us. He speaks for you and for me, One Who knows what we need, Who knows our own helplessness, and has made Himself our champion. That help is going on ceaselessly.

II. What are the fruits of His priesthood? What does He obtain for us ? Well, first of all, He obtains on our behalf mercy for our sins. It is an endless intercession, claiming on our behalf the Divine mercy of our Father, and His forgiveness. So in the hymn we plead :—

> Look, Father, look on His anointed face,
> And only look on us as found in Him.

Then His intercession takes up into itself the imperfection of our own prayers and of our own works. The best that we can do is poor and worthless ; but, caught up into the intercession of our great High Priest, the feeblest prayers have their value, and they prevail with our Father. The best that we can do in the way of life and good works, how poor a thing it is, how imperfect ! And yet, caught into the stream of His intercession, it gains worth, and merit from His merit, and becomes acceptable to our Father.

Yet again, His intercession upon the Throne of heaven pleads endlessly for us just the graces that we need for our daily life—grace which will help us to outgrow our weakness and our faults, and grow in likeness to the perfect life of Jesus. Then there descends upon that intercession the rain of His grace, which shall help us to escape above ourselves, and to come nearer Jesus.

III. What is the consequence and fruit of all this ? We have in the text, ' Let us therefore come boldly unto the throne of grace '. If the intercession of our Lord is to avail for us, if its fruit is to abound in us, then we must come to Him. There it all is—the immeasurable good of what Jesus has done and is doing on our behalf ; but it awaits our claiming. 'Come,' the Apostle says, 'and claim your share in the intercession of Jesus, in the merit of His life and His death. Come boldly to the throne of grace.' Do not let your past failures discourage you from coming near. It may have seemed that heaven has been deaf to your prayers that you have sent up. Do not think this, but come without discouragement, boldly, to the throne of grace. ' For,' he says, ' we have not an High Priest which cannot be touched with the feeling of our infirmities.' You come to an Infinite Compassion, to One Who knows, and Himself has felt, and is therefore able to deal with you. Come with boldness, cast yourself simply on His mercy and place yourself in His keeping, and that which you need shall be done.

THE GREAT HIGH PRIEST

'Seeing then that we have a great High Priest, that is passed into the heavens, Jesus the Son of God, let us hold fast our profession. For we have not an High Priest which cannot be touched with the feeling of our infirmities ; but was in all points tempted like as we are, yet without sin. Let us therefore come boldly unto the throne of grace, that we may obtain mercy, and find grace to help in time of need.'—Heb. iv. 14-16.

There is no portion of Holy Scripture which deals so especially with the consequences of the Ascension of our Lord Jesus Christ as does this Epistle to the Hebrews. I want you, therefore, to notice the three practical exhortations which the Apostle founds upon this Ascension of our Lord Jesus Christ.

I. In the eleventh verse he says: 'Let us labour therefore to enter into that rest'. Our Lord Jesus Christ is likened to Joshua. He has conquered our foes, He has overcome death, He hath opened the kingdom of heaven to all believers, and now He has sat down on the right hand of the Majesty on high. But these victories are not for Himself alone. Let us therefore labour to enter into that rest. It is sometimes a charge brought against the simple gospel of Jesus Christ, that it produces carelessness and indolence ; that the victory of our Lord and the introduction of our surety into the heavenly home is only an invitation to us to sit still upon our knees. My brethren, the argument is all the other way. Without a

Saviour who hath overcome death, and opened for us the gates of heaven, we might well sit down in despair.

II. The second practical exhortation he gives is in the fourteenth verse : ' Let us hold fast our profession '. He is speaking here to the Christian, he feels that sometimes the Christian may be inclined to give up his profession, but he urges him to hold on fast, to cling to it, to let nothing whatever check his hold upon that profession of his faith.

III. And then the third practical exhortation is this : ' Let us therefore come boldly unto the throne of grace, that we may obtain mercy, and find grace to help in time of need.' Here he is thinking not so much about the glory of the High Priest, as about the sympathy of the High Priest. Remember it is a throne ; therefore come with reverence and with Godly fear, for you are a sinner, a man of unclean lips. But it is a throne of grace ; so that, though your prayers may be unworthy, the faults in your prayers be overlooked ; though you yourself may be unworthy, your unworthiness will not stop His ear.—E. A. STUART, *The Great High Priest and other Sermons*, vol. XII. p. 33.

REFERENCE.—IV. 14-16.—C. M. Betts, *Eight Sermons*, p. 75.

' We have not an High Priest that cannot be touched with the feeling of our infirmities.'—HEB. IV. 15.

' EVERY believer,' says James Smetham, ' realises by experience that Christ is the only perfect sympathiser. "I'm not perfectly understood," says everybody in fact. But if you are a believer you are perfectly understood. Christ is the only one who never expects you to be other than *yourself*, and He puts in abeyance towards you all but what is like you. He takes your view of things, and mentions no other. He takes the old woman's view of things by the washtub, and has a great interest in wash-powder ; Sir Isaac Newton's view of things, and wings among the stars with him ; the artist's view, and feeds among the lilies ; the lawyer's, and shares the justice of things. But He never plays the lawyer or the philosopher or the artist to the old woman. He is above that littleness.'

REFERENCES.—IV. 15.—Spurgeon, *Sermons*, vol. xxxvi. No. 2148. W. J. Brock, *Sermons*, p. 97. H. Alford, *Sermons on Christian Doctrine*, p. 179. J. J. Blunt, *Plain Sermons* (3rd Series), p. 62. Marcus Dods, *Christ and Man*, p. 1. *Expositor* (4th Series), vol. iii. p. 30 ; *ibid.* (5th Series), vol. ii. p. 166. IV. 15, 16.—J. S. Maver, *Christian World Pulpit*, vol. liii. p. 412. F. J. A. Hort, *Village Sermons in Outline*, p. 53.

THE THRONE OF GRACE
' Let us therefore come boldly unto the throne of grace.'—HEB. IV. 16.

THERE is a science of prayer. In the words ' the Throne of Grace' may be found the beginning and the end of the same. To-day we deal with the beginning, and the point to be emphasised is that the soul approaches in its need not a throne of mere justice, nor a throne of criticism, but a Throne of Grace. It is not needful at the start to lay down the full method

and the perfect way of prayer. Our Lord Himself with loving boldness said at the beginning : ' Ask, and it shall be given you ; seek, and ye shall find ; knock, and it shall be opened unto you ; for every one that asketh receiveth, and he that seeketh findeth, and to him that knocketh it shall be opened '. It is after this manner that the Christian teacher should begin.

I. Prayer in the fullest sense, the prayer that is wrought in us by the Spirit and presented by the Christ of God—prayer that wins the King's ear—is the last triumph of the life of grace. Prayer in the noblest sense implies a concentration of all man's united energies. Coleridge shortly before his death said these words to a friend who has recorded them : ' I do not account a solemn faith in God as a real object to be the most arduous act of the reason and the will. Oh, no, my dear sir, it is to pray with all my heart and strength, with the reason and with the will, to believe that God will listen to your voice through Christ, and verily do the thing He pleaseth thereupon. This is the last, the greatest achievement of the Christian's warfare on earth. "Teach us to pray, O Lord." Here he burst into a flood of tears, and begged me to pray for him.' The highest energy the human heart is capable of is to pray, like St. Paul, with the spirit and the understanding. But few may reach this victory, and it is deeply consoling to remember that it is a Throne of Grace before which we kneel, and that though our prayers may be marred and faultful, yet our Mediator interprets them in the ears of our loving Father, while the Spirit helps our infirmities and gives life and power to the failing, dying heart.

II. While we recognise that there is such a thing as formal prayer, and even such a thing as the blasphemous mimicry and caricature of prayer, we remember also that the throne is a Throne of Grace, and that the weakest and most sinful human cry will reach it. May I pray when I doubt ? Monrad says : ' I once had an acquaintance—an intimately trusted friend I could scarcely call him—and as often as we met our conversation turned as a matter of course upon questions of deepest interest—questions that stirred our inmost feelings. "Do you think," he once said to me, "that it is right for us to pray to the Lord God without really believing in Him ?" I replied that if we do not believe in Him we shall scarcely be inclined to pray. "You are right," he answered, "for this reason it is something rare, yet so it is with me. I have a desire to fold my hands and say, 'If Thou existest, O God, hear me. If Thou hast a heart for the cares and anxieties of a poor mortal, incline Thine ear and hear what I would say to Thee.' But I know not whether I ought to pray thus, whether it is not sinful." On this I observed all depends on the motive. Some one might perhaps desire to speak thus in order in a sense proudly to challenge the Almighty, and, if he remains unpunished, to proclaim the impotence of God under the foolish notion that man is able to force the Almighty to a display of His power. But if no evil motive of this kind lay at the bottom of his wish, he need feel no scruple about carrying it into effect. "On thy responsibility be it," he exclaimed, and broke off the conversation.' It is right to pray even in deep doubt, it is right to express our dumb yearnings in a world we cannot read, for a God we cannot find. Many a soul is dimly searching and feeling after God that it may fill up the awful consciousness of blank and isolation. Let that soul turn to the Throne of Grace even though it cannot behold its brightness.—W. ROBERTSON NICOLL, *Sunday Evening*, p. 339.

'Let us therefore draw near with boldness to the throne of grace.'—HEB. IV. 16.

THE secret of goodness and greatness is in choosing *whom* you will approach and live with, through the crowding obvious people who seem to live with you. —BROWNING.

WHAT makes religion vital is not the stern proud *thinkings about it*; it is the 'drawing near unto God'; it is the 'coming boldly to the throne of grace'.—SMETHAM.

REFERENCES.—IV. 16.—W. L. Alexander, *Sermons*, p. 287. W. J. Brock, *Sermons*, p. 109. Spurgeon, *Sermons*, vol. xvii. No. 1024. *Expositor* (4th Series), vol. ii. pp. 132, 143 ; *ibid.* (5th Series), vol. v. p. 179. A. Maclaren, *Expositions of Holy Scripture—Hebrews*, p. 333. V. 1.—*Expositor* (6th Series), vol. viii. p. 328. V. 2.—Spurgeon, *Sermons*, vol. xxiv. No. 1407 ; vol. xxxviii. No. 2251 ; vol. xliii. No. 2529. V. 3.—A. Brown, *Christian World Pulpit*, vol. xliv. p. 372. V. 4.—G. Trevor, *Types and the Antitype*, p. 168. V. 5.—*Expositor* (6th Series), vol. x. p. 376. V. 7.—R. M. Benson, *Redemption*, p. 61. *Expositor* (5th Series), vol. ii. p. 256 ; *ibid.* vol. iii. p. 224 ; *ibid.* (6th Series), vol. v. p. 414. A. Maclaren, *Expositions of Holy Scripture—Hebrews*, p. 342. V. 7-10.—Spurgeon, *Sermons*, vol. xxxii. No. 1927. Marcus Dods, *Christ and Man*, p. 48. V. 7-11.—G. Body, *Christian World Pulpit*, vol. lvii. p. 214.

'Though He were a Son, yet learned He obedience by the things which He suffered.'—HEB. V. 8.

GOD had but one Son free from sin ; but none of all His sonnes free from correction.—HERRICK.

CONTRAST the erroneous view of the *Theologia Germanica* (xxx), which affirms that Christ's ' words and works and ways, His doings and refrainings, His speech and silence, His sufferings, and whatsoever happened to Him, were not forced upon Him, neither did He need them, neither were they of any profit to Himself'.

REFERENCES.—V. 8.—Spurgeon, *Sermons*, vol. xlvii. No. 2722. G. Body, *Christian World Pulpit*, vol. xlv. p. 193. Archbishop Cosmo Lang, *ibid.* vol. lv. p. 235. V. 8, 9.—A. T. Guttery, *ibid.* vol. lvi. p. 317. *Expositor* (4th Series), vol. i. p. 34 ; *ibid.* vol. ii. p. 16. V. 9.—Spurgeon, *Sermons*, vol. xx. No. 1172. *Expositor* (6th Series), vol. ii. p. 74. V. 9, 10. —R. M. Benson, *Redemption*, p. 152.

CHRISTIAN GROWTH

'Of whom we have many things to say, and hard to be uttered, seeing ye are dull of hearing.'—HEB. V. 11.

THIS writer addresses the Hebrews in very plain language. He calls them babes. He upbraids them

with being content with a milk diet. They had been some time alive, but they had not grown ; and no wonder, for they had never discovered that they had teeth. They ate no solid food ; they preferred what others had digested for them ; they preferred being dandled in the arms of others, and shrank from using their own limbs. That is to say, they were content with rudimentary knowledge of Christian truth and with traditional teaching, and made no effort to think for themselves and to advance into the infinite of spiritual realities.

I. In correction of this common fault of backwardness and indisposition to learn, this writer bids us observe two facts : (1) That *growth is expected in the Christian*. In fact, he tells us that if we are not growing we are dying. There is no third condition : he has in view only the alternative, either we are going on to perfection, or we are falling away. 'Let us go on unto perfection, *for* it is impossible to renew those who fall away.' This is the law of all life. Nothing is born mature. It passes through a period of growth, and it must grow or die. The parent who is delighted with the innocent helplessness of his child, and rejoices in its efforts at speech, becomes seriously alarmed if this lisping, tottering, help-requiring state threatens to become permanent.

II. The second fact regarding the Christian life which this writer wishes us to observe is that *this growth, which is essential, depends on the truth we receive*. He compares Christian truth to food ; that is, Christian teaching does for the inner man what food does for the body. The body cannot grow without food ; neither can the spirit come to maturity save by the reception of spiritual truth. But he divides Christian truth into two grand kinds, and these he represents by milk and solid food. Milk represents traditional teaching ; it is the product of that which has been received and digested by others, and is suitable for those who have no teeth of their own and no sufficiently strong powers of digestion. Like infants, they can only receive what others have thought, having no independent power of their own to investigate for themselves and form their own opinion about things. This milk, or traditional teaching, is admirably adapted to the first stage of Christian life, but cannot form mature Christians. The other kind of teaching he compares to solid food, which the individual must chew and digest for himself. It is true, physically, that poor and thin diet makes poor and thin blood ; that if a man is to spend much strength he must eat heartily. Spiritually it is equally true. Growth comes by nutrition. Without partaking of sound and wholesome truth the spirit cannot grow or be strong.

If we are not to be spiritual imbeciles, if we are to be strong and helpful men in Christ, we must seek nutriment in Christian truth. The vigorous and healthy soul does not need to be told this, as little as the strong, hard-working man needs to take tonics or be directed what to eat. But many of us do need, and most urgently, the direction here given us, to keep the mind feeling about for new ideas. The sea anemone is the emblem of the healthy Christian, fixed firmly to the rock, but with many feelers freely floating around to apprehend all that can be used.

What nutrition, then, are you giving to your spirit ? Is it such as is likely to secure your growth ? What do you read ? Tell me what a man reads and I will tell you his spiritual condition. Newspapers and magazines admirably serve their ends, but these ends are not spiritual nutrition. The Bible read carelessly and formally, so many verses a day, will work no charm any more than any other book so read. But the Bible read with expectation, interest, thought and personal application will yield nutriment of the most various and stimulating kind.

No language in the whole Bible is more stringent or alarming than that which this writer uses of those who fall away. So alarming is it, so firm in its prediction of inevitable perdition, that men have striven in every way to turn its edge. But in vain. The fact is, there *are* conditions of spiritual growth and health as there are conditions of physical growth ; and carelessness in the one case is as certainly followed by disaster or by death as carelessness in the other.— MARCUS DODS, *Christ and Man*, p. 214.

' Of whom we have many things to say, and hard of interpretation, seeing ye are become dull of hearing.'—HEB. v. 11.

'I AM at present,' says James Smetham in his *Letters* (p. 170), 'on the Epistle to the Hebrews. The great difference of such a subject from all others is that all the interests of Time and Eternity are wrapped up in it. The scrutiny of a title-deed to £100,000 a year is nothing to it. How should it be ? Is there a Christ ? Is He the heir of all things ? Was He made flesh ? Did He offer an all perfect sacrifice ? Did He supersede the old order of priests ? Is He the Mediator of a new and better Covenant ? What are the terms of that Covenant ? There are no questions like these. They raise, in their very investigation, the whole soul into the Empyrean. All other interests seem low, trivial, petty, momentary. . . . I am astonished at the imperative tone of this Epistle, and the element of holy scorn against those who refuse to go into those great questions carefully.'

REFERENCES.—V. 11, 12.—Marcus Dods, *Christian World Pulpit*, vol. lv. p. 139. V. 11-14.—*Expositor* (4th Series), vol. viii. p. 119.

' The first principles of the oracles of God.'—HEB. v. 12.

'THE wisdom from above has not ceased for us,' says Coleridge in the introduction to his *Lay Sermon ;* '"the principles of the oracles of God" are still uttered from before the altar! Oracles, which we may consult without cost ! Before an altar, where no sacrifice is required, but of the vices which unman us ! no victims demanded, but the unclean and animal passions, which we may have suffered to house within us, forgetful of our baptismal dedication—no victim, but the spiritual sloth, or goat, or fox, or hog, which lay waste the vineyard that the Lord had fenced and planted for Himself.'

REFERENCES.—V. 12-14.—Archbishop Temple, *Christian World Pulpit*, vol. lvi. p. 148. *Expositor* (5th Series), vol. v. p. 31. V. 13, 14.—Bishop Bethell, *Sermons*, vol. i. p. 386. V. 14.—Spurgeon, *Sermons*, vol. ix. No. 506. *Expositor* (4th Series), vol. i. p. 268.

THE FIRST PRINCIPLES OF CHRIST

' Repentance from dead works and faith towards God.'— HEB. VI. I.

THE combination of *repentance* and *faith* meets us in the earliest proclamation of the Gospel by our Lord Himself, and it continues to sound all through the pages of the New Testament. As a man's faith is set upon God so he repents of dead works.

I. How does such Faith in God Originate ?— Our author gives us the answer in the epithet of God which he introduces when he repeats this phrase and speaks of being ' cleansed from dead works to serve the living God '. 'The living God.' In that epithet lies the whole secret. It is the realisation that God is alive that calls out our faith. Faith cannot create itself, still less create its object ; it must always be the response to a revelation God makes. Our God is a living God—see what He has done ! see what He is doing!

II. Faith Depends most upon Experience.—There are special ways in which God reveals Himself to us to-day, and convinces us that He is a living God. (1) To some, perhaps to many, the revelation of God that comes home first and most keenly, is found in the love of our parents—not least of our mother —perhaps when they are taken from us and we see their character in the light of eternity. (2) To others, the most convincing revelation of God to-day is their own existence and personality ; that is to them the 'main miracle,' that 'I am I'. (3) To others again, the revelation of God's living will comes most securely not from within, but from the contemplation of the world without. (4) To others it is not so much the *life* or the purpose of the world that reveals the Maker as its *beauty ;* beauty of colour, beauty of form, beauty of sound. In ways like these our own daily reflection on experience may kindle our faith in a living God.—H. C. BEECHING, *Church Family Newspaper*, vol. xv. p. 220.

REFERENCES.—VI. 1.—H. P. Liddon, *University Sermons* (2nd Series), p. 98. *Expositor* (4th Series), vol. iv. pp. 59, 179. VI. 1-12.—C. Gutch, *Sermons*, p. 42. VI. 2.—E. W. Attwood, *Sermons for Clergy and Laity*, p. 407. *Expositor* (4th Series), vol. i. pp. 34, 209.

' Those who have tasted of the heavenly gift . . . and the good word of God, and the powers of the world to come.' HEB. VI. 4, 5.

THE *heavenly gift* is God's loving forgiveness of sins, the supreme boon of the Christian dispensation, in which all believers participate. The *good word of God* means the sure, kind promises made by Him to human faith for the future, and this is bound up with the experience, here and now, of *the powers of the world to come* which are already operating within the present age. Such a description of the normal Christian experience of God's Spirit is intelligible enough in the first century, when the strong eschatological hope of Christendom still throbbed within the Churches. But is the latter a reasonable element for ourselves? Is this 'l'avant-goût de l'éternité,' as Reuss calls it, this ardent eschatological expectation possible and desirable still? Cannot the taste of forgiveness which restores us to our place with God suffice by itself, without the other taste? Does not the modern outlook on the world compel us to drop the forward anticipation and to content ourselves with the present assurance of a heavenly Father's love such as Jesus taught? Instead of looking for a new heaven and earth, why should we not be satisfied with a God who has numbered the very hairs of our head? Would not this be at once more spiritual and more consonant with that view of the universe which we are bidden accept from modern science?

Dr. Kölbing, the distinguished Moravian scholar, raises this crucial question in a recent pamphlet on *Die bleibende Bedeutung der urchristlichen Eschatologie* (Göttingen, 1907, pp. 25 f.), and seeks to answer it in the negative. Whatever details of the primitive eschatology have a merely temporary value, he does not believe that we are obliged to curtail this description of the Christian position, as if 'eschatological faith, in the strict sense of the term, were merely the expression of a specifically Jewish and antiquated view of the universe'. His reasons are as follow.[1]

He begins by pointing out that, wherever the apocalyptic ideas of primitive Christianity may have been quarried, the religious source of its eschatology lay, as it still lies, in the sure knowledge of God's fatherly love to men which Jesus brought into the world. He then points out that this forward look of faith is justified for ourselves to-day by the believing man's experience of the world as a hindrance to the full development of spiritual life. 'In the light of the knowledge of God which Jesus has conferred on men, the Christian must ever and anon have the feeling that this earthly world has a variety of ways in which it can hinder any one who lies within its sphere from entering into fellowship with the Father in heaven.' The Christian can indeed experience the supernatural reality of God, but it is an experience which is exposed to thwarting doubts and recurring obstacles. The witness of history and the record of the Church are enough to prove this up to the hilt. Furthermore, as 'the Christian recognises that the dominating element in the spiritual life of Him who is Lord of the world is His holy and fatherly love,' he must also admit the conscious and unconscious opposition to God's moral will which starts up in society and in the individual. The progress of God's good reign is slow, and the actual facts seem often to contradict the idea of His royal love. 'Few are chosen,' and even the few meet difficulties of all sorts in the practice of their fellowship with God. What

[1] For a persuasive statement on the same lines, but with greater breadth, see Mr. Scott Lidgett's volume on *The Christian Religion* (1907), pp. 467 f.

can justify the Christian's confidence, as he faces such untoward facts, and 'overcomes the world,' but the glad certainty, now as in the primitive days of Christianity, that a new world of unclouded vision and unhindered service awaits God's children? This certainty of hope, with its perspective of the future, Dr. Kölbing argues, springs always from the faith of Jesus. It enables the weak and sinful here to glory already in the coming bliss, since such people know that God's forgiving and controlling grace can enable them, even through the trials and evil of the present, to inherit the world to come. 'If this is so, then we must decide that *to taste the powers of the world to come* is an element essential to the moral and religious faith of Christianity in God's holy love to sinful men. In other words, the eschatological character of primitive Christian faith is not a merely adventitious and transient element which was due to the Jewish view of the world; it possesses a permanent significance for the religious life of the Christian Church.' On this view, those who *taste the heavenly gift* of God's forgiveness do so, in the fullest sense, as they also *taste the good word* of God's promise for the future and *the powers of the world to come*, since the experience of forgiveness involves a reach and a range of faith in God's holy purpose which extend beyond the limits of a world-order where His power and love cannot fully come into play. The present experience thus stands in a vital relationship to the future hope.

> The stars come nightly to the sky,
> The tidal wave unto the sea,
> Nor time, nor space, nor deep, nor high,
> Can keep my own away from me.

And part of this *own* possession is the future. The present experience of the Spirit, with its assurance of Divine forgiveness and fellowship, not only transmutes the trials of to-day into opportunities of moral growth for the life of God, but provides a foretaste of that new order which will correspond, as this world cannot, with the just requirements of the believing soul.— JAMES MOFFATT.

REFERENCE.—VI. 4, 5.—*Expositor* (7th Series), vol. v. p. 477.

'It is impossible for those who were once enlightened, and have tasted of the heavenly gift, and were made partakers of the Holy Ghost, and have tasted the good word of God, and the powers of the world to come, if they shall fall away, to renew themselves again unto repentance.'—HEB. VI. 4-6.

'CONSIDER,' wrote Samuel Rutherford to the Presbyterians of Ireland in 1638, 'how fair before the wind some do ply with up-sails and white, even to the nick of "illumination" and "tasting of the heavenly gift"; and "a share and part of the Holy Ghost"; and "the tasting of the good word of God, and the powers of the world to come". And yet this is but a false nick of renovation, and, in short time, such are quickly broken upon the rocks, and never fetch the harbour, but are sanded in the bottom of hell. . . . A white skin over old wounds breaketh our under-coating conscience. False under water, not seen, is dangerous, and that is a leak and drift in the bottom of an enlightened conscience ; often falling and sinning against light.'

REFERENCES.—VI. 4-6.—C. Perren, *Sermon Outlines*, p. 182. Spurgeon, *Sermons*, vol. ii. No. 75. *Expositor* (4th Series), vol. vii. pp. 367, 443 ; *ibid*. vol. viii. p. 119. VI. 5. —G. F. Pentecost, *Marylebone Presbyterian Church Pulpit*, p. 3. John Watson, *Christian World Pulpit*, vol. xlvii. p. 113. *Ibid. The Inspiration of Our Faith*, p. 324.

NEVER TOO LATE TO MEND—IS IT?

' 'It is impossible to renew them again unto repentance.'—HEB. VI. 6.

'IMPOSSIBLE'—and yet we say it is 'never too late to mend'. 'God is good ; His mercy endureth for ever,'—that, happily, needs no discussion ; so far we are at one. But does universal love imply universal salvation? Is the love of God the only needed factor in the salvation of man? My sin cannot chill or change the love of God ; but what if it so change *me* that all that love never stirs me, never touches me, never wakens within me one answering throb? 'Never too late to mend'?—look where I will, I can find confirmation of it nowhere : contradiction, refutation of it everywhere.

I. It is not the doctrine of the New Testament. And when I say the New Testament, I mean the whole of the New Testament. The New Testament is a much sterner book than some of us like to think. There are shadows here that will not flee. Christ spoke of 'an eternal sin,' of which, if a man be guilty, he 'hath never forgiveness'. Note not merely the 'proof-texts' but the 'proof-trend' (as some one has named it), not merely the 'Biblical ripple,' but 'the Biblical gulf-stream' ; and if you do that, you will neither yourself believe, nor teach others to believe, that it is 'never too late to mend'.

II. Nature does not encourage us to believe that it is 'never too late to mend'. Gash a tree up to a certain point and kindly Nature will heal the wound ; but go beyond that point, and the tree will wither and die.

III. What say the great students of human nature? Milton pictured Satan a free agent, and yet saying :—

> All good to me is lost ;
> Evil, be thou my good.

Hear the guilty king in ' Hamlet ' ; prayer is useless :—

> What then? What rests?
> Try what repentance can : what can it not?
> Yet what can it *when one can not repent?*
> O wretched state ! O bosom black as death !
> O limed soul, that, struggling to be free,
> Art more engaged !

IV. And now if from these we turn to some of the awful facts in the life of men about us, will they bid us to hope that it is 'never too late to mend'? I have read of an habitual drunkard who said, 'If a glass of spirits were put before me, and I knew that the abyss was yawning between me and it, I must still take it'.

He who will not at last cannot.—G. JACKSON, *Table Talk of Jesus*, p. 253.

REFERENCES.—VI. 7.—A. Maclaren, *Expositions of Holy Scripture—Hebrews*, p. 349. VI. 8.—*Expositor* (4th Series), vol. ii. pp. 66, 382.

'But, beloved, we are persuaded better things of you, and things that accompany salvation, though we thus speak.' —HEB. VI. 9.

DR. NEALE wrote to his friend E. J. Boyce, whose sermons he was criticising : ' One thing in particular I admire : the manner in which you speak to your congregation, when mentioning their religious state. You are far more like St. Paul in that matter than you are like Owen. Owen said in one of his discourses, '' My brethren, I am well aware that a great many more of you that hear me now will be damned than will be saved ''. St. Paul said, '' But, beloved, we are persuaded better things of you, and things that accompany salvation, though we thus speak ''.'

REFERENCES.—VI. 9.—Spurgeon, *Sermons*, vol. iii. No. 152. J. Bateman, *Sermons Preached in Guernsey*, p. 112. A. Maclaren, *Expositions of Holy Scripture—Hebrews*, p. 359.

THE ASSURANCE OF SALVATION

'But, beloved, we are persuaded better things of you, and things that accompany salvation, though we thus speak. For God is not unrighteous to forget your work and labour of love, which ye have shewed toward His name, in that ye have ministered to the saints and do minister. And we desire that every one of you do shew the same diligence to the full assurance of hope unto the end. That ye be not slothful, but followers of them who through faith and patience inherit the promises.'—HEB. VI. 9-12.

I. WE learn from our text the proper spirit with which to regard the Christian course of salvation. There are two modes in which life can be observed. In our times, two rather high-sounding names have come to be common, and they fairly well express these contrasted sentiments ; we call them Optimism and Pessimism. Christianity has for the most part proved itself to be optimistic, and notwithstanding the fact that its theology and its commonly received creed have contained much that was terrible and full of pain, yet there has always been the side of bright and cheerful expectation, with the hope that in the final issue there would be a vast and enormously preponderating excess of good over evil, right over wrong, and blessedness over misery. Where the prevailing doctrine of Christianity has been kept nearest to the Scripture and has been less affected by theological and ecclesiastical developments, and a return has been made to earlier and more distinctly primitive faith and teaching, this has been especially the case, and the general spirit of Christian thought has been that expressed by the writer : ' We are persuaded better things of you, and things that accompany salvation, though we thus speak'. It is thus we should regard the condition of the Church, the spiritual outlook of our friends, and especially our own prospects.

II. And what are the grounds for this glad persuasion? (1) In the first place, this joyous hopefulness of the Christian is fixed upon God. (2) With that eminent practicality which marks the Christian teacher, our text shows us that this trust in God manifested in work and love toward His name is best shown in the ministrations of kindliness and brotherly love in which the believer engages toward the saints. (3) It is with wonderful insight, therefore, that our author refers to this ministration to the saints as the proof of the love which Christian people have for the Divine Name.

III. And the final source of this Christian optimism, the undying hope, is to be found in that activity and self-devotion which will bring those who possess it to share in all that is enjoyed by those who have already found the fulfilment of the promises. Three things mark Christian endeavour : Diligence, hopefulness, and continuance to the end. A great writer has said : 'I love the man who whistles as he works : no man will whistle as he works who does not give himself to his effort with completeness and devotion '. —LLEWELYN D. BEVAN, *Homiletic Review*, vol. LI. p. 60.

REFERENCES.—VI. 10.—J. C. Easterbrook, *The Riddle of Life and How to Read it*, p. 85. *Expositor* (6th Series), vol. iv. p. 447 ; *ibid.* vol. xi. p. 433. VI. 11.—A. Maclaren, *Expositions of Holy Scripture—Hebrews*, p. 367. VI. 11, 12.—H. Woodcock, *Sermon Outlines* (1st Series), p. 235. VI. 12.— W. J. Adams, *Christian World Pulpit*, vol. xliii. p. 166. W. J. Brock, *Sermons*, p. 147. J. Wright, *The Guarded Gate*, p. 161. A. Maclaren, *Expositions of Holy Scripture—Hebrews*, p. 377. VI. 17.—*Expositor* (7th Series), vol. v. p. 182.

'God, willing more abundantly to shew unto the heirs of promise the immutability of His counsel, confirmed it by an oath : that by His immutable things, in which it was impossible for God to lie, we might have a strong consolation.'—HEB. VI. 17, 18.

RATIONAL, sensible men, as they consider themselves, men who do not comprehend the very notion of loving God above all things, are content with such a measure of probability for the truths of religion, as serves them in their secular transactions ; but those who are deliberately staking their all upon the hopes of the next world, think it reasonable, and find it necessary, before starting on their new course, to have some points, clear and immutable, to start from ; otherwise, they will not start at all. They ask, as a preliminary condition, to have the ground sure under their feet ; they look for more than human reasonings and inferences, for nothing less than the 'strong consolation,' as the Apostle speaks, of 'those immutable things in which it is impossible for God to lie,' His counsel and His oath. Christian earnestness may be ruled by the world to be a perverseness or a delusion ; but, as long as it exists, it will presuppose certitude as the very life which is to animate it.—NEWMAN, *Grammar of Assent* (ch. VII.).

REFERENCES.—VI. 17, 18.—H. Woodcock, *Sermon Outlines* (1st Series), p. 17. Spurgeon, *Sermons*, vol. xv. No. 893. W. L. Watkinson, *Christian World Pulpit*, vol. lxxviii. p. 300. VI. 17-20.—C. O. Eldridge, *Preacher's Magazine*, vol. xix. p. 180. Spurgeon, *Sermons*, vol. xxii. No. 1294. VI. 18.—C. Perren, *Revival Sermons in Outline*, pp. 246, 247. Spurgeon, *Sermons*, vol. xxiii. No. 1352, and vol. xlvi. No. 2704. J. Beaumont, *Penny Pulpit*, No. 1706, p. 687. A. Maclaren, *Expositions of Holy Scripture—Hebrews*, p. 384.

WITHIN THE VEIL
' Within the veil.'—HEB. VI. 19.

'HOPE, the anchor of the soul,' is now one of the most familiar phrases in Christian thought and literature. It originated, however, with this inspired writer, and is an evidence of his inspiration ; for we do not naturally think of hope as giving steadfastness of life, but rather as giving it impetus. Any hope, if it be fixed on what is real, attainable, and good, is a God-sent angel ; but the hope spoken of here is better than every other, because this angel never leaves our side, nor ever will, even though we pass through the valley of the shadow of death. Instead of leading up to any disappointment it will end in a fruition beyond all conception. The evil, which death only can remove, hides from us our exalted Saviour, in whom our hope is fixed, and hides also all those whom He is gathering round Himself.

I. First, we should reflect on the fact here hinted at—that, as yet, heaven is veiled from us. It is quite true that, as compared with the Old Testament as well as with heathenism, the Lord Jesus has brought life and immortality to light by the Gospel ; but, beyond the certainty of heaven, and the assurance that Christ Himself is the centre and ruler of it, we know very little indeed. For some wise reason it was not the method of Christ and His Apostles to give us any specific or philosophical knowledge of heaven, even although that reticence might lead some to agnosticism and infidelity. Paul himself—though he was once caught up into the third heaven, and heard words which it was not lawful for a man to utter—made this confession : 'Now we see in a mirror darkly, but then face to face : now I know in part, but then shall I know even as also I have been known '. While John—through whom we have the Apocalypse itself, with its splendid imagery and mystic symbols —frankly says : 'It does no yet appear what we shall be ; but we know that when He shall appear we shall be like Him, for we shall see Him as He is '.

II. Now it appears to me that in these Scriptures we have (so far as the future world is concerned) appeals to our heart through our imagination ; and I wish to lay stress on this, because we have sometimes involved ourselves in greater darkness through mistaking figures for facts. Do not question for a moment the certainty of the home of bliss because the details of its economy are hidden behind the veil, and cannot yet be revealed to us as they are. Knowledge of details is not necessary in order to a living hope fixed in what lies before us, which, like an anchor, is holding us fast and drawing us nearer.— A. ROWLAND, *The Burdens of Life*, p. 261.

REFERENCE.—VI. 19.—A. Maclaren, *Expositions of Holy Scripture—Hebrews*, p. 394.

HE DESCENDED INTO HELL
(*For Easter-tide*)
' The forerunner.'—HEB. VI. 20.

IN this Easter meditation we shall not enter into controversies which, for complexity and bitterness, have hardly been equalled even in Christian theology. In one of Sydney Dobell's fine fragments, he makes an awakening soul say :—

> This is hell, then—
> And He descended into hell.

There have been manifold speculations as to Christ's open triumph over principalities and powers—as to His preaching to the spirits in prison, and much besides. Let it suffice us that He descended into Hades, the abode of the departed. Thus He took our journey over the 'tracts unknown' which lie between this world and that. Even there shall His hand lead us and His right hand hold us. He shared for the space of three days what is the experience of all the saints, save those who remain unto His coming. He submitted Himself to the whole law of the human lot—His spirit was free among the dead, while His body waited the appointed day. *Forasmuch as the children were partakers . . . He Himself took part of the same*, and so He holds the keys of all our possible experience. We have to think, then, of the words as illuminating the unknown way, and as teaching us what waits when the new gate opens into life, and we are in the unveiled presence of the Incarnate Word.

I. First, then, because His spirit has gone before, He can say to each believer, in the article of death, Follow Me. We have to pass 'across the wilds that no man knows' to the awful worlds of the future. It is the mysterious journey—not the end—from which many a humble, faithful soul shrinks. 'I have no fear of going to heaven,' said one, 'but *the crossing, the crossing!*' As we near the end, that great gulf between the familiar world and the hills of heaven stretches dark and wide at our feet. But 'He descended into Hades'. Christ died in the light. His body was anointed for burial by trembling and stained hands. But for His soul's journey He needed no chrism : He was going home. 'O God, when Thou wentest forth before Thy people, when Thou didst march through the wilderness . . . Thou didst confirm Thine inheritance when it was weary.'

II. His presence with the faithful dead is the presence of the Incarnate Christ. It is not enough to say that our Lord is conscious and supreme. The expression, indeed, is perhaps a tautology, for it is hard to see how He could be supreme without being conscious. What we can say is that He is incarnate and supreme. A spiritual presence of Christ in Paradise is not enough. If no more is vouchsafed, then Palestine nineteen hundred years ago was a place of greater opportunity. He was nearer the disciples who trusted Him during His earthly life than He is to those who have come up out of the great tribulation and have washed their robes in His blood. But it is not so. The faithful now behold Him clothed in the dear familiar raiment which is more than raiment, which is part of life, and are strengthened to wait the restitution of all things which God, who cannot lie, promised by His holy prophets since the world began.

III. This continual presence of Christ is primarily a friendship. Even here, without love, without friendship, there is no true life. The call of affection, and that only, awakens the soul. No man knows what he can do till he has learned to love. Love blows the trumpet of resurrection over the graves where his faculties are buried, and wakens them into energy and fruitfulness. Love teaches him how he can work, and think, and feel. But in the full sense, we have no friend but our Saviour. He, and He only, touches our natures at every point. Else why the deep craving for sympathy of which the world is full? Why are the closest ties so sharply sundered? These needs and pangs turn us to Christ ; but even so we give Him no perfect answer. It is only in death, only when sin has been finally purged out, that our souls yield themselves at every point to His grace.

He descended, our Forerunner, into Hades. He will return to claim from Death those bodies with which we trust Him on the sickbed, and of which He is possessor by an elder and a stronger right. He will return ere then, according to His word, to receive our souls. As the natural force abates, we shall be reinforced with life from its Prince and Fountain, and when we are called to take the great journey, another will go with us—One who knows the way.— W. ROBERTSON NICOLL, *Ten Minute Sermons*, p. 79.

REFERENCES.—VI. 20.—J. Baines, *Twenty Sermons*, p. 207. VII. 2.—Spurgeon, *Sermons*, vol. xxx. No. 1768. A. Maclaren, *Expositions of Holy Scripture—Hebrews*, p. 1. VII. 4.— Spurgeon, *Sermons*, vol. xxxi. No. 1835. VII. 7.—J. C. M. Bellew, *Christ in Life : Life in Christ*, p. 289. VII. 8.— *Expositor* (6th Series), vol. x. p. 359. VII. 11.—*Ibid*. vol. viii. p. 382. VII. 12.—T. Binney, *Penny Pulpit*, No. 1617, p. 331.

'Another priest who is made after the power of an endless life.'—HEB. VII. 15, 16.

If God dwells in the heart, and is vitally united to it, He will show that He is a God by the efficacy of His operation. Christ is not in the heart of a saint as in a sepulchre, or as a dead saviour that does nothing ; but as in His temple, and as one that is alive from the dead. For in the heart where Christ savingly is, there He lives and exerts Himself after *the power of that endless life* that He received at His Resurrection.—JONATHAN EDWARDS, *The Religious Affections* (pt. iii. ch. XII.).

REFERENCES.—VII. 14.—*Expositor* (5th Series), vol. iii. p. 450; *ibid*. vol. vi. p. 96. VII. 15, 16.—Archbishop Alexander, *Christian World Pulpit*, vol. xlvi. p. 17. VII. 16.—Bishop Boyd-Carpenter, *Christian World Pulpit*, vol. lii. p. 136. *Expositor* (5th Series), vol. v. p. 451; *ibid*. (7th Series), vol. vi. p. 430. VII. 18.—*Ibid*. (5th Series), vol. viii. p. 111. VII. 20-22.—Spurgeon, *Sermons*, vol. xxvii. No. 1597.

'By so much was Jesus made a surety of a better covenant.'— HEB. VII. 22.

His honour, and His great court in heaven, hath not made Him forget His poor friends on earth. In Him honours change not manners, and He doth yet desire your company. Take Him for the old Christ, and claim still kindness to Him, and say, 'O it is so ; He is not changed, but I am changed'. Nay, it is a part of His unchangeable love, and an article of the new covenant, to keep you that ye cannot dispone Him, nor sell Him. He hath not played fast and loose with us in the covenant of grace, so that we may run from Him at our pleasure. His love hath made the bargain surer than so ; for Jesus, as the cautioner, is bound for us.—SAMUEL RUTHERFORD, to Lady Kenmure (26th November, 1631).

REFERENCES.—VII. 22.—F. B. Cowl, *Preacher's Magazine*, vol. xviii. p. 380. VII. 23.—*Expositor* (4th Series), vol. i. p. 443. VII. 23-25.—Spurgeon, *Sermons*, vol. xxxii. No. 1915.

'This man, because He continueth ever, hath an unchangeable priesthood. . . . For such an High Priest became us, who is holy, harmless, undefiled, separate from sinners, and made higher than the heavens.'—HEB. VII. 24-26.

THE name of priest has been desecrated, till the very word, in some degree, carries with it the idea of something either spiritually despotic, or drily ecclesiastical and official ; yet what word, what thought is in reality so tender as that of a Man, *brought nearer than other men are, at once to man and to God* ? When applied to our Lord Himself, no other of His offices seems to bring and keep Him beside us in so intimate and human a relation as that of His 'unchangeable Priesthood'. 'He is a Priest for ever' ; one separate from sinners and undefiled ; and yet, through this very separation, drawn into the closest union with Humanity. Christ, when on earth, was upbraided for His freedom and accessibility. 'Behold, this man receiveth sinners, and eateth with them ;' and yet, like Joseph, the very type of bounty and brotherhood, He is one 'that is separated from His brethren,' drawing their souls after Him, while He withdraws from their presence. The heart desires one who is greater, purer, kinder, *freer* than itself, one standing aloof from its conscious falseness, its self-confessed littleness ; therefore is Christ, *because he is lifted up*, able to draw all men unto Him ; to draw as none other can do, close to Humanity, and to draw it close to Him.—DORA GREENWELL, in *Two Friends*.

THE POWER OF CHRIST TO SAVE

'He is able also to save them to the uttermost that come unto God by Him, seeing He ever liveth to make intercession for them.'—HEB. VIII. 25.

WE have here a brief but explicit statement, on the one hand, of the ability of Christ to save, and, on the other, of the ground on which that ability rests.

I. As to the ability of Christ to save—this is considered under two different aspects : as to its extent or range, and as to its intrinsic efficacy. (1) It extends to all those who come to God by Him. For though the word 'all' does not occur in the passage, it is of course implied. The phrase is precisely analogous to our Lord's own words : 'Him that cometh unto Me I will in no wise cast out,' which is equivalent to saying : 'Every one that cometh to Me shall certainly be received'. No doubt He has power to save even those who neglect or refuse to come. But this thought is not present to the mind of the writer, who is con-

templating the completeness of the salvation provided for those who come to God to obtain it, not the possibilities that are open to those who do not. (2) But Christ's ability to save, not only meets us at the threshold as it were of our approach to God, and assures of its sufficiency to bring us into His fellowship, it also assures us of His power to complete the process which He thus begins. He is able to save to the uttermost. This does not mean to the end of life, or up to the time of the Second Advent, though that is no doubt involved in the words. The idea rather is that His power is adequate to secure the perfect salvation of all who come to Him, so that nothing shall be required for its completeness which He is unable to supply. And this is the assurance that we need.

II. But we have still to consider the ground on which this saving ability of Christ rests. (1) It rests upon the fact of His ever living to make intercession. In this respect He presents a contrast to the Levitical priesthood. It passed from one to another as death removed the successive occupants of the office. But Christ abideth for ever, and there is no interruption to the continuity of His mediation. (2) Again, we may gather that the power of Christ's intercession springs from His atonement. This is, so to speak, the basis on which it proceeds, the great argument which makes it conclusive. And what can make it more so ? It is true our sins cry out for vengeance, but Christ's blood cries still louder for mercy. And its cry continues sustained, penetrating through all obstructions, resistless, clear, never failing to enter into the ears of God.—C. MOINET, *The Great Alternative and other Sermons*, p. 139.

'He is able to save them to the uttermost that come unto God by Him.'—HEB. VII. 25.

'IF the person,' says Guthrie of Fenwick, in *The Christian's Great Interest*, 'have a heart to come unto Him through Christ, then He is *able to save to the uttermost*. Yea, it is more provoking before God, not to close with Christ when the offer comes to a man, than all the rest of his transgressions are.'

REFERENCES.—VII. 25.—C. Perren, *Sermon Outlines*, p. 327. T. D. Barlow, *Rays from the Sun of Righteousness*, p. 110. J. Keble, *Sermons for Ascension Day to Trinity Sunday*, p. 42. T. Arnold, *Sermons*, vol. iii. p. 86. G. A. Sowter, *From Heart to Heart*, p. 219. J. Keble, *Sermons for Lent to Passion-tide*, p. 386. Spurgeon, *Sermons*, vol. ii. No. 84. J. Keble, *Sermons for Septuagesima to Ash Wednesday*, p. 421. W. Robertson Nicoll, *Sunday Evening*, p. 355. VII. 26.—*Expositor* (5th Series), vol. vii. p. 297 ; *ibid.* (7th Series), vol. vi. p. 423. A. Maclaren, *Expositions of Holy Scripture—Hebrews*, p. 10. VII. 27.—Spurgeon, *Sermons*, vol. xlvi. No. 2693. VIII. 1, 2.—A. Maclaren, *Expositions of Holy Scripture—Hebrews*, p. 20.

HEAVEN'S TEACHING ON EARTH'S DUTIES

'See, saith He, that thou make all things according to the pattern showed to thee in the mount.'—HEB. VIII. 5.

THE experience of Moses on Mount Sinai, to which our text refers, was a remarkable example of communion between God and man. We may thankfully accept it as a symbol of spiritual truth, and typical of recurring experience. Fellowship with God is not peculiar to any age, or clime, or race; and access to the Father is now far more generally enjoyed than in Mosaic times; for since then the world has seen and heard Him who said: 'I am the way, and the truth, and the life; no man cometh unto the Father, but by Me'. This verse reminds us—

I. That nothing is too trivial for God to notice. Moses was instructed in the mountain about the making of bowls, and dishes, and spoons, and staves, and tables. And if this fact suggests no other truth, at least it may remind us that the God of Jews and Christians is essentially unlike the God imagined by Epicureans—ancient and modern; for there is nothing too insignificant to be cared for by Him. Human knowledge, especially of late years, has been going in the direction of the trivial. While the Son of God was on earth, what small things He cared for! He who spoke with angels noticed children playing in the market-place. Now, if this be so, we ought not to wait before going to Him for help until some crushing sorrow comes to break us down.

II. We may speak to God about ordinary affairs in seasons of highest communion. If we are conscious that Christ goes with us, as He went with His disciples, to street, and market-place, and home, we may speak to Him about every grief and anxiety that comes.

III. Even slight deviations from Divine directions are forbidden. I fear we must acknowledge with shame that even professedly Christian people, in dealing with those outside the Church, have sometimes deliberately set aside the principles they profess; and the Sermon on the Mount has been condemned as impracticable and absurd. If it be true that even slight deviations from Divine directions are forbidden, we must guard ourselves against those forms of sin which we generally condone.

IV. What God calls us to do has more depending on it than we suppose. God expects of His servants what we, with less right, expect of ours—absolute fidelity and thoroughness in work, even though we do not see the object of it.—A. ROWLAND, *The Burdens of Life*, p. 209.

THE PATTERN IN THE MOUNT
HEB. VIII. 5.

HERE is a man who has left the multitude, with all its disturbing heats and clamours, and has sought the unperverting coolness of solitude, and on the cloud-capped height has found communion with his God. Now, one of the richest gifts with which God has dowered the race is the gift of mountain-men, men whose dwelling-place is on high, to whom the rarified atmosphere is their native air, who are finely perceptive of heavenly callings, and who are keen-eyed to discern the ideal tracings of the finger of God. There are the poets. What are these but mountain-men? And, then, there are the prophets, men again who have been cloistered on the heights with their God, and who descend into our mean discords with

'the voice of the great eternal' ringing in their mighty tones. There are mountain-moments in every life, when our tiny circle is immeasurably enlarged, when the cloud-rock breaks, and we see things as they are in the radiant glory of God.

I. Now in those mountain-moments we are all idealists. For what is an idealist? An idealist is one who sees the true idea of a thing. (1) In our mountain-moments we see the true idea of life. We see that the ideal life is a life of sublime fellowship, with sensitive perceptions and correspondences with the Highest. (2) And in these mountain-moments we see the true idea of the means of living. (3) And in these mountain-moments we see the true idea of society, as being a sacred fellowship, a gracious combination where competition does not poison or bruise, a fertile altruism in which the individual surely finds his appointed crown. (4) And so, too, we have the true idea of the fallen, the idea of the prodigal and the Magdalene, the pattern in the mount for her and him; God's design in heaven for thee and me. (5) And we have the true idea of little children, as princes and princesses of royal blood, who are called to sovereign eminence and service in the inheritance of the saints in light. The command is laid upon us as upon the men to whom the words were first spoken: 'See that thou make all things according to the pattern showed to thee in the mount'.

II. And how are we to set about the task? (1) Let us keep our imaginations freshly and vividly furnished with the ideal we wish to realise. A great friend of Westcott's wrote this great word about him: 'He was only strong because he saw, and *took time to see*'. Amid all our jostling and clamouring realities let us take time to contemplate the vision on the mount. (2) If we would retain the vision of the ideal, and be ministers of its incarnation, we must avoid all disgusting habits, whether the vulgarity be obtrusively bold or concealed beneath thin and superficial refinements. Above all, we must cultivate the fellowship and the friendship of the Lord Jesus Christ. In that glorious communion, in that supreme ministry of grace, it is possible for us to keep a clear eye and a ready and obedient hand.—J. H. JOWETT, *The British Congregationalist*, 4th June, 1908, p. 554.

'See that thou make all things according to the pattern shewed to thee in the mount.'—HEB. VIII. 5.

'EMERSON,' says Mr. Santayana in *Poetry and Religion* (p. 218), 'was not a prophet who had once for all climbed his Sinai or his Tabor, and having there beheld the transfigured reality, descended again to make authoritative report of it to the world. Far from it. At bottom he had no doctrine at all. The deeper he went and the more he tried to grapple with fundamental conceptions, the vaguer and more elusive they became in his hands.'

REFERENCES.—VIII. 5.—T. M. Morris, *Christian World Pulpit*, vol. li. p. 314. B. J. Snell, *The Virtue of Gladness*, p. 121. Bishop Westcott, *The Incarnation and Common Life*, p. 141. W. Moore Ede, *Christian World Pulpit*, vol. lviii. p. 332. *Expositor* (4th Series), vol. i. p. 437; *ibid.* (5th Series), vol. vi. p. 381. A. Maclaren, *Expositions of Holy Scripture—Hebrews*, p. 29. VIII. 6.—*Ibid.* vol. x. p. 237. VIII. 8.—W. H. Simcox, *The Cessation of Prophecy*, p. 168. VIII. 9.—*Expositor* (4th Series), vol. iii. p. 119.

THE ARTICLES OF THE NEW COVENANT

I. God's Writing on the Heart

'I will put My laws into their mind, and write them in their hearts.'—HEB. VIII. 10.

WE can scarcely estimate the shock to a primitive Hebrew Christian when he discovered that Judaism was to fade away. Now, the great object of this Epistle is to insist on that truth, and to calm the early Hebrew Christians under it, by showing them that the disappearance of the older system left them no poorer but infinitely richer, inasmuch as all that was in it was more perfectly in Christ's Gospel.

I. Let us first try to ascertain what exactly is the meaning of this great promise. These two clauses mean two things—the clear perception of the will of God, and the coincidence of that will with our inclinations and desires. (1) How is that wonderful change upon men to be accomplished? 'I will put, I will write.' Only He can do it. (2) It comes to substitute for all other motives to obedience the one motive of love. The secret of Christian morality is that duty is changed into choice, because love is made the motive for obedience. (3) This great promise is fulfilled in the Christian life, because to have Christ shrined in the heart is the heart of Christianity, and Christ Himself is our law. (4) This great promise is fulfilled, because the very specific gift of Christianity to man is the gift of a new nature, which is 'created in righteousness and holiness that flows from truth'. (5) This great truth has to be held with caution. (6) There is nothing in this promise which suspends the need for effort and for conflict.

II. Note the impassable gulf which this fulfilled promise makes between Christianity and all other systems. It is a *new* covenant, undoubtedly an altogether new thing in the world. For whatever other laws have been promulgated among men have had this in common, that they have stood over against the Will with a whip in one hand, and a box of sweets in the other, and have tried to influence desires and inclinations, first by the setting forth of duty, then by threatening, and then by promises to obedience. *There* is the inherent weakness of all which is merely law. But here is a system which says that it deals with the will as from within, and moves, and moulds, and revolutionises it. The peculiarity of the Gospel is that it gives both the knowledge of what we ought to be; and with and in the knowledge, the desire; and with and in the knowledge and the desire, the power to be what God would have us to be. St. Augustine penetrated to the very heart of this article when he prayed : 'Give what Thou commandest, and command what Thou wilt'.

III. Note the freedom and blessedness of this fulfilled promise. Not to do wrong may be the mark of a slave's timid obedience. Not to wish to do wrong is the charter of a son's free and blessed service.

IV. The condition of the fulfilment of this promise to us. What is there to do? First, and last, and midst, keep close to Jesus Christ. When the astronomer wishes to get the image of some far-off star, invisible to the eye of sense, he regulates the motion of his sensitive plate, so that for hours it shall continue right beneath the unseen beam. So we have to still our hearts, and keep their plates—the fleshy tables of them—exposed to the heavens. Then the likeness of God will be stamped there. Be faithful to what is written there. This is a promise for us all.—A. MACLAREN, *Triumphant Certainties*, p. 80.

THE ARTICLES OF THE NEW COVENANT

II. Their God, My People

'I will be to them a God, and they shall be to Me a people.'—HEB. VIII. 10.

'I AM thine : thou art mine,' is the very mother-tongue of love, and the source of blessedness. This mutual surrender, and, in surrender, reciprocal possession, is lifted up here into the highest regions. 'I will be their God, they shall be My people.' That was the fundamental promise of the Mosaic dispensation laid at Sinai, 'Ye shall be unto Me a people for a possession'. So, the writer here, falling back upon the marvellous prophecy of Jeremiah, regards this as being one of the characteristics of Christianity, that what was shadowed in Israel's possession of God and God's possession of Israel, is, in substance, blessedly and permanently realised in the relations of God to Christian souls, and of Christian souls to God.

I. 'I will be to them a God.' That is God's gift of Himself to us. The words go far deeper than the necessary Divine relation to all His creatures. (1) All that lies in that majestic monosyllable, which is shorthand for life, and light, and all perfectness, lived in a living person who has a heart, that word *God*, all that is included in that name, God will be to you and me, if we like to have Him for such. (2) It says, too, that all that Godhood, in all the incomprehensible sweep of its attributes, is on my side, if I will. (3) This giving of God to us by Himself is all concentrated in one historical act. He gave Himself to us when He spared not His only begotten Son.

II. And now we have to take the giving God and make Him our God.

III. We have to give ourselves to God. God comes first with the love that He pours over us poor creatures, and when 'we have known and believed the love that God hath to us,' then, and only then, do we throb back the reflected, ay, the kindred love. What is the surrender of the man who receives the love of God? In what region of my nature is that giving up of myself most imperative and blessed? In my will. The will is the man.

IV. God takes us for His. That is wonderful. It sometimes seems to me that it is more wonderful that God should take me for His than that He should give me Himself for mine.—A. MACLAREN, *Triumphant Certainties*, p. 90.

'For this is the covenant that I will make with the house of Israel after those days, saith the Lord; I will put My laws into their mind, and write them in their hearts.'—HEB. VIII. 10.

ON 22nd June, 1655, Cromwell wrote thus to Fleetwood: 'Dear Charles, my dear love to thee; and to my dear Biddy, who is a joy to my heart, for what I hear of the Lord in her. Bid her be cheerful, and rejoice in the Lord once and again: if she knows the covenant, she cannot but do so. For that transaction is without *her*; sure and stedfast, between the Father and the Mediator in His blood: therefore, leaning upon the Son, or looking unto Him, thirsting after Him, and embracing Him, we are His seed;—and the Covenant is sure to all the seed. The compact is for the seed; God is bound in faithfulness to Christ, and in Him to us: the Covenant is without *us*; a Transaction between God and Christ. Look up to *it*. God engageth in it to pardon us; to write His Law in our hearts; to plant His fear so that we shall never depart from Him. We, under all our sins and infirmities, can daily offer a perfect Christ, and thus we have peace and safety, and apprehension of love, from a Father in Covenant, who cannot deny Himself. And truly in this is all my salvation; and this helps me to bear my great burdens.'

REFERENCES.—VIII. 10.—Spurgeon, *Sermons*, vol. xliii. No. 2506. A. Maclaren, *Expositions of Holy Scripture—Hebrews*, p. 36; *ibid.* p. 46.

THE ARTICLES OF THE NEW COVENANT
III. *All shall know Me*

'They shall not teach every man his neighbour, and every man his brother, saying, Know the Lord: for all shall know Me, from the least to the greatest.'—HEB. VIII. 11.

IN old days there had been some direct communication between God and a chosen few, the spiritual aristocracy of the nation, and they spake the things that they had heard of God to the multitude who had had no such communication. My text says that all this is swept away, and that the prerogative of every Christian man is direct access to, communication with, and instruction from, God Himself.

I. I ask you to look with me at what this great promise means.

'They shall know Me.' We all know the difference between *hearsay* and *sight*. We all know the difference between *hearsay* and *experience*. To come still closer to the force of my text, we all know the difference between hearing about a man and making his acquaintance.

There is all the difference between knowing *about* God and knowing God; just the difference that there is between dogma and life, between theology and religion. We may have all articles of the Christian creed clear in our understandings, and may owe our possession of them to other people's teaching; we may even, in a sense, believe them, and yet they may

be absolutely outside of our lives. And it is only when they pass into the very substance of our being, and influence the springs of our conduct—it is only then that we know God. I maintain that this acquaintance with Him is what is meant in our text. The whole case for Christianity *cannot* be appreciated from outside. 'Taste and see.'

II. Notice how far this promise extends. 'They all, from the least to the greatest, shall know.' This is the true democracy of the Gospel—the universal possession of the life of Christ through the Spirit. (1) Now, if that be so, then it is by no means a truth to be kept simply for the purpose of fighting against ecclesiastical or sacerdotal encroachments and denials of it, but it ought to be taken as the candle of the Lord, by each of us, and in the light of it we ought to search very rigidly, and very often, our own Christian character and experiences. (2) But whilst thus the great promise of my text, in its very blessedness and fulness, does carry with it some solemn suggestions for searching self-examination, it also points in another direction. For consider what it excludes, and what it permits, in the way of brotherly help and guidance. It certainly excludes, on the one hand, all assumption of authority over the consciences and the understandings of Christian people, on the part either of churches or individuals, and it makes short work of all claims that there continues a class of persons officially distinguished from their brethren, and having closer access to God than they. (3) But brotherly help is not shut out.

III. The means by which this promise is fulfilled. (1) Jesus Christ's blood, the seal of the Covenant, is the great means by which this promise is fulfilled, inasmuch as in that death He sweeps away all the hindrances which bar us out from the knowledge of God. (2) By His mission and death there is given to the whole world, if it will receive it, and to all who exercise faith in His name, the gift of that Divine Spirit who teaches in the inmost spirit the true knowledge of His Son. (3) The one way by which every man and woman on earth may find him and herself included within that 'all, from the least to the greatest,' is simply trust in Christ Jesus.—A. MACLAREN, *Triumphant Certainties*, p. 98.

THE ARTICLES OF THE NEW COVENANT
IV. *Forgiveness the Fundamental Blessing*

'For I will be merciful to their unrighteousness, and their sins and their iniquities will I remember no more.'—HEB. VIII. 12.

THE introductory 'for' in my text shows that the fulfilment of all the preceding great promises depends upon and follows the fulfilment of this, the greatest of them. Forgiveness is the keystone of the arch. Strike it out, and the whole tumbles into ruin.

I. Forgiveness deals with man's deepest need. It is fundamental, because it grapples with the true evil of humanity, which is not sorrow, but is sin. The true notion and essence of forgiveness, as the Bible conceives it, is not the putting aside of consequences, but the flow of the Father's heart to the erring child. If a man has sinned, no Divine forgiveness will ever take the memory of his transgressions, nor their effects, out of his character. But the Divine forgiveness may so modify the effects as that, instead of past sin being a source of torment or a tyrant which compels to future similar transgressions, pardoned sin will become a source of lowly self-distrust, and may even tend to increase in goodness and righteousness. When bees cannot remove some corruption out of the hives they cover it over with wax, and then it is harmless, and they can build upon it honey-bearing cells. Thus it is possible that, by pardon, the consequences which must be reaped may be turned into occasions for good. But the act of the Divine forgiveness does annihilate the deepest and the most serious consequences of my sin; for hell is separation from God, the sense of discord and alienation between Him and me; and all these are swept away.

II. This forgiveness is attained through Christ, and through Him only.

The Christian teaching of forgiveness is based upon the conception of Christ's work and especially of Christ's death, as being the Atonement for the world's sin. Of course, my text itself does show that the very common misrepresentation of the New Testament evanelical teaching about this matter is a misrepresentation. It is often objected to that teaching that it alleges that Christ's sacrifice effected a change in the Divine heart and disposition, and made God love men whom He did not love before. The mighty 'I will' of my text makes no specific reference to Christ's death, and rather implies what is the true relation between the love of God and the death of Jesus Christ, that God's love was the originating cause, of which Christ's death was the redeeming effect.

III. This forgiveness is fundamental to all other Christian blessings.

A Christianity which does not begin with the proclamation of forgiveness is impotent. A Christianity which does not base forgiveness on Christ's sacrifice is impotent also. A Christianity which does not build holiness, delight in God's law, conscious possession of Him and possession by Him, and deep, blessed knowledge of Him on forgiveness, is woefully imperfect.—A. MACLAREN, *Triumphant Certainties*, p. 109.

REFERENCES.—VIII. 12.—Spurgeon, *Sermons*, vol. xxviii. No. 1685. A. Maclaren, *Expositions of Holy Scripture—Hebrews*, p. 62. IX. 1.—J. Caird, *Sermons*, p. 272. *Expositor* (6th Series), vol. iii. p. 136. IX. 1-10.—*Ibid.* (5th Series), vol. v. p. 379. IX. 4.—*Ibid.* (4th Series), vol. viii. p. 194. IX. 5.—*Ibid.* (6th Series), vol. viii. p. 337. IX. 7.—*Ibid.* (4th Series), vol. i. p. 88; *ibid.* (5th Series), vol. ii. p. 158; *ibid.* (7th Series), vol. v. p. 55.

ON MODERNISING CHRISTIANITY

'Until the time of reformation.'—HEB. IX. 10.

WHILE in a very real sense Christianity was a new religion in the days of St. Paul, in another, following his suggestion, it was a corrective, a revision and a modernisation of the old. The centuries have moved onward and our faith is no longer young. There are those among us who think that Christianity is now over-antiquated, that she is too old-fashioned, and that possibly there ought to be done for her what she in her youth did for the Jewish religion and for the cults of the pagan world. How far, then, and in what particulars is the Church bound to respect the time-spirit? Or, to phrase it differently, in what ways and within what restrictions is the modernising process allowable?

I. What are the changes needed? (1) Christianity should modernise her speech. Now, as on the day of Pentecost, every man has the right to hear the Gospel in the current language of the day, and the folly of talking in an unknown tongue is as pronounced now as when St. Paul condemned it. (2) Christianity, likewise, should modernise her thought. I do not say that she should abandon it, corrupt it, hide it, or in any way betray it. She can preserve it practically intact, and yet by rendering it less antiquated commend it to the time-spirit of the twentieth century. (3) Christianity ought further to modernise her activities. 'New occasions teach new duties,' and she, with open eyes for the vision, should not hesitate to employ whatever legitimate weapons are within her reach.

II. Let me point out some restrictions, some limitations, which may guard us from the excesses and from the extravagances that scandalise and vitiate the movement we are commending. (1) Christianity must be careful not so to modernise herself as to obscure her distinctive character. She is of the heavens, heavenly, and has no business to become earthy. It is no more necessary to be untrue to herself than it is for a man to be false to his deepest convictions. (2) Christianity, while preserving her character, must be mindful not so to modernise herself as to conceal her essential message. St. Paul gloried in the cross; and it will be a bitter day for humanity when the Church shall hide it, apologise for it, and explain away its only possible meaning as though it were her shame. (3) Christianity, finally, must be heedful not so to modernise herself as to becloud her supreme object. That the Church should strive for social amelioration, that she should do her utmost to improve temporal conditions, and that she should antagonise each specific evil and wrong of the time is cheerfully conceded. But she has a programme of her own. Her theory is: Cleanse the sources and the river will be pure; maintain the power in the power-house and traffic will keep on the move; supply and fill the reservoir and the homes of the citizens will not lack for water. This is her supreme object.—G. C. LORIMER, *The Modern Crisis in Religion*, p. 13.

REFERENCES.—IX. 10.—*Expositor* (4th Series), vol. i. p. 46; *ibid.* (5th Series), vol. vii. p. 398. IX. 11.—H. Alford, *Sermons on Christian Doctrine*, p. 193.

OUR LORD'S SACRIFICE

'But Christ being come an High Priest of good things to come, by a greater and more perfect tabernacle, not made with hands, that is to say, not of this building ; neither by the blood of goats and calves, but by His own blood He entered in once into the holy place, having obtained eternal redemption for us.'—Heb. ix. 11, 12.

I. The idea of sacrifice is almost co-extensive with the idea of God. The universality of the sacrificial idea can only be accounted for either by some primeval revelation from God, or by the fact that God, who endowed man with the religious instinct, implanted in him the notion of sacrifice.

Before the Fall, when man's conscience was unclouded by sin, sacrifice was the expression of love alone. Now that man's heart is stained by sin, sacrifice is the expression of penitence, and yet still of love ; for all true penitence is the utterance of love, telling God of sorrow, not for what the penitent has lost, not for the punishment incurred, but of that sorrow which is the expression of love in the presence of sin.

Sacrifice consists of an inward and an outward part, of which, while the inward may be the more important, the outward is absolutely necessary to perfect the sacrifice. True sacrifices are those inward feelings of love and obedience which form the very foundation of religion ; but those feelings are not in themselves proper sacrifices : in order that they may become so, they must find some external means of expression. A true sacrifice is one in which the religion of the heart is expressed by some outward symbol or rite acceptable to God.

In our Lord Jesus Christ the inward part was present from the first moment of His incarnate life (Heb. x. 9). It was the life of perfect love and unwavering obedience, which, as the inward part, found its outward expression in the death upon the cross, and made our Lord's a proper sacrifice—'a full, perfect, and sufficient sacrifice, oblation, and satisfaction for the sins of the whole world '.

II. In the Epistle to the Hebrews our Lord's sacrifice upon the cross is compared with the sacrifices under the Jewish law. Let us observe how perfectly our Lord fulfilled the sacrificial types, and where His sacrifice differs both from the Jewish sacrifices and the ritual of the Day of Atonement.

(a) There was the presentation of the victim by the offerer (Lev. i. 3). Two points here demand attention : the offering was to be without blemish, and it was to be a voluntary offering (Heb. ix. 14). It was, then, a voluntary offering ; and the act of presentation may be referred either to our Lord's high-priestly prayer (John xvii.), or to that prayer in the Garden of Gethsemane (Mark xiv. 26) ; or we may consider both these actions to belong to the presentation of the victim.

(b) The second stage in the offering of the Jewish sacrifice was the identification of the victim with the offerer (Lev. i. 4). By this action the offerer expressed his desire that the offering should be accepted in his place. The victim, however, was only a symbolic substitute for the offerer ; but our Lord was, in the truest sense, representative of the human race. The sacrificial offering offered by Christ is a real and equivalent substitute for all mankind, on whose behalf it is sacrificed.

(c) Then came the effusion of the blood. The offerer himself slew the victim. The priest took the blood and sprinkled it (Lev. iv. 5-7). The blood of each sin-offering was sprinkled against the veil, and symbolised the separation which sin had caused between God and man—that there was no free access to God. The blood of bulls and goats could not take away sin, and so the blood was sprinkled, but the veil remained unmoved. The precious blood of Jesus Christ cleanseth us from all sin, so when it was sprinkled the veil of the Temple was rent in twain, signifying that the barrier between God and man was removed, and access to God secured through the precious Blood of Christ.

(d) There was the burning upon the altar of certain parts of the victim, which thus went up as a sweet savour to God. And so our Lord (Eph. v. 2).

(e) There was a feast upon the sacrifice, and this is fulfilled by our Lord's gift of His Holy Body and Blood to be our food in the Eucharist. There we feast upon the Christian sacrifice.

III. Holy Scripture teaches us to associate the idea of life with the blood, and therefore forbade the Jews ever to eat blood (Lev. xvii. 10, 11). So that, as all sacrifice pointed to our Lord's sacrifice, this injunction pointed to the fact that it was the precious Blood which was to make atonement for sin, which was to redeem the world.

By this inauguration of the new dispensation, a new and living way is opened to the Throne of God, opened by the precious Blood. From that Blood each baptism gains its efficacy, from it each absolution derives its power ; the precious Blood of Christ —the means of redemption, applied to our souls through the Sacraments of the Church.—A. G. Mortimer, *Lenten Preaching.*

THE PRIESTHOOD OF CHRIST

'But Christ being come an High Priest of good things to come, by a greater and more perfect tabernacle, not made with hands, that is to say, not of this building ; neither by the blood of goats and calves, but by His own blood He entered in once into the holy place, having obtained eternal redemption for us.'—Heb. ix. 11, 12.

The priestly work of the Lord Jesus is the glorious theme of our text, but more especially the superiority of His Priesthood over that of Aaron. Four points of superiority are alluded to in the text. Superiority of the Person, the Place, the Plea, the Privileges.

I. The Superiority of the Person. The allusion in the text is to the high priest and to his work, especially on the Great Day of Atonement. The Levitical law made high priests of those who had infirmities, moral defects. Hence the high priest had to observe manifold and solemn rites of purification before he entered on the duties of the Great Day of

Atonement All these rites indicated his natural unfitness for the duties of his holy office. But Christ our High Priest had no need of ceremonial cleansing : He was clean already.

II. The Superiority of the Place where our High Priest Officiates. 'A greater and more perfect tabernacle." (1) 'Greater.' The figures of our arithmetic fail to describe its vastness. There will be as much room for the inhabitants to roam without colliding as there is in space for the stars to wander. (2) Not only greater but also a 'more perfect' tabernacle. No human art helped to build the tabernacle where our High Priest sits enthroned : no angel hand ever put a stone into it. The Builder and Maker is God.

III. The Plea of our High Priest is Superior to that of the Aaronic Priesthood. 'Not the blood of goats and calves, but by His own blood.' One man is of more value than all animals, but this was the blood of the God-man.

IV. Under Christ we have Superior Privileges. He is 'the High Priest of good things to come '. (1) The things under the law were only shadows : the good things under the Gospel are substantial and enduring. (2) Immediate access to God is one of the good things brought to us by Christ. (3) Christ hath obtained eternal redemption—eternal freedom. Freedom from what? (*a*) Freedom from the ceremonial law with all its burdensome and costly rites. (*b*) Christ hath obtained for us eternal freedom from sin.—RICHARD ROBERTS, *My Closing Ministry*, p. 224.

REFERENCES.—IX. 11, 12.—*Expositor* (4th Series), vol. ii. p. 280 ; *ibid.* (6th Series), vol. viii. p. 225. IX. 11-14.—*Ibid.* (4th Series), vol. i. p. 148. G. Body, *Christian World Pulpit*, vol. xlix. p. 185, and vol. lix. p. 192. A. Maclaren, *Expositions of Holy Scripture—Hebrews*, p. 72. IX. 12.—Spurgeon, *Sermons*, vol. xxxv. No. 2075. *Expositor* (6th Series), vol. x. p. 444 ; *ibid.* (7th Series), vol. v. p. 390. IX. 13, 14.—Spurgeon, *Sermons*, vol. xxv. No. 1481, and vol. xxxi. No. 1846.

'Christ through the eternal Spirit offered Himself without spot to God.'—HEB. IX. 14.

WE know not the truth of humanity—we know only its perversions while we are living the life of self and enmity and are as gods to ourselves. What it is to be a man, what we possess in humanity, we never know until we see humanity in Him who through the eternal Spirit offered Himself without spot to God.—MCLEOD CAMPBELL, *The Nature of the Atonement* (pp. 147, 148).

'To serve the living God.'—HEB. IX. 14.

'WE know,' says Faber, ' that the service of God is the grand thing, or rather that it is the only thing about us which is great at all.'

REFERENCES.—IX. 14.—Bishop Alexander, *Christian World Pulpit*, vol. xlviii. p. 134. W. M. Clow, *The Cross in Christian Experience*, p. 206. Walter Lock, *The Guardian*, 27th January, 1911. *Expositor* (4th Series), vol. i. pp. 34, 442 ; *ibid.* vol. ii. pp. 138-142 ; *ibid.* (5th Series), vol. ix. p. 405. IX. 15.—*Ibid.* (4th Series), vol. i. p. 34. IX. 15-28.—*Ibid.* p. 351.

IX. 16.—*Ibid.* (5th Series), vol. vii. p. 373. IX. 20.—Spurgeon, *Sermons*, vol. xxvi. No. 1567.

GETHSEMANE, THE ROSE GARDEN OF GOD

'Without shedding of blood is no——.'—HEB. IX. 22.

I DO not use the complete sentence. It is true even upon the lowest plane that without shedding of blood there is nothing, no mighty result, no achievement, no triumph. Every worthy deed costs something ; no high thing can be done easily. No great thing can be accomplished without the shedding of blood. Life is just our chance of making this great and strange discovery. Many of us never make it. We begin by trifling, by working with a fraction of our strength. We soon see that nothing comes of that. At last, if we are wise, we see that all the strength is needed. What have we besides this ? We must disrobe ourselves. We do it; yet our object remains ungained. What more have we to give ? We have our blood. So at last the blood is shed, the life is parted with, and the goal is reached. We are happy if we know that everything noble and enduring in this world is accomplished by the shedding of blood, not merely the concentration of the heart and soul and mind on one object, but the pruning and even the maiming of life. Young men are being taught this lesson now, and unless all signs are false they will be taught it more sternly in the future.

I. Blessing comes from blood-shedding ; that is, our power to bless in the highest sense comes from our shedding, as it were, great drops of blood. We need not shed them literally, though the Church has justly placed the martyrs first. The Church of Rome never prays for the martyrs, but makes request for their prayers. The martyrs it sees before Christ in robes of crimson, and the saints in white. The blood of the martyrs is the seed of the Church. We cannot atone, but we can bless. We cannot have a share in the one perfect Oblation, the Evening Sacrifice of the world, but we fill up that which is behind of the afflictions of Christ. Of every great servant of Christ it is true that the Lord says, ' I will show him how great things he must *suffer* for My Name's sake '. It would not be right to say that it is the suffering that counts, and not the labour. What is true is that the labour without the suffering does not count, that the two in a fruitful life are indissolubly joined. We are familiar with the great passages in which the Apostle is driven to use the awful language of the Passion, where he says, ' I am crucified with Christ, I die daily '. And it is true that all along the way there are sacrifice and blood-shedding. But I believe it is equally true that there is but one great Gethsemane in the lives of Christ's blessed servants. Many have none, and their work comes to little, but the elect have one that stands above all, one shedding of blood, one death, after which the rest seems easy. The Gethsemane may be, and often is, the rooting out of some cherished ambition that has filled the heart and occupied every thought. It may be the shattering of some song, the breaking of some dream. It may be, and often is, the great rending of the affections, the cutting of the soul free from some detaining human tenderness. Anyhow, the full agony cannot last more than a little, though the heart-ache may persist through a lifetime. 'Could ye not watch with Me *one hour?*' I sometimes think that blood-sheddings are far more common than we are apt to imagine, and that they take place in the most unlikely lives. In the memoir of Dr. Raleigh, a prosperous suburban minister with every earthly ambition realised, there is a significant passage. When he was at the zenith of his fame he said that ministers came and looked round at his crowded church, and envied his position. 'They do not know what it cost me to come to this.' So, in James Hamilton's life, we are permitted to see how he parted, for Christ's sake, with his great ambition. He wished to write a life of Erasmus, and devoted many years to preparation, but other claims came and baulked him of his long desire. He says : 'So this day, with a certain touch of tenderness, I restored the eleven tall folios to the shelf, and tied up my memoranda, and took leave of a project which has sometimes cheered the hours of exhaustion, and the mere thought of which has always been enough to overcome my natural indolence. It is well. It was a chance, the only one I ever had, of attaining a small measure of literary distinction, and where there is so much pride and haughtiness of heart it is better to remain unknown.' I think we may easily see where the Gethsemane was in Henry Martyn's life, and I think one may also see it in John Wesley's life, though I should not care to indicate it. But the heart knoweth its own bitterness. What we know is that the Gethsemanes in the Christian life come in the course of duty, and in obedience to God's will as it is revealed from day to day.

II. The bloom and perfection of life to the missionary come from the shedding of blood. Observe that I am not speaking here of the blessing to others, but of the blessing that is meant to come to ourselves in the great enrichment of the spiritual life that should follow, and abundantly make up for, the impoverishment and expenditure of the natural life. What comes after the parting with the natural life, after the shedding of blood, after the death to the world? Various things come, but what ought to come is the resurrection life, which the shedding of blood has made room for.

It does not always come even to the servants of God whose lives are faithful. Their work is fruitful, never without result, but they themselves have not the full blessing of the resurrection life.

(1) Often the Gethsemane of the soul means a brief tarrying in this world. It seems as if too much had gone, as if the spirit could not recover its energies. There are a few books peculiarly dear to the heart of the Church which I may call Gethsemane books. The chief are the lives of Brainerd, Martyn, and McCheyne. All of these died young, not without signs of the Divine blessing, but prematurely—rich and fervid

natures exhausted and burnt out. I do not overlook physical causes and reasons, but in each case there was a Gethsemane.

(2) Sometimes the earthly life parted with is not fully replaced by the resurrection life, and a long-drawn melancholy ensues. It is so, I venture to think, in the life of Charles Wesley. It will be granted by the most ardent admirers of that great saint and supreme Christian poet that the last thirty years of his life will not compare with those of his mighty, strenuous, ardent youth. They were sad years in the main, spent in comparative inaction, and with many weary, listless, discontented days. The text of Charles Wesley's later years, the text that must ever be associated with his name, was, 'I will bring the third part through the fire'. He thought that one-third part of Methodists would endure to the end. He never sought an abundant entrance for himself into the heavenly kingdom, never asked more than that 'I may escape safe to land—on a broken piece of the ship. This is my daily and hourly prayer, that I may escape safe to land.' Our Gethsemanes are not meant to end in gloom and melancholy. They are meant to give us, by the grace of God, a richer, even an eternal life in the place of that which we have lost. Our sufferings must be well used, for 'in this mortal journey wasted shade is worse than wasted sunshine'.

(3) No, the bloom of life should come out of death. The resurrection life should pour into the depleted veins, and fill them with strength and peace. That was eminently the experience of John Wesley. Branch after branch was withered, but every time the new life rushed through all the arid fibres, and they bloomed again. There is no book, I humbly think, in all the world like John Wesley's Journal. It is pre-eminently the book of the resurrection life lived in this world. It has very few companions. Indeed, it stands out solitary in all Christian literature, clear, detached, columnar. It is a tree that is ever green before the Lord.

When the world has become one great Gethsemane, we shall see over it all the flowers that grow, and grow only, in the garden where Christ's brow dropped blood. The Church of Christ must be in an agony, praying more earnestly, sweating, as it were, great drops of blood, before the world can be brought to Christ. We give nothing, until we give what it costs us to give, life. There is no life without death. Gethsemane is the rose garden of God.—W. Robertson Nicoll, *The Lamp of Sacrifice*, p. 55.

References.—IX. 22.—H. J. Wilmot-Buxton, *Sunday Sermonettes for a Year*, p. 134. M. Biggs, *Practical Sermons on Old Testament Subjects*, p. 43. Spurgeon, *Sermons*, vol. iii. No. 118, and vol. li. No. 2951. *Expositor* (6th Series), vol. vi. p. 462. IX. 23.—Bishop Bickersteth, *Sermons*, p. 182. IX. 24.—J. B. Mozley, *University Sermons*, p. 277.

'Now once in the end of the world hath He appeared, to put away sin by the sacrifice of Himself.'—Heb. ix. 26.

No fact in man's moral history is more certain than this, that the simple statement of Scripture, 'Christ has appeared to put away sin by the sacrifice of Himself,' has been found efficacious to reach down to the lowest depths of men's souls beyond any other truth ever uttered on this earth.—J. C. SHAIRP, *Studies in Poetry and Philosophy*, pp. **419, 420.**

REFERENCES.—IX. 26.—S. Bentley, *Parish Sermons*, p. 100. E. A. Stuart, *The One Mediator and other Sermons*, vol. xi. p. 201. Spurgeon, *Sermons*, vol. xiii. No. 759, vol. xvi. Nos. 911, 962, and vol. xxxviii. No. 2283. *Expositor* (4th Series), vol. vi. p. 139; *ibid.* (5th Series), vol. iv. p. 277. *ibid.* (6th Series), vol. vi. p. 458; *ibid.* vol. x. p. 319; *ibid.* (7th Series), vol. vi. p. 428. IX. 26-28.—Spurgeon, *Sermons*, vol. xxxvii. No. 2194.

' It is appointed unto men once to die, but after this the judgment.'—HEB. IX. 27.

SPEAKING of Plato's three great myths, Jowett, in his introduction to the *Gorgias*, observes that they ' are a substitute for poetry and mythology ; and they are also a reform of mythology. The moral of them may be summed up in a word or two : After death the Judgment ; and There is some better thing remaining for the good than for the evil '.

WE must die and give an account of our life ; here in all its simplicity is the teaching of sickness !— AMIEL.

I LOOKED then, and saw a man named *Evangelist*, coming to him, and asked, *Wherefore dost thou cry ?* He answered, Sir, I perceive by the Book in my hand, that I am condemned to die, and after that to come to Judgment, and I find that I am not willing to do the first, nor able to do the second.'—BUNYAN's *Pilgrim's Progress* (pt. 1).

'THE hope of a future life,' says Sir John Seeley in *Natural Religion* (pt. ii. ch. 3), ' is still strong in men's minds, and has, perhaps, been expressed with more ardour in this age than in any other. But the legal and penal ideas which used to be connected with it have almost disappeared. " In Memoriam " speaks in every line of a future state, but of a future judgment it is absolutely silent.'

REFERENCES.—IX. 27.—*Christian World Pulpit*, vol. xliii. p. 102. J. Keble, *Sermons for Advent to Christmas Eve*, p. 68. R. Scott, *Oxford Lent Sermons*, 1868, p. 113. G. W. Brameld, *Practical Sermons*, p. 15. F. E. Paget, *Helps and Hindrances to the Christian Life*, vol. i. p. 104. IX. 27, 28.— Spurgeon, *Sermons*, vol. viii. No. 430. IX. 28.—H. Bushnell, *Christ and His Salvation*, p. 352. X. 1.—T. F. Crosse, *Sermons* (2nd Series), p. 53. X. 1-3.—*Expositor* (6th Series), vol. viii. p. 338 ; X. 1-18.—*Ibid.* (4th Series), vol. i. p. 436. X. 2.—H. Bushnell, *Christ and His Salvation*, p. 260. X. 3. —*Expositor* (7th Series), vol. v. p. 348.

' For it is impossible that the blood of bulls and goats should take away sin.'—HEB. X. 4.

To a modern these words have an antiquated sound. The world of ideas which they suggest has passed so entirely away that we look back upon the stage they represent as a stage far below us, so far, indeed, that it is barely conceivable. But they were originally the apex of a long ascent. The quiet decisiveness and even scorn with which the writer sets down this conviction breathe a feeling of relief, after the long

centuries of persistent and unavailing sacrifices. Humanity is drawing breath after a prolonged nightmare. The primitive ritual of purification was based on the belief that the blood of animals could wipe away sin, ' because the animal that has been consecrated by contact with the altar becomes charged with a Divine potency, and its sacred blood, poured over the impure man, absorbs and disperses his impurity '. Thus, as Dr. Farnell continues (*The Evolution of Religion*, pp. 120 f.), the cognate idea of the pure heart was ' not necessarily wholly ethical,' as yet, but often ' co-existent with the ideas of sin that do not clearly recognize moral responsibility or the essential difference between deliberate wrong-doing and the ritualistic or accidental or involuntary sin.' ' The final point is reached when it is realized that the blood of bulls and of goats cannot wash away sin, that nothing external can defile the heart or soul, but only evil thought and evil will. This purged and idealised concept will then in the progressive religions revolt against its own parentage, and will prompt the eternal antagonism of the prophet against the ritual priest, of the Christ against the Pharisee.'—JAMES MOFFATT.

REFERENCES.—X. 5.—J. B. Mozley, *University Sermons*, p. 183. *Expositor* (4th Series), vol. ii. p. 42 ; *ibid.* (5th Series), vol. x. p. 62 ; *ibid.* (6th Series), vol. v. p. 62. X. 5-7.— R. M. Benson, *Redemption*, p. 1. G. Trevor, *Types and the Antitype*, p. 220. Spurgeon, *Sermons*, vol. xxxvii. No. 2202. X. 7.—R. J. Campbell, *New Theology Sermons*, p. 133. S. Baring-Gould, *Village Preaching for a Year*, pt. i. p. 66.

'Lo, I come to do Thy will.'—HEB. X. 9.

THE Man, Christ Jesus, was of all created beings— as far as we know their history—the only one who chose his own destiny, who foreknew and accepted its full conditions ; who saw a great need and responded to it : ' Lo ! I come ? My leave,' said the acute Frenchwoman, ' was not asked before I came into the world'—a saying in which all that the human heart can urge against God and His appointments lies hid. Why should I be called upon to endure, to forego so much ? Had the choice been permitted me, I might possibly have declined it. *Our Saviour's leave was asked.* His fulfilment of His Father's will was voluntary ; He saw the end from the beginning.— DORA GREENWELL, *The Patience of Hope*, pp. 12, 13.

REFERENCES.—X. 9.—Spurgeon, *Sermons*, vol. xlvi. No. 2698. X. 9, 10.—H. Drummond, *The Ideal Life*, p. 279.

' By the which will we have been sanctified through the offering of the body of Jesus Christ once and for all.'—HEB. X. 10.

WHEN man finds that if he would do God's will, however imperfectly, he must offer up this continual sacrifice, *the sacrifice of his own will*, his thoughts are irresistibly carried to rest upon that One offering up of a higher than any human will, by which Christ has perfected for ever them that are sanctified. The more deeply we feel the existing contradiction between God's will and that of His creature, the deeper becomes our sense of the need of somewhat to take it away, so that the heart draws near to a truth unapproachable by the intellect—*the necessary death of Christ.* — DORA GREENWELL, *The Patience of Hope,* pp. 29, 30.

REFERENCES.—X. 10.—Spurgeon, *Sermons,* vol. xxvi. No. 1527. H. Alford, *Quebec Chapel Sermons,* vol. i. p. 235. J. Budgen, *Parochial Sermons,* vol. ii. p. 32. X. 11, 12.—C. Bosanquet, *Tender Grass for the Lambs,* p. 73. X. 11, 14.—Spurgeon, *Sermons,* vol. xviii. No. 1034. X. 12.—C. Perren, *Sermon Outlines,* p. 245. W. P. Balfern, *Lessons from Jesus,* p. 263. A. Maclaren, *Expositions of Holy Scripture—Hebrews,* p. 76.

THE ONE OFFERING

'But this Man, after He had offered one sacrifice for sins for ever, sat down on the right hand of God ; from henceforth expecting till His enemies be made His footstool.'—HEB. X. 12, 13.

LOOK at these two verses, and see three things :—

I. The Work which our Lord has Accomplished. —His death was the great purpose of His Incarnation. He came from heaven to die because there was no one else who could possibly have died a sacrifice for sin. There was only one Being Whom we know of Who could have possibly made that sacrifice for sin ; it was the Incarnate Son of God, the Creator of the world Himself. If He was willing to become responsible for the sins of the world which He had created, then Justice, we conceive, might be satisfied with Him as the sacrifice for sin. That the Christ of God willed to do. He who was Very God of Very God—He willed to become the sacrifice for sin. Then mark :—

II. The Position which He is Occupying.—Having accomplished that work, the text tells us He 'sat down on the right hand of God '. Is it not strange to think that Jesus Christ 'sat down'? We look about us to-day, and is it not too much to say that more than one-half of the human race has never heard of that sacrifice which Jesus Christ made upon the cross. Do you not wonder then, that, He has 'sat down '? Jesus Christ made that atonement, that sacrifice for sin, because, as we have seen, there was none other who could make it. But God never does what we can do. We could not make the sacrifice, therefore Christ came, and made it ; but we can proclaim the message, and therefore He now rests.

Here, then, is the awful responsibility which rests upon us—that God has ordained that the work of the Saviour Himself shall be left so far incomplete, because it is the will of your Heavenly Father that you and I shall complete it. No generation ever had such splendid opportunities of doing this work as have we ourselves. The Christian nations, so called, of the world to-day are not only the most civilised, but they are also the most powerful. We, to whom God has given all this, are to go and evangelise the uncivilised and the weak nations of the world. Mark you, we have nothing to do with the conversion of the world —that is not our work, it is the work of God the Holy Ghost—but the evangelisation of the world is our work. 'This Gospel of the kingdom shall be preached in all the world for a witness unto all nations ; and then shall the end come' (St. Matt. XXIV. 14).

III. Mark, then, the Hope that He is Cherishing.— He Who is now seated on the right hand of God and waiting, He is expecting, He is 'expecting until His enemies be made His footstool'. And He is expecting that His Church will be so filled with gratitude because of the sacrifice He made, so filled with compassion because they have caught something of His Spirit—He is expecting that His Church will be so longing for His Coming, that they will hasten to perform His wish, and tell every creature that He has died.—E. A. STUART, *Assurance of Life.*

CHRIST'S EXPECTATION

'But this Man, after He had offered one sacrifice for sins for ever, sat down on the right hand of God ; from henceforth expecting till His enemies be made His footstool.' —HEB. X. 12, 13.

I WOULD ask you to look at these two verses, and see these three things. First, the work which He has accomplished ; secondly, the position which He is occupying ; and thirdly, the hope which He is cherishing.

I. First of all, then, the work which He has accomplished. Eighteen hundred years ago our Lord died upon the cross for all mankind. He came down from heaven, He took upon Himself our nature, He lived a life of sorrow and of suffering, and at last He died upon the cross. That death was the great purpose of His Incarnation. He came from heaven to die, because there was no one else who could possibly have died as a sacrifice for sin. He willed to become the sacrifice for sin.

II. And having accomplished that work, the text tells us He 'sat down'. That is the position which He is now occupying, He 'sat down on the right hand of God'. What does the Apostle mean? He means that, having accomplished that work, He now rests! He had finished the work which it was given to Him to do. God never does what *we* can do. We could not make the sacrifice, therefore Christ came and did it ; but we *can* proclaim the message, and therefore Christ sits down. Now think what this means. It means this ; that there is no miracle that God was unwilling to do to procure the salvation of man, for what miracle can be compared to the Incarnation of Christ ? there is no sacrifice which God is unwilling to make to procure the salvation of the world, for what sacrifice can be compared to the cross of Calvary? But when it comes to the proclamation of that Gospel, God is willing to sit down and wait ; willing to sit down all these centuries, because God is not willing to do your work and my work. Here is the awful responsibility which rests upon us.

III. And, Jesus Christ is expecting! He is expecting that His Church will be so filled with gratitude because of the sacrifice He made, He is expecting that His Church will be so filled with compassion because they have caught something of His spirit, He is expecting that His Church will be so longing for His coming that they will hasten to perform His wish and tell every creature that He has died!—

E. A. STUART, *His Dear Son and other Sermons*, vol. v. p. 25.

REFERENCES.—X. 12, 13.—J. Fletcher, *The Prophetic Vision of the Exalted Christ*, No. vii. Spurgeon, *Sermons*, vol. ii. No. 91. X. 14.—E. A. Stuart, *The New Commandment and other Sermons*, vol. vii. p. 89. T. Arnold, *Sermons*, vol. iii. p. 78. Spurgeon, *Sermons*, vol. v. No. 232. A. Maclaren, *Expositions of Holy Scripture—Hebrews*, p. 84. X. 15-18.—Spurgeon, *Sermons*, vol. xii. No. 714. X. 17.—Spurgeon, *Sermons*, vol. xxviii. No. 1685.

'**Having therefore boldness to enter into the holiest by the blood of Jesus.**'—HEB. X. 19.

IN the account of Wesley's Last Hours, written by one who was present, it is recorded that, one day towards the end, 'he slept most of the day, spoke but little, yet that little testified how much his whole heart was taken up in the case of the churches, the glory of God, and the things pertaining to that kingdom to which he was hastening. Ever in a low, but very distinct manner, he said, "There is no way into the holiest but by the blood of Jesus". Had he had strength at the time, it seemed as if he would have said more.'

REFERENCES.—X. 19, 20.—Spurgeon, *Sermons*, vol. xxxiv. No. 2015. X. 19-22.—H. Melvill, *Penny Pulpit*, No. 1606, p. 247. *Expositor* (4th Series), vol. ii. p. 141. X. 19-25.—J. G. Greenhough, *Christian World Pulpit*, vol. liv. p. 337. X. 19-31.—*Expositor* (4th Series), vol. ii. p. 131. X. 20.—A. B. Wilberforce, *Christian World Pulpit*, vol. xlix. p. 148.

LET US DRAW NEAR
'Let us draw near.'—HEB. X. 22.

TAKEN in its very simplest sense, the exhortation is very beautiful. It reminds us that we were once far off from God; that our sins had separated between us and God; and that the worst of it was that we were getting farther and farther away from God. We did not want to be brought near to God! But now the exhortation comes to us, 'Let us draw near to God'. It is almost as if we heard our Father speaking, 'Come near to Me, My children'. Now, I want you to notice the four things which the Apostle tells us we have, to enable us to draw near to God; and then the four things which we require so that we may draw nearer to Him.

I. The four things that we have. (1) The very Holiest is open to us. 'Having therefore, brethren, boldness to enter into the Holiest.' The Apostle tells us that we have access into the very Holiest by faith in Christ. Here you may taste your Father's love, here you may see something of your Father's holiness, here—in the holiest of all—you detest sin, you despise the world. And further, here you have perfect peace —you can worship, you can adore. (2) The Apostle tells us that not only is the way to the Holiest open, but he tells us that we have this boldness through the blood.' Mark you, not the boldness of irreverence, but the boldness of perfect confidence. (3) He goes on to tell you the third thing that you have, Jesus Christ has shown you how—'There is a new and a living way which He hath consecrated for you through

the veil, that is to say, His flesh'. Christ has shown us by His death, by His daily death, He has shown us how we are to get into the very Holiest. It is by self-sacrifice, it is by rending the flesh, it is by crucifying the flesh. (4) You have, high above all, a great High Priest.

II. And what is required? Well, just these four things. (1) You must have a perfect heart. (2) You must draw near in the fulness of faith—in the full assurance of faith. (3) You must have a heart sprinkled from an evil conscience. (4) And then, lastly, you must draw near with your body washed with pure water. Not only has the heart to be cleansed within, but the life has to be cleansed without. It is no use to say the heart is clean, if the life is impure. Look to your eating, to your drinking, your sleeping, labour, recreation; for these outward things have a very great deal to do with your spiritual life—E. A. STUART, *The New Creation and other Sermons*, vol. III. p. 9.

'**Let us draw near with a true heart, in full assurance of faith, having our hearts sprinkled from an evil conscience, and our bodies washed with pure water.**'—HEB. X. 22.

IN a note to 'The Church Porch,' in his edition of George Herbert's Poems, Dr. A. B. Grosart points out that 'in pre-Reformation times, a stoup or bowl of holy water (so-called) was placed at the entrance of churches to remind the worshipper to have his heart "*sprinkled* from an evil conscience," in order "to serve the living God." '

HEARE but a discourse of philosophy read, the invention, the eloquence and the pertinencie, doth presently tickle your spirit and moove you. There is nothing tickleth or pricketh your conscience; it is not to her men speake. Is it not true? Ariston said that Neither Bath nor Lecture are of any worth, except the one wash cleane and the other cleanse all filth away.—MONTAIGNE (*Florio*) vol. III. p. 9.

'**Let us draw near with a true heart, in full assurance of faith.**'—HEB. X. 22.

'WE need a more forward moving Christianity,' said Dr. John Duncan, 'with more of the πληροφορία πίστεως in it; which is not "in full assurance of faith," but "in the full sail of faith"—bearing right on with the wind; all canvas up.'

REFERENCES.—X. 22.—*Expositor* (5th Series), vol. ii. p. 24. X. 23.—Spurgeon, *Sermons*, vol. xxxii. No. 1897.

'**Let us consider one another to provoke unto love and to good works.**'—HEB. X. 24.

AGAIN, in the preface to *A Priest to the Temple*, Herbert remarks that 'it is a good strife to go as far as we can in pleasing Him who hath done so much for us'.

'Do you ask,' says Schleiermacher, 'how we can stir up one another to love? In no other way than this, that we ourselves show love towards him in whom we wish to excite it. If we consider one another with hearty, brotherly love, and try to understand one another without yielding to any unfavourable prejudice, so that we cast no look on our brother save that of a love which seeks to serve him, it cannot but be that he will become aware of that love, of its considerate efforts to do something suitable for him ; and when he does so, our love will not return to us empty, but will produce some fruit in his heart. Perhaps hitherto we have rather tried to move men to stronger expressions of love by severe words and harsh judgments, by representing the advantage they would desire from so doing, or the harm they would avoid. If so, let this be past and gone, with other errors. For nothing creates love save love itself.'

REFERENCES.—X. 25.—Bishop Creighton, *University and other Sermons*, p. 90. F. C. Spurr, *Christian World Pulpit*, vol. xlviii. p. 92. *Expositor* (4th Series), vol. ii. p. 194. X. 27.—F. E. Clark, *Christian World Pulpit*, vol. l. p. 230.

'Not forsaking the assembling of ourselves together, as the custom of some is.'—HEB. X. 29.

THE neglect of public worship, at which the writer hints, is due not so much to worldly indifference or to a fear of the risks involved in a church connection, as to the fascination of some other cult. The danger was that these Christians should regard Christianity as a semi-philosophic or religious sect or phase which could be exhausted and then left behind for something higher. The writer insists that it is not one of the contemporary schools or cults. It is final. Beyond its revelation, nothing higher can be looked for, and the Christian must resist any specious attempt to detach him from a close and permanent relationship to the church. Compare Harnack's remark (*History of Dogma*, vol. i. p. 151, note 1) : 'If we remember how the Greeks and Romans were wont to get themselves initiated into a mystery cult, and took part for a long time in the religious exercises, and then, when they thought they had got the good of it, for the most part or wholly to give up attending it, we shall not wonder that the demand to become a permanent member of a Christian community was opposed by many'. This is elaborated in the same writer's *Mission und Ausbreitung des Christentums* (1st ed. pp. 312 f., Eng. tr. II. pp. 50 f.), and Hatch has some apposite remarks upon it in his *Organisation of the Early Christian Churches* (pp. 29, 30). The historical point of the saying is unmistakable. But modern civilisation offers instances of the same tendency to regard the worship and revelation of Jesus as a phase which requires to be supplemented. There are people to-day who, from the same motives of vainglory and untrained curiosity, imagine that they have exhausted Christianity, or that they can secure and appropriate for higher ends its spiritual content. The words of this verse reiterate, as the rest of the Epistle does, the finality of Jesus Christ for men, and the truth that no advance of humanity can afford to dispense with Him.

For God has other words for other worlds,
But for this world the Word of God is Christ . . .
Who is there that can say, ' My part is done
In this : now I am ready for a law
More wide, more perfect for the rest of life ? '

Forsake not, do not abandon, your tie with other Christians, the writer pleads. It is a strain, in view of the centrifugal tendencies of the world, to maintain Christian fellowship, but it is a healthy strain, for this effort keeps you in touch with all that is central and satisfying in religion. A movement whose motto is ' A greater than Christ' may be imposing and seductive, but it has no future in this world of God and of his Christ.—JAMES MOFFATT.

REFERENCES.—X. 29.—*Expositor* (5th Series), vol. ii. p. 174. X. 30.—*Ibid.* vol. ix. p. 421 ; *ibid.* (6th Series), vol. vi. p. 388. X. 31.—Spurgeon, *Sermons*, vol. xii. No. 682. T. Arnold, *The Interpretation of Scripture*, p. 253. C. F. Aked, *The Courage of the Coward*, p. 171.

'It is a fearful thing to fall into the hands of the living God.'
—HEB. X. 31.

HERE also are ejaculations caught up at intervals, undated, in those final days : 'Lord, Thou knowest, if I do desire to live, it is to show forth Thy praise, and declare Thy works '. Once he was heard saying, ' It is a fearful thing to fall into the hands of the Living God !' This was spoken three times, says Harvey ; 'his repetitions usually being very weighty, and with great vehemency of spirit '. Thrice over he said this ; looking into the Eternal Kingdoms : ' a fearful thing to fall into the hands of the Living God !'—CARLYLE's *Cromwell*, vol. III. last chapter.

IT is a fearful thing, said the Hebrew, to fall into the hands of the living God ; and it is a fearful thing for a malefactor to fall into the hands of an ever-living poet. The injured Cæsars of Rome—Tiberius, for example, and Domitian—have not even yet been delivered by the most conscientious efforts of German and Anglo-German Cæsarists out of the prison whose keys are kept by Juvenal.—SWINBURNE, in *A Study of V. Hugo*, p. 141.

REFERENCES.—X. 32.—*Expositor* (6th Series), vol. iv. p. 447 ; *ibid.* vol. xi. p. 433.

HEB. X. 34.

WRITING on the great Ejection of 1662, Dr. Stoughton says : ' It required much effort in the minds of Puritan clergymen to brace themselves up to meet what was at hand. One prepared for the crisis by preaching to his congregation four successive Sundays from words to the Hebrews : " Ye took joyfully the spoiling of your goods, knowing in yourselves that ye have in heaven a better and an enduring substance ". Another, who had a wife and ten children—" eleven strong arguments," as he said, for conformity—remarked that his family must live on the sixth of Matthew : " Take no thought for your life, what ye shall eat, or what ye shall drink ; nor yet for your body, what ye shall put on ". A third, when asked what he would do with his family, replied : " Should I have as many children as that hen has chickens," pointing to one with a numerous brood, " I should not question but God would provide for them all ".'

REFERENCES.—X. 34.—Newman Smyth, *Christian World Pulpit*, vol. xliii. p. 97. *Expositor* (6th Series), vol. vii. p. 49. A. Maclaren, *Expositions of Holy Scripture—Hebrews*, p. 92. X. 35.—Spurgeon, *Sermons*, vol. xxi. No. 1263.

'For ye have need of patience, that, having done the will of God, ye may receive the promise.'—HEB. x. 36.

THERE is a proverb that it is the first step which is the most difficult in the achievement of any object, and the proverb has been altered by ascribing the main part of the difficulty to the last step. Neither the first nor the last has been the difficult step with me, but rather what lies between. The first is usually helped by the excitement and the promise of new beginnings, and the last by the prospect of triumph; but the intermediate path is unassisted by enthusiasm, and it is here we are so likely to faint.—MARK RUTHERFORD, *The Deliverance* (ch. v.).

WHAT duty is made of a single difficult resolve? The difficulty lies in the daily unflinching support of consequences that mar the blessed return of morning with the prospect of irritation to be suppressed or shame to be endured.—GEORGE ELIOT, in *Daniel Deronda*.

REFERENCES.—X. 36.—C. Parsons Reichel, *Sermons*, p. 220. T. F. Crosse, *Sermons*, p. 168. X. 37.—J. Keble, *Miscellaneous Sermons*, p. 394. X. 38.—Spurgeon, *Sermons*, vol. xv. No. 891, and vol. xlviii. No. 2809. H. Alford, *Sermons on Christian Doctrine*, p. 281. *Expositor* (4th Series), vol. iii. p. 120. X. 39.—A. Maclaren, *Expositions of Holy Scripture—Hebrews*, p. 98.

CHRISTIAN FAITH

'Now faith is the substance of things hoped for, the evidence of things not seen.'—HEB. XI. I.

I. What is Faith ?— Clearly the writer of the Epistle to the Hebrews does not look upon faith as opposed to reason. Faith is with him the basis of all intelligent knowledge of things, the key to the rational system of the universe. The world which we see is temporary, changing, unreal; but behind the unreality of the phenomenal world is the reality of law. What enables us to learn this? Reason, intelligence. What enables us to believe it? Faith. What enables us to act on this belief? Faith. On the one side are the world of the senses and the life of the senses; on the other the world of the reason and the life of the reason; and faith is the ally of reason against sense. Faith is that quality in men which more than anything else lifts them above the attractions of what is sensuous, pleasant, easy, attractive, to what is lofty and noble, which makes them trust the highest discoveries of reason and intellect, and yield to the principles of an austere morality.

II. But what is it that Creates Faith ?—I would answer religion, especially for us Christianity. Faith is a strong moral and personal force, which is called into being above all by devotion to a person, and that is what Christianity gives.—A. C. HEADLAM, *Church Family Newspaper*, vol. XIII. p. 906.

THE BEGINNING OF FAITH

'Faith is the substance of things hoped for, the evidence of things not seen.'—HEB. XI. I.

AS we hear these words we seem to penetrate down through all the differences and distinctions of outward forms and ceremonies to that which lies at the very root and foundation of religion—the sense that beyond and behind the visible there is an invisible; that all that we see is but a reflection, a broken image of an unseen Divine ideal; that all around us and above us and within us there are mighty agencies ever working, regulating, creating, controlling not only our own little lives, but the entire universe of things from eternity until now, and from now until eternity.

I. This is the Beginning of Faith.—Without such a consciousness religion does not and cannot exist. Before man can take any step at all in religion he must feel convinced of the reality of the unseen world and of spiritual things. He must not only have a mere vague belief in their possibility, but he must learn to feel as sure of this as he is of his own existence. And when once this assurance becomes realised, then, but not before, is the foundation solid on which to rear the superstructure of that definite creed, the materials for which are provided in that revelation of Himself which it hath pleased the High and Holy One Who inhabiteth Eternity to make to us Himself in the pages of the Book which is known to us as the Bible or Holy Scripture.

II. It follows as a Corollary to this that it is because such faith is either altogether wanting or very imperfectly developed that the attitude of so many minds towards the Holy Scriptures as a Divine revelation, towards the creeds which are the Church's authoritative interpretation of the teaching of those Holy Scriptures, is one of critical suspicion and aloofness, more or less hostile and incredulous. Many even of those who have in a hazy and half-hearted way received the Gospels as a Divine revelation, and who would resent the imputation that they were not Christians, yet shrink from any positive definition of belief, and they are affrighted when called upon to make public avowal that the Catholic Faith is this—that we worship one God in Trinity and Trinity in Unity; neither confounding the Persons nor dividing the substance, accompanied by the declaration that the holding of this faith is necessary to sound spiritual health. Such a tenet, they say, is incapable of demonstrated proof.

III. The Main Cause of Difficulty Lies in the Misapprehension of that which you say you cannot comprehend. It would be much more strange if you could comprehend it. In the book of Proverbs there are many striking sayings, and in the present connection I will adapt one to my text and say, 'Take this short piece of advice, "Go to the ant, thou sluggard; consider her ways and be wise"'. We all know what marvellous little creatures ants are, and how in their diminutive way they reproduce many of the features characteristic of human life — different classes of society, regulated industry, mutual help. These creatures must have considerable intelligence and more reasoning power, and yet within their confined space, to which of necessity their experience extends, what can they comprehend of the vast globe, with its oceans and its continents, on which they dwell, still less of the Being whose dominion stretches over all its lands and seas, Who could at a single blow overthrow the place of their habitation and bury them in its ruins? And yet the distance between the ant and the man is as nothing compared with that between man and his Creator. We cannot go beyond or outside God's own revelation of Himself to man as it is gradually unfolded in Holy Scripture.

PROGRESS IN RELIGIOUS CONVICTION

'Now faith is the substance of things hoped for, the evidence of things not seen.'—HEB. XI. I.

ALL religious conviction proceeds from God and cannot proceed from man, because whatever there is in man that is good is put into him by God.

I. The First Stage—Repentance.—The first stage in the progress of spiritual conviction is repentance ; a man has to find out that he is in the wrong before he can be set right. The foundation of all spiritual conviction rests in a knowledge of one's sins, because we shall never desire new things until we have found out our inability to do good or to act rightly without the grace of God. We must know our true selves to bring about this change ; to reach this stage in spiritual conviction. We see that spiritual conviction is to find out our true selves, and, by the grace of the Spirit of God we change our minds and we see our selves to be miserable sinners undeserving of anything but death, for 'the wages of sin is death'.

II. The Second Stage—Faith.—We will take for granted that we have all changed our minds about ourselves now, and we will pass on to examine the most glorious passage in spiritual conviction, which I trust every member of this congregation will be able to lay to heart. ' Now faith is the substance of things hoped for, the evidence of things not seen.' Why is faith absolutely necessary? The reason is given to us in this very chapter : we are told that without faith it is impossible to please God. No words can be stronger. When St. Paul is imprisoned in the city of Philippi, and there is a terrible earthquake, and the doors of the prison are opened, the Philippian jailor, a man who had never troubled his head about religion, fears that his prisoners are lost to him, and knowing that he will be put to death if this proves to be the case, determines to make an end of himself. Just as he is in the act St. Paul sees him, and says, ' Do thyself no harm, for we are all here'. No doubt the man had never met with such speech as that, and conviction takes hold of him, and he realises that he himself is a sinner, and what would have happened if he had put an end to himself in his condition. So he turns to the Apostles and says, ' Sirs, what must I do to be saved?' And St. Paul makes answer, 'Believe on the Lord Jesus Christ and thou shalt be saved'. If the Apostle had said, ' You must do some good work ; you must do something that is pleasing to God,' we should not have connected with it faith, which is the one thing necessary. Is it not true that faith is the one thing? I know that we must do the work, and we must wrestle and fight and pray, but

there is one thing needful when we have been convicted of our sin, and that is faith in the blessed work of our Saviour.

III. The Third Stage—Assurance.—Let us take the words just as they stand ! ' Faith is the substance of things hoped for.' What is substance? There is a great deal of difference between a mere speculation and reality. Substance is reality. We say that, as we are met together in the name of the Lord Jesus, He is present with us. Perhaps some of you say that you hope He is present. I can go further than that ; I can say that He is here. He is here in the spirit and we are in the body, and so cannot see Him ; there is the necessity for faith.

'Now faith is the substance of things hoped for, the evidence of things not seen.'—HEB. XI. I.

To walk staunchly by the best light one has, to be strict and sincere with oneself, not to be of the number of those who say and do not, to be in earnest—this is the discipline by which alone man is enabled to rescue his life from thraldom to the passing moment and to his bodily senses, to ennoble it, and to make it eternal. And this discipline has been nowhere so effectively taught as in the school of Hebraism. The intense and convinced energy with which the Hebrew, both of the Old and of the New Testament, threw himself upon his ideal of righteousness, and which inspired the incomparable definition of the great Christian virtue, faith—*the substance of things hoped for, the evidence of things not seen*—this energy of devotion to its ideal has belonged to Hebraism alone. —MATTHEW ARNOLD, preface to *Culture and Anarchy*.

' HE had faith in God,' says Dr. John Brown, in *Horæ Subsecivæ*, of Dr. Chalmers ; 'faith in human nature—faith, if we may say so, in his own instincts —in his ideas of men and things—*in himself;* and the result was, that unhesitating bearing up and steering right onward—" never bating one jot of heart or hope " so characteristic of him. He had " the substance of things hoped for ". He had " the evidence of things not seen ".'

CONTRAST Mr. R. H. Hutton's verdict upon George Eliot (*Modern Guides of English Thought in Matters of Faith*, p. 278): 'There were some of her characteristics which were in the deepest sense Christian ; but by this powerlessness to believe that of which she had no immediate evidence before her, whether in things human or Divine, George Eliot was exceptionally distinguished. The " substance of things hoped for " was to her no substance at all ; she had no buoyancy in her nature. " The evidence of things unseen " was a shadow—as to the various possible causes of which she could speculate at large with little confidence and no satisfactory result.'

THE true martyrs and all the saints, who by their holy practice under great trials declare that faith which is *the substance of things hoped for, and the evidence of things not seen*, can speak in the style of witnesses ; need not only say that they think the

Gospel is Divine, but say that it is Divine, giving it as their testimony because they have seen it to be so. . . . There is no true or saving faith, or spiritual conviction of the judgment of the truth of God, that has nothing in it of this manifestation of its internal evidence in some degree. The Gospel of the blessed God does not go abroad a-begging for evidence, so much as some think; it has its highest and most proper evidence in itself.—JONATHAN EDWARDS, *The Religious Affections* (pt. iii. ch. v.).

REFERENCES.—XI. 1.—J. T. O'Brien, *The Nature and the Effects of Faith*, p. 27. Archbishop Temple, *Christian World Pulpit*, vol. liii. p. 56. T. Arnold, *Sermons*, vol. ii. p. 1. J. Laidlaw, *Christian World Pulpit*, vol. xlix. p. 102. J. Cumming, *Penny Pulpit*, No. 1608, p. 263. E. J. Hardy, *Christian World Pulpit*, vol. lvi. p. 123. *Expositor* (5th Series), vol. i. p. 153; *ibid.* vol. vii. p. 392.

'By it the elders obtained a good report.'—HEB. XI. 2.

GOOD men are the stars, the planets of the age wherein they live, and illustrate the times. God did never let them be wanting to the world: as Abel, for an example of innocency, Enoch of purity, Noah of trust in God's mercies, Abraham of faith, and so of the rest. These, sensual men thought mad because they would not be partakers or practisers of their madness. But they, placed high on the top of all virtue, looked down on the stage of the world, and contemned the play of fortune.—BEN JONSON, *Discoveries* (LXXXVI.).

REFERENCE.—XI. 2.—J. Cumming, *Penny Pulpit*, No. 1633, p. 109.

'By faith we understand that the worlds were framed by the word of God, so that things which are seen were not made of things which do appear.'—HEB. XI. 3.

WE prescribe Him limits, we lay continuall siege unto His power by our reasons. We will subject Him to the vaine and weake appearances of our understanding: Him Who hath made both us and our knowledge. Because nothing is made out of nothing: God was not able to frame the world without matter. What? hath God delivered into our hands the keyes, and the strongest wards of His infinit puissance? Hath He obliged Himselfe not to exceede the bounds of our knowledge? Suppose, oh man, that herein thou hast been able to marke some signes of His effects. Thinkest thou He hath therein employed all He was able to doe, and that He hath placed all His power and ideas in this peece of worke? Thou seest but the order and policie of this little cell wherein thou art placed. The question is, whether thou seest it. His divinitie hath an infinit jurisdiction far beyond that. This peece is nothing in respect of the whole. —MONTAIGNE (*Florio*) II. 12.

REFERENCES.—XI. 3.—C. J. Graham, *Christian World Pulpit*, vol. lix. p. 147. J. Cumming, *Penny Pulpit*, No. 1659, p. 311. *Expositor* (4th Series), vol. ii. p. 250; *ibid.* vol. ix. p. 79; *ibid.* (5th Series), vol. iv. p. 156. XI. 3, 4.— W. J. Knox Little, *Christian World Pulpit*, vol. xlix. p. 212.

THE FAITH OF ABEL
'By faith Abel——.'—HEB. XI. 4.

THE author of the Epistle to the Hebrews begins the series of examples, by which he illustrates his conception of faith, with the case of Abel. There are various difficulties raised by the passage into which I need not enter, since I have discussed them elsewhere. Nor do I deal with the problems which the narrative of Genesis presents, since I am concerned not so much with it as with the view taken of it by the author. It is not clear in what he considered the superiority of Abel's sacrifice to lie, but probably it was for him less a question of quantity than of quality. In other words, while his language might well be interpreted to mean that Abel presented a more lavish sacrifice than the niggardly offering of Cain, it is perhaps rather more likely that he laid the stress on the fact that it was an animal and not a vegetable offering. The sacrificial efficacy of blood is prominent in his thought, and it is quite natural that the distinction in the material of the offerings should seem to give the clue to the acceptance of one and the rejection of the other.

While the death of the animal and the manipulation of its blood could not liberate man's conscience from the burden of his guilt or restore to him communion with God, it brought home to him the fact of guilt and the problem of reconciliation. It thus prepared the way for the supreme sacrifice of Christ by which the problem received its adequate and final solution. And its very inadequacy was itself an unconscious prophecy, for the tormenting sense of alienation from God which it expressed was itself a prediction that God would ultimately deal with the question in a radical way. The constant reminder which men received of their sins and their helplessness in dealing with them deepened the sense of sin and quickened the longing for an adequate redemption. It would not therefore be contrary to the general drift of the writer's argument to consider that he detected in Abel's selection of an animal victim the outcome of his faith.

I. This faith did not go without Divine recognition. The word of God bore witness to him. We read, 'And the Lord had respect unto Abel and to his offering'. The writer apparently understood this to mean that Abel's sacrifice secured the approval of God because it exhibited the quality of faith. This is suggested by what he says in connection with the next example, that without faith it is impossible to be pleasing unto Him. The problems which this raises were, perhaps, not before the writer's mind, though they can hardly fail to strike ourselves. At present, however, it is our task to look at things from his point of view. That witness was borne to those who had faith is a thought which has been already expressed in the words, 'By it the elders received a good report,' and much the same is said with reference to Enoch.

II. The author proceeds to tell us that through the faith he thus manifested he still speaks to us. In order to understand this we must bear in mind the writer's doctrine of Scripture. Scripture is for him the living and active word of God, so that its utterances belong not simply to the past but to the present.

And therefore, although from the point of view of the historian the speech of Abel might seem to belong to the past, to the author it belongs to the present in virtue of its record on the page of Scripture. The voice of Abel is the voice of his blood which called to God from the ground. It is a thought for which we have many parallels that blood spilt upon the earth cries for vengeance. We find it in Job's passionate appeal to the earth not to cover his blood and thus stifle his cry, and in Ezekiel's reference to the blood of Jerusalem which had been set on the bare rock by God that it should not be covered and thus go unredressed.

III. To ourselves no doubt the words of the author convey more naturally the impression that even though he is dead, Abel still speaks to us by his example. And though this does not quite hit his meaning, the thought itself is one which ought not to be forgotten. Shakespeare put into the mouth of the sophistical Antony the words :—

> The evil that men do lives after them,
> The good is oft interred with their bones.

H ppily that is not the case. While it is true that evil things and evil memory are a baleful legacy left by the wicked, yet it is also true that the memory of the just is an inspiration and their deeds are still potent for good after they have been taken from us. And thus the memory of those who, in the dim twilight of revelation, were faithful to the light they received and prepared for the coming of the dawn, has still its message for us whose lot is cast in a happier time and on whom the ends of the ages have come.— A. S. Peake, *The Heroes and Martyrs of Faith*, p. 30.

'He, being dead, yet speaketh.'—Heb. xi. 4.

Men cannot benefit those who are with them as they can benefit those who come after them; and of all the pulpits from which human voice is ever sent forth, there is none from which it reaches so far as from the grave.—Ruskin, *Seven Lamps of Architecture* (vi.).

References.—XI. 4.—J. Cumming, *Penny Pulpit*, No. 1681, p. 487. D. Young, *Christian World Pulpit*, vol. lvi. p. 350, and vol. liv. p. 54.

THE ESCAPE FROM DEATH

'By faith Enoch was translated,' etc.—Heb. xi. 5.

I. Although the author gives us no explicit help in solving the problem why the treatment of Enoch was so exceptional, we can perhaps detect to some extent the link that was in his mind between the faith of Enoch and his translation. Faith, I have said, is a conviction of the unseen realities. In the next place, it is a stronger power than hope, since it makes the future present. Even before the veil is removed, it, so to speak, abrogates it. It carries us in spirit within the veil, and makes us even now participate in the joys of the world to come. Then as the wings of faith grow more feeble, our strong flight draws to its close, and we find ourselves back again on the earthward side of the veil.

Perhaps, however, it might be possible, the writer may have thought, for that faith which gives us this transient experience of heaven to secure a permanent triumph. Thus a man whose faith was of unusual intensity might escape to the unseen realm without passing through death, and find in it his abiding home. The thought may seem fanciful, but it may be along these lines that we ought to look for our solution. The statement that he walked with God helps us rather more. It testifies to the close, unbroken intercourse between God and His servant which death could not destroy. The thought that faith conquers death comes out elsewhere in the chapter. Yet we are told of others, to whom this exceptional privilege was not vouchsafed, that they walked with God. I have accordingly no complete explanation to offer of the unique experience through which Enoch is said to have passed.

II. It was not unnatural that the words 'Enoch walked with God' should have led to the belief that God took him into His confidence, and revealed to him many mysteries. These mysteries, which touched the constitution of the universe, the fate of the wicked, the world's future history, were enshrined in an elaborate literature which began to grow up about him in the second century before our era. Quotation is made from it in Jude, but not elsewhere in the New Testament. It is possible that the original text of 1 Peter contained a reference to an experience of the patriarch. Some scholars have suggested that the preaching to the spirits in prison was really a preaching by Enoch to the angels imprisoned on account of the transgression recorded in the sixth of Genesis, and Dr. Rendel Harris has recently championed this view with great vigour.

The correction of the text involved is quite easy, and its acceptance would remove a really serious difficulty. My main reason for hesitating to accept it is that in the following chapter we have the statement that the Gospel was preached to the dead. I find it hard to believe that the two passages refer to entirely different events. But it is obvious that the latter has no reference to Enoch's preaching to the imprisoned angels, for this was a preaching of condemnation, and they could not be described as 'the dead'. Accordingly I think we must allow the passage in Jude to stand by itself in the New Testament. At the same time it is hardly likely that the author of the Epistle to the Hebrews can have been ignorant of this literature. Dr. Charles, in fact, thinks that our passage must depend in some way upon the book of Enoch, though this view does not rest on very strong grounds. But whether this be so or not, it is, at any rate, noteworthy that the author makes no allusion to Enoch's initiation into the secrets of God. He lays the stress on conduct rather than on knowledge. His silence reminds us that in our study of Scripture we should direct our attention not only to what it says but to what it does not say.

III. When we consider the story of Enoch's escape

from death and try to draw a practical lesson from it for ourselves, we must remember how different our attitude towards death is from that current among the Hebrews. The view which dominated their attitude throughout almost the whole of the Old Testament was of a very gloomy character. For them death was no mere incident, still less a granting of fuller light and more intimate fellowship with God. The dark and hopeless night closed in even after the happiest and the longest day and put a period to man's communion with God. The later Old Testament writings disclose to us the gradual lifting of the shadow and relief from the horror coming along various lines. The deepest thought which the saints of the Old Covenant achieved grew directly out of their religious experience. Their immediate sense of the love and the grace of God was so strong that their faith rose to the great conviction that this love was stronger than death.

Thus they could have anticipated Paul's ringing declaration that not death itself can separate us from the love of God. But Paul could add 'in Christ Jesus our Lord,' and thus give the weakest Christian a confidence which may have been a comparatively rare experience among the saints of the Old Covenant In creating this loftier Jewish doctrine I think that the story of Enoch had its part to play. In the forty-ninth Psalm the words 'For He will take me' are, I believe, a direct allusion to the words 'God took him' in Genesis.—A. S. PEAKE, *The Heroes and Martyrs of Faith*, p. 38.

REFERENCES.—XI. 5.—J. Bannerman, *Sermons*, p. 1. *Penny Pulpit*, No. 1687, p. 533. XI. 5, 6.—Spurgeon, *Sermons*, vol. xxii. No. 1307.

'Without faith it is impossible to please Him.'—HEB. xi. 6.

'FAITH,' says Lacordaire in one of his Paris Conferences, 'is not only a virtue—that is to say, a generous and efficacious effort towards what is good—it is the sacred portico through which all the virtues pass. There is no act of devotedness, no act of love, no honourable or holy action which was not at first an act of faith. . . . Therefore when St. Paul pronounced that sovereign sentence, "without faith it is impossible to please God," we may add—and men.'

REFERENCES.—XI. 6.—R. J. Campbell, *City Temple Sermons*, p. 1. J. Laidlaw, *Christian World Pulpit*, vol. xlix. p. 214. S. Cox, *Expositions*, p. 226. Spurgeon, *Sermons*, vol. iii. No. 107 ; vol. xxxv. No. 2100 ; vol. xliii. No. 2513, and vol. xlvii. No. 2740. J. Keble, *Sermons for Septuagesima to Ash Wednesday*, p. 75. S. Baring-Gould, *Village Preaching for a Year* (2nd Series), vol. ii. p. 33. J. Cumming, *Penny Pulpit*, No. 1690, p. 559. J. Stalker, *Christian World Pulpit*, vol. liv. p. 188. *Expositor* (5th Series), vol. i. p. 429. A. Maclaren, *Expositions of Holy Scripture—Hebrews*, p. 106.

HE CONDEMNED THE WORLD

'By faith Noah,' etc.—HEB. xi. 7.

NOAH had to maintain his faith in face of an unbelieving world. He alone among his contemporaries was pronounced righteous by God. The narrative gives us no hint of active opposition. It is often a

stimulant to a man's faith when he has to suffer persecution and hostility. He is thrown on his defence, his combative instincts are aroused. It may not always be easy to face a frowning world, but it is certainly much harder to face a scoffing world.

I. When we consider the lapse of time, the constant wear to which his faith was exposed from trivial incident and unheroic commonplace, the strain placed upon it from the prolonged and prosaic character of his task, the keen shafts of ridicule, and the wet blankets of indifference, we may rate highly the patience of his faith. The things of which he was warned were not seen as yet when the warning was given, but they still remained unseen through all the slow process of construction until the whole was complete. And still no sign was made as, amid the blank unconcern or the unrestrained hilarity of his doomed contemporaries, he entered into the ark. Then, when he was safe, the windows of heaven were opened, that the waters from the heavenly ocean above the firmament might pour through, and the fountains of the great submarine abyss might be broken up. Thus the waters which had been separated at Creation were mingled once more, and Chaos for a brief period resumed her ancient sway.

II. The writer tells us that thus Noah condemned the world. He does not mean that by constructing a shelter simply for himself and his family he doomed the rest of mankind to destruction. His thought is rather that the faith of Noah stood out in glaring contrast to the world's unbelief. Just as Lot seemed to those who were to marry his daughters as a mere jester when he told them that God would destroy Sodom, so Noah must have seemed to those who heard his prophecies of disaster. They could not believe his prediction of judgment, they met it all with incurable optimism. And so in our Lord's words, 'They ate, they drank, they married, they were given in marriage until the day that Noah entered into the ark, and the flood came, and destroyed them all'. And how often history repeats itself, how many there are whose blind infatuation has carried them gaily forward to the very brink of ruin, and cast them down to destruction in a moment!

III. Noah condemned the world by the spectacle of his unshrinking faith, but he made no impression upon it. And it is this quality in the world which makes the effort to reform some people seem so hopeless. I always feel that we have least hope of success with those whom we cannot get to take life seriously. Those who are set in their antagonism to goodness, who throw themselves into active opposition, are less to be despaired of. For with them there is a certain earnestness and seriousness, a concentration of purpose, though directed to wrong ends. In short, they have character, though it be bad character. And there are numerous examples to show what valiant and loyal soldiers of righteousness they may prove if they can once be brought into captivity to the obedience of Christ. But what are we to do with the flippant and the frivolous, in whose nature there is no depth, no reserve to which one can appeal? What can be done with the shallow, irresponsible people to whom the gravest moral and spiritual issues are less than an idle tale? There are many Sunday school teachers who would gladly prefer the bad boy, as he is called, to the frivolous boy, and too often the frivolous boy becomes a frivolous man.

It is now many years since I read a passage in Demosthenes which made a permanent impression on me. The great orator, looking back over the time when the power of Philip was steadily growing, says that the Greek States realised that trouble was coming, only, he adds, 'not upon themselves'. In other words, they could read the signs of the times with sufficient clearness to perceive that the power of Macedonia threatened the independence of the other Greek communities, but they could never bring themselves to believe that they would be the victims of the same disaster. Such is the unwillingness of human nature to face the stern realities of life, such men's incredulity that the disaster they see to be inevitable for others will overtake themselves.

By our noble seriousness we may condemn the world's frivolity. By our steadfast conviction of the unseen we may reprove its crass incredulity, and become heirs ' of the righteousness which is according to faith'.

'By faith Noah, being warned of God concerning things not seen as yet, moved with godly fear, prepared an ark to the saving of his house.'—HEB. XI. 7.

BELIEF in principles is the only intelligible interpretation I have ever been able to attach to the word faith. A man with faith in principles, even if they be not first-rate, is sure to succeed. The man who has no faith in them is sure to fail. Nothing finer, after all, can be said of faith than that which is said in the Epistle to the Hebrews, and no finer example can be given of it than that of Noah there given. Noah was warned of God that destruction would visit the impious race by which he was surrounded. He quietly set to work to build his ark. There is no record that it was built by miracle, and he must have been a long time about it. . . . Would it come true? Would he have to walk out again down those planks with the clean beasts and unclean beasts after him, amidst the inextinguishable laughter of all his pagan, God-denying neighbours? But in a week he heard the first growl of the tempest. He was justified, God was justified; and for evermore Noah stands on a Divine type of what we call faith. This is really it. What we have once *heard*, really heard in our best moments, by that let us abide. There are multitudes of moments in which intelligent conviction in the truth of principles disappears, and we are able to do nothing more than fall back on mere dogged determinate resolution to go on; not to give up what we have once found to be true.'—MARK RUTHERFORD in *The Deliverance*, pp. 162, 163.

REFERENCES.—XI. 7.—H. P. Liddon, *Sermons Preached on Special Occasions*, p. 243. Spurgeon, *Sermons*, vol. xxxvi. No. 2147. *Expositor* (6th Series), vol. vi. p. 319. A. Maclaren, *Expositions of Holy Scripture—Hebrews*, p. 112. XI. 8.—J. G.

Rogers, *Christian World Pulpit*, vol. xliii. p. 139. T. F. Crosse, *Sermons*, p. 213. W. H. Hutchings, *Sermon-Sketches*, p. 313. Spurgeon, *Sermons*, vol. xxi. No. 1242; vol. v. No. 261; vol. xxxvii. No. 2195. F. W. Aveling, *Christian World Pulpit*, vol. xlv. p. 21. A. S. Peake, *The Heroes and Martyrs of Faith*, p. 57.

THE TENT AND THE CITY

'By faith he [Abraham] sojourned in the land of promise, as in a strange country, dwelling in tents with Isaac and Jacob, the heirs with him of the same promise: for he looked for a city which hath foundations.'—HEB. XI. 9, 10.

THE faith which we profess should dominate us as Abraham was dominated. That man is not to be reckoned a religious man whose religion is shown in a few shining hours. Like the glow of health which spreads through a man's whole being, it must show itself in every deed and every day. The temple may manifest it, but so must the tent. Abraham, then, was a dweller in a tent; that fact had made a deep impression on the writer; and immediately he tells us the secret of that tent-life—he looked for a city whose builder and maker is God.

I. It is the tent which makes the city precious. We see at a glance that it was so with Abraham. It was the very insecurity of that tent-life, the isolation of it and its thousand perils, that made the dream of a city so infinitely sweet. After all the important thing is not what we live in; the supremely important thing is what we look for. If life is to be redeemed from sense and time, and brought under the powers that are eternal, the eyes must be opened somehow to God's city. How shall I open them? says the Almighty. How shall I make the unseen city precious? The answer to that lies in the tent of Abraham—so insecure, so perilous and so frail. From which I learn that much of life's harder discipline, and many a dark hour that men are called to, is given to humanity, by Abraham's God, that hearts may begin to hunger for the city. (1) For example think of sickness in that light. Is *it* not often the tent that makes the city precious? (2) In the same light also we may look on death. (3) Nor can I leave this subject without pointing out how it bears evangelically upon the fact of sin. Many a man is brought to see his need of Christ by the same experience as was vouchsafed to Abraham.

II. It is the city which explains the tent. You will never understand that tent, never know why Abraham chose it, until you are told the secret of his heart. It is his vision which interprets his conduct. You will never know a man until you know the hopes which animate him. It is because we are ignorant of the secret of our brother, and of all that is stirring and calling in his heart, that so often we judge him very falsely. It makes all the difference in the world what you and I are looking for. It is by what our hearts are set on and by what our thoughts are given to that the tent we dwell in is glorified or cursed.— G. H. MORRISON, *The Unlighted Lustre*, p. 122.

REFERENCES.—XI. 9, 10,—Spurgeon, *Sermons*, vol. xxxix. No. 2229. A. Maclaren, *Expositions of Holy Scripture—Hebrews*, p. 120.

'He looked for a city which hath foundations.'—HEB. XI. 10.

I AM a wanderer : I remember well
One journey, how I feared the track was missed,
So long the city I desired to reach
Lay hid ; when suddenly its spires afar
Flashed through the circling clouds ; you may conceive
My transport. Soon the vapours closed again,
But I had seen the city, and one such glance
No darkness could obscure : nor shall the present—
A few dull hours, a passing shame or two,
Destroy the vivid memories of the past.
　　　　　　　　　—BROWNING, *Paracelsus*.

'BY what methods,' asks Carlyle in his essay on Boswell's Johnson, ' by what gifts of eye and hand, does a heroic Samuel Johnson, now when cast forth into waste Chaos of Authorship, maddest of things, a mingled Phlegethon and Fleet-ditch, with its floating lumber, and sea-krakens, and mud-spectres—shape himself a voyage ; of the *transient* driftwood, and the *enduring* iron, build himself a sea-worthy Life-boat, and sail therein, undrowned, unpolluted, through the roaring "mother of dead dogs," onwards to an eternal Landmark and City that hath foundation ? This high question is ever the one answered in Boswell's Book . . . Glory to our brave Samuel ! He accomplished this wonderful problem ; and now through long generations, we point to him and say : Here also was a Man ; let the world once more have assurance of a Man ! '

THE vision of the prophets differed from the vision even of the greatest of the philosophers in the ever increasing clearness with which its reality was apprehended. The spirit of hope, so distinctive of the Jewish people, the invincible optimism which survived every disappointment, sustained them to the last. They laid hold of the future as their own possession with a confidence unapproached by any other nation, unless we may find a distant parallel in the exhilaration of tone with which the Roman poets forecast the imperial greatness of Rome. To the Greeks the future is dim and inscrutable. The future is the secret belonging to the gods, and it were presumptuous for man to seek to penetrate it. His duty is to seize the present with its limitless possibilities, and to use it with that rational energy and forethought which are born of an enlightened experience. It is a temper of mind wholly unlike that of the Jew, the loss of whose earthly country seemed to point him forward with a more victorious certitude to *the city which hath foundations*, to the heavenly Jerusalem.— PROF. BUTCHER in his *Harvard Lectures on Greek Subjects*, pp. 40, 41.

REFERENCES.—XI. 10.—J. A. Alexander, *The Gospel of Jesus Christ*, p. 458. XI. 12.—*Expositor* (5th Series), vol. iii. p. 271.

'These all died in faith.'—HEB. XI. 13.

'AND thus closes,' says Sir James Stephen, in his essay on the Clapham Sect, ' though it be far from exhausted, our chronicle of the worthies of Clapham, of whom it may be said, as it was said of those of whom

the world was not worthy, " these all died in faith ". With but very few exceptions, they had all partaken largely of those sorrows which probe the inmost heart, and exercise its fortitude to the utmost. . . . They died in the faith that for their descendants, at no remote period, was reserved an epoch glorious, though probably awful, beyond all former example. It was a belief derived from the intimations, as they understood them, of the prophet of Israel.'

ALL true good is Christian by its goal and by its origin, though neither may be seen by the doer, Christ, ' whom He hath appointed heir of all things ' (the goal), ' by whom also He made the worlds ' (the origin). The development of the race corresponds to this. There was a world travelling to Christ, of which it is said, 'These all died in faith '. They were judged by their direction.—DR. JOHN KER, *Thoughts for Heart and Life*, p. 107.

' These all died in faith, not having received the promises, but having seen them afar off, and were persuaded of them, and embraced them, and confessed that they were strangers and pilgrims on the earth.'—HEB. XI. 13.

SPEAKING, in the fourth chapter of his volume *On Compromise*, of these 'who attempt, in however informal a manner, to construct for themselves some working system of faith, in place of the faith which science and criticism have sapped,' Mr. Morley adds : ' In what ultimate form, acceptable to great multitudes of men, these attempts will at last issue, no one can now tell. For we, like the Hebrews of old, shall all have to live and die in faith, ' not having received the promises, but having seen them afar off, and being persuaded of them, and embracing them, and confessing that we are strangers and pilgrims on the earth '.

REFERENCES.—XI. 13.—T. Arnold, *Christian Life ; Its Hopes*, p. 231. T. Stephens, *Sermons by Welshmen*, p. 340. R. W. Church, *Village Sermons*, p. 268. *Expositor* (5th Series), vol. i. p. 143. A. Maclaren, *Expositions of Holy Scripture—Hebrews*, p. 129. XI. 13, 14.—Spurgeon, *Sermons*, vol. xxxi. No. 1825. XI. 13-16.—Archbishop Maclagan, *Christian World Pulpit*, vol. lviii. p. 337. J. J. Blunt, *Plain Sermons* (2nd Series), p. 216. XI. 14.—H. M. Butler, *Harrow School Sermons* (2nd Series), p. 282. A. Maclaren, *Expositions of Holy Scripture—Hebrews*, p. 138.

' Truly, if they had been mindful of that country from whence they came out, they might have had opportunity to have returned.—HEB. XI. 15.

IN DEFOE's *Seasonable Warning and Caution*, he expostulates thus with Britain on her tendency to relapse into Popery. ' Let us reason a little together on these Things, and let us inquire a little, why, and for what Reason, Britain so lately the glory of Europe ; so lately the Terror of France, the Bulwark of Religion, and the Destroyer of Popery, should be brought to be the Gazing-Stock of the World ? And why is it that her Neighbours expect to hear every hour that She is going back to Egypt, and having given up her Liberty, has made it her own Choice to submit to the Stripes of her Taskmasters, and make Bricks without Straw.'

REFERENCE.—XI. 15, 16.—Spurgeon, *Sermons*, vol. xviii. No. 1030.

'But now they desire a better country, that is, an heavenly.'—
HEB. XI. 16.

AFTER preaching (at Alnwick) I rode on to Newcastle. Certainly, if I did not believe there was another world, I should spend all my summers here; as I know no place in Great Britain comparable to it for pleasantness. But I seek another country, and therefore am content to be a wanderer upon the earth.— WESLEY'S *Journal* (4th June, 1759).

REFERENCES.—XI. 16.—J. J. Cox, *A Lent in London*, p. 93. J. J. Blunt, *Plain Sermons* (3rd Series), p. 26. Spurgeon, *Sermons*, vol. xlv. No. 2633. A. Maclaren, *Expositions of Holy Scripture—Hebrews*, p. 147.

'By faith Abraham, when he was tried, offered up Isaac.'—
HEB. XI. 17.

'THE faith of Abraham,' says Mr. Gladstone, 'with respect to this supreme trial, appears to have been centred in the one point, that he would trust God to all extremities, and in despite of all appearances. . . . He who had probably learned through the tradition of Enoch that God had modes of removal for his children other than death, may well have believed that some such method would at the critical moment be devised for Isaac; and what is commended in him by the Bible is not the intention to slay his own son with his own hand, but the ready assent to the privation he was to undergo in the frustration of the promise that the Messianic line should descend from him.'

DEATH-BED FAITH
HEB. XI. 20, 22.

THERE is a peculiar eminence attaching to a death-bed faith, to the faith which triumphs over the weakness of nature; and, while the vital forces are dying down to a glimmering spark, itself burns with a clear and steady flame. It is faith maintained under supreme difficulty. And whereas a death-bed repentance implies a previous life of sin, the kind of death-bed faith to which I am referring implies that faith has been the rule of life. It must have strong roots in a man's past to face unbroken the final storm. Hence, when the author singles out in the case of Isaac, Jacob, and Joseph the closing scene, he is tacitly saying to us that here we have a life of faith on which death placed a fitting crown. Indeed, he has already told us as much about two of them when he said that Abraham dwelt in tents, with Isaac and Jacob heirs with him of the same promise. Their faith in God's fulfilment of His promise had been manifested in this that, like Abraham, they clung to the nomad's mode of life, refusing to seek on earth a fixed abode. And in the case of Isaac, Jacob, and Joseph it is specially with the promise that the author is concerned.

I. Of the first we read, 'By faith Isaac blessed Jacob and Esau, even concerning things to come'. At first sight the statement is very puzzling, for the story in Genesis tells us that Isaac blessed Jacob in mistake for Esau. The whole story jars upon us as we read it. First of all, there is the favouritism betrayed by the parents towards their children. In the case of Isaac this quality, always reprehensible, seems to become even contemptible because of the reason which is given for it. Esau was a hunter, who gratified his father's selfish love for savoury food, and on this squalid basis his preference for Esau reposed. But Jacob turned away from the adventurous life which charmed his brother, and led a quieter, tamer life. In the author's significant words, 'He sod pottage'. He was what we should call a domesticated man; he dwelt in tents, we are further informed, and we can read between the lines that he had won his mother's heart, and become her favourite by stopping at home and helping her in the house-work.

We need have no hesitation in recognising that the faith of Isaac was at least displayed in this, that he held fast to the confidence that God's promise would be fulfilled. The fact that he made a mistake as to the Divine designation is not of such moment. It is true that we may put down his mistake to a lack of insight, yet his lack of insight is of an intellectual rather than of a spiritual kind. And there was much to suggest that Jacob could not be the heir to the promise. Yet it is true that he blessed Jacob by faith; for, when he was undeceived and learnt how he had been duped, he did not call back his blessing and substitute a curse. Indeed, the whole attitude of antiquity towards the curse and the blessing would have been against his doing so. Men of the ancient world thought of the curse and the blessing as passing beyond a man's control once he had uttered them. And Isaac also felt that, once the blessing had been pronounced, he could not recall it: it would surely work out its own accomplishment. 'I have blessed him, yea, and he shall be blessed.' We may indeed suppose that, in the exalted utterance with which he had blessed his son, he saw the evidence of an inspiration higher than his own. At any rate, he had the faith to recognise that Jacob, and not Esau, was the chosen of God. Yet he also blessed Esau. At first he shook under the shock of his discovery and saw, with cruel lucidity, all the pathos and tragedy of Esau's rejection. He could see no alleviation. And even the words of his blessing sound, at first, more like a curse. Far away from the fatness of the earth and the dew of heaven Esau's dwelling is to be, his living must be won by the sword, and he shall be in bondage to his brother. But the blessing comes at the end. He is at last to break loose and shake his brother's yoke from his neck.

II. From the case of Isaac the author passes to that of Jacob, and in this instance also he speaks only of the last scenes. If it is not paradoxical to say so, there are two things which seem surprising. One is that, Jacob being what he was, the author should have included him at all; the other that, having selected him for inclusion, he should say no more about him.

The story of Jacob leaves upon the modern reader, at any rate, a singularly unpleasant impression. In some ways he is one of the most repulsive characters in Biblical history.

Yet it would be a mistake were we to turn from

Jacob with loathing, and give him no credit for loftier qualities. The fact remains that Jacob, and not the more attractive Esau, was chosen to be the heir of the promise, and the reason for this we should seek to understand. And this leads me to the second point which I have described as surprising. When the author had once decided to include Jacob, we are astonished that he made so little of him. For while Jacob stands very low in the moral, he stands high in the religious scale, and peculiarly in the very quality which the author commends to our notice. With Isaac, the blessing, according to the view of antiquity, has something magical about it—it brings about what it predicts. But in Jacob's blessing a higher note is struck. The crossing of his hands is not caprice or favouritism, it is a reverent recognition of the Divine choice, in harmony with which he acts. Thus, at the close of a life which he describes as a pilgrimage, whose days have been few and evil, in Canaan a wanderer, for long years a sojourner in the East, and now a dweller in Egypt, he yet holds fast to his belief in the promise. Not only does he see for his descendants a return to Canaan, but a lofty destiny for the tribes of Ephraim and Manasseh.

III. It is the same interest which leads the author to select the closing scene in the life of Joseph. He too joined with his father in the belief that God would bring them out of Egypt, and, as the author tells us, he gave commandment concerning his bones. In that hour of triumph when they escaped from Egypt, he desired, so far as that could be, himself to participate. To our point of view, for which all lands are alike sacred, Joseph's desire appeals much less. For us, too, the physical tabernacle which we shed at death is not of such significance as it was in Egypt; perhaps in his request we may detect the influence of the Egyptian environment. There is one point of interest which may be touched on in closing. Jacob wishes to be buried in Canaan by his sons; Joseph, however, desires that his body may abide with his people till the Divine summons to leave Egypt should come to them. Perhaps nothing more is implied by this than that Jacob had ties with Canaan much closer than those of Joseph.—A. S. PEAKE, *The Heroes and Martyrs of Faith*, p. 82.

REFERENCES.—XI. 21.—J. Bannerman, *Sermons*, p. 41. Spurgeon, *ibid.* vol. xxiv. No. 1401. XI. 22.—*Ibid.* vol. xvi. No. 966. A. S. Peake, *The Heroes and Martyrs of Faith*, p. 99. XI. 23.—Spurgeon, *Sermons*, vol. xxiv. No. 1421.

THE CHOICE OF MOSES

'By faith Moses, when he was come to years, refused to be called the son of Pharaoh's daughter; choosing rather to suffer affliction with the people of God, than to enjoy the pleasures of sin for a season; esteeming the reproach of Christ greater riches than the treasures of Egypt: for he had respect unto the recompense of the reward.'—HEB. XI. 24-26.

IT is noticeable that the Old Testament heroes mentioned in this chapter are exhibited to us, not in the general tenor of their lives, but each at a single turning-point. The light is flashed always upon one moment in the story.

Here, then, one moment in the life of Moses, like the rest, is lifted into the light. We are made to see the crisis at which he decisively flung himself on God's side, so fixing the destinies of life.

I. Note first *the choice asked of Moses*. It was a choice rather to suffer affliction with the people of God than to enjoy the pleasures of sin for a season. To put it otherwise, his act was not the outcome of mere impassioned heat; it had a moral meaning; it was based on resolute and grave determination. The blow that struck down the petty tyrant may have fired the mine unexpectedly; nevertheless what the two parties before him stood for was clear enough. On the one side the people of God, unresisting, craven, trodden under foot, but with a destiny stretching out illimitably in the future; on the other side, sin, with its fleeting pleasures, in the court and life of Egypt. This was the parting of the ways for ever; and we have to think of him weighing the issue, reckoning the price—'this accomplished courtier, this child of luxury and pride, this man of letters and of mighty deeds'.

In the essentials of the matter it might have happened yesterday; perhaps it did happen yesterday, to you or me. Human nature changes little with the ages, and moral issues never vary. The distinctions of right and wrong, faced by these old fathers of grey time, are like the stars or the mountains to which they lifted up their eyes, and on which men look still and find them eternal and unchanging. Then or now, he who would buy everlasting life must pay for it with sacrifice. The gate that leads to life is narrow; which signifies at least this, that many things must be left outside that we would fain carry through. To a few the sacrifice is easy; by some happy gift of nature they find an instinctive joy in choosing Christ; but to many more, perhaps to most, the thing is hard. How often is a noble life built on the grave of a darling sin!

II. Note, secondly, *some features of Moses' act*.

(1) Mark, for one thing, that the sacrifice was made at the acme of his powers. He was forty. The harvest of life was just beginning to be reaped; youth's hasty fervours had subsided; he had arrived at that age when, as Froude observes, 'ambition becomes powerful in men, and takes the place of love of pleasure'. Is it not a great thing when those begin to serve God upon whom life has heaped its bounties lavishly?

(2) Then besides that, Moses made this surrender just when the people's lot was at its lowest.

Look on him now, at this turning point, and that word of his later promise glows wonderfully into meaning: 'A prophet shall the Lord your God raise up unto you, like unto me'; for in the silent grandeur of his self-abnegation he is indeed a far-shining type and symbol of a greater far than he, One who for our sakes became poor, that we through His poverty might be rich.

III. What is the dominating note in Moses' great act? How shall we name it briefly? In a word, it is *renunciation*. It is the casting away of that which is full of charm and sweetness, the adoption of a neglected and despised cause.

Note *the underlying motive of faith*. And here the first words of my text reach over and join hands firmly with the last: 'By faith Moses . . . had respect unto the recompense of the reward'. 'The reward'—some one will say; why, then, after all Moses was not wholly disinterested. Even his eye was fixed and bent upon the coming profit. It is as we said; unselfish religion is a dream.

But stay one moment. His eye was bent upon the future; that, of course, is part simply of what is meant by faith. But that very future, how must it appear? Could it promise anything to tempt ambition or gratify mere self? Nothing, as we have seen; nothing but labour, grief and disappointment, and at last a friendless grave. Yet none the less there was a great reward, a recompense past all computation. Look deeper, and it becomes plain that inwardly he was ever more and more possessed, inhabited by God; and for him that was enough. Yes! though in the end every human face withdrew, and not a hand was left to close his eyes, for this man it was enough that he had God and that God had him. — H. R. Mackintosh, *Life on God's Plan*, p. 15.

References.—XI. 24-26.—C. Perren, *Sermon Outlines*, p. 143. Spurgeon, *Sermons*, vol. xviii. No. 1063, and vol. xxxiv. No. 2030. J. Bunting, *Sermons*, vol. i. pp. 234, 243 and 258. E. H. Bickersteth, *Thoughts in Past Years*, p. 151. XI. 24-27.—A. Maclaren, *Expositions of Holy Scripture—Hebrews*, p. 156.

'Choosing rather to suffer affliction with the people of God than to enjoy the pleasures of sin for a season.'—Heb. xi. 25.

In the preface of his essay on Milton, De Quincey speaks of the sacrifice cheerfully made by the English poet in returning from Italy's pleasures to take part in his own country's service. 'The sacrifice was—that he renounced the heavenly spectacle of the Ægean Sea and its sunny groups of islands, renounced the sight of Attica, of the Theban districts, of Judea; next of that ancient river Nile, the river of Pharaoh and Moses, of the Pyramids, and the hundred-gated Thebes; finally he renounced the land of Syria, much of which was then doubtless unsafe for a Frank of any religion, and for a Christian of any nation. But he might have travelled in one district of Syria, *viz.*, Palestine, which for him had paramount attractions. All these objects of commanding interest to any profound scholar, Greece, the Grecian isles, Egypt, and Palestine, he surrendered to his sense of duty; not by any promise or engagement, but by the *act* then and there of turning his face homewards; well aware at the time that his chance was small indeed, under his peculiar prospects, of ever recovering his lost chance.'

'The pleasures of sin.'—Heb. xi. 25.

Only those who despise the pleasures can afford to despise the opinion of the world.—R. L. Stevenson.

'Accounting the reproach of Christ greater riches than the treasures of Egypt: for he looked unto the recompense of the reward.'—Heb. xi. 26.

A man will undergo great toil and hardship for ends that must be many years distant—such as wealth or fame—but none for an end that may be close at hand —as the joys of heaven.—Hawthorne.

References.—XI. 26.—R. Glover, *Christian World Pulpit*, vol. li. p. 150. J. Bunting, *Sermons*, vol. i. p. 276.

THE SECRET OF GREATNESS

'Moses endured as seeing Him Who is invisible.'—Heb. xi. 27.

What we call public men, men who are in the public eye, are well known to us all, yet in another sense they are unknown. In their official public life they are known to us, but in what is called the inner life, the hidden life of the soul, they are absolutely unknown. In this inner life they are known thoroughly and truly only to God. In it they hardly know themselves. And it is in this inner life that the power of God is made manifest. So long as man is true to his spiritual life and inspiration, so long will his public life be regulated by God. Moses was what is called a public man. All his actions in the sight of the people were dictated by God.

I. If we Look to the Inner Life of this Great Man we find the key to his greatness. I think we find the key to it in this text, 'He endured as seeing Him Who is invisible'. He lived by faith. He lived the hidden life of the soul. He was no mere organiser, no mere materialistic performer; he had an intense love for the spiritual life. He might have said with St. Paul, 'The things that are seen are temporal, and the things which are not seen are eternal'. Moses endured that life which you all know so well. He went on day after day, week after week, month after month, with all the trials and troubles and worries which then, as now, are the characteristics of a statesman's life. He endured. He endured because he had the power which comes of spiritual being. He saw Him who is invisible.

II. It is for us to see Him Who is Invisible.—We all believe, and rightly so, in making the very best use of our talents, but we must not lose sight of the great moving principle of the spiritual life which is found in the lives of these men of old, who were all lovers of the inner life of the soul. Let us pray that we may follow in their footsteps. In their lives and in their death they were devoted to the Lord Jesus. There is a far better death than the physical death; there is the death which makes man a new man. Let us pray to God that in the hour of death we may live—truly live. Let us pray that after we have gone through what man calls death we may leave this land of our earthly lives and dwell with Him in Paradise. In our Church life and in our life of our daily calling we must ever remember that He is before us. As we live our daily lives, what road are we on? Are we loving God and the hidden life of the soul? Do we realise that we are, through God, members of Christ and inheritors of the kingdom of Heaven? Do we look upon the prayers we utter as a matter of course? Yet prayer is our most great and glorious privilege, as it brings us into close union with Him. God moves in a mysterious way. He tries so many ways and means to bring us to Himself. And we on earth can please God as one family in Christ joined together with one heart and one voice in the service and praise of God, and endure joy, strength, and hope in this world of ours, as seeing Him Who is invisible.

'He endured as seeing Him Who is invisible.'—HEB. XI. 27.

WHAT is the outward discipline for him who, bidden to travel on the highways of life, can take no step heavenwards, unbeset or unobstructed by wealth, power, admiration, or popularity? How shall faith preserve her dominion over Him to whom the world is daily offering whatever can most kindle the imagination, engage the understanding, or gratify ambition? There is but one corrective. It is to be found in that unbroken communion with the indwelling God, in which Mr. Wilberforce habitually lived. He 'endured as seeing Him Who is invisible,' and as hearing Him Who is inaudible. When most immersed in political cares, or in social enjoyments, he invoked and obeyed the voice which directed his path, while it tranquillised his mind. That voice ... taught him to rejoice as a child in the presence of a Father whom he much loved and altogether trusted, and whose approbation was infinitely more than an equivalent for whatever restraint, self-denial, labour or self-sacrifice, obedience to his will might render necessary.—SIR JAMES STEPHEN, *Essays in Ecclesiastical Biography*.

THE conceptions of most of us are dull; the power of *presenting* the future to our minds (in the accurate and analysed sense of the expression), of making it present to us, of 'seeing Him Who is invisible,' is a faculty whose strength depends greatly on training, which is vouchsafed to different individuals in very different measure, and to most of us in very scanty measure.—W. RATHBONE GREG, *Enigmas of Life*, p. 248.

REFERENCES.—XI. 27.—H. H. Henson, *Godly Union and Concord*, p. 113. H. P. Liddon, *University Sermons* (2nd Series), p. 351.

'By faith the walls of Jericho fell down, after they had been compassed about for seven days.'—HEB. XI. 30.

'IT is surely very remarkable,' wrote Mr. Gladstone in his essay on Ingersoll, 'that, in the whole of this recital, the Apostle, "whose feet were shod with the preparation of the Gospel of peace," seems with a tender instinct to avoid anything like stress upon the exploits of warriors. Of the twelve persons having a share in the detailed expositions, David is the only warrior, and his character as a man of war is eclipsed by his greater attributes as a prophet, or declarer of the Divine counsels. It is yet more noteworthy that Joshua, who had so fair a fame, but who was only a warrior, is never named in the chapter, and we are simply told that "by faith the walls of Jericho fell down, after they had been compassed about seven times".'

'UP to his time,' says Newman, 'many instances as there were of the faith of saints, there is no instance recorded of the faith of a sinner. . . . Down to Joshua's day, no instance appears but of the faith of saints, but in the next verse, and in Joshua's history, we have a different specimen.'

'The time will fail me if I tell of Gideon.'—HEB. XI. 32.

SUCH men are raised to station and command,
When Providence means mercy to a land,
He speaks, and they appear; to Him they owe
Skill to direct, and strength to strike the blow,
To manage with address, to seize with power
The crisis of a dark decisive hour.
So Gideon earned a victory not his own,
Subserviency his praise, and that alone.
　　　　　　—COWPER, *Table Talk* (355 f.).

REFERENCES.—XI. 28.—A. S. Peake, *The Heroes and Martyrs of Faith*, p. 143. *Expositor* (7th Series), vol. v. p. 348. XI. 30.—H. P. Liddon, *University Sermons* (2nd Series), p. 222. XI. 31.—Spurgeon, *Sermons*, vol. iii. No. 119, and vol. xviii. No. 1061. A. Martin, *Winning the Soul*, p. 47. *Expositor* (5th Series), vol. vii. p. 98; *ibid.* (6th Series), vol. iii. p. 419.

'Of David and Samuel and the prophets.'—HEB. XI. 32.

'IT is not a little remarkable,' says Mr. Gladstone in the fifth chapter of his *Impregnable Rock of Holy Scripture*, 'that the enumeration by name of the great historic heroes of faith, in the Epistle to the Hebrews, ends in the person of King David, with the first youth of the monarchy. The only later instances referred to are the prophets, named as a class, who stood apart and alone, and were not as a rule leaders of the people, but rather witnesses in sackcloth against their iniquities. Taking the history from the Exodus to the exile as a whole, the latter end was worse than the beginning, the cup of iniquity was full; it had been filled by a gradual process; and one of the marks of that process was a lowering of the method, in which the chosen people were governed; it became more human and less Divine'.

REFERENCES.—XI. 32. — A. S. Peake, *The Heroes and Martyrs of Faith*, p. 152. XI. 32, 33.—*Ibid.* p. 161.

FAITH'S HEROIC DOING

'And what shall I more say? for the time would fail me to tell of Gideon and of Barak . . . and of the prophets,' etc.
　　　　　　—HEB. XI. 32-34.

COMPRESS it as much as he would the writer of the great history of the heroic deeds of faith felt that it was impossible to tell half the story. Time would fail even to run through the names of the Old Testament saints, and show how faith shaped the lives of those great workers, and laid the foundation of their heroic exploits.

I. The crowded canvas teaches that every life devoted to God is an illustration of the power of faith. The writer who wishes to inculcate this lesson of faith is able to lay his hand on every life of the Old Testament which was acceptable to God, and to show that it was an illustration of that principle. These are the names of men whose heroism sends a thrill of wonder through every heart. Each of the names that he mentions lives for evermore, and names that he has not been able even to mention rise to one's mind as the glorious passage rolls on. No truly acceptable life but is an illustration of the might of faith. Into all the various walks of life which God's providence calls us to tread we may bear the Spirit which will win us a place in the roll of faith's heroes.

II. The great deeds of faith include the loftiest achievements in every field. Set together here they dazzle mind and heart. All the great workers were men of faith; all these great deeds, for which the annals of the world have no parallel, were trophies of faith's mighty working. What realm of life is not lighted up by the heroic deeds of faith? The grandeur of these results overwhelm us. What light shines around the saddest and roughest road when we remember what faith has done! No trouble can overwhelm, no enemy can overthrow the life that has this foundation. Faith was strong for these great deeds because she had hold of the arm of God. She moved the arm that moved the world. Be strong in such thoughts for your life-struggle.—J. TELFORD, *The Preacher's Magazine*, vol. v. p. 269.

'The time would fail me to tell of . . . who through faith subdued kingdoms, wrought righteousness . . . turned to flight the armies of the aliens.'—HEB. XI. 32-34.

THERE is a remarkable chapter in the Epistle to the Hebrews, in which the writer unfolds to his countrymen what is in fact a National Portrait Gallery, as he enumerates, one by one, the heroes and saints of the Jewish history, and adds to his catalogue these inspiring words: 'And what shall I more say? for the time would fail me to tell of those . . . who through faith subdued kingdoms, wrought righteousness, obtained promises, stopped the mouths of lions, quenched the violence of fire, escaped the edge of the sword, out of weakness were made strong, waxed valiant in fight, turned to flight the armies of the aliens'. And finally he draws this conclusion from his long retrospect: 'Wherefore, seeing we are compassed about with so great a cloud of witnesses, let us lay aside every weight and the sin which doth so easily beset us, and let us run with patience the race that is set before us'. How much of the philosophy of history is condensed into that single sentence! It is suggestive to us of the ethical purpose which should dominate all our historical teaching. To what end do we live in a country whose annals are enriched by the story of great talents, high endeavours, and noble sacrifices, if we do not become more conscious of the possibilities of our own life, and more anxious to live worthily the inheritance which has come down to us?—SIR JOSHUA FITCH, *Educational Aims and Methods*, p. 28.

THE Cranmers, Hampdens, and Sidneys: the counsellors of our Elizabeth, and the friends of our other great deliverer, the third William—is it in vain that *these* have been our countrymen? Are we not the heirs of their good deeds? And what are noble deeds but noble truths realised? As Protestants, as Englishmen, as the inheritors of so ample an estate of might and right, an estate so strongly fenced, so richly planted, by the sinewy arms and dauntless hearts of our forefathers, we of all others have good cause to trust in the truth, yea, to follow its pillar of fire through the darkness and the desert, even though its light should but suffice to make us certain of its own presence.—COLERIDGE, *The Friend* (IX.).

THESE old Jewish heroes did fill my whole heart and soul. I learnt from them lessons which I never wish to unlearn. Whatever else I saw about them, this I saw—that they were patriots, deliverers from the tyranny and injustice from which the child's heart . . . instinctively, and, as I believe, by a Divine inspiration, revolts. Moses leading his people out of Egypt, Gideon, Barak, and Samson slaying their oppressors; David hiding in the mountains from the tyrant, with his little band of those who had fled from the oppression of an aristocracy of Nabals; John executing God's vengeance on the kings—they were my heroes, my models; they mixed themselves up with the dim legends about the Reformation martyrs, Cromwell and Hampden, Sidney and Monmouth, which I had heard at my mother's knee. Not that the perennial oppression of the masses, in all ages and countries, had yet risen on me as an awful, torturing, fixed idea. I fancied, poor fool! that tyranny was the exception, not the rule. But it was the mere sense of abstract pity and justice which was delighted in me. I thought that these were old fairy tales, such as never need be realised again. I learnt otherwise in after years. I have often wondered since why all cannot read the same lesson as I did in those old Hebrew Scriptures—that they, of all books in the world, have been wrested into . . . proofs of the Divine right of kings, the eternal necessity of slavery!— CHARLES KINGSLEY, *Alton Locke* (ch. I.).

IN his speech at the London banquet to Lloyd Garrison, 29th June, 1867, John Bright told of an article by Harriet Martineau upon 'The Martyr Age of the United States,' in which the great names connected with the abolitionist cause were chronicled, and then added: 'When I read that article and the description of those men and women there given, I was led, I know not how, to think of a very striking passage which I am sure must be familiar to most here, because it is to be found in the Epistle to the Hebrews. After the writer of that Epistle has described the great men and fathers of the nation, he says: "Time would fail me to tell of Gideon and of Barak . . . and of the prophets . . . who turned to flight the armies of the aliens'. I ask if this grand passage of the inspired writer may not be applied to that heroic band who have made America the perpetual home of freedom?'

THE man who accepts a crown *may be* more noble than he who lays one down and retires to the desert. Of the worthies who do things by faith, some are sawn asunder, and some subdue kingdoms. The look of the thing is nothing.—GEORGE MACDONALD, in *The Marquis of Lossie* (ch. XLII.).

THE GRAPES OF GOD

'Who through faith obtained promises.'—Heb. xi. 33.

THERE are three religious ideas, the connection of which with one another I will try to set forth : Promises, Faith, Prayer.

I. **Promises.**—What are the promises ? Those of you who are diligent readers of the Bible do not need to be told that a large proportion of God's Word consists of promises. All who can discern the inspiration of the Scriptures at all would allow that nowhere is Divinity more visible and unmistakable than in these passages. The very mind of God, the very heart of the Most High comes out in these promises, and it is not only by this that their Divinity can be recognised, but also by their humanity. In reading a book on the teaching of Jesus, I recently came across this remark : ' If Godly people keep books of promises, why do they not also keep books of commandments, especially the commandments of Jesus ? ' I venture to say that if you want the commandments to be well attended to, the best thing you can do is to attend well to the promises. If the promises of religion have free course and are glorified, there is little fear but the commandments will get their chance likewise.

II. **Faith.**—Faith is the second idea to connect in your minds with the promises. Faith is that in man which corresponds to promises in God. It is the human hand which grasps the promises as they hang down from on high, or rather, if I might say so, the mouth of the infant exactly fashioned so as to fit to the fountains of Divine nourishment. These promises are so numerous as to be practically innumerable, and if your faith is going on from one to another, exploring its depths and its sweetness, you have practically before you an endless progress, in which your faith will be as happy visiting promise after promise as a bee on a summer's day is in visiting flower after flower. I can imagine a thoughtful hearer saying : ' But is that not substituting a book for a person ? Is not Christ the object of faith ? It is to Christ and not to books we are to cling.' Most true ; I would preach that with all my heart if it were necessary, and yet it is in the texts that Christ presents Himself to our faith.

III. **Prayer.**—Prayer is just faith in action. If any of you have difficulties about exercising your faith, as I know many Christians have, you cannot do better than turn your effort into prayer ; that will do admirably. Just as our prayer lives and moves as it attaches itself to the promises, so our prayers receive a new life when we attach them to the promises, and you cannot have a better definition of prayer than the pleading of the promises.—J. STALKER, *Christian World Pulpit*, vol. LXXIV. p. 9.

'Stopped the mouths of lions.'—Heb. xi. 33.

GERARD ROUSSEL, the learned but timid Canon of Meaux, who was the friend of Bishop Briçonnet and Margaret of Angoulême, left Meaux for Strasbourg in 1525. He was too cautious to join with men like Farel, Zwingli, and Œcolampadius. To the last of these three reformers he wrote, after reciting the list of his opponents—the bishops, the doctors, the universities, the populace, the Parlement—*Quid faciet homuncio adversus tot leones ?* ' What shall a little man do against so many lions ? ' Prof. Baird, in quoting this letter, remarks : ' A reference to the book of Daniel might have enabled the Canon of Meaux to answer his own question '.

REFERENCES.—XI. 33.—Spurgeon, *Sermons*, vol. viii. No. 435. J. G. Rogers, *Christian World Pulpit*, vol. liv. p. 312. *Expositor* (6th Series), vol. x. p. 361.

HEROES AND MARTYRS

HEB. XI. 33, 34.

FROM the persons whom he has just mentioned, the Judges, David, Samuel and the Prophets, the author passes to their achievements, not confining himself to those whom he has mentioned, but embracing in his view the dazzling triumphs and the still more wonderful endurance exhibited by the heroes and martyrs of faith down the history of Israel till the time of the Maccabees. He had no pinched or contracted view of faith ; he includes in the range of it some things that we with our more secular habit of thought might be tempted to exclude.

I. First, there are the great military exploits of Israel's leaders. More than once he touches on this aspect of Hebrew history — ' subdued kingdoms,' ' waxed mighty in war,' ' turned to flight armies of aliens '. All of these sanctify the calling of the soldier as exhibiting faith, in a way which corresponds to the Old Testament rather than to the New Testament ideal.

Yet with all the imperfection which to ourselves seems to cling about this ideal, we ought not to blame the writer for reversion to a lower type. It would show a lack of historical imagination to expect Old Testament characters to conform to a New Testament standard as yet unrevealed. All we can expect is that they should place their life under the sanction of religion ; and, since war was to them part of the natural order of things, it provided a fitting field in which their faith might be exercised. We may, of course, feel that there is a difference between wars of conquest and wars in self-defence. But the Hebrews thought that religion justified their conquest of Canaan, and David no doubt imagined that his wars of aggrandisement raised the prestige of Israel's God. But we turn with more sympathy to the efforts made by Israel to shake off the Philistine yoke, or to the splendid and thrilling story of the Maccabean struggle to save the national religion from extinction.

II. We are on ground more congenial to ourselves in the phrase ' obtained promises '. For here, although military triumphs may be partly in mind, the thought is by no means limited to these. It is not simply that they received promises, but that they obtained their fulfilment. The making of the promise may be entirely independent in the first instance of the recipient's faith. It is God who takes the initiative in graciously setting before His servants some alluring prospect. But promises are naturally not unconditional, they imply believing response on the part of the recipient, and therefore if the promise is to be realised faith is necessary for its attainment. There is a sentence in Genesis with reference to the faith of Abraham which has left its mark deep upon the New Testament: 'Abraham believed God, and it was counted to him for righteousness'. It is true, of course, that lack of faith does not always cancel the fulfilment of the promise itself. The New Testament assures us that our lack of faith does not make void the faithfulness of God.

III. From the great conquests of faith the author passes to its even nobler triumphs of endurance. There is far less heroism displayed in exploits of daring valour. Here the flush of excitement, the conviction of success, the consciousness of admiring spectators, nerve the courage for a loftier flight. But in the experience of persecution the romantic and exhilarating supports of heroism are withdrawn. The hero can no longer feel the intoxication of conflict or 'drink delight of battle with his peers'. He has first to wait, and then to endure. And the torture of suspense is itself enough to make the strong quail in the agony of apprehension, especially when it is long drawn out, when everything is uncertain—the time, the manner, the intensity of the torment, when the mind has no fixed point of contemplation on which to rest. It is then that the battle may be almost lost before it is even joined. The tormentor well knows the horrors of suspense, and carefully calculates to break his victim's spirit before ever his body is brought into the torture-chamber. And when suspense and fearful apprehension have done their worst, when the courage is sapped and the imagination has played freely on the ghastly future, then physical torture is enlisted to complete the fiendish work which imagination has begun. Through it all the victim is quite helpless and passive ; he can do nothing, he can only suffer.

In our own soft and sentimental age, an age of vivid imagination, of nerves, anæsthetics, and cowardly shrinking from physical pain, the stories of the torture-chamber touch us with amazement if we are able to enter with sympathy into all the cruel misery they involved. We cannot help the reflection, if the old time of persecution were to come back, though in the more terrible form which the ingenuity of modern science on the one hand and the profounder knowledge of the human body on the other would make possible, how would the Churches of the present day meet the crisis? It can hardly be doubted that the first effect would be to sift the Churches to a faithful remnant, though it is not to be questioned that reserves of courage would be found in some where we should least expect it. But we should have at least this assurance, that the power of faith in which they triumphed would remain our chief hope; the firm hold on spiritual realities would be our surest safeguard against defeat of the spirit on the physical battle-field.—A. S. Peake, *The Heroes and Martyrs of Faith*, p. 186.

References.—XI. 34.—Spurgeon, *Sermons*, vol. xii. No. 697, and vol. xxxvii. No. 2209.

MARTYRDOM

' They were stoned, they were sawn asunder, were tempted, were slain with the sword.'—Heb. xi. 37.

The suffering of martyrdom was in some respects peculiar. It was a death, cruel in itself, publicly inflicted : and heightened by the fierce exultation of a malevolent populace. When we are in pain, we can lie in peace by ourselves. We receive the sympathy and kind services of those about us; and if we like it, we can retire altogether from the sight of others, and suffer without a witness to interrupt us. But the sufferings of martyrdom were for the most part public, attended with every circumstance of ignominy and popular triumph, as well as with torture. Criminals indeed are put to death without kindly thoughts from bystanders; still, for the most part, even criminals receive commiseration and a sort of respect. But the early Christians had to endure 'the shame' after their Master's pattern. They had to die in the midst of enemies who reviled them, and in mockery, bid them (as in Christ's case) come down from the cross. They were supported on no easy couch, soothed by no attentive friends ; and considering how much the depressing power of pain depends on the imagination, this circumstance alone at once separates their sufferings widely from all instances of pain in disease. The unseen God alone was their Comforter, and this invests the scene of their suffering with supernatural majesty, and awes us when we think of them. 'Yea, though I walk through the valley of the shadow of death, I will fear no evil ; *for Thou art with me.*' A martyrdom is a season of God's especial power in the eye of faith, as great as if a miracle were visibly wrought. It is a fellowship of Christ's sufferings, a commemoration of His death, a representation filling up in figure, 'that which is behind of His afflictions, for his Body's sake, which is the Church'. And thus, being an august solemnity in itself, and a kind of sacrament, a baptism of blood, it worthily finishes that long searching trial which I have already described as being its usual forerunner in primitive times.—J. H. Newman.

References.—XI. 37.—Spurgeon, *Sermons*, vol. xxvi. No. 1528. *Expositor* (6th Series), vol. x. p. 118.

' They were stoned, they were sawn asunder . . . they wandered in deserts and in mountains and in dens and caves of the earth.'—Heb xi. 37, 38.

Describing, in *Under the Syrian Sun* (vol. ii. pp. 357 f.), the martyrs of Babism in Persia, Mr. A. C. Inchbold observes that ' the Báb proclaimed the new faith, of which he openly avowed himself the Divine mouthpiece, during six years of persecution conducted on lines of a drastic, unparalleled severity. Among his immediate apostles and general adherents were counted many intellectual men of good position, and holding enlightened views. These people were hunted down like wild beasts, put to death by the most horrible torture that the ingenuity of fiendish man could devise. Like the Christian martyrs of old, "they were stoned, they were sawn asunder, were slain with the sword ; they wandered about in sheepskins and goatskins ; being destitute, afflicted, tormented ; they wandered in deserts and in mountains and in dens and caves of the earth ".'

IT is for the suppression of freedom that tortures have always been expressly used. For freedom of life and mind men and women have suffered more than for the filthiest crimes. 'They were tortured,' says the old writer, 'not accepting deliverance. Others had trial of cruel mockings and scourgings ; they were stoned, they were sawn asunder, were tempted, were slain with the sword ; they wandered about in sheepskins and goatskins, being destitute, afflicted, tormented.' And having reached that point, unable to restrain his admiration any longer, he throws in the words—' of whom the world was not worthy'. It was the same cause of freedom and the same heroic mind that filled the torture chambers of Europe from Domitian down to Bomba. Always the worst suffering has been reserved for liberty.—From *The Nation*, (4th May, 1907), p. 375.

REFERENCES.—XI. 38.—J. G. Rogers, *Christian World Pulpit*, vol. liv. p. 328. H. M. Butler, *Harrow School Sermons*, p. 411.

MAN PERFECTED THROUGH SUFFERING

'And these all, having obtained a good report through faith (having had witness borne to them, R.V.) received not the promise, God having provided some better thing for us, that they without us should not be made perfect.'—HEB. XI. 39, 40.

I. THE words teach that the fundamental gifts of the religious life can be received by the individual in isolation and obscurity. We may be ready to ask the question, Was it not hard that these early believers, who had so nobly satisfied God's demand upon their faith, should be shut out from their full and final blessedness for ages? Let it suffice to reply that they received, without a single exception, compensations that in the meantime more than fill d up the measure of their desires. (1) Their comparative ignorance and detachment did not bar them from the possession of this precious rudimentary grace. (2) In the absence of the fully accomplished promise, a witness of some sort was vital to their sustained fidelity. The God who had called them to His service could not well leave them destitute of it. (3) And then God could not leave an unnecessary burden on the conscience of His people.

II. The crowning gifts of the religious life can only be received in common with the completed Church of the elect. 'That they without us should not be made perfect.' (1) The life of nature is social, and its different parts are perfected together. God seems to delight in the magnificence of aggregate effects. And is it not so also in the spiritual world? Not till the golden chime is heard that proclaims the approach of God's ripe summer will the life of all the separate ages receive its highest glory and development. The higher you ascend in the scale of life, the more pronounced is this principle of interdependence. (2) With the setting up of the New Dispensation some new effusion of light and knowledge and spiritual victory has come to the Old Testament saints in the region of the unseen. Progress is not the monopoly of those who are in the flesh. Christ's mediatorial sacrifice was for patriarchs, prophets, and righteous men of old, and it has brought them abreast of us in privilege and insight and power. (3) Besides the richer effusion of joy that came to the first generation of God's servants through the work of God's Incarnate Son, their joy is further perfected with the progressive perfecting of human history. (4) The text suggests that there is a larger fulfilment of the Covenant in the last great day, for which the spirits of the Old and the New Dispensation must alike wait. The noble army of martyrs can only be fully crowned when the last pale recruit to their numbers shall have come in. (5) The fact that God should have determined to perfect the men of all ages together shows how much He thinks of those great principles of mutual association and fellowship which we sometimes esteem so little. He shows honour to those lowly disciples and followers of His Son whom we do not sufficiently honour. (6) God seems to be teaching us in this way the humility which can be best learned and exercised through fellowship. It is a check to our pride to be reminded that we can only be crowned in common with the rest. (7) And then by perfecting His servants together God seems to remind us of the graciousness and beauty of patience. Disembodied saints of the olden time are waiting for us, and we shall have to wait for them. (8) And then God has ordained that the perfecting of our destinies shall be in common, because He wishes to set forth His grace and power upon a scale of incomparable magnificence. The canvas on which God's hand is to work its consummate miracle must be stretched to its utmost dimensions.

REFERENCES.—XI. 39, 40.—Bishop Boyd-Carpenter, *Christian World Pulpit*, vol. lvi. p. 40, and vol. lix. p. 17. John Thomas, *ibid.* vol. lviii. p. 120. *Expositor* (5th Series), vol. vi. p. 160. XI. 40.—J. R. Bailey, *Christian World Pulpit*, vol. xlviii. p. 164.

A BESETTING SIN

(A Lenten Sermon)

' The sin which doth so easily beset us.'—HEB. XII. I.

SIN is a very difficult thing to define ; it is so complex, so subtle. The Greek word—which we translate for 'sin '—means 'missing the mark '. What a true name that is for any sin which any of us commit ! How sure it is, sooner or later, to 'miss the mark' for which we meant it. We do it with the idea that in some way or other it will give us pleasure. But does any sin, in the long run, give pleasure ?

Sins are very various, and of an infinite number of degrees.

I. But there is One Sin that is Predominant, it rules and characterises the whole man. It would be difficult to say how that particular sin began, and how it has attained its great power. No doubt it has a good deal to do with our physical temperament, even with our bodily state, our outward circumstances. And if you would trace its rise and its early course, you must go back to your early days. Since then, it has almost daily grown through a daily indulgence, if not in the act, the thought. And so it is that now—whether others know it or not, you know and God knows—that this sin has attained a very strong hold upon you. It meets you everywhere; everything seems to play into it; and though you have often fought against it, and often prayed about it, and been determined and in earnest to conquer it, still it is dominant, it meets you everywhere. It is *your besetting sin !*

II. Satan's Mode of Warfare with us is to Concentrate his Attack on one Spot in our character. He finds a weak point, and he plays upon it. Hence first, perhaps, by natural consequences, and afterwards by Satan taking advantage, the weak point turns into a positive sin. The sin recurs at intervals which become shorter and shorter, till it becomes 'the besetting sin' of our character. It grows stronger and stronger, until, as it ever must do, it turns into a habit; and when that sin is once dominant, Satan will even leave us alone in other things. He will let us be ever so good, that thereby he may give us a false estimate of ourselves, and make us careless of the one point where he is carrying on his deep wiles to ruin us for ever.

III. In Lent let each Ask Himself—'What is my besetting sin?' and to deal with the question very practically. Not to be satisfied with an indefinite, vague answer. 'What is *my* besetting sin?' Do you know what *your* besetting sin is? If you do not, ask God to show it to you, for it is the office of the Holy Spirit to 'convince of sin'. And if you have any friend or relation faithful enough, and wise enough, to help you, ask him to help you. It is a question, a solemn, religious matter to be dealt with before God, in your own room, in church, in your most sacred hours, with the great judgment day and eternity before you. Satan will try to confuse you, to complicate the question; but do not be satisfied till you have an answer which approves itself to your own conscience, which tallies with facts, which you can bring confidently to God, *confidently to God.*

(*a*) *When you know the occasions,* and the opportunities, and the persons, and the times, and the circumstances which have been specially dangerous to you in your past life, avoid them, if you can; if you cannot, put on a double guard at those times and seasons. Make a greater effort when you come to those points, and never venture into one of them before you put on your armour. Crush the first thought that may arise.

(*b*) *But do not be simply negative.* A vacuum is a very dangerous thing. Occupy the place in your heart where that sin was, with something, something very definite; something that will interest you; something that will employ you; something that will satisfy you; something very great and very good. If the house is empty the enemy will come back sevenfold, and take his old place, and you will find yourself worse off than before! Cultivate the opposite grace. Set about it in real earnestness, and be characterised by the virtues which you have hitherto failed to possess.

THE CHRISTIAN SOCIETY

'Compassed about with so great a cloud of witnesses.'—HEB. XII. I.

WHEN St. Paul spoke of Christians as being all members one of another, and as therefore bound to the duties of brotherly help and consolation, he was expressing a thought which lies at the very centre of Christianity. And I desire to draw your attention to this side of the revelation which we have received in Christ, as to the conception of Christianity as a social system, in which no man dare live to himself, in which no man can live to himself even if he would.

I. This conception of a mysterious bond uniting all men in one great fellowship is itself contained in the fact of the Incarnation. The brotherhood of all men is revealed in the Person of Him who calls all men His brethren. It may perhaps seem a trite thing to say, an obvious inference, hardly necessary to indicate to intelligent or Christian people. Nay, have we really learned the lesson yet? has the world, has the Church, really accepted this inference, and given it practical expression? No; we have not learnt yet the significance of the teaching of the Incarnation in relation to human society.

II. And so it appears that the lesson is not altogether easy to apply. And God, who is always better to us than we are to ourselves, has not left us to work it out for ourselves. For when Christ revealed His truth to men, He did not leave it there for them to appropriate, here a fragment, there a fragment, as they best could; but He left behind a Society which was to be at once its keeper and its symbol. The Church was to teach the truth; more than that, it was itself the expression of the great fundamental truth of the Incarnation, that all men are brethren in the sight of God, for they all have but one Redeemer who is the Brother of each.

III. The Church is, then, the Society through whose life we best realise at once our own relation to God and our own duties to our fellows. Let me suggest three lines of responsibility which we must face, if we be true to our inheritance. (1) We must face the *social* message of the Incarnation, which it is the Church's duty, our duty as members of the Church, to interpret to the world. (2) We must face the *doctrinal* message of the Incarnation in reference to our own intellectual attitude to our religion. We need to remind ourselves from time to time that, whatever side issues may be raised, the fact that God became man is the really important matter, the one answer to the puzzles of life here, the one hope for a future of holiness and service hereafter. (3) We need to face the message of the Incarnation in relation to our own spiritual life in a more personal fashion still. Called to be saints; all of us are so called. Social, intellectual, spiritual responsibilities — with what encouragements shall we face them? Let the Apostle answer, 'Compassed about with so great a cloud of witnesses' is our watchword.—J. H. BERNARD, *Via Domini: Sermons for Christian Seasons*, p. 285.

THE CLOUD OF WITNESSES

HEB. XII. I.

WE are compassed about with so great a cloud of witnesses—not merely the faithful of long past ages, but the saints of God in every period of the Church's history.

I. How clearly it reminds us that goodness is possible, and is within the reach of all. You and I have a life to live, a race to run, which is beset with many difficulties, many temptations, many sorrows. It is not, it cannot be, easy. But when we remember that this life has been lived, this race been run, by countless others, who have not lived and run in vain, is there no encouragement for us to press forward with fresh zeal and hope? They are God's true witnesses; they show us what He intended all men to be, and what by His all-prevailing grace we ourselves may yet be.

II. Their very presence with us is a continual call to lift up our hearts, and not to allow ourselves to become wholly engrossed in the things of this world. We know what a real danger that is. John Bunyan has drawn the character for us in one of his immortal pictures—the man that could look no way but downwards, with a muck-rake in his hand, and, standing over his head, an angelic being with a celestial crown in his hand and proffering him that crown for the muck-rake; 'but the man did neither look up nor regard, but raked to himself the straws, the small sticks, and dust of the floor'. How ready we are to fall into the same error! If nothing else will rouse us, may not the thought of our unseen witnesses do so? They supply us with the standard, not of earth, but of heaven, by which all our actions should be measured.

III. Be assured of their never-failing sympathy and love. We believe—do we not?—that our dead are now with Christ, and therefore that they are entering ever more fully into His mind and spirit. But if so, and if, as we are taught, Christ can still be 'touched with the feeling of our infirmities' (Heb. IV. 15), and is still pleading for us with an all-prevailing intercession before God (compare Heb. VII. 25), what more certain than that His people are engaged in the same great ministry of love? They have not, they cannot have, forgotten us.

IV. We rise up through His people to our Lord Himself; we look beyond them to Him who is 'the author and finisher of our faith'. One of the grandest of old Greek myths tells us how on stated days human souls follow in the train of the gods, and, rising above the world, gaze on the eternal and the absolute. It is only by strenuous effort that they can gain for a brief space this vision, and then they fall to earth again, and their life on earth corresponds with the range and clearness of the heavenly impressions they retain. 'For us,' says Bishop Westcott who recalls the story, 'the revelation of Christ has made this dream a truth.'—G. MILLIGAN, *The Divine Artist*, p. 97.

'We are compassed about with so great a cloud of witnesses.'
—HEB. XII. I.

'CONSIDER,' says Ruskin in the third volume of *Modern Painters* (ch. IV.), 'what are the legitimate uses of the imagination, that is to say, of the power of perceiving, or conceiving with the mind, things which cannot be perceived by the senses. Its first and noblest use is, to enable us to bring sensibly to our sight the things which are recorded as belonging to our future state, or as invisibly surrounding us in this. It is given us, that we may imagine the cloud of witnesses in heaven and earth, and see, as if they were now present, the souls of the righteous waiting for us; that we may conceive the great army of the inhabitants of heaven, and discover among those whom we most desire to be with for ever.'

LET us therefore turn our youthful imaginations into great picture-galleries and Walhallas of the heroic souls of all times and all places; and we shall be incited to follow after good, and be ashamed to commit any sort of baseness in the direct view of such 'a cloud of witnesses'. Would you know what faith means, leave Calvinists and Arminians to split straws about points of doctrine; but do you read and digest that splendid eleventh chapter of the Hebrews, and you will escape for ever from the netted snares of theological logomachy.—PROF. BLACKIE, in *Self-Culture*, p. 82.

THE blessing is ours of their love for great and noble things. We may not all be gifted with the divinest fires of their nobler insight and wider imagination, but we may learn to live as they did, and to seek a deeper grasp of life, a more generous sympathy. Overwhelmed we may be with self-tortures, and wants, and remorses, swayed by many winds, sometimes utterly indifferent from very weariness, but we may still return thanks for the steadfast power of the noble dead. It reigns unmoved through the raving of the storm; it speaks of a bond beyond death and beyond life.—MISS THACKERAY, in *Old Kensington*.

'The sin which doth so easily beset us.'—HEB. XII. I.

'MY heart,' says Augustine (*Confessions*, ch. I. of book seven), 'cried out vehemently against all my phantasms, and with this one blow I tried to beat off from my mind's eye the unclean troop which buzzed around it. And lo, being scarcely driven away, in the twinkling of an eye they again gathered thick around me, flew against my face, and beclouded it.'

REFERENCES.—XII. 1.—J. Parker, *The Gospel of Jesus Christ*, p. 117. Bishop Gore, *Christian World Pulpit*, vol.

xlix. p. 325. *Christianity in Daily Conduct*, p. 309. **Marcus Dods**, *Christian World Pulpit*, vol. xlv. p. 166. **J. W. Houchin**, *The Vision of God*, p. 92. **E. E. Jenkins**, *Christian World Pulpit*, vol. lii. p. 92. **J. Watson**, *Scottish Review*, vol. iii. p. 331. **B. J. Snell**, *Christian World Pulpit*, vol. xlviii. p. 1. **R. F. Horton**, *ibid.* p. 193. Archbishop Temple, *ibid.* vol. liii. p. 321. **A. Maclaren**, *Expositions of Holy Scripture—Hebrews*, p. 177; *ibid.* p. 186.

MANY MANSIONS

(For All Saints' Day)

'Therefore let us also, seeing we are compassed about with so great a cloud of witnesses, lay aside every weight, and the sin which doth closely cling to us, and let us run with patience the race that is set before us, looking unto Jesus, the author and perfecter of our faith.'—Heb. XII. 1, 2 (R.V.).

'In My Father's house are many mansions . . . I go to prepare a place for you.'—John XIV. 2.

Lord Beaconsfield, in his 'Venetia,' describes the aged tutor of the son and heir of a noble house as leading his pupil into the picture gallery of the castle. As he pointed out one portrait after another he reminds the youth that no single one of his ancestors had brought dishonour to the family name. He did this in order to stimulate and encourage him to walk in the steps of those who had gone before. The author of this Epistle, writing to Hebrew Christians tempted to apostatise from the faith, leads them to the portrait gallery of the heroes of faith. He compares them in number to the 'cloud' of spectators at the Isthmian games, looking down on the arena and watching with keenest interest the runners in a race. Bishop Lightfoot has told us that the Greek word for 'witnesses' is never used simply as spectators. Here they are those who bear testimony to a certain truth. They are not the Light, but they reflect the Light. 'Jesus Christ is to me,' said Tennyson one day, 'as is the sun to yonder flower.' 'So must it be to us,' said Canon Ainger, who authenticates the story, 'for power comes from the source, not from the colour, beauty, charm of the reflection.' 'And the Light was the life of men.'

I. Condition of the Glorified Saints.—'In My Father's house are many mansions; . . . I go to prepare a place for you.' Christ, in these words, is clearly speaking of the intermediate state. 'My Father's house' was the name which He gave to the Temple. He draws an analogy between the earthly and the heavenly sanctuary. The Temple had 'many mansions,' which were used for a threefold purpose.

(*a*) I need not say that the Temple was *a place of worship*. St. John, in the Apocalypse, speaks especially of this aspect of heaven. On the background of the Temple services he depicts the joyous praises of the glorified saints. In the Benedicite we chant: 'O ye spirits and souls of the righteous, bless ye the Lord: praise Him and magnify Him for ever'.

(*b*) Just as the Mosque of St. Sophia, in Constantinople, is not only a place of worship, but also a Mohammedan college, so the Temple was *a great school of instruction*. In its 'mansions,' its chambers and corridors, were the celebrated schools of Simeon and Hillel, and other Doctors of the Law. It was in the Temple that St. Paul sat at the feet of Gamaliel. It was in one of the 'mansions' of the Temple courts Joseph and Mary found the boy Jesus 'in the midst of the doctors, both hearing and asking them questions'. The dying Moses exclaimed, 'All the saints are in Thy hands, and they sat down at Thy feet'—the Eastern attitude of the scholar—'every one shall receive of Thy words'. The mightiest intellects have sat at the feet of Christ the Teacher, but the genius of a Pascal, the logic of a Butler, the splendid scholarship of a Lightfoot, or the spiritual insight of a Liddon have never learned on earth the truth of God as it is learned by the saints who are sitting at the feet of Jesus in the heavenly school.

(*c*) The Temple, like the Vatican, which with its many chambers is the dwelling of the Pontifical household, was *the home of a priesthood*. When a priest left his Levitical city, in the order of his course, and entered the gates of Jerusalem, he had not, like a stranger, to seek for lodgings. His 'mansion' or chamber was prepared for him within the precincts of the Temple. Our Lord specially refers to this fact. I ask you to notice that Christ used a technical term for 'mansion'. What the bungalow or rest-house is in India to-day the *mone* (the word used by Christ) was on the great roads of the Greek Empire—a place of rest and refreshment for the passing traveller. On the Roman roads these bungalows were called *mansiones*, and hence through the Latin Vulgate the word 'mansion' is found in our English version. Our Lord, by the use of this term, distinctly taught that the 'intermediate state' is not the final goal of human existence. The word *mone* implies both rest and progress. The saints in heaven are a stage nearer the final home, where in glorified bodies they shall stand in the presence of Him who is 'the Resurrection and the Life'. We cannot understand a disembodied spirit, and hence the universal instinct, when we think of reunion with loved ones whom we have lost, is to think of reunion in a resurrection state. The words of an old Scotch song often pass through my own mind, especially at this season of the Church's year:—

> Sweet the lav'rock's note and lang
> Lilting wildly up the glen:
> Will ye no' come back again?
> Will ye no' come back again?
> Better loved ye canna be.
> Will ye no' come back again?

We cannot bring our loved ones back again, but God can and will.

II. An Argument from Nature.—I must at once call your attention to a simple argument from nature founded on the words, 'I go to prepare a place for you'. Everywhere in the natural world we see a wonderful adaptation, even in the lowest forms of organic life, to their surroundings. When a little bird breaks its shell, its skin is one of the tenderest things in nature. The quill feathers of the parent bird, with which it flies, are hard, and would hurt and bruise the wee fledgeling if they touched it. So beneath these feathers there are others which are very soft—we call them down. They form a coverlet which comes between the hard feathers and the tender skin. 'Are ye not much better than they?' I ask parents who have lost little ones, if God thus provides for the little birds, can you doubt that in the nursery of heaven He will make the tenderest provision for these undeveloped intelligences? A Huguenot officer, seeing Admiral Coligny lying sorely wounded on the battlefield of Moncontour, whispered in his ear, 'Yet, God is very gentle'. Bereaved parents, do not forget the gentleness of God.

III. I must at once apply the chief thought which my first text suggests. The author of this Epistle bids us beware of the sin of unbelief, the entangling robe which most impedes our course. At this festival of All Saints, with all its hallowed memories, we are reminded of our own mortality. This faith of which I speak is a simple trust in One who alone can give peace in a dying hour. Let us once more, in the study of the Word, and in the use of the Ordinances which our beloved Church so richly supplies, rekindle the flickering embers of our faith at the altar-fires of heaven.—J. W. BARDSLEY, *Many Mansions*, p. 11.

ALL SAINTS' DAY

'Wherefore seeing we also are compassed about with so great a cloud of witnesses, let us lay aside every weight, and the sin which doth so easily beset us, and let us run with patience the race that is set before us, looking unto Jesus the Author and Finisher of our faith.'—HEB. XII. I, 2.

'SEEING that we are compassed about'—whether we see it or not it is a truth. There are so many people who seem to live quite unconscious of environment. And what is true of ordinary things is also true of the kingdom of God. Some Christians are so very unsympathetic to environment, and there are some whose eyes are open and they see Jesus at the right hand of God. It is like that beautiful Old Testament story of Elisha's servant.

But what are we compassed about with? The writer of this Epistle has before him the circus of Rome and the tiers, row upon row, filled with spectators. Those who strive, who are they? We can supply the answer ourselves. Who are the angels? They are spectators, they are observers. They take an interest in the contest, and their faces behold the face of our Father which is in heaven. And yet these are not the spectators St. Paul alludes to. He does not say that we are compassed about with a great cloud—mark the word 'cloud'—of spectators, observers; no, he says witnesses. And the word 'witness' means not a spectator, an observer, but one who testifies, a martyr. We might render it, 'We are compassed about with so great a cloud of martyrs'. They are not cold, critical observers of the struggle; no, they are those who themselves have struggled and fought, and run, and have won the victory.

Now mark the word 'wherefore'. The eleventh chapter, which precedes this, is the great chapter of the saints of old, who waxed valiant in the fight, who were stoned, tempted, sawn asunder, and who confessed that they were only strangers and pilgrims who sought a better country, and that a heavenly, who were destitute, tormented, afflicted, of whom the world was not worthy, of whom it is said, 'Wherefore God is not ashamed to be called their God'. The martyrs are the saints, the Church triumphant, witnessing the Church militant. Now you can understand the expression, 'Wherefore seeing we are compassed about with so great a cloud of witnesses'.

Then just let me follow the text out in the simplest way. What are we to do?

I. First of all we are to 'lay aside every weight, and the sin that doth so easily beset us'. The word 'us' is not in the original. It does not mean sin within us at all. We are to lay aside every weight and the sin which is always at us. That is the first thing to do. We are not to give in to the circumstances that are round about us, however evil they may be. Lay them all aside, strip yourself of them, and run free. It is the circumstances that are round about us that would prevent us gaining the crown. Now the circumstances of sin round about us steal away our faith. Who is there here who does not know in running the race the difficulty we have to maintain our faith clear to the end? The saints and martyrs are there all round, and of them it is written, 'These all died in faith'. The coldness, the atmosphere round about us, the indifference in high places, the criticism of the Word of God itself—lay them aside. You cannot run unless your faith is true.

II. And then the second point is this—run with patience the appointed course. There is where the happiness comes in. You yourself are placed on the course by God—it is all His choice. He made you, and He has made the conditions in which you have got to run. It is the appointed course. He has chosen the race for you. It is all His doing. You were born at the moment He chose, and you die the moment He chooses. Your times are in His hands. You are His from the beginning to the end of the course, entirely His, wholly His, completely His, wherever the circumstances of your life may be. And is not that a help? It is His course, His race, you are His runner.

III. And, then, last of all, 'Looking unto Jesus'. Keep your eye in the right direction. How strong here is the preposition! It is not looking unto exactly. There is a little word which in the Greek means looking into Jesus, right into Him, not looking only at His words, His works, His miracles, and His beautiful Life; something more than that, looking right into Him and reading His heart. When Peter fell cursing and swearing in the hall of the Judgment Seat, Christ looked at him. Peter saw it. How did Peter know that Christ was looking at him? Because Peter was looking at Christ. And when Christ looked at him and Peter looked at Christ, Peter looked right into His Heart and went out and wept bitterly. That is an example of looking into the Saviour.

Then comes the last beautiful expression of the text, 'the Author and Finisher of our faith'. Now, is not that a complete text? See how complete it is, coming after chapter XI. The Lord Jesus is the author of faith, and the end of faith, too. If we have faith in Jesus, He put it there. He is the Author of it. It is His faith in us. He is the Author of your faith, and He is the Finisher of your faith. He Who has begun the good work in you will continue it unto the day of His coming.

'Let us run . . . looking.'—Heb. xii. 1, 2.

'Spinoza,' says Professor Royce in his *Spirit of Modern Philosophy* (pp. 54, 55), 'is not a man of action; his heroism, such as it is, is the heroism of contemplation. . . . Unswervingly he turns from the world of finite hopes and joys; patiently he renounces every sort of worldly comfort; even the virtue that he seeks is not the virtue of the active man. There is one good thing, and that is the Infinite; there is one wisdom, and that is to know God; there is one sort of true love, and that is the submissive love of the saintly onlooker, who in the solitude of reflection sees everywhere an all-pervading law, an all-conquering truth, a supreme and irresistible perfection.'

References.—XII. 1, 2.—Marcus Dods, *Christ and Man*, p. 61. R. W. Church, *Village Sermons* (2nd Series), p. 346. R. Glover, *Christian World Pulpit*, vol. lix. p. 211. G. A. Bennetts, *Preacher's Magazine*, vol. xvii. p. 398. C. Gutch, *Sermons*, p. 280. J. C. M. Bellew, *Sermons*, vol. i. p. 197. F. D. Maurice, *Sermons*, vol. i. p. 63. Spurgeon, *Sermons*, vol. xxxiv. No. 2037. A. B. Davidson, *Waiting upon God*, p. 305. *Church Family Newspaper*, vol. xv. p. 960. XII. 1-29. —*Expositor* (4th Series), vol. ii. p. 194.

AUTHOR AND FINISHER
'The Author and Finisher of our faith.'—Heb. xii. 2.

Let the Apostle, an eloquent man and mighty in the Scriptures, read the Old Testament to us. We do not want a new Bible, we want a new reader. Who has this gift of vocal light and heart music who will read to us the Old Testament? That man is the writer of the Epistle to the Hebrews, which is the sublimest commentary on the Pentateuch ever written, the only true commentary on the Pentateuch. A man of such piercing insight and such long intellectual foresight, with such a gift of music, he comes into the house without opening the door. That is always true pastoral visitation—to enter the sickroom without a noise, to approach without a creak. Will the Apostle read to us the Old Testament? He will. 'By faith Abel.' I thought faith never occurred in the Old Testament. Yes, faith occurred, but not the word. Yet some persons only know things by the word. They only think a sermon is evangelical if it mentions the name of Jesus Christ five and twenty times; that they call Gospel preaching. It may be; it may not be. Oh, the fools that block our way to heaven! 'By faith Enoch . . . By faith Noah . . . By faith Abraham . . . By faith Rahab . . . By faith Isaac . . . By faith Jacob . . . By faith Joseph . . . By faith Moses . . .' Why, it was all faith, and we were told that faith was not so much as mentioned in the Old Testament; it now appears

that there is nothing else mentioned. He that hath ears to hear, let him hear.

I. No one man can hold all the faith. That is the lesson of the eleventh chapter of the Epistle to the Hebrews. By a certain aspect of faith Abel . . . ; by a certain phase of faith Enoch . . . ; by a certain degree of faith Isaac . . . ; by another degree of faith Moses humbled the pride of Egypt, scorned its offers, went away to sup with the people of God. Now let us read the text, and take out of it the word 'our,' that word you so much prized, let it go; it is not in the original language of the text. 'The Author and Finisher of faith'; not 'our' faith, which is but an aspect of the true faith, and in so far as it is a true aspect of the true faith is justly referred to the miracle-working power of the Holy Ghost. But the great text is Faith, not our faith, not His faith, but all the faith you can gather together multiplied by infinity; and Jesus is the Author and Finisher of faith—the new life, the life that refreshes itself in the life of God, the new mode of life. We have all read, speaking in the language of charity, the great work of Prof. Tyndall on *Heat as a Mode of Motion*. Who will write a kindred book relating to a higher science—faith a mode of motion, a mode of life, a mode of suffering, a mode of conquest? As the great Doctor found motion in heat, so we find the soul's motion in faith. We are saved by faith; faith is the gift of God.

II. You must distinguish between faith and the quantity of faith. Faith may be a quality rather than a magnitude. 'Great is thy faith' may be an expression which means, true and grand is the quality of thy faith. How much there is in quality! and how foolish, viewed in this light, is the absurd doctrine that all men are equal even in the sight of God! They are not. We are not equally whole men. Some man will touch me with his loving hand, and make a new creature of me in relation to passing circumstances. Another man will look at me, and add ten years to my life, my age, and the burden of my misery. 'Great is thy faith,' therefore, may be a reference quite as much to quality as to magnitude. Do not let us contemn men for want of faith, for in some aspects and directions they may have more faith than we. I have envied some people the way in which they can carry the burdens of life. I cannot do so; I go from Jerusalem to Jericho, and fall among temptations and assaults and hindrances, and I am left naked and half dead on the inhospitable roadside. But Jesus comes and recognises what is in me, knows me to be a man, a man saved, a man with the crimson upon him which flowed from one fount alone. We show our faith in different ways and in different degrees; but it may be the real saving faith after all.

III. Suppose we say that the subject is light rather than faith; how then would the illustration run? This little candle is not light, but a light; I can see that. This dim oil-lamp is not light, it is a light; this electric jet is not light, it is a light, an aspect of light, a part-light, it belongs to the great family called light. But you must understand the distinction and the difference between these. Now there is beyond all these aspects and phases of light the true light itself, God's light, not a twinkling star or a dying sun, but Light, the thing itself, the essential glory. That is the meaning of the text. By faith Abel, Enoch, Abraham, Isaac, Jacob, Moses, and all the rest of the grand heroes did this and that conquest; these were lights, each was a light, but God is Light, and all light comes from God. Do not mistake the little twinkling candle for light in the true sense of that term. It is just the same with yourself, and with Christians generally. I am but a little sparklet, hardly worthy to be called a sparklet; if you want to see light see Jesus, listen to Him, what saith He? 'I am the light of the world.' So we must make these broad and vital distinctions. Let each shine with his own lustre, let no lamp envy any other lamp, let no light depreciate any other light, let no preacher depreciate any other preacher. All the preachers are necessary; all the voices are not in the one voice; all the gamuts run up into one ineffable music.— Joseph Parker, *City Temple Pulpit*, vol. iv. p. 146.

LOOKING AND LOOKING OFF
(*For the New Year*)
'Looking unto Jesus.'—Heb. xii. 2.

Life is not given to us all at once as a full cup, to be slowly drained as the years pass, to become less palatable, less delightful, more flat, more weary. It is, on the contrary, given to us, and to all creation as it is needed, fresh from the hand of God. And, further, it is not meant to be dully continuous or gradually to sink away. It is to be new every morning, with fresh starts, fresh enrichments, and fresh hopes. It is one of the blessings of a new year that the break compels us to think of this. We cannot help dreaming between the end and the beginning, between the shining and the shading. Perhaps at first the thought of change, and loss, and disappointment is what suggests itself most powerfully. We say to ourselves that the past has taught the unwisdom of expecting, of darting thought and hope into the unknown future.

We keep our hold, and may make it faster on all that is really precious if we look up. We may run the race with patience, looking unto Jesus. The phrase in the original means not only looking but looking off. We have to look away from many things that draw the eyes, and look up to the Author and Finisher of our faith. So looking the cloud is lifted off our spirits, and we spring back to the old energy, and our youth is renewed like the eagle's.

I. This new year, however, it may find us, may, if we will, leave us richer, wiser, stronger, and calmer. Over much that will happen to us we have no control. But there is a great region which our own wills may possess and command, drive the winds as they list. If we seek more wisdom, it will be given to us. How few of us seek to press steadily towards a full posses-

sion of Christian truth! Many of our chief teachers, in their desire to reach those outside, have gone to the very circumference of Christianity. No doubt they may be nearer thus to those whom they are seeking to call. No doubt they do much, and very much, if they bring some of those who hear them even within the border. But why should they remain there as if there were nothing to be found further within? There is no truth of Christianity, however elementary, that does not show itself more mysterious, more beautiful, and more powerful in proportion as it is brooded over. There is no revelation that is not worth summering and wintering with. In order to know what we think we know, there must be concentration. There must be the looking off from many things, from many studies, from many labours, perhaps even from many Christian labours, before the final loveliness unveils itself. And besides, there are new truths in Christianity which we have not yet come to know, which we have perhaps regarded for years with doubt or suspicion, or even with dread, but which, mayhap, are to be the light and glory of our last years. To win possession of Christian truth there must be intellectual labour, though intellectual labour is not enough. The new discoveries about the Bible do not mean that we are to discard it, but that we are to study it more deeply and wisely until we understand, as we may now understand better, the true order and content of God's gracious converse with His people. Only it is ever to be remembered that the intellect can only guide us *to* spiritual truth. It is the Holy Ghost who must lead us *into* truth, lead us where the intellect leaves us, where human teachers cease to instruct us, where all light fails but His. We may master the lover's lexicon, but only love will teach us what love is, and sorrow what sorrow is, and death what death is. Even so, the Holy Ghost puts us in possession of the things of Christ by making them matter of our own experience. And the lessons we learn from Him are lessons never to be unlearned.

II. The new year may, if we will, bring with it a growth of strength. What are we to say about our moral progress? Do the wheat and the tares still twist and twine together in the garden of our souls? True, the wheat and the tares grow together unto the harvest. But it is the law of the life in Christ that as the wheat ripens, the tares gradually die out. Our business is to uproot them, to extirpate them, to make no treaty with them, to aim at no line of modified goodness, but to strive for perfection. We have learned to think soberly of what we can do, but looking off from our own weakness and up to Jesus we learn that we are not fighting alone.

We must look off from ourselves, cease that diseased introspection that so confuses and dims the Christian life. We must look away from the old desires that affrighted us, from the old matters on which we must speak to the Lord no more. We must cherish the great ambitions that are granted to all who seek, that may be found whatever our worldly circumstances may be. We must look upward and forward to that future so much larger and greater than our past has been, that future in which we shall attain more than the heights of our dreams, that future in which all the sins, and sorrows, and struggles of mortality shall vanish like a thing of nought. 'Oh, the winds of repentance, and reconciliation, and atonement that will blow from garden to garden of God in the tender twilights of His kingdom !'—W. ROBERTSON NICOLL, *Sunday Evening*, p. 83.

THE SHAME

'Despising the shame.'—HEB. XII. 2.

OUR Lord, going down into the chill passages that ended in the cross, and speaking with the full determination of eternal love, said : 'If any man will come after Me, let Him deny himself, and take up his cross, and follow Me'. We know, in part, the meaning of His words. We know that it is not our business to seek crosses or to make them. The cross lies in our path, and our duty is to lift it. The Christian has to deny self, and take up his cross cheerfully. 'Dragged crosses are very heavy, but carried crosses are very light.' Crosses lifted bravely and in the strength of Christ can be carried, even although it is true that every day brings its cross, not the same cross necessarily, but a cross always that has to be borne with gentle firmness through evil report and through good report up to the very end.

I. There are various ingredients in the cross. There is labour, there is pain, and there is shame. The cross of labour is the easiest to carry, if the labour is accomplished with some measure of recognition, of stimulus, of success. Many men need these. General Grant, writing of his great antagonist in the Civil War, said : 'Lee was a good man, a fair commander, who had everything in his favour. *He was a man who needed sunshine.*' He could go on with his task as long as he was treated like a demigod. It is small merit to work so long as work is delightful, so long as the air rings with plaudits. The exercise of power is very dear to certain natures, and may be no part at all of the Christian burden. So in the kingdom of God men have to sow in tears, and oftentimes wait through frustrated and broken years for the day when they shall reap in joy.

Another element in the Christian cross is pain. The cross may mean physical suffering. It may mean bereavement. It may mean great sacrifice of things prized and dear. But it is wonderful what even unassisted human nature can do in bearing pain. Stoicism was by no means a complete failure. All through the history of the world there have been palmary instances of men who with an end in view did not shrink from suffering, did not rebel or flinch, went steadily through great exactions and bitter agonies in order to reach their end.

But we venture to think that there is in the Christian cross something more than labour and pain, something far harder to encounter than any of these, something that tests finally, something that divides between the sheep and the goats. There is shame. In every cross there is something humiliating, something that lingers, something that stings like a whiplash, what is called in Scripture 'the shame,' the reproach of Christ. There are multitudes who cannot bear that. They cannot endure contempt ; they are strong enough for labour, strong enough, it may be, for pain, and yet not strong enough for shame.

II. Our Lord and His Apostles were fully aware of this, but even as the Lord Himself took the weight of shame, so His followers must. It was the shame of the cross that was our Lord's extreme trial. The deeper we go into the mystery of the Saviour's life, the more we shall understand this. It was the actual essential part of His discipline. He made acquaintance during His ministry with contempt and hatred and calumny, and after so many leagues of weary road He came in full sight of the tree. He was betrayed by His Apostle, sold for a slave's price, scourged, crowned with thorns, reckoned amongst the transgressors, made a spectacle to the world, and to angels and to men. Who shall declare His humiliation, tell what it all meant to Him as He hung naked there ? Even though from His cross He looked far and wide through time and eternity, over all kindreds and nations, even though He saw the sure fulfilment of His lifelong dream as He prayed that God would remember all His offering and accept His burnt sacrifice, nevertheless it was true that reproach broke His heart. He knew that it was shame that would most divide His followers from Him in the days to come, and in the cross that has struck its print so deep there is still nothing so terrible to flesh and blood. His Apostles encountered it and triumphed over it. St. Paul himself often employs the word. He speaks of crucifying the Son of God afresh and putting Him to an open shame. He knew that the followers of Christ could endure shame just in so far as they were His followers. Because He had borne shame for them, they were to bear shame for Him. Because He had not been ashamed of them, they were never to be ashamed of Him. Yet so hard was the battle that St. Paul speaks very soberly, very quietly, the words of his utmost triumph—'Nevertheless I am not ashamed'. He had said, 'I am not ashamed of the Gospel of Christ,' he had said, 'Hope maketh not ashamed,' he had blessed a brother who was not ashamed of the Apostle's chain. 'Let us go forth, therefore, unto Him without the camp, bearing His reproach.' *Unto Him* is the central word. What matters it though it be without the camp ? What matters it if it is unto Him ? What matters the reproach if He bore it ? As He did, for He endured the cross, despising the shame. The life of Jesus is to be made manifest in our mortal flesh. And the writer to the Hebrews uses the word Jesus, the name of Christ in His humiliation, the name so often used in scorn.'—W. ROBERTSON NICOLL, *Sunday Evening*, p. 111.

'Who for the joy that was set before Him endured the cross.'
Heb. xii. 2.

I mean by happiness, man's true well-being—that of
his higher, not his lower nature—that of his nature,
not for a moment, but for ever. With such happiness, duty, however stern, must always ultimately
coincide. I say, man was formed to desire such a
realisation of the possibilities of his nature, that to
bid him cease or slacken in this desire is a cruelty and
folly, and that the will of God ought never for an
instant to be conceived as hostile to such well-being.
If He were, why hear we of Redemption? And I may
point with reverence to the Incarnate Perfectness,
'who *for the joy that was set before Him* endured
the cross'; He would die to know the blessedness of
restoring to us our life. Only the most sublime self-
sacrifice could account for such a result or recompense;
and that recompense he did not refuse to keep constantly in view.'—Vaughan, *Hours with the Mystics*,
vol. ii. p. 284.

It is not alone the *amount* of suffering implied in
the treatment to which our Lord was subjected that
we must fail to estimate aright, unless we see that
suffering in the light of the life that was in Him. It
is still more as to the *nature* of that suffering that
we shall err. This we feel the moment we turn
from contemplating it as physical suffering on the
part of men and physical endurance on the part of
Christ, to contemplate it in its spiritual aspect as *the
form of the response of enmity to love*. There is
surely very special instruction for us here in the fact
that shame—indignity—is so marked a character of
the injuries inflicted on Christ. . . . Indignity and
contumely, that is to say, all that would most touch
that life which man has in the favour of man, and
which strikes more deeply than physical infliction,
because it goes deeper than the body, wounding the
spirit—is the most distinguishing feature of the evil
use made by sinful men of the power that they received over the Son of God when he was betrayed
into the hands of sinners. All along, the relation of
the *cross* to *shame* was ever present to the Lord's
mind.—M'Leod Campbell, *The Nature of the Atonement*, pp. 229 f.

THE OUTWARD LOOK

'Looking unto Jesus the Author and Perfecter of our faith.'—
Heb. xii. 2.

One of the main sources of strength of what we are
accustomed to call the evangelical view of Christianity
is its consistent emphasis of the *outward look*. To
my thinking, Thomas Carlyle was never a wiser and
stronger teacher than when he dealt with the endless
and useless torments which mankind has suffered in
its efforts to fulfil the Socratic precept 'know thyself'. 'Long enough has that poor self of thine
tormented thee. Thou wilt never get to know it,
I believe. Know what thou canst work at, and work
at it like a Hercules; that will be the better plan.'
It is nothing less than the honest truth that the self
cannot be known by self-analysis and self-examination.

I. If I had time to make the review, I think I
should be able to show you how strong and wise and
healthy is the objective note all through the Old
Testament—heard like a clarion in its greatest
passages. The call of the Psalmist is for an outgoing
of the soul in praise and prayer. They are the
noblest vehicles of public and private worship, because
committed to these Psalms the spirit of the worshipper
is lifted out of its broodings and disquietudes, and
self-pityings, and carried away in imagination and
faith towards its Maker and Redeemer. The message
of the Psalmist and Prophet is one everywhere; it is
the great cry that utters itself still from the pages
of Isaiah. 'There is no God but Me; a just God and
a Saviour; look unto Me, and be ye saved, all the
ends of the earth.'

II. When we turn to the New Testament we find
that this Gospel of the Outward Look is more and
more proclaimed. John the Baptist deals searchingly,
mercilessly with the sins of his day, but he concludes
by pointing his hearers—not only away from himself,
but away from themselves: 'Behold the Lamb of
God Who taketh away the sin of the world'. Christ
directed the gaze of the world from sin and its consequences to sin and its salvation.

III. Equally striking and consistent is the Gospel
of the Outward Look in the Apostle's preaching. I
think we cannot but be impressed with how little the
Apostles seemed to trouble about their own souls.
There is no counsel on which it is more necessary to
insist than to *rest* in the Lord, and wait patiently for
Him. Look out steadily, believingly, obediently to
the Christ of God; for in that look is self-forgetfulness, life, and peace.

IV. Nothing grows clearer to my mind than that,
in the religious life, to be self-centred is to fail. Introspection breeds pessimism and every morbid
phantasm of fear and folly. There is no safety for
any of us but in following Christ and in going about
doing good.—C. S. Horne, *The Soul's Awakening*,
p. 1.

References.—XII. 2.—Spurgeon, *Sermons*, vol. v. No.
236. W. J. Knox-Little, *Christian World Pulpit*, vol. xlv. p.
184. C. Perren, *Revival Sermons in Outline*, p. 330. *Expositor* (4th Series), vol. ii. p. 300; *ibid.* vol. x. p. 75; *ibid.* (5th
Series), vol. ii. p. 434. A. Maclaren, *Expositions of Holy
Scripture—Hebrews*, p. 199. XII. 3.—G. A. Sowter, *From
Heart to Heart*, p. 228. J. Keble, *Sermons for the Holy Week*,
p. 67. Spurgeon, *Sermons*, vol. xviii. No. 1073. *Expositor*
(6th Series), vol. x. p. 137.

'Ye have not yet resisted unto blood, striving against sin.'—
Heb. xii. 4.

Compare Charles Lamb's letter, of 23rd December,
1822, to Bernard Barton the Quaker, in which he
observes: 'You have no martyrs *quite to the fire*,
I think, among you; but plenty of heroic confessors,
spirit-martyrs, lamb-lions'.

What sayest thou, son? Cease to complain, when
thou considerest My passion and that of other saints.
Thou has not yet resisted unto blood. It is but little
which thou sufferest in comparison of those who

suffered so much, who were so strongly tempted, so grievously afflicted, so many ways tried and harassed. Thou oughtest therefore to call to mind the heavier woes of others, that thou mayest the easier bear thine own small troubles.—Thomas à Kempis, *Imitation of Christ* (iv. 19).

And who among the saints hath ever taken that castle without stroke of sword? The chief of the house, our elder Brother, our Lord Jesus, not being excepted, who won His own house and home, due to Him by birth, with much blood and many blows.— Samuel Rutherford, to Lady Kenmure (15th Nov. 1633).

Reference.—XII. 4.—A. Maclaren, *Expositions of Holy Scripture—Hebrews*, p. 209.

'My son, despise not thou the chastening of the Lord, nor faint when thou art rebuked of Him.'—Heb. xii. 5.

'When there is a keeping in any measure from a despising of the Lord's chastening,' Rev. H. Davidson wrote, in 1728, to Thomas Boston of Ettrick, 'yet I find no small difficulty to bear off from the other rock, a fainting under His rebukes. Faith's views, that it is the Lord, will prove quieting. A sight of His sovereignty, wisdom, righteousness, and faithfulness, works up the soul into a holy acquiescence in, and composure under, the eternal decree now revealed in the event.'

Sometimes the fire of adversity warms a cold heart, and then the story is not all sorrowful. The saddest story is that of some ice-bound souls, whom the very fires of adversity cannot reach.—Miss Thackeray, in *Old Kensington*.

Reference.—XII. 5.—Spurgeon, *Sermons*, vol. i. No. 48.

THE CHASTISEMENT OF THE CHRISTIAN
Heb. xii. 5, 6.

Retribution is necessary to salvation; chastisement and punishment must come before salvation. There are three great necessities for salvation.

I. A man must be brought into a certain state of mind and will; a certain mental attitude towards sin. So far as retribution shows that God is not Love, it is one of the most convincing proofs, if intelligently understood, that God is Love.

II. Man must be revealed to himself. And sometimes he is taught to know himself by a hard, painful process.

III. We must not be individuals. Our sympathies must be called out. A man may be great, but without sympathy he cannot be good. The only way to get a contrite heart is to get a broken heart.—Reuen Thomas, *British Congregationalist*, 30th August, 1906, p. 104.

'Whom the Lord loveth He chasteneth.'—Heb. xii. 6.

We all want religion sooner or later. I am afraid there are some who have no natural turn for it, as there are persons without an ear for music, to which, if I remember right, I heard one of you comparing what you called religious genius. But sorrow and misery bring even these to know what it means, in a

great many instances. May I not say to you, my friend, that I am one who has learned the secret of the inner life by the discipline of trials in the life of outward circumstance? I can remember the time when I thought more about the shade of a colour in a ribbon, whether it matched my complexion or not, than I did about my spiritual interests in this world or the next. It was needful that I should learn the meaning of the text, 'whom the Lord loveth He chasteneth'. Since I have been taught in the school of trial I have felt, as I never could before, how precious an inheritance is the smallest patrimony of faith.—O. W. Holmes, *The Poet at the Breakfast Table* (ch. vii.).

Reference.—XII. 6.—*Expositor* (4th Series), vol. iii. p. 118. XII. 7.—*Expositor* (6th Series), vol. x. p. 172.

Heb. xii. 8.

'I am better off now than I have been for years, God be thanked!' Charles Kingsley wrote in 1857 to Thomas Hughes. 'God grant, too, that I may not require to be taken down by some terrible trouble. I often fancy I shall be. If I am, I shall deserve it, as much as any man who ever lived. I say so now—justifying God beforehand, lest I should not have faith and patience enough to justify Him when the punishment comes.'

'Shall we not much rather be in subjection to the Father of our spirits and live.'—Heb. xii. 9.

'Small as the amount of prayer is,' says M'Leod Campbell, 'its usual character is a still sadder subject of thought than its usual amount. I mean its being so much a dealing with God simply as a Sovereign Lord, a Governor, and Judge, and so little a dealing with Him as the Father of our spirits.'

Reference.—XII. 9.—*Expositor* (6th Series), vol. viii. p. 38.

THE USES OF SUFFERING
'But He for our profit.'—Heb. xii. 10.

It is a great mistake, and one which deceives many, to suppose that suffering will, of itself, be any use. Suffering is never negative. But it often hardens. And suffering turned to no account, or turned to a bad account, is the most grievous of sins!

There must be a supernatural agency working with the suffering before it will be of any use to the sufferer. The Holy Ghost must do His own work in the soul.

Therefore, at the very threshold, ask two things: one, that the God of grace will work with the God of providence to make the trial effective to spiritual ends; and the other, that whatever be the special purpose for which the trial is sent, it may not pass away till you have learnt your lesson and the purpose is fulfilled.

This done, we may look for *the uses*.

I. **All Suffering is Intended to be to the Mind what Physical Pain is to the Body.**—When you feel a pain in any part of your body, it is sent for this purpose, to say to you, 'There is mischief going on here; attend to it'. It is the same to the soul, with every suffering which our heavenly Father ever sends us. It comes to say, 'There is something which needs correction'. There is something latent. But you must probe it, and examine it, and treat it seriously. The Holy Ghost, working in your conscience, will show you what it is.

II. **Sufferings are not always Intended for the same Uses.**—The suffering of Manasseh was for conversion; of Jacob, for correction; of Job, for humiliation; of David, for restoration; of St. Paul, for experience; of Christ—from a human point of view—for sympathy and pattern. So sufferings, coming in their various forms, come each to train another and another grace in the human mind. Every suffering has its own particular message to each particular heart. St. Paul has drawn us a chain: 'Tribulation' brings with it 'patience'; 'patience' brings with it a present 'experience' of God's love; the present 'experience' of God's love shows us the future: 'Tribulation worketh patience; and patience, experience; and experience, hope'.

III. **One Reason why Suffering is so Beneficial and so Essential to a high Christian Standard** is that it almost always separates us awhile, and brings us, if not into solitude, into more quietness and retirement. Suffering, in its very nature, is generally attended with isolation. This is what we want. To be more alone with ourselves and God; to be brought more face to face with our conscience and with Him; to be still enough to hear the whispers.

And it is a wonderful and most comforting thought—for every sufferer in the school of Christ—'My Master was chastened for His profit; and He, even He, "the Captain of my salvation," was "perfect through suffering".'

'He for our profit, that we may be partakers of His holiness.'
—Heb. xii. 10.

It is to keep a man awake, to keep him alive to his own soul and its fixed design of righteousness, that the better part of moral and religious education is directed; not only that of words and doctors, but the sharp ferule of calamity under which we are all God's scholars till we die.—R. L. Stevenson.

Evan had just been accusing the heavens of conspiracy to disgrace him. Those patient heavens had listened, as is their wont. They had viewed, and had not been disordered by his mental frenzies. It is certainly hard that they do not come down to us, and condescend to tell us what they mean, and be dumbfoundered by the perspicuity of our arguments. . . . Nevertheless, they to whom mortal life has ceased to be a long matter, perceive that our appeals for conviction are answered,—now and then very closely upon the call. When we have cast off the scales of hope and fancy, and surrender our claims on mad chance; when the wild particles of this universe consent to march as they are directed, it is given them to see—if they see at all—that some plan is working out: that the heavens, icy as they are to the pangs of our blow, have been throughout speaking to

our souls.—George Meredith, *Evan Harrington* (ch. x.).

Reference.—XII. 10.—A. Maclaren, *Expositions of Holy Scripture—Hebrews*, p. 216.

HEB. XII. II.

How the eternal Justice might see fit to deal with other souls, why he had been singled out for so peculiar and conspicuous a fate, Richard did not pretend to say. All that had become curiously unimportant to him. For he had ceased to call that fate a cruel one. It had changed its aspect. It had come suddenly to satisfy both his conscience and his imagination. With a movement at once of wonder and of deep-seated thankfulness, he, for the first time, held out his hands to it, accepting it as a comrade, pledging himself to use rather than to spurn it. He looked at it steadfastly, and, so looking, found it no longer abhorrent but of mysterious virtue and efficacy, endued with power to open the gates of a way closed to most men, into the heart of humanity, which, in a sense, is nothing less than the heart of Almighty God Himself. And this brought to him a sense of almost awed repose. It released him from the vicious circle of self, of sharp-toothed disappointment and leaden-heavy discouragement, in which he had so long fruitlessly turned. — Lucas Malet, in *Sir Richard Calmady* (bk. vi. ch. vi.).

References.—XII. 11.—J. G. Binney, *Christian World Pulpit*, vol. liii. p. 22. Spurgeon, *Sermons*, vol. ix. No. 528. XII. 13.—Spurgeon, *Sermons*, vol. xlix. No. 2854.

HOLINESS OF LIFE

(*For Ash Wednesday*)

'Follow peace with all men, and holiness, without which no man shall see the Lord.'—Heb. xii. 14.

Our subject is holiness; personal holiness which shows itself in the daily life; that personal possession of something which leads us day by day to live according to God's laws. No subject of greater moment could engage our attention on this the first day of Lent.

I. **A Life of Holiness is a Life not Ruled by the Body but by the Spirit,** and if our lives are ruled by the Spirit of God then we shall be holy. But if our life be ruled by the body and by the lust of the flesh and by our own evil desires, then we shall have no holiness and righteousness. We shall be of the earth earthy, for the rule of the body is antagonistic to the rule of the Holy Spirit.

II. **How shall we Obtain this Holiness?**—We can never lay claim to holiness until we have each one of us been cleansed of our own sins, and the right holiness of life is shown in the life of Christ. We are the possessors of the life of our Lord Jesus Christ, and we have received not only forgiveness of the past but cleansing. So the life of Christ is in our lives. We become partakers with Him, and His Spirit dwelleth in us. It is necessary for us to start from the only starting-point; we begin in Christ, we go on in Christ, and end in Christ when we become partakers of the joy of eternity. It is necessary for each one to come to Jesus Christ and to be partakers of eternal life through faith in a personal Saviour.

III. Our Bounden Duty.—It is bound upon us to aim at holiness and to possess it because we are not our own. We belong to God, we must do the works of God, and we must try and live the life of Christ because He has saved us by His own most precious blood. We know that many so-called Christians are leading a sham life so far as their religion is concerned. Their religion lacks sincerity. We know how sincere we ought to be, and how we ought always to cast out by the power of the Holy Spirit the sham and the hypocrisy both in our profession and in our practice. We ought to be very circumspect in our daily lives, and to be regular attenders at the house of God and take care to observe the Holy Sacrament.

IV. Yet it is not in Externals that Holiness Lies.—There must be form, but we must never leave out the inward and spiritual grace. Jesus Christ defined His Church in these words : ' the Kingdom of God is within you '. Such is holiness. It is something within. It is set up and cultivated by the Spirit in the heart, and because it is in the heart therefore it is in the life, and you do certain things because it is in your heart to do them. Holiness is something within ; it is that inward joy which shows itself in the life of Christ. Our hearts are inclined to fault, but when they are touched by the grace of God and the Holy Spirit enters and they are cleansed, then there is holiness. From the heart proceedeth good desires and right impulses, all these being the movement of the Holy Spirit.

'**Holiness, without which no man shall see the Lord.**'—HEB. XII. 14.

IF we wished to imagine a punishment for an unholy, reprobate soul, we perhaps could not fancy a greater than to *summon it to heaven*. Heaven would be hell to an irreligious man. We know how unhappy we are apt to feel at present, when alone in the midst of strangers, or of men of different tastes and habits from ourselves. How miserable, for example, would it be to have to live in a foreign land, among a people whose faces we never saw before, and whose language we could not learn. And this is but a faint illustration of the loneliness of a man of earthly dispositions and tastes, thrust into the society of saints and angels. How forlorn would he wander through the courts of heaven! He would find no one like himself; he would see in every direction the marks of God's holiness, and these would make him shudder. He would feel himself always in His presence. He could no longer turn His thoughts another way, as he does now, when conscience reproaches him. He would know that the Eternal Eye was ever upon him ; and the Eye of holiness, which is a joy and life to holy creatures, would seem to him an Eye of wrath and punishment.—J. H. NEWMAN.

'**Peace and holiness.**'—HEB. XII. 14.

HE that does a base thing in zeal for his friend, burns the golden thread that ties their hearts together.—JEREMY TAYLOR.

REFERENCES.—XII. 14.—G. Davidson, *Christian World Pulpit*, vol. xlv. p. 204. J. B. Mozley, *University Sermons*, p. 231. C. D. Bell, *The Saintly Calling*, p. 79. E. J. Boyce, *Parochial Sermons*, p. 257. Spurgeon, *Sermons*, vol. l. No. 2902. *Expositor* (4th Series), vol. iv. p. 58 ; *ibid.* (5th Series), vol. v. p. 137. XII. 14, 15.—Spurgeon, *Sermons*, vol. xvi. No. 940.

'**Lest any root of bitterness springing up trouble you.**'— HEB. XII. 15.

DESCRIBING his tour to South Africa with his wife and a cartographer, Mr. Theodore Bent, in *The Ruined Cities of Mashonaland* (p. 5), observes that ' we three left England at the end of January, 1891, and returned to it again at the end of January, 1892, having accomplished a record rare in African travel, and of which we are justly proud—namely, that no root of bitterness sprang up amongst us '.

REFERENCES.—XII. 15.—J. M. Neale, *Readings for the Aged* (4th Series), p. 42. *Ibid. Sermons Preached in Sackville College Chapel*, vol. i. p. 152.

THE SENSUALIST

'**Lest there be any fornicator,**[1] **or profane person, as Esau, who for one morsel of meat sold his birthright.**'—HEB. XII. 16.

ESAU was very far from being ' the lowest of the low '. On the contrary he possessed noble qualities, which make his ultimate fate all the more pitiful.

He is a big, generous, open-handed fellow, who forgives the brother who has done him the most deadly injuries and loads him with generosity. Does not such a man stand out in marked contrast to the scheming Jacob, who traps his brother in a moment of passion ? If Jacob be the religious man, and Esau the worldling, who would not choose the world?

I have put the case as strongly as I could, just because I know the Church is often said to pander to meanness when it is respectable, and pass by the essential goodness of Bohemianism. Thackeray puts it, in his contrast between Pitt Crawley and Rawdon. Du Maurier has ridden the thing to death in his whitewash of Trilby and blackwash of all the religious and moral people in his once famous novel. Nothing is more common and more easy than to depreciate religion and morality, and to exalt the easy virtues of modern Paganism.

Yet what has Scripture to say to this? It says uncompromisingly : 'Jacob have I loved : Esau have I hated'. There may indeed be a meanness about the former at the beginning. But if so it is not because of the man's religion. If a religious man is mean, it is not because he has too much religion : it is because he has too little. There was nothing mean about the man Christ Jesus.

Still, admitting Jacob's meanness, I do believe there is something about the Esau type of character which

[1] The better translation is, ' Lest there be any *sensual* or profane person '.

makes the Bible judgment to be ultimately true. Let us look at that character to-night, as it unfolds itself in the history. If you study it impartially you will come, I believe, to accept God's verdict : 'Jacob have I loved : Esau have I hated'.

I. What was there defective in Esau's character ? First and foremost, there was this—*he had no constancy of affection or purpose.*

Esau was, in fact, one of those men who keep all their goods in their shop window. When first they meet you they overwhelm you with kindness. They are what we somewhat vulgarly call 'gushing'. Soon, however, you discover that their first acquaintance is their best. They have nothing more to give you. You try to cultivate them : you find there is nothing to cultivate. There is no depth in their nature. They have no secret or solemn places in their life. There is no temple of God in their spirits. That is what the Bible means when it calls Esau *profane.*

II. So that brings us to the second and great element of weakness in Esau's character—*his sensuality, his lack of self-control, his inability to master the baser passions of his nature.*

It is on this the writer to the Hebrews concentrates when he calls him 'a sensual man, who for one morsel of meat sold his birthright'. There are times when the slumbering forces in our animal nature suddenly burst forth with volcanic fury, threatening devastation to all our future. Every man has in him certain appetites which he must conquer, if he is to win his life. That is the first problem of manhood. That is the great conflict of youth—to conquer my lower self, to crush the beast in me. Now I do not deny there are other than religious motives which can do this. Ambition can do it. Avarice has done it. But for a full and all-round victory only one thing avails—religion.

'No place for repentance'—we need not suppose from these words that Esau was lost eternally, that he found no pardon for his foolish act. There is only one sin that has no place for repentance—the sin of not repenting. What our text means is found in that other great scene in Esau's youth, when his blessing was stolen from him by Rebekah's craft, and he cried 'an exceeding bitter cry' : 'Hast thou not also another blessing ? Bless me, even me also, my father.' It would teach us that Jacob would never have been allowed to take the blessing of the first-born had it not been justly his already. Esau had forfeited the blessing when he sold the birthright.

So still there are sins which have no repentance. We do not say that you will not be saved from them by contrition and faith. What we do say is this—and life says it every day with terrible emphasis—that there are things which no repentance will ever buy back. You cannot restore the morning dewdrop to the shaken rose. You cannot get back the purity and unspoiled enthusiasm which early sensuality inevitably robs from the youthful soul. You cannot set yourself free from the net of evil relationships, or the stain of a blemished character which such a youthful 'indis-

cretion' may leave upon your life.—W. MACKINTOSH MACKAY, *Bible Types of Modern Men,* p. 269.

ESAUS WHO SELL THEIR BIRTHRIGHT

'Lest there be any fornicator, or profane person, as Esau, who for one morsel of meat sold his birthright.'—HEB. XII. 16.

THIS one act shows Esau. We know the man. He belongs to the class of men in whom passion and appetite rule, who are the slaves of every whim, and befooled by every fancy ; who fling away manhood and purity, conscience and God in rushing after some fool's paradise. That is the man. Lest there be a profane person, like Esau.

I. Now, What is God's Definition of Profanity ?—Our idea of profanity is irreverent speech. But God's idea of profanity goes deeper than that. Man may in his ungoverned thoughtless moments, in sudden anger, fling out words of impious daring which make us shudder ; and yet that man in his ordinary conduct may be above everything that is mean, false, tricky, and contemptible. He is not the profane person. And another man may never use words which would offend the most fastidious taste, or the most religious mind, and yet every day he may be selling his conscience, his pledged word, his honour, his trusting friend, or something equally precious, for a paltry price. He is the profane person.

II. The Mad Bargains of Life.—And such things are done every day ; terrible bargains with madness written on the face of them. We read of them in history, we read of them in the Bible, we find them in the lives of the men and women about us ; happy are we if we never blunder into them ourselves ! 'Lest there be among you a profane person, as Esau, who for one morsel of meat '—one morsel of meat !—there is a terrible emphasis on that word. We shudder at the greatness of the cost and the contemptibleness of the gain, for whatever you may gain by these bargains it is infinitesimal compared with the loss.

III. Irrevocable Loss.—What is there that can pay you for the loss of honesty, truthfulness, and purity ? It is not worth telling a lie for all the gold that passes through the mint. It is not worth breaking a pledge or betraying a trust for all the outward glory of Solomon. It is not worth sacrificing your principles and trailing your honour through the dust for all the huzzahs of the greatest crowd that have ever waved their hats in the air. You cannot buy these things back again. When these are lost the soul is lost. My last word is to Christians, Do not think that you have got beyond the danger.—J. G. GREENHOUGH, *Christian World Pulpit,* vol. LXII. p. 40.

'Any profane person, as Esau, who for one morsel of meat sold his birthright.'—HEB. XII. 16.

'PSYCHICAL pain,' said Heine flippantly, 'is more easy to endure than physical pain, and, had I to choose between a bad conscience and a bad tooth, I should choose the bad conscience.'

REFERENCES.—XII. 16.—F. C. Spurr, *Christian World Pulpit,* vol. lii. p. 323. F. W. Farrar, *Everyday Christian Life,* p. 174.

THE TEARS OF REMORSE

'He had no place of repentance, though he sought it carefully with tears.'—HEB. XII. 17.

ESAU was a fair representative of a man of the world. Considering the circumstances of his age, and his condition, he did nothing exceedingly wrong. He was 'more sinned against than sinning'. He was passionate; but he was not slow to forgive. He loved pleasure, and lived for it. He was a selfish man. We have no reason to say that he was a directly bad, or an immoral man. His conduct contrasts favourably with the conduct of his brother Jacob. Esau was never a deceiver. The great evil of Esau's life was that he thought little or nothing of spiritual things. He appears to have lived without any real sense of God and the Divine. God was not in all Esau's thoughts. This was Esau's sin.

'And Esau lifted up his voice, and wept.' Observe the state of Esau's mind at that moment. Esau never for a moment humbled himself before God. He never 'repented'. He never wished to 'repent'. He only wished to alter consequences.

It is necessary that this should be very clearly understood, because Esau's 'tears' have been made a handle to the thought that there may be on this earth those who wish to 'repent' and cannot. Never! Never was such a thing since the creation of the world, and never will be! One 'tear' that falls because we wish to 'repent,' and cannot 'repent,' is 'repentance'; and the forgiveness—that follows that 'tear'—is sure. But Esau's tears were not like that! They had nothing to do with 'repentance'. They were Remorse—only Remorse—impotent Remorse!

I. But what is Remorse?—Let us see—in the sad picture—some of its features.

(a) Remorse has nothing to do with sin—only with its results. The first and leading thought of real, Godly sorrow is a distressing feeling of sin—of sin as such; sin in itself — its wrongness, its blackness. The sin is the burden. But Remorse has to do with the accidents of sin.

(b) Remorse is essentially selfish. The heart is not pained because God is wronged—or because Christ is wounded—or because the Holy Spirit is grieved—or because a man is injured—but because we are hurt. It is only another form of egotism.

(c) Remorse is almost entirely fear. There is little or no love in it. The 'tear' is not the soft meltings of the affection, but the hard extortion of a dread.

(d) See, from the histories which we have of it, what Remorse is worth—what fruit it bears. A new life? Not once. Amendment? Not once. A certain right action? Not once (e.g., Saul and Samuel; Ahab and Elijah; Johanan and Jeremiah; Judas). Esau, who wept so importunately, rose from his tears and his pleadings in a fury and said, 'The days of mourning for my father are at hand; then will I slay my brother Jacob'. O fair and lovely show Remorse can wear! How it can weep, and talk of sin, and cry for mercy—while, take off the mask,

and what is its true face? Saul's pride—Ahab's obstinacy — Johanan's treachery — Judas's suicide—Esau's murder!

II. But cannot Remorse lead on to Repentance?—I think not. There is a state of heart, not unlike remorse at first view, which may be, and is, an element of Repentance. I call it Conviction. Conviction is not Repentance — for Conviction is not Conversion. Repentance is Conversion. Still, Conviction is necessary to Repentance. But Conviction is as wide from Remorse as grace is from nature, or as the tinsel is from the finest gold. Remorse is sorrow for sin's penalty—without God! Remorse is the severest torture of the human mind!

III. What is the Preventative, what is the Remedy of this Dismal End?—Penitence. Remorse is not Penitence. It is not part of Penitence. But Penitence may take its place. And Penitence, and only Penitence, can drive out Remorse. Was Esau ever in after life a Penitent? Were those bitter 'Tears of Remorse' ever changed for the sweet 'tears' of a holy sorrow? I do not know. Some token that he was not quite reprobate and cast out God gave him even then. 'Thy dwelling shall be the fatness of the earth, *and of the dew of heaven from above ;* and thou shalt serve thy brother,' yet one day 'thou shalt break his yoke from off thy neck' Even the hard Esau may have been saved when the 'tears' of mortification were changed for the 'tears' of a contrite heart and he 'found,' in a sense he never knew when he was at Isaac's feet, a 'place of repentance'.

'He found no place of repentance.'—HEB. XII. 17.

IN a letter, quoted in his biography (ch. IX.), Dr. Arnold of Rugby remarks: 'So far from finding it hard to believe that repentance can ever be too late, my only wonder is that it should ever be otherwise than too late, so instantaneous and lasting are the consequences of an evil once committed. I find it very hard to hinder my sense of this from quite oppressing me.'

REFERENCES.—XII. 17.—A. Maclaren, *Expositions of Holy Scripture—Hebrews*, p. 227.

THE SOUND OF A TRUMPET AND THE VOICE OF WORDS

'The sound of a trumpet and the voice of words.'—HEB. XII. 19.

ON 23rd February, 1791, John Wesley preached his last sermon at Leatherhead, in the dining-room of a magistrate, from the text, 'Seek ye the Lord while He may be found, call ye upon Him while He is near'. Thus that wonderful voice fell silent—that voice which they who heard entreated that the word should be spoken to them for evermore. He was then eighty-eight, and the long course of his earthly life, with its afflictions, its homelessness, its fatigue, and its constant triumph in Christ, was nearing the end. The next day he wrote his last letter, denouncing 'the execrable villainy' of slavery. He died on 2nd March. For many years he had lived in the second rest—that rest where Christ's yoke is easy and His burden light. Spiritual throes and pangs, earthly cares and fears, were far in the past, and it was with him as with his friend Fletcher of Madeley, of whom he testified that he died in an unspeakable calmness and serenity of spirit, 'a tranquillity in the Blood of Christ which keeps the souls of believers in their latest hour, even as a garrison keeps a city'. So he went home from the life which he himself had described as 'a few days in a strange land'.

I have chosen as a motto rather than a text a phrase from the passage in Hebrews where the terrors of Sinai are contrasted with the peace of Sion. At Sinai there was the sound of a trumpet and the voice of words—the tempest, the terror, the fire, and the quaking. But Sion is the home of all stable and tranquil things. We come to it now by faith, but only, as it were, in moonlight and in silence. No sound is heard but the voice of the blood of sprinkling, which speaketh better things than that of Abel. We shall come, if it please God, one day in the sunlight and the song.

For true preaching and true revival we need two things—the sound of a trumpet and the voice of words. The sound of a trumpet is in vain, if the voice of words does not follow it. The end is that false enthusiasm dying in grey ashes which no one denounced more fervently than John Wesley. There must be instruction after evangelisation, or all is in vain. It has been nobly said that 'life is spent in learning the meaning of great words, so that some idle proverb known for years and accepted perhaps as a truism comes home on a day like a blow'. But we never know the meaning of great words till the sound of a trumpet rouses the soul from slumber. The work of John Wesley is most fitly described in this twofold aspect as the sound of a trumpet and the voice of words.

I. He set the trumpet to his mouth and sounded it at a time when religion in England seemed dying or dead. Even in secular life there was a leisurely procession, with many sober pauses of which we know little now. In the Church there was a much denser stupor, a spiritual slumber so profound that Godly men openly despaired, and to others it seemed as if Christianity had waxed old, and was ready to vanish away. The voice of words continued, but they seemed to be spoken to no purpose. One of the greatest Christian thinkers of England, Bishop Butler, sat oppressed in his castle with hardly a hope surviving. He did not know that the day of the Lord had come, and that the prayers of the hearts that broke for the Lord's appearing had been answered.

For when John Wesley began his unparalleled apostolate, he sounded a trumpet in Sion. His words to the people were such short, sharp signal-calls as St. Augustine heard in the garden when the child said, 'Take, read'. He stood on his father's tomb and cried aloud, 'By grace are ye saved through faith'. He preached on the question, 'Why will ye die, O House of Israel?' till the people trembled and were still. He enlarged on the deep words, 'Repent, and believe the Gospel'. From the text, 'The Son of man hath power on earth to forgive sins,' he declared the great salvation. He spoke directly to the consciousness. The important point with him was consciousness, everywhere consciousness.

The sound of a trumpet. Our newer psychology, however little we may agree with its conclusions, has at least brought out the richness of what is called our subliminal consciousness. We know now that the mind of man is peopled, like a silent city, with a sleeping company of memories, associations, impressions, loves, hates, fears, relentings that may be wakened into fierce activity by some trumpet blast. Indeed, this subliminal consciousness may be so much more thronged than the working consciousness, that when it is called forth it may submerge the personality, and elect for itself a new king to reign over it. The crowd of insurgent spirits may overthrow the old monarchy. In the people to whom Wesley spoke there were God knows what memories, though the lamp of prophecy had been burning very low. There were in the darkened souls texts, prayers, psalms, hymns, words of love and yearning spoken by lips long mute. And these were heard again at the trumpet blast. The sound of the trumpet may come in some great experience, and will come again and again, even when the soul has been wakened from its sleep. Then, too, the voice of words is understood. Said a friend to me: 'I used to think the inscriptions on gravestones intensely commonplace. Since I buried my child and put a gravestone over her, there is not an inscription which has not been full of meaning to me.'

II. The voice of words. Wesley was a great teacher as well as a great evangelist, and no man did more for the training and schooling of his converts. No man attached greater importance to the voice of words, to constant and Scriptural instruction. We put in the forefront the great saving truths which he exalted with the whole Church of Christ. 'If we could once bring all our preachers, itinerant and local, uniformly and steadfastly to insist on these two points—Christ dying for us, and Christ reigning in us, we should shake the trembling gates of hell.' But his tranquillity to the very end was a tranquillity in the Blood of Christ.

He believed that the whole fruit of the Spirit—love, joy, peace—might be planted in the inmost soul and take deep root in the heart. But he believed that for the attainment of such perfection it was necessary to be obedient in all things to the law of Christ, and he did not shrink from the consequences.

The trumpet of revival, Wesley taught, must be the trump of God. All our fresh springs are in the Divine Spirit. Where the first life was found we must find the new supplies. The flaming, glowing heart that utters itself in words that let in the light and the life and love of God to the soul must be baptised with the Holy Ghost. Only that which is born of the Spirit is spirit, and the Spirit is given in answer to prayer.—W. ROBERTSON NICOLL, *The Lamp of Sacrifice*, p. 189.

THE CHRISTIAN'S ENVIRONMENT

'Ye are come unto Mount Sion, and unto the city of the living God, the heavenly Jerusalem, and to an innumerable company of angels.'—HEB. XII. 22.

THIS is a passage that makes one feel, with something akin to awe, the dignity and sublimity of the Christian calling. You read the passage, and as it lives before you there passes before the mind a stately procession of those beings with whom the Christian is in relationship, and there is also disclosed to the wondering gaze the possessions which the Christian inherits. 'Ye are come to these,' says the writer to the Hebrew Christians. He has just placed before them, by way of contrast, that from which they had passed. That *was* your inheritance and the inheritance of your fathers, and it was a religion of symbols or phenomena, a religion which appealed to the senses and through the senses to the soul. This *is* your inheritance, you are come now into spiritual affinities, heavenly relationships, eternal and unshakable possessions. 'Ye are come,' and not 'ye will come'; you already stand, if you can but realise it, at the centre of these great circles. Here is the present relationship and possession of the Christian.

I. It is intensely difficult, even to-day, for men to escape from bondage to the outward, to realise the unseen. This Epistle has still its work to do. What is religion to a great many people to-day? Church ordinances, the use of special Church buildings, the employment of and resort to a special ministry; swinging censers, chanting choirs, observance of days and functions. What is religion? Elaborate music, a preacher, the building of churches, the giving of money? No, ye are not come to these. They may be helps to religion, or the expression of religion, but they are not religion. Religion is an interior thing; a realisation of the presence of God the Father and the Judge; a surrender of the life in loving loyalty to His authority, the living only to do His will. Have we come to this? Are we enjoying this vision, realising our inheritance, living the life of the soul?

II. Here in this passage, in majestic outline, is set forth what it is to belong to the Church of Christ. Into all this wealth you have been admitted. See how the Church is described: 'The general assembly and church of the firstborn who are enrolled in heaven'. There is such a society in the world as the church of the firstborn, whose names God has enrolled. You joined the general assembly and church of the firstborn when you came to Jesus, the Mediator of the new covenant, and to the blood of sprinkling. Then your name was enrolled. Then you began to live, and your name was written in heaven. And all these privileges Jesus ushered you into. See what they are:—

(1) Brotherhood with holy souls living now.
(2) Brotherhood with all the holy dead, right back to the Apostles of the Lord. The holy dead have

come into their possessions earlier than we; but the fact that they have already come is the earnest that we shall come too.—CHARLES BROWN, *Light and Life*, p. 77.

REFERENCES.—XII. 22.—H. S. Holland, *God's City*, p. 3. H. J. Wilmot-Buxton, *Holy-tide Teaching*, p. 173. *Expositor* (5th Series), vol. ii. p. 342. XII. 22, 23.—A. Maclaren, *Expositions of Holy Scripture—Hebrews*, p. 236.

'Ye are come unto Mount Sion, . . . and to an innumerable company of angels.'—HEB. XII. 22-24.

'As to the vision of the other world,' observes Foster in his essay on *The Aversion of Men of Taste to Evangelical Religion* (ch. VIII.), 'you will observe a great difference between the language of sublime poetry and that of revelation, in respect to the nature of the sentiments and triumphs of that world, and still more perhaps in respect to the associates with whom the departing spirit expects soon to mingle. The dying magnanimity of poetry anticipates high converse with the souls of heroes, and patriots, and perhaps philosophers; a Christian feels himself going (I may accommodate the passage) to an innumerable company of angels, to the general assembly and church of the firstborn, to God the judge of all, to the spirits of just men made perfect, and to Jesus the Mediator of the new covenant.'

IN her reminiscences of her mother, Mrs. H. B. Stowe observes: 'There was one passage of Scripture always associated with her in our minds in childhood; it was this: "Ye are come unto Mount Sion, the city of the living God, to the heavenly Jerusalem, and to an innumerable company of angels; to the general assembly and church of the firstborn, and to the spirits of just men made perfect".

'We all knew that this was what our father repeated to her when she was dying, and we often repeated it to each other. It was to that we felt we *must* attain, though we scarcely knew how. In every scene of family joy or sorrow, or when father wished to make an appeal to our hearts which he knew we could not resist, he spoke of mother.

'I think it will be the testimony of all her sons that her image stood between them and the temptations of youth as a sacred shield; that the hope of meeting her in heaven has sometimes been the last strand which did not part in hours of fierce temptation; and that the remembrance of her holy life and death was a solemn witness of the truth of religion, which repelled every assault of scepticism, and drew back the soul from every wandering to the faith in which she lived and died.'

REFERENCES.—XII. 22-24.—Spurgeon, *Sermons*, vol. xxviii. No. 1689. C. D. Bell, *Hills That Bring Peace*, p. 339. XII. 23.—A. Maclaren, *Expositions of Holy Scripture—Hebrews*, p. 247. XII. 24.—*Ibid.* p. 257. M. Biggs, *Practical Sermons on Old Testament Subjects*, p. 31. Spurgeon, *Sermons*, vol. iv. No. 211, and vol. xii. No. 708. XII. 24, 25.—Spurgeon, *Sermons*, vol. xxxii. Nos. 1888 and 1889. XII. 25.—L. D. Bevan, *Christ and the Age*, p. 255. A. Maclaren, *Expositions of Holy Scripture—Hebrews*, p. 268. XII. 26.—E. M. Geldart,

Faith and Freedom, p. 132.　XII. 26, 27.—L. D. Bevan, *Christ and the Age*, p. 271.　XII. 26-28.—C. Williams, *Christian World Pulpit*, vol. xliv. p. 307.

THIS WORD 'YET ONCE MORE'

'This word, Yet once more, signifieth the removing.'—HEB xii. 27.

No book of the New Testament is more 'modern' than the Epistle to the Hebrews; none lies closer to the heart of the generation, or throbs with a deeper assent to its consciousness of change and its desire for the unchangeable. To the writer and the readers of the Epistle the changes looming on the Church and the world were so vast and awful that the vicissitudes of their own lives were lessened by their side. We are more keenly conscious of the blows of circumstances as they affect ourselves. We look back with yearning on a life like Wordsworth's, of whom it has been said that his bereavements were 'thinly scattered clouds in a "great sea of blue," seasons of mourning here and there among years which never lost their hold on peace, which knew no shame and no remorse, no desolation and no fear, whose days were never long with weariness nor their nights broken at the touch of woe'. To us this word 'Yet once more' signifieth the removing, but it is the removing of our own treasure and joy that strikes us with most piercing force. And yet we know that the foundations of our society and of our Church systems have been made to tremble.

I. 'The Hebrews,' for whom the Divine words were written, knew what comes to man as time runs out. They had experienced the steady, inevitable invasion of change in themselves and round them. It had even brought them insolence and violence, which they had borne well. But they were called on to face a worse trial—the ruin and overthrow of what God had built. They had to meet the death struggle of Judæa against Rome, the sweeping away of the sacred ritual of the Temple, the burning of the holy and beautiful house with fire, the abomination of desolation standing in the holy place. In the midst of this what wonder that faith trembled with the trembling order? What wonder that despair assailed and even took possession of the soul? What wonder that men asked in terror whether God's promise was broken—whether after all He was loving unto Israel—unto such as were of a clean heart?

II. There is one healing, and one only, for all hearts hurt by change. It is that God has done it. The consolation is administered here in a strange and daring fashion. Not content with proving that in the ascended Christ the Church possesses all, and more than all, that has been lost in the disappearance of the ritual of the old covenant, for

> In Him the shadows of the law
> Are all fulfilled and now withdraw,

the Apostle affirms that of this change God is the author. And if it seem incredible that He should thus shake His own temple, the Apostle answers the doubt by saying that He will yet shake His own

heavens. The shadow that lay full on the things of time is projected on eternity. 'Yet once more I shake not the earth only, but also heaven.' Once more only will He move the earth and the heaven. By a change which is not the culmination of the processes at work under our eyes, He will remove all that can pass away. Then the things that cannot be shaken—the eternal substance, be it what it may, of the temporal—will remain, and with it they who have not drawn back, and He, the Unchangeable, ruling amidst the immovable. But before that, change must crowd on change, and the Son of Man appear. For the awe-struck hearers of the Epistle forgotten words about earth and heaven perishing, waxing old, folded up, and changed were revived. It would calm them to see the way of change traced, its frontiers enlarged and yet limited, and its empire put securely in His hands who was bringing in the world over which no change can pass.

III. 'This word Yet once more' does not now overcome us. We can face 'the horrors of the last'. For others the warning may be fulfilled :—

> All that now delights thee from the day,
> On which it should be touched shall melt and pass away.

For them disillusionment may come on disillusionment, and regret follow regret. We have our place in the world that can never crumble into dust. The kingdom which cannot be moved is about us now. It glimmers through the show of things. We have been translated into the kingdom of God's dear Son, and the importunate and ever-shifting objects of sense do not blind us to its glories.—W. ROBERTSON NICOLL, *Ten Minute Sermons*, p. 193.

REFERENCES.—XII. 27.—A. Rowland, *Christian World Pulpit*, vol. xlvi. p. 248. Spurgeon, *Sermons*, vol. xii. No. 690. J. G. Rogers, *Christian World Pulpit*, vol. xlix. p. 280. J. Watson, *The Inspiration of Our Faith*, p. 335. E. Griffith-Jones, *Christian World Pulpit*, vol. lv. p. 92.

'With reverence and awe.'—HEB. xii. 28.

THOUGHT without Reverence is barren, perhaps poisonous ; at best, dies like cookery, with the day that called it forth ; does not live, like sowing, in successive tilths and wider-spreading harvests, bringing food and plenteous increase to all Time.—CARLYLE.

IN the biography of François Coillard, of the Zambesi, it is told how he once asked a friend in Paris, during 1897 : 'Do you ever regret having left the Church of Rome?' 'Never,' was the emphatic reply. 'In Protestantism I found an open Bible, the personal knowledge of our Lord Jesus Christ, and the forgiveness of my sins—three things I never found in Rome. But,' he added, 'I must confess there is one thing in Catholicism which I miss in our Reformation Churches, and that is adoration.' 'I miss it too,' said M. Coillard.

COMPARE Renan's indignant repudiation of Béranger's theology, in his essay on 'The Deity of the Bourgeois'. 'No, they cannot know thee, Holy Being, whom we behold not save in the serenity of a pure heart. The blasphemies of the man of genius must please thee more than the vulgar homage of complacent gaiety. The atheist is far rather he who so misjudges thee, than he that denies thee. The despair of a Lucretius or a Byron was more after thine own heart than this brazen-faced confidence of superficial optimism which insults while it adores thee.'

REFERENCES.—XII. 28.—L. D. Bevan, *Christ and the Age*, pp. 285, 299. E. J. Lyndon, *Preacher's Magazine*, vol. xix. p. 513. XII. 28, 29.—Spurgeon, *Sermons*, vol. xxviii. No. 1639.

'For our God is a consuming fire.'—HEB. XII. 29.

THE wrath of God properly understood, so far from being in conflict with the love of God, is the highest expression of it. How can God love any good without hating any evil ? ' Our God is a consuming fire ' —but the fire of the furnace which is hatred to the dross is love to the gold. And God's wrath against sin is not only love, but the on y love to the sinner. . . . Supposing it supposable, if God could and should remove from sin and disobedience their natural and penal consequences, would it be an act of love on His part to do so ? Would goodness continue to be blessedness if badness ceased to be accursedness ? ' *Our* God is a consuming fire,' and He is never so much ' our God ' as when He is consuming us. For it is only in God's wrath to our sin that we know God's love to ourselves.—DU BOSE, *Soteriology of the New Testament*, p. 51.

REFERENCES.—XII. 29.—R. J. Wardell, *Preacher's Magazine*, vol. xviii. p. 83. L. D. Bevan, *Christ and the Age*, p. 315.

'Let love of the brethren continue.'—HEB. XIII. I.

ONLY love rooted in sympathy and expressed in action to the point of a complete destruction of self-will is Christian love.—WAGNER's *Letters* (1880), p. 339.

REFERENCES.—XIII. 1.—T. C. Finlayson, *Christian World Pulpit*, vol. xlviii. p. 401. F. J. A. Hort, *Village Sermons in Outline*, p. 134.

'Let love of the brethren continue . . . let us go forth unto Him without the camp.'—HEB. XIII. I, 13.

PEOPLE are not most conscious of brotherhood when they continue languidly together in one creed, but when, with some doubt, with some danger perhaps, and certainly not without some reluctance, they violently break with the tradition of the past, and go forth from the sanctuary of their fathers to worship under the bare heaven.—R. L. STEVENSON, in *Men and Books*.

UNAWARE OF ANGELS

'Some have entertained angels unawares.'—HEB. XIII. 2.

IN a recent novel, where great power is on the whole misdirected, there is one sentence that cannot easily be forgotten. A stern old mother has a daughter given to writing. The mother disapproves, but when the daughter dies we are told that what her mother used to speak of as verses she always afterwards called poems. That is what death does for our loved ones. It changes their verses into poems. Were we to write for ever we could not say a word more. Everything is then transfigured and stands out in a new

light, a light in which we could not see it while the dear ones were yet with us.

> In this dim world of clouding cares
> We rarely know, till wildered eyes
> See white wings lessening up the skies,
> The angels with us unawares.

But we know them then.

I. The Ideal was once among us, and we beheld His glory, and did not know it for the glory of the Only Begotten of the Father, full of grace and truth. While He tabernacled among men they doubted Him, questioned Him, criticised Him, scorned Him. It was not till He was taken from them that the full truth burst upon their sight. He knew that it would be so. As He neared the Great Altar where He offered up the Perfect Sacrifice, He said that He would send the Spirit to reprove the world of righteousness, ' because I go to My Father, *and ye see Me no more*. In a hush of love and reverence He was laid in His new tomb, and since that hour He has been the Hope, the Glory, the Ideal, and the Crown of our fallen humanity.

II. It was so, as each of us knows, with our own beloved. However much we cared for them, however deeply we understood them, however we looked up to them, we know them better now. Even here we understood their truth and pity and patient loving kindness, but now everything comes more nearly and dearly home. In a measure our eyes were holden, but they have been open long since. Now that the past is cast upon a ground of wonder it seems comprehensible, and we marvel that we were so dull. The loves that have been taken from us, the venerating regard of childhood, the passion of youth, the restful affection of mature years, the trust of lost little children, the kind, true friendships that we hoped would bridge all the changes over—we know how to prize them as we sit with our yearning and sometimes remorseful thoughts. Were they faultless ? Perhaps they were not, but whatever there was of frailty, imperfection, ignorance, was no true part of their redeemed being, and has all fallen from them now. Others may recall such things, but we cannot. Our forgetfulness is even as the forgetfulness of God, Who casts our sins behind His back, and neither remembers them nor, if we may dare to say it, can remember them. So much besides is clear to us that in the old time we never saw. They were dead in Christ while they were living here, and their life was hid with Christ in God. Now it seems to issue from Christ and to be part of Christ's glory.

But all this is true in Christ and in Christ only. It is in Him that the dead are living and the lost are found. It is in Him that

> We give blind grief and blinder sense the lie,
> And say, ' They did not live to die '.

It is in Him that the golden hope of immortality, so often clouded, springs unbaffled from its sleep. In Him the soul's prevision in its moments of intensest life is true, the very truth of truths. It is through Him we know that we cannot idealise the dead, that they are more lovely and gracious than our loveliest and most gracious dreams. In Him the promises of God are Yea, and in Him Amen. And so it is to Him, to His Cross, and His Resurrection that all our hopes are nailed.—W. ROBERTSON NICOLL, *Sunday Evening*, p. 53.

THE LARGER HOSPITALITY

'Be not forgetful to entertain strangers ; for thereby some have entertained angels unawares.'—HEB. XIII. 2.

READING this verse for the first time, it almost seems as if this plea for hospitality were based upon a selfish motive. Are we to do good that we may win good? Not so. If a man be hospitable on the bare chance of entertaining angels, he is no hospitable man. But if a man be hospitable from loftiest motives, sooner or later, God will bring angels to his door. Our text tells the joy of every open home and heart and mind. It reads the doom of every closed door. Shut it and bar it! You will shut out a hundred vagabonds. One day you will shut out an angel. And it were better to be deceived a score of times than miss a heavenly messenger like that. I want to take this thought and run it out into three realms.

I. And first, the realm of home. Are all the angels dead? Have none in the garb of strangers ever appeared on your horizon? To answer that, we have to ask, What is an angel? An angel is a messenger of God. And every word that ever cheered you from a stranger's lips, and every thought that ever reached you from a stranger's heart, and every Christlike sight that ever touched you in a stranger's home, these have been angel ministries to you—the messengers of God. Entertain strangers. It is the noblest hospitality. Sooner or later you shall find, by the tokens of a larger heart and fuller life, that you have been entertaining angels unawares.

II. Now, look at the realm of experience. For years life is one uneventful drudgery ; we wake, we eat, we work, we tire, we sleep. But the day comes when at our doors there stands a stranger. Perhaps it is poverty. Perhaps it is sickness. Perhaps it is death. How will you treat that stranger? that is the question. Some men rebel. And some grow bitter. And some despair ; but they are brave, and plod along without a prayer, without a hope, till men say, 'See how resigned they are!' They do not know it is the resignation of a broken heart. There is a nobler way. Be not forgetful to entertain the stranger : you shall be entertaining angels unawares. God's blessings come in strange disguises.

III. Lastly, I want to take our text into the realm of thought. It is amazing what cold entertainment the world has always given to great thoughts, when first they came as strangers. But do not quarrel with the world. Perhaps that same inhospitality is yours and mine—if not to-day, to-morrow. 'Prove all things ; hold fast that which is good,' that is the Christian attitude.—G. H. MORRISON, *Flood-Tide*, p. 271.

Be not forgetful to entertain strangers ; for thereby some have entertained angels unawares.'—HEB. XIII. 2.

I WAS a little acquainted,' says Boswell in his *Tour to the Hebrides* (Saturday, 21st August), 'with Mr. Forbes, the minister of the parish. I sent to inform him that a gentleman desired to see him. He returned for answer, "that he would not come to a stranger". I then gave my name, and he came. I remonstrated to him for not coming to a stranger ; and, by presenting him to Dr. Johnson, proved to him what a stranger might sometimes be. His Bible inculcates, "be not forgetful to entertain strangers," and maintain the same motive. He defended himself by saying, "He had once come to a stranger, who sent for him ; and he found him *a little worth person !*"'

REFERENCES.—XIII. 2.—S. A. Tipple, *The Admiring Guest*, p. 166. H. J. Bevis, *Sermons*, p. 120. *Expositor* (4th Series), vol. x. p. 71. XIII. 3.—C. O. Eldridge, *Preacher's Magazine*, vol. xviii. p. 37.

'Let marriage be held in honour among all, and let the bed be undefiled.'—HEB. XIII. 4.

DISCUSSING the origin of the Canons of Nicæa (*History of the Eastern Church*, lect. v.), Dean Stanley relates how ' a proposition was made, enjoining that all married clergy (according to one report, including even sub-deacons) were to separate from their wives. The opposition came from a most unexpected quarter. From amongst the Egyptian bishops stepped out into their midst, looking out of his one remaining eye, and halting on his paralysed leg, the old hermit-confessor, Paphuntius or Paphunte. With a roar of indignation rather than with a speech, he broke into the debate : 'Lay not this heavy yoke upon the clergy. Marriage is honourable in all, and the bed undefiled. By exaggerated strictness you will do the Church more harm than good. All cannot bear such an ascetic rule . . .' His speech produced a profound sensation. His own austere life of unblemished celibacy gave force to every word that he uttered ; he shared that rare excellence of appreciating difficulties which he himself did not feel, and of honouring a state of life which was not his own.

NEITHER LEFT NOR FORSAKEN

' I will never leave thee, nor forsake thee.'—HEB. XIII. 5.

I. ' I WILL never leave thee.' The nearest and the dearest even cannot say this to us. Life is full of partings, and we come to feel at last, with Ruskin, ' That word good-bye shakes me from head to foot '. Even when the closest relationship has been reached, when two have walked side by side through life, and have shared every variety of existence, when the warmer passion has passed and is replaced by something deeper and truer, till the duality of being becomes a unity, one must die, and the other, stranded and helpless, must go on living. It is the constant experience that such partings leave behind them something more than sorrow, something of compunction, which may even be remorse. It is the universal testimony that the strength of a dear bond is never known till it is broken, till the ancient depths are stirred, till the vanished faces appear upon the background of the young spring skies. The heart reaches far back and vainly into the forgotten years, and longs to recover them, not so much to fill them more fully with love as with the signs and tokens of love. But there is a far greater tragedy than that of the death parting. There is such a thing as living together and yet drifting farther and farther apart. The heart may stray, and a river broader and deeper than Jordan may lie between those who outwardly are close together. Better to look with love and reverence and yearning and gratitude and repentance across the straits of death than to feel that in the home the cruel grave of the dead love has been dug and filled. But our Lord's promise means that no matter how we are impoverished we have left to us His presence and His heart. No matter how sorely broken we may be with the assaults of life, no matter by what separations we may be left lonely, He never leaves us, and never forsakes us. When that becomes a weight which was once no weight at all, when we have less and less to do with things around us, when, as the phrase has it, our day is over, there is One Who remains, One on whom our dying eyes may rest, one hiding place from the wind, one covert from the tempest.

II. For the promise is not only 'I will not leave thee;' it is also 'I will never forsake thee'. We change ourselves. This is at once the misery and the blessedness of life. We shall all be changed, says the Apostle, to those who had already changed much. Think how we have altered from our childhood in body and mind, in thought and in feeling. All our life has been made up of stages of one long change, and what would happen if Christ changed, too? But Jesus Christ is the same yesterday, to-day, and for ever. His love burns on through the storms as steadily as a lamp in a windless place. We have suffered cruelly from the loss of the living and the loss of the dead. Friend and lover have gone far from us and have found others to care for; but He never changes. He bears with our falling, with our wandering, with our forgetfulness, and His love is as ardent and forgiving and helpful at the last as it was at first. It is not only that He never leaves us; it is that He neither leaves us nor forsakes us.

So it is with trial. It is this the writer to the Hebrews is thinking of, and we can almost see the sudden light leaping into those steadfast eyes, that had faced the worst which time could do, as he spoke. He had told his fellow-Christians to imitate the faith of the martyrs—whose faith imitate, considering the end of their conversation, considering how it brought them to that—to the hard bed, with its pillow of sharp thorns, on which the Redeemer fell asleep. They died the death of the Righteous, and their last end was like His, and they found Him as good as His word. We vex and weary ourselves thinking what we shall do, how long we shall be able to work, what will happen when we are perforce idle, how we shall bear the pains and partings that are to be. He wants to put an end to all this by His promise that

whatever befalls we shall neither be left nor forsaken. He tells us to do the duty of the moment in the moment, and for the rest to hold by him. And when the last bonds are loosened, and we are delivered from our earthly troubles, we shall be for ever with the Lord, and we shall be like Him, for we shall see Him as He is. The blessedness of that vision, who can tell but those who stand before Him?—W. ROBERTSON NICOLL, *Sunday Evening*, p. 97.

'Be ye free from the love of money: content with such things as ye have: for himself hath said, I will in no wise fail thee, neither will I in any wise forsake thee.'—HEB. XIII. 5.

I FIND that the Spirit of God taught the writers of the New Testament to apply to us all in general, and to every single person in particular, some gracious words which God in the Old Testament spake to one man upon a special occasion in a single and temporal instance. Such are the words which God spake to Joshua; 'I will never fail thee, nor forsake thee,' and upon the stock of that promise St. Paul forbids covetousness and persuades contentedness, because those words were spoken by God to Joshua in another case.—JEREMY TAYLOR, *Holy Dying* (ch. v. sec. 5).

BUT now I began to exercise myself with new thoughts; I daily read the word of God, and applied all the comforts of it to my present state. One morning, being very sad, I opened the Bible upon these words, 'I will never, never leave thee, nor forsake thee'. Immediately it occurred that these words were to me; why else should they be directed in such a manner, just at the moment when I was mourning over my condition, as one forsaken of God and man? Well then, said I, if God does not forsake me, of what ill consequence can it be, or what matters it, though the world should all forsake me; seeing on the other hand, if I had all the world, and should lose the favour and blessing of God, there would be no comparison in the loss?—DEFOE, *Robinson Crusoe*, pt. i. (ch. III.).

MOST people have had a period or periods in their lives when they have felt thus forsaken; when, having long hoped against hope, and still seen the day of fruition deferred, their hearts have truly sickened within them. This is a terrible hour, but it is often that darkest point which precedes the rise of day; that turn of the year when the icy January wind carries over the waste at once the dirge of departing winter, and the prophecy of coming spring. The perishing birds, however, cannot thus understand the blast before which they shiver; and as little can the suffering soul recognise, in the climax of its affliction, the dawn of its deliverance. Yet, let whoever grieves still cling fast to love and faith in God: God will never deceive, never finally desert him. 'Whom He loveth, He chasteneth.' These words are true, and should not be forgotten.—CHARLOTTE BRONTË, *Shirley* (chap. xx.).

REFERENCES.—XIII. 5.—Spurgeon, *Sermons*, vol. viii. No. 477; vol. xxxii. No. 1880. XIII. 5-6.—A. Maclaren,

After the Resurrection, p. 291. Spurgeon, *Sermons*, vol. xxiv. No. 1449. A. Maclaren, *Expositions of Holy Scripture—Hebrews*, p. 277.

'Imitate their faith.'—HEB. XIII. 7.

IMITATION : it enters into the very fastnesses of character ; and we, our souls, ourselves, are for ever imitating what we see and hear, the forms, the sounds, which haunt our memories, our imaginations.—PATER, *Plato and Platonism*, p. 272.

REFERENCES.—XIII. 7.—T. Arnold, *The Interpretation of Scripture*, p. 310. J. M. Neale, *Sermons Preached in Sackville College Chapel*, vol. iv. p. 98. XIII. 7, 8.—G. Campbell Morgan, *Christian World Pulpit*, vol. lvii. p. 3.

DISCIPLESHIP

'Jesus Christ is the same yesterday and to-day, yea and for ever.'—HEB. XIII. 8.

WHAT do the Gospels certify to have been the character of original Christianity ? The answer is on the surface. Original Christianity was a discipleship to Jesus Christ.

I. The followers of Christ are in the Gospels commonly described as His disciples. Discipleship implied the frank acceptance of Christ's personal claims, and the power which won that acceptance was the power of Christ's personal influence. But what did discipleship practically involve ? Obviously, at the time to these first disciples, peril, loss, temporal ruin. Nothing could be sterner or more threatening than the prospect which He unfolded before His disciples. Discipleship goes deeper than the external circumstances of life. 'Jesus Christ is the same yesterday and to-day, yea and for ever'. The terms of His service reflect His changelessness.

II. Discipleship is the abiding aspect of Christianity. Churches and creeds, as such, have no immunity from the law of change, but if the essence of Christianity be not the membership of a church, nor yet the acceptance of a system of belief, but rather discipleship to a living Person, then it seems possible to hope that Christianity may possess an indestructible life. Discipleship, in the common experience of mankind, terminates in one of two ways. On the one hand, the disciple may outstrip his teacher, learn all he has to teach, and advance into regions where he has no message. On the other hand, the disciple may lose confidence in the teacher, shake off the spell of his personal influence, set himself free from his moral and intellectual control. Can either of these contingencies happen in the case of the Christian discipleship ? Are there any signs that Christians have outgrown the teachings of the Master ? Is the world growing weary of the Ideal presented in the Gospel ? As far as I can see, the evidence points in the opposite direction.

III. The changes of Christianity which, at first sight, perplex and distress us, are not only intelligible, but even necessary, when Christianity is conceived as a discipleship. For discipleship must always include the notion of advance. In truth, not to advance is to cease to be a disciple.

IV. Finally, it is in realising our Christian profes-

sion as before all things a discipleship to Christ that we shall recover fraternity. The nearer we draw to our Master, the nearer we draw also to one another. —H. H. HENSON, *Christian World Pulpit*, vol. LXI. p. 17.

THE UNCHANGEABLE CHRIST

HEB. XIII. 8.

I. The Christian Conception of God Involves Immutability. — Capricious divinities abound in the history of the race. They are the creatures of imagination. The idea of a changeable God is an absurdity to the Christian mind. The Divine nature suffers no variableness. The Divine purpose is unchangeable also. (1) The physical universe suggests Divine immutability. The universe is under the dominion of law which is absolutely universal, penetrating all spheres, space and time. Behind the law is the law-giver in Whom is no variableness, neither shadow of turning. (2) This is supported by the moral law. Righteousness, justice, truth, goodness, love, these are the same everywhere—in God, and in man ; and every moral being everywhere. (3) The unchangeableness of God is emphasised in the Scriptures.

II. The Unchangeable Christ is the Gospel we Preach.—He is the Author, Finisher, and essence thereof. The permanency of the Gospel is secured in Him who is from everlasting to everlasting the same. The unity of truth is secured in Christ. The Gospel is essentially the same in all ages, and under all conditions of life. It is preached to the barbarian, and to the civilised, everywhere the same Christ the Saviour of man. This is quite consistent with variety of forms, expressions, and methods. All truth is in Christ, the garment in which it is clothed is of many colours. Unity of essence, and diversity of expression are not inconsistent. The old Gospel is always new. Divers and strange doctrines present themselves on every hand, but there is no substitute for the old Gospel. We may speak in other terms. The pronunciation of some words is not precisely the same, but the unchangeable Christ abides. The worlds revolve around Him still.

THE UNCHANGING CHRIST

HEB. XIII. 8.

I. WE must take account of the supreme claim which is enshrined in the declaration that, amid all the chances and changes of the world, Jesus Christ is always the same. This could not be true if He were but as the great saints and heroes of history. They assuredly change dramatically. We alter our minds about them ; the reason and conscience of men goes away from them ; they cease to appear worthy of homage ; they come to be the symbols of delusion, and the beacons of warning. Of none of them could it be truly said that they change not as the ages pass. But when we come to the Master, whom Apostles and saints worshipped and strove as best they could to follow, we have reached fixity at last. His supremacy remains secure and unchallenged through all the revolutions of thought and sentiment. There is but one explanation of this sole and unchallenged prerogative of unchanging power. It is the core of the Christian creed, the truth on which the Church stands, by which the Christian lives. Jesus Christ is not as the rest. He is the unique, the only-begotten of the Father, God Incarnate.

II. We must observe that this supremacy, absolute and immutable, is independent of ecclesiastical systems, and of specific theologies. The emphasis placed on the various parts of the scheme of Christian doctrine is constantly changing. Yet through all the changes the one assured and unalterable factor is precisely the sole and incommunicable supremacy of Christ.

III. This unchanging and unique supremacy of Jesus Christ is not disallowed by the larger view of religion, which is now everywhere laying hold of men's minds. It is not the Church alone, but all mankind, speaking through its infinite variety of spiritual utterances, which says to Christ with St. Peter: 'Lord, to whom shall we go? Thou hast the words of eternal life.'

IV. Finally, if we turn from every outward sphere and enter within the sanctuary of our own minds, and there face the anxiety which rises on our thought from the knowledge of our own weakness and falsehood, it is still the same fact on which we must build our hopes. Being what I know myself to be, we ask, How dare I make the profession of Christianity at all? The only justification in reason and in religion for the venture of discipleship is found, not in ourselves, but in the unchanging Christ. 'Jesus Christ is the same yesterday, and to-day, yea, and for ever.' Courage, then, though memories of failure hang darkly on our minds, and our hearts fail us as we listen to the Babel of conflicting voices, and are shocked by the reckless vehemence of unloving zeal, or chilled by the questionings of an age which has forgotten God!

THE EVER-LIVING CHRIST

'Jesus Christ is the same yesterday, and to-day, yea and for ever.'—HEB. XIII. 8 (R.V.).

IN the context the author of this Epistle exhorts the Hebrew Christians not to forget their guides and leaders who had spoken unto them the Word of God. Some, like St. Stephen and St. James, had won a martyr's crown. Many had been scattered by persecution as fallen leaves before the autumn wind. But let them remember, said he, this grand and blessed truth: ministers may die or be removed, but 'Jesus Christ'—the object of their faith and the subject of their preaching—'is the same yesterday, and to-day, yea and for ever.'

Over the vast gateway of the deserted city of Futtypore Sikri, in Northern India, is an Arabic inscription to this effect: 'This world is but a bridge; pass over, build not thy dwelling there'. The statement is true; the exhortation is wise. And yet in that sentence lurks a great sorrow. The antidote to that sorrow lies in the words of the Psalmist: 'Lord, Thou hast been our dwelling-place in all generations,' and in the words of my text, 'Jesus Christ is the same yesterday, and to-day, yea and for ever'.

For a moment observe the names of our Lord which we have here. Jesus, His personal name; Christ, or the 'anointed one,' the name which speaks of His official capacity—which tells that He was set apart by God for the complete and perfect salvation of His people, and which opens out to us His offices of Prophet, Priest and King.

I. Prophet.—The title of Prophet was given to Christ as the great Revealer and Teacher of the will of God. Moses predicted that this Prophet was to be a man like unto himself. 'Unto Him shall ye hearken.' All the leaves of prophecy, like one great sunflower, turn to Christ the Light. Like its author, the Bible is the same 'yesterday and to-day'. 'Other books,' writes the Archbishop of Armagh, 'pass away; but of that the silver cord shall never be loosed, nor the golden bowl broken, nor the mourners that go about the streets proclaim that at last the great book is dead and carried to the charnel-house of dead religions.' The Prophet teaches, as I have said, not only by the written word, but by a Divinely appointed ministry. Because Christ ever lives the Gospel ministry will never die.

II. Priest.—Christ is 'a Priest for ever after the order of Melchisedec'. By the sacrifice of Himself upon the cross the God-Man took the 'Divine anathema against sin upon His own immaculate head'. He suffered 'the just for the unjust'. 'We have redemption through His blood, even the forgiveness of sins, according to the riches of His grace.' The atonement proclaims an accepted world, a reconciled Father, a redeemed humanity. In these days, when an ethical revival is the great need of the Church and the world, and when by the law of reaction there is a growing danger of the divorcement of duty from dogma—yes! and when the hearts of men are craving for a morality which they do not possess—we must summon them afresh to the cross of Christ as the fulcrum of a moral life and the mainspring of holiness.

Earthly ministers, like the Mosaic priests, are by succession. The time comes when we must die or be removed. Our voices are hushed, and the footfall of our steps is no longer heard in the street. It is my comfort to speak of one whose Priesthood is unchangeable: who, seated amid the heavenly glories, ever pities, ever intercedes, ever pardons, ever helps, ever blesses.

III. King.—If the Jew in the old dispensation looked for a Messiah who was to reign as King and not for a Messiah who was to suffer as Priest, we in this dispensation continually think of Christ as Priest almost to the forgetfulness of Christ as King. Do not forget that Christ is King as well as Priest. Turn your thoughts ofttimes from the pathetic beauty of the sunset on Calvary to the glorious sunrise on Olivet. Amid the clouds of night let us look for the brightness of the coming dawn.

This kingdom is yours if you will but accept its conditions.—J. W. BARDSLEY, *Many Mansions*, p. 349.

'Jesus Christ is the same yesterday, and to-day, yea and for ever.'—HEB. XIII. 8.

Is it conceivable that the God who made the seven stars and Orion, and who is without variableness or shadow of turning, played off caprices on the narrow seaboard of Asia Minor in the centuries before our era, which, having come to another mind, or being weary, He has ceased to enact in modern days, cowed and overfaced by steam and penny newspapers reeled off without stopping? Is the strength of Israel lying or repenting now the world has waxed older and wiser and more scientific, and is clothed in cloth, and builds magnificent clubrooms in Pall Mall, where His name goes for nothing?—JAMES SMETHAM, *Letters*, p. 347.

REFERENCES.—XIII. 8.—Reuen Thomas, *Christian World Pulpit*, vol. xlviii. p. 107. H. H. Henson, *Godly Union and Concord*, pp. 1 and 269. A. Coote, *Twelve Sermons*, p. 12. T. Rider, *Christian World Pulpit*, vol. lii. p. 40. J. Cartwright, *Preacher's Magazine*, vol. xviii. p. 180. Bishop Nickson, *The Record*, vol. xxvii. p. 1084. A. H. Stanton, *Christian World Pulpit*, vol. liii. p. 7. Spurgeon, *Sermons*, vol. iv. No. 170; vol. xv. No. 848, and vol. xl. No. 2358. F. E. Paget, *Helps and Hindrances to the Christian Life*, vol. i. p. 36. J. M. Neale, *Sermons Preached in Sackville College Chapel*, vol. iv. p. 290. C. Vince, *The Unchanging Saviour*, p. 1. A. Maclaren, *Expositions of Holy Scripture—Hebrews*, p. 285. XIII. 8, 9.—W. Alexander, *Primary Convictions*, p. 3. XIII. 9.—*Expositor* (4th Series), vol. ii. p. 143. A. Maclaren, *Expositions of Holy Scripture—Hebrews*, p. 294. XIII. 10, 15.—*Ibid.* p. 303. XIII. 11, 12.—J. Bannerman, *Sermons*, p. 219. XIII. 12.—Spurgeon, *Sermons*, vol. xlvi. No. 2660. XIII. 13.—*Ibid.* vol. x. No. 577.

'Jesus . . . suffered without the gate. Let us go forth therefore unto Him without the camp.'—HEB. XIII. 12, 13.

In early times the graveyards and cemeteries were always outside the towns or villages, partly—and here is shown our forefathers' likeness to us—for the greater healthiness, partly—and here is shown their romance, which we have lost—in realisation that all men are strangers and pilgrims upon earth, and because of the great sacrifice 'offered without the camp'.—J. H. SHORTHOUSE.

'Here have we no continuing city, but we seek one to come.'—HEB. XIII. 14.

FROM this text Becket preached in the chapter-house of Canterbury Cathedral in December, 1170, on returning from France after his hollow reconciliation with Henry II. 'The cathedral,' says Dean Stanley, 'was hung with silken drapery; magnificent banquets were prepared; the churches resounded with organs and bells; the palace-halls with trumpets; and the Archbishop preached in the chapter-house on the text, "Here we have no abiding city, but we seek one to come". On Christmas Day, he preached from the words, "on earth, peace to men of good-will". He began by speaking of the sainted fathers of the Church of Canterbury, the presence of whose bones made doubly hallowed the consecrated ground. "One martyr," he said, "they had already—Alfege,

murdered by the Danes, whose tomb stood on the north side of the high altar. It was possible," he added, "that they would soon have another." The people who thronged the nave were in a state of wild excitement; they wept and groaned; and an audible murmur ran through the church. "Father, why do you desert us so soon? to whom will you leave us?" But as he went on with his discourse, the plaintive strain gradually rose into a tone of fiery indignation. "You would have thought," says Hubert of Bosham, who was present, "that you were looking at the prophetic beast, which had at once the face of a man and the face of a lion."'—STANLEY'S *Memorials of Canterbury*, pp. 66, 67.

'Here have we no continuing city.'—HEB. XIII. 14.

LIFE is not designed to minister to a man's vanity. He goes upon his long business most of the time with a hanging head, and all the time like a blind child. Full of rewards and punishments as it is—so that to see the day break or the moon rise, or to meet a friend, or to hear the linnet call when he is hungry, fills him with surprising joys—this world is yet for him no abiding city. Friendships fall through, health fails, weariness assails him; year after year, he must thumb the hardly varying record of his own weakness and folly. It is a friendly process of detachment.—R. L. STEVENSON, in *A Christmas Sermon*.

AND so it came about that John Gladwyn Jebb left both Mexico and this land where we have 'no abiding city,' almost as naked of the world's goods as when he entered it. . . . He was too sanguine, too romantic, too easily deluded by others, and too mystical—a curious vein of mysticism was one of his most striking characteristics—for this nineteenth century. As a crusader, or as a knight-errant, doubtless, he would have been a brilliant success, but as a manager of companies and a director of business matters it must be confessed that he was a failure. Would that there existed more of such noble failures—the ignoble are sufficiently abundant—for then the world might be cleaner than it is. It matters little now: his day is done, and he has journeyed to that wonderful Hereafter of which during life he had so clear a vision, and that was so often the subject of his delightful and suggestive talk.—RIDER HAGGARD, in *The Life and Adventures of J. G. Jebb*, pp. xxiv, xxv.

HEB. XIII. 14.

PERHAPS one fact which lies at the root of all the actions of the Turks, small and great, is that they are by nature nomads. It is their custom to ornament the walls of their houses with texts instead of pictures, and, if they quoted from the Bible instead of the Koran, no words would better characterise their manner of life than 'Here have we no continuing city'.—SIR CHARLES ELIOT, *Turkey in Europe*, p. 89.

REFERENCES.—XIII. 14.—R. W. Church, *Village Sermons* (2nd Series), p. 10. E. M. Geldart, *Faith and Freedom*, p.

117. E. T. J. Marriner, *Sermons Preached at Lyme Regis*, p. 63. F. Bourdillon, *Plain Sermons for Family Reading* (2nd Series), p. 225.

THE SACRIFICE OF PRAISE

'By Him therefore let us offer the sacrifice of praise to God continually.'—HEB. XIII. 15.

'THE sacrifice of praise.' We are apt to pass over the words and miss their deep meaning. The sacrifice of praise is not the mere natural expression of joy. The word carries a red stain. Praise in a world like this, and from creatures such as we are, must often be sacrificial if it is to be continual. Continued thanksgiving carried through a life of faith is a sacrifice which may be laid upon the altar where the Perfect Oblation was offered up for the sins of the whole world.

When the father of Principal Cairns died, after protracted suffering, there was a short pause till each of the family circle had realised what had happened. Then the mother in a broken voice asked that 'the books' might be laid on the table, and gave out the verse :—

> The storm is changed into a calm
> At His command and will;
> So that the waves that raged before
> Now quiet are and still.

It was her voice that raised the tune. Then she asked her eldest son to read a chapter of the Bible, and afterwards to pray. When they knelt down the son made a strong effort to steady his voice, but failed utterly, and 'the dear mother herself lifted up the voice of thanksgiving for the victory that had been won'. That was the sacrifice of praise.

I. To understand the words fully we turn back to the place where they are used, the last chapter in Hebrews. 'We have an altar,' says the Apostle. That Altar is Christ upon His Cross. It is an Altar whereof those who remain in Judaism and serve the tabernacle have no right to eat. But what is denied to them is the privilege of Christian believers. They feast upon the sacrifice. 'He that eateth Me, even he shall live by Me.' Christ for us becomes Christ in us. By eating of the sacrifice, the supernatural life is sustained, and the years are turned into one long thanksgiving. Our Altar stood without the gate of Jerusalem. 'The bodies of those beasts, whose blood is brought into the sanctuary by the High Priest for sin, are burned without the camp. Wherefore Jesus also, that He might sanctify the people with His own Blood, suffered without the gate.' Even as the Christian Church of those days was cast out of the Jewish Synagogue, so the Christian Church is to be separated from the world that it may be united to Him. It is detached from the visible order that it may be united with the invisible. Its true home is not here, not even without the camp, where its Altar stands. That is a stage on the way to the stable city beyond the sea of death, where the eternal order holds, which we seek,' 'for here we have no continuing city, but we seek one to come'. So then, being outside the gate, and exiles by the Christian Altar, we are to offer up our sacrifices, not the sacrifice of propitiation, but the sacrifice of praise. It is a sacrifice, seeing that it has to be offered continually. It is also a sacrifice, seeing that it is the fruit of lips that make confession of His name. Confession when the Apostle wrote meant much, and it is not well with us if it means little now.

II. To offer the sacrifice of praise, is to bless the Lord at *all* times, to give thanks in everything, to make the mornings, noons, and midnights of life one Eucharist. How different is the sacrifice of praise from the mere exultation of youth! Youth, with its profuse illusions, demands happiness as its right, and even if it recognises God as the giver of joy, turns away from Him when the shadow falls. Youth demands victory, and cannot wait. It grows weary in a long and losing fight. But if we have learned to offer the sacrifice of praise upon the Altar, we need not covet youth. God has provided some better thing for us. We know it even when we see ourselves grey haired and wrinkled in the mirror, and feel that the battle is as much as ever we can fight, and the race as much as ever we can run. We have learned to give thanks as the tide of battle rolls this way and that. The inner life wells up as the outer sinks into the ground. There is within us something better than the light-heartedness of youth, a joy, a buoyancy, a confidence which the world cannot give and cannot take away. We have learned to drink in the sunlight when exposed to it, and give back that light in the brightness of the night. To offer the sacrifice of praise is to give thanks, as the Lord gave thanks when He took the bread and blessed it and brake it. He gave thanks for the wayfaring behind and the Cross before.

III. We learn, too, as life goes on that the Christian sacrifice of praise means much more than the acceptance of sorrow in the hope that it may pass and be succeeded by gladness. There is less meaning for the Christian Church than there was for the Jewish in the words, 'Weeping may endure for a night, but joy cometh in the morning'. It is Jewish rather than Christian to watch the unbidden guest Sorrow with impatience and wretchedness, taking comfort in the thought that her presence must pass with the dreary night, that at morning she will be gone, and we shall find Joy in her room. There is an element of truth in that view. Mornings of joy, even in this life, sometimes follow nights of weeping. When the worst comes to the worst, men say things mend, and they say also that it is always darkest before dawn. But we have come to know that Sorrow does not pass even though Joy enters, and those who can offer the sacrifice of praise do not even pray that she should pass. They learn to make room for the two angels, the veiled angel and the shining. Both are welcome guests, both are sent from God, both will work for us a gracious ministry if we will only suffer it. For the veiled angel we are to praise God, though it must be the sacrifice of praise.—W. ROBERTSON NICOLL, *Sunday Evening*, p. 367.

REFERENCES.—XIII. 15.—Spurgeon, *Sermons*, vol. xxxiv. No. 2048. J. Keble, *Sermons for Christmas and Epiphany*, p. 337.

'Let us offer a sacrifice of praise to God. . . . But to do good and to communicate forget not.'—HEB. XIII. 15, 16.

'HIS tenderness,' says George Eliot, of Adam Bède, 'lay very close to his reverence, so that the one could hardly be stirred without the other.'

REFERENCES.—XIII. 15, 16.—C. S. Laird, *Preacher's Magazine*, vol. v. p. 79. A. Maclaren, *Expositions of Holy Scripture—Hebrews*, p. 323. XIII. 16.—*Expositor* (5th Series), vol. ix. p. 222 XIII. 17.—E. H. Bickersteth, *Thoughts in Past Years*, p. 39. J. H. Holford, *Memorial Sermons*, p. 228. G. Matheson, *The Sunday Review*, vol. i. p. 105. XIII. 18.—J. C. M. Bellew, *Sermons*, vol. i. p. 36. J. Keble, *Sermons for Septuagesima to Ash Wednesday*, p. 411. W. Robertson Nicoll, *Ten Minute Sermons*, p. 181. *Expositor* (5th Series), vol. x. p. 25.

THE FIVE SCHOLARS OF LAUSANNE

'Now the God of peace, Who brought again from the dead our Lord Jesus, that great Shepherd of the sheep, through the blood of the everlasting covenant, make you perfect in every good work to do His will.'—HEB. XIII. 20.

THESE words are associated with the martyrdom of the Five Scholars of Lausanne, whose names are among the most honoured in the French martyrology. They were executed at Lyons on 16th May, 1553. Earnest appeals had been made on their behalf by the Swiss Cantons, but Henry II. refused to pardon them. Their progress to the place of execution was marked by the recital of psalms, the benediction, 'The God of peace, that brought again from the dead,' etc., and the Apostles' Creed, and after mutual embraces and farewells, their last words, as their naked bodies, smeared with grease and sulphur, hung side by side over the flames, were : 'Be of good courage, brethren, be of good courage'. Dr. H. M. Baird says : 'Their mission to France had not been in vain. It is no hyperbole of the historian of the Reformed Churches, when he likens their cells to five pulpits, from which the word of God resounded through the entire city and much further. The results of their heroic fortitude, and of the wide dissemination of copies of the confession of their Christian faith, were easily traced in the conversion of many within and without the prison, while the memory of their joyful constancy on their way to the place of execution—which rather resembled a triumphal than an ignomini-ous procession—and in the flames, was embalmed in the heart of many a spectator.'

HEB. XIII. 20.

THIS text has an association also with the great Ejection of 1662. Dr. Stoughton says :—

'Pepys, who liked to see and hear everything which was going on, walked to old St. Dunstan's Church, at seven o'clock in the morning, but found the doors unopened. He took a turn in the Temple Gardens until eight, when, on coming back to the church, he saw people crowding in at a side door, and found the edifice half-filled, ere the principal entrance had been opened. Dr. Bates, minister of the church, took for his text, "Now the God of peace, that brought again from the dead our Lord Jesus, that great Shepherd of the sheep, through the blood of the everlasting covenant, make you perfect". "He making a very good sermon," reports the Secretary, "and very little reflections in it to anything of the times." After dinner, the gossip went to St. Dunstan's again, to hear a second sermon from the same preacher upon the same text. Arriving at the church, about one o'clock, he found it thronged, and had to stand during the whole of the service. Not until the close of this second homily did the preacher make any distinct allusion to his ejectment, and then it was in terms the most concise and temperate. "I know you expect I should say something as to my nonconformity. I shall only say thus much, it is neither fancy, faction, nor humour that makes me not to comply, but merely for fear of offending God. And if after the best means used for my illumination, as prayer to God, discourse, study, I am not able to be satisfied concerning the lawfulness of what is required ; if it be my unhappiness to be in error, surely men will have no reason to be angry with me in this world, and I hope God will pardon me in the next."'

REFERENCES.—XIII. 20.—H. Alford, *Easter-tide Sermons*, p. 32. Spurgeon, *Sermons*, vol. v. No. 277. *Expositor* (4th Series), vol. i. p. 34 ; *ibid.* (6th Series), vol. xi. p. 60. A. Maclaren, *Expositions of Holy Scripture—Hebrews*, p. 332. XIII. 20, 21.—*Ibid.* (4th Series), vol. ix. p. 239. Spurgeon, *Sermons*, vol. xx. No. 1186, and vol. xxiii. No. 1368. XIII. 22.—*Expositor* (6th Series), vol. xi. p. 435. XIII. 24.—*Ibid.* (5th Series), vol. iii. p. 393 ; *ibid.* vol. x. p. 159. XIII. 25. —*Ibid.* (4th Series), vol. ii. p. 143.

THE EPISTLE OF JAMES

'THE Epistle of St. James,' said Père Gratry, 'may be called the Epistle of equality.' He used the expression 'that amazing Epistle of St. James'.

REFERENCES.—I. 1.—J. Stalker, *Christian World Pulpit*, vol. liii. p. 370. R. W. Dale, *The Epistle of James*, p. 1. *Expositor* (4th Series), vol. i. p. 65. I. 1-4.—*Ibid.* p. 260. I. 2-4.—Spurgeon, *Sermons*, vol. xxix. No. 1704. I. 2-7.—J. B. S. Watson, *Christian World Pulpit*, vol. lxi. p. 246. I. 2-8.—J. A. Alexander, *The Gospel of Jesus Christ*, p. 555. I. 2-11.—R. W. Dale, *The Epistle of James*, p. 9.

'Knowing this, that the proof of your faith worketh patience.'
—JAMES I. 3.

IT sometimes seems a little strange how, after having earnestly prayed to be delivered from temptation, and having given ourselves with shut eyes into God's hand, from that time every thought, every outward influence, every acknowledged law of life, seems to lead us on from strength to strength.—MRS. GASKELL, in *Ruth* (ch. XXIII.).

NEVER expect thy flesh should truly expound the meaning of the rod. It will call love, hatred; and say, God is destroying, when He is saving. It is the suffering party, and therefore not fit to be the judge.—BAXTER, *Saints' Rest* (ch. X.).

IF the passion have ended, not in a marriage but in a disappointment, the nature, if it have strength to bear the pressure, will be more ennobled and purified by that than by success. Of the uses of adversity which are sweet, none are sweeter than those which grow out of disappointed love; nor is there any greater mistake in contemplating the issues of life, than to suppose that baffled endeavours and disappointed hopes bear no fruits, because they do not bear those particular fruits which were sought and sighed for.—SIR HENRY TAYLOR, *Notes on Life*, pp. 76, 77.

REFERENCE.—I. 3.—*Expositor* (6th Series), vol. i. p. 122.

'That ye may be perfect and entire.'—JAMES I. 4.

A GREAT man is always willing to be little. When he sits on the cushion of advantages, he goes to sleep. When he is pushed, tormented, dejected, he has a chance to learn something. . . . In general, every evil to which we do not succumb is a benefactor. As the Sandwich Islander believes that the strength and valour of the enemy he kills passes into himself, so we gain the strength of the temptation we resist. —EMERSON, on *Compensation*.

'Wanting nothing.'—JAMES I. 4.

'IN my younger years,' said Richard Baxter, 'my trouble for sin was most about my actual failings in thought, word, or action. But now I am much more troubled for *inward defects*, and omission or want of the vital duties or graces of the soul. Had I all the riches of the world, how gladly would I give them for a fuller knowledge, belief, and love of God and everlasting glory! These wants are the greatest burden of my life.'

REFERENCES.—I. 4.—W. F. Shaw, *Sermon Sketches for the Christian Year*, p. 103. T. Sadler, *Sunday Thoughts*, p. 273. J. M. Neale, *Readings for the Aged* (4th Series), p. 111. *Ibid. Sermons Preached in Sackville College Chapel*, vol. i. p. 355. H. D. Rawnsley, *Church Family Newspaper*, vol. xv. p. 1104. *Expositor* (5th Series), vol. v. p. 35. A. Maclaren, *Expositions of Holy Scripture—James*, p. 351.

ST. PHILIP AND ST. JAMES

'If any of you lack wisdom, let him ask of God, that giveth to all men liberally, and upbraideth not; and it shall be given him.'—JAMES I. 5.

THIS is one of the many beautifully-practical thoughts which so fill and characterise St. James, whose festival, together with that of St. Philip, we celebrate to-day.

I. **What is Wisdom?**—'Wisdom' is not knowledge, though it involves knowledge, for the most learned persons are often the least wise. 'Wisdom' is the right use of knowledge. Or take it thus. 'Wisdom' is that union of the heart and head when right affections guide the exercise of talent. Or, 'wisdom' is power to balance materials of good thought. It is the ability to direct intelligently and usefully the words we speak or the acts we do. Or, a step higher still, 'wisdom' is the reflection of the mind of God. Christ is the reflection of the mind of God. Therefore Christ is 'wisdom'. And the most Christlike is the most wise. If you wish to understand 'wisdom,' study Christ.

II. **The Guilt of Foolishness.**—The memory of most of us need go very little way back to show the necessity for this understanding of God. What a very humbling thing it is to look back and think—I do not now say how sinfully—but how very foolishly we have again and again spoken and acted. And is foolishness much less than sin? Is foolishness not sin? Is it not the 'idle word' for which we shall 'give account'? Was it not the 'fool' who said in his heart, 'There is no God'? and the 'fool' who said to his soul, 'Soul, thou hast much goods'? Was not it the 'foolish man' that 'built upon the sand'? And were not the 'foolish virgins' the virgins lost? If 'wisdom' were not a thing covenanted, then might a man not be responsible for being unwise. But now that God has promised to 'give wisdom' to every one who 'asks' for it, it is no longer venial to be foolish. The silly word you say, and the foolish act you do, is left guilty, and without excuse.

III. Asking for Wisdom.—To obtain 'wisdom,' the first thing you have to do is to recognise it to be a gift. 'Wisdom' seems to be such a natural development of mind that we cannot easily get rid of the idea that if we only think enough—think long enough, and think deeply enough we shall think ourselves into wisdom. But to the 'wisdom' such as God gave Joseph in the sight of Pharaoh—that 'wisdom' of which some asked, 'Whence hath this man wisdom'?—the wisdom 'which is first pure'—the 'wisdom' no science, no self-discipline, no effort will secure—the road is prayer, only prayer, communion with the Unseen.

' **If any of you lack wisdom, let him ask of God.**'—JAMES i. 5.

'DOCTOR,' said the invalid again, 'will you read me just four verses in the Bible?' 'Why, yes, my boy, as many as you wish to hear.' 'No, only four.' His free hand moved for the book that lay on the bed, and presently the Doctor read: *My brethren, count it all joy when ye fall into divers temptations; knowing this, that the trying of your faith worketh patience. But let patience have her perfect work that ye may be perfect and entire, wanting nothing. If any of you lack wisdom, let him ask of God, Who giveth to all liberally, and upbraideth not; and it shall be given him.* 'There,' whispered the sick man, and rested with a peaceful look in all his face. 'It—doesn't mean wisdom in general, Doctor—such as Solomon asked for?' 'Doesn't it?' said the other meekly. 'No, it means the wisdom necessary to let—patience—have her perf—— I was a long time—getting anywhere near that!'—G. W. CABLE, *Dr. Sevier*, pp. 450, 451.

WHEN Thomas Scott determined, for conscientious reasons, to give up his ministry in the English Church, he describes (*Force of Truth*, ch. II.) how he set about an inquiry into the scriptural basis of the Articles. 'And the first passage, I remember, which made me suspect that I might be wrong,' in refusing to examine them thus, 'was James i. 5, "If any of ye lack wisdom, let him ask of God, that giveth to all men liberally, and upbraideth not; and it shall be given him". On considering these words with some attention, I became conscious that, though I had thought myself wise, yet assuredly I had obtained none of my wisdom in this manner; for I had never offered one prayer to that effect during the whole course of my life.'

' **That giveth to all men liberally, and upbraideth not.**'—JAMES i. 5.

THE Aryan nations, before their separation, cherished a belief in a hero or god to whom they owed all their comforts in life: it was he that made the sun shine and the dawn keep her time; and it was to him they looked for the weather they wanted. The first breeds of animals useful to man, whether domestic or wild, were believed to have been obtained by him through craft or violence from the jealous powers who wished to keep them from the human race. . . . The habit of imagining both gods and demons to be jealous of the human race is familiar to all in the literature of various ancient nations.—RHYS, *Celtic Heathenism*, p. 302.

REFERENCES.—I. 5.—Spurgeon, *Sermons*, vol. xiii. No. 735. F. B. Cowl, *Preacher's Magazine*, vol. xviii. p. 237. J. Learmount, *British Congregationalist*, 4th July, 1907, p. 18. *Expositor* (4th Series), vol. ii. p. 263. A. Maclaren, *Expositions of Holy Scripture—James*, p. 360. I. 5, 6.—J. Keble, *Sermons for Advent to Christmas Eve*, p. 321. I. 6, 7.—Spurgeon, *Sermons*, vol. xliii. No. 2537.

THE VACILLATIONS OF FAITH

'But let him ask in faith, nothing doubting: for he that doubteth is like the surge of the sea driven by the wind and tossed. For let not that man think that he shall receive anything of the Lord: a double-minded man, unstable in all his ways.'—JAMES i. 6-8.

IN the writings of the Apostle Paul, as well as in the sayings of our Lord Himself, we are reminded of the fact that the faith which achieves great things and uplifts the devout life to the highest excellence set before it, must be an established principle of the soul, and not a passing mood only.

I. The faith that is evanescent is an affectation, and can no more pass as a just constituent of fruitful worship and service than any other kind of vamped-up sentiment. The complete sincerity of faith is proved by its imperturbable persistence. Faith means the deepest thought we have of God; and when that thought swings from side to side like the pendulum, one moment viewing God as true, benign, compassionate, covenant-keeping, and the next letting Him pass out of sight or viewing Him in more or less contradictory aspects, God is not thought of according to His due.

II. The faith that is only momentary cannot satisfy the heart of the Eternal. The life of some winged insects is said to be measured by the hour only, and, unlike bees and ants, they have no need to lay up food supplies which will last through long wintry months. God does not belong to an order of beings whose requirements can be met by what is transient and volatile, and it is impossible to satisfy His mighty insistency by a mood of faith unstable as the morning dew.

III. The blessings we seek in believing supplication are permanent in their duration, and faith is the condition of their tenure as well as of their first attainment. 'For by faith ye stand.' The double-minded man who never knows himself, who has never found out his own equation in spiritual things, who drifts before moods as gaily as the nautilus spreads its painted sails to the winds, who believes when genial influences combine to make it easy so to do, and morbidly disbelieves at the first temptation which comes to test his faith, is a failure as a suppliant and touches the lowest depths of vanity and frustration when he bends the knee in vacuous prayer.

IV. If we would cherish into an established habit the faith that seeks to spring up and possess our souls, we must never wantonly expose ourselves to influences hostile to faith. And, above all, we must draw near to God in the ways appointed for building up faith.

V. If our prayers are to be marked by unswerving and triumphant confidence, strong qualities must go to the making of our faith, qualities which will stand the strain of waiting and the rebuffs which meet us when we have gone forth to await the fulfilment of our desires. (1) Such an attribute is conscience, less mutable by far than other parts of man s being. God's breath is in it, and the breath of One in whom there is no variation, neither shadow cast by turning, protects this faculty from the weaknesses of its kindred faculties. (2) And in the best sense of the word reason must also enter into our faith if it is to escape the reproach of fitfulness. (3) And then when the conscience and the judgment are assured concerning the great hearer of prayer and the fitness of the things for which we ask, we must put into our prayers that power of will which is one of the most distinctive attributes of our being, and thus will the undivided and coherent man be made to pray.

REFERENCES.—I. 6-8.—*Expositor* (4th Series), vol. iii. p. 32.

JAMES I. 7.

DR. MARCUS DODS wrote at the age of twenty-nine to his friend the Rev. S. R. Macphail: 'Be persuaded that God will deliver you from sin, wait on Him, do not sink, do not scoff, do not suffer a shadow of doubt about it. I do not obey my own voice, but yet my past years say, if there is one verse of the Bible that is true it is about the waverer, "Let not that man think that he will receive anything from the Lord". Is it not, Simeon, the turning-point with us all when we can give God His place, believe in Him wholly. *Early Letters*, p. 323.

'A double-minded man is unstable in all his ways.'—JAMES I. 8.

IN all religious processions through the city the heralds went first to bid the people cease their work and attend to the ceremony; for just as the Pythagoreans are said to forbid the worship of the gods in a cursory manner, and to insist that men shall set out from their homes with this purpose and none other in their minds, so Numa thought it wrong that the citizens should see or hear any religious ceremony in a careless, half-hearted manner, and made them cease from all worldly cares and attend with all their hearts to the most important of all duties, religion; so he cleared the streets of all the hammering and cries and noises which attend the practice of ordinary trades and handicrafts, before any holy ceremony.—PLUTARCH, *Life of Numa* (xiv.).

REFERENCE.—I. 9, 10.—*Expositor* (4th Series), vol. iii. p. 195.

'Let the rich rejoice in that he is made low.'—JAMES I. 10.

WOULD it not be wiser for people to rejoice at all that they now sorrow for, and *vice versâ*? To put on bridal garments at funerals, and mourning at weddings? For their friends to condole with them when they attained riches and honour, as only so much care added?—HAWTHORNE.

ADVERSITY had been so far his friend that it had taken from him all hope of the social success for which people crawl and truckle, and restored him, through failure and doubt and heartache, the manhood which his prosperity had so nearly stolen from him.—W. D. HOWELLS, *The Rise of Silas Lapham* (XXVII.).

LIFE will be dearer and clearer in anguish,
Than ever was felt in the throbs of delight.
　　　　　　　　　—LORD HOUGHTON.

REFERENCES.—I. 10, 11.—*Expositor* (4th Series), vol. iii. p. 264. I. 11.—*Ibid.* (6th Series), vol. x. p. 445.

THE BLESSEDNESS OF ENDURING TEMPTATION

'Blessed is the man that endureth temptation; for when he is tried, he shall receive the crown of life, which the Lord hath promised to them that love Him.'—JAMES I. 12.

THE text does not mean that we ought to be glad if temptation comes, nor that temptation is a blessed thing in itself; but that the Christian is blessed who endures it, and who comes out of it approved and strengthened.

I. Let us try to discover the meaning of 'temptation' spoken of here. The English word has become so associated with the idea of incitement to evil that it does not fully express what is meant, nor even express it correctly. True, a 'trial' or 'trouble' is sometimes also a 'temptation' in that sense, as we know too well. But no trouble is ever sent by God with the intention of inciting to sin. Perhaps some paraphrase such as this may help us: 'Blessed is the man that endureth the test which comes through God—sent troubles, for when he has passed through the testing time, and been approved, he shall receive the crown of life which the Lord hath promised to them that love Him.' Trials do for us what stormy winds do in nature, for both fulfil God's word and carry out His design.

II. Now the variety of our capacities requires variety in the means used to test and develop them. Hence, in the second verse, we read of 'divers' temptations. (1) Trial often comes through prosperity and comfort. For example, those about you may be singularly gentle and yielding. Now this has been one of God's tests to you, though you have never recognised it. How far have you been considerate, trying to find out the wishes which will not be openly expressed? (2) On the other hand, if those about you are cold and irresponsive; if they never reward you with a smile or a word of thanks, do what you may for them; if your quiet acts of self-sacrifice are not so much as noticed, if your love is met by indifference, or even by unkindness, God is testing you by this.

III. What, then, are some of the purposes wrapped up in God's design? His main purpose, according to this chapter, is to strengthen, to test, and to develop faith by its exercise; because faith is the root-virtue from which patience and courage spring. Blessed is the man that endureth the temptation of struggle and effort, for he shall receive the crown of life.

IV. The promise referred to here was given by the Lord Jesus Himself, who, in His personal experience, knew the hardness of our conflict and the painfulness of our sufferings ; and it involves the assurance that He Himself is watching over us, measuring our strength, proportioning our trials and duties to the powers of endurance, innate and inspired, so that He will not suffer us to be tempted above that we are able. — A. ROWLAND, *Open Windows and other Sermons*, p. 48.

REFERENCES.—I. 12.—W. Wynn, *Christian World Pulpit*, vol. liv. p. 102. Spurgeon, *Sermons*, vol. xxxi. No. 1874. T. F. Crosse, *Sermons* (2nd Series), p. 213. Brooke Herford, *Courage and Cheer*, p. 217. R. W. Church, *Village Sermons* (3rd Series), p. 223. C. Bosanquet, *Blossoms from the King's Garden*, p. 111. W. L. Watkinson, *The Supreme Conquest*, p. 142. *Expositor* (4th Series), vol. iii. p. 443 ; *ibid.* vol. ix. p. 4. A. Maclaren, *Expositions of Holy Scripture—James*, p. 368. I. 12-18.—R. W. Dale, *The Epistle of James*, p. 22.

' I am tempted of God.'—JAMES I. 13.

THIS is the excellent foppery of the world, that, when we are sick in fortune,—often the surfeit of our own behaviour,—we make guilty of our disasters the sun, the moon, and the stars : as if we were villains by necessity ; fools by heavenly compulsion ; drunkards, liars, and adulterers by an enforced obedience of planetary influence ; and all that we are evil in, by a Divine thrusting on.—SHAKESPEARE, *King Lear* (Act i. Sc. 2).

' For God cannot be tempted with evil, neither tempteth He any man.'—JAMES I. 13.

COMPARE the conversation between Socrates and Adeimantos in Plato's *Republic* (379, 13) :—

'Then that which is good is not the cause of all things, but only of what is as it should be, being guiltless of originating evil.'

'Exactly so.'

'If that be so, then God, inasmuch as He is good, cannot be the cause of all things, according to the common doctrine. On the contrary, He is the author of only a small part of human affairs ; of the larger part He is not the author : for all evil things far outnumber all good things : and the good things we must ascribe to no other than God, while we must seek elsewhere, and not in Him, the causes of the evil things.'

REFERENCES.—I. 13.—*Expositor* (5th Series), vol. v. p. 323. I. 13-15.—G. W. Brameld, *Practical Sermons*, p. 69. *Expositor* (4th Series), vol. iv. p. 42.

' Every man is tempted, when he is drawn away of his own lust and enticed.'—JAMES I. 14.

OH the hourly dangers that we here walk in ! Every sense and member is a snare ; every creature, every mercy, and every duty is a snare to us. We can scarcely open our eyes, but we are in danger of envying those above us, or despising those below us ; of coveting the honours and riches of some, or beholding the rags and beggary of others with pride and unmercifulness. If we see beauty, it is a bait to lust ; if deformity, to loathing and disdain.

How soon do slanderous reports, vain jests, wanton speeches, creep into the heart ! How constant and strong a watch does our appetite require ! Have we comeliness and beauty ? What fuel for pride ! Are we deformed ? What an occasion of repining ! Have we strength of reason, and gifts of learning ? Oh how prone to be puffed up, to hunt after applause, and despise our brethren. Are we unlearned ? How apt we are to despise what we have not ! Are we in places of authority ? How strong is the temptation to abuse our trust, make our will law, and cut out all the enjoyments of others, by the rules and model of our own interest and policy ! Are we inferiors ? How prone to grudge at others' pre-eminence, and bring their actions to the bar of our judgment ! Are we rich and not too much exalted ? Are we poor and not discontented ? Are we not lazy in our duties, or make a Christ of them ? Not that God hath made all these things our snares, but through our own corruption they become so to us. Ourselves are the greatest snare to ourselves.—BAXTER, *Saints' Rest*, pp. 60, 61.

'THERE is a popular belief respecting evil spirits,' says Scott in a note to the fifteenth chapter of *The Abbot*, 'that they cannot enter an inhabited house unless invited, nay, dragged over the threshold.'

'TEMPTATION is a cause of possible sin,' says Ritschl, ' originating in an impulse, the satisfaction of which appears on first thoughts to be in itself legitimate. . . . It is, therefore, a signal mistake to refer the well-known saying of James, as is generally done, to evil and desire. Christ also was exposed to temptation, simply because temptation is always bound up with an inclination which is at the outset morally legitimate or permissible. For no man of moral worth will find a temptation in a situation in which he from the first recognises Satan.'

REFERENCES.—I. 16, 17.—J. H. Jowett, *The Examiner*, 7th June, 1906, p. 558.

GOD AS THE ETERNAL GIVER
(*A Sermon to Oxford Undergraduates*)

' Every good gift and every perfect boon is from above, and cometh down from the Father of light, With whom is no variableness, neither shadow that is cast by turning.'—JAMES I. 17.

I. WHAT is the description, the character, of God, as depicted in the Bible ? What should we have to take as the title of the Bible if it was a story for which we were asked to find a title ? I say there is only one title we could select, and it would be : 'God as the Eternal Giver'. Open the Bible, and begin with the book of Genesis. We cannot stop to go into it, but there, in picture form, it describes the Eternal Giver giving gifts to mankind—sunshine, air, the gift of life ; and

How good is man's life, the mere living
How fit to employ
All the heart, and the soul, and the senses
For ever in joy.

He gives further the gift of love, the love of man for

woman, and woman for man, and parents for children, and children for parents. All that is described in the opening chapters. Then comes the second part, which comprises all the Old Testament and the beginning of the New Testament. And what is that? The gift of the Eternal Son—nothing short of that. And we ask you—we who are in the middle of the battle—to hold fast down here to the true Christian religion, and not to barter it away for any religion which merely speaks of a good man named Jesus Christ Who once lived on earth. The Christian religion as prophesied in the Old Testament, and depicted in the New, is the giving of the Eternal Son of God and nothing else. It is prophesied all through the Old Testament, and then described in the simplest and most touching language at the beginning of the New Testament.

Is that all? Have we now got to the end of the giving of God? Not at all. 'It is expedient for you that I go away, for if I go not away the Comforter will not come; but if I depart I will send Him to you.' Prophesied all through the latter part of the Gospel, and described at the beginning of the Acts of the Apostles, is the third giving, the giving of the Eternal Spirit. With tongues of fire and a rushing mighty wind the great doors of heaven open again and down comes the third great gift of God, the Eternal Spirit, which He has given to the end of time.

II. But is He—that brings us to the second question—is He the same God to-day? Have we this Eternal Giver to turn to? A moment's reflection will show you that every one of those gifts which is described as given in the Bible, He gives perpetually.

III. Now come one more stage with me. It is impossible to describe to you what this third proposition means to many of us. We have still got our imagination to deal with—our imagination which tells us that this is too good to be true. Is it impossible to believe that the great God is like this? Do you remember that splendid saying of David's when he looked on Saul lying there in his melancholy madness and felt a Divine desire to help him come into his heart, and he says, 'Would I suffer for him whom I love? so wouldst thou; so wilt thou?' There has never been any answer to that. A little lad at Euston was filling all those thousands of men in the station with admiration, because, without thinking of what he did, or thinking anything of it, he threw himself forward to pick up two children off the line as an express came rushing in, and though the train actually touched him, he pulled the children out of the way as a matter of course. If a lad would do that, and God would not do it, then the little lad is greater than God. But the creature cannot surpass the Creator. If there is a God at all He must be capable of self-sacrifice. The Eternal Giver described in the Bible must be loving and working to-day. The more you think of it, the more you are convinced that the Bible description must be true, and that this is the God that you and I are asked to serve and love and worship for ever and ever.

IV. And if this is so, what is the difference it makes to our lives? (1) The first difference is this: if we really believe it we are bound to do something which we find very often the hardest thing to do. We must love God. That is the difficulty of religion. And if we love God it changes life. The weariness will vanish from religion; it will become a labour of love.

(2) And secondly, how can we tread under foot His gifts, if we believe He gives us them Himself. Put on the shoes of service.

(3) And thirdly, what a difference it makes to our prayers. I believe many of us even now have no idea what prayer is. Prayer is not trying to change the will of God to suit our whims. We may be quite sure that the Eternal Giver is much more anxious than you or I are for our highest interests. He always wants to give us the best. Every morning His hands are full of hope and love and wisdom for us. But by prayer we enable Him to give us what He wants to give us, and which He cannot do for a cold, apathetic, sluggish nature that does not want to improve. Therefore prayer is a most delightful co-operation with God in which two friends, as it were, work together for a common object. And intercession is like unto it.

(4) And, lastly, ought there not to be, if this picture of the Eternal Giver is true, a great deal more likeness in the faces and characters of the sons of the Eternal Giver to their Father. You know how fathers and mothers love to see their likeness in their children. Well, now, I fully believe that the reason that Christianity progresses so slowly, that we are not more impressive to the world, and able to make a far quicker impression, is that the sons of the Eternal Giver are so unlike their Father. That is what Christ prayed for in His great prayer, that we were to be one, that the world might believe that the Father sent Him. The world does not believe at all fully yet in that, and that is because the sons of the Eternal Giver do not give themselves away with the generosity that is to be expected of those that believe in the Bible story.—A. F. WINNINGTON-INGRAM (Bishop of London), *Church Times*, 28th October, 1910.

'The Father of lights.'—JAMES I. 17.

IN optics, if you make a hole in the shutter at noon, or stick a square bit of blackness on the pane, and make the rays from the hole or around the square to pass through a prism, then we have, if we let them fall on whiteness or catch them right, those colours we all know and rejoice in, that Divine *spectrum*. . . . The white light of heaven—*lumen siccum*—opens itself out, as it were, tells its secret, and lies like a glorious border on the Edge o' Dark (as imaginative Lancashire calls the twilight, as we Scotchmen call it, the gloamin'), making the boundaries between light and darkness a border of flowers, made out by each. Is there not something to think of in 'The Father of lights,' thus beautifying the limits of

His light and of His darkness, which to Him alone is light, so that here burns a sort of 'dim, religious light'—a sacred glory, where we may take off our shoes and rest and worship?—Dr. John Brown, *In Clear Dream and Solemn Vision.*

'With whom is no variableness, neither shadow of turning.'
JAMES I. 17.

God is a Being of perfect simplicity and truth, both in deed and word, and neither changes in Himself nor imposes upon others, either by apparitions, or by words, or by sending signs, whether in dreams or in waking moments.—Plato's *Republic* (382).

'If I only knew that God was as good as that woman, I should be content.' 'Then you don't believe that God is good?' 'I didn't say that, my boy. But to know that God was good and kind and fair—heartily, I mean, and not halfways with if's and but's—my boy, there would be nothing left to be miserable about.'—George Macdonald, *Robert Falconer.*

Speaking of the spirit of the age, in his essay on Dr. Marshall, Dr. John Brown, in *Horæ Subsecivæ*, notes how 'this great social element, viewless, impalpable, inevitable, untameable as the wind, is—like the great laws of nature—of which indeed it is one—for ever at its work; and like its Divine author and guide, goes about continually doing good. . . . This is that tide in the affairs of men—*a Deo, ad Deum*—that onward movement of the race in knowledge, in power, in work, and in happiness, which has gladdened and cheered all who believe, and who, through long ages of gloom and misery and havoc, have still believed that truth is strong, next to the Almighty. . . . It is a tide that has never turned; unlike the poet's, it answers the behest of no waning and waxing orb, it follows the eve of Him who is without variableness or the shadow of turning.'

Thou hadst not to do with an unconstant creature, but with Him 'with whom is no variableness, nor shadow of turning'. His love to thee will not be as thine was on earth to Him, seldom, and cold, up and down.—Baxter, *Saints' Rest* (ch. I.).

REFERENCES.—I. 17.—A. C. Turberville, *The Pulpit*, vol. i. p. 6. R. C. Trench, *Sermons New and Old*, p. 163. R. Flint, *Sermons and Addresses*, p. 28. F. St. John Corbett, *The Preacher's Year*, p. 88. C. Kingsley, *The Good News of God*, p. 229. *Expositor* (6th Series), vol. viii. p. 39. I. 18.—J. H. Snowdon, *Christian World Pulpit*, vol. xlv. p. 292. J. Keble, *Sermons for the Saints' Days*, p. 224. T. Binney, *Kings' Weigh-House Chapel Sermons*, p. 206. J. Budgen, *Parochial Sermons*, vol. i. p. 124. *Expositor* (4th Series), vol. iii. p. 183. A. Maclaren, *Expositions of Holy Scripture—James*, p. 376. I. 18-21.—Bishop Gore, *Christian World Pulpit*, vol. lvi. p. 22.

'He begat us with the word of truth. . . . Wherefore . . . be ye doers of the word.'—JAMES I. 18-22.

The new moral birth is sacred—as sacred as the child within the mother's womb—it is a kind of blasphemy against the Holy Ghost to conceal it. And when I use the word "moral" here—or anywhere above—I do not, I hope, mean that dull pinch-

lipped conventionality of negation which often goes under that name. The deep-lying ineradicable desires, fountains of human action, the life-long aspirations, the lightning-like revelations of right and justice, the treasured hidden ideal, borne in flame and darkness, in joy and in sorrow, in tears and in triumph, within the heart—these are, as a rule, anything but conventional.—Edward Carpenter, *England's Ideal*, p. 73

'Let every man be swift to hear, slow to speak, slow to wrath.'—JAMES I. 19.

Speaking of the discipline of self-restraint and the stoical repression of feelings in Japan, Dr. Nitobé, in his volume on *Bushido* (pp. 106 f.), observes that in Japan 'when a man or woman feels his or her soul stirred, the first instinct is quietly to suppress the manifestation of it. In rare instances is the tongue set free by an irresistible spirit, when we have eloquence of sincerity and fervour. It is putting a premium on a breach of the third commandment to encourage speaking lightly of spiritual experiences. It is truly jarring to Japanese ears to hear the most sacred words, the most secret heart experiences, thrown out in promiscuous audiences. "Dost thou feel the soil of thy soul stirred with tender thoughts? It is time for seeds to sprout. Disturb it not with speech; but let it work alone in quietness and secrecy"—writes a young Samurai in his diary.

'To give in so many articulate words one's inmost thoughts and feelings—notably the religious—is taken among us as an unmistakable sign that they are neither very profound nor very sincere. "Only a pomegranate is he"—so runs a popular saying—"who, when he gapes his mouth, displays the contents of his heart."'

Compare the advice of Polonius in *Hamlet* (Act i. Sc. 3) :—

Give every man thy ear, but few thy voice.

Surly judges there have been who did not much admire the 'Bible of Modern Literature,' or anything you could distil from it, in contrast with the ancient Bibles; and found that in the matter of speaking, our far best excellence, when that could be obtained, was excellent silence, which means endurance and exertion, and good *work* with lips closed.—Carlyle, *Latter-Day Pamphlets* (v.).

While in thy lips thy words thou dost confine,
Thou art their lord; once uttered, they are mine.—
Archbishop Trench.

'All the ground near Sir Archibald's,' between Aberdeen and Inverness, 'is as well cultivated as most in England. About seven I preached. The kirk was pretty well filled, though upon short notice. Certainly this is a nation "swift to hear, and slow to speak," though not "slow to wrath". — Wesley's *Journal* (7th June, 1764).

Johnson.—What I most envy Burke for is his being constantly the same. He is never what we call humdrum; never unwilling to begin to talk, nor in haste to leave off. BOSWELL.—Yet he can listen. JOHNSON.—No; I cannot say he is good at that. So desirous is he to talk, that, if one is speaking at this end of the table, he'll speak to somebody at the other end.—BOSWELL's *Tour to the Hebrides* (15th Aug.)

REFERENCES.—I. 19.—J. J. Blunt, *Plain Sermons*, p. 220. *Expositor* (5th Series), vol. vi. p. 9. I. 19, 20.—W. H. Evans, *Sermons for the Church's Year*, p. 292. I. 19-21.—*Expositor* (4th Series), vol. iv. p. 279. I. 19-27.—R. W. Dale, *The Epistle of James*, p. 36.

'The wrath of man worketh not the righteousness of God.'—JAMES I. 20.

IF a bad-tempered man can be admirably virtuous, he must be under extreme difficulties. . . . For it is of the nature of such temper to interrupt the formation of healthy mental habits, which depend on a growing harmony between perception, conviction and impulse. There may be good feelings, good deeds — for a human nature may touch endless varieties and blessed inconsistencies in its windings —but it is essential to what is worthy to be called high character, that it may be safely calculated on. —GEORGE ELIOT, *Essays of Theophrastus Such* (VI.).

REFERENCE.—I. 20.—*Expositor* (6th Series), vol. xii. p. 28.

'Receive with meekness the ingrafted word, which is able to save your souls.'—JAMES I. 21.

THE stream of custom and our profession bring us to the Preaching of the Word, and we sit out our hour under the sound; but how few consider and prize it as the great ordinance of God for the salvation of souls, the beginner and the sustainer of the Divine life of grace within us! And certainly, until we have thus thought of it, and seek to feel it thus ourselves, although we hear it most frequently, and let slip no occasion, yea, hear it with attention and some present delight, yet still we miss the right use of it, and turn it from its true end, while we take it not as that *ingrafted word which is able to save our souls.*— LEIGHTON.

REFERENCES.—I. 21.—A. B. O. Wilberforce, *Christian World Pulpit*, vol. xlix. p. 296. J. Keble, *Sermons for Easter to Ascension Day*, p. 386. I. 21, 22.—Spurgeon, *Sermons*, vol. xxxi. No. 1847.

'Be ye doers of the word, and not hearers only.'—JAMES I. 22.

IN the one volume of *Sesame and Lilies*—nay, in the last forty pages of its central address to English-women—everything is told that I know of vital truth, everything urged that I see to be needful of vital act —but no creature answers me with any faith or any deed. They read the words, and say they are pretty, and go on in their own ways.—RUSKIN, *Fors Clavigera* (LVIII.).

WHEN President Roosevelt opened the Bible to kiss it, on taking the oath at his inauguration, this text was found to be the place he chose.

REFERENCES.—I. 22.—E. A. Stuart, *His Dear Son and other Sermons*, vol. v. p. 17. F. W. Farrar, *Sin and its Conquerors*, p. 58. F. B. Cowl, *Preacher's Magazine*, vol. xvii. p. 188. I. 22-24.—H. S. Holland, *Christian World Pulpit*, vol. liv.

p. 49. I. 22-25.—Spurgeon, *Sermons*, vol. xxv. No. 1467. *Expositor* (4th Series), vol. i. p. 25; *ibid.* vol. iii. pp. 183, 448. I. 23.—F. St. John Corbett, *The Preacher's Year*, p. 92. I. 23-25.—Spurgeon, *Sermons*, vol. xxxi. No. 1848.

'He beholdeth himself and goeth his way, and straightway forgetteth what manner of man he was.'—JAMES I. 24.

'FEW people,' says Matthew Arnold, in *The French Play in London*, 'who feel a passion think of learning anything from it. A man feels a passion, he passes through it, and then he goes his way and straightway forgets, as the Apostle says, what manner of man he was. Above all, this is apt to happen with us English, who have, as an eminent German professor is good enough to tell us, "so much genius, so little method". The much genius hurries us into infatuations; the little method prevents our learning the right and wholesome lesson from them.'

THE LAW OF LIFE IN CHRISTIANITY— LIBERTY

'The perfect law of liberty.'—JAMES I. 25.

THERE is no more inspiring word in human speech than Freedom, Liberty. It expresses an instinctive craving of the human heart. It awakens a responsive echo in the human breast.

Curiously enough, it has often been a taunt levelled at the Church—and with a certain measure of justification—that it stands in opposition to this noble and legitimate instinct of the human heart. If that is true, then a great error has been committed in direct antagonism to the spirit of the Gospel. The Gospel was announced by the Lord in terms of liberty: 'The Spirit of the Lord is upon Me . . . to preach deliverance to the captive . . . to set at liberty them that are bruised'. The Christ appeared as the Liberator, the Emancipator.

> He came to break oppression,
>   To set the captive free,
> To take away transgression
>   And rule in equity.

NOTE the third line—'to take away transgression' —for it is of the essence of the Christian conception of liberty, and we must return to it. But it is important to notice generally that the Christian religion is in entire accord with this noble aspiration of the human heart. If Christianity is to understand itself aright, it must see that liberty is of the very essence of its own constitution. Freedom is the law of the Christian life. The flower of the Christian life can never blossom in its perfection till it expands in the congenial atmosphere of perfect liberty.

I. It is important to notice that there are two kinds of freedom. There is an outer freedom and an inner, just as there is an outer and an inner bondage. The outer is in each case the more obvious. The slavery that holds the body captive is more quickly detected than the tyranny that enthralls the spirit. A man's limbs may be free. He may have every right of the freeborn and yet have the spirit of a slave, held captive in the tyranny of custom or dread, or degrading habit. A man, on the other hand, may be a prisoner, with a spirit indomitable, with a liberty within, which tyrants cannot quell. Men contend for their right to more than Burns sings of in his Scottish pæan of freedom. They want ultimately, like the Pilgrim Fathers, 'Freedom to worship God'. This is, in its highest terms, the one right man has from nature, as Mazzini maintains, even if he have no other. He has the right of 'liberating himself from every obstacle impeding his free fulfilment of his own duties'. But that is something spiritual. It demands, in the first instance, the emancipation of the inner man. It is men with the free spirit who fight for freedom.

II. Notice the significance of this for Christianity and of Christianity for this. The Gospel is what man needs if he will be free. It is the Gospel which becomes 'the religion of ethical liberation, for in its very centre lies the belief in the unfettering of the will for good by the forgiveness of sins'. Martin Luther, who never beats about the bush, gives a very straight answer to the question, Where lie the roots of liberty? In a brief treatise on 'The Liberty of a Christian Man,' a most concise and illuminating statement of the essence and spirit of Christianity, he says, in a word, that the foundation of all true freedom lies in the deliverance of the soul from the bondage of sin through faith in the finished work of Christ.

Where did Luther learn this? It was the truth of Christ, which Rome had concealed from the eyes of men for centuries in order to impose on them the tyranny of her own will and serve her own base ends. Luther learned it from Paul and a greater than Paul, Paul's Master, our Lord.

III. Liberty is a right of man from God's hand, a right which has been discovered for us by Christ. But, as Dr. John Ker says, 'there is great danger in contending for freedom, either civil or religious, of our making it the end instead of the means'. Anthony Trollope had a novel called *What will He do with It?* That is the question for every man who has gained his freedom. What will he do with it? If it is not recognised speedily that freedom is more than anything else a constant opportunity, it will degenerate into licence. If men do not realise that there is a law of liberty, they will become mere libertines, who, wearing the name of freedom, are the most degraded slaves. No, there are great calls awaiting a man, the call of truth, the call of righteousness, as soon as he gains his freedom. And as Dr. Denney says, 'A man must be perfectly free'—why?—'that the whole weight of his responsibilities may come upon him. Liberty is the correlative of responsibility?' A free man must address himself to the knowing of the truth that he may form proper judgments. He must consider the will of God that he may choose and pursue worthy ideals. Self kicks at these, as though they were new fetters, an infringement of freedom of thought, a restraint on the natural impulses. It were well for a man in this temper to consider the prayer with

which the late Master of Balliol, Professor Edward Caird, used every morning to open his class for the study of Moral Philosophy : 'Almighty and most merciful God, who hast created us for Thyself so that we can find rest only in Thee, grant unto us purity of heart and strength of purpose, so that no selfish passion may hinder us from knowing Thy will, and no weakness from doing it, that in Thy light we may see light, and in Thy service find perfect freedom, through the spirit of Christ'. 'For,' says St. Francis de Sales, 'the liberty of beloved children . . . is a thorough detachment from all things in order to follow God's recognised will.'— R. J. DRUMMOND, *Faith's Certainties*, p. 255.

'Whoso looketh into the perfect law of liberty, and continueth therein.'—JAMES I. 25.

As the most far-sighted eye, even aided by the most powerful telescope, will not make a fixed star appear larger than it does to an ordinary and unaided sight, even so there are heights of knowledge and truth sublime which all men in possession of the ordinary human understanding may comprehend as much and as well as the profoundest philosopher and the most learned theologian. Such are the truths relating to the *logos* and its oneness with the self-existent Deity, and of the humanity of Christ and its union with the *logos*. It is idle, therefore, to refrain from preaching on these subjects, provided only such preparations have been made as no man can be a Christian without. The misfortune is that the majority are Christians in name, and by birth only. Let them but once, according to St. James, have looked down steadfastly into the *law* of liberty or freedom in their own souls (the will and the conscience), and they are capable of whatever God has chosen to reveal.—COLERIDGE.

IN a letter to a country rector (*Life*, ch. VIII.) Kingsley avows that 'the highest idea of man is to know his Father, and look his Father in the face, in full assurance of faith and love; and that out of that springs all manful energy, all self-respect, all self-restraint, all that the true Englishman has, and the Greek and Spaniard have not. And I say this is what St. James means when he speaks of "the perfect law of liberty". I say that this Protestant faith, which teaches every man to look God in the face for himself, has contributed more than anything else to develop family life, industry, freedom, in England, Scotland, and Sweden.'

'The perfect law of liberty.'—JAMES I. 25.

ALL civilisation is the yoking of man, and the vicissitudes of history arise out of the trial of various yokes, and the abuse of them by lawless and unyoked power, the rebellions against their misuse involving also rebellion against yokes as such. We have need of Law *and* Gospel. Better Law only than no yoke, and the Gospel is no Gospel if it does not both presuppose and include Law.—DR. HORT, *Hulsean Lectures*, p. 203.

REFERENCES.—I. 25.—W. Morison, *Christian World Pulpit*, vol. lvii. p. 132. Archbishop Lang, *Christian World Pulpit*, vol. lix. p. 384. A. Maclaren, *Expositions of Holy Scripture—James*, p. 386.

'And bridleth not his tongue.'—JAMES I. 26.

'THE thing here supposed and referred to,' says Butler in his great Sermon on The Government of the Tongue, 'is talkativeness : a disposition to be talking, abstracted from the consideration of what is to be said ; with very little or no regard to, or thought of doing, either good or harm. . . . And this unrestrained volubility and wantonness of speech is the occasion of numberless evils and vexations in life. It begets resentment in him who is the subject of it ; sows the seed of strife and dissension amongst others ; and inflames little disgusts and offences, which if let alone would wear away of themselves.'

WHILE thou so hotly disclaimest the devil, be not guilty of diabolism. Fall not into one name with that unclean spirit, nor act his nature whom thou so much abhorrest ; that is, to accuse, calumniate, backbite, whisper, detract, or sinistrously interpret others. Degenerate depravities, and narrow-minded vices ! not only below St. Paul's noble Christian but Aristotle's true gentleman. Trust not with some that the Epistle of St. James is apocryphal, and so read with less fear that stabbing truth, that in company with this vice 'thy religion is in vain'. Moses broke the tables without breaking of the law ; but where charity is broke, the law itself is shattered, which cannot be whole without love, which is the fulfilling of it.'—SIR THOMAS BROWNE, *Christian Morals* (pt. I. sec. 16).

CANON CARUS, in his memoir of Charles Simeon, quotes a reminiscence of the latter's quick temper. 'We were one day sitting at dinner at Mr. Hankinson's, when a servant behind him stirred the fire in a way so *unscientific* that Mr. S. turned round and hit the man a thump in the back to stay his proceedings. When he was leaving me, on horseback, after the same visit, my servant had put the wrong bridle upon his horse. He was in a hurry to be gone, and his temper broke out so violently that I ventured to give him a little humorous castigation. His cloak-bag was to follow him by coach ; so I feigned a letter in my servant's name, saying how high his character stood in the kitchen, but that they could not understand how a gentleman who preached and prayed so well, should be in such passion about nothing, and wear no *bridle* upon his tongue.'

'This man's religion is vain.'—JAMES I. 26.

'IF the religious spirit,' says Mr. Morley in *Compromise* (pp. 178, 179), leads to a worthy and beautiful life, if it shows itself in cheerfulness, in pity, in charity and tolerance, in forgiveness, in a sense of the largeness and the mystery of things, in a lifting up of the soul in gratitude and awe to some supreme power and sovereign force, then whatever drawback may be in the way of superstitious dogma, still such a spirit is on the whole a good thing. If not, not. It would be better without the superstition : even with the superstition, it is good. But if the religious spirit is only a fine name for narrowness of understanding, for shallow intolerance, for mere social formality, for a dread of losing that poor respectability which means thinking and doing exactly as the people around us think and do, then the religious spirit is not a good thing, but a thoroughly bad and hateful thing.'

REFERENCES.—I. 26.—Bishop Butler, *Human Nature and Other Sermons*, p. 54. J. Keble, *Sermons for Easter to Ascension Day*, p. 416.

UNSPOTTED FROM THE WORLD

'And to keep himself unspotted from the world.'—JAMES I. 27.

As men and women grow older they change. Of all the changes that they undergo, those of their moral natures are often the most painful to watch. The boy changes into the man, and there is something lost which never seems to come back again. He has a hard conscience now, instead of a tender one ; he is scornful about sacred things ; no longer earnest and enthusiastic, but flippant and cynical ; he tolerates evils he used to hate ; makes excuses for passions he once thought horrible ; he qualifies and limits the absolute standards of truth and purity. He has changed. His life has lost that clear ring, its white lustre. He is no longer unspotted.

In regard to this we all have a dim idea that if we could have taken that life and isolated it, we could have kept its freshness and purity. We grant that there is evil in the heart, but we do not believe that the mere fermentation of that evil in itself could have come to all this. Out of the aggregate of the many influences which we call 'the world,' have come the evil forces that have changed and soiled this life. It has not been himself. He has walked through mire, and the filth has gathered on his skirts ; through pestilence, and the poison has crept into his blood. Not merely the evil heart within has shown its wickedness, but the evil around us has fastened upon us. We have not merely been spotted, but 'spotted by the world'. Our own experience confirms the Bible conception of 'the world,' and so we listen. And here the Bible steps in and describes lives shaped by this cosmos, this total of created things.

I. 'Lives spotted by the world.' The stained lives. Who does not know what this means ? There is the outward stain—the stain upon the reputation. How few reputations remain so pure as to be fit patterns for others to follow ! There are the stains upon our conduct, the impure and untrue acts which visibly cloud the fair surface of our best activity. And then, worst of all, there is the stain upon the heart, of which none but the man himself knows anything. These are the stains which we accumulate.

II. And now, in view of all this, we come to our religion ; and we hear St. James telling us, in unsparing words, what 'pure religion and undefiled before God' is. Mark, then, how intolerant religion is. She starts with what men declare to be impossible. She refuses to bring down her standards. She insists that men must come up to her. She proclaims absolute standards. She will not say, 'Your case is a hard one, and for that reason I will waive a part of my demands; for you, religion shall mean not to do this sin or that sin'. Before every man, in the thickest of the world's contagions, she stands and cries with unwavering voice, 'Come out, be separate, keep yourself unspotted from the world'. There is something sublime in this unsparingness. It almost proves that our religion is Divine when it undertakes for man so Divine a task. And our religion is not true unless it have this power in it, unless the statesman, the merchant, the man or woman in society, do indeed find it the power of purity and strength. We must bring our faith to this test. Unless our religion does this for us, it is not the true religion that St. James talked of, and that the Lord Jesus came to reveal and to bestow.

III. We go for our assurance to the first assertion of the real character of Christianity in the life of Jesus. The life of Jesus was meant to be the pattern of the lives of all who call themselves His followers. His was a real human life, and yet the very sinlessness of Jesus has made Him seem to many not to be Man, instead of being the type of what manhood was intended to be, and what all men must come to be. The very principle of the Incarnation, that without which it loses all its value, surely is this, that Christ was Himself the first Christian; that in Him was displayed the power of that grace by which all believers were to be helped and saved. And so for this reason the life of Jesus was lived in the closest contact with His fellow-men. He passed through the highest temptations to which our nature is exposed; He walked through the same muddy streets of sordid care; He penetrated the same murky atmosphere of passion that we have to go through, and thence He came out pure, and unspotted from the world; thus He is really God manifest in the flesh. As He came forth spotless, so by His power we must come out unstained at last, and 'walk with Him in white'.

IV. As we study the life of Jesus we are taught that religion is, by its very nature, positive. Jesus was never guarding Himself, but always invading the lives of others with His holiness. He did not shut Himself up, as it were, in the castle of His life, guarding every loophole, but He made it an open centre of operations from which the surrounding territory was to be subdued. So we learn from Him that our truest safety, our true spotlessness from the world must come, not negatively, by the garments being drawn back from every worldly contact, but positively, by the garments being so essentially pure that they fling pollution off.

V. We must ever bear in mind the purpose of the Incarnation; we must grasp the bewildering thought of a personal love for our single souls; we must find its meaning in those precious words, 'Christ died for me.' Then will the soul, full of profoundest gratitude, look round to see what it has to give to the Saviour in return, and it will find it has nothing to give—save itself. It is its own no longer; it is given

away to Christ. It lives His life—Who redeemed it —and not its own. Thus, it is by walking in this new sense of consecration to Him, it will walk unharmed; it will be kept 'unspotted from the world' by Christ. More than this; it is by a Christ-like dedication to the world that Christ really saves us from the world. You go to your Lord and say, 'O Lord, this world is tempting me, and I fear its stains. Shall I run away from it?' And the Voice comes, as from the opened sky, 'No, go up close to the world, and help it; feel for its wickedness; pity it; sacrifice yourself for it; so shall you be safest from its infection, and not sacrifice yourself to it'. It is possible so to be given up to Christ and our fellows, that the lust, falsehood, cruelty, injustice, and selfishness of the world shall not hurt us; it is possible to walk through the fire and not be burned. But it depends always and wholly upon whether He walks there with us. Let us not trust ourselves, for we are weakness. Trust Him, work for all who need us; so shall we go through all impurity and be gathered safe home at last into the Father's House.—BISHOP PHILLIPS BROOKS.

'Pure religion and undefiled is. . . .'—JAMES I. 27.

How much it is misunderstood may be seen from the fact that, though the word itself, religion, stands for one of the most beautiful and simple things in the world, there yet hangs about it an aroma which is not wholly pleasing. What difficult service that great and humble name has seen! With what strange and evil meanings it has been charged! How dinted and battered it is with hard usage! how dimmed its radiance, how stained its purity! . . . To express the religion of Christ in precise words would be a mighty task; but it may be said that it was not merely a system, nor primarily a creed; it was a message to individual hearts, bewildered by the complexity of the world and the intricacy of religious observances. Christ bade men believe that their Creator was also a Father; that the only way to escape from the overwhelming difficulties presented by the world was the way of simplicity, sincerity, and love; that a man should keep out of his life all that insults and hurts the soul, and that he should hold the interests of others as dear as he holds his own.— A. C. BENSON, *From a College Window*, pp. 307 f.

ONE of the hardest burdens laid upon the other good influences of human nature has been that of improving religion itself.—JOHN STUART MILL.

'To visit the fatherless and widows in their affliction, and to keep himself unspotted from the world.'—JAMES I. 27.

SHORTLY after being made a bishop, Jean Pierre Camus of Belley, consulted St. Francis de Sales upon the difficulty which he felt of keeping chaste amid the temptations into which his love of charity led him inevitably. St. Francis replied: 'You must distinguish between persons whose position obliges them to take charge of others, and such as lead a private life which involves no responsibility save for themselves. The first must commit chastity to the care of charity, and if it be real, it will answer to the trust, serving as a wall and rampart; but private persons do well to subject their charity to chastity, and maintain great reserve and caution in their actions. Those in responsible positions are often obliged to expose themselves to temptations inseparable from their duties, and so long as they do not tempt God by presumption, His grace will guard them.'

THE outward service (θρησκεία) of ancient religion, the rites, ceremonies, and ceremonial vestments of the old law, had morality for their substance. They were the old *letter*, of which morality was the spirit; the enigma, of which morality was the *meaning*. But morality itself is the service and ceremonial (cultus exterior, θρησκεία) of the Christian religion. The scheme of grace and truth that *became* through Jesus Christ, the faith that *looks down into* the perfect law of liberty, has *light for its garment; its very robe is righteousness.*' On this the twenty-third aphorism in *Aids to Reflection*, Coleridge has this comment: 'Herein the Apostle places the pre-eminence, the peculiar and distinguishing excellence, of the Christian religion. The ritual is of the same kind, though not of the same order, with the religion itself—not arbitrary and conventional, as types and hieroglyphics are in relation to the things expressed by them; but inseparable, consubstantiated (as it were) and partaking therefore of the same life, permanence, and intrinsic worth with its spirit and principle.

I MYSELF can hardly conceive a working Ethical society of which the aim would not include in essentials the Apostle's definition of the pure service of religion. We might characterise it as the aim of being in the world and yet not of it, working strenuously for the improvement of mundane affairs, and yet keeping ourselves, as the Apostle says, 'unspotted of the world'—that is, in modern phrase, keeping clear of the compromises with sordid interests and vulgar ambitions which the practical standards of all classes and sections of society are too apt to admit. —SIR LESLIE STEPHEN, *Practical Ethics*, p. 14.

'To visit the fatherless and widows in their affliction.'—JAMES I. 27.

WHEN the time called Christmas came, while others were feasting and sporting themselves, I looked out poor widows from house to house, and gave them some money.—Fox's *Journal* (1645).

THINKERS of the most different schools and sects would probably agree that true charity demands of us money, but also something more than money: personal service, sacrifice of time and thought.—SIR LESLIE STEPHEN, *Practical Ethics*, p. 7.

SON, if lofty be the lintels of thy house, and thy friend be sick, say not, What shall I send him? but go on foot and see him with thy eyes; for that is better for him than a thousand talents of gold and silver.—From *The Story of Ahikar*.

IN describing the great Welshman, Lewis Morris, of the eighteenth century, George Borrow (*Wild Wales*, ch. XL.) praises his 'noble generosity and sacrifice of self for the benefit of others. Weeks and months he was in the habit of devoting to the superintendence of the widow and fatherless.'

AT the last day He is to ask us not what sins we have avoided, but what righteousness we have done, what we have done for others, how we have helped good and hindered evil: what difference it has made to this world, and to our country and our family and friends, that we have lived. The man who has been only pious and not useful will stand with a long face on that great day, when Christ puts to him his questions.—R. L. STEVENSON, to the Samoan Students.

'And to keep himself unspotted from the world.'—JAMES I. 27.

THE moment we care for anything deeply, the world —that is, all the other miscellaneous interests— becomes our enemy. Christians showed it when they talked of keeping oneself 'unspotted from the world'; but lovers talk of it just as much when they talk of the 'world well lost'.—G. K. CHESTERTON.

A WHITE bird, she told him once, looking at him gravely, a bird which he must carry in his bosom across a crowded public place—his own soul was like that.—PATER, *Marius the Epicurean*, vol. I.

To have one chance in life, in eternity, for a white name, and to lose it!—JAMES LANE ALLEN, *The Mettle of the Pasture*, p. 404.

AFTER I had spent a month in surveying the curiosities of this city [Venice], and had put on board a ship the books which I had collected in Italy, I proceeded through Verona and Milan, and along the Leman lake to Geneva. The mention of this city brings to my recollection the slandering More, and makes me again call the Deity to witness, that in all those places in which vice meets with so little discouragement, and is practised with so little shame, I never once deviated from the paths of integrity and virtue, and perpetually reflected that, though my conduct might escape the notice of men, it could not elude the inspection of God.—MILTON, *The Second Defence*.

I FIRMLY believe that it is in keeping our honour spotless that we best perform our duty, both to ourselves and to others—of course I mean honour in its purest and highest sense. Our chief business in this world is with ourselves: 'Keep yourselves unspotted from the world'. This I know is not at this time a fashionable doctrine.—J. H. SHORTHOUSE.

REFERENCES.—I. 27.—Spurgeon, *Sermons*, vol. xxxix. No. 2313. H. Rix, *Sermons, Addresses and Essays*, p. 73. J. Laidlaw, *Christian World Pulpit*, vol. xlix. p. 214. B. J. Snell, *The Widening Vision*, p. 113. H. S. Holland, *Christian World Pulpit*, vol. xlix. p. 408. T. Arnold, *The Interpretation of Scripture*, p. 261. W. Ogg, *Christian World Pulpit*, vol. lviii. p. 408. *Expositor* (4th Series), vol. iv. p. 456; *ibid.* (5th Series), vol. ix. p. 220. A. Maclaren, *Expositions of Holy Scripture—James*, p. 397.

'My brethren, hold not the faith of our Lord Jesus Christ, the Lord of glory, with respect of persons.'—JAMES II. I.

THE sermon was chiefly occupied with proving that God is no respecter of persons ; a mark of indubitable condescension in the clergyman, the rank in society which he could claim for himself duly considered. But, unfortunately, the church was so constructed, that its area contained three platforms of position, actually of differing level ; the loftiest, in the chancel, on the right hand of the pulpit, occupied by the gentry ; the middle, opposite the pulpit, occupied by the tulip-beds of their servants ; and the third, on the left of the pulpit, occupied by the common parishioners. Unfortunately too, by the perpetuation of some old custom, whose significance was not worn out, all on the left of the pulpit were expected, as often as they stood up to sing—which was three times—to turn their backs to the pulpit, and so face away from the chancel where the gentry stood.— GEORGE MACDONALD, *David Elginbrod* (chap. XII.).

REFERENCES.—II. 1.—*Expositor* (5th Series), vol. vi. p. 2. A. Maclaren, *Expositions of Holy Scripture—James*, p. 406. II. 1-13.—R. W. Dale, *The Epistle of James*, p. 54.

'If there come unto your assembly a man with a gold ring, in goodly apparel, and there come in also a poor man in vile raiment.'—JAMES II. 2.

'I FOUND my way to the church,' [in Pont Sainte Maxence], says Stevenson in his *Inland Voyage*, 'for there is always something to see about a church, whether living worshippers or dead men's tombs ; you find there the deadliest earnest, and the hollowest deceit.'

'Ye have respect to him that weareth the gay clothing.'— JAMES II. 3.

WHOEVER passes up Broadway finds his attention arrested by three fine structures—Trinity Church, that of the Messiah, and Grace Church. . . . In the old world, the history of such edifices, though not without its shadow, had many bright lines. Mysterious orders, of which we know only that they were consecrated to brotherly love and the development of mind, produced the genius which animated the architecture ; but the casting of the bells and suspending them in the tower was an act in which all orders of the community took part ; for when those cathedrals were consecrated, it was for the use of all. Rich and poor knelt together upon their marble pavements, and the imperial altar welcomed the obscurest artisan. This grace our churches want—the grace which belongs to all religions, but is peculiarly and solemnly enforced upon the followers of Jesus. The poor to whom He came to preach can have no share in the grace of Grace Church. In St. Peter's, if only as an empty form, the soiled feet of travel-worn disciples are washed ; but such feet can never intrude on the fane of the holy Trinity here in republican America, and the Messiah may be supposed still to give as excuse for delay, 'The poor ye have always with you'. We must confess this circumstance is to us quite destructive of reverence and value for these buildings. We are told that, at the late consecration, the claims

of the poor were eloquently urged ; and that an effort is to be made, by giving a side chapel, to atone for the luxury which shuts them out from the reflection of sunshine through those brilliant windows. It is certainly better that they should be offered the crumbs from the rich man's table than nothing at all, but it is surely not the way that Jesus would have taught to provide for the poor.—MARGARET FULLER.

IF anywhere democracy seems natural, it should be in the eyes of God ; and yet, if Americans show anywhere social demarcations, it is in the province of religion. This is true, not only of different churches where the expense of membership is so unequal that in large cities rich and poor are farther apart on Sundays than on week-days, but it is true of the sects themselves.—HUGO MÜNSTERBERG, *The Americans*, p. 500.

'Hath not God chosen the poor of this world rich in faith and heirs of the kingdom.'—JAMES II. 5.

Is the last and most admirable invention of the human race only an improved muck-rake ? Is this the ground on which Orientals and Occidentals meet ? Did God direct us so to get our living, digging where we never planted—and He would, perchance, reward us with lumps of gold ?—THOREAU, *Life Without Principle*.

COMPARE also, for a comment on this verse, the twenty-ninth chapter of *The Vicar of Wakefield*.

THE very discipline of poverty makes the heart and spirit and body strong for love. It is the poor who know the intensity of human affection—the poor and patient who have to labour and toil for that prize to the uttermost farthing which ransoms the simplest delight.—JOHN OLIVER HOBBES, in *The Vineyard* (ch. VI.).

'WE shall never do anything without the poor,' wrote Vinet to a friend, when the Free Church of the Vaud Canton was being formed. 'Nothing is great, nothing is strong, save what begins with the poor.'

'Ye have despised the poor.'—JAMES II. 6.

ALL the darker and sterner aspect of the age which we have been viewing, its social revolt, its moral and religious awakening, the misery of the peasant, the protest of the Lollard, are painted with a terrible fidelity in the poem of William Langland. . . . His world is the world of the poor : he dwells on the poor man's life, on his hunger and toil, his rough revelry and his despair, with the intensity of a man who has no outlook beyond it. The narrowness, the misery, the monotony of the life he paints reflect themselves in his verse.—GREEN, *Short History of the English People*, pp. 248, 249.

'That worthy name by the which ye are called.'—JAMES II. 7.

I DARE not call myself a Christian. I have hardly met the man in all my life who deserved that name. —MAX MÜLLER.

IT has been suggested that every man should be called a Christian who fulfils two conditions. The first is, that he believes the universe as a whole to be something rational and righteous—something which has ever our approval and admiration. The second is, that he finds himself in so much sympathy with the life and character of Jesus, that he desires to consecrate his religious feelings and convictions by associating them with the name of Jesus. Of all the attempts to define the outer limits within which the word Christian may be applied, this is perhaps the most successful.—J. M. E. McTaggart, *Studies in Hegelian Cosmology*, p. 246.

Reference.—II. 7.—J. Halsey, *Christian World Pulpit*, vol. lvii. p. 260.

'Thou shalt love thy neighbour as thyself.'—James ii. 8.

To the plain man the most important feature of justice is that it consists in his practical recognition of the truth that *another man's equal good is equally important with his own.* — Dr. Sophie Bryant, *Studies in Character*, p. 32.

The correlative to loving our neighbours as ourselves is hating ourselves as we hate our neighbours.— O. W. Holmes, *The Professor at the Breakfast Table* (xi.).

'If ye fulfil the royal law, according to the scripture, Thou shalt love thy neighbour as thyself, thou shalt do well.'— James ii. 8.

To hope or to fear for another is the sole thing which can give to humanity the fulfilled consciousness of its own being.—Eugénie de Guérin.

References.—II. 8.—*Expositor* (6th Series), vol. iv. p. 101. II. 8, 9.—R. J. Campbell, *City Temple Sermons*, p. 92. II. 10.—H. R. Heywood, *Sermons and Addresses*, p. 50. R. J. Campbell, *City Temple Sermons*, p. 245. Brooke Herford, *Courage and Cheer*, p. 15. II. 12.—H. Bonner, *Sermons and Lectures*, p. 52. J. Keble, *Sermons for the Sundays After Trinity*, p. 331.

MERCY AND JUDGMENT

'Mercy rejoiceth against judgment.'—James ii. 13.

They are both true; they are both great facts in human history and experience. Long ago a man said: 'My song shall be of mercy and judgment'. Surely he was a great anthem maker who could bring them both into tune. He did it, and he was right.

I. Do not suppose that we can escape this matter of judgment by some metaphysical argument: man! the matter is in thee, in thy soul, in thy blood; why shirk it, why flinch from the fact? How many there are who want to escape the Church and all that the Church means by getting up some little bubbling frothy argument about abstractions and a species of pseudo-metaphysics. If they would but look right into the very centre of their own hearts they may see murder. That is one aspect of judgment—self-torment. We have many fine speeches about the possibility of God pardoning the sinner. Do not talk about that; first talk about the sinner pardoning himself. That is the difficulty even after Divine pardon. God has pardoned us through the cross of His dear Son, He has looked at us through the crimson medium of Calvary, and He has said mayhap, My son, thy sins which are many are all forgiven thee.

Yes, but, Thou Almighty One, I cannot forgive myself; I am glad with a kind of grim gladness that I have been forgiven away in the eternities, but I cannot forgive myself; I did the wrong deed, and Thou must qualify me, so to say, to forgive myself; I would accept heaven's kind pardon, but I cannot forgive my own soul. How is that to be met? I want to feed some little child because I neglected my own, but I seem to make no progress in feeding the child, the very food seems to be lost upon it: can I not have just one full round hour with my own child that I might try to make up to it what I neglected to give? That would be a kind of pardon; I thank Thee for Thy great pardon, now come to me and give me that kind of grace which will enable me to do on my side what Thou hast done on Thine.

People want to know if there is a hell. Certainly. Where is it? In you; that is where it is; in me, preacher of the Word; like all other preachers, his very soul is steeped in holy Scripture, and yet hot hell is in the man. Woe betide the soul that puzzles itself with such frivolities as, Is heaven a state or is heaven a place? No earnest mind can ask such questions; they are outside the fiery bounds of mere frivolity and curiosity.

Sometimes certain sufferings can only be expressed in terms of duration. They are poor terms, in themselves they are empty little words, but if we pile them sufficiently together they enable the soul to express its most agonistic and self-tormenting emotion. Therefore we say, 'The worm that dieth not'. I know it! 'The fire that is not quenched.' I feel it! Do not take me out to some valley near Jerusalem, and say it was a figure; take me into my own soul, where there are deeper valleys than there ever were in Jerusalem; I feel the gnawing of the worm undying, and I feel the torment that cannot be stilled but by the total Trinity—Father, Son, and Holy Ghost.

II. 'Mercy rejoiceth against judgment.' There are some persons who do not like to hear about judgment. They will never make any progress, and they are people not to be trusted; they are as Ephraim, a cake unturned; there is no reality of wisdom in such people; 'Mercy rejoiceth against judgment'. Mercy says, I must follow all the sin and all the misery, and I must teach all these people to say, Where sin abounded grace did much more abound. I have a great message, quoth mercy, and I must be out and tell it to the sons of distress and the daughters of weeping misery. What is the message of mercy? Does it abolish the law? No, mercy says, I came not to destroy the law, but to fulfil it. Mercy faces judgment, mercy recognises judgment; mercy never says, Never mind the law, do not think about the law. That is not the voice of Gospel mercy. We are taken by mercy itself to Sinai, with all its rocks and rocky lines, and then taken away until we come into green slopes, even the slopes of Mount Zion. We must pass through both experiences, some in this degree, some in that. Sin is not the same thing to every soul.

III. Judgment is a matter within human limits which can be measured and satisfied. If it is a legal judgment, a man can bend his back and accept his punishment, and then stand up and challenge society to remind him of his expiated guilt. But there is another judgment that is not of the nature of social crime, but that spiritual judgment of the heart itself which is conducted in the sight of the living righteous God. Mercy is not mere sentiment; it is not a gush, it is a salvation. What does it save us from? That is a minor question, though a great one. What does it save us into? That is another interrogation, wide as heaven, lasting as duration. Have we sufficiently thought of the negative aspect of the gift of Christ? What is that negative aspect? It touches me to the quick; it is purely negative, but most suggestive and helpful as an initial idea. What is it? 'That we might not perish.' We can begin with that idea, it is initial, it will do to start with; it is only negative, but of great value. 'He gave His only begotten Son, that whosoever believeth in Him should not perish.' That is a minus quantity, though it is important, Is there not a positive quantity? There is, and it follows immediately upon the very words that have been quoted—'but have everlasting life'.—JOSEPH PARKER, *City Temple Pulpit*, vol. IV. p. 243.

'Mercy rejoiceth against judgment.'—JAMES II. 13.

REJOICE against it—*in the face of it*, that must mean. It is a fine figure, mercy looking full in the face of judgment, and not bating a particle of its joy.—DR. JOHN KER's *Letters*, p. 84.

REFERENCES.—II. 14-23.—A. Maclaren, *Expositions of Holy Scripture—James*, p. 415. II. 14-26.—R. W. Dale, *The Epistle of James*, p. 67.

'If a brother or sister be naked, and destitute of food, and one of you say unto them, Depart in peace, be ye warmed and filled: notwithstanding ye give them not those things which are needful to the body, what doth it profit?'—JAMES II. 15, 16.

I SEEM to remember a poor old grateful kind of a creature, blinking, and looking up with his no eyes in the sun—

Is it possible that I could have steeled my purse against him?

Perhaps I had no small change.

Reader, do not be frightened at the hard words, imposition, imposture—*give and ask no questions.*—CHARLES LAMB, on *The Decay of Beggars*.

REFERENCES.—II. 15-17.—*Expositor* (5th Series), vol. ix. p. 224; *ibid.* (6th Series), vol. v. p. 297.

'And one of you say unto them.'—JAMES II. 16.

THE fundamental error of France lies in her psychology. France has always believed that to say a thing is the same as to do it, as though speech were action.—AMIEL.

'Faith, if it have not works, is dead, being alone.'—JAMES II. 17.

NOTHING in mediæval history is to me more strange and appalling than their general acceptance of these truths as mathematical certainties, as things laid alongside of their actual life, without ever touching or quickening their spiritual consciousness. I have seen something of this in a less repulsive form among the poor of our own day,—belief and conscience running as in two parallel lines which never meet; also, amongst people of the last generation, a belief in revelation, and a respect for it, which is not vivifying, and yet is belief, if not faith.—DORA GREENWELL, *Two Friends*, p. 84.

REFERENCES.—II. 17.—J. Johns, *Preacher's Magazine*, vol. xvii. p. 324. II. 18.—T. Arnold, *The Interpretation of Scripture*, p. 269. *Expositor* (7th Series), vol. v. p. 547. II. 18-26.—T. Mann, *Christian World Pulpit*, vol. xliv. p. 219.

TYPES OF UNAVAILING FAITH

'The devils also believe and tremble.'—JAMES II. 19.

I. THE faith of devils is grounded in compulsion rather than in free moral choice. They believe in spite of themselves. Belief is thrust upon them, and for that very reason cannot influence character, or work towards moral ends. No faith can guide the life and mould the destiny unless it first enlist the will on its side. The scene in which the Pharisees and Sadducees came tempting our Lord, and desiring Him to show them a sign from heaven, still repeats itself, with slight changes. When we join ourselves to the company of the Sadducees, and seek irrefutable signs from heaven, murmuring that the methods by which Jesus presents God and immortality to us fall short of absolute proof, is it not clear that we are demanding a necessary and inevitable faith—a faith from which all those moral qualities which go with the personal choice is excluded? In other words, that we desire a faith which is one and the same in its basis with the faith of devils, and have therefore no true idea of its proper function in the spiritual life? Such a faith, if enforced upon men in the present stage of their spiritual development, would not answer the purpose for which God has made this principle the key to our training and salvation. Room for the moral element must always be found in the faith, which saves into a pure and blessed life. The chief virtue of faith in God's sight is that it enlists the will into its activities. The wish to believe is the high feature in our faith which distinguishes it from the bastard faith of devils.

II. Another note of futility in this faith of the devils is that it does not include the affections. This, of course, is implied in the statement that true faith must be free, for the highest love is spontaneous and unconstrained. If the faith is to effectually shape the life and character, it must command our human sympathies as well as secure the assent of the reason, and the processes are intertwined. When we go on to say this futile faith, so dramatically described by St. James, lacks every element of trust, it is but another form of declaring that love has no place in its exercise. Independence towering into arrogant impiety is the dominant trait of the diabolic character, as it is briefly hinted in the Scriptures.

III. The outward test of the insufficiency of a

devil's faith is that it lacks those holy and gracious works by which the saving efficacy of all belief is verified. The practical life is a self-recording mechanism by which we may read the quality of the forces which are working within us. The faith that does not melt the character and cast it into worthier moulds, has no place in the redemptive economies of our Lord and Saviour.

IV. St. James reminds us that this intellectual veneer of faith cannot disguise the malady of a condemned spirit. 'The devils believe and tremble.' Unless our belief has those elements in it which bring the whole life into conformity with the Divine, we must continue strangers to the deep, satisfying peace which is the heritage of saints.

'The devils also believe and tremble.'—JAMES II. 19.

THERE is an opinion which may be said simply to identify religion with orthodoxy, with the holding for true what is true. No doubt right doctrine is a very important matter, but does that make it religion? Put it to the religious consciousness, and the answer is, No. It is the belief 'with the heart' that is wanted; and where that is not, religion is not. Else even the very devils would be religious; for they, as we are told, go further even than is required of them, and add to orthodoxy the fear of God.—F. H. BRADLEY, Ethical Studies, p. 300.

THE devils, we are told, believe and tremble. But it is hard to convince people that nothing short of this can be true Christian faith. So because they are sometimes terrified by the thought of God, they fancy they believe, though their hearts are far away from Him.—Guesses at Truth (2nd Series).

SUPERSTITION is the only religion of which base souls are capable.—JOUBERT.

ROUSSEAU, with his offensive vanity and literary pride, had a curious respect for Christ. With a good bit of the devil in him, he believed and trembled. But I believe that he believed that sentence in his vague and cloudy panegyric on Christ to be true: 'If the son of Sophroniscus was a hero, the son of Mary was a God'. The 'faith of devils' lies latent in many a mind for an emergency. As one prayed when his ship was sinking, 'O God, if there be a God, have mercy on my soul, if I have a soul'.—DR. JOHN DUNCAN, Colloquia Peripatetica, p. 140.

REFERENCES.—II. 19.—Archbishop Magee, Sermons at St. Saviour's, Bath, p. 218. Expositor (4th Series), vol. ii. p. 26; ibid. (5th Series), vol. i. p. 143.

'Faith without works is dead.'—JAMES II. 20.

AN opinion, I should say, gains vividness rather from constant application to conduct than from habitual opposition.—SIR LESLIE STEPHEN, on Toleration.

REFERENCES.—II. 20.—J. H. Jellet, The Elder Son, p. 227. II. 21-23.—Bishop Bethell, Sermons, vol. i. p. 100.

'By works was faith made perfect.'—JAMES II. 22.

GORDON was no 'saint' in the usual meaning which the world attaches to the name. He was utterly removed from the class of religious Church Militant who, as passing residents in some French or Italian city, are prone to hurl their hymns on the Sabbath morning at the heads of the native heretics; neither had he the smallest fellowship with another large class of persons who would divide religion into two parts—the muscular and the Methodist, one half John Bull and the other John Knox. Absolutely without parallel in our modern life, Gordon stands out the foremost man of action of our time and nation, whose ruling principle was faith and good works. No gloomy faith, no exalted sense of self-confidence, no mocking of the belief of others, no separation of his sense of God from the everyday work to which his hand has to be put; but a faith which was a living, moving, genial reality with him, present always and everywhere, shining out in every act of his life.—SIR WM. BUTLER, Life of General Gordon, p. 80.

GOD'S FRIENDS
'He was called the friend of God.'—JAMES II. 23.

WHEN and by whom was he so called? There are two passages in the Old Testament in which an analogous designation is applied to the patriarch, but probably the name was one in current use amongst the people, and expressed in a summary fashion the impression that had been made by the history of Abraham's life. As many of us are aware, this name, 'the Friend,' has displaced the proper name, Abraham, on the lips of all Mohammedan people to this day; and the city of Hebron, where his corpse lies, is commonly known simply as 'the Friend'. I wish to bring out two or three of the salient elements and characteristics of friendship as exercised on the human level, and to use these as a standard and test of our religion and relation to God.

I. Friends trust and love one another. Mutual confidence is the mortar which binds the stones in society together, into a building. (1) Unless I trust God I cannot be a friend of God's. (2) Let us remember where the sweet reciprocation and interchange of love begins. 'We love Him because He first loved us.' It was an old fancy that, wherever a tree was struck by lightning, all its tremulous foliage turned in the direction from which the bolt had come. When the merciful flash of God's great love strikes a heart, then all its tendrils turn to the source of the life-giving light, and we love back again, in sweet reverberation to the primal and original love.

II. Friends have frank, familiar intercourse with one another. (1) If we are friends and lovers of God, we shall delight in intercourse with Him. (2) If we are friends of God we shall have no secrets from Him. (3) Tell God all, if you mean to be a friend of His. (4) If we are God's lovers, He will have no secrets from us.

III. Friends delight to meet each other's wishes. (1) If we are God's lovers and friends, we shall find nothing sweeter than bowing to His will and executing His commandments. (2) And God, the heavenly Friend, will do what we wish.

IV. Friends give gifts to each other. (1) If we are God's lovers, God will give us Himself, in so far as we can receive Him; and all other gifts in so far as they are good and needful. (2) If we are God's friends and lovers we shall give Him, in glad surrender, our whole selves.

V. Friends stand up for each other. (1) If we are God's friends and lovers He will take up our cause. (2) If we are God's friends and lovers we have to take up His cause.—A. MACLAREN, *Triumphant Certainties*, p. 172.

REFERENCES.—II. 23.—Spurgeon, *Sermons*, vol. xxxiii. No. 1962. A. Maclaren, *Expositions of Holy Scripture—James*, p. 421. II. 24.—Bishop Bethell, *Sermons*, vol. i. p. 79. II. 25.—Spurgeon, *Sermons*, vol. xviii. No. 1061. *Expositor* (5th Series), vol. vii. p. 98.

'As the body without the spirit is dead, so faith without works is dead also.'—JAMES II. 26.

I WOULD treat of faith as it is actually found in the soul; and I say it is as little an isolated grace, as a man is a picture. It has a depth, a breadth, and a thickness; it has an inward life which is something over and above itself; it has a heart and blood and pulses and nerves, though not upon the surface. All these indeed are not *spoken of*, when we make mention of faith; nor are they painted on the canvas; but they are implied in the word, because they exist in the thing. . . . St. James, after warning his brethren against 'holding the faith' of Christ 'in respect of persons,' that is, in an *unloving* spirit, as the context shows, proceeds to say that it is '*perfected* by works,' and that 'without works' it is 'dead,' as a body without the soul. That is, as the presence of the soul changes the nature of the dust of the earth, and makes it flesh and blood, giving it a life which otherwise it could not have, so love is the modelling and harmonising principle on which justifying faith depends, and in which it exists and acts.—NEWMAN, *Lectures on Justification*, pp. 265, 266.

REFERENCES.—II. 26.—*Expositor* (5th Series), vol. vi. p. 335. R. W. Church, *Village Sermons* (2nd Series), p. 161. III. 1-6.—R. W. Dale, *The Epistle of James*, p. 84. III. 1-13.—A. Maclaren, *Expositions of Holy Scripture—James*, p. 431.

'If a man offend not in word, the same is a perfect man and able also to bridle the whole body.'—JAMES III. 2.

SHE gossiped, like all the rest of Old Chester; but by some mysterious method, Susan Carr's gossip gave the listener a gentler feeling towards his kind. When she spoke of her neighbour's faults, one knew that somehow they were simply virtues gone to seed; and what was more remarkable, her praise had no sting of insinuation in it, no suggestion that she could speak differently if she chose.—MARGARET DELAND, *Philip and His Wife*, p. 44.

REFERENCES.—III. 2.—J. Keble, *Sermons for Christmas and Epiphany*, p. 483. III. 4.—T. F. Crosse, *Sermons*, p. 226. S. Gregory, *How to Steer a Ship*, p. 1. H. Bushnell, *Christ and His Salvation*, p. 140. III. 4-15.—T. Spurgeon, *Christian World Pulpit*, vol. xlix. p. 344.

'Behold, how great a matter a little fire kindleth.'—JAMES III. 5.

THESE fires are one of the saddest features of the mountain districts. The ravages of the past are visible in almost every valley; and every year fresh areas of living green are being swept by the pitiless flames and left a melancholy wilderness. The ease with which a forest fire is started is astounding, and only rivalled by the rapidity of its progress, when once it gains a hold upon the trees, and by the extent of the destruction ere the blaze is quenched. A single lighted match thrown carelessly upon the ground, a shower of sparks from a passing locomotive, a camp-fire insufficiently extinguished, may be the origin. And from this tiny cause, 'how great a matter a little fire kindleth'.—JAMES OUTRAM, *In the Heart of the Canadian Rockies*, p. 147.

THESE fires are one of the great dangers of California. I have seen from Monterey as many as three at the same time, by day a cloud of smoke, by night a red coal of conflagration in the distance. A little thing will start them, and, if the wind be favourable, they gallop over miles of country faster than a horse.—R. L. STEVENSON, in *The Old Pacific Capital*.

REFERENCES.—III. 5.—O. Bronson, *Sermons*, p. 229. III. 5, 6.—J. J. Blunt, *Plain Sermons*, p. 123.

'And the tongue is a fire, a world of iniquity.'—JAMES III. 6.

AN Apostle speaks of the tongue both as a blessing and as a curse. It may be the beginning of a fire, he says, a 'universitas iniquitatis,' and, alas! such did it become in the mouth of gifted Abelard. His eloquence was wonderful; he dazzled his contemporaries, says Fulco, 'by the brilliancy of his genius, the sweetness of his eloquence; the ready flow of his language, and the subtlety of his knowledge'. People came to him from all quarters;—from Rome, in spite of mountains and robbers; from England, in spite of the sea; from Flanders and Germany; from Normandy, and the remote districts of France; from Angers and Poitiers; from Navarre by the Pyrenees, and from Spain, besides the students of Paris itself; and among those who sought his instructions now or afterwards, were the great luminaries of the schools in the next generation. . . . It was too much for a weak head and heart, weak in spite of intellectual power; for vanity will possess the head, and worldliness the heart, of the man, however gifted, whose wisdom is not an effluence of the Eternal Light.—NEWMAN, *University Sketches* (ch. XVI.).

'The tongue is a fire.'—JAMES III. 6.

In the eighth pit of punishment, within the Eighth Circle of the *Inferno*, Dante describes the doom of evil counsellors in imagery drawn from this verse. Each is swathed in a fiery tongue, which burns them with agonising fury just as their tongues on earth set on fire the world.

'Which setteth on fire the wheel of nature.'—JAMES III. 6.

KNOWLEDGE, the discipline by which it is gained, and the tasks which it forms, have a natural tendency to refine the mind, and to give it an indisposition, simply natural, yet real, nay, more than this, a disgust and abhorrence, towards excesses and enormities of evil . . . a simple hatred of that miserable tone of conversation which, obtaining as it does in the world, is a constant fuel of evil, heaped up round about the soul.—Newman, *The Idea of a University*, p. 187.

The chief end I purpose to myself in all my labours is to vex the world rather than to divert it.—Swift (in a letter to Pope).

'All sins,' said St. Francis de Sales, 'come under the head of thought, word, and deed; and faults in word are the most common and often the most dangerous for several reasons. First, because sins of thought only injure oneself, and give no scandal or bad example to others; God alone sees and is displeased with them, and moreover a loving repentance and ready turning to Him blots them out; whereas sins of the tongue go further, the evil word once uttered can only be recalled by a humble retractation, and even thus a brother's heart may have been poisoned by it. Again, notorious acts of sin are liable to public punishment; but evil speaking, unless it is exceptionally gross and slanderous, is subject to no check. Thirdly, sins of the tongue are specially dangerous because people do so little in the way of restitution or reparation for them.'

'For every kind of things in the sea is tamed, and hath been tamed of mankind.'—James III. 7.

Our learned Dr. Hakewill, in his *Apology of God's Power and Providence*, quotes Pliny to report that one of the emperors had particular fish ponds, and, in them, several fish that appeared and came when they were called by their particular names. And St. James tells us, that all things in the sea have been tamed by mankind. And Pliny tells us, that Antonia, the wife of Drusus, had a lamprey at whose gills she hung jewels or ear-rings.—Izaak Walton, *The Complete Angler* (The Fourth Day).

Reference.—III. 7-12.—R. W. Dale, *The Epistle of James*, p. 96.

'The tongue can no man tame; it is an unruly evil, full of deadly poison.'—James III. 8.

Our intercourse with others renders itself mainly into government of the tongue. I do not know which of these two things is the most astonishing, the unexpected importance of the place assigned to this duty in Holy Scripture, or the utter unconcern which even good men often feel about it. For the most part we have gone far along our road in devotion and done ourselves many an irreparable mischief, before we bestow half the carefulness on the government of our tongue, which it not only deserves but imperiously requires.—F. W. Faber, *Growth in Holiness*, pp. 91, 92.

A very great part of the mischiefs that vex the world arise from words. People soon forget the meaning, but the impression and the passion remain.—Burke.

'Most people,' says Plutarch (*Life of Timoleon*, xxxii.), 'seem to feel hard words more than hard deeds, and are more upset by insults than by actual injuries. What we do to an enemy in war is done from necessity, but the evil we say of him seems to arise from an excess of spite.'

In a letter to his son Philip, Sir Henry Sidney warns him that 'a wound given by a word is oftentimes harder to be cured than that which is given with the sword. Be rather a hearer and bearer away of other men's talk than a beginner and procurer of speech. . . . Think upon every word before you utter it, and remember how nature hath ramparted up, as it were, the tongue with teeth, lips, yea, and hair without the lips, and all betokening reins or bridles for the loose use of that member.'

THE RUIN OF A MASTERPIECE
(*A Temperance Sermon*)

'Therewith curse we men, which are made after the similitude of God.'—James III. 9.

St. James is speaking here in his searching, practical way about the use of the tongue and the sins of the tongue. He reminds us that it is possible for the same tongue to speak or sing the praises of God, and to say bitter or cruel things against men. The wrongness of saying these things about men, he says, lies in this: that man is so sacred, and has so much in his nature of affinity to God, that to curse man is to curse a being made after the similitude of God. To speak harsh and bitter and loveless things about man is thus an offence against what is great and holy in the estimation of his Maker.

I. St. James reminds us that bad words against men —words that can hurt and injure and assault men— are bad because man is so great, because his nature is so sacred. Does not that work out all round the circle of our duty to human nature and to ourselves? This drink curse—what does it invade? What does it deteriorate? What does it drag down lower than the dust? What does it ruin and wreck? Not the beasts that perish, but men that are after the similitude of God. The injury is an injury upon what its Author designed to be a masterpiece of His perfect and Divine skill. The nature of the most miserable victim of drink was made after the similitude of God. The greater the thing wrecked, the more awful, the more pathetic, the more deplorable, the more tremendous is the wreck. If a cottage falls down by the sinking of a coal-pit under it, it is a great pity; but suppose the earth should heave and Westminster Abbey go down; that would be terrific, and the greatness of the Temple alone could measure the boundless greatness of the evil of the ruin. Man was designed by the Architect of all to be the shadow and the image of His own nature, with a will which is the true centre of causation, the shadow of the will of God, with a reason which can respond to the thought of the Divine mind, with a love which makes him most akin to the Divine nature. That is a temple, and shall all that temple be wrecked and ruined, infinitely debased and bemired by a vice which plants itself on the border-line between the body and the spirit, between the physical and the psychical, and lays its horrible hands upon both, wrecking the physique and making the spiritual nature worse than ruined—an antagonism to its Lord? It is this greatness and significance of man that makes the greatness of his fall and the greatness of his sin and the greatness of the peril to his soul, and the greatness of the call for all who would be on the side of good against evil, right against wrong, heaven against hell.

II. Have none of you appeals very near at hand? Such is the curse of drink in England that there are not many homes which have not some one or other of their kinship more or less a victim to this abominable peril and curse and temptation. I believe I must be speaking to hundreds in this congregation who, if it were the right thing to do, could say, Yes, I have a relative; I have a friend who has fallen or is falling a victim to it—perhaps one with a fine intellect, a delicate imagination, and noble powers for usefulness; perhaps, on the other hand, one who began life all unsuspecting and unwarned, and now finds the temptation has coiled like a serpent round the life, stifling every hope of better things. Be it so or be it not so with any one of you, you know the public facts. You know what is meant all over this city by the countless centres of temptation that flare their light across the street, that invite the tired and the disgusted and the down-trodden within their doors, and send them out again a step lower down the slope that leads to the final wreck. And these are the men and the women who were made after the similitude of God!

III. There is one last thought. The greatness of man made the greatness of his fall, and the greatness of his fall called down the greatness of His Redeemer and his Redeemer's work. It was because God had made us to be so like Himself, and man made such a ruin of the work, that the Eternal Son of the Father for us men and for our salvation came down from heaven. His delights were with the sons of men; His mighty compassions overflowed upon the sons of men as they had made themselves, whom God had made to be so great. Behold the greatness of Christ, and the greatness of His claim that we should take our place upon His side. But forget not that this all-mighty Christ, the Lord, is in the field against the evil.—Bishop Handley Moule, *Christian World Pulpit*, vol. LXXVI. p. 361.

'Therewith curse we men.'—James III. 9.

In *Rob Roy* (pt. i. ch. XIII.) Andrew Fairservice remarks: 'I have heard wives flyte in England and Scotland—it's nae marvel to hear them flyte ony gate —but sic ill-scrapit tongues as thae Hieland carlines' —and sic grewsome wishes, that men should be slaughtered like sheep—and that they may lapper their hands to the elbows in their heart's blude—sic awsome language as that I never heard oot o' a human thrapple;—and, unless the deil wad rise among them to gie them a lesson, I thinkna that this talent at cursing could be amended.'

We are told that, at the breaking up of the Council of Trent, the legate pronounced the words 'Anathema to all heretics,' and then the whole assembly rose, and the hall re-echoed from every lip, 'Anathema! Anathema!' It was well suggested by an American bishop of our own day, that if the Angel of Peace could have appeared at that moment, and whispered in the ears of the infuriated Romanists the Scriptural warning, 'Bless and curse not,' there might have been a flush of shame on every cheek.—F. W. Robertson, *Essays and Addresses*, p. 248.

Reference.—III. 9.—*Expositor* (4th Series), vol. iii. p. 140.

'Out of the same mouth proceedeth blessing and cursing. My brethren, these things ought not to be so.'—James III. 10.

I have several times seen the stiletto and the rosary come out of the same pocket.—Coleridge.

Ruskin, in the fiftieth number of *Fors Clavigera*, quotes the following from a correspondent's letter: 'Could you but hear the blasphemous and filthy language our rosy village bairns use as soon as they are out of the parson's earshot, even when leaving the Sabbath School! . . . I know that the children are well taught six days a week, yet there is little fruit of good behaviour among them, and an indecency of speech which is amazing in rural children. On Christmas morn a party of these children, boys and girls, singing carols, encountered my young daughter going alone to the church service. The opportunity was tempting, and as if moved by one vile spirit, they screamed at her a blast of the most obscene and profane epithets that vicious malice could devise. She knew none of them; had never harmed them in her life. She came home with her kind, tender heart all aghast. 'Why do they hate me so?' she asked. Yet a short time after the same children came into the yard, and began with the full shrill powers of their young lungs:—

Why do I love Jesus?

the refrain

Because He died for me,

with especial gusto.'

A grandson of the late Rev. Dr. Primrose (of Wakefield, vicar), wrote me a little note from his country living this morning, and the kind fellow had the precaution to write 'No thorn' upon the envelope, so that ere I broke the seal, my mind might be relieved of any anxiety lest the letter should contain one of those lurking stabs which are so painful to the present gentle writer.—Thackeray, *Roundabout Papers*.

The printed word is a tongue—a tongue that reaches very far; and for this reason all that is said of the tongue relates also to the printed word: 'Therewith bless we God, and therewith curse we men, made after the likeness of God?'—Tolstoi (to Peter Verigin).

Thomas Boston remarks that he was 'particularly surprised with "one thing at Ettrick," *viz.*, the prevalency of the sin of profane swearing; and was amazed to find blessing and cursing proceeding out of the same mouth ; praying persons, and praying in their families too, horrid swearers at times ; so that by the month of November I behoved to set myself to preach directly against that sin.'

REFERENCES.—III. 10.—J. M. Neale, *Readings for the Aged* (3rd Series), p. 1 ; *ibid. Sermons Preached in Sackville College Chapel*, vol. i. p. 11.

'With meekness of wisdom.'—JAMES III. 13.

ERSKINE of Linlathen, in 1832, wrote to M. Gaussen : ' My dear Brother, although I have had much enjoyment in meeting you once more in this world, yet I have also suffered much, chiefly because I am sensible that in witnessing for God's truth to you, I often sinned against the law of love and meekness and patience'. This apology was drawn out by the writer's memory of many keen theological discussions between himself and his friend during the latter's visit to Scotland.

'If ye have bitter envying and strife in your hearts, glory not.' —JAMES III. 14.

'I REMEMBER Miss Brontë once telling me,' writes Mrs. Gaskell, 'that it was a saying round about Haworth, "Keep a stone in thy pocket seven year; turn it and keep it seven year longer, that it may be ever ready to thine hand when thine enemy draws near".'

By religion we live in God : all these quarrels lead to nothing but life with men or with cassocks.— AMIEL.

'TALKING of Goldsmith, Johnson said, he was very envious. I defended him,' says Boswell, ' by observing that he owned it frankly upon all occasions. Johnson : "Sir, you are enforcing the charge. He had so much envy that he could not conceal it. He was so full of it that he overflowed. He talked of it, to be sure, often enough. Now, sir, what a man avows, he is not ashamed to think ; though many a man thinks what he is ashamed to avow. We are all envious naturally ; but by checking envy, we get the better of it ! "'

REFERENCE.—III. 13-18.—R. W. Dale, *The Epistle of James*, p. 107.

'This wisdom descendeth not from above, but is earthly, sensual, devilish.'—JAMES III. 15.

'STERNE,' wrote Dr. William Robertson, of Irvine, 'Sterne is a blackguard, morally speaking ; a pleasant enough sort of person in other respects. His *Sentimental Journey* must, with all its wickedness, have impressed me much, for although I have not read it, I am sure for a good many years its successive stages and incidents are about as familiar as those of our own tour along the Rhine. That monk, that imaginary prisoner, that dead ass, that melancholy girl, Marie, I think, that grace before meat, I am sure I shall never forget them in the world. I wish I may be able to forget them in the next, for there's a dash of the " earthly, sensual, and devilish " in them, that makes them unsuitable companions for a better world.'

REFERENCE.—III. 15.—*Expositor* (4th Series), vol. ii. p. 43.

'Where envying and strife is, there is confusion and every evil work.'—JAMES III. 16.

ONE thing is certain in our Northern land,
Allow that birth or valour, wealth or art,
Give each precedence to their possessor,
Envy, that follows on such eminence,
As came the lyme-hound on the roebuck's track,
Shall pull them down, each one.
                    SIR DAVID LYNDSAY.

SPEAKING of Oxford in the eighteenth century, Mr. Cotter Morison (*Gibbon*, p. 6) observes : 'The strange thing is that, with all their neglect of learning and morality, the colleges were not the resort of jovial if unseemly boon companionship ; they were collections of quarrelsome and spiteful litigants, who spent their time in angry law-suits. The indecent contentions between Bentley and the Fellows of Trinity were no isolated scandal.'

'IN former days,' wrote Vinet during the religious squabbles at Basle, 'God seemed to be an intimate personal friend. To-day, controversial theology has come to separate us from Him.'

HE is a wonderful man that can thread a needle when he is at cudgels in a crowd ; and yet this is as easy as to find Truth in the hurry of disputation.— JOSEPH GLANVILL.

THE people of Alexandria, a various mixture of nations, united the vanity and inconsistency of the Greeks with the superstition and obstinacy of the Egyptians. The most trifling occasion, a transient scarcity of flesh or lentils, the neglect of an accustomed salutation, a mistake of precedency in the public baths, or even a religious dispute, were at any time sufficient to kindle a sedition among that vast multitude, whose resentment was furious and implacable.—GIBBON, *Decline and Fall* (ch. x.).

MR. BADMAN's envy was so rank and strong, that if it at any time turned its head against a man, it would hardly ever be pulled in again. He would watch over that man to do him mischief, as the cat watches over the mouse to destroy it ; yea, he would wait seven years, but he would have an opportunity to hurt him, and when he had it, he would make him feel the weight of his envy.—BUNYAN.

To hate indistinctly is soothing, and suffices for some time ; but in the end there must be an object. Hate without object is like shooting without a mark. What makes the sport interesting is a heart to pierce. There must be a man, a woman—some one to ruin. —VICTOR HUGO.

REFERENCES.—III. 16.—W. R. Inge, *All Saints' Sermons*, p. 40. F. B. Cowl, *Preacher's Magazine*, vol. xviii. p. 190.

'The wisdom that is from above is first pure, then peaceable, gentle and easy to be intreated, full of mercy and good fruits, without partiality, and without hypocrisy.'—JAMES III. 17.

IN describing the anointing (v. 14) of the Regent, Mary of Guise, Mr. Andrew Lang (*History of Scotland*, II. 67) remarks that 'the Apostle least loved of Knox, St. James, was her warrant. The same author writes: " The wisdom that is from above is first pure, then peaceable, gentle and easy to be intreated, full of mercy and good fruits, without partiality, and without hypocrisy". Little, indeed, of this wisdom prevailed in either party at this period. In the Regent at her death we see this spirit, and almost in her alone. "She embraced, and with a smiling countenance kissed the nobles, one by one, and to those of inferior rank who stood by she gave her hand to kiss, as a token of her kindness and dying charity." '

In a letter from Cambridge written during 1885, Dr. Mandell Creighton points out to a younger friend : ' We should all of us try to feel something of the Divine love towards man, in spite of his weaknesses. " Men my brothers" should be a thought constantly before us. I freely admit that what is called "society" is a sore trial to one's charity. The failings of the natural man are not so revolting as the meannesses of the cultivated and pretentious world. The empty head and the cold heart are unpleasant to see ; yet most heads are not entirely empty, and most hearts are not entirely cold. There is often a great deal of mute misery concealed under an affectation of frivolity. One can try to understand and help all sorts of people, and no one is quite hopeless. All answer in some degree to a call to them to bring out the best that is in them.'

' WHAT we need at present for our Church's well-being,' wrote Newman in his *Prophetical Office*, ' is not invention, nor originality, nor sagacity, nor even learning in our divines, at least in the first place, though all gifts of God are in a measure needed, and never can be unseasonable, when used religiously, but we need peculiarly a sound judgment, patient thought, discrimination, a comprehensive mind, an abstinence from all private fancies and caprices and personal tastes,—in a word, Divine wisdom.' Newman recurs to this text in his *University Sketches* (ch. xv.) : ' The Church does not think much of any " wisdom " that is not *desursum*, that is, revealed ; nor unless, as the Apostle proceeds, it is "primum quidem *pudica*, deinde *pacifica* ". These may be called the three vital principles of the Christian student, faith, chastity, love ; because their contraries, *viz.*, unbelief or heresy, impurity, and enmity are just the three great sins against God, ourselves, and our neighbours, which are the death of the soul.'

In his first speech to the Little Parliament of 1653, Cromwell declares : ' It's better to pray for you than to counsel you in that matter, that you may exercise the judgment of mercy and truth ! It's better, I say, to pray for you than to counsel you ; to ask wisdom from heaven for you ; which I am confident many thousands of saints do this day and have done and will do, through the permission of God and His assistance. I say it's better to pray than advise : yet truly I think of another Scripture which is very useful, though it seems to be for a common

application to every man as a Christian—wherein he is counselled to ask wisdom ; and he is told what that is. That's "from above," we are told ; it's " pure, peaceable, gentle, and easy to be intreated, full of mercy and good fruit" ; it's "without partiality and without hypocrisy". Truly my thoughts run much on this place, that to the execution of judgment (the judgment of truth, for that's the judgment) you must have wisdom "from above" ; and that's "pure". That will teach you to exercise the judgment of truth ; it's "without partiality". Purity, impartiality, sincerity ; these are the effects of "wisdom," and these will help you to execute the judgment of truth.'

'First pure, then peaceable.—JAMES III. 17.

COMPARE the maxim which Newman used almost as a proverb : ' Holiness rather than peace '.

IN Wesley's *Journal* for Friday, 31st January, 1766, it is noted : ' Mr. Whitefield called upon me. He breathes nothing but peace and love. Bigotry cannot stand before him, but hides its head wherever he comes.'

' I REJOICE that I have avoided controversies,' wrote Darwin in his autobiography, ' and this I owe to Lyell, who many years ago, in reference to my geological works, strongly advised me never to get entangled in a controversy, as it rarely did any good and caused a miserable loss of time and temper.'

' TRUE wisdom is not only " pacifica," it is " pudica " ; chaste as well as peaceable. Alas for Abelard ! a second disgrace, deeper than ambition, is his portion now. . . . A more subtle snare was laid for him than beset the heroic champion or the all-accomplished monarch of Israel ; for sensuality came upon him under the guise of intellect, and it was the high mental endowments of Eloisa, who became his pupil, speaking in her eyes and thrilling on her tongue, which were the intoxication and the delirium of Abelard '.—NEWMAN, *University Sketches* (ch. XVI.).

'Without partiality.'—JAMES III. 17.

I HAVE known, and still know, many Dissenters, who profess to have a zeal for Christianity ; and I dare say they have. But I have known very few Dissenters indeed, whose hatred to the Church of England was not a much more active principle of action with them than their love for Christianity. The Wesleyans in uncorrupted parts of the country are nearly the only exceptions. There never was an age since the days of the Apostles in which the Catholic spirit of religion was so dead, and put aside for the love of sects and parties, as at present.—COLERIDGE, *Table Talk* (28th December, 1831).

'Full of mercy and good fruits.'—JAMES III. 17.

WHY is the Giver of the Divine the permitter of those tremendous passions, which are not without their glory, but which wreck so many human lives ? Perhaps the reason may be found in the sacredness of pity. Evil and agony are the manure from which spring some of the whitest lilies that have ever bloomed beneath that enigmatic blue which roofs the terror and the triumph of the world. And while human beings know how to pity, human beings will always believe in a merciful God.—Robert Hichens, in *The Call of the Blood*.

Nothing gives me so much the idea of God on earth as intelligence and kindness. I dearly love, above all things, to meet these two things united, and to enjoy them intimately. — From Eugénie de Guérin's *Journal*.

Reference.—III. 17.—C. Gutch, *Sermons*, p. 66.

' The fruit of righteousness is sown in peace of them that make peace.'—James iii. 18.

'Also the good Bishop labours night and day to preserve peace,' says the Prior in the sixteenth chapter of *Quentin Durward*, 'as well becometh a servant of the altar; for it is written in Holy Scripture, *Beati pacifici*. But ——' here the good Prior stopped, with a deep sigh.

'Whence came wars and fightings among you? Came they not hence, even of your lusts that war in your members'?—James iv. i.

At the corner of old maps of the world, of the fifteenth century, may be noted a large, blank space, without form and without name, whereon these three words are inscribed: *Hic sunt leones*. This sombre corner exists also in man. The passions prowl around and mutter, somewhere within us, and it may be said also of one dark spot in our souls: 'Here are lions'.—Victor Hugo.

'Politics, domestic and foreign, are very discouraging,' wrote Sydney Smith in a letter in 1827. 'Jesuits abroad, Turks in Greece, No-Poperists in England! A panting to burn B; B fuming to roast C; C miserable that he cannot reduce D to ashes; and D consigning to eternal perdition the three first letters of the alphabet.'

References.— IV. 1.—E. W. Attwood, *Sermons for Clergy and Laity*, p. 488. IV. 1-6.—R. W. Dale, *Christian World Pulpit*, vol. xlvii. p. 193. IV. 1-16.—R. W. Dale, *The Epistle of James*, p. 121. IV. 2, 3.—Spurgeon, *Sermons*, vol. xxviii. No. 1682. IV. 3.—*Preacher's Magazine*, vol. xviii. p. 370. C. G. Finney, *Penny Pulpit*, No. 1559, pp. 105, 113. —*Expositor* (5th Series), vol. ii. p. 178.

'The friendship of the world is enmity with God.'— James iv. 4.

Our whole life is startlingly moral. There is never an instant's truce between virtue and vice.—Thoreau, *Walden*.

'Whosoever will be the friend of the world is the enemy of God.'—James iv. 4.

The friendship of the world ought to be a 'pearl of great price,' for its cost is very serious.—John Foster, *On the Aversion of Men of Taste to Evangelical Religion* (vii.).

It is as possible for a man to worship a crocodile, and yet be a pious man, as to have his affections set upon this world, and yet be a good Christian.'— William Law.

References.—IV. 4.—H. Bonar, *Short Sermons for Family Reading*, p. 263.

' God resisteth the proud.'—James iv. 6.

'Sometimes of late,' wrote Carlyle to his mother, 'I have bethought me of some of your old maxims about pride and vanity. I do see this same vanity to be the root of half the evil men are subject to in life. Examples of it stare me in the face every day. The pitiful passion, under any of the thousand forms which it assumes, never fails to wither out the good and worthy part of a man's character, and leave him poor and spiteful, an enemy to his own peace and that of all about him. There never was a wiser doctrine than that of Christian humility, considered as a corrective for the coarse, unruly selfishness of man's nature.'

Satan suggested to-day that I could never have a high place in heaven: and this proud imagination vexed me till the Lord showed me reason to be contented if I got to heaven at all.—Dr. A. A. Bonar, *Diary*, p. 16.

'But giveth grace unto the humble.'—James iv. 6.

Pride and humility are the two master-powers, the two kingdoms in strife for the eternal possession of man.—William Law.

References.—IV. 6.—W. R. Inge, *All Saints' Sermons*, 1905-07, p. 143. Bishop Winnington Ingram, *A Mission of the Spirit*, p. 178. *Expositor* (4th Series), vol. ix. p. 101.

'Submit yourselves therefore to God.'—James iv. 7.

Speaking in *Mark Rutherford's Deliverance* (ch. vi.) of the 'duty of duties to suppress revolt and to submit sometimes calmly and cheerfully to the Creator,' the writer adds: 'This surely, under a thousand disguises, has been the meaning of all the forms of worship which we have seen in the world. Pain and death are nothing new, and men have been driven into perplexed scepticism and even insurrection by them, ever since men came into being.'

Perfect reverence, or *willing* submission, implies love—mere deference to power is quite another thing, and not religion at all.—W. B. Rands, *Memoirs of Henry Holbeach*, ii. p. 66.

' Resist the devil and he will flee from you.'—James iv. 7.

As it is said that ferocious animals are disarmed by the eye of man, and will dare no violence if he but steadily look at them, so is it when right looks upon wrong. Resist the devil, and he will flee from you; offer him a bold front, and he runs away. He goes, it may be, uttering threats of rage, but yet he goes! So is it that all the great, efficient men of the world are made.—Bushnell.

Rich, indeed, in moral instruction was the life of Charles Lamb; and perhaps in one chief result it offers to the thoughtful observer a lesson of consolation that is awful, and of hope that ought to be immortal, *viz*. in the record which it furnishes, that by meekness of submission, and by earnest conflict with evil, in the spirit of cheerfulness, it is possible ultimately to disarm or to blunt the very heaviest of curses—even the curse of lunacy.—DE QUINCEY, *Charles Lamb.*

REFERENCES.—IV. 7.—J. E. Wakerley, *Preacher's Magazine*, vol. v. p. 34. Spurgeon, *Sermons*, vol. xxii. No. 1276. J. Bunting, *Sermons*, vol. i. p. 151. IV. 7, 8.—G. Bellett, *Parochial Sermons*, p. 124. IV. 7-10.—Spurgeon, *Sermons*, vol. xxiv. No. 1408.

'Draw nigh to God and He will draw nigh to you. Cleanse your hands, ye sinners ; and purify your hearts, ye doubleminded.'—JAMES IV. 8.

MAN flows at once to God when the channel of purity is open.—THOREAU.

'He will draw nigh to you.'—JAMES IV. 8.

So high as a tree aspires to grow, so high it will find an atmosphere suited to it.—THOREAU.

REFERENCE.—IV. 8.—Spurgeon, *Sermons*, vol. xlviii. No. 2795.

'Be afflicted, and mourn, and weep ; let your laughter be turned to mourning, and your joy to heaviness.'—JAMES IV. 9.

'Our sadness,' wrote Thoreau in one of his letters, 'is not sad, but our cheap joys. Let us be sad about all we see and are, for so we demand and pray for better.'

'If thou judge the law, thou art not a doer of the law, but a judge.'—JAMES IV. 11.

THOSE who themselves need the charitable judgment of other people should above all things be lenient in their own judgments. For my part I consider the best and most finished type of man to be the person who is always ready to make allowances for others, on the ground that never a day passes without his being in fault himself, yet who keeps us clear of faults as if he never pardoned them in others.'—PLINY THE YOUNGER.

REFERENCE.—IV. 11.—J. Weller, *Christian World Pulpit*, vol. xlvii. p. 356.

'Who art thou that judgest another ? . . . pray one for another.'—JAMES IV. 12 and v. 16.

I WONDER what proportion our secret intercession bears to our open criticism. I should fear it was very little ; for I cannot help fancying that if we prayed more we should feel that we prayed so little, that we should not dare, for shame's sake, to talk at all.—F. W. FABER, *All for Jesus*, p. 124.

'There is one lawgiver ; who art thou that judgest another ?'—JAMES IV. 12.

LISTEN to an hour of conversation in any Christian company. How much of it turns almost of necessity, as it would seem, on the action and characters of others ! The meaning of judging others appears to be this : the judgment-seat of our Divine Lord is, as it were, already set upon the earth. But it is empty. It is waiting for Him. We meanwhile, unmannerly and unbidden, keep ascending the steps, enthroning ourselves upon the seat, and anticipating and mimicking His judgment of our brethren.—F. W. FABER, *Growth in Holiness*, pp. 91, 92.

REFERENCES.—IV. 12.—*Expositor* (5th Series), vol. vi. p. 5. IV. 13, 14.—Bishop Bethell, *Sermons*, vol. i. p. 302. IV. 13-15.—C. M. Betts (*Eight Sermons*), p. 26. IV. 13-17.—Spurgeon, *Sermons*, vol. xxxviii. No. 2242.

THE TWO AGNOSTICISMS

'Ye know not what shall be on the morrow.'—JAMES IV. 14.

HERE is an instance of real agnosticism. We find that instance in the period of time which we glibly talk of as to-morrow. No man has seen to-morrow, no man can see to-morrow, to-morrow is not within the visual line, and is not within the line of calculation unless the line be approached religiously. We have no right to speak about to-morrow as if we had any lien upon it or any right to its possession and enjoyment. We can only enter the sanctuary called to-morrow by the gate Beautiful, the gate of God's temple, the portal of the sanctuary of the Eternal. When we speak of to-morrow we should speak in an undertone ; when we speak of the coming time we should whisper to ourselves lest we disturb some avenging ghost who is jealous of being spoken about without the customary and established sanctions. This is to change the whole range and tenor of conversation. We have to be religious even in making appointments.

I. Let us personalise the morrow ; let us no longer think of it as some mere grade or shadow of time, let us rather regard it as a personality, a presence, looking at us though we cannot look at it ; and the contention of the religious thinker is that to-morrow is in its own way and degree as great a mystery as God. That is the reflection which rebukes me when I want to settle down upon the swamp which by a falsification of realities I call the rock of agnosticism. I will take you away from the metaphysical and the supposedly distant and transcendental, and I will shut you up with your own days ; you have to-day and yesterday and to-morrow, I will bring you into the court and ask you, Have you seen to-morrow ? do you know what shall be on the morrow ? are you sure there will be a to-morrow ? are you sure you will live to see it ? Let us no longer have the drivel talk about not being able to know God even if there is a God until we are prepared to apply our own foolish reasoning to the spirit, the spectre, called to-morrow, unseen, invisible. It may come—so may God !

II. If I reject God upon the grounds which have been indicated I shall also reject the next harvest that is supposed to be coming. I want to show by these simple illustrations how vast an area is covered by the not-knowing and the supposed not-knowableness of God. Has any man seen next harvest ? Yesterday has not pledged to-morrow ; ten million harvests have not pledged the next harvest, and even if it were bound by a written and sealed oath, so far as men are concerned nobody can say that by some operation of so-called nature the whole world may not be blown away in white ashes, so that there shall be neither husbandman nor farmer, neither sower of seed nor swinger of scythe and sickle.

III. Even suppose that we do not know to-morrow, it is unwise to exclude it from our thought. Even suppose that we do not know God, and cannot know God unto perfection, we are not therefore made wise by extruding Him from the temple of our thought. The not-knowable may be the true wisdom, and we are not able to know what we do know until we properly appreciate the not-knowable.

I believe that God has revealed Himself to the mind and heart of man; I do not believe that man has found out God, but I believe that God has found out man.—JOSEPH PARKER, *City Temple Pulpit*, vol. I. p. 20.

WHAT IS YOUR LIFE?

'Whereas ye know not what shall be on the morrow. For what is your life? It is even as a vapour, that appeareth for a little time, and then vanisheth away.'—JAMES IV. 14.

THERE may be said to be two ways of looking at life, each of which finds favour just now with a wide circle of people. First, the theory that life is everything and eternity nothing, and secondly, The theory that life is nothing and eternity everything. Now, those who hold the first of these, object to the time-view of life altogether. The strength of this school is in their great view of life : their weakness and error, in their little view of time. The second view is the more antiquated, perhaps the more illiterate. Life, with it, is nothing at all. Eternity is the great thing. The strength of this school is that it recognises eternity : its weakness, and its great error, that it refuses to think of life and spoils the thought of eternity for those who do. The man who is really concerned to live well must possess himself continually of the thought that he is not to live long.

If we were to go over the conceptions of life which have been held by great men in succeeding ages of the world, we should find scarce anything new, scarce anything which the Bible had not used before. There lie scattered throughout this Book no fewer than *eighteen* of these answers, and all in metaphor, to the question, ' What is your life ?' It is.

A tale that is told.	A sleep.
A pilgrimage.	A vapour.
A swift post.	A shadow.
A swift ship.	A flower.
A handbreadth.	A weaver's shuttle.
A shepherd's tent removed.	Water spilt on the ground.
A thread cut by the weaver.	Grass.
	Wind.
A dream.	

Nothing.

Generally speaking, the first thing to strike one about these images is that they are all quick things—there is a suggestion of brevity and evanescence about them, and this feeling is so strong that we might fancy there was only one answer to the question, What is your life? namely, Your life is *short*. But if we look closer at them for a moment, shades of difference will begin to appear, and we shall find the hints of other meanings as great and striking and quite as necessary to complete the conception of ' your life '. Three of these metaphors give this answer :—

I. Your life is a very little thing. (1) A shadow.

It is unreal, it is illusory. (2) A shepherd's tent removed. (3) A tale that is told.

II. There is next another set of metaphors which bring out the more common answer that life is a short thing. It is a handbreadth : a weaver's shuttle; nothing; an eagle hasting to the prey; a swift post; a swift ship.

III. The next thought is so closely allied to this that one can scarcely separate it but for convenience. It suggests the idea of transitoriness.

IV. Life is an irrevocable thing. Our book has a wonderful metaphor for this—' water spilt upon the ground which cannot be gathered up again '.

V. Life is an uncertain thing.—HENRY DRUMMOND, *The Ideal Life and other Addresses*, p. 235.

HUMAN LIFE, PERISHING AND IMMORTAL

' What is your life? For ye are a vapour, that appeareth for a little time and then vanisheth away.'—JAMES IV. 14.

' The world passeth away, and the lust thereof; but he that doeth the will of God abideth for ever.'—I JOHN II. 17.

THESE passages indicate the solemn and arresting paradox which is presented by every child of man. On the one hand, he is a fragile and transient phenomenon ; on the other he may be the co-worker with his Creator, and sharer of His immortality. That paradox, thus stated, only exists, of course, for those who regard humanity from the religious point of view ; but, though in less awful form, it must needs present itself to every reflective observer of human life. Religion does but offer an explanation of an enigma which itself admits of no dispute. For the contrast between the grandeur of man's designs and the permanence of his achievements, on the one hand, and his physical weakness and the pitiful shortness and insecurity of his life on the other, cannot be avoided or explained away. Very powerfully, yet with characteristic quaintness, the certainty of death was pressed on his hearers by the most eloquent of Deans of St. Paul's, in a sermon which was preached in Whitehall on the first Friday in Lent, 1630. It was the last sermon which Donne preached, and men afterwards commented on the singular fitness of the subject, and the extraordinary solemnity of the preacher : 'This whole world is but an universal churchyard, but one common grave, and the life and motion, that the greatest persons have in it, is but as the shaking of buried bodies in their graves by an earthquake. That which we call life is but a week of deaths, seven days, seven periods of our life spent in dying; a dying seven times over, and there is an end. Our birth dies in infancy, and our infancy dies in youth, and youth and the rest die in age ; and age also dies, and determines all.'

I. This note of sombre severity is now rarely heard. The modern preacher has caught so much of the secularist tendency of the time as to avoid everything which might seem to suggest some belittlement of the urgent claims of the present. Yet I must needs think there is an element of weakness in this avoidance of those solemn and elementary facts, which are, when all is said, the grand determining postulates of the religious life. For indeed, the claims of the present are not likely to be appraised rightly until they are seen in connection with a vivid and abiding consciousness of the transiency of all terrestrial things, nor is the real importance of the present perceived until it is seen in relation to a future which stretches illimitably beyond the grave. Forgotten myriads who have lived on this earth before us seem to offer their piteous and unavailing protest; and we perforce make our own their melancholy words: 'Our name shall be forgotten in time, and no man shall remember our works; and our life shall pass away as the traces of a cloud, and shall be scattered as a mist, when it is chased by the beams of the sun, and overcome by the heat thereof. For our allotted time is the passing of a shadow, and our end retreateth not.'

II. Turn to the more inspiring message of St. John. He, perhaps, is also living in a great city; but, unlike St. James, he has been carried far from the scenes of his youth, and is ending his life among men of alien speech, and strange worship. Ephesus, as he knows it, is one of the most famous cities of the Empire. It is a flourishing seat of world-wide commerce: an important political centre; above all, one of the sacred places of paganism to which from far and near pilgrims gather for worship. Wealth abounds and the culture which wealth enables. Ephesus is glorious with buildings and statues. A magnificent and sensual superstition utters itself in the great temple of Artemis and excites the minds, while it pollutes the lives of a numerous and fanatical population. In Ephesus also, scarcely regarded amid so many larger and more arresting features, there is a Christian Church in which Apostles have preached and saints have lived and died. St. John is the last of the comrades of Christ; and, ere he in turn passes from sight, he sets his pen to paper in order to give a final message to his brethren in the Faith. He feels the strange power of the mighty moving city; he fears the attraction of its crowded various life; he sees through its pompous and confident prosperity; and he points his children in Christ to the veiled and greater life which has been brought to them through the Gospel.

III. 'Follow Me.' These are words that shatter all our pessimism as we stand amid dead and dying things. So much is the mark of decay upon it. So much of what once was vigorous and vital is now felt to be decadent. There is so much to regret in what is slowly and inevitably vanishing. The backward currents drag at our feet. They suck us down towards the melancholy seas that moan out their sorrow for all that has been lost. We might so easily surrender ourselves to the sad refrain of the preacher: 'All go to one place. Nothing stays. All are of the dust. And all turn to dust. As the one dieth so dieth the other. Vanity of vanities.'

If our hopes were limited by earthly horizons we could hardly fail to yield to the cold clutch of death. We should lose heart. We should go under with that which perishes. We should have the sentence of death in ourselves.

But through it all a voice rings like a trumpet, 'Follow Me'. 'Follow on.' There is more to come than has ever yet been seen. There is a new task to open on us, a new race to be run, a new day to dawn, a new victory to be won. Christ holds in Himself the potency of a better and fairer earth than all that we are losing. He can bring into being a purer humanity than we have yet dreamed of. There shall be cities built free from ancient wrongs, and sweet and clean and wholesome boys and girls shall be playing in their streets without a fear. There shall be a day when they shall not hurt or slay in all God's Holy Mountain. There are golden years ahead and a new heaven and a new earth. Let the past go, there is better to come.

This is no vague fancy without reason or support. For Christ is already King and Lord. Already He is on the throne and holds the keys of death and hell. Already He possesses the powers that can achieve what He promises. He is sufficient for it all. We have our grounds for trusting Him. We know His redeeming efficiency in our bodies and in our souls. He can do all things; for He can do for others what He has done for us.—H. HENSLEY HENSON, *Christian World Pulpit*, vol. LXXIX. p. 22.

'Ye know not what shall be on the morrow.'—JAMES IV. 14.

LIFE is a series of surprises, and would not be worth taking or keeping, if it were not. God delights to isolate us every day, and hide from us the past and the future.—EMERSON, on *Experience*.

'IT is one of the most solemn things I do,' he said to one of his children, who asked him why, in the title-page of his MS. volume of sermons, he always wrote the date only of its commencement, and left a blank for that of its completion, 'to write the beginning of that sentence and think that I may perhaps not live to finish it.'—STANLEY's *Life of Dr. Arnold*, II. 269.

IT costs me many a pang when I reflect that I shall probably never have resolution enough to take another journey to see this best and sincerest of friends, who loves me as much as my mother did! but it is idle to look forward—what is next year—a bubble that may burst for her or for me before even the flying year can hurry to the end of its almanack!—HORACE WALPOLE's *Letters* (7th September, 1769).

COMPARE the abrupt close of Sir Walter Scott's *Journal*, which breaks off suddenly at the moment of his illness in 1832, with the unfinished sentence: 'We slept reasonably, but on the next morning——'

'For what is your life? It is even a vapour.'—JAMES IV. 14.

I CANNOT laud this life, it looks so dark;
Σκιᾶς ὄναρ—dream of a shadow, go:
God bless you, I shall join you in a day.
    —TENNYSON, 'To Rev. W. H. Brookfield'.

'A vapour that appeareth for a little time, and then vanisheth away.'—JAMES IV. 14.

ALL that belongs to the body is a stream, and what pertains to the soul is a dream and vapour, and life is a warfare and a stranger's sojourn, and after-fame is oblivion.—MARCUS AURELIUS.

IN looking back, it sometimes appears to me as if I had in a manner slept out my life in a dream or shadow on the side of the hill of knowledge, where I have fed on books, on thoughts, on pictures, and only heard in half-murmurs the trampling of busy feet, or the noises of the throng below.—HAZLITT, on *The Fear of Death.*

REFERENCES.—IV. 14.—Spurgeon, *Sermons,* vol. xxx. No. 1773. J. Parker, *City Temple Pulpit,* vol. i. p. 20. W. J. Knox-Little, *Christian World Pulpit,* vol. xlix. p. 201. L. D. Bevan, *Sermons to Students,* p. 187. Reuen Thomas, *Christian World Pulpit,* vol. lii. p. 211. F. St. John Corbett, *The Preacher's Year,* p. 112. C. Perren, *Revival Sermons in Outline,* p. 237. J. N. Friend, *Preacher's Magazine,* vol. xviii. p. 220. J. Aspinall, *Parish Sermons* (2nd Series), p. 199. H. H. Henson, *Christian World Pulpit,* vol. lxii. p. 1.

'If the Lord will.'—JAMES IV. 15.

LORD, when in any writing I have occasion to insert these passages, God willing, God lending me life, etc., I observe, Lord, that I can scarce hold my hand from encircling these words in a parenthesis, as if they were not essential to the sentence, but may as well be left out as put in. Whereas, indeed, without them all the rest is nothing; wherefore hereafter I will write these words full and fairly, without any enclosure about them. Let critics censure it for bad grammar, I am sure it is good divinity.—THOMAS FULLER.

'To him that knoweth to do good and doeth it not, to him it is sin.'—JAMES IV. 17.

'THIS year,' wrote Dr. Andrew Bonar once in his Diary, 'omissions have distressed me more than anything.'

REFERENCE.—IV. 17.—G. W. Brameld, *Practical Sermons* (2nd Series), p. 267.

'Go to, now, ye rich men, weep and howl.'—JAMES V. 1.

'I HAD an hour's baiting from Mrs. —— yesterday. She got upon political preaching—abused it very heartily—acknowledged that religion had to do with man's political life, but said a clergyman's duty is to preach obedience to the powers that be—was rather puzzled when I asked her whether it were legitimate to preach from Jas. v. 1, "Go to, now, ye rich men, weep and howl," etc.—asked whether it was possible for old women and orphans to understand such subjects; to which I replied, "No; and if a clergyman refuse to touch on such subjects, which belong to real actual life, the men will leave his church; and, as is the case in the Church of England, he will only have charity orphans, who are compelled to go, and old women to preach to".'—F. W. ROBERTSON's *Life* (letter CXIII.).

REFERENCE.—V. 1-6.—*Expositor* (5th Series), vol. ii. p. 373.

'Your gold and silver is cankered, and the rust of them shall eat your flesh as it were fire.'—JAMES V. 3.

'THE wilderness had caressed him,' says Mr. Joseph Conrad of an unscrupulous West African trader, 'and lo! he had withered; it had taken him, loved him, embraced him, got into his veins, consumed his flesh, and sealed his soul to its own, by the inconceivable ceremonies of some devilish initiation. He was its spoiled and pampered favourite. Ivory? I should think so. Heaps of it, stacks of it. You should have heard him say, "My intended, my ivory, my station, my river, my——" everything belonged to him. It made me hold my breath in expectation of hearing the wilderness burst into a prodigious peal of laughter, that would shake the fixed stars in their courses. Everything belonged to him—but that was a trifle. The thing was to know what he belonged to, how many powers of darkness claimed him for their own. That was the reflection that made me creepy all over.'

'Ye have heaped treasure together for the last days.'—JAMES V. 3.

THERE is a payment which Nature rigorously exacts of men, and also of Nations, and this I think when her wrath is sternest, in the shape of dooming you to possess money. To possess it; to have your bloated vanities fostered into monstrosity by it, your foul passions blown into explosion by it, your heart and perhaps your very stomach ruined with intoxication by it; your poor life and all its manifold activities stunned into frenzy and comatose sleep by it—in one word, as the old Prophet said, your soul for ever lost by it. . . . Nature, when her scorn of a slave is divinest, and blazes like the blinding lightning against his slavehood, often enough flings him a bag of money, silently saying: 'That! away: thy doom is that'.—CARLYLE, *Latter-Day Pamphlets* (v.).

'Behold, the hire of the labourers who have reaped down your fields, which is of you kept back by fraud, crieth.'—JAMES V. 4.

D. COMMENCED life after a hard course of study as usher to a knavish fanatic schoolmaster at a salary of eight pounds per annum, with board and lodging. Of this poor stipend he never received above half in all the laborious years he served this man. He tells a pleasant anecdote, that when poverty, staring out at his ragged knees, had sometimes compelled him, against the modesty of his nature, to hint at arrears, Dr. —— would take no immediate notice, but after supper, when the school was called together for even-song, he would never fail to introduce some instructive homily against riches, and the corruption of the heart occasioned through the desire of them—ending with 'Lord, keep thy servant, above all things, from the heinous sin of avarice,' etc. . . . which, to the little auditory, sounded like a doctrine full of Christian prudence and simplicity, but to poor D. was a receipt in full for that quarter's demand at least.—CHARLES LAMB, on *Oxford in the Vacation.*

OFTEN the religious are the weary; and perhaps nowhere else does a perpetual vision of Heaven so disclose itself to the weary as above lonely toiling fields.—JAMES LANE ALLEN in *The Reign of Law*, p. 36.

' The cries of them that have reaped are entered into the ears of the Lord of Sabaoth.'—JAMES V. 4.

THERE is not an imprisoned worker looking out from these Bastilles but appeals, very audibly in Heaven's High Court, against you and me, and every one who is not imprisoned, ' Why am I here ? ' His appeal is audible in Heaven ; and will become audible enough on Earth too, if it remains unheeded here. His appeal is against you, foremost of all ; you stand in the front-rank of the accused ; you, by the very place you hold, have first of all to answer him and heaven.—CARLYLE, *Past and Present* (pt. II. ch. 6).

' Ye have lived in pleasure on the earth, and been wanton ; ye have nourished your hearts, as in a day of slaughter.'— JAMES V. 5.

THE days are gone by when the Seigneur ruled and profited. ' Le Seigneur,' says the old formula, ' enferme ses manants comme sous porte et gonds, du ciel à la terre. Tout est à lui, forêt chenue, oiseau dans l'air, poisson dans l'eau, bête au buisson, l'onde qui coule, la cloche dont le son au loin roule.' Such was his old state of sovereignty, a local god rather than a mere king. And now you may ask yourself where he is, and look round for vestiges of my late lord, and in all the countryside there is no trace of him but his forlorn and fallen mansion. . . . But on the plain where hot sweat trickles into men's eyes, and the spade goes in deep and comes up slowly, perhaps the peasant may feel a movement of joy at his heart when he thinks that these spacious chimneys are now cold, which have so often blazed and flickered upon gay folk at supper, while he and his hollow-eyed children watched through the night with empty bellies and cold feet.—R. L. STEVENSON, *Forest Notes*.

REFERENCE.—V. 5.—B. J. Snell, *The Widening Vision*, p. 129.

' Ye have condemned, ye have killed the righteous one : He doth not resist you.'—JAMES V. 6.

HISTORY . . . is rather a record of excessive patience in the various nations of the earth than of excessive petulance.—JOHN MORLEY, *Compromise*, p. 146.

' I DO not see at all,' Eugénie de Guérin writes in her *Journal*, ' how the spirit of revolt and the spirit of Christianity can ever form an alliance. Were there *revolts* against authority among the first Christians, who suffered oppressions severer than any which Christians have to suffer nowadays ? The Theban legion, the Thundering legion—did they draw the sword ? Had they not the right to do it, if Poland has now the right ? The martyrs do not seem, then, to have read God and Liberty, as M. de Lamennais reads these words. For the martyrs never raised a hand against the enemies of God and Liberty. I have been accustomed to think that the Spirit of Christianity consists in submission to God and to rulers, of whatever kind, and however they treat us ; that the only weapon to be opposed to their tyranny

is prayer, and then, if necessary, to suffer death un-resisting and forgiving the slayer, as Jesus Christ Himself forgave.'

THE DIVINE HUSBANDMAN
' Behold, the husbandman waiteth for the precious fruit of the earth, and hath long patience for it, until he receive the early and latter rain.'—JAMES V. 7.

I. THE husbandman waiteth. And see how out of the mouth of two witnesses this word shall be established—how it shall be shown that it is His title Whose Name is above every name. ' Let my Beloved come into His garden and eat His pleasant fruits '— says the spotless Bride in the Canticles : ' she supposing Him to be the gardener '—it is the glorious penitent in the Gospel. So the perfection of holiness and the perfection of penitence join in telling us this one thing : that He whom we serve, though not as we would, Whom we love, though not as we shall, Whom we seek and shall some day find, that He among all His other marvellous titles, is the Husbandman of all husbandmen, the Gardener of all gardeners.

II. And here we have Him waiting—waiting for what ? The precious fruit of the earth. It is of no material fruit of this world that He is speaking. Of flowers He is indeed telling ; but they are flowers which can only flourish round the true Rose of Sharon in a lovelier climate than this. Fruit He is indeed requiring : but fruit like that which the Tree of Life bears in the midst of the Paradise of God. And yet it springs from earth ; it is brought forth by ourselves—vile earth and miserable sinners. Job speaks of this in somewhat a different manner, but yet to the same effect : ' Iron is taken out of the earth, and brass is molten out of the stone '. That true iron, the courage of the martyrs, and the endurance of the confessors, came from frames subject to like passions with ourselves. Brass, the material of God's Altar, fit for spiritual sacrifice, is molten,' in the fire of affliction, out of the stone, the hard stone of these unfeeling hearts of ours.

III. For this precious fruit that dear Lord is content to wait ' And hath long patience for it '. So He had indeed. All the patience of those thirty-three years of humility and suffering—all the patience of the bitter ascent up Mount Calvary, all the patience of the cross, all the patience of those forty hours in the grave.

IV. All the earth is indeed filled with the seed of precious fruit, the sleeping bodies of the servants of the Lamb. In this sense also ' the earth is the Lord's and the fulness thereof '. And for these also He who Himself lay in the same earth is waiting : knowing where every particle of that which was once His temple is laid up, watching over it in whatever transformation it undergoes—seeing with that loving eye those His treasures in little quiet country churchyards, in great battle-fields, in the depths of the ocean, and foreknowing, too, the day when ' the bones which He had humbled shall rejoice,' when ' the valleys also shall stand so thick with corn that they shall laugh and sing,' when 'the little hills shall rejoice on every side'. The first-fruits of this harvest is now expecting the rest.—J. M. NEALE, *Sermons for the Church Year*, vol. I. p. 25.

'Be patient, therefore, brethren.'—JAMES V. 7.

WAITING pure is perhaps the hardest thing for flesh and blood to do well.—GEORGE MACDONALD, *Donal Grant* (ch. XIII.).

AFTER all, patience is very strong. Making a mistake at the outset of life is like beginning to wind a skein of silk at the wrong end. It gives us infinite trouble, and perhaps is in a tangle half through, but it often gets smooth and straight before the close. Thus, many a man has so conquered himself, for duty's sake, that the work he originally hated, and therefore did ill, he gets in time to do well, and consequently to like. In the catalogue of success and failure, could such be ever truthfully written, it would be curious to note those who had succeeded in what they had no mind to, and failed in that which they considered their especial vocation. A man's vocation is that to which he is 'called'; only sometimes he mistakes the voice calling. But the voice of duty there is no mistaking, nor its response; in the strong heart, the patient mind, the contented spirit, especially the latter, which, while striving to the utmost against what is not inevitable, when once it is proved to be inevitable, accepts it as such and struggles no more. Still, to do this requires not only human courage, but superhuman faith; the acknowledgment of a Will diviner than ours, to which we must submit, and in the mere act of submission find consolation and reparation.—MRS. CRAIK, *Sermons Out of Church*, pp. 237, 238.

'The early and the latter rain.'—JAMES V. 7.

BY the stream through Tolworth Common spotted persicaria is rising thickly, but even this strong-growing plant is backward and checked on the verge of the shrunken stream. The showers that have since fallen have not made up for the lack of the April rains, which in the most literal sense cause the flowers of May and June. Without those early spring rains the wild flowers cannot push their roots and develop their stalks in time for the summer sun. The sunshine and heat finds them unprepared.—RICHARD JEFFERIES, *Toilers of the Field*, pp. 310, 311.

REFERENCES.—V. 7, 8.—Spurgeon, *Sermons*, vol. xvii. No. 1025. F. D. Maurice, *Sermons*, vol. v. p. 1. G. A. Sowter, *Sowing and Reaping*, p. 62. V. 7-9.—*Expositor* (4th Series), vol. x. p. 138.

'Be ye also patient.'—JAMES V. 8.

DR. MARCUS DODS was only twenty-four when he wrote: 'Patience is the great Œdipus that every Sphinx opens up to. The present is not complete without the future, so for the future I wait, and in the present will try to find, not comfort and satisfaction, but work and contentment.'—*Early Letters*, p. 96.

'The coming of the Lord draweth nigh.'—JAMES V. 8.

SYDNEY DOBELL, in 1855, spoke of 'the second advent of our Lord' as 'the "high argument" on which I hope to spend my life. It has been—almost since poetry first stirred in me—the chosen theme of my hope, preparation, and ambition, but I do not intend to begin—I should think it presumption to begin—till I am past forty years old.'

'Grudge not one against another, brethren.'—JAMES V. 9.

NATIONAL enmities have always been fiercest among borderers.—MACAULAY, *History of England* (ch. XIII.).

REFERENCES.—V. 10.—*Expositor* (5th Series), vol. vi. p. 380. V. 10-17.—*Ibid*. vol. ii. p. 190.

'We count them happy which endure.'—JAMES V. 11.

HAPPY ye, whether the waiting be for short time or long time, if only it bring the struggle. One sure reward have ye, though there may be none else—the struggle: the marshalling to the front of rightful forces—will, effort, endurance, devotion; the putting resolutely back of forces wrongful; the hardening of all that is soft within, the softening of all that is hard; until out of the hardening and the softening results the better tempering of the soul's metal, and higher development of those two qualities which are best in man and best in his ideal of his Maker—strength and kindness, power and mercy.—JAS. LANE ALLEN, in *The Reign of Law*, p. 50 f.

WOMEN, in a state of exaltation from excited feelings, imagining, because duty often requires self-sacrifice, that when they are sacrificing themselves they must needs be doing their duty, will often be capable of taking a resolution, when they are not capable of undergoing the consequences with fortitude. For it is one sort of strength that is required for an act of heroism; another, and a much rarer sort, which is available for a life of endurance.—SIR HENRY TAYLOR, *Notes on Life*, p. 80.

'WE have been too long in the secret ourselves,' says Newton in the preface to Cowper's poems, 'to account the proud, the ambitious, or the voluptuous, happy.'

REFERENCES.—V. 11.—F. Bourdillon, *Plain Sermons for Family Reading*, p. 171. Spurgeon, *Sermons*, vol. xxxi. No. 1845.

'Above all things, my brethren, swear not at all.'—JAMES V. 12.

ONE thing was notable about these women, from the youngest to the eldest, and with hardly an exception. In spite of their piety, they could twang off an oath with Sir Toby Belch in person. There was nothing so high or so low, in heaven or earth or in the human body, but a woman of this neighbourhood would whip out the name of it, fair and square, by way of conversational adornment. My landlady, who was pretty and young, dressed like a lady and avoided *patois* like a weakness, commonly addressed her child in the language of a drunken bully. And of all the swearers that I ever heard, commend me to an old lady in Gondet, a village of the Loire. I was making a sketch, and her curse was not yet ended when I had finished it and took my departure. It is true she had a right to be angry; for here was her son, a hulking fellow, visibly the worse for drink before the day was well begun. But it was strange to hear her unwearying flow of oaths and obscenities, endless like a river, and now and then rising to a passionate shrillness, in the clear and silent air of the morning. In city slums the thing might have passed unnoticed; but in a country valley and from a plain and honest countrywoman, this beastliness of speech surprised the ear.—R. L. STEVENSON, *A Mountain Town in France.*

DESCRIBING the life of the agricultural girl, in *Field-Farming Women*, Richard Jefferies observes: ' Her mother shouts at her in a shrill treble perpetually; her father enforces his orders with a harsh oath and slap. The pressure of hard circumstances, the endless battle with poverty, render men and women both callous to each other's feelings and particularly strict to those over whom they possess unlimited authority. But the labourer must not be judged too harshly: there is a scale in these matters; a proportion as in everything else; an oath from him, and even a slap on the ear, is really the counterpart of the frown and emphasised words of a father in a more fortunate class of life; and the children do not feel it, or think it exceptionally cruel, as the children of a rich man would. Undoubtedly, however, it does lessen the bond between child and parent.'

' *Above all things,* my brethren, swear not.' If, as is generally assumed, this refers to the custom of using profane oaths in common conversation, how remote from modern ideas is the place assigned to this vice, which perhaps affects human happiness as little as any other that can be mentioned, in the scale of criminality, and how curiously characteristic is the fact that the vice to which this supremacy of enormity is attributed continued to be prevalent during the ages when theological influences were most powerful, and has in all good society faded away in simple obedience to a turn of fashion which proscribes it as ungentlemanly!—LECKY, *Map of Life*, pp. 51, 52.

COMPARE further the second chapter of Law's *Serious Call.*

' Let your yea be yea, and your nay, nay.'—JAMES v. 12.

WHILE one man quarrels in a drunken brawl, the other will use his strength to overthrow tyrants and consolidate a nation. It was the glory of Garibaldi that while he achieved the latter task, he had used no deceit. Machiavellianism was to him enough to condemn a cause as a miserable one; his yea was yea, and his nay, nay, but was he then blunt and rugged? No.—HOLMAN HUNT, *History of Pre-Raphaelitism*, vol. II. p. 245.

' Is any among you afflicted ? '—JAMES v. 13.

NEVER give way to melancholy; nothing encroaches more; I fight against it vigorously. One great remedy is, to take short views of life. Are you happy now? Are you likely to remain so till this evening? or next week? or next month? or next year? Then why destroy present happiness by distant misery, which may never come at all, and you may never live to see it? For every substantial grief has twenty shadows, and most of them shadows of your own making.—SYDNEY SMITH.

REFERENCES.— V. 13. — C. S. Horne, *Christian World Pulpit*, vol. xlviii. p. 257. V. 14.—J. R. Gregory, *Preacher's Magazine*, vol. x. p. 23. V. 14, 15.—*Expositor* (6th Series), vol. x. p. 135.

THE PRAYERS OF LUTHER AT COBURG
' Effectual fervent prayer.'—JAMES v. 16.

DURING the months when the Diet of Augsburg was sitting in 1530, Luther was left behind by the Elector John the Constant in the fortress of Coburg. His companion, Veit Dietrich, tells us that he spent much of his time in prayer. In a letter to Melanchthon dated 30th June, Veit Dietrich wrote: ' I cannot sufficiently admire the remarkable firmness, cheerfulness, faith and hope of the man in these most bitter times. These he nourishes steadily by more diligent meditation on God's Word. Not a day passes on which he does not devote at least three hours to prayer, and those the hours most suitable for study. Once I happened to hear him praying. Good God, what spirit, what faith there was in his words! He pleaded with such reverence as if he felt himself to be talking with God, with such hope and faith as if he were speaking with a father and a friend. ' I know,' he said, ' that Thou art our God and Father. I am sure, therefore, that Thou wilt destroy the persecutors of Thy children. If not, the danger is Thine as well as ours. The whole of this business is Thine; we have been compelled to meet it; defend us therefore.' I, standing apart, heard him praying with a clear voice in almost these very words. My soul also burned with a strange ardour as he spoke so familiarly, so solemnly, so reverently with God, and as he prayed he pleaded promises from the Psalms like one who was sure that all the things for which he asked would come to pass.'—*Corpus Reformatorum*, vol. II. No. 755, col. 159.

' Confess your faults one to another.'—JAMES v. 16.

Is there not such a thing as the doing of penance out of the Church, in the manly fashion? . . . Boldly to say we did a wrong will clear our sky for a few shattering peals.—MEREDITH, *The Amazing Marriage* (ch. XLIII.).

Now for the first time she remembered without indifference the affectionate kindness Dinah had shown her, and those words of Dinah in the bedchamber— that Hetty must think of her as a friend in trouble. Suppose she was to go to Dinah and ask her to help her? Dinah did not think about things as other people did: she was a mystery to Hetty, but Hetty knew she was always kind. She couldn't imagine Dinah's face turning away from her in dark reproof or scorn, Dinah's voice willingly speaking ill of her, or rejoicing in her misery, as a punishment. Dinah did not seem to belong to that world of Hetty's, whose glance she dreaded like scorching fire. But even to her Hetty shrank from beseeching and confession: she could not prevail on herself to say, 'I will go to Dinah'; she only thought of that as a possible alternative, if she had not courage for death. —George Eliot, *Adam Bede* (xxxvii.).

We want some means of availing ourselves of the experience of other people. Of course we can do so to some extent by conversation with experienced persons or by reading good biographies. Yet many people have no friends from whom they can get much real moral help, and are unable to find their experiences exactly like those recorded in books. ... How much help some suggestive thoughts of others might at times give to us, whether in the way of encouragement or warning! There seems a field open for spiritual experts who, like skilled physicians, might use their knowledge to recommend to one sick person a remedy that has proved effectual in a similar case. In one of Borrow's books there is a graphic sketch of a man who went half his life in misery because he believed he had committed the unpardonable sin, till it was suggested to him that many other people were probably in the like predicament. Had he opened his mind to an experienced spiritual adviser, he might have obtained relief much earlier. Miss Alice Gardner, *The Conflict of Duties*, p. 226.

JAMES v. 16.

The most considerable difference I note among men is not in their readiness to fall into error, but in their readiness to acknowledge their inevitable lapse.— Huxley.

'And pray one for another.'—James v. 16.

A friend of mine told me that he had been at different times sensible of spiritual blessings bestowed on him through the prayers of particular persons at a distance. He was conscious of a special blessing, and he had a most distinct impression that that blessing came to him through the prayers of a particular person; and on asking the person afterwards, he learned that he had been praying for that very blessing on him. I like such a story exceedingly. I like to think of God ... binding souls so close as to make them channels to each other of the water of life.—Erskine of Linlathen (in a letter to his cousin, 11th March, 1829).

'The effectual fervent prayer of a righteous man availeth much.' James v. 16.

'This, dear madam,' wrote Burns on New Year's Day, 1789, to Mrs. Dunlop, 'is a morning of wishes, and would to God that I came under the Apostle James' description: *the prayer of a righteous man availeth much*. In that case, madam, you should welcome in a year full of blessings.'

References.—V. 16.—S. Pearson, *Christian World Pulpit*, vol. l, p. 140. W. J. E. Bennett, *Sermons Preached at the London Mission*, 1869, p. 91. H. S. Lunn, *Christian World Pulpit*, vol. liv. p. 267. V. 16-18.—W. H. Simcox, *The Cessation of Prophecy*, p. 65.

THE ARGUMENT OF INSTANCES
'Elias . . . prayed.'—James v. 17.

This gives us the argument and the defence of a great example. Observe who it was that prayed; not a little obscure, uninfluential man, but a great prophet, whose other name was fire, who lived on high mountains and overheard the soft, rolling, thrilling anthems of heaven. There comes before us no man who has to make good his claim, who has to win our confidence by displaying before us some deeds heroic and beneficent; the man with whom we are now face to face is a man of established fame in Israel, indeed one of the very greatest sons of time. As he stands there, austere, determinate, tremendous in energy and in fiery zeal, I hear concerning him that 'Elias prayed'.

I. If Elias prayed, and all these great men prayed, this throws upon us an immense responsibility. We ought to take care how we vote against these men. We should hold our mouths in resolute patience until the whole case has been gone over in the most scrutinising and penetrating manner before we say we will not pray. Can we take the responsibility of defying and despising all that we have learned from history? The prayer would not be altered if only the poorest creatures had prayed, the altar would lose nothing if it had only been surrounded by forsaken women and orphaned children and poor begging creatures that had to pick up their food from door to door, it would still be the altar; in this case, however, it is surrounded by such men as Moses and David and Solomon and Nehemiah and Hezekiah and Elias; all the lion souls of history, the great heroic men that led the civilisation of their age. Are we going to take the responsibility of rebuking our sires and ancestors, and pouring out the expectoration of our irrational contempt upon the whole current and upward movement of the religious thought of the centuries?

II. 'Elias prayed.' This cheers us by the most complete encouragement. The way has been made clear to us, we may speak now that these great voices have spoken; by the utterance of such prayers it seems as if a pathway had been cut in the very air itself along which and above which and in association with which our smallest souls may move. These men came back with great answers; God seemed for the time being to put the key of power upon the girdle of each, and enable each to open the door of heaven and take just what he wanted.

III. 'Elias prayed.' That would be a grand stopping-place, but there is not room enough there for all that the soul requires, so we come into the higher sanctuary, and find that 'Jesus prayed'. He is never so truly near me as when he says, Let us pray. He would not always permit us to be with Him in prayer; the greatest spiritual acts of devotion and sacrifice must be completed in solitude: and Jesus went up into a mountain to pray; and Jesus left the disciples behind Him, and went forward, and fell on His face, and prayed: the cold mountains and the midnight air witnessed the fervour of His prayer.

Jesus prayed a second time; Elias prayed again; there are amended prayers, enlarged prayers, self-corrected prayers, so that we may go back in Gethsemane and say amid all the gathering glooms, Lord, let me recall that last prayer, and let me say in ampler language, language with infinitely more meaning in it, Not my will, but Thine be done. That prayer is always answered; that indeed is the Lord's prayer, the first answer the cross, the second the crown.—Joseph Parker, *City Temple Pulpit*, vol. vii. p. 79.

'Elias was a man subject to like passions as we are.'—James v. 17.

WHAT hinders us in comparing former events in the Church with what we now see, is that we are wont to regard St. Athanasius or St. Theresa and others as crowned with glory, and acting in regard to us as gods. Now that time has cleared our vision we see that they are so. But when this great saint was persecuted he was a man called Athanasius, and St. Theresa was a nun. 'Elias was a man subject to the same passions as ourselves,' says St. Peter [?], to disabuse Christians of that false notion. But we must reject the examples of the saints as disproportioned to our state. They were saints, say we, they are not like us.—Pascal.

REFERENCES.—V. 17.—C. Perren, *Sermon Outlines*, p. 267. R. W. Church, *Village Sermons* (3rd Series), p. 249.

PRAYER AND TEMPERAMENT

'Elias was a man subject to like passions as we are, and he prayed earnestly that it might not rain; and it rained not on the earth by the space of three years and six months. And he prayed again, and the heaven gave rain and the earth brought forth her fruit.'—James v. 17, 18.

THIS incident belongs to what we call the pre-scientific age.

These words assume God's power as the hearer of prayer over all the forces of the firmament.

I. Alas! nowadays the message of science is often used to check man's inclination to pray. It is a current axiom that natural law is unalterable. Are we face to face with a group of cast-iron necessities which allow of no mutual subordinations? We know that it is not so. One physical law is sometimes subjected to another, and all bow together to God's interpretation of the moral interests of the universe. God could not so arrange the mechanisms of lifeless matter as to make them involve the negation of man's fellowship with Himself. If prayer cannot be answered God is a force and nothing more, and moral motives are in His esteem trifling as the fine summer dust which settles upon the crank of the engine, without checking its movement.

II. But the moral difficulties that threaten to thwart our prayers are more stupendous and appalling than those suggested by the study of natural law. It is these which St. James has in view in the text before us. He is looking at prayer in its relation to human character rather than as it concerns the established order of the physical universe. Our own antecedent unworthiness to be heard and answered, is the supreme problem that troubles us as we come before God. This inspired writer tells us that the problem is not intractable. It has been solved in the prevailing supplications of men who are compounded of kindred elements. In heartening ourselves by this thought let us not assume that the efficacy of prayer is independent of all moral forces. There must be a core of genuine righteousness within us if our cries are to be heeded.

III. In the fulness of God's grace and compassion all drawbacks of temperament and character have been already reckoned with. It is to a throne of mercy we come, not to a throne about which the unsullied angels of light cluster,—and this means creatures of passion may draw near. Prayer becomes priceless through the name in which it is presented, however poor and mean and ignoble the petitioner himself.

'If any of you do err from the truth, and one convert him.'—James v. 19.

IT is characteristic of a good man neither to go wrong himself, nor to let his friend go wrong.

REFERENCES.—V. 19, 20.—Spurgeon, *Sermons*, vol. i. No. 45. C. Perren, *Revival Sermons in Outlines*, p. 339. Spurgeon, *Sermons*, vol. xix. No. 1137.

'He which converteth a sinner from the error of his way shall save a soul from death.'—James v. 20.

'To save a soul.' I can't somehow realise the idea that *I* should ever be so honoured of God. To save my own soul, and wear through the long fight without losing my own crown, and without bringing disgrace on the cause of Christ, these have seemed the limit of my hope. I can go on working; I can give a little; I can add my labour to the heap in the hope that among other agencies I may help rather than retard the work of Christ. But to 'save a soul,' as the direct result of my own direct effort, has scarce ever entered into my contemplation.—James Smetham, *Letters*, p. 112.

WE know how the sentiments of affection and charity suggest repeated attempts to save these erring brothers, and how keenly the tender-hearted feel that, after all hope of better things is gone, the claim on their affections still remains, and they must see that the morally worthless who are near and dear to them at least, shall be maintained in some fitting way. Love dies hard, and even if it be dead in all happier and brighter senses, a brother in distress is still a brother whose pains smart again, and ought to smart in our sympathies. They cannot cease to smart thus without our moral degradation.—Dr. Sophie Bryant, *Studies in Character*, p. 38.

WHEN the power of reclaiming the lost dies out of the Church, it ceases to be the Church.—Sir John Seeley, *Ecce Homo* (ch. xx.).

'If any one shows me a good man,' said Mazzini, 'I say, How many souls has he saved?'

IF any of those who were awakened by my ministry did after that fall back (as sometimes too many did),

I can truly say their loss hath been more to me than if one of my own children, begotten of my body, had been going to its grave. . . . I have counted as if I had goodly buildings and lordships in those places where my children were born; my heart hath been so wrapped up in the glory of this excellent work, that I counted myself more blessed and honoured of God by this than if He had made me the Emperor of the Christian World, or the Lord of all the glory of the Earth without it. O these words, *He that converteth a sinner from the error of his way doth save a soul from death.* . . . These, I say, with many others of a like nature, have been great refreshment to me.—BUNYAN, *Grace Abounding*, p. **286**.

THERE are men who think—men—the plucking of sinners out of the mire a dirty business!—MEREDITH.

'And shall hide a multitude of sins.'—JAMES V. 20

THE man of perfect virtue, wishing to be established, seeks also to establish others.—*Chinese Analects* (VI. 28).

REFERENCE.—V. 20.—J. Keble, *Miscellaneous Sermons*, p. **156**.

THE FIRST EPISTLE OF PETER

PETER

REFERENCES.—I.—*Expositor* (4th Series), vol. iii. p. 149 ; *ibid.* vol. viii. p. 285. I. 1.—*Ibid.* vol. ix. p. 258 ; *ibid.* (6th Series), vol. vi. p. 229. A. Maclaren, *Expositions of Holy Scripture—Peter*, p. 1. I. 1-6.—C. Brown, *Trial and Triumph*, p. 3. I. 2.—Spurgeon, *Sermons*, vol. viii. No. 434. *Expositor* (6th Series), vol. vi. p. 55. I. 3.—Bishop Wilberforce, *Sermons*, p. 103. W. M. Sinclair, *Church Family Newspaper*, vol. xiv. p. 272. I. 3-5.—Spurgeon, *Sermons*, vol. xvi. No. 948. I. 3-6.—G. T. Newton, *Preacher's Magazine*, vol. xvii. p. 322. I. 4.—D. L. Moody, *The Fulness of the Gospel*, p. 116. I. 5.—A. Maclaren, *After the Resurrection*, p. 170. R. W. Dale, *Christian World Pulpit*, vol. xlviii. p. 330. J. A. Alexander, *The Gospel of Jesus Christ*, p. 211. A. Maclaren, *Christian World Pulpit*, vol. lix. p. 329. *Expositor* (4th Series), vol. x. p. 198. A. Maclaren, *Expositions of Holy Scripture—Peter*, p. 7. I. 6.—*Ibid.* p. 17. Spurgeon, *Sermons*, vol. iv. No. 222.

THE TRIAL OF FAITH

'For a season if need be, ye are in heaviness, through manifold temptations ; that the trial of your faith, being much more precious than of gold that perisheth, though it be tried with fire, might be found unto praise and honour and glory at the appearing of Jesus Christ.'—I PETER I. 6, 7.

WHAT is faith? Faith is the heart setting to its seal that God is true. Faith is an appropriating grace. Faith is an apprehending grace. True faith has a quick ear, a clear eye, a ready hand, and a Divine capacity for the word of God. One is tempted to ask, Why does our heavenly Father permit the faith of His poor children to be tried? The answer is in our text, because the trial of your faith is much more 'precious than of gold that perisheth, though it be tried with fire'. I need not tell you that the trial of faith arises from the difficulties which present themselves to our experience in connection with the things which faith has to deal with.

I. When one thinks of what one is, and of what one has done and what one is capable of doing, *self* is certainly the great difficulty—*the greatest difficulty* of the believer. *Self*—one might lecture for an hour upon the variety of the phases of self which try the faith of the children of God ; all are comprised in self ; alas ! it is Satan's masterpiece, one could almost say, a pity it was ever heard out of hell—self.

II. The providence of God often presents a great trial to faith ; some have so many trials, so many difficulties, so many sorrows, that it would almost seem as if God had nothing else to do but to catch the tears that fall day by day from His poor children's eyes and put them into His bottle.

III. Again, the difficulties of our way in the wilderness are a great trial of faith : ' We wrestle not against flesh and blood, but against principalities and powers, against spiritual wickedness in heavenly places '.

IV. Another great trial of the faith of the children of God, and one they very often experience, is the hiding of the Father's face.

V. Another great difficulty to faith is unanswered prayer.

VI. Another great trial of faith is, when we seem to wait upon the Lord in prayer, and the answer comes at last, but it is not the answer that we want, and the very last thing under the heavens that we expect perhaps ; indeed the answer wellnigh breaks the heart.

VII. The last thing I would mention as a trial of faith is, when God's dealings with us seem to run counter to His promises. If you judge God's dealings by His promises, faith will always come off triumphant ; but if you judge of the promises by the dealings you will walk by sight, not by faith, and always be in difficulty. Remember these things, remember the least faith is true faith, and cannot fail. Remember that the most useful, the most successful, the most triumphant of God's servants, have always been those whose faith has been most tested.—MARCUS RAINSFORD, *The Fulness of God*, p. 142.

REFERENCES.—I. 6, 7.—R. W. Dale, *The Epistle of James*, p. 192. I. 7.—Spurgeon, *Sermons*, vol. xxxiv. No. 2055. *Expositor* (4th Series), vol. ii. p. 66. A. Maclaren, *Expositions of Holy Scripture—Peter*, p. 27. I. 7-12.—C. Brown, *Trial and Triumph*, p. 17.

I PETER I. 8.

THE inconceivable loveliness of Christ! It seems that about Him there is a sphere where the enthusiasm of love is the calm habit of the soul, that without words, without the necessity of demonstrations of affection, heart beats to heart, soul answers soul, we respond to the Infinite Love, and we feel his answer in us, and there is no need of words.—HARRIET BEECHER STOWE.

THIS verse is the text of Jonathan Edwards' treatise on *The Religious Affections*.

REFERENCES.—I. 8.—J. Stalker, *Christian World Pulpit*, vol. li. p. 24. W. P. Balfern, *Glimpses of Jesus*, p. 1. H. Smith, *Preacher's Magazine*, vol. v. p. 369. C. S. Macfarland, *Christian World Pulpit*, vol. lviii. p. 266. A. Maclaren, *Expositions of Holy Scripture—Peter*, p. 34. I. 8, 9.—Spurgeon, *Sermons*, vol. xii. No. 698. I. 9.—*Expositor* (5th Series), vol. v. p. 31. I. 9-12.—Spurgeon, *Sermons*, vol. xxvi. No. 1524. I. 10.—W. M. Sinclair, *Words from St. Paul's*, p. 17. *Expositor* (6th Series), vol. v. p. 15. I. 10-12.—*Ibid.* vol. vi. p. 54. H. Smith, *Preacher's Magazine*, vol. xix. p. 84. R. W. Dale, *Fellowship with Christ*, p. 57. A. Maclaren, *Expositions of Holy Scripture—Peter*, p. 41. I. 11.—A. Tucker, *Preacher's Magazine*, vol. xvii. p. 178. *Expositor* (4th Series), vol. v. p. 28 ; *ibid.* (5th Series), vol. iii. p. 446 ; *ibid.* vol. ix. p. 74 ; *ibid.* (6th Series), vol. xii. p. 234. I. 12.—*Ibid.* vol. iv. p. 195 ; *ibid.* vol. vi. p. 316. Bishop Westcott, *The Incarnation* and Common Life, p. 341. T. Binney, *King's Weigh-House Chapel Sermons* (2nd Series), p. 132. Spurgeon, *Sermons*, vol. xlvi. No. 2697.

THE HOPE OF YOUTH

'Hope to the end for the grace that is to be brought unto you.'
—1 PETER I. 13.

THESE words contain in a small compass the great characteristics of St. Peter; they sum up the main points in his character, and explain why he was chosen to be the chief of the Apostles. Hope marked St. Peter to the end of his own career. At the beginning he was impetuous, courageous, restless; he showed the weakness as well as the strength of his temperament. He was rash in act and speech alike; but he was simple, sincere, and eminently human, attracting us even when he was weakest.

I. Now these are the characteristics which we recognise as the distinguishing marks of youth. He was strong where youth is strong, weak where youth is weak; and for this reason, because he had the temper of youth, he was chosen as the rock on which Christ's Church was to be built. He carried to the end the great characteristics of the boyish mind, which were developed but not abandoned.

II. Learn from Peter how youth can change to manhood without losing any of its grace, its vigour or its simplicity. Nay, rather it is on keeping these qualities unchanged to the end that the power and influence of later life depends. You need to keep always some measure of the impetuosity of youth, its high aspirations, its enthusiasms, its lofty ambitions, its absence of self-seeking, its disinterestedness, hopefulness, and belief in itself. Live in hopefulness, in the sense of a mission, of preparation for your Master's call, of submission to Christ.—BISHOP CREIGHTON, *University and other Sermons*, p. 153.

REFERENCES.—I. 13.—A. Maclaren, *Christian World Pulpit*, vol. lvii. p. 332. R. J. Wardell, *Preacher's Magazine*, vol. xviii. p. 127. Spurgeon, *Sermons*, vol. xxxii. No. 1909, and vol. xlv. No. 2649. J. B. Brown, *The Divine Life in Man*, p. 344. *Expositor* (6th Series), vol. iv. p. 346. A. Maclaren, *Expositions of Holy Scripture—Peter*, p. 51. I. 13-18.—F. D. Maurice, *Sermons*, vol. v. p. 183. I. 13-21.—C. Brown, *Trial and Triumph*, p. 31. I. 14.—J. S. Maver, *Christian World Pulpit*, vol. lv. p. 286. I. 15, 16.—H. Drummond, *The Ideal Life*, p. 279. *Expositor* (5th Series), vol. v. p. 137. I. 16.—J. A. Beet, *Preacher's Magazine*, vol. xviii. p. 395.

REDEMPTION AND JUDGMENT

'And if ye call on the Father who without respect of persons judgeth according to every man's work, pass the time of your so sojourning here in fear: Forasmuch as ye know that ye were not redeemed with corruptible things . . . but with the precious blood of Christ, as of a lamb without blemish and without spot.'—1 PETER I. 17-19.

THERE is no room for doubt that in the Christian religion the two ideas of redemption and of judgment are altogether inseparable. This passage of St. Peter, for example, joins closely together the revelation of mercy, the offer of redemption, and the power of the Precious Blood to cleanse, with the high calling to holiness, the demand for obedience, and the pro-

mise of judgment. And over and over again in the New Testament there is the same connection in the Apostolic preaching. They preached, not that now at last, after a time of law and righteousness, there had dawned a day of toleration and of ease for God's creatures; they preached in broad contrast to this, that whereas in ages past God had been long-suffering, now the day of His righteous judgment approached swiftly. 'The times of ignorance,' says St. Paul, 'God winked at, but now commandeth all men everywhere to repent, because he hath appointed a day in the which He will judge the world in righteousness by that Man Whom He hath ordained, whereof He hath given assurance unto all men, in that he hath raised Him from the dead'. We who live under the Gospel, under mercy, live in the approaching light of the Day of Judgment. In the beauty and tenderness of our Lord's birth, 'God made Himself an awful rose of dawn,' the dawn that leads to the full blaze of the Sun of Righteousness.

This is the Christian religion, or rather an integral part of it. In this faith men of old time found moral strength, partly because the expectation of judgment threw light upon the problems of conduct; and partly because, believing in Jesus, not as they fancied Him, but as He revealed Himself, they found the power of His Holy Spirit enabling them to do those things which He required.

We in our time, preferring to dream about a gentle Saviour not revealed, are obliged to go without those high powers of the world to come which He came to give us, Who is not only our Saviour, but our Judge.

I. Now in these last years, the saving doctrine of approaching judgment has found a new antagonist. It was always resisted by the moral sloth which belongs to our nature; it was always hard for us to look forward to that great day of account—easier and pleasanter to believe that it would never come. But nowadays we have what seems like a support for our sloth in a certain characteristic of modern thought. There is a notion that it is unreasonable to expect that God will some day act decisively.

The Gospel that tells us that one day the Holy City, the New Jerusalem, will come down complete from heaven, teaches us that now the kingdom of heaven is amongst us and within; the same revelation that teaches us that Christ our Lord and Judge will one day suddenly present His Bride perfect before the Father in His marriage feast, teaches us also that He labours day by day, moment by moment, in myriads of hearts, to rid her, wrinkle by wrinkle, of all her blemishes, that she may, at last, stand perfect in that Presence.

II. There is no lack of recognition in sacred thought of the truth of uniformity, of continuous growth; but there is a gross lack of recognition in secular thought of the reality of catastrophe and change. And so we have persuaded ourselves that whatsoever judgment of God there be, it is a judgment which is working itself out smoothly now; that we already know the worst; that the slight prick of conscience, that the passing ache of an offended taste for goodness, is the judgment of God, and that we may slide on, registering our own condemnation, and so find when the last great books are opened nothing fresh for us to hear.

This is wholly contrary to the faith of our Lord Jesus Christ; and it is wholly contrary to our common experience; for what is the teaching—the first surface teaching—of all our common life? Surely it is the teaching of tremendous changes. We go forward through life from crisis to crisis, and we all of us move towards a day—the day of death—when we shall discover something which, whatever it is, will be a vast and momentous change. We have been misled, by a fine-spun reflection upon the ultimate meanings of things, to neglect their plain and manifest character. Natural history teaches us that animals and plants are all the same at last, and it teaches us so truly, according to a certain method of study. It teaches us that we cannot well mark or define the difference between animal and plant life considered in their first elements. But in practice there is a vast distinction between meeting a tree, for example, and meeting a tiger. We have given up, for the sake of the fine-spun results of a difficult reflection, our common-sense and practical knowledge of the momentous differences which meet us in experience.

III. You talk of uniformity of experience, but the man who is hungry and who has no prospect of food or work will not believe you if you tell him that he is on the way to become healthy and strong; the man who is just in the depths of bereavement with a broken heart will not believe you if you tell him that he is only on the way to inevitable joy and happiness. If you build squalor round our people you will in vain persuade yourself to believe that dirt and crowding and darkness are sure to lead people, if they go on long enough, to health and freedom and nobility and the greatness of the guarded family life. No, in fact, we understand that negligence is not the way to preparedness, that cowardice is not the way to safety, that moral slackness does not lead us to moral contentment or to moral achievement; that sin is not virtue in the making. Sin leads not to virtue, but to more sin and to everlasting death.

And so we must look forward to the great day and pray that now we may be preserved in the smallest of our crises, that at last we may stand without blame before Him when He cometh and shows to us His glory. Our prayer should be: Vouchsafe, O Lord, to keep us this day, this hour, without sin. Judge yourselves now, and you shall not be judged. Pray Him now for grace and you shall meet Him then at last with joy, for you shall see Him as He is, being conformed to His likeness, not in the swiftness of a last conversion, but in the solidity of a life of obedience.

IV. There are other doctrines profounder than this, but we hold them in vain if we do not grasp this moral issue. There are other Christian thoughts finer and more interesting than this, but we sing in vain the songs of Zion if we are not meanwhile marching step by step towards heaven. There are modes of teaching which give greater recognition to the mystery of our life. Our life is indeed surrounded with mystery. Temperament has unknown capacities; heredity has huge and awful powers; circumstance becomes more and more wonderful as the veil is lifted, so that we see something of the good and the evil powers outside sense which lie around our path. But it is in vain that we dream of the mystery, if we do not mark and walk along the lighted track. There is between the gulfs of darkness one lighted track, the track of duty. It is the narrow path.—FATHER WAGGETT, *Church Times*, 4th December, 1908.

REFERENCES.—I. 17-21.—*Expositor* (5th Series), vol. vi. p. 2. I. 18, 19.—*Ibid.* (4th Series), vol. v. p. 185. I. 19.—H. J. Wilmot-Buxton, *Sunday Sermonettes for a Year*, p. 203. J. T. Stannard, *The Divine Humanity*, p. 97. Spurgeon, *Sermons*, vol. xi. No. 621.

'See that ye love one another with a pure heart fervently.'—
I PETER I. 22.

DR. MARCUS DODS wrote at the age of sixteen to his sister Marcia: 'Sometimes it strikes me with a kind of sudden rapture how these words "with a pure heart fervently" shall be fulfilled in our love to one another hereafter. How good must He be, Who knowing our enmity, has given us such power of affection, natures so capable of intense delight. Could one only always believe this goodwill of God, how easy it would be to love, serve, and enjoy Him. What are the minds that can see, and not see this love, the hearts that can feel, and not feel this?'—*Early Letters*, p. 176.

REFERENCES.—I. 22.—T. Binney, *King's Weigh-House Chapel Sermons*, p. 206. *Expositor* (5th Series), vol. vii. p. 31. A. Maclaren, *Expositions of Holy Scripture—Peter*, p. 76. I. 22 to II. 3.—C. Brown, *Trial and Triumph*, p. 47. I. 23-25.—Spurgeon, *Sermons*, vol. vii. No. 398, and vol. xvii. No. 999. J. Clifford, *Christian World Pulpit*, vol. xlvii. p. 298. H. Alford, *Quebec Chapel Sermons*, vol. iii. p. 324. I. 24.—J. Budgen, *Parochial Sermons*, vol. i. p. 66. I. 24, 25.—W. J. Brock, *Sermons*, p. 135. II. 1, 2.—*Expositor* (4th Series), vol. ii. p. 299. II. 1-3.—Spurgeon, *Sermons*, vol. viii. No. 459. II. 2.—J. Budgen, *Parochial Sermons*, vol. ii. p. 177. *Expositor* (4th Series), vol. ii. p. 300. II. 2, 3.—T. Arnold, *Christian Life: Its Hopes*, p. 122. II. 3.—Spurgeon, *Sermons*, vol. xxxvi. No. 2168. *Expositor* (5th Series), vol. vi. p. 376. II. 4.—Spurgeon, *Sermons*, vol. xxiii. No. 1334. II. 4, 5.—I. E. Page, *Preacher's Magazine*, vol. xvii. p. 515. Spurgeon, *Sermons*, vol. xxiii. No. 1376. A. Maclaren, *Expositions of Holy Scripture—Peter*, p. 86. II. 4-10.—C. Brown, *Trial and Triumph*, p. 61.

THE LIVING STONES OF THE TEMPLE

'Ye also, as living stones, are built up a spiritual house, to be a holy priesthood, to offer up spiritual sacrifices, acceptable to God through Jesus Christ.'—I PETER II. 5.

I. EACH individual in the Church of God has to submit himself to the Master Builder's hand. For some He designs notable places in His spiritual house on earth, and still more in the house eternal in the heavens. For others here on earth there are obscurer positions—some, indeed, quite hidden away from the notice of men. There is one essential difference between the material stones and the spiritual. The material stones are dead, lifeless. The spiritual stones must be living. There must be energy, power, progress about them.

II. If there is to be the gradual preparing and fitting into the spiritual fabric of the living stones, how is it to be effected? Surely by training and discipline.

III. To belong to a holy priesthood, implies, as the text teaches us, the offering up of spiritual sacrifices. Our sacrifices offered to God must be of ourselves; each in our measure must try to follow Him who offered Himself.—H. A. Redpath, *Church Family Newspaper*, vol. xiv. p. 860.

References.—II. 5.—W. G. Horder, *Christian World Pulpit*, vol. lii. p. 365. J. Keble, *Sermons for the Saints' Days*, p. 415. H. Woodcock, *Sermon Outlines* (1st Series), p. 175. J. Keble, *Sermons for Christmas and Epiphany*, p. 316. *Expositor* (5th Series), vol. iii. p. 127. A. Maclaren, *Expositions of Holy Scripture—Peter*, p. 92. II. 5-9.—B. J. Snell, *Sermons on Immortality*, p. 90. II. 6.—Spurgeon, *Sermons*, vol. xxiv. No. 1429.

MIGHTY TO SAVE—MIGHTY TO KEEP

'Unto you, therefore, which believe, He is precious.'
—1 Peter ii. 7 (R.V.).

Let me point out some of the ways in which our Lord is so precious unto His people.

I. He is Precious unto us in Life.—(1) Because of His cleansing blood. (2) Because of His Divine advocacy. (3) Because of His all-sustaining grace. 'No confidence in the flesh,' full confidence in our King, is the secret of every conquering life.

II. He is also Precious unto us in the Hour of Death.—(1) Because of His supporting promises. Instinctively the mind turns from all other books to the One Book in that dark hour. Sir Walter Scott said, 'Bring me the book'. 'What book?' asked his attendant. 'There is only one book for a dying man,' was the substance of the great author's reply. (2) Because of His satisfying presence. It is reasonable to shrink from death. The love of life is a Divine instinct. We can only meet death fearlessly when we realise that 'He is with us,' and that the solitude of death is filled with Jesus.

III. He is also Precious unto us in the Day of Judgment.—Jesus will be precious to His people because of His mantling righteousness. The spotless robe of Christ shall envelop the believer, and God shall look upon him as righteous, even as Christ is righteous. Because of His rich reward. Many shall be the rewards 'to him that overcometh'. To sit on His throne, with golden crown and harp and palm; to rule over 'cities'; to be a 'pillar' in the temple of God—these are some of the blessings awaiting us; but there is a reward far transcending all these; for its height, its depth, we cannot fathom. It is the blessed 'Enter thou into the *joy* of thy Lord'. How rapturous will be that joy!

IV. Christ shall be Precious unto us Through Eternity.—Heaven is not so much a place as a person. To be 'with Christ,' to be 'at home with the Lord,' was the heaven St. Paul longed for. Wherever Jesus is, there will we find heaven. We might become satiated with the many glorious sights of the celestial city, but never can we have enough of Jesus, our Lord and our God.—T. J. Madden, *Addresses to all Sorts and Conditions of Men*, p. 112.

References.—II. 7.—C. A. Berry, *Christian World Pulpit*, vol. xlix. p. 113. J. Bateman, *Sermons Preached in Guernsey*, p. 101. Spurgeon, *Sermons*, vol. v. No. 242; vol. xvi. No. 931; vol. xxxvi. No. 2137, and vol. lii. No. 3014. J. C. Hill, *Christian World Pulpit*, vol. lii. p. 398. *Expositor* (5th Series), vol. ix. p. 37.

1 Peter ii. 7, 8.

On the base of the statue erected to Stein by the German nation, the following words, a play on his name, are inscribed: *Des guten Grundstein, des bösen Eckstein, der deutschen Edelstein* (a cornerstone of goodness, a stumbling-block for evil, a precious stone to Germany).

Reference.—II. 7, 8.—Spurgeon, *Sermons*, vol. xxi. No. 1224.

A ROYAL PRIESTHOOD

'Ye are a royal priesthood.'—1 Peter ii. 9.

I. To whom were these words addressed? To a caste? To the clergy? To ministers of the Word? Certainly not. 'To the strangers scattered abroad throughout Pontus, Galatia, Cappadocia, Asia, and Bithynia,' *i.e.* to disciples of Christ of no note or standing in the Church. This is the priesthood which the great Apostle recognises. It is well worthy of attention that this same Apostle, whose name and authority have been so unwarrantably pressed into the service of priestly assumption and papal usurpation, should be so careful to disclaim anything that would separate him from his brethren. In writing to elders, he calls himself an elder; in writing to these strangers, he says, 'Ye are a royal priesthood'. How has it come to pass then that in this enlightened century and in this Bible-loving England the utterly unscriptural belief in a priestly caste should have advanced by leaps and bounds? May it not be because we who claim to be in all respects loyal to the New Testament keep the true priesthood too much in the background? A priesthood is a necessity to sinful men. If men do not see the genuine priest, they will flock to the false one. We must bring forward the true to take the place of the false; we must exalt our great High Priest, who has passed into the heavens, and show that through Him alone we have access to God, that by His sacrifice alone our sins can be forgiven, and through the merits of His intercession alone can we obtain the Holy Spirit, and with Him all good things. We must assert the rights of the whole people of Christ to the priestly prerogative and privilege, telling them with the same emphasis as the great Apostle himself, 'Ye are a royal priesthood'. What, then, is this high dignity that belongs to the people of Christ? What this is may best be seen by recalling the functions of the priesthood. They were three—sacrifice, intercession, benediction. Our priesthood, like our Saviour's, begins with sacrifice, the yielding up of ourselves to be the Lord's. This gives us access through our great High Priest, by Whom we have received the atonement ; with that access comes the privilege of prevailing intercession ; and out of these again arises the third prerogative, that of scattering abroad the blessings of the kingdom.

II. Now that we have seen what is meant by the priesthood of believers, let us inquire what would be the practical consequence of making it a reality. Let us exalt the High Priest of our profession in all His priestly acts—in sacrifice, intercession, and benediction ; and when men discover that the priestly office is not vacant, that it is filled by One who is a priest for ever in the power of an endless life, no mere minister will dare take this honour to himself, and no Church will dare to sanction the usurpation. Let Christian people not only claim it, but exercise it. If we do, where will the caste of the priesthood be ? It will be abolished.—J. MONRO GIBSON, *The Glory of Life*, p. 87.

REFERENCES.—II. 9.—H. W. Webb-Peploe, *The Record*, vol. xxvii. p. 769. H. Woodcock, *Sermon Outlines* (1st Series), p. 148. J. M. Gibson, *Christian World Pulpit*, vol. l. p. 248. Spurgeon, *Sermons*, vol. xlviii. No. 2765. H. N. Bate, *Church Family Newspaper*, vol. xv. p. 452. *Expositor* (5th Series), vol. iii. p. 191 ; *ibid.* (6th Series), vol. i. p. 367 ; *ibid.* vol. iv. p. 278. A. Maclaren, *Expositions of Holy Scripture—Peter*, p. 101. II. 10.—*Ibid.* vol. v. p. 87.

1 PETER II. 11.

IN the diary of F. Coillard, of the Zambesi, for 23rd March, 1860, there is the following entry : 'Everything with the Basutos is very simple. An ox-skin covers them by day, and wraps them up by night; some reeds and a little grass suffice to make them a shelter against the changes of the weather. I remember how many remarks were made about my little cottage.... Some one observed that "the white men built as if they were never going to die". How very just and sensible—I might even say *Christian* —was this remark ! Certainly the Basuto style of building is very well designed to remind us that we are only travellers, for when they move they take their houses with them, and if a woman dies they leave her house to fall to ruins.'

1 PETER II. 11.

WHEN one is a wanderer, one feels that one fulfils the true condition of humanity.—MAURICE DE GUÉRIN.

REFERENCES.—II. 11.—R. M. Benson, *Redemption*, p. 351. II. 11-20.—C. Brown, *Trial and Triumph*, p. 75. II. 12.— R. W. Church, *Village Sermons* (3rd Series), p. 204. II. 13, 14.—H. H. Henson, *Christian World Pulpit*, vol. lxi. p. 257. II. 15.—*Preacher's Magazine*, vol. x. p. 135. J. J. Blunt, *Plain Sermons*, p. 80. II. 15, 16.—*Ibid.* p. 37.

1 PETER II. 16.

THE free man is he who is *loyal* to the Laws of this Universe ; who in his heart sees and knows, across all contradictions, that injustice *cannot* befall him here ; that except by sloth and cowardly falsity evil is not possible here. The first symptom of such a man is not that he resists and rebels, but that he obeys.—CARLYLE, *Latter-Day Pamphlets*, vi.

REFERENCE.—II. 16.—Bishop Boyd-Carpenter, *Christian World Pulpit*, vol. xlv. p. 313.

THE COMMON CORONATION
'Honour all men.'—1 PETER II. 17.

ONE of the foremost duties of the Church of God is to vindicate the essential greatness of human nature. Let us, then, attempt to show how in the light of certain facts and of the teaching of the Christian faith, human nature is worthy of high honour, despite the existence of so much in human life that is calculated to provoke cynicism and contempt.

I. The triviality of human circumstance obscures man's essential greatness. Looking into history we are startled by the discovery that the very greatest of mankind lived once as mere mortals, having habitually to do with the smallest concerns and the most modest business of human life. Just as the dignity of human life is vindicated by its great men in those intellectual masterpieces which were perfected in monotony and drudgery, so that dignity receives higher and fuller demonstration still in its good men in the splendid moral results which they attain by and through the paltriest circumstances. Give life its true interpretation, and we see the importance and large possibilities of the humblest lot. When the rough screens of beggarly circumstance drop away, the marvellous moral artistry that God has wrought in dark corners will astonish men and angels.

II. The essential greatness of man is obscured by his manifold sufferings and humiliations. It is absurd to think meanly of us because of our painful estate ; the truer test of what we are being the temper in which we deal with adverse circumstance. That temper is often heroic. Sackcloth is on the skin, but scarlet is on the soul ; battered out of shape by the shocks of doom, men are still gold.

III. The essential greatness of man is obscured by his moral fault. (1) In the most deeply degraded of our fellows we recognise *the action of conscience*. In the very depths of sin and shame this Divine faculty asserts itself, and indirectly proclaims the grandeur of the sinner. The man of colour confessing, 'I know that I am a man because I feel that I am a sinner,' uttered a great truth. (2) Human nature in its deepest degradation is still *the object of Divine, redeeming love.*

IV. The essential greatness of man is not questioned by any discoveries of modern science. The vast grasp and magnificent results of modern science bear fresh and powerful testimony to the unique and transcendent eminence of man.—W. L. WATKINSON. *The Bane and the Antidote*, p. 285.

'Honour the King.'—1 PETER II. 17.

IN the Church of St. Laurence, Ludlow, there is a memorial to the Salwey family, of Puritan fame, with their motto 'Pro rege saepe, pro republica semper' 'for the King often, for the country always'. With this we may compare the words of Robert Atkins, one of the clergy ejected in 1662: 'Let him never be accounted a sound Christian that doth not both fear God and honour the King. I beg that you would not interpret our Nonconformity to be an act of unpeaceableness and disloyalty. We will do anything for His Majesty but sin. We will hazard anything for him but our souls. We hope we could die for him, only we dare not be damned for him. We make no question, however we may be accounted of here, we shall be found loyal and obedient subjects at our appearance before God's tribunal.

1 Peter II. 17.

I MAY say the root of Radicalism is *Honour all men*, separated from its context, *Fear God*. I may say also the root of Conservatism is *Honour the King*, separated from its context, *Fear God*.—McLEOD CAMPBELL.

ONLY in looking heavenward, take it in what sense you may, not in looking earthward, does what we can call union, mutual love, society, begin to be possible.—CARLYLE, *Sartor Resartus*, bk. III. ch. II.

'CHAUCER,' says Lovell, 'could look to God without abjectness, and on man without contempt.'

REFERENCES.—II. 17.—H. S. Holland, *Christian World Pulpit*, vol. lviii. pp. 163, 169 and 342. W. F. Shaw, *Sermon Sketches for the Christian Year*, p. 60. J. Budgen, *Parochial Sermons*, vol. ii. p. 343. H. R. Heywood, *Sermons and Addresses*, p. 150. F. W. Farrar, *Everyday Christian Life*, p. 234. H. S. Holland, *Vital Values*, p. 82. Bishop Creighton, *Christian World Pulpit*, vol. li. p. 408. *Expositor* (5th Series), vol. vii. p. 459. II. 20, 21.—G. Body, *Christian World Pulpit*, vol. lvii. p. 164.

JESUS OUR EXAMPLE—IN SUFFERING

'For even hereunto were you called: because Christ also suffered for us, leaving us an example, that ye should follow His steps.'—1 PETER II. 21.

I. THERE are two strange mysteries in human life which confront us at every step—the mystery of sin and the mystery of suffering. And they are most closely correlated. Suffering is the penance of sin not only in the sense of punishment, but also as its remedy, for by suffering we are sanctified. Suffering is the penance of sin, and yet not necessarily of our own individual sin, for it is probably true that those who suffer most are those who are most free from sin. And why is this? Surely it is because suffering is the penance for *all* sin, and those who are living the most holy lives, and are therefore closest to our Lord, have the blessed privilege of fellowship in His Passion, which implies suffering for others. Looked upon in this way, suffering ceases to be an evil. We need, at the outset then, to strive to realise this. Try then, as one of the most important lessons of spiritual life, to realise the *privilege* of suffering. Do not take the world's warped view of suffering.

II. But let us turn to our Lord's life and see how He is our great Example in suffering. From the cradle to the grave our Blessed Lord's life was one long life of suffering. I shall not therefore attempt to follow it throughout, but shall take three points in it which bring before us the three classes of suffering we have to bear. (1) We suffer in mind. From the point of view of religion there is the suffering of doubt, which comes at times like a cloud between almost every Christian and God. We suffer from perplexity. And we suffer in mind lastly and perhaps most often, in what may be called the 'worries' of life, the irritations, the trifling troubles of every day. We turn to our Lord 'My God, my God, why hast Thou forsaken Me?' The words tell of a sorrow of mind, tell of an intensity of mental suffering which was, without doubt, the greatest that any human mind has ever known. And so, in your hour of mental trouble, think of our Lord on the cross. (2) But then we have to suffer in body, through sickness or accident. How is our Lord our Example in pain and sorrow and suffering of body? Not in any sickness which came through His own sin, but in that pain and suffering which came from the sin of the world. When we are called upon to bear pain, then let us look up at the Cross and in our bodily pain unite ourselves with our Lord, offering our pains in union with His sufferings, offering them to God the Father. (3) And then, lastly, there is the third division of suffering, the suffering of the human soul: the suffering in our affections, the keenest, the deepest, the hardest of all to bear. Throughout His life He suffered, 'being grieved at the hardness of men's hearts'.

None can ever know the power of the Resurrection life of Christ who has not first tasted the chalice of His woes.—A. G. MORTIMER, *Lenten Preaching*, p. 142.

REFERENCES.—II. 21.—J. C. M. Bellew, *Sermons*, vol. i. p. 93. W. M. Sinclair, *Words from St. Paul's* (2nd Series), p. 176. E. W. Attwood, *Sermons for Clergy and Laity*, p. 138. A. M. Fairbairn, *Christian World Pulpit*, vol. xlv. p. 241. H. J. Wilmot-Buxton, *Sunday Sermonettes for a Year*, p. 152. C. M. Betts, *Eight Sermons*, p. 39. J. J. Blunt, *Plain Sermons* (2nd Series), p. 95. *Expositor* (4th Series), vol. v. p. 186; *ibid.* vol. viii. p. 358; *ibid.* (5th Series), vol. vi. p. 385; *ibid.* (6th Series), vol. viii. p. 225. A. Maclaren, *Expositions of Holy Scripture—Peter*, p. 107.

1 Peter II. 21.

IN the deepest sense, the Son of God has left us an example that we should walk in His steps. In the highest path that our spirits are called to tread, that is to say, in our intercourse with the Father of Spirits, the foot-prints of Jesus are to guide us; our confidence is to be the fellowship of His confidence; our worship, the fellowship of His worship: for sonship is that worship, in spirit and in truth, which the Father seeketh.—McLEOD CAMPBELL.

REFERENCES.—II. 21-24.—F. Bourdillon, *Plain Sermons for Family Reading*, p. 101. II. 21-25.—C. Brown, *Trial and Triumph*, p. 91. II. 22.—*Expositor* (5th Series), vol. ii. p. 168.

1 Peter II. 24.

IN his sixth Epistle to the Florentines, Dante makes a remarkable application of this verse to Henry VII.

'These facts,' he protests, 'remain to be impressed on your minds: that this standard-bearer of the Roman Empire, the Divine and triumphant Henry, thirsting not for his private advantage, but for the public good of the world, undertook each arduous emprise for us, partaking our hardships of his own freewill, so that to him after Christ, the prophet Isaiah pointed the finger of prophecy, when by the revelation of the Holy Spirit he foretold: "Surely he hath borne our griefs, and carried our sorrows".'

References. — II. 24.—A. Goodrich, *Christian World Pulpit*, vol. xlvi. p. 170. W. G. Bryan, *Seven Sermons on the Sacraments*, p. 66. Spurgeon, *Sermons*, vol. xix. No. 1143; vol. xlviii. No. 2790; vol. l. No. 2887. Phillips Brooks, *Christian World Pulpit*, vol. xlvii. No. 245. *Expositor* (4th Series), vol. iii. p. 275.

I PETER II. 25.

THE public signing of the Covenant, probably on 2nd March, by the stern but weeping populace, on a flat stone in the kirkyard of the dispossessed Franciscans, has been duly celebrated in Scottish art and letters. 'What they felt,' says Mr. Gardiner, in the same strain as Rothes, 'was the joy of those who had been long led astray, and had now returned to the Shepherd and Bishop of their souls.'—A. LANG, *History of Scotland*, vol. III. p. 32.

References.—II. 25.—A. Tucker, *Preacher's Magazine*, vol. v. p. 366. G. Body, *Christian World Pulpit*, vol. xlvii. p. 168. T. F. Crosse, *Sermons* (2nd Series), p. 144. J. Keble, *Sermons for Easter to Ascension Day*, p. 303. III. 1.—*Expositor* (6th Series), vol. x. p. 280. III. 1-12.—C. Brown, *Trial and Triumph*, p. 107. III. 3.—*Expositor* (6th Series), vol. vi. p. 212.

IN THE SIGHT OF GOD
'In the sight of God.'—I PETER III. 4.

GOD sees; the eyes of the Lord run to and fro throughout the whole earth, to show Himself mighty on behalf of them that trust in Him. His eyes are weapons, His eyes are lightnings, His smile makes the morning, His frown makes the night; He is a great God above all gods; He stands where other gods cannot climb.

Peter says in this text, Let it be in the hidden man of the heart; let it be in the meek and quiet spirit; let it be in one sense invisible that it may in another sense be more visible; let your good works have a good background. Spirit sees spirit. Spirit cannot communicate with flesh; they have no dealings one with the other in the deepest spiritual sense. God is a spirit; therefore God communicates with the spirit of man, which is akin to His own. How He does this He has never condescended to explain; but that communication is made to us from the spiritual world is certain; otherwise many ideas, suggestions, impulses, and mental operations can never be accounted for. There are many passages in the Old Testament which we cannot understand until we have read the New Testament, and brought the new lamp to shed a light on the old mystery. And so there are many things about this human sight, and the Divine sight looking at it, spirit of man looking for Spirit of God, and Spirit of God trying what image it can create whereby to represent itself, and lighting upon the gentle-breasted dove. A wondrous thing that God should have had to look about, so to say, amongst His own creatures to pick up one here and one there which will most nearly represent some Divine idea. And so, who is this fair, young, beautiful creature, His face a mystery? who is He? Represent Him to me by some other life. The voice says, Behold the Lamb. Lamb and dove; they seem to bring their own meaning with them; there is not in them one drop of bad black blood, all so gentle as to be all but spiritual, and so symbolical that it must be behind each of them a sacrament.

I. God is continually rebuking both our hearing and our seeing; He says to us in effect, You have sight, but must not stretch it beyond its proper limits; and you can hear noise, you cannot yet hear music, but hearing the noise is a preparation for hearing the music; you think you can hear the music now, but you hear no music; the true music is to come; it is a thought rather than a thing, a film rather than a substance; but in so far as you use your faculties within due limits and in a reverential spirit you are advancing—Oh, hear it and be glad!—advancing to the time of song, and music, and rapture, and ecstasy.

II. In Peter's expression we find the element of valuation—the valuation, it may be, of property. There are two valuations, the valuation which man assigns, and the valuation which God fixes. Peter says that a meek and a quiet spirit is in the sight of God of great price. In the sight of man it is ridiculed. Who cares for meekness? who appreciates quietness? who is there that does not regard repose as a sign of feebleness? whereas repose may be the last expression of power, quietness may be reserved thunder. Moses was meek, the meekest man in all the earth, but who could be so angry when his spirit was turned? The lamb is peaceful, docile, yet one great poet speaks of 'the wrath of the Lamb'. 'In the sight of God of great price.' Then a man may be rich without knowing it; he may have qualities and attributes of character which are jewellery without price, far surpassing rubies, and diamonds, and all the things thou canst desire out of the silver mine and the gold mine. A man may be rich, and have no jewel casket; and man may be very rich, and never have been in a jeweller's shop? a woman may be most rich, the wealthiest, sweetest mother, without having any things that are called lovely, and beautiful, and precious. And so a man may be a poor man and not know it.

III. There is another sense in which this word 'in the sight of God' is used—'Whether it be right in the sight of God to hearken unto you more than unto God, judge ye'. That is the law which settles everything. There are so many people who think themselves law-abiding who are law-breaking, but they do not know it, and they do not mean it; gentle, modest people, but not deficient in pharisaic zeal, I want to obey the great law which includes and transfigures all the little laws in the degree in which they are true and wise.—JOSEPH PARKER, *City Temple Pulpit*, vol. VII. p. 213.

REFERENCES.—III. 6.—Spurgeon, *Sermons*, vol. xxvii. No. 1633. *Expositor* (6th Series), vol. vi. p. 235. III. 7.—Spurgeon, *Sermons*, vol. xx. No. 1192. W. H. Brookfield, *Sermons*, p. 87.

THE CHRISTIAN IN SOCIETY

'Be ye all of one mind, having compassion one of another, love as brethren, be pitiful, be courteous.'—i PETER III. 8.

THIS passage sums up the duties of a Christian towards the circle immediately around him in his daily life.

I. First, 'be ye all of the same mind'. From the love of Christ follows first and most plainly Christian unanimity; unanimity in its strictest sense of agreement, or rather identity of convictions on fundamental points; about that there can be no doubt. We must be of the same mind, or rather we must see that we are of the same mind, that it is impossible that any, even the meanest, who calls upon Christ's name in any, even the most inarticulate, accents should not be one in heart and soul with us, should not be to us in very truth a brother.

II. If we are Christ's at all, we must recognise our fellow-countrymen in Christ; recognise them as countrymen wherever we find them, and in however miserable a plight, recognise them freely and heartily and honestly, and by so doing we shall come at once to the next step of the Apostle's admonition, 'have compassion one of another,' feel with one another. To feel with our brethren—how great a thing it is; great both for them and us; great for them, for how the crushed and wounded soul revives before the look that tells it its woes are not unheeded; how the despairing spirit clings with an agonised grasp to the words that tell him he is not absolutely alone in the world, till hope comes back, and life becomes strong to it once more. Such is the office of Christian love in each society and circle. But it can only work these results, if thorough, if built upon a loss of self in Christ.

III. Pitifulness and courtesy are to be the accompaniments of his daily life, and by means of them his Christian love is to shine forth to all who come in contact with him. (1) Pitifulness is more subtle than sympathy; for sympathy is the capacity for entering into another's joys or sorrows, and feeling with them so as to halve the sorrow and double the joy; pitifulness is that deep-seated tenderness of heart and soul which draws to itself the weary and heavy-laden, which commands the confidence of the broken-hearted. (2) Courtesy is the development of Christian love in the smallest detail of daily life and conduct; it is the perpetual recognition of our duties towards every one we meet; it is the perpetual sense of the dignity of humanity, of the honour due to all God's creatures, of the infinite grandeur of every

human soul.—BISHOP CREIGHTON, *University and other Sermons*, p. 16.

i PETER III. 8.

'COMPASSION,' says Butler finely, 'is a call, a demand of nature, to relieve the unhappy; as hunger is a natural call for food.'

'Be courteous.'—i PETER III. 8.

WE should take pains to be polite to those whom we love. Politeness preserves love, is a kind of sheath to it.—MARK RUTHERFORD.

REFERENCES.—III. 8.—F. W. Farrar, *Christian World Pulpit*, vol. xlv. p. 369. H. C. Beeching, *Seven Sermons to Schoolboys*, p. 50. T. Binney, *King's Weigh-House Chapel Sermons* (2nd Series), p. 226. R. G. Soans, *Sermons for the Young*, p. 1. F. J. A. Hort, *Village Sermons in Outline*, p. 145. Archbishop Maclagan, *Christian World Pulpit*, vol. lviii. p. 219. III. 8-12.—*Expositor* (5th Series), vol. iii. p. 349.

THE LOVE OF LIFE

'He that will love life.'—i PETER III. 10.

I. WHAT is really meant by Life? There are two words in the New Testament which, from the necessities of our language, are alike rendered 'life'. One of these words ($\beta\iota\circ\varsigma$) signifies the principle of animal life, the things by which it is preserved or gladdened, and its span. The other word ($\zeta\omega\acute{\eta}$) belongs to a higher sphere. It is the new life given in germ at Baptism, which may be stunted or strengthened, as grace is used or abused; and which, after the Resurrection, is to be suitably clothed upon. Thus, the first refers to man's natural existence as one of the animal creation; the second to man's supernatural existence as a son of God. Christ was incarnate to impart this. 'The first man Adam was made a living soul; the last Adam was made a quickening (life-creating) spirit' (1 Cor. xv. 45). 'I am come,' said Christ, 'that they might have life.' The question, then, for Christians really is not whether life, the higher, future existence, is worth living; but whether existence under mere animal or external conditions is worth living? The latter, no doubt, is an intricate question, and something may be said in favour of a negative reply. We may be reminded of the transitoriness of human existence; the vanity of our expectations; the objects of our hopes crushed in the iron hand of necessity; the loss of those we love; the protracted humiliation of the breaking up of the machine, accompanied perhaps by some bodily torture; together with this, a weariness of life; nay, often this last comes long before old age. One young spirit, who passed by the terrible gate of suicide into the other world, wrote: 'The good things come off so seldom'. Of all forms of madness, 'Seeing things exactly as they are' seemed to Voltaire the most appalling and hopeless. Very much may, of course, be said in mitigation of this pessimism. 'Life rightly used has happiness for each of its stages.' The sweetness of domestic love; the pleasures of society and friendship; the preponderance of health over sickness and pain; the activities, the pleasing surprises that often come to the weariest lot; the beauties of Nature which exhilarate the body, and interest the mind of man. 'We bless Thee for our creation, preservation, and all the blessings of this life.'

II. On the question, Is existence, elevated into the higher and supernatural life, worth living? we Christians can have no doubt.

(1) Present acceptance makes life worth living. Finished final salvation is not offered in the twinkling of an eye. But present acceptance is promised to all who come to God through Christ. This makes any existence tolerable. 'A tranquil God tranquillises all things, and to see His peacefulness is to be at peace.'

(2) There are times of exquisite pleasure in communion with God. These compensate for the languor of old age and for the slow 'martyrdom of life'. They support the believer under the cross: he began by carrying it; it ends by carrying him.

(3) There is the truest pleasure in work for God. The study of His Word is a perpetual delight. The Church's sacramental life is full of joy. The teaching of the young, the ministry to the sick, the rescue of the fallen, the quickening and elevation of Service and Worship—these have pleasures of their own which give animation and variety to life. But how about that sorrow which is inseparable from religion—the sorrow of Repentance? A great theologian has said that 'that kind of sorrow is its own consolation'; 'He hath given a new kind of tears upon earth, which make those happy who shed them'. 'Oh, that we could understand that the mystery of grace gives blessedness with tears!'

(4) That life is worth living is proved by the view which Jesus took of it. 'My delights were with the sons of men' (Prov. VIII. 31). Christ was no pessimist about human life. He saw of what man was capable—what holiness and victory, as well as what sin and defeat. He yearned, from the cradle to the grave, for the Holy Week and Easter, that He might bear the sweetness of the burden.

No doubt human life is tragic and pathetic; yet there is a magic smile on the face of the drama, after all. In the midst of life's most poignant sorrows riven hearts are alone with God, and white lips say, 'Thy will be done'. For they know that after a while the point of view will change. The life of them that sleep in Jesus will stand out as a beautiful whole. Precious words will remain. Wherever they lie, all is well. 'Them that sleep in Jesus will God bring with Him.'—ARCHBISHOP ALEXANDER.

REFERENCES.—III. 10, 11.—A. S. Brooke, *Christian World Pulpit*, vol. lvi. p. 135. III. 12.—J. Keble, *Sermons for Sundays After Trinity*, pt. i. p. 166. III. 13-22.—C. Brown, *Trial and Triumph*, p. 125. III. 14, 15.—J. Keble, *Sermons for Sundays After Trinity*, pt. i. p. 176. A. Maclaren, *Expositions of Holy Scripture—Peter*, p. 116. III. 15.—E. J. Hardy, *Christian World Pulpit*, vol. lv. p. 104. T. Arnold, *Sermons*, vol. iii. p. 148. J. Bunting, *ibid.* vol. i. p. 309. C. J. Ridgeway, *The King and His Kingdom*, pp. 174 and 185. III. 15, 16.—J. Stalker, *Christian World Pulpit*, vol. xlix. p. 364. III. 16.—*Expositor* (5th Series), vol. vii. p. 368.

III. 17.—*Ibid.* (4th Series), vol. i. p. 142. III. 18.—W. P. Du Bose, *The Gospel According to St. Paul*, p. 143. J. D. Thompson, *Christian World Pulpit*, vol. xlviii. p. 42. R. Flint, *Sermons and Addresses*, p. 184. S. Baring-Gould, *Village Preaching for a Year* (2nd Series), vol. i. p. 192. W. J. Brock, *Sermons*, p. 285. Spurgeon, *Sermons*, vol. xliv. No. 2573. R. J. Campbell, *British Congregationalist*, 11th July, 1907, p. 29. *Expositor* (4th Series), vol. v. p. 187; *ibid.* (6th Series), vol. iv. p. 156. III. 18-20.—*Ibid.* vol. iii. p. 259. III. 19.—*Ibid.* vol. ii. p. 287; *ibid.* (5th Series), vol. vii. p. 222. Basil Wilberforce, *Christian World Pulpit*, vol. lvii. p. 369. R. F. Horton, *The Hidden God*, p. 81. H. J. Wilmot-Buxton, *Sunday Sermonettes for a Year*, p. 84. III. 20, 21.—J. Keble, *Village Sermons on the Baptismal Service*, p. 56.

A GOOD CONSCIENCE

'The answer of a good conscience.'—I PETER III. 21.

I. WE have to take note of a marvellous faculty, instinctive in human nature, which we have learned to call conscience, and having called it conscience have often dismissed out of our minds; a faculty which is recognised by everyone, however they may explain it; a faculty which enables us to know the difference between right and wrong, as the eye knows the difference between black and white. Every one of us knows that conscience exists.

II. And the second point which we must note is that conscience, although it is a gift of God to men, must, like all gifts, be educated and enlightened. There are some who seem to think that when they have done a thing conscientiously the question is over. It is not over at all. The question is, Ought they to have done that thing, however conscientiously? Has the conscience entrusted to them by God been sufficiently enlightened with all the light which is possible for them in order to make it act as God would have it act? If we are to gain the first essential element of Christian joy, the answer of a good conscience, we have to use every possible means in our power to keep our consciences enlightened.

III. Have we got it? (1) Have you the answer of a good conscience with regard to your city and business life? (2) Or, again, there are some who complain that they have no joy or happiness in their homes. Whose fault is it? Have you the answer of a good conscience, or is it your temper which is at the bottom of the unhappiness of your home?—BISHOP WINNINGTON-INGRAM, *Under the Dome*, p. 61.

REFERENCES.—III. 21.—*Expositor* (6th Series), vol. iv. p. 13. III. 22.—J. Keble, *Sermons for Ascension Day to Trinity Sunday*, p. 1. Spurgeon, *Sermons*, vol. xxxii. No. 1928. III. 24.—*Expositor* (6th Series), vol. v. p. 313. IV. 1.—F. D. Maurice, *Sermons*, vol. i. p. 333. F. J. A. Hort, *Village Sermons in Outline*, p. 226. J. M. Neale, *Sermons preached in Sackville College Chapel*, vol. i. p. 237. *Expositor* (4th Series), vol. v. p. 187; *ibid.* vol. viii. p. 358; *ibid.* (6th Series), vol. iv. p. 13. IV. 1, 2.—W. P. Du Bose, *The Gospel According to St. Paul*, p. 143. IV. 1-3.—Spurgeon, *Sermons*, vol. xliii. No. 2549. IV. 1-8.—A. Maclaren, *Expositions of Holy Scripture—Peter*, p. 123. IV. 1-11.—C. Brown, *Trial and Triumph*, p. 141. IV. 3.—S. A. Tipple, *The Admiring Guest*, p. 108. IV. 6.—*Expositor* (4th Series), vol. ii. p. 287; *ibid.* vol. iii. p. 370. IV. 7.—C. Vince, *The*

Unchanging Saviour, p. 315. T. F. Crosse, *Sermons* (2nd Series), p. 225. J. Barker, *Plain Sermons*, p. 62. Bishop Barry, *A Sermon Preached at St. Paul's Cathedral*, 17th April, 1894. Bishop Westcott, *Village Sermons*, p. 203. *Expositor* (6th Series), vol. vi. p. 53. IV. 7, 8.—J. J. Blunt, *Plain Sermons*, p. 228. IV. 8.—W. H. Hutchings, *Sermon-Sketches*, p. 1. J. Keble, *Sermons for Ascension Day to Trinity Sunday*, p. 93.

MANIFOLD GRACE

'The manifold grace of God.'—1 PETER IV. 10.

THE whole verse reads thus, 'Let every man that has received the gift even so minister the same one to another as good stewards of the manifold grace of God'. What is 'manifold'? Many? No. The word 'many' would be misleading, though it does enter into the larger and truer interpretation of the term. Manifold in this case means variegated, many in colour and light and bloom and beauty. Manifold is not in this relation a question of quantity or quality, but of variety; every colour a poem, all the colours belonging to one another and totalling up into one ineffable whiteness. Every man hath received the gift, therefore let him minister the same, and let one give to another, and let every man bring his colour to every other man's colour, and let all the world see how variegated in charm and hue is the total grace or gift of God. Every man holds his own colour of grace as a steward. Your colour is not mine, mine is not the colour held by some other man, but every man hath received his gift of God, his shade of colour. The shades of colour do not look well when they are taken away from one another; therefore they should be arranged into poems of brightness and bloom and fragrance; for God is the giver of them all. The holders of the variegated grace of God are only stewards.

I. This word 'manifold' occurs in many places, and it applies to good things and to bad things alike. There is nothing in the descriptive word itself, it is only when it is related to some substantive that it acquires a character or indicates a special utility of its own. Who expected to find this expression in Nehemiah, the busiest of the books, the wall-building book, the Balbus before the time. 'In Thy manifold mercies thou forsookedst them not' (Neh. IX. 19). The mercy is one, the mercies are ten thousand. Always distinguish between the substantial central quality and its radiations or offshoots or incidental distributions of forces. Mercy comes in many forms.

II. In that most wondrous of the psalms in many respects, the 104th, we read in the twenty-fourth verse, 'O Lord, how manifold are Thy mercies!' Why not say, How great is Thy mercy! That should be said, that has been said, but most of us are still in the lower school, and we have not quite got into the way of amalgamating and unifying the divers plurals and bringing them into one sublime and glowing unity. The Apostle Paul, most wondrous of writers and speakers, in one unconscious effort united the plurals and the singular in one grand expression, Ephesians III. 10—that album of wisdom, that temple of the uppermost and innermost piety. Paul there speaks of 'the manifold wisdom of God'. It is another variety of the text, 'the manifold grace of God'—the grace split up into attributes, into lines, separate individuality accentuated, and yet all gathering themselves up into grace, wisdom, love.

III. I must recall an idea just referred to, namely, that the word manifold is applied not only to things good, Divine, beautiful, but to other things. 'I know your manifold transgressions and sins' (Amos. v. 12). Every man sins in his own way, and every man condemns the sins of every other man. That is how we come to have the little clay idol called Personal Respectability—that miserable imp, that worst species of infidelity, if exaggerated and unduly applied and construed. Every man tries to make himself respectable by remarking upon the want of respectability in the man who is sitting next him : as who should say, You observe how critical I am, and how different I am from this person, although we are seated near to one another and are actually in the closest bodily proximity; yet how different I am from him! But the other man is saying exactly the same thing! That is the awkward part of the criticism. Mind yourself, take heed unto thyself. Pulling down another man's house does not make your own any more secure.

So then the word 'manifold' may be applied not only to the grace of God, the wisdom of God, and the mercy of God, but to the transgressions and the sins of men and to the temptations through which all souls that are being educated for heaven must needs pass. Be ye stewards of the grace which God has committed to you. It is a grace of wealth, a grace of leisure or of patience or of tenderness; you are gifted with the love of mankind, you have yearning hearts after the Lord; you have a great skill in seeing the best side of every man's character, and working upon the lost from the point of hope and the centre of possible restoration. Oh, do not look at the weed, look at the flower; do not look at the hardships, but look at the enjoyments. Wondrous is the mercy, the grace of God.—JOSEPH PARKER, *City Temple Pulpit*, vol. II. p. 13.

REFERENCES.—IV. 10.—J. Parker, *City Temple Pulpit*, vol. ii. p. 13. R. W. Church, *Village Sermons*, p. 126. A. E. Tonkin, *Christian World Pulpit*, vol. xliv. p. 323. H. M. Butler, *Harrow School Sermons* (2nd Series), p. 46. *Expositor* (6th Series), vol. vii. p. 275.

'THE ABILITY WHICH GOD GIVETH'

1 PETER IV. 11.

I. 'THE ability which God giveth': a religious ability, a spiritual faculty, a way of looking at things and doing things that is not common, that traces itself back to the sanctuary and the altar, and comes forth with some redness of blood upon it. This is a mystery we cannot put into words; yet we feel it. We feel fire, though we may not be able to understand all its composition and trace all its history.

'As every man hath received the gift.' That is the fundamental principle. We receive gifts; we do not invent them, we do not create them in any sense. All true gifts are gifts of God; from the Father of lights there cometh down every good and every perfect gift.

'As every man hath received the gift, let him be a good steward.' What of? 'Of the manifold grace of God.' The word 'manifold' means in that case many-coloured—the vermilion and the indigo and all the colours. It is a many-coloured grace. There is nothing monotonous in God. He never gives to two men the same gift. If they are openly and patently the same gift they are not so inwardly and spiritually; each has a note of its own, a comment of its own, a subtle expressive accent, that no other man can steal or successfully duplicate.

II. Here, then, we are called into the great doctrine of responsibility. What is the animating thought in the Apostle's mind? One likes to get back to the original impulse. There is a secret within a secret. You do this or that not because of the manifold reasons which are on the surface; all these may be only excuses, not reasons, not conclusions of the logical faculty, but something put forth that will do for the moment. What is the original impulse in Peter's fervent mind? The same impulse that was in Paul's still greater intellect. He said: Do all these things, for 'the end of all things is at hand'. Anybody can see beginnings—but to see the end! The Apostles grandly caught the spirit of their Master. They said, Jesus Christ will be here presently; He is at hand, He is almost visible; neglect no duty, discharge every obligation, regard life as a solemn responsibility, and be up! That is true; that is the spirit in which we ought to work. Work while it is called day, for the night cometh wherein no man can work. It is night in one aspect, it is the kingdom of morning in another. You shake hands with your friends and say, We will meet you to-morrow. Your friend is not at the trysting-place. How is this? Here is a telegram for you. What does it say? He died an hour after he parted from you. Is the tenure of life so brittle as that? Exactly; we are tenants at will; we have no lease; it is, so to say, a word-of-mouth arrangement, and one of the mouths has nothing to say about it, which is the Lord's mouth.

III. What, then, have we to do with regard to this doctrine, that all things are coming swiftly and suddenly to an end? What is the monition arising out of the declaration that the kingdom of God is at hand? It is this, that we are to do all our work as if it were the only work we have to do. Death is at the door; there is but a step between thee and death; thou knowest not what a day may bring forth. That is the atmosphere in which we have to work. We do not like it, but we did not create it, and we cannot abolish it; we can, so to say, utilise and sanctify it.

IV. 'As every man hath received the gift.' Here is individual endowment. Is that a fact? Yes, that is a fact. That is your opportunity and mine. I

have been envying the endowments of a man or woman—poet, statesman, preacher—and the Lord says, Why envy? The man who has the five gifts did not give them to himself; the five talents were given by the Lord; now it is for you to remember that you—your own very, very self—you have a gift. That should make men of us. Seeing that the image and the superscription of that gift is God's, how can we account ourselves penniless, how can we shiver as if we were orphaned and poor and driven out upon the face of the earth as mean mendicants? The question for each man to consider is, What is my one particular gift? I must burnish it, or use it, or, changing the figure, I must plant it, and set it in relation to all that spiritual chemistry which is proceeding throughout the whole creation, and who knows but that from that little root there may come something, perhaps beautiful, perhaps nutritious, perhaps fragrant?—JOSEPH PARKER, *City Temple Pulpit*, vol. iv. p. 280.

REFERENCES.—IV. 11.—W. M. Sinclair, *Christ and our Times*, p. 245. T. Arnold, *Sermons*, vol. ii. p. 143. J. Parker, *City Temple Pulpit*, vol. iv. p. 280. IV. 12, 13.—W. J. Knox-Little, *Christian World Pulpit*, vol. xlix. p. 232. IV. 12-19.—C. Brown, *Trial and Triumph*, p. 157. IV. 13.—J. Caird, *Sermons*, p. 167. IV. 14.—*Expositor* (5th Series), vol. v. p. 382. IV. 14-16.—*Ibid.* vol. vi. p. 144. IV. 15.—J. Parker, *City Temple Pulpit*, vol. vi. p. 97. J. G. Rogers, *Christian World Pulpit*, vol. liv. p. 296. J. Parker, *ibid.* vol. liii. p. 296. IV. 16-19.—W. H. Simcox, *The Cessation of Prophecy*, p. 114.

THE FORLORN RESCUE

'Scarcely saved.'—1 PETER IV. 18.

THE righteous are vividly conscious of the fact that more than once they escaped by a hair's breadth. Such are the weakness and folly of human nature that our salvation is rendered possible only in the infinite power and grace of God. The evolutionist knows that in the great struggle of nature competitive forms are so evenly balanced against each other that the slightest advantage determines the successful plant or animal. Darwin's words are these: 'A grain in the balance may determine which individuals shall live and which shall die; which variety or species shall increase in number, and which shall decrease or finally become extinct'. 'A grain in the balance.' Very astonishing is the vast part that the grain plays in deciding the mighty fortunes of nature. The presence or absence of the grain in the balance is equally decisive in society. That which determines between the successful and the unsuccessful, the rich and the poor, the famous and the forgotten, is often singularly insignificant—a mere particle. So the moral triumph of man repeatedly seems due to superiority in strength by just a degree. 'Scarcely saved.'

I. The special lesson we would now enforce is the immense importance of any gain whatever in the religious life. Many Christian people do not appreciate this fact, and accordingly despise the minute accessions of light and strength secured by daily study, vigilance, and effort. The minute gain of daily faithfulness is in its significance immense. Truth, a trifle more clearly discerned; faith, enhanced as by a grain of mustard seed; love, clinging by an added tendril; and hope, the anchor of the soul, somewhat more surely biting the solid ground, mean much in the history of a soul.

II. Let us take to heart the fact that the working out of our salvation is a serious thing, attended by infinite difficulty. We are familiar with peril in our natural life. There is far more tension of awareness in our natural life than at first appears. Yet the peril of the soul is certainly not less; and the best are conscious that they have nothing of which to boast. The most thrilling rescues of fire-ladder or life-boat are dull metaphors of the wonderful deliverances of the soul from sin and hell. Heaven must have held its breath several times over the best of us. Let us, then, take care that henceforth we put our whole soul into the work of its own salvation; despising nothing, neglecting nothing. There is no telling in our spiritual life with what vast consequences microscopic gains are fraught, or what tragedies the lack of those gains may entail. The atom becomes a spiritual rock which guarantees our salvation; the grain turns in our favour the balances of eternity.— W. L. WATKINSON, *The Ashes of Roses*, p. 52.

REFERENCES.—IV. 18.—H. Windross, *Preacher's Magazine*, vol. x. p. 558. Spurgeon, *Sermons*, vol. liii. No. 3047.

GOD'S FAITHFULNESS

'Wherefore let them that suffer according to the will of God commit the keeping of their souls to Him in well-doing, as unto a faithful Creator.'—1 PETER IV. 19.

FAITHFULNESS is the most beautiful thing which we have on earth. How, then, does this most touching characteristic appear in God? You will notice the special form in which St. Peter brings home his great conviction and appeal. In order to speak of faithfulness in God, especially as a faithful Creator, he might have taken the uniformity of nature, or he might have taken the faithfulness in history. But St. Peter chooses by preference another great field upon which may be tested the faithfulness of God. He chooses the land of Trouble. What a wonderful land that is! Just as nothing is so foolish as to underrate difficulties about religion, so nothing is so shallow as to underrate the crushing burden of the troubles which men and women have on earth sometimes to bear.

I. I ask those who have explored the land of Trouble whether they cannot witness to these three things: (1) First, that although the fire of suffering is sometimes very hot indeed—for, remember, He sits as a refiner and purifier of silver, and it wants a great deal of heat to purify silver—yet if a man does pray that prayer, 'Not my will, but Thine be done,' if he has prepared himself in Gethsemane, then he is conscious of an unseen and mysterious strength which is given him in the time of trouble; he is conscious of a great strong hand, as it were, holding him; he is conscious of some power which is temper-

ing the fire so that he can just bear it. (2) Is it not true that in the darkness of the land of Trouble comes also a mysterious form—Jesus Christ? (3) And, as in the beginning the Holy Spirit, the Spirit of order, brought the *kosmos*—order—out of chaos, so now that same Holy Spirit takes His part in the time of trouble.

II. But one word as to the conditions of receiving the faithfulness of God. St. Peter, with his wonderful touch, gives three of them. (1) Those that suffer must suffer according to the will of God. (2) The suffering of others must be according to the will of God. (3) And, lastly, 'in well-doing'. No morbid retrospect, no craving after a lost Paradise—if it is lost—no wrapping one's self up in selfish sorrow. No, the soul must fling itself forward in 'well-doing,' in good works. It must throw itself all the more forward for the sorrow of the past. The soul that does so inherits and deserves the faithfulness of God.— BISHOP WINNINGTON-INGRAM, *Under the Dome*, p. 115.

REFERENCES.—IV. 19.—Newman Smyth, *Christian World Pulpit*, vol. l. p. 43. V. 1.—Spurgeon, *Sermons*, vol. xlv. No. 2610. V. 2.—*Expositor* (5th Series), vol. i. p. 469. V. 3.—*Ibid.* (6th Series), vol. i. p. 397.

ST. ANDREW'S DAY

'And when the Chief Shepherd shall appear, ye shall receive a crown of glory that fadeth not away.'—1 PETER V. 4.

ST. ANDREW'S DAY has been set apart by the authorities of our Church for the consideration of the great subject of Foreign Missions, and I desire to bring it before you in the light of the Second Advent, for to-morrow, as you know, is Advent Sunday. 'When the Chief Shepherd shall appear.' As I hear that message it tells me three things.

I. There is a Chief Shepherd.—First it tells me that there is a Chief Shepherd. As we think of our great cities and of the millions of souls living in them, some of them so sad, so lonely, so tempted, it should be everything to us to know that there is a Chief Shepherd Who knows and cares for every one of them; that even those whom we cannot reach ourselves, He knows and tries to protect and care for. When, again, we think of the 800,000,000 of heathen and 180,000,000 of Mohammedans, it is everything to know that this world is not left to itself. There is a Chief Shepherd, and the claim which He makes is ringing unto the ends of the earth. 'All souls are Mine,' saith the Lord of Hosts, 'all souls are Mine'.

II. The Chief Shepherd is Near.—And then, secondly, this message tells us that the Chief Shepherd is near. When you read your New Testament in the Revised Version you will find that all those passages which speak of His appearing are translated when He is 'manifested,' and the old idea, founded I suppose on the parable of the man who went into a far country, that Jesus is a long way off somewhere is shown by those passages to be entirely erroneous. He is in the midst of us. There is one standing in our midst Whom we see not but Who is close by, and the word 'manifested' means that at the Second

Advent the veil will be taken from our eyes at a flash and we shall see Him Who is in the midst of us all the time. It is as if we came into this Church blindfolded, and suddenly, in a flash, the bandage is taken from our eyes and we see the Chief Shepherd Who was there all the time. The Chief Shepherd is not only alive, but near.

> Closer is He than breathing,
> Nearer than hands and feet.

III. We shall see the Chief Shepherd.—And here is the third point, that the one certain thing about our lives, be they long or short, be they sad or merry, is that we shall see the Chief Shepherd. Our eyes shall see Him. The one certain truth is that the Chief Shepherd will see us and that we shall see Him, and the only question that will matter in life will be not 'What do I think of Jesus Christ?' but 'What does He think of me?'

IV. A Message for Workers.—I need hardly point out what a message that is for all who are working for God. If we forget that our sole task in life is to gather in the thousands of souls, not only here but throughout the whole world, we shall incur the displeasure of the Chief Shepherd, because we only live to gather in souls for whom He died, and whom He loves. 'All souls are Mine,' saith the Lord of Hosts. Then every day, every night, with every power we have, before He comes again and before we see Him, let us seek to gather that great flock in all parts of the world. All through the beautiful Ordination service for a priest, it is his pastoral work which is impressed upon him again and again.

(a) *Can the Chief Shepherd rely upon you?* He says, 'Upon this rock I will build My Church; and the gates of hell shall not prevail against it'. He is building on you. The one hope of having a really missionary, loyal-hearted, honourable, God-fearing Church is on the laity who believe, and I want to ask you whether you are failing the Chief Shepherd in that place where He has placed you? In that warehouse or office, are you a man He can depend upon, a man of God, the one who witnesses, who is perfectly certain to be firm and will not have bad language used in the presence of boys or in his own presence, who stands up for truth and honesty in all dealings. Remember that Jesus Christ, the Chief Shepherd, Whom you have to see one day, and Who sees you now, looks to you as a rock man.

(b) *Are you gathering.* Then again, 'He that is not with Me is against Me, and he that gathereth not with Me scattereth'. If that does not mean that a man is not a Christian who takes no part in missionary work, I do not know what it means. Jesus Christ said of the world, 'All souls are mine'. He says of you, 'He that is not with Me is against Me; and he that gathereth not with Me scattereth'. When the Chief Shepherd shall appear, we shall find what He expected us to do. You dare not meet Him empty-handed. If in the spirit of pastoral work and pastoral service you live your life, when the Chief Shepherd

shall appear you shall receive a crown of glory **that** fadeth not away.

'When the Chief Shepherd shall appear.'—1 Peter v. 4.

WE know how it will be; to shepherds He will become the Chief Shepherd, to sailors the steersman, to travellers the guide, to soldiers the commander; He will bless the seed for the peasants, and He will sit at table with us, a daily invited guest, in the breaking of bread.—ADOLF DEISSMANN.

REFERENCES.—V. 4.—*Expositor* (4th Series), vol. ix. p. 4. V. 5.—*Christianity in Daily Conduct*, p. 45. W. H. Evans, *Short Sermons for the Seasons*, p. 101. H. Alford, *Quebec Chapel Sermons*, vol. ii. pp. 15, 30. F. D. Maurice, *Sermons*, vol. ii. p. 171. A. Maclaren, *After the Resurrection*, p. 182. V. 6.—Spurgeon, *Sermons*, vol xxix. No. 1733. J. M. Neale, *Sermons Preached in Sackville College Chapel*, vol. i. p. 134. *Ibid. Readings for the Aged* (4th Series), p. 26. V. 6, 7.—T. Arnold, *Sermons*, vol. ii. p. 173. J. J. Blunt, *Plain Sermons*, p. 105. F. J. A. Hort, *Village Sermons* (2nd Series), p. 167.

ATRA CURA
'All your care.'—1 Peter v. 7.

ATRA Cura—Black Care—was familiar to the light-hearted Roman poet. It was impossible to ride away from it; wherever the traveller went, it went with him.

After all these years of Christ the hard tyranny of circumstance is unloosened. Perhaps it never pressed so heavily as of late. Every morning there rises the great army of the careworn to take up the daily toils with sinking heart. Every day competition grows more savage, and success more difficult.

I. Atra Cura—Black Care—we find it everywhere —even in the gatherings of Christians. How is it going, they ask too anxiously, with the cause of truth and righteousness? There are hours when all but the bravest are overborne for the moment by the fierceness of the conflict—almost afraid to believe that the eternal summer draws nearer, and that the kingdom of God must come. When the grey clouds drift over the sky and the winds beat loudly and fiercely, there is no peace save for the soul that has learned to rise above the region of storms.

II. The argument against care, so frequently urged by our Lord and His Apostles, is always an argument for faith. When Christ began His ministry He pointed upward from the love that watched over the falling sparrow. If God was with the tiny dying bird, how much surer was His keeping of the children. And when at the last, under the shadow of the cross, Jesus sat reasoning with His disciples, He was still pleading for faith. *Let not your heart be troubled . . . believe.* He told them in slow, tender words that they were not to be afraid, for He was always to be with them. St. Paul argued downward from redemption to providence: God who spared not His own Son would not grudge bread. This then is the cure for care: a belief in the constant dumb tending of the Invisible.

III. This promise of unsleeping love does not mean that we are to escape the discipline of life. Rather, it signifies that we are to undergo it. Only the pain and darkness that may sometimes wrap us harshly round are not suffered to invade the central peace of the spirit. Such as they are, we are to have help in bearing them. Our Lord has never promised that we shall keep what money we have or that we shall gain more. He may see us to be too deeply involved in the complexities of living. In His wise love He may take us out of circumstances which make a true and spiritual life impossible, and set us in the great currents of humanity again. Perhaps Jesus never meant that life should grow all of one pattern and stuff. But if men come to think otherwise, true believers will have no temptation to resist them. Nothing material is to have supremacy over us. There is a deep sense in which Christians still must live outside their worldly possessions, and confess themselves to be strangers and pilgrims on the earth. —W. ROBERTSON NICOLL, *Ten-Minute Sermons*, p. 27.

'Casting all your care upon Him.'—1 PETER V. 7.

MR. A. C. BENSON remarks on this text: 'The strongest and best things in the world seem to me to be peace and tranquillity, and the same hidden power seems to be leading me thither ; and to lead me all the faster whenever I try not to fret, not to grieve, not to despair. " Casting all your care upon Him, for He careth for you," says the Divine Word ; and the more that I follow intuition rather than reason, the nearer I seem to come to the truth.'

REFERENCES.—V. 7.—Spurgeon, *Sermons*, vol. viii. No. 428. S. Gregory, *How to Steer a Ship*, p. 53. J. Keble, *Sermons for the Sundays After Trinity*, p. 474. G. B. F. Hallock, *Christian World Pulpit*, vol. lvi. p. 175. C. O. Eldridge, *Preacher's Magazine*, vol. xvii. p. 315. F. Bourdillon, *Plain Sermons for Family Reading*, p. 197.

1 PETER V. 8.

RUTH was half-way towards the impatient Mr. Bellingham when her old friend called her back. He longed to give her a warning of the danger that he thought she was in, and yet he did not know how. When she came up, all he could think of to say was a text ; indeed, the language of the Bible was the language in which he thought whenever his ideas went beyond practical everyday life into expressions of emotion or feeling. 'My dear, remember the devil goeth about as a roaring lion, seeking whom he may devour ; remember that, Ruth.' The words fell on her ear, but gave no definite idea. The utmost they suggested was the remembrance of the dread she felt as a child when this verse came into her mind, and how she used to imagine a lion's head with glaring eyes peering out of the bushes, in a dark shady part of the wood, which, for this reason, she had always avoided, and even now could hardly think of without a shudder. She never imagined that the grim warning related to the handsome young man who awaited her with a countenance beaming with love, and tenderly drew her hand within his arm.—MRS. GASKELL's *Ruth* (ch. IV.).

REFERENCES.—V. 8.—W. F. Shaw, *Sermon Sketches for the Christian Year*, p. 83. J. Bunting, *Sermons*, vol. ii. p. 47.

C. Bosanquet, *Blossoms from the King's Garden*, p. 139. S. A. Brooke, *Christian World Pulpit*, vol. xlv. p. 16. *Expositor* (6th Series), vol. iv. p. 190. V. 8, 9.—F. D. Maurice, *Sermons*, vol. i. p. 299. Spurgeon, *Sermons*, vol. vii. No. 419. H. M. Butler, *Harrow School Sermons*, p. 320. V. 9.—J. Keble, *Sermons for Sundays After Trinity*, pt. i. p. 74. F. Bourdillon, *Plain Sermons for Family Reading* (2nd Series), p. 180. V. 10.—J. J. West, *Penny Pulpit*, No. 1490, p. 57. Spurgeon, *Sermons*, vol. vi. No. 292, and vol. xxix. No. 1721. *Expositor* (4th Series), vol. i. p. 34. V. 10, 11.—J. Vaughan, *Fifty Sermons* (9th Series), p. 326.

'Silvanus, our faithful brother, as I account him.'— 1 PETER V. 12.

THIS is Peter's mature judgment on the character of his friend ; it is no hasty certificate, signed in a moment of good-nature. He had learned, from his own experience, how responsible a thing it is to permit ourselves to drift into friendships or associations with other people promiscuously. Hence these deliberate words may serve as a text for a sermon upon our responsibility for the influence exerted by others upon us, as well as for the ties of friendship which we form, and which quicken us into an activity for better or for worse.

(*a*) Peter knew how disastrous it was to let any sudden or strong influence determine one's actions. For the sake of personal safety he had allowed the maid-servant in the hall of judgment to control or at least affect his actions and utterances for the moment. For the sake of peace he had permitted the Jewish Christians at Antioch to divert him from the path of principle. (*b*) On the other hand, he had profited by the friendship of his brother Andrew (John I. 41), and by association with John and Paul, so that both the lapses and achievements of his life had been largely due to the influence of other people upon his character.

His personal history had thus made him careful and prudent by this time about human influence. Any impulsive, warm-hearted nature like his is too apt to admit the sway of other people from time to time without sufficient reflection, and this receptiveness may turn out fatally as well as happily. 'The friends thou hast, *and their adoption tried*' are the only ones who are, like Silvanus, to be held fast to the soul with hooks of steel. They must be judged trustworthy, and that judgment cannot rest upon the impression of the moment.—JAMES MOFFATT.

REFERENCES.—V. 12.—A. Maclaren, *Expositions of Holy Scripture—Peter*, p. 138 ; *ibid.* p. 146. *Expository Sermons on the New Testament*, p. 241. *Expositor* (7th Series), vol. vi. p. 287. V. 12, 13.—*Ibid.* (5th Series), vol. x. p. 319. For an Exposition of the whole Chapter see Rev. Charles Brown's *Trial and Triumph*, p. 172.

ST. MARK'S DAY
'Marcus, my son.'—1 PETER V. 13.

THE exact time when a religious festival was instituted in honour of St. Mark cannot now be positively determined ; it is nevertheless generally thought to have occurred about the ninth century, for it has been annually observed since then by the Greek, Latin, and other Churches with profound reverence, and finally on 25th April, because then, according to tradition, St. Mark suffered martyrdom at Alexandria in Egypt, where he fixed his chief residence.

But doubt does not end here: it attaches even to the Evangelist himself. Three other Marks are mentioned in Holy Scripture, while St. Mark changes his Hebrew name—John—to that by which he is now familiarly known in the Church. This was a common practice when Evangelists and Apostles were desirous of visiting the Gentile world on embassies of mercy; but it has generally added to the perplexity of deciding satisfactorily concerning some persons who have taken a leading part in sacred affairs. It is so in this instance. There are, however, some particulars respecting St. Mark which leave no room for doubt. His mother's name was Mary; and it was at her house the Apostles and other Christian brethren were hospitably received, and to which St. Peter repaired after his deliverance from prison by the angel of the Lord (Acts xii. 5-17).

I. St. Peter makes special and interesting allusions to him as Marcus in his earlier Epistle. He was a good man. St. Peter calls him his 'son,' just as St. Paul calls Timothy his 'son'—a phrase of Christian endearment which means that as St. Paul was the spiritual father of Timothy, so St. Peter was the spiritual father of Mark.

II. That he possessed a missionary spirit is clear. At first he was the devoted companion of St. Paul and St. Barnabas in some of their long journeys to propagate Christianity (Acts xii. 25; xiii. 5); but he withdrew himself in Pamphylia, because St. Paul contended with St. Barnabas about his going farther with them, and he, 'departing from them, returned to Jerusalem'. Soon after this, he joined himself to St. Peter, for he loved him as Timothy loved St. Paul. We next read of him as being with St. Peter in Babylon (1 Peter v. 13). Subsequently he visited Rome, at the express wish of St. Paul, in company with Timothy (2 Tim. iv. 11); but how long he remained in this famous city we cannot ascertain. Tradition says that he left it for Alexandria, where he planted a Church, and died and was buried. If all these things are true of him, and we can scarcely doubt them, then St. Mark loved not only his spiritual father, but the souls of men, and especially Him Who died to save them from perishing.

III. Finally we think of him as the writer of the second Gospel. This he did between the years fifty-six and sixty-three. As he was for a long time the intimate acquaintance of St. Peter, he heard from his lips the chief events of the life of Christ, and also the substance of His wonderful discourses. The unbroken testimony of the Fathers is—that St. Mark was the interpreter of St. Peter, and that he wrote under his eye and with his help. Another fact is equally certain —the right of his Gospel among the inspired books has never been questioned, nor that he was the writer of it. He loved the truth as the truth was in Jesus, and therefore gladly penned it for the everlasting welfare of mankind.

The acts and memories of such a man are fragrant as Eden, and wholesome in their influences, albeit over such a man there hangs the thick veil of mystery, and consequently he will never be fully known, either in bodily presence or saintly virtue, until he is seen 'face to face' in heaven, and all mysteries are cleared away for ever.

THE SECOND EPISTLE OF PETER

2 PETER

REFERENCES.—I. 1.—Spurgeon, *Sermons*, vol. xvi. No. 931. A. Maclaren, *Expositions of Holy Scripture—Peter*, p. 170. I. 1-4.—Spurgeon, *Sermons*, vol. x. No. 551. *Expositor* (6th Series), vol. x. p. 284. I. 3.—C. O. Eldridge, *Preacher's Magazine*, vol. xvii. p. 316. A. Maclaren, *Expositions of Holy Scripture—Peter*, p. 178.

STEPS TO A DIVINE GOAL

'Whereby are given unto us exceeding great and precious promises: that by these ye might be partakers of the Divine nature, having escaped the corruption that is in the world through lust.'—2 PETER I. 4.

I. PETER reminds us of the end to be achieved by those manifold assurances to which the Divine fidelity is pledged. 'That through these ye may become partakers of the Divine nature.' What a profound and original conception is this that God has expressly given to His people—promises through which they may reach a vital participation in His own sacred and glorious nature. In all human society there is an unhappy tendency to exclusiveness and self-absorption. Men want to save up for themselves and their children the best fruit of their thought and toil, to establish monopolies, to fence off their privileges from common use. The end of human law is to prevent the dispersion of the benefits which certain groups of men have made their own; whilst the end of all Divine law is to diffuse the gladness, the honour, and the power which once belonged to God alone. What a sublime contrast to our mean, grudging exclusiveness is presented in the free, illimitable expansiveness of God's self-communicating love. He wishes us not only to love after the pattern of His love, to set before ourselves the same objects and the same pursuits, to yearn with affections like His own, to share in the glory of His mighty acts; but to possess an interblended life, to feel His vitality uniting itself to our central consciousness, to be organic channels which hold the movements of His nature just as in the tissues and vessels of the child the royal life of the house to which he belongs is surging.

II. The Apostle specifies a condition which lies upon the threshold of this great ascent. 'Having escaped the corruption which is in the world through lust.' Participation in a Divine life and attachment to an evil world cannot be coincident, and the one state necessarily excludes the other. Escape from the corruption that is in the world through lust is the bigger half of the problem which confronts us in our upward progress. God cannot unveil to us the glory of His loving Fatherhood, nor can we prove the high dignity of our sonship, in the base and unworthy associations which sometimes detain us. We are not sin-proof angels, and we may allow ourselves to be so saturated in the tempers and traditions of the world, that our most sacred capabilities will be profaned, and the foregleams of Divine greatness in us eclipsed.

III. St. Peter reminds us of the part played by these inspired promises in uplifting human character and destiny. The promises are described as 'great and precious,' because they contemplate ends of startling vastness, and bring men, through the faith of which they are the warrant, to priceless honour and blessedness. They are precious as the blood in which the redemptive covenant is founded, precious as the priceless faith they create in meek and contrite hearts.

'Great and precious promises.'—2 PETER I. 4.

WHEN Isaac Watts was dying, and almost worn out by his infirmities, 'he observed, in conversation with a friend, that he remembered an aged minister used to say that the most learned and knowing Christians, when they come to die, have only the same plain promises of the Gospel for their support as the common and the unlearned; "and so," he said, "I find it. It is the plain promises, that do not require much labour and pains to understand them, for I can do nothing now but look unto my Bible for some promise to support me, and live upon that." He discoursed much of his dependence upon the atoning sacrifice of Christ: and his trust in God, through the Mediator, remained unshaken to the last. "I should be glad," he said, "to read more, yet not in order to be confirmed more in the truth of the Christian religion or in the truth of its promises; for I believe them enough to venture an eternity on them."'

'There are given unto us exceeding great and precious promises.'—2 PETER I. 4.

THIS text is closely associated with the spiritual history of John Wesley. For 26th May, 1738, he opened his Greek Testament at these words. His later note shows how he interpreted them: 'Being renewed in the image of God, and having communion with Him, so as to dwell in God and God in you'. In the afternoon of the same day he heard the anthem at St. Paul's Cathedral, 'Out of the deep have I called unto Thee, O Lord'.

REFERENCES.—I. 4.—Spurgeon, *Sermons*, vol. xvi. No. 931. R. F. Horton, *The Examiner*, 5th July, 1906, p. 649. D. L. Ritchie, *Christian World Pulpit*, vol. lxxviii. p. 244. *Expositor* (4th Series), vol. ii. p. 435; *ibid.* vol. iv. p. 119. A. Maclaren, *Expositions of Holy Scripture—Peter*, p. 189.

FAITH AND VIRTUE

'Add to your faith virtue.'—2 PETER I. 5.

THIS familiar verse has been altered considerably in the Revised Version, where it is given in the form: "In your faith supply virtue, and in your virtue knowledge, and in your knowledge temperance,' and so on. Some one has said that this rendering proved how little the Revisers knew of English prose; but however that may be, at all events their translation does give us a clue to the writer's real meaning. The older form has the preposition 'to' throughout—'add to your faith virtue,' and the rest; so that virtue, knowledge, and temperance, were made to appear as separate, detached things, each of which could be tied or stuck on to the others. '*In* your faith supply virtue' means something different. It means that faith is the root from which virtue grows up. These graces, in short, are not ready-made articles, which we can appropriate and use mechanically, like the dressed and polished blocks of stone one sees in a builder's yard. Instead, they are as closely related as the members of a live body. They flourish together, and they decay together; so near is the affinity and sympathy between them. A man who lacked any one of them entirely could have no real share in any other; just as a chain, one link of which is broken, will bear no weight whatever, be the other links ever so strong. He who has no patience, or no temperance, or no brotherly love is not merely an imperfect Christian; he is not a Christian at all.

So that it would be a good deal more true—though of course every metaphor breaks down somewhere—to say that the reciprocal connections of these graces are like those between the parts of a living tree. The twig sprouts from the branch, the branch runs down into the trunk, and the trunk stands broad-based upon the roots. In the same way, these verses give us the family tree of the Christian graces. Very likely the writer had no thought of the time-order in which they appear; time has comparatively little to do with such matters. He sets them before us rather in the order of their natural relationship. Each acts upon all, and all commence simultaneously. Brotherly kindness is near the foot of the list, and temperance is near the top; yet they were born the same hour.

I. Note, first, that *faith is the root from which the graces spring*. By faith, I need hardly remind you, the writer means faith in the Lord Jesus Christ. The trustful apprehension of God's unspeakable gift, of the mercy which rose over the world like a bright dawn when the Redeemer came—that is what he intends by the word. This is worth mentioning; for it is not uncommon to speak of faith abstractly, as no more than a hopeful, positive, serious way of regarding life. But when the New Testament writers say 'faith,' they mean quite definitely, faith in contact with its proper object, Christ, and becoming only through that contact a strong triumphant thing. Now and then religion is talked of as though it were but the reaching out of an empty hand gropingly and

tentatively into vacancy, like some timid insect waving helpless feelers in the air. That is not our situation. True, there was a time, a time of long grief and pain consumed in experiment and exploration; but it was closed at last; closed, too, not half so much by man's finding God as by God's finding and redeeming man. In Jesus the Father has come amongst us, near enough to be touched, near enough to be grasped; and that touch, that grasp, is faith.

If there is no faith towards the Lord Jesus Christ, no consent of the will, no outgoing of the heart, no yielding of the whole nature, then the great result cannot follow. It is useless to look up to, and covet, this beautiful cluster of graces if we are unwilling to fulfil the conditions and to commence at the commencement. Christ's gifts are ours only as we take Christ Himself.

II. Note that *faith is essentially prospective*. The Greek word translated 'supply' is a very full and suggestive one. It is a word with a history. It takes us back to the days in old Athens when it was reckoned a high honour by a citizen to be asked to defray the expenses of a public ceremony. Translate that idea into the language of religion, and bring it down to date, and it means, does it not, that God is willing to launch us into the Divine life, and to sustain us in it, but we must help to meet the cost? For of course the Christian life cannot be lived without expenditure; expenditure of a moral and spiritual kind, which goes on all the time. Are you willing to take a share in that? God gives us Christ, and all the grace enclosed in that dear name; He gives us the cross; He gives the open grave of Easter morning; will you undertake to supply virtue, knowledge, patience? Surely religion is to cost us something. Not simply in money, real as its claim on money is; but in effort, in prayer, in vigilance, in renunciation. These stand for the expenses of the Christian discipleship, and every follower of the Son of God must meet them. True, in order to afford them we may have to pinch ourselves somewhere else. Far too often religion is thought of as a realm in which the rules of common sense may be flouted with impunity; but here also people who try find that impossible. If we waste our love and enthusiasm on lower things, how little is there left for God and Christ!

III. Note, lastly, *what we are bidden to supply—virtue*. Plainly the word 'virtue' cannot bear in this passage its widest and most general meaning. That is to say, it cannot stand for the whole class, the entire round, of moral and spiritual excellences. Otherwise, if its scope were really so wide as this, it would be superfluous to say further on, 'to your knowledge add temperance, and to your temperance, patience'; for these qualities would have been already implied. When we look at the word more closely, therefore, and recollect that 'virtue' in its antique sense denoted something vigorous, manly, strong, we may bring it to a point by naming it *moral courage*. To your faith add moral courage

—that is the real message of our text.—H. R. MACKINTOSH, *Life on God's Plan*, p. 228.

2 PETER I. 5 f.

THE progress of which St. Peter speaks is a development from within. It is not the impartation to a certain quality of a thing not originally there; it is the unfolding from it of a thing which is latently there. It is the bringing out into bloom that life of the flower which sleeps already in the bud; the expansion into meridian glory of the sunshine slumbering in the dawn. It is an exhortation to expand the life of the germ, to remember what possibilities are folded within the germ. This faith, in itself so small a thing, is declared to be the seed of all other things.—GEORGE MATHESON, *Landmarks of Christian Morality*, pp. 147, 148.

REFERENCES.—I. 5.—E. White, *Christian World Pulpit*, vol. xlvi. p. 323. H. R. Heywood, *Sermons and Addresses*, p. 184. Basil Wilberforce, *Sanctification by the Truth*, pp. 129, 138. A. Maclaren, *Expositions of Holy Scripture—Peter*, p. 198. I. 5, 6.—J. Keble, *Sermons for Sundays After Trinity*, pt. i. p. 1. I. 5-7.—J. Iverach, *Christian World Pulpit*, vol. xlvi. p. 91. I. 6.—A. B. O. Wilberforce, *Christian World Pulpit*, vol. xlv. p. 218. Basil Wilberforce, *Sanctification by the Truth*, pp. 150, 160, 170. I. 6, 7. J. Keble, *Sermons for Sundays After Trinity*, pt. i. p. 10. I. 7.—Basil Wilberforce, *Sanctification by the Truth*, p. 180.

THE MAN WHO CANNOT SEE FAR ENOUGH

'He that lacketh these things is blind, and cannot see afar off.'—2 PETER I. 9.

'*The Short-sighted Man*' is our subject, and the Apostle brings him before us rather strikingly. The word oculists use for physical short-sightedness is 'Myopia'. It is a term which signifies the flattening of the lens of the eye in such a way that the vision of the distant is blurred and dim. Now this is exactly the Greek word the Apostle uses here when he says of this man, 'He cannot see afar off'. In a word, he is suffering from spiritual Myopia. Though keen enough in descrying things that are near, he is spiritually incapable of appreciating things that are far away.

As in the case of the long-sighted man, so here this defect of vision may assume two forms. It may have regard to the past or the future. It may be a blindness in the vision of memory or in the vision of anticipation. A man may be blind by forgetfulness or heedlessness.

I. It is the first of these the writer of this Epistle has specially in his mind. 'He that lacketh these things,' he says, speaking of the graces of a holy life, 'is blind,' inasmuch as '*he hath forgotten that he was purged from his old sins*'.

It was so with the man of our text. There was a time in his life when his heart throbbed with a great emotion, when Christ was a reality in his soul, when he looked in vision to the cross, and felt as he did so that the guilt of his sins was rolled away, that he was 'purged from his old sins'. Christ crucified has died out of his life. Faith in the evangelic Gospel has be-

come faint and far away. Love to the Saviour has grown cold. He has 'forgotten that he was cleansed from his old sins'. He has become dim, short-sighted in his vision of a great past.

What is the cure for spiritual short-sightedness? Is it not just the uplifting of the eyes? The 'man with the muck-rake' would never have grovelled in the dirt had his eye caught sight of the golden crown above his head. 'I will lift mine eyes unto the hills from whence cometh mine aid.' The great hills of God with their distant horizons and elevations—these are what are needed to give coolness and healing to the eyes contracted with the things of earth.

II. But while our text has a message for those who cannot see afar into their past, it has one no less insistent for those *who cannot look out into the dim distances of the future*.

God has not left us without a rough sketch-plan of our future. 'I will show thee the path of life,' He says to the obedient soul; and though there may be many surprises in that path, its general direction is governed by great spiritual laws that never change.

I remember a man once telling me of a terrible time of physical distress in his life. Business worries and overwork robbed him of all his nervous resilience. Sleep forsook him. Madness stared him in the face. He left his business, and went from place to place in the weary search for health. But during all that time one resolve kept firm in his heart. He would never use narcotics of any kind to procure forgetfulness of his misery or the rest that nature denied. He was advised to do it again and again, even by skilled advisers. But to all he said, 'No! I foresee what the end of that will be. I shall become a slave to some terrible habit, and die a coward's death. Let me die, if die I must, fighting.' So he fought and won. Who is ever beaten when he fights so? I never knew one. He came back a stronger man both in body and mind and soul.

Far-sightedness has also another value. It may be an inspiration in discouragement as well as a deterrent in danger. It may spur on the runner as well as caution the foolhardy. As in the Greek games the laurel lifted high encouraged the racer, so in life's conflict the vision of the distant prize urges on the competitor and revives his ardour.—W. MAC-INTOSH MACKAY, *Bible Types of Modern Men*, p. 163.

RELIGIOUS NEAR-SIGHTEDNESS

'He that lacketh these things is blind, and cannot see afar off, and hath forgotten that he was purged from his old sins.'—2 PETER I. 9.

To know what these deficiencies that maim a man's religious life are, we must turn back to the category of qualities needing cultivation that Peter gives us. 'To faith add virtue.' Virtue, or inward strength, connects itself with the will, for it is through the will it works. 'To virtue knowledge.' It is through all the channels of the intellectual life that knowledge is received and treasured. 'And to knowledge temperance.' Temperance is concerned with the government of the passions; and God, in cleansing a man from his past pollutions, seeks the subjection of well-ruled passions to His service. 'To temperance patience.' Patience connects itself with the sensibilities, through which we are made to suffer. In cleansing a man, God seeks the after-harmony of all his sensibilities with the Divine will. 'And to patience godliness.' In separating a man from evil, God seeks for the response of all the religious faculties to His operations. 'And to godliness brotherly kindness and charity.' These qualities link themselves with the sphere of the affections. The Apostle describes the lack of these things, first, under the metaphor of a grave defect in one of the leading physical senses ; and, secondly, under the figure of a lapse in the working of the intellectual powers.

I. He who is wanting in one or all of these high qualities lacks the primary organ of perfect spiritual perception. 'He is blind.' How many of us have inadequate views of what salvation means! Some people see nothing in salvation but deliverance from wrath and tempest and everlasting fire. A miserably defective view that is ! God does not save us to put us on to some secure level of moral mediocrity and to leave us here, but to bring us into fellowship with Himself. 'He that lacketh those things is blind.' And now Peter softens the expression and substitutes a somewhat milder term. At best the blindness is half-blindness. 'He cannot see afar off.' He discerns the near, but is quite at fault when he comes to deal with the distant.

II. Again, St. Peter describes the lack of these higher Christian excellences under the figure of an intellectual lapse. 'Having forgotten the cleansing from his old sin.' The worth of a conversion may be lost through imperfect recollection. The very bases of all high and holy relationship to God, and of all noble, spiritual possibilities, are lost when a man forgets that he was purged from his old sin, and illustrates the forgetfulness in the neglect of these high excellences of character.

III. These words imply that the memory of past grace will be a living and effectual inspiration to us at each successive step of our perfecting. An unbroken and ever grateful remembrance of the love God showed to us when He first saved us will inspire us to meet the loftiest demands of our Christian life and obligation. All imperfection has its root in ingratitude and indifference to past grace.

EMANCIPATION FROM THE PAST
2 PETER I. 9.

LET us at once recognise the inevitable struggle by which emancipation from the past is achieved, and yet insist on the glorious possibility of complete redemption.

I. The condemnation of the past must be dealt with. The solemn truth that 'God requireth that which is past' is registered in our conscience, and urged by it. The thoughtless regard forgiveness as the simplest, easiest, and least costly of acts ; and old sins are dropped into oblivion indifferently with old almanacs. Yet, awakening to the truth of things, we are at once acutely conscious of the extreme seriousness of the pride, self-will, and wickedness which poisoned the years that have gone. For the first time sin becomes a reality. Conscience knows nothing of the facility of absolution. Science finds no place for clemency. Government does not find it easy to forgive. When we come to think deeply and truly, to give conscience a chance, to reason out our action as in the sight of God, we know that nothing short of a miracle can purge our guilt, and set us free from the dead, unrighteous past clamouring for our blood. That miracle has been wrought in Christ. The whole of revelation testifies that God did not find it easy to forgive. The elaborate system of temple worship and sacrifice depicted in the Old Testament symbolised the majesty of moral law and the immense difficulty of showing mercy to the sinner. And this is the tremendous problem which the New Testament sets itself to solve. Leave the old life and the old sins in the depths of God's love, Christ's merit, the Holy Spirit's grace. Then ours is the peace that passeth understanding, and we shall not be confounded.

II. The energy of indwelling evil is a portentous difficulty to be mastered. No sooner do we seriously challenge the evil of our nature than it acquires a vitality and force which surprise and confound us. Once more we come to a miracle of grace. The schism, strife, and sorrow of human nature are healed in the truth and love of Christ Jesus. The spirit of life in Christ Jesus makes us free from the law of sin and death.—W. L. WATKINSON, *The Supreme Conquest*, p. 36.

SPIRITUAL SHORT-SIGHTEDNESS
'Seeing only what is near.'—2 PETER I. 9.

THESE people of whom the Apostle speaks were in a word *short-sighted* people. They had accepted the Gospel when it was first preached, but they had never taken religion seriously. They had not given diligence to add virtue to faith, knowledge to virtue, and temperance to knowledge, and patience to temperance, and godliness to patience, and love to godliness. There had been no serious striving after sanctification. They had made no attempt to pluck up and root out and cast forth the pleasant vices of the flesh to which they had once been addicted. They had never made an effort at the daily self-denial, and the daily bearing of the cross, and the daily purification.

I. First, let me speak of *short-sightedness and sin*. Sin brings with it an immediate gratification. The Bible recognises this quite frankly. It speaks of the *pleasures* of sin. Sin at the moment means delight ; ultimately it means death. At the moment it promises pleasure ; in the long run it means the worm that dieth not, and the fire that is not quenched. And men sin because they blind themselves to all that seems far off and remote, to the regret, and remorse, and shame, and hell that sin entails ; and have eyes only for what is nearest—the immediate gratification. The covetous man sees his growing heap of gold, and not his lean and shrivelled soul. The drunkard sees satisfaction for his appetite, and not the drunkard's grave. The profligate sees gratification for his burning lust, and not the profligate's hell. Short-sightedness is the mother of sin. Men sin because they only see what is near.

II. Secondly, let me speak of *short-sightedness and worldliness*. Really *worldliness* is only one form of sin, and on the principle that the greater includes the less, all that I have said about *sin* applies also to worldliness.

The reason for the prevalent and well-nigh universal sin of *worldliness* is *spiritual short-sightedness*. The prizes that earth offers are palpable, tangible, immediate. They engross men's attention, they absorb their thought, they fill the horizon of their desire. Heaven and the smile of Christ, and the well-done of God, seem remote, far off, uncertain. Money, pleasure, fame, banish them from the mind, and to the acquisition of these things men devote themselves, seeing only 'what is near'.

Our safety lies in the *long look*. Let no one persuade you that the thought of heaven is the mark of the dreamy and unpractical man. Charles Kingsley was one of the most strenuous and practical of men, but heaven was never absent from his thought Dr. Dale was the last man in the world against whom a charge of sentimentality could be brought, but how large a place heaven occupied in his thinking may be gathered by the space allotted to hymns about the better country in the book which he compiled. The thought of heaven is no dreamy unpractical thing; it is the means by which we are to emancipate ourselves from slavery to the transient and the perishing.

III. Thirdly, let me say a word about *short-sightedness* and *despair*. We sometimes fall into despondency and something like despair in our Christian service. There come times to us all when we feel like Elijah when under the juniper tree, and we say like him, 'Lord, let me die, for I have laboured for nought, and in vain'. What is the cause and origin of our despondency? Short-sightedness. We have only looked at the things which are near.

And the remedy for that hopelessness and despair is the *long look*. 'Lift up your eyes on high,' says the old Book. We despair when we see only the things that are near—the sin, the vice, the indifference and callousness of men; but we gain courage and hope when we see God.—J. D. JONES, *Elims of Life*, p. 124.

FORGETTING THE CLEANSING

2 PETER I. 9.

'HE that lacketh these things.' What things? The radiant treasures are named in a previous verse: faith, virtue, knowledge, temperance, patience, godliness, love of the brethren, love. Let us grasp the order of the Apostle's thought. 'Having forgotten the cleansing.' That is not the ultimate consequence;

it is the primary cause. The 'lack' and the 'blindness' do not create the forgetfulness, they are created by it.

I. 'Having forgotten.' Forgotten what? 'The cleansing.' In the New Testament there is a recognised gradation in the importance of duties. Some of the commandments are described as 'least' and others as 'greatest'. There is a similar gradation in the importance of truths. 'I delivered unto you first of all' the truths concerning the 'cleansing'; 'first of all,' as of primary and unspeakable import. 'Christ died for our sins'; 'first of all,' as radical and alphabetic, in which everything which seeks to be positive and enduring must take its root. 'He was delivered for our offences, and was raised again for our justification.' You know the exalted eminence which these truths occupied in the teachings of the Apostle Paul. 'First of all,' proclaimed the Apostle Paul, 'Christ died for our sins.' 'First of all,' repeats the Apostle Peter, 'Christ hath once suffered for sins, the just for the unjust, that He might bring us to God.' 'First of all,' cries the Apostle John, 'the blood of Jesus Christ His son cleanseth us from all sin.' Now, what did they claim for the work? They claimed that the truth was a Gospel of *power*, 'the power of God unto salvation'. Let the primary truths have the primary place; let them be princes in the conscious life; and the princes of consciousness will appear as principles in conduct, filling life with moral passion and enthusiasm, and converting a reluctant drudgery into an exultant freedom.

II. But, now, obliterate the energising truth. What then? The practical will become the impracticable. You cannot expunge the theology and retain the morality. Dethrone the cleansing, and you chill the passion for perfectness; exalt the cleansing, and moral enthusiasm becomes abounding. We have abundant confirmation of the sequence in the history of the Christian centuries.

III. What is the ultimate issue? 'Blindness.' What we cease to crave for we cease to see. When moral passion cools, moral ideals fade, or we see 'only what is near'. Life having lost its background, loses its foreground. That is the order and succession of this appalling degeneracy—forgetfulness of grace, moral laxity, lost ideal. Turn the matter round. If we are to see clearly, if we are to behold the heavenly, to appreciate it, to be responsive to the allurements of the ideal and the eternal, our moral life must have passionate enthusiasm, and for a passionate enthusiasm the consciousness needs to be possessed by the great energising truths of the cleansing.—J. H. JOWETT, *Apostolic Optimism*, p. 247.

REFERENCES.—I. 1-9.—J. D. Jones, *Elims of Life*, p. 124. *Expositor* (6th Series), vol. vi. p. 55.

2 PETER I. 10.

I BELIEVE that we are all called and elected to eternal life, but that we may frustrate the counsel of God, and that therefore we are exhorted to make our calling and election sure, not to make ourselves sure that we are called and elected, but to make our undoubted calling and election firm, solid, as Æschines said of the democracy. The democracy existed, but it might be made sure, or it might be sapped by the factious oligarchy.—T. ERSKINE, *Letters*, p. 396.

REFERENCES.—I. 10.—H. W. Webb-Peploe, *The Record*, vol. xxvii. p. 797. Bishop Welldon, *The Gospel in a Great City*, p. 141.

HOLY DILIGENCE AND HOLY AMBITION

'Wherefore the rather, brethren, give diligence to make your calling and election sure: for if ye do these things ye shall never fall: For so an entrance shall be ministered unto you abundantly into the everlasting kingdom of our Lord and Saviour Jesus Christ.'—2 PETER I. 10, 11.

WHAT do Peter's words: 'Make your calling and election sure' mean? Was he suspicious of the people to whom he was writing? Had he any doubt about their election and their calling? Both his Epistles were written to precisely the same people, for in his second Epistle he says: 'This second Epistle, beloved, I now write unto you'. He was writing 'to the strangers scattered throughout Pontus, Galatia, Cappadocia, Asia and Bithynia, elect according to the foreknowledge of God,' so that he had no doubt about their election, and he did not seem to have any doubt about their calling, for he said, 'ye are a chosen generation, a royal priesthood, a holy nation, a peculiar people: that ye should show forth the praises of Him Who hath called you'. He was writing to men and women who had received the effectual call of the Holy Ghost.

I. How are we to make sure of our calling? By finding out what are the characteristics of God's call. (1) God's call is to holiness, and if we are able to say that we long for holiness we may be sure that we have received the call of God. (2) It is also a call that leads to the glorifying of the Lord Jesus, and if in any humble measure Jesus is being glorified in us, then our calling has been made sure.

II. There is holy ambition in the text. There is to be the abundant entrance.—A. G. BROWN, *The Baptist*, vol. LXXI. p. 420.

REFERENCES.—I. 10, 11.—Spurgeon, *Sermons*, vol. iii. No. 123. R. F. Horton, *Christian World Pulpit*, vol. lix. p. 297. C. D. Bell, *The Name Above Every Name*, p. 193. T. Binney, *King's Weigh-House Chapel Sermons*, p. 138. I. 11.—*Expositor* (4th Series), vol. i. p. 34. I. 11, 15.—A. Maclaren, *Expositions of Holy Scripture—Peter*, p. 206. I. 12, 17.—*Ibid.* (6th Series), vol. x. p. 285. I. 15.—H. Melvill, *Penny Pulpit*, No. 1597, p. 175. *Expositor* (5th Series), vol. vi. p. 270. I. 16.—*Ibid.* (6th Series), vol. vi. p. 49; *ibid.* (7th Series), vol. v. p. 505. D. Heagle, *That Blessed Hope*, p. 27.

THE THREE TABERNACLES

'For we have not followed cunningly devised fables, when we made known unto you the power and coming of our Lord Jesus Christ, b t were eye-witnesses of His Majesty, when we were with Him in the holy mount.'—2 PETER I. 16, 18.

THE body of Moses, about which St. Michael the Archangel had contended with Satan, the. body which had been buried by God in a valley over against Bethpeor, no man knowing its resting-place, appeared in glory. The body of Elias, which had been taken up in a chariot of fire and horses of fire, returned once more to earth. The giver of the law and the greatest of Prophets, came to bear' witness to Him that was Maker of the Law, and the inspirer of the prophets. Now was fulfilled that which was written by Isaiah—'Then the moon shall be confounded, and the sun ashamed, when the Lord of Hosts shall reign in Mount Sion and in Jerusalem, and before His ancients gloriously'.

I. And what did they talk of? 'They appeared in glory and spake of His decease.' To talk of death in the height of this glory! To talk of a shameful death, a death of agony, amidst such brightness as the world had never before seen! Yes, but the text does not end so. They 'spake of His decease which He should accomplish'. What a wonderful word! When do we speak thus? We say that a man accomplishes deliverance from death, but to accomplish death itself, who would thus talk? And still further, 'they spake of his decease which He should accomplish in Jerusalem'. Now Jerusalem means the vision of peace. For it was by His death that He reconciled man to God. And that indeed was a glorious subject for a season of glory. This was a brighter and better vision than Moses had, when he got him to the top of Pisgah, and beheld all the land which God had promised to His people. This was a nobler prospect than Elijah had, when the chariot was bearing him up above the clouds and his mantle fell from off him.

II. St. Peter would speak, 'It is good for us to be here, and let us make three tabernacles. No, good Peter. This is not what we want. We want not three tabernacles but one mansion. We want no tabernacles that can be taken down and removed; we want a house not made with hands, that can never be shaken. And we only want one. There is but one hiding-place from the wind, one covert from the tempest, one ark. Our Lord Jesus Christ is all this; and He is one.—J. M. NEALE, *Sermons in Sackville College Chapel*, vol. IV. p. 85.

THE GOSPEL OF CERTAINTY

'For we have not followed cunningly devised fables, when we made known unto you the power and coming of our Lord Jesus Christ, but were eye-witnesses of His Majesty. For He received from God the Father honour and glory, when there came such a voice to Him from the excellent glory, This is My Beloved Son, in whom I am well pleased. And this voice which came from heaven we heard, when we were with Him in the holy mount. We have also a more sure word of prophecy; whereunto ye do well that ye take heed, as unto a light that shineth in a dark place, until the day dawn, and the day-star arise in your hearts: knowing this first, that no prophecy of the Scripture is of any private interpretation. For the prophecy came not in old time by the will of man; but holy men of God spake as they were moved by the Holy Ghost.'—2 PETER I. 16-21.

IN our text Peter sets forth the lines of evidence in favour of Christianity. They are three: Oral Testimony, Scripture, and Personal Experience. 'A threefold cord is not quickly broken.'

I. As to Oral Testimony. He says: 'We have not followed cunningly devised fables, when we made known unto you the power and coming of our Lord

Jesus Christ : *but were eye-witnesses of His Majesty*.'
(1) Such evidence has valid weight. We are all the
while accepting it. Ninety-nine per cent. of our
knowledge comes by hearsay. We receive the testimony of eye-witnesses unless there is a special reason
for rejecting it. (2) Such evidence, in favour of
Christianity, has a vast cumulative value for us. There
are some hundreds of millions of people living to-day
who are prepared to testify as to their personal experience in the saving power of the Gospel. It is
submitted that so great a body of testimony is of
overwhelming weight. The only question is as to the
character of the witnesses. Can their credibility be
impeached ? Peter and his fellow-apostles were men
of humble origin but unquestioned honesty, who had
everything to lose and nothing to gain by their championship of the crucified Nazarene ; and with their
blood they sealed their devotion to Him. And what
shall be said of those who constitute the Universal
Church of to-day ? Let a thousand be taken at ran-
dom from any fellowship of believers, and a thousand
from without ; and let a just comparison be made between them. We will abide the issue. It was by
such comparison that Alexander Pope, himself an unbeliever, was moved to make this historical definition :
' A Christian is the highest style of man '.

II. The next line of evidence is Scripture ; of which
Peter says : ' We have also *a more sure word of prophecy*, whereunto ye do well that ye take heed, as
unto a light that shineth in a dark place '. It is obvious that there must be somewhere a final criterion
of truth. It cannot be supposed that the Heavenly
Father would set His children adrift without a chart
for their direction. This is the ground and rationale
of the Scriptures. They were intended to be our ultimate and infallible rule of faith. And they are so
received, despite all controversy, by the Universal
Church. (1) The Apostle justifies his confidence in
the Scriptures by adding that they ' come not by the
will of man ; but holy men spoke as they were moved
by the Holy Ghost '. (2) Still further, the Apostle
says that the Scriptures so written are not ' of any
private interpretation '. The word rendered ' private '
is literally ' one's own '. This means that no man is
his own interpreter.

III. One more line of evidence is named by Peter :
to wit, Personal Experience. Personal experience
adds final confirmation to oral testimony and Scripture. All voices, human and Divine, are ineffective
until by vital appropriation we make the Gospel an
indwelling fact. The truth is put beyond all peradventure when the day star arises in our hearts. One
thing is better, and only one—to see Him in the
brightness of His heavenly glory.—D. J. BURRELL.
The Gospel of Certainty, p. 9.

REFERENCES.—*Expositor* (6th Series), vol. vi. p. 53. I. 17-
20.—Bishop Gore, *Christian World Pulpit*, vol. liv. p. 88. I.
18.—C. S. Robinson, *Simon Peter*, p. 279. *Expositor* (5th
Series), vol. viii. p. 467 ; *ibid.* (7th Series), vol. v. p. 367. I. 19.
—E. T. J. Marriner, *Sermons Preached at Lyme Regis*, p. 19. I.
19-21.—*Expositor* (6th Series), vol. vi. p. 54 ; *ibid.* vol. x. p. 286.

WATER FROM THE FOUNTAIN

' Knowing this first, that no prophecy of the Scripture is of any
private interpretation.'—2 PETER I. 20.

THE idea of the passage is this : it is a very difficult
passage, but this is the gist and pith of it : No
prophecy is a dream of the prophet ; in fact, the
prophet has little or nothing to do with it ; he is a
mere instrument through which the revelation comes,
and when he is out of his prophetic mood, he is conscious that great presences have passed before his
vision, that great questions have been stated, and
great visions have been seen. He is a mere instrument. The organ is not the music ; it is but the
instrument through which the music is expressed.

I. Now see what flows from this interpretation of
the text. First of all, the prophecy is not human
literature. It is something more, it is a quantity
beyond. It leads me away and away, over fields and
pastures, through forests and vineyards, farther and
farther, until I lose it for a moment in heaven itself.
The Bible is an immeasurable book ; it begins, but
never ends. Are you making this use of the Bible ?
Do you say, ' It is literature, and being literature, it
ought to be measured by the dictionary and the
grammar ? ' What can they measure ? They are
poor instruments ; they can go but a very little way
in the interpretations of Divine visions and revelations. Know that your vision is right when it leads
you into self-forgetfulness, self-sacrifice, and the very
passion of devotion. Where are our passionate men
to-day, men all fire, all heat, all earnestness ? If the
Bible were only literature, it would be, of course,
measured by the lexicon and by the grammar ; but it
is not mere literature, but as I have already said,
literature and something more, and what that something more is the Holy Ghost must teach us.

II. And then, secondly, this proposition that the
Bible is not mere human literature is proved by its
quality. There is none like it ; I never tasted water
like this. I know this Bible river by the quality of
its waters, and its general content. Some people
read out of the Bible all its meaning, and they are
likely to blame the vision of the seers who read into
it what they imagine is foreign matter. My brother
preachers, we must get into the spirit, into the
original poetry and thought of the Bible, before we
can really understand it ; and when I am there, I am
in the secret places of the tabernacles of the Most
High, and the waters of criticism good or bad never
rise to that mighty, wondrous level. You strive
after the spirit, and you need have no fear, and will
have no fear, that the Bible has had its day. Salvation is not of grammar, but of sympathy.

I do not want to know what David said, I want to
know what the Spirit meant by the mouth of David.
We must not say, David did not write this Psalm, or
David could not have written this Psalm ; David was
dead five hundred years before that was done. I am
not content with these things, I want to know what
the Lord, the Holy Spirit, meant by these words,
when He spake them through the mouth of the

Prophet, and no man can help me unless he be in that same spirit.—JOSEPH PARKER, *City Temple Pulpit*, vol. VI. p. 214.

REFERENCES.—I. 21.—M. Biggs, *Practical Sermons on Old Testament Subjects*, p. 1. H. D. M. Spence, *Voices and Silences*, pp. 49, 65. H. E. Ryle, *Christian World Pulpit*, vol. lv. p. 241. H. Melvill, *Penny Pulpit*, No. 1591, p. 123. J. R. Cohu, *The Sermon on the Mount*, p. 154. II. 1.—*Expositor* (4th Series), vol. v. p. 188 ; *ibid.* (5th Series), vol. ii. p. 236 ; *ibid.* (6th Series), vol. iii. p. 106 ; *ibid.* vol. x. p. 56 ; *ibid.* (7th Series), vol. v. p. 171. A. Maclaren, *Expositions of Holy Scripture—Peter*, p. 215. II. 4.—G. W. Allen, *Christian World Pulpit*, vol. xliii. p. 70. Spurgeon, *Sermons*, vol. xxxi. No. 1820. *Expositor* (6th Series), vol. vi. p. 70 ; *ibid.* vol. x. p. 286. II. 5.—*Ibid.* (4th Series), vol. ii. p. 253. II. 6.— *Ibid.* (5th Series), vol. vi. p. 380. II. 8.—*Ibid.* p. 290. II. 9.—*Ibid.* p. 213. Spurgeon, *Sermons*, vol. xli. No. 2441. II. 11.—*Expositor* (6th Series), vol. vi. p. 221. II. 11-13.— *Ibid.* vol. x. p. 289. II. 15, 16.—B. J. Snell, *Christian World Pulpit*, vol. li. p. 153. II. 15-18.—*Expositor* (6th Series), vol. x. p. 290. II. 17.—H. Bonner, *Sermons and Lectures*, p. 218. II. 21.—*Expositor* (5th Series), vol. vi. p. 91 ; *ibid.* vol. viii. p. 470.

2 PETER II. 22.

'I ENTERED on this farm,' Burns wrote to Dr. Moore (2nd Aug. 1787), 'with a full resolution, "Come, go to, I will be wise !" I read farming books, I calculated crops, I attended markets, and in short, in spite of the devil and the world and the flesh, I believe I should have been a wise man, but the first year, from unfortunately buying bad seed, the second from a late harvest, we lost half our crops. This overset all my wisdom, and I returned, "like the dog to his vomit, and the sow that was washed, to her wallowing in the mire".'

REFERENCES.—II. 22.—*Expositor* (6th Series), vol. viii. p. 328. III.—*Ibid.* (5th Series), vol. ii. pp. 94, 99. III. 1.— *Ibid.* (6th Series), vol. v. p. 459. W. G. Horder, *Christian World Pulpit*, vol. xliii. p. 187. III. 3, 4.—R. W. Church, *Village Sermons* (2nd Series), p. 239. A. Ainger, *Sermons Preached in the Temple Church*, p. 210.

2 PETER III. 4.

THE sense of security more frequently springs from habit than from conviction, and for this reason is often subsists after such a change in the condition as might have been expected to suggest alarm. The lapse of time during which a given event has not happened is, in the logic of habit, constantly alleged as a reason why the event should never happen, even when the lapse of time is precisely the added condition which makes the event imminent.—GEORGE ELIOT, *Silas Marner* (ch. v.).

REFERENCES.—III. 4.—H. M. Butler, *Harrow School Sermons* (2nd Series), p. 292. J. Martineau, *Endeavours after the Christian Life*, p. 94. III. 6, 7.—*Expositor* (4th Series), vol. ii. p. 288.

THE SLOWNESS OF GOD

'One day is with the Lord as a thousand years, and a thousand years as one day.'—2 PETER III. 8.

I. FIRST, let us think of the sphere of nature—of this wonderful universe in which God has placed us. Like a scroll upon its bosom *this* is written, that with the Lord a thousand years are as one day. It was Augustine who said this of God : God is patient because He is eternal. He takes His time because all time is His. There are a thousand years within His day. And that is a lesson we are learning now, with a fulness that was undreamed of once—how slow and sure and splendidly persistent God has been in fashioning the world.

II. Think again of the sphere of revelation. Does not that same mark of slowness meet us there ? The one thing God has never done, is to be in a hurry to reveal Himself. Suppose you were to ask a child this question, How do you think that God will speak to men ? Would not the answer be of sudden voices pealing from the silence of the sky ? Well as a matter of fact God *has* spoken to men, for that is just what we mean by revelation : but His speaking has been as different from that as a strain of music from the din of thunder. Not suddenly, in one stupendous moment, has God declared the riches of His grace. That would have been cruelty and not kindness, for men would have been blinded by the glare. It has been here a little, there a little ; one syllable to-day and one to-morrow, until at last these broken syllables blended in the Incarnate Word.

III. The slowness of God, again, is often manifest in regard to the great matter of our duty. Not all in a moment, but rather step by step, does God reveal the pathway of our duty. Think, for example, of the case of Paul when he was on his missionary journey. First he wished to go southward to Galatia, and the Spirit of God forbade him to go there. Then his heart turned northward to Bithynia : would it not be a joy to preach the Gospel there ? But once again his will was crossed, and the Spirit of God suffered him not. We understand to-night why that was so : he was being led to the great hour at Troas. He was travelling to the man of Macedonia, and to the summons from the shore of Europe. But the point to note is that Paul did not know that ; nor could he tell why doors were being shut : he could only leave it in the hand of God, who seeth the end from the beginning. How easy it would have been for God to let Paul know why he was being baffled. But it was not thus that heaven dealt with Paul, and it is not so that heaven deals with us. God leads us forward one step at a time, giving us light and strength for that one step, and only as we take it and are strong does He reveal the pathway of our duty.

IV. There is only one other sphere that I would mention, and that is the sphere of judgment upon sin. Sometimes God is very swift in penalty ; at other times, inexorably slow. There are sins which instantly condemn a man, and make him a social outcast in a day. They cannot be hidden, and, being cried abroad, they shatter the character and blight the home. But if there be sins that go before to judgment, I think there are far more that follow after, and such sins may track a man for years before at the long last they track him down. Seek ye the

Lord while He may be found; call ye upon Him while He is near.—G. H. MORRISON, *The Return of the Angels*, p. 167.

REFERENCES.—III. 8.—Spurgeon, *Sermons*, vol. viii. No. 447. J. Keble, *Sermons for the Sundays after Trinity*, p. 419; *ibid. Sermons for Advent to Christmas Eve*, p. 58. III. 9.—W. M. Sinclair, *Christian World Pulpit*, vol. xliv. p. 228. III. 10, 11.—Spurgeon, *Sermons*, vol. xix. No. 1125. III. 13.—F. D. Maurice, *Sermons*, vol. vi. p. 257. S. Baring-Gould, *Village Preaching for a Year*, vol. i. p. 329. F. W. Farrar, *Everyday Christian Life*, pp. 13, 31. III. 13, 14.—G. A. Smith, *Christian World Pulpit*, vol. xlviii. p. 232. III.

14.—A. Maclaren, *Expositions of Holy Scripture—Peter*, p. 224. III. 14, 15.—J. Keble, *Sermons for Christmas to Epiphany*, p. 214. III. 15.—*Ibid. Sermons for Advent to Christmas Eve*, pp. 198, 209, 219. Spurgeon, *Sermons*, vol. xxxiii. No. 1997. III. 15, 16.—E. J. Hardy, *Christian World Pulpit*, vol. lvi. p. 83. T. Arnold, *The Interpretation of Scripture*, p. 196. III. 16.—F. Hastings, *Christian World Pulpit*, vol. xlvi. p. 261. III. 17.—Spurgeon, *Sermons*, vol. xliii. No. 2533. III. 17, 18.—G. W. Brameld, *Practical Sermons* (2nd Series), p. 149. III. 18.—W. S. Stewart, *Christian World Pulpit*, vol. xlv. p. 236; vol. xlvii. p. 106. E. A. Bray, *Sermons*, vol. ii. p. 181. Spurgeon, *Sermons*, vol. viii. No. 427; vol. xlvi. No. 2700. A. Maclaren, *Expositions of Holy Scripture—Peter*, p. 234.

THE FIRST EPISTLE OF JOHN

THE FIRST EPISTLE OF JOHN

THE man who loves his fellows is never a spent force. . . . It is said of the Apostle John that in his last enfeebled days he was wont to have himself carried to church on a litter, that from it, as from the most revered of pulpits, he might whisperingly preach to the people. Such as John could never be a spent force.—JAMES MCKECHNIE, MEREDITH'S Allegory, *The Shaving of Shagpat*, p. 242.

'That which was from the beginning, which we have heard, which we have seen with our eyes, which we have looked upon, and our hands have handled, of the Word of life.' —I JOHN I. I.

THE ancient philosophers, too, spoke of a wise man who was the type and exemplar of all goodness, about whom strange paradoxes were affirmed—that he was a king, that he might be happy on the rack, and the like. This was their mode of describing philosophy. But they never supposed that Socrates or Chrysippus, or any other great teacher, really fulfilled this ideal. They did not 'see with their eyes,' nor 'touch with their hands,' the Word of Life. Nevertheless the Greek ideal, which is not confined to the Stoics, but is found to a certain extent in Aristotle and Plato, does throw a distant light on the relation of Christ to His disciples in the first ages. For it seems to show that in all ages mankind have been seeking for something more than ideas; they have wanted a person like themselves in whom they might see truth and goodness face to face.—BENJAMIN JOWETT.

I DO not know what Christians generally make of that first Epistle of John. As far as I notice, they usually read only from the eighth verse of the first chapter to the second of the second; and remain convinced that they may do whatever they like all their lives long, and have everything made smooth for them by Christ. And even of the poor fragment they choose to read, they miss out always the first words of the second chapter. . . . But whatever modern Christians and their clergy choose to make of this Epistle, there is no excuse for any rational person, who reads it carefully from beginning to end, yet pretends to misunderstand its words. However originally confused, however afterwards interpolated or miscopied, the message of it remains clear in its three divisions: (1) That the Son of God is come in the flesh (ch. IV. 2; v. 20, and so throughout); (2) That He hath given us understanding that we may know Him that is true (III. 19; IV. 13; v. 19-20); and (3) That in this understanding we know that we have passed from death to life, because we love the brethren (III. 14). All which teachings have so passed from deed and truth into mere monotony of unbelieved phrase, that no English now is literal enough to bring the force of them home to my readers' minds.— RUSKIN, *Fors Clavigera* (LXXXI.).

For an Exposition of the Epistles see: *Fellowship in the Life Eternal: An Exposition of the Epistles of St. John*, by G. G. Findlay.

REFERENCES.—I. 1-2.—J. R. Gregory, *Preacher's Magazine*, vol. iv. p. 268. I. 1-3—*Expositor* (5th Series), vol. i. p. 145.

'And the life was manifested, and we have seen.'—I JOHN I. 2.

'NOTHING,' says Herbert Spencer in *Education* (ch. II.), 'requires more to be insisted on than that vivid and complete impressions are all essential. No sound fabric of wisdom can be woven out of rotten raw-materials.'

REFERENCES.—I. 2.—Newman Smyth, *Christian World Pulpit*, vol. xliii. p. 392. J. N. Bennie, *The Eternal Life*, p. 1. R. J. Campbell, *Christian World Pulpit*, vol. lvi. p. 211. J. T. Stannard, *The Divine Humanity*, p. 12. C. Kingsley, *The Good News of God*, p. 19. H. Bonar, *Short Sermons for Family Reading*, pp. 20, 26. *Expositor* (5th Series), vol. v. p. 254. I. 2, 3.—Archbishop Cosmo Lang, *Church Times*, vol. lix. p. 817.

THE INDWELLING GOD

'Our fellowship is with the Father and with His Son Jesus Christ.'—I JOHN I. 3.

I. How are we to conceive of the indwelling God ? All nature is a revelation of God, and nature must be interpreted by what is highest in man. When we think of man we think not only of his will, his mind, and his goodness, but of something higher still of which he is capable—the quality of love. God therefore cannot be less. He can only be infinitely more than all we can conceive of love in its utmost intensity and self-sacrifice. In Him wisdom, will, goodness, love, reach to the highest imaginable point of intensity and reality, and this God is every moment within you—closer than your breathing, nearer than your very selves, 'so close that He is not even so far off as to be near'.

II. What is the right relationship with this indwelling God ? What is the relationship that we may conceive Him to desire for us ? What God is yearning for is that we may enter into fellowship with Himself. We are made for this fellowship with God; it is the law of our being. Are you not conscious as you think of this necessary fellowship between you and the indwelling God of at least two obstacles to our attaining to it? (1) The first is our ignorance. (2) The second obstacle is our sin.—ARCHBISHOP COSMO LANG, *Church Family Newspaper*, vol. XIV. p. 792.

FELLOWSHIP WITH CHRIST
(For St. John the Evangelist's Day)

'Truly our fellowship is with the Father and with His Son, Jesus Christ.'—1 John i. 3.

Is it surprising that fellowship should be the keynote of this Epistle? Do we not find the explanation in that beautiful description recorded in the Gospel for the day, that St. John was 'the disciple whom Jesus loved?'

True fellowship is the union of a common service of love for Christ's sake. What really is the triumph of Christianity in each life, in the Church, and in the world? It is getting each one to serve the others with his best.

I. Our Fellowship in Christ is Based on Relationships.—It is 'with the Father'. We are, as Christians, not a separated, scattered family; we are all with the Father; we are all at home; we are sons and daughters, brothers and sisters, in the actual relations of family life, and our Father is with us. They who have present fellowship with the Father make up the 'whole family in heaven and in earth'. St. John wanted those disciples to whom he wrote to have full fellowship with him; but he knew that they could only gain it as they had what he had, 'fellowship with the Father'.

II. Our Fellowship in Christ is Based on Character.—'With His Son, Jesus Christ.' God smiled out of heaven upon His Son, and said, 'This is My beloved Son, in Whom I am well pleased'. It was Christ's *character* with which He was so pleased. Christ bade His disciples 'follow Him'; but He did not merely mean, 'attend upon Me; or step into My footprints'. He meant, 'Be like Me; do like Me; have My mind; breathe My spirit; work My works; be changed into My image; be such sons of the Father as I am'. St. John so carefully says, 'Fellowship with the Son,' to remind us that the spirit of sonship is essential both to fellowship with the Father and with each other. Be a son with Christ, and it will be easy to keep in brotherhood. Keep in full fellowship with the Son, by being good and sonlike as He was, and there need be no fear about our fellowship with one another.

'Truly our fellowship is with the Father, and with His Son, Jesus Christ.'—1 John i. 3.

If we cannot commune with our friends, we can at least commune with Him to whom they are present, who is infinitely with them as with us. He is the true bond of union between the spirit-world and our souls; and one blest hour of prayer; when we draw near to Him and feel the breadth and length and depth and height of that love of His that passeth knowledge, is better than all those incoherent, vain, dreamy glimpses with which longing hearts are cheated. They who have disbelieved all spiritual truth, who have been Sadduceeic doubters of either angel or spirit, may find in modern spiritualism a great advance. But can anyone who has ever really had communion with Christ, who has said with John, 'Truly our fellowship is with the Father and the

Son'—can such an one be satisfied with what is found in the modern circle?—Harriet Beecher Stowe.

References.—I. 3.—Spurgeon, *Sermons*, vol. vii. No. 409; vol. l. No. 2905. I. 3, 4.—A. H. Moncur Sime, *Christian World Pulpit*, vol. lvii. p. 84. F. W. Farrar, *Truths to Live By*, p. 16.

ST. JOHN THE EVANGELIST'S DAY

'These things write we unto you, that your joy may be full.'— 1 John i. 4.

St. John, whose festival we commemorate to-day, gives in our text his reason for writing the Epistle. The Apostle, who lay on the breast of the Master at supper, and who describes himself as he 'whom Jesus loved,' carried ever after with him the atmosphere of sweet and holy rest. It breathes in all his writings; the spirit of one who knows his God, who has felt the Divine love, and can with confidence look forward to the future. He speaks with simple directness of the fellowship that the believer should have in Christ. He shows, as he has proved in his own life, the connection between sound doctrine and holy living, between faith and practice. The love of Jesus Christ is his greatest experience, and this love has kindled a corresponding flame in his own heart which is as the main-spring of all his actions. He would have all believers know this love, and experience a like peace and rest. He writes these things 'that their joy may be full'.

I. Joy in God.—As we have seen, St. John saw an intimate connection between right believing and right living, and his right faith and right conduct brought him that piece of mind and gladness which should ever be a heritage of the Christian. A special note of his message is its calm assurance and confidence in the Divine love, and this confidence he feels should also be the portion of every believer in Jesus Christ. In emphasis of his message, twenty-seven times, in this short Epistle, the word 'know' occurs. His desire is that we should have the joy and gladness, the great benefit to our souls, of knowing that as God's children we are in His keeping; that our spiritual progress is carefully guarded and fostered by him; that He concerns Himself to sustain and protect His people. And from this knowledge of the goodness of God and His unremitting love will spring joy and confidence. Was it not part of the very purpose of the Son of God in coming to this earth to change sin and sorrow into gladness and joy? His life and death of sorrow were that we might have happiness. He rose with healing in His wings that pain and suffering might be relieved. His will is that his children may know by faith the very real joy of His presence in their hearts, and look forward to that greater joy and gladness when they shall see Him face to face, and shall dwell in His presence for ever.

II. Joy in a wholehearted Service of Love.—This was doubtless the Apostle's own experience. In the midst of a long and arduous life of toil for the Master, during periods of bitter and cruel persecution of the Church, he still maintains this note of full confidence—of the glory of perseverance for a cause bound to be ultimately victorious. And love was the motive power; the sense and knowledge of the individual care and love of the Son of God for him, and a deep concern for the souls for whom Jesus came to die. And what a transforming power such love for and personal knowledge of God brings! How it changes and alters the character, bringing in the joy of conscious strength! The weak man is made strong; the nervous man confident; the vacillating is given decision of character. Moses, shy and apprehensive, fleeing from vengeance, is changed into the bold and purposeful leader. Now rebuking Pharaoh upon his throne, again withstanding the people and pronouncing judgment upon their unfaithfulness. Jeremiah, bewailing his youth and inexperience, is changed into the prophet conscious that he is God's mouthpiece, condemning sin and foretelling further punishment. Zacchæus, the taxgatherer, is changed from the oppressor of the poor to the conscientious follower of Christ, righting past wrongs and giving liberally of his means. Saul of Tarsus, the bigoted oppressor of the brethren, proud of his position and intellectual attainments, is changed into St. Paul, the earnest missionary and humble-minded follower of Christ. 'The people that do know their God shall be strong, and do exploits.' A life of strong, purposeful service for Christ is a life of true joy, such as the idler in the vineyard can never know. It matters not where our field of service lie: whether in the home circle, the place of business, the workshop, or in more directly spiritual work among the young, teaching them their inheritance in the kingdom, or in service in the house of God; whenever we do it from motives of love, anxious for Divine commission and enabling power, it becomes to us a service of truest heart-satisfaction and joy.

'And these things we write, that our joy may be fulfilled.'—
I JOHN I. 4.

'THERE comes a period of life,' says Maeterlinck, ' when we have more joy in saying the thing that is true than in saying the thing that is merely wonderful'.

HAPPINESS quite unshared can scarcely be called happiness; it has no taste.—CHARLOTTE BRONTË.

REFERENCES.—I. 4.—Expositor (4th Series), vol. vii. p. 97. 1. 5.—Ibid. vol. ii. p. 322. R. J. Wardell, Preacher's Magazine, vol. xviii. p. 83. R. W. Church, Village Sermons, p. 296. F. W. Farrar, Truths to Live By, p. 31.

'If we say we have fellowship with him, and walk in darkness, we lie, and do not the truth.'—I JOHN I. 6.

THE great and real source of doubt in which all lesser doubts seem to be swallowed up, is the apathy and indifference of Christian men, saying one thing and doing another. . . . No intellectual arguments have any power to pacify such doubts; the only answer to them is the removal of the grounds upon which they rest.—BENJAMIN JOWETT.

REFERENCES.—I. 6.—F. W. Farrar, Truths to Live By, p. 47. I. 6, 7.—Spurgeon, Sermons, vol. xxxiii. No. 1986.

THE CLEANSING BLOOD OF CHRIST

'And the blood of Jesus Christ, His Son, cleanseth us from all sin.'—I JOHN I. 7.

WHILE there are happily many signs of return to a deeper and more Evangelic conception of Christianity, there are also symptoms that disquiet and dishearten. Among these we place the acceptance, so far as it has gone, among Evangelical teachers, of Bishop Westcott's exegesis of the text, 'The blood of Jesus Christ, His Son, cleanseth us from all sin'. By Dr. Westcott the cleansing action is explained not in connexion with propitiation and acceptance, but as the internal purification of will and thought and heart by the life-power of our Lord in His people. In other words, the blood is practically the life or spirit of Jesus Christ working in His members. Even the literary sense might teach that the Apostle meant something far deeper than that. But while human nature remains what it is, there will be a strong tendency to put forward the impartation of spiritual life and a subjective moral deliverance, and to throw into the far background all that has to do with the satisfaction of Christ, the broken law, the sense of guilt and remorse, and the reversal of Divine condemnation.

I. When we look at the text, 'The blood of Jesus Christ His Son, cleanseth us from all sin,' and keep in view the analogy of the Apostle's writings and the tenor of the New Testament, we can hardly fail to come to the conclusion so ably advocated by Dr. Moule as against Westcott by a long array of Scriptural passages from the Old and New Testament. Dr. Moule shows that the blood of Jesus Christ God's Son is the blood of death, the seal of the covenant, the cruor of atoning sacrifice. The idea of life does not enter at all. Fellowship with God and walking in the light can never take sin away. No emotion, no feeling, no attainment, no height of spirituality, can remove our guilt. Our guilt was taken away by the great Propitiation, when He suffered without the gate, and knew the withdrawings of God. We have our peace not from the reigning Saviour, but from the bleeding Saviour, not from the King in His glory, but from the Redeemer in His shame. For this text speaks of a complete cleansing. We are cleansed from all sin. Even though the body of sin crucified within us is dying its slow, difficult death, there is a great sense in which we are even now delivered from all evil. Through the blood-shedding of Christ we have remission of sins now, and are truly forgiven as we shall be when the light of the glory of God falls on the resurrection face. So far as sin is a matter of guilt before God, it is taken away even to the last relic of evil, and we walk with God in the light, having our conversation above the skies. Is it impossible to understand this? Are the words of the hymn dark to us?

He beheld her broken-hearted,
Ruined and undone;
Yet enthroned among the angels,
Brighter than the sun.

When we fall again, when the imagination plays traitor, and the affections parley, and the soul is betrayed, still we claim again the merit of the atoning sacrifice, and are cleansed from all sin. No doubt it is true that the Spirit uses the doctrine of the Atonement to the fostering of holiness, and turns the sinner's face to God. But evermore what cleanses us is that which remained of Christ when the fire had passed over Him, even the enduring merits of His great sacrifice sprinkled upon us through the Holy Ghost.

II. In full keeping with this are all the references in St. John's books. When we turn to the Apocalypse we find ourselves instantly in the presence of the Lamb slain and immaculate in the midst of the throne of God. Jesus was the Lamb of God's Passover, not merely consecrated, not merely bruised and smitten, but put to death—slain. The blood that cleanses is not the blood of a martyr, but the blood of the Lamb. The blood of a martyr could no more take away sin than the blood of bulls and goats, but through the blood of the Lamb we have eternal redemption. We overcome the Arch-enemy by the blood of the Lamb. If we face the Accuser with argument drawn from our works and our feeling, we shall infallibly be overthrown. But the wounds of Jesus plead for us, and we overcome him by the blood of the Lamb and the word of His testimony. Therefore said one : ' Lie asoak in the Atonement, put thy broken heart to sleep over the breast of Christ, hard by His wound '. If we do this, through the blood of the Lamb, Who has paid our debt, fought our battle, endured in our stead, we are righteous in God's presence even now. Sin is removed from the conscience, and the day approaches fast when all sin will end. For when the Sabbath of eternity breaks, there will come with it the last sprinkling with hyssop, and we shall be cleansed so—clean every whit. Meanwhile it is through this blood that the olden curse of the race is gone, that the doom of the past is taken away, that the remaining perils of this mortal life are overruled, that we are to be brought through the terrors of the end, the falling of the star Wormwood, the final dreadful struggle between good and evil, the last trials of the sons of God.

III. Another book, the teaching of which on this great theme is frequently misunderstood, is the Epistle to the Hebrews. We read there that the sacrifices offered year by year continually could not make the comers thereunto perfect. For if they could, the sacrifices would have been offered no more, because the worshippers once purged would have had no more conscience of sin. Wherefore since the law could not help, Christ came saying, ' Thou didst not will the offering of beasts. Thou didst prepare Me a body, and I am come to do Thy will and offer Myself in that body.' He did offer the true and final oblation for sin, and having made it He sat down at the right hand of God. He entered into the holiest with His own blood, and perfected for ever them that are sanctified. We are sanctified through the offering of the body of Jesus Christ once for all. Once purged we have no more conscience of sin. His death and the offering of His blood, His entrance into the very communion and presence of the Being of God, opens the sanctuary on high for all believers. They are said repeatedly to be purged, sanctified, made perfect. The slightest examination of these passages should show that the reference cannot be to an internal purification. The Apostle speaks of a single act of purging or purifying the conscience. That cannot refer to sin as a moral condition of the mind, but to sin in that sense in which it is taken away by sacrifice. It means that the heart is sprinkled from an evil conscience, that the obstacle to fellowship raised by the sins of the people has been taken away by the Propitiation, and that no sense of guilt is left in the heart that has received a free and unburdened pardon. So, in the same way, when it is said that we have been sanctified through the offering of the body of Jesus once for all, the idea of sanctification is not of a gradual change of mind from defilement to purity, not a progressive relation at all, but the bringing of the people into the relation to God of a worshipping people. And in the same way the perfection to which the Author of Salvation has brought us is not the endowment with every quality of excellence, nor the removal of every tendency to sin. It means that we have been brought within the Covenant relation, and that, being there, we shall come at last into the full and true fellowship of God.—W. ROBERTSON NICOLL, *Sunday Evening*, p. 305.

' If we walk in the light, as He is in the light, we have fellowship one with another.'—I JOHN I. 7.

'THERE is no such firm, such attaching bond, as that of prayer and a common work for Christ,' says Dora Greenwell in *Two Friends* (pp. 103, 104). ' *A common work tends to a common life*, fuller than the individual can ever live. Even in natural things there is no fulness except through participation ; and I myself have been long persuaded that we do not fully live unto Christ except through mutual communion. How significant is that saying of St. John's, " If we walk in the light, as He is in the light, we have fellowship one with another ".

THE predominance of light as a figure and as a symbol in Clifford's writing will be remarked : he associates it with the right and all things good so constantly and naturally that it is one of the marks of his style. He had physically a great love of light, and chose to write, when he could, in a clear and spacious room, with the windows quite free of curtains. — SIR FREDERICK POLLOCK, on Prof. W. K. Clifford.

' And the blood of Jesus Christ his Son cleanseth us from all sin.'—I JOHN I. 7.

WHEN James Chalmers of New Guinea was a young careless fellow at Inveraray in 1859, he was led to the light finally, out of great depression, by the text: *the blood of Jesus Christ His Son cleanseth us from all sin*. It helped him to believe that salvation was possible for him, and so 'some gladness came,' followed by assurance soon afterwards.

About ten or eleven o'clock one day, as I was walking under a hedge (full of sorrow and guilt, God knows), and bemoaning myself for this hard hap, suddenly this sentence bolted in upon me : *the blood of Christ remits all guilt.* At this I made a stand in my spirit : with that, this word took hold upon me, *the blood of Jesus Christ his Son cleanseth us from all sin.* Now I began to conceive peace in my soul, and methought I saw as if the Tempter did leer and steal away from me, as being ashamed of what he had done. At the same time also I had my sin, and the blood of Christ thus represented to me, that my sin, when compared to the blood of Christ, was no more to it than this little clot or stone before me is to this vast and wide field that here I see. This gave me good encouragement for the space of two or three hours.—Bunyan, *Grace Abounding* (143, 144).

References.—I. 7.—E. A. Stuart, *The Great High Priest and other Sermons*, vol. xii. p. 17. W. Redfern, *The Gospel of Redemption*, p. 165. W. M. Sinclair, *The Record*, vol. xxvii. p. 780. F. W. Farrar, *Truths to Live by*, p. 74. R. J. Campbell, *New Theology Sermons*, p. 217. Spurgeon, *Sermons*, vol. xi. No. 663, and vol. iv. No. 223. *Expositor* (4th Series), vol. v. p. 122; *ibid.* (5th Series), vol. vi. p. 158. A. Maclaren, *Expositions of Holy Scripture—1 John*, p. 253.

ASSUMPTIONS OF SINLESSNESS

'If we say that we have no sin, we deceive ourselves, and the truth is not in us.'—1 John i. 8.

Let us consider the bearing of the text—

I. On our conceptions of truth. Truth is a wide word, but I use it here in St. John's sense as equivalent to the truth of the Gospel—the truth which regulates the kingdom of God. Some of these truths, to speak of it as consisting of many component parts, underlie the faith of the Church as such, and are embraced by all its branches. It is through these we become Christians, though some of them we may state in different terms, and apprehend from different sides, as Scripture itself does. But there are others, over and above, which it is difficult and indeed impossible to harmonise, and others, again, which it is not too much to say have not yet been fully understood. That we should do our best to understand and combine them into a consistent system, or creed, is not only natural and right, but we cannot do otherwise if we are earnest students of Holy Writ. But we must remember that our conclusions about many subjects, and points of doctrine, must be held provisionally, and with minds open to conviction and further light. God has not given us an infallible judgment, nor promised to guide us to an absolutely right verdict, in regard to all matters in dispute. An infallible judgment can only exist in perfect or sinless character.

II. Consider the bearing of the text in relation to guidance in practical conduct. When we know the Gospel we wish to act in accordance with it. In other words, we desire not only to be led into right views of truth, but also into right conceptions of duty. In reality these two are one. To think truly will secure our acting rightly. If we always knew the truth completely, with that sympathetic knowledge which is a characteristic of Christian faith, we should always act rightly—at least so far as the spirit and intention of our act is concerned. How does God answer our prayer for guidance? He gives us what the Scriptures call grace, inward enlightenment, or strength, according as the occasion may require. Without it sin works unqualified by any Divine control, with it sin is always under restraint. Hence no act or perception on the part of a Christian man is wholly the result of grace, but more or less of grace and more or less of sin. This being so there will always remain some liability to error even when grace is specially granted. The liability will, no doubt, decrease as we grow in the grace and knowledge of Christ, but it will never wholly disappear.—C. Moinet, *The Great Alternative and other Sermons*, p. 171.

'If we say that we have no sin, we deceive ourselves, and the truth is not in us.'—1 John i. 8.

'If we say that we have no sin, we deceive ourselves, and the truth is not in us.' But although we have sin still abiding in us, and, like the bias in a bowl, warping us to the world, yet that vital seminal principle of the grace of God in Christ always keeps its ground, its life, and tendency towards heaven, and wears out, wastes, and gradually subdues the contrary tendency of sin and corruption.—Sir Matthew Hale.

Reference.—I. 8.—F. W. Farrar, *Truths to Live By*, p. 47.

THE SENSE OF SIN

'If we say that we have no sin, we deceive ourselves, and the truth is not in us. If we confess our sins, He is faithful and righteous to forgive us our sins and to cleanse us from all unrighteousness.'—1 John i. 8, 9.

'If we say we have no sin.' Yes, but who would say it? How rarely we come upon anyone who would stand before his fellows in private or in public and claim to have no sin.

I. But there are other vehicles of expression besides words. Language has many modes. (1) Our prayers can say it. The very silence in our prayers can make it appear that we are not conscious of sin. (2) And surely our pride can say it. (3) And our very walk can testify to our fellows our conscious immunity from sin. (4) And, further than all this, I think that sometimes our very posture in the house of God testifies that the sense of sin is absent.

II. But in whatever way the assumption is made, we may deduce two inferences such as are drawn by the Apostle himself. (1) First of all 'the truth is not in us'. That is to say, the high standard is absent. (2) And the second and consequent inference is this, that we are self-deceived. 'We deceive ourselves.'

III. When we bring in the truth, the truth as it is in Jesus, and measure all the issues of our being by its exacting demands, our imperfections troop out in countless multitude. What, then, shall we do with them? 'If we confess.' But confess to whom? (1) Let us first of all confess them to ourselves. 'To thine own self be true.' (2) And there are some sins which we might very well confess to our brother. We are bound to confess them to our brother if we have done our brother a wrong. We can never find health and peace so long as personal injury is unconfessed and unrepaired. (3) But these confessions are only preparatory to the all-essential one of confession to the Lord.

IV. And what will be the issues of such confession? (1) Forgiveness. Freedom in the power of Jesus Christ our Lord. (2) And with the freedom there will come purity. The Lord will cleanse the life He has just emancipated.—J. H. JOWETT, *The British Congregationalist*, 10th January, 1907, p. 36.

REFERENCES.—I. 8, 9.—J. M. Neale, *Sermons Preached in Sackville College Chapel*, vol. ii. p. 308. Bishop Gore, *Christian World Pulpit*, vol. li. p. 169. J. Keble, *Sermons for Lent to Passion-tide*, pp. 63, 73. I. 8-10.—Spurgeon, *Sermons*, vol. xxi. No. 1241. I. 8, 20.—*Expositor* (4th Series), vol. vi. p. 66. I. 9.—Hugh Price Hughes, *Christian World Pulpit*, vol. liv. p. 225. J. Bunting, *Sermons*, vol. ii. p. 439. W. H. Evans, *Sermons for the Church's Year*, p. 78. S. Pearson, *Christian World Pulpit*, vol. l. p. 140. Spurgeon, *Sermons*, vol. v. No. 255. *Expositor* (5th Series), vol. viii. p. 373. I. 10.—R. J. Campbell, *Sermons Addressed to Individuals*, p. 259. I. 12-14.—A. H. Moncur Sime, *Christian World Pulpit*, vol. lv. p. 341. I. 15.—H. S. Holland, *ibid.* vol. li. p. 321.

'If any man sin, we have . . . Jesus Christ.'—1 JOHN II. 1.

'I FEEL, when I have sinned, an immediate reluctance to go to Christ,' says McCheyne. 'I am ashamed to go. I feel as if it would do no good to go—as if it were making Christ a minister of sin, to go straight from the swine-trough to the best robe—and a thousand other excuses; but I am persuaded they are all lies, direct from hell. John argues the opposite way: "If any man sin, we have an Advocate with the Father". Jer. III. 1, and a thousand other Scriptures, are against it. I am sure there is neither peace nor safety from deeper sin but in going directly to the Lord Jesus Christ. This is God's way of peace and holiness. It is folly to the world and the beclouded heart, but it is *the way*. . . . The weight of my sin should act like the weight of a clock; the heavier it is, it makes it go the faster.

'An Advocate with the Father.'—1 JOHN II. 1.

LUTHER said in his Table-Talk: 'When Duke Henry [Henry the Pious of Saxony] lay dying, many things were spoken to him of the Lord Christ, and he was asked if he wished to die resting on Him. He replied, "I am sure I could have no better procurator".'—E. KROKER, *Luther's Tischreden*, No. 538, p. 270.

'An Advocate with the Father.'—1 JOHN II. 1.

DR. DAVIDSON, in Ian Maclaren's *Afterwards*, said to his faithful friend and elder Drumsheugh, on the last night of his life: 'You and I, Drumsheugh, will have to go a long journey soon, and give an account of our lives in Drumtochty. Perhaps we have done our best as men can, and I think we have tried; but there are many things we might have done otherwise, and some we ought not to have done at all. It seems to me, now, the less we say on that day of the past the better. . . . We shall wish for mercy, rather than justice, and'—here the doctor looked earnestly over his glasses at his elder, 'we would be none the worse, Drumsheugh, of a friend to . . . say a good word for us both in the great court.'

'A've thocht that masel'—it was an agony for Drumsheugh to speak—'mair than aince. Weelum MacLure wes—eitlin' (feeling) aifter the same thing the nicht he slippit awa', an' gin ony man cud hae stude on his ain feet—yonder, it was—Weelum.'

REFERENCES.—II. 1.—F. W. Macdonald, *Christian World Pulpit*, vol. lviii. p. 100. St. V. Beechey, *The Excuses of Non-communicants*, p. 30. J. M. Bleckley, *The Christian Armour*, p. 242. C. Stanford, *Symbols of Christ*, p. 287. Spurgeon, *Sermons*, vol. ix. No. 515. *Expositor* (4th Series), vol. viii. p. 123; *ibid.* (5th Series), vol. x. p. 330.

THE MERCY-SEAT OF GOLD

'My little children, these things write I unto you, that ye may not sin. And if any man sin, we have an Advocate with the Father, Jesus Christ the righteous; and He is the propitiation for our sins; and not for ours only, but also for the whole world.'—1 JOHN II. 1, 2.

'My little children'—the language of venerable age. The language of ineffable love! The language of great authority! In these words we have :—

I. A Brief Epitome of the Gospel of our Lord Jesus Christ.—There are just five points in that epitome. (1) Behind all that we know of God there is a Father's heart. (2) Man, sinner as he is, is allowed to plead his cause in the Court of Mercy. (3) The Advocate is provided. (4) He advocates our cause upon the basis of His propitiation. (5) Man, by God's blessing, may live a stainless life.

II. A Glimpse of the Lord Jesus as the Representative Man.—He was the second Adam, the Lord from heaven, and His work of redemption is co-extensive with the havoc brought by Adam's fall and sin. Topsy, in *Uncle Tom's Cabin*, says: 'Why should I be punished? I never ate that apple!' Certainly: neither Topsy nor anyone else will go to hell because Adam ate that apple, because whatever loss accrued to the race from that act of sin has been more than made good by the act of righteousness of the One Man Jesus Christ. Why then are men lost? (1) Because they contract themselves out of the benefits of Christ's death. (2) Christ's death is for us all, but every man has, by faith, to take what God gives.—F. B. MEYER, *In the Beginning God*, p. 179.

ST. JOHN THE EVANGELIST'S DAY

'If any man sin, we have an Advocate with the Father, Jesus Christ the righteous; and He is the propitiation for our sins.'—1 JOHN II. 1, 2.

THE text brings to our minds the sinner, the Father, and the Saviour.

I. The Sinner.—'If any man sin.' This, then, is clearly a message for you and for me. St. John, the

Apostle of Love, is not one whit behind the other Apostles in bringing before us the exceeding sinfulness of sin, and also its universality. ' If we say that we have no sin, we deceive ourselves.

II. The Father.—It is the presence of sin in our hearts which has come between us and God. We know that God is *Love ;* but that is only one attribute of the Divine character. God is *holy*, and His holiness is such that He cannot bear to behold iniquity. Moreover, God is *just*, and His justice demanded that sin must be punished.

III. The Saviour.—But St. John tells us in this beautiful text how God's love, and holiness, and justice all meet in Jesus Christ. He is our *Advocate* (all our prayers are offered through Him); His very name, *Jesus*, means that He is our Saviour; He is also *Christ* (the Anointed of God); the *Righteous* (for He knew no sin); and all these characteristics fit Him to be the *Propitiation* for our sins. But we need to remember that ' the first and direct regard of the Atoning Sacrifice is not towards man but towards God. It aims, indeed, with Divine precision, by a short, sublime circuit of love and blessing at man's heart; showing man not by word only but by unspeakably moving deed what God would do, I dare to say what God would suffer, for his salvation. But the direct aspect of the Sacrifice is towards God, as violated Holiness. It is such as to set God's love free along the line of His law ; "that He may be just *and* the Justifier," the Accepter, of the sinner who closes with Him. He who is the Propitiation is, as such, our "Advocate *towards the Father*" (1 John II. 1). The notion of "Reconciliation," in the diction of the Bible, looks probably in this direction. "Be ye reconciled to God," interpreted by nontheological passages where kindred phraseology is used as between man and man (see 1 Sam. xxix. 4 ; and compare Pearson, p. 365), means not, "Bring your wills to meet half-way a Father cruelly misunderstood, and purely indulgent"; but, "Hasten while you may to claim the amnesty of the Atonement at the feet of your holy King". Not for one moment does the Bible allow us so to mistake this aspect of the Atonement as to dream of a fierce and hostile Deity wishing to condemn but bought off by the woes of a sinless Victim. It is the Father Himself who finds the Ransom, Who gives His Beloved, Who lays on Him the iniquity of us all. From the infinite recess of Paternal Love comes forth the Lamb that is to be slain. But then the Lamb bleeds on an altar that looks towards the dread shrine of that awful Holiness which means the eternal moral Order personal in God. Jesus Christ crucified is the Gift of God as Love, that we may stand scatheless, welcomed, adopted, beloved, before God as Fire.'

References.—II. 1, 2.—T. Barker, *Plain Sermons*, p. 84. C. D. Bell. *The Saintly Calling*, p. 59. F. W. Farrar, *Truths to Live By*, p. 92. D. L. Moody, *The Fulness of the Gospel*, p. 41. R. J. Campbell, *The Examiner*, 17th May, 1906, p. 473. A. Pinchard, *Church Family Newspaper*, vol. xv. p. 890. *Expositor* (6th Series), vol. viii. p. 321. II. 2.—*Ibid.* (4th Series), vol. v. pp. 122, 189, 362. II. 2-7.—*Ibid.* (6th Series), vol. x. p. 451.

SAVING KNOWLEDGE

' Hereby do we know that we know Him, if we keep His commandments.'—1 JOHN II. 3.

LET us do our duty as it presents itself : this is the secret of true faith and peace. We have power over our deeds, under God's grace ; we have no direct power over our habits. Let us but secure our actions, as God would have them, and our habits will follow. Suppose a religious man, for instance, in the society of strangers ; he takes things as they come, discourses naturally, gives his opinion soberly, and does good according to each opportunity of good. His heart is in his work, and his thoughts rest without effort on his God and Saviour. This is the way of a Christian ; he leaves it to the ill-instructed to endeavour after a (so-called) spiritual frame of mind amid the bustle of life, which has no existence except in attempt and profession. True spiritual-mindedness is unseen by man, like the soul itself, of which it is a quality ; and as the soul is known by its operations, so it is known by its fruits.—J. H. NEWMAN.

References.—II. 3.—F. W. Farrar, *Truths to Live By*, p. 108. II. 3, 4.—Spurgeon, *Sermons*, vol. xvi. No. 922. II. 3-6.—*Expositor* (6th Series), vol. viii. p. 455.

' Whoso keepeth his word, in him verily hath the love of God been perfected.'—1 JOHN II. 5.

THE commandment of Christ, which the Apostle has especial respect to when he here speaks of our keeping His commandments, is that great commandment of His which respects deeds of love to our brethren, as appears by the following verses. Grace is said to be perfected or finished in holy practice, as therein it is brought to its proper effect and to that exercise which is the end of its principle ; the tendency or design of grace is reached, and its operation completed and crowned. As the tree is made perfect in the fruit ; it is not perfected in the seed's being planted in the ground ; it is not perfected in the first quickening of the seed, and in its putting forth root and sprout ; nor is it perfected when it comes up out of the ground ; nor is it perfected in bringing forth leaves ; nor yet in putting forth blossoms ; but, when it has brought forth good ripe fruit, then it is perfected, therein it reaches its end, the design of the tree is finished ; all that belongs to the tree is completed and brought to its proper effect in the fruit. So is grace in its practical exercise. — JONATHAN EDWARDS, *The Religious Affections* (III. 12).

References.—II. 5.—*Expositor* (5th Series), vol. v. p. 36. II. 6.—J. Edwards, *Preacher's Magazine*, vol. x. p. 514. F. W. Farrar, *Truths to Live By*, p. 122. Spurgeon, *Sermons*, vol. xxix. No. 1732. II. 7, 8.—A. Maclaren, *Expositions of Holy Scripture*—1 *John*, p. 261. II. 7-11.—*Expositor* (6th Series), vol. ix. p. 226. II. 10, 11.—F. W. Farrar, *Truths to Live By*, p. 138.

THE FORGIVENESS OF SINS

' I write unto you, little children, because your sins are forgiven you for His name's sake.'—1 JOHN II. 12.

THERE are clearly two things that this text invites us to think about.

I. The forgiveness of sins as the fundamental experience of the Christian life.

II. The ground of forgiveness, the name of Jesus in connection with the forgiveness of sins.—J. DENNEY, *The Scottish Review*, vol. IV. p. 471.

REFERENCES.—II. 12.—Spurgeon, *Sermons*, vol. xxix. No. 1711. II. 13.—*Ibid.* T. Sadler, *Sermons for Children*, p. 121. A. P. Stanley, *Sermons for Children*, p. 10. II. 13, 14.—Spurgeon, *Sermons*, vol. xxix. Nos. 1715, 1751.

STRONG MEN

'I have written unto you, young men, because ye are strong, and the word of God abideth in you, and ye have overcome the wicked one.'—1 JOHN II. 14.

WE hear a good deal in these days about *strong men*. It is a wise thing to discipline the human body so that it may be a healthy and active servant of the will and reason of man. But to have a strong *body* is not to be a strong *man*. True manhood does not lie in the developed muscle. We hear, also, a good deal about education—about the training of the human intellect—in these days. As with some men the body seems to be everything, so with other men the brain seem to be everything. What an example Mr. Gladstone was to the young men of this generation as regards the development of body and brain! The student and the tree-feller! Man has a tripartite nature—body, brain, and soul or spirit. Man is not merely 'a thinking animal,' he is a moral being. It was *moral strength* St. John had in his mind when he said : 'I have written unto you, young men, because ye are strong'. And it was by their moral and spiritual vigour they had conquered the wicked one—even Satan. What is the secret of moral and spiritual strength?

I. Faith in God.—What made Luther strong before the Emperor Charles and those perjured accusers? Faith in God.

II. The Word of God.—See how St. John connects the strength of our young manhood with the bread of God's truth : 'Because ye are strong, and the Word of God abideth in you'. We have now learned the secret of manhood's true strength ; let us consider next the true purpose for which we are endowed with this strength.

III. Victory.—The words of the Apostle are remarkable : 'Ye *have* conquered' (not ye will conquer) 'the wicked one'. Was Satan, were the powers of evil, already conquered? I think there is a reference here to the time of their conversion, when these young men threw off all allegiance to Satan, and turned to serve the living and true God. Whatever conflict now remained was to be waged against a beaten and baffled enemy. The conflict does not end with conversion : it is only beginning in earnest. This age is the epiphany of youth ; the cry everywhere is for young, strong manhood. The Church of God wants it—wants *you*.—T. J. MADDEN, *Tombs or Temples*, p. 128.

REFERENCES.—II. 14.—Archbishop Temple, *Christian World Pulpit*, vol. liv. p. 350. J. Laidlaw, *Studies in the*

Parables, p. 299. Spurgeon, *Sermons*, vol. xiv. No. 811. *Expositor* (4th Series), vol. vi. p. 67. A. Maclaren, *Expositions of Holy Scripture*—1 *John*, p. 269.

'Love not the world, neither the things that are in the world.'
—1 JOHN II. 15.

HIS colonising idealism was not proof against the strain of idly watching others reap from active participation in the great struggle with Spain a larger personal reward than himself. Desire for wealth grew upon him as the passions of youth cooled, and the hope that some of the profits which Spain had acquired from her settlements in the New World might fill his own coffers besieged his brain. Anxiety to make out of an energetic pursuit of colonisation a mighty fortune, was coming into conflict with the elevated aspirations of early days.—SIDNEY LEE, on Sir Walter Raleigh, in *Great Englishmen of the Sixteenth Century* (p. 133 f.).

'Love not the world.'—1 JOHN II. 15.

THE Church of Rome seems to succeed by canonising the world.—WESTCOTT.

WHAT is *the world*, as described to us in the New Testament, Sir John Seeley asks (in *Natural Religion*, pt. ii. ch. I.)? 'It is a kind of conspiracy of prejudices, or union of all that is stagnant, inert, mechanical, and automatic, into a coherent tyrannous power and jealous consentient opinion. *Conventionalism*, indeed, is the modern name for that which stands here for the opposite of religion ; and we can judge from this in what way religion itself was conceived, for the opposite of conventionalism is freshness of feeling, enthusiasm.'

LOVE not Pleasure, love God ! This is the everlasting year, wherein all contradiction is solved ; wherein whoso walks and works, it is well with him.—CARLYLE, in *Sartor Resartus*.

'EVEN those who most love the world do not love the same world,' says Dora Greenwell in *The Covenant of Hope* (pp. 35, 36). 'The ambitious man, the covetous one, the pleasure-seeker, stare at each other in wonder, perhaps in pity, while the man who has placed his aim in everyday comfort and respectability gazes at all three with an inquiring *cui bono ?*'

'ONE of the most painful things I feel in continental travel,' Dr. John Ker wrote once in a letter, 'is the appearance that life everywhere has of mere pleasure-seeking. Not that anyone should object to pleasure, but it is here so much the chief and evident end that it destroys one's sense of the reality of life. It is as painful in its way as the misery in our lanes and alleys, for there one has sometimes a gleam of a moral purpose.'

REFERENCES.—II. 15.—F. W. Farrar, *Truths to Live By*, p. 153. H. Rix, *Sermons, Addresses and Essays*, p. 57. H. R. Gamble, *The Ten Virgins*, p. 17. B. J. Snell, *The Widening Vision*, p. 113. R. W. Church, *Village Sermons*, p. 150 ; *ibid.* (2nd Series), p. 326. II. 15, 16.—W. H. Hutchings, *Sermon Sketches*, p. 7.

OTHER-WORLDLINESS AND UNWORLDLINESS

'Love not the world, neither the things that are in the world. If any man love the world, the love of the Father is not in him. For all that is in the world, the lust of the flesh, and the lust of the eyes, and the pride of life, is not of the Father, but is of the world. And the world passeth away, and the lust thereof, but he that doeth the will of God abideth for ever.'—1 JOHN II. 15-17.

I. It is important to notice at the outset that it is not the world but the love of it which is condemned. Those who are addressed are spoken to as having already overcome the evil one. It is clearly, then, the good things of the world the Apostle has now in view, the things which are attractive, and which being in themselves innocent, may be properly enjoyed, but only within certain limits, lest they should prove too engrossing. What is forbidden, then, is the love of these things. It is engrossing love which is forbidden, love which shuts out the love of the Father. There is another thing to be observed in order to get the full thought of the Apostle. In the verse which follows, he passes from the grand word 'love' to the poor wreck of it which remains in the horrible word 'lust'. When love of the things that are in the world becomes a master passion, it ceases to be love, because it has degenerated into lust.

II. So far what is condemned; now what is commended? What is the alternative to this love of the world, and this lust of the things that are in the world? It is given in a short but most emphatic and suggestive sentence: 'He that doeth the will of God abideth for ever'. There is not the slightest hint of abandoning the world. We are to do our duty in the world, and not to separate ourselves from it. The alternative to worldliness is not other-worldliness, but *doing the will of God*. Not only are we to stay in the world, but we are to abide in the calling which God has assigned us, unless there be some very special reason for making a change. There is abundant wisdom in the recommendation of the Apostle: 'Let every man abide in the same calling wherein he was called'.—J. MONRO GIBSON, *A Strong City*, p. 39.

REFERENCE.—II. 15-17.—*Expositor* (5th Series), vol. vi. p. 225.

'The lust of the eyes.'—1 JOHN II. 16.

SPEAKING of evil curiosity, in his *Confessions* (x. 35), Augustine calls it 'a vain and inquisitive desire, cloaked under the title of knowledge and science, not of delighting in the flesh but of acquiring experience through the flesh. And because this is situated in the appetite for knowledge, and the eyes are chief among the senses as the source of knowledge, it is called in the Divine language, "the lust of the eyes". For, while "to see," properly speaking, belongs to the eyes alone, yet we use this term also of the other senses, when employed in the search for knowledge. We do not say, "hark, how it flashes," or "smell how it glares," or "taste how it shines," or "feel how bright it is". We say, in all these cases, "see"—not only, "see how it shines," but "see how it sounds, how it smells, how it tastes, how hard it is". Thus the general

experience of the senses is called "the lust of the eyes," inasmuch as the office of seeing, wherein the eyes hold the first place, is adopted by the other senses also, when engaged in the search for knowledge.'

AMBITION does not carry its marks of disgrace upon it like many openly shameful sins. It springs up insensibly, takes root, spreads its branches under plausible pretexts, and we only begin to be conscious of it after the heart is poisoned. . . . But on the other hand do not go out of mere lack of ambition and bury yourself in a workshop regulating clocks, instead of serving God and His world.—FÉNELON (to the Vidame d'Amiens).

Now and then I think of the days when I mimicked the Stoics and called my body—A VILE CARCASE, my spirit—A DREAM, A SMOKE; when I howled at the cities of the earth—You are dust-heaps! and to the heavens—You are ether! I never meant it. No one ever does mean these things. The pride of life and the desire of the eyes is mighty in all men, and while one is strong the time is the time of love.—JOHN OLIVER HOBBES, *The School for Saints* (ch. VI.).

REFERENCES.—II. 16.—J. Keble, *Sermons for Septuagesima to Ash Wednesday*, p. 230. *Expositor* (4th Series), vol. iii. p. 209.

'The world passeth away.'—1 JOHN II. 17.

BUILD your nest upon no tree here; for ye see God hath sold the forest to death; and every tree whereupon we would rest is ready to be cut down, to the end that we may fly and mount up, and build upon the Rock.—S. RUTHERFORD.

'He that doeth the will of God.'—1 JOHN II. 17.

THE point is not to feel an attraction for holiness but to will whatever God wills.—FÉNELON.

REFERENCES.—II. 17.—R. Higinbotham, *Sermons*, p. 43. A. Maclaren, *After the Resurrection*, p. 142. J. Martineau, *Endeavours After the Christian Life* (2nd Series), p. 52. A. Maclaren, *Expositions of Holy Scripture—First Epistle of John*, p. 279. II. 18.—F. T. Bassett, *Things That Must Be*, p. 27. F. W. Farrar, *Truths to Live By*, p. 167. *Expositor* (6th Series), vol. vii. p. 269. II. 18-23.—*Ibid.* (5th Series), vol. vii. p. 107. II. 18-27.—*Ibid.* vol. v. p. 241. II. 19.—*Ibid.* (4th Series), vol. iv. p. 23.

'Ye have an unction from the holy one, and ye know all things.'—1 JOHN II. 20.

IN the journals of Caroline Fox, the writer describes a serious conversation between Derwent Coleridge and the old Quaker banker Lloyd, from which the latter 'suddenly broke off, saying, "But thou wilt not understand what I mean by the *unction*". Whenever he (*i.e.* Coleridge) now hears the word, this remark recurs to his mind, and with it the peculiarly deep and solemn feeling it inspired, and the recognition of that spiritual meaning which friends attach to the word unction, that which is indeed spirit and life.'

REFERENCES.—II. 21.—R. F. Horton, *Christian World Pulpit*, vol. liii. p. 177. *Expositor* (4th Series), vol. iv. p. 23.

THE ANOINTING WITH THE HOLY SPIRIT

'The Anointing which ye have received of Him.'—1 JOHN II. 27.

THERE is no need for me to prove or attempt to prove that the Holy Ghost is a person. In the Greek, though the name for the Holy Ghost is neuter, it is followed by a personal pronoun *autos*, which could not be used unless the Holy Spirit was a person. On the day of Pentecost the Holy Spirit came to give power for the preaching of the Gospel.

I. You ask me if the day of Pentecost was a specimen day. I answer: Yes, and for two reasons —(1) On the day of Pentecost the Priest in the Temple presented twelve loaves, the specimen and the result of the harvest; and inasmuch as God chose the day of Pentecost for the outpouring of the Holy Spirit, He surely meant us to understand that the day of Pentecost was a specimen day, and that what He did that day He was prepared to do every day; and He would have done it if the Church had not choked and frustrated His plans. (2) In Acts II. 39, you have these words of Peter: 'This promise is unto you, and to your children, and to all that are afar off, even as many as the Lord our God shall call'.

II. Now a step farther. You say to me: 'Sir, tell me how I may get this power myself'. I will. What are the conditions? (1) You cannot have the power of the Holy Ghost without having the Holy Ghost Himself. (2) You must be cleansed. (3) You must live for the glory of Christ as your supreme end. (4) Your preaching and teaching must be in harmony with the Word of God. (5) The Holy Spirit must be received by faith.—F. B. MEYER, *The Soul's Ascent*, p. 263.

THE COURAGE OF LOVE

'And now, little children, abide in Him, that, when He shall appear [if He shall be manifested, R.V.] we may have confidence, and not be ashamed before Him at His coming.' —1 JOHN II. 28.

IN any intimate friendship, and in proportion to its intimacy, there is likely to be a mutual assimilation of thought, and similarity of expression. Moreover, if the one nature be more receptive, and the other more creative and original, the stronger will be the impress of the master mind. Now, in the case of the unique relation between Jesus the Master and John the beloved disciple, we have strength on the one side and receptivity on the other at their maximum. Therefore it is not surprising to find that John's teaching is a very close reproduction of the teaching of Jesus, not only in its essential truth—for this we should in any case expect—but also in the mode of representation, and even in the details of phraseology. We have as our subject: The Hidden Life and its Manifestation.

I. The distinction holds good if we confine our attention for the moment to this present time. (1) Undoubtedly the hidden life is the very essence of religion. A mere profession of religion has, indeed, satisfied myriads, and satisfies myriads still; but no one who seriously studies the question can doubt that the profession, without the inward reality, is vain and worse than vain. But quite as strongly does this saying condemn the vague mysticism that would content itself with some sentiment of tender regard for Jesus, not caring to inquire too closely into His claims. 'Abide in Me'—what claims are here! (2) But this hidden life, though opposed to the pretentious profession of mere religious formality, and having its seat and centre deeper down than the mere opinions and sentiments of our nature, has its own proper manifestation among men. For we live an outward as well as an inward life, and if we are true the outward will answer to the inward.

II. There is another distinction, however, made more prominent in the words before us, as between this life and the next. Here our life in Christ is a hidden life, in the sense that, though its power is visibly at work, making all new in our aims and actions, yet the privilege that seems properly to pertain to it, the position that it should confer, are not yet revealed. Sometimes there seems to be a painful contradiction between our confessed relationship to Christ and the events which are permitted to befall us in the world: but in any case our condition here is one of obscurity, of poverty, of suspense. 'Beloved, now are we children of God'; then why is it 'not yet made manifest' (1 John III. 2)? We confess Him: why does not He confess us? (1) It is implied here that we need a full inward preparation, before we can properly sustain that weight of privilege, with its attendant responsibilities. (2) But *His* coming '—this is the thought that is prominent. —J. F. LOCKYER, *The Preacher's Magazine*, vol. VII. p. 295.

REFERENCES.—II. 28.—Spurgeon, *Sermons*, vol. xxxv. No. 2105. W. H. Evans, *Short Sermons for the Seasons*, p. 10. II. 29.—Newman Smyth, *Christian World Pulpit*, vol. xlvii. p. 204.

SONS OF GOD

'Behold what manner of love the Father hath bestowed upon us, that we should be called the sons of God.'—1 JOHN III. 1.

I. The grandest Title.—Men will do much and endure many things for the sake of worldly honour. A man will work hard and deny himself, that he may obtain a title, or receive some cross or order from the hands of his sovereign. But these things do not last, the honour of a peerage cannot prolong a life, and the Victoria Cross, or the glittering order, must be laid on a coffin one day. The grandest title is that which the Father bestows upon us—the sons of God. It means that God is our Father, one God and Father of us all; that we are members of one great family, the Church; with great privileges and blessings here, and the blessed hope of everlasting life to cheer us onward, the blessed hope that one day we shall be with Jesus, and see Him as He is. Our heritage, as the children of God, is our faith in each Person of the Blessed Trinity, in the Holy Catholic Church, in the forgiveness of sins, the resurrection of the body, and the life everlasting.

II. We must be Brave and Loyal.—We must

remember whose sons we are, and be brave in our *faith*. Someone says, 'Since Christ has made the Christian course a warfare, of all men living, a coward is the most unfit to be a Christian'. Yet what miserable cowards some so-called Christians are! They are well enough while the sun of prosperity shines, but when persecution and trial arise for sake of the Gospel, they come out in their true colours. When the struggle comes between duty and self-pleasing, between what we like, and what is right, many, like the children of Ephraim, turn themselves back in the day of battle. When the fighting comes, when the Cross is offered, when the shadows of Gethsemane and Calvary darken round us, too many forsake Jesus and follow no more after Him.

III. We must be Brave in the Public Discharge of our Religious Duties.—In the olden days of Rome, the Gauls defeated the Romans and sacked their city, only the Capitol held out against the enemy, which was defended by a noble Roman youth. He had been accustomed on a certain day in every year to offer sacrifice for his family on one of the hills of Rome. The day came round, and found the hill in possession of the enemy. Still the brave Roman determined to do what he believed was his duty. He took the necessary materials for the sacrifice, cautiously left the Capitol, which was surrounded by the enemy, reached the accustomed spot, performed his religious duties, and returned in safety, though he carried his life in his hands. If we are surrounded by foes and hindrances, if our companions and neighbours put obstacles in the way of religious duty, if the devil sends temptations to make us neglect the service of God, let us remember whose sons we are, and offer the sacrifice of praise and thanksgiving, though an host of men be encamped against us.

IV. We must Love one another, Because we are one Family, the Sons of God.—'Pity is akin to love,' and pity makes us kind. Kindness is the outward and visible sign of the inward spiritual grace of love.—H. J. WILMOT-BUXTON, *Notes of Sermons for the Year*, pt. I. p. 94.

CHRIST AND HUMAN BROTHERHOOD

I JOHN III. I.

GOD's greatness we cannot grasp, God's wisdom is unsearchable, but God's love is something that any heart can hold and any mind picture. It is higher than the heavens and deeper than all seas, yet it is so homely and so human and so near that to realise it you have but to take some dear child of your own upon your knees, and express in tender kisses what you are to that child and what the child is to you.

I. There is no kind of love which we understand so well as parental love. For it was the first love we knew, and every day of our early life gave us sweet and forcible lessons in it; and the pictures which it left upon our memory are never blotted out, though the faces which imprinted them have passed into the great darkness. The love of the Almighty for us is wonderful. It is well-nigh incredible. Yet you see a human copy of it every time that you see a mother bending over a baby's cradle. Both are unaccountable, but both are facts. 'Behold, what manner of love the Father hath bestowed upon us, that we should be called the children of God.'

II. Upon whom is this grace bestowed? We are all His children by right; there is something of His image in all. There are possibilities of large Divine growth in all, and there is a place in His almighty heart of love for all. But only they who know it and rejoice in it are children in actuality and possession. The rest are children in possibility, but outcasts in fact.

III. It is the one thing which makes us great. We talk about levelling up. That is the one fact which levels us up. All other greatness is a fictitious thing alongside that of the sons of God.

IV. It is the one foundation of human equality. Apart from the fact that we are all alike dear to God, all alike His immortal children, there is no such thing as human equality. Whatever we are, strong or feeble, brilliant or commonplace, capable of the highest work or only fit for drudgery, we have the same place at His feet, we have the same share in His love; we are all His immortal offspring.

V. It is the one root and bond of human brotherhood. It is only at the feet of the all-loving Father that we learn the facts and the obligations of brotherhood. And without that all the grand humanitarian sentiments which are so much boasted of would perish as sparks go out when they are flung off from the parent fire.—J. G. GREENHOUGH, *The Cross in Modern Life*, p. 63.

'Behold what manner of love the Father hath bestowed on us, that we should be called children of God.'—I JOHN III. I.

LITTLE children easily believe their parents, easily believe wonderful things, things concerning which neither their senses nor their experience give them any warranty. The sons of God are 'little children,' because they easily believe all the wonderful things which God has spoken. 'Behold, what manner of love the Father hath bestowed upon us!' *Behold* it! get into it, let it kindle your affections. 'Beloved,' look into this love. . . . The world regards you as its children, and never suspects that God's crown-jewels are concealed within your earthly nature. The world did not suspect it in Christ's case. 'The world knoweth you not because *it knew Him not*.' It could not add to your safety, nor to your joy, that the world should know you. Only, the more your Divine sonship is hidden from observation, the more you should muse upon it, equally for God's praise and your own bosom-gladness.—PULSFORD, *Supremacy of Man* (ch. IV.).

REFERENCES.—III. 1.—Spurgeon, *Sermons*, vol. xxxii. No. 1934. J. Keble, *Sermons for Christmas and Epiphany*, p. 367. C. Perren, *Revival Sermons in Outline*, p. 282. F. W. Farrar, *Truths to Live By*, p. 184. *Expositor* (5th Series), vol. ix. p. 304. A. Maclaren, *Expositions of Holy Scripture*—1 John, p. 289. III. 1, 2.—R. J. Drummond, *Faith's Certainties*, p. 149. III. 1-3.—C. O. Eldridge, *Preacher's Magazine*, vol. xvii. p. 179.

REALITY REDUPLICATES

'We shall be like Him, for we shall see Him as He is.'—
1 JOHN III. 2.

'WE would see Jesus.' In the days of His flesh men did see Him, but their eyes were dim, and the veil that covered Him was unrent. Nevertheless there were those who pierced through to the reality, and on whose souls He left some print of His own.

I. For full vision there needed not the light only, but the vision that could bear it. Once when He gathered His saints to the mountain for anticipation of His sacrifice His glory burst through—'the glory which He had with the Father before the world was'. The light was too keen and bright, and they descended the mountain bewildered, with the Companion to whom men should do whatsoever they listed.

They came nearer Him perhaps after He had risen from the dead in the body He has taken for ever. Even then the veil was drawn, though drawn thin and fine. The glory was subdued and attempered till it was supportable, and by the sea of Tiberias, while they gazed in silence, the vision sank deep, and none dared ask Him, 'Who art Thou?' knowing that it was the Lord. The nearer and clearer the vision, the deeper the mark it leaves, and the triumphs of the Cross after our Lord had risen bear witness to this.

But a day is coming when all believers shall behold their Lord as He is. The naked soul will front the uncreated Light undazzled, unafraid, rejoicing, receiving. 'We shall see Him as He is.' Then we shall be like Him. The reality will double itself on every side. The likeness already begun will be made perfect and eternal.

II. Consider how the same law acts in every life. It is reality that doubles itself—makes disciples, wins causes, is served by willing martyrs. Our life is much of it sham, little of it real. Our pretensions to knowledge, to talent, to goodwill towards men, to many other things, are vain enough, but the least among God's elect knows in his bitterest hour of the thin but unbreakable thread that joins him to Christ. That is the supreme possession. Our imposture, conscious or unconscious, may deceive for the time, but it deceives much less than we think, and it has a brief hour. How many of us flatter ourselves that our falsities are so like the real that men do not see through them. Vainest delusion! We are taken to pieces; our make-up is torn off by rough hands; the tinsel and the theatricalities do not serve us even for some short hours of artificial light. Then? Surely there is something more in us than that. When the most merciless censor has had his will, he must yield to all the redeemed something—something of courage, fidelity, love, aspiration. That is the abiding self, and that influences. Goodness, though in things mainly evil; truth, though in things mainly false, is evermore impressive. Or rather, it is reality that impresses, that reduplicates, whether it be for good or evil.

How wonderful that day will be when we shall see Christ, when we shall truly behold the True! It will come, for 'when He shall appear we shall see Him'. All things that troubled the clearness of the heart will be over. The eyes will be no more overcast and dark. They will deepen and glow as the first radiance of His face shines over them, and speedily, joyfully, all the nature will pass into the likeness of the unveiled glory of the Lord.—W. ROBERTSON NICOLL, *Ten Minute Sermons*, p. 313.

'We know that when He shall appear, we shall be like Him, for we shall see Him as He is.'—1 JOHN III. 2.

THIS is one of those texts that we hear and quote so often without seeing more than its first and external beauty. Just as a man might walk over one of the prairies of California, admiring the richness of the grass, and the loveliness of the prairie lily, ignorant all the time of the gold that will some day be excavated from the soil under his feet.

I. 'We shall be like Him.' Therefore we are not like Him now.

II. 'We shall be like Him.' Yes, if we are even now growing like Him. Slowly and with many a break, many a drawback, many a hindrance in this world; rapidly and unbrokenly and without difficulty in the rest of Paradise which must precede His appearing. Just like a lake, so driven of the wind and tossed that though the sun is shining brightly on it, there is no further reflection of his rays than a few spots here and there of broken gold; but as the wind dies away it gradually settles into smoother undulations, and the broken fragments become wavy pillars of light, and then for a moment at a time you catch the figure of an almost perfect sun, and the moments lengthen out and the disturbances shorten, till at length there is scarcely an agitation—and finally a perfect image, so dazzlingly bright that the eye cannot rest upon it—so it is here. 'Then shall the righteous shine forth as the sun in the kingdom of their Father.'—J. M. NEALE, *Sermons for the Church Year*, vol. I. p. 18.

'Beloved, now are we children of God, and it is not yet made manifest what we shall be. We know that, if He shall be manifested, we shall be like Him, for we shall see Him as He is.'—1 JOHN III. 2.

AT the very close of her life, Mrs. Oliphant is described as having enjoyed 'perfect ease in body and mind. All care and worry seemed to leave her. She said she felt as if she were lying somewhere waiting to be lifted up; or again, as if she were lying in the deep grass of some flowery meadow near the gate, waiting for our Lord to pass by. . . . She said she could not think of God as the Almighty God of all the world, but just as her Father, and that at this moment even the thought of her children seemed to cease in the thought of Him. . . . The names of her boys were on her lips almost at the last, though she had said repeatedly, "I seem to see nothing but God and our Lord".'

THE perplexing doubts about the universe, in which I newly found myself in youth, have led to deeper faith in the immanent Divine Spirit, transforming death from a movement in the dark into a movement in Omnipotent Goodness ; trusted when it withdraws us from this embodied life, still unable to picture what lies in the future. 'It is not yet made manifest what we shall be'.—Prof. Campbell Fraser's *Biographia Philosophica*, p. 334.

'It doth not yet appear what you shall be.' There is no object which you have ever seen to which we can point, and say, You shall be like that. In the whole visible universe there is no beauty, brightness, nor glory, of which you can say, That is the pattern of our future glory.

You have seen the blushing morning, and the golden evening ; you have seen the soft beauty of the moon and the glory of the sun ; but you have seen nothing like what you shall be. You have seen our wintry trees change and change, under vernal influence, until they became pictures of beauty, and you have seen glory inwrapped in dark clouds ; and immense as is the distinction between leafless trees and blooming trees, or between leaden clouds and those of a golden sunset, the distinction is yet greater between what you now are and what you shall be.— Pulsford.

'God forgive me if I am wrong,' said Kingsley, speaking of death, 'but I look forward to it with an intense and reverent curiosity.'

Lately in my many sad musings it has been brought very clearly before my mind how often all the horrible tension, the dread, the anxiety which there are no words strong enough to describe—which devoured me, but wh ch I had to conceal often behind a smiling face— would yield in a moment, in the twinkling of an eye, at the sound of a voice, at the first look, into an ineffable ease, and the overwhelming happiness of relief from pain, which is, I think, our highest human sensation, higher and more exquisite than any positive enjoyment in this world. It used to sweep over me like a wave, sometimes when I opened a door, sometimes in a letter—in all simple ways. I cannot explain, but if this should ever come to the eye of any woman in the passion and agony of motherhood, she will more or less understand. I was thinking lately, or rather, as sometimes happens, there was suddenly presented to my mind, like a suggestion from some one else, the recollection of these ineffable happinesses, and it seemed to me that it meant that which would be when one pushed through that last door and was met—oh, by what, by whom?—by instant relief. The wave of sudden ease and warmth and peace and joy.—Mrs. Oliphant.

'It is not to be wondered at,' Dean Stanley writes in the tenth chapter of his biography of Dr. Arnold, 'that the boys of his Form remarked with peculiar interest, that the last subject which he had set them for an exercise was Domus Ultima ; that the last translation for Latin verses was from the touching lines on the death of Sir Philip Sidney, in Spenser's Ruins of Time ; that the last words with which he

closed his last lecture on the New Testament were in commenting on the passage of St. John : " It doth not yet appear what we shall be ; but we know that when He sha l appear we shall be like Him, for we shall see Him as He is " . . . " Yes," he added, with marked fervency, " the mere contemplation of Christ shall transform us into His likeness." '

References.—III. 2.—T. Binney, *King's Weigh-House Chapel Sermons* (2nd Series), p. 316. Phillips Brooks, *The Law of Growth*, p. 346. Spurgeon, *Sermons*, vol. iv. No. 196. vol. ii. Nos. 61 and 62, and vol. lii. No. 3004. C. Parsons Reichel, *ibid*. p. 119. Bishop Stubbs, *Christian World Pulpit*, vol. xlv. p. 385. S. H. Fleming, *Fifteen-Minute Sermons for the People*, pp. 168, 172, 176. H. D. Rawnsley, *Christian World Pulpit*, vol. xlviii. p. 155. J. A. Alexander, *The Gospel of Jesus Christ*, p. 102. Reuen Thomas, *Christian World Pulpit*, vol. l. p. 173. H. M. Butler, *Harrow School Sermons* (2nd Series), p. 150. F. St. John Corbett, *The Preacher's Year*, pp. 37, 96. W. Ince, *Christian World Pulpit*, vol. liv. p. 106. C. Cuthbert Hall, *ibid*. vol. lxii. p. 12. *Expositor* (6th Series), vol. iv. p. 275. III. 2, 3.—A. Ainger, *Sermons Preached in the Temple Church*, p. 13. S. Chadwick, *Mundesley Conference Report for* 1910, p. 401.

'And everyone that hath this hope set in him purifieth himself, even as he is pure.'—1 John iii. 3.

I say not that we are to be looking away to heaven, as being disgusted with the world ; much less to be praising heaven's adorable purity in high words of contrast, as if to excuse or atone for the lack of all purity here. I only say that we are to be much in the meditation of Christ as glorified, surrounded with the glorified ; to let our mind be hallowed by its pure converse and the themes in which it dwells ; to live in the anticipation of what is most pure in the universe, as being what we most love and long for in the universe ; and so we are to be raised by our longings, and purified with Christ by the hopes we rest on His person.—Bushnell.

References. — III. 3. — C. Vince, *The Unchanging Saviour*, p. 238. F. W. Farrar, *Truths to Live By*, p. 197. W. J. Hocking, *Christian World Pulpit*, vol. xliv. p. 356. J. M. Bleckley, *The Christian Armour*, p. 256. S. Udny, *Christian World Pulpit*, vol. lvii. p. 102. *Expositor* (6th Series), vol. v. p. 220 ; *ibid*. vol. xii. p. 419. A. Maclaren, *Expositions of Holy Scripture—1 John*, p. 310. III. 4.— Lyman Abbott, *Christian World Pulpit*, vol. xlvi. p. 346. Bishop Wilberforce, *Sermons*, p. 143. J. D. Thompson, *Christian World Pulpit*, vol. xlviii. p. 3. H. P. Liddon, *Sermons Preached on Special Occasions*, p. 52. R. J. Campbell, *A Faith for To-day*, p. 107. F. W. Farrar, *Truths to Live By*, p. 61. R. J. Campbell, *Christian World Pulpit*, vol. lvi. p. 360. *Expositor* (4th Series), vol. viii. p. 161 ; *ibid*. (6th Series), vol. xii. p. 54. III. 4, 5.—Spurgeon, *Sermons*, vol. xliii. No. 2509.

THE PROBLEM OF SIN

'Whosoever abideth in Him sinneth not : whosoever sinneth hath not seen Him, neither known Him.'—1 John iii. 6.

I suppose some time or another all of us have met professing, earnest Christians who said that they never sinned, who said 'My conversion was so real, so true, that I never sin.' The verse that I have read seems to suggest that a true Christian, one who abides in Christ, never sins, but if we look beneath the surface we shall see its true meaning.

I. Duality of Nature.—We have a duality of nature. We who have been baptised, who have put on Christ, have a Divine nature, and also, alas! a poor fallen nature, natures which are as different as white from black, natures which again and again are in bitter antagonism, in conflict. St. Paul, whose Christianity, whose conversion, whose sonship no one in the world could question, acknowledged this duality of natures when he said, 'For the good that I would I do not: but the evil which I would not, that I do'. Now here it seems to me is the explanation of St. John's words. We know that St. John never regarded a Christian as one who did not sin. Why we hear it every time we attend Holy Communion. 'If any man sin, we have an Advocate with the Father.' St. John knew that the converted soul sinned, yet he also said that the converted, the regenerate man, the baptised, the Son of God, as such in his Divine nature could not possibly sin. As long as a man abides in Christ sin is an impossibility. When he loses his temper, when he says that sharp thing about somebody else, when he is a little bit insincere, then he turns his back, he blots out his vision; for the moment he knows not Christ, he acts as a poor fallen man, not as a son of God, not as a regenerate being, not in his Divine nature, but as a child of Adam. Is not that true? Is not sin impossible so long as there is true communion with God? As long as I look at Christ, as long as I keep my eyes towards Him, as long as I am conscious of His Presence in me, as long as I am true to Him and remember my Divine nature, I cannot sin. But the very word trespass means a leaving for the moment, a separation from God.

II. Steady Growth in Grace.—First of all the growth must be in power over our weaker self. Step by step we should prove stronger in temptation within and without. Gradually our better nature—that is our Divine nature, the nature that we receive from the Father—should be gaining the mastery and pressing down the lower nature. And surely the way to do this is to practise the Presence of Christ. We know how sometimes when we fix these natural eyes upon some object, and then we close our eyes or even look at other objects, still we see that object on which we have been intent. So should it be as we focus our spiritual vision upon Christ: we should carry back into the city, back into our homes, back into all our difficult world Christ Himself.

References.—III. 7.—A. Maclaren, *Expositions of Holy Scripture*—1 John, p. 320. III. 8.—Spurgeon, *Sermons*, vol. xxix. No. 1728. R. W. Hiley, *A Year's Sermons*, vol. ii. p. 288. S. Cox, *Expositions*, p. 287. S. Baring-Gould, *Village Preaching for a Year*, vol. i. p. 146. III. 8, 9.—S. Cox, *Expositions*, p. 273.

'For this is the message which ye heard from the beginning, that we should love one another.'—1 John III. 11.

I know not if it be because I shall soon leave this earth, and the rays that are already reaching me from below the horizon have disturbed my sight, but I believe our world is about to begin to realise the words, 'Love one another,' without, however, being concerned whether a man or a God uttered them.—Alex. Dumas, in 1893.

The worlds in which we live at heart are one,
The world 'I am,' the fruit of 'I have done';
And underneath these worlds of flower and fruit,
The world 'I love'—the only living root.
　　　　　—Henry van Dyke.

References.—III. 13.—W. M. Sinclair, *Christ and Our Times*, p. 33. J. Keble, *Sermons for Sundays After Trinity*, pt. i. p. 42. A. Bradley, *Sermons Chiefly on Character*, p. 187.

LOVE TO CHRIST'S BRETHREN: A TEST OF SELF-EXAMINATION.

1 John III. 14.

I. Note first, the mighty change described. Spiritual death is a terrible reality. And that is the state of all men by nature. If you once realise this, then it will be clear to you that God alone can awaken the dead soul and bid it live and work and watch and pray. Christianity is not a matter of opinion, it is a matter of vital experience. When a man is regenerated he receives a new life.

II. The knowledge of this mighty change. 'We *know*.'

III. The ground of that knowledge, 'Because we love the brethren,' *i.e.* those who truly believe in the Lord Jesus Christ. They are the household of faith, and in a very real sense the brethren of Christ. True believers form a brotherhood. They differ in the colour of their skin, in their nationality, in their language, and in a multitude of other ways, but they are all one in Christ Jesus.—F. Harper, *The Preacher's Magazine*, vol. vii. p. 177.

References.—III. 14.—W. R. Inge, *All Saints' Sermons*, 1905-07, p. 113. Spurgeon, *Sermons*, vol. xliv. No. 2556. *Expositor* (4th Series), vol. i. p. 205.

'Whosoever hateth his brother is a murderer.'—1 John III. 15.

I believe that bitterness is always ready to break bounds in the heart of man; it flows freely in the channel that indignation scoops out for it. One must have been a long while in the school of Jesus Christ, one must have learned from him to tread many things under foot, in order to run no further risk of self-deception, and of indulging hatred under the guise of indignation.—Vinet.

For man to be redeemed from revenge—that is for me the bridge to the highest hope, and a rainbow after long storms.—Nietsche.

References.—III. 15.—C. Moinet, *The Great Alternative and other Sermons*, p. 185. H. Alford, *Quebec Chapel Sermons*, vol. iii. p. 339. F. B. Cowl, *Preacher's Magazine*, vol. xviii. p. 47.

'Hereby know we love, because He laid down His life for us: and we ought to lay down our lives for the brethren.'—1 John III. 16.

A fisherman gave Coleridge an account of a boy that had been drowned the day before, and that they had tried to save him at the risk of their own lives. He said 'he did not know how it was that they ventured, but, sir, we have a *nature* towards one another'. This expression, Coleridge remarked to me, was a fine illustration of that theory of disinterestedness which I (in common with Butler) had adopted.— Hazlitt, *My First Acquaintance with Poets.*

1 John iii. 16.

THE expenditure of life for Him is not always in one brilliant act of sacrifice, but far oftener in the glad surrender of life's hours successively until all the years are full. I have thought a hundred times of trying to preach on that standing text—once, I believe, I did try, and was ashamed of myself afterwards—'Hereby perceive we the love, because He laid down His life for us, and we ought to lay down our lives for the brethren'. We ought—we ought to lay it down—that is the principle for every Christian. I confess I have been again and again fairly paralysed when thinking of preaching on that text. But many Christian lives have in their degree been honest sermons upon it.—PRINCIPAL RAINY.

REFERENCES.—III. 16.—Spurgeon, *Sermons*, vol. xlvi. No. 2656; vol. li. No. 2959. Basil Wilberforce, *Sanctification by the Truth*, p. 51. Lyman Abbott, *Christian World Pulpit*, vol. xlviii. p. 238. III. 16-18.—W. Hubbard, *ibid.* vol. xliv. p. 26. III. 18.—G. G. Bradley, *ibid.* vol. liii. p. 8. A. P. Stanley, *Sermons for Children*, p. 10. III. 19.—J. S. Bartlett, *Sermons*, p. 224. III. 19-21.—J. J. Blunt, *Plain Sermons*, p. 266.

'God is greater than our heart, and knoweth all things.'—
1 John iii. 20.

'CHEERFULNESS and lightness of heart,' says Newman, 'are not only privileges, but duties. Cheerfulness is a great Christian duty. That sorrow, that solicitude, that fear, that repentance, is not Christian which has not its portion of Christian joy; for "God is greater than our heart," and no evil, past or future, within or without, is equal to this saying, that Christ has died and reconciled the world unto himself,' and again : '"God is greater than our heart, and knoweth all things". It is this feeling of simple and absolute confidence and communion which soothes and satisfies those to whom it is vouchsafed. We know that even our nearest friends enter into us but partially and hold intercourse with us only at times; whereas the consciousness of a perfect and enduring presence, and it alone, keeps the heart open.... The contemplation of Him, and nothing but it, is able fully to open and relieve the mind, to unlock, occupy, and fix our affections. Created natures cannot open us, or elicit the ten thousand mental senses which belong to us, and through which we really live. None but the presence of our Maker can enter us.'

REFERENCE.—III. 20.—J. Keble, *Sermons for Advent to Christmas Eve*, pp. 123, 137.

'Beloved, if our heart condemn us not, we have boldness toward God.'—1 John iii. 21.

THE secret of pleasure in life—as distinct from its greatest triumphs of transcendent joy—is to live in a series of small, legitimate successes. By legitimate I

mean, such as are not accompanied by self-condemnation.—SIDNEY DOBELL.

REFERENCES.—III. 21.—Spurgeon, *Sermons*, vol. xxxi. No. 1855. J. Keble, *Sermons for Advent to Christmas Eve*, p. 151. *Expositor* (4th Series), vol. i. p. 40. III. 22-24.—Spurgeon, *Sermons*, vol. xix. No. 1103. III. 23.—*Ibid.*, vol. ix. No. 531.

'Believe not every spirit.'—1 John iv. 1.

WE are all discerners of spirits. That diagnosis lies aloft in our life or unconscious power. The intercourse of society—its trade, its religion, its friendships, its quarrels—is one wide, judicial investigation of character.—EMERSON, on *The Over-Soul.*

'Beloved, believe not every spirit, but prove the spirits, whether they are of God.'—1 John iv. 1.

A POOR man, in our day, has many gods foisted on him; and big voices bid him, 'Worship or be—!' in a menacing and confusing manner. What shall he do? By far the greater part of said gods, current in the public, whether canonised by Pope or Populus, all were dumb apises and beatified Prime-oxen;— nay, some of them, who have articulate faculty, are devils instead of gods. A poor man that would save his soul alive is reduced to the sad necessity of sharply trying his gods whether they are divine or not; which is a terrible pass for mankind, and lays an awful problem upon each man. The man must do it, however. At his own peril he will have to do this problem too, which is one of the awfulest; and his neighbours, all but a most select portion of them, portion generally *not* clad in official tiaras, can be of next to no help to him in it, nay, rather will infinitely hinder him in it, as matters go.—CARLYLE, *Latter-Day Pamphlets* (VIII.).

REFERENCES.—IV. 1.—W. G. Horder, *Christian World Pulpit*, vol. lvii. p. 235. IV. 2, 3.—J. T. L. Maggs, *Preacher's Magazine*, vol. xviii. p. 295. IV. 4.—W. C. E. Newbolt, *Church Family Newspaper*, vol. xv. p. 12. IV. 6.— G. Bellett, *Parochial Sermons*, p. 1.

'Love is of God.'—1 John iv. 7.

GOD desires neither narrow hearts nor empty heads for His children, but those whose spirit is of itself indeed free, yet rich in the knowledge of Him, and who regard this knowledge of God as the only valuable possession.—HEGEL.

'THE true sage,' says Maeterlinck, 'is not he who sees, but he who, seeing furthest, has the deepest love for mankind. He who sees without loving is only straining his eyes in the dark.'

I NEVER yet cast a true affection on a woman; but I have loved my friend, as I do virtue, my soul, my God. From hence, methinks, I do conceive how God loves man; what happiness there is in the love of God.—SIR THOMAS BROWNE, *Religio Medici* (pt. ii. sec. 5).

REFERENCES.—IV. 7.—Archbishop Alexander, *Christian World Pulpit*, vol. liv. p. 20. J. Keble, *Sermons for Sundays After Trinity*, pt. i. p. 223. T. Binney, *King's Weigh-House Chapel Sermons*, p. 206. IV. 7, 8.—H. S. Holland, *Christian World Pulpit*, vol. lvi. p. 107.

THE MASTER KEY
'God is Love.'—1 JOHN IV. 8.

HERE is all we want. Here we have three words, which are three syllables, and they are bigger words than all the piled words of the most elaborate dictionary ever constructed. These are the words out of which all the other words come.

The use of this text is not to be found in its own verbal exposition. This is a text that is to be carried all over the Bible; this is the commentator of the whole Scripture. Turn over a page—where is the lamp? That is Bible reading. You fail to expound the Scripture because you have lost the lamp. Do not suppose, then, that 'God is love' is a text that can be explained in one discourse or explained in all the discourse ever poured from the fluent tongue of eloquence. Never read a chapter without lighting the lamp and putting it just over the chapter you are reading. What is your lamp? God is love.'

I. The lamp! We might take it with us now and look at a few passages in the light of this gleaming candle of God. Take this awful text: 'In the day thou eatest thereof thou shalt surely die'. He threatens the man whom He has made! He does not. The lamp! now read under the light of the lamp, and you will find that this is no threat, this is no uplifting of the arm of Jehovah, as who should say, Take care what you are about, or one mistake on your part and you are a dead man. God never learned that savagery of tone; God speaks in another music. These were hard words, no doubt, to the man who heard them for the first time. When you point out to your dear little child that if he goes into a certain place he will be injured, you are not threatening the boy; we cannot say, Why speak to the dear little boy in that tone? You properly reply that the tone is an expression of solicitude, anxiety, tenderest love, saying in all the music of the parental heart, Take care! If you go down there you will be perhaps injured, something may meet you there that will frighten you; if you once go into that den or jungle where the wild beast is you will be torn to pieces: take care not to go in that direction. That is not threatening; that is loving, caring-for, going-out-after, with tender desire and anxiety. So I take my lamp text, 'God is love,' and hold it all above the story of Eden, and behold, I know that God has made all things good and designed all things in love, and that the very voice of warning is a new accent in the music of sweetest, tenderest care.

II. Let us hold the lamp over another text that is almost too terrible to read. May I read it in a genteel assembly? shall I not be hissed out of the pulpit I degrade if I read this text?—'The wicked shall be turned into hell, and all the nations that forget God.' I admit that it is possible so to utter these words as to import into them a false meaning and a false tone, but I insist that it is also possible so to read them as to make them about as tender words as can be found in the whole compass of inspired revelation. This is not wrath, it is pleading, it is the expression of solicitous love: as who should say, My dear soul, do you really know what wickedness is? do you know what it means, what it involves, and what it really must come to in the bitter end? Here, in one of those so-called rough imprecatory passages, wherein God is supposed to be very wrathful and very stormy, here, we find the very heart of love; in the midst of all this warning there is one large tender tear that wets the cheek of God. Do not believe those persons, therefore, who point out the imprecations and denunciations, and wish you to believe that all these things are indications of the wrath of God. Hear me, they are not; they are indications of the love of God; God in His mercy thinks it right to tell us what the harvest of sin-sowing is, and if He had never told us, how could He judge us? and if He had never told us and attempted to judge us, what a standing-ground we would have for self-vindication, how we might charge Him with injustice for having kept back the secret of the evolution of moral processes. We go to the judgment with our eyes open, we go to perdition with the Scriptures written in plainest language of entreaty and love.

III. The lamp! What is this?—'It shall be more tolerable for Tyre and Sidon in the day of judgment than for you.' 'God is love.' He does not judge promiscuously or indiscriminately; there is not one lot for all; if a man has begun with much, much will be required of him, and if he has begun with little, he will be judged accordingly.

IV. So I come back to my little Bible, my three syllabled Bible, the Bible that holds all the Bible. When I come upon a great and awful mystery I call for the lamp, and it has a way of throwing its beams down into its deepest cavities. I have held it over the grave. This epigrammatic sentence fits all graves, it fits all cemeteries; it is the word that is written on its portals of the churchyard, 'God is love'.—JOSEPH PARKER, *City Temple Pulpit*, vol. III. p. 233.

REFERENCES.—IV. 8.—F. W. Farrar, *Christian World Pulpit*, vol. xlv. p. 321. W. C. Wheeler, *Sermons and Addresses*, p. 125. W. J. Hocking, *Christian World Pulpit*, vol. xlvi. p. 61. Lyman Abbott, *Ibid.*, vol. liv. p. 109. R. J. Campbell, *Ibid.*, vol. lvi. p. 321. M. Gardner, *Ibid.*, vol. lxx. p. 407.

LOVE'S SUPREME DISCLOSURE
'God is love. In this was manifested the love of God toward us, because that God sent his only-begotten Son into the world, that we might live through Him.'—1 JOHN IV. 8, 9.

LOVE, as John tells us again and again, is to be seen and known only in what it does. We shall therefore look at this love of God disclosing itself in lovely deeds, and rise step by step to see the supreme disclosure in the Cross of Christ.

I. The first and simplest thing to say about love is this—it is a *social passion*. There cannot be love without at least two, a lover and a beloved. The man who had never seen the face of a fellow-man could not know the meaning of love. The faculty of love would be dormant in him, and be felt only as an unsatisfied yearning. If God be love, He must have loved from all eternity. Before the angels were created, or the universe had being, God was love. God never dwelt in a still and awful loneliness.

II. The second simple thing to say about love is this—*love is creation*. Love must create, and it must create well-being. Love cannot be inactive. It must plan and toil and spend its resources and exert its energy. It must devise order, goodness, beauty, joy. Here we have the mighty motive of creation. Love is the source and creation is the stream. God does not love the world simply because He created it. He created this world of life and beauty and order because He is love. It is always love that builds a home. It is always love that makes a garden. It is always love that peoples a wilderness. The first words of the Bible are a revelation of love: 'In the beginning God created the heaven and the earth'.

III. The third simple thing to say about love is this—*that love is providence*. Love cannot be content with creation. It must pass on to care, and God's care is His providence. Your little son makes himself a rudely shapen boat. Its designing has filled his heart and busied his hand for hours. At length he launches his little mimic craft by some beach. Does he set his venture afloat and then turn his back upon it, heedless of its fate? Mark how he waits and watches and risks himself lest his little vessel come to untimely shipwreck. Love created it, and love hangs over it in absorbing care. And so God did not create the universe, and make all things beautiful in their season, and set His spirit in man, and then turn His back and vanish into silence. He does not sit afar off on the world's edge to see it go. The world is not a piece of clockwork, finished once for all, and set agoing by an almighty mechanic. It is a living and growing organism. God's eyes are ever watching it. His fingers are ever working upon it, His hands ever devising new beauty in it.

IV. The fourth thing and the great thing to say about love is this—*love is grace*. This is where love makes its supreme disclosure. What is grace out love dealing with sin? What can God, who is love, do for the sinner but pour Himself out in costly sacrifice to redeem him?

V. The fifth thing to say about love is—*love is discipline*. Love's supreme disclosure is the Cross, but love which redeems must pass on to discipline. Love's redeeming work was not done when Christ had burst the gates of hell. The dominion of sin was broken, but its fascination and power were not wholly annulled. No man who has accepted the forgiveness of God, and put himself under the mastership of Christ, can be ignorant that the power of indwelling sin is his most humbling experience. There is a work of God for man. There is also a work of God in man. Therefore God disciplines His redeemed. He chastens by mercy and by judgment, through limiting privation and burdening care, by the shadow on the heart and the thorn in the flesh, to purify and to perfect in righteousness.

VI. The sixth thing to say about love is—*love is heaven*. In New Testament teaching that is the issue of love's work in the Cross and by the discipline of God. Love can never be satisfied without the loved one's presence and fellowship. 'I go to prepare a place for you, that where I am ye may be also,' was the last assurance of incarnate love. To that message all the New Testament writers make a yearning response.—W. M. Clow, *The Cross in Christian Experience*, p. 41.

'God is Love. In this was manifested the love of God toward us, because that God sent his only-begotten Son into the world, that we might live through Him.'—1 John iv. 8, 9.

Of the reality of God's love St. John had no doubt; neither need we have any, though some do doubt it, thinking that God's justice and hatred of sin interfere with His love. But justice does not interfere with love in God. Justice and love are compatible in man, and much more so in God. The cross of Christ reveals and establishes the harmony between righteousness and mercy. There justice gets its own, and love has its way, and God is a 'just God and a Saviour,' and 'grace reigns through righteousness'. Christ's cross is not the cause but the consequence of God's love. The text asserts God's love before He sent Christ; affirms Christ's mission to be the manifestation of God's love. There need be no doubt, then, as to the fact, that God loves us, has loved us. But more than this, the text not only implies that God is loving and loves us, but asserts that He is love. Love is the sum and harmony of all His attributes, His essence.

I. The Manifestation of God's Love.—God's love is manifested in creation, in preservation, and in all the blessings of this life, but above all in redemption.

(*a*) God *sent* His Son. He did not merely allow or consent to His coming. He Himself sent His Son, gave Him His commission and authority.

(*b*) God sent *His only-begotten Son*. He who was sent by God as a gift of love was no less than His only-begotten Son. Then God's love is as great as the divine glory of His Son. God sends no servant, no archangel, but His equal and co-eternal Son Who, as His only-begotten, and sharing that nature which is love, could best manifest God's love.

(*c*) God sent His Son *into the world*. The destination of the Son, His being sent into a fallen and sinful world, a world disordered and corrupt, a world which during thousands of years had not grown better but worse, manifested God's love. Christ's personal history and experience in the world manifested how great was the love of God that sent Him to such a world and to such treatment in it.

(*d*) God sent His Son . . . that *we might live through Him*. The purpose of Christ's mission, involving His death as a sacrifice for sin, His giving His life to redeem ours, manifested God's love. They for whom He sent His Son were sinners, guilty, helpless, unloving.

II. Some Thoughts which Emerge.—(1) Here is the spring and motive of love to God and the love to man which is its evidence.

(2) If God has given His only-begotten Son for our life, with Him also He shall freely give us all things.

(3) How precious is the soul of man! It is the subject of God's love, and Christ was sent to give it true life.

(4) We must become sons of God, born sons, if we are to manifest His love.

(5) To reject God's love thus manifested must be the greatest sin and misery, and it is self-inflicted misery as it is wilful sin.

REFERENCES.—IV. 8-10, 16.—G. Body, *Christian World Pulpit*, vol. lix. p. 137. IV. 9.—C. Bradley, *Faithful Teaching*, p. 12. J. R. Illingworth, *University and Cathedral Sermons*, p. 87. *Expositor* (5th Series), vol. vii. p. 42. IV. 9, 10.—J. Cumming, *Penny Pulpit*, No. 1587, p. 91.

LEARNING TO LOVE GOD

'Herein is love, not that we love God, but that He loved us and sent his Son to be the propitiation for our sins.'—1 JOHN IV. 10.

LOVE to God, like the rain and the snow, must come down from heaven. St. John, the Apostle of love, tells us love is of God; and yet I think that God has placed within your reach, and mine, certain means by which we may learn to love God, or learn to love Him better than we do already. Let me remind you what some of these are.

I. First, Thirst. Canon Mozley, one of the ablest men in the Church of England in the nineteenth century, has a remarkable sermon on the strength of wishing, and in that sermon he points out that the Bible teaches us that, if a man wishes for any great spiritual gift, sooner or later that gift will be his, provided it be the supreme wish of his heart; and he quotes some great words of Bishop Wilson of Sodor and Man, that we receive grace in proportion as we desire it. Do we desire to love God? Then, sooner or later, that desire will be satisfied, if it is the supreme desire of the heart. And that for two reasons—God never implants a desire in a man's heart to mock him, but that sooner or later He may satisfy it. And that desire will find its voice in prayer, and to prayer the great promise is made, 'Ask and it shall be given'.

II. The second, Faith. St. John, the apostle of love, the disciple whom Jesus loved, tells us in this very chapter how he came to love God : 'We have known and believed the love that God hath to us'. The whole secret of loving God is to believe that God loves us; not to try to force ourselves to love God, but to accept the great truth that God loves us. And God has given our faith what I will venture to call two footholds upon which we may plant our feet and be perfectly sure that God loves us. The first is the cradle of Bethlehem ; and the second the Cross of Calvary.

III. The third, Service. Samuel Taylor Coleridge, in his 'Aids to Reflection,' says that if you would restore a commonplace truth to its first lustre you must translate it into action. Here is a great truth that God loves us. Go and act as if it were true.

Amongst your friends is one who, in popular language, is going wrong. Try and save him, write to him, talk to him, pray for him, consider what you can do to rescue him from ruin. Do it because God loves you and loves him. In your neighbourhood is a family sorely pressed with poverty. Try and help them ; feed the hungry, clothe the naked, lift up the fallen ; do what you can to stand by them in their time of trouble, and do it because God loves you and loves them. The cause of Jesus Christ wants your service, wants your heart. Give, work, because God loves you and loves all men ; and as you act out the love of God, or because God loves you and them, your love will grow. Love can only live by loving ; and by serving love will grow.

Lastly, there is love for the creature. I believe that God is training us all by the sweet pure love of home life to love Him. There are some people who say, Take care that you do not love your husband, or your wife, or your lover, or your friend, or your child, too much. If you love them in God, and for God, you can never love them too much. Nay, God will train you to love Him through loving your dear ones at home. And in the love that the husband has for the wife, or the wife has for the husband, we have a dim reflection of the love wherewith the heavenly Bridegroom loves His Church and every member of His Church, and the husband and the wife will say : If our love is so strong and deep and ennobling, what must be the love wherewith Christ loves us? And so we will rise, I say, on the stepping-stones of human love to realise God's love to us, and to love Him back. First faith, then service, then love to the creature : these are some means which God has put within our power to enable us to love Him better.—BISHOP CHAVASSE, *Christian World Pulpit*, vol. LXXVIII. p. 97.

REFERENCES.—IV. 10.—R. J. Campbell, *Christian World Pulpit*, vol. liii. p. 198. Spurgeon, *Sermons*, vol. xli. No. 2394 ; vol. xlii. No. 2248. H. T. Potten, *British Congregationalist*, 20th September, 1906, p. 177. *Expositor* (4th Series), vol. vi. p. 347. A. Maclaren, *Expositions of Holy Scripture—1 John*, p. 329. IV. 10, 11.—Spurgeon, *Sermons*, vol. xxix. No. 1707.

'Beloved, if God so loved us, we ought also to love one another.'—1 JOHN IV. 11.

BLESSED is he that loveth Thee, and his friend in Thee, and his enemy for Thee.—AUGUSTINE, *Confessions* (IV. 9)

REFERENCES.—IV. 11.—S. Gregory, *How to Steer a Ship*, p. 103. Archbishop Benson, *Living Theology*, p. 71. IV. 12.—R. W. Church, *Village Sermons* (2nd Series), p. 221.

'If we love one another, God dwelleth in us. Hereby we know that we dwell in Him, and He in us.'—1 JOHN IV. 12, 13.

SIR, there may be artificial pride in this humility ; but for me, I neither know what He is, nor His Son's Name, nor where He dwelleth. I hear a report of Christ great enough, and that is all. Oh! what is nearness to Him? What is that, to be 'in God,' to 'dwell in God'? What a house that must be ! How far are some from their house and home? . . .

When shall we attain to a living in only, only God !—
S. RUTHERFORD to Colonel Gilbert Ker.

'And we have known and believed.'—1 JOHN IV. 16.

IN his essay on Boswell's *Life of Johnson*, Carlyle defines the few higher natures of every age as people who 'examine and determine, not what others do, but what it is right to do. . . . These are properly our Men, our great Men; the guides of the dull host—which follows them as by an irrevocable decree. They are the chosen of the world; they had this rare faculty not only of "supposing" and "inclining to think," but of *knowing* and *believing*; the nature of their being was, that they lived not by Hearsay, but by clear Vision.'

REFERENCES.—IV. 14.—U. R. Thomas, *Christian World Pulpit*, vol. l. p. 310. Spurgeon, *Sermons*, vol. xl. No. 2383. IV. 14, 15.—*Expositor* (6th Series), vol. v. p. 290. IV. 15.— C. S. Macfarland, *The Spirit Christlike*, p. 157. *Expositor* (5th Series), vol. vii. p. 210. IV. 16.—R. M. Grier, *Christian World Pulpit*, vol. xlvi. p. 28. C. D. Bell, *The Power of God*, p. 13. Bishop Gore, *Christian World Pulpit*, vol. l. p. 49. Spurgeon, *Sermons*, vol. v. No. 253. G. F. Pentecost, *Christian World Pulpit*, vol. li. p. 232. IV. 16-18.—C. Kingsley, *The Good News of God*, p. 256.

THE SERVANT AS HIS LORD

'As He is, so are we in this world.'—1 JOHN IV. 17.

LARGE truths may be spoken in little words. Profundity is often supposed to be obscurity, but the deepest depth is clear. John, in his gospel and epistles, deals with the deepest realities, and with all things in their eternal aspects, but his vocabulary is the simplest in the New Testament. What can be simpler than 'As He, so are we in this world?' And what can go beyond the thought that lies in it, that a Christian is a living likeness of Christ?

I. A Christian is Christ's living likeness. That is a startling thing to say, and all the more startling if you notice that John does not say 'As He *was*, in this earthly life of humiliation and filial obedience, but 'as He is,' in His heavenly life and reign and glory. Now *there* is the difference between the teaching of such classes of religionists as represent Christ's humanity as all in all, and preach to us that He, in His earthly life, is the pattern to whom we are to seek to conform our lives, and the true evangelical teaching. We are like Him, if we are His, in this that we are joined to God, that we hold fellowship with Him, that our lives are all permeated with the Divine, that we are saturated with the presence of God, that we have submitted ourselves to Him and to His will, that 'not my will, but Thine, be done' is the very inmost meaning of our hearts and our lives. I have put an emphasis upon the 'is' instead of the 'was,' as it applies to Jesus Christ. I would further put an emphasis upon the 'are,' as it applies to us. 'So *are* we.' John is not saying what Christian men ought to strive to be, but he is saying what all Christian men, by virtue of their Christian character, *are*. 'So are we, *in this world*.' The 'world'—or, to use modern phraseology, 'the

environment'—conditions the resemblance. But notice further, how that limitation carries with it another message. *There* is Christ in the heavens, veiled and unseen. Here are you on earth, His representative.

II. Such a likeness to Jesus Christ is the only thing that will enable a man to lift up his head in the Day of Judgment. Whilst unquestionably the beginning of salvation, and the condition of forgiveness here, and of acceptance hereafter, are laid in trust in Jesus Christ, that trust is sure to work out a character which is in conformity with His requirements and moulded after the likeness of Himself. It is only when faith works in us, through love and communion, characters like Jesus Christ's, that we shall be able to stand—though even then we shall have to trust to Divine and infinite mercy, and to the sprinkling of His blood before the Throne of God.

III. The process by which this likeness is secured. Our love is made perfect by dwelling in God, and God in us; in order that we may be thus conformed to Christ's likeness, and so have boldness in that great day. 'Abide in Me, and I in you.' But, remember, such abiding is no idle waiting, no passive confidence.—A. MACLAREN, *Triumphant Certainties*, p. 286.

REFERENCES. — IV. 17. — Bishop Winnington-Ingram, *Under the Dome*, p. 236. R. F. Horton, *Christian World Pulpit*, vol. lii. p. 225. A. Maclaren, *Expositions of Holy Scripture*—1 *John*, p. 338. IV. 17, 18.—R. W. Church, *Village Sermons* (3rd Series), p. 258.

FEAR AND LOVE

'There is no fear in love ; but perfect love casteth out fear : because fear hath torment.'—1 JOHN IV. 18.

FEAR and love—these two—and the greater of these is love. We are all agreed that love is the mightiest lever in the universe; but it is very possible that we are not all of one mind as to the use of *fear* in religion. And has it any legitimate use? Our answer is decidedly in the affirmative. The Bible speaks of two kinds of fear—the filial and the slavish. We fear God, and we fear the devil; but we do not fear the one in the same sense as we fear the other. Filial fear is a duty; but slavish fear is a sin. The one attracts us *to* God; but the other drives us away *from* Him. Fear's thunders, unless followed by love's enrapturing melodies, have a baneful influence upon the human soul; and this we shall endeavour to show.

I. Fear has a tendency to produce a Morality of Policy, unless supplemented by Love. The terrified soul strives to be virtuous, not from any love for virtue *per se*, but from fear of sin's punishment. We must strive to hate sin as sin, and love virtue as virtue, independently of the punishment or reward.

II. Incessant appeals to Fear have a sadly enervating influence upon the moral nature. Fear paralyses the soul, deprives it of its moral vigour, and positively hinders effort. Fear weakens the physical frame, and paves the way for any disease that may be hovering about. And is not this true of the intellect? Fear may drive the soul out of Egypt; but we need a more benignant power to lead it into Canaan.

III. Incessant appeals to Fear tend to promote unbelief. A dreaded God will eventually become a God despised, hated and denied.

IV. Incessant appeals to Fear tend to make spiritual worship impossible. Love delights to commune with its object; but a dreaded object will put a summary end to all pleasurable communion. A dreaded God cannot be heartily and devoutly worshipped. You can no more love Him than you can caress a volcano!

V. Incessant appeals to Fear may lead to a forced Obedience which is practically worthless. 'A man convinced against his will is of the same opinion still.' When the judgments were removed, Pharaoh forgot all his promises. Forced obedience, generated by fear, is little better than disobedience. In the face of all that we have said, some may be tempted to ask, 'What, then, is the use of fear in religion? Has it any use at all'. Our reply is that fear must be used to pave the way for something better than itself; in itself, it must be the herald and forerunner of love. Sinai must be the precursor of Calvary. It is so in the Bible, it is so in Providence, and it must be so in the spiritual history of the individual.— J. Ossian Davies, *Old Yet Ever New*, p. 179.

LOVE AND FEAR
1 John iv. 18.

John has been speaking of boldness, and that naturally suggests its opposite—fear. He has been saying that perfect love produces courage in the day of judgment, because it produces likeness to Christ, who is the judge. In my text he explains and enlarges that statement. For there is another way in which love produces boldness, and that is by its casting out fear. These two are mutually exclusive. There are three things here that I wish to notice—the empire of fear, the mission of fear, and the expulsion of fear.

I. **The Empire of Fear.**—Fear is a shrinking apprehension of evil as befalling us, from the person or thing which we dread. (1) There are conditions of human nature, in which the God who ought to be our dearest joy and most ardent desire becomes our ghastliest dread. The root of such an unnatural perversion of all that a creature ought to feel towards its loving Creator lies in the simple consciousness of discordance between God and man, which is the shadow cast over the heart by the fact of sin. (2) Arising from that discomforting consciousness of discord there come, likewise, other forms and objects of dread. For if I am out of harmony with Him, what will be my fate in the midst of a universe administered by Him and in which all are His servants? (3) Then there rises up another object of dread, which, in like manner, derives all its power to terrify and to hurt from the fact of our discordance with God; and that is 'the shadow feared of man,' that stands shrouded by the path and waits for each of us. There is something else that casts out fear than perfect love, and that is, perfect levity. A man who is in discord with God has reason to be afraid, and I come to you with the old exhortation of the prophet, 'Be troubled, ye careless ones'.

II. **The Mission of Fear.**—'Fear hath torment.' 'Torment' does not convey the whole idea of the word. It means suffering, but suffering for a purpose: suffering which is correction; suffering which is disciplinary; suffering which is intended to lead to something beyond itself. The intention of fear is to lead to that which shall annihilate it by taking away its cause. (1) Let the dread direct me to its source, my own sinfulness. (2) Let the discovery of my own sinfulness direct me to its remedy, the righteousness and the Cross of Jesus Christ.

III. **The Expulsion of Fear.**—If I go to Jesus Christ as a sinful man, and get His love bestowed upon me, then, as the next verse to my text says, my love springs in response to His to me, and in the measure in which that love rises in my heart will it frustrate its antagonistic dread. Remember that it is '*perfect* love' which 'casts out fear'. A little love has not mass enough in it to drive out thick, clustering fears.—A. Maclaren, *Triumphant Certainties*, p. 296.

'**Perfect love casteth out fear.**'—1 John iv. 18.

Cromwell wrote in 1652 to his son-in-law, General Fleetwood:—

'Salute your dear wife from me. Bid her beware of a bondage spirit. Fear is the natural issue of such a spirit, the antidote is love. The voice of fear is: If I had done this, if I had avoided that, how well it had been with me! I know this hath been her vain reasoning; poor Biddy!'

Love argueth in this verse, What a Christ have I; what a Father in and through Him! What a name hath my Father; merciful, gracious, long-suffering, abundant in goodness and truth; forgiving iniquity, transgression and sin. . . . This commends the love of God; it is Christ dying for men *without* strength, for men whilst sinners, whilst enemies. . . . Acts of obedience are not perfect, and therefore yield not perfect grace. Faith, as an act, yields it not; but 'only' as it carries us into Him, who is our perfect rest and peace; in whom we are accounted of, or received by the Father, even as Christ Himself. This is our high calling. Rest we here, and here only.

'**Perfect love casteth out fear.**'—1 John iv. 18.

Other fears and sorrows, grievances of body and mind, are troublesome for the time; but this is for ever, eternal damnation, hell itself, a plague, a fire; an inundation hurts one province alone, and the loss may be recovered; but this superstition involves all the world almost, and can never be remedied. Sickness and sorrows come and go, but a superstitious soul hath no rest.—Burton's *Anatomy of Melancholy*.

Charles Kingsley's eldest son once wrote that '"Perfect love casteth out fear" was the motto on which my father based his theory of bringing up his children; and this theory he put in practice from their babyhood till when he left them as men and women. From this, and from the interest he took in all their pursuits, their pleasures, trials, and even the petty details of their everyday life, there sprung up a "friendship" between father and children that increased in intensity and depth with years.'

'IN a sense, we were afraid of him,' Thomas Arnold writes of his father, Dr. Arnold of Rugby, in *Passages in a Wandering Life* (p. 9); 'that is, we were very much afraid, if we did wrong, of being found out and punished, and still worse, of witnessing the frown gathering on his brow. Yet in all of us on the whole love cast out fear; for he never held us at a distance, was never impatient with us; always, we knew, was trying to make us good and happy.'

'CAN there be true love without wholesome fear? And does not the old Elizabethan "My dear dread" express the noblest voluntary relation in which two human souls can stand to each other? Perfect love casteth out fear. Yes: but where is love perfect among imperfect beings, save a mother's for her child. For all the rest, it is through fear that love is made perfect; fear which bridles and guides the lover with awe—even though misplaced — of the beloved one's perfections; with dread—never misplaced—of the beloved one's contempt.'—CHARLES KINGSLEY, *Essays*, p. 344.

THERE comes a time when neither Fear nor Hope are necessary to the pious man; but he loves righteousness for righteousness' sake, and love is all in all. It is not joy but escape from future perdition that he now feels; nor is it hope for some untold happiness in the future: it is a present rapture of piety and resignation and love—a present that fills eternity. It asks nothing, it fears nothing; it loves and it has no petition to make. God takes back His little child to Himself—a little child that has no fear, and is all trust.—ALEXANDER SMITH.

FEAR AND LOVE
'He that feareth is not made perfect in love.'—1 JOHN IV. 18.

IN heaven, love will absorb fear; but in this world, *fear and love must go together.* No one can love God aright without fearing Him; though many fear Him, and yet do not love Him. Self-confident men, who do not know their own hearts, or the reasons they have for being dissatisfied with themselves, do not fear God, and they think this bold freedom is to love Him. Deliberate sinners fear but cannot love Him. But devotion to Him consists in love and fear, as we may understand from our ordinary attachment to each other. No one really loves another who does not feel a certain reverence towards him. When friends transgress this sobriety of affection, they may indeed continue associates for a time, but they have broken the bond of union. It is mutual respect which makes friendship lasting. So again, in the feelings of inferiors towards superiors. Fear must go

before love. Till he who has authority shows he has it and can use it, his forbearance will not be valued duly; his kindness will look like weakness. We learn to contemn what we do not fear; and we cannot love what we contemn. So in religion also. We cannot understand Christ's mercies till we understand His power, His glory, His unspeakable holiness, and our demerits; that is, until we first fear Him.— J. H. NEWMAN.

REFERENCES.—IV. 18.—S. Cox, *Expositions*, p. 364. E. M. Geldart, *Echoes of Truth*, p. 143. F. de W. Lushington, *Sermons to Young Boys*, p. 60. *Expositor* (4th Series), vol. ii. p. 213. A. Maclaren, *Expositions of Holy Scripture*—1 *John*, p. 347.

THE RAY AND THE REFLECTION
'We love Him, because He first loved us.'—1 JOHN IV. 19.

THE correct reading of my text, as you will find in the Revised Version, omits 'Him' in the first clause, and simply says 'we love,' without specifying the object. That is to say, for the moment John's thought is fixed rather on the inward transformation effected—from self-regard to love—than on considering the object on which the love is expended. When the heart is melted, the streams flow wherever there is a channel. The river, as he goes on to show us, parts into two heads, and love to God and love to man are, in their essence and root-principle, one thing. So my text is the summary of all revelation about God, the ultimate word about all our relations to Him, and the all-inclusive directory as to our conduct to one another.

I. The ultimate word about God. 'He first loved us.' Properly and strictly speaking, that 'first' only declares the priority of the Divine love towards us over ours towards Him. But we may fairly give it a wider meaning, and say—first of all, ere Creation and Time—first of all things was God's love: last to be discovered because most ancient of all. (1) Consider, for a moment, the relation which all the other perfections of the Divine nature have to this central and foundation one. There is the central blaze: the rest is but the brilliant periphery that encloses it. (2) Are we not warranted in believing that in that which we call the love of God there do abide the same elements as characterise the thing that bears the same name in our human experience? The spectrum has told us that the constituents of the mighty sun in the heavens are the same as the constituents of this little darkened earth. And there are the same lines in the Divine spectrum that there are in ours.

II. Here we have the ultimate word as to our religion. (1) A simple trust in the love of God, as manifested in Jesus Christ, our Lord, is the only thing which will so deal with man's natural self-regard and desire to make himself his own object and centre, as to substitute for that the victorious love of God. (2) If we love Him, it will be the motive power and spring of all manner of obedience and glad services. St. Augustine's paradox, rightly understood, is a magnificent truth, 'Love! and do what you will'.

III. Here is the ultimate word about our conduct to men. The only victorious antagonist to the self-regarding temperament of average men, and the only power which will change philanthropy from a sentiment into a self-denying and active principle of conduct, is to be found in the belief of the love of God in Jesus Christ, and in answering love to Him.—A. Maclaren, *Triumphant Certainties*, p. 305.

'We love Him, because He first loved us.'—1 John iv. 19.

It was in his happier state of mind that Law was found by Wesley, and in this spirit he said to him: 'You would have a philosophical religion, but there can be no such thing. Religion is the most plain, simple thing in the world. It is only, *we love Him, because He first loved us*'.—Southey.

The religious idea is essentially not an individualist perception, not a single fact which stands separate and palpable, but an organic and organising principle, which binds man to man, and of which the Church is the embodiment and evidence. 'How can a man love God,' it is said, 'if he love not his brother also?' How, it may be added, can one see and realise God, unless he see and realise the community and solidarity of man? On the coherence and coincidence of these two aspects all religion depends: it is this which, when it is alive, makes it always propagandist; for you feel that it cannot be really true for you unless it is true for others also.—Prof. William Wallace, *Gifford Lectures*, pp. 47, 48.

'He that loveth not his brother whom he hath seen, cannot love God whom he hath not seen.'—1 John iv. 20.

'But,' said Vinet half-sadly, half-ironically, in his diary, 'it is just the brother one sees whom it is so difficult to love'.

References.—IV. 19.—H. S. Holland, *Christian World Pulpit*, vol. liv. p. 168. W. H. Evans, *Short Sermons for the Seasons*, p. 96. R. J. Campbell, *City Temple Sermons*, p. 122. Spurgeon, *Sermons*, vol. v. No. 229; vol. xvii. No. 1008; vol. xxii. No. 1299, and vol. xlvii. No. 2730. A. Maclaren, *Expositions of Holy Scripture—1 John*, p. 355. IV. 20.—J. M. Whiton, *Summer Sermons*, p. 53. H. S. Holland, *Christian World Pulpit*, vol. xlv. p. 329. Bishop Riley, *Church Family Newspaper*, vol. xv. p. 536. IV. 20, 21.—J. C. M. Bellew, *Christ in Life: Life in Christ*, p. 315. IV. 21.—J. S. Boone, *Sermons*, p. 190. V. 1.—Spurgeon, *Sermons*, vol. xvii. No. 979. V. 1-5.—*Expositor* (6th Series), vol. v. p. 287.

GOD'S COMMANDMENTS

'His commandments are not grievous.'—1 John v. 3.

We shall do well to remind ourselves at the beginning of life that we are already in a wonderful world, that the pathway of our lives will lead us through the intricacies of a Divine system, which is intended progressively to reveal itself to us, and to bring us nearer to our intended perfection and to God. Let me try to point out two or three of the chief groups of forces which form part of this Divine system.

I. The Fellowship of Love.—First, then, as touching the very beginning of our existence here, there is what has been called the fellowship of Love. Love is a great force, or set of forces, most delicate, most subtle, most intricate, most Divine; and yet how little considered, how imperfectly prepared for, by most of us! Marriage is indeed a wonderful part of the Divine system, and full of progressively developing power and blessing, instituted by God in Paradise, before sin had confused and dulled the pleasures He had prepared for us; chosen as the symbol of the great mystery of God; given freely to all, rich as well as poor, with no respect of persons. How imperfectly do we prepare for it! I do not speak of that miserable refined system of human barter, when parents, for the sake of politics or some worldly scheme, sell their children for their own advancement, and condemn them to the slavery of a loveless marriage; but rather I am thinking of the hundreds of thoughtless men and women who enter upon this Divine mystery, yield themselves to the intricacies of these heavenly forces, without reasonable consideration, without any serious thought, without one word of prayer. We are shocked when the results come before us, day after day, alas! in our daily journals, and we read of the heartless forsaking, or brutal treatment, of one who should be as another self, the symbol of the Bride of Christ. We are shocked, too, hardly less, at the frequent applications of richer men to be freed from a union that they might have hoped would have had strength to stand even the shock of death.

II. The Fellowship of Rights.—Here is another fellowship, another set of forces, very powerful, which God has prepared for us among the intricacies of the Divine system in which we live, closely connected with the progressive development of family life. It has been called the fellowship of Rights. No man can live to himself: we are all bound together; the family becomes the germ of the State. Ethics, as it has been said, must be regarded again, as of old, as the vestibule of politics: it is not possible to continue exhorting children of any class with mere moral maxims of individual morality; they must become conscious as they live on of the intricacies of the combined forces of political and national life—forces which God has prepared for us, and intended to assist humanity in its progress towards perfection and nearness to Himself.

III. The Fellowship of Grace.—There is yet a third fellowship, a third group of forces, a third example of the intricacies of the Divine system in which we may now be—the fellowship of Grace; *i.e.*, in simple language, though perhaps not more easily understood, the Church.

Here is a Divine system, which is the perfection of the fellowships of Love and of Rights: it is a universal Brotherhood; it is the kingdom of heaven.—Bishop Edward King, *The Love and Wisdom of God*, p. 121.

THE GRACIOUSNESS OF THE LAW

'For this is the love of God, that we keep His commandments: and His commandments are not grievous.'—1 JOHN v. 3.

I. Every Commandment is a Salvation.—How is it that the commandments appear grievous? Because they cross our unnatural and inordinate desires. To resent the laws of Sinai is more foolish than to complain of the steel bars of the menagerie which come between us and the wild beasts. The grievousness is in ourselves, and the commandment is a glorious salvation from the evil within us which we have most to fear. Not only are the commandments not grievous, they are gracious. There are two kinds of grace—preventing grace and reclaiming grace. The grace that absolves our sins, covers our guilt, brings into our bosom abiding peace, is precious indeed. Yet preventing grace is not less precious. One of the grandest revelations of this preventing grace is seen in the clear and authoritative publication of the law. The commandment is not grievous, any more than the lighthouse—it is a warning, guiding, saving beacon.

II. Every Commandment is an Inspiration.—Science assures us of the efficacy of light; it is not light only, but force—quickening, cleansing, compelling force. And the truth in Jesus is not merely dry light for the intellect, but vital force availing for interior purity and practical obedience. When we are born of God and filled with faith and love, the keeping of the commandment is easy and delightful. When the Master showed the immense sublimity of the law of forgiveness, the disciples did not ask that it should be modified to their weakness, but that through increased faith and force they might be equal to it in all its length and breadth.

III. Every Commandment is a Benediction.—Not a salvation only, but a beatitude. No astronomer has yet been able to observe any evidence of a comet possessing a fixed axis of revolution, and most probably because they have not yet acquired this law, comets are so unorganised and so eccentric in their orbits; free from a fixed axis of revolution they wander at large with erratic movement, yet they remain chaotic, and do not develop into beautiful and fruitful planets. Yes; it is only as the love of God becomes the fixed axis of our being, and a close obedience to law the rule of our life, that we are fashioned into the full glory of our nature and enter upon its vast destiny of blessedness.—W. L. WATKINSON, *The Ashes of Roses*, p. 235.

'His commandments are not grievous.'—1 JOHN v. 3.

CONTRAST Shelley's bitter note to *Queen Mab*: 'Religion and morality, as they now stand, compose a practical code of misery and servitude: the genius of human happiness must tear every leaf from the accursed book of God ere man can read the inscription on his heart'.

'IN my life, an exceptionally happy one from a worldly point of view,' says Tolstoï, 'I can number such a quantity of sufferings endured for the sake of "the world" that they would be enough to furnish a martyr for Jesus. . . . Let any sincere man pass his life in review, and he will perceive that never, not once, has he suffered through practising the doctrine of Jesus; the chief part of the miseries of his life have proceeded solely from his following, contrary to his inclinations, the spell of the doctrine of the world.'

HAVE we not all of us moods, in which an allusion to God makes us impatient; and is not this fact alone the nearest of any fact to a deep-sea sounding of our corruption? It is hard to see what God has done to deserve all this. . . . It is the very necessity of our case as creatures, that we must be under a law; and could we be under laws less numerous, less onerous, than those under which we are laid by the perfection of God? Easy laws, few laws, and laws which it is our own interest to keep—these are the characteristics of the dominion of God.—F. W. FABER.

REFERENCES.—V. 3.—J. W. Houchin, *The Vision of God* p. 72. J. Keble, *Sermons for Septuagesima to Ash Wednesday*, p. 200. V. 3, 4.—J. J. Blunt, *Plain Sermons* (2nd Series), p. 160.

THE FACT OF THE RESURRECTION
(*For Easter Sunday*)

'This is the victory that overcometh the world, even our faith.—1 JOHN v. 4.

TO-DAY, the octave day of Easter, the joy of the Apostolic colleagues is fulfilled. Ever since the Apostles saw the Lord, they have been glad; but through the past week a shadow of sorrow has been cast over their happiness, because, do what they would, for so the original implies, they could not persuade one of their colleagues to believe their statement that Christ had risen again. But to-day Jesus appeared to Thomas as well as again to the other disciples, and he who, for the very joy of the thing, had been unable to accept his brethren's testimony, gives utterance, on the appearance of the risen Lord to him, to the fullest and truest expression of faith which had as yet been delivered, as he worshipped Him and said, 'My Lord and my God'. As we all know, alas! faith in these days is very much at discount. Men claim the right of doing with the science of religion that which no sane man would ever think of doing with any other science. They claim the right to overthrow all authority and all inquiry and research that has gone before, they try to persuade us to begin again from the very beginning as if there were no treasures of the Church in ages past. There is not one of us, therefore, who can afford to dispense with the encouragement and help which the Easter festival brings us with regard to our faith.

I. In the first place, the fact of the Resurrection, as a well-authenticated event in history, is the sure foundation for our faith, for it abundantly proved all that went before it, and it, and it alone, fully accounts for all that follows after it. Easter proves the truth of the Catholic creed which says that God the Son was conceived by the Holy Ghost, born of the Virgin Mary, for it was not possible that He Who gives life, and in Whom is life, should be holden of the pains of death. The miracle is rather on Good Friday afternoon than on Easter morning, for the Resurrection is but the taking again of that which man could not deprive our Lord of, but which He laid down of His own free will, and which He, with that power that He tells us He had, took up again. Such a power could not, of course, possibly belong to any but God, and it is in this proof that the Resurrection gives us that we listen gladly to the statement of St. Paul when, as in the Second Lesson to-day, he tells us, 'If Christ be not raised, your faith is vain ; ye are yet in your sins'. And as with all that comes before Easter, so also with the history of the world, as of the Church, it is only in the truth of the fact of the Resurrection that we can find any satisfactory solution of the problems which are set before us. And seeing that it is by the Resurrection from the dead that Jesus is declared to be 'the Son of God with power according to the spirit of holiness,' we without hesitation, we with undying thankfulness, ever lifting up our hearts in praise to God for His goodness and mercy towards us, accept the whole faith given by God through His Son, and feel, as we believe, that 'this is the victory that overcometh the world, even our faith'.

II. But again the Resurrection is not only a fact ; it is also a revelation, that is to say, an unveiling of things unknown and not understood before. It is the revelation of a spiritual force here, and also a revelation of the unseen world beyond. During the great forty days that our Lord remained on earth, He showed that His whole human being was glorified, transformed by the Resurrection. And it is in this revelation of the Resurrection that we learn about new modes of human life. We see how we also can live through death and have a home beyond. We understand how, even in this life, we are bound to live the higher and spiritual existence, the life identified with the Resurrection life of Christ our Lord. It is in this revelation that we now have union with those who have gone before, and that we look forward to the time when we, too, shall be changed. How great is the influence of this revelation on our faith it is impossible to exaggerate. We feel—it is within each one of us as an instinct— that this life is not the end of everything. Other religions, other, I mean, than that of Christ, teach us this truth quite plainly, but it is only in the Resurrection of Jesus Christ we can certainly know the reality of that which instinct forewarns us of, and once more we say, 'This is the victory that overcometh the world, even our faith'.

III. But the Resurrection, because it is a fact and because it is a revelation, is also a call. To believe in the fact, in any way to have been conscious of the power of the revelation, is to receive a call as truly, as fully, as searchingly, as plainly, as responsibly as when our Blessed Lord first said to the Apostles,

'Go ye, therefore, and make disciples of all nations'. It is impossible for people really to know Jesus and the power of His Resurrection without being filled with zeal and ardour for the conversion of the world, and this zeal is manifested at home and abroad. It matters not where it is. What does matter is that you and I, who profess every day of our life that we do believe that on the third day He rose again from the dead, should be as those who have heard the call to go forth and bring others to the knowledge and love of God. It is the truth of the Resurrection, or rather, shall we say, it is the love for the risen Lord, that has made men and women in this very day give up all for the love of their Saviour. Go where you will, and you will find people working for Christ, not a dead Christ, not a powerless Christ, not a mere historic Christ of the past, but a living Christ, the Almighty Christ, the historic Christ, and oh ! more, far more, than that, even Jesus Christ, the same yesterday, to-day, and for ever. Year by year the Easter call comes fresh to you and to me. And as we go forth, and in our lives, and by our words, and by our alms, and fastings, and prayers, preach the glorious Gospel of the Resurrection, and see at home and abroad one soul here and another soul there—for never let us despise a single soul— joining that glad procession until it becomes a great multitude which no man can number, shall we, once again, with all joy, humility, and thankfulness, say, 'This is the victory that overcometh the world, even our faith'.

THE FAITH THAT OVERCOMES

'For whatsoever is born of God overcometh the world : and this is the victory that overcometh the world, even our faith.'—1 JOHN V. 4.

I. THE first thing which strikes us in the character of our faith is that it bears the impress of man as well as of God—of God *in* and *through* man. Christianity is essentially *personal* : it centres in a Saviour's life.

II. Our faith is not only personal; it is essentially historical. True it is that more than eighteen hundred years have passed since He Who was called contemptuously 'the Nazarene' proclaimed Himself to be 'the Son of God, the Saviour of the World,' but we must remember that since the commission to the twelve His words have ever had their full effect.

III. Our faith, which is personal and historical, is also essentially practical. Every mystery which is revealed to us is only so far set forth as to guide our conduct without satisfying our curiosity. The victory of faith is as manifold as its nature. (*a*) In the first place, it is a victory over fleshly, material evils, both in the individual and in society. It has power to vanquish the selfishness of man. (*b*) Yet again, our faith is also a victory over intellectual as well as over material evils. Its history shows us how far it can appropriate all that is good and great in the progress of nations. The eternal truths of revelation remain unchanged, but they are clothed from time to time in that outward form which makes them most effectual in influencing the temper of the age. (c) Yet, once again, our faith is also a victory over spiritual evils. The Christian life is the necessary commentary on the Christian creed. The sincerity of our belief is measured by the efficiency of our practice.—Bishop Westcott, *Village Sermons*, p. 172.

'This is the victory that overcometh the world, even our faith.'
—1 John v. 4.

Public and private exercises are religious and good as the simple voice of, or as means to the strengthening of, the religious will. That will consists in the faith that overcomes the world, by turning it into the Christian world which for faith it is.—F. H. Bradley, *Ethical Studies*, p. 304.

'Vinet,' wrote Scherer, 'had acquired by personal experience a great confidence in the power of truth, and this is a second characteristic of his religious idea. What does it matter that men are hostile and indifferent? The Gospel which has reached his heart cannot fail to reach others. Christianity is true, therefore it is a force. All that it needs is liberty. Leave it to itself, offer neither hindrance nor support, and it will conquer the world.'

References.—V. 4.—T. H. Ball, *Persuasions*, p. 226. J. Monro Gibson, *Christian World Pulpit*, vol. liii. p. 340. J. Keble, *Sermons for Easter to Ascension Day*, p. 201. R. C. Cowell, *Preacher's Magazine*, vol. xvii. p. 326. R. W. Hiley, *A Year's Sermons*, vol. i. p. 209. Spurgeon, *Sermons*, vol. i. No. 14. J. Bowstead, *Practical Sermons*, vol. i. p. 314. J. E. Watts Ditchfield, *Mundesley Conference Report*, 1910, p. 388. *Expositor* (5th Series), vol. v. p. 142. A. Maclaren, *Expositions of Holy Scripture—Epistles of John*, p. 1. V. 4, 5. —T. Arnold, *Sermons*, vol. ii. p. 8. Spurgeon, *Sermons*, vol. xlvii. No. 2757. V. 5, 6.—H. Bonar, *Short Sermons for Family Reading*, p. 348.

CONFLICT AND CONQUEST

'Who is he that overcometh the world, but he that believeth that Jesus is the Son of God.'—1 John v. 5.

In the season of Lent it is needful that our minds should be prepared for the important duties that devolve upon us, and there is no subject more useful for meditation than the Christian warfare. The Church, therefore, in her wisdom, has appointed the Lenten season as a time for fasting and prayer in order that the faithful may be led to a higher spiritual life.

I. Our Conflict is with the World.—Our Lord has told us who the prince of this world is, and we therefore understand that we are opposed by all the powers and forces of evil, marshalled and put in array by Satan himself. When we regard the mighty forces brought against us, the vast multitude of the host, and the discipline of the array, we are led seriously to consider our position—whether we are able, with our small and disunited band, to wage war with such an enemy as this. Naturally, we find ourselves perfectly unable; the conflict is too grievous; we are overmatched and outnumbered; what can we do? The consideration of this teaches us our entire dependence upon God. We turn to His Holy Word for help, and we read that help can be gained sufficient to our need, and, if we earnestly seek it, strength will be imparted to fight and to overcome.

II. Who is He that 'Overcometh the World'?—The answer of our text is this: 'He that believeth that Jesus is the Son of God'. One who not only has enlisted in Christ's army, but also still remains a Christian soldier. By overcoming the world we must here understand overcoming the temptations of the 'world, the flesh, and the devil'. How grievous these temptations are, we know; how frequently we are even ourselves overcome, we know. But of this we may be sure: if we are thoroughly equipped for the fight our eventual triumph will be certain and complete. We need to gird on the 'whole armour of God'. The *whole armour*, not a *part* merely. This is where the mistake is often made. A Christian is negligent in prayer; or he is weak in faith; or he is not regular in attendance upon the ministrations of God's Holy Church; he does not keep a guard upon his words or his actions; he is not ready to forgive and forget an injury; he gives way to pride, or malice, or conceit: in fact, he is not fully prepared for the spiritual warfare. If there are any defects in his panoply the enemy takes advantage of those unprotected parts, and he falls; but when he is clad in the whole armour, well riveted and linked together, then he is ever victorious, and overcomes the world. We must be thorough Christians if we hope to overcome.

III. What is the Nature of this Faith?—It is of a threefold nature:—

(a) *A faith that leads a sinner to prostrate himself*, as a true penitent, at the foot of his Saviour's cross, not daring even to look up, but simply to cry aloud for pardon in those words of the publican, 'Lord, be merciful to me a sinner'.

(b) *A faith that lays hold of that cross*, as the Christian, with bended knees, clings to it, being determined, by the help of God, never to depart from it again.

(c) *A faith that enables him to bear that cross during life*, humbly and devotedly, 'counting all things but loss,' for the sake of Him who died thereon. This is how the Christian overcomes the world; this is belief in the Son of God.

Trusting, then, in Christ, we gain help sufficient for every need, and strength to encounter every foe.

'Who is he that overcometh the world, but he that believeth that Jesus is the Son of God?'—1 John v. 5.

He who has a faith, we know well, is twice himself. The world, the conventional order of things, goes down before the weapons of faith, before the energy of those who have a glimpse, or only think they have a glimpse, of the eternal or normal order of things.— Sir John Seeley, *Natural Religion*, p. 34.

References.—V. 6.—*Expositor* (5th Series), vol. x. p. 60. V. 6-8.—*Ibid.* vol. vii. p. 301; *ibid.* (7th Series), vol. v p. 416.

THE SPIRITUAL DOCTRINE OF GOD

(*Trinity Sunday*)

'For there are three that bear record in heaven, the Father, the Word, and the Holy Ghost: and these three are one.'—I JOHN v. 7.

ONE of the most significant and valuable changes in the habits of theological thinking is the change from the deductive and metaphysical to the inductive and psychological method. In simpler language, it was formerly the rule to establish a doctrine apart from our human experience, and then to adapt life and thought to the doctrine; it is now the rule to take our human experience with us when we are trying to understand or state all doctrines.

In no case is this latter method more advantageous, and indeed necessary, than in regard to the doctrine of the Holy Trinity. If we try to build it up out of proof-texts from Scripture, and abstract reasoning and speculation, we shall succeed only in bewildering ourselves. The abstract doctrine of the Trinity is scholastic, mechanical, and fictitious. The popularised form of such a conception will be either some form of tritheism, or it will be a mere paradox with no meaning at all.

I. But it was not in this abstract fashion that the doctrine originally came. It did not arise from our text, for that text was absent from the original documents and did not appear till the fifth century. The doctrine, as Clarke says, 'Sprang up in experience, not in speculation'. It was because men found the one God manifesting Himself to them in three ways that they tried to conceive and state their thoughts of Him accordingly. The abstract formulations and controversies were drawn partly from Scripture; partly from the need of combating heresies which stated the being of God in terms which were not true to the Christian experience; and partly from the Greek spirit which sought to rationalise and harmonise all human knowledge. But none of these was the source of the doctrine, which arose out of the deepest hours of communion between the souls of believers and God.

II. When we ask not what God is in Himself, but what He is to us, the answer of experience is, that we know Him as Father, as Son, and as Holy Spirit. It is interesting to remember that this is the order in which the revelation has been historically made. The earliest phase of it was that of the patriarchal times. Then, in the nomad society, fatherhood was the dominant idea. It governed law, custom, and all the affairs and relations of life. So men, looking up towards the Divine through their own experience, naturally found Him as the Father—the highest expression of their ruling and guiding conception. Later, when national history grew tragic with sin and punishment, defeat and exile shattering the nation's complacent life, and conscience embittering the misery of their hearts, there came a second phase. The suffering Servant, the stricken and afflicted One bearing on His own heart the sins of many, and by His stripes healing them, revealed the Son. When Jesus had been crucified, His disciples saw in Calvary the complete revelation of all that towards which the prophets had been groping. Here was another view of God, and the life of the world demanded it and was satisfied by it. Yet these were not all. From the first there had been a sense of the Divine inspiring and guiding the ordinary life of man, quickening his interests and working through him in his enthusiasms. In the days of the Apostles this inspiring and quickening became so distinct and so powerful a phenomenon, that they could explain it no otherwise than by a third view of God as Holy Spirit. Thus in historic order, God revealed Himself to man threefold.

In the experience of the individual the same thing is true, and though no religious experience is coerced into following any unbroken order of sequence, yet in general the order is the same.

III. Heine, in a memorable passage, has elaborated this conception, and with that we may leave the subject. We must leave it in mystery; but through the mystery the great thought of the Holy Trinity shines, sufficient for the needs of life, though still eluding the efforts of the strongest intellect. We cannot master these conceptions and force them into a unity of thought. We shall be wise if we let them master us, and guide us into a life of worship and obedience.

'Ah, my child,' says Heine, 'while I was yet a little boy, while I yet sat upon my mother's knee, I believed in God the Father, who rules up there in heaven, good and great; who created the beautiful earth, and the beautiful men and women thereon; who ordained for sun, moon, and stars their courses.

'When I got bigger, my child, I comprehended yet a great deal more than this, and comprehended, and grew intelligent; and I believe on the Son also, on the beloved Son, who loved us and revealed love to us; and for His reward, as always happens, was crucified by the people.

'Now, when I am grown up, have read much, have travelled much, my heart swells within me, and with my whole heart I believe on the Holy Ghost. The greatest miracles were of His working, and still greater miracles doth He even now work; He burst in sunder the oppressor's stronghold, and He burst in sunder the bondsman's yoke. He heals old death-wounds, and renews the old right; all mankind are one race of noble equals before Him. He chases away the evening clouds and the dark cobwebs of the brain, which have spoilt love and joy for us, which day and night have lowered on us.'—JOHN KELMAN, *Ephemera Eternitatis*, p. 144.

REFERENCES.—V. 7, 8.—E. W. Attwood, *Sermons for Clergy and Laity*, p. 210. *Expositor* (7th Series), vol. v. p. 129. V. 8.—J. Keble, *Sermons for Lent to Passion-tide*, p. 172; *ibid. Sermons for Easter to Ascension Day*, p. 160. Spurgeon, *Sermons*, vol. xx. No. 1187.

'If we receive the witness of men, the witness of God is greater.'—I JOHN v. 9.

ON the contrast of credulity and faith, see Spencer's *Sociology* (p. 117), where he points out that 'one would hardly suppose, *à priori*, that untruthfulness would habitually co-exist with credulity. Rather our inference might be that, because of the tendency above enlarged upon, people most given to making false statements must be people most inclined to suspect statements made by others. Yet, somewhat anomalously, as it seems, habitual veracity generally goes with inclination to doubt evidence; and extreme untrustworthiness of assertion often has, for its concomitant, readiness to accept the greatest improbabilities on the slenderest testimony.'

REFERENCES.—V. 9, 10.—Spurgeon, *Sermons*, vol. xxi. No. 1213. V. 10.—G. S. Barrett, *Christian World Pulpit*, vol. li. p. 179. H. Woodcock, *Sermon Outlines* (1st Series), p. 134. C. G. Finney, *Penny Pulpit*, No. 1554, p. 69. Bishop E. H. Browne, *Sermons on the Atonement*, p. 114. F. W. Farrar, *Truths to Live By*, p. 47. Spurgeon, *Sermons*, vol. xx. No. 1207; vol. xxi. No. 1250, and vol. xxiv. No. 1428.

' And the witness is this, that God hath given to us eternal life, and this life is in His Son.'—1 JOHN V. 11.

How the brave sun doth peep up from beneath,
Shows us his golden face, doth on us breath;
Yea, he doth compass us around with glories,
Whilst he ascends up to his highest stories,
Where he his banner over us displays
And gives us light to see our works and ways.
Nor are we now, as at the peep of light,
To question is it day or is it night;
The night is gone, the shadows fled away,
And now we are most certain that 'tis day.
And then it is when Jesus shows His face,
And doth assure us of His love and grace.
                    —BUNYAN.

ONE has spoken of difficulty in joining, in anticipation, 'himself and glory in one thought'. The greater difficulty is to join ourselves and eternal life in one thought now, although God has already in Christ so connected us in the very truth of things. But, as I have said, we are alike slow of heart to receive Christ's revelation of ourselves, and to receive His revelation of God—to believe that God has given to us eternal life in His Son, and to believe that God is love.—McLEOD CAMPBELL, *The Nature of the Atonement* (ch. VII.).

'These things have I written unto you . . . that ye may know ye have eternal life.'—1 JOHN V. 13.

I SHALL never envy the honours which wit and learning obtain in any other cause, if I can be numbered among the writers who have given ardour to virtue, and confidence to truth.—DR. JOHNSON.

REFERENCES.—V. 11.—T. F. Crosse, *Sermons*, p. 114. V. 11, 12.—H. D. Rawnsley, *Church Family Newspaper*, vol. xiv. p. 287. V. 12.—Spurgeon, *Sermons*, vol. xiii. No. 755. *Expositor* (4th Series), vol. i. p. 203. V. 13.—C. S. Macfarland, *The Spirit Christlike*, p. 141. E. A. Stuart, *His Dear Son and other Sermons*, vol. v. p. 97. Spurgeon, *Sermons*, vol. xxx. No. 1791, and vol. xxxiv. No. 2023. V. 13-15.—Spurgeon, *Sermons*, vol. x. No. 596. V. 14.—F. J. A. Hort, *Village Sermons in Outline*, p. 48.

' And this is the confidence that we have in Him, that, if we ask anything according to His will, He heareth us. And if we know that He hear us, whatsoever we ask, we know that we have the petitions that we desired of Him.'— 1 JOHN V. 14, 15.

THIS is one of the texts which require very little understanding and very great believing. It seems to go so entirely against the evidence of our senses. Whatsoever we ask, we receive! Why, which is there of us who has not asked again and again for something that we longed for, and yet has never received it at all! How many mothers have prayed for a dear child's life: and the child was taken: just as David did when Nathan had said to him, 'the child that is born to thee shall surely die'. How many men have asked earnestly to be delivered from some disease, as St. Paul from his blindness—but no, they have carried it with them to their graves. How many poor people have been oppressed (the children of Israel were by the Egyptians) by some cruel, griping, hard-hearted man, and has prayed to be delivered from him, but they never were! Then what does the text mean? Whatsoever we ask, we receive. And yet we know that we do not receive.

I. Now, the way in which some good men have explained this is, that whatever we ask we shall receive if it be good for us: that if we do not receive, it is only because it is not good for us—and that it is made up to us in some other way. Now I do not doubt that there is *some* truth in this, we may be sure, from our Lord's promise, that if we ask for a fish, he will not give us a scorpion—if we ask, that is, for something that seems wholesome and useful, He will not, because of our mistake, bestow on us something which is dangerous and a poison.

II. But still, there is a great deal more in the promise than this explanation gives it. 'Whatsoever we ask, we have the petitions.' First notice how many promises of the same kind there are, 'Ask, and it shall be given you; seek, and ye shall find; knock, and it shall be opened unto you.' 'Whatsoever ye shall ask of My Father in My Name, that will I do'. ' If two of you shall agree as touching anything in My Name, it shall be done for them of My Father which is in heaven; and all things whatsoever ye shall ask in prayer, believing, ye shall receive. If you ask with all your power, determined to have, and believing that you will have, you will have. But then, how very, very few have this faith? The Apostles wrought their miracles only because they had more faith. If we had their faith we could do what they did. There is no other difference. There are all sorts of special answers to prayer; from the commonest answer to the highest miracle. Holy men have divided all answers to prayer into two heads; a grace or ordinary answer, and a miracle. A grace is an answer which does not break through what we call the laws of nature, that is, the laws by which God governs the world, but which nevertheless is very singular and remarkable. A miracle does break through these laws.

III. But then, you will notice, there are two conditions which our Lord makes when He promises to give us that which we ask. In the first place we must ask earnestly; in the second, we must believe that we shall have that for which we ask. But then this very faith is the gift of God. Here, as in everything else, of Him, and through Him and to Him, are all things. He gives us the desire to pray, at first; He gives us the belief that we shall have what we pray for; and having given us both these things, He crowns His gifts by giving us the thing we do pray for.—J. M. NEALE, *Sermons in Sackville College Chapel*, vol. II. p. 23.

HOW PRAYER IS ANSWERED

1 JOHN V. 14, 15.

J. M. NEALE gives the following illustration on this passage : 'Here is an instance of a very remarkable grace. It happened little more than a fortnight ago. There was a young soldier in the French army who when he went to the war, had most earnestly asked for the prayers of his mother. He dwelt on this over and over again; it was the last request he made her when he left his home; and in every letter she received from him there was still this same earnest request, Do not forget to pray for me. I daresay that she did not forget what he had asked every morning and evening. But one Wednesday afternoon—it was about four o'clock—this mother had it most strongly impressed upon her mind—she could not tell why or how, but so it was, that her son was in great danger, and that she ought to pray for him at once. And accordingly she did so, and went on praying for him, still having the same feeling, for more than two hours. In process of time she had a letter from the same son to say that in all these hours he had been in the extremity of danger, he had been picked out to serve in the forlorn hope of the French army in the battle of Balaclava. In that time he had seen the soldiers who stood next to his right and left sides shot down sixteen times; his own cap had been torn away, and his trousers were nearly torn to pieces with splinters of flints, hit up out of the ground by spent bullets; but he himself was not in the least injured; had not even received a scratch. Now this I do not call, strictly speaking, a miracle. It is rather an example of a "grace". Anyhow it is a wonderful proof how God can and does hear prayer.'—*Sermons in Sackville College Chapel*, vol. II. p. 27.

REFERENCES.—V. 14, 15.—J. E. Page, *Preacher's Magazine*, vol. xvii. p. 318. R. Rainy, *Christian World Pulpit*, vol. liii. p. 387. C. D. Bell, *The Power of God*, p. 140. R. J. Campbell, *A Faith for To-day*, p. 309. J. M. Neale, *Sermons Preached in Sackville College Chapel*, vol. ii. p. 23. R. J. Campbell, *Christian World Pulpit*, vol. lvii. p. 51. *Ibid. The Examiner*, 24th May, 1906, p. 509. *Ibid. City Temple Sermons*, p. 38. V. 14-17.—S. Cox, *Expositions*, p. 239. V. 15.—*Expositor* (4th Series), vol. iii. p. 382. V. 16.—S. Cox, *Expositions*, p. 253. V. 16, 17.—H. Bonar, *Short Sermons for Family Reading*, p. 340.

TRIUMPHANT CERTAINTIES—I

'We know that whosoever is born of God sinneth not ; but he that is begotten of God keepeth himself, and that wicked one toucheth him not.'—1 JOHN v. 18.

JOHN closes his letter with a series of triumphant certainties, which he considers as certified to every Christian by his own experience.

I. Of whom is the Apostle speaking here? 'We know that whosoever is born of God'—or, as the Revised Version reads it, '*begotten* of God'—'sinneth not'. Let me recall to you the Master's words with which He all but began His public ministry. 'Except a man be born again he cannot see the kingdom of God.' There is the root of all that this Epistle is so full of, the conception of a regeneration, a being born again, which makes men, by a new birth, sons of God, in a fashion and in a sphere of their nature in which they were not the sons of the Heavenly Father before that experience. (1) This sonship of God, which is the result of being born, is mediated and received by us through our faith. (2) This new birth, and the new Divine life which is its result, co-exist along with the old nature in which it is planted, and which it has to coerce and subdue, sometimes to crucify, and always to govern. The new life has to grow. But growth is not the only word for its development. That new nature has to fight for its life.

II. What is asserted about this Divine life? 'Whosoever is born of God sinneth not.' I take the text to mean—not that a Christian is, or must be, in order to vindicate his right to be called a Christian, sinless, but that there is a power in him, a life-principle in him which is sinless, and whatsoever in him is born of God overcometh the world and 'sinneth not'. (1) This notion of a Divine life-power, lodged in, and growing through, and fighting with the old nature, makes the hideousness and the criminality of a Christian man's transgressions more hideous and more criminal. (2) The one task of Christians ought to be to deepen and to strengthen the life of God which is in their souls, by faith.

III. What is the ground of John's assertion about him 'that is born of God?' 'Whosoever is born of God sinneth not,' because round his weakness is cast the strong defence of the Elder Brother's hand.'—A. MACLAREN, *Triumphant Certainties*, p. 1.

REFERENCES.—V. 18.—A. Maclaren, *Expositions of Holy Scripture—Epistles of John*, p. 12. V. 18-21.—*Expositor* (5th Series), vol. ix. p. 81.

TRIUMPHANT CERTAINTIES—II

'We know that we are of God, and the whole world lieth in wickedness.'—1 JOHN v. 19.

THERE are few things which the average Christianity of to-day wants more than a participation in that joyous confidence and buoyant energy which throb in the Apostle's words; and for lack of this triumphant certitude many a soul has been lamed, its joy clouded, its power trammelled, and its work in the world thwarted.

I. Look at the Christian certainty of belonging to God. 'We know that we are of God.' (1) The first conception in the phrase is that of life derived, communicated from God Himself. (2) The second of the ideas in this expression is, the continual dependence of that derived life upon God. (3) It is correspondent with its source, 'Ye are of God,' kindred with Him and developing a life which, in its measure, being derived and dependent, is cognate with, and assimilated to, his own. This is the prerogative of every Christian soul. The man that has that life *knows* it. That word 'know' has been usurped, or at all events illegitimately monopolised by certain forms of knowledge. But surely the inward facts of my own consciousness are as much facts, and are certified to me as validly and reliably as are facts in other regions which are attested by the senses, or arrived at by reasoning.

II. We have here the Christian view of the surrounding world. John learned from Jesus to use that phrase 'the world,' not as meaning the aggregate of material things, but as meaning the aggregate of godless men. The measure of our conscious belonging to God is the measure of our perception of the contrast between us and the ways of the men about us.

III. Consider the consequent Christian duty. (1) Cultivate the sense of belonging to a higher order than that in which you dwell. (2) Be careful to avoid infection. (3) Look on the world as Christ looked on it. (4) Work for the deliverance of your brethren from the alien tyrant. Notice the difference between the two clauses in the text. 'We are *of* God'; that is a permanent relation. 'The world lieth *in* the wicked one'; that is not necessarily a permanent relation. The world is not *of* the wicked one; it is '*in*' him, and that may be altered. As in the old stories, knights hung their dishonoured arms upon trees, and laid their heads in the lap of an enchantress, so men have departed from God, and surrendered themselves to the fascinations and the control of an alien power. But the world may be taken out of the sphere of influence in which it lies. And that is what you are here for.—A. Maclaren, *Triumphant Certainties*, p. 11.

'We know that we are of God, and that the whole world lieth in the evil one.'—1 John v. 19.

He lets the world have its way; not from the hopelessness of the sceptic or the indifference of the epicurean, but because he knows that his own way, however lamely and blindly he pursues it, is yet that to which all the world's ways converge, and that it is the way that leadeth unto eternal life.—T. H. Green.

Marcus Aurelius—than whom perhaps none ever craved more earnestly for justice, or possessed a soul more wisely impressionable, more nobly sensitive—Marcus Aurelius never asked himself what might be happening outside that admirable little circle of light wherein his virtue and consciousness, his Divine meekness and piety, had gathered those who were near

him, his friends and servants. Infinite iniquity, he knew full well, stretched around him on every side; but with this he had no concern. To him it seemed a thing that must be, mysterious and sacred as the mighty ocean. . . . It did not lessen his courage; on the contrary, it enhanced his confidence, his concentration, and spurred him upwards, like the flame that, confined to a narrow area, rises higher and higher, alone in the night, urged by the darkness.—Maeterlinck, in *The Buried Temple*.

References.—V. 19.—Bishop Gore, *Christian World Pulpit*, vol. l. p. 251. *Expositor* (6th Series), vol. viii. p. 37. A. Maclaren, *Expositions of Holy Scripture—Epistles of John*, p. 21.

THE CERTAINTIES OF OUR WARFARE

1 John v. 19, 20.

This has been called the Epistle of Love, and it well deserves that title; but it might be almost more appropriately called the Epistle of Certainties. There is the ring of absolute assurance from the opening words to the finish. Nor was the language of this Apostle at all singular and exceptional. As he wrote and spoke so felt and so testified all those first witnesses of Christ.

I. The strength and prevailing power of the early disciples were in their certainties. It was the age of the sceptic, a period of almost universal uncertainty. Men were everywhere boastfully declaring or mournfully confessing that nothing was or could be known about the higher powers and a future life. And then these Apostles went forth with triumphant certainty on their lips, holding in their hands the clue to all the great mysteries. No wonder that men gathered around them.

II. It was the certainties of the Apostolic Church that made it a missionary Church. The audacity of that early faith was sublime. There was no hesitation because there was no doubt. They could neither fear nor hold back nor sit still, in the absolute assurance that possessed them. 'We know that we are of God, and the whole world lieth in wickedness.' And herein lies the lesson which I wish to press upon you: for in saying this I am saying what is true of every Church that is alive and earnest and aggressive. In this respect the old order never changes.

III. The measure of our certainty is the measure of our power. In all forward work especially the one essential is the absolute assurance that we hold proved truths, that our weapons have been forged in God's own furnace, that our directions have been given by the Holy Ghost, and the promises which inspire us uttered by Divine lips, and that He in whose name we go forth is the only true God and eternal life. The Church has surely had enough of the pruning hook and the dissecting knife. She wants to use the sword again in her real warfare. She wants to feel her feet again planted on apostolic certainties.

IV. We come back, then, ever to this confession of the Apostle, for to question it is to make missionary enterprise, if not a laughing-stock, at least a much-ado-about-nothing. 'We are of God, and the whole world lieth in wickedness.' Here in Christian lands we cannot always confidently say who are of God and who are of the wicked one. But the words are still true in their uttermost significance, of those who know Christ and those who know Him not. These are the certainties of the Christian heart, never to be let go or explained away; and these form the basis and inspiration of missionary purpose and work. And to this I have but to add one word. Surely the measure of our assurance is the measure of our obligation. The more absolutely we know these things the heavier is our burden of responsibility.—J. G. GREENHOUGH, *The Cross in Modern Life*, p. 120.

REFERENCE.—V. 19, 20.—J. G. Greenhough, *Christian World Pulpit*, vol. xlix. p. 328.

TRIUMPHANT CERTAINTIES—III

'And we know that the Son of God is come, and hath given us an understanding, that we may know Him that is true, and we are in Him that is true, even in His Son Jesus Christ.'—I JOHN v. 20.

THIS third of John's triumphant certainties is connected closely with the two preceding ones. It is so, as being in one aspect the ground of these, for it is 'because the Son of God is come' that men are born of God, and are of Him. It is so in another way also, for properly the words of our text ought to read not '*And* we know,' rather '*But* we know'. They are suggested, that is to say, by the preceding words, and they present the only thought which makes them tolerable. 'The whole world lieth in the wicked one. But we know that the Son of God is come.' Falling back on the certainty of the Incarnation and its present issues, we can look in the face the grave condition of humanity, and still have hope for the world and for ourselves.

I. The Christian's knowledge that the Son of God is come. (1) When John says 'The Son of God is come' he is not speaking about a past fact only, but about a fact which, beginning in a historical past, is permanent and continuous. In one aspect, no doubt, Jesus Christ had come and gone, before any of the people to whom this letter was addressed heard it for the first time, but in another aspect, if I may use a colloquial expression, when Jesus Christ came, He 'came to stay'. (2) The words of my text, in their assurance of possessing something far more solid than an opinion or a creed, in Christ Jesus and our relation to Him, are warranted, on the consideration that the growth of the Christian life largely consists in changing belief that rests on testimony into knowledge grounded in vital experience.

II. Note the new power of knowing God given by the Son who is come. John says that one issue of that Incarnation and permanent presence of the Lord Christ with us is that 'He hath given us an understanding that we may know Him that is true'. I do not suppose that he means thereby that any absolutely new faculty is conferred upon men, but that new direction is given to old ones, and dormant

powers are awakened. In the Incarnation Jesus Christ gave us God to see; by His present work in our souls He gives us the power to see God. This gift, thus given by the Incarnate and present Christ, is not an intellectual gift only, but something far deeper. To know about God is theology, to know Him is religion.

III. Note the Christian indwelling of God, which is possible through the Son who is come. 'We are *in* Him that is true.' Christ in us is the deepest truth of Christianity. And that God is in us, if Christ is in us, is the teaching not only of my text but of the Lord Himself, when He said, 'We will come unto him and make our abode with him'.—A. MACLAREN, *Triumphant Certainties*, p. 21.

THE lesson which St. John enforces, and which it was most easy for those to enforce, in whom a single human love had concentrated at once all that they counted most real in their whole life, human or Divine —'He that loveth not his brother whom he hath seen, how can he love God whom he hath not seen?' —was a lesson quite foreign to the minds of the greater number of the Psalmists. The authors of these wonderful poems certainly found it much easier to love God than to love man, and their only theme of perpetual wonder was how it had been possible for God Himself to love man.—R. H. HUTTON, *Contemporary Thought and Thinkers*, vol. II. (XXII.).

ALL sorts of means are kept at work to make the children obedient and simple and noble. Joy and sorrow are servants in God's nursery; pain and delight, ecstasy and despair, minister in it; but amongst them there is none more marvellous in its potency than that mingling of all pains and pleasures to which we specially give the name of love.—GEORGE MACDONALD, *The Marquis of Lossie* (ch. XLIII.).

The Son of God hath given us an understanding.'—I JOHN v. 20.

IN the ninth of his introductory aphorisms in *Aids to Reflection*, Coleridge writes thus: 'None then, not one of human kind, so poor and destitute, but there is provided for him, even in his present state, a house not built with hands. Aye, and spite of the philosophy (falsely so called) which mistakes the causes, the conditions, and the occasions of our becoming conscious of certain truths and realities for the truths and realities themselves—a house gloriously furnished. Nothing is wanted but the eye, which is the light of this house, the light which is the eye of this soul. This seeing light, this enlightening eye, is Reflection. It is more indeed than is ordinarily meant by that word; but it is what a Christian ought to mean by it, and to know too, whence it first came, and still continues to come—of what light even this light is but a reflection'. To the word 'Reflection' in this passage, a note is appended explaining that it is the true meaning of the Greek term διανοιά in 1 John v. 20, whose full force is exhibited by the definition: 'a power of discernment by Reason'.

REFERENCES.—V. 20.—R. Rainy, *Christian World Pulpit*, vol. liii. p. 387. Archbishop Cosmo Lang, *Christian World*

Pulpit, vol. lix. p. 372. A. Maclaren, *Expositions of Holy Scripture—Epistles of John*, p. 29.

THE LAST WORDS OF THE LAST APOSTLE

'This is the true God, and eternal life. Little children, keep yourselves from idols.'—1 JOHN v. 20, 21.

THESE words are probably not only the close of this Epistle, but the last words, chronologically, of Scripture.

I. Here we have the sum of all that we need to know about God. (1) What or whom does John mean by 'this'? When he says, 'This is the true God' he means to say, 'This God of whom I have been affirming that Jesus Christ is His sole revealer, and of whom I have been declaring that through Jesus Christ we may know Him and dwell abidingly in Him, 'this'—and none else—'is the true God'. (2) What does John mean by 'true'? By that expression he means, whenever he uses it, some person or thing whose nature and character correspond to his or its name, and who is essentially and perfectly that which the name expresses. The God revealed in Jesus Christ, and with whom a man through Jesus Christ may have fellowship of knowledge and friendship, answers to all that men mean when they speak of a God. (3) Consider what it is that the world owes to Jesus Christ, in its knowledge of God.

II. Here we have the sum of His gifts to us. The revelation which John would lay upon our hearts, is that, in His own essential self, the God revealed in Jesus Christ, and brought into living fellowship with us by Him, is 'eternal life'. By 'eternal life' he means something a great deal more august than endless existence. He means a life which not only is not ended by time, but which is above time, and not subject to its conditions at all.

III. We have here the consequent sum of Christian effort. 'Little children keep yourselves from idols,' seeing that 'this is the true God,' the only One that answers to your requirements, and will satisfy your desires. What does John mean by an idol? He means anything, or any person, that comes into the heart and takes the place which ought to be filled by God, and by Him only. And how is it to be done? 'Keep yourselves.' But it is not only our own effort that is needed, for just a sentence or two before the Apostle had said : 'He that is born of God'—that is Christ—'keepeth us'. So our keeping of ourselves is essentially our letting Him keep us.—A. MACLAREN, *Triumphant Certainties*, p. 31.

REFERENCES.—V. 20, 21.—Spurgeon, *Sermons*, vol. xli. No. 2396. A. Maclaren, *Expositions of Holy Scripture—Epistles of John*, p. 39.

MODERN IDOLATRY

'Little children, guard yourselves from idols.'—1 JOHN v. 21.

THESE are John's last words to those whom, in his affectionate, old man's way, he addresses as 'little children'; probably if the books of the Bible were arranged in the order in which they were written, they would be seen to be the last words of Scripture also. 'Idol' in his vocabulary means anything that comes between us and God, anything that takes for us the place of God. His words are a warning against idolatry in its widest and largest meaning.

I. Who among us is an idolater? What a man trusts in, that is his God. You may never have bowed the knee to an idol made with hands, and as far back as you can remember you may have daily bowed the knee to God, and yet you may be an idolater. Whom do I serve? In the outer sphere of life, in the eyes of men, God. But 'in my spirit,' whom? what? For remember, as Dr. Maclaren has truly said. 'A man's true worship is not the worship which he performs in the public temple, but that which he offers down in that little private chapel where nobody goes but himself.' The deities that are shrined *there*, these be thy gods, be thy offerings otherwhere what they may. Let us take the Bible in our hand and search out some of the dark corners of our hearts.

II. 'Whose God is their belly.' That is idolatry in its most repulsive, disgusting form. Gluttony, Drunkenness, Lust—to bow down before those is to worship the Beast, and to bear his mark in our foreheads. Swift and terrible is the retribution.

III. 'Covetousness, which is idolatry.' Does not that word smite some of us? Of all forms of modern idolatry none is more fatal than this.

IV. 'And Hezekiah brake in pieces the brazen serpent that Moses had made : for unto those days the children of Israel did burn incense to it : and he called it Nehushtan.' Now we are in another world altogether. What does this mean? That it is possible for us to turn even the sacred things of religion into idols that come between us and God.

V. Beauty holds us to-day with a spell our fathers never knew. Literature, too, has brought its priceless treasures to our very door. To say that art and literature must not be as gods to us, is not to deny them their place in our life : it is to deny them the first place. I claim the first place for my Lord. Make Him first in everything. Nay, He can take no other place.—G. JACKSON, *First Things First*, p. 191.

REFERENCES.—V. 21.—A. P. Stanley, *Sermons for Children*, p. 10. F. B. Cowl, *Preacher's Magazine*, vol. xviii. p. 335.

'Little children keep yourselves from idols.'—1 JOHN v. 21.

WE have surely never such need to show humiliation as when we are in the presence of a fallen idol. It is not the god, which was no god, that suffers, but its former worshipper, who sees what appeared divinity, corruption, and what looked like strength, rottenness. And, in at least some slight degree, this terrible contemplation must be made by all mortals who place their entire faith in mere flesh and blood : who love the creature, which has beauty that we may desire it, more than the Creator whom no man hath at any time seen. One who wrote of human affection with a tenderness and understanding past comparison —who knew its infinite power and no less infinite weakness—one who has taught that by loving man we best learn how to love his Maker, has also warned us—'Keep yourselves from idols'.—JOHN OLIVER HOBBES, *A Study in Temptations* (ch. XVIII.).

THE SECOND EPISTLE OF JOHN

2 JOHN

REFERENCES.—1.—*Expositor* (6th Series), vol. xii. p. 413. 3.—A. Maclaren, *Expositions of Holy Scripture*—1, 2, 3 *John*, p. 47. 4.—T. Sadler, *Sermons for Children*, p. 48.

'And now I beseech thee . . . that we love one another.'—
2 JOHN 5.

LET our one unceasing care be to better the love that we offer our fellow-creatures. One cup of this love that is drawn from the spring on the mountains is worth a hundred taken from the stagnant wells of ordinary charity.—MAETERLINCK.

'Look to yourselves that we lose not those things which we have wrought, but that we receive a full reward.'—2 JOHN 8.

'WE are all taught by interest,' says Stevenson in his first essay on John Knox. 'And if the interest be not merely selfish, there is no wiser preceptor under heaven, and perhaps no sterner.'

REFERENCES.—I. 5.—T. Arnold, *The Interpretation of Scripture*, p. 293. I. 7, 9.—*Expositor* (6th Series), vol. v. p. 292. I. 8.—T. Binney, *King's Weigh-House Chapel Sermons*, p. 240.

THE MAN WHO LOSES HIS PAST

'Look to yourselves, that ye lose not those things which ye[1] have wrought.'—2 JOHN 8.
'In his days did Hiel, the Bethelite, build Jericho.'—1 KINGS XVI. 34.

THE rebuilding of Jericho is the first step, historically, towards the destruction of Jerusalem. The taking of it had been the key to the conquest of Joshua. The raising again of its ruined towers was the sign of national decay and approaching death. Like the pointer on the barometer, nothing in itself, it signified everything.

It is another Israel than followed Joshua. Omri and Ahab occupy the thrones of David and Solomon. Religion is decaying. Idolatry is advancing. The memory of Jericho is faint and far away. 'In *these* days did Hiel, the Bethelite, build Jericho.'

But if faint in memory, the curse of Joshua has not lost power. As soon as the foundation is laid, it shows its power. The eldest son of the founder dies. We can fancy the neighbours recalling the old curse, and dissuading the rash man from his work. But all in vain. He perseveres. The gates are set up. Once more the prophecy is fulfilled. The youngest child dies amid the inauguration of the new city.

But the loss was not Hiel's only. It was national. A victory had been lost. The old towers of Jericho once more lifted their heads, a witness to national decay. The record of faith had been destroyed. The defeated enemy had returned.

I. This is the thought I wish to dwell upon, '*the*

[1] Marginal Reading.

man who has lost his past'. 'Look to yourselves,' says the Apostle in our other text, 'that ye lose not the things ye have wrought, but that every man receive a full reward'. Every man, like every nation, has great moments in his history; triumphs of faith, times when the veil which lies upon him is removed, and he sees with open face the glory of God. 'These things,' says John, 'are yours'. They are things you have wrought. They have entered into your sinews and muscles, as the swinging blows on the anvil have entered into the blacksmith's arm. But these victories may be lost. The iron muscles may become fatty and feeble. Conquered Jericho may be built again. Things you have wrought may be lost for ever.

It is sad for a man to be false to any experience, sad to have to say that any great moment in his past was a delusion and a mistake; but when that comes to be the case of his great religious experiences, of the deepest moments of his life, it is sadder than death.

Yet such people are not always conscious of their loss. It has come like the rebuilding of Jericho, slowly and gradually. No visible foe has done it. No: they have done it themselves. Silently, like the Temple of God, have the walls of worldliness risen around their souls. God has spoken, perhaps in family trial, as was the case with Hiel, perhaps in the still small voice of conscience; but the message has been disregarded. They have not been faithful to their past. They have 'lost the things they had wrought'.

II. There is a curious contrast *in the way men grow old*. Have you ever noticed it? Here is a man who grows harder as the winter of life draws near. His life is one long process of disillusionising. He is always finding men out, so that now he believes in no one—and as a result no one believes in him. He has a great contempt for women. He thinks men are naturally selfish. Life is a struggle for survival. There is no such thing as disinterested love. At the bottom of every action man is thinking of himself.

Why should growing old mean to some losing faith in one's fellow-men, interest in life, joy and hope; finding the heart close in with bitterness till death comes as a welcome release? And why to another does old age mean a growing younger, a mellowing and a softening, a larger life, a brighter faith, a clearer hope? It is because the one has lost something the other has held. The one has lost that first faith in God which is the ground of all faith in man. The other has held to it, held firmly amidst sorrow, discouragement and temptation, and thus found it in the end what every one who holds it will find it, 'a full reward'.—W. Mackintosh Mackay, *Bible Types of Modern Men*, p. 17.

'Receive him not into your house.'—2 John 10.

Choose your companions with care, for there are people just as contagious as a disease. At first you cannot tell them even when you see them; he looks to be a man like everybody else, and, suddenly, without being aware of it yourself, you will start to imitate him in life. You look around—and you find you have contracted his scabs.—Maxim Gorky.

'I would not write to you with paper and ink.'—2 John 12.

'If it be the least pleasure,' Pope wrote to Swift, 'I will write once a week most gladly; but can you abstract the letters from the person who writes them, so far as not to feel more vexation in the thought of our separation than satisfaction in the nothings he can express.'

'I trust to come to you and speak face to face, that your joy may be full.'—2 John 12.

I do indeed look back with much wonder and thankfulness to the intercourse with you which inaugurated this year for me. There is so much in the interchange of conviction, even if we receive nothing fresh.—F. D. Maurice, to Erskine of Linlathen.

To become a pleasure-yielding person is a social duty. —Spencer.

THE THIRD EPISTLE OF JOHN

3 JOHN

REFERENCES.—I. 1.—T. Binney, *King's Weigh-House Chapel Sermons* (2nd Series), p. 205. *Expositor* (5th Series), vol. vi. p. 82.

WISHING

'I wish above all things that. . . .'—3 JOHN 2.

'I WISH above all things that. . . .' I purposely leave the sentence unfinished, in the guise of a dim interrogation, in order that each of us may supply the missing piece. How do I finish the imperfect pile? The nature of the insertion will determine the quality of the contribution which I make to the common life. Let me give one or two suggestions of worthy ways in which perhaps we may complete the sentence, wishes that will be fruitful in moral and spiritual progress.

I. Let us wish for a renewal of the secret intimacies of family worship.

II. Let us wish for an enrichment of the fellowship of the Christian Church.

III. And let us wish for the creation of a more fervent evangelisation.—J. H. JOWETT, *British Congregationalist*, 11th July, 1907, p. 32.

THE THIRD EPISTLE OF JOHN

'Beloved, I pray that in all things thou mayest prosper and be in health, even as thy soul prospereth.'—3 JOHN 2.

'I BELIEVE,' wrote Edward Thring to R. L. Nettleship, 'that one of the most obvious tests to a truth lover that he is really loving truth and not a sham, not a Duessa, is the perpetual growth of capacity. Every year has been to me a softening of the impressible nature, and a clearing of the eye in all fields of Divine goodness, quite irrespective of the hard, hot, choking work of the external world and its attacks. I feel more and more how all right spirit life is a gladness and glory increasing; how Divine goodness is speaking in all tones that reach the heart with joy or sorrow, awe or ecstasy, everywhere and in all things, if we can but hear it; how completely the spirit within can be in communion with light independent of external circumstances, and yet how external circumstances and creation are the medium through which God speaks.'

'Greater joy have I none than this, to hear of my children walking in the truth.'—3 JOHN 4.

ALL joy worth the name is in equal love between unequals.—COVENTRY PATMORE.

REFERENCES.—I. 2.—J. Caird, *Sermons*, p. 218. C. Perren, *Revival Sermons in Outline*, p. 189. J. G. Greaves, *Christian World Pulpit*, vol. xlv. p. 394. A. Maclaren, *Expositions of Holy Scripture—Epistles of John*, p. 54. I. 4.—A. P. Stanley, *Sermons for Children*, pp. 10, 76. T. H. Bell, *Persuasions*, p. 119. C. Bradley, *The Christian Life*, p. 269. Spurgeon, *Sermons*, vol. xix. No. 1148. *Expositor* (6th Series), vol. viii. p. 323.

'Whatsoever thou doest to the brethren, and to strangers which have borne witness of thy love.'—3 JOHN 5, 6.

THERE can be no true love without devotion; devotion is the exercise of love, by which it grows.—R. L. STEVENSON.

REFERENCES.—I. 5-8.—*Expository Sermons on the New Testament*, p. 276. J. Bunting, *Sermons*, vol. ii. p. 170.

'Who bear witness to thy love before the Church.'—3 JOHN 6.

I HAD expected to find in the Church the inexpugnable citadel of Faith; but I have found in it no less the home of Love.—MANNING.

REFERENCES.—I. 6-8.—H. Elvet Lewis, *Christian World Pulpit*, vol. lix. p. 400. 7. A. Maclaren, *Expositions of Holy Scripture—3 John*, p. 61.

'Diotrephes loveth to have the pre-eminence.'—3 JOHN 9.

'HE expects,' said Bentham of James Mill, 'to subdue everybody by his domineering tone, to convince everybody by his positiveness. His manner of speaking is offensive and overbearing.'

REFERENCES.—I. 11.—*Expositor* (6th Series), vol. xii. p. 50. I. 12.—A. Maclaren, *Expositions of Holy Scripture—3 John*, p. 79.

'Greet the friends by name.'—3 JOHN 14.

No one would care to live without friends, though he had all other good things. . . . We need friends, when we are young, to keep us from error; we need them, when we are old, to tend to us and carry out the plans we are unable to execute ourselves; and we need them in the prime of life to keep us in noble deeds—'two together'—for thus are we more effective both in thought and in act.—ARISTOTLE.

'The friends salute thee. Greet the friends by name.'—3 JOHN 14.

'I FIND all things on earth, even truth and joy, sooner than friendship.'—JEAN PAUL. This for the motto —to examine and attest the fact, and then to explain the reason. First, then, there are the extraordinary qualifications demanded for true friendship, arising from the multitude of causes which make men delude themselves and attribute to friendship what is only a similarity of pursuit, or even a dislike of feeling oneself alone in anything. But, secondly, supposing the friendship to be as real as human nature ordinarily permits, yet how many causes are at constant war against it, whether in the shape of violent irruptions or unobserved yet constant wearing away by dyspathy, etc.—COLERIDGE.

THE EPISTLE OF JUDE

JUDE

REFERENCES.—I. 1.—H. J. Wilmot-Buxton, *Holy-Tide Teaching*, p. 188. Spurgeon, *Sermons*, vol. viii. No. 434. *Expositor* (5th Series); vol. vii. p. 368. I. 1, 2.—Spurgeon, *Sermons*, vol. xli. No. 2412.

JUDE 3.

HE that bids us 'contend for the Faith once delivered to the Saints,' tells us that we should do it by 'avoiding the spirit of Cain, Corah, and Balaam'; and by 'building up *ourselves* in the most holy Faith,' not pinning it upon other men's sleeves. Praying 'in the Holy Ghost,' not mumbling over matins. Keeping 'ourselves in the love of God,' not destroying men because they will not be of our Faith. 'Waiting for the mercy of Jesus Christ'; not cruel, but merciful.—CROMWELL's *Declaration to the People of Ireland* (1650).

'Faith once delivered.'—JUDE 3.

THE participation which we have of the knowledge of truth, whatsoever she is, it is not by our owne strength we have gotten it; God hath sufficiently taught it us in that he hath made choice of the simple, common, and ignorant to teach us His wonderfull secrets. Our faith hath not been purchased by us : it is a gift proceeding from the liberality of others. It is not by our discourse or understanding that we have received our religion.—MONTAIGNE (*Florio*), ii. 12.

REFERENCES.—I. 3.—J. Clifford, *The Christian Certainties*, p. 107. R. W. Dale, *Fellowship with Christ*, p. 88. Spurgeon, *Sermons*, vol. xxvii. No. 1592. H. S. Seekings, *Preacher's Magazine*, vol. xvii. p. 321. W. M. Sinclair, *Simplicity in Christ*, p. 27. F. B. Woodward, *Sermons* (2nd Series), p. 133. J. G. Rogers, *Christian World Pulpit*, vol. liv. p. 347. H. Allen, *Penny Pulpit*, No. 1640, p. 165. J. Keble, *Sermons for the Saints' Days*, p. 424. *Church Family Newspaper*, vol. xiv. p. 832. *Expositor* (5th Series), vol. i. p. 144. A. Maclaren, *Expositions of Holy Scripture—Jude*, p. 87. I. 4, 8. —*Ibid.* vol. vi. p. 203. I. 5-7.—*Ibid.* p. 377. I. 6.—J. Budgen, *Parochial Sermons*, vol. ii. p. 86. 7.—*Expositor* (4th Series), vol. i. p. 33.

'Michael the archangel, when contending with the devil.'—JUDE 9.

IN Luther's *Table Talk* this passage occurs, 'I often think with amazement what a battle there must be between the devils and angels. I think that the angels must often give way for a time, while they fight for us' [Ich halt, das die Engel auch offtmals ein weil unterligen, cum certant pro nobis].—E. KROKER, *Luther's Tischreden*, p. 295, No. 586.

REFERENCE.—I. 11.—B. J. Snell, *Christian World Pulpit*, vol. li. p. 153.

MASKED PERILS OF SPIRITUAL LIFE AND FELLOWSHIP

'Hidden rocks in your love-feasts.'—JUDE 12.

THE ungodly men who had crept unawares into the Christian community are likened by the Apostle to sunken rocks which amid smooth seas and under fair skies prove fatal to the mariner. But these hidden rocks present themselves in moods, theories, and sentiments, as well as in false brethren ; and against these subtlest perils we must diligently watch. We seek now to indicate several of these submerged reefs.

I. The quest of spiritual power whilst forgetting the uses of such power is one of these hidden rocks. Miss J. M. Fry made the following statement at a recent religious gathering : 'Many persons are actuated by mere vanity in desiring the attainment of spiritual power '. We understand how wealth may be desired for mere vanity : not with an appreciation of its uses, but out of the passion of possession and the desire of display. Intellectual power be coveted from the same motive. Spiritual power should be sought so that the ignoble elements of our nature may be effectually purged, that the sanctification of our faculties may be complete, and that all our work for God and man may be efficient. To lose sight of these practical uses is to fall into a subtle snare of refined selfishness and vanity.

II. The cultivation of character in the artistic spirit is a snare of the spiritual life. He who has understood the teaching of Christ never forgets that the good is the beautiful, and that the two must be sought in this order. He remembers that loveliness of character is first a question of essence and not of form. To cultivate moral beauty in the spirit of art and fashion is to make shipwreck on the coral reef of a silver sea.

III. Sensuous enjoyment may insinuate itself into spiritual culture so as to become a peril. It might be thought that there is little to fear from sensuality in a fervent spiritual life : it would seem so essentially coarse and vulgar as not to be susceptible of concealment or decoration. But it is not so. The 'love-feast' became an orgie, and the heavenly love of the individual saint may imperceptibly degenerate into dangerous sentimentalism and profane passion.

IV. To cultivate fervent devoutness apart from practical life is another peril of the spiritual. Contact with the realities of the worldly life is necessary to the health, and sanity of the soul, to the strength and soundness of our piety.

V. Talking too much about our spiritual life may prove to its detriment. A French critic writes:

'Beware of an artist who talks too well of his art. He wastes his art in talk.' And it is as certainly true in regard to religion. There is much that is sacred and secret about the experiences of the soul, and it is dangerous to violate its delicacy.—W. L. WATKINSON, *The Ashes of Roses*, p. 224.

AUTUMN TREES WITHOUT FRUIT
'Autumn trees without fruit.'—JUDE 12 (R.V.)

IN the Revised Version of the New Testament the expressive phrase, 'Autumn trees without fruit,' takes the place of the obscure rendering, 'Trees whose fruit withereth, without fruit'. Possibly the thought underlying this almost contradictory combination of terms is that of a tree yielding fruit that never comes to perfection, but remains on the boughs, shrivelled, good for nothing but to be burned. The new rendering is, however, a great gain. It presents, concisely and graphically, the main thought of the writer in words that cannot be misunderstood: 'Autumn trees without fruit' are trees without fruit at the very time when they ought to be full of fruit. St. Jude's words are a picturesque description of character. In his days such trees were growing in the innermost enclosure of the garden of the Lord. But there are 'autumn trees without fruit' outside the Church as well as within its borders.

I. The glory of the autumn is that it is the fruit-bearing season, when our eyes are gladdened by the sight of

> Vines with clustering branches growing,
> Plants with goodly burden bowing.

Amidst the abounding autumnal increase, a fruitless tree in an orchard is an anomaly, a surprise. Why has the tree no fruit in autumn? It would be easy to draw out the parable in detail, and to show how each reason finds an analogy in some fault of character. It is, however, more important to remind those whose lives are in the spring-time, that the teaching of this text is rather for them than for those whose years are in the sear and yellow leaf. How often the tree is fruitless in autumn on account of some disaster that befell it in the spring or early summer!

II. A twofold judgment must be passed on 'autumn trees without fruit,' whatever be the cause of their barrenness. (1) An autumn tree without fruit is a grievous loss, a bitter disappointment to its owner. (2) An autumn tree without fruit is also a failure in itself, inasmuch as the great purpose of its existence is unfulfilled. In both these respects it is a striking but sorrowful emblem of every human life that yields no fruit of praise to God and blessing unto men.

III. From a verse in St. Jude's short epistle the conditions of fruitfulness may be learnt: 'Ye, beloved, rooting yourselves in your most holy faith, praying in the Holy Spirit, keep yourselves in the love of God'. (1) The roots of a tree need moisture and nourishment, also room to grow. (2) Prayer is an essential condition of fruitfulness. (3) Finally, to keep ourselves in the love of God is essential to our

bearing fruit that is ripe and sweet and mellow.— J. G. TASKER, *God's Garden*, p. 115.

REFERENCES.—I. 12.—H. Woodcock, *Sermon Outlines* (1st Series), p. 5. Spurgeon, *Sermons*, vol. xiv. No. 797. *Expositor* (6th Series), vol. ix. p. 98. I. 12-18.—*Ibid.* (5th Series), vol. vi. p. 203. I. 13.—*Ibid.* (4th Series), vol. ii. p. 288. I. 14, 15.—Spurgeon, *Sermons*, vol. xxii. No. 1307. I. 19.—Spurgeon, *Ibid.*, vol. iv. No. 167. *Expositor* (4th Series), vol. ii. pp. 43, 44. I. 20.—M. Johnson, *Christian World Pulpit*, vol. lviii. p. 309. Spurgeon, *Sermons*, vol. xii. No. 719. I. 20, 21.—T. Arnold, *The Interpretation of Scripture*, p. 277. H. Alford, *Quebec Chapel Sermons*, vol. i. p. 395. C. D. Ball, *The Saintly Calling*, p. 163. A. Maclaren, *Expositions of Holy Scripture—Jude*, p. 97.

ST. SIMON AND ST. JUDE, APOSTLES
'Keep yourselves in the love of God.'—JUDE 21.

OUR text is taken from the Epistle of St. Jude, this being the day on which we commemorate St. Simon and St. Jude. It is not of their work that I desire to speak; let us concentrate our minds upon the exhortation of our text. This brief injunction is charged with tenderness, though not with that alone. In the same breath it whispers of the love of God, *and* of the responsibility of man. This very short Epistle is for vigour surpassed, perhaps, by no portion of any other. Its matter and tenor are most striking, and in large part awfulness is the tone of it. Short as it is, it finds room for some statements not found elsewhere in Scripture, or only darkly intimated, such as those respecting the angels who lost their first estate, and Michael the archangel, and the fresh particulars respecting Enoch and Balaam. Its warnings are of the most thrilling and unqualified character. As we read through the short, sharp, incisive sentences we wonder how they must have smitten the ear of those to whom they were originally addressed. Yet the outcome of all is a sentence breathing tenderest solicitude and the warmth of love itself. It seems that a fearful apostasy was in the very air all around, and the writer of the Epistle trembled with fear lest it should find a harbour in the heart of those whom he now so earnestly warns. And he sums up all in these sentences of pleading counsel, 'Ye, beloved, building up yourselves in your most holy faith, praying in the Holy Ghost, keep yourselves on the love of God, looking for the mercy of our Lord Jesus Christ unto eternal life'. There are many places and relationships in our human life, *in* which it is honourable and a privilege to be—how suggestive to bring them one and all into comparison with *this* position, the position of being 'in the love of God'. This is supremely best.

I. **What the Love of God is.**—Far, infinitely far from being a word only, or a vague profession, it is so great a necessity, that if it were once withdrawn in every sense, our own hold on life would be lost. Through many a channel it streams. There is the love which He has for all He has made; for us, as He made us, and as He would see us again. It is a creative, parental, guardian love. How good it is to be—at present still inalienably—in *this* love! There is the pitying love which He has for us as sinners, for a whole saddened, suffering, sinful world—and this love, so real, so commanding, overweighs all. How good to have the resort and refuge of *this* love ! There is the fostering, welcoming love, which He has, to receive and to help first repentant conviction, first penitent tearfulness, first practical endeavour, first symptoms of the returning prodigal. Oh, how good to have the help of *this* love ! There is the love which He has to those who have strayed from the Lord, who have fallen, who have denied Him ! and whom He would receive again, with tenfold pitying grace. There is the love which He has to a company of brethren and sisters in the truth, in Christ. Oh, how needed is *this* love !

II. The Fulness of Sense in which We may be in it.—The love of God is so vast, that there is no risk of not being entirely surrounded by it, safely wrapped in it—bathed in it. The love of the creature has danger in it ; but in and to the love of God, you may literally give yourself up, 'spirit, soul, and body,' with a safe and a blessed abandon. The love of God has no fickleness, no uncertainty about it. 'The gifts and calling of God are without repentance.' Nothing 'shall be able to separate us from the love of God, which is in Christ Jesus.'

III. We may Keep in it for Ever.—Of all else that is innocent, honourable, good, and great, in which we may rest, we have to say (as when some morning awakes us), it is time to be getting up ! But never, never so, if our place of folding is 'in the love of God'. In it, work and rest, sleep and wake, day to day, and night to night, while you live even here below ; and when you last lie down to sleep 'in' it, let the morn awake you, it will be still to find you 'in' it ; 'in' it satisfied ; 'in' it 'clad in bright and deathless bloom ;' 'in' it, for ever supremely blest ! So then, 'keep yourselves in the love of God'—in the one only way of doing so, by giving yourself afresh to Him Who alone can 'keep you'.

REFERENCES.—I. 21.—J. W. Brown, *Christian World Pulpit*, vol. xxxvii. p. 8. Spurgeon, *Sermons*, vol. xxii. No. 1286. J. Binney, *King's Weigh-House Chapel Sermons*, p. 218. I. 22, 23.—*Expositor* (6th Series), vol. iv. p. 200. I. 23.— C. Perren, *Revival Sermon in Outlines*, p. 260.

SECURITY AND GLORY

'Now unto Him that is able to keep you from falling, and to present you faultless before the presence of His glory with exceeding joy, to the only wise God our Saviour, be glory and majesty, dominion and power, both now and ever. Amen.—JUDE 24, 25.

I. THE first thought for our consideration is God's provision for our security and glory. 'Unto Him

that is able to keep you from falling.' The more accurate translation, which you will find in the revised version of the New Testament : 'To guard you from stumbling.' The word here translated 'keep' is a strong word. It is even impregnated with a strong military flavour, and suggests the picture of an armed force. In the centre stands one whose life is threatened by fierce and hostile bands, but by his side stands an invincible Warrior pledged to protect him from all evil. 'To guard you from stumbling.' That does not mean that we can expect at present to be guarded in such a way that we shall be absolutely sinless. The stumbling here spoken of is akin to falling, and marks failure of a very grievous type. It is such a stumble as leaves our life halt and maimed, takes the power out of us, and renders us a prey to the evil one. Such stumbling as this God can save us from. The exercise of this power depends on the human response to it. 'He is able.' Why then are there some that stumble ? Not because God's power is deficient, but because they withdraw themselves outside the circle of His power. 'And to make you stand before the presence of His glory faultless in exceeding joy.' The word translated 'blameless' does not necessarily mean 'without sin'. It is sometimes used in the Scriptures of men that are true and pure in heart, though there may be defects in the details of their life and conduct. But in its present position it can mean nothing but 'sinlessness'.

II. The passage next introduces us to the fundamental petition of this guarded and glorified life. 'Unto Him—the only wise God our Saviour—be glory and majesty, dominion and power.' (1) This ascription of glory is not made to God simply as God, the Creator of heaven and earth. It is to God our Saviour that Jude invites us to sing. (2) 'Glory !' that is the infinite essential perfection of God, God as He is in His own eternal brightness, in the glory of His person and His essential nature. (3) 'Dominion !' The word here translated 'dominion' means 'power over'. (4) 'And power !' The word here translated power means the power that belongs to rightful authority. Of course in a certain sense, glory and majesty, dominion and power belong to God already. But in another sense, they are not fully realised until they are loyally acknowledged from one end of the universe to the other, until every soul joins in the praise, and God is glorified by all His creatures. —JOHN THOMAS, *Myrtle Street Pulpit*, vol. III. p. 145.

REFERENCES.—I. 24, 25.—Spurgeon, *Sermons*, vol. xi. No. 634 ; vol. xxxix. No. 2296 ; and vol. lii. No. 2994. A. Maclaren, *Expositions of Holy Scripture—Jude*, p. 105.

THE BOOK OF REVELATION

THE BOOK OF REVELATION

I LIKE to think (wrote Bishop King of Lincoln) that the glorious visions of the Apocalypse were given in a time of suffering, at the end of a life. We may expect 'good wine' at the last. How unlike the way of the world !—*Spiritual Letters*, p. 110.

REFERENCE.—I. 1-3.—C. Anderson Scott, *The Book of Revelation*, p. 1.

'Blessed are they that hear the words of the prophecy, and keep the things which are written therein.'—REV. I. 3.

IT is a great mistake to think that because you have read a masterpiece once or twice, or ten times, therefore you have done with it. Because it is a masterpiece, you ought to live with it, and make it part of your daily life.—JOHN MORLEY.

REFERENCES.—I. 3.—T. C. Fry, *Christian World Pulpit*, vol. xlvi. p. 45. I. 3-20.—*Expositor* (6th Series), vol. ii. p. 347. I. 4.—H. S. Holland, *Christian World Pulpit*, vol. xliii. p. 360. I. 4, 5.—A. Maclaren, *Expositions of Holy Scripture—Revelation*, p. 114. I. 4-6.—C. Anderson Scott, *The Book of Revelation*, p. 20.

THE GREAT ENFRANCHISEMENT

'Unto Him that loveth us, and loosed us from our sins by His blood ; and He made us to be a Kingdom, to be priests unto His God and Father ; to Him be the glory and the dominion for ever and ever.'—REV. I. 5.

I. 'UNTO Him that loveth us.' That is the background in which we find the base and the warrant for all our confidence and faith. God loves! The beginning is not to be found in us, in our inclinations and gropings and resolvings and prayers. The primary element is the inclination of God. When did He begin to love? 'I have loved thee with an everlasting love.' Up from the everlasting. This is the Biblical account of our origin, of the primary movement that gave our being its birth :—' He first loveth '. Nobody comes into the world God-hated. Loveth! The affection is continuous : not spasmodic, but unbroken ; there is no abatement of its volume. 'God so loved that He *gave* ' ! Love is an importation, a giving, sacrifice unconscious of itself. Love is tremendous energy, hungrily keen for the detection of need, that it might fill the gaping gap out of its own resources.

II. What next does He discover, from Whom there is nothing concealed ? He beholds His children in the bondage of corruption and night. They are the captives of sin and of death. One of the clearest and calmest thinkers of our time, a man who sees far into the secret springs of human life, has given his judgment that the most real terrors that afflict men are the guilt of sin and the fear of death.

III. How can we obtain deliverance ? The primary need of man is not accomplishment but character, and for this we require not the washing of culture but the washing of regeneration. When education and culture have reached their utmost limits, and the mental powers are refined into exquisite discernment, the two black, gruesome birds of the night remain—guilt and death, and only the Eternal Son can disturb them, and cause them to flee away. Here comes in the energetic, sleepless ministry of the Eternal Love.

IV. 'And He made us to be a Kingdom, to be priests unto His God and Father.' He 'loosed' and then He ennobled. Now we are made a Kingdom, we become citizens, endowed with a sublime franchise the possessors of unspeakable privileges and rights. We are made a 'kingdom of priests '. Every child has the right to share the sovereignty of Jesus, and to enjoy free access into the most secret place of the Father's presence. This is the issue of the primal loving.—J. H. JOWETT, *Apostolic Optimism*, p. 237.

'Jesus Christ, who is the faithful witness, the firstborn of the dead, and the ruler of the kings of the earth.'—REV. I. 5.

'THE Faithful Witness' demands faith ; 'the First Begotten of the dead' incites hope ; 'the Prince of the kings of the earth' challenges obedience. Now faith may be dead, hope presumptuous, obedience slavish. But 'He that loved us' thereby wins our love ; and forthwith by virtue of love faith lives, hope is justified, obedience is enfranchised.—C. G. ROSSETTI.

'To Him that loved us.'—REV. I. 5.

'I AM in the habit,' wrote Charles Simeon to a friend in 1827, 'of accounting religion as the simplest of all concerns : "To Him that loved us, and washed us from our sins in His own blood, and hath made us kings and priests unto our God, to Him be glory and dominion for ever and ever," expresses the very frame of mind in which I wish both to live and die.'

REFERENCES.—I. 5.—R. Flint, *Sermons and Addresses*, p. 39. *Expositor* (4th Series), vol. v. p. 124 ; *ibid.* (5th Series), vol. ii. p. 24 ; *ibid.* (7th Series), vol. v. p. 148. I. 5, 6.—Spurgeon, *Sermons*, vol. xxix. No. 1737, and vol. xxxvii. No. 2230. G. Littlemore, *Christian World Pulpit*, vol. lvi. p. 38. H. Melvill, *Penny Pulpit*, No. 1707, p. 695. Bishop Gore, *Christian World Pulpit*, vol. lx. p. 49. J. Stuart Holden, *The Pre-eminent Lord*, p. 163.

'Priests unto God and His Father.'—REV. I. 6. (cf. xx. 6).

THE whole function of Priesthood was, on Christmas morning, at once and for ever gathered into His person who was born at Bethlehem ; and thenceforward, all who are united with Him, and who with Him make sacrifice of themselves ; that is to say, all members of the Invisible Church become, at the instant of their conversion, Priests ; and are so called in 1 Pet. ii. 5 and Rev. i. 6 and xx. 6, where, observe, there is no possibility of limiting the expression to the Clergy ; the conditions of Priesthood being simply having been loved by Christ, and washed in His blood.—RUSKIN, *On the Old Road*, ii. sec. 196.

REFERENCES.—I. 6.—E. E. Genner, *A Book of Lay Sermons*, p. 91. A. Maclaren, *Expositions of Holy Scripture—Revelation*, p. 135.

BACK TO CHRIST
(For Advent)
'Behold, He cometh.'—REV. i. 7.

I NEED hardly remind you that these words give us our Advent message. ' Back to Christ,' that is the motto of to-day. We commemorate in this season that the Lord has come, that the Lord will come, that the Lord is here. Many have been His comings since He came a child to Nazareth, many they will be before He comes in that last wonderful way of which we know not how to speak, except in such parables as He Himself has given. And we proclaim by our Eucharist this morning to those who have faith and heart to understand, 'The Lord is here to-day, the same as ever'.

I. **Imparting Gifts.**—The message of advent links itself with the message of St. Andrew's Day, 'We have found the Messiah'. So spoke St. Andrew to his brother Peter ; and that, again, is linked with that other saying that follows it so closely of Philip, ' Come and see ' (the Christ). For why do we wish that Christian missions should go out? Is it not because we have something so precious that it must be given away ? It is the nature of all the precious things upon earth that they must not be kept, but given away. Nothing is too precious too give away. That which you want to have for yourself, that which you cannot enjoy with another is not precious. Think what are the most valuable things. Take two only.

(*a*) *The gift of knowledge.*—What do you want to do when you know? To impart. And why? Because in teaching you know that you know much better than you thought, and because you have the sympathy of another who knows ; but best of all because knowledge is too good a thing to keep to yourself.

(*b*) *The gift of love.*—What does love consist of but giving love? And love grows by being given away. These two things, knowledge and love, they are what we have of Jesus Christ, and so the divine call ' Back to Christ ' is linked with the call of St. Andrew's Day, ' Come and see '. So it is that we want to teach, or to cause other people to teach, because we have something so precious that we must give it away.

II. **Back to Christ.**—Are there any hearts here which are not stirred, are there any hearts here which do not know that Christ is so precious, that the knowledge and love of Christ are such precious

things that they must needs publish them, that they must needs give them to others ? Let me be a missionary to these hearts for one or two moments. Let me ask them humbly to go back to Christ. Back to Christ as He was, as you may read of Him, as you may almost follow His steps up and down the country of Galilee, as you may hear Him speak, as you may see Him die. Go back to Him and see what kind of Friend He was. Understand, again, what it was in Him that saved men and women, how He would never despair of anyone who had despaired of themselves, of anyone who would come and not place the confidence of their heart where they had so often placed it and misplaced it before, upon their own hopeless frailty, but upon His strength. ' Believe in Me,' He said throughout His life, ' and thou shalt be saved.' What is the message for men and women who despair, what is the message for men and women who are tired of their perpetual shortcomings ? Not in yourself, but in the power which is outside you and yet which is so near, so near that from the outside It can come into the inside and there reanimate you. That is the message which He brought when He came to give life, namely, His own life, that men might live by it as He lived. And then again, as you come back to Christ, you see how, partly in condescension to our frailty, partly because of our Lord's prevision of the dulness of human nature to understand mere words, partly because He knew that no language could convey what was meant as a simple symbol might, He enshrined that very truth, that very promise, that very essence of His healing power, in the simplest of symbols, the symbol, namely, of our eating and drinking, by which our bodily life is sustained. He handed down for all those who followed Him to hand on, this great truth, enshrined in the Sacrament, so much more expressive than any words, that by Him we live. Go back to Christ and learn at the altar that by Him you may live and live His life. And why ? Because last of all He claimed —and He has substantiated His claim in all these thousands of years and millions of believers—He claimed that in Him dwelt the Godhead, and He was one with the Father.

' Behold, He cometh with the clouds ; and every eye shall see Him.'—REV. i. 7.

EARTH must fade away from our eyes, and we must anticipate that great and solemn truth, which we shall not fully understand till we stand before God in judgment, that to us there are but two beings in the whole world, God and ourselves. The sympathy of others, the pleasant voice, the glad eye, the smiling countenance, the thrilling heart, which at present are our very life, all will be away from us, when Christ comes in judgment. Every one will have to think of himself. Every eye shall see *Him ;* every heart will be full of *Him.* He will speak to every one ; and every one will be rendering to Him his own account. —NEWMAN.

REFERENCES.—I. 7.—Spurgeon, *Sermons*, vol. xxxiii. No. 1989. *Expositor* (4th Series), vol. x. pp. 292, 344. I. 8.—

A. G. Mortimer, *The Church's Lessons for the Christian Year*, pt. iii. p. 43. E. A. Bray, *Sermons*, vol. ii. p. 280.

REV. I. 9.

'SIR,' said Dr. Johnson to Boswell in Skye, 'when a man retires into an island, he is to turn his thoughts entirely to another world.'

REV. I. 9.

THERE is a prolonged conflict to be maintained with temptation to sin, with weariness, with the persistent pressure upon the mind and heart of those transient excitements and interests which make us forget the invisible and eternal kingdom.—R. W. DALE.

REFERENCES.—I. 9.—R. W. Hiley, *A Year's Sermons*, vol. iii. p. 244. *Expositor* (6th Series), vol. viii. p. 394.

'WHICH IS CALLED PATMOS'

'I John . . . was in the isle that is called Patmos for the word of God, and for the testimony of Jesus Christ. I was in the Spirit.'—REV. I. 9, 10.

'I JOHN . . . was in the isle that is called Patmos for the word of God, and for the testimony of Jesus Christ. I was in the Spirit.' He does not say, 'I was in Patmos,' he says, 'In the isle which is called Patmos'—by those who care to give it a name. The scenery of daily life in which the Apostle was moving had passed from his sight. He was in the Spirit. Whatever the earthly name might be, the reality was the gate of heaven, for when the Spirit was there the loneliness was no loneliness and the desolation was no desolation. Even so, though in a lesser way, did Egypt cease to be Egypt when Joseph was there. The poet has written, 'Never the place and the time and the loved one altogether'. But if the loved one be there the place and the time are hardly thought of. The place may be transfigured, perhaps, in some strange fashion, and the hour grow golden, but more likely both vanish quite from the thought. To the Apostle the thought of earthly love and human companionship was exchanged for something higher, for a name and a place better than of sons and daughters. He was in the Spirit, the Spirit of Christ was with him, and because the Spirit was there Christ was there. It was through the revelation of the Holy Spirit that he heard the great voice of a trumpet saying, 'I am Alpha and Omega,' and saw one like unto the Son of Man in the midst of the seven golden candlesticks. What was Patmos then, the little island in the Ægean Sea? What was anything? St. John's eyes were engaged with another vision. He recalled perhaps the place where He saw the Lamb of God dying on a far-off stormy even. He may have thought of the new grave in the spring garden where the Lord had lain, or of the morning when He stood upon the shore, risen from the last abysses. Thoughts of the ecstasy of life and the passion of death would meet and mingle in the Apostle's mind as he saw the glory and triumph of the First and the Last. Then he felt that he was not in the world of poetry and dream, but amidst the everlasting realities. Then he knew the glorious fulfilment of the promise he had written when Christ spoke of the coming Comforter Whom the world could not receive because it saw Him not. He was in the Spirit.

I. It is no mere influence that creates and sustains such feelings. It is only the presence of a person—of a dear companion. In proportion as love and sympathy are perfected, circumstances sink into insignificance, and we rise into the timeless life. So it was here. And this is the first truth concerning the Holy Ghost that needs to be grasped, that the Holy Ghost is a Person, and that He is a Divine Person. The unveiling of the Adorable Life of the Holy Trinity is, and must be, gradual. We are subjects in the Kingdom of the Holy Ghost, of Whom it may be said that in a manner He rules the world through this dispensation of His power. The final revelation of the Divine life was given when the Holy Ghost came. Christ, and Christ alone, is the subject of the Holy Spirit's teaching; but Christ has returned to the Father, and has sent the Paraclete in virtue of His ascended Manhood, that He may overcome the world.

II. How wonderful, then, that the Third Person of the Blessed Trinity is the least known, the least loved, the least worshipped. Yet it is not so wonderful. It is hard to realise a merely spiritual presence. The Son of God became man, and we have the story of His Incarnation. More than that, we have the Holy Spirit to interpret the story, so that Christ is not merely the Lord of the ancient tale, but the Lord Who holds word with us now. The Holy Spirit does not speak of Himself, and therefore we do not think or speak as we should of Him. And yet He is the Source of every gracious thought and memory and hope and trust that come to our mind. By bringing before us the life and death and resurrection of the Lord Jesus, He arms us with the same mind, so that as we think of how the feet of Christ took the hard journey, in which they trampled down the enemies of our salvation, till the iron broke through them and nailed them to the cross, we at last deliver our comings and goings to the same Crucifixion.

III. Yes, though He does not speak of Himself, though He glorifies Christ, yet He makes His claim upon us, His absolute and eternal claim. It is made in a manner to which there is no human parallel. We do know, blessed be God, how the high soul of a brother or a sister in Christ may keep us from falling, may help us to ascend, may mould us somewhat after the pattern of its own spiritual beauty. But the Holy Ghost is not satisfied until He takes possession of the house and fills it with His Presence and His Glory.—W. ROBERTSON NICOLL, *Sunday Evening*, p. 189.

REFERENCES.—I. 9-20.—C. Anderson Scott, *The Book of Revelation*, p. 34. A. Maclaren, *Expositions of Holy Scripture—Revelation*, p. 144.

ON THE OBSERVANCE OF DAYS
(*For the New Year*)

'I was in the Spirit on the Lord's Day.'—REV. I. 10.

THE wonderful book of the Revelation introduces us suddenly to a most picturesque and most pathetic situation. It is Sunday in Patmos, where John is an exile condemned to work in the mines. Sunday was a great day with those early Christians—the Lord's Day, the Christian festival of the Resurrection. For that brilliant fact shone behind them but a little distance off, and once a week they laid aside all other thoughts, and lived over again in loving imagination the events that had changed the world for them.

Sunday was not a holiday in the mines, but the spirit of this redeemed man is free, and he has access to the spiritual world. While his feet and hands toil at their dreary tasks, he passes into an ecstatic state, suspending his connection with this material world, and leading him into the other land, unseen of any eyes but his.

In this exalted state the boundaries both of time and space are thrown down, and he moves free in a larger world. He is back again in the morning light of the day of Christ's rising. Again he runs to the empty tomb with Peter; again the woman whom they have left solitary by that empty tomb comes and tells them what she has seen; and again amid the evening shadows he himself hears the words, 'Peace be unto you'. Similarly he escapes from the narrow confines of the island, and shares the life of the infant Church scattered along the coast-lines of the Great Sea. He is their brother and companion, both in the tribulation and in the kingdom of Jesus Christ; with them both in darkness and in glory. He is with them, too, in that patience of the saints which both the tribulation and the kingdom has taught them— that wonderful patience of the early Church, which had learned to be patient with life, both in its present trial and its deferred hope.

Such was the spirit of the day for John—partly commemoration of the past, partly fellowship with the far distant, in the brotherhood of the patient Church. It was a day of mingled sorrow and exultation, in every sense a very special day.

I. We still keep certain days apart, and break the monotony of the year with their recurring calls to remember and to love. There is sometimes heard a grudge against making much of one day above another, but surely that is but a frowsy way of thinking.

There are others who in a different spirit ask: ' Why select one day above another? Are not all days equally days of the Lord? Rather let us raise the tone of every day till it reaches festival height.' This looks indeed like religion, but it is not human nature. Those who are always at high pressure grow inevitably strained and unnatural. It is quite true that every day is a day of the Lord, for every day is ' full of things offering themselves for our wonder, and understanding, and love, and every person we meet is a traveller between life and death'. So all the interests of life are religious; but we are human, and none of us is capable of bearing more than a certain strain. Such attempts overstrain life to a tension that is neither desirable nor wholesome.

II. In a word, the spirit is tidal, and 'the soul wins its victories as the sea wins hers'. The occasional and fluctuating element in life is not only justifiable but essential to healthy human nature. The tides of the spirit are known to us all—the great reactions, the swinging tides of feeling, interest, and energy. These are from above, coming down upon us, unlike the pedestrian guides of common sense and principle which direct us evenly on our way. This does not apply merely to the ebb and flow of sweet or tender feeling, though it includes that also. Rather one thinks of the occasional heightening of life all round, the intensification of its powers in moments when it ' means intensely, and means good '.

We have here a principle which gives its true meaning to the observance of Sunday. Unfortunately the whole question has come to be associated either with laws and forcible restraints, or with the mere idea of rest, and the cessation of the daily routine. Both of these are negative conceptions of the day, relating to what we must not do on it. Really such restrictions exist not for their own sake, but in order to make room for the positive Sunday life. That life consists of much that is keenest and most worthy in human nature—the fellowship of friends, thoughts of the absent, memories of the dead, aspirations after better life, communion with God. For the sake of these things of the Spirit it is worth while to resist the encroachment of week-day interests. And the resistance must be firm, for much is ever waiting to be completed, and overlapping fragments of workaday life will make it impossible without watchfulness to be in the Spirit on the Lord's Day.—JOHN KELMAN, *Ephemera Eternitatis*, p. 1.

THE LORD'S DAY

'On the Lord's day.'—REV. I. 10.

IF you have ever stood and watched the sea raging and foaming immediately after a great storm, lashing itself with fury, as it were; and then, after the storm has subsided and passed away, you have stood again, perhaps, and watched the sea as it lies out far away at low tide, in that lull and peace which so often succeeds upon a violent storm, you cannot but, I think, be conscious of a peculiar sense of peace; peace without which does not minister to that peace within. Or, if we transfer our metaphor from nature to humanity—you may, perhaps, have traversed one of those busy streets of London on a Saturday night, when the barrows are there line upon line, and the salesmen are at their busiest trying to part with their wares; all noise and hubbub, strain, excitement, and activity. And then, on the next morning, Sunday, you see nothing left of all the activity of the previous evening but the wreckage, and the scavengers cleaning it up. What a sense of peace this produces upon the soul. The barrows gone, the men gone, the wares gone, the noise gone—and in place of it a wonderful stillness and peace—a peace which speaks to the soul of the things of God, which reminds us of His immediate presence, and which causes us to remember that it is the day of God—God's own special day dedicated to Him. And as we watch the change I have tried to describe, we see, as it were, a resurrection going on—a resurrection reminding us of the first resurrection which was really but a foretaste of the general resurrection to come.

I. Our Sunday is the Foretaste of our General Welfare.—But the peace which I have described is not one, or should not be one of inaction. It should mean that whilst parting with much which we are accustomed to encounter in our day by day life, we thereby make room for an activity of another kind, a spiritual activity. And the state in which we find ourselves is not a solitary state. Peace, we know, comes to us as individuals and as a purely subjective message; but we must remember that that is not all. There is a community of hosts in all worship, a community of spirit. 'God is a Spirit; and they that worship Him must worship Him in spirit and in truth.' That is the highest to which man can attain: to answer to the will of the Father, to be His, to worship Him, and to love Him. And whilst this is the case, or should be, in our everyday life, and whilst every day should be consecrated and dedicated to God, whether in our work, our recreation, our time of physical refreshment or what not; yet there is one day which comes to us with special force as being set apart, reserved, and kept holy for the very special service and worship of Almighty God.

II. There are many Difficult Questions Concerning this Point of Sunday Observance.—There is a great deal that may be said, but let us try and pare it down as much as we can.

(*a*) *Hard and fast rules are impossible.* What is good or best for one may not be good or best for everybody else.

(*b*) *What we do with our Sundays is more important than what we refrain from doing.* If we think Sunday is to be a day, in the first place, when we can put away this and that, and refrain from doing this and the other simply because we rather like it, then we are mistaken; if we think this, we are reducing it to a far lower level than we should. We refrain from doing things merely in order that we may do other things. Life is so full—we cannot be doing nothing; we must be thinking of something even if we are not engaged in any special form of activity; and, this being so, if we refrain from doing this or that it should be in order that we may find room and space and time for doing better and higher things.

III. Two General Principles Stand Out yet more Prominently.—Each individual may shape his own life; but all will agree, I think, on one point—

(*a*) *That man does need at least one day's rest in seven.*

(*b*) *Sunday should be a day properly proportioned.* If we once give way to enjoyment, pure and simple, in the afternoon, there is danger that we may encroach upon the morning, that time which should be specially set apart for the worship of Almighty God. It is in the morning that we have

our great and central act of worship and thanksgiving. In the early days the Christian was known by his attendance at the Lord's own service.

THE LORD'S DAY

'I was in the Spirit on the Lord's day.'—Rev. i. 10.

This expression, 'The Lord's Day,' bears distinctly the stamp of Christ. Its occurrence here reminds us of the great change that Christianity has accomplished. The day of the week devoted to rest has been changed, and is associated with Christ Himself. On that day He appeared in heavenly majesty to His exiled seer, and gave him the messages to the Churches. John says, 'I was in the Spirit,' literally, 'I became in the Spirit'. But surely we are not to understand that John's spiritual condition was miraculous. If it was exceptional it was only so in degree, and not in kind. The fact of being 'in the Spirit' will issue in the largest blessings.

I. This is an ideal to be aimed at, for the Lord's Day will not necessarily bring the Lord's Day Spirit. Thank God it brings much and it comes surely. It brings rest, and opportunity for rest. But to be 'in the Spirit on the Lord's Day' is another matter. 'The process of the suns' cannot give you that; social customs and religious institutions, much as they may help, cannot guarantee it. It depends not on the day, but on you. It cannot be put on like a Sunday garment, it springs from the heart. Therefore it must be cultivated; it must be trained and nourished, like all the spiritual possibilities of man.

II. Being 'in the Spirit on the Lord's Day' is an experience to be enjoyed. Think of some of its advantages. (1) Whatever blessing and inspiration there may be in the services of the sanctuary you will receive. (2) Then think how much more independent you will be in regard to the kind and quality of what we call the means of grace. Your favourite preacher may be absent from the pulpit, or you may have to worship in some plain, rural sanctuary, with nothing to charm the sense, but you may see wondrous visions of God, and your soul be thrilled with the touch of Christ. (3) Being 'in the Spirit on the Lord's Day' will make the Sabbath a delight to you.

III. If you are 'in the Spirit on the Lord's Day' you are sure to do good. You will help to make an atmosphere in the Church. One question only remains. How is this Sabbatic spirit to be attained? Of course, the answer is, we must live the spiritual life, we must enter into God's rest. Ours must be that Divine fellowship that sanctifies all days.— R. Baldwin Brindley, *The Darkness Where God Is*, p. 151.

References.—I. 10.—C. H. Grundy, *Luncheon Lectures at St. Paul's Cathedral*, p. 57. A. M. Fairbairn, *Christian World Pulpit*, vol. lii. p. 56. A. P. Stanley, *Sermons on Special Occasions*, p. 77. A. Rowland, *Christian World Pulpit*, vol. lx. p. 44. *Expositor* (5th Series), vol. v. p. 51; *ibid.* (6th Series), vol. iii. p. 275; *ibid.* (7th Series), vol. vi. p. 105.

THE GOLDEN CANDLESTICK

'I saw seven golden candlesticks; and in the midst of the seven candlesticks one like unto the Son of Man.'—REV. I. 12, 13.

IN this vision two things are very prominent—the golden candlesticks and the Son of Man walking in the midst. There can be no question as to the meaning of the symbolism of the golden candlesticks. Our Lord settles that in the 20th verse : 'The seven candlesticks which thou sawest are the seven Churches'. There is an allusion undoubtedly to the candlestick in the Holy Place in the tabernacle of Moses, which was made at God's command after a Divine pattern. We now propose to trace the analogy between the golden candlestick, the lamp-stand of the Mosaic tabernacle, and the Church of the living God. Let us consider :—

I. The position occupied by the golden candlestick. It was not in the Holiest Place, but in the first tabernacle, called the Sanctuary, or the Holy Place. (1) One characteristic of the place was darkness. This fitly represents the condition of the world where God has placed His Church. But darkness is a figure of speech signifying ignorance. (a) The world is ignorant of God. (b) Man is ignorant of himself. (c) Man is ignorant of the way of recovery. (2) The Sanctuary of old, although dark, was nevertheless holy. Dark as may be the world, it is the sacred property of Him who redeemed it with His precious blood.

II. The purpose for which Christ placed His Church in this dark world. The Church is here compared not to anything merely ornamental, but to the homely candlestick or lamp-stand. The Church is not simply a thing of beauty, a mere ornament set up for admiration, but something to render service, a power to lift the world out of darkness into the marvellous light of God.

III. The candlestick had its *pipes* to convey the oil to the extremities of the branches. The pipes symbolise the means of grace, the ordinances of the Church ; these are the appointed channels through which God communicates blessings to humble waiting souls.

IV. Through the golden pipes flowed the Holy Oil, yielding at the top of each branch a pure flame. There can be no doubt whatsoever that the oil symbolises the Holy Spirit.

V. Who supplies the Holy Oil for the golden candlestick ? 'The Son of Man' as the High Priest is the minister of the sanctuary, and evermore supplies the Church with the Holy Spirit.

VI. But with all these one thing more is wanting, without which the holy lamp yields no light ; we must have *Fire* to retouch and rekindle the seven lamps. As the lamps were rekindled by contact with altar fire, so the Holy Spirit works through the means of the truth of the Gospel.

VII. There is, however, one point in which the analogy fails. In the tabernacle of Moses there was **only *one*** golden candlestick, whereas John in his vision saw seven. This is not without its significance. Under Moses religion was Jewish, limited, local ; Christianity, on the other hand, has the stamp of universality.—RICHARD ROBERTS, *My Closing Ministry*, p. 34.

REFERENCES.—I. 12.—A. H. Bradford, *Christian World Pulpit*, vol. l. p. 120. H. S. Holland, *ibid*. vol. li. p. 345. *Expositor* (6th Series), vol. x. p. 154. I. 12-14.—J. Bannerman, *Sermons*, p. 365. I. 12-17.—Spurgeon, *Sermons*, vol. vii. No. 357.

THE NOTE OF THE HEROIC

' His eyes were as a flame of fire.'—REV. I. 14.

IT is notable that in this vision of the ascended Saviour the eyes should have been, as it were, a flame of fire. That is hardly the characteristic we should have expected after hearing of hair that was as white as snow. The snow-white hair suggests to us venerable age ; it hints at the passing of unnumbered years, with the inevitable quenching of the fire of youth ; but when we should look for eyes that were very gentle, or that were filled with the wise tenderness of age, we find that His eyes were as a flame of fire. Now that contrast at once suggests to me this thought. In Christ there is not only a beauty as of silvered age ; there is also a fire and a heroism as of youth.

I. Now we cannot turn to the earthly life of Jesus without being struck with one marvellous union there. I refer to the union of what was beautiful and gracious, with all that was in the truest sense heroic. He was gentle, charitable, courteous, kind, a perfect pattern of moral beauty. But the wonder of that beauty is magnified a hundredfold when we remember the heroism with which it went hand in hand. If to be true to one's mission and to stand alone ; if to be faithful, and joyful, and quiet, and undaunted ; if to challenge all the powers of hell to combat ; if to march forward without a falter to a cross—if that be heroism in its noblest meaning, then Jesus of Nazareth must have been heroic.

II. In some degree, then, as we grow like to Christ, that union of qualities will be found in us. It is one distinctive mark of that new character that has been built up through the powers of the Gospel, that there is ample room in it for all that is gracious, and at the same time for all that is heroic. We should be poor disciples of a compassionate Lord unless we have eyes that can soften into pity. But we shall be poor soldiers in the warfare mystical unless these eyes are as a flame of fire.

III. It is notable, too, that as the spiritual life of Christendom has deepened, as it has grown richer with the passing of the ages, it has brought with it a deeper and truer conception of what spiritual heroism really is. I close with two remarks. The first is that there is always danger for a Church when the note of the heroic passes from its life. And the second is, I appeal to the young men on the ground of the heroism of Christ Jesus. Mr. FitzGerald, the translator of Omar Khayyám, in an exquisite little piece he calls 'Euphranor,' has some suggestive words on chivalry. He says that the charm of chivalry was just its note of heroism ; and if it appealed—as it certainly did appeal—to the bravest and noblest and most gallant man, it was just because it put the accent there. May I not do the same with Jesus Christ? I think it is a true appeal to opening manhood.—G. H. MORRISON, *Sunrise : Addresses from a City Pulpit*, p. 300.

REFERENCES.—I. 16.—Spurgeon, *Sermons*, vol. xxxiii. No. 1976, and vol. xliii. No. 2498. *Expositor* (6th Series), vol. ix. p. 316.

AT HIS FEET AS DEAD

'And when I saw Him, I fell at His feet as dead.'—REV. I. 17.

'Now that He ascended,' said the Apostle, 'what is it but that He first descended to the lowest parts of the earth?' There was first the humiliation, then the exaltation; first the descent, then the ascent. Yet it is equally true that while He was descending, He was all the time ascending, and that at the very lowest point of His descent He was already upon His throne. There are strange glimpses of His own consciousness at the supreme moment of crisis. Now, He said, is the Son of Man glorified. This when He was almost forsaken and on the very verge of His last Passion. He taught it to His disciples; He showed them how, and how only, their ambition to be greatest could be reached. The greatest had to be the servant of all, and while serving all was in possession of his greatness. Christ went lower, and yet lower, in quest of His crown, and it waited Him in the lowest parts of the earth. And when it seemed that there was for Him no more of earthly honour and earthly love, He suddenly found all things transfigured in the light of the eternal world. When He yielded His life in the infinite willinghood with which He went to His sacrifice, He knew that from His cross He would draw all men unto Him. As He sank lower and lower still, all things ministered strangely to His ascension. While He lay in the new tomb, with closed eyes, amidst the sweet fragrance of the myrrh and aloes which He left behind Him, He was the very heart of the world. When He rose radiant in the dark and returned to the old surroundings for forty days—days full, to the brim, of peace—He was conscious all the time that His kingship had been attained. There was indeed the visible enthronement. He led His disciples as far as Bethany. He lifted up His hands and blessed them, and they watched Him for a little as He bore His way upward. Then the cloud stretched itself beneath Him—a pure floor on which His feet might rest. And at last He took His seat above all principalities and powers on the right hand of God the Father Almighty. What was visible was only the outward manifestation of what had already come to Him as His reward, of what had been coming nearer and nearer as He descended deeper and deeper into the ocean of suffering. And so it is with all the great spiritual careers. Take Wesley, take St. Francis, and mark how they were ascending while they were descending, and how, the farther they went in their abandonment of the world, they came closer and closer to the Divine Lord and Lordship.

What is true externally is eminently true of the internal life. To the world this inner experience may seem only a silver thread, scarce discoverable but by the eye of God. To those who know it the outer life is little by comparison even when the stream both of the outer and the inner seems full and broad. They scarce gaze upon the passing scene, scarce hear the din of the endless battle. The inner life transfigures the outer life, and gives its own hue to all the external universe. Those who are ignorant of this have never advanced one step in the life of the soul. For them no deep fountain of intellect and feeling has been unsealed. But ere the secret is fully known sharp arrows must pierce the soul, hard teachings must make it wise, life's best blood must seal the sacrifice. The believer must learn to live earnestly and without despair through all, seeking no home till 'home is everywhere'. Let us trace the process of the soul's schooling for the Divine degree.

I. The beginning is to sit at the feet of Jesus and learn of Him, and many go no farther. Yet even that is a great step in the life of the soul. It has hitherto groped in darkness, and has been exiled from the truth. Now it seizes it with the most earnest grasp, and lives in it with the deepest joy. It suddenly awakens to the true aims of existence.

II. The soul makes great advance when it lies at the feet of Christ, worn, sick, wounded, and proves His healing power. When the carelessness of youth passes, when the great trials of life come, we fall at His feet in our trouble and He gives us rest. Working, fainting, striving, finding that there is always something to be done, although no heart is left for us to do it, we come to Him for strength. From the first hopeless sorrow, after the long month where each day wears the night's dull face, when we have ' to clasp to the heart resigned the fatal must,' we seek Christ in our despair and He helps us to hope once more.

III. The life not wholly surrendered may be lived grandly, but it is with a higher beauty that it perishes before God. When we are crushed, emptied, dead at His feet, it is then we begin to live. Then our weakness becomes our strength and our death our life. For it is in that hour that He enters in to live our life for us, He lays His right hand upon us saying, ' Fear not,' and there passes into us all His fulness, so that we are able to say with His servant of old, ' I live, yet not I, but Christ liveth in me '. Christ is within us not merely as a second conscience, but as another and as the subduing life. Then we know what the Word means when it says that He is made of God unto us wisdom, and righteousness, and sanctification, and redemption. The password is found that admits to full and free initiation.—W. ROBERTSON NICOLL, *Sunday Evening*, p. 331.

FEAR NOT
'Fear not.'—Rev. i. 17.

My purpose is to ask your attention to the seven 'Fear nots' of the New Testament.

(1) We take our first 'Fear not!' from St. Luke VIII. 15 : 'But when Jesus heard it, He answered him, saying, Fear not! believe only, and she shall be made whole'. This is a 'Fear not!' teaching us that we are never to give up hope. If there were ever a seemingly hopeless case, it was this of Jairus's daughter ; but when Christ is concerned, or concerns Himself about us, we need never despair. 'Fear not!'

(2) Then the second 'Fear not!' is in St. Matthew x. 28 : 'Fear not them which kill the body, but are not able to kill the soul'. This is the 'Fear not!' which defies persecution. There is not much opening for violent persecution in this our day, but the enemies of Christ know well enough how to inflict pain upon Christians, upon those who refuse to stay with them. But how little our enemies can do to us. They cannot touch you. Suppose they even mangled and murdered your body, that is not touching you, and after they have done that, there is no more they can do. Therefore, I say, 'Fear not! be bold for Christ, stand up for Jesus in all times, in all situations, and in every place. Fear not! confess Christ and He will bless thee.'

(3) The third 'Fear not!' you will find in St. Luke XII. 32 : 'Fear not! little flock ; for it is your Father's good pleasure to give you the kingdom'. Here we have the 'Fear not!' that drives away anxiety with regard to our earthly supplies. No man, by worrying, can add a cubit to his stature. No man, by worrying or by growing anxious, can help lift a single burden of this life. Let us, therefore, henceforth learn to trust God, not only for the supply of our spiritual needs, but also for the supply of our temporal need.

(4) The next 'Fear not!' is in the Acts of the Apostles (XXVII. 24) : 'Fear not, Paul, . . . lo! God hath given thee all them that sail with thee'. Now this 'Fear not!' is a most important one. It is a 'Fear not!' even when almost certain failure seems to be staring us in the face. God is always better than our fears. Our worst troubles are those troubles that never come at all, those things which we are always afraid are coming, and which do not come. Let us therefore look up and 'Fear not!'

(5) Then we will pass back again to St. Luke v. 10 : 'And Jesus said unto Simon, Fear not! from henceforth thou shalt catch men'. Now this is a 'Fear not!' for all weary Christian workers. The disciples said in a desponding tone, 'We have toiled all the night, and have taken nothing'—words that are often on the lips of weary Christian workers. The Master said to His disciples, 'Work away!' they did so, and were rewarded with a tremendous haul ; and so the Master will come to every weary, discouraged Christian worker, and say, 'My brother, My sister, fear not, work away. Fear not, faint not, henceforth thou shalt catch men.'

(6) The sixth 'Fear not!' is also in St. Luke's Gospel (II. 10) : 'And the angel said unto them, Fear not! for behold, I bring you good tidings of great joy, which shall be to all people'. This is a 'Fear not!' for each penitent sinner. In a few days we shall look once again upon the Star of Bethlehem, and as we see that Babe there, we realise that God is not against us. We realise that God is for us : nay, more, God is with us—our 'Emmanuel'.

(7) And then we come to the 'Fear not!' of our text (Rev. I. 17). In this text our Master gives us three reasons, three solid facts why we should at once cease to fear. The first reason why Christ may well bid us 'Fear not!' is on account of His eternal existence : 'I am the first and the last'. He is the living Saviour. The second reason is on account of His victory. He says, 'Behold! I am alive for evermore'. Note that word 'Behold!' It means that, in spite of all that death and hell and the devil can do, Christ, nevertheless, is alive for evermore. They tried to destroy our Master, but He conquered them all, and so His message is to each one of us, 'Fear not!' The third reason is this : He has the right to do so, because He has the power and authority, all power and authority over the unseen universe. He says, 'I have the keys of hell and of death'. Keys there mean authority, power, possession. Christ declares that He has the power, therefore death and the grave can only open as He pleases. One day Christ will shut the door of death, because He came to destroy the work of the devil. One day He will shut the door, and when Christ hath shut it, no man openeth it.

REVERENCE
'And when I saw Him, I fell at His feet as dead.'—Rev. i. 17.

John was a prisoner in the isle of Patmos when he had this revelation of Jesus Christ. There are some things we cannot learn in Babylon that become plain to us in sea-girt Patmos. There are some sights we are blind to in the markets ; our eyes are only opened in the mines. 'It is adversity,' says Bacon in his priceless essays, 'which carrieth the greater benediction, and the clearer revelation of God's favour.' I want to take this falling-down of John as a true instance of a truly reverent spirit. John saw, John worshipped, John adored.

I. I do not think that the most cheerful optimist would dare to assert this was a reverent age. We are all busy ; few of us are reverent. Yet without reverence life is a shallow thing, and true nobility of character is impossible ; and without reverence we shall be strangers to the end to all that is best and worthiest in religion. Can we explain the comparative absence of this grace ? I think we can. It springs from certain features of our modern life. (1) And the first of these is the wear and hurry of it. It is not easy for an overdriven man to keep a reverent heart. (2) The lack of reverence, too, I cannot doubt, is partly due to the spirit of inquiry of to-day. We are never afraid to criticise, but we have almost forgotten to adore. (3) But this present lack of reverence has another source; it is the dying-out from heart and conscience of the fear of God. 'Ah, Rogers,' said Dr. Dale of Birmingham to his old friend—'ah, Rogers, no one fears God now'.

II. Now what is reverence? It is the practical recognition of true greatness. It is my attitude of heart and mind when I am confronted by the truly worthy and the truly great. Where does individual irreverence begin? I think that generally it begins at home. When I have ceased to reverence myself it is the hardest thing in the whole world to reverence my brother man, to reverence God. Now there are two things in the life of Jesus that arrest me. (1) And the first of these is His reverence for God. (2) But still more arresting than the reverence of Jesus for His God is the reverence that Jesus had for men.

III. So as I think on reverence, and link it with the supreme reverence of Jesus, I learn three lessons that may guide us to a more reverent life. (1) If we are ever to grow reverent again, we must know more. Jesus was reverent because His knowledge was perfect; we are irreverent because our knowledge is shallow. (2) We must trust more. I cannot reverence a *man* whom I distrust. I cannot reverence a *God*. It wants deep faith to make me reverent. (3) We must love more. Love reveals, love sees, love breaks the bars, love reads the secrets both of man and God. And when I have seen my brother's secret story, and when I have seen into the deep things of God, I never can be irreverent again.—G. H. MORRISON, *Flood-tide*, p. 103.

'I fell at His feet as one dead.'—REV. I. 17.

MR. BAGEHOT, after describing the religious opinions of the First Edinburgh Reviewers, sums up his essay in these words: 'A certain class of Liberal divines have endeavoured to petrify into a theory a pure and placid disposition. . . . With misdirected energy, these divines have laboured after a plain religion; they have forgotten that religion has its essence in awe, its charm in infinity, its sanction in dread; that its dominion is an inexplicable dominion; that mystery is its power. There is a reluctance in all such writers; they creep away from the unintelligible parts of the subject; they always seem to have something behind; not to like to bring out what they know to be at hand. They are in their nature apologists; and as George III. said, "I did not know the Bible needed an apology". As well might the thunder be ashamed to roll, as religion hesitate to be too awful for mankind. The invective of Lucretius is truer than the placid patronage of the divine.'

REFERENCES.—I. 17.—Spurgeon, *Sermons*, vol. xxvi. No. 1533. *Expositor* (5th Series), vol. i. p. 193.

THE GROUND OF FEARLESSNESS

'Fear not; I am the first and the last, and the Living One; and I was dead, and behold, I am alive for evermore, and I have the keys of death and of Hades.'—REV. I. 17, 18 (R.V.).

THE 'Fear nots' of Scripture are part of the inheritance of the Christian. For the Word of God stands, and a promise once made is made for ever. It is to be observed that when He says to John 'Fear not,' He directs the feeling and thought not to anything in John himself, or to anything in his circumstances: on the contrary, He directs the mind of John to Himself. The ground of confidence is altogether in the Lord Himself. This is one of the commonplaces of Christian experience. The meaning of the text grows on us as we dwell on it. As we hear the striking words, and let their meaning and their particulars sink into our minds, a wonderful vista of great meanings opens to our view. 'Fear not, for I am the Living One; fear not, for I became dead: fear not, for I have the keys of death and of Hades. As we think the matter out into detail, we find ourselves thinking of life, of death, and of what comes after death.

I. 'Fear not to live; I am the Living One.' It might be possible for us to say thoughtlessly, Is it necessary to dwell on this, for who fears to live? It is not life which any one fears; it is the difficulties, perplexities, the hindrances of life which one fears and dreads. To every thoughtful man life has its responsibilities, its cares, and its possibilities. As we reflect on this, as we think out the situations and possibilities that open out to us as life proceeds and new horizons are disclosed, we feel the gracious power of this word. 'Fear not to live; for I am the Living One.' It is as if the Lord said, 'Fear not to live; I share your life. Through me you will be able to grasp the opportunities of life, you will rise to the height of your calling, and when duty calls you will be able to answer all its demands. You will be able to say, 'I live, yet not I, but Christ liveth in me'.

II. 'Fear not to die; for I was dead.' He knew all the secrets of death: every step in the valley of the shadow of death had been trodden by Him. In virtue of that experience and of that victory over death, the risen Lord can say to His people, 'Fear not to die; for I was dead'.

III. 'Fear not what comes after death; for I have the keys of death and Hades.' We may take home the consolation of the Master's words, and gather together the wealth of our inheritance. We may live, we may die, we may appear before the judgment-seat with confidence; for Christ liveth who was dead, and is alive for evermore. Apart from Christ there is no power and no right in any one to expect deliverance from the fear of life, the fear of death, or the fear of what comes after death.—J. IVERACH, *The Other Side of Greatness*, p. 136.

REFERENCES.—I. 17, 18.—Bishop Boyd-Carpenter, *Christian World Pulpit*, vol. l. p. 81. C. A. Berry, *Vision and Duty*, p. 191. Spurgeon, *Sermons*, vol. xviii. No. 1028.

THE LIVING LORD

'I am He that liveth, and was dead; and behold I am alive for evermore.'—REV. I. 18.

'He is risen, as He said.'—ST. MATTHEW XXVIII. 6.

EACH of these two texts tells us of the truth of the Resurrection in the testimony of Jesus Christ Himself. I want you to ask yourselves, on what grounds do you believe in the Resurrection of Jesus Christ? There is a great deal of collateral evidence. For instance, there is the evidence of His enemies. There is the testimony of his friends. There is the testimony of what St. Paul witnesses: 'He was seen of above five hundred brethren at once, of whom the greater part remain unto this present, but some are fallen asleep . . . and last of all He was seen of me also.'

I. Sure Testimony.—But that is not the testimony I want to impress upon you this morning. The best testimony that Christ is risen from the dead is that of Jesus Christ Himself. St. John had it from His own lips in that wonderful vision, and the angel beside the empty grave announced it to the frightened women, 'He is risen, as He said'. You will remember that He told His Disciples, quietly taking them apart to tell them a truth, that He should be delivered to the Gentiles, scourged, spitted upon, put to death, and the third day He should rise again. So the testimony He gave His Disciples is the testimony I want you to receive as His disciples this Easter morning, 'He is risen, as He said'. Christ has spoken and the matter is settled. We accept it by faith—faith in the Word of God Himself, 'He is risen, as He said,' and that is enough.

I know that poets have sung of the Elysian fields beyond the grave. I know that philosophers have speculated on the immortality of the soul, and I know that what the poets have sung, and what the philosophers have speculated upon is worthy of consideration, and may amount to a probability. But do not rest the doctrine of Christ's Resurrection on a probability. We must be absolutely certain. We must know in Whom we have believed, and be persuaded that He is able to keep those committed to Him unto the last day. There must be no 'perhaps' no 'inference,' no 'it may be'. It must not be a matter of opinion but a matter of certainty—the certainty of faith in the Word of God; 'He is risen, as He said'. To doubt the Resurrection of Christ is to make Christ a liar.

II. Dead, Buried, Risen.—The force of the Resurrection all depends, of course, upon the great fact of Calvary. He was born in order that He might be able to die, and He died; and because He died, He rose again, the circumstances of His death being detailed to us that we might be quite certain. And whenever we say the Creed we enter into the detail; we say, 'Was crucified, dead——'. Are you quite certain He was dead? Yes, 'buried'—that makes quite sure that He was dead. Yes, He was dead, and the third day He rose again, 'as He said'. I could take you to the cemetery, and say to you, Look at these graves; beneath these graves is the dust of those we love. You know that? Yes. You are certain that they are there? Yes, they are buried there; their dust, just their dust is there, and one day they shall all rise again, and we shall be united again in Christ. Those who sleep in Christ shall rise again from the dead, and Christ will bring them with Him. That is our religion.

III. A Gospel worth Receiving.—This is a Gospel worth preaching, is it not? And this is a Gospel worth receiving, is it not? We do not preach it on the faith of the word of man, but it is on the faith of the Word of God. 'He is risen, as He said,' and opened the Kingdom of Heaven to all believers. Believest thou this? And this morning you will ratify here in church your faith in the Resurrection of Christ, and of all who sleep in Him. And wherefore these words to you? Because to men and women, wounded but not weak, the Cross is something more than a refuge; it has changed bereavement into joy.

THE RESURRECTION CHANGE
(For Easter Day)

'I am He that liveth and was dead; and behold I am alive for evermore.'—REV. I. 18.

THE glories of Easter! The Queen of Festivals! Our worship is full of the blessed truth that 'Jesus Christ is risen to-day'. What shall be our theme as we stand beside the empty tomb? There are many aspects of the Resurrection which might well engage our attention. We will think of the great changes effected by it.

I. A Change in Our Blessed Lord Himself.

(a) *The resurrection of the body* means the rising again in some way of that which died and was buried. We carry our dead to the sepulchre, and a lonely and a desolate thing does it appear to leave them in the dull hole which we have dug in the earth, while we go back to the light, and the warmth, and the cheery voices of life. Yet is this but a heathen view. The dust, which was human, hath in it something which involves the development out of itself of a further life.

(b) *But, while the teaching of the New Testament establishes a real organic connection* between that which died and that which rises again, it intimates also a mighty change. Does not the text (also 1 Cor. xv. 37-44) indicate this?

(c) *Hence, we may learn to take another and a more blessed aspect of death itself.* True, death entered into the world by sin; humanity, that is, was subjected to it as the penalty of transgression. But it has become in Christ the instrument also by which these bodies are changed so as to bear the splendour of the everlasting morning.

II. A Change in our Lord's Relations with His Followers.

(a) *If He forbids Mary's touch because He has not yet ascended, He thereby manifestly implies that when He had ascended, then should she touch Him without rebuke.* His ascension would not separate Him from but bring Him nearer to His faithful ones.

(b) *Thus Christ draws on the believer from a lower to a higher love;* from a carnal to a spiritual touch; from a clinging to Him with the limbs of the body, to an embracing Him with the arms of the soul.

(c) *Do you ask, 'How can I touch my ascended Lord?'* The reply is ready.

1. He touches Christ, who, when crushed with the felt burden of sin, conscious of a force of evil continually mastering him, after vain attempts to get rid of his slavery by mere strength of will, or the maxims of worldly prudence, casts himself into the whole system of Christ's religion, clasping unto him alike Christ's commandments and Christ's promises, and looking and calling on Him for health and salvation.

2. Yea, there is a more palpable touching of the Divine Lord still. What is the Blessed Sacrament but the ordinance in which He offers Himself at a given moment, by a definite act, to the spiritual touch, to draw healing virtue out of Him?

REFERENCES.—I. 18.—A. G. Mortimer, *The Church's Lessons for the Christian Year*, pt. ii. p. 343. Spurgeon, *Sermons*, vol. xv. No. 894; vol. xlvi. No. 2689. J. Stalker, *Christian World Pulpit*, vol. xlvii. p. 280. W. H. Hutchings, *Sermon Sketches*, p. 111. A. Ainger, *Sermons Preached in the Temple Church*, p. 310. W. P. Balfern, *Glimpses of Jesus*, p. 272. F. J. A. Hort, *Village Sermons* (2nd Series), p. 139. J. Farquhar, *The Schools and Schoolmasters of Christ*, p. 12. *Expositor* (4th Series), vol. iii. p. 246; *ibid.* (7th Series), vol. vi. p. 427.

'These things saith he that holdeth the seven stars in his right hand, he that walketh in the midst of the seven golden candlesticks.'—REV. II. I.

COMPARE Milton's magnificent apostrophe, in *The Remonstrant's Defence*: 'Who is there that cannot trace Thee now in Thy beamy walk through the midst of Thy sanctuary, amidst those golden candlesticks, which have long suffered a dimness amongst us through the violence of those that had seized them, and were more taken with the mention of their gold than of their starry light; teaching the doctrine of Balaam, to cast a stumbling-block before Thy servants, commanding them to eat things sacrificed to idols, and forcing them to fornication? Come, therefore, O Thou that hast the seven stars in Thy right hand, appoint Thy chosen priests according to their orders and causes of old, to minister before Thee, and duly to press and pour out the consecrated oil into Thy holy and ever-burning lamps. Thou hast sent out the spirit of prayer upon Thy servant all over the land to this effect, and stirred up their vows as the sound of many waters about Thy throne.'

REFERENCES.—II. 1.—R. E. Hutton, *The Crown of Christ*, p. 341. *Expositor* (6th Series), vol. xi. p. 65. A. Maclaren, *Expositions of Holy Scripture—Revelation*, p. 170. II. 1-7.— C. Anderson Scott, *The Book of Revelation*, p. 49.

THINGS JESUS KNOWS ABOUT US
'I know.'—REV. II. 2.

HAVE you noted how often the Risen Saviour says 'I know' in the letters to the seven churches? Seven times the avowal sounds out. Tremendous in their suggestiveness are those 'I knows'. What are the things Jesus knows about us?

I. Jesus knows the activities of His people. In five out of the seven letters this formula is found: 'I know thy works'. He cites at least two features of those energies and so reveals His intimate knowledge of them. He knows their *quantity*. 'I know thy works and thy toil' (ver. 2, R.V.). He knows the *quality* of our activities, 'I know . . . thy patience'. Patient activities, 'That thou canst not bear evil men'. Detestation of wickedness. 'And didst try them which call themselves Apostles, and they are not, and didst find them false,' moral and spiritual discrimination. Do these qualities grace our service? (1) Christ knows any deterioration which may mark our activities. (2) But if He knows deterioration He is also aware of all development.

II. Jesus knows the Christian characteristics of His people. (1) In ch. II. 19 the Risen One says, 'I know . . . thy *love*' (R.V.). (2) 'I know . . . thy love, and *faith*'. (3) 'I know . . . thy ministry.' If there be faith and love there is sure to be 'ministry'. (4) He recalls their 'patience'. What Miss Rossetti calls 'endurance outliving impulse' is a pearl of great price in the Lord's most precious sight. (5) Jesus knows the faultiness of His people, as well as their excellent features. 'But I have this against thee' (ver. 20, R.V.).

III. Jesus knows the trials of His people. That is a sweet word in ch. II. 9, 'I know thy . . . tribulation'. What balm that assurance brings! Perhaps scarcely any one else knows it, but if He knows what matters that?

IV. Jesus knows the abode of His people. In ch. II. 13, we read, 'I know . . . where thou dwellest'. He visits our abode, floods it with sunshine in summer, and lights the household fire in winter. Jesus guards our homes.—DINSDALE T. YOUNG, *The Enthusiasm of God*, p. 93.

'I know thy works, and thy toil, and thy patience.'—REV. II. 2.

IN his introduction to Plato's *Republic*, Jowett notes how 'the want of energy is one of the main reasons why so few persons continue to improve in later years. They have not the will, and do not know the way. They 'never try an experiment,' or take up a point of interest for themselves; they make no sacrifices for the sake of knowledge; their minds, like their lives, at a certain age become fixed. Genius has been defined as 'the power of taking pains'; but hardly any one keeps up his interest in knowledge throughout a whole life.

THE greatest part of the good work of the world is done either in pure and unvexed instinct of duty, 'I have stubbed Thornaby waste,' or else, and better, it is cheerful and helpful doing of what the hand finds to do, in surety that at evening time, whatsoever is right the Master will give.—RUSKIN.

'Thou canst not bear them which are evil.'—REV. II. 2.

THIS fierceness against sin, which we are so proud of being well quit of, is the very life of a church; the toleration of sin is the dying of its lamp.— RUSKIN, *Fors Clavigera*, LXXXIV.

'I know thy works.'—Rev. ii. 2 f.

In the following address to each church, its 'work' is spoken of as the state of its heart. Of which the interpretation is nevertheless quite simple, that the thing looked at by God first, in every Christian man, is his work; without that, there is no more talk or thought of him.'—Ruskin, *Fors Clavigera*, lxxxiv.

References.—II. 2.—*Expositor* (5th Series), vol. vi. p. 146; *ibid.* (6th Series), vol. vi. p. 400. II. 2-4.—J. M. Neale, *Sermons on the Apocalypse*, p. 1. II. 2, 3, 6.—*Expositor* (5th Series), vol. v. p. 242. II. 3.—Spurgeon, *Sermons*, vol. xviii. No. 1069.

'I have this against thee.'—Rev. ii. 4.

All the dear graces are first reckoned up to the honour of the Church of Ephesus : endurance and patience and for His Name's sake, labouring and not fainting. 'Nevertheless,' our dear Lord goes on, 'I have *this* against thee, because thou hast left thy first love.'

And now see how much we learn by comparing Ephesus with Thyatira.

Ephesus clung to the faith, hating apostates and heretics; the Lord says, 'How thou hast tried them which say they are Apostles and are not, and hast found them liars'. But then, this great, this over-powering accusation. 'Thou hast left thy first love.'

Thyatira had the opposite sin. She suffered the woman Jezebel which calleth herself a prophetess, but she loved, and she showed her love by her works; and the last, He that knoweth all things, knew to be more than the first. On the one side faith, with decreasing love; on the other, increasing love, with more cowardly faith.'—J. M. Neale.

DECAYING LOVE

'Nevertheless I have somewhat against thee, because thou hast left thy first love.'—Rev. ii. 4.

The Church at Ephesus was favoured with apostolic letters from two different Apostles, the one from Paul, the other from John. We know of no other Church that was so favoured. We propose to direct our thoughts to St. John's letter to the Ephesians.

I. The letter, although written by John, was dictated by the Lord Jesus Himself. The words are not the words of John, but of the Divine Master, the Conqueror of death and hell: who was dead, but who hath ascended on high, and is alive for evermore. When writing our letters we reserve our signature for the close; Jesus Christ begins His letters by first announcing His name. To Ephesus He announces Himself as 'He that holdeth the seven stars in His right hand, who walketh in the midst of the seven golden candlesticks'.

II. Having introduced Himself by these Divine names and titles, Jesus Christ now commends the excellences of the Ephesian Church. 'I know thy works.' We have here three commendable qualities specified. (1) The life was right. 'Thou hast borne, and hast patience, and for My name's sake hast laboured, and hast not fainted' (ver. 3). (2) The doctrine was right. (3) The discipline was right.

'Thou hast tried them which say they are apostles, and are not, and hast found them liars' (ver. 2).

III. Christ now reveals, and reproves her fault. 'I have against thee, that thou didst let go thy first love.' Our Lord estimates the Ephesian Church, not by her external toil or patience, but by her inward motive, the state of her heart towards Himself. The solemn admonitory lesson taught by the Ephesian Church, is that with incessant activities in the service of Christ and of humanity, there may be at the same time a daily decline of personal piety.

IV. Our Lord now instructs the Church what to do to avoid final apostasy (ii. 5). The advice is threefold. Remember, repent, reform. (1) Remember therefore from whence thou art fallen. (2) 'Repent.' Having by a faithful scrutiny ascertained the heights which you once occupied, and the depths into which you have now fallen; and contrasting your present coldness with your former ardour, repent, mourn with bitterness of soul over the change. (3) Reformation. 'Do thy first works.'—Richard Roberts, *My Jewels*, p. 147.

References.—II. 4.—Spurgeon, *Sermons*, vol. iv. No. 217. II. 4, 5.—*Ibid.* vol. xxxii. No. 1926.

'Remember then whence thou art fallen, and repent, and do the first works.'—Rev. ii. 5.

Compare a fragment of Euripides' last drama, 'Archelaus,' thus Englished by Prof. Gilbert Murray :—

> Sweetness of days and rest and dallying
> Have never lifted any fallen thing,
> City nor house.

Monday, 5th April.—I was surprised, when I came to Chester, to find that there also morning preaching was quite left off, for this worthy reason : 'Because the people will not come, or, at least, not in the winter'. If so, the Methodists are a fallen people. Here is proof. They have 'lost their first love'; and they never will or can recover it till they 'do the first works'.—Wesley's *Journal*.

'Remember whence thou art fallen, and repent.'—Rev. ii. 5.

We imagine that when souls have had a fall, they immediately look up and contrast their present with their preceding position. This does not occur. The lower their fall, the less generally their despair, for despair is a business of the will, and when they come heavily down upon their humanity, they get something of the practical seriousness of nature. If they fall very low, the shock and the sense that they are still on their feet make them singularly earnest to set about the plain plan of existence—getting air for their lungs and elbow-room. Contrast, that mother of melancholy, comes when they are some way advanced upon the *upward* scale.—George Meredith, in *Sandra Belloni*, xxxiv.

'Or else I will remove thy candlestick out of its place.'—Rev. ii. 5.

To terrify a man at the possibilities of his neglected nature, is to do something towards the redemption of that nature.—George Macdonald.

'This thou hast, that thou hatest the works of the Nicolaitans, which I also hate.'—Rev. ii. 6.

MEN will never love where they ought to love, who do not hate where they ought to hate.—BURKE.

'He that hath an ear, let him hear what the Spirit saith to the churches.'—Rev. ii. 7.

'I HAD also great openings concerning the things written in the Revelation,' says George Fox, 'and when I spoke of them, the priests and professors would say that was a sealed book, and would have kept me out of it : but I told them, Christ could open the seals, and that they were the nearest things to us ; for the Epistles were written to the saints that lived in former ages, but the Revelations were written of things to come.'

I AM not of the opinion of those gentlemen who are against disturbing the public repose ; I like a clamour whenever there is an abuse. The fire-bell at midnight disturbs your sleep, but it keeps you from being burned in your bed.—BURKE.

'He that overcometh.'—Rev. ii. 7.

ONLY evil grows of itself ; for goodness we want effort and courage.—AMIEL.

IN *Malcolm*, George Macdonald makes Alexander Graham, the dominie, speak as follows to a pupil : 'That's the battle of Armageddon, Sheltie, my man. It's aye ragin', ohn gun roared and bayonet clashed. Ye maun up an' do yer best in't, my man. Gi'en ye dee fechtin' like a man, ye'll flee up wi' a quaiet face an' wide open een ; an' there's a great Ane 'at'll say to ye, "Weel dune, laddie". But gi'en ye gie in to the enemy, he'll turn ye intill a creepin' thing 'at eats dirt ; an' there'll no be a hole in a' the crystall wa' o' the New Jerusalem near eneuch to the grun' to lat ye creep throu'.' The battle is, of course, that between good and evil.

REFERENCES.—II. 7.—G. E. Biber, *The Seven Voices of the Spirit*, pp. 1, 15. *Expositor* (5th Series), vol. v. p. 96. A. Maclaren, *Expositions of Holy Scripture—Revelation*, p. 187. II. 8.—R. E. Hutton, *The Crown of Christ*, p. 357. *Expositor* (4th Series), vol. iii. p. 251. II. 8-11.—C. Anderson Scott, *The Book of Revelation*, p. 66.

FAITHFUL UNTO DEATH

'Be thou faithful unto death, and I will give thee a crown of life.'—Rev. ii. 10.

THAT does not mean merely, 'Be faithful until death calls you away'. It means far more than that ; it means, 'Be faithful, even though it *costs* you your life'. There are a few thoughts I would present to you.

I. The first is the view we have here of the Christian life apparently defeated. That is the underlying idea that underlies it all. The apparent and the real are often different from one another. Here is a people receiving highest commendation from the Lord Jesus Christ, and yet their whole career seems to be an utter failure. Have you not seen the life of the true man a comparative failure ? Is there not something wrong somewhere ? Or are we to take it

that the Christian life can be defeated, that it can be a failure, that it may make its progress in clouds, and end in darkness ?

II. That is just what I wish to show you it cannot do, because the next thought here for our consideration is the real success of this apparently defeated life. 'Be thou *faithful*.' Faithfulness is victory. When the world kills off the faithful man because it cannot bend his will and take him away from his loyalty, it is not the man that is defeated, it is the world. The truly strong life is the life that can defy circumstances, that can make every failure a stepping-stone to a nobler resolve, that can maintain its integrity when all the world is against it.

III. The next thought here is the spring, the sustaining spring of the Christian life which we once more find in the suggestive words, 'Be thou faithful'. 'Be thou faithful,' or *loyal* ; that means, of course, loyal to Jesus Christ. He asks for your loyalty, your personal loyalty to Him, and in that loyalty you shall conquer ; because the Christian life is sustained by faith in a personal life, a personal power, and a personal love. We are not supported by abstractions.

IV. Then lastly we come to the reward of faithfulness, 'And I will give thee a crown of life'. (1) Notice the contrast ! Notice the compensation ! 'Be thou faithful unto *death*, and I will give thee a crown of *life*.' The life that is won through the sacrifice of this life is a life eternal, profound, joyous, infinitely great and glorious—a life in some wonderful way like the life of God Himself. (2) Notice the giver, 'I will give thee'. Jesus Christ is to be the rewarder of man. It is from Him the gift must come, because after all, it is a *gift*.—JOHN THOMAS, *Myrtle Street Pulpit*, vol. iii. p. 1.

'Be thou faithful.'—Rev. ii. 10.

'AT that time,' says Dumas in *Les Trois Mousquetaires*, 'it was vital to have men like De Tréville round one. Many might take for their device the epithet of "strong," which formed the second part of his motto, "*Fidelis et fortis*," but very few gentlemen could lay claim to the "faithful," which constituted the first. Tréville was one of these latter. His was one of those unique organisations which are endowed with an obedient intelligence like a dog, with a blind valour, with a quick eye and a prompt hand.'

'Fear not the things which thou art about to suffer : ye shall have tribulation ten days.'—Rev. ii. 10.

THE history of persecution is a history of endeavours to cheat nature, to make water run uphill, to twist a rope of sand.—EMERSON.

'ALL of us are weak in the period of growth, and are of small worth before the hour of trial. This fellow,' says George Meredith of a young Englishman, 'had been fattening all his life on prosperity ; the very best dish in the world ; but it does not prove us. It fattens and strengthens us, just as the sun does. Adversity is the inspector of our constitutions ; she simply tries our muscle and powers of endurance, and should be a periodical visitor. But, until she come, no man is known.

IT is laid in the unalterable constitution of things: none can aspire to act greatly, but those who are of force greatly to suffer.—BURKE.

REFERENCES.—II. 10.—T. Puddicome, *Preacher's Magazine*, vol. v. p. 223. R. G. Soans, *Sermons for the Young*, p. 120. R. Brewin, *Preacher's Magazine*, vol. x. p. 515. H. Moore, *Christian World Pulpit*, vol. lvii. p. 230. J. W. Veevers, *Preacher's Magazine*, vol. xix. p. 464. D. Macleod, *Christian World Pulpit*, vol. lix. p. 75. F. B. Cowl, *Preacher's Magazine*, vol. xviii. p. 190. J. Learmount, *British Congregationalist*, 20th June, 1907, p. 622. A. Rowland, *The Exchanged Crowns*, p. 1. H. Windross, *The Life Victorious*, p. 125. *Expositor* (4th Series), vol. ix. p. 4. II. 11.—G. E. Biber, *The Seven Voices of the Spirit*, p. 35. J. M. Neale, *Sermons Preached in Sackville College Chapel*, vol. iv. p. 143. A. Maclaren, *Expositions of Holy Scripture—Revelation*, p. 196. II. 12.—R. E. Hutton, *The Crown of Christ*, p. 369. II. 12, 13.—Spurgeon, *Sermons*, vol. xxxiv. No. 2007. II. 12-17.—C. Anderson Scott, *The Book of Revelation*, p. 81.

I KNOW WHERE THOU DWELLEST

'I know thy works, and where thou dwellest, even where Satan's seat is.'—REV. II. 13.

I. NOTICE, in the first place, that it is possible to be a Christian anywhere. Pergamos was the place where Satan's seat was; and yet even in that city there was a Christian Church, concerning many of whose members the Lord could say that 'they had held fast His name, and had not denied His faith'. Christianity is not a thing of locality, but of character. As Jonathan Edwards said: 'The grace of God can live where neither you nor I could'; and they who work in the streets and lanes of the cities are often cheered by coming in unexpected places on humble Christians who are walking with God as truly as Enoch did. And what is true of places is equally so of occupations. Now, if this be so, if it be true that a man may be a Christian anywhere, what follows: (1) This, that we must not be prejudiced against a man because of the locality in which we find him, or the work in which he is engaged. (2) It follows that we ought never to excuse ourselves for our lack of Christianity by pleading the force of circumstances, or the nature of our business, or the character of the place in which we reside.

II. The words of my text suggest the truth that it is harder to be a Christian in some places than in others. There are households in which it seems to be the most natural thing in the world for a child to grow up into the beauty of holiness; and there are others in which everything like loyalty to Christ would meet with the bitterest opposition, and could be maintained only by strenuous exertions. If that be true, what follows: (1) This, the Lord knows that it is true, and He will estimate our work by our opportunity. (2) We ought to learn to be charitable in our judgments of others.

III. The harder the place in which we are, we should be the more earnest by prayer and watchfulness to maintain our Christian character. Where

the danger is greatest, the vigilance should be most wary. What is really the hardest place in the Christian life? It is not always that in which there is the greatest external resistance to Christianity. All history shows that the greatest danger to the Christian is not in that which openly assails him. An avowed antagonist he meets as an antagonist. But when the ungodly meet him as friends, then he is in real peril.

IV. The greater the difficulty which we overcome in the maintenance of our Christian characters, the nobler will be our reward.—W. M. TAYLOR, *The Silence of Jesus and other Sermons*, p. 90.

HAVING DONE ALL, TO STAND

'I know thy works, and where thou dwellest, even where Satan's seat is; and thou holdest fast My name, and hast not denied My faith, even in those days wherein Antipas was my faithful martyr, who was slain among you, where Satan dwelleth.'—REV. II. 13.

I. ANTIPAS was 'My faithful martyr'. Now, is it not remarkable that this glorious title, *My martyr, My faithful martyr*, given to no other Saint, should not for ever have kept alive the memory of Antipas, what he did, how he suffered? And yet absolutely nothing is known of him. In the later martyrologies, indeed, we have a long history of his passion, but clearly only as a legend, written by one who knew no more of the facts than ourselves. I do not believe that Antipas was the name of any individual martyr. The word πᾶς in Greek means every one. As Antichrist, being interpreted, is he that resists Christ, so Antipas means he that resists every one; that is who simply, by himself, stands up against a world of evil-doers. Antipas in this sense, every martyr of every age has been or must be; and singularly enough, one such martyr of Pergamum history tells us of. You have heard of the letter written by the Church of Lyons in France to the Churches in Asia, seventy years later than the Epistles of St. John, concerning the glorious martyrs there in a local persecution; when the slave St. Blandina, being bound in a chair of red-hot iron, thence encouraged her fellow-worshippers to hold out; when the aged Bishop St. Pothinus died under the buffeting of the mob;—then one of the foremost soldiers in this brave fight, then one of the first athletes in this brave race, was Attalus, a Pergamene. I have seen the dungeon in which they were confined; a dungeon to which you can only obtain access by crawling in like a worm.

II. How did this Church of Pergamum stand firm where Satan dwelt? Look at those two clauses, 'And thou holdest fast My name, and hast not denied My faith'. That is one of the texts that at first sight seem so disappointing in their conclusion. Having done all, *to stand*. To hold your own, and that all; the whole result, simply *not to yield*. And take another example. 'Therefore seeing we have received this ministry,—this ministry of binding and loosing —this ministry according to the voice of which the Incarnate Word is given to us under the similitude of bread and wine—this ministry of which He Himself is the great High Priest,—seeing we have received this ministry—and as further, *as we have obtained mercy*,—now, surely it must be, we shall carry the whole world before us! And, alas! it is only, *we faint not!* Not to faint, the highest results of the great gifts that God can bestow upon man!—J. M. NEALE, *Sermons on the Apocalypse*, p. 6.

I KNOW WHERE THOU DWELLEST
REV. II. 13.

So is it rendered in the Revised Version. The words *thy works* are omitted, and the passage stands thus —I know where thou dwellest. Now what say you to this? It is very sweet to know that the Master knows where we live. Sweeter still is it, a great deal, that He comes to see us. And yet, what think you?—that the Lord should know us at home. But the words mean a great deal more than that. It is much more than the watchfulness of an eager love. The context shows that it is a backward glance at the life which He Himself had lived on earth. The preface to the address indicates the thought that runs through it. ' I am alive, and was dead, and behold, I am alive for evermore.' It is as if He bade us not to think that He is far away from us and out of our reach, but that as He is one with us in closest relationship, bone of our bone, and flesh of our flesh, so He is one with us in closest intimacy ; that in all the round of the daily life, and in all that we have to do and to be, He knows by His own life as well as by His love. It is of this tenderest sympathy that we are to avail ourselves.

I. 'I know where thou dwellest.' It is spoken to those who are in the home of poverty. With what tenderness and sympathy are the words spoken as the memory of His own life—*I know*. From what depth of experience does He speak! Why there should be such poverty in the world is a mystery; whether such poverty should be at all is a matter that Church and State ought to ask very earnestly. But so long as poverty shall last, so long shall the Master send this message of His love to His poor followers: 'I know where thou dwellest'.

II. The word is for those who are beset with hindrance and temptation. Alas! how many are ready to say that nobody knows the struggle they have, the temptations that beset them. One knows, Who hath all power in heaven and in earth—'I know, I know where thou dwellest'. But it may be that in some hearts these words bring no comfort, stirring rather a sigh. What of the fallen? What can the glorious Lord of heaven know of the slave of lust and the victim of intemperance? For such these words can be spoken: 'I know where thou dwellest'.

The blessed Master declares that He knows our address. But then this knowledge leads to the only climax that can satisfy Him. 'Behold I stand at the door and knock. If any man hear My voice and open the door, I will come in and sup with him, and he with Me.' That and that only is His satisfaction

and ours.—M. G. PEARSE, *Naaman the Syrian and other Sermons*, p. 154.

OBSCURE SERVANTS OF GOD
' Antipas, My faithful martyr.'—REV. II. 13.

ANTIPAS is a name only—almost as impersonal as an echo. And yet he floats down the stream of centuries, as some memorial of southern climes might be carried down a great river. *Unknown but not unnecessary* is the epitaph that might be written on the tombstones of some mentioned in the Bible; of many more who have walked in the way of duty, and got their names written in the Book of Life. With our own experience and observation of 'the heart of man and human life,' what can we make certain about this man with nothing but a name? This, at any rate, this, if nothing else :—

I. The truth was a real thing to him because he realised it. A truth is not true until it is realised. A man is not saved by what he holds, but by what he is held. (1) I believe in God. So did Antipas. We are all theists. And yet any man who realised the awfully solemn and truly blessed meaning of this would live as in a temple. (2) I believe in the Word of God. So did Antipas. So do you. Your father believed in the Word of God and what a life he lived, what a man he was! An army of such men would sweep across a continent, and leave light and hope, like the trail of an outgoing vessel, behind them. (3) I believe in the sacred presence—the divinity that lies behind all life : the godlike that redeems it from insignificance. So did Antipas. Shakespeare, Milton, Wordsworth, Spenser, Young, Browning, Tennyson, believed in it ; and the glow is seen on every third page they wrote. We may recall these names when told that brain is not on the side of supernaturalism. Nor are the painters one whit behind the chiefest of the Apostles of world-remembered song. And as to the musicians, it is the commonest of commonplaces that living music is Biblical music.

II. He realised the truth, because he lived it. He found it true by experiment. There are certainties in our holy religion. I trust, I hope, I desire, must sometimes give place to I know. We cannot live on dreams. We starve on ideas only. We cannot all think alike. Some are reached through the intellect, others through the emotions. But whether through the intellect or the emotions it must reach the life. We must be changed into its image.

III. He did not fail of his reward. ' Antipas, my faithful martyr.' Here is the Divine recognition of unknown services. Unknown to earth, known to heaven. Our faithful duty is recognised. Kindness done receives grateful acknowledgment. In the world beyond the bounds of time and sense every Antipas shall hear his name read ; and know that the Divine purposer has not forgotten the work he did, the pain he suffered, in accomplishing the Divine purpose.—J. H. GOODMAN, *The Lordship of Christ*, p. 235.

‘I know where thou dwellest, even where Satan's throne is.’—
Rev. II. 13.

MANY of the best intellectual lives known to us have been hampered by vexatious impediments of the most various and complicated kinds; and when we come to have accurate and intimate knowledge of the lives led by our intellectual contemporaries, we are always quite sure to find that each of them has some great thwarting difficulty to contend against. . . . However circumstances may help us or hinder us, the intellectual life is always a contest or a discipline.—P. G. HAMERTON.

REFERENCES.—II. 13.—S. Horton, *Christian World Pulpit*, vol. liv. p. 12. J. M. Neale, *Sermons on the Apocalypse*, p. 6. B. J. Snell, *Christian World Pulpit*, vol. li. p. 153.

‘The teaching of Balaam.’—Rev. II. 14.

WE become Balaams when our influence lowers the tone of any who are about us.—C. G. ROSSETTI.

REFERENCES.—II. 14.—*Expositor* (5th Series), vol. vi. p. 203; *ibid.* (6th Series), vol. iii. p. 108.

THE OVERCOMING MAN

‘To him that overcometh will I give to eat of the hidden manna, and will give him a white stone, and in the stone a new name written, which no man knoweth saving he that receiveth it.’—Rev. II. 17.

LET us look at this thought—*the Overcoming Man and his crown*, or Christian character the reflection of Christian struggle. Let us look at it in connection with three great battles of the soul—the battle with *doubt*, the battle with *sin*, the battle with *sorrow*.

I. First of all, there is the man who has a hard battle to find God.

What a difference there is between some men and others in this respect! Some have no ‘ordeal of faith’: they drift into the kingdom like a ship on a full tide and an even keel. Others again have years of agony ere their souls find rest. In older days this struggle usually took the form of a search after pardon. The question of questions was this—‘Can God pardon me, a chief of sinners like me?’

If you wrestle through your doubts to God, you will fight your way to a grander faith. Out of that experience God will give you a name such as no one but you could have. It is, I believe, the case, that no man has ever nobly defended a truth who was not at first its doubter or denier. ‘Out of the eater comes forth meat: out of the strong sweetness.’

There are two ways by which the traveller can reach Land's End from Penzance: one the highroad on the stage-coach, the other struggling up and down the mighty cliffs that flank the last of England's shores. Who shall doubt which is the easier? But who shall say that he is the richer in experience who comes by the easier? The way to God's highest revelations is always hard. It is only the soul that has greatly overcome that learns the greatness of God's ‘new name’.

II. The same is true of the struggle with sin; of the man who has a hard time *in his conflict with evil.*

III. Last, and perhaps most beautiful of all, we see here an illustration of the man *who has a hard*

time *in the school of suffering.* ‘Experience,’ said a great preacher, ‘teaches fools, but she graduates saints.’ Her graduation ceremony, it must be admitted, is often the close of a long and hard curriculum. If you read the record of our great writers, both secular and sacred, you will be surprised to find of how many of them it was true that they were great sufferers. Of more than poets it is true that ‘they learnt in suffering what they taught in song’. The fragrant name they possess in literature was won out of ‘great tribulation’. The hymns we sing with such comfort to others were born out of bitter hours of pain and disappointment. Our hymnology is largely a martyrology. The men whose words will never die, often died themselves prematurely, or if they lived, lived in what was a living death.

Nor is it different with character, of which indeed literature is but the expression and flower. It is the man who has had a weary struggle with pain and disappointment who wins the new and tender name of ‘a son of consolation’. It is the man who has been chastened by sore affliction, and he alone, who can enter into the holy of holies of perfect trust. ‘What are these which are arrayed in white robes?’ ‘These are they that came out of great tribulation.’ Of them it is specially true that they receive ‘a white stone and a new name which no man knoweth saving he that receiveth it’.—W. MACKINTOSH MACKAY, *Bible Types of Modern Men*, p. 299.

THE WHITE STONE

‘He that hath an ear, let him hear what the Spirit saith unto the Churches: To him that overcometh will I give to eat of the hidden manna, and will give him a white stone, and in the stone a new name written, which no man knoweth saving he that receiveth it.’—Rev. II. 17.

I. MANY mediæval writers have said, that the white stone refers to the Greek custom of marking happy days by throwing a white stone into a box: unhappy days by throwing in a black stone; and according as, at the end of the year, the black or the white were most numerous, so was the year considered happy or unhappy. So, they say, a white stone means the one, long, endless glad day of eternity. But there is this fatal objection. St. John nowhere in the whole of his writings draws a metaphor from heathen games or customs. It was not so with St. Paul; he is constantly alluding to them.

II. What other meaning for this white stone? All the promises to the seven Churches have reference to some special period of the history of the Church of Israel. This then has too; and as we read in the same verse about the hidden manna, so it must have something to do with the time when they were in the wilderness.

Next, the word here translated *stone* may just as well mean *gem*; and *white* is more than merely white; it is glistering or sparkling; but a white glistering gem is surely a diamond.

Now think of the Tabernacle service and of the High Priest's vestments. The most famous of these was the breast-plate. The breast-plate was a piece of linen, exactly twice as long as it was broad. Folded in the middle, then, it became square; the sides were sewn together, and it became a square bag. Now the Jews are agreed that, in this bag, the Urim and Thummim was kept. *Was kept;* for they were one and the same thing; and hence sometimes called Urim only. The two words by interpretation mean Light and Illumination. Whatever it was, it was something at which the High Priest, and he only, looked when consulting the oracle. And what was it? There is a very old tradition that it was a stone on which the incommunicable Name of God—Jehovah—was engraved. But what kind of stone?

On the outside of the breast-plate were fastened twelve precious stones, the names of which you may read in Exodus. It is to be supposed that whatever was kept in the purse was more valuable than anything that formed the outside of the purse. Now—most remarkably—among the twelve stones, the diamond is not mentioned; although the Jews were very well acquainted with it. Urim and Thummim, then, was probably a peerless diamond, engraved with Jehovah's name.

III. It is the great promise to him that overcometh that he shall be made, in the highest and most glorious sense, a Priest in the heavenly temple where is the beatific vision. If any, under the old law, should be privileged to eat of the hidden manna, the manna laid up in the golden pot within the ark, who but the High Priest, that alone knew where it was concealed? If any should be able to read what was written on the Urim, who but the same High Priest, that alone knew what it was, and by his very office was bound to consult it?—J. M. Neale, *Sermons on the Apocalypse*, p. 18.

A NEW NAME

'To him that overcometh will I give to eat of the hidden manna, and will give him a white stone, and in the stone a new name written, which no man knoweth saving he that receiveth it.'—Rev. ii. 17.

I. What is meant by the bestowment of a new name? A glance at some of the historical records of the Old Testament will make it clear to us. When Abram was ninety years old, the Lord appeared to Him, and said: 'Thy name shall not any more be called Abram, but thy name shall be Abraham; for the father of a multitude of nations have I made thee'. Next, you will remember the occasion of Jacob's wrestling with the angel at the brook Jabbok. And when Jacob had struggled and prevailed, the angel said: 'Thy name shall be called no more Jacob, but Israel; for thou hast striven with God and with men, and hast prevailed'. Again, you will remember that when Daniel and his three friends at Babylon were chosen to enter into the royal service, they received new names from the prince of the eunuchs. We may usefully bring these three kinds of application to bear upon the passage before us. (1) The conquering life, as in the case of Abraham, will receive a new revelation of itself. We do not at present know our own true name, and even still less does the world

know it. (2) The receipt of the new name, as in the case of Jacob, involves an accession of life and power. (3) Further, as we saw in the case of Daniel and his friends, the conferring of a new name involves the designation to new power and office. Higher life means higher service.

II. So far we have dealt with the promise in its general application, but are now directed by our Lord's word to the important question of individual distinctions: 'which no man knoweth saving he that receiveth it'. These words remind us of the proverb: 'Every heart knoweth its own bitterness, and a stranger doth not intermeddle with his joy'. The meaning is clear. Just as life is divided from life here, and each heart has its own world of possession, so it shall be in the higher life to come. The victors are not crowned in the mass, but singly. There is indeed one general life of holiness and godlikeness which all possess in common. This is what the Lord means in iii. 12: 'I will write upon him My new name'. But this common possession is linked with profound differences. The pure heaven that shines above all is precisely the same, but not so the image of it reflected in each that stands in the glory. Each shall receive the fulness of his own life, no less and no more. The nobler and larger our service here, the grander will be our new name, and the deeper the wells of joy that are to be peculiarly our own.—John Thomas, *Myrtle Street Pulpit*, vol. iii. p. 268.

THE WHITE STONE

'A white stone.'—Rev. ii. 17.

We are told that all the ground about Pergamos is even to this day covered with white stones and therefore the Christians of that city could not stir out without being reminded of the promise 'to him that overcometh'. And what is this white stone? The Church has generally believed that it means the body which Christ's true servants will receive at the resurrection day. For just as nothing is more lasting than a stone, as it cannot be destroyed, as it cannot be worn away, so our bodies will be raised incorruptible, and never more subject to sickness or decay. And a white stone, because they will be glorious and shining; just as the face of our Lord in His transfiguration became white and shining, so as no fuller on earth can whiten. 'I will give him a white stone,' then, is the same thing as saying, 'I will give him a new and glorious body, when this corruptible shall have put on incorruption, and this mortal shall have put on immortality.'—J. M. Neale, *Sermons in Sackville College Chapel*, vol. iv. p. 17.

'I will give him a white stone, and upon the stone a new name written, which no one knoweth but he that receiveth it.'—Rev. ii. 17.

Some glances of real beauty may be seen in their faces who dwell in true meekness. There is a harmony in the sound of that voice to which Divine love gives utterance, and some appearance of right order in their temper and conduct whose passions are regulated; yet those do not fully show forth that inward life to those who have not felt it; this white stone and new name is only known rightly by such as receive it.—Woolman's *Journal*.

References.—II. 17.—M. G. Glazebrook, *Prospice*, p. 149. W. P. Workman, *A Book of Lay Sermons*, p. 145. W. T. Davison, *Christian World Pulpit*, vol. liii. p. 117. F. D. Maurice, *Sermons*, vol. iv. p. 163. C. Perren, *Sermon Outlines*, pp. 179, 339. G. E. Biber, *The Seven Voices of the Spirit*, p. 63. A. Maclaren, *Expositions of Holy Scripture—Revelation*, p. 205. II. 18.—R. E. Hutton, *The Crown of Christ*, p. 381. F. W. Farrar, *Christian World Pulpit*, vol. l. p. 45. *Expositor* (6th Series), vol. ix. p. 372. II. 18-29.—C. Anderson Scott, *The Book of Revelation*, p. 97.

'I know that thy last works are more than the first.'—
Rev. II. 19.

Principal Shairp, speaking of Wordsworth's well-rounded life, lays stress on 'the moral fortitude' which 'appears in the firmness with which he kept his purpose, and the industry with which he wrought it out. Undiscouraged by neglect, undeterred by obloquy and ridicule, in the face of obstacles that would have daunted almost any other man, he held on his way unmoved, and wrought out the gift that was in him till the work was complete. Few poets have ever so fully uttered the thing that was given them to speak.'

In his monograph on Voltaire, Mr. John Morley has occasion to speak of the thirty-third year of life, 'that earlier climacteric when the men with vision first feel conscious of a past, and reflectively mark its shadow. It is then that they either press forward eagerly with new impulse in the way of their high calling, knowing the limitations of circumstance and the hour, or else, fainting, draw back their hand from the plough, and ignobly leave to another or to none the accomplishment of the work. The narrowness of the cribbed deck that we are doomed to tread, amid the vast space of an eternal sea with fair shores dimly seen and never neared, oppresses the soul with a burden that sorely tries its strength, when the fixed limits first define themselves before it. Those are the strongest who do not tremble beneath this grey ghostly light, but make it the precursor of an industrious day.'

'If there is anything of interest in my story,' writes Mark Pattison in his *Memoirs*, 'it is as a story of mental development. . . . I have never ceased to grow, to develop, to discover, up to the very last. While my contemporaries, who started so far ahead of me, fixed their mental horizon before they were thirty-five, mine has been ever enlarging and expanding. . . . Slow as the steps were, they have been all forward.'

'There are lives,' says Mr. P. G. Hamerton, 'such as that of Major Pendennis, which only diminish in value as they advance—when the man of fashion is no longer fashionable, and the sportsman can no longer stride over the ploughed fields. The old age

of the Major Pendennises is assuredly not to be envied; but how rich is the age of the Humboldts! I compare the life of the intellectual to a long wedge of gold—the thin end of it begins at birth, and the depth and value of it go on indefinitely increasing.'

Contrast Bagehot's verdict on Macaulay. 'His mind shows no trace of change. What he is he was; and what he was, he is. He early attained a high development, but he has not increased it since; years have come, but they have whispered little; as was said of the second Pitt, "He never grew, he was cast". His first speeches are as good as his last; his last scarcely richer than his first. . . . The events of twenty years have been full of rich instruction on the events of twenty years ago, but they have not instructed him.'

References.—II. 19.—F. W. Farrar, *Christian World Pulpit*, vol. xlix. p. 385. J. Vaughan, *Fifty Sermons* (9th Series), p. 39. A. Maclaren, *Expositions of Holy Scripture—Revelation*, p. 215.

'Thou sufferest that woman Jezebel to teach and to seduce my servants.'—Rev. II. 20.

Immoral life in one leader of the people is more pernicious than a whole streetful of impurities in the lower quarters of the community, seeing that streams, foul or fair, cannot flow upward.—Landor.

'Thou sufferest that woman Jezebel.'—Rev II. 20.

There is a mercy which is weakness, and even treason against the common good.—George Eliot.

I think the world is like Captain Esmond's company I spoke of anon; and could you see every man's career in life, you would find a woman clogging him; or clinging round his march and stopping him; or cheering him and goading him; or beckoning him out of her chariot, so that he goes up to her, and leaves the race to be run without him; or bringing him the apple, and saying 'Eat,' or fetching the daggers and whispering 'Kill'. Yonder lies Duncan, and a crown, and an opportunity.'—Thackeray.

References.—II. 20-22.—*Expositor* (5th Series), vol. vi. p. 203.

'And I gave her space to repent; and she repented not.'—
Rev. II. 21.

For my part, I believe that remorse is the least active of all a man's moral senses—the very easiest to be deadened when wakened; and in some never wakened at all. We grieve at being found out, and at the idea of shame or punishment, but the mere sense of wrong makes very few people unhappy in Vanity Fair.—Thackeray.

Reference.—II. 23.—C. Perren, *Revival Sermons in Outline*, p. 314.

THE DEPTHS OF SATAN
'The deep things of Satan.'—Rev. II. 24.

It is clear that the 'depths of Satan' stand in some sort of contrast with the 'depths of God' (1 Corinthians II. 10). There are in God great deeps, vast abysses in which the strongest intellect may search without coming on any limits. There are also in

Satan 'deeps'; and they are of such a kind that the deeps of God are the only reality with which they can be put into comparison. But we should be losing all sense of proportion if we were to imagine that the depths of Satan in any way balanced the depths of God, if we were to admit for a moment that there was any equality or even colourable pretence to claim an equality. Let us look into the four depths of Satan, Pride, Despair, Lust and Unbelief.

I. Pride. Milton, as became his Titanic spirit, devoted all his strength to representing the depth of Pride. 'Better to rule in hell than serve in heaven,' is Satan's fixed idea. Satan is the spirit that sets himself up, as against God. Into that depth of moral and spiritual absurdity he sweeps men.

II. The depth of Despair. Man, under Satan's rule, is always passing in a violent transition from self-confidence, defiance and pride, to a servile despondency which admits of no comfort.

III. But of all the depths of Satan none is more mysterious or horrible than the one which is referred to in the text under the image of Jezebel (II. 20). The enemy of souls seizes the natural functions of the body, the very functions on which the life and continuance of the race depend, and manages to pervert them into instruments of lust.

IV. The most seductive depth of Satan, however, in our day is Unbelief. Great is the glamour of Unbelief! It flatters itself with a superiority of knowledge and of intellect. It laughs at the dreams of the earth's raw youth. And yet it is all illusion. God is not less necessary or certain : Christ is not less plainly the Way, the Truth, and the Life, because Mephistopheles, the 'spirit that denies,' has led away many deluded minds into this denial. Christ came to destroy the works of the Devil (1 John III. 8). The destruction has begun and proceeds.— R. F. HORTON, *The Trinity*, p. 171.

REFERENCE.—II. 24.—R. J. Horton, *Christian World Pulpit*, vol. lix. p. 153.

'That which ye have, hold fast till I come.'—REV. II. 25.

How respectable the life that clings to its objects! Youthful aspirations are fine things, your theories and plans of life are fair and commendable : but will you stick ? Not one, I fear, in that Common full of people, or in a thousand but one : and when you tax them with treachery, and remind them of their high resolutions, they have forgotten that they made a vow. The individuals are fugitive, and in the act of becoming something else, and irresponsible. The race is great, the ideal fair, but the men whiffling and unsure. The hero is he who is immovably centred.—EMERSON.

IN the battle of life are we all going to try for the honours of championship? If we can do our duty, if we can keep our place pretty honourably through the combat, let us say *Laus Deo !* at the end of it, as the firing ceases, and the night falls over the field. . . . We may not win the baton or epaulettes,

but God give us strength to guard the honour of the flag.—THACKERAY.

'And he that overcometh, and keepeth My works unto the end, to him will I give authority over the nations.'—REV. II. 26.

'I WAS both surprised and grieved,' writes Wesley in his *Journal*, 'at a genuine instance of enthusiasm. J. B. of Tunfield Leigh, who had received a sense of the love of God, a few days before, came riding through the town, hallooing and shouting and driving the people before him ; telling them God had told him he should be a king, and should tread all his enemies under his feet. I sent him home immediately to his work, and advised him to cry day and night to God that he might be lowly in heart, lest Satan should again get an advantage over him.'

REFERENCES.—II. 26-28.—A. Maclaren, *Expositions of Holy Scripture—Revelation*, p. 223. II. 26-29.—G. E. Biker, *The Seven Voices of the Spirit*, p. 83. II. 27.—*Expositor* (4th Series), vol. iii. p. 118.

THE GIFT OF THE MORNING STAR

'And I will give him the morning star.'—REV. II. 28.

OVER the grave of a dead captain of freedom it was said : 'Above the changing fortunes of the cause of which he was the leader, he moved as untroubled as the stars in their orbits. He was never elated by success ; never disheartened by temporary disasters and failures. *Of ultimate success he was always certain.*'

Thus was fulfilled the promise made 'to him that overcometh and keepeth My works unto the end,' *I will give him the morning star.* Those who refuse to do treason to conviction and principle, who will not weakly comply with the fashions about them —receive the morning star. That star is much more than the promise ; it is the earnest of the future light of victory. For those who receive it, the battle in a true sense is past. They are conquerors all the time they fight.

I. It is this realisation of victory which has distinguished all great leaders and made them what they are. What is it that makes men spiteful, irritated, ungenerous ? Nothing but the fear of defeat. Victors are magnanimous ; they can afford to be so, and so can he who knows already the triumph of his cause. It may be laid down with certainty that all great leaders have been magnanimous. Sneering, sarcasm, sharp retort, slander—such things have brought men into temporary prominence, but they have never made a name, won a battle, or even permanently advanced a cause. It is the lot of leaders to provoke fierce hatred ; to live often under the cloud of almost universal distrust. Their names are at times as 'lightning rods for storms to strike on '. Being human, they may be betrayed into occasional bitterness by injustice, or more likely by their clear perception of the awful contrast between the real and the ideal. And they may lawfully know how to puncture wind bags. But one of their sure marks is reverence for man. They never forget that the mass live in a world of mist and shadow. They do not lose their faith in human nature. They believe to the end that when the human soul can be parted from the 'discouraging clouds of confusion,' from the tumults and passions of the hour, it is ready to give heed to the voice of eternal truth and justice.

II. There is unity in the lives where this light has been kindled—the unity of a regal purpose. If all the lives that start on a high level of faith and hope maintained the promise of their beginning, redemption would indeed be nigh. But with most it is far otherwise. They may have seen visions and dreamed dreams in their time, but visions and dreams have faded, and the lofty ardour of youth has gone with them. Now they have given over the fight, perchance have deserted to the other camp ; at best they remain timid, irresolute, full of hesitations and misgivings. But those with the earnest of the light are undismayed. They are heroically constant. What wonder if men gather round them and follow them !

Nothing is more strange and affecting, and yet nothing is more true, than that those who take the most vehement part in the conflicts of this world and the keenest interest in its affairs are nevertheless detached from it. They are all the while sons of the high mother city which is free. It is this which makes them magnanimous, patient, resolute ; it is this which makes them willing to leave the struggle before victory is proclaimed, and even when it seems as if the infantry of trust were being repulsed. They have achieved a great liberty. While they live they dwell with God ; when they die they depart in peace, because their eyes have seen His salvation.—W. Robertson Nicoll, *Ten-Minute Sermons*, p. 139.

THE MORNING STAR

'And I will give him the morning star.'—Rev. II. 28.

I love the stillness of the text ; receive that text as an assurance that the Lord is the distributor of the prizes and the rewards, and He has promised in these wondrous letters to the Seven Churches of Asia that one day He will have a grand prize distribution :—I will give, I will give, I will give,—as if He would distribute His universe amongst those who have turned it into an altar. It is wondrous music. 'To him that overcometh I will give to eat of the tree of life.'· Observe, it is to him that overcometh. Expect war, expect strenuous contest ; the Lord is watching the contestants, and He is breathing down the hot thunderous air this Gospel message : To him that overcometh. . . . Cheer thee, strike again, contest once more, now again ! hearts up ! to him that overcometh will I give a great festival ; I will pluck the fruit from the tree of life, and he shall have abundance. Nothing for the coward, nothing for the runaway, nothing for him who would magnify his weakness into a kind of piety ; but everything to him that overcometh ; he that endureth unto the end shall be saved.

I. What I like best, because my heart needs it most, is the promise made unto the faithful in Thyatira :—'I will give him the morning star'. The Lord would seem not to keep any of the universe to Himself ; He divides His creation with His children. What have you done ? By Thy grace I have fought strong temptations, and I have won. Come thou, sit down under the shadow of the tree of life, and I will pluck fruit for thee. What hast thou done ? I have had a strenuous time, every nerve has been strained, temptations were poured upon me like fiery darts. Sit down ; thou shalt be recruited with the manna of God. And what hast thou done ? I have endeavoured to keep Thy Word in difficult positions and situations ; I have been sore pressed to disobey Thee, but by Thy grace, and by Thy grace alone, I have overcome. Stand ! I will give thee the morning star, sign of royalty, signet of the King, pledge of more. Morning is the poetry of the day. Who can count its jewels of dew ? Morning means more than it seems to mean, for it means vanished night. Where is the night ? Gone ! Where that darksome, fearsome, midnight ? Fled away ! Where is it ? None can tell. The morning star has nothing to do with nightly gloom. The nightmare is past, the sorrowful travelling alone is ended, solitude is a conquered enemy, and the man who has overcome by the grace of Jesus Christ shall have the morning star. Is it a living star ? Yes. Have I not heard of it in another relation ? Is the morning star but some flash of perishing radiance ? Oh no ! it is clothed with personality. Tell me how. 'I am the bright and the morning star.' It is a star within the star, a Redeemer, a personality. The stars are embodiments of God. I will pluck for the faithful and true, the valiant and the conquering, heaven's chief jewel, and he shall wear it on his glowing heart. I will give him the morning star.

II. 'Morning.' Jesus Christ never associates Himself with night. Do not let the pessimists overcome you ; have in you a light that will burn out their darkness. Jesus Christ is the light of life, the light of the world ; you are so constituted it may be—I speak to the few, not to the many—as to be soon nervously depressed, and those grim pessimists would soon persuade you to give up your faith in God. Pessimists never did anything for the world. We cannot judge them by their fruits, for fruits they have none ; they are men who darken the soul, their very shadow is descending night ; in their voices there is no music, on their face there is no illuminating smile. Jesus Christ always associates Himself with the morning :—'When the morning was come.' And God has always associated Himself with the morning : 'Come up early in the morning,' said He to Moses ; and He has always been talking about the morning. Christianity is associated with morning fulness, morning impulses, morning ideas and conceptions and brightness ; and not with night-reflections and pessimistic meditations and the killing of the heart by self-impeachment. Always Jesus Christ is associated with the morning light, the white gleam on the eastern hills, the opening portal, the rising of the sun.

III. He who has the morning star has the noon. I wish that idea could penetrate our minds, and hold them ; then should we be strong men, and no longer panic-driven and dumb because of fear. He who has the morning star has in that star the pledge that he shall have the noon, the midday, the zenith gleam. He who has Christ has heaven. If we really believed the promises of the Cross, we should now be in the upper sanctuary, there should be no separation, no distance, no sensible disseverance of soul from soul.

IV. 'I will give him the morning star.' Everything else goes out but the Christian faith—which, in other words, is, everyone goes down but Jesus Christ, and the man to whom Jesus Christ has given Himself— Himself who is the bright and morning star. O soul of man, put away from thee the idea of old age ! It does not belong to the new temple, the new sanctuary, the final revelation in Christ Jesus. Bid it begone ; old age is not among the jewels of God. But the morning star is chief of those jewels. If thou wouldst always be young, be good ; if thou wouldst not know when old age cometh, be stooping to serve some little child, and thou wilt not know that old age has come, and gone, and left thee—a child !—JOSEPH PARKER, *City Temple Pulpit*, vol. II. p. 119.

SEVEN

'And unto the angel of the Church in Sardis write : These things saith He that hath the seven Spirits of God, and the seven stars, I know thy works, that thou hast a name that thou livest, and art dead.'—REV. III. 1.

I THINK, of all fearful passages in Holy Scripture, the Epistles to the Churches of Sardis and Laodicea are the most fearful. Sardis was looked on as a model Church, no doubt prided herself and was envied by others, for her spiritual endowments, gift of tongues and the like. Imagine then, how like a thunderbolt it must have fallen upon them, when they came together on the Sunday that followed the receipt of this epistle, and the Bishop read the words of Him that cannot be deceived and cannot err, for his own most terrible condemnation and theirs : 'Thou hast a name that thou livest, and art dead '.

I. The Lord's Title.—The number seven recurs and recurs in the Apocalypse. The seven candlesticks, the seven lamps of fire, the seven seals ; seven horns and eyes of the Lamb ; seven angels and seven trumpets ; seven seals ; seven thunders ; seven heads of the dragon ; seven crowns on those heads ; seven heads of the wild beast ; seven mountains ; the seven kings ; sevenfold ascription of praise ; seven invitations to come ; and the division of the whole book into seven visions.

What especially does seven mean : it means and it is, the sign of God's covenant relation to man, and especially to His Church, Jewish or Gentile.

II. Have three and four any Mystical Meaning of their Own ?—Most surely yes. Three sets forth God ; four, the world. These numbers, brought into

contact and relation, express, in seven, the token of the covenant betwixt the two.

I need not show you that three is the number of God. But now about four. Not to speak of the four elements and the four seasons, which are not mentioned in Holy Scripture, we have the four winds. In Ezekiel, 'Come from the four winds'. In St. Matthew : 'They shall gather together His elect from the four winds of heaven'. In the Apocalypse 'Four angels standing on the four corners of the earth,' holding the four winds of the earth. See in Revelation, the four living creatures, emblems of all created life, and in Ezekiel, with four feet and four wings ; the four beasts in Daniel, lion, bear, leopard and monster, representing the four great world-powers successively to arise ; the four metals in the great world-image ; gold, silver, brass, iron ; the same metals again when the offerings of regenerated earth are catalogued in Isaiah. 'For brass I will bring gold, and for iron I will bring silver, and for wood brass and for stones iron.' The four Gospels, type of the preceding through the whole world ; the sheet St. Peter saw knit at the four corners, full of all manner of beasts ; the four horns in Zechariah, the sum-total of all the world powers as arrayed against the Eternal ; sword, famine, evil beasts, pestilence ; and compare that with St. John's vision, when power was given to the rider on the ghastly horse to kill with sword, and with hunger, and with death (that is disease), and with the beasts of the earth. The enumeration of diseases by St. John, 'impotent, blind, halt, withered' ; and finally, the repeated enumeration of the inhabitants of the world, by 'kindreds and tongues, and people and nations'.

Thus you see how the world is reconciled to God in this most mysterious number ; and what the God of Grace orders, the God of nature typifies. What is the sign of the covenant between God and man but the rainbow with its seven colours.—J. M. NEALE, *Sermons on the Apocalypse*, p. 28.

LISTLESSNESS

' Thou hast a name that thou livest, and art dead.'—REV. III. 1.

I. WHAT strikes me first of all as the great characteristic in common of these two unhappy churches [Sardis and Laodicea] is the absence of all mention of external trouble or inward temptation. Ephesus is vexed by Nicolaitanes ; Smyrna shall have tribulation ten days ; Pergamum is twice said to dwell 'where Satan's throne is' ; 'where Satan dwelleth'. Thyatira is tempted by 'that woman Jezebel' to the lusts of the flesh ; Philadelphia is harassed ' by them of the synagogue of Satan, who say they are Jews and are not, but do lie '. But dead Sardis and miserable Laodicea have no fears, no trouble, no enemy. Satan knew too well to harass them. They were, as the Prophet says, settled upon their lees. What is true of Churches is true of individuals. Therefore there may be comfort or there may be warning here. Who would not rather be tempted with Philadelphia than have the peace of Sardis ? And notice this

Next to Smyrna and Philadelphia, to whom not one word of blame is said, perhaps Thyatira comes highest; she whose last works of love were more than the first; that is a glorious advance. She it is who is attacked by the most loathsome temptation; that of 'that woman Jezebel'. Now, whether this were really the founder of a sect, or merely a personification of the Gnostics, still the trial to the Church was the same. They taught that it was a small thing for a man to despise the temptations of the flesh, if he fled from them and avoided them. No, they said; the true, the glorious victory was to remain superior to such pleasures while tasting them to the full; to give up the senses to all they could desire, while the spirit remained in a calm, pure region above them. This, they said, was defying Satan in his own kingdom and stronghold.

And a masterpiece of Satan's that was; and thousands it drew away to hell. And singularly enough, the very name, Jezebel, has an analogy with the teaching. We know, from the Old Testament, the kind of life she led; we know from other history that she, before her marriage to Ahab, was the priestess of Astarte, the Venus of the Sidonians, and yet her name is said in the Old Phœnician, to mean *pure*; just as Agnes in Greek.

II. Temptations, let them be what they may, if only they are resisted, are the mark of growth; it is that terrible stagnation, when nothing has to be resisted, that all true servants of our dear Lord ought earnestly and His dearest servants *most* earnestly, to pray against.

III. Sardis, at this time, was not only one of the most luxurious, but one of the most populous of the cities of Asia Minor. Notice then: our Lord will not allow the few names, insignificant in the eyes of the world though they might be, to think that they are overlooked by Him. And only a few *names*, rather than a few? Surely with reference to that Book of Life in which the names of all who have fought the fight well—who have run the race well, are even 'now enrolled'. But see how our dear Lord takes care that, even in the general condemnation, even when He so speaks of the Church as dead, He is careful that His own dear servants, few though they be, should feel that they are not overlooked by Him. It is the old story over again, 'Wilt thou destroy the city for lack of five?' And the five, though they were not to be found, yet had they been found, would have been precious in the Lord's sight.
—J. M. NEALE, *Sermons on the Apocalypse*, p. 38.

'Thou hast a name that thou livest, and art dead.'—REV. III. 1.

'THERE was no such thing as a dead particle in his faith,' said Dr. Martineau once of a friend; 'it was instinct with life in every fibre.'

IN the correspondence of Zachary Macaulay, when he was governor of Sierra Leone, the following entry occurs:—'To Lady Huntingdon's Methodists, as a body, may with great justice be addressed the first verse of the third chapter of the Revelation. The

lives of many of them are very disorderly, and rank antinomianism prevails among them.'

REFERENCES.—III. 1.—R. E. Hutton, *The Crown of Christ*, p. 401. A. Maclaren, *Christian World Pulpit*, vol. xlix. p. 305; *ibid.*, *Expositions of Holy Scripture—Revelation*, p. 232. III. 1-3.—H. S. Holland, *Christian World Pulpit*, vol. lix. p. 33. III. 1-6.—C. Anderson Scott, *The Book of Revelation*, p. 113.

'I have found no works of thine fulfilled before my God.'—REV. III. 2.

YOUTH has an access of sensibility, before which every object glitters and attracts. We leave one pursuit for another, and the young man's year is a heap of beginnings. At the end of a twelvemonth he has nothing to show for it—not one completed work.—EMERSON.

REFERENCES.—III. 3.—F. D. Maurice, *Sermons*, vol. ii. p. 35. J. Keble, *Sermons for the Sundays after Trinity*, p. 441. J. Keble, *Sermons for Christmas and Epiphany*, p. 248. *Expositor* (5th Series), vol. x. p. 152.

TRUE HEROISM

'Thou hast a few names even in Sardis which have not defiled their garments; and they shall walk with me in white: for they are worthy.'—REV. III. 4.

THE words that introduce the message to the Church in Sardis prepare us to see that the central thought of the message itself is the operation of spiritual power. 'These things saith He that hath the seven spirits of God and the seven stars.' The 'seven spirits of God' symbolise the fulness of Divine power, and the seven stars the earthly subject through which this power is prepared to operate. It is with the *victorious* life we now deal, that we may learn the lesson how to live, and learn it in the most inspiring way, namely, by the vision of those that have lived and gloriously triumphed. We shall consider:—

I. The character of earth's best manhood. 'Thou hast a few names even in Sardis which have not defiled their garments.' We do not mean to say that these commended few in Sardis were the *élite* of the whole earth, that they were paragons of perfection, and had reached the highest summit of human virtue. The important matter is that they were the *élite* of the society in which they lived. The true test of a man's power is the way in which he does battle with his environment, and rises above the common level of his surroundings. There is no heroism in the world like that of the man who lives in the world and grandly reveals that he is not of the world.

II. In considering the character of earth's best manhood, we could not possibly fail to think of the 'Perfect Man,' and, therefore, the 'Perfect Man,' Jesus Christ. And it needs no long consideration to realise that 'the relation of earth's best manhood in general to that of Jesus Christ' is a question of transcendent importance. There are two tendencies of thought that go far to rob us of our best inheritance in Jesus Christ. One tendency is that which makes Jesus Christ only another name for God. The other tendency is that which reduces Jesus Christ to the earth-born level of poor imperfect men like ourselves, only knowing life's secret a little better than most other men and threading its ways with greater skill.

III. By union with Christ a character of sterling worth is developed. The statement in our text is very clear and emphatic. 'For they are worthy.' We must take care in this connection not to confound things that are distinct. It is not by merit that we obtain salvation; it is in salvation that we find our merit. God's kingdom comes to us, though we are utterly unworthy of the glorious gift; but, when we have received the kingdom, it invests us with high worth and dignity.—JOHN THOMAS, *Myrtle Street Pulpit*, vol. II. p. 13.

REFERENCES.—III. 4.—Spurgeon, *Sermons*, vol. ii. No. 68. J. W. Veevers, *Preacher's Magazine*, vol. xix. p. 274. A. Maclaren, *Expositions of Holy Scripture—Revelation*, p. 243.

WHITE RAIMENT

(*A Whitsunday Address*)

'He that overcometh, the same shall be clothed in white raiment.'—REV. III. 5.

THROUGHOUT the greater part of Christendom, to-day is celebrated under the name of Whitsunday. It is the Sunday commemorative of the day of Pentecost, when the Holy Ghost descended on the Church. From the earliest times that Pentecostal Sunday was a favourite one for the sacrament of baptism. Its memories of the outpouring of the Spirit made it peculiarly appropriate for that. And it was thus it got its name of Whitsunday, from the white garments of the little children, who, on that day so hallowed by its unction, were brought to the font to be baptised. It is white-sunday; the day of the white robes; the day when the church was beautiful in white. It is the only Sunday in the year which enshrines a particular colour in its name. And so I venture to speak to you this evening on some of the suggestions of that colour, which is so often mentioned in the Bible, and always with an element of symbolism.

I. First, then, I ask you to observe that white is emblematical of purity. It is the symbol of purity in every language; the outward sign of it in every ritual.

Now I dare say there are some who feel a sense of shame when they hear that. If white be the sign and sacrament of purity—God help them, they shall never wear it. Is there no young man who has been living foolishly since he awoke to the liberty of manhood? Is there no young woman who is very different from what she was a dozen years ago? 'Character,' said Mr. Moody once, 'character is what a man is in the dark,' and if we knew what you were in the dark, would there be any hope of white apparel? I answer most emphatically, yes. That is the gospel I am here to preach. It is not to the heart of childlike innocence that the white raiment

of our text is promised. It is to every one who overcomes; who rises from his past, and is ashamed; who cries, from the very margin of despair, 'Create within me a clean heart, O God'.

II. Then once again, I want you to observe that white was the colour which indicated victory. It was so, not only in the Bible, but also in the literature of Greece and Rome. To-day, we do not so regard it. It is not significant of triumph now. The white flag is the symbol of submission, and the white feather is the badge of cowardice. But in the ancient world of Jew and Pagan there was no such sinister suggestion in it: it was not the colour of the coward then; white was the colour of the conquerer.

Do you see then another facet of our text—he that overcometh shall be clothed in white? It means that the battles which are won in secret, shall some day be the vesture which we wear. Our hardest conflicts are not fought in public; our hardest conflicts are on a hidden field. Out of our hidden triumphs God is weaving the robe that is to deck us by and by.

III. Once again, I ask you to observe that white is the colour which expresses joy. It does so because it is the colour of light, and there is something gladsome in the light. We do not speak about the *day* of sorrow; we speak and sing about the *night* of sorrow. 'The night is dark, and I am far from home,' is the utterance of one in heaviness. But light is gladsome, and it heartens us, and it summons forth the music of the birds, and so there has always been the thought of joy in the radiance which is the badge of day.

And so our text hints at this other truth—a truth which we can never lay to heart too much. It tells us, in the symbol of apocalypse, that overcoming is the road to joy.

IV. Once again I want you to remember that white is the livery of heavenly service. It is the garb which all the angels wear, and the angels are the ministers of God. Has not our Master taught us thus to pray, 'Thy will be done on earth as it is done in heaven'? The type and pattern of perfect service is the unceasing ministry of angels. Flying abroad upon the wings of help, the angels were always habited in white. And so the colour came to speak of service; of instant and questioning obedience; of readiness to do the will of God, though the path of ministry was to a grave.—G. H. MORRISON, *The Return of the Angels*, p. 119.

WHITE AND SCARLET

'He that overcometh, the same shall be clothed in white raiment.'—REV. III. 5.

THIS, it is true, was not the way in which the martyrs overcame; but if God grant us to come within a thousand degrees of them in glory, it will be enough. They have a more glorious portion. 'The shield of the mighty men,' says Nahum, 'is made red, the valiant men are in scarlet.' The mighty men are the martyrs; the scarlet is the glorious colours of their own blood. And so again, Solomon, speaking of the Church, says: 'She shall not be afraid when the cold cometh, for her house hold are clothed in scarlet'. That is, she shall have no cause to fear when others are falling away from God ; seeing that she has so many who have given their lives to prove the strength of their love to Him.—J. M. NEALE, *Sermons in Sackville College Chapel*, vol. iv. p. 22.

REFERENCE.—III. 5.—A. Maclaren, *Expositions of Holy Scripture—Revelation*, p. 250.

'These things saith he that is holy, he that is true.'—REV. III. 7.

OUR knowledge of the moral part of the divine character, of His veracity—as well as of His justice— comes from our own moral nature. We feel that God is holy, just as we feel that holiness *is* holiness ; just as we know by internal consciousness that goodness is good in itself, and by itself ; just as we know that God in Himself is pure and holy. We feel that God is true, for veracity is a part of holiness and a condition of purity. But if we did not think holiness to be excellent in itself, if we did not feel it to be a motive unaffected by consequences and independent of calculation, our belief in the divine holiness would fade away, and with it would fade our belief in the divine veracity also.'—From BAGEHOT's essay on *The Ignorance of Man*.

REFERENCE.—III. 7.—R. E. Hutton, *The Crown of Christ*, p. 417.

THE OPEN DOOR

'The open door.'—REV. III. 7, 8.

I. NOTICE, first that when it is translated ' Thou hast a little strength,' which would rather be an acknowledgment of power than weakness, it ought to be ' Thou hast little strength '. ' My strength is made perfect in weakness.'

You must join the two verses together, ' I have set before thee an open door, and no man can shut it,' with His title who has thus opened it, ' He that hath the key of David upon his shoulder '. And you may take the door in two senses. The power of spreading the gospel among the surrounding heathen, as St. Paul speaks, ' A great door and effectual is opened unto me '. Or, it may be, that more blessed door, the entrance to be abundantly ministered unto the kingdom of heaven. Either way, the reason that follows is one of those divine arguments so infinitely above the reasonings of man. ' I have set before thee an open door, and no man can shut it, *for* thou hast little strength.' What, impossible to be conquered, because we are weak ? Even so ; because that very weakness enlists omnipotence on our side. It was, no doubt, from reasoning after the manner of men, that our translators put in contrary to the Greek, that word *a*. Not so the Holy Ghost. It is something after the same method of argument as that sublime passage of Tertullian : ' The Son of God went about healing disease and infirmity ; it is possible because it is unlikely, and died on the cross for us ; it is probable because it is incredible ; and rose again the third day ; it is certain because it is impossible '. And take the opposite side of the

picture, and see how St. Paul speaks of that, with the bitterest irony he ever allows himself to use : ' Now ye are full, now ye are rich ; ye have reigned as Kings without us ; and I would to God *ye did reign*, that we also might reign with you '.

II. ' I have set before thee an open door.' That is, in the other sense, that gate which is of one solid pearl and which leads into the King's city, that city whose light is like unto a stone most precious, even like a jasper stone, clear as crystal ; that gate through which nothing shall in any wise enter that defileth.

III. The key which opens the kingdom of heaven, and government which is exalted above all powers, both in heaven and earth, is none else than the Cross. That is the key, and the only key, which unlocks this door ; and a singular thing it is, how the old type has kept its place physically, when the metaphorical meaning has long been forgotten. Did you ever see an elaborate key in which the wards were not made crosswise ? And notice this, on account of that special promise to Eliakim [The key of the house of David will I lay upon his shoulder] the Jews connected the idea of a key with that of the coming of the Messiah. Further, mediæval saints tell us why it should have pleased our Lord to submit to the necessity of bearing His cross on one shoulder ; namely, that is, that we, bearing it after Him, must bear whatever our special cross is, for ourselves.— J. M. NEALE, *Sermons on the Apocalypse*, p. 53.

REFERENCES.—III. 7-13.—C. Anderson Scott, *The Book of Revelation*, p. 126. A. B. Davidson, *Waiting upon God*, p. 331. III. 7-22.—G. Campbell Morgan, *Christian World Pulpit*, vol. lviii. p. 358. III. 8.—J. Keble, *Sermons for Easter to Ascension Day*, p. 25. J. Duckworth, *A Book of Lay Sermons*, p. 171. J. M. Neale, *Sermons on the Apocalypse*, p. 46. III. 8, 10.—Spurgeon, *Sermons*, vol. xxx. No. 1814. III. 8-11.—R. Glover, *Christian World Pulpit*, vol. l. p. 68. III. 10.—A. Maclaren, *Expositions of Holy Scripture—Revelation*, p. 259.

FAINT YET PURSUING

'Behold, I come quickly ; hold fast that thou hast, that no man take thy crown.'—REV. III. 11.

I. NOTICE that the same command is given to two of the seven Churches, and in both cases is joined to the same declaration. To Thyatira it is written, ' That which ye have already hold fast till I come . To Philadelphia, ' Behold, I come quickly ; hold that fast what thou hast,' *till I come*. I wish we had these words constantly in our hearts ; a hard struggle to carry on, a hard race to run, but then it is only ' Till I come '. Whatsoever thy hand findeth to do, do it with all thy might—because the night is at hand when no man can work—because it is only ' Till I come '. There is but a short time to do deeds of love ; there is but a short time to fight the good fight of faith ; there is but a short time to exercise hope. ' Behold, I come quickly. . . . So much the more as ye see the day approaching.'

II. ' That no man take thy crown.' St. Bernard says : ' It is well said ; *thy* crown. For to all that have contended here, although in different fights, to all that have run well here, although in different races, a special crown is appropriated ; as the martyrs shall wear a diadem of ruby, the confessor of gold, so also for chastity is there a crown of snow-white brilliancy.'

And not so only, but as the cunning artificer decks the crown which he has in hand with many and various jewels, according to the riches and the pleasure of him for whom it is made, so each good work done by the elect in this world forms as it were a separate gem in the diadem of their blessedness on high. Each therefore has his crown ; as each has his own sorrows and trials in this valley of misery, so each has his own reward and coronation in the kingdom of glory; according to the saying, 'The heart knoweth his own bitterness, and a stranger doth not intermeddle with his joy'.—J. M. NEALE, *Sermons on the Apocalypse*, p. 62.

'Behold, I come quickly.'—REV. III. II.

THERE is less sand in your glass now than there was yesternight. This span-length of ever-posting time will soon be ended. But the greater is the mercy of God the more years ye get to advise upon what terms, and upon what conditions, ye cast your soul in the huge gulf of never-ending eternity. The Lord hath told you what ye should be doing till He come. . . . All is night that is here, in respect of ignorance and daily ensuing troubles, one always making way to another, as the ninth wave of the sea to the tenth ; therefore sigh and long for the dawning of that morning, and the breaking of that day of the coming of the Son of Man, when the shadows shall flee away. Persuade yourself the King is coming : read the letter sent before Him, 'Behold, I come quickly'. Wait with the wearied nightwatch for the breaking of the eastern sky, and think that ye have not a morrow.—From one of SAMUEL RUTHERFORD's *Letters* to Lady Kenmure.

THE ALIENATED CROWN
'Hold fast that which thou hast, that no man take thy crown.'
—REV. III. II.

EACH Church and each separate disciple has a distinctive vocation, and in the counsels of God, a specific and unmistakable prize associates itself with the faithful fulfilment of that vocation. The fact that the crown lost by one passes to another, brings to mind the good faith of God and the largeness of His plans. So imperatively benign are the Divine purposes, that there can be no diminution in their scope. The Lord will never take back what He has once resolved to give for the blessing and enrichment of His people. This exhortation implies that the partial and temporary failure of the individual does not imply the final failure of the race.

I. We need to concern ourselves first of all with the personal significance of these words, although they were addressed to the representative of a Church, and have a collective application. Many incidents of the Scriptures illustrate and enforce them. Great in character as was Moses, and invested with enduring honour, he failed to attain all the glory it was God's will to put upon him. The lesson comes home to us

again as we read the history of David. And in the New Testament we find yet more striking and tragic illustrations. Judas was one whose crown was taken by a worthier disciple. The promise of great things hides itself in lives which, to the outward eye, are unpromising, meagre, poverty-stricken. God could not create men to put before them from the beginning the prospect of a crownless immortality. Did not some of us in the days of our youth give the promise of an eminent usefulness we have since failed to realise? Others then promised less, but they more than surpass us now. The crown meant for us is passing to more royal souls.

II. This solemn warning reminds us of our national perils, as well as of the losses which sometimes threaten us in our life of individual piety and service. (1) Many signs seem to show that the crown of honour England has worn as a Christian nation may pass to less luxurious peoples of simple creed and strenuous life. It is impossible to contemplate, without a sad shrinking of heart, the idea that our free citizens are governed to a greater extent than they know by the representatives of demoralising trades. (2) Whilst the Christian communities in our midst have grown in intelligence and self-respect, they are in danger of losing some of the high distinctions they once possessed as Christ's representatives to the people He seeks to befriend and save.

REFERENCES. — III. 11.—J. Keble, *Sermons for Easter to Ascension Day*, pp. 262, 272. W. E. Beet, *Preacher's Magazine*, vol. xix. p. 248. III. 11-13.—Bishop Wilberforce, *Sermons*, p. 91.

A PILLAR IN THE HOUSE OF GOD
'Him that overcometh will I make a pillar in the house of My God.'—REV. III. 12.

As we hear these words let us do as did the seer of this vision, let us turn to see Him Who speaks to us. To you and me it is spoken by the high King of heaven. To you and me is offered the blessedness that shall never end.

I. See to whom this great word is spoken. 'Him that overcometh will I make a pillar in the house of My God.' Does there rise before us a hero like David, fearless, splendid in his courage, hurling with unerring aim the pebble from the sling? Nay, listen again, 'I know thee, that thou hast a little strength'. The word is spoken for the lowest and the least. Is it then for some sublime achievement, some unearthly endurance that this high reward is given? No, the achievement was a very simple one of which the world heard nothing and no record was kept upon earth. 'Thou hast kept My word and hast not denied My name.' So, then, every one of us may come and hear this glorious promise from the lips of our great Captain and Saviour: 'Him that overcometh will I make a pillar in the house of My God'.

II. And more than this. He who speaks is not only the great and glorious Captain of the Lord's host ; not only the tender and pitiful brother who for us men and for our salvation came into this world to live and to die and to rise again—He Himself is the force by which we are to overcome. Look then at the overcoming love which is ours in Christ. All the holy influences that come to us, the gracious promptings and whispers of His Almighty love, are the prophecies and pledges of His might in which we may overcome.

III. The little strength becomes a pillar by overcoming. He who becomes a pillar, in the temple of God must first be rooted and grounded in Jesus Christ. Christ is our life. 'If a man abide not in Me he is cast forth and withered.' 'Him will I make a pillar. Not by.and by, but now and here.'—M. G. Pearse, *The Preacher's Magazine*, vol. ix. p. 337.

PILLARS—OR CATERPILLARS!

Rev. iii. 12.

What the Church of God requireth is 'pillars'—pillars strong and steadfast. What, alas! the Church possesseth to her damage is 'caterpillars' innumerable. It is obvious to all who will but see that havoc is being made of the Church of the Living God by this great army of 'caterpillars'—the crawling, creeping Christians who are of the earth, earthy. These fill too frequently positions of power in the organisations of the visible Church, and hence the cry on all sides of failure, damage, and defeat. We turn with grateful hearts to the 'pillars,' to the true workers, the real supporters of the Church of God. 'Him that overcometh,' the conquering man, the victorious saint, 'will I make a "pillar" in the temple of My God'.

I. We want *granite pillars*, strong and durable, in those days of ecclesiastical and social quakings, if the Church is not 'to be moved away from the hope of the Gospel'. The most popular theology is the theology of *indefiniteness*. The symbolism of this theology is, 'I know not anything'. In Ephesians iv., where St. Paul is speaking of the 'perfecting of the saints,' he lays it down as a condition that, without definite, dogmatic teaching, the Church cannot be edified, and he warns them against being 'tossed to and fro, and carried about with every wind of doctrine'. We are pleading for firmness in holding fast the *essentials*.

II. We want *marble pillars*—shafts of beauty in the corridors of His House of Prayer, beautiful with the beauty of holiness. We are persuaded that the greatest, the most telling power in the world is the power of a blameless life. What men think over is not words nor works, but the man's life—his character; not what he says, nor what he does, but what he *is*, is the criterion.

These, then, are the two pillars: granite and marble—strength and beauty, the Jachin and the Boaz of this glorious temple. The Church requireth both. Firmness, strength, stability: for the times demand these. Purity, truth in the inward parts, and the beauty of holiness: for this generation lacketh these. —T. J. Madden, *Addresses to All Sorts and Conditions of Men*, p. 126.

References.—III. 12.—Bishop Kennion, *Christian World Pulpit*, vol. lvii. p. 104. J. Keble, *Village Sermons on the Baptismal Service*, p. 227. A. Maclaren, *Expositions of Holy Scripture—Revelation*, p. 275. III. 12, 13.—G. E. Biber, *The Seven Voices of the Spirit*, p. 137.

THE LAODICEAN CHURCH

'Unto the angel of the church of the Laodiceans write: These things saith the Amen, the faithful and true witness, the beginning of the creation of God.'—Rev. iii. 14.

No thoughtful person can read the letters of our ascended Lord to the seven Churches in Asia without observing that there is a great diversity in the condition and character of these Churches. Four of the Churches had a mixture of good and evil; something to commend and something to condemn. *Two* of the Churches have nothing in them but good. There is *one* Church, however, of which nothing good is said, *all evil*, not a single virtue left; not one at least is named in the letter to Laodicea. To this, the worst, the most degraded, the only Christless Church of the seven, would we now direct attention. Let us consider :—

I. The condition of the Church of the Laodiceans. (1) The Church's estimate of herself: 'I am rich and increased with goods, and have need of nothing'. Self-sufficiency, and that self-sufficiency based on her material wealth. (2) Christ's estimate of the Laodicean Church: 'Thou art wretched, and miserable, and poor, and blind, and naked'. 'Thou art neither cold nor hot; I would thou wert cold or hot. So then because thou art lukewarm, and neither cold nor hot, I will spue thee out of My mouth.' Why does He prefer a state of utter coldness to lukewarmness? absolute indifference to hypocrisy? (*a*) May it not be because there is more *honesty* in the man who is utterly indifferent to religion, and avows it, than in the hypocrite. (*b*) A second reason may be, that there is more likelihood of the conversion of the cold than of the lukewarm. The humiliating, damning feature in the condition of this Church is that she is without Christ, without a Saviour.

II. The appeal of Christ. (1) The appeal is based on Christ's character. To arrest the attention of the lukewarm Laodiceans, He announces the authority and truthfulness of Him who speaks to them. (2) The appeal is based on the All-sufficiency of Christ. (3) The appeal suggests conditions. 'Buy.' (4) The appeal is based upon promises.—Richard Roberts, *My Closing Ministry*, p. 56.

References.—III. 14.—Spurgeon, *Sermons*, vol. xii. No. 679. R. E. Hutton, *The Crown of Christ*, p. 427. F. W. Farrar, *Christian World Pulpit*, vol. xliii. p. 353. *Expositor* (6th Series), vol. iii. p. 125. III. 14-21.—Spurgeon, *Sermons*, vol. xx. No. 1185. E. J. Boyce, *Parochial Sermons*, p. 107. III. 14-22.—C. Anderson Scott, *The Book of Revelation*, p. 141.

'I would thou wert cold or hot.'—Rev. iii. 15.

Unhappily in matters political the curse of a flabby amorphous eclecticism is upon too many of us; watching the conflict of principles or policies in a dazed and bewildered frame of mind, we persuade ourselves that we are philosophically impartial when we are only indolently indifferent. 'Which train are you going by, sir—up or down?' 'I'll wait and see!' and both engines rush out and leave the unhappy vacillator to his reveries, till by and by the platform is cleared, and the station is shut up for the night, and the gas lamps are turned down; and there is no moon, and no stars, and no shelter, and the wind is rising.—DR. JESSOPP, in the *Trials of a Country Parson.*

MR. BAGEHOT somewhere speaks of 'those *unabsorbed*, purposeless, divided characters which seem to puzzle us. They complicate human life, and they do so the more effectually that they typify and represent so much of what every man feels and must feel within himself. In each man there is so much which is unmoral, so much which has nothing to do with hell or heaven; which occupies a middle place not recognised in any theology; which is hateful both to the impetuous "friends of God" and His most eager enemies.'

REFERENCES.—III. 15.—H. J. Wilmot-Buxton, *Sunday Sermonettes for a Year*, p. 88. H. R. Gamble, *Church Family Newspaper*, vol. xv. p. 72. *Expositor* (5th Series), vol. ix. p. 47. III. 15, 16.—Spurgeon, *Sermons*, vol. xlviii. No. 2802. III. 15-19.—A. Maclaren, *Expositions of Holy Scripture— Revelation*, p. 283.

'Thou art lukewarm.'—REV. III. 16.

LUKEWARMNESS implies that a great deal has gone before, that a height has been climbed, and that from cowardice, human respect, or weariness, we have come down from it. Like certain phenomena in geology, it is at once our evidence of a former state of things, and of the catastrophe which overthrew it. He who was never fervent can never be lukewarm. . . . It is a great grace, a prophecy of a miraculous cure, to find out that we are lukewarm; but we are lost if we do not act with vigour the moment we make this frightful discovery. It is like going to sleep in the snow, almost a pleasant tingling feeling at the first, and then—lost for ever.—F. W. FABER.

THEN hath the Tempter come upon me, also with such discouragements as these: 'You are very hot for mercy, but I will cool you; this frame shall not last always: Many have been as hot as you are for a spurt, but I have quenched their zeal'. And with this, such and such who were fallen off would be set before mine eyes. Then I should be afraid that I should do so too. But, thought I, I am glad this comes into my Mind. 'Well, I will watch, and take what heed I can. Though you do,' said Satan, 'I shall be too hard for you; I will cool you insensibly, by degrees, by little and little. What care I,' saith he, 'though I be seven years in chilling your heart if I can do it at last? Continual rocking will lull a crying child asleep. I will ply it close, but I will have my end accomplished.'—BUNYAN, *Grace Abounding*, sec. 110.

'Thou sayest, I am rich, and have gotten riches, and have need of nothing; and knowest not that thou art wretched, and miserable, and poor, and blind, and naked.'—REV. III. 17.

WHAT if it has pleased God that I should have been born and bred and have lived ever since in the tents of Esau? What if—by no choice of my own—my relations and friends should have been the hunters and the fighters? What if, during a weakly youth, I was forced to watch—for it was always before my eyes—Esau rejoicing in his strength, and casting away his birthright for a mess of pottage? . . . And what if, when I tried, I found that Esau would listen to me; that he had a heart as well as Jacob? What if he told me at the same time that he could not listen to Jacob's private chaplains; that he did not understand them, nor they him; that he looked on them with alternate fear and contempt? If I said to myself more and more clearly as the years rolled on, I will live for Esau and with Esau; if I be called a gluttonous man and a wine-bibber, the friend of publicans and sinners, there is One above us who was called the same, and to Him I commit myself and my work; it is enough for me that He knows my purpose, that on Crimean battle-fields and Indian marches, poor Esau has died with a clearer conscience and a lighter heart for the words which I have spoken to him. If I have said this, whom have I wronged? I have no grudge against Jacob and his preachers; only when I read the seventeenth verse of the third chapter of Revelation, I tremble for him, and for England, knowing well that on Jacob depends the well-being of England, whether physical, intellectual, or spiritual, and that my poor Esau is at best food for powder.—From a letter written in defence of his methods and life.

'THE accession of George I.,' says Sir Leslie Stephen, 'marked the beginning of a period of political stagnation which lasted for nearly half a century. The country prospered and waxed rich. Harvests were abundant; towns began to grow; and the seeds of much that was good and much that was evil in our later history were sowed. . . . The governing classes enjoyed the power which they had acquired by the Revolution, and were content to keep what they had gained. They would oppress nobody actively; on the other hand they would introduce no reforms. Their highest virtue was in leaving things alone. . . . The church retained obnoxious privileges on the condition of making very little use of them; and the nation indolently drifted towards the unknown future, carelessly contented for the most part.'

REFERENCES.—III. 17.—*Expositor* (5th Series), vol. vi. pp. 259, 332. III. 17, 18.—Spurgeon, *Sermons*, vol. xxviii. p. 1677. III. 17-19.—Bishop Pereira, *The Record*, vol. xxvii. p. 444. III. 17-20.—Bishop Percival, *Christian World Pulpit*, vol. xlix. p. 142. III. 18.—F. J. Madden, *Tombs or Temples*, p. 38. III. 19.—Spurgeon, *Sermons*, vol. iii. No. 164.

'Behold, I stand at the door and knock.'—REV. III. 20.

AT Kelso, some will long remember his remarks in visiting a little girl, to whom he said, 'Christ gives last knocks. When your heart becomes hard and careless, then fear lest Christ may have given a *last knock.*'—BONAR'S *Life of M'Cheyne*, p. 143.

THE CLOSED DOOR

'Behold, I stand at the door and knock.'—REV. III. 20.

LET us look at these words with reference to the Person Who speaks them, and consider, in its various aspects, the striking picture which they represent.

I. The Closed Door.—It was closed in the case of the Laodiceans by lukewarmness. But there are other things which are effectual in closing the doors of our hearts.

(a) *Sin in its numberless forms.* The sin that is practised *openly* in defiance of God; the sin that *hides itself* from the light, and which none but God can see; that '*easily besetting sin,*' so nurtured and encouraged as at last to become a part of our nature, that sin of *unfaithfulness* that finds a refuge in broken vows and careless indifference to all God's Ordinances.

(b) *The love of the world.* The craving after the goods of this life, which tends to spread itself over the whole entrance, so as to shut out all influences that aim at the life beyond.

(c) *Pride.* The pride of intellect, for instance, that does not scruple to assert that true knowledge lies in Sight and not in Faith; because, forsooth, the laws of finite man have no power to grasp the Infinity of God!

(d) *Self-righteousness,* which depends upon its own powers for the attainment of the spiritual life.

All these tend to close the door of a man's heart. Which of us has the door closed against Christ?

II. There is One Standing at the Door.—Who is He? He is a King; the same King that St. John describes in the former part of this book as 'Alpha and Omega, the beginning and the ending, which is, and which was, and which is to come, the Almighty'. Is not this a matter for wonder that such as He should stand and knock for entrance at the door of our sinful hearts? Wonderful indeed! And yet not so wonderful, if we consider that this is He Who left His Father's Throne and came down from Heaven to take our nature upon Him, that we might have boldness through Him to come near to the Throne of Grace. Surely, then, He has the right of all others to demand admittance.

(a) *Mark his wondrous condescension.* He has bidden us come to Him; to ask, and we shall have; to seek, and we shall find; to knock, and it shall be opened unto us. And yet, so great is His love, He comes to us that He may bring us to Himself, lest in our blindness we neglect our own salvation, and the Day of Redemption pass by, and leave us unredeemed.

(b) *Mark His wondrous patience.* He comes to His own; but His own receive Him not. He comes to those whom He has redeemed, by manifold sufferings, by agony and Bloody Sweat, by a bitter death upon the Cross; but He finds no hand stretched out to welcome Him. His 'Israel' will not hear, His people will not consider. He comes as a Friend; but lo! the door is shut; there is no one to watch for His coming, there is no one ready to receive Him. Nay, even when He has knocked, He has been refused admittance; and yet—He waits there still! He has stood by while others have been admitted—the world with all its empty vanities; the flesh with all its selfish desires; sin with its fair outside and deceptive promises; Satan himself with his legions of evil angels. He has looked through the open door, and seen the house within filled with destroyers and enemies, and He has not turned away, although these have been preferred before Him. He stands there still.

III. As He Stands He Knocks.—And each of us has heard these knockings, although in different ways, sometimes without asking who it is that knocks, sometimes without hearing the answer; sometimes without fully understanding what the sound has meant. And why? Probably through indifference; or, perhaps, because we have not wished to be disturbed; or, perhaps, because the weeds and brambles of the world have overgrown the door so thickly that the sound or the knock cannot penetrate. And all this time we have fancied ourselves *secure, because we have heard no sound!*

IV. How has He knocked?—In many various ways.

(a) *By the joys and sorrows that have been our lot* all through life, whereby He would remind us that He is the Author of all joy, and the Comforter of every sorrow.

(b) *By changes in the world around us,* and among those best known to us, whereby He would point us to Himself when our unsatisfied souls cry out for something strong to rest upon.

(c) *By the Ordinances of His Church* whereby He calls us into communion with Himself, and feeds us with the spiritual Food which alone can strengthen the spiritual life.

(d) *By the Seasons of the Church's Year* which point to *His* all-holy Life as the pattern and example of *our* life, and by the Seasons of the natural year which teach the lessons of life and death, bidding us look beyond to the Cause of all things, and recognise in Him the source both of Resurrection and Life.

All these are so many ways in which He has knocked for entrance; and in whatever particular we have neglected our duty toward any or each of these, it has been to shut the door of our hearts against Him, and to refuse to hear His Voice, however plainly He has spoken.

V. He Calls as well as Knocks.—He lifts up His voice and *speaks* to us, lest we should not know Who it is that seeks admission, and says, 'Behold, *I* stand at the door and knock.' And this He does in two ways.

(a) *By His Holy Word,* by which He proves the truth of His Mission and appeals to man's conscience, bidding him weigh his own soul in one scale and the world in the other, and then consider with himself what advantage he shall gain if he barter the one for the other.

(b) *By means of that living Voice within,* bidding us seek the sweet influence of God's Good Spirit to *nourish* the new-born life, lest the tares of the world choke it, and the heat of temptation wither it, and it bring no fruit to perfection. So does the patient loving Jesus stand and wait at the door of our hearts, seeking an entrance that He may fill us with 'all joy and peace in believing' ; so does He call week after week, and month after month, by all the means His Love has furnished for our souls' good ; and so does he still wait and watch, if peradventure the careless soul inside will at last hearken and open the door, and admit Him.

VI. He is Ready also to Depart.—He will not tarry for ever. He stands patiently now; He has waited and watched long and anxiously, and He will wait still, as long as there is hope; but *He will not compel an entrance.* All gifts of grace are His, and may be yours for the asking. He will grant you *preventing* grace, that may awaken and predispose you in all your words and thoughts and deeds ; and *assisting* grace, that may help you forward in your heavenward path, and give you power to bend your will to His.

But His Spirit will not always strive with man.

REFERENCES.—III. 20.—H. S. Holland, *Christian World Pulpit*, vol. lix. p. 21. F. D. Maurice, *Sermons*, vol. iv. p. 185. H. R. Heywood, *Sermons and Addresses*, p. 12. J. Bunting, *Sermons*, vol. i. p. 110. A. Maclaren, *The Wearied Christ*, p. 91. *Expositor* (6th Series), vol. iii. p. 341. A. Maclaren, *Expositions of Holy Scripture—Revelation*, p. 302. III. 21.—*Ibid.* p. 312. R. J. Campbell, *City Temple Sermons*, p. 134. *Ibid. The Examiner*, 28th June, 1906, p. 625. *Expositor* (5th Series), vol. v. p. 184. III. 21, 22.—G. E. Biber, *The Seven Voices of the Spirit*, p. 157. III. 22.—A. G. Brown, *Preacher's Magazine*, vol. i. p. 37.

ELEVATION AND VISION

'After these things I saw, and behold, a door opened in heaven, and the first voice which I heard, a voice as of a trumpet speaking with me, one saying, Come up higher, and I will show thee the things which must come to pass hereafter.'—REV. IV. I.

IT is a serious error to suppose that we can rightly apprehend the highest truths whilst we live on a low plane of thought and conduct, and yet it is a very common error. Those who grovel in the dust, nay, who wallow in the sensual mire, yet believe themselves competent to discuss the most solemn problems of existence and destiny : they conclude that the truths concerning God—His existence, laws, government, revelation and purpose—are apprehended and understood mentally like theories of mechanics and mathematics. It is a profound mistake.

I. To see eternal realities with open vision we must preserve a pure and sensitive soul. Recently in some experiments in colour photography it was attempted to reproduce the colours of the spectrum. The experiment succeeded so far as the bars of colour in the interval between the violet and the red were concerned : but the camera failed to represent the ultra hues, the film was not sufficiently sensitive to seize the hidden mystery of colour, and a couple of blotches alone witnessed to the existence of the unseen rays. Thus a coarsened soul in its dark misgivings bears witness to unseen things, yet it lacks the subtlety to discern and realise the glorious realities of the transcending universe. Our spirit must be uplifted by fellowship with God, made sensitive by purity, refined by love, kept steady by a great hope and confidence, or it cannot reflect and realise eternal verities. It is not so much by intellectual acuteness as by truth and purity in the inward parts that we lay hold of the things of God.

II. To apprehend justly and influentially eternal truths our life must be lofty in its spirit and aim. The real explanation of our dubiety and despair is not to be sought in our intellectual defects and limitations, but rather in the narrowness, egotism, and debasement of our thoughts, ideals, and strivings. We need to get on a higher plane of thinking, sympathy, and purpose. 'Come up higher and I will show thee.' Is not that the call of God to us? We are told that from the bottom of a pit the stars are visible at noonday, but to those who are content to dwell in the murky depths of low thinking, feeling, and action, the lights of the upper universe are lost in impenetrable obscuration. Character is the chief source of illumination ; noble conduct best augments the inner light ; life aspiring to high standards rather than logic divines the secrets of eternity.—W. L. WATKINSON, *The Ashes of Roses*, p. 104.

REFERENCES.—IV. 1.—H. S. Holland, *Vital Values*, p. 58. W. Morison, *Christian World Pulpit*, vol. xliv. p. 379. J. Keble, *Sermons for Ascension Day to Trinity Sunday*, p. 354. W. H. Simcox, *The Cessation of Prophecy*, p. 82. Spurgeon, *Sermons*, vol. xv. No. 887. IV. 1, 2.—H. J. Bevis, *Sermons*, p. 155. IV. 2.—*Expositor* (4th Series), vol. v. p. 124.

THE RAINBOW AND THE THRONE

'And immediately I was in the spirit, and behold a throne was set in heaven . . . and there was a rainbow round about the throne, in sight like unto an emerald.'—REV. IV. 2, 3.

I WANT to dwell on the rainbow round the throne like to an emerald. Do you see any mystical meanings in that rainbow? I shall tell you what it suggests to me.

I. In the first place it speaks to me of this, that the permanent is encircled by the fleeting.

Whenever a Jew thought of the throne of God, he pictured one that was unchangeable. 'Thy throne, O God, is an everlasting throne,' was the common cry of psalmist and of prophet. Other thrones might pass into oblivion ; other kingdoms flourish and decay. There was not a monarchy on any hand of Israel, but had risen and had fallen, like a star. But the throne of God, set in the high heaven, where a thousand years are as a day, *that* throne from all eternity had been, and to all eternity it would remain. Such was the throne which the Apostle saw, and round about it he descried a rainbow. It was engirdled with a thing of beauty, which shines for a moment, and in shining vanishes. The permanent was encircled by the transient. The eternal was set within the momentary. The sign and symbol of unchanging power was rooted in the heart of what was fleeting.

II. Another truth which is suggested here is that power is perfected in mercy. The rainbow has been symbolical of mercy, ever since the days of Noah and the flood. God made a covenant with Noah, you remember, that there should never be such a flood again. Never again, so long as earth endured, was there to fall such desolating judgment. And in token of that, God pointed to the bow, painted in all its beauty on the storm-cloud—that rainbow was to be for ever the sign and sacrament that He was merciful.

III. The heavenly setting of mystery is hope.

As the Apostle gazed upon the throne, there was one thing that struck him to the heart. 'Out of the throne came voices, thunderings and lightnings.' Whose these voices were, he could not tell. What they were uttering, he did not know. Terrible messages pealed upon his ear, couched in some language he had never learned. And with these voices was the roll of thunder; and through it all, the flashing of the lightning; and John was awed, for in the throne of God he was face to face with unutterable mystery. Then he lifted his eyes, and lo, a rainbow, and yet it was different from earthly rainbows. It was not radiant with the seven colours that John had counted on the shore of Patmos. It was like an emerald— what colour is an emerald? It was like an emerald; it was *green*. Around the throne, with its red flame of judgment, there was a rainbow, and the bow was green. Does that colour suggest anything to you? To me it brings the message of the Spring. You never hear a poet talk of *dead* green; but you often hear one talk of *living* green. It is the colour of the tender grass, and of the opening buds upon the trees. It is the colour of rest for weary eyes. It is the colour of hope for weary hearts.—G. H. MORRISON, *The Return of the Angels*, p. 317.

REFERENCES.—IV. 3.—D. M. Pratt, *Christian World Pulpit*, vol. liii. p. 186. H. S. Seekings, *Preacher's Magazine*, vol. xvii. p. 505. G. R. Fetherston, *A Garden Eastward*, p. 15.

'And upon the thrones I saw four and twenty elders.'— REV. IV. 4.

'IN Brescia,' says Prof. Villari, during the Lent of 1486, 'Savonarola, with the Book of Revelation for his theme, found it easier to stir the sympathies of his hearers. His words were fervent, his tone commanding, and he spoke with a voice of thunder; reproving the people for their sins, denouncing the whole of Italy, and threatening all with the terrors of God's wrath. He described the forms of the twenty-four elders, and represented one of them as rising to announce the future calamities of the Brescians. Their city, he declared, would fall a prey to raging foes; they would see rivers of blood in the streets; wives would be torn from their husbands, virgins ravished, children murdered before their mothers' eyes; all would be terror and fire and bloodshed. His sermon ended with a general exhortation to repentance, inasmuch as the Lord would have mercy on the just. The mystic image of the elder made a deep impression on the people. The preacher's voice seemed really to resound from the other world; and his threatening predictions awakened much

alarm. During the sack of Brescia, in 1572, by the ferocious soldiery of Gaston de Foix, when, it is said, that about six thousand persons were put to the sword, the inhabitants remembered the elder of the Apocalypse and the Ferrarese preacher's words'.

THE whole state of man is a state of culture; and its flowering and completion may be described as Religion or Worship. There is always some religion, some hope and fear extended into the invisible— from the blind boding which nails a horseshoe to the mast or the threshold, up to the song of the elders in the Apocalypse.—EMERSON.

REFERENCES.—IV. 4, 10, 11.—Spurgeon, *Sermons*, vol. viii. p. 441. C. Anderson Scott, *The Book of Revelation*, p. 155. IV. 6, 7.—A. P. Stanley, *Sermons on Special Occasions*, p. 291.

THE EMBLEMS OF THE EVANGELISTS

'And before the throne there was a sea of glass like unto crystal: and in the-midst of the throne, and round about the throne, were four beasts full of eyes before and behind. And the first beast was like a lion, and the second beast like a calf, and the third beast had a face as a man, and the fourth beast was like a flying eagle. And the four beasts had each of them six wings about him; and they were full of eyes within: and they rest not day and night, saying, Holy, holy, holy, Lord God Almighty, which was, and is, and is to come.'—REV. IV. 6-8.

THESE four beasts—what are they? The devout fancy of the Christian Fathers regarded them as emblems of the four Evangelists—St. Matthew, St. Mark, St. Luke, and St. John—those supreme benefactors of the Christian Church who have bequeathed to all generations that priceless legacy, the story, from their several standpoints, of that Life of matchless love which was the revelation of the unseen God and Father. There is some variation in the application of the imagery, but I shall follow what seems to me the aptest and truest interpretation—that of St. Augustine.

I. St. Matthew the Lion.—Of course the key to this emblem is the old fancy that the lion is the King of the Beasts. And you see the appropriateness of the emblem?

St. Matthew wrote his Gospel as an appeal to unbelieving Israel in the dark days when that terrible, crushing disaster had befallen the nation—the destruction of Jerusalem by the Roman general Titus and the dispersion of the people over the face of the earth. When they were broken, scattered, and despairing, St. Matthew, the Jewish Evangelist, wrote his Gospel, not to upbraid them with their unbelief, but to make a last gracious appeal to them, and to prove to them, after the manner of demonstration which the Jewish mind appreciated, that the Lord Jesus, whom their fathers in their blindness had rejected, was none other than the King of Israel—the Promised Saviour, the Holy Messiah, the Son of David's royal house, whom the prophets had foretold, and whom, generation after generation, believing men had been dreaming of and praying for and longing after.

St. Matthew gathers up all the promises of God

and all the hopes of His people, and shows how they are fulfilled and realised in the King and Saviour.

II. St. Mark the Man.—And how apt this emblem is! St. Mark has no theological thesis, no apologetic purpose. He simply tells the story of our Lord's ministry, and he never stops to point a moral or deduce a consequence.

If St. Matthew depicts Jesus as the Son of David, the King of Israel, St. Mark depicts Him as the Son of Man, the prophetic Servant of the Lord : ' Behold, My servant, whom I uphold, Mine elect, in whom My soul delighteth ; I have put My Spirit upon Him : He shall bring forth judgment to the Gentiles '.

III. St. Luke the Calf.—And here is something puzzling. The calf is the sacrificial victim, and if there be any book in the New Testament which has nothing to say of sacrifices—of victims and priests and altars and shedding of blood, it is the Gospel according to St. Luke. St. Luke was a Greek, a physician of Antioch, and he knew nothing about Jewish typology and symbolism, and there is nothing about sacrifices in his Gospel. And yet those ancient mystics found his emblem in the calf.

It is certainly puzzling ; but just consider it, and you will perceive the appropriateness of it. What is sacrifice ? It is not a priest. It is not a victim. It is not a reeking altar. Oh, no ! it is the giving of oneself for others. It is Love, and Love is the keynote of St. Luke's Gospel.

His Gospel reveals him as a Christian gentleman with a chivalrous compassion for every feeble and defenceless thing. And that is sacrifice—that, and not the priest or the bleeding victim or the crimson altar. And what makes the Sacrifice on Calvary is not the Cross, the nails, the spear ; it is the Love which brought Jesus to that awful doom and moved Him to bear it all for our sinful sakes. And St. Luke's is the sacrificial Gospel because it is the Gospel of the Love of God in Christ Jesus our Lord.

IV. St. John the Eagle.—And this hardly needs explanation. There is a radical difference between St. John and the other Evangelists. The latter tell us about Jesus as He appeared among the children of men, and you discover by and by, as the story proceeds, that this Man was something more than a man, and you reach at last the conviction that He was God. But St. John begins at the other end. Remember his immortal Prologue. He starts by saying : ' Now here is what I am going to tell you about— not the story of a human life but the story of a divine manifestation. The Word was made flesh, and dwelt among us ; and we beheld His glory.' That is St. John's starting-point ; and the starting-point makes such a difference. He lifts us at once above Bethlehem. He never says a word about the inn or the manger : he carries us away up to the Throne of God and brings us down thence in company with the Incarnate Saviour.

It is like an eagle's flight. I saw an eagle once in the Western Highlands. It had alighted in the neighbourhood of a shepherd's flock, and he scared it away lest it should plunder his lambs, and it took

wing and soared up into the blue sky, growing less and less until it seemed but a dim speck, scarce as big as a skylark. The old fable says that the eagle is the only creature whose eye can look undazzled on the blazing sun ; and there could be no fitter emblem of St. John. He lifts us above the noise and strife of earth, and sets us amid the blaze of the heavenly glory.—DAVID SMITH, *Man's Need of God*, p. 149.

REFERENCES.—IV. 6-8.—H. S. Holland, *Christian World Pulpit*, vol. l. p. 40. A. P. Stanley, *Sermons on Special Occasions*, p. 57.

' And the first creature was like a lion . . . and the third creature had a face as of a man.'—REV. IV. 7.

' IN times of opposition,' says Milton at the close of the *Apology for Smectymnuus*, ' when either against new heresies arising, or old corruptions to be reformed, this cool unpassionate mildness of positive wisdom is not enough to damp and astonish the proud resistance of carnal and false doctors, then (that I may have leave to soar awhile, as the poets use) Zeal, whose substance is ethereal arming in complete diamond, ascends his fiery chariot, drawn with two blazing meteors, figured like beasts, but of a higher breed than any the zodiac yields, resembling two of those four which Ezekiel and St. John saw ; the one visaged like a lion, to express power, high authority, and indignation ; the other, of countenance like a man, to cast derision and scorn upon perverse and fraudulent seducers ; with these the invisible warrior, Zeal, shaking loosely the slack reins, drives over the heads of scarlet prelates, and such as are insolent to maintain traditions, bruising. their stiff necks under his flaming wheels.'

' Holy, holy, holy, is the Lord God Almighty.'—REV. IV. 8.

I ASSERT for myself that I do not behold the outward creation, and that to me it is hindrance and not action. ' What,' it will be questioned, ' when the sun rises, do you not see a disc of fire, somewhat like a guinea ? ' ' Oh, no, no ! I see an innumerable company of the heavenly host crying, *Holy, holy, holy, is the Lord God Almighty*. I question not my corporeal eye, any more than I would question a window, concerning a sight. I look through it, and not with it.'— WILLIAM BLAKE.

REFERENCES.—IV. 8.—F. St. John Corbett, *The Preacher's Year*, p. 106. H. J. Bevis, *Sermons*, p. 165. R. W. Hiley, *A Year's Sermons*, vol. i. p. 283. J. J. Blunt, *Plain Sermons* (3rd Series), p. 204. J. Keble, *Sermons for Ascension Day to Trinity Sunday*, p. 374. Bishop Wilberforce, *Sermons*, p. 231. H. Alford, *Quebec Chapel Sermons*, vol. i. p. 1. J. Vaughan, *Fifty Sermons* (9th Series), p. 112. IV. 9-11.—C. Kingsley, *The Good News of God*, p. 325.

For an Exposition of chapter v. see A. B. Davidson's *Waiting Upon God*, p. 351. V. 2.—Bishop Gore, *Christian World Pulpit*, vol. liii. p. 384.

THREE VIEWS OF MAN'S DESTINY

1. *Pessimism*

' I wept much, because no man was found worthy to open and to read the book.'—REV. V. 4.

THIS is a mysterious passage in a mysterious book, but the fact that interpretation may easily become ridiculous should not debar us from the beauty and the power of one of the greatest and most picturesque of Scriptural poetic images. God is on His throne, but He is left undescribed, and we see only His hand holding a sealed book.

What concerns us especially is the group of three figures which represent three of the main attitudes of man to destiny. There is the weeping man, the pessimist, who sees only the sadness of the mystery, and tends towards despair and cynicism. Then there is the elder of Judah with the lion of his tribe, the optimist whose one resource is that of energy. Finally there is the true key to destiny; the lamb as it has been slain, emblem of love and sacrifice. We may consider these in three successive studies.

The pessimist comes first, represented by the weeping man of the text. This man may stand for many thousands who have stood in bitterness before the unsolved riddle of human life. The apparent waste—the heartless and unreasonable waste—of the wealth of human hearts and lives, force upon him the questions, What does God mean by making a world like this? and, What is He going to do with it?

These questions find no answer. No man is strong enough to break the seals and open the book. No nation is strong enough. All these pathetic 'efforts to understand things' fill the writer's mind with an overwhelming sense of futility. He can make nothing of it, and he abandons the attempt with tears.

There were other elements in this grief besides baffled curiosity. We all learn sooner or later that many things in this strange world are beyond our understanding, and we come to terms with the mystery of things with as good a grace as we can. But there are special elements here, which in some degree enter into the experience of all such seekers, and which give to pessimism its keenest point.

I. First of all, the dreamer had been promised a knowledge of the future, and in this refusal there was something like a claim dishonoured. And in us all there is the feeling that in some sense we have a right to know. We are not asking for complete explanations, but surely we may expect light enough to live by. We are here not of our own choice, and we are willing to accept the situation and make the best of it. But, so tangled is the skein of life, it often happens that with the best intentions men make the most serious mistakes. We want some sure guidance, and above all we want some assurance that it is not all in vain, and that our destinies are not, as they sometimes seem to be, the sport of chance. We are willing to work cheerfully or to suffer patiently if we can only understand. But this looks like the demand for day labour while light is denied us, and it is no wonder though we weep.

II. Second, a discovery is here given of how much is required for such knowledge as we crave. 'No man is *worthy* to open the book.' The hindrance to understanding, the veil between our souls and

truth is our own sin, and conscience further embitters the great unanswered question. The mystery of life often seems to press most sorely on the good, but it does not break their hearts. They find some meaning in things that consoles them and gives them rest. But the unworthy have no such consolation. It is they who weep most bitterly before the face of destiny, and rebel against the way in which the unintelligible world is made. When we are caught in the mills of God, the nether millstone on which any soul is ground is ever its own unworthiness.

III. The lessons of all this are plain. When we are confronted with the blank and bitter mystery of things it is not well to brood sullenly on the sense of a dishonoured claim. The book is unreadable, and we have no real right to understand. Neither science nor religion professes to answer all our questions. Our theories give no full explanation, our visions are but glimpses at the best, but 'led blindfold through the glimmering camp of God'. And, further, when we are tempted to despair and to rebel and to malign the world, it is well to ask ourselves, Am I *worthy* to open the book? What grossness, what pride, what folly enter even into our desire to understand? What use have we made of the light vouchsafed to us? For doubt is surprising only when the life is pure, and they who know most are those who are 'holding the mystery of the faith in a pure conscience'.—John Kelman, *Ephemera Eternitatis*, p. 230.

Reference.—V. 4.—E. A. Askew, *The Service of Perfect Freedom*, p. 8.

THREE VIEWS OF MAN'S DESTINY
2. *The Gospel of Healthy-mindedness.*

'Weep not: behold, the Lion of the tribe of Juda . . . hath prevailed to open the book.'—Rev. v. 5.

The elder's view of the Messiah is 'the Lion of the tribe of Judah,' and his boast is that Christ, in that capacity, has been able to unseal and open the book of human destiny. At least one of the older commentators has recognised in this elder the figure of the patriarch Jacob, and has referred the text back to the splendid words of Genesis XLIX. 9—'Judah is a lion's whelp; from the prey, my son, thou are gone up: he stooped down, he crouched as a lion, and as an old lion; who shall rouse him up?'

I. It would seem that from early times the lion had been a sort of insignia of Judah, a national emblem like the Scottish and the Persian lion. Dr. Dods has said in this connexion, 'There is enough in the history of Judah himself, and in the subsequent history of the tribe, to justify the ascription to him of all lion-like qualities—a kingly fearlessness, confidence, power, and success; in action a rapidity of movement, and a might that make Him irresistible, and in repose a majestic dignity of bearing'. The same writer goes on to contrast the 'rushing onset of the lion with the craft of the serpent, the predatory instinct of the wolf and the swiftness of the hind'. This, especially in times of oppression and adversity, gives a very fair idea of the conception of Messiah cherished by the elders of Israel. To their passionate patriotism He was the mirror and emblem of national strength and triumph.

History has borne out the lordly boast. Judea has been not merely a personal but a national force in the arena of the world's destinies. All nations have taken their part in the grand sum-total of history, but it is Judea that has led the way, both in the understanding and in the shaping of the destinies of the world. Disraeli has boasted that 'the most popular poet in England is the sweet singer of Israel,' and that 'the divine image of the most illustrious of the Hebrews' has been again raised amid the homage of kneeling millions in the most civilised of the kingdoms of Europe. When we think of what Jesus Christ has meant already in human history, we are constrained to confess that that gallant little nation, perched on its high ridge of rock, has indeed unsealed the book. By the earliest Christian missions, by the Crusades, and by the unceasing play of Christianity upon the West, she gave its future to savage Europe. Later, when the New World opened its gates to the Old, it was Puritan Christianity that gave its noblest qualities to the American race. To-day, when for Africa and Asia the seals are being opened in so swift and dramatic succession, the issues of the future again depend wholly on the Judean— it will be Christ or a godless civilisation more ominous than their past heathenism.

II. But the Lion of the tribe of Judah may also be taken as the representative type of a clearly defined ideal of character. It is the oriflamme of the Gospel of healthy-mindedness, and the doctrine of the strenuous life. This lion-like attack on destiny is indeed a magnificent imagination. It tells of direct attack that scorns diplomatic cunning, of will and main force whose self-reliance waits neither for the backing of friends nor of circumstances. It tells us of a certain band of warriors against fate who by sheer force and rush of onset have carried destiny by storm.

These are the men of *sturm und drang*, who master and enlist the great forces of the world. For the most part they are plain men, not assuming virtues of greater delicacy than they can understand. Always they are strong men, who are not wearied but braced by labour and endurance. They are simple men, unembarrassed by the subtle questionings which distract others. They cut through the knots which others strive in vain to disentangle, and their only refuge from discouragements and fears is the refuge of action. Men of this spirit may do superhuman things, taking the citadels of destiny by assault. Destiny goes down before Will, and the Weird itself (so runs the ancient Saxon song) will help 'an undoomed man if he be brave'. Not even the sense of sin and failure, nor the disheartening memory of the irrevocable past, is able wholly to daunt such spirits. There is in strong and courageous vitality, a strange power of healing and of purifying, which baffles the powers of darkness.

III. Jesus Christ rides at the head of that company of heroes. He is not the opponent, but the truest of all exponents of the Gospel of the healthy mind. He matched His strength against the religious hierarchy of Jerusalem, against the vast Empire of Rome, against the world, and He has won His battle all along the line. In the progress of the Christian conscience we see Him pitted against the slaveries, oppressions, injustices of two thousand years. In the progress of Christian civilisation we see Him combating the forces of sorrow, poverty, disease, and death. In the progress of religious thought we see Him conquering prejudice, hypocrisy, and errors of the mind and heart and will.—JOHN KELMAN, *Ephemera Eternitatis*, p. 236.

THE BREAKING OF THE SEALS

'And one of the elders saith unto me, Weep not: behold the Lion of the tribe of Juda, the Root of David, hath prevailed to open the book, and to loose the seven seals thereof. And I beheld, and, lo, in the midst of the throne and of the four beasts, and in the midst of the elders, stood a Lamb as it had been slain, having seven horns and seven eyes, which are the seven spirits of God sent forth into all the earth.'— REV. v. 5, 6.

I. THE impotency of unaided humanity to enter into the secret of God. This fact is proclaimed in this dramatic scene with marked emphasis. 'And no man in heaven, nor in earth, neither under the earth, was able to open the book, *neither to look thereon.*' Translating the dramatic picture, it is the grave truth that the Scriptures so constantly emphasise, that lies at the very base of the Christian doctrine of salvation, that fallen man had no power in himself to regain the heights from which he had fallen. Fallen man cannot with his own hands open the roll of the eternal secret of life; he cannot even look at it.

II. The Lion-power that accomplishes the task for humanity. 'Behold the Lion of the tribe of Juda, the Root of David, hath prevailed to open the book and to loose the seven seals thereof.' The description here given is very suggestive. On the one hand there is a strong savour of human nature in the terms employed. The Deliverer partakes of the nature of Juda, and of David, and the types of national and individual human life. This mighty love is in some sense human, and yet He is immeasurably more than man. He is the 'Lion' of the tribe of Juda, that is, He is the actual world-conqueror, of whom that tribe was only a type or shadow. The 'Root of David' expresses the same relation of this hero to earth's typical individual, that is the type of its noblest life. So the nature of this Deliverer belongs essentially to the world invisible and eternal. He towers immeasurably above all that is best in human life, both national and individual.

III. The Lamb-sacrifice in the heart of the Lion-power. The transcendently glorious nature of the Hero presented to us, and his entering into closest union with human life, are not sufficient to account for His power of leading mankind into the Divine secret, of restoring man to God. The heart of the

Lion-power is Lamb-sacrifice. In more ordinary language, the incarnation of Christ apart from His atonement is not sufficient to account for the redemption of the world. *The Lamb that was slain* emphatically points out the *death of Christ*, as in a special sense the sacrificial act that bore away the sin of the world. Note the measureless power and infinitely exalted position here ascribed to the Lamb. 'A Lamb having seven horns and seven eyes.' This is, of course, a symbolic way of ascribing to Him perfection of power and universal dominion, and of asserting that out of His life all spiritual power goes forth into all the world. In full harmony with this description the Lamb is represented as sharing with Him that sitteth upon the throne the worship of the whole creation.—JOHN THOMAS, *Myrtle Street Pulpit,* vol. II. p. 181.

THREE VIEWS OF MAN'S DESTINY
3. *Love and Sacrifice*
'A Lamb as it had been slain.'—REV. v. 6.

THE lion of the elder is a true aspect of Christ, and yet there is a more excellent way. It is the way of the saint, the divine seer and evangelist, who comes to rest upon the vision of 'the Lamb standing as it had been slain,' as the innermost secret of life and the true key of human destiny. For there is a limit to the power of will and courage, and sooner or later even the boldest attack teaches us by its imperfect success that we mortals must 'approach destiny respectfully'.

So now we have the lamb substituted for the lion. And it is ἀρνίον—'the little lamb'—quoted from Isaiah LIII. 7, but purposely changed to the diminutive. This is the favourite thought of that tender and far-seeing spirit who took up the beautiful imagery of the twenty-third Psalm, and understood so well the meaning of the words 'thy gentleness hath made me great,' when he told how the Baptist had spoken of Jesus as the Lamb of God.

I. A great principle is embodied here. There is a Syrian mountain whose black basalt breaks the lofty table-land above the sea of Galilee. At that mountain the Crusaders lost Palestine after one of the fiercest of their battles. On the same spot, according to tradition at least, Jesus won the world by His Sermon on the Mount. It is the merest commonplace, alike of science and of human nature, that the humblest approach gains the richest results. Nature resists man's violence, but yields inevitably in the end to his loving patience. In character, self-assertion and the endeavour to make an impression have accomplished much; persecution, punishment and coercion have done much; but love has done far more than these. Love is the key to destiny. Force may succeed outwardly, and yet be but a magnificent failure. Love never fails: it does its appointed work.

II. It was this which was the life-long task and achievement of Jesus. In Him the world has seen love at once revealing and making destiny. For what was it in Him that led men to understand themselves and to change into better manhood? What was it that made that nobler life seem no longer an impossible ideal, but their own rightful heritage? It was not His courage nor His strength, not His absoluteness nor His denunciation. It was simply His love—that same love which cured the sickness of the land and burst open the tombs of its dead.

That aspect of the life of Christ gives us a great counsel to which we shall take heed if we be wise. When we have tried to force success by sheer daring and strenuousness and have failed, nothing is more natural than to become embittered. But this reminds us that we have not yet exhausted our resources. One power remains in reserve, the power of love. Those are wise who, in the dark hour of defeat, guard the springs of the heart and refuse to be embittered.

III. But in that master-picture of Isaiah's which is here presented, there is a further meaning. It is not only the lamb, but the lamb slain that we see; not only love but sacrifice. The lamb has death-wounds on its body, as it stands in the first pathos of death, slain though not yet fallen. This is indeed the kind of love that conquers destiny. There are many kinds of love—placidly selfish love, good-humoured and easy-going affection, that knows nothing of sacrifice. But this is by far too great a task for such love. The book of destiny remains for ever closed to selfishness.

So we come in sight of the ancient truth, old indeed as the world though but slowly apprehended, that man must sacrifice to destiny.

Behind all such sacrifices, interpreting them and inspiring them, stands the great self-sacrifice of Jesus Christ. As we see Him moving on towards Calvary we tremble as we realise how the fate of the world turned on that cross. By accepting it He revealed the meaning of man's destiny, and he conquered it for man. The lamb slain prevailed to open the book. The revealing power of the cross has showed how through suffering man is made perfect, and changed the mystery of pain to the hope of glory, the bitter cry to the shout of victory, and the victims of life to the sons of God.—JOHN KELMAN, *Ephemera Eternitatis,* p. 242.

'And I beheld, and lo, in the midst of the throne and of the four beasts, and in the midst of the elders, a Lamb.'—REV. v. 6.

ONCE I was troubled to know whether the Lord Jesus was Man as well as God, and God as well as Man; and truly, in those days, let men say what they would, unless I had it with evidence from Heaven, all was nothing to me, I counted not myself set down in any truth of God. Well, I was much troubled about this point, and could not tell how to be resolved; at last, that in Revelation v. came into my mind, *And I beheld, and lo, in the midst of the throne and of the four beasts, and in the midst of the elders, stood a Lamb.* In the midst of the Throne, thought I, there is His Godhead; in the midst of the Elders, there is His Manhood; but, oh! methought this did glisten! it was a goodly touch, and gave me sweet satisfaction.—BUNYAN, *Grace Abounding*, sec. 122.

REFERENCES.—V. 6.—Charles Brown, *God and Man*, p. 115. C. J. Clark-Hunt, *The Refuge of the Sacred Wounds*, p. 61. *Expositor* (6th Series), vol. viii. p. 344; *ibid.* vol. xii. p. 44. A. Maclaren, *Expositions of Holy Scripture—Revelation*, p. 322. V. 6, 7.—Spurgeon, *Sermons*, vol. xxxv. No. 2095. V. 8.—V. S. S. Coles, *Christian World Pulpit*, vol. lvii. p. 234. Spurgeon, *Sermons*, vol. xviii. No. 1051. V. 8-10.—Spurgeon, *Ibid.* vol. xxxix. No. 2321.

THE LAMB AND THE BOOK

'Thou art worthy to take the book and to open the seals thereof: for thou wast slain, and hast redeemed us to God by thy blood.'—REV. v. 9.

THE meaning of that scene is unmistakable and instantly clear. It sets forth this truth, that Jesus, the Lamb of God who was slain at Calvary, alone has the power to disclose and to interpret the mind and purpose and ways of God. It was when the Lamb had taken the book and was about to break the first seal that they sung the new song, saying, 'Thou art worthy to take the book, and to open the seals thereof: for thou wast slain, and hast redeemed us to God by thy blood'.

Let me illustrate this great truth that the crucified Christ unseals the book of God. God has more than one book, and yet all His books give us the one revelation. Let us see how Christ breaks the seals, and what He gives us to read on pages which otherwise had been dark to men.

I. Look, to begin with, at *the sealed book of Scripture*. It should be a commonplace to us that we cannot read the Old Testament except in Christ's light. Only by an effort of the imagination can we realise how closely sealed and how dark with mystery the Old Testament would have been if Christ had not died and risen again.

The truth is as clearly illustrated by the New Testament scriptures. There are some to-day to whom the New Testament is still a sealed book. One has only to take up such a book as Martineau's *Seat of Authority in Religion* to find that so clear, so penetrating, so spiritual a mind cannot read the plainest pages of the book. The depth of its moral wisdom, the divineness of its message, and the power of its appeal to the conscience bear in upon his mind and move him to impassioned praise. But the meaning and purpose of the book are hidden from him. The simplest peasant could be his teacher, and would stand amazed that learning and genius should so miss what lies so plainly revealed. Had Martineau looked up at the Cross and seen the Lamb who was slain to redeem, all would have been clear. Read the Gospels and the Epistles in the light of that death for sin, and every word and deed is translated. The cradle of Bethlehem, the carpenter's shop at Nazareth, the Jordan water at baptism, the wilderness of temptation, the garden of Gethsemane, and all the riches of grace in sermon and parable and miracle, stand out as the life-story that leads to the Cross. It is the Lamb that was slain that unfolds, interprets, and expounds the New Testament.

II. Look, in the second place, at *the sealed book of nature*. In the light of Christ's Cross we see that life in nature is sacrificial and redeeming. In the light of Christ's Cross we see that the pain and agony and death, which so abound, are only the inevitable condition that life may continue, the species be perpetuated, and the high and beneficent ends of nature gained. Modern science is reading the purpose and the meaning of nature in the light of the truth taught by the death of Christ.

III. Look, in the third place, at *the sealed book of history*.

In every century since our historians stand before the sealed book. In every generation the hearts of Christian people fail them for fear. This twentieth century has only just begun. We are scarcely across its threshold, and yet east and west, the red horse of war, the black horse of famine, and the pale horse of death have gone forth. The cries of terror and of pain are ascending to God. A great part of the struggle between the nations, and the consequent waste of precious life and pain of tender hearts, is actually due to the advance of the Cross. It is the civilisation of Christendom coming into conflict with the ideals of heathendom. It is the leaven of the thoughts of the gospel fermenting in Eastern minds. Within the Church itself there is also bewilderment and pain. There are questions which find no answer, problems which reach no solution, doctrines that seem to be shaken. Who shall unfold this page of mystery? Who shall break the seal of this secret? The Lamb that was slain.

IV. Look, in the fourth place, at *the sealed book of our own lives*.

Stand below the Cross, and look up at the Lamb that was slain, and mark the course and issue of His passion and His death, and you will realize why the pages of your book are dark with sorrow and wet with tears. Out of life's battle comes conquest over self. Out of life's dark hours come light and strength and peace. Out of life's meek acceptance of death, there comes life for ourselves and others.—W. M. CLOW, *The Cross and Christian Experience*, p. 139.

REFERENCES.—V. 9.—W. H. Simcox, *The Cessation of Prophecy*, p. 158. *Expositor* (5th Series), vol. vii. p. 374; *ibid.* (6th Series), vol. ix. p. 44.

'Thou hast redeemed us to God by thy blood out of every kindred, and tongue, and people, and nation; and hast made us unto our God kings and priests.'—REV. v. 9, 10.

IT is a delight to a soldier or traveller to look back on his escapes when they are over; and for a saint in heaven to look back on his sins and sorrows upon earth, his fears and tears, his enemies and dangers, his wants and calamities, must make his joy more joyful. Therefore the blessed, in praising the Lamb, mention His redeeming them out of every nation and kindred and tongue; and so, out of their misery and wants and sins, and making them kings and priests unto God. But if they had nothing but content and rest on earth, what room would there have been for these rejoicings hereafter ?—RICHARD BAXTER.

REFERENCES.—V. 9, 10.—Spurgeon, *Sermons*, vol. xxi. No. 1225. Bishop Gore, *Christian World Pulpit*, vol. lx. p. 49. *Expositor* (4th Series), vol. iv. p. 426. V. 9-13.—T. Jones, *Christian World Pulpit*, vol. li. p. 394. V. 10.—C. Perren, *Revival Sermons in Outline*, p. 194. Spurgeon, *Sermons*, vol. i. No. 10. V. 11.—*Expositor* (4th Series), vol. iii. p. 256.

'Worthy is the Lamb that hath been slain to receive the power.'
—REV. V. 12.

IN one of his letters, Dr. John Ker describes the effect produced on him by reading Carlyle's *Reminiscences*. 'We may be thankful,' he writes, 'that we have a better standard in the Infinite Strength that stooped to weakness, to pity and to raise it. I should be far from saying that Carlyle had not the Christian in him, but he wanted one part of it, and it is proof of an entirely original and Divine being, that the Reminiscences of the fishermen of Galilee give us One who had the most perfect purity, with the most tender pity—an unbending strength that never despised weakness.

'One of the false things of the day is to exalt power (including intellect in a form of power) at the expense of the moral and spiritual. It belongs to materialism, and in a degree to pantheism, and it is the direct opposite of Christianity, which makes Christ lay power aside, in order to make the centre of the universe self-sacrifice and love; and that their power should gravitate to this centre, because it is the only safe one. " Worthy is the Lamb that was slain to receive power." When we begin to see this, we feel in our deepest nature that it is Divine—that this must be true if the universe has any meaning, and the soul a worthy end. It gets obscured sometimes, but it will come out again.

REFERENCE.—VI. 1-8.—*Expositor* (4th Series), vol. x. p. 292.

'He went forth conquering and to conquer.'—REV. VI. 2.

THE motto of the Moravian Church is ' Vicit Agnus noster, eum sequamur'. ('Our Lamb has conquered, let us follow Him.')

'And behold a pale horse : and his name that sat on him was Death.'—REV. VI. 8.

DEATH appears mounted on a horse, not on a throne; he arrives, he passes by.—C. G. ROSSETTI.

DR. JOHN BROWN, in the second series of *Horæ Subsecivæ*, describes a sermon by Dr. Chalmers on the reign of death, and on death as a tremendous necessity. Towards the end, 'in a few plain sentences, he stated the truth as to sin entering, and death by sin, and death passing upon all. Then he took fire once more, and enforced, with redoubled energy and richness, the freeness, the simplicity, the security, the sufficiency of the great method of justification. How astonished and impressed we all were! He was at the full thunder of his power; the whole man was in an agony of earnestness. . . . And when he sat down, after warning each one of us to remember who it was, and what it was, that followed death on

his pale horse, and how alone we could escape—we all sunk back into our seats.'

'To kill with famine.'—REV. VI. 8.

COMPARE Shelley's vivid description in the tenth canto of *The Revolt of Islam*, XVIII. f.

REFERENCES.—VI. 8.—E. A. Askew, *The Service of Perfect Freedom*, p. 109. *Expositor* (5th Series), vol. x. p. 121.

'How long ?'—REV. VI. 9 f.

AFTER quoting Lacretelle's description of a bloody riot in May, 1750—'Some of the rioters were hanged on the following days'—Carlyle proceeds : 'O ye poor naked wretches! and this then is your inarticulate cry to heaven, as of a dumb tortured animal, crying from uttermost depths of pain and debasement? Do these azure skies, like a dead crystalline vault, only reverberate the echo of it on you? Respond to it only by " hanging on the following days "?—not so : not for ever! Ye are heard in Heaven. Also the answer will come—in a horror of great darkness, and shakings of the world, and a cup of trembling which all the nations shall drink.'—*French Revolution*, bk. I. II.

THAT general opinion, that the world grows near its end, hath possessed all ages past as nearly as ours. I am afraid that the souls that now depart cannot escape that lingering expostulation of the saints under the altar, *Quousque Domini* (How long, O Lord)? and groan in the expectation of the great jubilee.—SIR THOMAS BROWNE, *Religio Medici*.

REFERENCES.—VI. 9.—*Expositor* (4th Series), vol. iii. p. 251. VI. 9-11.—C. Gotch, *Sermons*, p. 265.

REV. VI. 10, 11.

HERE it is plain that the departed have the power of prayer. The souls under the altar 'cried with a loud voice, saying, How long, O Lord?' It appears, further, that they retain a consciousness of their former life on earth, for they say, 'How long, O Lord, holy and true, dost Thou not judge and avenge *our* blood on them that dwell on the earth?' It appears, too, from this passage that the souls of the departed are capable of receiving knowledge, for 'it was *said unto them* that they should rest yet for a little season'. It appears, too, from this passage that they are, while in Paradise, capable of receiving additional comfort and glory, for it says, 'white robes were given to every one of them'.

I. The thought of the life of the souls in Paradise may help to reconcile us to bear the loss which their departure must in many ways bring upon us. For when we think even of the little that we know of their perfect and increasing happiness we would not wish them back again. Their life above is, as the Apostle tells us, 'far, far better' than our life here below. It is true 'we know in part' only, as the Apostle says, what the joys of that blessed life in Paradise must be ; but we know enough to make us thankful for those 'who depart hence in the Lord'. At present when we read the book of nature, or even the book of Revelation, we are but as persons reading in a book with crumpled, or missing, leaves; there is much which we desire to fill in, 'we only know in part'; but hereafter, there above, we shall 'know even as we have been known'; there we shall see, as it were, all the disordered leaves of our present knowledge arranged in perfect order, in the one volume of God's most perfect will, bound with the bond of His eternal love :—

> Nel suo profondo vidi che s'interna,
> Legato con amore in un volume,
> Ciò che per l'universo si squaderna.
> —Dante, *Paradiso*, c. xxxiii. 85.

II. At present, it is true, we only see 'in part,' but if we look with the eye of faith on the wonders with which God has surrounded us in this world, and remember that they are His handiwork, then we shall be able to read the book of nature in the spirit of Christ's parables, and learn something of the ways of God. Every spring-time shows us a resurrection after the apparent death of winter—the trees and flowers were 'not dead, but sleeping'. It is a constant miracle of wonder and delight to me to watch through the early days of spring the still, dark, and dead-like stems of the trees in our orchards. It seems so unlikely that the dark, dull stem should ever be the channel for a life of beauty and of self-production. Inch after inch, as the eye rises from the ground, there seems no hope of any future glory, and yet, when the appointed time has come, we see the miracle of its organic life performed, and blossom after blossom is unfolded, and then the full fruit is formed. To all the life-power is conveyed, undisturbed by the separate perfection of each. Each bud, and blossom, and fruit receives its due allotment through the living organism; there is no forgetfulness and no confusion. Millions, and millions of millions, at last receive the beauty and the fruitfulness of which in the days of its early growth there was no sign or hope. So, if we could see above the myriad stars, we might behold the souls in Paradise clothed with a beauty and a glory of which the life on earth could give us no true conception, but which is theirs, quite naturally, according to the supernatural laws by which God will perfect the beauty and the fruitfulness of the branches of the True Vine.—Bishop Edward King, *The Love and Wisdom of God*, pp. 332-334.

References.—VI. 16.—Bishop Lightfoot, *Cambridge Sermons*, p. 193. T. F. Crosse, *Sermons* (2nd Series), p. 238. J. Keble, *Sermons for Advent to Christmas Eve*, p. 175. H. Bushnell, *Christ and His Salvation*, p. 314. *Expositor* (5th Series), vol. v. p. 339 ; *ibid.* (6th Series), vol. vi. p. 404. VII. 4.—H. H. Henson, *Godly Union and Concord*, p. 144.

THE SAINTS OF GOD

(For All Saints' Day)

'After this I beheld, and, lo, a great multitude, which no man could number, of all nations, and kindreds, and people, and tongues, stood before the throne, and before the Lamb, clothed with white robes, and palms in their hands.'—Rev. vii. 9.

These are the saints of God. They have been men and women like ourselves. They were diverse in character, they had come from all nations, they were equally diverse in experience, they had had helps, but they had had trials and difficulties. Many of them had their faults, but they are the saints of God. They are one in this, that their testimony is to the triumph of the Lamb.

I. **All Saints' Festival.**—All of us have an interest in All Saints' festival, for most of us have known some saints, and all of us hope to be saints. Though, of course, the festivals more directly and closely connected with the great events in the life of our Blessed Lord—Christmas, Easter, Ascension—must always hold the first place in our minds, and though they claim over all mankind the sovereignty and power of Jesus Christ, because He claimed mankind through them, yet do we not know that all that is good and true in us comes from Him, and we are honouring Him in the celebration of the festival of All Saints? If we see light as we look up and think of all that it means, we do not forget that He is the Light that lighteth every man that cometh into the world, He is the true King of Saints, He, glory be to His name, is the Elder Brother of every good man and woman, every good boy and girl. It is good for us sometimes —is it not?—to turn away from the thoughts of the sins of men, and to behold them in the white robes. It helps us, does it not, and it inspires hope among us, for all of us may have an inheritance among them. I know that to some it is almost a hindrance to think about the mediæval saints because they cannot well enter into the meaning of their surroundings and the general character of their lives, and one could well wish that the roll of saints on our Church calendar were extended to much later times, that we might include in it those who seem in our own day to have stood up so strongly for Christ and have lived as the saints of old. We certainly cannot forget Livingstone and General Gordon, we cannot forget Lord Shaftesbury or Lord Lawrence, we cannot forget Bishop Patteson and his noble martyrdom, or Bishop Hannington in his manly march to death, or the tender ministrations of the devoted Sister Dora or the self-abnegation of Father Damien. All these fill our minds with ennobling ideals. They have stood so near to our own time that we seem to be in touch with them, and if we think of them we are reminded of the saints of God. There are two marks especially which are characteristic of the saints of God.

II. **The Purity of the Saints.**—The first is their purity. Their victory may be over the passions of their own nature, it may involve struggle itself, but it is clear enough that purity is the mark of God's saints. Yet we do wrong if we fail to recognise that in the Holy Scriptures that great word means something more than we generally associate with it. It does mean singleness of aim, it does mean sincerity of purpose: 'If therefore thine eye be single, thy whole body shall be full of light'. It was said of Sir Isaac Newton by one who knew him well, 'His was the whitest soul I have ever known,' and it was said of Dean Stanley by Dr. Vaughan in the sermon that he preached after his funeral, 'I who have known him longest have never known him other than pure'. But, I say, that word goes further than we commonly mean, and it is plain enough that such men as these were free from all double-mindedness. They were single-hearted, and such are the pure in heart who see God. Yes, purity is one of the marks of the saints of God. We may be conscious of our need of it, but it is stated of those who are standing round the throne of God, that they have washed their robes in the Blood of the Lamb. I take that to mean that in the self-sacrifice of the Blessed Lord they have so learned to love Him, to become one with Him, and to be imbued with His spirit that their own selfish and sinful aims have lost all power over them, they have been cleansed from them, they have been washed from them, and realising the love of Christ Who loved them and gave Himself for them, they have found their home, their forgiveness, and their peace with God. And to this may we not each of us attain? We need not despair. The roll of God's saints includes many that have washed their robes and made them white after they had been stained with sin. Our hope, our redemption, our sanctification are just the same as were the hope of all those saints of God. Christ, Who indeed said, 'No man cometh to the Father except by Me,' said also, 'Whosoever cometh unto Me I will in no wise cast out'. It is in Him that the saints have found their power of purity.

III. The Purposefulness of the Saints. — The second mark of these saints of God is their purposefulness. No man can ever drift into sanctity. No man can go to sleep a sinner and wake up a saint. He may forget what is past, but he needs cleansing from it. No man can serve God without an effort. No man can do his duty without really meaning to. In all respects the best work in the world is done by men of purpose. Of course it involves self-discipline, it involves the restraint of foolish imaginations, it often means the curbing of many natural impulses; but is it not the case that too often we fritter away our best ideals and we never seem in any way to realise them? Our very energies fail us because we have not sufficiently concentrated our minds on any true end. But God's saints have felt the constraining love of Christ. This has made each one of them pull himself together and set his face steadfastly towards the goal.

THE SAINTS IN PAST TIME A COMFORT IN PRESENT WEAKNESS

'After this I beheld, and, lo, a great multitude, which no man could number.'—Rev. VII. 9.

It is a frequent trouble or trial with almost every thoughtful Christian to feel disappointed with the measure of success that the Gospel has had in the world. And the simplest, and, in a measure, the truest answer to this feeling of disappointment is, that we are to estimate its success, not by the extent, but by the degree and intensity of its influence.

I. In the first place, ought not the Christian to be disappointed? Shall he complain, if the world has not realised the desires of his charity. How can he, when he knows that they have even more cruelly disappointed the love of his Lord Himself?

II. But though the Christian's rightful lot and proper feeling is one of disappointment, he is not without comfort under it. And next to that great comfort, of knowing that the sorrows of Christian love are a share of the sorrows of Christ, the greatest comfort is faith in the Communion of Saints. Though the elect in any one age and country and society are few, the elect of all time are a great multitude; the elect in all past time are many enough to encourage us; the elect in the time to come will be many enough to be worth our while to work for. Each single soul that is saved, at death or at the final coming of the Lord, belongs thenceforth not to the crooked and perverse generation in which its lot was cast, but to the general assembly and Church of the first-born; it is not a single isolated member of a feeble minority, but a soldier in a mighty army, a citizen of a kingdom able to conquer the world. This is one difference between a servant of God and another man, that one belongs to a society and the other does not. Think what a truly innumerable company it is! Clearly then we have no need to faint, when we are compassed with so great a cloud of witnesses.—W. H. Simcox, *The Cessation of Prophecy*, p. 215.

References.—VII. 9.—H. J. Wilmot-Buxton, *Holy-Tide Teaching*, p. 195. T. F. Crosse, *Sermons*, p. 220. *Expositor* (4th Series), vol. i. p. 48. A. Maclaren, *Expositions of Holy Scripture—Revelation*, p. 331. VII. 9, 10.—*Christian World Pulpit*, vol. xliv. p. 174. D. W. Simon, *Twice Born and other Sermons*, p. 194. H. P. Liddon, *University Sermons* (2nd Series), p. 55. E. T. J. Marriner, *Sermons Preached at Lyme Regis*, p. 85. F. O. Maurice, *Sermons*, vol. ii. p. 306. T. Arnold, *Interpretation of Scripture*, p. 302. H. M. Butler, *Harrow School Sermons*, p. 188. R. C. Trench, *Sermons New and Old*, p. 232. F. J. A. Hort, *Village Sermons* (2nd Series), p. 224. VII. 13.—S. Baring-Gould, *Village Preaching for Saints' Days*, p. 209. J. S. Bartlett, *Sermons*, p. 272. J. M. Neale, *Sermons Preached in Sackville College Chapel*, vol. iv. p. 1.

HEAVEN THROUGH TRIBULATION

'And one of the elders answered, saying unto me, What are these which are arrayed in white robes? Whence came they? And I said unto him, Sir, thou knowest. And he said to me, These are they which came out of great tribulation, and have washed their robes, and made them white in the blood of the lamb.'—Rev. VII. 13, 14.

Reading men and women know that this word 'tribulation' has a wonderful history. There is always a vision at the root of every word; and until you see the hidden picture you do not know the meaning of the word. Tribulation. We see a threshing machine, an instrument for cleansing corn and wheat, for separating straw and dust from wheat, called *Tribulum*. God borrowed the word from the husbandmen of the East, and put it into this Book.

I. Tribulation is God's way of separating earthliness from the heaven of His people. Tribulation means trouble, but it means trouble sanctified, trouble that has done us good, that sends us to our knees, to our Bibles. It takes great tribulation to sanctify a sinner; but God will not let one item of tribulation come upon him that is not needed. He has His eye day and night upon His saints.

II. These are they which came out of great tribulation, but that is not all—tribulation alone will not do it. They washed their robes. The blood of Christ alone can atone. Sin is such a tremendous evil that it will take nothing less than a tremendous lotion to wash it away—nothing less than the blood of God Himself. They serve Him day and night in His Temple. The whole of heaven is one temple, for God is the Temple of it, and the Lamb is the Light thereof. Oh, if it is so good to be here, what must it be to be there?—A. WHYTE, *The Sunday School Chronicle*, vol. xxxiv. p. 315.

REFERENCE.—VII. 13, 14.—Spurgeon, *Sermons*, vol. xviii. No. 1040.

SAVED TO SERVE

'And one of the elders answered, saying unto me, What are these which are arrayed in white robes? and whence came they? And I said unto him, Sir, thou knowest. And he said to me, These are they which came out of great tribulation, and have washed their robes, and made them white in the blood of the Lamb. Therefore are they before the throne of God, and serve Him day and night in His Temple.'—REV. VII. 13-15.

I. The gorgeous visions and somewhat clouded vistas of the Apocalypse are sometimes difficult of interpretation. The passage before us, however, is on the whole simple and clear; men with a spiritual understanding have little or no difficulty with it. It is the vision of the redeemed victorious Church, numbered in it the men and women whom we knew, who dealt with us here and strengthened and comforted our lives, but who have now gone from our mortal sight. What blessed work they do who can say? Milton in one of his majestic moments, which was also one of his humblest moods, speaking of the heavenly host said: 'Thousands at His bidding speed and post o'er land and ocean without rest. They also serve who only stand and wait.' Whatever their work, it is work without weariness, it is service without labour, it is toil without tears, it is the glad service of those who are at Home, and see and know as they are known.

II. Now surely here is a great truth which the Church on earth needs to learn. This vision of the Church redeemed proclaims the great truth that God saves men to serve. Those garments of the saints mean honour, victory; yes, but also service. In the Kingdom of God all are enrolled and equipped for active service, and no man can lazily loiter in pride or selfishness or ease, and be counted worthy.

III. Crowned to serve? Yes. But that is a thought that the world has great difficulty in understanding. Is it easy for the Church? It is the kind of truth that ennobles life, and opens up visions, and shows us how worth living life is, and that following Christ—even as He was as a servant and minister, giving His life a ransom for many—is the one thing that makes life heroic and worthy of a man's toil and struggle. And the Church must learn it.

IV. How do we think of it personally in relation to Christ's Church on earth? It is a great honour for us to have been called of God to see the face of Christ; it is also a great responsibility. Our cleansing in Christ clothes us with the uniform of active service. There are a great many people who have not got any joy in their religion, because they have missed this truth. There is much faith that is very feeble, and it brings little or no joy to the heart, or to the home, or to the Church, because it is not sweetened and strengthened by work.—D. L. RITCHIE, *Peace the Umpire and other Sermons*, p. 157.

FROM STRESS TO TRIUMPH

REV. VII. 13-17.

I. Two features in the past history of the victorious hosts are briefly indicated. (1) The elder who draws near to interpret the vision speaks of the discipline through which the multitude has passed—a lesson not without its significance to this saint in exile. 'These are they which came out of the great tribulation.' The weird imagery of this book seems to suggest that the stages of the tribulation are so ordered that it achieves the ends of a great spiritual discipline. The convulsions which rend the earth are one and all determined by movements before the throne of God in heaven. The saints are sealed ere the restless forces of destruction rush forth upon their errands, and the trials which are to prove high qualities take place under the eye of a watching God and amidst the ministries of His messengers. (2) The interpreting elder sketches the past history of the redeemed multitude in its ethical inwardness. The life once lived upon earth was a life of purifying faith in the Divine sacrifice. 'They washed their robes and made them white in the blood of the Lamb.' Admitted to the holiest sanctuary of all worlds, they minister before God as priests and kings. But it is through the blood of propitiation that they have won access to this high standing-ground.

II. This vision brings into view the higher destiny upon which God's redeemed servants have entered. Four elements combine in the gladness of this beatific life. (1) The life of the glorified first presents itself to the mind of John as a grand victory in which uncounted hosts participate. The sense of a well-won victory, the victory of the highest of all causes, pulsates in the life of the glorified. 'Salvation to our God which sitteth on the throne, and to the Lamb.' (2) The elder goes on to describe the redeemed as raised to a priesthood of worship and service. This is the central absorbing employment of the new state upon which they have entered. 'Therefore are they before the throne of God, and they serve Him day and night in His temple.' (3) These triumphant saints are still in fellowship with the Good Shepherd who laid down His life for the sheep. This thought is brought out in the Revised

Version: 'The Lamb in the midst of the throne shall be their shepherd'. Between Himself and those who have been made white by His sacrificial blood there is a bond no change can weaken or destroy. (4) The last touch in this picture sets forth the Eternal God as the Comforter of His saved people. 'And God shall wipe away every tear from their eyes.' Not only is He the object of worship upon the throne, He comes nearer still to the redeemed multitude, healing all the smarts of earth, and dispersing the last memory of pain. When God puts His hand upon the fountain of mortal tears, the fountain is sealed up for ever.

'They washed their robes, and made them white in the blood of the Lamb.'—REV. VII. 14.

DID you ever observe the force of double symbols? Sometimes they increase the light they cast, like twin stars. There is that fine one in the Apocalypse, 'Who have washed their robes, and made them white in the blood of the Lamb'. Isn't that wonderfully expressive? Ah yes, and they'll be prouder of their redness than of their whiteness.—DR. JOHN DUNCAN, in *Colloquia Peripatetica.*

'THINK, Madam,' wrote Samuel Rutherford to Lady Kenmure, after a great sorrow in her family, 'it is a part of your glory to be enrolled among those whom one of the elders pointed out to John, "These are they which came out of great tribulation, and have washed their robes, and made them white in the blood of the Lamb." Behold your Forerunner going out of the world all in a lake of blood, and it is not ill to die as He did.'

REFERENCES.—VII. 14.—Spurgeon, *Sermons*, vol. xxii. No. 1316. J. Laidlaw, *Studies in the Parables*, p. 269. A. Smellie, *The Scottish Review*, vol. vi. p. 443. *Expositor* (4th Series), vol. v. p. 125; *ibid.* vol. vi. p. 251; *ibid.* (5th Series), vol. vi. p. 218.

'Nor any heat.'—REV. VII. 14-16.

THE summer of 1826 was, I believe, the hottest and driest in the nineteenth century. Almost no rain fell from May till August. I recollect the long continued sultry haze over the mountains of Lorne, Loch Etive daily a sea of glass, the smoke of kelp-burning ascending from its rocky shores, and the sunsets reflecting the hills of Mull and Morven in purple and crimson and gold. I can picture a sultry Sunday in that year in the quaint, rudely furnished, crowded parish church, then beside the manse, and the welcome given to the sublime imagery of the Apocalypse in the words which formed the text: 'These are they which came out of great tribulation, and have washed their robes, and made them white in the blood of the Lamb. They shall hunger no more, neither thirst any more; neither shall the sun light on them, nor any heat.'—PROF. CAMPBELL FRASER, *Biographia Philosophica*, p. 17.

Compare the use of these verses also in Mrs. Gaskell's *North and South*, XI. XIII. and XVII.

REFERENCE.—VII. 15.—A. Smellie, *The Scottish Review*, vol. vi. p. 163.

THE DIGNITY OF SERVICE

'Therefore are they before the throne of God, and serve Him day and night in His temple: and He that sitteth on the throne shall dwell among them. . . . For the lamb which is in the midst of the throne shall feed them, and shall lead them unto living fountains of waters: and God shall wipe away all tears from their eyes.'—REV. VII. 15, 17.

THIS is one of the glimpses of the better life which John gives us in this book of celestial visions. Heaven is a place of sweet activities. The redeemed are serving God day and night before His throne. The Lamb in the midst of the throne is still occupied as when on earth He said: 'I am among you as He that saveth'. All these, from the highest to the lowest, are busy in the ministry of love. And we take it that that is the pattern in the mount after which God would have us fashion all things in the earthly life, and so in the text we get a sermon not so much about heaven as about the work and interests of the present day.. We learn:—

I. That the highest life is a life of perpetual service. In God's view rank is determined by the measure of service. It is strange how the world has set aside and reversed this principle in its conceptions of rank and dignity. We speak of service with a sort of disdain, and of servants as ignoble and inferior persons. We are nearest heaven in proportion as we serve.

II. The highest life is a life of service in the temple, or rather of temple service. The highest life on earth is a life made up entirely of temple service—a life in which we do all things from the least to the greatest in the same spirit in which we sing hymns and offer prayers, honestly, reverently, and purely, as in the sight of God and our Master Jesus Christ. What we need more and more to feel is that we are always in the temple; that though we do not see God's face, we are for ever in His sight; that we serve before His throne, and that He takes careful and loving knowledge of everything. It is possible even on earth to be like those who serve Him day and night in His temple.

III. The highest life is a life of work inspired by love, by love and not by necessity. In all that we do there may be the willing, thankful, rejoicing spirit, a feeling of infinite indebtedness to God for His great gifts and His great love, which gives, as it were, wings to the feet that are engaged in common labour. According to the measure of your love will you be near to those who serve as they behold His face.—J. G. GREENHOUGH, *The Cross in Modern Life*, p. 209.

'They shall hunger no more.'—REV. VII. 16.

'No one who has never wanted food knows what life is,' said Wilderspin. . . . 'No one knows the real primal meaning of that pathetic word Man—no one knows the true meaning of Man's position here among the other living creatures of this world, if he has never wanted food. Hunger gives a new seeing to the eyes.'—THEODORE WATTS-DUNTON, *Aylwin.*

REFERENCES.—VII. 16, 17.—Spurgeon, *Sermons*, vol. xxx. No. 1800, and vol. xxxvi. No. 2128.

PARADISE

'The Lamb which is in the midst of the Throne shall feed them (or "be their Shepherd"), and shall guide them unto living waters; and God shall wipe away all tears from their eyes.'—Rev. vii. 17.

When evening came, the Oriental shepherd gathered his flock around him, and, in imagery borrowed from the flocks feeding on Olivet, we are told that he puts himself at the head of his sheep and slowly mounts the hill, tenderly carrying the weakest in his arms, and leading them gently on until they reach the permanent Fold which stood on the high ground of the Mount of Olives.

It is a true picture of the way in which Jesus deals with us when the evening of life comes to us. Then the Good Shepherd comes and calls us home. Do we ask in trembling anxiety when will death come to us? Where will it be? In what shape will it present itself? There is no answer to these questions. I remember once, at the unveiling of a memorial to some colliers who had perished in an explosion, a pitman spoke with much pathos of the way a collier would say good-bye to his wife and children each morning when he started for his daily toil, not knowing if he would ever return home alive again. Surely we might each say the same thing of ourselves. However short the absence from home may be, who can tell if he will be permitted to return again? Such thoughts should not be put away as alarming; it is our wisdom to realise the possible nearness of death much more then we usually do.

But what is Death? We ask the question in trembling anxiety, and Jesus does tell us something in answer. Death is certainly not destruction, it is no cessation of being; it is not even a suspension of being; it is a changed condition of life: 'Absent from the body, present with the Lord'; 'Whether we live or die, we are the Lord's'. Death is a birth into new conditions of life. We are told of our Blessed Lord, that 'He was put to death in the flesh, but quickened in the Spirit'; that which seemed like falling into a deep unconscious sleep was, in Jesus, the passing into quickened energy of life, As with our Forerunner, so will it be with us—death is our birth into the life of Paradise.

He is the Comforter, Nourisher, Guide and Teacher of the Saints at rest, for this is the best definition of life in Paradise—it is a life of rest. This is its characteristic feature as it is brought before us in the Bible. 'The souls of the righteous are in the Hand of God, and there shall no evil touch them; in the sight of the unwise they seem to die, but they are at peace.' And again, 'I heard a voice from heaven saying unto me, Write, Blessed are the dead which die in the Lord . . . that they may rest from their labours'.

Let us consider some of the elements of that rest. I. The waiting souls in Paradise enjoy the rest of those who have escaped for ever from weariness. Here on earth the sun smites upon us with its burning heat, and we become very weary. How tired one gets of life sometimes! The strain of even an ordinary existence is so great, not only from its outward circumstances, but from its continual inward conditions. But the souls in Paradise are at rest. No longer does the corruptible body weigh down the incorruptible soul; no longer have they to bear the heavy burden of this mortal flesh; no longer does 'the sun light upon them, nor any heat'; they enjoy the deep, abiding, and refreshing rest of Paradise.

II. They have the rest of freedom from life's anxieties. There is no care there; 'they shall hunger no more, neither thirst any more'; they are freed from anxiety as to their own perseverance, from the terrible anxiety of living under conditions of known spiritual peril. Theirs is the rest of temptation escaped; the rest that comes after the battle has been fought out to its extremest limits; it is the rest of attained security.

III. They enjoy the rest of spiritual satisfaction. Here, it is our very beatitude to know unsatisfied desire: 'Blessed are they that hunger and thirst after righteousness;' and well we know by experience the truth of this beatitude, for our progress is marked by increasing desire, and every Eucharist adds to the intensity of the longing of the soul after God.

IV. There is also the rest of Service. We carry with us into Paradise consciousness, memory, and the power of communion with the Lord. It must therefore surely follow that if we are present with the Lord, sharing His Love, blending our will with His high purpose, the rest of Paradise must be the rest of activity; and one undoubted sphere of that activity is the Ministry of Intercession. The saints within the veil are ever bearing us upon their hearts, as they think of us as being on the perilous journey of earthly life; and their supplications blend with the Mighty Sacrifice offered by the Great High Priest at the Golden Altar, as He intercedes for His Church on earth.

V. Yet, once again, and sweetest thought of all, the waiting souls are living in the rest of Hope. There is a restlessness even in their rest, and through it they know the crowning joy of Paradise, as they cry from beneath the Altar, 'How long, O Lord, how long?' In this life of hope they have foretastes of the greater joys that await them in heaven; they look for the joy of Resurrection when they shall live once more an embodied life, but in a resurrection body, conformed to the glory of the risen Lord; they look for the joy of 'His appearing,' for that fulness of bliss which they shall know when they shall wake up after His likeness and be satisfied with it. They have the anticipation of all that awaits them in the glorious Resurrection life of the Saints, and ever, under the power of the grace of Jesus, does this joyful hope grow clearer as the entranced spirits enter deeper into the secrets of their future life in heaven.

—George Body, *The Good Shepherd*, p. 99.

THE FEEDING OF THE LAMB

' The Lamb which is in the midst of the throne shall feed them.
—Rev. vii. 17.

The first words which John ever heard of Jesus were words that described Him as a Lamb. When John was a disciple of the Baptist's, drinking in inspiration from that stern teacher, he had heard these words fall from the Baptist's lips, 'Behold the Lamb of God which taketh away the sin of the world'. What experiences John had had and what a vast deal he had suffered when he came to write this book of Revelation! Yet in Revelation some seven and twenty times John repeats the sweet expression Lamb of God—the first words he had ever heard of Christ. How blessed is a life when from its first stage to its last there runs through it one regulating thought!

I. Christ in heaven to-day is the very Christ who walked by the banks of Jordan. I think we all need to be assured of that, for we are very prone to disbelieve it. We know that He is no longer rejected and despised, and we know that the body of His humiliation has been glorified, until insensibly we transfer these changes from His outward nature to His heart, as though death and resurrection had altered that. So do we conceive Christ as far away from us, separated from the beating of the human heart; glorious, yet not so full of tender brotherhood as in the days of Capernaum and Bethany. That error is combated by the vision of the Lamb in heaven. Purity, gentleness, and sacrifice are there.

II. Another thought which our text suggests is this, that we shall need Christ in heaven as much as we do here. The Lamb which is in the midst of the throne shall feed them—even in heaven there shall be no feeding without Christ. We all know in some measure how great and how constant is our need of Christ on earth. Are we not prone to imagine that in the world beyond the need of being nourished by Christ Jesus will be less? However such an idea may arise within us, remember that it is not the conception of the Bible. All that we owe to Him on earth is but a tithe of what we shall owe to Him when we awake. It is suggested, too, by the words of the original that this feeding shall be a perpetual process. The love of God will expand and deepen endlessly so that every fresh hour will have its sweet surprise.

III. Lastly, and most significant of all, will you note the position in which the Lamb is standing. In the very centre and seat of power He has His place: He is the Lamb in the midst of the throne. That means that the redeemed shall be fed not only gently, but by one who stands in the place of sovereign power.—G. H. MORRISON, The Unlighted Lustre, p. 259.

'God shall wipe away every tear.'—REV. VII. 17.

'How can we conceive,' James Smetham once wrote, 'of a complete joy, if those we love are not there with us? I dare hardly turn my eyes this way. It is like the beginning of our agony to think of eternal separation; it seems as if it would fill eternity with tears. What is that view of Truth that will wipe all tears away? What that consent to the Divine Rectitude which cannot permit a diminished joy even when the wicked are silent in darkness? I need help for such thoughts as these—God bring all we

love safe within that circle of glory. God grant we may have no loves on earth that will not be everlasting.'

HER sympathy for man is not the 'child of golden hope,' but of deep and tender pity. The grave will right many wrongs, the future will bring in a peaceful, better time—what more can science or its religion promise? Not that God will wipe away the tears from every eye; for its heaven is only the vision of the ideal, and never can be a fact.—DR. WILLIAM BARRY, on George Eliot.

IN a letter to his father, written out of a fit of youthfull melancholy, Burns alludes to this passage thus: 'I am more pleased with the 15th, 16th, and 17th verses of the seventh chapter of Revelation, than with any ten times as many verses in the whole Bible, and would not exchange the noble enthusiasm with which they inspire me for all that this world has to offer. As for this world, I despair of ever making a figure in it. Indeed I am altogether unconcerned at the thoughts of this life.'

REFERENCES.—VII. 17.—Spurgeon, Sermons, vol. xi. No. 643. J. Morlais Jones, Christian World Pulpit, vol. lvi. p. 356. J. Keble, Sermons for the Sundays After Trinity, p. 229. Ibid. Miscellaneous Sermons, p. 340.

REV. VIII. I.

MR. A. C. BENSON writes: 'I think that there are few verses of the Bible that give one a more sudden and startling thrill than the verse at the beginning of the eighth chapter of the Revelation. "And when he had opened the seventh seal there was silence in heaven about the space of half an hour." The very simplicity of the words, the homely note of specified time, is in itself deeply impressive. But further, it gives the dim sense of some awful and unseen preparation going forward, a period allowed in which those that stood by, august and majestic as they were, should collect their courage, should make themselves ready with bated breath for some dire pageant.'

REFERENCES.—VIII. 1.—W. F. Shaw, Sermon Sketches for the Christian Year, p. 66. VIII. 11.—J. Keble, Sermons for the Saints' Days, p. 362.

'Woe, woe, woe, for them that dwell on the earth, by reason of the other voices of the trumpet of the three angels, who are yet to sound.'—REV. VIII. 13.

COMPARE Mrs. Oliphant's analysis of Botticelli's special trait, in her Makers of Florence (p. 353). 'It is,' she observes, 'to be seen in his pictures of all subjects, even in his "Venus"—a cloud somewhere shadowing the sun, a perception dim and terrible of griefs that must come, howsoever they may be disguised, or how distant soever they may be for the moment. This is the very soul and sentiment of his work, his highest inspiration in art.'

'And he opened the pit of the abyss.'—REV. IX. 2.

MILTON alludes to this passage in the great apostrophe towards the close of his Reformation in England, where he invites the Triune God on behalf of England's peace and purity. 'Look upon this, Thy poor and almost spent and expiring Church, leave her not thus a prey to these importunate wolves, that wait and think long till they devour Thy tender flock; these wild boars that have broke into Thy vineyard, and left the print of their polluting hoofs upon the souls of Thy servants. O let them not bring about their damned designs, that stand now at the entrance of the bottomless pit, expecting the watchword to open, and let out those dreadful locusts and scorpions, to reinvolve us in that pitchy cloud of infernal darkness, where we shall never more see the sun of Thy truth again, never hope for the cheerful dawn, never more hear the bird of morning sing. Be moved with pity at the afflicted state of this our shaken monarchy, that now lies labouring under her throes, and struggling against the grudges of more dreaded enemies.'

If God permit the lid of evil to be lifted as a test or as a punishment, the key remains in His hand to secure that lid again when He will. But if I lift any lid of evil, I have no power to shut off the dire escape from myself or from others: death and defilement I may let loose, but I cannot recapture.— C. G. ROSSETTI.

'And there came out of the smoke locusts upon the earth: and unto them was given power, as the scorpions of the earth have power.'—REV. IX. 3 f.

COLERIDGE, in his second Lay Sermon, sees political empirics, demagogues, and 'noisy and calumnious zealots' in the figures which 'St. John beheld in the apocalyptic vision as a compound of locust and scorpion. They are not,' he continues, 'of one place or of one season. They are the perennials of history; and though they may disappear for a time, they exist always in the egg, and need only a distempered atmosphere and an accidental ferment to start up into life and activity.' In a subsequent note he toys with the fancy that no other images 'could form more appropriate and significant exponents of a seditious and riotous multitude, with the mob-orators, their heads or leaders, than the thousands of pack-horses with heads resembling those of a roaring wild beast, with smoke, fire, and brimstone (that is, empty, unintelligible, incendiary, calumnious, and offensively foul language) issuing from their mouth'.

THE FICTIONS OF SIN
'On their heads were as it were crowns like gold.'— REV. IX. 7.

THESE mystical locusts have been very differently construed by various scholars, but it will be better and safer for us to agree that they personify the lusts and passions which destroy the soul, and which therefore destroy all things. The text suggests that sin effects great things, that it promises great things, and yet fails to give what it promises. The crown it boasts is not real, solid, golden, but a mere figure of speech —'as it were'. There is a terrible irony in sin.

I. There is no reality in the *greatness* that men seek in the spirit of selfishness and lust. Take a selfish conqueror, of whom Napoleon is the type.

Take a selfish poet, and let Byron be our typical instance. Whatever is built on egotism, violence, covetousness, or any other form and quality of unrighteousness, inherits only an apparitional crown.

II. There is no reality in the *wealth* that is obtained unrighteously or used selfishly. (1) Look at *illegitimate* wealth—wealth gotten by immoral means. (2) And there is much the same deception and disappointment in all *unspiritual* wealth. Balzac built himself a splendid mansion, but when it was finished he had no money left wherewith to furnish it, and so he proceeded to furnish it in imagination: here, according to a ticket, hung a great picture, there stood a rich cabinet, yonder a superb table—the place fluttered with labels, but the realities were missing. It is much the same with the selfish, unspiritual rich. They have certificates, title deeds, receipts, parchments, bank books declaring the soundness of their investments, the reality of their estate, but their wealth is no fact in their deepest life, there is no corresponding sentiment in their brain and heart. Have no unrighteous wealth; it will only deceive and curse you.

III. There is no reality in the *pleasure* that sin promises. Seek genuine, solid satisfactions. During his last days Verlaine, the brilliant French poet, was occupied in covering the squalid furniture of his squalid rooms with gold paint. The reason of the poor fellow was gone, and it pleased his wild eye and disordered fancy to reckon the worthless furniture of his miserable lodging as the golden furniture of palaces. So the distempered soul drugged with the opium of vanity and passion looks upon base, vulgar, ugly, and ruinous things and habits as altogether beautiful and precious. But Verlaine's yellow furniture did not sell for gold, and the day inevitably comes when those who have lived a worldly and godless life awake to the vanity of the things and pursuits for which they gave and suffered so much. It is in the truth and grace and power of God in Christ that we realise all the rich and enduring satisfactions of the heart. There is no 'as it were' in Him. No mimic crown, no ghostly garland, no mocking prize. —W. L. WATKINSON, *The Blind Spot*, p. 267.

THE CRAFT AND CRUELTY OF SIN
'And they had hair as the hair of women, and their teeth were as the teeth of lions.'—REV. IX. 8.

CONSPICUOUS in the Apocalypse are many strange creatures—locusts like horses, great dragons having seven heads and ten horns, a beast rising out of the sea having seven heads and ten horns, 'and the beast was like unto a leopard, and his feet were as the feet of a bear, and his mouth as the mouth of a lion'. The grotesque imagery of the Apocalypse has a moral significance which, above all things, must be fully understood and applied. These mixed, bizarre, inconceivable creatures—exaggerated scorpions, red dragons, huge locusts, and serpents represent the various forms and powers of evil, and they must be so interpreted. Let us therefore expound the text in this special light, and broadly consider its teachings on the craft and cruelty of sin.

I. The Craft of Sin.—'They had hair as the hair of women.' The soft, silken, shiny hair stands for the speciousness and persuasiveness of temptation. Evil circumvents us with deep and delicate snares, until even those who walk warily hardly walk surely. (1) Sometimes it affects the guise of *love*. (2) Sin often identifies itself with *beauty*. (3) Evil often assumes the *festal aspect*. (4) Sin often glides in as *fashion*. (5) Sin is sometimes incarnated as *glory*. (6) Finally, sin appeals to us in the guise of *virtue* and *religion*. The master-stroke of evil is to play itself off as holiness and devotion. Yet let us not forget that the secret of sin's fascination is in the distempered soul itself.

II. The Cruelty of Sin.—'Their teeth were as the teeth of lions.' How sharp and startling is the contrast presented in the text—woman's hair, lion's teeth! Yes; and how sharp and startling is the contrast between the beginnings and the endings of transgression! There is no cruelty like the cruelty of sin, and no suffering like that which it occasions. (1) Let us believe in the reality and seriousness of spiritual peril. We need to get the sobering thought into our heart, and we shall get it into our heart if we live much with Christ. (2) Let us seek salvation in the Spirit and grace of God, made manifest in Jesus Christ. Such is the power of evil in the world, and such the guile of our own heart, that we can never successfully deal with temptation by mere knowledge and natural firmness. We must be illuminated, inspired, and fortified by the spirit of God freely acting through our whole being.—W. L. WATKINSON, *The Bane and the Antidote*, p. 149.

REFERENCES.—IX. 12.—*Expositor* (6th Series), vol. ix. p. 462. IX. 14.—*Ibid.* p. 316. IX. 20.—*Ibid.* (7th Series), vol. vi. p. 275. X. 5, 6.—J. C. M. Bellew, *Sermons*, vol. i. p. 293. *Expositor* (5th Series), vol. iv. p. 156.

'The mystery of God shall be finished, according to the good tidings which He declared to the prophets.'—REV. x. 7.

COMPARE Savonarola's outburst, with a similar oxymoron, in his Advent addresses to the Florentines in 1494. After a scathing exposure of Rome's iniquities, he cries: 'Hasten the chastisement and the scourge, that we may quickly return to Thee. . . . The only hope that now remains to us, is that the sword of God may soon smite the earth.'

REFERENCE.—X. 8.—A. Whyte, *Christian World Pulpit*, vol. xliii. p. 403.

'It was in my mouth sweet as honey; and when I had eaten it, my belly was made bitter.'—REV. x. 10.

ALTHOUGH Divine inspiration must certainly have been sweet to those ancient prophets, yet the irksomeness of that truth which they brought was so unpleasant unto them, that everywhere they call it a burden. Yea, that mysterious book of revelation, which the great evangelist was bid to eat, as it had been some eye-brightening electuary of knowledge and foresight, though it were sweet in his mouth, and in the learning, it was bitter in his belly, bitter in the denouncing. Nor was this hid from the wise poet Sophocles, who in that place of his tragedy where Teiresias is called to resolve King Œdipus in a matter which he knew would be grievous, brings him in bemoaning his lot, that he knew more than other men. . . . But when God commands to take the trumpet, and blow a dolorous or a jarring blast, it lies not in man's will what he shall say, or what he shall conceal.—MILTON.

REFERENCES.—X. 10.—R. F. Horton, *Christian World Pulpit*, vol. lxi. p. 273. *Expositor* (6th Series), vol. x. p. 356. XI. 2.—S. Baring-Gould, *Village Preaching for a Year*, vol. ii. p. 290. XI. 3-13.—*Expositor* (6th Series), vol. x. p. 12. XI. 5.—R. J. Drummond, *Faith's Certainties*, p. 383.

'The two witnesses.'—REV. XI. 7.

LORD, I read of the two witnesses, 'and when they shall have finished their testimony, the beast that ascendeth out of the bottomless pit shall make war against them and shall overcome them and kill them'. They could not be killed whilst they were doing, but when they had done their work; during their employment they were invincible. No better armour against the darts of death than to be busied in Thy service.—THOMAS FULLER.

THE CITY: ITS SIN AND SAVIOUR

'The great city, which spiritually is called Sodom and Egypt, where also our Lord was crucified.'—REV. XI. 8.

THE fact that our Lord was crucified nigh unto the sacred city is a suggestive fact we shall do well to ponder.

I. The Sinfulness of the City.—Which spiritually is called Sodom and Egypt. Not that the obscenity and visible horror of Sodom were features of Jerusalem, but the sacred city resembled Sodom in its internal and vicious condition. Egypt was the land of slavery and persecution, and Israel had spiritually taken the place of Egypt, reproduced the characteristics of Egypt. The point specially to be observed is, that Jerusalem had become thus infamous through the abuse of religious privilege. It was a religious city that was spiritually called Sodom and Egypt; perverted religious opportunity made it pre-eminent in iniquity and retribution. All evils come to their worst in great cities; the evils exist in petty forms and inconspicuous colours in rustic scenes, but the wealth, liberty, numbers, and rivalry of a great city bring them out broadly and luridly. It is a forcing-bed where every vice attains abnormal growth. And when the benign influences of religion are rejected, the wickedness is in the same proportion aggravated.

II. The Saviour of the City.—'Where also our Lord was crucified.' Christ crucified is the one antidote for the city's wickedness and woe, even when that city is Jerusalem. We are not going to cleanse, enlighten, uplift, and idolise our cities without God; and then it will only be through God as He has been pleased to reveal Himself in His redeeming Son. Every sin that blasts the city is condemned in the cross; every inspiration that saves it flows from the cross. Calvary testifies to the everlasting righteousness of God, to His mercy to the penitent, to His sympathy and grace with up-struggling humanity. Only in the cross do we get at the root of the mischief; only there do we find the essential blessing. God is in Christ crucified, reconciling the world unto Himself; and only as sinners find their way to the foot of the cross are Babylon, Sodom, and Egypt transformed into the City of God. 'And he carried me away in the Spirit to a great and high mountain, and showed me that great city, the holy Jerusalem, descending out of heaven from God.'—W. L. WATKINSON, *The Ashes of Roses*, p. 68.

REFERENCES.—XI. 12.—Spurgeon, *Sermons*, vol. ix. No. 488. XI. 15.—C. J. Ridgeway, *The King and His Kingdom*, p. 29. W. Watson, *Christian World Pulpit*, vol. lvi. p. 389. Bishop Dowden, *Religion in Relation to the Social and Political Life of England*, No. 6. T. Arnold, *Sermons*, vol. iv. p. 310. F. T. Bassett, *Things that Must Be*, p. 72. *Expositor* (5th Series), vol. ii. p. 349. XI. 16, 17.—W. H. Hutchings, *Sermon Sketches*, p. 18. XI. 18.—*Expositor* (6th Series), vol. x. p. 362.

THE ARK AND ITS NEW SANCTUARY

'And there was seen in His temple the ark of His covenant.'
—REV. XI. 19.

I. THIS vision of the ark in heaven suggests that the worship of God is henceforth to direct itself towards a new centre. Under the old dispensation the ark was a witness to the root-principles of true worship. It contained within itself the mementoes of those facts and truths from which the Covenant tie between God and His people was woven, and which must ever be kept in mind by those who would enjoy fellowship with God. (1) This vision implies that the worship of a humanity regenerated by the discipline of judgment will find its centre and resting-place in the selfsame principles which were foreshadowed by the ordinances of the first tabernacle. The proclamation by great voices in heaven. 'The kingdoms of this world are become the kingdoms of our Lord and of His Christ,' herald a new and better theocracy; and as the ark of the Covenant was the keystone of the old, so are the truths illustrated by its emblems essentials of the new. (2) This glimpse of an ark in the celestial temple suggests that the new centre of worship is catholic and not national. (3) The vision seems to indicate the growing religious capacity of the race. John implies in this vision that all worship will at last pour itself forth where God has fixed the true mercy-seat, and the places on earth accounted holy will be left behind by the soaring faith of the believer.

II. The Covenant ark in heaven is the pledge of victory and external salvation to the chosen people. Napoleon Bonaparte once said: 'A man must feel himself a child of fortune if he is to brace his soul to fortitude'. That cynical and godless man had probably ceased to feel himself a pet of the Fates when he began to blunder, and brought about, in due time, his own irretrievable overthrow. In presence of the ark of God's Covenant in the ever-open temple, the servant of Jesus Christ may always realise that a resistless providence is on his side, and that he can suffer no final defeat. The Covenant ark in heaven is a landmark of the inheritance which God has promised to them that love Him. The ark of the Covenant seen by John precedes the pilgrim saints into the new land of promise, and asserts their birthright in 'the city whose builder and maker is God'. It puts the patriarchs in possession of that better country which they never found on earth. If we are servants of the Covenant, and in accord with its demands, it is already claiming our inheritance for us. The symbolic ark has been carried amidst exulting songs into its last resting-place. It has passed into the realms of light, and, in view of the one Church in heaven and on earth, waits there till the last weary fainting warrior, the last pale footsore woman, the last halting child, has crossed the flood, and every jot and tittle of the Covenant promise has been fulfilled.

REFERENCES.—XI. 19.—Spurgeon, *Sermons*, vol. xxvii. No. 1621; vol. xli. No. 2427. XII. 1-5.—Bishop Gore, *Christian World Pulpit*, vol. xliv. p. 33. XII. 2.—*Expositor* (4th Series), vol. ii. p. 290.

ST. MICHAEL AND ALL ANGELS

'Michael and his angels.'—REV. XII. 7.

TRADITION says that the Feast of St. Michael and all Angels was first celebrated in the fourth century; but history states that its general observance did not occur until the eighth century, when it became an annual festival. Since then the Eastern Church has observed it on 8th November; the Anglican Church on 29th September.

The belief in angelic creatures has been a favourite article in the universal creed, but the most unequivocal and direct evidence of their existence and ministry is to be found in the Bible. Fifteen, at least, of the inspired writers have described them.

I. Of the vast number of the holy angels there is very little doubt. The Jewish Rabbis state that 'nothing exists without an attendant angel, not even a blade of grass'. The great Aquinas asserts that 'there are more angels than all substances together, celestial and terrestrial, animate and inanimate'. St. Gregory calculates that 'there are so many angels as there are elect'. Charles Kingsley maintains that 'in every breeze there are living spirits, and God's angels guide the thunder-clouds'. But what saith the Scripture? On its pages their number is variously stated. As Jacob was on his way back to his native land 'the angels of God met him'. In his last benediction Moses speaks of 'ten thousand'. When Elisha prayed that his servant's eyes might be opened, 'he saw, and behold the mountain was full of horses and chariots of fire round about'. In his vision of the Ancient of Days, Daniel beheld 'thousand thousands ministering unto Him, and ten thousand times ten thousand standing before Him'. St. John did but echo this language in one of his gorgeous descriptions of Heaven when he described the angels as a vast assembly 'which no man could number'. At the advent of Jesus there appeared 'a multitude of the heavenly host,' and one dark eventide, near Gethsemane, He declared to Peter that if He prayed to His Father He would give Him 'more than twelve legions of angels'.

II. But all the angels are not of the same rank. Michael, for example, is represented in Scripture as being the next in rank to the Angel-Jehovah. In the Book of Daniel he is spoken of as 'one of the chief princes' in the celestial hierarchy, and in the Book of St. John as 'the archangel'.

III. A word may now be added about the ministry of angels. They were ever the servants of Jesus during His incarnate life, as they are now in His glorified life ; and sometimes God has employed them to punish the wicked. The Collect for this Festival speaks of the succour and defence which they may render to us, and it is well to remember that they are God's ministers, and 'do His pleasure'. 'Babes,' says Manton, 'have their guardian angels' ; and Bengel asserts that 'the angels take care of the little ones ; and so much the more the less they are able to protect themselves' ; while Keble ascribes the 'first soft smile' of sleeping infancy to their presence, and, in his own poetic and beautiful manner, represents their smile as 'a gleam from heaven's deep sea of love'. And a Greater than these has said that the angels of the little ones do always behold the Face of their Father in Heaven.

It may be true that holy angels render service to unholy men ; but, according to the Bible, they are specially 'sent forth to do service for the sake of them that shall inherit salvation'. Nor do they forget the body which enshrined the soul. They guard its sleeping-place, as they did the sepulchre of Jesus, until the early dawn of the resurrection, when they will give up their trust.

REFERENCES.—XII. 7.—R. E. Hutton, *The Crown of Christ*, p. 281. H. S. Holland, *Christian World Pulpit*, vol. xlviii. p. 209. XII. 8.—W. H. Barlow, *Christian World Pulpit*, vol. xlix. p. 372.

'The accuser of our brethren.'—REV. XII. 10.

THE character in which he [Blake] abhors and renounces Satan is that of 'the accuser of sins'. The monarch of hell might be the antagonist of many things accounted sacred, and might exercise wild volcanic forces in many inconvenient directions, and yet incur small blame from Blake ; but it is a different matter when the same personage accuses others of sins. . . . *There* lies the fatal flaw in Satan. 'Every religion that preaches vengeance for sin is the religion of the enemy and avenger, and not of the forgiver of sin ; and their God is Satan named by the Divine name.'—W. M. ROSSETTI, upon Blake.

REFERENCES.—XII. 10.—*Expositor* (4th Series), vol. v. p. 291 ; *ibid.* (6th Series), vol. viii. p. 327.

'They overcame him by the blood of the Lamb.'—REV. XII. 11.

BISHOP DANIEL WILSON preached from this text at St. Bride's Church in 1846, on behalf of the Church Missionary Society. He only paid one visit to England during his quarter of a century's episcopate in India and his sermon was the chief event of his furlough. His heads were (1) the mighty foe, (2) the means of resisting him, (3) the issue of the conflict. At the close he used this expression : 'Then may we humbly hope that being washed, covered, plunged, hidden in the blood of the Lamb, we shall pass as one of our commentators [Dr. Gill] sublimely speaks, "under the purple covering triumphantly to glory".'

REFERENCES.—XII. 11.—Spurgeon, vol. xxi. No. 1237 ; vol. xxxiv. No. 2043. XII. 12.—Spurgeon, *Sermons*, vol. xxv. No. 1502.

'And the earth helped the woman.'—REV. XII. 16.

I LIKE to see the *earth* helping the *woman*. I do not plead very earnestly for any particular church, but I would have a well-formed machinery fixed in every country—ducts of irrigation—through which the predominant religion, whatever it is, may diffuse its streams of Christian instruction.—CHALMERS, in 1830.

REFERENCE.—XII. 16.—Bishop Boyd-Carpenter, *Christian World Pulpit*, vol. lv. p. 337.

'And the dragon went to make war with . . . those who keep the commandments of God, and have the testimony of Jesus Christ.'—REV. XII. 17.

IN his *Holy War*, Bunyan describes the various Captains of the Devil's army against Mansoul, one of whom is 'Captain Pope ; his standard-bearer bare the red colours, and his scutcheon was the stake, the flame, and the good man in it'.

'And I saw a beast coming up out of the sea . . . and all the world wondered after the beast.'—REV. XIII. 1-3.

LOUIS NAPOLEON was a symbol and creature of his time, which divided with him the crime of the *coup d'état*. He had his day, and paid his debt at the end of it to the retributory powers. But while his day lasted, and he seemed to thrive, he was an ugly object in the eyes of those who believed in some sort of providence.—FROUDE.

'THE same day,' writes Carlyle in his account of the French orgies in 1793, 'while this brave Carmagnole-dance has hardly jigged itself out, there arrive Procureur Chaumette and Municipals and Departmentals, and with them the strangest freightage : a New Religion ! Demoiselle Candeille of the opera, a woman fair to look upon, when well rouged ; she, borne on palanquin shoulder-high, with red woollen nightcap, in azure mantle, garlanded with oak, holding in her hand the Pike of the Jupiter-*Peuple*, sails in, heralded by white young women girt in tricolor. Let the world consider it ! This, O National Convention, wonder of the Universe, is our New Divinity ; *Goddess of Reason*, worthy, and alone worthy, of revering. Her henceforth we adore. Nay, were it too much to ask of our august National Representation that it also went with us to the *ci-devant* Cathedral called of Notre-Dame, and executed a few strophes in worship of her? . . . Other mysteries, seemingly of a Cabiric or Paphian character, we leave under the Veil, which appropriately stretches itself "along the pillars of the aisles"—not to be lifted aside by the hand of History.'

REFERENCES.—XIII. 1, 2.—F. T. Bassett, *Things that Must Be*, p. 1. XIII. 2, 5, 6.—H. Edwards, *Penny Pulpit*, No. 1499, p. 129.

'The whole earth wondered after the beast.'—REV. XIII. 3.

MALMESBURY gives us the beginning of the marriage story;—how the prince reeled into chapel to be married; how he hiccuped out his vows of fidelity— you know how he kept them; how he pursued the woman whom he had married; to what a state he brought her; with what blows he struck her; with what malignity he pursued her; what his treatment of his daughter was; and what his own life. *He the first gentleman in Europe!* There is no stronger satire on the proud English society of that day, than that they admired George.—THACKERAY, on 'George the Fourth'.

'Who is like unto the beast?'—REV. XIII. 4

THERE is as great vice in praising, and as frequent, as in detracting.—BEN JONSON.

THERE never was a mean and abject mind that did not admire an intrepid and dexterous villain.— BURKE.

REFERENCE.—XIII. 5-8.—*Expositor* (6th Series), vol. xii. p. 103.

'And all that dwell upon the earth shall worship him, whose names are not written in the book of life of the Lamb slain from the foundation of the world.'—REV. XIII. 8.

ON a certain time, as I was walking in the fields, the Lord said unto me: *Thy name is written in the Lamb's book of life, which was before the foundation of the world*. And as the Lord spake it, I believed, and saw it in the new birth.—Fox's *Journal*.

REFERENCES.—XIII. 8.—*Expositor* (5th Series), vol. iv. p. 277; *ibid.* vol. v. p. 416.

'Here is the patience and the faith of the saints.'— REV. XIII. 10.

HE was an absolute sepulchre in the swallowing of oppression and ill-usage. It vanished in him. There was no echo of complaint, no murmur of resentment from the hollows of that soul. The blows that fell upon him resounded not, and no one but God remembered them.—GEORGE MACDONALD, in *Robert Falconer*.

COMPARE, for the idea of impatience and irritation as fatal to character, the description of the French put by Lord Lytton, in *My Novel*, into the mouth of Mr. Caxton. 'Sir, their whole political history, since the great meeting of the Tiers Etat, has been the history of men who would rather go to the devil than be bitten by a flea. It is the record of human impatience, that seeks to force time, and expects to grow forests from the spawn of a mushroom.'

As Dr. Birkbeck Hill rightly observes of Gibbon: 'After the long war that he had waged against the stifling of truth by the Church of Rome, his fall was deep indeed, when, under the terror inspired by the French Revolution, he urged some Portuguese gentlemen not to give up, at such a crisis, the Inquisition'.

CONTRAST Dr. Johnson's theory, in his well-known note to the first scene of 'Henry the Fourth' (first part): 'The lawfulness and justice of the holy wars have been much disputed, but perhaps here is a principle on which the question may be easily determined. If it be part of the religion of the Mahommedans to extirpate by the sword all other religions, it is, by the law of self-defence, lawful for men of every other religion, and for Christians among others, to make war upon Mahommedans, simply as Mahommedans, as men obliged by their own principles to make war upon Christians, and only lying in wait till opportunity shall promise them success.'

THE BEAST WITH LAMB'S HORNS

'Another beast . . and he had two horns like a lamb.'— REV. XIII. 11.

I AM not at present concerned with the precise recognition of this beast. I only want to lay hold of this predominant fact: the beast wore some characteristics that are suggestive of Him that sitteth on the Throne. But here I am told that the deceiver has some of the Redeemer's characteristics! He is a beast, but with 'horns like a lamb'. The beast mimics the Lamb. Let us consider this nefarious ministry of mimicry.

I. The Devil makes us trifle with moral destiny. 'The serpent said unto the woman, Ye shall not surely die'. Sin does not spell death! Is the deceptiveness effective? Let us consult our hearts. We are deluded by the horns, and we become the victims of the beast.

II. And the Devil assumes the colour of the general surroundings. He hides himself in the common standards.

III. And the Devil allures us by æsthetic appeals. The Devil can besiege the senses and captivate by the pleasurable sensations.

IV. And the Devil deludes us by the mirage of material satisfaction. He disguises the dry desert, and it bewitches us as an apparent land of springs. He makes us thirst and haste, and, lo! we discover sand! 'He showed him all the kingdoms of the world, and the glory of them.' How fascinating, and yet how delusive!—J. H. JOWETT, *The British Congregationalist*, p. 118.

REFERENCES.—XIII. 11.—*Expositor* (4th Series), vol. iv. p. 325. XIII. 12.—*Ibid.* (5th Series), vol. i. p. 351. XIII. 13. —*Ibid.* vol. viii. p. 183. XIII. 14.—*Ibid.* (4th Series), vol. vii. p. 412. XIII. 15.—*Ibid.* vol. ii. p. 285. XIII. 18.— *Ibid.* (6th Series), vol. i. p. 394. XIV. 1-3.—Spurgeon, *Sermons*, vol. iii. No. 110. XIV. 2, 4, 6.—J. C. M. Bellew, *Sermons*, vol. iii. p. 64.

A NEW SONG

(*For Holy Innocents' Day*)

'And they sung as it were a new song before the throne.'—
REV. XIV. 3.

WHY, when heaven is yet ringing with the bright message of peace, does the wailing of Ramah, of Bethlehem, shriek in upon it with discordant jar? Perhaps the words of to-day's Epistle may suggest our attitude while feeling after the teaching of the Holy Spirit on this festival.

The Apostle in his vision is contemplating a great company standing with the Lamb on Mount Zion, worshipping before the throne, and from that throne proceeds a voice as of many waters, and the voice of a great thunder.

I. **It may be that the Teaching of Holy Innocents' Day is part of the New Song of the Church** which comes forth from the throne of God. For it is the song of infant wailing, an inarticulate cry, the song of those 'whose only language is a cry,' a cry of pain, of anguish, and of misery. All who came near Christ more or less suffered by approaching Him, just as if earthly trouble and pain went out of Him, as some precious virtue, for the good of their soul. Surely this is part of the new song of Holy Innocents' Day, the true meaning of suffering in the economy of the world.

II. **The Song that Mounts up before the Throne To-day is also a Song without Words.**—It tells of no great achievements, no mighty actions. It tells of nameless fame, of passionless renown, of the glorious blessing of innocency as one of the choicest treasures of heaven. There is no other strain like it. Imperfection mingles with the song and the glory of the greatest martyrs. But they are without fault before the throne of God. The honour bestowed on little children—the honour which belongs to innocency—is another distinguishing mark of Christianity, the new song which the Church has tried to learn. Is the Holy Innocents' Day put there simply to daunt us, and to kindle remorse, and aggravate our loss? No, we can in a sense make ourselves young again. We can go straight to our Father's home, and ask Him to teach us even in this weary world, 'Lord, what wouldst Thou have me to do?'

'And they sing as it were a new song before the throne.'—
REV. XIV. 3.

WHAT a blessing it is that there are things so good and delightful that no repetition of them can convert them into bores! Were there not some such things, eternity would be but a melancholy prospect for us. The song of heaven is called a new song, although I suppose its elements must always be the same, to express its unwearying nature. The affections are always new.—ERSKINE of Linlathen, in a letter to his sister.

REFERENCES.—XIV. 3.—H. Woodcock, *Sermon Outlines* (1st Series), p. 45. Bishop Wilberforce, *Sermons*, p. 169. *Expositor* (5th Series), vol. viii. p. 463; *ibid.* vol. x. p. 153.

'These are they which follow the Lamb whithersoever He goeth. These were redeemed from among men, being the firstfruits unto God and to the Lamb.'—REV. XIV. 4.

CHRISTMAS Day is followed by three other holy days: St. Stephen, St. John, and the Innocents. Now, why is this? Why are these three holy days put thus close together, and made to follow immediately after Christmas? And why, of all the New Testament Saints, should these three be chosen to be, as it were, the train of followers appointed to wait on the Saviour at His Birth?

I. They are examples of the fruits of the Incarnation; instances of the work of restoration, and cleansing, and refining, by Christ of that nature which in Adam had been ruined; instances of what His Coming in the Flesh could do to make men like Himself, and fit for His Glory. Thus the Festival of St. Stephen, a man like ourselves, yet raised so high as to shed his blood for the truth, and pray for his murderers; of St. John, also like one of us, yet so sanctified that he spake of the love of God as only the Lord Himself spoke of it; of the Innocents, like other children, yet whose deaths as speechless infants, the saddest of all fates here, turned the curse and penalty of Adam's sin into a crown of glory—these were joined on to Christmas Day as the marks and trophies of His Christmas victory.

II. They show us that Christ's blessing is not confined to one way of serving Him, to one sort of people, but is meant for all sorts and conditions and ages; that He has a place in His kingdom for young and old, for small and great. His saints will include men cut off in their prime, yet who have in a few days fulfilled the work of many; men like St. John, who have filled a long life with the glory and love of God; and also those whom the world despises, as weak and poor, children in age and in understanding, but gentle and sanctified enough to be His witnesses, and to suffer in quietness and silence.

III. They remind us that there are many different ways of serving Christ; many different gifts; many different ways of glorifying Him; yet all are of God, all belong to His one great purpose of saving and sanctifying man, all help on towards His kingdom. St. Stephen's death (premature, from a worldly point of view) does not make St. John's long life and peaceful end less acceptable, less becoming to the beloved disciple of a crucified Master. Early to die, or long to live, are both ways which lead to glory.

IV. They exemplify those special graces (in human type) of which He came down on earth to show the perfect pattern, and which were all united in His person. They show us reflections—faint, indeed, but real—in human souls like our own, of the glories of the Sun of Righteousness. They show us that man can, like Christ, gladly lay down his life for the sake of God, and his brethren; that man can love, after the example, and in the way, in which Christ loved; they show us the type among men of that perfect innocence and humility which was in Him. If we want to be like Christ, we must be like St. Stephen,

St. John, and the Holy Innocents, in those special graces for which we commemorate them.—R. W. Church, *Village Sermons.*

HOLY INNOCENTS' DAY

'These are they which follow the Lamb whithersoever He goeth.'—Rev. xiv. 4.

To-day we commemorate the deaths of the little children slaughtered at Bethlehem to allay the unworthy fear of Herod. The blood-shedding of these little ones, martyrs in deed if not in will, strikes almost a discordant note amid our Christmas festivities. Our hearts are still full of the gladness of the coming of the Child-King. In our ears we still hear the ring of childish laughter, we can still see the brightness of the children's eyes, as they feel that so much of all the Christmas merry-making has been organised in love, that they may have their part in the rejoicing at the birthday of the King In the midst of it all we are pointed to this tragedy of old, the slain little ones, victims to the cruel hatred and fear of an unworthy king. We realise that it is all part of the great strife for our salvation which our Lord waged. These little victims were but the first sacrificed by the powers of evil to retard the progress of the kingdom of light. Cruelty and hatred compassed the death of the King Himself, and since then saints have suffered, blood has been shed, tears have flowed, and martyrs have witnessed by their deaths.

I. The Tragedy of Child-Suffering.—It reminds us, too, of the ever-present tragedy of child-suffering —the suffering which results from the misdoing, cruelty, or neglect of adult people. How sad it all is, and we realise that, like the tragedy of Holy Innocents' Day, it is all the fruit of sin! How many victims are sacrificed, year by year, by the neglect or positive ill-treatment of vicious and cruel parents! Parents so sodden by drink and other demoralising indulgence that natural affection has died within them, or only shines fitfully, making the periods of neglect, violence, and cruelty all the more horrible by contrast. Thank God, much is now being done to alleviate the suffering of little children. We may do much to alleviate this suffering, to stop this continual moral and actual slaying of little innocents, by supporting by every means in our power the carrying of the Gospel, the work of our Church, in the dark places in our cities. This is the true remedy: to lift up Jesus, the Friend for little children ; to reach parents by our Temperance Societies and other reforming parish agencies ; and so sweeten and make wholesome the home influences. And this is work which we can do much to aid, both by personal service and by giving of our means.

II. A Message of Comfort.—*We find a message of comfort* as we turn again to the Epistle for to-day, showing us the state of happiness of little ones gathered by the Good Shepherd into His fold. 'These are they which follow the Lamb whithersoever He goeth; these were redeemed from among men, being the firstfruits unto God and to the Lamb.'

In some of the colonial churches this Epistle is used in place of the usual lesson in the Burial Service at the funerals of little children, and it certainly contains a message of hope and consolation for stricken hearts, bereaved of little loved ones. 'They follow the Lamb.' We, too, seek to follow Him, but, alas! cumbered by our earthly nature, how unworthy is our following! How many are our failures and mistakes! They dwell in His very presence. 'In their mouth is found no guile ; for they are without fault before the throne of God.' Could there be happier conditions of existence or of service? The thought of their perfect bliss may well set ringing again in our hearts the Christmas bells of rejoicing and gladness. Surely every Christian heart must in time learn that the little one, taken in the freshness of its innocency and purity, uncontaminated by the world, is not to be mourned as one lost, but rather to be rejoiced over as a little lamb safely carried to the fold by the kind Shepherd. 'Of such is the kingdom of heaven.' Thus we see that the message of Holy Innocents' Day need not be a sad one to us at all. To the bereaved it may be a joyous and glad one, as they regard these little ones as the 'firstfruits unto the Lamb'. The first of the many little 'children of God' since brought safely to the joy of the presence of their Lord. And it will be a glad one to us all if we learn to follow the Lamb through all the dark paths of life, as they in their happier condition follow Him, bearing the marks of purity, guilelessness and obedience.

' These are they which were not defiled with women ; for they are virgins.'—Rev. xiv. 4.

I am obliged to mention, though I do it with great reluctance, another deep imagination which at this time, the autumn of 1816, takes possession of me— there can be no mistake about the fact ; *viz.*, that it would be the will of God that I should lead a single life. This anticipation, which has held its ground almost continuously ever since—with the break of a month now and a month then, up to 1829, and after that date without any break at all—was more or less connected in my mind with the notion that my calling in life would require such a sacrifice as celibacy involved : as, for instance, missionary work among the heathen, to which I had a great drawing for some years. It also strengthened my feeling of separation from the visible world.—Newman's *Apologia pro Vita Sua.*

This was also a text over which Milton says he 'did not slumber,' taking it as an incentive to purity, which struck 'doubtless at fornication; for marriage must not be called a defilement'.

' These are they which follow the Lamb whithersoever He goeth.'—Rev. xiv. 4.

When Joseph John Gurney was adopting more and more strictly the principles of Quakerism, he wrote in defence of his conduct : 'It will be difficult to the outward man to become more of a Friend, but it is the path of the cross; and of those who had the

Father's name written on their foreheads, St. John heard a voice from heaven saying, "These are they which follow the Lamb *whithersoever* He leadeth them".'

In the last chapter of *Jane Eyre*, Charlotte Brontë applies the same text to the resolute character of St. John Rivers in his missionary career. ' A more resolute, indefatigable pioneer never wrought amidst rocks and dangers. Firm, faithful, and devoted ; full of energy and zeal and truth, he labours for his race. . . . His is the ambition of the high master-spirit, which aims to fill a place in the first rank of those who are redeemed from the earth—who stand without fault before the throne of God ; who share the last mighty victories of the Lamb; who are called and chosen and faithful.'

Keble makes this verse the text of his lines on 'The Holy Innocents' Day'.

' These are they which follow the Lamb whithersoever He goeth.'—Rev. xiv. 4.

John Evelyn, in his Diary, quotes this verse in describing the last hours of his dear son : 'Such a child I never saw ; for such a child I bless God, in whose bosom he is ! May I and mine become as this little child, who now follows the child Jesus, that Lamb of God, in a white robe, whithersoever He goes ; even so, Lord Jesus, *fiat voluntas tua.* Thou gavest him to us, Thou hast taken him from us, blessed be the name of the Lord ! That he had anything acceptable to Thee was from Thy grace alone, seeing from me he had nothing but sin, but that Thou hast pardoned ! Blessed be my God for ever ! Amen.'

References.—XIV. 4.—Spurgeon, *Sermons*, vol. xlii. No. 2456. *Expositor* (7th Series), vol. vi. p. 177.

THE IDEAL CHRISTIAN LIFE

' These are they which follow the Lamb whithersoever He goeth. These were purchased from among men, to be the firstfruits unto God and unto the Lamb. And in their mouth was found no lie : they are without blemish.'— Rev. xiv. 4, 5 (R.V.).

This is a picture, furnished by revelation, of a redeemed society. Its fulness is realised in the life which is to come ; its beginnings are here and now. Although, therefore, the vision of life which is painted for us here belongs in its fulness to the future, we may see its outlines in the present, see now the characteristics of the life here sketched for us ; and we ought to be striving after this ideal every day.

I. In the first place, it is a complete following of Christ. Following Christ is the alpha and omega of the Christian life, and without it there can be no Christian life. To follow Him in the general sense is to live in His spirit, the spirit of trust and obedience towards God, and of loving interest and service towards men, which He manifested. And to follow Him in the particular sense is to say every day with honest and earnest purpose, 'Lord, what wilt Thou have me to do?' not, 'What are others doing,' but, 'What is the will of My Master for me?' Nothing

is clearer to a student of the ways of Christ with men than that His will differs for different people.

II. We come upon the secret of this absolute following : 'These were purchased'. The atonement of Christ is not a cold legal transaction, by virtue of which a certain number of souls are passed over from the power of evil to the power of good ; it is not thus that men are bought ; but by goodness, by love, by the infinite grace of Christ the will is won over, the love of man for God is created, the devotion of the heart is purchased.

III. We see the result of following Christ manifested in the character of these elect souls. 'In their mouth was found no lie : they are without blemish.' Christ imparts this purity to those who follow Him. A more perfect following of Christ, a more perfect union with Him, will mean a more perfect purity. There is nothing that the Bible more strongly insists upon than that we shall be true. And they are without spot, they are pure and clean. Nothing pains a man who is truly seeking to follow Christ, nothing gives him such agony of soul, as the spots and stains that are in his thoughts and desires, on his inner life, spots which he sometimes thinks are gone, which break out again and again, visible it may be to no eye but his own and God's. But it is not impossible, and we are not to lose the desire. It may take a lifetime to achieve it, but it will certainly be achieved by the man who earnestly seeks it, and seeks it in the right way.—Charles Brown, *Light and Life*, p. 23.

References.—XIV. 4, 5.—Spurgeon, *Sermons*, vol. xxxix. No. 2324. XIV. 6.—W. Landels, *Christian World Pulpit*, vol. xlv. p. 363. R. F. Horton, *Christian World Pulpit*, vol. lvi. p. 216. *Expositor* (4th Series), vol. i. p. 34.

' The angel with the everlasting Gospel.'—Rev. xiv. 6, 7.

From this passage Edward Bickersteth preached his great sermon at the Jubilee of the Church Missionary Society in 1848, in St. Anne's Church, Blackfriars. He dwelt on the Gospel as everlasting (1) in contrast with perishing empires ; (2) in contrast to the pretensions of vain philosophy ; (3) in its suitableness to the most urgent wants of mankind ; (4) in the eternal blessings it conveys; (5) in the obligation of every Christian to diffuse it.

Reference.—XIV. 7.—N. D. Hillis, *Christian World Pulpit*, vol. lvii. p. 328.

' If any man worshippeth the beast and his image, he shall drink of the wine of the wrath of God.'—Rev. xiv. 9, 10.

I believe it to be quite one of the crowning wickednesses of this age that we have starved and chilled our faculty of indignation, and neither desire nor dare to punish crimes justly. We have taken up the benevolent idea, forsooth, that justice is to be preventive instead of vindictive ; and we imagine that we are to punish, not in anger, but in expediency ; not that we may give deserved pain to the person in fault, but that we may frighten other people from committing the same fault. . . . But all true justice is vindictive to vice, as it is rewarding to virtue. Only —and herein it is distinguished from personal revenge—it is vindictive of the wrong done, not of the wrong done to *us*. It is the rational expression of deliberate anger, as of deliberate gratitude; it is not exemplary or even corrective, but essentially retributive; it is the absolute art of measured recompense, giving honour where honour is due, and shame where shame is due, and joy where joy is due, and pain where pain is due.—Ruskin, *Lectures on Art*, iii.

References.—XIV. 9-11.—*Expositor* (4th Series), vol. ii. p. 290; *ibid.* (6th Series), vol. iii. p. 457. XIV. 12.—J. A. Alexander, *The Gospel of Jesus Christ*, p. 487. *Expositor* (5th Series), vol. i. p. 143. XIV. 12, 13.—Spurgeon, *Sermons*, vol. xxi. No. 1219. H. M. Butler, *Harrow School Sermons* (2nd Series), p. 71.

'Their works do follow them.'—Rev. xiv. 13.

After describing the scene at Cromwell's death-bed, Carlyle quotes this verse to round off his hero's career :—
'*Blessed are the dead that die in the Lord; blessed are the valiant that have lived in the Lord. Amen, saith the Spirit*—Amen. *They do rest from their labours and their works follow them.*
'*Their works follow them.* As, I think, this Oliver Cromwell's have done and are still doing! We have had our "Revolutions of Eighty-eight," officially called "glorious," and other Revolutions not yet called glorious; and somewhat has been gained for poor Mankind. Men's ears are not now slit-off by rash Officiality; Officiality will, for long henceforth, be more cautious about men's ears. The tyrannous star-chambers, branding-irons, chimerical kings and surplices at All-hallowtide, they are gone, or with immense velocity going. Oliver's works do follow him! The works of a man, bury them under what guano-mountains and obscene out-droppings you will, do not perish, cannot perish. What of Heroism, what of Eternal Light was in a Man and his Life, is with very great exactness added to the Eternities.'

If the blessedness of the dead *that die in the Lord* were only in resting in the grave, then a beast or a stone were as blessed; nay, it were evidently a curse and not a blessing. For was not life a great mercy? Was it not a greater mercy to serve God and do good—to enjoy all the comforts of life, the fellowship of the saints, the comfort of ordinances, and much of Christ in all—than to be rotting in the grave? Therefore some further blessedness is there promised. —Richard Baxter.

In *The Friend* (essay xiv.) Coleridge pronounces the following eulogy upon Dr. Andrew Bell, founder of the 'Madras' or monitorial system of education, 'Would I frame to myself the most inspiriting representation of future bliss which my mind is capable of comprehending, it would be embodied to me in the idea of Bell receiving, at some distant period, the appropriate reward of his earthly labours, when thousands and ten thousands of glorified spirits, whose reason and conscience had through his efforts been unfolded, shall sing the song of their own redemption, and pouring forth praises to God and to

their Saviour, shall repeat his "new name" in Heaven, give thanks for his earthly virtues, as the chosen instrument of Divine mercy to themselves, and not seldom, perhaps, turn their eyes towards him, as from the sun to its image in the fountain, with secondary gratitude and the permitted utterance of a human love.'

I have certainly seen sometimes engraved over your family vaults, and especially on the more modern tablets, those comfortful words, *Blessed are the dead which die in the Lord*. But I observe that you are usually content, with the help of the village stonemason, to say *only* this concerning your dead; and that you but rarely venture to add the *yea* of the Spirit, *that they may rest from their labours, and their works do follow them*. Nay, I am not even sure that many of you clearly apprehend the meaning of such followers and following, nor, in the most pathetic funeral sermons, have I heard the matter made strictly intelligible to your hope. . . . And yet it is a text which, seeing how often we would fain take the comfort of it, surely invites explanation. The implied difference between those who die in the Lord, and die—otherwise; the essential distinction between the labour from which those blessed ones rest, and the work which in some mysterious way follows them . . . ought, it seems to me, to cause the verse to glow on your (lately, I observe, more artistic) tombstones, like the letters on Belshazzar's wall; and with the more lurid and alarming light, that this *following* of the works is distinctly connected, in the parallel passage of Timothy, with *judgment* upon the works.—Ruskin, *Fors Clavigera*, xlv.

References.—XIV. 13.—Archbishop Temple, *Christian World Pulpit*, vol. lix. p. 65. J. Baines, *Twenty Sermons*, p. 75. C. Gutch, *Sermons*, p. 290. J. Keble, *Sermons for the Holy Week*, p. 241. *Expositor* (5th Series), vol. vi. p. 14. *Ibid.* (6th Series), vol. x. p. 359. XIV. 13, 14.—J. G. Greenhough, *Christian World Pulpit*, vol. lix. p. 86. XIV. 14-20. —Spurgeon, *Sermons*, vol. l. No. 2910.

'And another angel came out of the temple, crying to him that sat on the cloud, Send forth thy sickle, and reap, for the harvest of the earth is over-ripe.—Rev. xiv. 15.

I must, in passing, mark for you that the form of the sword or sickle of Perseus, with which he kills Medusa, is another image of the whirling happy vortex, and belongs especially to the sword of destruction and annihilation; whence it is given to the two angels (Rev. xiv. 15), who gather for destruction, the evil harvest and evil vintage of the earth.—Ruskin, *The Queen of the Air*, sec. 30.

References.—XIV. 18.—*Expositor* (5th Series), vol. ix. p. 139. XV. 1.—*Ibid.* (5th Series), vol. x. p. 200. XV. 2, 3.— S. H. Fleming, *Fifteen-Minute Sermons for the People*, p. 52. A. Maclaren, *Expositions of Holy Scripture—Revelation*, p. 341. XV. 2-4.—J. H. Holford, *Memorial Sermons*, p. 166.

THE SONG OF TRIUMPH

'And they sing the song of Moses the servant of God, and the song of the Lamb.'—Rev. xv. 3.

I. The life of the redeemed is here represented as a 'Service of Song'. This will afford matter neither for merriment nor surprise, if we reflect for a moment or two on the function of song. Music is a language, and frequently the only language that can give expression to the highest thoughts of the mind, or the deepest feelings of the heart. For words cannot utter what is greatest in us. Looks may do it, glances, gestures, smiles and tears may do it, but it is never so well or so effectually done as when the gifted sons and daughters of song come to our aid. (1) It is further to be noticed that all life, as it approaches perfection, becomes melodious. (2) There is no music like the music of triumph, and no songs like those which celebrate deliverance.

II. I take it as beautifully significant, that the burden of this song should be what it is, and that it should be called 'The Song of Moses and of the Lamb'. Moses, the much tried servant of God, the heroic leader of a stiff-necked people ; and the Lamb, the eternal symbol of sacrificial suffering and sorrow. For it is a mistake to suppose that noble sorrow, nobly borne, silences the voice of song. Shelley says, 'Our sweetest songs are those that tell of saddest thought'. It is partly true, it is mainly sentimental. But this is wholly true, that sorrow—when, as I say, it is nobly borne, when the pathetic 'How long?' passes into no form of rebellion and self-will—is important to hang or keep the harp upon the willows. Song breaks from it as the phœnix from the flame.

III. It is further suggested by this vision of the redeemed, that the conquerors of all ages take part in this song. The radiant hope here 'set before us' is, that *all* who have overcome will unite in the eternal song. They shall come from the east and from the west, from the north and from the south, with the marks of conflict still upon them, and there, standing upon the 'Sea of glass,' with the golden fires as of a grand sunset flashing across its smooth surface, they shall roll to highest heaven 'the song of Moses and of the Lamb'. Think of that, my heavily-laden friend ! The very thing that weighs upon thee most, thou shalt set it to music some day.

IV. Let us expect conflict. There is something more than a happy alliteration in the well-worn phrase. 'No cross, no crown.'

V. Only let us look for victory from the right source. 'Looking unto Jesus' is the only safe attitude for the best and bravest of us.—J. Thew, *Broken Ideals*, p. 61.

Rev. xv. 3.

COMPARE a sentence written by Mrs. H. B. Stowe during the dark hours of the war between the South and North : 'If this struggle is to be prolonged till there be not a home in the land where there is not one dead, till all the treasure amassed by the unpaid labour of the slave shall be wasted, till every drop of blood drawn by the lash shall be atoned by blood drawn by the sword, we can only bow and say, "Just and true are thy ways, thou King of Saints".'

REFERENCES.—XV. 3.—H. Melvill, *Penny Pulpit*, No. 1656, p. 289. H. Alford, *Quebec Chapel Sermons*, vol. ii. p. 295. Spurgeon, *Sermons*, vol. iii. No. 136. *Expositor* (6th Series), vol. v. p. 137.

'Great and marvellous are Thy works.'—Rev. xv. 3, 4.

DR. JOHN BROWN, in his letter to Dr. Cairns, tells of his uncle 'astonishing us all with a sudden burst. It was a sermon upon the apparent *plus* of evil in this world, and he had driven himself and us all to despair—so much sin, so much misery—when, taking advantage of the chapter he had read, the account of the uproar at Ephesus in the Theatre, he said, "Ah, sirs ! what if some of the men who, for *about the space of two hours cried out, Great is Diana of the Ephesians,* have for the space of eighteen hundred years and more been crying day and night, *Great and marvellous are Thy works, O Lord God Almighty ; just and true are all Thy ways, Thou king of saints ; who shall not fear Thee, O Lord, and glorify Thy Name ; for Thou only art holy".'

THE GLORY THAT SHALL BE REVEALED

'And they sing the song of Moses the servant of God, and the song of the Lamb, etc.'—Rev. xv. 3-6.

I. IN the text we hear of those songs and of that music, of those victors, those happy palm bearers, who are keeping the true Feast of Tabernacles ; who with joy and gladness have been brought and have entered into the King's palace. And we hear too of the mighty tribulation through which they passed ; how they got the victory over the fourfold enemy, over the wild beast and over his image and over his mark, and over the number of his name. That Anti-Christ, who, conquered, the warfare of the Church will be accomplished, her iniquity pardoned ; that image, no doubt some devilish caricature of the miracle of the Resurrection ; and his mark and his name the impressing of which, whatever it may be, will bring on the final persecution. It is worth while to notice how, from the very beginning, Satan has seemed to exult in imitating God's miracles ; as when Jannes and Jambres cast down their rods and they were turned into serpents ; or changed water into blood, or brought forth frogs upon the land. So, as the greater number of holy writers piously believe, that deadly wound of the wild beast which was healed, will be a diabolical parody of the Resurrection. For it goes on directly, 'All the world wondered after the wild beast' as if it were the crowning, the stupendous miracle which clinched his authority. And notice as we are marked in our foreheads with the Lord's sign, so will his unhappy servants be with the mark of the wild beast ; and as the promise to him that overcometh was the white stone and the new name, the Lord's new and everlasting name, written on it, so must the others have the wild beast's name ; or (and time only will show what is the difference) the mark of his name.

II. And about the sea of glass. Notice ; there was but One, who, in this world, walked even on the sea ; His one follower, who so desired to walk—we know how his attempt ended. But, put the whole mystery together—the boundlessness of the sea, the transparency of the glass, the brilliance of the fire. I remember once when in one of the narrow sea-straits that divide the little islands of Denmark, I was voyaging this way and that way a whole summer day, with nothing to do but to lean over the boatside, and to watch how the glorious rays of the sun shot in through the pure green sea, working out those ripples of gold and emerald which no earthly words can describe ; how the sight brought to my mind the true sea, that sea, glorious in its boundlessness and in its depth, but which yet has the element of fire added to it, and perhaps some little thing more of the future kingdom was then made known to me.

III. Then, they shall not pass over it ; then they shall not say, ' Lord, *if* it be Thou, bid me that I come to Thee upon the water'. No, then they shall stand on the infinite abysses of God's judgments ; shall see how all things *have* worked together for good to them that love God ; shall perceive how all the waves of this troublesome world were bearing them onwards to the calm of the Everlasting Port ; and that, with the clearness of the glass ; that, with the love of the fire, they *stand* on the sea of glass. —J. M. NEALE, *Sermons on the Apocalypse*, p. 71.

' Who shall not fear, O Lord, and glorify Thy name ?'—REV. XV. 4.

' She glorified herself and waxed wanton.'—REV. XVIII. 7 (R.V.).

THESE are the only two passages in which the word *glorify* is used in the book of Revelation ; once, to describe the Christian, once, to describe the pagan, attitude. For the latter see R. W. Church's *Cathedral and University Sermons*, pp. 25 f. (' Can we believe that He whose words were so terrible against the pride of Egypt and Babylon, against that haughty insolence in men, on which not only Hebrew prophet, but the heathen poets of Greece looked with such peculiar and profound alarm—that He will not visit it on those who, in their measure, are responsible for its words and temper, when it takes possession of a Christian nation ? ')

' Go ye, and pour out the seven vials of the wrath of God upon the earth.'—REV. XVI. 1.

IN the thirty-seventh chapter of *Shirley*, Charlotte Brontë applies this passage to Napoleon's final campaign in Russia, in 1812 :—

' This summer, Bonaparte is in the saddle : he and his host scour Russian deserts. . . . He marches on old Moscow : under old Moscow's walls, the rude Cossack waits him. Barbarian stoic ! he waits without fear of the boundless ruin rolling on. He puts his trust in a Snow-cloud ; the Wilderness, the Wind, and the Hail-storm are his refuge ; his allies are the elements—Air, Fire, Water. And what are these ? Three terrible archangels ever stationed before the throne of Jehovah. They stand clothed in white, girdled with golden girdles ; they uplift vials, brimming with the wrath of God. Their time is the day of vengeance ; their signal the word of the Lord of hosts.'

' And the second angel poured out his vial upon the sea.'—REV. XVI. 3.

HUGH MILLER, in the second chapter of *My Schools and Schoolmasters*, describes the tales told by his uncle Alexander, who had served in the navy under Nelson, Duncan, and Sir Ralph Abercromby. Late in life, when the old warrior had been reading Keith's *Signs of the Times*, and when ' he came to the chapter in which that excellent writer describes the time of hot naval warfare which immediately followed the breaking out of war, as the period in which the second vial was poured out on the sea, and in which the waters *became as the blood of a dead man, so that every living soul died in the sea*, I saw him bend his head in reverence as he remarked, " Prophecy, I find, gives to all our glories but a single verse, and it is a verse of judgment ! " '

' They poured out the blood of saints and prophets, and blood hast thou given them to drink.'—REV. XVI. 6.

THE blood of man should never be shed but to redeem the blood of man. It is well shed for our family, for our friends, for our God, for our country, for our kind. The rest is vanity ; the rest is crime. —BURKE.

REFERENCE.—XVI. 6.—E. M. Geldart, *Echoes of Truth*, p. 283.

' Yea, O Lord Almighty, true and righteous are thy judgments.'—REV. XVI. 7.

WRITING to Sir Charles Bunbury in 1870 upon the Franco-Prussian war, Charles Kingsley declared : ' There can be no doubt that the French programme of this war was to disunite Germany once more, and to make her weak and at the mercy of France. . . . The emperor fancied that after deceiving the French people—after governing them by men who were chosen because they could and dared deceive, that these minions of his, chosen for their untruthfulness, would be true, forsooth, to him alone ; that they would exhibit, unknown, in a secret government, virtues of honesty, economy, fidelity, patriotism, which they were forbidden to exercise in public, where their only function was to nail up the hand of the weather-glass, in order to ensure fine weather, as they are doing to this day in every telegram. So he is justly punished, and God's judgments are, as always, righteous and true.'

REFERENCE.—XVI. 9.—Spurgeon, *Sermons*, vol. xxxiv. No. 2054.

' That the way of the kings of the East might be prepared.'— REV. XVI. 12.

WHAT was it that filled the ears of the prophets of old but the distant tread of foreign armies, coming to do the work of justice.—GEORGE ELIOT, in *Romola*.

ARMAGEDDON

' And He gathered them together into a place called in the Hebrew tongue Armageddon.'—REV. XVI. 16.

IT would be foreign to our purpose to enter into the controversy as to the precise location of Armageddon. Place is neither here nor there. The important point is, that there is to be ultimately somewhere a great decisive conflict between the powers of good and evil ; the outcome of which will be the complete overthrow of the Prince of Darkness, and the undisputed reign of our Lord and Saviour Jesus Christ. It will be profitable to mark the manifestations of evil in these last days, and then on the other hand to observe some of the sure tokens of the triumph of Christ.

I. The Manifestations of Evil.—(1) Let us note at the outset the aggravated forms of Avarice which prevail in these days. The scramble for wealth is universal with all its attending selfishness and brutality. (2) Observe also the defiant front of Intemperance in our time. It is the enemy of our home life, our social life, our political life. (3) As to sensuality. (4) Another of the current forms of malignant evil is Bibliophobia, or hatred of the Scriptures as the Word of God. This is the fashionable form of infidelity. (5) Sabbath desecration. (6) As to persecution. (7) War.

II. Observe Some of the Sure Tokens of the Triumph of Christ.—(1) The Scriptures as Divine truth have a deeper hold than ever on the hearts of Christian people. The old Book is cherished as it never was cherished before ; is studied more earnestly ; is believed in more cordially. 'The Word of the Lord is tried.' It has been vindicated, triumphantly vindicated, as a true volume from beginning to end. (2) Christ is served in His Church more loyally and effectively than ever. We are approaching a realisation of the dream of Wesley. 'All at it, always at it, altogether at it.' (3) The personality and power of the Holy Ghost are recognised in the Church as never before.—D. J. Burrell, *The Gospel of Certainty*, p. 217.

Rev. XVII. 6.

Mercy and love are sins in Rome and hell.—Beaumont and Fletcher, 'Bonduca,' Act iv. Scene 4.

THE LAMB'S WAR WITH THE BEAST
'These shall make war with the Lamb, and the Lamb shall overcome them.'—Rev. XVII. 14.

It is strange that the most mysterious book of the Bible should be especially singled out as the Revelation. Yet though no book is less patient of a detailed and pedantic exposition, none is more full of the triumph and the tears of God's Word, none is richer in lessons to guide us in the stern and fluctuating conflict of our Lord with Satan. There is a roll of martyrs in the Christian Church, and over against it a roll of apostates. There are stories of great stones rolled to the door of sepulchres and removed by angel hands, of life and victory, but also of failure and disappointment and every form of death. The battle is often pictured here as a war between the Lamb and the beast. The beast may be taken to denote the rebellion of the animal, the untamed, the sensual, the violent element, blatant and blasphemous.

I. A powerful and painful little book, lately published, under the title, *From the Abyss*, sketches a typical working man, John Smith by name. The writer foresees a not distant day when by the help of the policeman and the Peabody buildings the ape and tiger instincts will be eliminated in man. He thinks that lives now insurgent and unconfined will become

confined and acquiescent, that the block-dweller of the future will pass from the great deep to the great deep, vacant, cheerful, undisturbed by envy, aspiration, or desire. John Smith represents half a million people. He lives in a four-roomed cottage at Camberwell, with a wife and five children, and a lodger. Six days of the week he goes early to his work at bricklaying ; he returns at night to his pipe and supper, and, perhaps, goes round to the public-house to hear the news. On Sunday he sleeps late, but he has Sunday dinner, a stroll in Peckham Rye, and he closes his day with his companions at the 'Blue Dragon'. So long as work is good, and pay regular, he does not lift his voice in complaint. Intellectual interests he has none. He will not listen to lectures. He will read a newspaper, but the news does not stir him. He cannot be galvanised into utterance. He drifts to his work daily, dumbly contented if work is easy and lucrative, dumbly resentful if it is not, but dumb always. To the Churches he is practically invulnerable. He has no quarrel with religion, but what faith he has is merely in a Deity of universal tolerance. He is commonplace, respectable, and fairly virtuous. Yet he is an immortal spirit journeying between two eternities through a world of tragical meaning, to the significance of which he seems destined to be blind. There are, we are told, in this vast city hundreds of thousands of such, and the trouble about them is not that they are unhappy, but that being what they are they should be so happy. Against this apparent death of the spiritual needs and cravings, against this life under the low sky, against this apparent numbness of heart and conscience, the Lamb wages His war.

II. 'These shall make war with the Lamb, and the Lamb shall overcome them.' This is our task—the awakening of the soul. How shall we do it ? How shall we stir that heavy sleeper ? How shall we rouse it into the tumult of yearnings and aspirings ? How shall we break the force of the opiates that have drugged it till it seems dead, till the sole object in life seems to be to eat well, to drink well, to sleep well, to work as little as possible, and to keep out of the way of trouble ? This is a harder task than to meet the soul awake and aware, clamorous, craving, exacting, rebellious, wild for home. Well, we will labour with all our might to destroy the social conditions that make a decent life impossible. Is it true that in many cases here in London there is a strength of circumstance that even the Gospel cannot quell and dominate, cesspools in which they who live must sin and perish ? Is it true that there are thousands of children defrauded of their childhood, born to an inheritance of vice and wretchedness, damned from the beginning ? We must change that at any cost, and that Church has strayed from the Master which is not in earnest sympathy and in mutual sacrifice with those inspired by a passion of pity to take away what Emerson calls this accursed mountain of sorrow. But as Christians we go very much further. Our problem is not solved when every dweller in London has four rooms. The problem of John Smith would still remain to us. It would not be solved even if we could transfer the East End to the West End, or even if we could mingle and equalise the privileges and opportunities of the two. The deliverance from materialism is not to be achieved in this manner, and it is the deliverance from materialism that we supremely care for. I come back to the point that we must awaken the soul. The Lamb sees the soul, and because He sees we should see also. There is an old legend which perhaps you remember. The Saviour and His disciples were walking along the way when they came upon a dead dog. The disciples did not conceal their disgust ; the Saviour said, 'How white its teeth are !' And He always finds in the most degraded that touch of hallowing beauty, that germ of spirit and life, through which His redemption may come.

III. 'The Lamb shall overcome them.' What ideas are associated with the Lamb ? How does He awaken, how does He cast out devils, how does He raise the dead ? For answer, we read of His knowledge, His love, His power, His sacrifice. In the soldiers of the Lamb these in measure must be reproduced.

Mark Rutherford tells us of a friend who longed to try for himself a mission in one of the slums about Drury Lane. 'I sympathised with him, but I asked him what he had to say. I remember telling him that I had been into St. Paul's Cathedral, and that I pictured the Cathedral full and myself in the pulpit, and I was excited when imagining the opportunity offered me to deliver some message to three thousand or four thousand persons in such a building. But in a minute or two I discovered that my sermon would be very nearly as follows : 'Dear friends, I know no more than you. I think we had better go home.'' But because the Lamb has prevailed to open the book and to loose the seals thereof, we may speak without faltering, without fear, with the ring of certainty.

The Lamb is another name for love. In that Lamb love was shown stripped of the veils that hide. The love of the Lamb is the spring of our love, the love of Christ that no sin can weary, and no lapse of time can change, all-redeeming, all-glorifying, changing even death and despair to the gates of heaven. That love may win fresh triumphs in the wilderness through our love.—W. ROBERTSON NICOLL, *The Lamp of Sacrifice*, p. 134.

REFERENCE.—XVII. 14.—C. Bradley, *The Christian Life*, p. 347.

'Fallen, fallen is Babylon the great.'—REV. XVIII. 2.

HERE we are at Treves. I need not tell you all I have felt here and at Fleissen. At first the feeling that one is standing over the skeleton of the giant iniquity—old Rome—is overpowering. And as I stood last night in that amphitheatre, amid the wild beasts' dens, and thought of the Christian martyrdoms and the Frank prisoners, and all the hellish

scenes of agony and cruelty that place had witnessed, I seemed to hear the very voice of the Archangel whom St. John heard in Patmos, crying, *Babylon the Great is fallen ;*—no more like the sound of a trumpet, but only in the still whisper of the night breeze, and through the sleeping vineyards, and the great still smile of God out of the broad, blue heaven.—KINGSLEY.

'Come forth, my people, out of her.'—REV. XVIII. 4.

FLY from Rome, for Babylon signifieth confusion, and Rome has confused all the Scriptures, confused all vices together, and confused everything. Fly, then, from Rome, and come to repentance.—SAVONAROLA, to the Florentines, in 1496.

COMPARE also Carlyle's use of the text in his diatribe against the landed aristocracy, in *Past and Present*. After accusing them of indolence and oppression, he pauses for a moment to reflect : 'Exceptions !—ah yes, thank Heaven, we know there are exceptions. Our case were too hard, were there not exceptions, and partial exceptions not a few, whom we know, and whom we do not know. Honour to the name of Ashley,—honour to this and the other valiant Abdiel, found faithful still, who would fain, by work and by word, admonish their Order not to rush upon destruction ! These are they who will, if not save their Order, postpone the wreck of it. All honour and success to these. The noble man can still strive nobly to save and serve his Order ;—at lowest, he can remember the precept of the Prophet : 'Come out of her, my people, come out of her'.

REFERENCES.—XVIII. 7, 8.—*Expositor* (4th Series), vol. ii. p. 292. XVIII. 8.—*Ibid.* (6th Series), vol. v. p. 114.

THE MANHOOD TRAFFIC

'The merchants of the earth shall weep and mourn over her ; for no man buyeth their merchandise any more, the merchandise of gold and silver, and precious stones, and of pearls, and fine linen, and purple, and silk, and scarlet, and all thyine wood, and all manner vessels of ivory, and all manner vessels of most precious wood, and of brass, and iron, and marble, and cinnamon, and odours, and ointments, and frankincense, and wine, and oil, and fine flour, and wheat, and beasts, and sheep, and horses, and chariots, and slaves [margin, or bodies], and souls of men.' REV. XVIII. 11-13.

THIS passage is built up after the analogy of Ezekiel's prophecies concerning Tyre, in conjunction with which they should be read (see Ezek. XXVII., XXVIII.) ; and the merchandise of the city of Rome in the Apostle's time has undoubtedly formed the groundwork of this enumeration.

I. The text declares that one of the causes of the ruin of this Babylon was her extravagant luxury. The history of the world is full of solemn lessons concerning the enervating influence of luxury. It is scarcely too much to say that luxury was the chief destroyer of all the great empires of antiquity. We are constantly discovering a proneness to fall away into the ease-taking and self-pampering which ruined the great empires of ancient Babylon, of Media and Persia, of Greece and Rome. Christ-like self-renunciation is a virtue which cannot grow in the soil of luxurious living.

II. But it is to the two last items in this extraordinary inventory that I wish to call your attention, *viz.*, slaves and souls of men. As the margin informs us the literal translation is bodies and souls of men. There are ways of making merchandise of manhood beside the coarse and palpable one of selling men for slaves. (1) I very much fear, thanks to the cruel, heartless, atheistic political economy which this country learnt from Jeremy Bentham, John Stuart Mill, and company, that very much of our commerce is practically a traffic in the blood, and bones, and nerves, and souls of men. No commerce is healthy, except that whose fundamental law is, 'Thou shalt love thy neighbour as thyself'. (2) The drink traffic, the opium traffic, and whoremongering are other manifestations of this awful trade in the bodies and souls of men. If the Church would do her Master's work she must arise and be the champion of the poor, the enemy of all sweating, the inexorable foe of all manhood traffic.—G. A. BENNETTS, *The Preacher's Magazine*, vol. IV. p. 509.

REFERENCE.—XVIII. 14.—*Expositor* (6th Series), vol. xii. p. 283.

'A great millstone.'—REV. XVIII. 21.

COMPARE the use of this verse in Tennyson's poem, 'Sea Dreams'.

REFERENCES.—XIX.—*Expositor* (5th Series), vol. x. p. 292. XIX. 1.—H. S. Holland, *God's City*, p. 59.

'He hath judged the great harlot.'—REV. XIX. 2.

THE real force of demonstration for Girolamo Savonarola lay in his own burning indignation at the sight of wrong; in his fervent belief in an Unseen Justice that would put an end to the wrong, and in an Unseen Purity to which lying and uncleanness were an abomination. To his ardent, power-loving soul, believing in great ends, and longing to achieve those ends by the exertion of its own strong will, the faith in a supreme and righteous Ruler became one with the faith in a speedy Divine interposition that would punish and reclaim.—GEORGE ELIOT, in *Romola*.

REFERENCES.—XIX. 3.—F. E. Paget, *Helps and Hindrances to the Christian Life*, p. 177. XIX. 4.—F. S. Bartlett, *Sermons*, p. 296.

'Praise our God, all ye His servants, and ye that fear Him, both small and great.'—REV. XIX. 5.

A VERY dear and saintly person, years ago called home, once in my hearing exulted at this appearance of the small number that fear God: viewing it as a vast encouragement. Even they will be there, not on sufferance, but taken account of, brought forward, called upon to enhance the acceptable rapture.—C. G. ROSSETTI.

REFERENCES.—XIX. 5.—J. Keble, *Sermons for the Saints' Days*, p. 453. XIX. 6.—E. H. Eland, *Christian World Pulpit*, vol. liii. p. 294. XIX. 7-8.—Spurgeon, *Sermons*, vol. xxxv. No. 2096. XIX. 8.—H. Howard, *The Raiment of the Soul*, p. 1. XIX. 9.—Spurgeon, *Sermons*, vol. xli. No. 2428. *Expositor* (6th Series), vol. x. p. 179. XIX. 10.— J. Smith, *The Integrity of Scripture*, p. 193. XIX. 11.—

H. M. Butler, *Harrow School Sermons* (2nd Series), p. 266. C. A. Scott, *The Book of Revelation*, p. 287. XIX. 11-16.— H. S. Holland, *Christian World Pulpit*, vol. lvii. p. 49. Spurgeon, *Sermons*, vol. xxv. No. 1452.

'In righteousness He doth judge and make war.'—REV. XIX. 11-14.

A BATTLE is constantly going on, in which the humblest human creature is not incapable of taking some part, between the powers of good and those of evil, and in which every, even the smallest, help to the right side has its value in promoting the very slow and often almost insensible progress by which good is gradually gaining ground from evil, yet gaining it so visibly at considerable intervals as to promise the very distant, but not uncertain final victory of God. To do something during life, on even the humblest scale, if nothing more is within reach, towards bringing this consummation ever so little nearer, is the most animating and invigorating thought which can inspire a human creature.—J. S. MILL, at the close of his *Three Essays on Religion*.

REFERENCES.—XIX. 12.—Spurgeon, *Sermons*, vol. v. No. 281. XIX. 13.—F. T. Bassett, *Christ in Eternity and Time*, p. 98. *Expositor* (4th Series), vol. vi. p. 67; *ibid.* vol. vii. p. 99.

'And the armies which are in heaven followed him, clothed in fine linen, white and pure.'—REV. XIX. 14.

COMPARE the use made of this verse by Mr. Shorthouse at the close of *Sir Percival*.

REFERENCES.—XIX. 16.—W. Gladden, *Christian World Pulpit*, vol. lvi. p. 27. XIX. 20.—F. T. Bassett, *Things That Must Be*, p. 51. *Expositor* (4th Series), vol. ii. p. 292. XX. 1-9.—E. T. J. Marriner, *Sermons Preached at Lyme Regis*, p. 39. XX. 4-6.—Spurgeon, *Sermons*, vol. vii. No. 391.

THE THOUSAND YEARS' REIGN OF CHRIST

'And I saw thrones, and they sat upon them, and judgment was given unto them: and I saw the souls of them that were beheaded for the witness of Jesus, and for the word of God, and which had not worshipped the beast, neither his image, neither had received his mark upon their foreheads, or in their hands; and they lived and reigned with Christ a thousand years.'—REV. XX. 4.

I. FIRST we shall show that the literal interpretation of the passage before us is altogether wrong and untenable. (1) The first proof of this is a very obvious one. We are dealing with a *symbolic* book. From the glorious description of the Saviour in the first chapter to the last picture of the Holy Jerusalem the book is one great series of panoramic displays of symbolic pictures. It is not intended to narrate literal events, whether belonging to the past, the present, or the future. (2) The next proof of my contention that you cannot possibly take this passage literally is that the literal interpretation of the passage is not only not supported by the other parts of Holy Scripture, but even flatly contradicted by them. (3) Then, again, the moral results expected by some from a visible appearing of Christ are altogether at variance with the statements of the other Scriptures, and with everything we know of the laws of the kingdom of God.

II. Now we proceed to seek the true interpretation

of the passage. In order to get at the true interpretation we have to observe two rules. One is: We must try to discover from the book itself how it uses its symbols. The other is: We must see to it that our own interpretation agrees with the clear utterances of the New Testament. (1) The one fact of interpretation we have to note is that numbers are always used in this book to represent principles or ideas, and not in their arithmetical character. To give one example: the number seven signifies completeness; the number three symbolises Divinity or Deity. Ten is the symbol for 'kingship'. What then is the meaning of 'a thousand'? A thousand is ten raised to the third power, and therefore signifies, the book being its own interpreter, the kingdom of God. It symbolises the Divine kingdom in its perfect and absolute completeness.

III. Let us in the last place sum up the lessons of this symbolic picture. (1) The first lesson is that the kingdom of God is absolutely guaranteed once and for ever in Jesus Christ. (2) The next lesson we are here taught is, that believers even now in their true and inner life are the real kings and judges of the world. 'I saw thrones and they sat on them and judgment was given unto them.' (3) The last lesson is that our present life in the kingdom is an earnest and guarantee of our complete future glory. 'Blessed are they that have part in the first resurrection; over them the second death hath no power.' — JOHN THOMAS, *Myrtle Street Pulpit*, vol. II. p. 231.

REFERENCES.—XX. 4.—*Expositor* (4th Series), vol. iii. pp. 251, 363; *ibid.* vol. x. p. 297.

'The camp of the saints, and the beloved city.'—REV. xx. 9.
THERE is nothing real or useful that is not a seat of war.—EMERSON.

'ON the western slope of the Guadarrama mountains,' writes Froude in his essay on Saint Teresa, 'midway between Medina del Campo and the Escurial, stands the ancient town of Avila. From the windows of the railway carriage can be seen the massive walls and flanking towers, raised in the eleventh century in the first heat of the Spanish crusade. The fortifications themselves tell the story of their origin. The garrison of Avila were soldiers of Christ, and the cathedral was built into the bastions, in the front line of defence, as an emblem of the genius of the age.'

REFERENCE.—XX. 9.—*Expositor* (4th Series), vol. x. p. 347.

'And I saw a great white throne, and Him that sat upon it, from whose face the earth and the heaven fled away.'— Rev. xx. 11.
AT Hinely Hill, writes Wesley in his *Journal* for 1749, 'a large congregation met in the evening. I expounded part of the twentieth chapter of the Revelation. But O what a time was this! It was as though we were already standing before the "great white throne". God was no less present with us in prayer; when one just by me cried with a loud and bitter cry, I besought God to give us a token that all things work together for good. He did so; He wrote pardon upon her heart, and we all rejoiced unto Him with reverence.'

DR. BONAR, in his *Life of M'Cheyne*, describes the latter's final preaching at Newcastle in 1842. 'He preached in the open air, in a space of ground between the Cloth Market and St. Nicholas Church. Above a thousand souls were present, and the service continued until ten, without one person moving from the ground. The moon shone brightly, and the sky was spangled with stars. His subject was, "The Great White Throne". In concluding his address, he told them that "they would never meet again till they all met at the judgment-seat of Christ; but the glorious heavens over their heads, and the bright moon that shone upon them, and the old venerable church behind them, were his witnesses that he had set before them life and death". Some will have cause to remember that night through eternity.'

REFERENCES.—XX. 11.—Spurgeon, *Sermons*, vol. xii. No. 701, and vol. xlii. No. 2473. *Expositor* (6th Series), vol. v. p. 326. XX. 11, 12.—Bishop Gore, *Christian World Pulpit*, vol. lviii. p. 353.

'And I saw the dead, small and great, standing before the throne.'—REV. XX. 12.

STAND *before God*—past kneeling, past praying; not to be converted, but sentenced. *Now*, not *then*, is the day of salvation: not *then* except for the already saved.—C. G. ROSSETTI.

'WHEN I see kings lying by those who deposed them,' writes Addison in his reflections upon Westminster Abbey (*Spectator*, No. xxvi.), 'when I consider rival wits placed side by side, or the holy men that divided the world with their contests and disputes, I reflect with sorrow and astonishment on the little competitions, factions, and debates of mankind. When I read the several dates of the tombs, of some that dy'd yesterday, and some six hundred years ago, I consider that great day when we shall all of us be contemporaries and make an appearance together.'

'And the dead were judged out of the things written in the books.'—REV. XX. 12.

WHO are we to measure the chances and opportunities, the means of doing, or even judging, right and wrong awarded to men; and to establish the rule for meting out these punishments and rewards? We are as insolent and unthinking in judging of men's morals as of their intellects. . . . Our measure of rewards and punishments is most partial and incomplete, absurdly inadequate, utterly worldly, and we wish to continue it into the next world. Into that next and awful world we strive to pursue men, and to send after them our impotent party verdicts of condemnation or acquittal. We set up our paltry little rods to measure heaven immeasurable. —THACKERAY, in *Pendennis* (LXI.).

JUDGMENT BY THE TWOFOLD RECORD

'And the books were opened: and another book was opened which is the Book of Life: and the dead were judged out of these things which were written in the books according to their works.'—REV. XX. 12.

AT the time he received and wrote his visions, the writer of the Apocalypse had steeped himself in the phraseology and similitudes of the Prophet Daniel. This metaphor of the open books which enters into the vision of judgment is to be found in the writings of the captive noble. The metaphor may have been suggested to Daniel by his acquaintance with the work and procedure of the official historiographers in Eastern courts. The metaphor is intended to teach that God has His own secret processes for verifying those facts of life and conduct which will be crucial to His final judgment upon each member of the human race.

I. Saints and sinners alike are forgetful of their own acts, and more or less blind to the character which is the sum of those acts, although for very different reasons. (1) Genuine goodness is at the very antipodes to all self-consciousness. A true saint has not only a very short memory for his own holy acts, he never thinks of them as his own acts at all. (2) The good deeds of a truly virtuous and holy mind will be so normal and spontaneous that they will pass unnoticed and unrecorded. True goodness forgets its own achievements. (3) And then how prone is the bad man to forget his evil deeds! His habits not infrequently blunt and narcotise memory, together with all the other intellectual powers. And the more evil there is in his life, the less likely he is to recall it. (4) And then the Book of Remembrance is necessary to check and counterpoise those distorting freaks of the imagination which are apt to arise whenever we seek to judge ourselves.

II. This reference to the books that were opened seems to carry with it an important doctrinal signification. (1) The Book of Remembrance is kept to vindicate the grace and wisdom and forgiving favour of the Lamb in inserting the names of His chosen ones in the Book of Life. (2) The central place given in the judgment to the Book of Life teaches that one of the stern conditions of salvation is that the name shall be written there through the grace and atoning favour of the Lamb. A man cannot be saved by the things recorded in the Book of Remembrance alone. It is because our names are written in the Lamb's Book of Life that the holy and acceptable works we may come to do acquire their title to reward. (3) On the other hand, let us not overlook the solemn fact that our destiny will be just as profoundly affected by the plain chronicle of the daily life as by the fact that we were once pardoned through the grace of the Redeemer, and enrolled as subjects of His kingdom.

REFERENCES.—XX. 12.—Spurgeon, Sermons, vol. vii. No. 391. C. Perren, Revival Sermons in Outline, p. 192. H. J. Bevis, Sermons, p. 290. W. H. Hutchings, Sermon Sketches, p. 31. J. Keble, Sermons for Advent to Christmas Eve, pp. 36, 47. Bishop Alexander, The Great Question, p. 95. XX. 12, 13.—J. Keble, Sermons for Advent to Christmas Eve, p. 99. J. M. Neale, Sermons Preached in Sackville College Chapel, vol. iv. p. 234. XX. 14.—N. D. Hillis, Christian World Pulpit, vol. lvii. p. 328. Expositor (4th Series), vol. ii. p. 424. XXI.—Expositor (5th Series), vol. ii. p. 94; ibid. vol. x. p. 455.

'No more sea.'—REV. XXI. 1.

WHILE I think of it, why is the sea (in that apologue of Attár once quoted by Falconer) supposed to have lost God? Did the Persians agree with something I remember in Plato about the sea and all in it being of an inferior nature, in spite of Homer's 'Divine ocean,' etc.—FITZGERALD'S Letters, i. p. 320.

'And I saw a new heaven and a new earth.'—REV. XXI. 1 f.

WILL not one of the properties of the spiritual body be, that it will be able to express that which the natural body only tries to express? Is this a sensual view of heaven?—then are the two last chapters of the Revelations most sensual. They tell not only of the perfection of humanity, with all its joys and wishes and properties, but of matter! They tell of trees and fruit and rivers—of gold and gems and all beautiful and glorious material things. . . . Why is heaven to be one vast lazy retrospect? Why is not eternity to have action and change, yet both, like God's, compatible with rest and immutability? This earth is but one minor planet of a minor system: are there no more worlds? Will there not be incident and action springing from these when the fate of the world is decided?—KINGSLEY.

REFERENCES.—XXI. 1.—C. Anderson Scott, The Book of Revelation, p. 287. R. J. Campbell, City Temple Sermons, p. 234. C. D. Bell, The Power of God, p. 168. W. L. Watkinson, Christian World Pulpit, vol. liii. p. 393. T. J. Madden, Tombs or Temples? p. 85. J. H. Burkitt, Christian World Pulpit, vol. lii. p. 374. A. G. Mortimer, The Church's Lessons for the Christian Year, pt. i. p. 187. A. H. Bradford, Christian World Pulpit, vol. xliv. p. 401. R. C. Cowell, Preacher's Magazine, vol. xvii. p. 372. R. W. Hiley, A Year's Sermons, vol. i. p. 85. Expositor (4th Series), vol. ii. p. 381. A. Maclaren, Expositions of Holy Scripture—Revelation, p. 355. XXI. 1-3.—H. S. Holland, Christian World Pulpit, vol. xliii. p. 293. XXI. 1-5.—T. Barker, Plain Sermons, p. 149. XXI. 1-7.—Expositor (4th Series), vol. ii. p. 293.

THE NEW JERUSALEM
(For Septuagesima)

'I saw the holy city, new Jerusalem, coming down out of heaven from God, made ready as a bride adorned for her husband.'—REV. XXI. 2.

ON this Sunday, Septuagesima, we have the beginning and the end of the Bible brought before us in the Lessons both of the Morning and of the Evening Services; the First Lessons being taken from the opening chapters of the Book of Genesis, the Second from the concluding chapters of the book of the Revelation. And whilst the beginning of the Bible speaks of the world being prepared for man and of man making his appearance on its stage, the close of it sets before us visions of a future awaiting man and the world which he has subdued to be his dwelling-place.

I. The book of the Revelation is professedly a collection of visions; it is full of imagery. And imagery sets us seeking interpretations of it. But it is not always easy to interpret; and the Revelation, or the Apocalypse—the two names mean the same thing, unveiling or drawing a curtain aside—has been subjected to a great variety of more or less ingenious interpretation. Some of the visions were no doubt intended to indicate definite historical events of the age in which the book was issued; but others set forth spiritual realities belonging to the nature and purposes of God and the development of the kingdom of Christ, in forms which were intended to fasten on the imagination and so to feed the spiritual life. Thus a curtain is drawn aside, and we have a vision of the Court of heaven. We see a throne, and there is One sitting on the throne, but He is hidden in splendour; worshipping Him are four living creatures, which are symbols of the animated Creation, and twenty-four Elders, twelve representing the old dispensation and twelve the new—as it were the twelve Patriarchs and the Twelve Apostles in a celestial form. These and all other existing things are shown to us paying homage after their kind to their Eternal Maker. Then the Lamb is introduced —a lamb as though it had been slain—and this figure remains throughout the book the symbol of Him Who had offered Himself up in sacrifice to the Father, and had been exalted to the right hand of God.

II. It is to this class of imagery that the visions of the concluding chapters belong. They exhibit scenes which represent the triumph of the kingdom of Christ. They are intended, as I said, to interest the imagination and so to supply nourishing food to Christian faith and hope. They set forth spiritual realities and relations which have a bearing on our present life; and it is in this character, and not as enigmatic predictions of historical events, that they are to be valued and studied.

III. Here, where the Church is described under the figure of a golden city, we have a sort of final vision of what we are to look forward to as a completion of the Divine work, a fulfilment of the Divine purpose. It is a vision of mankind ordered according to God's will. This form of mankind is God's creation; it comes down out of heaven from God, and it has the glory of God. It has a civic character, is of the nature of a commonwealth, having diverse offices and functions and classes in it. It is in a supreme degree orderly, like a city built after a definite plan. It is the outcome of the Old and New Covenants: it preserves the memory of the Twelve Tribes, the Twelve Apostles are the foundation on which its wall is built. It has all manner of splendour and preciousness. It lives in the light of God. The nations walk in that light; the kings of the earth bring their glory into the presence of God. National life is not superseded; but all the actions of men are just and harmonious, and therefore there is nothing but happiness in the world. Nearly everything in the imagery of these chapters represents perfection; all is of the absolute best, under the light of God, in joyful devotion to God. But there is a hint of what is not yet as it should be, where the seer beholds the river of water of life proceeding from the throne of God and of the Lamb, and the tree of life growing

on the river's banks; for the leaves of the tree are for the healing of the nations. So the nations want healing. We may take this as implying that the ideal form of mankind, divinely ordered, divinely enlightened and quickened, divinely blessed, has to work itself out by degrees into actual and victorious existence.

IV. In endeavouring to draw from these shining chapters at the close of the Bible what we can receive as their instructive significance, we are led to observe that here, as elsewhere in the New Testament, there is a mysterious slurring over of the line which divides this mortal life from the other life beyond the grave. To Christians of a great number of the later generations nothing was very important but the passing of that terrible line. Christian hope looked entirely away from this earth to the region of the departed; all glory was associated with that unseen world. But a change, with far-reaching effects, has passed over the theology of our English race. Since the publication of a memorable book on *The Kingdom of Christ*, by F. D. Maurice, just seventy years ago, the sermons and writings of our accepted teachers have drawn away, at first very slowly but of late quite rapidly and completely, from dwelling on the contrasted miseries and felicities of individuals in the life beyond the grave, and have directed attention to that kingdom of God which Christ came to establish, and which He has opened to all believers. And the rediscovery of this heavenly kingdom which is to subdue the kingdoms of the earth to itself has coincided with the springing up of a generous longing, independent of professed Christian belief, and bent on building from the earth upwards, for a world from which all the pains and disadvantages of poverty are to be banished. That clarion-song of Blake's—

> I will not cease from mental fight,
> Nor shall my sword sleep in my hand,
> Till we have built Jerusalem
> In England's green and pleasant land—

has never been the cry of so many hearts and minds as at the present time. Those who have been made disciples to the kingdom of heaven cannot exclude the abolition of the miseries of poverty from their hopes. But the commandment which they have received bids them look for a city which shall come down from heaven. They are to seek first the kingdom of the heavenly Father and His righteousness. They are to pray and labour that this kingdom may come; they are to be remembrancers of the Lord, giving Him no silence till He establish and till He make Jerusalem a praise in the earth. Which if they do, it is promised that the things which the Gentiles seek shall be added to them. And the seer of the Revelation is true to the teaching of Him Who through sacrifice was exalted to be King of kings and Lord of lords. He pictures a world blessed by the coming down of a city from heaven. The scene is not that of a remote Paradise on high, to which the favoured few have gone up, but that of a city on its way from heaven to earth; it is beheld from a mountain-top; the nations walk in the light of it: the leaves of its tree of life are for the healing of the nations.—J. LLEWELYN DAVIES, *The Guardian*, 10th February, 1909.

'And I saw the New Jerusalem, coming down from God out of heaven, prepared as a bride adorned for her husband.' —REV. XXI. 2.

THE New Jerusalem, as we witness it, is no more exempt from corruption than was the Old. That early Christian poet who saw it descending in incorruptible purity 'out of heaven from God,' saw, as poets use, an ideal. He saw that which perhaps for a point of time was almost realised, that which may be realised again. But what we see in history behind us and in the world about us is, it must be confessed, not like 'a bride adorned for her husband'. We see something that is admirable, and much that is great and wonderful, but not this splendour of maiden purity. The bridal dress is worn out, and the orange-flower is faded. First the rottenness of dying superstitions, then barbaric manners, then intellectualism preferring system and debate to brotherhood, strangling Christianity with theories and framing out of it a charlatan's philosophy which madly strives to stop the progress of science—all these corruptions have in the successive ages of its long life infected the Church, and many new and monstrous perversions of individual character have disgraced it. . . . But the triumph of the Christian Church is that it is *there*—that the most daring of all speculative dreams, instead of being found impracticable, has been carried into effect, and, when carried into effect, instead of being confined to a few select spirits, has spread itself over a vast space of the earth's surface, and, when thus diffused, instead of giving place after an age or two to something more adapted to a later time, has endured for two thousand years, and, at the end of two thousand years, instead of lingering as a mere wreck spared by the tolerance of the lovers of the past, still displays vigour and a capacity of adjusting itself to new conditions, and lastly, in all the transformations it undergoes, remains visibly the same thing and inspired by its Founder's universal and unquenchable spirit.

It is in this and not in any freedom from abuses that the Divine power of Christianity appears.—SIR JOHN SEELEY, in *Ecce Homo*.

'And I saw the holy city.'—REV. XXI. 2.

WHAT will it be at last to see a 'holy' city! for Londoners, for Parisians, for citizens of all cities upon earth, to see a holy city!—C. G. ROSSETTI.

REFERENCES. — XXI. 2. — J. Adderley, *Christian World Pulpit*, vol. xlvi. p. 22. R. J. Wardell, *Preacher's Magazine*, vol. xviii. p. 411. J. Watson, *The Inspiration of our Faith*, p. 262. T. Phillips, *Christian World Pulpit*, vol. lxviii. p. 1. Bishop Welldon, *The Gospel in a Great City*, p. 168. R. J. Drummond, *Faith's Certainties*, p. 323. XXI. 2-7.—*Expositor* (6th Series), vol. v. p. 323. XXI. 3.—H. S. Holland, *Christian World Pulpit*, vol. lxi. p. 393.

THE ELIMINATION OF THE LAW OF ANTA- GONISM

'And I heard a great voice out of heaven saying, Behold, the tabernacle of God is with men, and He will dwell with them, and they shall be His people, and God Himself shall be with them, and be their God. And God shall wipe away all tears from their eyes; and there shall be no more death, neither sorrow, nor crying, neither shall there be any more pain; for the former things are passed away.' —REV. XXI. 3, 4.

I. THE law of antagonism is unnatural.

II. It is the purpose of God in Jesus Christ to abolish the law of antagonism. The Spirit of Christ shall never cease to work in the race until there is no more useless antagonism, misdirected antagonism, destructive antagonism, but there shall act instead the affinities, the attractions, the forces of a higher law, and the reign of blood and iron shall be over for ever. But the question may be urged, What shall guarantee our safety and growth when the fiery law is abolished? The prevalence of the spirit of Jesus Christ.

III. We mark the signs that the law of antagonism is being eliminated. (1) We see signs of change to a happier state of things in our relation to nature. (2) We see signs of change to a happier state of things within society itself. (3) Signs of change to a happier state of things are visible also in international life. Salvator Rosa long ago painted his picture, 'Peace burning the Instruments of War'. This generation, may not witness that glorious bonfire, but many signs signify that ere long it shall be kindled, lighting the footsteps of the race into the vaster glory that is to be. Let us first ourselves get the spirit of Christ. Let us profoundly believe in the golden year. It will come. This vision of the Revelation is no mockery.—W. L. WATKINSON, *The Transfigured Sackcloth*, p. 223.

REFERENCES.—XXI. 4.—D. Brown, *Christian World Pulpit*, vol. lviii. p. 341. Bishop Wilberforce, *Sermons*, p. 155. F. de W. Lushington, *Sermons to Young Boys*, p. 39. Dinsdale T. Young, *The Gospel of the Left Hand*, p. 139. *Expositor* (5th Series), vol. vi. p. 102.

A NEW YEAR'S SERMON

'He that sat upon the throne said, Behold, I make all things new.'—REV. XXI. 5.

THE first Sunday of the New Year is a day of hope, of promise, of anticipation. It is true indeed that the stream of time flows onwards uninterruptedly; the periods which mark its course are in a sense the mere creations of human convenience. But who does not feel moved to take stock, so to say, of his life; who does not imagine that it is somehow possible to make a fresh start upon the anniversary of his birth, or of his marriage, or upon Christmas Day, or Easter Day, or at the beginning of a New Year?

For Christianity is the religion of hope; it touches the hard rock of human nature, as it were, with a magic wand, and immediately there breaks forth the fresh bubbling water of a regenerate life. The one word wholly incompatible with the Christian faith and the Christian spirit is 'despair'.

I. There is hope for the individual.

Read the story of the Lord Jesus Christ in the Gospels, and see how His presence breathed a new life, wherever He moved, into sad, downcast, penitent, abandoned souls. The publican or tax-gatherer, the alien Samaritan woman, the leper, the Magdalene, the thief upon the cross—He gave them all hope.

II. There is hope, too, for society.

Do we hear any faithless voices to-day protesting that this England of ours is going to the dogs because of Free Trade, or unemployment, or the physical degeneration of the people, or the decadence of patriotic spirit and virtue? Such despondency is un-Christian, it is rebellious against the Providence of God. It denies the possibility of His 'fulfilling Himself in many ways'. But the future is, as the past was, in His keeping. His name is not 'I was,' but 'I am'. It may be impossible to fight against the spirit of the age, but is not that spirit the breath of His Almighty Will? In human history the great tendencies, the great achievements, are all the direct and visible results of God's working; it is only small results which are even apparently wrought by man. Not less true is it of the present than of the future life that God 'is not the God of the dead, but of the living'.

III. 'He that sat upon the throne said, Behold, I make all things new.' The promise stands as part of the vision which St. John in his Apocalypse enjoyed and revealed. But it is a promise of heaven, not of earth. The Holy City, the new Jerusalem which the Apostle beheld, does not rise from the earth heavenwards; it 'comes down from God out of heaven'. Vain is it therefore to suppose that any change of social or political environment will effect the regeneration of society. In all the actual or possible circumstances of the State human nature remains and will remain the same, the same in its greatness and its littleness, the same in its aspirations and temptations, the same in its essential and inalienable needs.

The millennium, if it comes at all, will not begin in any Hall of Science or Socialism; it will begin and can only begin in regenerate human hearts. 'The Kingdom of God,' says the Saviour, 'is within you'.

Men need reform, but the most needed of all reforms is self-reform.

The new heaven and the new earth will be realised, so far as they are possible upon earth, only when Jesus Christ has become Lord over the hearts and consciences of men. It is He who sits upon the throne; it is He who says, 'Behold, I make all things new'.—Bishop Welldon, *The Gospel in a Great City*, p. 18.

THE INCARNATION
(*For Christmas*)
'Behold, I make all things new.'—Rev. xxi. 5.

Each festival of the Church declares a special truth and offers a peculiar grace.

I. **The Festival of Christmas Declares the Incarnation** of the Eternal Word and offers the grace of renewal. The Incarnation is the starting-point of a new order of things, and the whole of human life is affected by it. As a help to the better understanding of the great truth, it is well that we should distinguish between Personality and Human Nature. Personality is that which we share with no one else; human nature is that which we share with every other member of the human race; human nature is that which unites; personality is that which separates; human nature is communicative; but no one can part with his personality or share it with another.

II. **What, then, took place when the Eternal Word took Flesh and became Man?**—This: He took the nature of Adam in all its fulness; but instead of His human nature being centred round a new Personality, it was taken up into the Personality of the Eternal Word. The Son of God took to Himself that which would unite Him to the human race; He took human nature, but not a human personality. We do not see in the Lord Jesus Christ the prominence of any one characteristic, such as we are accustomed to find in the saints. He belonged to no one human race or nation. Pilate was right when he said, 'Behold the Man'; and the Apostle reminds us that there is neither Jew nor Gentile, but that all are one in Christ Jesus.

III. **If any ask 'Why Perplex us with these Subtleties of Dogma?'** it is enough to say that the very life of the Church and of every individual Christian is bound up in a right faith in Jesus Christ. Again and again we find that those who came to Him when He was on earth had to face the question 'What think ye of Christ?' More than half the heresies of the past have arisen because men will not, or do not, know Jesus Christ. It is such a help to us when we see that the Incarnation starts a new era for mankind. 'In Christ,' wrote St. Paul, 'man is a new creature;' and as the Incarnation is appropriated by the individual soul, the communicated nature comes not as a dole, but it is ours by way of personal endowment. Therein is our hope, our power of renewal, certain.

IV. **If we Know the Gift of God** we shall listen to the voice of Christ as He stands in our midst. 'Come unto Me'—such is His invitation—'and I will give you rest.' We are looking into this New Year; with the past forgiven—undone it cannot be —our hearts will be set at liberty and we can run in the way of God's Commandments. Then we shall become indeed new creatures, and our inner life may be renewed day by day by the power of the Holy Ghost.

THE DIVINE POET
'Behold, I make all things new.'—Rev. xxi. 5.

I. This chapter is already full of the word and the wine and the music new: 'A new heaven and a new earth'; the 'new Jerusalem, coming down from God out of heaven'; 'behold, I make all things new'.

And not before the time. The world is weary of its wickedness and groaning and restlessness; we have had tears enough and death enough and sorrow and crying and pain ineffable: great God, awake and make all things new! This is the promise of these opening verses: 'And God shall wipe away all tears from their eyes; and there shall be no more death, neither sorrow, nor crying, neither shall there be any more pain: for the former things are passed away. And He that sat upon the throne said'—and said by right—'Behold, I make all things new,' and the past shall be forgotten like a dream without memory. Enough! These are grand words; they thrill us by their power, we are caught up into somewhat of their stature and majesty. The New Testament is bound to bring us new things by its very name; it is a new testament: there was a Testament before it. This is the real newness—the continuation and the completion of something which has gone before. This is not a first writing, it is a second writing, and new, not in its God, not in its redeeming purpose, but new in many an application, new in many a realisation by the soul of the higher life and the grander possibility.

II. Note the personality of the text. The Speaker is alive; the Speaker is individualised from all other speakers; the Speaker is appalling in His awesome solitude. He would seem to have no companion now; yea, rather, it would seem as if the threefold Personality had become united in one name. No more we hear of 'Let us make,' we are now confronted by an intenser term, 'Behold, I make all things new'. It would seem as if each Person in the Divine Trinity had times of special expression and times of special relation to nature and to man and to providence and to destiny: now it is the Father; and the other Persons of the Trinity are concealed, as it were, behind His glory: now it is the Son, the only begotten Son, the Saviour of the world: and, finally, it is the Paraclete, the Holy Spirit, who rules the whole mystery of human development. And what if now the Three should in a peculiar and definite sense be One—as if the Three-One should all be speaking in, 'Behold, I make all things new'.

III. Has the word 'make' any special significance in this passage? Certainly; it is the keyword. God represents Himself as the maker, the poet; for in the deepest classical sense the poet is the maker, not the statistician, not the geometer, not the man who deals in magnitudes and quantities and numbers and ever-changing relations of an arithmetical or superficial kind: these men are not makers; the poets 'make'—God is the Poet. He makes, He makes all things, He makes all things new. God is the fountain of wealth, God is the author of precious stones, God is the maker of harvest-fields and vineyards; God pours out the sea, God causes the stars to spill their glory on the meaner worlds. Associate the idea of the poet with the term worker or maker. God is the beginner of all things: all things are in God; there is not a pebble on all the seashore that

He did not let fall there—a diamond in His eyes, mere sand in ours, for vulgarity debases whatever it looks on. God is the unceasing poet, the unceasing maker. He never makes a June that lasts longer than a month, but He makes millions of Junes, millions of springs, millions of autumn days, with their brown and gold and play and flash of exquisite beauty. He makes them as a lapidary might make the stone shapely; He makes them as the poet might startle the common wind into music. See the Poet Divine in every summer day, in every sparklet of dew, in every dawn, in every babe, in every morning promise.

IV. Note that the proclamation by the very necessity of its terms is full of hope. 'Behold, I make all things new.' In the Divine economy things seem linked together in festoons and masses and unities. When one thing is made new all things seem to be made new.

Christianity is the religion of hope, the religion of renewal, the religion of development. It has never uttered its final word; it begins its eloquence, it never finishes it in any sense that means finality or the exhaustion of God. 'Behold, I make all things new.'—JOSEPH PARKER, *City Temple Pulpit*, vol. I. p. 2.

'And He that sat upon the throne said, Behold, I make all things new.'—REV. XXI. 5.

JACQUES LEFÈVRE, the father of French Protestantism, used to say to his pupil, William Farel, 'William, the world is going to be renewed, and you will behold it'. Farel frequently recalls in letters this impressive prophecy. In his Commentary on St. Paul's Epistles, Lefèvre wrote: 'The signs of the times announce that a renewal is near, and while God is opening new ways for the preaching of the Gospel, by the discoveries and conquests of the Portuguese and Spaniards in all parts of the world, we must hope that He will visit His Church and raise it from the degradation into which it has fallen'.

REFERENCES.—XXI. 5.—Spurgeon, *Sermons*, vol. xxxi. No. 1816. A. Coote, *Twelve Sermons*, p. 27. Bishop Alexander, *The Great Question*, p. 284. H. P. Chapman, *Church Family Newspaper*, vol. xvi. p. 28. C. S. Horne, *Christian World Pulpit*, vol. lxvii. p. 4. *Expositor* (7th Series), vol. vi. p. 371.

'I AM ALPHA AND OMEGA'

'I am Alpha and Omega, the beginning and the end.'—REV. XXI. 6.

THERE is no great mystery about the title. The smallest Sunday school child knows that it is simply the first and the last letter of the Greek alphabet. It is as if He said, 'I am the A and the Z'.

I. He is the Alpha and the Omega in the great alphabet of time. Look back as far as you can; go back as far as ever thought can pierce, and yet you can hear the echo from some far-off distance, 'I am'. Then look forward to the future. Think of the time when the little rill of time will lose itself in the great ocean of Eternity; imagine the universe blotted out, the lamps of heaven quenched, the firmament rolled together as a scroll—but Jesus Christ will ever be still the same, 'yesterday, to-day, and for ever'. He is the Omega, the last. He Who was the Architect, will also be the Builder, and will bring it to a perfect end. ' I am confident that He which hath begun the good work in you will finish it.' He Who began will complete—in spite of all opposition, and in spite of all sin.

II. He is not only the Alpha and the Omega in point of time, but He is the Alpha and the Omega in point of rank. He is the Alpha. He was made higher than the angels. In whatever character you regard Jesus Christ, we claim the Alpha for Him. And yet He became the Omega. He, Who was the equal with God, becomes obedient unto death, even the death of the Cross; and died for our sins upon the Tree.

III. So once more He is the Alpha and the Omega in the great scheme of salvation. The origination of salvation must be with Him. So He must also be the Omega; He will be the Omega for the salvation of the world. We do not believe in some gradual evolution towards a day of glory; we believe sin will never be really cast out until He comes—we believe that evil will never be really extirpated until He comes.

IV. He must be the Alpha and the Omega of your salvation. (1) First let Him be the Alpha and the Omega of your trust. (2) We would urge you that He may be the Alpha and the Omega of your love. (3) He must be our Alpha and our Omega in all our teaching and in all our work. My Christ is first, my Christ is last, my Christ is all in all !—E. A. Stuart, *His Dear Son and other Sermons*, vol. v. p. 113.

References.—XXI. 6.—Spurgeon, *Sermons*, vol. xxvi. No. 1549.

MAN, THE CONQUEROR
' He that overcometh shall inherit all things, and I will be his God, and he shall be My son.'—Rev. xxi. 7.

I. *Life, a warfare*, is the first reflection forced on you by the words 'He that overcometh,' that is, there is something to overcome. In every Church, in every city in Asia Minor, there must be a contest. For the man who will not contend there is no promise in this book. One of the most familiar phrases on the lips of teachers and moralists, whether they teach through fiction or dry philosophy, is 'the battle of life'.

Whatever of mystery there be about it, it is a fact that the highest life is not reached without severest conflict. Whatever truth there may be in the theories of the quietists concerning rest and peace in the Christian life, this is always true—it is never lived without conflict. It is fighting all the way. If Christ calls you to anything by example and word He calls you to battle with the world, the flesh, and the devil. The man who will not fight can never live the Christian life.

II. The second thing is, that *life may be a great victory*. The word is not 'To him that fighteth,' as though the fighter might be defeated and get a kind

of solatium for his reward, but 'To him that over-cometh,' seeming to say that overcoming is certain to him who will fight. And it is. There is no hope-lessness for the moral warrior. Victory is the great possibility. The circumstances and conditions of the seven Churches in Asia differed widely. Some, like Sardis, seem to have been mastered. But the same great door of hope is opened to all, and the one word to all is 'overcometh'. Jesus Christ never led any-body to defeat yet. If you have been defeated it is because you have lost touch with Him.

III. *Life is designed to be a great inheritance.* He that overcometh shall inherit what? All things. All that you can cram into the word 'life': joy, peace, pleasure, satisfaction. Not hereafter but here. Who is the man that enjoys nature, for whom every spring brings a new world, who finds the relationships of life teeming with interest? The man with the pure heart. Who is the man who enjoys the world? Not the man who is mastered by it and made its slave, but the man who conquers it.

IV. Lastly, *life was intended to be a high and holy fellowship.* I was intended not merely to know and feel that there was a God, but to say, 'My God' and to know that God says to me 'My Son'. To live the life of a son of God is the highest part of my inheritance.—Charles Brown, *God and Man*, p. 43.

References.—XXI. 7.—J. Keble, *Sermons for the Saints' Days*, p. 68. C. Brown, *God and Man*, p. 43.

' But for the fearful, and unbelieving, and abominable, and murderers, and fornicators, and sorcerers, and idolaters, and all liars, their part shall be in the lake that burneth with fire and brimstone ; which is the second death.'—Rev. xxi. 8.

Mr. Yorke, the impetuous manufacturer in *Shirley*, 'believed fully that there was a judgment to com If it were otherwise, it would be difficult to imagine how all the scoundrels who seemed triumphant in this world, who broke innocent hearts with impun-ity, abused unmerited privileges, were a scandal to honourable callings, took the bread out of the mouths of the poor, browbeat the humble, and truckled meanly to the rich and proud—were to be properly paid off, in such coin as they had earned. But,' he added, 'whenever he got low-spirited about such like ongoings, and their seeming success in this mucky lump of a planet, he just reached dawn t'owd book' (pointing to a great Bible in the bookcase), 'opened it like at a chance, and he was sure to light of a verse blazing with a blue brimstone low that set all straight. He knew,' he said, 'where some folk was bound for, just as weel as if an angel wi' great white wings had come in ower t' door-stone and told him.'

' The fearful.'—Rev. xxi. 8.

Courage, says John Stuart Mill in his essay upon Nature, 'is from first to last a victory achieved over one of the most powerful emotions of human nature. . . . It may fairly be questioned if any human being is naturally courageous. Many are naturally pug-nacious, or irascible, or enthusiastic, and these passions when strongly excited may render them insensible to fear. But take away the conflicting emotions, and fear reasserts its dominion: consistent courage is always the effect of cultivation.'

'The lake that burneth with fire and brimstone.'—Rev. xxi. 8.

In private we read Paley's *Evidences* or Leslie on *Deism*. These two stuck by me, and did my head good. I took in the whole argument, and I thank God that nothing has ever shaken it. If history is a foundation of certainty, Christianity, even by human evidence, is certain. This has been with me through life, in every state and age and intellectual condition. The book of Revelation I read at Tretteridge and the 'lake that burneth with fire and brimstone' never even faded in my memory. They were vivid and powerful truths and motives which forwarded and governed me; I owe to them more than will ever be known till the last day.—Cardinal Manning's *Journal*.

I had always a fear of judgment and of the pool burning with fire. The verse in Apocalypse xxi. 8 was fixed in my whole mind from the time I was eight or nine years old, *confixit carnem meam timore*, and kept me as boy and youth and man in the midst of all evil, and in all occasions remote and proximate; and in great temptations; and in a perilous and unchecked liberty.—Cardinal Manning.

THE WORK OF THE BRIDE OF CHRIST

'The Bride, the Lamb's wife.'—Rev. xxi. 9.

The Church, the Bride of Christ, is not called into existence simply for itself, but it is called into existence for the sake of the Bridegroom. The work of the Bride of Christ: 'Ye shall be witnesses unto Me'. 'Ye shall make disciples of all the nations.' In other words, a husband and wife ought to be one in thought, in character, in work. And that is the idea, that the Church of Christ should be one in thought, in character, and in work with Him. Now what is Jesus Christ's character? That should be the character of His Bride, and the different parts of the Bride. The different members of the Church should have the character of Jesus Christ.

What is the thought of Jesus Christ? That should be the thought of the Church, the different parts of the Church. What is the work of Jesus Christ? That should be the work of the Church, the different parts of the Church. One in thought, character, work, one in Him.

I. The Work of the Bride.—Just think of the love of Jesus Christ for the world! Can we estimate it? Can we picture it? Can we even imagine it? And yet if we are one with Him and His Bride, there ought to be in us that same spirit of love and devotion, that keenness for the work, that characterised Him. He came down on earth to seek and to save that which was lost. It is said that Michael Angelo one day went to call on Raphael, before Raphael had made his great name, in his earlier days, and Raphael was not at home. And Michael

Angelo went into his house and saw there a picture Raphael had commenced, and it was like nearly all the work of Raphael in that day, very cramped, very small, apparently insignificant. And Angelo looked at it and then he wrote underneath on the canvas, 'Larger, larger, larger,' and signed it. And Raphael came home, saw Angelo had been to visit him, and he looked at the canvas and saw the words, 'Larger, larger, larger'. And that was the turning-point in the artistic career of the great artist Raphael. And it seems to me that Jesus Christ will come and write on our churches, aye, and in different Christians' hearts and lives, 'Larger, larger, larger'. We have such puny, small conceptions of things, instead of the great conception that Jesus Christ would have us have, the great conception of character He would have us have, the great idea of work and usefulness and sphere of labour which Jesus Christ would have us possess. Be larger in prayer. We want—do we not?—showers of blessing to come down upon our Church. As one preacher said recently in a sermon, showers of blessing depend equally upon us along with God. You look at the shower coming down. Where is that rain coming from? The clouds. How did it get to the clouds? The sun drew it up from the earth. The sun drew the water up from the earth and it got into the clouds, and it descends in fertilising showers. The more our prayers are gathered up in the heavens, the more they descend in showers. If there is a famine, if there is no rain, depend upon it it is because the Sun has not gathered from the earth the prayers of God's people. Therefore, if we want showers of blessing, we want as a Church to be engaged in prayer. How wonderful it is, that we can influence God, and influence others by prayer! St. Augustine says, in one of his works, that the Church owes the mighty and wonderful example of St. Paul to the prayer of dying Stephen. It is the prayer of the Bride of Christ going up to God, which gives showers of blessing. God cannot deny the Bride of His Son anything. The Church of the living God has power with God. Let us be a praying people, praying for the blessing of God to come down upon our heads.

II. The Position of the Bride.—Let us just remember this, the position of the Bride of Christ, the privilege of the Bride of Christ. When you are united to Jesus Christ in the closest of all ties as His Bride, think what a claim you have upon Him, think what a claim He has upon you. If you are His Bride, what has He a right to expect from you? Loyalty to Himself, nothing coming between. What have you a right to expect from Him? Everything. Think of the Queen, because she is the wife of the King, think of her privileges, her prerogatives! She occupies a different position from that of any other lady in the land. The wife of the King! You are the Bride of Christ.

III. The Ambition of the Bride.—Just as a wife looks up to the husband, so the Church must look up to Jesus Christ. Jesus only! that is the cry of the

Church, that is the cry of the Christian. Jesus only! If that could only appeal to our heart, what a difference it would make to our life! Then other things would not move us. We should simply have Jesus the Bridegroom, Jesus the Husband, Jesus the Master, Jesus the Lord. Think of the great love wherewith He hath loved us. Can you tell me what the love of Christ is? and yet it is this love that will come into our hearts. Think on all we might be if one with Jesus Christ, one in Jesus Christ? The glory of it, the possibility of it! Let us never rest till we have the realisation of it!

'I will shew thee the bride, the wife of the Lamb.'—Rev. XXI. 9.

Hugh Miller, in *My Schools and Schoolmasters*, tells of an old Highlander, Donald Roy, who, as each of his three grand-daughters married, 'added to his other kindnesses the gift of a gold ring. They had been brought up under his eye sound in the faith; and Donald's ring had, in each case, a mystic meaning;—they were to regard it, he told them, as the wedding-ring of their *other Husband*, the Head of the Church, and to be faithful spouses to Him in their several households.'

The action of a future world as a control upon our deeds and a stimulus to our desires, depends upon its being such, upon our believing it such at least, as we can conceive of and aspire to. If it is to operate upon us it must be picturable by us. Only through our idea of it can it influence our lives. Why then quarrel with our conceptions because necessarily imperfect, and probably much more—as all finite ideas of the Infinite, all material description of the Spiritual, must be? Heaven will be, if not what we desire now, at least what we desire then. If it be not contracted to our human dreams, those dreams will be expanded to its vast reality. If it be not fitted for us, we shall be prepared for it. In the true sense, if not in our sense, it will be a scene of serene felicity, the end of toil, the end of strife, the end of grief, the end of doubt; a Temple, a Haven, and a Home!—W. Rathbone Greg.

Reference.—XXI. 9-27.—Spurgeon, *Sermons*, vol. xlv. No. 2648.

'And he shewed me that great city, the holy Jerusalem, descending out of heaven from God.'—Rev. XXI. 10.

No architect's designs were furnished for the New Jerusalem, no committee drew up rules for the Universal Commonwealth. If in the works of Nature we can trace the indications of calculation, of a struggle with difficulties, of precaution, of ingenuity, then in Christ's work it may be that the same indications occur. But these inferior and secondary powers were not consciously exercised; they were implicitly present in the manifold yet single creative act. The inconceivable work was done in calmness; before the eyes of men it was noiselessly accomplished, attracting little attention. Who can describe that which unites man? Who has entered into the formation of speech which is the symbol of their union? Who can de-

scribe exhaustively the origin of civil society? He who can do these things can explain the origin of the Christian Church. For others it must be enough to say, 'the Holy Ghost fell on those that believed'. No man saw the building of the New Jerusalem, the workmen crowded together, the unfinished walls and unpaved streets; no man heard the clink of trowel and pickaxe; it descended *out of heaven from God*.—Sir John Seeley.

References.—XXI. 10.—Archbishop Benson, *Christian World Pulpit*, vol. xlv. p. 264. XXI. 10-12.—Bishop Wordsworth, *Church Family Newspaper*, vol. xv. p. 172.

'And her light was like unto a stone most precious, even like a jasper stone. . . . And the foundations were garnished with all manner of precious stones.'—Rev. XXI. 11, 19-21.

How beautiful these gems are! It is strange how deeply colours seem to penetrate one, like scent. I suppose that is the reason why gems are used as spiritual emblems in the Revelation of St. John. They look like fragments of heaven.—George Eliot, in *Middlemarch*.

That elegant Apostle, which seemed to have a glimpse of heaven, hath left but a negative description thereof: which neither eye hath seen, nor ear hath heard, nor can enter into the heart of man: he was translated out of himself to behold it; but, being returned unto himself, could not express it. St. John's description of emeralds, chrysolites, and precious stones, is too weak to express the material heaven we behold. Briefly, therefore, where the soul hath the full measure and complement of happiness; where the boundless appetite of that spirit remains completely satisfied that it can neither desire addition nor alteration; that, I think, is truly heaven; and this can only be in the enjoyment of that essence, whose infinite goodness is able to terminate the desires of itself, and the unsatiable wishes of ours. Wherever God will thus manifest Himself, there is heaven.—Sir Thomas Browne, *Religio Medici*.

It is not to be denied that the favourite delineations of heaven are almost wholly suggested or coloured by the book of Revelation, in which the descriptions, magnificently splendid and sometimes sublime, are yet, if we except seven verses of the twenty-first chapter, almost wholly material. And not only so, but the material elements are by no means the noblest that might have been chosen. The New Jerusalem is painted as something between a gorgeous Palace, and a dazzling Conventicle. . . . The writer's conception of what befitted the Temple of the Lord and the dwelling of the redeemed embraced rather the rare curiosities than the common loveliness of nature; palaces and jewels and precious stones—not gentle streams, and shady groves, and woodland glades, and sunny valleys, and eternal mountains, and the far-off murmur of a peaceful ocean. *His* heaven was a scene of magnificent ornamentation rather than of solemn beauty; of glory, not of love and bliss. It might kindle his fancy; it chills ours. —W. Rathbone Greg.

Yas, they's life an' happiness a-plenty in cheerful labour in the open fields, an' a mighty slim chance for the doctor. Why, they's even wealth in it ef it's lived right: not riches, maybe, but wealth. . . . Why, the way I read Scripture, it seems to me we're given to understand that heaven is a home of wealth. 'Many mansions' sounds that a-way, I'm shore; an' golden streets shows thet they won't anything be considered too good for use. An' sometimes I've thought that maybe it meant to give us to understand that simple riches—like gold—was to be trod under foot. An' all the Revelational jewels, why, they seem to be set either in the walls, or doors, or somewhere, not let loose in piles, to be swapped or squabbled over. No riches to possess, but they's wealth to enjoy.—RUTH M'ENERY STUART, in *Century Magazine*, April, 1903.

REFERENCES.—XXI. 11.—J. Waddington, *Penny Pulpit*, No. 1680, p. 479.

GATES ON EVERY SIDE

'On the east, three gates; on the north, three gates; on the south, three gates; on the west, three gates.'—REV. XXI. 13.

WHEN St. John saw the holy city, the new Jerusalem, coming down from God out of heaven, it is clear that the entrance-gates made a deep impression on his mind. Over and over again he comes back to the theme, speaking of their number, their substance, their beauty, and the names written upon them. He tells us, for example, that the city had twelve gates and at the gates twelve angels. Next he relates that the twelve gates were twelve pearls; every several gate was of one pearl. And once more, in this text, we learn that there were three on every side, looking away to the four quarters of the compass, on the east and the north and the south and the west.

It is all a picture, of course; a picture, not in colours but in poetry; a picture of the great love of God the Father. God will have all men to be saved; and the twelve gates, facing each possible approach to the city, are an emblem of that. The doors of the Father's house look out to all the winds of heaven, and they are shut neither night nor day; for the love of God is open and the heart of God is waiting. Like the entrance to a great city hospital, they are never closed. However late a wanderer may arrive, however long after the rest he may stumble in, broken and weary, he will find that he has been expected, and that kind hands are ready to receive him. The penitent never takes God unawares. The prodigal is always seen a great way off. God's care is not pre-occupied, or His mind too full to think of us. Come when or how we may, there are gates of pearl open on every side.

It is a great and moving thought that men find their way to Christ from every quarter. Yet the gates on every side call up still another suggestion; they recall the variety of *motives* by which men are led to faith. Men come from every direction, but they also come for every kind of reason.

I. Men come *from a sense of duty*. For there is a large class of persons who, though totally unaffected by emotional appeals, are yet filled with a powerful desire to do right. These people before long are confronted with the personality of Jesus; His words stick in their conscience. Soon they feel that to refuse to submit their will to Christ's is to evade responsibility and evade obligation. So the pressure on conscience grows. The necessity arises of choosing between the higher life and the lower, of seizing the one real opportunity of life, or making the great refusal.

This may not be the commonest impulse, or the easiest path; yet without question it is an impulse and a path which God Himself has appointed, and if it be followed sincerely it leads to Him. Only, if it is to do anything for us, we must be in deadly earnest, refusing to be content with a desire, and pressing with resolution on to the reality. We must make up our mind to be thorough, taking to ourselves Prof. Drummond's advice to University students: 'Don't be amphibian, trying to lead two lives; be out and out'. If conscience is urging us to Christ, then we must go all the way with conscience.

II. Others come *from vague discontent with an empty life*. They long for some purpose or ideal worth battling for; they covet an experience adequate to the enthusiasm they know they are ready to give.

III. Still others come to God *for shelter*. What these people—a great unnumbered multitude—seek in God is refuge.

Christianity, it has been said, is not a sorrowful religion, but it is a religion for the sorrowful. The Gospel would be no Gospel, and Christ would not be Christ, were there in Him no glad tidings for the friendless and the sad.

IV. Still further, others come *from fear of moral ruin*. They have learnt that they are no match for their own nature; they have discovered how little the anchors of prudence can be trusted when the storms of passion rise.

Take the gate you are nearest to; they all lead into the city that hath foundations, whose builder and maker is God.

V. Finally, many come to God *to be forgiven*. All come to this ere long; all must so come; but also many set out from it. A writer has lately said that the feeling of guilt is dead to-day; if that be true, it will pass. There is a soul of honesty in men and women that may be trusted to keep alive the feeling of accountability, so long as there is a God in heaven and failing, wandering mortals on the earth.

Let my concluding word be this, that no one entrance among them all has an exclusive claim against the others. *They all lead in;* and it is the redeeming love of God that has opened every one.—H. R. MACKINTOSH, *Life on God's Plan*, p. 29.

XXI. 13.—J. H. Jowett, *Christian World Pulpit*, vol. xlix. p. 387. F. L. Goodspeed, *Christian World Pulpit*, vol. lx. p. 10.

THE PROPORTIONS OF LIFE

'The length and the breadth and the height of it are equal.'—
REV. XXI. 16.

AT first glance this figure seems absurd. We could understand a city being equal in its length and breadth. Many fine cities of the world have been built in an almost perfect square. But this city that John saw was equal, not only in its length and breadth, but in its height as well. And it is almost impossible to picture that. I think that the truth that John 'is struggling here to utter is just the perfect symmetries of glory. John may be speaking of the city here, but he is really thinking of the citizens. There will be nothing ill-developed or unsymmetrical. But you will mark, that if the perfect life is to be quite symmetrical, that does not mean it is to be all the same. In the endless life there is no sameness, there is no dull and cheerless and wearisome monotony, but a carrying out of individual character on its own lines to its own completeness until the length and the breadth and the height of it are equal.

I. Now one of the first things that impresses us in human life is the want of proportion in men's actual characters. All character has got a threefold aspect. There are the duties of a man towards himself. There are the outgoings of his life towards his brother. There are the upgoings of his heart towards his God. And we only need to look within a little, or to think of the men we know, the men we love best, to feel that here, whatever it may be yonder, the length and the breadth and the height are never equal. And there can be little question that just that want of symmetry is often essential to what men call success.

II. Now over against our ill-proportioned characters, there stands the perfect symmetry of the character of Jesus. All that is best in the thousand hearts of men, and all that is noblest in the separate types, meets and is crowned in the Redeemer. In the midst of the blinding specialism of the age, and all the contracting and narrowing tendencies abroad, there is no such help to a fully-rounded character as a constant friendship with Jesus Christ.—G. H. MORRISON, *Flood-Tide*, p. 12.

REFERENCES.—XXI. 16.—G. Matheson, *Christian World Pulpit*, vol. li. p. 325. *Expositor* (5th Series), vol. vi. p. 341. XXI. 17.—F. W. Farrar, *Everyday Christian Life*, p. 82. XXI. 18.—T. E. Ruth, *Baptist Times and Freeman*, vol. lv. p. 39. XXI. 21.—J. Dodd Jackson, *Christian World Pulpit*, vol. liv. p. 198. J. Waddington, *Penny Pulpit*, No. 1680, p. 479.

DEUS MEUS ET OMNIA

'I saw no Temple therein.'—REV. XXI. 22.

I. LET us confess that if we now for the first time heard these words—heard them, too, after the ravishing description of our true home which precedes them, they would fall rather blank on the ear. What! we, whose highest and best times have been in the Temple of God on earth, we, who believe that the most glorious services below are but the poorest shadows, the most wretched photographic negatives of the perpetual Liturgy there; to be told at last, 'I saw no Temple therein'. What is the use of all the art, all the skill, all the labour, all the cost, to make our Churches less unworthy of the indwelling of Him whom Heaven and the heaven of heavens cannot contain? What is the use of those great speeches which glow like a warm coal at one's very heart. 'The house which I am about to build shall be wonderful great,' and the resolution of the Spanish Chapter, 'Let us build such a Cathedral that they who come after us may take us to have been mad when we imagined it,' if, after all, when these things are passed away, 'I saw no Temple therein'.

II. But then, O the depth of the riches, both of the wisdom and knowledge of God! This is not the only instance in which, as regards that our future home, what must in one point of view be taken so differently, is, if looked at aright, so glorious.

'They rest not day nor night.' That we know is said of the glorious city; said of it too, as concerning one of its chief glories and blessings. But is it not also true of the city of misery? They rest not day nor night. So, over and over again, we find that the 'very excellent things' spoken, or to be spoken, of the City of God, are things which, except for the perfect happiness of the place, must be anything but blessings; they must be curses. 'The gates of it shall not be shut at all.' Would that be any happiness, here on earth, to us in our warfare? 'For there shall be no night there.' Would that be any blessing to us, here on earth, wearied as we often are: as our dear Lord, according to His manhood, was before us? But the most remarkable lesson we have is in the most glorious self-contradiction, to say it with all reverence, in Isaiah, when that fifth Evangelist, setting forth to us those things which eye hath not seen nor ear heard, neither hath it entered into the heart of man to conceive, says: 'The sun shall be no more thy light by day; neither for brightness shall the moon give light unto thee; but the Lord shall be unto thee an everlasting light and thy God thy glory.' And then: 'Thy sun shall no more go down; neither shall thy moon withdraw itself, for the Lord shall be thine everlasting light, and the days of thy mourning shall be ended'.

III. So we come back to that 'I saw no Temple therein'. And, lest any man should say, 'This is a hard saying; who can bear it?' St. John gives us the reason, 'For the Lord God Almighty and the Lamb are the temple of it'. That is, the one Temple and the all Temple, that which cannot be seen, even then, with the bodies of our resurrection, is this and this only, the Beatific Vision.

What the Beatific Vision is, we can only fancy by knowing what it is not. And keeping all this in view, small regret shall we have in 'I saw no temple therein,' when the Beatific Vision itself will be our Temple. It is that God who is love, filling His happy servants with the outpouring of that love, it is the God who is light, satisfying them with the perfect brilliancy of that light. And always remember, that unto that height of glory our Human Nature has entered; that there, in its fullest blaze, a Man is seated at the right hand of the Father; that eyes, in every point fashioned as our eyes, behold Him there, whose face, however far off, we could not see and live.—J. M. NEALE, *Sermons on the Apocalypse, etc.*, p. 102.

REFERENCES.—XXI. 22.—J. Bannerman, *Sermons*, p. 310. R. M. Benson, *Redemption*, p. 388. XXI. 23.—Spurgeon, *Sermons*, vol. x. No. 583. Archbishop Magee, *Christ the Light of all Scripture*, p. 3.

'And the nations shall walk in the light thereof.'—REV. XXI. 24.

'THE soul that lives,' says Richard Baxter, 'ascends frequently and runs familiarly through the streets of the Heavenly Jerusalem, visiting the patriarchs and prophets, saluting the Apostles, and admiring the army of the martyrs; so do thou lead on thy heart and bring it to the palace of the great King.'

REFERENCES.—XXI. 24.—Bishop Westcott, *Christian World Pulpit*, vol. lv. p. 360. Bishop Festing, *Christian World Pulpit*, vol. lvii. p. 407. H. S. Holland, *ibid.* vol. lxi. p. 393. XXI. 25.—W. P. S. Bingham, *Sermons on Easter Subjects*, p. 149. W. H. Savile, *Church Family Newspaper*, vol. xv. p. 196.

'And there shall in no wise enter into it he that maketh a lie.' —REV. XXI. 27.

'VERACITY,' observes John Stuart Mill, in his essay upon Nature, 'might seem, of all virtues, to have the most plausible claim to being natural, since, in the absence of motives to the contrary, speech usually conforms to, or at least, does not intentionally deviate from, fact. Accordingly, this is the virtue with which writers like Rousseau delight in decorating savage life, and setting it in advantageous contrast with the treachery and trickery of civilisation. Unfortunately this is a mere fancy picture, contradicted by all the realities of savage life. Savages are always liars. They have not the faintest notion of truth as a virtue. They have a notion of not betraying to their hurt, as of not hurting in any other way, persons to whom they are bound by some special tie of obligation; their chief, their guest, perhaps, or their friend; these feelings of obligation being the taught morality of the savage state, growing out of its characteristic circumstances. But of any point of honour respecting truth for truth's sake, they have not the remotest idea; no more than the whole East, and the greater part of Europe, and in the few countries which are sufficiently improved to have such a point of honour, it is confined to a small minority, who alone, under any circumstances of real temptation, practise it.'

'A TRUTHFUL man,' said Tennyson, 'usually has all the virtues.'

'They which are written in the Lamb's book of life.'—REV. XXI. 27.

IN the *Life of Dean Stanley* (vol. II. p. 314), there is an anecdote of two soldiers who, on their way home from gunnery practice at Shoeburyness, spent a day in London and found themselves at Westminster Abbey, just as the gates were locked. A gentleman noticed them turning away in disappointment and invited them to accompany him. Taking the keys from the beadle, he showed them the sights of the abbey, and as they paused opposite one monument to a soldier he took occasion to remark, 'You wear the uniform of her Majesty, and would like, I daresay, to do some heroic deed worthy of a monument like this'. They both said, Yes, they should—when, laying his hand on each of them, he continued, 'My friends, you may both have a more enduring monument than this, for this will moulder into dust and be forgotten; but you, if your names are written in the Lamb's book of life, will abide for ever'. 'We neither of us,' said the soldiers, 'understood what he meant. But we looked into his grave, earnest, loving face, with queer feelings in our hearts, and moved on. . . . And as we travelled home, we talked about our visit to the abbey and puzzled much as to the meaning of the Lamb's book of life.' Eventually, those words of the Dean proved the turning-point in the lives of the two men and of their wives.

REFERENCES.—XXI. 27.—Spurgeon, *Sermons*, vol. xxvii. No. 1590. F. de W. Lushington, *Sermons to Young Boys*, p. 39. XXII.—*Expositor* (5th Series), vol. x. p. 464.

'A pure river of water of life, proceeding out of the throne of God and of the Lamb.'—REV. XXII. 1.

You are seeking your own will, my daughter. You are seeking some other good than the law you are bound to obey. But how will you find good? It is not a thing of choice: it is a river that flows from the foot of the Invisible Throne, and flows by the path of obedience.—Savonarola to Romola, in GEORGE ELIOT's *Romola*.

'Clear as crystal.'—REV. XXII. 1.

'CLEAR as crystal'—not concealing, but revealing. For in the day of eternity all faithful children shall be as that Father of the faithful of whom the Lord once said: 'Shall I hide from Abraham that thing which I do?'—C. G. ROSSETTI.

THROUGH the care of my parents I was taught to read nearly as soon as I was capable of it; and as I went from school one day, I remember that while my companions were playing by the way, I went forward out of sight, and sitting down I read the twenty-second chapter of Revelations: 'He showed me a pure river of water of life, clear as crystal, proceeding out of the throne of God and of the Lamb,' etc. In reading it my mind was drawn to seek after that pure habitation which I then believed God had prepared for His servants. The place where I sat, and the sweetness that attended my mind, remain fresh in my memory.— JOHN WOOLMAN's *Journal*.

REFERENCES.—XXII. 1.—H. A. Paul, *Penny Pulpit*, No. 1612, p. 295. XXII. 1, 2.—W. L. Watkinson, *The Fatal Barter*, p. 20. XXII. 1-5.—J. Bowstead, *Practical Sermons*, vol. ii. p. 282. XXII. 1-11.—A. Maclaren, *Expositions of Holy Scripture—Revelation*, p. 366.

IN THE MIDST OF THE STREET
REV. XXII. 2.

WAS there ever half so beautiful a street as that seen by the aged eyes of the seer of Patmos? In a loving description of the new Jerusalem, the city that descended from God out of heaven, he noticed that in the midst of the street there was a river, and on either side of the river there were trees—trees of life. A tree in the street! And what a tree! Ever young and fair, bearing fruit all the year round, and dressed in leaves which were able to heal the sick and torn nations of the world as soon as they entered this street of the city of God and plucked thereof. Beautiful street of a beautiful city! If only our unbelieving eyes could catch a sight of such a street with the magic, beneficent tree in the midst of it, how eagerly we too would run to pluck its leaves and heal our distracted hearts!

I. But what is it that keeps us back? Why do we not see the city? And why do we not eat of the fruit of this tree of life? Is it because they are so far away? Perhaps they are not so far as we think. For this city, remember, is not in the heavens; it is a city that came down out of heaven upon the earth. Call it, if you like, a dream city; but it is a dream of this world, and not of the skies. For, note, there are nations to be healed. The work of the world is not yet done. Its nations are sick; the mind and the heart are not sound; they need healing. And they find it on the leaves of the tree in the street of the city of God. So it would seem as if the vision that sustained the aged heart of this true seer was that of some heavenly city in this world. True, there lies upon this city a wondrous light, such as never was on sea or land; and no city that has ever been built by human hands can compare with it for the nobility of its inhabitants. But it seems, after all, to be a city set up upon the earth, inhabited not by spirits but by living men, with the living God among them.

II. Wherever men are gathered together, there is some not altogether ignoble life. For the existence of cities, when you come to think of it, is a recognition, however unconscious, of the brotherhood of men and of their need of one another. Every one who is honestly working is doing something for that great organism which we call society; each, in doing his own work, is serving the others—it may be unwittingly—and blessing the whole. Where two or three are gathered together in the name of Jesus, there He is in the midst of them, to bless them; and where hundreds and thousands are gathered together in the interests of a common civilisation, we may well believe that Jesus is not far away, though there is not a little on which He could only look with eyes of sorrow. And we may well believe that there is a tree of life somewhere in the midst.

III. The obligations of religion to the street and to all that ramified social life which the street implies, are very great. Jesus loved the street. There were indeed times when He had to bid His disciples go apart into a desert place and rest awhile; but it was that they might enter on their work again with strength renewed. He left the wilderness in which He sojourned for a while after the call to His ministry, to work among the busy haunts of men in the cities on the shore of the lake of Galilee. The city, its needs and its redemption, were ever in His thoughts. He would fain have gathered her people together as a hen gathers her brood under her wings. He did not shirk the responsibilities of the unlovely street. To Him it was not unlovely; it was the field on which He believed that, in the far-off day, there would be a golden harvest.

The tree of life was in the midst of the street, and its leaves were for the healing of the nations.—J. E. MACFADYEN, *The City With Foundations*, p. 237.

REFERENCES.—XXII. 2.—G. A. Gordon, *Christian World Pulpit*, vol. xlvi. p. 72. Spurgeon, *Sermons*, vol. xxi. No. 1233. Bishop Chadwick, *Christian World Pulpit*, vol. liii. p. 355; vol. lx. p. 283. *Expositor* (5th Series), vol. ii. p. 60; *ibid.* vol. vi. p. 277. XXII. 3.—Spurgeon, *Sermons*, vol. xxvii. No. 1576. J. M. Neale, *Sermons on the Apocalypse*, p. 79. XXII. 3, 4.—R. Higinbotham, *Sermons*, p. 16.

THE HEAVENLY SERVICE

'His servants shall serve Him . . . and they shall reign for ever and ever.'—REV. XXII. 3-5.

IN the first Paradise there was service in the dressing and keeping of the garden. One might say that there was more than service, in that the garden had to be *kept* as against some hostile influence; that there was working and watching, if not working and warfare, for man in Eden. We have now a harder work, a more earnest watching, a sorer conflict, for we are weaker as fallen, and the enemy is bolder. Every one of God's children has to work and watch and fight until his rest be won.

In the second Paradise there is no watching or warfare, because there is no enemy, no curse. Service alone is the task of heaven; not toilsome, for the taint of the curse no longer vitiates it; not mechanical, but spiritual; cheerful also, and perfect, because there is nothing to depress or mar it in the presence of the healing leaves of the tree of life.

Four things make the service perfect in matter and spirit:—

I. **His Servants shall see His Face.**—There is no hiding or darkening or overclouding of God's face; nothing to intercept the brightness of His countenance, and the full, clear tokens of His favour; no painful mysteries, no dark dispensations, no forsakings. The vision of God's face will make the service full of joy and strength and spirit, and banish all feeling of toil and drudgery and discontent.

II. **His Name shall be in their Foreheads.**—They are His servants here and now doing His work. But their service, like themselves and Him whom they serve, is not always recognised where it is rendered. God's name is on their foreheads now: He reads it there; angels read it there in their ministry. But the world does not see it; and it is often illegible or invisible to the servants themselves. They have not all or always that full assurance of faith which is so mighty a stimulus and so great a strength for God's service. It is not easy to maintain integrity and do work as God's servants amid the promiscuous company of the visible Church, which disturbs and deadens holy feeling and certitude, embarrasses activity, throws hesitancy and suspicion upon Christian life and work here; but there, where no forehead shall bear any other name than God's; where His name shall be visible and legible wherever it is written|; where each shall know himself and know his brother as marked by the common and only name; where each shall have the full assurance that he is God's servant and is surrounded only by God's servants—there, there will be nothing to paralyse, disconcert, or hinder that service with which God's servants shall serve Him.

III. There shall be no Night there.—No night for rest or refreshment to interrupt the service and renew flagging energy; no night of ignorance as to God's will, or of sin to obscure their perception of duty, or of sorrow to distract their attention. No natural, artificial, borrowed, or secondary light needed, for pushing on delayed, or overtaking neglected, work; no light that can go out or fail, to the hindering of the service. What a service that must be which is carried on for ever in the unfading and unsetting light of God Himself by men who know Him and their duty, no longer through means and ordinances and providences circuitously, but directly and immediately, as they see light in His light!

IV. They shall Reign for Ever and Ever.—They serve, but they also reign. They contemplate their service and execute it as from Christ's throne on which they reign with Him. They have reached their kingdom through overcoming by the blood of the Lamb and the word of their testimony, through faithfulness over a few things. They will welcome their kingly state, their rule over many things, not as giving them exemption from all service, but as inspiring and fitting them for a nobler service and a more perfect fidelity to duty. They will feel that the dignity to which they have been promoted, the higher capacities with which they have been invested, and the unbounded confidence which has been placed in them, bind them to a loftier and more extensive and more successful service; to a service in which there is nothing petty, or mean, or sordid; to a service where no trace can be found of paltry motives, and jealousies, and resentments, such as touch the loyalty of mere subjects or servants; to a service which, in its largeness and frankness, and fearlessness and loyalty, is worthy of those who are, not only servants, but kings reigning for ever and ever.

REFERENCES.—XXII. 4.—Spurgeon, *Sermons*, vol. xiv. No. 824. A. R. Ashwell, *God in His Work and Nature*, p. 46.

'There is no night there.'—REV. XXII. 5.

J. M. NEALE wrote of the death of Charles Simeon: 'I cannot tell you how much I am grieved for his loss. I should think there was a great deal of sorrow to-night in Cambridge. I was going to say, What a glorious night for him! but there is no night there.'

REFERENCES.—XXII. 5.—W. H. Evans, *Short Sermons for the Seasons*, p. 170. S. Bentley, *Parish Sermons*, p. 127. C. Bradley, *Faithful Teaching*, p. 178.

'Blessed is he that keepeth the words of the prophecy of this book.'—REV. XXII. 7 f.

WHEN you have read, you carry away with you a memory of the man himself; it is as though you had touched a loyal hand, looked into brave eyes, and made a noble friend; there is another bond on you thenceforward; binding you to life and to the love of virtue.—R. L. STEVENSON.

REFERENCES.—XXII. 8-21.—C. Anderson Scott, *The Book of Revelation*, p. 322. XXII. 9.—Reuen Thomas, *Christian World Pulpit*, vol. xlviii. p. 139. *Expositor* (6th Series), vol. v. p. 123. XXII. 10-12.—T. Arnold, *Sermons*, vol. ii. p. 118.

REV. XXII. 11.

FROM this text George Gilfillan heard Dr. Chalmers preach in Edinburgh on 9th October, 1831.

'Being near-sighted, and the morning rather dim, we could not catch a distinct glimpse of his features, we saw only a dark mass of man bustling up the pulpit stairs, as if in some dread and desperate haste. We heard next a hoarse voice, first giving out the psalm in a tone of rapid familiar energy, and after it was sung and prayer was over, announcing the text, "He that is unjust let him be unjust still (*stull*, he pronounced it), he that is filthy (*fulthy*, he called it), let him be filthy still, and he that is righteous, let him be righteous still, and he that is holy let him be holy *stull*". And then, like an eagle leaving a mountain cliff, he launched out at once on his subject, and soared on without any diminution of energy or flutter of wing for an hour and more. The discourse . . . had two or three magnificent passages, which made the audience for a season one soul—a burst, especially, we remember, in reference to the materialism of heaven—"There may be palms of triumph, I do not know—there may be floods of melody," etc., and then he proceeded to show that heaven was more a state than a place.'

REFERENCE.—XXII. 11.—Archbishop Magee, *Christ the Light of all Scripture*, p. 147.

'Behold, I come quickly; and my reward is with me, to render to each man according to his work.'—REV. XXII. 12.

PIETY cannot maintain itself if God makes no difference between the godly and the wicked, and has nothing more to say to the one than to the other; for piety is not content to stretch out its hands to the empty air, it must meet an arm descending from heaven. It must have a reward, not for the sake of the reward, but in order to be sure of its own reality, in order to know that there is a communion of God with men, and a road which leads to it.—WELLHAUSEN.

REFERENCES.—XXII. 12.—Bishop Alexander, *The Great Question*, p. 187. E. A. Bray, *Sermons*, vol. i. p. 320. XXII.

13.—Spurgeon, *Sermons*, vol. ix. No. 546. A. J. Mason, *Christian World Pulpit*, vol. lix. p. 28. J. M. Neale, *Sermons on the Apocalypse*, p. 92. Phillips Brooks, *The Mystery of Iniquity*, p. 310.

'Blessed are they that wash their robes, that they may have the right to come to the tree of life.'—Rev. xxii. 14.

UNDER the head of spiritual self-seeking ought to be included every impulse towards psychic progress, whether intellectual, moral, or spiritual in the narrow sense of the term. It must be admitted, however, that much that commonly passes for spiritual self-seeking in this narrow sense is only material and social self-seeking beyond the grave. In the Mohammedan desire for paradise and the Christian aspiration not to be damned in hell, the materiality of the goods sought is undisguised. In the more positive and refined view of Heaven, many of its goods, the fellowship of the saints and of our dead ones, and the presence of God, are but social goods of the most exalted kind. It is only the search of the redeemed inward nature, the spotlessness from sin, whether here or hereafter, that can count as spiritual self-seeking pure and undefiled.'—PROF. JAMES, *Textbook of Psychology*, p. 185.

REFERENCES.—XXII. 14.—J. Keble, *Miscellaneous Sermons*, p. 267. A. Maclaren, *Expositions of Holy Scripture—Revelation*, p. 380. XXII. 14, 15.—G. W. Brameld, *Practical Sermons* (2nd Series), p. 63. *Expositor* (6th Series), vol. viii. p. 338.

'I am . . . the bright and morning star.'—Rev. xxii. 16.

IN Dr. Andrew Bonar's diary for 18th September, 1849, there is this entry : 'This morning early I had awakened and looked out. It was about four o'clock. The morning star was shining directly before our window in a bright sky. One part of the window was misty with frost, the other clear, and through the clear part the star shone most beautifully. I thought of Christ's words, ὁ ἀστὴρ ὁ λαμπρὸς ὁ πρωϊνός (Rev. xxii. 16). Christ is all this in this world to me till the day break. I fell asleep, and when I next awoke the sun was shining through my room. Shall it not be thus at the Resurrection ? Our shadowy views of Christ are passed, and now He is the Son of Righteousness'.

DOES not every *fresh* morning that succeeds a day of gloom and east wind, seem to remind us that for a living spirit, capable, because living, of renovation, there can be no such thing as 'failure,' whatever a few past years may seem to say ?—F. W. ROBERTSON, *Letters*.

REFERENCES.—XXII. 16.—*Expositor* (7th Series), vol. v. p. 14.

'The Spirit and the Bride say, Come.'—Rev. xxii. 17.

YET some Christians traverse the world like walking funerals rather than like wedding-guests ! (Know thyself.)—C. G. ROSSETTI.

REFERENCES.—XXII. 16.—J. Johnston, *Penny Pulpit*, No. 1509, p. 209. J. C. M. Bellow, *Sermons*, vol. i. p. 15. *Expositor* (5th Series), vol. iii. p. 450.

THE HOLY SPIRIT AND CHRISTIAN MISSIONS

'And the Spirit and the Bride say, Come. And let him that heareth say, Come.'—REV. XXII. 17.

I. IT either is or is not true that the Spirit of God works in the heart of every man on the face of the earth. It is or is not true that God leaves not Himself without witness in every heart, that there is a light which lighteth every man, that the nations which have not 'the law,' or 'revelation,' as generally understood, have the law or revelation written on their hearts. It either is or is not true that when truth, as truth is in Jesus, is faithfully preached, the Holy Spirit convicts the world of sin, of righteousness and of judgment. And if these things are true, according to New Testament conceptions, the scattering of the seed of the kingdom throughout the whole is sowing in a prepared field.

But a belief in the Holy Spirit implies more than this. It implies a living link between all human spirits, because the same Divine Spirit speaks to all. Carlyle's Irish widow in Edinburgh, when charitable relief for herself and her children had been refused, proved her sisterhood to those who disowned her, when the typhus fever, of which she died, spread and killed seventeen others in the neighbourhood. There are many ways of proving the solidarity of the race, but one of the soundest and most abiding is the fact that under the strangest disguises the human heart has the same needs, the same kinship to the Divine, and is more or less effectively taught by the same Divine Spirit.

All the efforts man can put forth for the extension of the kingdom are needed, but it is the touch of the Divine which inspires, transforms, vivifies. Any overpowering force which would compel all Christians always to put first things first in spiritual work would revive the Church to-day and regenerate the world to-morrow.

This may be seen if we think out the direct operation of the Spirit in relation to (1) religious convictions, (2) Christian motives, and (3) the spirit and temper of Christian enterprise. So many of the religious ideas that are current to-day are not deep convictions, and they need to be made such. So many genuine convictions are held in reserve in the background of the mind, and they need to be made living, active, fiery, penetrative. Christian motives operate, but languidly and imperfectly.

Only the Divine Spirit Himself can so stir and shake the Church to its very depths that truisms may be translated into truths that will prove mighty to the pulling down of strongholds and the bringing of every thought into captivity to the obedience of Christ.

II. The Holy Spirit alone furnishes the secret of true unity. Unity in the ranks of the Christian army as it goes forth to bloodless victory ; unity amongst the kingdoms of this world when at last they become the kingdom of our Lord and of His Christ. Christians at least profess always to be seeking for unity, but a large proportion steadfastly refuse to adopt the only promised means for obtaining it.

The New Testament Churches were at one because they enjoyed 'the unity of the Spirit'; they were bidden not to make it, but to keep it (Eph. IV. 3). St. Paul obviously meant a oneness which the Holy Spirit Himself effected by His indwelling, the 'one Spirit' mentioned in the next verse. It is true he mentions 'one body,' and the mystical body of Christ cannot be multiplied or divided. But it is the living Head who makes it one, and the indwelling Breath of God that keeps it one. St. Paul would never have separated the two halves of Irenæus' sentence, 'Where the Spirit is, there the Church is; and where the Church is, there the Spirit is and all true liberty'. But if he had been compelled to take either alone, he would have chosen the former half—the root which would bring the fruits, not the fruit which is unable to exist without the roots. If the Church was truly one at first, it was not in virtue of a uniformly defined creed, or a universally accepted code, or an exactly identical mode of government in all the Churches, but because all acknowledged one Father, one Lord and one Spirit who was the very bond of fellowship with the Father and the Son and the bond of union in the members one with another.—W. T. Davison, *The Indwelling Spirit*, p. 195.

THE BRIDE OF CHRIST

'The Spirit and the Bride say, Come.'—Rev. xxii. 17.

There are some very curious ideas in men's minds as to what the Church is. The Scriptural idea of the Christian Church is something more than a building. It is nothing less than a body, which is styled the Bride of Christ. Christ the Bridegroom, the Church the Bride. And if people would only realise the Scriptural conception of the Christian Church, then I think that the Christian Church would begin to do its work, to realise its place, and to become what Jesus Christ would have it be. It is because the Christian Church has never yet, as a whole, risen to its high ideal as the Bride of Christ that it is so weak, so poor, so feeble.

Now let us look at it. The Church the Bride of Jesus Christ. What is the character of the Bride of Jesus Christ?

I. **United in its Parts.**—It must be a Bride united to Christ by the very closest possible ties. It is a Bride which must be united to the Father, God. It is a Bride in which there is no division, in which there is unity of character, of purpose, and of aim. Our Lord prayed earnestly for those who composed His Church, the Bride of Himself, 'that they all may be one, as Thou, Father, art in Me, and I in Thee'. No less an ideal than the unity of the Father and the Son must be the ideal which Christians must aim at developing in their midst, every Church member united to other members of the Church even as God the Father and Son are united as one.

II. **Holy in its Entirety.**—We are told, in the Epistle to the Ephesians, the Church must be without 'spot, or wrinkle, or any such thing'. We are told in that very same chapter of the Lord Jesus Christ, the wonderful Bridegroom, that He will sanctify and cleanse His Church, His Bride. The Lord Jesus Christ will come and take His Church, sanctify it, set it apart, comfort, consecrate it, make it holy, pure, spotless, fit to be the Bride even of Himself. Oh, the marvellous character that the Christian Church ought to possess! If every one of us could sometimes sit down and turn to 1 Corinthians XIII. and read through that marvellous description of love—'love thinketh no evil,' and so on, right through from the beginning to end—that is just the picture of what the Bride of Christ should be, the character of the Church of the living God.

III. **It should be Alive.**—The Church which is the Bride of Jesus Christ can only be manned by living men—live men in the pulpit, live men in the pew, live men as officers. The Bride of Christ must thrill with life, with power.

IV. **Animated by Loyalty.**—The Church of Christ united, holy, alive, will be animated with loyalty to the common Head, aye, and loyalty to the different parts. If there is anything the matter with one's eye, the hand immediately goes up to it, to see whether it can put it right. You see the analogy St. Paul uses—the analogy of the body—to show how every part is depending on every other part, and so the Christian Church is animated with loyalty, not only to Jesus Christ, but that very loyalty to Jesus Christ implies loyalty to each other, loyalty to each other's character and life. Never detract, then, from the merits of another, but rather add to them, 'in love preferring one another'. You may always tell how close the Church is to Jesus Christ by how close it is to its different parts.

References.—XXII. 17.—Spurgeon, *Sermons*, vol. v. No. 279; vol. viii. No. 442; vol. xxiii. No. 1331; vol. xxvii. No. 1608, and vol. xlvi. No. 2685. Lyman Abbott, *Christian World Pulpit*, vol. xliv. p. 88. E. M. Geldart, *Faith and Freedom*, p. 94. Basil Wilberforce, *Christian World Pulpit*, vol. xlv. p. 38. F. D. Maurice, *Sermons*, vol. v. p. 221. J. Keble, *Miscellaneous Sermons*, p. 209. T. H. Ball, *Persuasions*, p. 23. J. Bannerman, *Sermons*, p. 382. G. W. Brameld, *Practical Sermons*, p. 168. J. Vaughan, *Fifty Sermons* (9th Series), p. 212. A. Maclaren, *Expositions of Holy Scripture—Revelation*, p. 391. XXII. 18, 19.—*Expositor* (6th Series), vol. v. p. 208; *ibid.* vol. vi. p. 124. XXII. 20, 21.—H. Bonar, *Short Sermons for Family Reading*, p. 456.

THE GRACE OF CHRIST

'The grace of our Lord Jesus Christ be with you all.'—Rev. XXII. 21.

What is Grace? In ordinary parlance, grace is beauty; and, etymologically, grace means that which gives joy, that which is delightful. The grace of our Lord Jesus Christ was the quality of His life. I would note the salient characteristics of this grace, the beautiful grace of our Lord Jesus Christ.

I. And the first note is, holiness. The beauty of holiness was on Christ, and indeed He was the only man to Whom the word 'holy' can be applied without any reservation at all.

II. Great was His loving-kindness. He was utterly disinterested. And the charm of His character is enduring.

III. He was so humble—meek and lowly of spirit. Servant of servants, washing the disciples' feet. Holy, loving, humble, forgiving—that is the grace of our Lord Jesus, and that grace is the best thing in life, is the loveliest quality in our human nature.

—B. J. SNELL, *The Examiner*, 12th July, 1906, p. 673.

'The grace of the Lord Jesus be with the saints.'—REV. XXII. 21.

GRACE is needed to make a man into a saint. Whoever doubts this knows neither what a saint is nor a man.—PASCAL.

THE last words of Mr. Honest were: Grace Reigns. So he left the world.—BUNYAN.

OUTLINES FOR THE CHURCH YEAR

ADVENT

Advent exhortation, An, 382.
Back to Christ, 982.
Broken hearted, The, 26.
Christ the Judge, 229.
Christ the light giver, 685.
Christian hope, 506.
Coming of the end, The, 575.
Faithfulness and fear, 529.
Intermediate goal, The, 531.
Latest trumpet of the seven, The, 581.
Presence of Christ, The, 151.
Second Advent, The, 499, 771.
Sleepers, Wake, 684.
That blessed hope, 807.

CHRISTMAS DAY

Angelic greeting, The, 11.
Angels' song, The, 14.
Bread for the hungry, 240.
Child Jesus, The, 12.
Chimes of Christmas, The, 14.
Christmas Lessons, 12.
Coming of the Saviour, The, 631.
Equanimity, 727.
Glad tidings, 11.
Go unto Bethlehem, 15.
Great joy, 10.
Holly, Yew, and Laurel, 193.
Hour, and the Divine deliverer, The, 632.
Incarnation, The, 191, 630, 1041.
Love of the cradle, The, 7.
Manger bed, The, 8.
Manger unveiling, The, 9.
Manifestation of the invisible God, The, 192.
Message of the angel, The, 14.
Mission of Christ, The, 631.
Philanthropy of God, The, 809.
Pilgrimage to Bethlehem, The, 16.
Purpose of the birth, The, 12.
Revelation in a Son, 823.
Shepherds and the angels, The, 9.
Shepherds, The, 9.
Sign, The ; a Babe, 14.
Word made flesh, The, 190.

ST. STEPHEN'S DAY

First Christian martyr, The, 393.
Martyrdom of St. Stephen, 392, 393.
St. Stephen's vision, 391.
Supreme moments, 392.
Vision of Christ, The, 391.

ST. JOHN THE EVANGELIST'S DAY

Disciple whom Jesus loved, The, 358, 359, 361, 362.
Fellowship with Christ, 945, 949.

THE HOLY INNOCENTS

Holy Innocents' Day, 1029.
New song, A, 1028.

EPIPHANY

Quiet life, The, 22.
Steps of His most blessed life, The, 23.

LENT

A besetting sin, 864.
Armour of God, The, 697.
Call to repentance, The, 98.
Comfort in temptation, 551.
Conflict with sin, The, 640.
Forgiveness, 84.
Holiness of life, 874.
On the threshold of Lent, 139.
Preparation for Lent, 2.
Sorrow for sin, 614.
Temptation, 549.
Trinity of temptation, The, 697.

PALM SUNDAY

Value of a pageant, The, 144.

GOOD FRIDAY

Atonement, 609.
Christ crucified, 512.
Christ's finished work, 340.
Compelling passages, 343.
Considerateness of Jesus, The, 336.
Cross of Jesus, The, 648.
Crucified through weakness, 620.
Death of Christ, The, 571.
Divine power of the Cross, The, 332.
'Father, forgive them,' 166-168.
'Father, into Thy hands I commend My spirit,' 171-173.
Fifth word from the Cross, The, 339, 340.
Gethsemane, the rose-garden of God, 844.
Great expiation, The, 517.
He died for all, 606.
Herod the Tetrarch, 163.
Incomparable glory of the Cross, The, 647.
Inscription on the Cross, The, 334, 335.
'I thirst,' 338.
'It is finished,' 341, 342.
Jesus providing for His own, 337.
Looking for the wrong thing, 163.
'Lord, remember me,' 168-170.
Mary, the mother of Jesus, 335.
Meekness of the Cross, The, 711.
Message that convinces, The, 515.
'My Kingdom is not of this world,' 331.
One offering, The, 847.
Our Lord's sacrifice, 843.
Pains of thirst, The, 338.
Power of the Cross, The, 512, 735.
Preaching Christ crucified, 514.
Prevailing voice, The, 164.
Priesthood of Christ, The, 843.
Revealing Cross, The, 166.
Silence of Jesus, The, 333.
Sin, 609.
'To-day shalt thou be with Me in Paradise,' 170, 171.
Two St. Maries at the Cross, The, 336.
Watershed, The, 512.
With Me in Paradise, 162.
Women of Jerusalem, The, 165.
Word of tender care, The, 337.

EASTERTIDE

'Alive from the dead,' 456.
Beneficent intrusions, 351.
Body in the light of the resurrection, The, 535.
Burning heart, The, 181.
Christ, a quickening Spirit, 175.
'Christ died and rose,' 503.
Christ our life, 751.
Christian gladness, 352.
Doubt of Thomas, The, 353.
Easter commands, 364.
Easter Day, 344, 585.
Easter message, The, 174.
Evidences for the resurrection, 572.
Fact of the resurrection, The, 966.
First words of the risen Lord, The, 348.
From death unto life, 603.
Hands and side, 352.
Hands of Jesus, The, 183.
Happiness of Easter, The, 69.
He would have gone further, 178.
Holden eyes, 176.
Hope and service, 586.
Life after death, 291.
Life manifested through death, 603.
Love and grief, 345.
Mary's commission, 350.
Mistaken suppositions, 347.
Our Companion, 175.
Power of Christ's resurrection, The, 718, 720.
Realised presence, The, 182.
Resurrection and personal experience, The, 719.
Resurrection Body, The, 577.
Resurrection of life, The, 272.
Resurrection, The, 573, 750.
Risen Lord, The, 179.
Rising of Christ, The, 346.
Sadness of the disciples, 176.
Supper at Emmaus, The, 180.
Supposing Him to be the gardener, 346.
'Touch Me not,' 348, 350.
Victory over sin, The, 584.
Witnesses for Christ, 183.
Wound prints, 351.

ASCENSIONTIDE

Ascended Lord, The, 317.
Ascending with Him, 655.
Ascension Day, 820, 829.
Ascension of our Lord, The, 370.
Ascension, The, 186.
Ascensiontide, 349.
Clouds that hide Christ, 369.
Crowned Christ, The, 819.
Expectation, 185.
High latitudes, 656.
New point of view, A, 369.
Promise of the Father, The, 365.
'This same Jesus,' 370.
Waiting, 365.

WHITSUNTIDE

Anointing with the Holy Spirit, The, 953.
Baptism of the Spirit, The, 366.
Body a temple, The, 534.
Coming of the Holy Ghost, The, 525.
Coming of the Spirit, The, 375, 376.
Day of Pentecost, The, 374.
Divine indwelling, The, 526.
Earthly life of the Holy Ghost, The, 316.
Enthusiasm of the Spirit, The, 689.
Fire of the Spirit, The, 768.
Fruition of fuller life, The, 683.
Fruit of the Spirit, The, 640, 642.
Grieve not the Spirit, 678.
Holy Spirit in the dispensation, The, 378.
Holy Spirit's love, The, 509.
Inspiration and outlook, 378.
Joy the fruit of the Spirit, 642.
Lesson of Pentecost, The, 374.
Ministry of a transfigured Church, The, 375.
Office and work of the Holy Ghost, The, 420, 463.
Plenitude of the Spirit, The, 687.
Spirit-filled life, The, 688.
Spirit of power, The, 374.
Spiritual power, 367.
There is a Holy Ghost, 419.
Unity of the Spirit, The, 669-672.
White raiment, 1003.
Whit-Sunday, 377.
Witness for Jesus, 368.
Witness of personal service, The, 367.
Witnessing Church, A, 367.
Witnessing Spirit, The, 389.

HOLY TRINITY SUNDAY

Man's how and Christ's how, 211.
Revelation of God to man, The, 192.
Serpent in the wilderness, The, 216.
Spiritual doctrine of God, The, 969.

SAINTS' DAYS

ST. ANDREW

Character of St. Andrew, The, 194.
Missionary spirit, The, 196.
Modesty of true greatness, The, 195.
Our business and how to do it, 196, 197.
St. Andrew's Day, 931.
World's benefactors, The, 195.

ST. THOMAS THE APOSTLE

Doubt of Thomas, The, 353-357.
St. Thomas, 270.

CONVERSION OF ST. PAUL

Christian metamorphosis, The, 707.
Conversion of Saul, The, 396, 397.
Conversion of St. Paul, 626.
Magnifying Christ, 704.
Making of an Apostle, The, 396.
Secret of St. Paul's life, The, 706.
St. Paul's love for Christ, 626.
St. Paul's sacrifices, 717.
What is it to be a Christian? 627.
Worship and service, 409.

ST. MATTHEW'S DAY

Unknown Apostle, The, 611.
See also, 372-374.

ANNUNCIATION OF THE BLESSED VIRGIN MARY

Angels' greeting to the Virgin Mary, The, 3.
Handmaid of the Lord, The, 4.
Reverence due to the Virgin Mary, The, 5.

ST. MARK'S DAY

John, whose surname was Mark, 407.
St. Mark's Day, 933.

ST. PHILIP AND ST. JAMES

Ethiopian convert, The, 395.
Gospel feast, The, 232, 233.
How Nathaniel came to Christ, 198.
St. Philip and St. James, 889.
Story of conversion, A, 394.

ST. BARNABAS

Character of St. Barnabas, The, 403.
Man of generosity, The, 398.
Proprietorship or stewardship, 387.
St. Barnabas' exhortation, 402.
St. Barnabas the Apostle, 402, 408.

ST. JOHN THE BAPTIST

Baptist's message to Jesus, The, 40.
Coming man, The, 41.
Friends of the Bridegroom, 221.
God-sent men, 189.
Gospel according to John the Baptist, The, 193.

Great man, A, 42.
Man called John, A, 189.

ST. PETER

Angel and the sandals, The, 406.
Benign shadows, 388.
Boldness of Peter and John, The, 383, 384.
Departing of the angel, The, 406.
Desertion and drudgery, 358.
Look of Christ, The, 160.
Lord's look, The, 161.
'Lovest thou Me,' 360.
Penitence, 161.
Peter's denial, 159.
Practical type, The, 357.
St. James the Apostle, 404.
St. Peter asleep, 404.
St. Peter's deliverance, 405.
St. Peter's weakness and strength, 95.
Simon Peter, 160.
Strengthen the brethren, 157.
Vision of the great sheet, The, 400.

ST. BARTHOLOMEW

Hidden life, The, 157.

ST. MICHAEL AND ALL ANGELS

Ministering spirits, 815.
St. Michael and his angels, 1025.
Unaware of angels, 881.

ST. LUKE THE EVANGELIST

Character of St. Luke, The, 798.
Holy alliance, A, 803.
Luke, the Beloved Physician, 759.
'Only Luke is with me,' 802.
St. Luke the Evangelist, 758.
St. Luke's Gospel, 1.
What we owe to St. Luke, 811.

ST. SIMON AND ST. JUDE

Keep yourselves in the love of God, 979.

ALL SAINTS' DAY

All Saints' Day, 868.
Asleep in Jesus, 764.
Called to be saints, 436.
Many mansions, 867.
Marks of the saintly life, The, 368.
Saints of God, The, 702, 1017.
Sleeping in Jesus, 765.
Them that sleep in Him, 764.
What is a Saint? 325.

INDEX TO OUTLINES

ABEL, The faith of, 852.
Abiding in Christ, 306.
Ability which God giveth, The, 929.
Adaptation, Concurrent, 734.
Adorning the doctrine, 806.
Advent exhortation, An, 382.
— The Second, 499.
Affliction, Texts explained by, 180.
Afflictions of Christ, That which is behind the, 740.
Agnosticism, Positivism and Materialism, 187.
Agnosticisms, The two, 910.
Algebraic religion, 538.
Alive from the dead, 456.
Alliance, A holy, 803.
All Saints' Day, 436, 868.
Almsgiving, 399.
Alpha and Omega, I am, 1042.
Alternatives, 242.
Altruism, Christian, 710.
" Always," 585.
Analysis, Spiritual, 282.
Andrew, The character of St., 194.
Andrew's Day, St., 931.
Angel, Departing of the, 406.
— in man, The, 390.
— Message of the, 14.
— of the pool, The, 227.
— and the sandals, The, 406.
Angel's greeting to the Virgin Mary, The, 3.
— song, The, 14.
Angels, Unaware of, 881.
Anger, Apostolic, 649.
Animal Sunday, 469.
Annunciation of the Blessed Virgin Mary, 3.
Anointing with the Holy Spirit, The, 953.
Antagonism, The elimination of the law of, 1040.
— Limitations of the law of, 550.
Apocalyptic outlook, Christ's, 147.
Apostle, The making of an, 396.
— The unknown, 611.
Apostles, St. Simon and St. Jude, 33.
Apostolic paradox, The, 612.
— succession, 529.
— teaching, The unity of, 572.
Approachableness of Christ, The, 109.
Appropriations, Christ's, 303.
Ark and its New Sanctuary, The, 1025.
Armageddon, 1033.
Armour of God, The, 695, 697.
— — — The whole, 699.
— — light, The, 499.
Ascended Lord, The, 317.
Ascending with Him, 655.
Ascension, The, 186.
— Day, 820, 829.
— of our Lord, The, 370.
— tide, 349.
Ashamed of Christ, 55.
Asleep in Jesus, 764.
Association, The Power of, 501.
Assurance, The abounding, 742.

Athletes, Advice to young, 544.
Atonement, 609.
— An aspect of the, 262.
Atra Cura, 932.
Author and Finisher, 869.
Authority? By what, 149, 418.
— The seat of, 131.
Autumn trees without fruit, 979.
Awake, Fully, 58.

BACK to Christ, 982.
Backwater of life, The, 799.
Baptism of the Spirit, The, 366.
Baptist's message to Jesus, The, 40.
Barnabas the Apostle, St., 402, 408.
— character of St., 403.
— exhortation, St., 402.
Battle, The spiritual, 641,
Bearing one another's burdens, 644.
Beasts with lamb's horns, The, 1027.
Beggar, A blind, 139.
Belief and confession, 482.
Believers, The perseverance of, 266.
Benediction, Valediction and, 621.
Benefactors, The world's, 195.
Best wine last, The, 205.
Bethany, 268.
— Sisters: a lesson in quietude, 74.
Bethesda, The house of mercy, 227.
Bethlehem, Go unto, 15.
— Pilgrimage to, 16.
Betrayal, Contrasts of the night of, 554.
Beware of the dogs, 716.
Bible, Duty of studying the, 828.
— Neglect of reading the, 415.
— reading, A, 437, 824.
Birth, Mystery of the New, 213.
— Purpose of the, 13.
— Two aspects of the New, 212, 214.
Birth-mark, The, 251.
Birthright, Esaus who sell their, 876.
Bithynia and Jerusalem, 413.
Blessed hope, That, 807.
Blessedness, The Divine, 442.
Blessing, The present, 482.
Blind beggar, A, 139.
— Christ and the man born, 253.
— spot, The, 88.
Blindness and judgment, 257.
— of the Pharisee, The, 43.
Blood of Christ, The cleansing, 946.
Blunderers, Well-meaning, 103.
Body, God and the, 579.
— Discerning the Lord's, 556.
— in the light of the Resurrection, The, 535.
— Redemption of the, 487.
— The Resurrection, 579.
— Resurrection of the, 427.
— a temple, The, 534.
— The temple of His, 205.
Boldness, 383.
Bondage and freedom, 635.
Born of the Flesh and born of the Spirit, 211.
Bread, Daily, 82.
— for the hungry, 240.

Bread of life, The, 237, 240.
Brethren, Love to Christ's, 957.
Bride of Christ, The, 1052.
— — — Work of the, 1044.
Broken-hearted, The, 26.
Brotherhood, Christ and human, 954.
— The great human, 678.
Brother's inheritance, His, 91.
Burning and the shining, The, 230.
Business and how to do it, Our, 196.
— Religion in, 763.

CANDIDATES, The three, 64.
Candlestick, The golden, 986.
Candour of Christ, The, 329.
Care conquered by God's peace, Man's 729.
— The word of tender, 337.
Castaway, A, 546.
Centurion, The good, 38.
Certainties, Triumphant, 971, 973.
Certainty, The gospel of, 940.
Character, Acclimatisation of, 735.
— and creed, 286.
— Depth in, 37.
— Three estimates of one, 38.
— Spiritual, 530.
Charisma, The, 783.
Chastisement of the Christian, The, 873.
Child, Destiny of the holy, 18.
— Jesus, The, 12.
— — Education of the, 22.
Childhood, First words of the, 20.
Childlike character, The, 567.
Childliness, The lessons of, 681.
Children, To the dear, 682.
— of God, 465.
Choice, The personal, 551.
Choir invisible and their music, The, 113.
Christ is all, and in all, 753.
— The approachableness of, 109.
— of the boundless future, The, 479.
— The candour of, 329.
— The charm of, 615.
— The Church's conception of, 665.
— and city life, 145.
— and the Creation, 738.
— The demand of, 156.
— must depart, Why, 311.
— the door, 258.
— The ever-living, 885.
— The first principles of, 833.
— In, 461.
— The indispensable, 236.
— The indwelling, 664.
— the Judge, 229.
— the life, 237.
— our life, 250, 751.
— The look of, 160.
— The manliness of, 384.
— and His mission, 284.
— The motives of, 285.
— The presence of, 151.
— a quickening spirit, 175.
— sanctifying Himself, 328.

Christ, Suffering with, 17.
— The suffering of, 177.
— The unchangeable, 884.
— What unites to, 157.
— to us? What is, 18.
— the way, the truth, and the life, 294.
— the world's light, 247.
Christian faith, The God of, 290.
— faith, Sum and substance of the, 289.
— knowledge, 470.
— life, The, 676.
— — Beginning and development of the, 744.
— — a fight, a race, a trust, 800.
— — The ideal, 1030.
— — worth more than all things else, The, 433.
— The marks of a, 723.
— ministry, The, 557, 600.
— social life of the, 202.
— The spiritual biography of a, 453.
— What it is to be a, 627.
— Why ought I to be a, 31.
— worship, 380.
Christianity and business, 490.
— and Judaism, 813.
— a revelation, 658.
— The world's indictment of, 600.
Christmas, The chimes of, 14.
— Day, 8, 9, 11.
— lessons, 12.
Christ's appearing, The love of, 800.
— expectation, 847.
— finished work, 340.
— must, 216.
— working, Some features of, 228.
Church, the Body of Christ, The, 675.
— a family, The, 663.
— of God, The, 387.
— The nourished and cherished, 691.
— and social questions, The, 725.
Citizenship, The earthly and the heavenly, 724.
— The heavenly, 726.
City life, Christ and, 145.
— The self-doomed, 146.
— Its sin and Saviour, The, 1024.
Cleansing, Forgetting the, 939.
Clouds that hide Christ, 369.
Collection, Concerning the, 582.
Comfort, 593.
— in present weakness, The Saints in past time, 1018.
— in sorrow, 320.
Coming to oneself, 114.
Commandment, A new, 288.
Commandments, God's, 965.
Communion, A call to, 359.
Companion, Our, 175.
Completing passages, 343.
Compromise, No, 454.
Concentration, Spiritual, 721.
Conduct, The canon of, 692.
— the test of character, 457.
Conflict and conquest, 968.
Conquest, The supreme, 477.
Conscience, A good, 928.
— A ministry that satisfies the, 593.
Consecration, Entire, 65.
— of Jesus, The, 327.
Consider, 823.
Considerateness of Jesus, The, 336.
Consolation of Christ, The, 289.
Continuance, The triumph of, 599.

Contrasted destinies, 128.
Controversy, Against, 709.
Conversion, A story of, 394.
Corner-stone, The head, 310.
Coronation, The common, 924.
Courage, A call to Christian, 790.
— of love, The, 953.
Courtesy born of Jesus, The, 703.
Covenant, Articles of the New, 840, 841.
Cradle, Love of the, 7.
Cross, Attraction of the, 282.
— Divine Power of the, 332.
— Incomparable glory of the, 647.
— Inscription on the, 334, 335.
— of Jesus, The, 648.
— Offence of the, 638.
— Power of the, 512, 735.
— Preaching of the, 511.
— the proof of the love of God, The, 452.
— The revealing, 166.
— Stumbling-block of the, 638.
Crown, The alienated, 1005.
Crowned Christ, The, 819.
Crucified, Christ, 512.
— through weakness, 620.
Crusaders, Christian, 779.
Culture, The cross and, 743.
Curfew, God's mild, 667.
Cut to the quick, 619.

Dark—and Jesus not yet come, 235.
Day of Christ, Brightness of the, 299.
— The Lord's, 984, 985.
Days, On the observance of, 983.
Dayspring, The, 6.
Dead, At His feet as, 987.
Death-bed faith, 857.
Death of Christ, The, 571.
— The Christian idea of, 705.
— Emancipation from the fear of, 821.
— The escape from, 853.
— Free from, 456.
— Life after, 291.
— and the life of grace, The taste of, 820.
— Life out of, 280.
— unto life, From, 603.
Debt, The royal, 690.
Decaying love, 992.
Deep things of God, The, 522.
Defeat, The peace of, 425.
Defence and defiance, 696.
Delays, The doctrine of, 134.
— Profitable, 184.
Deliverance from the power of sin, 714.
Deliverer, The hour, and the Divine, 632.
Demas, 801.
Departure, The expediency of Christ's, 311.
Dependence, Sympathy and, 74.
Depression, Paul under, 802.
Depths of God, The, 521.
Desert flowers, 50.
Desertion and drudgery, 358.
Destiny, Three views of man's, 1011, 1012, 1014.
Deus Meus et Omnia, 1047.
Development, Life's, 580.
Devotional type, The, 75.
Diana of the Ephesians, 421.
Died for all, He, 606.
Diligence and holy ambition, Holy, 940.
Disciple whom Jesus loves, The, 361.

Discipleship, 884.
— Hidden, 344.
— The three candidates for, 62.
Disillusionment, 114.
Divine glory of Christ, The, 752.
Doctrinal fickleness, 673.
Doctrine of God, The spiritual, 969.
— and life, 791.
Door, Christ the, 258, 259.
— The closed, 1008.
— The narrow, 100.
— The open, 259.
Dost thou believe? 256.
Doubt, Reasons for, 429.
Drawing and coming, 239.
Draw near, Let us, 848.
Drifting, 817.
— from Christ, 816.
Duty, A Christian's, 767.
Dwellest, I know where thou, 994, 995.
Dying, Jesus, the helper of the, 173.

Earthen vessels, The treasure in, 602.
Easter commands, 364.
— Day, 344, 585.
— The happiness of, 69.
— Message, The, 174.
— -tide, 503.
Easy way out of it all, The, 379.
Economy, Suggestions towards a new kind of, 24.
Education of the Child Jesus, 22.
Elder brother spirit, The, 120.
Election, The doctrine of, 484.
Elevation and vision, 1009.
Emmaus, The supper at, 180.
End, Coming of the, 575.
Enemies, The testimony of His, 309.
Enfranchisement, The great, 981.
Enlargement through service, 614.
Enthusiasm, 371.
— of the spirit, The, 689.
Entombment, Escaping, 380.
Environment, The Christian's, 879.
— The law of moral, 795.
Envying, 642.
Epaphras: "A heart at leisure from itself," 715.
Equals, Our duty towards our, 119.
Equanimity, 727.
Esaus who sell their birthright, 876.
Eternal and the temporal, The, 605.
Ethiopian convert, The, 395.
Euodia and Syntyche, 727.
Evangelists, Emblems of the, 1010.
Evidence that counts, The, 244.
Evil, The consciousness of, 446.
— The evolution of, 797.
— The extinction of, 208.
— The transformation of, 617.
Example, Our, 713.
— The perfect, 287.
Excellent way, The more, 704.
Excuses, 104.
Expectation, 185.
Expiation, The great, 517.
Eyes, Holden, 176.

Failure, Faith triumphant in, 29.
— of success, The, 105.
Faint yet pursuing, 1004.
Faith, 134.
— The beatitude of, 356.
— The beginning of, 850.
— The blessing of, 356.

Faith, Christian, 850.
— Christ's view of, 206.
— on the earth, 135.
— The effect of, 594.
— that overcomes, The, 967.
— Saving, 271.
— Self-enlarging, 231.
— without sight, 357.
— Sum and substance of the Christian, 289.
— The trial of, 920.
— triumphant in failure, 29.
— Types of unavailing, 902.
— The vacillations of, 890.
— and virtue, 936.
— the way of peace, 450.
Faithful unto death, 993.
— saying, The, 778, 779.
Faithfulness and fear, 529.
— God's, 931.
Faith's heroic doing, 860.
Family, God's, 662.
— The loved, 268.
Fashion, 540.
Father, Forgive them ; for they know not what they do, 166.
— Going to the, 296.
— and the three sons, The, 116.
— Our, 79.
Fatherhood of God, The, 464.
Father's business, The, 19, 20.
Fear and love, 962, 964.
— not, 988.
Fearlessness, The ground of, 989.
Feast, The Gospel, 232.
— Will He not come to the, 276.
Feelings, Religious use of excited, 51.
Feet, At His, 43.
Fellow-workers in Christ, 508.
Fellowship with Christ, 945.
Fig-tree, The barren, 98.
Finding, The joy of, 121.
Finish, Not able to, 108.
Finished, It is, 341, 342.
Fire Christ flung on earth, The, 97.
First ideas, The persistent influence of, 315.
Fishes, Two miraculous draughts of, 28, 29.
Flowers, Desert, 50.
Following Christ, 280.
Folly, The question of, 99.
Fool, Our Lord's, 92.
— St. Paul's, 578.
Foolishness, Two estimates of, 527.
Fools, but as wise, Not as, 686.
Forbearance, The virtue of, 755.
Foreknowledge and Predestination, 475.
Forewarned, Forearmed, 594.
Forgetting the things behind, 722.
Forgive them, Father, 167.
Forgiveness, 83, 754.
— of sins, 410, 949.
Forsaken, Neither left nor, 882.
Forsaking all, 109.
Forty, Over, 385.
Foundation of God, The, 796.
Fragments, Gather up the, 234.
Frankness, of Jesus Christ, The, 292.
Freedom of the pure, The, 249.
— True, 598.
Friend in need, A, 793.
Friends of the Bridegroom, 221.
— of Christ, The, 308, 309.
— of God, 447, 903.

Friends of Jesus, Outside, 199.
Friendship with Christ, The purpose of, 309.
— — God, 307.
— Jesus our example : In, 309.
Fruit of the light, The, 683.
— of the Spirit, The, 640, 642.
Fuller life, The fruition of, 683.
Fulness of God, The, 666.
Fundamental things, Some of the, 486.
Funeral service, A, 765.

GARDENER, Supposing Him to be the, 346.
Gates on every side, 1046.
Generosity, The man of, 398.
Geometry of life, The, 565.
Gethsemane, The rose garden of God, 844.
Gift, The greatest, 86.
Gifts, The best, 559.
Girdings, The two, 361.
Giver, God as the eternal, 892.
Glad tidings, 11.
Gladness, Christian, 352.
Glass darkly, Through a, 564.
Glory, Called unto, 772.
— to glory, From, 597.
— The hope of, 741.
— Security and, 980.
— that shall be revealed, The, 1032.
— Vision of the, 275.
' Go Hence,' The call to, 303.
Goal, The intermediate, 531.
Godhead, Mystery of the, 622.
God made visible, 781.
— -sent men, 189.
God's ways, The sureness of, 373.
Golden mean, The, 729.
Good, Of the chief, 474.
— the enemy of the best, The, 717.
— and evil, The war between, 494.
Good-bye to God, Bidding, 428.
Gospel of Christ as an obligation, The, 543.
— of the glory, The, 775.
— Glory and power of the, 438.
— Heart of the, 218.
— Omissions of the, 362.
— The unalterable, 623.
— What is the, 570.
Grace of Christ, The, 1052.
— The energy of, 652.
Graces, Three great Christian, 761.
Grand God and the lowly path, The, 444.
Grapes of God, The, 862.
Gravitation, Spiritual, 615.
Greatness, The secret of, 859.
— Thoughts on God's, 297.
Greeting, The, 115.
Grieving the Spirit, 680.
Groping after God, 417.
Growth, Christian, 832.
Guidance, Divine, 426.
Guild of God, The, 523.

HABITATIONS, Temporal and spiritual, 738.
Half-hearted, To the, 757.
Hallowed be Thy name, 80.
Handmaid of the Lord, The, 4.
Hands beautiful, 182.
— of God, Into the, 173.
— of Jesus, The, 183.

Hands and side, 352.
— into Thy, 171.
Happiness of Easter, The, 69.
— of God, The, 776.
Harvest, God's, 67.
— The law of, 263.
— thanksgiving, 611.
He would have gone further, 178.
Healing the sick, 53.
— and suffering, 381.
Hearing, Prayerful, 50.
Heart, The burning, 181.
Heathen, Cry of the, 414.
Heaven, 723.
— prepared for those prepared for heaven, 519.
Heavenly calling, The, 666.
— places, In the, 653.
Heights, On the, 745.
Hell, He descended into, 836.
Herod the Tetrarch, 163.
Heroes and martyrs, 862.
Heroic, Note of the, 986.
Heroism, True, 1002.
Hidden life, The, 157.
High latitudes, 656.
— Priest, The great, 830.
Him with Whom we have to do, 829.
Hindrances, 637.
Hireling shepherd, The, 261.
History in perspective, 547.
Holiness of life, 874.
Holly, yew, and laurel, 193.
Holy Ghost, Coming of the, 525.
— — Earthly life of the, 316.
— — Office and work of the, 420.
— — There is a, 419.
— orders, The mystery of, 328.
— Spirit and the Church, The, 184.
— — in this dispensation, The, 378.
— — as a factor in our prayers, The, 473.
— Spirit's love, The, 508.
Homeless life, The, 163.
Homesickness of the soul, The, 114.
Homing of the people, The, 245.
Honour retrieved, 407.
Hope, 471.
— Christian, 506.
— and service, 586.
Hospitality, The larger, 882.
Hour, A transient, 159.
Hours, Number of the, 269.
How, Man's and Christ's, 210.
Human life, Perishing and Immortal, 911.
Husbandman, The Divine, 914.
Hypocrisy, Profession without, 629.

I THIRST, 338.
Idolatry, Modern, 974.
Ill-temper, 120.
Imitation of Jesus, The, 287.
Imperialism, Christian, 489.
Inattention, The fatal power of, 126.
Incarnation, The, 191, 630, 1041.
— of God, The, 436.
Individuality, 616.
— in Christian life and work, The place and power of, 627.
— The ideal of true, 247.
Indwelling, The Divine, 526.
— God, The, 944.
Influence, Is it good or bad ? 783.
Injurious, 776.

Innocents' Day, Holy, 1029.
Inquiring soul, Christ preaching to an, 209.
Inquiry, Reality in religious, 330.
Inscription on the cross, The threefold, 335.
Inspiration and outlook, 378.
Instances, The argument of, 917.
Intellectual type, The, 207.
Intercession, 701.
Interferences, Unwarrantable, 276.
Intrusions, Beneficent, 351.
Invisible, Revelation of the, 441.
Irrepressible in Christian testimony, The, 385.
Isolation, The splendid, 326.

James, The martyrdom of St., 404.
James's Day, St. Philip and St., 197.
Jerusalem, The new, 1038.
Jesus, The Child, 12.
— Christ in the daily life, 204.
— — as Master, 286.
— The considerateness of, 336.
— at the grave, 273.
— The Helper of the dying, 173.
— Living the life of, 241.
— The originality of, 244.
— providing for His own, 337.
— said about His first coming, What, 249.
— Seeking for, 235.
— This same, 370.
— We would see, 278.
Jewels, Imperishable, 566.
John the Baptist, Gospel according to, 193.
— the Evangelist's Day, St., 362, 945, 949.
— A man called, 189.
— St, 358.
Joy, The Angels', 112.
— of Christ, The, 307.
— Christian, 306.
— The double, 226.
— the fruit of the Spirit, 642.
— Great, 10.
— in heaven, 111.
— of the Lord, The, 69.
— The obligation of, 767.
— and Peace in believing, 506.
Judaism, Christianity and, 813.
Judge, Christ the, 229.
Judgment, 443, 531.
— Mercy and, 901.
— Redemption and, 921.
— by the twofold record, 1037.

Key, The master, 959.
Kingdom of Christ, The, 331.
— come, Thy, 80.
— Gift of the, 94.
Knowledge, Christian, 470.
— and love, 541.
— Saving, 949.
Knows about us, Things Jesus, 991.

Lamb and the book, The, 1015.
— Feeding of the, 1021.
Lamb's war with the beast, The, 1034.
Lame man healed, The, 386.
Laodicean Church, The, 1006.
Last words of the last Apostle, The, 974.
Lasts, What, 562.
Law, Fulfilling the, 496.

Law, Graciousness of the, 966.
— and love, 154.
— a schoolmaster, The, 629.
— sin, and death, 583.
Laws of the inner life, The, 461.
Lawyer's question, The, 70.
Lazarus, Why Jesus wept at the grave of, 272.
— Prayer at the resurrection of, 275.
Legacies, Christ's, 301.
Lent, Fourth Sunday evening in, 82.
— Fifth Sunday evening in, 84.
— On the threshold of, 139.
Leper, The grateful, 130.
Lesson and our teacher, Christ our, 677.
Liberty which Christ gives, The, 598.
— Christian, 636.
— the law of life in Christianity, 895.
Life, The abundant, 260.
— The brevity of our Lord's, 251.
— which is to come, Promise of the, 782.
— after death, 291.
— out of death, 280.
— hid with Christ, 750.
— The hidden, 157.
— The homeless, 63.
— Jesus Christ in the daily, 204.
— and light, 187, 188, 323.
— The love of, 927.
— manifested through death, 603.
— The promise of, 790.
— only, This, 574.
— The quiet, 22.
— What is your, 911.
Light, Christ the world's, 247.
— Walking in the, 269.
Light-giver, Christ the, 685.
Lilies grow, How the, 93.
Limitations and freedom, 636.
Listening, Always, 76.
Listlessness, 1001.
Little forgiveness, Little love, 44.
— while, A, 316.
Living the life of Jesus, 241.
— Lord, The, 989.
Loneliness, 321.
Look, The Lord's, 161.
Looking and looking off, 870.
— on the other side, 710.
— for the wrong thing, 163.
Lord Jesus, Our, 591.
Lord's Day, The, 984, 985.
— Supper, Fitness for the, 556.
— — and personal faith, The, 555.
— — Social value of the, 553.
Lost, Gospel for the, 111.
— life, A saved soul and a, 170.
— property, 142.
— Seeking the, 110, 142.
Lot's wife, 132, 133.
Love, 566.
— of Christ, The great, 307.
— Christian, 775.
— The course of true, 217.
— The depth of, 665.
— and fear, 963.
— in four dimensions, 219.
— God, Learning to, 961.
— of God, The, 661.
— — Inseparable, 478.
— — Never-failing, 479.
— and grief, 345.
— for Jesus, 360.

Love for Jesus, God's, 263.
— Law and, 154.
— The mystery of, 218.
— The perfecting power of, 755.
— The self-sacrifice of, 284.
— The tears of, 43.
Lovely, Things that are, 733.
Love's supreme disclosure, 959.
Luke, the beloved physician, 759.
— the Evangelist, St., 758, 798, 802.
— What we owe to St., 811.
Luther at Coburg, The prayers of, 916.

Magnet, The world's, 283.
Magnetism of the uplifted Lord, The, 282.
Magnifying Christ, 704.
Malefactor, The penitent, 169.
Man, The coming, 41.
— the conqueror, 1043.
— of God, The, 797.
— after God's own heart, The, 409.
— A great, 42.
— as king, 819.
— The perfect, 673.
— The true end of, 762.
— Who is best worth talking about, The, 780.
— The worth of, 112.
Manger unveiling, The, 9.
Manhood, Christian, 562.
Manifestation of the invisible God, The, 192.
Manifold grace, 929.
Manliness of Christ, The, 384.
— True, 588.
Man's course, God shaping, 426.
— need of God and God's need of man, 110.
Mansions, Many, 290, 867.
Maries at the cross, The two St., 336.
Mark's Day, St., 933.
Marriage, 201.
Martyr, The first Christian, 393.
Martyrdom, 863.
— of Stephen, The, 393.
Martyrs, Heroes and, 862.
Marvel not, 212.
Mary the mother of Jesus, 335.
Mary's commission, 350.
Materialism, National repentance, 748.
Matrimony, Holy, 202.
Matthias, St., 372.
Meekness of the cross, The, 711.
Melanchthon's last public message, 698.
Memorable places, 274.
Memory, 127.
Men, God-sent, 189.
Mend? Is it never too late to, 835.
Mercy, 35.
— and judgment, 901.
— -seat of gold, The, 949.
Message that convinces, The, 515.
Metamorphosis, The Christian, 707.
Michael and All Angels, St., 815, 1025.
Midnight, The message for, 85.
Mighty to save—mighty to keep, 923.
Mind of Christ, The, 712, 713.
Ministry, Beginning of the, 25.
— The Christian, 557, 600.
— Measuring a, 423.
Miracle, The eclipse of, 298.
— The standard, 654.
Mirror and the vision, The, 30.
Mission of Christ, The, 631.

Missionary commission of the Church, The, 353.
— motives, 385.
— spirit, The, 196.
— for to-day, The, 53.
Missions, 72.
— The Holy Spirit and Christian, 1051.
— The policy of concentration in foreign, 107.
— Our relation to foreign, 121.
Modern world, Christ's view of the, 90.
Modernizing Christianity, On, 842.
Modesty of true greatness, The, 195.
Moments, Supreme, 392.
Morality, Christian, 639.
Morning star, Gift of the, 999.
Moses, The choice of, 858.
Motives, Mixed, 277.
Motto, Our, 808.
Mount, The pattern in the, 839.
Mustard seed, The grain of, 189.
Mystery, 564.

NAME above every name, The, 386,
— A new, 997.
— No other, 382.
Nathanael came to Christ, How, 198.
Nation, The inner life of a, 663.
Natural man, The, 522.
— and the spiritual, The, 580.
Nature transformed by grace, 197.
Nearness of God, The, 417.
Near-sightedness, Religious, 937.
Need, Christ meets every, 511.
— of God, Man's, 110.
— of man, God's, 110.
Negatives, Judging by, 220.
Neglecting the great salvation, 817.
Neighbour? Who is my, 71.
Neighbourliness, The law of Christian, 72.
New life, The model of our, 445.
— point of view, A, 369.
New Year, An address for the, 744.
— Year's Sermon, A, 1040.
Night, The ministry of, 208.
Nobody—somebody—everybody, 52.
Nothing or everything, 334.

OBEDIENCE, The lesson of, 203.
Obligation, The sense of, 123.
Obscure servants of God, 995.
Offering, The one, 847.
One needful thing, 75.
Optimism, Apostolic, 491.
— The true, 474.
Order and steadfastness, 743.
Originality of Jesus, The, 244.
Orphaned for an hour, 761.
Otherness, 711.
Outsider, Claim of the, 758.
Outsiders, 568.
Outward look, The, 872.
Overcoming man, The, 996.
Own place, His, 372.

PAGEANT, The value of a, 144.
Pain of the world, The, 470.
Paradise, 1021.
— To-day shalt thou be with Me in, 170.
— With Me in, 162.
Pardon of sin, The, 227.
Parent's responsibilities, Neglect of, 21.
Past, Burial of the, 63.

Past, Emancipation from the, 938.
— The man who loses his, 975.
Patience, 772.
— with slow growth, 48.
— Sound in, 805.
Patient master and the slow scholars, The, 295.
— waiting for Christ, 773.
Patmos, Which is called, 983.
Patriotism and intercession, 659.
— in religion, 39.
Paul, conversion of St., 397, 626.
— and Silas, 415.
— in the storm, 433.
Paul's charge, St., 423.
— life, The secret of St., 706.
— love for Christ, St., 626.
— sacrifices, St., 717.
— strange ambition, 720.
— vision of Christ's body, St., 431.
Pay, When they had nothing to, 43.
Peace, 147.
— The gift of, 300, 301.
— Secrets of, 322.
— the umpire, 756.
— within and without, 493.
Penitence, 44, 161.
Penitent thief, The, 171.
Penitents, Christ remembering, 168.
Pentecost, The day of, 374.
— The lesson of, 374.
Perfect but not perfected, 722.
— type in Christ, The, 745.
Perfecting, Daily, 604.
Perfection, Christian, 621.
Perils of spiritual life and fellowship, Masked, 978.
Perplexity, The point of, 317.
Perseverance, Patient, 152.
Persuaded, Not yet, 129.
Peter asleep, St., 404.
— and John, The boldness of, 383.
Peter's deliverance, St., 405.
— denial, 159.
— weakness and strength, St., 95.
Petition, The second, 81.
Pharisee, Blindness of the, 43.
— and the publican, The, 136.
Philanthropy of God, The, 809.
Philip and St. James, St., 889.
— — — James's day, St., 197.
Physician, The Good, 400.
Pillar in the House of God, A, 1005.
Pillars—or caterpillars! 1006.
Plainly, Tell us, 265.
Pleasing Christ, 684.
Pleasure, The use and abuse of, 796.
Plenitude of the Spirit, The, 687.
Ploughman, The spiritual, 65.
Poet, The Divine, 1041.
Porter openeth, To him the, 257.
Possessions of the Christian life, The unlimited, 612.
Power of God, The, 440.
— manifested, 761.
— The Spirit of, 374.
— Spiritual, 367.
Practical type, The, 357.
Praise, The sacrifice of, 887.
Praising God, 380.
— people, The duty of, 552.
Pray, Teach us to, 77.
— without ceasing, 767.
Prayer is answered, How, 971.
— Christ's lessons in, 76.

Prayer, God the offerer of, 472.
— The Holy Mount of, 57.
— Jesus our example in, 78.
— The Lord's, 79.
— The metamorphic power of, 57.
— and its response, 31.
— of the scorned, The, 136.
— and temperament, 918.
Prayerful hearing, 50.
Prayers of Luther at Coburg, The, 916.
Preaching, Christ crucified, 514.
— The justification of Christian, 742.
Precedents, Misused, 61.
Pre-eminent Lord, The, 739.
Preferences, The higher, 749.
Preparation for the best, 2.
— Progress needs, 32.
Presence of Christ, The, 151.
— The real, 556.
— The realised, 182.
Priesthood of Christ, The, 843.
— A royal, 923.
Prince and his saving gifts, The, 389.
Prize was won at an Old Athletic Festival, How the, 544.
Progress through decay, 603.
— needs preparation, 32.
Promise of the Father, The, 365.
Prophecies of Jesus, The, 234.
Proportions of life, The, 1047.
Proprietorship or stewardship, 387.
Provision, Superabundant, 233.
Publican, Pharisee and the, 136.
Publican's prayer, The, 137.
Pure, Danger and pain of the, 302.
— Freedom of the, 249.
Putting on Christ, 500.

QUESTION, The lawyer's, 70.
— A vital, 255.
Quiet life, The, 22.
— mind, The, 693.
Quietness, The ambition of, 763.
Quietude, A lesson in, 74.

RACE and the fight, The, 545.
Raiment, White, 1003.
Rainbow and the throne, The, 1009.
Raised with Christ, 746.
Rank, 575.
Ray and the reflection, The, 964.
Readiness of the gospel of peace, The, 700.
Reality Reduplicates, 955.
Receptivity, The grace of, 532.
Recognised, though afar off, 116.
Reconciliation in Christ, 607.
— after conversion, 608.
Redeemed life God's workmanship, The, 657.
Redemption, The Divine source of, 778.
— and judgment, 921.
Reigning in life, 453.
Reincarnation of Christ, The, 634.
Religion, Patriotism in, 39.
Religious conviction, Progress in, 851.
Remorse, The tears of, 877.
Renewal, Constant, 604.
Repentance, The call to, 98.
Request, The disciples', 77.
Rescue, The forlorn, 930.
Response, Prayer and its, 31.
Responsibility, Individual, 645.
— Personal, 644.
Rest, Our Lord in work and, 222.

Rest, From strain to, 243.
Resting-places, Many, 290.
Resurrection, The, 573, 750.
— body, The, 577.
— of the body, The, 151.
— change, The, 990.
— Evidences for the, 572.
— Fact of the, 966.
— The Gospel of Christ's, 571.
— Impersonal, 238.
— Implications of the, 416.
— and the life, The, 272.
— and personal experience, 719.
— The power of Christ's, 718, 720.
— Witnesses of the, 364.
Retribution, 127.
Revelation, By, 624.
— of God to man, The, 192.
— Progressive, 652.
Reverence, 988.
Rich and yet poor, 92.
Ridicule, The weapon of, 52.
Righteous Father revealed by Christ, The, 329.
— and the good, The, 451.
Righteousness of God, The, 440.
Rights and duties, Our, 495.
Risen with Christ, 746.
— life, The, 747.
— Lord, The, 179.
— — First words of the, 348.
Rising of Christ, The, 346.
Rivalry and service, 59.
Robe, The, 117.
— The best, 118.
Rocks, Biblical, 546.
Ruin of a masterpiece, The, 905.

Sabbath, The men without a, 101.
— of the Son, The, 826.
Sacramental remembrance and testimony, The, 555.
— thoughts, 155.
Sacrifice of God the Father, The, 424.
— The living, 486.
— Our Lord's, 843.
— St. Paul's view of, 560.
— of praise, The, 887.
Sadness of the disciples, The, 176.
Saint? What is a, 325.
Saintly life, Marks of the, 368.
Saints of Cæsar's household, The, 136.
— Called to be, 510.
— of God, The, 702, 1017.
— Weapons of the, 601.
Salvation, Assurance of, 415, 835.
— for the chief of sinners, 777.
— The Trinity in, 211.
Sanctification, 507.
— Complete, 770.
Sanctifying Himself, Christ, 328.
Satan, The depths of, 998.
Satisfaction, The desire for, 137.
Saul, The conversion of, 396.
Save, The power of Christ to, 838.
Saved soul and a lost life, A, 170.
Saviour, Assured knowledge of the personal, 792.
— Coming of the, 631.
— An Old Testament portraiture of the, 505.
Seals, Breaking of the, 1013.
Second Advent, The, 771.
Secret stairs, God's, 811.
Secrets made known, 528.

Security and glory, 980.
See far enough, The man who cannot, 937.
Seed, The word as, 46.
— among thorns, 48.
Seeing Jesus, 278.
Seeker, The best, 141.
Seeking for Jesus, 235.
— the lost, 110.
Seeming to have, 49.
Seen . . . not seen, 605.
Self-centred or Christ-centred, 91.
— -denial, The law of, 54.
— examination, A test of, 957.
— -inquiry in religion, 412.
Selfishness of society, The, 103.
Sensualist, The, 875.
Serpent lifted up, The, 215.
— in the wilderness, The, 216.
Serpents and scorpions, 68.
Servant, The form of a, 714.
— as his Lord, The, 962.
Serve, Saved to, 1019.
Service, The dignity of, 1020.
— Enlargement through, 614.
— Four points of good, 204.
— The heavenly, 1049.
— Hope and, 586.
— in a lowly sphere, 537.
— to man, 287.
— of men, The, 66.
— Quality of, 434.
— Rivalry and, 59.
— The witness of personal, 367.
Setting suns, 27.
Seven, 1001.
— Words from the cross, The, 167.
Shadows, Benign, 388.
Shame, The, 871.
— and sorrow, Ah the bitter, 608.
Sheep, The other, 262.
Shepherd, The good, 262.
— The hireling, 261.
— and the sheep, The, 258.
— Voice of the true, 266.
Shepherd's power over His life, The, 264.
Shepherds and the angels, The, 9.
— of Bethlehem, The, 9.
Short-sightedness, Spiritual, 938.
Sight of God, In the, 926.
— Spiritual, 138.
Sign: A babe, The, 14.
Silence of Jesus, The, 333.
Simon Peter, 160.
— and St. Jude, Apostles, St., 33, 979.
Simplicity, A plea for, 617.
Simply to Thy cross I cling, 449.
Sin, 996.
Sin as alienation from God, 657.
— A besetting, 864.
— Christ condemning, 462.
— The conflict with, 640.
— Conviction of, 314.
— The craft and cruelty of, 1023.
— The fictions of, 1023.
— and grace, 454.
— The malignity of, 459.
— The problem of, 956.
— The sense of, 948.
— in the world, The most popular, 131.
Sinlessness, Assumptions of, 948.
Sitting by the well, Our Lord, 223.
Sleep in Him, Them that, 764.

Sleeper, The Sunday, 422.
Sleepers, Wake, 684.
Sleeping through Jesus, 765.
Slowness of God, The, 942.
Snares, Modern, 781.
Social questions, The Church and, 725.
Society, The Christian, 865.
— — — in, 927.
— The selfishness of, 103.
Soldier, The Christian, 794.
Son and heir! 633.
— of Man comes for, What the, 143.
— — — Mission of the, 62.
— Revelation in a, 823.
Song, A new, 1028.
— of triumph, The, 1031.
Sons of God, 953.
— — — revealed, The, 468.
Sorrow, Comfort in, 320.
— for sin, 614.
Soul, Winning the, 152.
Soul's vision and hearing of Jesus, The, 256.
Souls, Winning and saving, 152.
Sower, A, 45.
— Parable of the, 47.
Sowers, 46.
Sowing and reaping, 645, 646.
Spendest more, Whatsoever thou, 72.
Spirit, Baffling of the, 412.
— Coming of the, 375, 376.
— Fire of the, 768.
— Grieve not the, 678.
— and letter, 596.
— One, 671.
— The religion of, 462.
— Unity of the, 670.
— Universality of the, 558.
Spirit-born, Life of the, 214.
— filled life, The, 688.
Spiritual forces, 411.
— life, Reality of the, 788.
— times, Behind the, 420.
— to the worldly life, Relation of the, 491.
Spirituality, and civilisation, 788.
Stability of faith, The, 587.
Stand, Having done all to, 994.
Standard, Lowering the, 223.
Star, The morning, 1000.
Stephen, Martyrdom of St., 392.
Stephen's death, St., 390.
— vision, St., 391.
Steps to a Divine goal, 935.
— of His most blessed life, The, 23.
Steward, The unjust, 122.
Stone that grinds to powder, The, 150.
— The white, 996, 997.
Stones of the temple, The living, 922.
Strain to rest, From, 243.
Strait betwixt two, A, 708.
— How to be in a, 708.
Strategy, The invincible, 494.
Street, In the midst of the, 1049.
Strength, The prayer for, 281.
— Spiritual, 589.
— and weakness, 518.
— The weakness of, 548.
Strengthen the brethren, 157.
Stress to triumph, From, 1019.
Strive to enter in, 100.
Strong men, 951.
Submission, The glory of, 690.
Success, The failure of, 105.

Suffering, Bodily, 741.
— with Christ, 17.
— The dignity of, 619.
— Jesus our example in, 925.
— The joy of, 613.
— Man perfected through, 864.
— The uses of, 873.
Sufferings of Christ, The, 177.
— and the glory, The, 466.
Sufficiency, Our, 595.
Sunday observance, 173.
Suns, Setting, 27.
Suppositions in life, False, 786.
— Mistaken, 347.
Sympathy, 435.
— and dependence, 74.

Tabernacles, The three, 940.
Teacher, The Man and the, 784.
— and His message, The Divine, 314.
— Sanctifying of the, 327.
Teaching on earth's duties, Heaven's, 838.
— Definite religious, 388.
Tears of Jesus, The, 146, 273.
— of love, The, 43.
— Meaning of the, 146.
Tell us plainly, 265.
Temper, Bad, 680.
Temperance, The Christian idea of, 643.
Temple of His body, The, 205.
Temples, Christ and his human, 526.
Temptation, 84, 549.
— The blessedness of enduring, 891.
— Comfort in, 551.
— The trinity of, 697.
Tenderheartedness, Evangelical grace of, 681.
Tent and the city, The, 855.
Tents, The eternal, 124.
Testimony, Personal, 255.
Thankfulness, 756, 768.
Thanks at the Supper Table, Christ giving, 156.
That I may know Him, 294.
Therefore, 268.
Thief, The penitent, 171.
Things which God reveals to them that love Him, The, 520.
Think about, What to, 731.
— Time to, 732.
Thirst, Divine, 340.
— The pains of, 338.
Thomas, St., 270, 355.
— the Apostle, St., 270, 354.
— The doubt of, 353, 354.
Thorns, Seed among, 48.
Thought and action, 431.
— The discipline of, 733.
Thoughts, Protected, 730.
— The regulation of, 732.
— Right, 730.
— The rule of our, 828.
Thousand years' reign of Christ, The, 1036.
Throne of grace, The, 831.
Thy will be done, 81.
Till and until, 672.
Time, The appointed, 60.
— The brevity of, 538.
— The interpreting influence of, 285.
— Knowing the, 498.

Time, The providence of, 59..
— The tyranny of, 152.
Timothy's life and mission, 789.
Touch me not, 348, 350.
Trading servants, The, 143.
— — Rewards of the, 144.
Traffic, The manhood, 1035.
Transfiguration, The, 56.
— Mount of the, 56.
Transfigured Church, Ministry of a, 375.
Transformation, 488.
— into the Lord's image, 598.
Transiency of the unreal, The, 49.
Transient hour, A, 159.
Transition, The great, 185.
Trial by fire, The, 524.
Tribulation, Heaven through, 1018.
Tribunals, The three, 530.
Trinity, Fifteenth Sunday after, 648.
— Twenty-fifth Sunday after, 111.
Trumpet of the seven, The latest, 581.
— and the voice of words, The sound of a, 877.
Trusts, The two, 792.

Unavailing faith, Types of, 902.
Unchanging Christ, The, 884.
Unclothed and clothed upon, 677.
Undeveloped lives, 279.
Union, Aspects of the mystical, 692.
— of Christ and the believer, The, 305.
Unity, A plea for, 668.
— not uniformity, 669.
Unprofitable made profitable, The, 810.
Unreal, Transiency of the, 49.
Unreality, 610.
Unrecognised Christ, The, 295.
Unselfishness, A study in, 804.
Unspoken inquiries, 319.
Unto the Lord, 502.
Upward look, The, 747.

Valediction and benediction, 621.
Veil, Within the, 836.
Vessel, The ministering, 602.
Victories, Not victors, 595.
Victory, 582.
— The further side of, 477.
— over sin, 583, 584.
Viper on the hand, The, 434.
Virgin Mary, Reverence due to the, 5.
Virtue, Contrasts in, 44.
— The pre-eminent Christian, 488.
Vision of Christ, The, 391.
— of the great sheet, The, 400.
— Loyalty to, 432
— Mirror and the, 30.
— The pre-requisite of, 57.
Visions, 414.
Visitation, 5, 148.
Vocations, Suppressed, 769.
Voice, The prevailing, 164.

Wages or gift, 458.
Waiting, 365.
— for Christ, 51.
Walking in the light, 269.
Warfare, The certainties of our, 972.
— The Christian, 696.
Warning, Words of, 106.
Watch—yourselves, your opportunities, 687.

Water from the fountain, 941.
Watershed, The, 512.
Waverers, 66.
Weakness, Crucified through, 620.
— The educative power of, 618.
Wealth, The depth of God's, 485.
— that never fails, 659.
Weariness, The cure for, 646.
Well, Jacob's, 224.
— Our Lord sitting by the, 223.
Well-doing, Equipped for, 808.
What is this? 318.
Whit-Sunday, 377, 463.
White already, 225.
— raiment, 1003.
— and scarlet, 1003.
— stone, The, 996, 997.
Will, Authority of the, 230.
— Dedication of the, 225.
— Power of the, 694.
Wisdom, Spiritual, 124.
Wishing, 977.
— I caught myself, 480.
Witness of the Church, The moral, 313.
— of the Spirit, The, 465.
Witnesses for Christ, 183.
— The cloud of, 866.
— for Jesus, 368.
Witnessing Church, A, 367.
— spirit, The, 389.
Woman, The rights of, 553.
Womanhood, A school for, 805.
Women in the Church, The rights of, 569.
— of Jerusalem, The, 165.
Word from the cross, The fifth, 339.
— made flesh, The, 190.
— of God, Personality of the, 177.
— Hearing the, 28.
— as seed, The, 46.
Words of the childhood, The first, 20.
— of life, 241.
— from the cross, The seven, 167.
— of the risen Lord, The first, 348.
Work, Christ's finished, 340.
— Jesus our example, In, 253.
— Our, 123, 324.
— and rest, Our Lord in, 222.
— The sacredness of, 228.
Workers with God, 524.
Working, Some features of Christ's, 228.
Workman and his overseer, The, 795.
Works, Greater, 296.
World, He condemned the, 854.
— How to use the, 539.
— Unspotted from the, 897.
Worldliness and unworldliness, Other, 952.
— ? What is, 326.
Worship and service, 409.
Worth of man, The, 112.
— while? Is it, 430.
Woundprints, 351.
Wrong thing, Looking for the, 163.

'Yet once more' This word, 880.
Youth, The hope of, 921.

Zaccheus: The advantage of disadvantages, 140.